Robert Frank

29 Sep 70

ULYSSES S. GRANT

Ulysses S. Grant

MEMOIRS AND SELECTED LETTERS
Personal Memoirs of U. S. Grant
Selected Letters 1839–1865

THE LIBRARY OF AMERICA

Texts of the letters are reprinted from THE PAPERS OF
ULYSSES S. GRANT, edited by John Y. Simon, Volumes 1–14, copyright
1967–1985, by The Ulysses S. Grant Association, published by
Southern Illinois University Press. Reprinted by
permission of the publisher.

Facsimile on pages 742–43 courtesy of The New-York Historical Society.

Distributed to the trade in the United States
and Canada by the Viking Press.

Library of Congress Catalog Number: 90-60013
For cataloging information, see end of Notes.
ISBN 0–940450–58–5

The Library of America–50

Manufactured in the United States of America

MARY DRAKE McFEELY
AND
WILLIAM S. McFEELY
WROTE THE NOTES AND SELECTED
THE LETTERS FOR THIS VOLUME

Grateful acknowledgment is made to the National Endowment for the Humanities, the Ford Foundation, and the Andrew W. Mellon Foundation for their generous support of this series.

Contents

Personal Memoirs of U. S. Grant, Vol. I   1

Personal Memoirs of U. S. Grant, Vol. II.   393

Selected Letters 1839–1865   867

Appendix: Notes to the Doctor
    written while completing the Memoirs
    at Mount McGregor, June–July 1885.   1109

Chronology.   1121

Note on the Texts   1162

Notes   1171

PERSONAL MEMOIRS

OF

U. S. GRANT.

IN TWO VOLUMES.

VOL. I.

U. S. Grant
Bvt. 2d. Lt. 4th Infy.

These volumes are
dedicated to the American
Soldier and Sailor.

U. S. Grant.

New York City
May 23d 1885.

Preface.

"Man proposes and God disposes." There are but few important events in the affairs of men brought about by their own choice.

Although frequently urged by friends to write my memoirs I had determined never to do so, nor to write anything for publication. At the age of nearly sixty-two I received an injury from a fall, which confined me closely to the house while it did not apparently affect my general health. This made study a pleasant pastime. Shortly after, the rascality of a business partner developed itself by the announcement of a failure. This was followed soon after by universal depression of all securities, which seemed to threaten the extinction of a good part of the income still retained, and for which I am indebted to the kindly act of friends. At this juncture the editor of the *Century Magazine* asked me to write a few articles for him. I consented for the money it gave me; for at that moment I was living upon borrowed money. The work I found congenial, and I determined to continue it. The event is an important one for me, for good or evil; I hope for the former.

In preparing these volumes for the public, I have entered upon the task with the sincere desire to avoid doing injustice to any one, whether on the National or Confederate side, other than the unavoidable injustice of not making mention often where special mention is due. There must be many errors of omission in this work, because the subject is too large to be treated of in two volumes in such way as to do justice to all the officers and men engaged. There were thousands of instances, during the rebellion, of individual, company, regimental and brigade deeds of heroism which deserve special mention and are not here alluded to. The troops engaged in them will have to look to the detailed reports of their individual commanders for the full history of those deeds.

The first volume, as well as a portion of the second, was written before I had reason to suppose I was in a critical condition of health. Later I was reduced almost to the point of death, and it became impossible for me to attend to anything for weeks. I have, however, somewhat regained my strength, and am able, often, to devote as many hours a day as a person should devote to such work. I would have more hope of satisfying the expectation of the public if I could have allowed myself more time. I have used my best efforts, with the aid of my eldest son, F. D. Grant, assisted by his brothers, to verify from the records every statement of fact given. The comments are my own, and show how I saw the matters treated of whether others saw them in the same light or not.

With these remarks I present these volumes to the public, asking no favor but hoping they will meet the approval of the reader.

U. S. GRANT.

MOUNT MACGREGOR, NEW YORK, *July* 1, 1885.

Contents.

VOLUME I.

PREFACE. 5

Chapter I.
ANCESTRY—BIRTH—BOYHOOD 17–27

Chapter II.
WEST POINT—GRADUATION 28–35

Chapter III.
ARMY LIFE—CAUSES OF THE MEXICAN WAR
—CAMP SALUBRITY 36–45

Chapter IV.
CORPUS CHRISTI—MEXICAN SMUGGLING—
SPANISH RULE IN MEXICO—SUPPLYING
TRANSPORTATION. 46–53

Chapter V.
TRIP TO AUSTIN—PROMOTION TO FULL
SECOND-LIEUTENANT—ARMY OF OCCUPATION . 54–59

Chapter VI.
ADVANCE OF THE ARMY—CROSSING THE
COLORADO—THE RIO GRANDE. 60–64

Chapter VII.
THE MEXICAN WAR—THE BATTLE OF PALO
ALTO—THE BATTLE OF RESACA DE LA PALMA
—ARMY OF INVASION—GENERAL TAYLOR—
MOVEMENT ON CAMARGO 65–73

Chapter VIII.
ADVANCE ON MONTEREY—THE BLACK FORT—
THE BATTLE OF MONTEREY—SURRENDER OF
THE CITY   74–82

Chapter IX.
POLITICAL INTRIGUE—BUENA VISTA—
MOVEMENT AGAINST VERA CRUZ—SIEGE AND
CAPTURE OF VERA CRUZ.   83–88

Chapter X.
MARCH TO JALAPA—BATTLE OF CERRO GORDO
—PEROTE—PUEBLA—SCOTT AND TAYLOR . . .   89–95

Chapter XI.
ADVANCE ON THE CITY OF MEXICO—BATTLE OF
CONTRERAS—ASSAULT AT CHURUBUSCO—NE-
GOTIATIONS FOR PEACE—BATTLE OF MOLINO
DEL REY—STORMING OF CHAPULTEPEC—SAN
COSME—EVACUATION OF THE CITY—HALLS OF
THE MONTEZUMAS   96–110

Chapter XII.
PROMOTION TO FIRST LIEUTENANT—CAPTURE
OF THE CITY OF MEXICO—THE ARMY—MEXI-
CAN SOLDIERS—PEACE NEGOTIATIONS   111–118

Chapter XIII.
TREATY OF PEACE—MEXICAN BULL FIGHTS—
REGIMENTAL QUARTERMASTER—TRIP TO
POPOCATAPETL—TRIP TO THE CAVES OF
MEXICO   119–128

Chapter XIV.
RETURN OF THE ARMY—MARRIAGE—ORDERED
TO THE PACIFIC COAST—CROSSING THE
ISTHMUS—ARRIVAL AT SAN FRANCISCO.   129–134

Chapter XV.
SAN FRANCISCO—EARLY CALIFORNIA
EXPERIENCES—LIFE ON THE PACIFIC COAST—
PROMOTED CAPTAIN—FLUSH TIMES IN
CALIFORNIA 135–140

Chapter XVI.
RESIGNATION—PRIVATE LIFE—LIFE AT GALENA
—THE COMING CRISIS 141–151

Chapter XVII.
OUTBREAK OF THE REBELLION—PRESIDING AT
A UNION MEETING—MUSTERING OFFICER OF
STATE TROOPS—LYON AT CAMP JACKSON
—SERVICES TENDERED TO THE GOVERNMENT . . 152–159

Chapter XVIII.
APPOINTED COLONEL OF THE 21ST ILLINOIS—
PERSONNEL OF THE REGIMENT—GENERAL
LOGAN—MARCH TO MISSOURI—MOVEMENT
AGAINST HARRIS AT FLORIDA, MO.—GENERAL
POPE IN COMMAND—STATIONED AT MEXICO,
MO. 160–167

Chapter XIX.
COMMISSIONED BRIGADIER-GENERAL—COMMAND
AT IRONTON, MO.—JEFFERSON CITY—CAPE
GIRARDEAU—GENERAL PRENTISS—SEIZURE OF
PADUCAH—HEADQUARTERS AT CAIRO 168–176

Chapter XX.
GENERAL FREMONT IN COMMAND—MOVEMENT
AGAINST BELMONT—BATTLE OF BELMONT—A
NARROW ESCAPE—AFTER THE BATTLE 177–186

Chapter XXI.
GENERAL HALLECK IN COMMAND—COMMANDING
THE DISTRICT OF CAIRO—MOVEMENT ON FORT
HENRY—CAPTURE OF FORT HENRY 187–195

Chapter XXII.
INVESTMENT OF FORT DONELSON—THE NAVAL
OPERATIONS—ATTACK OF THE ENEMY—
ASSAULTING THE WORKS—SURRENDER OF THE
FORT 196–213

Chapter XXIII.
PROMOTED MAJOR-GENERAL OF VOLUNTEERS—
UNOCCUPIED TERRITORY—ADVANCE UPON
NASHVILLE—SITUATION OF THE TROOPS—
CONFEDERATE RETREAT—RELIEVED OF THE
COMMAND—RESTORED TO THE COMMAND—
GENERAL SMITH 214–221

Chapter XXIV.
THE ARMY AT PITTSBURG LANDING—INJURED
BY A FALL—THE CONFEDERATE ATTACK AT
SHILOH—THE FIRST DAY'S FIGHT AT SHILOH—
GENERAL SHERMAN—CONDITION OF THE
ARMY—CLOSE OF THE FIRST DAY'S FIGHT—
THE SECOND DAY'S FIGHT—RETREAT AND
DEFEAT OF THE CONFEDERATES 222–236

Chapter XXV.
STRUCK BY A BULLET—PRECIPITATE RETREAT OF
THE CONFEDERATES—INTRENCHMENTS AT
SHILOH—GENERAL BUELL—GENERAL
JOHNSTON—REMARKS ON SHILOH 237–247

Chapter XXVI.
HALLECK ASSUMES COMMAND IN THE FIELD—
THE ADVANCE UPON CORINTH—OCCUPATION
OF CORINTH—THE ARMY SEPARATED 248–257

Chapter XXVII.
HEADQUARTERS MOVED TO MEMPHIS—ON
THE ROAD TO MEMPHIS—ESCAPING JACKSON—
COMPLAINTS AND REQUESTS—HALLECK
APPOINTED COMMANDER-IN-CHIEF—RETURN
TO CORINTH—MOVEMENTS OF BRAGG—
SURRENDER OF CLARKSVILLE—THE ADVANCE
UPON CHATTANOOGA—SHERIDAN COLONEL OF
A MICHIGAN REGIMENT. 258–269

Chapter XXVIII.
ADVANCE OF VAN DORN AND PRICE—PRICE
ENTERS IUKA—BATTLE OF IUKA 270–277

Chapter XXIX.
VAN DORN'S MOVEMENTS—BATTLE OF
CORINTH—COMMAND OF THE DEPARTMENT OF
THE TENNESSEE 278–282

Chapter XXX.
THE CAMPAIGN AGAINST VICKSBURG—
EMPLOYING THE FREEDMEN—OCCUPATION
OF HOLLY SPRINGS—SHERMAN ORDERED
TO MEMPHIS—SHERMAN'S MOVEMENTS
DOWN THE MISSISSIPPI—VAN DORN CAPTURES
HOLLY SPRINGS—COLLECTING FORAGE
AND FOOD. 283–291

Chapter XXXI.
HEADQUARTERS MOVED TO HOLLY SPRINGS—
GENERAL MCCLERNAND IN COMMAND—
ASSUMING COMMAND AT YOUNG'S POINT—
OPERATIONS ABOVE VICKSBURG—
FORTIFICATIONS ABOUT VICKSBURG—THE
CANAL—LAKE PROVIDENCE—OPERATIONS AT
YAZOO PASS 292–302

Chapter XXXII.
THE BAYOUS WEST OF THE MISSISSIPPI—
CRITICISMS OF THE NORTHERN PRESS—
RUNNING THE BATTERIES—LOSS OF THE
INDIANOLA—DISPOSITION OF THE TROOPS . . . 303–314

Chapter XXXIII.
ATTACK ON GRAND GULF—OPERATIONS BELOW
VICKSBURG 315–323

Chapter XXXIV.
CAPTURE OF PORT GIBSON—GRIERSON'S
RAID—OCCUPATION OF GRAND GULF—
MOVEMENT UP THE BIG BLACK—BATTLE OF
RAYMOND 324–331

Chapter XXXV.
MOVEMENT AGAINST JACKSON—FALL OF
JACKSON—INTERCEPTING THE ENEMY—BATTLE
OF CHAMPION'S HILL 332–348

Chapter XXXVI.
BATTLE OF BLACK RIVER BRIDGE—CROSSING
THE BIG BLACK—INVESTMENT OF VICKSBURG—
ASSAULTING THE WORKS 349–356

Chapter XXXVII.
SIEGE OF VICKSBURG 357–367

Chapter XXXVIII.

Johnston's Movements—Fortifications at
Haines' Bluff—Explosion of the Mine—
Explosion of the Second Mine—Preparing
for the Assault—The Flag of Truce—
Meeting with Pemberton—Negotiations
for Surrender—Accepting the Terms—
Surrender of Vicksburg 368–383

Chapter XXXIX.

Retrospect of the Campaign—Sherman's
Movements—Proposed Movement upon
Mobile—A painful Accident—Ordered to
Report at Cairo 384–391

Maps and Illustrations.

VOLUME I.

*Brevet Second Lieutenant U. S. Grant at the Age
   of 21 Years, from an old Daguerreotype taken
   at Bethel, Clermont County, Ohio, in 1843.
   Engraved on Steel by A. H. Ritchie, N.A.* . . *Frontispiece*

Fac-simile of Handwriting . . . . *Dedication*

*Birthplace at Point Pleasant, Clermont County,
   Ohio. Etched by Wm. E. Marshall*   23

Map of Monterey and its Approaches   79

Map of the Valley of Mexico   107

Map of the Battle-field near Belmont.   181

*Map showing the relative Positions of Fort Henry
   and Fort Donelson*   193

Map of Fort Donelson.   199

*Fac-simile of General Buckner's Dispatch relating
   to Terms of Capitulation, General Grant's
   reply, "I propose to move immediately upon
   your Works," and General Buckner's answer
   accepting the Terms for the Surrender of Fort
   Donelson, all from the Original Documents.* . .   209–211

Map of the Field of Shiloh   229

Map of the Country about Corinth, Mississippi. . . .   253

Map of the Battles of Iuka and Corinth   273

Map of the Vicksburg Campaign   311

Map — Bruinsburg, Port Gibson and Grand Gulf. . .   319

Map of the Country about Jackson, Mississippi   335

Map of the Battle of Champion's Hill   343

Map of Battle-field of Big Black River Bridge   351

Map of the Siege of Vicksburg   361

*Map — Line of Defences Vicksburg to Haines' Bluff
   and Black River Bridge*   371

Chapter I.

ANCESTRY — BIRTH — BOYHOOD.

M Y FAMILY is American, and has been for generations, in all its branches, direct and collateral.

Mathew Grant, the founder of the branch in America, of which I am a descendant, reached Dorchester, Massachusetts, in May, 1630. In 1635 he moved to what is now Windsor, Connecticut, and was the surveyor for that colony for more than forty years. He was also, for many years of the time, town clerk. He was a married man when he arrived at Dorchester, but his children were all born in this country. His eldest son, Samuel, took lands on the east side of the Connecticut River, opposite Windsor, which have been held and occupied by descendants of his to this day.

I am of the eighth generation from Mathew Grant, and seventh from Samuel. Mathew Grant's first wife died a few years after their settlement in Windsor, and he soon after married the widow Rockwell, who, with her first husband, had been fellow-passengers with him and his first wife, on the ship *Mary and John*, from Dorchester, England, in 1630. Mrs. Rockwell had several children by her first marriage, and others by her second. By intermarriage, two or three generations later, I am descended from both the wives of Mathew Grant.

In the fifth descending generation my great grandfather, Noah Grant, and his younger brother, Solomon, held commissions in the English army, in 1756, in the war against the French and Indians. Both were killed that year.

My grandfather, also named Noah, was then but nine years old. At the breaking out of the war of the Revolution, after the battles of Concord and Lexington, he went with a Connecticut company to join the Continental army, and was present at the battle of Bunker Hill. He served until the fall of Yorktown, or through the entire Revolutionary war. He must, however, have been on furlough part of the time — as I believe most of the soldiers of that period were — for he married in Connecticut during the war, had two children, and was a widower at the close. Soon after this he emigrated to

Westmoreland County, Pennsylvania, and settled near the town of Greensburg in that county. He took with him the younger of his two children, Peter Grant. The elder, Solomon, remained with his relatives in Connecticut until old enough to do for himself, when he emigrated to the British West Indies.

Not long after his settlement in Pennsylvania, my grandfather, Captain Noah Grant, married a Miss Kelly, and in 1799 he emigrated again, this time to Ohio, and settled where the town of Deerfield now stands. He had now five children, including Peter, a son by his first marriage. My father, Jesse R. Grant, was the second child—oldest son, by the second marriage.

Peter Grant went early to Maysville, Kentucky, where he was very prosperous, married, had a family of nine children, and was drowned at the mouth of the Kanawha River, Virginia, in 1825, being at the time one of the wealthy men of the West.

My grandmother Grant died in 1805, leaving seven children. This broke up the family. Captain Noah Grant was not thrifty in the way of "laying up stores on earth," and, after the death of his second wife, he went, with the two youngest children, to live with his son Peter, in Maysville. The rest of the family found homes in the neighborhood of Deerfield, my father in the family of Judge Tod, the father of the late Governor Tod, of Ohio. His industry and independence of character were such, that I imagine his labor compensated fully for the expense of his maintenance.

There must have been a cordiality in his welcome into the Tod family, for to the day of his death he looked upon Judge Tod and his wife, with all the reverence he could have felt if they had been parents instead of benefactors. I have often heard him speak of Mrs. Tod as the most admirable woman he had ever known. He remained with the Tod family only a few years, until old enough to learn a trade. He went first, I believe, with his half-brother, Peter Grant, who, though not a tanner himself, owned a tannery in Maysville, Kentucky. Here he learned his trade, and in a few years returned to Deerfield and worked for, and lived in the family of a Mr. Brown, the father of John Brown—"whose body lies mouldering in the

grave, while his soul goes marching on." I have often heard
my father speak of John Brown, particularly since the events
at Harper's Ferry. Brown was a boy when they lived in the
same house, but he knew him afterwards, and regarded him
as a man of great purity of character, of high moral and physical courage, but a fanatic and extremist in whatever he advocated. It was certainly the act of an insane man to attempt the
invasion of the South, and the overthrow of slavery, with less
than twenty men.

My father set up for himself in business, establishing a tannery at Ravenna, the county seat of Portage County. In a few
years he removed from Ravenna, and set up the same business
at Point Pleasant, Clermont County, Ohio.

During the minority of my father, the West afforded but
poor facilities for the most opulent of the youth to acquire an
education, and the majority were dependent, almost exclusively, upon their own exertions for whatever learning they
obtained. I have often heard him say that his time at school
was limited to six months, when he was very young, too
young, indeed, to learn much, or to appreciate the advantages
of an education, and to a "quarter's schooling" afterwards,
probably while living with Judge Tod. But his thirst for education was intense. He learned rapidly, and was a constant
reader up to the day of his death—in his eightieth year.
Books were scarce in the Western Reserve during his youth,
but he read every book he could borrow in the neighborhood
where he lived. This scarcity gave him the early habit of
studying everything he read, so that when he got through
with a book, he knew everything in it. The habit continued
through life. Even after reading the daily papers—which he
never neglected—he could give all the important information
they contained. He made himself an excellent English scholar,
and before he was twenty years of age was a constant contrib-
utor to Western newspapers, and was also, from that time
until he was fifty years old, an able debater in the societies for
this purpose, which were common in the West at that time.
He always took an active part in politics, but was never a
candidate for office, except, I believe, that he was the first
Mayor of Georgetown. He supported Jackson for the Presidency; but he was a Whig, a great admirer of Henry Clay,

and never voted for any other democrat for high office after Jackson.

My mother's family lived in Montgomery County, Pennsylvania, for several generations. I have little information about her ancestors. Her family took no interest in genealogy, so that my grandfather, who died when I was sixteen years old, knew only back to his grandfather. On the other side, my father took a great interest in the subject, and in his researches, he found that there was an entailed estate in Windsor, Connecticut, belonging to the family, to which his nephew, Lawson Grant—still living—was the heir. He was so much interested in the subject that he got his nephew to empower him to act in the matter, and in 1832 or 1833, when I was a boy ten or eleven years old, he went to Windsor, proved the title beyond dispute, and perfected the claim of the owners for a consideration—three thousand dollars, I think. I remember the circumstance well, and remember, too, hearing him say on his return that he found some widows living on the property, who had little or nothing beyond their homes. From these he refused to receive any recompense.

My mother's father, John Simpson, moved from Montgomery County, Pennsylvania, to Clermont County, Ohio, about the year 1819, taking with him his four children, three daughters and one son. My mother, Hannah Simpson, was the third of these children, and was then over twenty years of age. Her oldest sister was at that time married, and had several children. She still lives in Clermont County at this writing, October 5th, 1884, and is over ninety years of age. Until her memory failed her, a few years ago, she thought the country ruined beyond recovery when the Democratic party lost control in 1860. Her family, which was large, inherited her views, with the exception of one son who settled in Kentucky before the war. He was the only one of the children who entered the volunteer service to suppress the rebellion.

Her brother, next of age and now past eighty-eight, is also still living in Clermont County, within a few miles of the old homestead, and is as active in mind as ever. He was a supporter of the Government during the war, and remains a firm believer, that national success by the Democratic party means irretrievable ruin.

In June, 1821, my father, Jesse R. Grant, married Hannah Simpson. I was born on the 27th of April, 1822, at Point Pleasant, Clermont County, Ohio. In the fall of 1823 we moved to Georgetown, the county seat of Brown, the adjoining county east. This place remained my home, until at the age of seventeen, in 1839, I went to West Point.

The schools, at the time of which I write, were very indifferent. There were no free schools, and none in which the scholars were classified. They were all supported by subscription, and a single teacher—who was often a man or a woman incapable of teaching much, even if they imparted all they knew—would have thirty or forty scholars, male and female, from the infant learning the A B C's up to the young lady of eighteen and the boy of twenty, studying the highest branches taught—the three R's, "Reading, 'Riting, 'Rithmetic." I never saw an algebra, or other mathematical work higher than the arithmetic, in Georgetown, until after I was appointed to West Point. I then bought a work on algebra in Cincinnati; but having no teacher it was Greek to me.

My life in Georgetown was uneventful. From the age of five or six until seventeen, I attended the subscription schools of the village, except during the winters of 1836–7 and 1838–9. The former period was spent in Maysville, Kentucky, attending the school of Richardson and Rand; the latter in Ripley, Ohio, at a private school. I was not studious in habit, and probably did not make progress enough to compensate for the outlay for board and tuition. At all events both winters were spent in going over the same old arithmetic which I knew every word of before, and repeating: "A noun is the name of a thing," which I had also heard my Georgetown teachers repeat, until I had come to believe it—but I cast no reflections upon my old teacher, Richardson. He turned out bright scholars from his school, many of whom have filled conspicuous places in the service of their States. Two of my cotemporaries there—who, I believe, never attended any other institution of learning—have held seats in Congress, and one, if not both, other high offices; these are Wadsworth and Brewster.

My father was, from my earliest recollection, in comfortable circumstances, considering the times, his place of residence, and the community in which he lived. Mindful of his own lack of facilities for acquiring an education, his greatest desire in maturer years was for the education of his children. Consequently, as stated before, I never missed a quarter from school from the time I was old enough to attend till the time of leaving home. This did not exempt me from labor. In my early days, every one labored more or less, in the region where my youth was spent, and more in proportion to their private means. It was only the very poor who were exempt. While my father carried on the manufacture of leather and worked at the trade himself, he owned and tilled considerable land. I detested the trade, preferring almost any other labor; but I was fond of agriculture, and of all employment in which horses were used. We had, among other lands, fifty acres of forest within a mile of the village. In the fall of the year choppers were employed to cut enough wood to last a twelve-month. When I was seven or eight years of age, I began hauling all the wood used in the house and shops. I could not load it on the wagons, of course, at that time, but I could drive, and the choppers would load, and some one at the house unload. When about eleven years old, I was strong enough to hold a plough. From that age until seventeen I did all the work done with horses, such as breaking up the land, furrowing, ploughing corn and potatoes, bringing in the crops when harvested, hauling all the wood, besides tending two or three horses, a cow or two, and sawing wood for stoves, etc., while still attending school. For this I was compensated by the fact that there was never any scolding or punishing by my parents; no objection to rational enjoyments, such as fishing, going to the creek a mile away to swim in summer, taking a horse and visiting my grandparents in the adjoining county, fifteen miles off, skating on the ice in winter, or taking a horse and sleigh when there was snow on the ground.

While still quite young I had visited Cincinnati, forty-five miles away, several times, alone; also Maysville, Kentucky,

BIRTH-PLACE OF GENERAL U.S. GRANT.

POINT PLEASANT, OHIO.

Etched by W.T. Merchant.

often, and once Louisville. The journey to Louisville was a big one for a boy of that day. I had also gone once with a two-horse carriage to Chilicothe, about seventy miles, with a neighbor's family, who were removing to Toledo, Ohio, and returned alone; and had gone once, in like manner, to Flat Rock, Kentucky, about seventy miles away. On this latter occasion I was fifteen years of age. While at Flat Rock, at the house of a Mr. Payne, whom I was visiting with his brother, a neighbor of ours in Georgetown, I saw a very fine saddle horse, which I rather coveted, and proposed to Mr. Payne, the owner, to trade him for one of the two I was driving. Payne hesitated to trade with a boy, but asking his brother about it, the latter told him that it would be all right, that I was allowed to do as I pleased with the horses. I was seventy miles from home, with a carriage to take back, and Mr. Payne said he did not know that his horse had ever had a collar on. I asked to have him hitched to a farm wagon and we would soon see whether he would work. It was soon evident that the horse had never worn harness before; but he showed no viciousness, and I expressed a confidence that I could manage him. A trade was at once struck, I receiving ten dollars difference.

The next day Mr. Payne, of Georgetown, and I started on our return. We got along very well for a few miles, when we encountered a ferocious dog that frightened the horses and made them run. The new animal kicked at every jump he made. I got the horses stopped, however, before any damage was done, and without running into anything. After giving them a little rest, to quiet their fears, we started again. That instant the new horse kicked, and started to run once more. The road we were on, struck the turnpike within half a mile of the point where the second runaway commenced, and there there was an embankment twenty or more feet deep on the opposite side of the pike. I got the horses stopped on the very brink of the precipice. My new horse was terribly frightened and trembled like an aspen; but he was not half so badly frightened as my companion, Mr. Payne, who deserted me after this last experience, and took passage on a freight wagon for Maysville. Every time I attempted to start, my new horse would commence to kick. I was in quite a dilemma for a time.

Once in Maysville I could borrow a horse from an uncle who lived there; but I was more than a day's travel from that point. Finally I took out my bandanna—the style of handkerchief in universal use then—and with this blindfolded my horse. In this way I reached Maysville safely the next day, no doubt much to the surprise of my friend. Here I borrowed a horse from my uncle, and the following day we proceeded on our journey.

About half my school-days in Georgetown were spent at the school of John D. White, a North Carolinian, and the father of Chilton White who represented the district in Congress for one term during the rebellion. Mr. White was always a Democrat in politics, and Chilton followed his father. He had two older brothers—all three being school-mates of mine at their father's school—who did not go the same way. The second brother died before the rebellion began; he was a Whig, and afterwards a Republican. His oldest brother was a Republican and brave soldier during the rebellion. Chilton is reported as having told of an earlier horse-trade of mine. As he told the story, there was a Mr. Ralston living within a few miles of the village, who owned a colt which I very much wanted. My father had offered twenty dollars for it, but Ralston wanted twenty-five. I was so anxious to have the colt, that after the owner left, I begged to be allowed to take him at the price demanded. My father yielded, but said twenty dollars was all the horse was worth, and told me to offer that price; if it was not accepted I was to offer twenty-two and a half, and if that would not get him, to give the twenty-five. I at once mounted a horse and went for the colt. When I got to Mr. Ralston's house, I said to him: "Papa says I may offer you twenty dollars for the colt, but if you won't take that, I am to offer twenty-two and a half, and if you won't take that, to give you twenty-five." It would not require a Connecticut man to guess the price finally agreed upon. This story is nearly true. I certainly showed very plainly that I had come for the colt and meant to have him. I could not have been over eight years old at the time. This transaction caused me great heart-burning. The story got out among the boys of the village, and it was a long time before I heard the last of it. Boys enjoy the misery of their companions, at least village boys in that day did, and in later life I have found that all adults are not free from the peculiarity. I kept the horse until he was four years old, when he went blind, and I sold him for twenty dollars. When I went to Maysville to school, in 1836, at the age of fourteen, I recognized my colt as one of the blind horses working on the tread-wheel of the ferry-boat.

I have described enough of my early life to give an impression of the whole. I did not like to work; but I did as much of it, while young, as grown men can be hired to do in these days, and attended school at the same time. I had as many privileges as any boy in the village, and probably more than most of them. I have no recollection of ever having been punished at home, either by scolding or by the rod. But at school the case was different. The rod was freely used there, and I was not exempt from its influence. I can see John D. White— the school teacher—now, with his long beech switch always in his hand. It was not always the same one, either. Switches were brought in bundles, from a beech wood near the school house, by the boys for whose benefit they were intended. Often a whole bundle would be used up in a single day. I never had any hard feelings against my teacher, either while attending the school, or in later years when reflecting upon my experience. Mr. White was a kind-hearted man, and was much respected by the community in which he lived. He only followed the universal custom of the period, and that under which he had received his own education.

Chapter II.

IN THE WINTER of 1838–9 I was attending school at Ripley, only ten miles distant from Georgetown, but spent the Christmas holidays at home. During this vacation my father received a letter from the Honorable Thomas Morris, then United States Senator from Ohio. When he read it he said to me, "Ulysses, I believe you are going to receive the appointment." "What appointment?" I inquired. "To West Point; I have applied for it." "But I won't go," I said. He said he thought I would, *and I thought so too, if he did.* I really had no objection to going to West Point, except that I had a very exalted idea of the acquirements necessary to get through. I did not believe I possessed them, and could not bear the idea of failing. There had been four boys from our village, or its immediate neighborhood, who had been graduated from West Point, and never a failure of any one appointed from Georgetown, except in the case of the one whose place I was to take. He was the son of Dr. Bailey, our nearest and most intimate neighbor. Young Bailey had been appointed in 1837. Finding before the January examination following, that he could not pass, he resigned and went to a private school, and remained there until the following year, when he was reappointed. Before the next examination he was dismissed. Dr. Bailey was a proud and sensitive man, and felt the failure of his son so keenly that he forbade his return home. There were no telegraphs in those days to disseminate news rapidly, no railroads west of the Alleghanies, and but few east; and above all, there were no reporters prying into other people's private affairs. Consequently it did not become generally known that there was a vacancy at West Point from our district until I was appointed. I presume Mrs. Bailey confided to my mother the fact that Bartlett had been dismissed, and that the doctor had forbidden his son's return home.

The Honorable Thomas L. Hamer, one of the ablest men Ohio ever produced, was our member of Congress at the time, and had the right of nomination. He and my father had been members of the same debating society (where they were generally pitted on opposite sides), and intimate personal friends from their early manhood up to a few years before. In politics they differed. Hamer was a life-long Democrat, while my father was a Whig. They had a warm discussion, which finally became angry—over some act of President Jackson, the removal of the deposit of public moneys, I think—after which they never spoke until after my appointment. I know both of them felt badly over this estrangement, and would have been glad at any time to come to a reconciliation; but neither would make the advance. Under these circumstances my father would not write to Hamer for the appointment, but he wrote to Thomas Morris, United States Senator from Ohio, informing him that there was a vacancy at West Point from our district, and that he would be glad if I could be appointed to fill it. This letter, I presume, was turned over to Mr. Hamer, and, as there was no other applicant, he cheerfully appointed me. This healed the breach between the two, never after reopened.

Besides the argument used by my father in favor of my going to West Point—that "he thought I would go"—there was another very strong inducement. I had always a great desire to travel. I was already the best travelled boy in Georgetown, except the sons of one man, John Walker, who had emigrated to Texas with his family, and immigrated back as soon as he could get the means to do so. In his short stay in Texas he acquired a very different opinion of the country from what one would form going there now.

I had been east to Wheeling, Virginia, and north to the Western Reserve, in Ohio, west to Louisville, and south to Bourbon County, Kentucky, besides having driven or ridden pretty much over the whole country within fifty miles of home. Going to West Point would give me the opportunity of visiting the two great cities of the continent, Philadelphia and New York. This was enough. When these places were visited I would have been glad to have had a steamboat or railroad collision, or any other accident happen, by which I might have received a temporary injury sufficient to make me ineligible, for a time, to enter the Academy. Nothing of the kind occurred, and I had to face the music.

Georgetown has a remarkable record for a western village. It is, and has been from its earliest existence, a democratic town. There was probably no time during the rebellion when, if the opportunity could have been afforded, it would not have voted for Jefferson Davis for President of the United States, over Mr. Lincoln, or any other representative of his party; unless it was immediately after some of John Morgan's men, in his celebrated raid through Ohio, spent a few hours in the village. The rebels helped themselves to whatever they could find, horses, boots and shoes, especially horses, and many ordered meals to be prepared for them by the families. This was no doubt a far pleasanter duty for some families than it would have been to render a like service for Union soldiers. The line between the Rebel and Union element in Georgetown was so marked that it led to divisions even in the churches. There were churches in that part of Ohio where treason was preached regularly, and where, to secure membership, hostility to the government, to the war and to the liberation of the slaves, was far more essential than a belief in the authenticity or credibility of the Bible. There were men in Georgetown who filled all the requirements for membership in these churches.

Yet this far-off western village, with a population, including old and young, male and female, of about one thousand— about enough for the organization of a single regiment if all had been men capable of bearing arms—furnished the Union army four general officers and one colonel, West Point graduates, and nine generals and field officers of Volunteers, that I can think of. Of the graduates from West Point, all had citizenship elsewhere at the breaking out of the rebellion, except possibly General A. V. Kautz, who had remained in the army from his graduation. Two of the colonels also entered the service from other localities. The other seven, General McGroierty, Colonels White, Fyffe, Loudon and Marshall, Majors King and Bailey, were all residents of Georgetown when the war broke out, and all of them, who were alive at the close, returned there. Major Bailey was the cadet who had preceded me at West Point. He was killed in West Virginia, in his first engagement. As far as I know, every boy who has entered West Point from that village since my time has been graduated.

I took passage on a steamer at Ripley, Ohio, for Pittsburg, about the middle of May, 1839. Western boats at that day did not make regular trips at stated times, but would stop anywhere, and for any length of time, for passengers or freight. I have myself been detained two or three days at a place after steam was up, the gang planks, all but one, drawn in, and after the time advertised for starting had expired. On this occasion we had no vexatious delays, and in about three days Pittsburg was reached. From Pittsburg I chose passage by the canal to Harrisburg, rather than by the more expeditious stage. This gave a better opportunity of enjoying the fine scenery of Western Pennsylvania, and I had rather a dread of reaching my destination at all. At that time the canal was much patronized by travellers, and, with the comfortable packets of the period, no mode of conveyance could be more pleasant, when time was not an object. From Harrisburg to Philadelphia there was a railroad, the first I had ever seen, except the one on which I had just crossed the summit of the Alleghany Mountains, and over which canal boats were transported. In travelling by the road from Harrisburg, I thought the perfection of rapid transit had been reached. We travelled at least eighteen miles an hour, when at full speed, and made the whole distance averaging probably as much as twelve miles an hour. This seemed like annihilating space. I stopped five days in Philadelphia, saw about every street in the city, attended the theatre, visited Girard College (which was then in course of construction), and got reprimanded from home afterwards, for dallying by the way so long. My sojourn in New York was shorter, but long enough to enable me to see the city very well. I reported at West Point on the 30th or 31st of May, and about two weeks later passed my examination for admission, without difficulty, very much to my surprise.

A military life had no charms for me, and I had not the faintest idea of staying in the army even if I should be graduated, which I did not expect. The encampment which preceded the commencement of academic studies was very wearisome and uninteresting. When the 28th of August came—the date for breaking up camp and going into barracks—I felt as though I had been at West Point always, and that if I staid to graduation, I would have to remain always. I did not take hold of my studies with avidity, in fact I rarely ever read over a lesson the second time during my entire cadetship. I could not sit in my room doing nothing. There is a fine library connected with the Academy from which cadets can get books to read in their quarters. I devoted more time to these, than to books relating to the course of studies. Much of the time, I am sorry to say, was devoted to novels, but not those of a trashy sort. I read all of Bulwer's then published, Cooper's, Marryat's, Scott's, Washington Irving's works, Lever's, and many others that I do not now remember. Mathematics was very easy to me, so that when January came, I passed the examination, taking a good standing in that branch. In French, the only other study at that time in the first year's course, my standing was very low. In fact, if the class had been turned the other end foremost I should have been near head. I never succeeded in getting squarely at either end of my class, in any one study, during the four years. I came near it in French, artillery, infantry and cavalry tactics, and conduct.

Early in the session of the Congress which met in December, 1839, a bill was discussed abolishing the Military Academy. I saw in this an honorable way to obtain a discharge, and read the debates with much interest, but with impatience at the delay in taking action, for I was selfish enough to favor the bill. It never passed, and a year later, although the time hung drearily with me, I would have been sorry to have seen it succeed. My idea then was to get through the course, secure a detail for a few years as assistant professor of mathematics at the Academy, and afterwards obtain a permanent position as professor in some respectable college; but circumstances always did shape my course different from my plans.

At the end of two years the class received the usual furlough, extending from the close of the June examination to the 28th of August. This I enjoyed beyond any other period of my life. My father had sold out his business in Georgetown—where my youth had been spent, and to which my day-dreams carried me back as my future home, if I should ever be able to retire on a competency. He had moved to Bethel, only twelve miles away, in the adjoining county of Clermont, and had bought a young horse that had never been in harness, for my special use under the saddle during my furlough. Most of my time was spent among my old school-mates—these ten weeks were shorter than one week at West Point.

Persons acquainted with the Academy know that the corps of cadets is divided into four companies for the purpose of military exercises. These companies are officered from the cadets, the superintendent and commandant selecting the officers for their military bearing and qualifications. The adjutant, quartermaster, four captains and twelve lieutenants are taken from the first, or Senior class; the sergeants from the second, or Junior class; and the corporals from the third, or Sophomore class. I had not been "called out" as a corporal, but when I returned from furlough I found myself the last but one—about my standing in all the tactics—of eighteen sergeants. The promotion was too much for me. That year my standing in the class—as shown by the number of demerits of the year—was about the same as it was among the sergeants, and I was dropped, and served the fourth year as a private.

During my first year's encampment General Scott visited West Point, and reviewed the cadets. With his commanding figure, his quite colossal size and showy uniform, I thought him the finest specimen of manhood my eyes had ever beheld, and the most to be envied. I could never resemble him in appearance, but I believe I did have a presentiment for a moment that some day I should occupy his place on review— although I had no intention then of remaining in the army. My experience in a horse-trade ten years before, and the ridicule it caused me, were too fresh in my mind for me to communicate this presentiment to even my most intimate chum. The next summer Martin Van Buren, then President of the United States, visited West Point and reviewed the cadets; he did not impress me with the awe which Scott had inspired. In fact I regarded General Scott and Captain C. F. Smith, the Commandant of Cadets, as the two men most to be envied in the nation. I retained a high regard for both up to the day of their death.

The last two years wore away more rapidly than the first two, but they still seemed about five times as long as Ohio years, to me. At last all the examinations were passed, and the members of the class were called upon to record their choice of arms of service and regiments. I was anxious to enter the cavalry, or dragoons as they were then called, but there was only one regiment of dragoons in the Army at that time, and attached to that, besides the full complement of officers, there were at least four brevet second lieutenants. I recorded therefore my first choice, dragoons; second, 4th infantry; and got the latter. Again there was a furlough—or, more properly speaking, leave of absence for the class were now commissioned officers—this time to the end of September. Again I went to Ohio to spend my vacation among my old schoolmates; and again I found a fine saddle horse purchased for my special use, besides a horse and buggy that I could drive—but I was not in a physical condition to enjoy myself quite as well as on the former occasion. For six months before graduation I had had a desperate cough ("Tyler's grip" it was called), and I was very much reduced, weighing but one hundred and seventeen pounds, just my weight at entrance, though I had grown six inches in stature in the mean time. There was consumption in my father's family, two of his brothers having died of that disease, which made my symptoms more alarming. The brother and sister next younger than myself died, during the rebellion, of the same disease, and I seemed the most promising subject for it of the three in 1843.

Having made alternate choice of two different arms of service with different uniforms, I could not get a uniform suit until notified of my assignment. I left my measurement with a tailor, with directions not to make the uniform until I notified him whether it was to be for infantry or dragoons. Notice did not reach me for several weeks, and then it took at least a week to get the letter of instructions to the tailor and two more to make the clothes and have them sent to me. This was a time of great suspense. I was impatient to get on my uniform and see how it looked, and probably wanted my old school-mates, particularly the girls, to see me in it.

The conceit was knocked out of me by two little circumstances that happened soon after the arrival of the clothes, which gave me a distaste for military uniform that I never recovered from. Soon after the arrival of the suit I donned it, and put off for Cincinnati on horseback. While I was riding along a street of that city, imagining that every one was looking at me, with a feeling akin to mine when I first saw General Scott, a little urchin, bareheaded, barefooted, with dirty and ragged pants held up by a single gallows—that's what suspenders were called then—and a shirt that had not seen a wash-tub for weeks, turned to me and cried: "Soldier! will you work? No, sir—ee; I'll sell my shirt first!!" The horse trade and its dire consequences were recalled to mind.

The other circumstance occurred at home. Opposite our house in Bethel stood the old stage tavern where "man and beast" found accommodation. The stable-man was rather dissipated, but possessed of some humor. On my return I found him parading the streets, and attending in the stable, barefooted, but in a pair of sky-blue nankeen pantaloons—just the color of my uniform trousers—with a strip of white cotton sheeting sewed down the outside seams in imitation of mine. The joke was a huge one in the mind of many of the people, and was much enjoyed by them; but I did not appreciate it so highly.

During the remainder of my leave of absence, my time was spent in visiting friends in Georgetown and Cincinnati, and occasionally other towns in that part of the State.

Chapter III.

ON THE 30th of September I reported for duty at Jefferson Barracks, St. Louis, with the 4th United States infantry. It was the largest military post in the country at that time, being garrisoned by sixteen companies of infantry, eight of the 3d regiment, the remainder of the 4th. Colonel Steven Kearney, one of the ablest officers of the day, commanded the post, and under him discipline was kept at a high standard, but without vexatious rules or regulations. Every drill and roll-call had to be attended, but in the intervals officers were permitted to enjoy themselves, leaving the garrison, and going where they pleased, without making written application to state where they were going for how long, etc., so that they were back for their next duty. It did seem to me, in my early army days, that too many of the older officers, when they came to command posts, made it a study to think what orders they could publish to annoy their subordinates and render them uncomfortable. I noticed, however, a few years later, when the Mexican war broke out, that most of this class of officers discovered they were possessed of disabilities which entirely incapacitated them for active field service. They had the moral courage to proclaim it, too. They were right; but they did not always give their disease the right name.

At West Point I had a class-mate—in the last year of our studies he was room-mate also—F. T. Dent, whose family resided some five miles west of Jefferson Barracks. Two of his unmarried brothers were living at home at that time, and as I had taken with me from Ohio, my horse, saddle and bridle, I soon found my way out to White Haven, the name of the Dent estate. As I found the family congenial my visits became frequent. There were at home, besides the young men, two daughters, one a school miss of fifteen, the other a girl of eight or nine. There was still an older daughter of seventeen, who had been spending several years at boarding-school in St. Louis, but who, though through school, had not yet returned home. She was spending the winter in the city with connections, the family of Colonel John O'Fallon, well known in St. Louis. In February she returned to her country home. After that I do not know but my visits became more frequent; they certainly did become more enjoyable. We would often take walks, or go on horseback to visit the neighbors, until I became quite well acquainted in that vicinity. Sometimes one of the brothers would accompany us, sometimes one of the younger sisters. If the 4th infantry had remained at Jefferson Barracks it is possible, even probable, that this life might have continued for some years without my finding out that there was anything serious the matter with me; but in the following May a circumstance occurred which developed my sentiment so palpably that there was no mistaking it.

The annexation of Texas was at this time the subject of violent discussion in Congress, in the press, and by individuals. The administration of President Tyler, then in power, was making the most strenuous efforts to effect the annexation, which was, indeed, the great and absorbing question of the day. During these discussions the greater part of the single rifle regiment in the army—the 2d dragoons, which had been dismounted a year or two before, and designated "Dismounted Rifles"—was stationed at Fort Jessup, Louisiana, some twenty-five miles east of the Texas line, to observe the frontier. About the 1st of May the 3d infantry was ordered from Jefferson Barracks to Louisiana, to go into camp in the neighborhood of Fort Jessup, and there await further orders. The troops were embarked on steamers and were on their way down the Mississippi within a few days after the receipt of this order. About the time they started I obtained a leave of absence for twenty days to go to Ohio to visit my parents. I was obliged to go to St. Louis to take a steamer for Louisville or Cincinnati, or the first steamer going up the Ohio River to any point. Before I left St. Louis orders were received at Jefferson Barracks for the 4th infantry to follow the 3d. A messenger was sent after me to stop my leaving; but before he could reach me I was off, totally ignorant of these events. A day or two after my arrival at Bethel I received a letter from a class-mate and fellow lieutenant in the 4th, informing me of the circumstances related above, and advising me not to open any letter post marked St. Louis or Jefferson Barracks, until the expiration of my leave, and saying that he would pack up my things and take them along for me. His advice was not necessary, for no other letter was sent to me. I now discovered that I was exceedingly anxious to get back to Jefferson Barracks, and I understood the reason without explanation from any one. My leave of absence required me to report for duty, at Jefferson Barracks, at the end of twenty days. I knew my regiment had gone up the Red River, but I was not disposed to break the letter of my leave; besides, if I had proceeded to Louisiana direct, I could not have reached there until after the expiration of my leave. Accordingly, at the end of the twenty days, I reported for duty to Lieutenant Ewell, commanding at Jefferson Barracks, handing him at the same time my leave of absence. After noticing the phraseology of the order—leaves of absence were generally worded, "at the end of which time he will report for duty with his proper command"—he said he would give me an order to join my regiment in Louisiana. I then asked for a few days' leave before starting, which he readily granted. This was the same Ewell who acquired considerable reputation as a Confederate general during the rebellion. He was a man much esteemed, and deservedly so, in the old army, and proved himself a gallant and efficient officer in two wars—both in my estimation unholy.

I immediately procured a horse and started for the country, taking no baggage with me, of course. There is an insignificant creek—the Gravois—between Jefferson Barracks and the place to which I was going, and at that day there was not a bridge over it from its source to its mouth. There is not water enough in the creek at ordinary stages to run a coffee mill, and at low water there is none running whatever. On this occasion it had been raining heavily, and, when the creek was reached, I found the banks full to overflowing, and the current rapid. I looked at it a moment to consider what to do. One of my superstitions had always been when I started to go any where, or to do anything, not to turn back, or stop until the thing intended was accomplished. I have frequently started to go to places where I had never been and to which I did not know the way, depending upon making inquiries on the road, and if I got past the place without knowing it, instead of turning back, I would go on until a road was found turning in the right direction, take that, and come in by the other side. So I struck into the stream, and in an instant the horse was swimming and I being carried down by the current. I headed the horse towards the other bank and soon reached it, wet through and without other clothes on that side of the stream. I went on, however, to my destination and borrowed a dry suit from my—future—brother-in-law. We were not of the same size, but the clothes answered every purpose until I got more of my own.

Before I returned I mustered up courage to make known, in the most awkward manner imaginable, the discovery I had made on learning that the 4th infantry had been ordered away from Jefferson Barracks. The young lady afterwards admitted that she too, although until then she had never looked upon me other than as a visitor whose company was agreeable to her, had experienced a depression of spirits she could not account for when the regiment left. Before separating it was definitely understood that at a convenient time we would join our fortunes, and not let the removal of a regiment trouble us. This was in May, 1844. It was the 22d of August, 1848, before the fulfilment of this agreement. My duties kept me on the frontier of Louisiana with the Army of Observation during the pendency of Annexation; and afterwards I was absent through the war with Mexico, provoked by the action of the army, if not by the annexation itself. During that time there was a constant correspondence between Miss Dent and myself, but we only met once in the period of four years and three months. In May, 1845, I procured a leave for twenty days, visited St. Louis, and obtained the consent of the parents for the union, which had not been asked for before.

As already stated, it was never my intention to remain in the army long, but to prepare myself for a professorship in some college. Accordingly, soon after I was settled at Jefferson Barracks, I wrote a letter to Professor Church—Professor of Mathematics at West Point—requesting him to ask my designation as his assistant, when next a detail had to be made. Assistant professors at West Point are all officers of the army, supposed to be selected for their special fitness for the particular branch of study they are assigned to teach. The answer from Professor Church was entirely satisfactory, and no doubt I should have been detailed a year or two later but for the Mexican War coming on. Accordingly I laid out for myself a course of studies to be pursued in garrison, with regularity, if not persistency. I reviewed my West Point course of mathematics during the seven months at Jefferson Barracks, and read many valuable historical works, besides an occasional novel. To help my memory I kept a book in which I would write up, from time to time, my recollections of all I had read since last posting it. When the regiment was ordered away, I being absent at the time, my effects were packed up by Lieutenant Haslett, of the 4th infantry, and taken along. I never saw my journal after, nor did I ever keep another, except for a portion of the time while travelling abroad. Often since a fear has crossed my mind lest that book might turn up yet, and fall into the hands of some malicious person who would publish it. I know its appearance would cause me as much heart-burning as my youthful horse-trade, or the later rebuke for wearing uniform clothes.

The 3d infantry had selected camping grounds on the reservation at Fort Jessup, about midway between the Red River and the Sabine. Our orders required us to go into camp in the same neighborhood, and await further instructions. Those authorized to do so selected a place in the pine woods, between the old town of Natchitoches and Grand Ecore, about three miles from each, and on high ground back from the river. The place was given the name of Camp Salubrity, and proved entitled to it. The camp was on a high, sandy, pine ridge, with spring branches in the valley, in front and rear. The springs furnished an abundance of cool, pure water, and the ridge was above the flight of mosquitoes, which abound in that region in great multitudes and of great voracity. In the valley they swarmed in myriads, but never came to the summit of the ridge. The regiment occupied this camp six months before the first death occurred, and that was caused by an accident.

There was no intimation given that the removal of the 3d and 4th regiments of infantry to the western border of Louisiana was occasioned in any way by the prospective annexation of Texas, but it was generally understood that such was the case. Ostensibly we were intended to prevent filibustering into Texas, but really as a menace to Mexico in case she appeared to contemplate war. Generally the officers of the army were indifferent whether the annexation was consummated or not; but not so all of them. For myself, I was bitterly opposed to the measure, and to this day regard the war, which resulted, as one of the most unjust ever waged by a stronger against a weaker nation. It was an instance of a republic following the bad example of European monarchies, in not considering justice in their desire to acquire additional territory.

Texas was originally a state belonging to the republic of Mexico. It extended from the Sabine River on the east to the Rio Grande on the west, and from the Gulf of Mexico on the south and east to the territory of the United States and New Mexico—another Mexican state at that time—on the north and west. An empire in territory, it had but a very sparse population, until settled by Americans who had received authority from Mexico to colonize. These colonists paid very little attention to the supreme government, and introduced slavery into the state almost from the start, though the constitution of Mexico did not, nor does it now, sanction that institution. Soon they set up an independent government of their own, and war existed, between Texas and Mexico, in name from that time until 1836, when active hostilities very nearly ceased upon the capture of Santa Anna, the Mexican President. Before long, however, the same people—who with permission of Mexico had colonized Texas, and afterwards set up slavery there, and then seceded as soon as they felt strong enough to do so—offered themselves and the State to the United States, and in 1845 their offer was accepted. The occupation, separation and annexation were, from the inception of the movement to its final consummation, a conspiracy to acquire territory out of which slave states might be formed for the American Union.

Even if the annexation itself could be justified, the manner in which the subsequent war was forced upon Mexico cannot. The fact is, annexationists wanted more territory than they could possibly lay any claim to, as part of the new acquisition

Texas, as an independent State, never had exercised jurisdiction over the territory between the Nueces River and the Rio Grande. Mexico had never recognized the independence of Texas, and maintained that, even if independent, the State had no claim south of the Nueces. I am aware that a treaty, made by the Texans with Santa Anna while he was under duress, ceded all the territory between the Nueces and the Rio Grande; but he was a prisoner of war when the treaty was made, and his life was in jeopardy. He knew, too, that he deserved execution at the hands of the Texans, if they should ever capture him. The Texans, if they had taken his life, would have only followed the example set by Santa Anna himself a few years before, when he executed the entire garrison of the Alamo and the villagers of Goliad.

In taking military possession of Texas after annexation, the army of occupation, under General Taylor, was directed to occupy the disputed territory. The army did not stop at the Nueces and offer to negotiate for a settlement of the boundary question, but went beyond, apparently in order to force Mexico to initiate war. It is to the credit of the American nation, however, that after conquering Mexico, and while practically holding the country in our possession, so that we could have retained the whole of it, or made any terms we chose, we paid a round sum for the additional territory taken; more than it was worth, or was likely to be, to Mexico. To us it was an empire and of incalculable value; but it might have been obtained by other means. The Southern rebellion was largely the outgrowth of the Mexican war. Nations, like individuals, are punished for their transgressions. We got our punishment in the most sanguinary and expensive war of modern times.

The 4th infantry went into camp at Salubrity in the month of May, 1844, with instructions, as I have said, to await further orders. At first, officers and men occupied ordinary tents. As the summer heat increased these were covered by sheds to break the rays of the sun. The summer was whiled away in social enjoyments among the officers, in visiting those stationed at, and near, Fort Jessup, twenty-five miles away, visiting the planters on the Red River, and the citizens of Natchitoches and Grand Ecore. There was much pleasant intercourse between the inhabitants and the officers of the army. I retain very agreeable recollections of my stay at Camp Salubrity, and of the acquaintances made there, and no doubt my feeling is shared by the few officers living who were there at the time. I can call to mind only two officers of the 4th infantry, besides myself, who were at Camp Salubrity with the regiment, who are now alive.

With a war in prospect, and belonging to a regiment that had an unusual number of officers detailed on special duty away from the regiment, my hopes of being ordered to West Point as instructor vanished. At the time of which I now write, officers in the quartermaster's, commissary's and adjutant-general's departments were appointed from the line of the army, and did not vacate their regimental commissions until their regimental and staff commissions were for the same grades. Generally lieutenants were appointed to captaincies to fill vacancies in the staff corps. If they should reach a captaincy in the line before they arrived at a majority in the staff, they would elect which commission they would retain. In the 4th infantry, in 1844, at least six line officers were on duty in the staff, and therefore permanently detached from the regiment. Under these circumstances I gave up everything like a special course of reading, and only read thereafter for my own amusement, and not very much for that, until the war was over. I kept a horse and rode, and staid out of doors most of the time by day, and entirely recovered from the cough which I had carried from West Point, and from all indications of consumption. I have often thought that my life was saved, and my health restored, by exercise and exposure, enforced by an administrative act, and a war, both of which I disapproved.

As summer wore away, and cool days and colder nights came upon us, the tents we were occupying ceased to afford comfortable quarters; and "further orders" not reaching us, we began to look about to remedy the hardship. Men were put to work getting out timber to build huts, and in a very short time all were comfortably housed—privates as well as officers. The outlay by the government in accomplishing this was nothing, or nearly nothing. The winter was spent more agreeably than the summer had been. There were occasional parties given by the planters along the "coast"—as the bottom lands on the Red River were called. The climate was delightful.

Near the close of the short session of Congress of 1844–5, the bill for the annexation of Texas to the United States was passed. It reached President Tyler on the 1st of March, 1845, and promptly received his approval. When the news reached us we began to look again for "further orders." They did not arrive promptly, and on the 1st of May following I asked and obtained a leave of absence for twenty days, for the purpose of visiting St. Louis. The object of this visit has been before stated.

Early in July the long expected orders were received, but they only took the regiment to New Orleans Barracks. We reached there before the middle of the month, and again waited weeks for still further orders. The yellow fever was raging in New Orleans during the time we remained there, and the streets of the city had the appearance of a continuous well-observed Sunday. I recollect but one occasion when this observance seemed to be broken by the inhabitants. One morning about daylight I happened to be awake, and, hearing the discharge of a rifle not far off, I looked out to ascertain where the sound came from. I observed a couple of clusters of men near by, and learned afterwards that "it was nothing; only a couple of gentlemen deciding a difference of opinion with rifles, at twenty paces." I do not remember if either was killed, or even hurt, but no doubt the question of difference was settled satisfactorily, and "honorably," in the estimation of the parties engaged. I do not believe I ever would have the courage to fight a duel. If any man should wrong me to the extent of my being willing to kill him, I would not be willing to give him the choice of weapons with which it should be done, and of the time, place and distance separating us, when I executed him. If I should do another such a wrong as to justify him in killing me, I would make any reasonable atonement within my power, if convinced of the wrong done. I place my opposition to duelling on higher grounds than any here stated. No doubt a majority of the duels fought have been for want of moral courage on the part of those engaged to decline.

At Camp Salubrity, and when we went to New Orleans Barracks, the 4th infantry was commanded by Colonel Vose, then an old gentleman who had not commanded on drill for a number of years. He was not a man to discover infirmity in the presence of danger. It now appeared that war was imminent, and he felt it was his duty to brush up his tactics. Accordingly, when we got settled down at our new post, he took command of the regiment at a battalion drill. Only two or three evolutions had been gone through when he dismissed the battalion, and, turning to go to his own quarters, dropped dead. He had not been complaining of ill health, but no doubt died of heart disease. He was a most estimable man, of exemplary habits, and by no means the author of his own disease.

Chapter IV.

CORPUS CHRISTI — MEXICAN SMUGGLING — SPANISH RULE
IN MEXICO — SUPPLYING TRANSPORTATION.

EARLY IN SEPTEMBER the regiment left New Orleans for Corpus Christi, now in Texas. Ocean steamers were not then common, and the passage was made in sailing vessels. At that time there was not more than three feet of water in the channel at the outlet of Corpus Christi Bay; the debarkation, therefore, had to take place by small steamers, and at an island in the channel called Shell Island, the ships anchoring some miles out from shore. This made the work slow, and as the army was only supplied with one or two steamers, it took a number of days to effect the landing of a single regiment with its stores, camp and garrison equipage, etc. There happened to be pleasant weather while this was going on, but the land-swell was so great that when the ship and steamer were on opposite sides of the same wave they would be at considerable distance apart. The men and baggage were let down to a point higher than the lower deck of the steamer, and when ship and steamer got into the trough between the waves, and were close together, the load would be drawn over the steamer and rapidly run down until it rested on the deck.

After I had gone ashore, and had been on guard several days at Shell Island, quite six miles from the ship, I had occasion for some reason or other to return on board. While on the *Suviah* — I think that was the name of our vessel — I heard a tremendous racket at the other end of the ship, and much and excited sailor language, such as "damn your eyes," etc. In a moment or two the captain, who was an excitable little man, dying with consumption, and not weighing much over a hundred pounds, came running out, carrying a sabre near-ly as large and as heavy as he was, and crying that his men had mutinied. It was necessary to sustain the captain with-out question, and in a few minutes all the sailors charged with mutiny were in irons. I rather felt for a time a wish that I had not gone aboard just then. As the men charged with mutiny submitted to being placed in irons without resistance,

I always doubted if they knew that they had mutinied until they were told.

By the time I was ready to leave the ship again I thought I had learned enough of the working of the double and single pulley, by which passengers were let down from the upper deck of the ship to the steamer below, and determined to let myself down without assistance. Without saying anything of my intentions to any one, I mounted the railing, and taking hold of the centre rope, just below the upper block, I put one foot on the hook below the lower block, and stepped off. Just as I did so some one called out "hold on." It was too late. I tried to "hold on" with all my might, but my heels went up, and my head went down so rapidly that my hold broke, and I plunged head foremost into the water, some twenty-five feet below, with such velocity that it seemed to me I never would stop. When I came to the surface again, being a fair swimmer, and not having lost my presence of mind, I swam around until a bucket was let down for me, and I was drawn up without a scratch or injury. I do not believe there was a man on board who sympathized with me in the least when they found me uninjured. I rather enjoyed the joke myself. The captain of the *Suviah* died of his disease a few months later, and I believe before the mutineers were tried. I hope they got clear, because, as before stated, I always thought the mutiny was all in the brain of a very weak and sick man.

After reaching shore, or Shell Island, the labor of getting to Corpus Christi was slow and tedious. There was, if my memory serves me, but one small steamer to transport troops and baggage when the 4th infantry arrived. Others were procured later. The distance from Shell Island to Corpus Christi was some sixteen or eighteen miles. The channel to the bay was so shallow that the steamer, small as it was, had to be dragged over the bottom when loaded. Not more than one trip a day could be effected. Later this was remedied, by deepening the channel and increasing the number of vessels suitable to its navigation.

Corpus Christi is near the head of the bay of the same name, formed by the entrance of the Nueces River into tidewater, and is on the west bank of that bay. At the time of its first occupancy by United States troops there was a small

Mexican hamlet there, containing probably less than one hundred souls. There was, in addition, a small American trading post, at which goods were sold to Mexican smugglers. All goods were put up in compact packages of about one hundred pounds each, suitable for loading on pack mules. Two of these packages made a load for an ordinary Mexican mule, and three for the larger ones. The bulk of the trade was in leaf tobacco, and domestic cotton-cloths and calicoes. The Mexicans had, before the arrival of the army, but little to offer in exchange except silver. The trade in tobacco was enormous, considering the population to be supplied. Almost every Mexican above the age of ten years, and many much younger, smoked the cigarette. Nearly every Mexican carried a pouch of leaf tobacco, powdered by rolling in the hands, and a roll of corn husks to make wrappers. The cigarettes were made by the smokers as they used them.

Up to the time of which I write, and for years afterwards—I think until the administration of President Juarez—the cultivation, manufacture and sale of tobacco constituted a government monopoly, and paid the bulk of the revenue collected from internal sources. The price was enormously high, and made successful smuggling very profitable. The difficulty of obtaining tobacco is probably the reason why everybody, male and female, used it at that time. I know from my own experience that when I was at West Point, the fact that tobacco, in every form, was prohibited, and the mere possession of the weed severely punished, made the majority of the cadets, myself included, try to acquire the habit of using it. I failed utterly at the time and for many years afterward; but the majority accomplished the object of their youthful ambition.

Under Spanish rule Mexico was prohibited from producing anything that the mother-country could supply. This rule excluded the cultivation of the grape, olive and many other articles to which the soil and climate were well adapted. The country was governed for "revenue only;" and tobacco, which cannot be raised in Spain, but is indigenous to Mexico, offered a fine instrumentality for securing this prime object of government. The native population had been in the habit of using "the weed" from a period, back of any recorded history of this continent. Bad habits—if not restrained by law or public opinion—spread more rapidly and universally than good ones, and the Spanish colonists adopted the use of tobacco almost as generally as the natives. Spain, therefore, in order to secure the largest revenue from this source, prohibited the cultivation, except in specified localities—and in these places farmed out the privilege at a very high price. The tobacco when raised could only be sold to the government, and the price to the consumer was limited only by the avarice of the authorities, and the capacity of the people to pay.

All laws for the government of the country were enacted in Spain, and the officers for their execution were appointed by the Crown, and sent out to the New El Dorado. The Mexicans had been brought up ignorant of how to legislate or how to rule. When they gained their independence, after many years of war, it was the most natural thing in the world that they should adopt as their own the laws then in existence. The only change was, that Mexico became her own executor of the laws and the recipient of the revenues. The tobacco tax, yielding so large a revenue under the law as it stood, was one of the last, if not the very last, of the obnoxious imposts to be repealed. Now, the citizens are allowed to cultivate any crops the soil will yield. Tobacco is cheap, and every quality can be produced. Its use is by no means so general as when I first visited the country.

Gradually the "Army of Occupation" assembled at Corpus Christi. When it was all together it consisted of seven companies of the 2d regiment of dragoons, four companies of light artillery, five regiments of infantry—the 3d, 4th, 5th, 7th and 8th—and one regiment of artillery acting as infantry—not more than three thousand men in all. General Zachary Taylor commanded the whole. There were troops enough in one body to establish a drill and discipline sufficient to fit men and officers for all they were capable of in case of battle. The rank and file were composed of men who had enlisted in time of peace, to serve for seven dollars a month, and were necessarily inferior as material to the average volunteers enlisted later in the war expressly to fight, and also to the volunteers in the war for the preservation of the Union. The men engaged in the Mexican war were brave, and the officers of the regular army, from highest to lowest, were educated in their profession. A more efficient army for its number and armament, I do not believe ever fought a battle than the one commanded by General Taylor in his first two engagements on Mexican—or Texan soil.

The presence of United States troops on the edge of the disputed territory furthest from the Mexican settlements, was not sufficient to provoke hostilities. We were sent to provoke a fight, but it was essential that Mexico should commence it. It was very doubtful whether Congress would declare war; but if Mexico should attack our troops, the Executive could announce, "Whereas, war exists by the acts of, etc.," and prosecute the contest with vigor. Once initiated there were but few public men who would have the courage to oppose it. Experience proves that the man who obstructs a war in which his nation is engaged, no matter whether right or wrong, occupies no enviable place in life or history. Better for him, individually, to advocate "war, pestilence, and famine," than to act as obstructionist to a war already begun. The history of the defeated rebel will be honorable hereafter, compared with that of the Northern man who aided him by conspiring against his government while protected by it. The most favorable posthumous history the stay-at-home traitor can hope for is—oblivion.

Mexico showing no willingness to come to the Nueces to drive the invaders from her soil, it became necessary for the "invaders" to approach to within a convenient distance to be struck. Accordingly, preparations were begun for moving the army to the Rio Grande, to a point near Matamoras. It was desirable to occupy a position near the largest centre of population possible to reach, without absolutely invading territory to which we set up no claim whatever.

The distance from Corpus Christi to Matamoras is about one hundred and fifty miles. The country does not abound in fresh water, and the length of the marches had to be regulated by the distance between water supplies. Besides the streams, there were occasional pools, filled during the rainy season, some probably made by the traders, who travelled constantly between Corpus Christi and the Rio Grande, and some by the buffalo. There was not at that time a single habitation, cultivated field, or herd of domestic animals, between Corpus Christi and Matamoras. It was necessary, therefore, to have a wagon train sufficiently large to transport the camp and garrison equipage, officers' baggage, rations for the army, and part rations of grain for the artillery horses and all the animals taken from the north, where they had been accustomed to having their forage furnished them. The army was but indifferently supplied with transportation. Wagons and harness could easily be supplied from the north; but mules and horses could not so readily be brought. The American traders and Mexican smugglers came to the relief. Contracts were made for mules at from eight to eleven dollars each. The smugglers furnished the animals, and took their pay in goods of the description before mentioned. I doubt whether the Mexicans received in value from the traders five dollars per head for the animals they furnished, and still more, whether they paid anything but their own time in procuring them. Such is trade; such is war. The government paid in hard cash to the contractor the stipulated price.

Between the Rio Grande and the Nueces there was at that time a large band of wild horses feeding; as numerous, probably, as the band of buffalo roaming further north was before its rapid extermination commenced. The Mexicans used to capture these in large numbers and bring them into the American settlements and sell them. A picked animal could be purchased at from eight to twelve dollars, but taken at wholesale, they could be bought for thirty-six dollars a dozen. Some of these were purchased for the army, and answered a most useful purpose. The horses were generally very strong, formed much like the Norman horse, and with very heavy manes and tails. A number of officers supplied themselves with these, and they generally rendered as useful service as the northern animal; in fact they were much better when grazing was the only means of supplying forage.

There was no need for haste, and some months were consumed in the necessary preparations for a move. In the meantime the army was engaged in all the duties pertaining to the officer and the soldier. Twice, that I remember, small trains were sent from Corpus Christi, with cavalry escorts, to San Antonio and Austin, with paymasters and funds to pay off small detachments of troops stationed at those places. General Taylor encouraged officers to accompany these expeditions. I accompanied one of them in December, 1845. The distance from Corpus Christi to San Antonio was then computed at one hundred and fifty miles. Now that roads exist it is probably less. From San Antonio to Austin we computed the distance at one hundred and ten miles, and from the latter place back to Corpus Christi at over two hundred miles. I know the distance now from San Antonio to Austin is but little over eighty miles, so that our computation was probably too high.

There was not at the time an individual living between Corpus Christi and San Antonio until within about thirty miles of the latter point, where there were a few scattering Mexican settlements along the San Antonio River. The people in at least one of these hamlets lived underground for protection against the Indians. The country abounded in game, such as deer and antelope, with abundance of wild turkeys along the streams and where there were nut-bearing woods. On the Nueces, about twenty-five miles up from Corpus Christi, were a few log cabins, the remains of a town called San Patricio, but the inhabitants had all been massacred by the Indians, or driven away.

San Antonio was about equally divided in population between Americans and Mexicans. From there to Austin there was not a single residence except at New Braunfels, on the Guadalupe River. At that point was a settlement of Germans who had only that year come into the State. At all events they were living in small huts, about such as soldiers would hastily construct for temporary occupation. From Austin to Corpus Christi there was only a small settlement at Bastrop, with a few farms along the Colorado River; but after leaving that, there were no settlements except the home of one man, with one female slave, at the old town of Goliad. Some of the houses were still standing. Goliad had been quite a village for the period and region, but some years before there had been a Mexican massacre, in which every inhabitant had been killed or driven away. This, with the massacre of the prisoners in the Alamo, San Antonio, about the same time, more than three hundred men in all, furnished the strongest justification the Texans had for carrying on the war with so much cruelty.

In fact, from that time until the Mexican war, the hostilities between Texans and Mexicans was so great that neither was safe in the neighborhood of the other who might be in superior numbers or possessed of superior arms. The man we found living there seemed like an old friend; he had come from near Fort Jessup, Louisiana, where the officers of the 3d and 4th infantry and the 2d dragoons had known him and his family. He had emigrated in advance of his family to build up a home for them.

Chapter V.

TRIP TO AUSTIN—PROMOTION TO FULL SECOND
LIEUTENANT—ARMY OF OCCUPATION.

WHEN OUR PARTY left Corpus Christi it was quite large, including the cavalry escort, Paymaster, Major Dix, his clerk and the officers who, like myself, were simply on leave; but all the officers on leave, except Lieutenant Benjamin— afterwards killed in the valley of Mexico—Lieutenant, now General, Augur, and myself, concluded to spend their allotted time at San Antonio and return from there. We were all to be back at Corpus Christi by the end of the month. The paymaster was detained in Austin so long that, if we had waited for him, we would have exceeded our leave. We concluded, therefore, to start back at once with the animals we had, and having to rely principally on grass for their food, it was a good six days' journey. We had to sleep on the prairie every night, except at Goliad, and possibly one night on the Colorado, without shelter and with only such food as we carried with us, and prepared ourselves. The journey was hazardous on account of Indians, and there were white men in Texas whom I would not have cared to meet in a secluded place. Lieutenant Augur was taken seriously sick before we reached Goliad and at a distance from any habitation. To add to the complication, his horse—a mustang that had probably been captured from the band of wild horses before alluded to, and of undoubted longevity at his capture—gave out. It was absolutely necessary to get forward to Goliad to find a shelter for our sick companion. By dint of patience and exceedingly slow movements, Goliad was at last reached, and a shelter and bed secured for our patient. We remained over a day, hoping that Augur might recover sufficiently to resume his travels. He did not, however, and knowing that Major Dix would be along in a few days, with his wagon-train, now empty, and escort, we arranged with our Louisiana friend to take the best of care of the sick lieutenant until thus relieved, and went on.

I had never been a sportsman in my life; had scarcely ever gone in search of game, and rarely seen any when looking for it. On this trip there was no minute of time while travelling between San Patricio and the settlements on the San Antonio River, from San Antonio to Austin, and again from the Colorado River back to San Patricio, when deer or antelope could not be seen in great numbers. Each officer carried a shot-gun, and every evening, after going into camp, some would go out and soon return with venison and wild turkeys enough for the entire camp. I, however, never went out, and had no occasion to fire my gun; except, being detained over a day at Goliad, Benjamin and I concluded to go down to the creek—which was fringed with timber, much of it the pecan—and bring back a few turkeys. We had scarcely reached the edge of the timber when I heard the flutter of wings overhead, and in an instant I saw two or three turkeys flying away. These were soon followed by more, then more, and more, until a flock of twenty or thirty had left from just over my head. All this time I stood watching the turkeys to see where they flew—with my gun on my shoulder, and never once thought of levelling it at the birds. When I had time to reflect upon the matter, I came to the conclusion that as a sportsman I was a failure, and went back to the house. Benjamin remained out, and got as many turkeys as he wanted to carry back.

After the second night at Goliad, Benjamin and I started to make the remainder of the journey alone. We reached Corpus Christi just in time to avoid "absence without leave." We met no one—not even an Indian—during the remainder of our journey, except at San Patricio. A new settlement had been started there in our absence of three weeks, induced possibly by the fact that there were houses already built, while the proximity of troops gave protection against the Indians. On the evening of the first day out from Goliad we heard the most unearthly howling of wolves, directly in our front. The prairie grass was tall and we could not see the beasts, but the sound indicated that they were near. To my ear it appeared that there must have been enough of them to devour our party, horses and all, at a single meal. The part of Ohio that I hailed from was not thickly settled, but wolves had been driven out long before I left. Benjamin was from Indiana, still less populated, where the wolf yet roamed over the prairies.

He understood the nature of the animal and the capacity of a few to make believe there was an unlimited number of them. He kept on towards the noise, unmoved. I followed in his trail, lacking moral courage to turn back and join our sick companion. I have no doubt that if Benjamin had proposed returning to Goliad, I would not only have "seconded the motion" but have suggested that it was very hard-hearted in us to leave Augur sick there in the first place; but Benjamin did not propose turning back. When he did speak it was to ask: "Grant, how many wolves do you think there are in that pack?" Knowing where he was from, and suspecting that he thought I would over-estimate the number, I determined to show my acquaintance with the animal by putting the estimate below what possibly could be correct, and answered: "Oh, about twenty," very indifferently. He smiled and rode on. In a minute we were close upon them, and before they saw us. There were just *two* of them. Seated upon their haunches, with their mouths close together, they had made all the noise we had been hearing for the past ten minutes. I have often thought of this incident since when I have heard the noise of a few disappointed politicians who had deserted their associates. There are always more of them before they are counted.

A week or two before leaving Corpus Christi on this trip, I had been promoted from brevet second-lieutenant, 4th infantry, to full second-lieutenant, 7th infantry. Frank Gardner,* of the 7th, was promoted to the 4th in the same orders. We immediately made application to be transferred, so as to get back to our old regiments. On my return, I found that our application had been approved at Washington. While in the 7th infantry I was in the company of Captain Holmes, afterwards a Lieutenant-general in the Confederate army. I never came in contact with him in the war of the Rebellion, nor did he render any very conspicuous service in his high rank. My transfer carried me to the company of Captain McCall, who resigned from the army after the Mexican war and settled in Philadelphia. He was prompt, however, to volunteer when the rebellion broke out, and soon rose to the rank of major-

*Afterwards General Gardner, C.S.A.

general in the Union army. I was not fortunate enough to meet him after he resigned. In the old army he was esteemed very highly as a soldier and gentleman. Our relations were always most pleasant.

The preparations at Corpus Christi for an advance progressed as rapidly in the absence of some twenty or more lieutenants as if we had been there. The principal business consisted in securing mules, and getting them broken to harness. The process was slow but amusing. The animals sold to the government were all young and unbroken, even to the saddle, and were quite as wild as the wild horses of the prairie. Usually a number would be brought in by a company of Mexicans, partners in the delivery. The mules were first driven into a stockade, called a *corral*, inclosing an acre or more of ground. The Mexicans,—who were all experienced in throwing the lasso,—would go into the *corral* on horseback, with their lassos attached to the pommels of their saddles. Soldiers detailed as teamsters and blacksmiths would also enter the *corral*, the former with ropes to serve as halters, the latter with branding irons and a fire to keep the irons heated. A lasso was then thrown over the neck of a mule, when he would immediately go to the length of his tether, first one end, then the other in the air. While he was thus plunging and gyrating, another lasso would be thrown by another Mexican, catching the animal by a fore-foot. This would bring the mule to the ground, when he was seized and held by the teamsters while the blacksmith put upon him, with hot irons, the initials "U. S." Ropes were then put about the neck, with a slip-noose which would tighten around the throat if pulled. With a man on each side holding these ropes, the mule was released from his other bindings and allowed to rise. With more or less difficulty he would be conducted to a picket rope outside and fastened there. The delivery of that mule was then complete. This process was gone through with every mule and wild horse with the army of occupation.

The method of breaking them was less cruel and much more amusing. It is a well-known fact that where domestic animals are used for specific purposes from generation to generation, the descendants are easily, as a rule, subdued to the same uses. At that time in Northern Mexico the mule, or his ancestors, the horse and the ass, was seldom used except for the saddle or pack. At all events the Corpus Christi mule resisted the new use to which he was being put. The treatment he was subjected to in order to overcome his prejudices was summary and effective.

The soldiers were principally foreigners who had enlisted in our large cities, and, with the exception of a chance drayman among them, it is not probable that any of the men who reported themselves as competent teamsters had ever driven a mule-team in their lives, or indeed that many had had any previous experience in driving any animal whatever to harness. Numbers together can accomplish what twice their number acting individually could not perform. Five mules were allotted to each wagon. A teamster would select at the picket rope five animals of nearly the same color and general appearance for his team. With a full corps of assistants, other teamsters, he would then proceed to get his mules together. In two's the men would approach each animal selected, avoiding as far as possible its heels. Two ropes would be put about the neck of each animal, with a slip noose, so that he could be choked if too unruly. They were then led out, harnessed by force and hitched to the wagon in the position they had to keep ever after. Two men remained on either side of the leader, with the lassos about its neck, and one man retained the same restraining influence over each of the others. All being ready, the hold would be slackened and the team started. The first motion was generally five mules in the air at one time, backs bowed, hind feet extended to the rear. After repeating this movement a few times the leaders would start to run. This would bring the breeching tight against the mules at the wheels, which these last seemed to regard as a most unwarrantable attempt at coercion and would resist by taking a seat, sometimes going so far as to lie down. In time all were broken in to do their duty submissively if not cheerfully, but there never was a time during the war when it was safe to let a Mexican mule get entirely loose. Their drivers were all teamsters by the time they got through.

I recollect one case of a mule that had worked in a team under the saddle, not only for some time at Corpus Christi, where he was broken, but all the way to the point opposite

Matamoras, then to Camargo, where he got loose from his fastenings during the night. He did not run away at first, but staid in the neighborhood for a day or two, coming up sometimes to the feed trough even; but on the approach of the teamster he always got out of the way. At last, growing tired of the constant effort to catch him, he disappeared altogether. Nothing short of a Mexican with his lasso could have caught him. Regulations would not have warranted the expenditure of a dollar in hiring a man with a lasso to catch that mule; but they did allow the expenditure "of the mule," on a certificate that he had run away without any fault of the quartermaster on whose returns he was borne, and also the purchase of another to take his place. I am a competent witness, for I was regimental quartermaster at the time.

While at Corpus Christi all the officers who had a fancy for riding kept horses. The animals cost but little in the first instance, and when picketed they would get their living without any cost. I had three not long before the army moved, but a sad accident bereft me of them all at one time. A colored boy who gave them all the attention they got—besides looking after my tent and that of a class-mate and fellow-lieutenant and cooking for us, all for about eight dollars per month, was riding one to water and leading the other two. The led horses pulled him from his seat and all three ran away. They never were heard of afterwards. Shortly after that some one told Captain Bliss, General Taylor's Adjutant-General, of my misfortune. "Yes; I heard Grant lost five or six dollars' worth of horses the other day," he replied. That was a slander; they were broken to the saddle when I got them and cost nearly twenty dollars. I never suspected the colored boy of malicious intent in letting them get away, because, if they had not escaped, he could have had one of them to ride on the long march then in prospect.

Chapter VI.

A T LAST the preparations were complete and orders were issued for the advance to begin on the 8th of March. General Taylor had an army of not more than three thousand men. One battery, the siege guns and all the convalescent troops were sent on by water to Brazos Santiago, at the mouth of the Rio Grande. A guard was left back at Corpus Christi to look after public property and to take care of those who were too sick to be removed. The remainder of the army, probably not more than twenty-five hundred men, was divided into three brigades, with the cavalry independent. Colonel Twiggs, with seven companies of dragoons and a battery of light artillery, moved on the 8th. He was followed by the three infantry brigades, with a day's interval between the commands. Thus the rear brigade did not move from Corpus Christi until the 11th of March. In view of the immense bodies of men moved on the same day over narrow roads, through dense forests and across large streams, in our late war, it seems strange now that a body of less than three thousand men should have been broken into four columns, separated by a day's march.

General Taylor was opposed to anything like plundering by the troops, and in this instance, I doubt not, he looked upon the enemy as the aggrieved party and was not willing to injure them further than his instructions from Washington demanded. His orders to the troops enjoined scrupulous regard for the rights of all peaceable persons and the payment of the highest price for all supplies taken for the use of the army.

All officers of foot regiments who had horses were permitted to ride them on the march when it did not interfere with their military duties. As already related, having lost my "five or six dollars' worth of horses" but a short time before I determined not to get another, but to make the journey on foot. My company commander, Captain McCall, had two good American horses, of considerably more value in that country, where native horses were cheap, than they were in the States. He used one himself and wanted the other for his servant. He was quite anxious to know whether I did not intend to get me another horse before the march began. I told him No; I belonged to a foot regiment. I did not understand the object of his solicitude at the time, but, when we were about to start, he said: "There, Grant, is a horse for you." I found that he could not bear the idea of his servant riding on a long march while his lieutenant went a-foot. He had found a mustang, a three-year-old colt only recently captured, which had been purchased by one of the colored servants with the regiment for the sum of three dollars. It was probably the only horse at Corpus Christi that could have been purchased just then for any reasonable price. Five dollars, sixty-six and two-thirds per cent. advance, induced the owner to part with the mustang. I was sorry to take him, because I really felt that, belonging to a foot regiment, it was my duty to march with the men. But I saw the Captain's earnestness in the matter, and accepted the horse for the trip. The day we started was the first time the horse had ever been under saddle. I had, however, but little difficulty in breaking him, though for the first day there were frequent disagreements between us as to which way we should go, and sometimes whether we should go at all. At no time during the day could I choose exactly the part of the column I would march with; but after that, I had as tractable a horse as any with the army, and there was none that stood the trip better. He never ate a mouthful of food on the journey except the grass he could pick within the length of his picket rope.

A few days out from Corpus Christi, the immense herd of wild horses that ranged at that time between the Nueces and the Rio Grande was seen directly in advance of the head of the column and but a few miles off. It was the very band from which the horse I was riding had been captured but a few weeks before. The column was halted for a rest, and a number of officers, myself among them, rode out two or three miles to the right to see the extent of the herd. The country was a rolling prairie, and, from the higher ground, the vision was obstructed only by the earth's curvature. As far as the eye could reach to our right, the herd extended. To the left, it extended equally. There was no estimating the number of animals in it; I have no idea that they could all have been corralled in the State of Rhode Island, or Delaware, at one time. If they had been, they would have been so thick that the pasturage would have given out the first day. People who saw the Southern herd of buffalo, fifteen or twenty years ago, can appreciate the size of the Texas band of wild horses in 1846.

At the point where the army struck the Little Colorado River, the stream was quite wide and of sufficient depth for navigation. The water was brackish and the banks were fringed with timber. Here the whole army concentrated before attempting to cross. The army was not accompanied by a pontoon train, and at that time the troops were not instructed in bridge building. To add to the embarrassment of the situation, the army was here, for the first time, threatened with opposition. Buglers, concealed from our view by the brush on the opposite side, sounded the "assembly," and other military calls. Like the wolves before spoken of, they gave the impression that there was a large number of them and that, if the troops were in proportion to the noise, they were sufficient to devour General Taylor and his army. There were probably but few troops, and those engaged principally in watching the movements of the "invader." A few of our cavalry dashed in, and forded and swam the stream, and all opposition was soon dispersed. I do not remember that a single shot was fired.

The troops waded the stream, which was up to their necks in the deepest part. Teams were crossed by attaching a long rope to the end of the wagon tongue, passing it between the two swing mules and by the side of the leader, hitching his bridle as well as the bridle of the mules in rear to it, and carrying the end to men on the opposite shore. The bank down to the water was steep on both sides. A rope long enough to cross the river, therefore, was attached to the back axle of the wagon, and men behind would hold the rope to prevent the wagon "beating" the mules into the water. This latter rope also served the purpose of bringing the end of the forward one back, to be used over again. The water was deep enough for a short distance to swim the little Mexican mules which the army was then using, but they, and the wagons, were pulled through so fast by the men at the end of the rope ahead, that no time was left them to show their obstinacy. In this manner the artillery and transportation of the "army of occupation" crossed the Little Colorado River.

About the middle of the month of March the advance of the army reached the Rio Grande and went into camp near the banks of the river, opposite the city of Matamoras and almost under the guns of a small fort at the lower end of the town. There was not at that time a single habitation from Corpus Christi until the Rio Grande was reached.

The work of fortifying was commenced at once. The fort was laid out by the engineers, but the work was done by the soldiers under the supervision of their officers, the chief engineer retaining general directions. The Mexicans now became so incensed at our near approach that some of their troops crossed the river above us, and made it unsafe for small bodies of men to go far beyond the limits of camp. They captured two companies of dragoons, commanded by Captains Thornton and Hardee. The latter figured as a general in the late war, on the Confederate side, and was author of the tactics first used by both armies. Lieutenant Theodric Porter, of the 4th infantry, was killed while out with a small detachment; and Major Cross, the assistant quartermaster-general, had also been killed not far from camp.

There was no base of supplies nearer than Point Isabel, on the coast, north of the mouth of the Rio Grande and twenty-five miles away. The enemy, if the Mexicans could be called such at this time when no war had been declared, hovered about in such numbers that it was not safe to send a wagon train after supplies with any escort that could be spared. I have already said that General Taylor's whole command on the Rio Grande numbered less than three thousand men. He had, however, a few more troops at Point Isabel or Brazos Santiago. The supplies brought from Corpus Christi in wagons were running short. Work was therefore pushed with great vigor on the defences, to enable the minimum number of troops to hold the fort. All the men who could be employed, were kept at work from early dawn until darkness closed the labors of the day. With all this the fort was not completed until the supplies grew so short that further delay in obtaining more could not be thought of. By the latter part of April the work was in a partially defensible condition, and the 7th infantry, Major Jacob Brown commanding, was marched in to garrison it, with some few pieces of artillery. All the supplies on hand, with the exception of enough to carry the rest of the army to Point Isabel, were left with the garrison, and the march was commenced with the remainder of the command, every wagon being taken with the army. Early on the second day after starting the force reached its destination, without opposition from the Mexicans. There was some delay in getting supplies ashore from vessels at anchor in the open roadstead.

Chapter VII.

THE MEXICAN WAR—THE BATTLE OF PALO ALTO—THE
BATTLE OF RESACA DE LA PALMA—ARMY OF INVASION
—GENERAL TAYLOR—MOVEMENT ON CAMARGO.

WHILE GENERAL TAYLOR was away with the bulk of his
army, the little garrison up the river was besieged. As
we lay in our tents upon the sea-shore, the artillery at the fort
on the Rio Grande could be distinctly heard.

The war had begun.

There were no possible means of obtaining news from the
garrison, and information from outside could not be otherwise than unfavorable. What General Taylor's feelings were
during this suspense I do not know; but for myself, a young
second-lieutenant who had never heard a hostile gun before, I
felt sorry that I had enlisted. A great many men, when they
smell battle afar off, chafe to get into the fray. When they say
so themselves they generally fail to convince their hearers that
they are as anxious as they would like to make believe, and as
they approach danger they become more subdued. This rule
is not universal, for I have known a few men who were always
aching for a fight when there was no enemy near, who were
as good as their word when the battle did come. But the
number of such men is small.

On the 7th of May the wagons were all loaded and General
Taylor started on his return, with his army reinforced at Point
Isabel, but still less than three thousand strong, to relieve the
garrison on the Rio Grande. The road from Point Isabel to
Matamoras is over an open, rolling, treeless prairie, until the
timber that borders the bank of the Rio Grande is reached.
This river, like the Mississippi, flows through a rich alluvial
valley in the most meandering manner, running towards all
points of the compass at times within a few miles. Formerly
the river ran by Resaca de la Palma, some four or five miles
east of the present channel. The old bed of the river at Resaca
had become filled at places, leaving a succession of little lakes.
The timber that had formerly grown upon both banks, and
for a considerable distance out, was still standing. This timber

was struck six or eight miles out from the besieged garrison, at a point known as Palo Alto—"Tall trees" or "woods."

Early in the forenoon of the 8th of May as Palo Alto was approached, an army, certainly outnumbering our little force, was seen, drawn up in line of battle just in front of the timber. Their bayonets and spearheads glistened in the sunlight formidably. The force was composed largely of cavalry armed with lances. Where we were the grass was tall, reaching nearly to the shoulders of the men, very stiff, and each stock was pointed at the top, and hard and almost as sharp as a darning-needle. General Taylor halted his army before the head of column came in range of the artillery of the Mexicans. He then formed a line of battle, facing the enemy. His artillery, two batteries and two eighteen-pounder iron guns, drawn by oxen, were placed in position at intervals along the line. A battalion was thrown to the rear, commanded by Lieutenant-Colonel Childs, of the artillery, as reserves. These preparations completed, orders were given for a platoon of each company to stack arms and go to a stream off to the right of the command, to fill their canteens and also those of the rest of their respective companies. When the men were all back in their places in line, the command to advance was given. As I looked down that long line of about three thousand armed men, advancing towards a larger force also armed, I thought what a fearful responsibility General Taylor must feel, commanding such a host and so far away from friends. The Mexicans immediately opened fire upon us, first with artillery and then with infantry. At first their shots did not reach us, and the advance was continued. As we got nearer, the cannon balls commenced going through the ranks. They hurt no one, however, during this advance, because they would strike the ground long before they reached our line, and ricochetted through the tall grass so slowly that the men would see them and open ranks and let them pass. When we got to a point where the artillery could be used with effect, a halt was called, and the battle opened on both sides.

The infantry under General Taylor was armed with flint-lock muskets, and paper cartridges charged with powder, buck-shot and ball. At the distance of a few hundred yards a man might fire at you all day without your finding it out.

The artillery was generally six-pounder brass guns throwing only solid shot; but General Taylor had with him three or four twelve-pounder howitzers throwing shell, besides his eighteen-pounders before spoken of, that had a long range. This made a powerful armament. The Mexicans were armed about as we were so far as their infantry was concerned, but their artillery only fired solid shot. We had greatly the advantage in this arm.

The artillery was advanced a rod or two in front of the line, and opened fire. The infantry stood at order arms as spectators, watching the effect of our shots upon the enemy, and watching his shots so as to step out of their way. It could be seen that the eighteen-pounders and the howitzers did a great deal of execution. On our side there was little or no loss while we occupied this position. During the battle Major Ringgold, an accomplished and brave artillery officer, was mortally wounded, and Lieutenant Luther, also of the artillery, was struck. During the day several advances were made, and just at dusk it became evident that the Mexicans were falling back. We again advanced, and occupied at the close of the battle substantially the ground held by the enemy at the beginning. In this last move there was a brisk fire upon our troops, and some execution was done. One cannon-ball passed through our ranks, not far from me. It took off the head of an enlisted man, and the under jaw of Captain Page of my regiment, while the splinters from the musket of the killed soldier, and his brains and bones, knocked down two or three others, including one officer, Lieutenant Wallen,—hurting them more or less. Our casualties for the day were nine killed and forty-seven wounded.

At the break of day on the 9th, the army under Taylor was ready to renew the battle; but an advance showed that the enemy had entirely left our front during the night. The chaparral before us was impenetrable except where there were roads or trails, with occasionally clear or bare spots of small dimensions. A body of men penetrating it might easily be ambushed. It was better to have a few men caught in this way than the whole army, yet it was necessary that the garrison at the river should be relieved. To get to them the chaparral had to be passed. Thus I assume General Taylor reasoned. He halted the army not far in advance of the ground occupied by the Mexicans the day before, and selected Captain C. F. Smith, of the artillery, and Captain McCall, of my company, to take one hundred and fifty picked men each and find where the enemy had gone. This left me in command of the company, an honor and responsibility I thought very great.

Smith and McCall found no obstruction in the way of their advance until they came up to the succession of ponds, before described, at Resaca. The Mexicans had passed them and formed their lines on the opposite bank. This position they had strengthened a little by throwing up dead trees and brush in their front, and by placing artillery to cover the approaches and open places. Smith and McCall deployed on each side of the road as well as they could, and engaged the enemy at long range. Word was sent back, and the advance of the whole army was at once commenced. As we came up we were deployed in like manner. I was with the right wing, and led my company through the thicket wherever a penetrable place could be found, taking advantage of any clear spot that would carry me towards the enemy. At last I got pretty close up without knowing it. The balls commenced to whistle very thick overhead, cutting the limbs of the chaparral right and left. We could not see the enemy, so I ordered my men to lie down, an order that did not have to be enforced. We kept our position until it became evident that the enemy were not firing at us, and then withdrew to find better ground to advance upon.

By this time some progress had been made on our left. A section of artillery had been captured by the cavalry, and some prisoners had been taken. The Mexicans were giving way all along the line, and many of them had, no doubt, left early. I at last found a clear space separating two ponds. There seemed to be a few men in front and I charged upon them with my company. There was no resistance, and we captured a Mexican colonel, who had been wounded, and a few men. Just as I was sending them to the rear with a guard of two or three men, a private came from the front bringing back one of our officers, who had been badly wounded in advance of where I was. The ground had been charged over before. My exploit was equal to that of the soldier who boasted that he had cut off the leg of one of the enemy. When asked why he did not cut off his head, he replied: "Some one had done that before." This left no doubt in my mind but that the battle of Resaca de la Palma would have been won, just as it was, if I had not been there.

There was no further resistance. The evening of the 9th the army was encamped on its old ground near the Fort, and the garrison was relieved. The siege had lasted a number of days, but the casualties were few in number. Major Jacob Brown, of the 7th infantry, the commanding officer, had been killed, and in his honor the fort was named. Since then a town of considerable importance has sprung up on the ground occupied by the fort and troops, which has also taken his name.

The battles of Palo Alto and Resaca de la Palma seemed to us engaged, as pretty important affairs; but we had only a faint conception of their magnitude until they were fought over in the North by the Press and the reports came back to us. At the same time, or about the same time, we learned that war existed between the United States and Mexico, by the acts of the latter country. On learning this fact General Taylor transferred our camps to the south or west bank of the river, and Matamoras was occupied. We then became the "Army of Invasion."

Up to this time Taylor had none but regular troops in his command; but now that invasion had already taken place, volunteers for one year commenced arriving. The army remained at Matamoras until sufficiently reinforced to warrant a movement into the interior. General Taylor was not an officer to trouble the administration much with his demands, but was inclined to do the best he could with the means given him. He felt his responsibility as going no further. If he had thought that he was sent to perform an impossibility with the means given him, he would probably have informed the authorities of his opinion and left them to determine what should be done. If the judgment was against him he would have gone on and done the best he could with the means at hand without parading his grievance before the public. No soldier could face either danger or responsibility more calmly than he. These are qualities more rarely found than genius or physical courage.

General Taylor never made any great show or parade, either of uniform or retinue. In dress he was possibly too plain, rarely wearing anything in the field to indicate his rank, or even that he was an officer; but he was known to every soldier in his army, and was respected by all. I can call to mind only one instance when I saw him in uniform, and one other when I heard of his wearing it. On both occasions he was unfortunate. The first was at Corpus Christi. He had concluded to review his army before starting on the march and gave orders accordingly. Colonel Twiggs was then second in rank with the army, and to him was given the command of the review. Colonel and Brevet Brigadier-General Worth, a far different soldier from Taylor in the use of the uniform, was next to Twiggs in rank, and claimed superiority by virtue of his brevet rank when the accidents of service threw them where one or the other had to command. Worth declined to attend the review as subordinate to Twiggs until the question was settled by the highest authority. This broke up the review, and the question was referred to Washington for final decision.

General Taylor was himself only a colonel, in real rank, at that time, and a brigadier-general by brevet. He was assigned to duty, however, by the President, with the rank which his brevet gave him. Worth was not so assigned, but by virtue of commanding a division he must, under the army regulations of that day, have drawn the pay of his brevet rank. The question was submitted to Washington, and no response was received until after the army had reached the Rio Grande. It was decided against General Worth, who at once tendered his resignation and left the army, going north, no doubt, by the same vessel that carried it. This kept him out of the battles of Palo Alto and Resaca de la Palma. Either the resignation was not accepted, or General Worth withdrew it before action had been taken. At all events he returned to the army in time to command his division in the battle of Monterey, and served with it to the end of the war.

The second occasion on which General Taylor was said to have donned his uniform, was in order to receive a visit from the Flag Officer of the naval squadron off the mouth of the Rio Grande. While the army was on that river the Flag Officer sent word that he would call on the General to pay his respects on a certain day. General Taylor, knowing that naval officers habitually wore all the uniform the "law allowed" on all occasions of ceremony, thought it would be only civil to receive his guest in the same style. His uniform was therefore got out, brushed up, and put on, in advance of the visit. The Flag Officer, knowing General Taylor's aversion to the wearing of the uniform, and feeling that it would be regarded as a compliment should he meet him in civilian's dress, left off his uniform for this occasion. The meeting was said to have been embarrassing to both, and the conversation was principally apologetic.

The time was whiled away pleasantly enough at Matamoras, while we were waiting for volunteers. It is probable that all the most important people of the territory occupied by our army left their homes before we got there, but with those remaining the best of relations apparently existed. It was the policy of the Commanding General to allow no pillaging, no taking of private property for public or individual use without satisfactory compensation, so that a better market was afforded than the people had ever known before.

Among the troops that joined us at Matamoras was an Ohio regiment, of which Thomas L. Hamer, the Member of Congress who had given me my appointment to West Point, was major. He told me then that he could have had the colonelcy, but that as he knew he was to be appointed a brigadier-general, he preferred at first to take the lower grade. I have said before that Hamer was one of the ablest men Ohio ever produced. At that time he was in the prime of life, being less than fifty years of age, and possessed an admirable physique, promising long life. But he was taken sick before Monterey, and died within a few days. I have always believed that had his life been spared, he would have been President of the United States during the term filled by President Pierce. Had Hamer filled that office his partiality for me was such, there is but little doubt I should have been appointed to one of the staff corps of the army—the Pay Department probably—and would therefore now be preparing to retire. Neither of these speculations is unreasonable, and they are mentioned to show how little men control their own destiny.

Reinforcements having arrived, in the month of August the movement commenced from Matamoras to Camargo, the head of navigation on the Rio Grande. The line of the Rio Grande was all that was necessary to hold, unless it was intended to invade Mexico from the North. In that case the most natural route to take was the one which General Taylor selected. It entered a pass in the Sierra Madre Mountains, at Monterey, through which the main road runs to the City of Mexico. Monterey itself was a good point to hold, even if the line of the Rio Grande covered all the territory we desired to occupy at that time. It is built on a plain two thousand feet above tide water, where the air is bracing and the situation healthy.

On the 19th of August the army started for Monterey, leaving a small garrison at Matamoras. The troops, with the exception of the artillery, cavalry, and the brigade to which I belonged, were moved up the river to Camargo on steamers. As there were but two or three of these, the boats had to make a number of trips before the last of the troops were up. Those who marched did so by the south side of the river. Lieutenant-Colonel Garland, of the 4th infantry, was the brigade commander, and on this occasion commanded the entire marching force. One day out convinced him that marching by day in that latitude, in the month of August, was not a beneficial sanitary measure, particularly for Northern men. The order of marching was changed and night marches were substituted with the best results.

When Camargo was reached, we found a city of tents outside the Mexican hamlet. I was detailed to act as quartermaster and commissary to the regiment. The teams that had proven abundantly sufficient to transport all supplies from Corpus Christi to the Rio Grande over the level prairies of Texas, were entirely inadequate to the needs of the reinforced army in a mountainous country. To obviate the deficiency, pack mules were hired, with Mexicans to pack and drive them. I had charge of the few wagons allotted to the 4th infantry and of the pack train to supplement them. There were not men enough in the army to manage that train without the help of Mexicans who had learned how. As it was the difficulty was great enough. The troops would take up their march at an early hour each day. After they had started, the tents and cooking utensils had to be made into packages, so that they could be lashed to the backs of the mules. Sheet-iron kettles, tent-poles and mess chests were inconvenient articles to transport in that way. It took several hours to get ready to start each morning, and by the time we were ready some of the mules first loaded would be tired of standing so long with their loads on their backs. Sometimes one would start to run, bowing his back and kicking up until he scattered his load; others would lie down and try to disarrange their loads by attempting to get on the top of them by rolling on them; others with tent-poles for part of their loads would manage to run a tent-pole on one side of a sapling while they would take the other. I am not aware of ever having used a profane exple-tive in my life; but I would have the charity to excuse those who may have done so, if they were in charge of a train of Mexican pack mules at the time.

Chapter VIII.

ADVANCE ON MONTEREY—THE BLACK FORT—THE
BATTLE OF MONTEREY—SURRENDER OF THE CITY.

THE ADVANCE from Camargo was commenced on the 5th of September. The army was divided into four columns, separated from each other by one day's march. The advance reached Cerralvo in four days and halted for the remainder of the troops to come up. By the 13th the rear-guard had arrived, and the same day the advance resumed its march, followed as before, a day separating the divisions. The forward division halted again at Marin, twenty-four miles from Monterey. Both this place and Cerralvo were nearly deserted, and men, women and children were seen running and scattered over the hills as we approached; but when the people returned they found all their abandoned property safe, which must have given them a favorable opinion of *Los Grengos*—"the Yankees." From Marin the movement was in mass. On the 19th General Taylor, with his army, was encamped at Walnut Springs, within three miles of Monterey.

The town is on a small stream coming out of the mountain-pass, and is backed by a range of hills of moderate elevation. To the north, between the city and Walnut Springs, stretches an extensive plain. On this plain, and entirely outside of the last houses of the city, stood a strong fort, enclosed on all sides, to which our army gave the name of "Black Fort." Its guns commanded the approaches to the city to the full extent of their range. There were two detached spurs of hills or mountains to the north and north-west of the city, which were also fortified. On one of these stood the Bishop's Palace. The road to Saltillo leaves the upper or western end of the city under the fire of the guns from these heights. The lower or eastern end was defended by two or three small detached works, armed with artillery and infantry. To the south was the mountain stream before mentioned, and back of that the range of foot-hills. The plaza in the centre of the city was the citadel, properly speaking. All the streets leading from it were swept by artillery, cannon being intrenched behind temporary parapets. The house-tops near the plaza were converted into infantry fortifications by the use of sand-bags for parapets. Such were the defences of Monterey in September, 1846. General Ampudia, with a force of certainly ten thousand men, was in command.

General Taylor's force was about six thousand five hundred strong, in three divisions, under Generals Butler, Twiggs and Worth. The troops went into camp at Walnut Springs, while the engineer officers, under Major Mansfield—a General in the late war—commenced their reconnoissance. Major Mansfield found that it would be practicable to get troops around, out of range of the Black Fort and the works on the detached hills to the north-west of the city, to the Saltillo road. With this road in our possession, the enemy would be cut off from receiving further supplies, if not from all communication with the interior. General Worth, with his division somewhat reinforced, was given the task of gaining possession of the Saltillo road, and of carrying the detached works outside the city, in that quarter. He started on his march early in the afternoon of the 20th. The divisions under Generals Butler and Twiggs were drawn up to threaten the east and north sides of the city and the works on those fronts, in support of the movement under General Worth. Worth's was regarded as the main attack on Monterey, and all other operations were in support of it. His march this day was uninterrupted; but the enemy was seen to reinforce heavily about the Bishop's Palace and the other outside fortifications on their left. General Worth reached a defensible position just out of range of the enemy's guns on the heights north-west of the city, and bivouacked for the night. The engineer officers with him—Captain Sanders and Lieutenant George G. Meade, afterwards the commander of the victorious National army at the battle of Gettysburg—made a reconnoissance to the Saltillo road under cover of night.

During the night of the 20th General Taylor had established a battery, consisting of two twenty-four-pounder howitzers and a ten-inch mortar, at a point from which they could play upon Black Fort. A natural depression in the plain, sufficiently deep to protect men standing in it from the fire from the fort, was selected and the battery established on the crest nearest the enemy. The 4th infantry, then consisting of but six reduced companies, was ordered to support the artillerists while they were intrenching themselves and their guns. I was regimental quartermaster at the time and was ordered to remain in charge of camp and the public property at Walnut Springs. It was supposed that the regiment would return to its camp in the morning.

The point for establishing the siege battery was reached and the work performed without attracting the attention of the enemy. At daylight the next morning fire was opened on both sides and continued with, what seemed to me at that day, great fury. My curiosity got the better of my judgment, and I mounted a horse and rode to the front to see what was going on. I had been there but a short time when an order to charge was given, and lacking the moral courage to return to camp—where I had been ordered to stay—I charged with the regiment. As soon as the troops were out of the depression they came under the fire of Black Fort. As they advanced they got under fire from batteries guarding the east, or lower, end of the city, and of musketry. About one-third of the men engaged in the charge were killed or wounded in the space of a few minutes. We retreated to get out of fire, not backward, but eastward and perpendicular to the direct road running into the city from Walnut Springs. I was, I believe, the only person in the 4th infantry in the charge who was on horseback. When we got to a place of safety the regiment halted and drew itself together—what was left of it. The adjutant of the regiment, Lieutenant Hoskins, who was not in robust health, found himself very much fatigued from running on foot in the charge and retreat, and, seeing me on horseback, expressed a wish that he could be mounted also. I offered him my horse and he accepted the offer. A few minutes later I saw a soldier, a quartermaster's man, mounted, not far away. I ran to him, took his horse and was back with the regiment in a few minutes. In a short time we were off again; and the next place of safety from the shots of the enemy that I recollect of being in, was a field of cane or corn to the north-east of the lower batteries. The adjutant to whom I had loaned my horse was killed, and I was designated to act in his place.

This charge was ill-conceived, or badly executed. We belonged to the brigade commanded by Lieutenant-Colonel Garland, and he had received orders to charge the lower batteries of the city, and carry them if he could without too much loss, for the purpose of creating a diversion in favor of Worth, who was conducting the movement which it was intended should be decisive. By a movement by the left flank Garland could have led his men beyond the range of the fire from Black Fort and advanced towards the northeast angle of the city, as well covered from fire as could be expected. There was no undue loss of life in reaching the lower end of Monterey, except that sustained by Garland's command.

Meanwhile Quitman's brigade, conducted by an officer of engineers, had reached the eastern end of the city, and was placed under cover of the houses without much loss. Colonel Garland's brigade also arrived at the suburbs, and, by the assistance of some of our troops that had reached house-tops from which they could fire into a little battery covering the approaches to the lower end of the city, the battery was speedily captured and its guns were turned upon another work of the enemy. An entrance into the east end of the city was now secured, and the houses protected our troops so long as they were inactive.

On the west General Worth had reached the Saltillo road after some fighting but without heavy loss. He turned from his new position and captured the forts on both heights in that quarter. This gave him possession of the upper or west end of Monterey. Troops from both Twiggs's and Butler's divisions were in possession of the east end of the town, but the Black Fort to the north of the town and the plaza in the centre were still in the possession of the enemy. Our camps at Walnut Springs, three miles away, were guarded by a company from each regiment. A regiment of Kentucky volunteers guarded the mortars and howitzers engaged against Black Fort. Practically Monterey was invested.

There was nothing done on the 22d by the United States troops; but the enemy kept up a harmless fire upon us from Black Fort and the batteries still in their possession at the east end of the city. During the night they evacuated these; so that on the morning of the 23d we held undisputed possession of the east end of Monterey.

Twiggs's division was at the lower end of the city, and well covered from the fire of the enemy. But the streets leading to the plaza—all Spanish or Spanish-American towns have near their centres a square called a plaza—were commanded from all directions by artillery. The houses were flat-roofed and but one or two stories high, and about the plaza the roofs were manned with infantry, the troops being protected from our fire by parapets made of sand-bags. All advances into the city were thus attended with much danger. While moving along streets which did not lead to the plaza, our men were protected from the fire, and from the view, of the enemy except at the crossings; but at these a volley of musketry and a discharge of grape-shot were invariably encountered. The 3d and 4th regiments of infantry made an advance nearly to the plaza in this way and with heavy loss. The loss of the 3d infantry in commissioned officers was especially severe. There were only five companies of the regiment and not over twelve officers present, and five of these officers were killed. When within a square of the plaza this small command, ten companies in all, was brought to a halt. Placing themselves under cover from the shots of the enemy, the men would watch to detect a head above the sand-bags on the neighboring houses. The exposure of a single head would bring a volley from our soldiers.

We had not occupied this position long when it was discovered that our ammunition was growing low. I volunteered to go back* to the point we had started from, report our position to General Twiggs, and ask for ammunition to be forwarded. We were at this time occupying ground off from the street, in rear of the houses. My ride back was an exposed one. Before starting I adjusted myself on the side of my horse furthest from the enemy, and with only one foot holding to

---

*General Garland expressed a wish to get a message back to General Twiggs, his division commander, or General Taylor, to the effect that he was nearly out of ammunition and must have more sent to him, or otherwise be reinforced. Deeming the return dangerous he did not like to order any one to carry it, so he called for a volunteer. Lieutenant Grant offered his services, which were accepted.—PUBLISHERS.

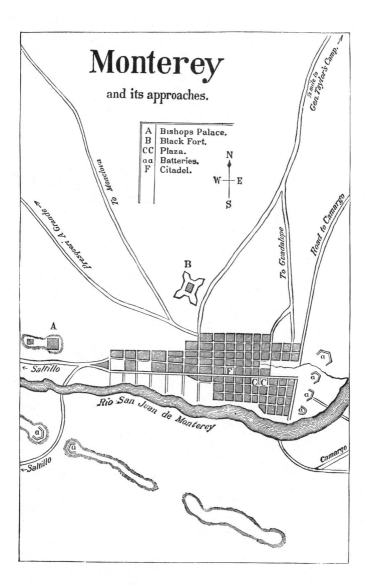

Monterey

and its approaches.

A	Bishops Palace.
B	Black Fort.
CC	Plaza.
αα	Batteries.
F	Citadel.

½ mile to Gen. Taylor's Camp.

To Monclova

To Guadalupe

Road to Camargo

Presidio. A. Grande.

B

A

← Saltillo

F

C C

α

α

α

Rio San Juan de Monterey

α

α

← Saltillo

Camargo

the cantle of the saddle, and an arm over the neck of the horse exposed, I started at full run. It was only at street crossings that my horse was under fire, but these I crossed at such a flying rate that generally I was past and under cover of the next block of houses before the enemy fired. I got out safely without a scratch.

At one place on my ride, I saw a sentry walking in front of a house, and stopped to inquire what he was doing there. Finding that the house was full of wounded American officers and soldiers, I dismounted and went in. I found there Captain Williams, of the Engineer Corps, wounded in the head, probably fatally, and Lieutenant Territt, also badly wounded, his bowels protruding from his wound. There were quite a number of soldiers also. Promising them to report their situation, I left, readjusted myself to my horse, recommenced the run, and was soon with the troops at the east end. Before ammunition could be collected, the two regiments I had been with were seen returning, running the same gauntlet in getting out that they had passed in going in, but with comparatively little loss. The movement was countermanded and the troops were withdrawn. The poor wounded officers and men I had found, fell into the hands of the enemy during the night, and died.

While this was going on at the east, General Worth, with a small division of troops, was advancing towards the plaza from the opposite end of the city. He resorted to a better expedient for getting to the plaza—the citadel—than we did on the east. Instead of moving by the open streets, he advanced through the houses, cutting passage-ways from one to another. Without much loss of life, he got so near the plaza during the night that before morning, Ampudia, the Mexican commander, made overtures for the surrender of the city and garrison. This stopped all further hostilities. The terms of surrender were soon agreed upon. The prisoners were paroled and permitted to take their horses and personal property with them.

My pity was aroused by the sight of the Mexican garrison of Monterey marching out of town as prisoners, and no doubt the same feeling was experienced by most of our army who witnessed it. Many of the prisoners were cavalry, armed with lances, and mounted on miserable little half-starved horses that did not look as if they could carry their riders out of town. The men looked in but little better condition. I thought how little interest the men before me had in the results of the war, and how little knowledge they had of "what it was all about."

After the surrender of the garrison of Monterey a quiet camp life was led until midwinter. As had been the case on the Rio Grande, the people who remained at their homes fraternized with the "Yankees" in the pleasantest manner. In fact, under the humane policy of our commander, I question whether the great majority of the Mexican people did not regret our departure as much as they had regretted our coming. Property and person were thoroughly protected, and a market was afforded for all the products of the country such as the people had never enjoyed before. The educated and wealthy portion of the population here, as elsewhere, abandoned their homes and remained away from them as long as they were in the possession of the invaders; but this class formed a very small percentage of the whole population.

Chapter IX.

POLITICAL INTRIGUE—BUENA VISTA—MOVEMENT
AGAINST VERA CRUZ—SIEGE AND CAPTURE OF
VERA CRUZ.

THE MEXICAN WAR was a political war, and the administration conducting it desired to make party capital out of
it. General Scott was at the head of the army, and, being a
soldier of acknowledged professional capacity, his claim to the
command of the forces in the field was almost indisputable
and does not seem to have been denied by President Polk, or
Marcy, his Secretary of War. Scott was a Whig and the administration was democratic. General Scott was also known to
have political aspirations, and nothing so popularizes a candidate for high civil positions as military victories. It would not
do therefore to give him command of the "army of conquest."
The plans submitted by Scott for a campaign in Mexico were
disapproved by the administration, and he replied, in a tone
possibly a little disrespectful, to the effect that, if a soldier's
plans were not to be supported by the administration, success
could not be expected. This was on the 27th of May, 1846.
Four days later General Scott was notified that he need not go
to Mexico. General Gaines was next in rank, but he was too
old and feeble to take the field. Colonel Zachary Taylor—a
brigadier-general by brevet—was therefore left in command.
He, too, was a Whig, but was not supposed to entertain any
political ambitions; nor did he; but after the fall of Monterey,
his third battle and third complete victory, the Whig papers at
home began to speak of him as the candidate of their party
for the Presidency. Something had to be done to neutralize
his growing popularity. He could not be relieved from duty
in the field where all his battles had been victories: the design
would have been too transparent. It was finally decided to
send General Scott to Mexico in chief command, and to authorize him to carry out his own original plan: that is, capture
Vera Cruz and march upon the capital of the country. It was
no doubt supposed that Scott's ambition would lead him to
slaughter Taylor or destroy his chances for the Presidency, and

83

yet it was hoped that he would not make sufficient capital himself to secure the prize.

The administration had indeed a most embarrassing problem to solve. It was engaged in a war of conquest which must be carried to a successful issue, or the political object would be unattained. Yet all the capable officers of the requisite rank belonged to the opposition, and the man selected for his lack of political ambition had himself become a prominent candidate for the Presidency. It was necessary to destroy his chances promptly. The problem was to do this without the loss of conquest and without permitting another general of the same political party to acquire like popularity. The fact is, the administration of Mr. Polk made every preparation to disgrace Scott, or, to speak more correctly, to drive him to such desperation that he would disgrace himself.

General Scott had opposed conquest by the way of the Rio Grande, Matamoras and Saltillo from the first. Now that he was in command of all the forces in Mexico, he withdrew from Taylor most of his regular troops and left him only enough volunteers, as he thought, to hold the line then in possession of the invading army. Indeed Scott did not deem it important to hold anything beyond the Rio Grande, and authorized Taylor to fall back to that line if he chose. General Taylor protested against the depletion of his army, and his subsequent movement upon Buena Vista would indicate that he did not share the views of his chief in regard to the unimportance of conquest beyond the Rio Grande.

Scott had estimated the men and material that would be required to capture Vera Cruz and to march on the capital of the country, two hundred and sixty miles in the interior. He was promised all he asked and seemed to have not only the confidence of the President, but his sincere good wishes. The promises were all broken. Only about half the troops were furnished that had been pledged, other war material was withheld and Scott had scarcely started for Mexico before the President undertook to supersede him by the appointment of Senator Thomas H. Benton as lieutenant-general. This being refused by Congress, the President asked legislative authority to place a junior over a senior of the same grade, with the view of appointing Benton to the rank of major-general and then placing him in command of the army, but Congress failed to accede to this proposition as well, and Scott remained in command: but every general appointed to serve under him was politically opposed to the chief, and several were personally hostile.

General Scott reached Brazos Santiago or Point Isabel, at the mouth of the Rio Grande, late in December, 1846, and proceeded at once up the river to Camargo, where he had written General Taylor to meet him. Taylor, however, had gone to, or towards Tampico, for the purpose of establishing a post there. He had started on this march before he was aware of General Scott being in the country. Under these circumstances Scott had to issue his orders designating the troops to be withdrawn from Taylor, without the personal consultation he had expected to hold with his subordinate.

General Taylor's victory at Buena Vista, February 22d, 23d, and 24th, 1847, with an army composed almost entirely of volunteers who had not been in battle before, and over a vastly superior force numerically, made his nomination for the Presidency by the Whigs a foregone conclusion. He was nominated and elected in 1848. I believe that he sincerely regretted this turn in his fortunes, preferring the peace afforded by a quiet life free from abuse to the honor of filling the highest office in the gift of any people, the Presidency of the United States.

When General Scott assumed command of the army of invasion, I was in the division of General David Twiggs, in Taylor's command; but under the new orders my regiment was transferred to the division of General William Worth, in which I served to the close of the war. The troops withdrawn from Taylor to form part of the forces to operate against Vera Cruz, were assembled at the mouth of the Rio Grande preparatory to embarkation for their destination. I found General Worth a different man from any I had before served directly under. He was nervous, impatient and restless on the march, or when important or responsible duty confronted him. There was not the least reason for haste on the march, for it was known that it would take weeks to assemble shipping enough at the point of our embarkation to carry the army, but General Worth moved his division with a rapidity that would have

been commendable had he been going to the relief of a beleaguered garrison. The length of the marches was regulated by
the distances between places affording a supply of water for the
troops, and these distances were sometimes long and sometimes short. General Worth on one occasion at least, after having made the full distance intended for the day, and after the
troops were in camp and preparing their food, ordered tents
struck and made the march that night which had been intended for the next day. Some commanders can move troops
so as to get the maximum distance out of them without fatigue, while others can wear them out in a few days without
accomplishing so much. General Worth belonged to this latter
class. He enjoyed, however, a fine reputation for his fighting
qualities, and thus attached his officers and men to him.

The army lay in camp upon the sand-beach in the neighborhood of the mouth of the Rio Grande for several weeks,
awaiting the arrival of transports to carry it to its new field of
operations. The transports were all sailing vessels. The passage was a tedious one, and many of the troops were on ship-
board over thirty days from the embarkation at the mouth of
the Rio Grande to the time of debarkation south of Vera
Cruz. The trip was a comfortless one for officers and men.
The transports used were built for carrying freight and possessed but limited accommodations for passengers, and the
climate added to the discomfort of all.

The transports with troops were assembled in the harbor of
Anton Lizardo, some sixteen miles south of Vera Cruz, as
they arrived, and there awaited the remainder of the fleet,
bringing artillery, ammunition and supplies of all kinds from
the North. With the fleet there was a little steam propeller
dispatch-boat—the first vessel of the kind I had ever seen,
and probably the first of its kind ever seen by any one then
with the army. At that day ocean steamers were rare, and
what there were were side-wheelers. This little vessel, going
through the fleet so fast, so noiselessly and with its propeller
under water out of view, attracted a great deal of attention. I
recollect that Lieutenant Sidney Smith, of the 4th infantry, by
whom I happened to be standing on the deck of a vessel
when this propeller was passing, exclaimed, "Why, the thing
looks as if it was propelled by the force of circumstances."

Finally on the 7th of March, 1847, the little army of ten or twelve thousand men, given Scott to invade a country with a population of seven or eight millions, a mountainous country affording the greatest possible natural advantages for defence, was all assembled and ready to commence the perilous task of landing from vessels lying in the open sea.

The debarkation took place inside of the little island of Sacrificios, some three miles south of Vera Cruz. The vessels could not get anywhere near shore, so that everything had to be landed in lighters or surf-boats; General Scott had provided these before leaving the North. The breakers were sometimes high, so that the landing was tedious. The men were got ashore rapidly, because they could wade when they came to shallow water; but the camp and garrison equipage, provisions, ammunition and all stores had to be protected from the salt water, and therefore their landing took several days. The Mexicans were very kind to us, however, and threw no obstacles in the way of our landing except an occasional shot from their nearest fort. During the debarkation one shot took off the head of Major Albertis. No other, I believe, reached anywhere near the same distance. On the 9th of March the troops were landed and the investment of Vera Cruz, from the Gulf of Mexico south of the city to the Gulf again on the north, was soon and easily effected. The landing of stores was continued until everything was got ashore.

Vera Cruz, at the time of which I write and up to 1880, was a walled city. The wall extended from the water's edge south of the town to the water again on the north. There were fortifications at intervals along the line and at the angles. In front of the city, and on an island half a mile out in the Gulf, stands San Juan de Ulloa, an enclosed fortification of large dimensions and great strength for that period. Against artillery of the present day the land forts and walls would prove elements of weakness rather than strength. After the invading army had established their camps out of range of the fire from the city, batteries were established, under cover of night, far to the front of the line where the troops lay. These batteries were intrenched and the approaches sufficiently protected. If a sortie had been made at any time by the Mexicans, the men serving the batteries could have been quickly reinforced without great exposure to the fire from the enemy's main line. No serious attempt was made to capture the batteries or to drive our troops away.

The siege continued with brisk firing on our side till the 27th of March, by which time a considerable breach had been made in the wall surrounding the city. Upon this General Morales, who was Governor of both the city and of San Juan de Ulloa, commenced a correspondence with General Scott looking to the surrender of the town, forts and garrison. On the 29th Vera Cruz and San Juan de Ulloa were occupied by Scott's army. About five thousand prisoners and four hundred pieces of artillery, besides large amounts of small arms and ammunition, fell into the hands of the victorious force. The casualties on our side during the siege amounted to sixty-four officers and men, killed and wounded.

Chapter X.

MARCH TO JALAPA—BATTLE OF CERRO GORDO—
PEROTE—PUEBLA—SCOTT AND TAYLOR.

GENERAL SCOTT had less than twelve thousand men at Vera Cruz. He had been promised by the administration a very much larger force, or claimed that he had, and he was a man of veracity. Twelve thousand was a very small army with which to penetrate two hundred and sixty miles into an enemy's country, and to besiege the capital; a city, at that time, of largely over one hundred thousand inhabitants. Then, too, any line of march that could be selected led through mountain passes easily defended. In fact, there were at that time but two roads from Vera Cruz to the City of Mexico that could be taken by an army; one by Jalapa and Perote, the other by Cordova and Orizaba, the two coming together on the great plain which extends to the City of Mexico after the range of mountains is passed.

It was very important to get the army away from Vera Cruz as soon as possible, in order to avoid the yellow fever, or vomito, which usually visits that city early in the year, and is very fatal to persons not acclimated; but transportation, which was expected from the North, was arriving very slowly. It was absolutely necessary to have enough to supply the army to Jalapa, sixty-five miles in the interior and above the fevers of the coast. At that point the country is fertile, and an army of the size of General Scott's could subsist there for an indefinite period. Not counting the sick, the weak and the garrisons for the captured city and fort, the moving column was now less than ten thousand strong. This force was composed of three divisions, under Generals Twiggs, Patterson, and Worth. The importance of escaping the vomito was so great that as soon as transportation enough could be got together to move a division the advance was commenced. On the 8th of April, Twiggs's division started for Jalapa. He was followed very soon by Patterson, with his division. General Worth was to bring up the rear with his command as soon as transportation enough was assembled to carry six days' rations for his troops with the necessary ammunition and camp and garrison equipage. It was the 13th of April before this division left Vera Cruz.

The leading division ran against the enemy at Cerro Gordo, some fifty miles west, on the road to Jalapa, and went into camp at Plan del Rio, about three miles from the fortifications. General Patterson reached Plan del Rio with his division soon after Twiggs arrived. The two were then secure against an attack from Santa Anna, who commanded the Mexican forces. At all events they confronted the enemy without reinforcements and without molestation, until the 18th of April. General Scott had remained at Vera Cruz to hasten preparations for the field; but on the 12th, learning the situation at the front, he hastened on to take personal supervision. He at once commenced his preparations for the capture of the position held by Santa Anna and of the troops holding it.

Cerro Gordo is one of the higher spurs of the mountains some twelve to fifteen miles east of Jalapa, and Santa Anna had selected this point as the easiest to defend against an invading army. The road, said to have been built by Cortez, zigzags around the mountain-side and was defended at every turn by artillery. On either side were deep chasms or mountain walls. A direct attack along the road was an impossibility. A flank movement seemed equally impossible. After the arrival of the commanding-general upon the scene, reconnoissances were sent out to find, or to make, a road by which the rear of the enemy's works might be reached without a front attack. These reconnoissances were made under the supervision of Captain Robert E. Lee, assisted by Lieutenants P. G. T. Beauregard, Isaac I. Stevens, Z. B. Tower, G. W. Smith, George B. McClellan, and J. G. Foster, of the corps of engineers, all officers who attained rank and fame, on one side or the other, in the great conflict for the preservation of the unity of the nation. The reconnoissance was completed, and the labor of cutting out and making roads by the flank of the enemy was effected by the 17th of the month. This was accomplished without the knowledge of Santa Anna or his army, and over ground where he supposed it impossible. On the same day General Scott issued his order for the attack on the 18th.

The attack was made as ordered, and perhaps there was not a battle of the Mexican war, or of any other, where orders issued before an engagement were nearer being a correct report of what afterwards took place. Under the supervision of the engineers, roadways had been opened over chasms to the right where the walls were so steep that men could barely climb them. Animals could not. These had been opened under cover of night, without attracting the notice of the enemy. The engineers, who had directed the opening, led the way and the troops followed. Artillery was let down the steep slopes by hand, the men engaged attaching a strong rope to the rear axle and letting the guns down, a piece at a time, while the men at the ropes kept their ground on top, paying out gradually, while a few at the front directed the course of the piece. In like manner the guns were drawn by hand up the opposite slopes. In this way Scott's troops reached their assigned position in rear of most of the intrenchments of the enemy, unobserved. The attack was made, the Mexican reserves behind the works beat a hasty retreat, and those occupying them surrendered. On the left General Pillow's command made a formidable demonstration, which doubtless held a part of the enemy in his front and contributed to the victory. I am not pretending to give full details of all the battles fought, but of the portion that I saw. There were troops engaged on both sides at other points in which both sustained losses; but the battle was won as here narrated.

The surprise of the enemy was complete, the victory overwhelming; some three thousand prisoners fell into Scott's hands, also a large amount of ordnance and ordnance stores. The prisoners were paroled, the artillery parked and the small arms and ammunition destroyed. The battle of Buena Vista was probably very important to the success of General Scott at Cerro Gordo and in his entire campaign from Vera Cruz to the great plains reaching to the City of Mexico. The only army Santa Anna had to protect his capital and the mountain passes west of Vera Cruz, was the one he had with him confronting General Taylor. It is not likely that he would have gone as far north as Monterey to attack the United States troops when he knew his country was threatened with invasion further south. When Taylor moved to Saltillo and then advanced on to Buena Vista, Santa Anna crossed the desert confronting the invading army, hoping no doubt to crush it and get back in time to meet General Scott in the mountain passes west of Vera Cruz. His attack on Taylor was disastrous to the Mexican army, but, notwithstanding this, he marched his army to Cerro Gordo, a distance not much short of one thousand miles by the line he had to travel, in time to intrench himself well before Scott got there. If he had been successful at Buena Vista his troops would no doubt have made a more stubborn resistance at Cerro Gordo. Had the battle of Buena Vista not been fought Santa Anna would have had time to move leisurely to meet the invader further south and with an army not demoralized nor depleted by defeat.

After the battle the victorious army moved on to Jalapa, where it was in a beautiful, productive and healthy country, far above the fevers of the coast. Jalapa, however, is still in the mountains, and between there and the great plain the whole line of the road is easy of defence. It was important, therefore, to get possession of the great highway between the sea-coast and the capital up to the point where it leaves the mountains, before the enemy could have time to re-organize and fortify in our front. Worth's division was selected to go forward to secure this result. The division marched to Perote on the great plain, not far from where the road debouches from the mountains. There is a low, strong fort on the plain in front of the town, known as the Castle of Perote. This, however, offered no resistance and fell into our hands, with its armament.

General Scott having now only nine or ten thousand men west of Vera Cruz, and the time of some four thousand of them being about to expire, a long delay was the consequence. The troops were in a healthy climate, and where they could subsist for an indefinite period even if their line back to Vera Cruz should be cut off. It being ascertained that the men whose time would expire before the City of Mexico could possibly fall into the hands of the American army, would not remain beyond the term for which they had volunteered, the commanding-general determined to discharge them at once, for a delay until the expiration of their time would have compelled them to pass through Vera Cruz during the season of the vomito. This reduced Scott's force in the field to about five thousand men.

Early in May, Worth, with his division, left Perote and marched on to Puebla. The roads were wide and the country open except through one pass in a spur of mountains coming up from the south, through which the road runs. Notwithstanding this the small column was divided into two bodies, moving a day apart. Nothing occurred on the march of special note, except that while lying at the town of Amozoque— an easy day's march east of Puebla—a body of the enemy's cavalry, two or three thousand strong, was seen to our right, not more than a mile away. A battery or two, with two or three infantry regiments, was sent against them and they soon disappeared. On the 15th of May we entered the city of Puebla.

General Worth was in command at Puebla until the latter end of May, when General Scott arrived. Here, as well as on the march up, his restlessness, particularly under responsibilities, showed itself. During his brief command he had the enemy hovering around near the city, in vastly superior numbers to his own. The brigade to which I was attached changed quarters three different times in about a week, occupying at first quarters near the plaza, in the heart of the city; then at the western entrance; then at the extreme east. On one occasion General Worth had the troops in line, under arms, all day, with three days' cooked rations in their haversacks. He galloped from one command to another proclaiming the near proximity of Santa Anna with an army vastly superior to his own. General Scott arrived upon the scene the latter part of the month, and nothing more was heard of Santa Anna and his myriads. There were, of course, bodies of mounted Mexicans hovering around to watch our movements and to pick up stragglers, or small bodies of troops, if they ventured too far out. These always withdrew on the approach of any considerable number of our soldiers. After the arrival of General Scott I was sent, as quartermaster, with a large train of wagons, back two days' march at least, to procure forage. We had less than a thousand men as escort, and never thought of danger. We procured full loads for our entire train at two plantations, which could easily have furnished as much more.

There had been great delay in obtaining the authority of Congress for the raising of the troops asked for by the administration. A bill was before the National Legislature from early in the session of 1846–7, authorizing the creation of ten additional regiments for the war to be attached to the regular army, but it was the middle of February before it became a law. Appointments of commissioned officers had then to be made; men had to be enlisted, the regiments equipped and the whole transported to Mexico. It was August before General Scott received reinforcement sufficient to warrant an advance. His moving column, not even now more than ten thousand strong, was in four divisions, commanded by Generals Twiggs, Worth, Pillow and Quitman. There was also a cavalry corps under General Harney, composed of detachments of the 1st, 2d, and 3d dragoons. The advance commenced on the 7th of August with Twiggs's division in front. The remaining three divisions followed, with an interval of a day between. The marches were short, to make concentration easier in case of attack.

I had now been in battle with the two leading commanders conducting armies in a foreign land. The contrast between the two was very marked. General Taylor never wore uniform, but dressed himself entirely for comfort. He moved about the field in which he was operating to see through his own eyes the situation. Often he would be without staff officers, and when he was accompanied by them there was no prescribed order in which they followed. He was very much given to sit his horse side-ways—with both feet on one side—particularly on the battle-field. General Scott was the reverse in all these particulars. He always wore all the uniform prescribed or allowed by law when he inspected his lines; word would be sent to all division and brigade commanders in advance, notifying them of the hour when the commanding general might be expected. This was done so that all the army might be under arms to salute their chief as he passed. On these occasions he wore his dress uniform, cocked hat, aiguillettes, sabre and spurs. His staff proper, besides all officers constructively on his staff—engineers, inspectors, quartermasters, etc., that could be spared—followed, also in uniform and in prescribed order. Orders were prepared with great care and evidently with the view that they should be a history of what followed.

In their modes of expressing thought, these two generals contrasted quite as strongly as in their other characteristics. General Scott was precise in language, cultivated a style peculiarly his own; was proud of his rhetoric; not averse to speaking of himself, often in the third person, and he could bestow praise upon the person he was talking about without the least embarrassment. Taylor was not a conversationalist, but on paper he could put his meaning so plainly that there could be no mistaking it. He knew how to express what he wanted to say in the fewest well-chosen words, but would not sacrifice meaning to the construction of high-sounding sentences. But with their opposite characteristics both were great and successful soldiers; both were true, patriotic and upright in all their dealings. Both were pleasant to serve under—Taylor was pleasant to serve with. Scott saw more through the eyes of his staff officers than through his own. His plans were deliberately prepared, and fully expressed in orders. Taylor saw for himself, and gave orders to meet the emergency without reference to how they would read in history.

Chapter XI.

ADVANCE ON THE CITY OF MEXICO—BATTLE OF
CONTRERAS—ASSAULT AT CHURUBUSCO—NEGOTIATIONS
FOR PEACE—BATTLE OF MOLINO DEL REY—STORMING
OF CHAPULTEPEC—SAN COSME—EVACUATION OF THE
CITY—HALLS OF THE MONTEZUMAS.

THE ROUTE followed by the army from Puebla to the City of Mexico was over Rio Frio mountain, the road leading over which, at the highest point, is about eleven thousand feet above tide water. The pass through this mountain might have been easily defended, but it was not; and the advanced division reached the summit in three days after leaving Puebla. The City of Mexico lies west of Rio Frio mountain, on a plain backed by another mountain six miles farther west, with others still nearer on the north and south. Between the western base of Rio Frio and the City of Mexico there are three lakes, Chalco and Xochimilco on the left and Texcoco on the right, extending to the east end of the City of Mexico. Chalco and Texcoco are divided by a narrow strip of land over which the direct road to the city runs. Xochimilco is also to the left of the road, but at a considerable distance south of it, and is connected with Lake Chalco by a narrow channel. There is a high rocky mound, called El Peñon, on the right of the road, springing up from the low flat ground dividing the lakes. This mound was strengthened by intrenchments at its base and summit, and rendered a direct attack impracticable.

Scott's army was rapidly concentrated about Ayotla and other points near the eastern end of Lake Chalco. Reconnoissances were made up to within gun-shot of El Peñon, while engineers were seeking a route by the south side of Lake Chalco to flank the city, and come upon it from the south and south-west. A way was found around the lake, and by the 18th of August troops were in St. Augustin Tlalpam, a town about eleven miles due south from the plaza of the capital. Between St. Augustin Tlalpam and the city lie the hacienda of San Antonio and the village of Churubusco, and south-west of them is Contreras. All these points, except St. Augustin Tlalpam, were intrenched and strongly garrisoned. Contreras is situated on the side of a mountain, near its base, where volcanic rocks are piled in great confusion, reaching nearly to San Antonio. This made the approach to the city from the south very difficult.

The brigade to which I was attached—Garland's, of Worth's division—was sent to confront San Antonio, two or three miles from St. Augustin Tlalpam, on the road to Churubusco and the City of Mexico. The ground on which San Antonio stands is completely in the valley, and the surface of the land is only a little above the level of the lakes, and, except to the south-west, it was cut up by deep ditches filled with water. To the south-west is the Pedregal—the volcanic rock before spoken of—over which cavalry or artillery could not be passed, and infantry would make but poor progress if confronted by an enemy. From the position occupied by Garland's brigade, therefore, no movement could be made against the defences of San Antonio except to the front, and by a narrow causeway, over perfectly level ground, every inch of which was commanded by the enemy's artillery and infantry. If Contreras, some three miles west and south, should fall into our hands, troops from there could move to the right flank of all the positions held by the enemy between us and the city. Under these circumstances General Scott directed the holding of the front of the enemy without making an attack until further orders.

On the 18th of August, the day of reaching San Augustin Tlalpam, Garland's brigade secured a position within easy range of the advanced intrenchments of San Antonio, but where his troops were protected by an artificial embankment that had been thrown up for some other purpose than defence. General Scott at once set his engineers reconnoitring the works about Contreras, and on the 19th movements were commenced to get troops into positions from which an assault could be made upon the force occupying that place. The Pedregal on the north and north-east, and the mountain on the south, made the passage by either flank of the enemy's defences difficult, for their work stood exactly between those natural bulwarks; but a road was completed during the day and night of the 19th, and troops were got to the north and west of the enemy.

This affair, like that of Cerro Gordo, was an engagement in which the officers of the engineer corps won special distinction. In fact, in both cases, tasks which seemed difficult at first sight were made easier for the troops that had to execute them than they would have been on an ordinary field. The very strength of each of these positions was, by the skill of the engineers, converted into a defence for the assaulting parties while securing their positions for final attack. All the troops with General Scott in the valley of Mexico, except a part of the division of General Quitman at San Augustin Tlalpam and the brigade of Garland (Worth's division) at San Antonio, were engaged at the battle of Contreras, or were on their way, in obedience to the orders of their chief, to reinforce those who were engaged. The assault was made on the morning of the 20th, and in less than half an hour from the sound of the advance the position was in our hands, with many prisoners and large quantities of ordnance and other stores. The brigade commanded by General Riley was from its position the most conspicuous in the final assault, but all did well, volunteers and regulars.

From the point occupied by Garland's brigade we could see the progress made at Contreras and the movement of troops toward the flank and rear of the enemy opposing us. The Mexicans all the way back to the city could see the same thing, and their conduct showed plainly that they did not enjoy the sight. We moved out at once, and found them gone from our immediate front. Clarke's brigade of Worth's division now moved west over the point of the Pedregal, and after having passed to the north sufficiently to clear San Antonio, turned east and got on the causeway leading to Churubusco and the City of Mexico. When he approached Churubusco his left, under Colonel Hoffman, attacked a tête-de-pont at that place and brought on an engagement. About an hour after, Garland was ordered to advance directly along the causeway, and got up in time to take part in the engagement. San Antonio was found evacuated, the evacuation having probably taken place immediately upon the enemy seeing the stars and stripes waving over Contreras.

The troops that had been engaged at Contreras, and even then on their way to that battle-field, were moved by a causeway west of, and parallel to the one by way of San Antonio and Churubusco. It was expected by the commanding general that these troops would move north sufficiently far to flank the enemy out of his position at Churubusco, before turning east to reach the San Antonio road, but they did not succeed in this, and Churubusco proved to be about the severest battle fought in the valley of Mexico. General Scott coming upon the battle-field about this juncture, ordered two brigades, under Shields, to move north and turn the right of the enemy. This Shields did, but not without hard fighting and heavy loss. The enemy finally gave way, leaving in our hands prisoners, artillery and small arms. The balance of the causeway held by the enemy, up to the very gates of the city, fell in like manner. I recollect at this place that some of the gunners who had stood their ground, were deserters from General Taylor's army on the Rio Grande.

Both the strategy and tactics displayed by General Scott in these various engagements of the 20th of August, 1847, were faultless as I look upon them now, after the lapse of so many years. As before stated, the work of the engineer officers who made the reconnoissances and led the different commands to their destinations, was so perfect that the chief was able to give his orders to his various subordinates with all the precision he could use on an ordinary march. I mean, up to the points from which the attack was to commence. After that point is reached the enemy often induces a change of orders not before contemplated. The enemy outside the city outnumbered our soldiery quite three to one, but they had become so demoralized by the succession of defeats this day, that the City of Mexico could have been entered without much further bloodshed. In fact, Captain Philip Kearney—afterwards a general in the war of the rebellion—rode with a squadron of cavalry to the very gates of the city, and would no doubt have entered with his little force, only at that point he was badly wounded, as were several of his officers. He had not heard the call for a halt.

General Franklin Pierce had joined the army in Mexico, at Puebla, a short time before the advance upon the capital commenced. He had consequently not been in any of the engagements of the war up to the battle of Contreras. By an unfortunate fall of his horse on the afternoon of the 19th he was painfully injured. The next day, when his brigade, with the other troops engaged on the same field, was ordered against the flank and rear of the enemy guarding the different points of the road from San Augustin Tlalpam to the city, General Pierce attempted to accompany them. He was not sufficiently recovered to do so, and fainted. This circumstance gave rise to exceedingly unfair and unjust criticisms of him when he became a candidate for the Presidency. Whatever General Pierce's qualifications may have been for the Presidency, he was a gentleman and a man of courage. I was not a supporter of him politically, but I knew him more intimately than I did any other of the volunteer generals.

General Scott abstained from entering the city at this time, because Mr. Nicholas P. Trist, the commissioner on the part of the United States to negotiate a treaty of peace with Mexico, was with the army, and either he or General Scott thought—probably both of them—that a treaty would be more possible while the Mexican government was in possession of the capital than if it was scattered and the capital in the hands of an invader. Be this as it may, we did not enter at that time. The army took up positions along the slopes of the mountains south of the city, as far west as Tacubaya. Negotiations were at once entered into with Santa Anna, who was then practically *the Government* and the immediate commander of all the troops engaged in defence of the country. A truce was signed which denied to either party the right to strengthen its position, or to receive reinforcements during the continuance of the armistices, but authorized General Scott to draw supplies for his army from the city in the meantime.

Negotiations were commenced at once and were kept up vigorously, between Mr. Trist and the commissioners appointed on the part of Mexico, until the 2d of September. At that time Mr. Trist handed in his ultimatum. Texas was to be given up absolutely by Mexico, and New Mexico and California ceded to the United States for a stipulated sum to be afterwards determined. I do not suppose Mr. Trist had any discretion whatever in regard to boundaries. The war was one of conquest, in the interest of an institution, and the probabilities are that private instructions were for the acquisition of territory out of which new States might be carved. At all events the Mexicans felt so outraged at the terms proposed that they commenced preparations for defence, without giving notice of the termination of the armistice. The terms of the truce had been violated before, when teams had been sent into the city to bring out supplies for the army. The first train entering the city was very severely threatened by a mob. This, however, was apologized for by the authorities and all responsibility for it denied; and thereafter, to avoid exciting the Mexican people and soldiery, our teams with their escorts were sent in at night, when the troops were in barracks and the citizens in bed. The circumstance was overlooked and negotiations continued. As soon as the news reached General Scott of the second violation of the armistice, about the 4th of September, he wrote a vigorous note to President Santa Anna, calling his attention to it, and, receiving an unsatisfactory reply, declared the armistice at an end.

General Scott, with Worth's division, was now occupying Tacubaya, a village some four miles south-west of the City of Mexico, and extending from the base up the mountain-side for the distance of half a mile. More than a mile west, and also a little above the plain, stands Molino del Rey. The mill is a long stone structure, one story high and several hundred feet in length. At the period of which I speak General Scott supposed a portion of the mill to be used as a foundry for the casting of guns. This, however, proved to be a mistake. It was valuable to the Mexicans because of the quantity of grain it contained. The building is flat roofed, and a line of sand-bags over the outer walls rendered the top quite a formidable defence for infantry. Chapultepec is a mound springing up from the plain to the height of probably three hundred feet, and almost in a direct line between Molino del Rey and the western part of the city. It was fortified both on the top and on the rocky and precipitous sides.

The City of Mexico is supplied with water by two aqueducts, resting on strong stone arches. One of these aqueducts draws its supply of water from a mountain stream coming into it at or near Molino del Rey, and runs north close to the west base of Chapultepec; thence along the centre of a wide road, until it reaches the road running east into the city by the Garita San Cosme; from which point the aqueduct and road both run east to the city. The second aqueduct starts from the east base of Chapultepec, where it is fed by a spring, and runs north-east to the city. This aqueduct, like the other, runs in the middle of a broad road-way, thus leaving a space on each side. The arches supporting the aqueduct afforded protection for advancing troops as well as to those engaged defensively. At points on the San Cosme road parapets were thrown across, with an embrasure for a single piece of artillery in each. At the point where both road and aqueduct turn at right angles from north to east, there was not only one of these parapets supplied by one gun and infantry supports, but the houses to the north of the San Cosme road, facing south and commanding a view of the road back to Chapultepec, were covered with infantry, protected by parapets made of sand-bags. The roads leading to garitas (the gates) San Cosme and Belen, by which these aqueducts enter the city, were strongly intrenched. Deep, wide ditches, filled with water, lined the sides of both roads. Such were the defences of the City of Mexico in September, 1847, on the routes over which General Scott entered.

Prior to the Mexican war General Scott had been very partial to General Worth—indeed he continued so up to the close of hostilities—but, for some reason, Worth had become estranged from his chief. Scott evidently took this coldness somewhat to heart. He did not retaliate, however, but on the contrary showed every disposition to appease his subordinate. It was understood at the time that he gave Worth authority to plan and execute the battle of Molino del Rey without dictation or interference from any one, for the very purpose of restoring their former relations. The effort failed, and the two generals remained ever after cold and indifferent towards each other, if not actually hostile.

The battle of Molino del Rey was fought on the 8th of September. The night of the 7th, Worth sent for his brigade and regimental commanders, with their staffs, to come to his quarters to receive instructions for the morrow. These orders contemplated a movement up to within striking distance of the Mills before daylight. The engineers had reconnoitred the ground as well as possible, and had acquired all the information necessary to base proper orders both for approach and attack.

By daylight on the morning of the 8th, the troops to be engaged at Molino were all at the places designated. The ground in front of the Mills, to the south, was commanded by the artillery from the summit of Chapultepec as well as by the lighter batteries at hand; but a charge was made, and soon all was over. Worth's troops entered the Mills by every door, and the enemy beat a hasty retreat back to Chapultepec. Had this victory been followed up promptly, no doubt Americans and Mexicans would have gone over the defences of Chapultepec so near together that the place would have fallen into our hands without further loss. The defenders of the works could not have fired upon us without endangering their own men. This was not done, and five days later more valuable lives were sacrificed to carry works which had been so nearly in our possession on the 8th. I do not criticise the failure to capture Chapultepec at this time. The result that followed the first assault could not possibly have been foreseen, and to profit by the unexpected advantage, the commanding general must have been on the spot and given the necessary instructions at the moment, or the troops must have kept on without orders. It is always, however, in order to follow a retreating foe, unless stopped or otherwise directed. The loss on our side at Molino del Rey was severe for the numbers engaged. It was especially so among commissioned officers.

I was with the earliest of the troops to enter the Mills. In passing through to the north side, looking towards Chapultepec, I happened to notice that there were armed Mexicans still on top of the building, only a few feet from many of our men. Not seeing any stairway or ladder reaching to the top of the building, I took a few soldiers, and had a cart that happened to be standing near brought up, and, placing the shafts against the wall and chocking the wheels so that the cart could not back, used the shafts as a sort of ladder extending to within three or four feet of the top. By this I climbed to the roof of the building, followed by a few men, but found a private soldier had preceded me by some other way. There were still quite a number of Mexicans on the roof, among them a major and five or six officers of lower grades, who had not succeeded in getting away before our troops occupied the building. They still had their arms, while the soldier before mentioned was walking as sentry, guarding the prisoners he had *surrounded*, all by himself. I halted the sentinel, received the swords from the commissioned officers, and proceeded, with the assistance of the soldiers now with me, to disable the muskets by striking them against the edge of the wall, and throw them to the ground below.

Molino del Rey was now captured, and the troops engaged, with the exception of an appropriate guard over the captured position and property, were marched back to their quarters in Tacubaya. The engagement did not last many minutes, but the killed and wounded were numerous for the number of troops engaged.

During the night of the 11th batteries were established which could play upon the fortifications of Chapultepec. The bombardment commenced early on the morning of the 12th, but there was no further engagement during this day than that of the artillery. General Scott assigned the capture of Chapultepec to General Pillow, but did not leave the details to his judgment. Two assaulting columns, two hundred and fifty men each, composed of volunteers for the occasion, were formed. They were commanded by Captains McKinzie and Casey respectively. The assault was successful, but bloody.

In later years, if not at the time, the battles of Molino del Rey and Chapultepec have seemed to me to have been wholly unnecessary. When the assaults upon the garitas of San Cosme and Belen were determined upon, the road running east to the former gate could have been reached easily, without an engagement, by moving along south of the Mills until west of them sufficiently far to be out of range, thence north to the road above mentioned; or, if desirable to keep the two attacking columns nearer together, the troops could have been turned east so as to come on the aqueduct road out of range of the guns from Chapultepec. In like manner, the troops designated to act against Belen could have kept east of

Chapultepec, out of range, and come on to the aqueduct, also out of range of Chapultepec. Molino del Rey and Chapultepec would both have been necessarily evacuated if this course had been pursued, for they would have been turned.

General Quitman, a volunteer from the State of Mississippi, who stood well with the army both as a soldier and as a man, commanded the column acting against Belen. General Worth commanded the column against San Cosme. When Chapultepec fell the advance commenced along the two aqueduct roads. I was on the road to San Cosme, and witnessed most that took place on that route. When opposition was encountered our troops sheltered themselves by keeping under the arches supporting the aqueduct, advancing an arch at a time. We encountered no serious obstruction until within gun-shot of the point where the road we were on intersects that running east to the city, the point where the aqueduct turns at a right angle. I have described the defences of this position before. There were but three commissioned officers besides myself, that I can now call to mind, with the advance when the above position was reached. One of these officers was a Lieutenant Semmes, of the Marine Corps. I think Captain Gore, and Lieutenant Judah, of the 4th infantry, were the others. Our progress was stopped for the time by the single piece of artillery at the angle of the roads and the infantry occupying the house-tops back from it.

West of the road from where we were, stood a house occupying the south-west angle made by the San Cosme road and the road we were moving upon. A stone wall ran from the house along each of these roads for a considerable distance and thence back until it joined, enclosing quite a yard about the house. I watched my opportunity and skipped across the road and behind the south wall. Proceeding cautiously to the west corner of the enclosure, I peeped around and seeing nobody, continued, still cautiously, until the road running east and west was reached. I then returned to the troops, and called for volunteers. All that were close to me, or that heard me, about a dozen, offered their services. Commanding them to carry their arms at a trail, I watched our opportunity and got them across the road and under cover of the wall beyond, before the enemy had a shot at us. Our men under cover of the arches kept a close watch on the intrenchments that crossed our path and the house-tops beyond, and whenever a head showed itself above the parapets they would fire at it. Our crossing was thus made practicable without loss.

When we reached a safe position I instructed my little command again to carry their arms at a trail, not to fire at the enemy until they were ordered, and to move very cautiously following me until the San Cosme road was reached; we would then be on the flank of the men serving the gun on the road, and with no obstruction between us and them. When we reached the south-west corner of the enclosure before described, I saw some United States troops pushing north through a shallow ditch near by, who had come up since my reconnaissance. This was the company of Captain Horace Brooks, of the artillery, acting as infantry. I explained to Brooks briefly what I had discovered and what I was about to do. He said, as I knew the ground and he did not, I might go on and he would follow. As soon as we got on the road leading to the city the troops serving the gun on the parapet retreated, and those on the house-tops near by followed; our men went after them in such close pursuit—the troops we had left under the arches joining—that a second line across the road, about half-way between the first and the garita, was carried. No reinforcements had yet come up except Brooks's company, and the position we had taken was too advanced to be held by so small a force. It was given up, but retaken later in the day, with some loss.

Worth's command gradually advanced to the front now open to it. Later in the day in reconnoitring I found a church off to the south of the road, which looked to me as if the belfry would command the ground back of the garita San Cosme. I got an officer of the voltigeurs, with a mountain howitzer and men to work it, to go with me. The road being in possession of the enemy, we had to take the field to the south to reach the church. This took us over several ditches breast deep in water and grown up with water plants. These ditches, however, were not over eight or ten feet in width. The howitzer was taken to pieces and carried by the men to its destination. When I knocked for admission a priest came to the door, who, while extremely polite, declined to admit

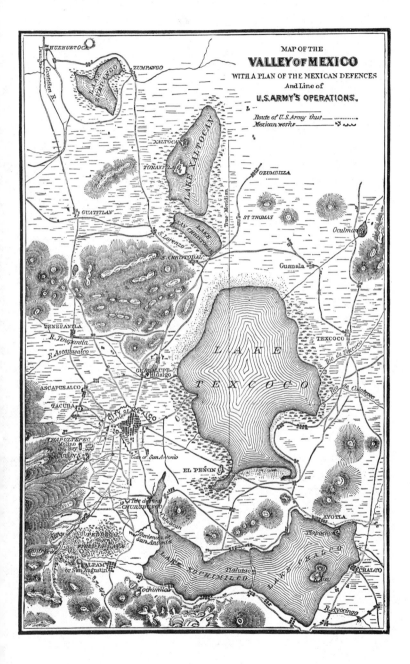

MAP OF THE
VALLEY OF MEXICO
WITH A PLAN OF THE MEXICAN DEFENCES
And Line of
U.S. ARMY'S OPERATIONS.

Route of U.S. Army thus ....
Mexican works _____

us. With the little Spanish then at my command, I explained to him that he might save property by opening the door, and he certainly would save himself from becoming a prisoner, for a time at least; and besides, I intended to go in whether he consented or not. He began to see his duty in the same light that I did, and opened the door, though he did not look as if it gave him special pleasure to do so. The gun was carried to the belfry and put together. We were not more than two or three hundred yards from San Cosme. The shots from our little gun dropped in upon the enemy and created great confusion. Why they did not send out a small party and capture us, I do not know. We had no infantry or other defences besides our one gun.

The effect of this gun upon the troops about the gate of the city was so marked that General Worth saw it from his position.* He was so pleased that he sent a staff officer, Lieutenant Pemberton—later Lieutenant-General commanding the defences of Vicksburg—to bring me to him. He expressed his gratification at the services the howitzer in the church steeple was doing, saying that every shot was effective, and ordered a captain of voltigeurs to report to me with another howitzer to be placed along with the one already rendering so much service. I could not tell the General that there was not room enough in the steeple for another gun, because he probably would have looked upon such a statement as a contradiction from a second lieutenant. I took the captain with me, but did not use his gun.

The night of the 13th of September was spent by the troops under General Worth in the houses near San Cosme, and in line confronting the general line of the enemy across to Belen. The troops that I was with were in the houses north of the road leading into the city, and were engaged during the night in cutting passage-ways from one house to another towards the town. During the night Santa Anna, with his army—except the deserters—left the city. He liberated all the convicts confined in the town, hoping, no doubt, that they would inflict upon us some injury before daylight; but several hours

---

*Mentioned in the reports of Major Lee, Colonel Garland and General Worth.—PUBLISHERS.

after Santa Anna was out of the way, the city authorities sent a delegation to General Scott to ask—if not demand—an armistice, respecting church property, the rights of citizens and the supremacy of the city government in the management of municipal affairs. General Scott declined to trammel himself with conditions, but gave assurances that those who chose to remain within our lines would be protected so long as they behaved themselves properly.

General Quitman had advanced along his line very successfully on the 13th, so that at night his command occupied nearly the same position at Belen that Worth's troops did about San Cosme. After the interview above related between General Scott and the city council, orders were issued for the cautious entry of both columns in the morning. The troops under Worth were to stop at the Alameda, a park near the west end of the city. Quitman was to go directly to the Plaza, and take possession of the Palace—a mass of buildings on the east side in which Congress has its sessions, the national courts are held, the public offices are all located, the President resides, and much room is left for museums, receptions, etc. This is the building generally designated as the "Halls of the Montezumas."

Chapter XII.

O N ENTERING the city the troops were fired upon by the
released convicts, and possibly by deserters and hostile
citizens. The streets were deserted, and the place presented
the appearance of a "city of the dead," except for this firing by
unseen persons from house-tops, windows, and around corners. In this firing the lieutenant-colonel of my regiment, Garland, was badly wounded, Lieutenant Sidney Smith, of the
4th infantry, was also wounded mortally. He died a few days
after, and by his death I was promoted to the grade of first
lieutenant. I had gone into the battle of Palo Alto in May,
1846, a second lieutenant, and I entered the city of Mexico
sixteen months later with the same rank, after having been in
all the engagements possible for any one man and in a regiment that lost more officers during the war than it ever had
present at any one engagement. My regiment lost four commissioned officers, all senior to me, by steamboat explosions
during the Mexican war. The Mexicans were not so discrimi-
nating. They sometimes picked off my juniors.

General Scott soon followed the troops into the city, in
state. I wonder that he was not fired upon, but I believe he
was not; at all events he was not hurt. He took quarters at
first in the "Halls of the Montezumas," and from there issued
his wise and discreet orders for the government of a conquered city, and for suppressing the hostile acts of liberated

---

NOTE.—It had been a favorite idea with General Scott for a great many
years before the Mexican war to have established in the United States a soldiers' home, patterned after something of the kind abroad, particularly, I
believe, in France. He recommended this uniformly, or at least frequently, in
his annual reports to the Secretary of War, but never got any hearing. Now,
as he had conquered the state, he made assessments upon the different large
towns and cities occupied by our troops, in proportion to their capacity to
pay, and appointed officers to receive the money. In addition to the sum thus
realized he had derived, through capture at Cerro Gordo, sales of captured

convicts already spoken of—orders which challenge the respect of all who study them. Lawlessness was soon suppressed, and the City of Mexico settled down into a quiet, law-abiding place. The people began to make their appearance upon the streets without fear of the invaders. Shortly afterwards the bulk of the troops were sent from the city to the villages at the foot of the mountains, four or five miles to the south and south-west.

Whether General Scott approved of the Mexican war and the manner in which it was brought about, I have no means of knowing. His orders to troops indicate only a soldierly spirit, with probably a little regard for the perpetuation of his own fame. On the other hand, General Taylor's, I think, indicate that he considered the administration accountable for the war, and felt no responsibility resting on himself further than for the faithful performance of his duties. Both generals deserve the commendations of their countrymen and to live in the grateful memory of this people to the latest generation.

Earlier in this narrative I have stated that the plain, reached after passing the mountains east of Perote, extends to the cities of Puebla and Mexico. The route travelled by the army before reaching Puebla, goes over a pass in a spur of mountain coming up from the south. This pass is very susceptible of defence by a smaller against a larger force. Again, the highest point of the road-bed between Vera Cruz and the City of Mexico is over Rio Frio mountain, which also might have been successfully defended by an inferior against a superior force. But by moving north of the mountains, and about thirty miles north of Puebla, both of these passes would have been avoided. The road from Perote to the City of Mexico, by

---

government tobacco, etc., sums which swelled the fund to a total of about $220,000. Portions of this fund were distributed among the rank and file, given to the wounded in hospital, or applied in other ways, leaving a balance of some $118,000 remaining unapplied at the close of the war. After the war was over and the troops all home, General Scott applied to have this money, which had never been turned into the Treasury of the United States, expended in establishing such homes as he had previously recommended. This fund was the foundation of the Soldiers' Home at Washington City, and also one at Harrodsburgh, Kentucky.

The latter went into disuse many years ago. In fact it never had many soldiers in it, and was, I believe, finally sold.

this latter route, is as level as the prairies in our West. Arriving due north from Puebla, troops could have been detached to take possession of that place, and then proceeding west with the rest of the army no mountain would have been encountered before reaching the City of Mexico. It is true this road would have brought troops in by Guadalupe—a town, church and detached spur of mountain about two miles north of the capital, all bearing the same general name—and at this point Lake Texcoco comes near to the mountain, which was fortified both at the base and on the sides: but troops could have passed north of the mountain and come in only a few miles to the north-west, and so flanked the position, as they actually did on the south.

It has always seemed to me that this northern route to the City of Mexico, would have been the better one to have taken. But my later experience has taught me two lessons: first, that things are seen plainer after the events have occurred; second, that the most confident critics are generally those who know the least about the matter criticised. I know just enough about the Mexican war to approve heartily of most of the generalship, but to differ with a little of it. It is natural that an important city like Puebla should not have been passed with contempt; it may be natural that the direct road to it should have been taken; but it could have been passed, its evacuation insured and possession acquired without danger of encountering the enemy in intricate mountain defiles. In this same way the City of Mexico could have been approached without any danger of opposition, except in the open field.

But General Scott's successes are an answer to all criticism. He invaded a populous country, penetrating two hundred and sixty miles into the interior, with a force at no time equal to one-half of that opposed to him; he was without a base; the enemy was always intrenched, always on the defensive; yet he won every battle, he captured the capital, and conquered the government. Credit is due to the troops engaged, it is true, but the plans and the strategy were the general's.

I had now made marches and been in battle under both General Scott and General Taylor. The former divided his force of 10,500 men into four columns, starting a day apart, in moving from Puebla to the capital of the nation, when it was known that an army more than twice as large as his own stood ready to resist his coming. The road was broad and the country open except in crossing the Rio Frio mountain. General Taylor pursued the same course in marching toward an enemy. He moved even in smaller bodies. I never thought at the time to doubt the infallibility of these two generals in all matters pertaining to their profession. I supposed they moved in small bodies because more men could not be passed over a single road on the same day with their artillery and necessary trains. Later I found the fallacy of this belief. The rebellion, which followed as a sequence to the Mexican war, never could have been suppressed if larger bodies of men could not have been moved at the same time than was the custom under Scott and Taylor.

The victories in Mexico were, in every instance, over vastly superior numbers. There were two reasons for this. Both General Scott and General Taylor had such armies as are not often got together. At the battles of Palo Alto and Resaca-de-la-Palma, General Taylor had a small army, but it was composed exclusively of regular troops, under the best of drill and discipline. Every officer, from the highest to the lowest, was educated in his profession, not at West Point necessarily, but in the camp, in garrison, and many of them in Indian wars. The rank and file were probably inferior, as material out of which to make an army, to the volunteers that participated in all the later battles of the war; but they were brave men, and then drill and discipline brought out all there was in them. A better army, man for man, probably never faced an enemy than the one commanded by General Taylor in the earliest two engagements of the Mexican war. The volunteers who followed were of better material, but without drill or discipline at the start. They were associated with so many disciplined men and professionally educated officers, that when they went into engagements it was with a confidence they would not have felt otherwise. They became soldiers themselves almost at once. All these conditions we would enjoy again in case of war.

The Mexican army of that day was hardly an organization. The private soldier was picked up from the lower class of the inhabitants when wanted; his consent was not asked; he was poorly clothed, worse fed, and seldom paid. He was turned adrift when no longer wanted. The officers of the lower grades were but little superior to the men. With all this I have seen as brave stands made by some of these men as I have ever seen made by soldiers. Now Mexico has a standing army larger than that of the United States. They have a military school modelled after West Point. Their officers are educated and, no doubt, generally brave. The Mexican war of 1846–8 would be an impossibility in this generation.

The Mexicans have shown a patriotism which it would be well if we would imitate in part, but with more regard to truth. They celebrate the anniversaries of Chapultepec and Molino del Rey as of very great victories. The anniversaries are recognized as national holidays. At these two battles, while the United States troops were victorious, it was at very great sacrifice of life compared with what the Mexicans suffered. The Mexicans, as on many other occasions, stood up as well as any troops ever did. The trouble seemed to be the lack of experience among the officers, which led them after a certain time to simply quit, without being particularly whipped, but because they had fought enough. Their authorities of the present day grow enthusiastic over their theme when telling of these victories, and speak with pride of the large sum of money they forced us to pay in the end. With us, now twenty years after the close of the most stupendous war ever known, we have writers—who profess devotion to the nation—engaged in trying to prove that the Union forces were not victorious; practically, they say, we were slashed around from Donelson to Vicksburg and to Chattanooga; and in the East from Gettysburg to Appomattox, when the physical rebellion gave out from sheer exhaustion. There is no difference in the amount of romance in the two stories.

I would not have the anniversaries of our victories celebrated, nor those of our defeats made fast days and spent in humiliation and prayer; but I would like to see truthful history written. Such history will do full credit to the courage, endurance and soldierly ability of the American citizen, no matter what section of the country he hailed from, or in what ranks he fought. The justice of the cause which in the end prevailed, will, I doubt not, come to be acknowledged by every citizen of the land, in time. For the present, and so long as there are living witnesses of the great war of sections, there will be people who will not be consoled for the loss of a cause which they believed to be holy. As time passes, people, even of the South, will begin to wonder how it was possible that their ancestors ever fought for or justified institutions which acknowledged the right of property in man.

After the fall of the capital and the dispersal of the government of Mexico, it looked very much as if military occupation of the country for a long time might be necessary. General Scott at once began the preparation of orders, regulations and laws in view of this contingency. He contemplated making the country pay all the expenses of the occupation, without the army becoming a perceptible burden upon the people. His plan was to levy a direct tax upon the separate states, and collect, at the ports left open to trade, a duty on all imports. From the beginning of the war private property had not been taken, either for the use of the army or of individuals, without full compensation. This policy was to be pursued. There were not troops enough in the valley of Mexico to occupy many points, but now that there was no organized army of the enemy of any size, reinforcements could be got from the Rio Grande, and there were also new volunteers arriving from time to time, all by way of Vera Cruz. Military possession was taken of Cuernavaca, fifty miles south of the City of Mexico; of Toluca, nearly as far west, and of Pachuca, a mining town of great importance, some sixty miles to the northeast. Vera Cruz, Jalapa, Orizaba, and Puebla were already in our possession.

Meanwhile the Mexican government had departed in the person of Santa Anna, and it looked doubtful for a time whether the United States commissioner, Mr. Trist, would find anybody to negotiate with. A temporary government, however, was soon established at Queretaro, and Trist began negotiations for a conclusion of the war. Before terms were finally agreed upon he was ordered back to Washington, but General Scott prevailed upon him to remain, as an arrangement had been so nearly reached, and the administration must approve his acts if he succeeded in making such a treaty as had been contemplated in his instructions. The treaty was finally signed the 2d of February, 1848, and accepted by the government at Washington. It is that known as the "Treaty of Guadalupe Hidalgo," and secured to the United States the Rio Grande as the boundary of Texas, and the whole territory then included in New Mexico and Upper California, for the sum of $15,000,000.

Soon after entering the city of Mexico, the opposition of Generals Pillow, Worth and Colonel Duncan to General Scott became very marked. Scott claimed that they had demanded of the President his removal. I do not know whether this is so or not, but I do know of their unconcealed hostility to their chief. At last he placed them in arrest, and preferred charges against them of insubordination and disrespect. This act brought on a crisis in the career of the general commanding. He had asserted from the beginning that the administration was hostile to him; that it had failed in its promises of men and war material; that the President himself had shown duplicity if not treachery in the endeavor to procure the appointment of Benton: and the administration now gave open evidence of its enmity. About the middle of February orders came convening a court of inquiry, composed of Brevet Brigadier-General Towson, the paymaster-general of the army, Brigadier-General Cushing and Colonel Belknap, to inquire into the conduct of the accused and the accuser, and shortly afterwards orders were received from Washington, relieving Scott of the command of the army in the field and assigning Major-General William O. Butler of Kentucky to the place. This order also released Pillow, Worth and Duncan from arrest.

If a change was to be made the selection of General Butler was agreeable to every one concerned, so far as I remember to have heard expressions on the subject. There were many who regarded the treatment of General Scott as harsh and unjust. It is quite possible that the vanity of the General had led him to say and do things that afforded a plausible pretext to the administration for doing just what it did and what it had wanted to do from the start. The court tried the accuser quite as much as the accused. It was adjourned before completing its labors, to meet in Frederick, Maryland. General Scott left the country, and never after had more than the nominal command of the army until early in 1861. He certainly was not sustained in his efforts to maintain discipline in high places.

The efforts to kill off politically the two successful generals, made them both candidates for the Presidency. General Taylor was nominated in 1848, and was elected. Four years later General Scott received the nomination but was badly beaten, and the party nominating him died with his defeat.*

---

*The Mexican war made three presidential candidates, Scott, Taylor and Pierce—and any number of aspirants for that high office. It made also governors of States, members of the cabinet, foreign ministers and other officers of high rank both in state and nation. The rebellion, which contained more war in a single day, at some critical periods, than the whole Mexican war in two years, has not been so fruitful of political results to those engaged on the Union side. On the other side, the side of the South, nearly every man who holds office of any sort whatever, either in the state or in the nation, was a Confederate soldier; but this is easily accounted for from the fact that the South was a military camp, and there were very few people of a suitable age to be in the army who were not in it.

Chapter XIII.

TREATY OF PEACE—MEXICAN BULL FIGHTS—
REGIMENTAL QUARTERMASTER—TRIP TO POPOCATAPETL
—TRIP TO THE CAVES OF MEXICO.

THE TREATY OF PEACE between the two countries was signed by the commissioners of each side early in February, 1848. It took a considerable time for it to reach Washington, receive the approval of the administration, and be finally ratified by the Senate. It was naturally supposed by the army that there would be no more fighting, and officers and men were of course anxious to get home, but knowing there must be delay they contented themselves as best they could. Every Sunday there was a bull fight for the amusement of those who would pay their fifty cents. I attended one of them—just one—not wishing to leave the country without having witnessed the national sport. The sight to me was sickening. I could not see how human beings could enjoy the sufferings of beasts, and often of men, as they seemed to do on these occasions.

At these sports there are usually from four to six bulls sacrificed. The audience occupies seats around the ring in which the exhibition is given, each seat but the foremost rising higher than the one in front, so that every one can get a full view of the sport. When all is ready a bull is turned into the ring. Three or four men come in, mounted on the merest skeletons of horses blind or blind-folded and so weak that they could not make a sudden turn with their riders without danger of falling down. The men are armed with spears having a point as sharp as a needle. Other men enter the arena on foot, armed with red flags and explosives about the size of a musket cartridge. To each of these explosives is fastened a barbed needle which serves the purpose of attaching them to the bull by running the needle into the skin. Before the animal is turned loose a lot of these explosives are attached to him. The pain from the pricking of the skin by the needles is exasperating; but when the explosions of the cartridges commence the animal becomes frantic. As he makes a lunge towards one horseman, another runs a spear into him. He turns towards his last tormentor when a man on foot holds out a red flag; the bull rushes for this and is allowed to take it on his horns. The flag drops and covers the eyes of the animal so that he is at a loss what to do; it is jerked from him and the torment is renewed. When the animal is worked into an uncontrollable frenzy, the horsemen withdraw, and the matadores—literally murderers—enter, armed with knives having blades twelve or eighteen inches long, and sharp. The trick is to dodge an attack from the animal and stab him to the heart as he passes. If these efforts fail the bull is finally lassoed, held fast and killed by driving a knife blade into the spinal column just back of the horns. He is then dragged out by horses or mules, another is let into the ring, and the same performance is renewed.

On the occasion when I was present one of the bulls was not turned aside by the attacks in the rear, the presentations of the red flag, etc., etc., but kept right on, and placing his horns under the flanks of a horse threw him and his rider to the ground with great force. The horse was killed and the rider lay prostrate as if dead. The bull was then lassoed and killed in the manner above described. Men came in and carried the dead man off in a litter. When the slaughtered bull and horse were dragged out, a fresh bull was turned into the ring. Conspicuous among the spectators was the man who had been carried out on a litter but a few minutes before. He was only dead so far as that performance went; but the corpse was so lively that it could not forego the chance of witnessing the discomfiture of some of his brethren who might not be so fortunate. There was a feeling of disgust manifested by the audience to find that he had come to life again. I confess that I felt sorry to see the cruelty to the bull and the horse. I did not stay for the conclusion of the performance; but while I did stay, there was not a bull killed in the prescribed way.

Bull fights are now prohibited in the Federal District—embracing a territory around the City of Mexico, somewhat larger than the District of Columbia—and they are not an institution in any part of the country. During one of my recent visits to Mexico, bull fights were got up in my honor at Puebla and at Pachuca. I was not notified in advance so as to be able to decline and thus prevent the performance; but in both cases I civilly declined to attend.

Another amusement of the people of Mexico of that day, and one which nearly all indulged in, male and female, old and young, priest and layman, was Monte playing. Regular feast weeks were held every year at what was then known as St. Augustin Tlalpam, eleven miles out of town. There were dealers to suit every class and condition of people. In many of the booths *tlacos*—the copper coin of the country, four of them making six and a quarter cents of our money—were piled up in great quantities, with some silver, to accommodate the people who could not bet more than a few pennies at a time. In other booths silver formed the bulk of the capital of the bank, with a few doubloons to be changed if there should be a run of luck against the bank. In some there was no coin except gold. Here the rich were said to bet away their entire estates in a single day. All this is stopped now.

For myself, I was kept somewhat busy during the winter of 1847–8. My regiment was stationed in Tacubaya. I was regimental quartermaster and commissary. General Scott had been unable to get clothing for the troops from the North. The men were becoming—well, they needed clothing. Material had to be purchased, such as could be obtained, and people employed to make it up into "Yankee uniforms." A quartermaster in the city was designated to attend to this special duty; but clothing was so much needed that it was seized as fast as made up. A regiment was glad to get a dozen suits at a time. I had to look after this matter for the 4th infantry. Then our regimental fund had run down and some of the musicians in the band had been without their extra pay for a number of months.

The regimental bands at that day were kept up partly by pay from the government, and partly by pay from the regimental fund. There was authority of law for enlisting a certain number of men as musicians. So many could receive the pay of non-commissioned officers of the various grades, and the remainder the pay of privates. This would not secure a band leader, nor good players on certain instruments. In garrison

there are various ways of keeping up a regimental fund sufficient to give extra pay to musicians, establish libraries and
ten-pin alleys, subscribe to magazines and furnish many extra
comforts to the men. The best device for supplying the fund
is to issue bread to the soldiers instead of flour. The ration
used to be eighteen ounces per day of either flour or bread;
and one hundred pounds of flour will make one hundred and
forty pounds of bread. This saving was purchased by the commissary for the benefit of the fund. In the emergency the 4th
infantry was laboring under, I rented a bakery in the city,
hired bakers—Mexicans—bought fuel and whatever was necessary, and I also got a contract from the chief commissary of
the army for baking a large amount of hard bread. In two
months I made more money for the fund than my pay
amounted to during the entire war. While stationed at Monterey I had relieved the post fund in the same way. There,
however, was no profit except in the saving of flour by converting it into bread.

In the spring of 1848 a party of officers obtained leave to
visit Popocatapetl, the highest volcano in America, and to take
an escort. I went with the party, many of whom afterwards
occupied conspicuous positions before the country. Of those
who "went south," and attained high rank, there was Lieutenant Richard Anderson, who commanded a corps at Spottsylvania; Captain Sibley, a major-general, and, after the war,
for a number of years in the employ of the Khédive of Egypt;
Captain George Crittenden, a rebel general; S. B. Buckner,
who surrendered Fort Donelson; and Mansfield Lovell, who
commanded at New Orleans before that city fell into the
hands of the National troops. Of those who remained on our
side there were Captain Andrew Porter, Lieutenant C. P.
Stone and Lieutenant Z. B. Tower. There were quite a number of other officers, whose names I cannot recollect.

At a little village (Ozumba) near the base of Popocatapetl,
where we purposed to commence the ascent, we procured
guides and two pack mules with forage for our horses. High
up on the mountain there was a deserted house of one room,
called the Vaqueria, which had been occupied years before by
men in charge of cattle ranging on the mountain. The pasturage up there was very fine when we saw it, and there were still

some cattle, descendants of the former domestic herd, which had now become wild. It was possible to go on horseback as far as the Vaqueria, though the road was somewhat hazardous in places. Sometimes it was very narrow with a yawning precipice on one side, hundreds of feet down to a roaring mountain torrent below, and almost perpendicular walls on the other side. At one of these places one of our mules loaded with two sacks of barley, one on each side, the two about as big as he was, struck his load against the mountain-side and was precipitated to the bottom. The descent was steep but not perpendicular. The mule rolled over and over until the bottom was reached, and we supposed of course the poor animal was dashed to pieces. What was our surprise, not long after we had gone into bivouac, to see the lost mule, cargo and owner coming up the ascent. The load had protected the animal from serious injury; and his owner had gone after him and found a way back to the path leading up to the hut where we were to stay.

The night at the Vaqueria was one of the most unpleasant I ever knew. It was very cold and the rain fell in torrents. A little higher up the rain ceased and snow began. The wind blew with great velocity. The log-cabin we were in had lost the roof entirely on one side, and on the other it was hardly better than a sieve. There was little or no sleep that night. As soon as it was light the next morning, we started to make the ascent to the summit. The wind continued to blow with violence and the weather was still cloudy, but there was neither rain nor snow. The clouds, however, concealed from our view the country below us, except at times a momentary glimpse could be got through a clear space between them. The wind carried the loose snow around the mountain-sides in such volumes as to make it almost impossible to stand up against it. We labored on and on, until it became evident that the top could not be reached before night, if at all in such a storm, and we concluded to return. The descent was easy and rapid, though dangerous, until we got below the snow line. At the cabin we mounted our horses, and by night were at Ozumba.

The fatigues of the day and the loss of sleep the night before drove us to bed early. Our beds consisted of a place on the dirt-floor with a blanket under us. Soon all were asleep; but long before morning first one and then another of our party began to cry out with excruciating pain in the eyes. Not one escaped it. By morning the eyes of half the party were so swollen that they were entirely closed. The others suffered pain equally. The feeling was about what might be expected from the prick of a sharp needle at a white heat. We remained in quarters until the afternoon bathing our eyes in cold water. This relieved us very much, and before night the pain had entirely left. The swelling, however, continued, and about half the party still had their eyes entirely closed; but we concluded to make a start back, those who could see a little leading the horses of those who could not see at all. We moved back to the village of Ameca Ameca, some six miles, and stopped again for the night. The next morning all were entirely well and free from pain. The weather was clear and Popocatapetl stood out in all its beauty, the top looking as if not a mile away, and inviting us to return. About half the party were anxious to try the ascent again, and concluded to do so. The remainder—I was with the remainder—concluded that we had got all the pleasure there was to be had out of mountain climbing, and that we would visit the great caves of Mexico, some ninety miles from where we then were, on the road to Acapulco.

The party that ascended the mountain the second time succeeded in reaching the crater at the top, with but little of the labor they encountered in their first attempt. Three of them—Anderson, Stone and Buckner—wrote accounts of their journey, which were published at the time. I made no notes of this excursion, and have read nothing about it since, but it seems to me that I can see the whole of it as vividly as if it were but yesterday. I have been back at Ameca Ameca, and the village beyond, twice in the last five years. The scene had not changed materially from my recollection of it.

The party which I was with moved south down the valley to the town of Cuantla, some forty miles from Ameca Ameca. The latter stands on the plain at the foot of Popocatapetl, at an elevation of about eight thousand feet above tide water. The slope down is gradual as the traveller moves south, but one would not judge that, in going to Cuantla, descent enough had been made to occasion a material change in the climate and productions of the soil; but such is the case. In the morning we left a temperate climate where the cereals and fruits are those common to the United States; we halted in the evening in a tropical climate where the orange and banana, the coffee and the sugar-cane were flourishing. We had been travelling, apparently, on a plain all day, but in the direction of the flow of water.

Soon after the capture of the City of Mexico an armistice had been agreed to, designating the limits beyond which troops of the respective armies were not to go during its continuance. Our party knew nothing about these limits. As we approached Cuantla bugles sounded the assembly, and soldiers rushed from the guard-house in the edge of the town towards us. Our party halted, and I tied a white pocket handkerchief to a stick and, using it as a flag of truce, proceeded on to the town. Captains Sibley and Porter followed a few hundred yards behind. I was detained at the guard-house until a messenger could be dispatched to the quarters of the commanding general, who authorized that I should be conducted to him. I had been with the general but a few minutes when the two officers following announced themselves. The Mexican general reminded us that it was a violation of the truce for us to be there. However, as we had no special authority from our own commanding general, and as we knew nothing about the terms of the truce, we were permitted to occupy a vacant house outside the guard for the night, with the promise of a guide to put us on the road to Cuernavaca the next morning.

Cuernavaca is a town west of Cuantla. The country through which we passed, between these two towns, is tropical in climate and productions and rich in scenery. At one point, about half-way between the two places, the road goes over a low pass in the mountains in which there is a very quaint old town, the inhabitants of which at that day were nearly all full-blooded Indians. Very few of them even spoke Spanish. The houses were built of stone and generally only one story high. The streets were narrow, and had probably been paved before Cortez visited the country. They had not been graded, but the paving had been done on the natural surface. We had with us one vehicle, a cart, which was probably the first wheeled vehicle that had ever passed through that town.

On a hill overlooking this town stands the tomb of an ancient king; and it was understood that the inhabitants venerated this tomb very highly, as well as the memory of the ruler who was supposed to be buried in it. We ascended the mountain and surveyed the tomb; but it showed no particular marks of architectural taste, mechanical skill or advanced civilization. The next day we went into Cuernavaca.

After a day's rest at Cuernavaca our party set out again on the journey to the great caves of Mexico. We had proceeded but a few miles when we were stopped, as before, by a guard and notified that the terms of the existing armistice did not permit us to go further in that direction. Upon convincing the guard that we were a mere party of pleasure seekers desious of visiting the great natural curiosities of the country which we expected soon to leave, we were conducted to a large hacienda near by, and directed to remain there until the commanding general of that department could be communicated with and his decision obtained as to whether we should be permitted to pursue our journey. The guard promised to send a messenger at once, and expected a reply by night. At night there was no response from the commanding general, but the captain of the guard was sure he would have a reply by morning. Again in the morning there was no reply. The second evening the same thing happened, and finally we learned that the guard had sent no message or messenger to the department commander. We determined therefore to go on unless stopped by a force sufficient to compel obedience.

After a few hours' travel we came to a town where a scene similar to the one at Cuantla occurred. The commanding officer sent a guide to conduct our party around the village and to put us upon our road again. This was the last interruption: that night we rested at a large coffee plantation, some eight miles from the cave we were on the way to visit. It must have been a Saturday night; the peons had been paid off, and spent part of the night in gambling away their scanty week's earnings. Their coin was principally copper, and I do not believe there was a man among them who had received as much as twenty-five cents in money. They were as much excited, however, as if they had been staking thousands. I recollect one poor fellow, who had lost his last tlaco, pulled off his shirt and, in the most excited manner, put that up on the turn of a card. Monte was the game played, the place out of doors, near the window of the room occupied by the officers of our party.

The next morning we were at the mouth of the cave at an early hour, provided with guides, candles and rockets. We explored to a distance of about three miles from the entrance, and found a succession of chambers of great dimensions and of great beauty when lit up with our rockets. Stalactites and stalagmites of all sizes were discovered. Some of the former were many feet in diameter and extended from ceiling to floor; some of the latter were but a few feet high from the floor; but the formation is going on constantly, and many centuries hence these stalagmites will extend to the ceiling and become complete columns. The stalagmites were all a little concave, and the cavities were filled with water. The water percolates through the roof, a drop at a time—often the drops several minutes apart—and more or less charged with mineral matter. Evaporation goes on slowly, leaving the mineral behind. This in time makes the immense columns, many of them thousands of tons in weight, which serve to support the roofs over the vast chambers. I recollect that at one point in the cave one of these columns is of such huge proportions that there is only a narrow passage left on either side of it. Some of our party became satisfied with their explorations before we had reached the point to which the guides were accustomed to take explorers, and started back without guides. Coming to the large column spoken of, they followed it entirely around, and commenced retracing their steps into the bowels of the mountain, without being aware of the fact. When the rest of us had completed our explorations, we started out with our guides, but had not gone far before we saw the torches of an approaching party. We could not conceive who these could be, for all of us had come in together, and there were none but ourselves at the entrance when we started in. Very soon we found it was our friends. It took them some time to conceive how they had got where they were. They were sure they had kept straight on for the mouth of the cave, and had gone about far enough to have reached it.

Chapter XIV.

RETURN OF THE ARMY—MARRIAGE—ORDERED TO THE
PACIFIC COAST—CROSSING THE ISTHMUS—ARRIVAL
AT SAN FRANCISCO.

M Y EXPERIENCE in the Mexican war was of great advantage to me afterwards. Besides the many practical lessons it taught, the war brought nearly all the officers of the regular army together so as to make them personally acquainted. It also brought them in contact with volunteers, many of whom served in the war of the rebellion afterwards. Then, in my particular case, I had been at West Point at about the right time to meet most of the graduates who were of a suitable age at the breaking out of the rebellion to be trusted with large commands. Graduating in 1843, I was at the military academy from one to four years with all cadets who graduated between 1840 and 1846—seven classes. These classes embraced more than fifty officers who afterwards became generals on one side or the other in the rebellion, many of them holding high commands. All the older officers, who became conspicuous in the rebellion, I had also served with and known in Mexico: Lee, J. E. Johnston, A. S. Johnston, Holmes, Hebért and a number of others on the Confederate side; McCall, Mansfield, Phil. Kearney and others on the National side. The acquaintance thus formed was of immense service to me in the war of the rebellion—I mean what I learned of the characters of those to whom I was afterwards opposed. I do not pretend to say that all movements, or even many of them, were made with special reference to the characteristics of the commander against whom they were directed. But my appreciation of my enemies was certainly affected by this knowledge. The natural disposition of most people is to clothe a commander of a large army whom they do not know, with almost superhuman abilities. A large part of the National army, for instance, and most of the press of the country, clothed General Lee with just such qualities, but I had known him personally, and knew that he was mortal; and it was just as well that I felt this.

The treaty of peace was at last ratified, and the evacuation of Mexico by United States troops was ordered. Early in June the troops in the City of Mexico began to move out. Many of them, including the brigade to which I belonged, were assembled at Jalapa, above the vomito, to await the arrival of transports at Vera Cruz: but with all this precaution my regiment and others were in camp on the sand beach in a July sun, for about a week before embarking, while the fever raged with great virulence in Vera Cruz, not two miles away. I can call to mind only one person, an officer, who died of the disease. My regiment was sent to Pascagoula, Mississippi, to spend the summer. As soon as it was settled in camp I obtained a leave of absence for four months and proceeded to St. Louis. On the 22d of August, 1848, I was married to Miss Julia Dent, the lady of whom I have before spoken. We visited my parents and relations in Ohio, and, at the end of my leave, proceeded to my post at Sackett's Harbor, New York. In April following I was ordered to Detroit, Michigan, where two years were spent with but few important incidents.

The present constitution of the State of Michigan was ratified during this time. By the terms of one of its provisions, all citizens of the United States residing within the State at the time of the ratification became citizens of Michigan also. During my stay in Detroit there was an election for city officers. Mr. Zachariah Chandler was the candidate of the Whigs for the office of Mayor, and was elected, although the city was then reckoned democratic. All the officers stationed there at the time who offered their votes were permitted to cast them. I did not offer mine, however, as I did not wish to consider myself a citizen of Michigan. This was Mr. Chandler's first entry into politics, a career he followed ever after with great success, and in which he died enjoying the friendship, esteem and love of his countrymen.

In the spring of 1851 the garrison at Detroit was transferred to Sackett's Harbor, and in the following spring the entire 4th infantry was ordered to the Pacific Coast. It was decided that Mrs. Grant should visit my parents at first for a few months, and then remain with her own family at their St. Louis home until an opportunity offered of sending for her. In the month of April the regiment was assembled at Governor's Island, New York Harbor, and on the 5th of July eight companies sailed for Aspinwall. We numbered a little over seven hundred persons, including the families of officers and soldiers. Passage was secured for us on the old steamer *Ohio*, commanded at the time by Captain Schenck, of the navy. It had not been determined, until a day or two before starting, that the 4th infantry should go by the *Ohio*; consequently, a complement of passengers had already been secured. The addition of over seven hundred to this list crowded the steamer most uncomfortably, especially for the tropics in July.

In eight days Aspinwall was reached. At that time the streets of the town were eight or ten inches under water, and foot passengers passed from place to place on raised footwalks. July is at the height of the wet season, on the Isthmus. At intervals the rain would pour down in streams, followed in not many minutes by a blazing, tropical summer's sun. These alternate changes, from rain to sunshine, were continuous in the afternoons. I wondered how any person could live many months in Aspinwall, and wondered still more why any one tried.

In the summer of 1852 the Panama railroad was completed only to the point where it now crosses the Chagres River. From there passengers were carried by boats to Gorgona, at which place they took mules for Panama, some twenty-five miles further. Those who travelled over the Isthmus in those days will remember that boats on the Chagres River were propelled by natives not inconveniently burdened with clothing. These boats carried thirty to forty passengers each. The crews consisted of six men to a boat, armed with long poles. There were planks wide enough for a man to walk on conveniently, running along the sides of each boat from end to end. The men would start from the bow, place one end of their poles against the river bottom, brace their shoulders against the other end, and then walk to the stern as rapidly as they could. In this way from a mile to a mile and a half an hour could be made, against the current of the river.

I, as regimental quartermaster, had charge of the public property and had also to look after the transportation. A contract had been entered into with the steamship company in New York for the transportation of the regiment to California, including the Isthmus transit. A certain amount of baggage was allowed per man, and saddle animals were to be furnished to commissioned officers and to all disabled persons. The regiment, with the exception of one company left as guards to the public property—camp and garrison equipage principally—and the soldiers with families, took boats, propelled as above described, for Gorgona. From this place they marched to Panama, and were soon comfortably on the steamer anchored in the bay, some three or four miles from the town. I, with one company of troops and all the soldiers with families, all the tents, mess chests and camp kettles, was sent to Cruces, a town a few miles higher up the Chagres River than Gorgona. There I found an impecunious American who had taken the contract to furnish transportation for the regiment at a stipulated price per hundred pounds for the freight and so much for each saddle animal. But when we reached Cruces there was not a mule, either for pack or saddle, in the place. The contractor promised that the animals should be on hand in the morning. In the morning he said that they were on the way from some imaginary place, and would arrive in the course of the day. This went on until I saw that he could not procure the animals at all at the price he had promised to furnish them for. The unusual number of passengers that had come over on the steamer, and the large amount of freight to pack, had created an unprecedented demand for mules. Some of the passengers paid as high as forty dollars for the use of a mule to ride twenty-five miles, when the mule would not have sold for ten dollars in that market at other times. Meanwhile the cholera had broken out, and men were dying every hour. To diminish the food for the disease, I permitted the company detailed with me to proceed to Panama. The captain and the doctors accompanied the men, and I was left alone with the sick and the soldiers who had families. The regiment at Panama was also affected with the disease; but there were better accommodations for the well on the steamer, and a hospital, for those taken with the disease, on an old hulk anchored a mile off. There were also hospital tents on shore on the island of Flamingo, which stands in the bay.

I was about a week at Cruces before transportation began to come in. About one-third of the people with me died, either at Cruces or on the way to Panama. There was no agent of the transportation company at Cruces to consult, or to take the responsibility of procuring transportation at a price which would secure it. I therefore myself dismissed the contractor and made a new contract with a native, at more than double the original price. Thus we finally reached Panama. The steamer, however, could not proceed until the cholera abated, and the regiment was detained still longer. Altogether, on the Isthmus and on the Pacific side, we were delayed six weeks. About one-seventh of those who left New York harbor with the 4th infantry on the 5th of July, now lie buried on the Isthmus of Panama or on Flamingo island in Panama Bay.

One amusing circumstance occurred while we were lying at anchor in Panama Bay. In the regiment there was a Lieutenant Slaughter who was very liable to sea-sickness. It almost made him sick to see the wave of a table-cloth when the servants were spreading it. Soon after his graduation, Slaughter was ordered to California and took passage by a sailing vessel going around Cape Horn. The vessel was seven months making the voyage, and Slaughter was sick every moment of the time, never more so than while lying at anchor after reaching his place of destination. On landing in California he found orders which had come by the Isthmus, notifying him of a mistake in his assignment; he should have been ordered to the northern lakes. He started back by the Isthmus route and was sick all the way. But when he arrived at the East he was again ordered to California, this time definitely, and at this date was making his third trip. He was as sick as ever, and had been so for more than a month while lying at anchor in the bay. I remember him well, seated with his elbows on the table in front of him, his chin between his hands, and looking the picture of despair. At last he broke out, "I wish I had taken my father's advice; he wanted me to go into the navy; if I had done so, I should not have had to go to sea so much." Poor Slaughter! it was his last sea voyage. He was killed by Indians in Oregon.

By the last of August the cholera had so abated that it was

deemed safe to start. The disease did not break out again on the way to California, and we reached San Francisco early in September.

Chapter XV.

SAN FRANCISCO at that day was a lively place. Gold, or placer digging as it was called, was at its height. Steamers plied daily between San Francisco and both Stockton and Sacramento. Passengers and gold from the southern mines came by the Stockton boat; from the northern mines by Sacramento. In the evening when these boats arrived, Long Wharf—there was but one wharf in San Francisco in 1852—was alive with people crowding to meet the miners as they came down to sell their "dust" and to "have a time." Of these some were runners for hotels, boarding houses or restaurants; others belonged to a class of impecunious adventurers, of good manners and good presence, who were ever on the alert to make the acquaintance of people with some ready means, in the hope of being asked to take a meal at a restaurant. Many were young men of good family, good education and gentlemanly instincts. Their parents had been able to support them during their minority, and to give them good educations, but not to maintain them afterwards. From 1849 to 1853 there was a rush of people to the Pacific coast, of the class described. All thought that fortunes were to be picked up, without effort, in the gold fields on the Pacific. Some realized more than their most sanguine expectations; but for one such there were hundreds disappointed, many of whom now fill unknown graves; others died wrecks of their former selves, and many, without a vicious instinct, became criminals and outcasts. Many of the real scenes in early California life exceed in strangeness and interest any of the mere products of the brain of the novelist.

Those early days in California brought out character. It was a long way off then, and the journey was expensive. The fortunate could go by Cape Horn or by the Isthmus of Panama; but the mass of pioneers crossed the plains with their ox-teams. This took an entire summer. They were very lucky when they got through with a yoke of worn-out cattle. All other means were exhausted in procuring the outfit on the Missouri River. The immigrant, on arriving, found himself a stranger, in a strange land, far from friends. Time pressed, for the little means that could be realized from the sale of what was left of the outfit would not support a man long at California prices. Many became discouraged. Others would take off their coats and look for a job, no matter what it might be. These succeeded as a rule. There were many young men who had studied professions before they went to California, and who had never done a day's manual labor in their lives, who took in the situation at once and went to work to make a start at anything they could get to do. Some supplied carpenters and masons with material—carrying plank, brick, or mortar, as the case might be; others drove stages, drays, or baggage wagons, until they could do better. More became discouraged early and spent their time looking up people who would "treat," or lounging about restaurants and gambling houses where free lunches were furnished daily. They were welcomed at these places because they often brought in miners who proved good customers.

My regiment spent a few weeks at Benicia barracks, and then was ordered to Fort Vancouver, on the Columbia River, then in Oregon Territory. During the winter of 1852–3 the territory was divided, all north of the Columbia River being taken from Oregon to make Washington Territory.

Prices for all kinds of supplies were so high on the Pacific coast from 1849 until at least 1853—that it would have been impossible for officers of the army to exist upon their pay, if it had not been that authority was given them to purchase from the commissary such supplies as he kept, at New Orleans wholesale prices. A cook could not be hired for the pay of a captain. The cook could do better. At Benicia, in 1852, flour was 25 cents per pound; potatoes were 16 cents; beets, turnips and cabbage, 6 cents; onions, 37½ cents; meat and other articles in proportion. In 1853 at Vancouver vegetables were a little lower. I with three other officers concluded that we would raise a crop for ourselves, and by selling the surplus realize something handsome. I bought a pair of horses that had crossed the plains that summer and were very poor. They recuperated rapidly, however, and proved a good team to break up the ground with. I performed all the labor of breaking up the ground while the other officers planted the potatoes. Our crop was enormous. Luckily for us the Columbia River rose to a great height from the melting of the snow in the mountains in June, and overflowed and killed most of our crop. This saved digging it up, for everybody on the Pacific coast seemed to have come to the conclusion at the same time that agriculture would be profitable. In 1853 more than three-quarters of the potatoes raised were permitted to rot in the ground, or had to be thrown away. The only potatoes we sold were to our own mess.

While I was stationed on the Pacific coast we were free from Indian wars. There were quite a number of remnants of tribes in the vicinity of Portland in Oregon, and of Fort Vancouver in Washington Territory. They had generally acquired some of the vices of civilization, but none of the virtues, except in individual cases. The Hudson's Bay Company had held the North-west with their trading posts for many years before the United States was represented on the Pacific coast. They still retained posts along the Columbia River and one at Fort Vancouver, when I was there. Their treatment of the Indians had brought out the better qualities of the savages. Farming had been undertaken by the company to supply the Indians with bread and vegetables; they raised some cattle and horses; and they had now taught the Indians to do the labor of the farm and herd. They always compensated them for their labor, and always gave them goods of uniform quality and at uniform price.

Before the advent of the American, the medium of exchange between the Indian and the white man was pelts. Afterward it was silver coin. If an Indian received in the sale of a horse a fifty dollar gold piece, not an infrequent occurrence, the first thing he did was to exchange it for American half dollars. These he could count. He would then commence his purchases, paying for each article separately, as he got it. He would not trust any one to add up the bill and pay it all at once. At that day fifty dollar gold pieces, not the issue of the government, were common on the Pacific coast. They were called slugs.

The Indians, along the lower Columbia as far as the Cascades and on the lower Willamette, died off very fast during the year I spent in that section; for besides acquiring the vices of the white people they had acquired also their diseases. The measles and the small-pox were both amazingly fatal. In their wild state, before the appearance of the white man among them, the principal complaints they were subject to were those produced by long involuntary fasting, violent exercise in pursuit of game, and over-eating. Instinct more than reason had taught them a remedy for these ills. It was the steam bath. Something like a bake-oven was built, large enough to admit a man lying down. Bushes were stuck in the ground in two rows, about six feet long and some two or three feet apart; other bushes connected the rows at one end. The tops of the bushes were drawn together to interlace, and confined in that position; the whole was then plastered over with wet clay until every opening was filled. Just inside the open end of the oven the floor was scooped out so as to make a hole that would hold a bucket or two of water. These ovens were always built on the banks of a stream, a big spring, or pool of water. When a patient required a bath, a fire was built near the oven and a pile of stones put upon it. The cavity at the front was then filled with water. When the stones were sufficiently heated, the patient would draw himself into the oven; a blanket would be thrown over the open end, and hot stones put into the water until the patient could stand it no longer. He was then withdrawn from his steam bath and doused into the cold stream near by. This treatment may have answered with the early ailments of the Indians. With the measles or small-pox it would kill every time.

During my year on the Columbia River, the small-pox exterminated one small remnant of a band of Indians entirely, and reduced others materially. I do not think there was a case of recovery among them, until the doctor with the Hudson Bay Company took the matter in hand and established a hospital. Nearly every case he treated recovered. I never, myself, saw the treatment described in the preceding paragraph, but have heard it described by persons who have witnessed it. The decimation among the Indians I knew of personally, and the hospital, established for their benefit, was a Hudson's Bay building not a stone's throw from my own quarters.

The death of Colonel Bliss, of the Adjutant General's department, which occurred July 5th, 1853, promoted me to the captaincy of a company then stationed at Humboldt Bay, California. The notice reached me in September of the same year, and I very soon started to join my new command. There was no way of reaching Humboldt at that time except to take passage on a San Francisco sailing vessel going after lumber. Red wood, a species of cedar, which on the Pacific coast takes the place filled by white pine in the East, then abounded on the banks of Humboldt Bay. There were extensive saw-mills engaged in preparing this lumber for the San Francisco market, and sailing vessels, used in getting it to market, furnished the only means of communication between Humboldt and the balance of the world.

I was obliged to remain in San Francisco for several days before I found a vessel. This gave me a good opportunity of comparing the San Francisco of 1852 with that of 1853. As before stated, there had been but one wharf in front of the city in 1852—Long Wharf. In 1853 the town had grown out into the bay beyond what was the end of this wharf when I first saw it. Streets and houses had been built out on piles where the year before the largest vessels visiting the port lay at anchor or tied to the wharf. There was no filling under the streets or houses. San Francisco presented the same general appearance as the year before; that is, eating, drinking and gambling houses were conspicuous for their number and publicity. They were on the first floor, with doors wide open. At all hours of the day and night in walking the streets, the eye was regaled, on every block near the water front, by the sight of players at faro. Often broken places were found in the street, large enough to let a man down into the water below. I have but little doubt that many of the people who went to the Pacific coast in the early days of the gold excitement, and have never been heard from since, or who were heard from for a time and then ceased to write, found watery graves beneath the houses or streets built over San Francisco Bay.

Besides the gambling in cards there was gambling on a

larger scale in city lots. These were sold "On Change," much as stocks are now sold on Wall Street. Cash, at time of purchase, was always paid by the broker; but the purchaser had only to put up his margin. He was charged at the rate of two or three per cent. a month on the difference, besides commissions. The sand hills, some of them almost inaccessible to foot-passengers, were surveyed off and mapped into fifty vara lots—a vara being a Spanish yard. These were sold at first at very low prices, but were sold and resold for higher prices until they went up to many thousands of dollars. The brokers did a fine business, and so did many such purchasers as were sharp enough to quit purchasing before the final crash came. As the city grew, the sand hills back of the town furnished material for filling up the bay under the houses and streets, and still further out. The temporary houses, first built over the water in the harbor, soon gave way to more solid structures. The main business part of the city now is on solid ground, made where vessels of the largest class lay at anchor in the early days. I was in San Francisco again in 1854. Gambling houses had disappeared from public view. The city had become staid and orderly.

Chapter XVI.

M Y FAMILY, all this while, was at the East. It consisted now of a wife and two children. I saw no chance of supporting them on the Pacific coast out of my pay as an army officer. I concluded, therefore, to resign, and in March applied for a leave of absence until the end of the July following, tendering my resignation to take effect at the end of that time. I left the Pacific coast very much attached to it, and with the full expectation of making it my future home. That expectation and that hope remained uppermost in my mind until the Lieutenant-Generalcy bill was introduced into Congress in the winter of 1863–4. The passage of that bill, and my promotion, blasted my last hope of ever becoming a citizen of the further West.

In the late summer of 1854 I rejoined my family, to find in it a son whom I had never seen, born while I was on the Isthmus of Panama. I was now to commence, at the age of thirty-two, a new struggle for our support. My wife had a farm near St. Louis, to which we went, but I had no means to stock it. A house had to be built also. I worked very hard, never losing a day because of bad weather, and accomplished the object in a moderate way. If nothing else could be done I would load a cord of wood on a wagon and take it to the city for sale. I managed to keep along very well until 1858, when I was attacked by fever and ague. I had suffered very severely and for a long time from this disease, while a boy in Ohio. It lasted now over a year, and, while it did not keep me in the house, it did interfere greatly with the amount of work I was able to perform. In the fall of 1858 I sold out my stock, crops and farming utensils at auction, and gave up farming.

In the winter I established a partnership with Harry Boggs, a cousin of Mrs. Grant, in the real estate agency business. I spent that winter at St. Louis myself, but did not take my family into town until the spring. Our business might have become prosperous if I had been able to wait for it to grow.

As it was, there was no more than one person could attend to, and not enough to support two families. While a citizen of St. Louis and engaged in the real estate agency business, I was a candidate for the office of county engineer, an office of respectability and emolument which would have been very acceptable to me at that time. The incumbent was appointed by the county court, which consisted of five members. My opponent had the advantage of birth over me (he was a citizen by adoption) and carried off the prize. I now withdrew from the co-partnership with Boggs, and, in May, 1860, removed to Galena, Illinois, and took a clerkship in my father's store.

While a citizen of Missouri, my first opportunity for casting a vote at a Presidential election occurred. I had been in the army from before attaining my majority and had thought but little about politics, although I was a Whig by education and a great admirer of Mr. Clay. But the Whig party had ceased to exist before I had an opportunity of exercising the privilege of casting a ballot; the Know-Nothing party had taken its place, but was on the wane; and the Republican party was in a chaotic state and had not yet received a name. It had no existence in the Slave States except at points on the borders next to Free States. In St. Louis City and County, what afterwards became the Republican party was known as the Free-Soil Democracy, led by the Honorable Frank P. Blair. Most of my neighbors had known me as an officer of the army with Whig proclivities. They had been on the same side, and, on the death of their party, many had become Know-Nothings, or members of the American party. There was a lodge near my new home, and I was invited to join it. I accepted the invitation; was initiated; attended a meeting just one week later, and never went to another afterwards.

I have no apologies to make for having been one week a member of the American party; for I still think native-born citizens of the United States should have as much protection, as many privileges in their native country, as those who voluntarily select it for a home. But all secret, oath-bound political parties are dangerous to any nation, no matter how pure or how patriotic the motives and principles which first bring them together. No political party can or ought to exist when one of its corner-stones is opposition to freedom of thought and to the right to worship God "according to the dictate of one's own conscience," or according to the creed of any religious denomination whatever. Nevertheless, if a sect sets up its laws as binding above the State laws, wherever the two come in conflict this claim must be resisted and suppressed at whatever cost.

Up to the Mexican war there were a few out and out abolitionists, men who carried their hostility to slavery into all elections, from those for a justice of the peace up to the Presidency of the United States. They were noisy but not numerous. But the great majority of people at the North, where slavery did not exist, were opposed to the institution, and looked upon its existence in any part of the country as unfortunate. They did not hold the States where slavery existed responsible for it; and believed that protection should be given to the right of property in slaves until some satisfactory way could be reached to be rid of the institution. Opposition to slavery was not a creed of either political party. In some sections more anti-slavery men belonged to the Democratic party, and in others to the Whigs. But with the inauguration of the Mexican war, in fact with the annexation of Texas, "the inevitable conflict" commenced.

As the time for the Presidential election of 1856—the first at which I had the opportunity of voting—approached, party feeling began to run high. The Republican party was regarded in the South and the border States not only as opposed to the extension of slavery, but as favoring the compulsory abolition of the institution without compensation to the owners. The most horrible visions seemed to present themselves to the minds of people who, one would suppose, ought to have known better. Many educated and, otherwise, sensible persons appeared to believe that emancipation meant social equality. Treason to the Government was openly advocated and was not rebuked. It was evident to my mind that the election of a Republican President in 1856 meant the secession of all the Slave States, and rebellion. Under these circumstances I preferred the success of a candidate whose election would prevent or postpone secession, to seeing the country plunged into a war the end of which no man could foretell.

With a Democrat elected by the unanimous vote of the Slave States, there could be no pretext for secession for four years. I very much hoped that the passions of the people would subside in that time, and the catastrophe be averted altogether; if it was not, I believed the country would be better prepared to receive the shock and to resist it. I therefore voted for James Buchanan for President. Four years later the Republican party was successful in electing its candidate to the Presidency. The civilized world has learned the consequence. Four millions of human beings held as chattels have been liberated; the ballot has been given to them; the free schools of the country have been opened to their children. The nation still lives, and the people are just as free to avoid social intimacy with the blacks as ever they were, or as they are with white people.

While living in Galena I was nominally only a clerk supporting myself and family on a stipulated salary. In reality my position was different. My father had never lived in Galena himself, but had established my two brothers there, the one next younger than myself in charge of the business, assisted by the youngest. When I went there it was my father's intention to give up all connection with the business himself, and to establish his three sons in it: but the brother who had really built up the business was sinking with consumption, and it was not thought best to make any change while he was in this condition. He lived until September, 1861, when he succumbed to that insidious disease which always flatters its victims into the belief that they are growing better up to the close of life. A more honorable man never transacted business. In September, 1861, I was engaged in an employment which required all my attention elsewhere.

During the eleven months that I lived in Galena prior to the first call for volunteers, I had been strictly attentive to my business, and had made but few acquaintances other than customers and people engaged in the same line with myself. When the election took place in November, 1860, I had not been a resident of Illinois long enough to gain citizenship and could not, therefore, vote. I was really glad of this at the time, for my pledges would have compelled me to vote for Stephen A. Douglas, who had no possible chance of election. The contest was really between Mr. Breckinridge and Mr. Lincoln;

between minority rule and rule by the majority. I wanted, as between these candidates, to see Mr. Lincoln elected. Excitement ran high during the canvass, and torch-light processions enlivened the scene in the generally quiet streets of Galena many nights during the campaign. I did not parade with either party, but occasionally met with the "wide awakes"— Republicans—in their rooms, and superintended their drill. It was evident, from the time of the Chicago nomination to the close of the canvass, that the election of the Republican candidate would be the signal for some of the Southern States to secede. I still had hopes that the four years which had elapsed since the first nomination of a Presidential candidate by a party distinctly opposed to slavery extension, had given time for the extreme pro-slavery sentiment to cool down; for the Southerners to think well before they took the awful leap which they had so vehemently threatened. But I was mistaken.

The Republican candidate was elected, and solid substantial people of the North-west, and I presume the same order of people throughout the entire North, felt very serious, but determined, after this event. It was very much discussed whether the South would carry out its threat to secede and set up a separate government, the corner-stone of which should be, protection to the "Divine" institution of slavery. For there were people who believed in the "divinity" of human slavery, as there are now people who believe Mormonism and Polygamy to be ordained by the Most High. We forgive them for entertaining such notions, but forbid their practice. It was generally believed that there would be a flurry; that some of the extreme Southern States would go so far as to pass ordinances of secession. But the common impression was that this step was so plainly suicidal for the South, that the movement would not spread over much of the territory and would not last long.

Doubtless the founders of our government, the majority of them at least, regarded the confederation of the colonies as an experiment. Each colony considered itself a separate government; that the confederation was for mutual protection against a foreign foe, and the prevention of strife and war among themselves. If there had been a desire on the part of any single State to withdraw from the compact at any time while the number of States was limited to the original thirteen, I do not suppose there would have been any to contest the right, no matter how much the determination might have been regretted. The problem changed on the ratification of the Constitution by all the colonies; it changed still more when amendments were added; and if the right of any one State to withdraw continued to exist at all after the ratification of the Constitution, it certainly ceased on the formation of new States, at least so far as the new States themselves were concerned. It was never possessed at all by Florida or the States west of the Mississippi, all of which were purchased by the treasury of the entire nation. Texas and the territory brought into the Union in consequence of annexation, were purchased with both blood and treasure; and Texas, with a domain greater than that of any European state except Russia, was permitted to retain as state property all the public lands within its borders. It would have been ingratitude and injustice of the most flagrant sort for this State to withdraw from the Union after all that had been spent and done to introduce her; yet, if separation had actually occurred, Texas must necessarily have gone with the South, both on account of her institutions and her geographical position. Secession was illogical as well as impracticable; it was revolution.

Now, the right of revolution is an inherent one. When people are oppressed by their government, it is a natural right they enjoy to relieve themselves of the oppression, if they are strong enough, either by withdrawal from it, or by overthrowing it and substituting a government more acceptable. But any people or part of a people who resort to this remedy, stake their lives, their property, and every claim for protection given by citizenship—on the issue. Victory, or the conditions imposed by the conqueror—must be the result.

In the case of the war between the States it would have been the exact truth if the South had said,—"We do not want to live with you Northern people any longer; we know our institution of slavery is obnoxious to you, and, as you are growing numerically stronger than we, it may at some time in the future be endangered. So long as you permitted us to control the government, and with the aid of a few friends at the North to enact laws constituting your section a guard against the escape of our property, we were willing to live with you. You have been submissive to our rule heretofore; but it looks now as if you did not intend to continue so, and we will remain in the Union no longer." Instead of this the seceding States cried lustily,—"Let us alone; you have no constitutional power to interfere with us." Newspapers and people at the North reiterated the cry. Individuals might ignore the constitution; but the Nation itself must not only obey it, but must enforce the strictest construction of that instrument; the construction put upon it by the Southerners themselves. The fact is the constitution did not apply to any such contingency as the one existing from 1861 to 1865. Its framers never dreamed of such a contingency occurring. If they had foreseen it, the probabilities are they would have sanctioned the right of a State or States to withdraw rather than that there should be war between brothers.

The framers were wise in their generation and wanted to do the very best possible to secure their own liberty and independence, and that also of their descendants to the latest days. It is preposterous to suppose that the people of one generation can lay down the best and only rules of government for all who are to come after them, and under unforeseen contingencies. At the time of the framing of our constitution the only physical forces that had been subdued and made to serve man and do his labor, were the currents in the streams and in the air we breathe. Rude machinery, propelled by water power, had been invented; sails to propel ships upon the waters had been set to catch the passing breeze—but the application of steam to propel vessels against both wind and current, and machinery to do all manner of work had not been thought of. The instantaneous transmission of messages around the world by means of electricity would probably at that day have been attributed to witchcraft or a league with the Devil. Immaterial circumstances had changed as greatly as material ones. We could not and ought not to be rigidly bound by the rules laid down under circumstances so different for emergencies so utterly unanticipated. The fathers themselves would have been the first to declare that their prerogatives were not irrevocable. They would surely have resisted secession could they have lived to see the shape it assumed.

I travelled through the Northwest considerably during the winter of 1860–1. We had customers in all the little towns in south-west Wisconsin, south-east Minnesota and north-east Iowa. These generally knew I had been a captain in the regular army and had served through the Mexican war. Consequently wherever I stopped at night, some of the people would come to the public-house where I was, and sit till a late hour discussing the probabilities of the future. My own views at that time were like those officially expressed by Mr. Seward at a later day, that "the war would be over in ninety days." I continued to entertain these views until after the battle of Shiloh. I believe now that there would have been no more battles at the West after the capture of Fort Donelson if all the troops in that region had been under a single commander who would have followed up that victory.

There is little doubt in my mind now that the prevailing sentiment of the South would have been opposed to secession in 1860 and 1861, if there had been a fair and calm expression of opinion, unbiased by threats, and if the ballot of one legal voter had counted for as much as that of any other. But there was no calm discussion of the question. Demagogues who were too old to enter the army if there should be a war, others who entertained so high an opinion of their own ability that they did not believe they could be spared from the direction of the affairs of state in such an event, declaimed vehemently and unceasingly against the North; against its aggressions upon the South; its interference with Southern rights, etc., etc. They denounced the Northerners as cowards, poltroons, negro-worshippers; claimed that one Southern man was equal to five Northern men in battle; that if the South would stand up for its rights the North would back down. Mr. Jefferson Davis said in a speech, delivered at La Grange, Mississippi, before the secession of that State, that he would agree to drink all the blood spilled south of Mason and Dixon's line if there should be a war. The young men who would have the fighting to do in case of war, believed all these statements, both in regard to the aggressiveness of the North and its cowardice. They, too, cried out for a separation from such people. The great bulk of the legal voters of the South were men who owned no slaves; their homes were generally in the hills and poor country; their facilities for educating their children, even up to the point of reading and writing, were very limited; their interest in the contest was very meagre—what there was, if they had been capable of seeing it, was with the North; they too needed emancipation. Under the old régime they were looked down upon by those who controlled all the affairs in the interest of slave-owners, as poor white trash who were allowed the ballot so long as they cast it according to direction.

I am aware that this last statement may be disputed and individual testimony perhaps adduced to show that in ante-bellum days the ballot was as untrammelled in the South as in any section of the country; but in the face of any such contradiction I reassert the statement. The shot-gun was not resorted to. Masked men did not ride over the country at night intimidating voters; but there was a firm feeling that a class existed in every State with a sort of divine right to control public affairs. If they could not get this control by one means they must by another. The end justified the means. The coercion, if mild, was complete.

There were two political parties, it is true, in all the States, both strong in numbers and respectability, but both equally loyal to the institution which stood paramount in Southern eyes to all other institutions in state or nation. The slave-owners were the minority, but governed both parties. Had politics ever divided the slave-holders and the non-slave-holders, the majority would have been obliged to yield, or internecine war would have been the consequence. I do not know that the Southern people were to blame for this condition of affairs. There was a time when slavery was not profitable, and the discussion of the merits of the institution was confined almost exclusively to the territory where it existed. The States of Virginia and Kentucky came near abolishing slavery by their own acts, one State defeating the measure by a tie vote and the other only lacking one. But when the institution became profitable, all talk of its abolition ceased where it existed; and naturally, as human nature is constituted, arguments were adduced in its support. The cotton-gin probably had much to do with the justification of slavery.

The winter of 1860–1 will be remembered by middle-aged people of to-day as one of great excitement. South Carolina promptly seceded after the result of the Presidential election was known. Other Southern States proposed to follow. In some of them the Union sentiment was so strong that it had to be suppressed by force. Maryland, Delaware, Kentucky and Missouri, all Slave States, failed to pass ordinances of secession; but they were all represented in the so-called congress of the so-called Confederate States. The Governor and Lieutenant-Governor of Missouri, in 1861, Jackson and Reynolds, were both supporters of the rebellion and took refuge with the enemy. The governor soon died, and the lieutenant-governor assumed his office; issued proclamations as governor of the State; was recognized as such by the Confederate Government, and continued his pretensions until the collapse of the rebellion. The South claimed the sovereignty of States, but claimed the right to coerce into their confederation such States as they wanted, that is, all the States where slavery existed. They did not seem to think this course inconsistent. The fact is, the Southern slave-owners believed that, in some way, the ownership of slaves conferred a sort of patent of nobility—a right to govern independent of the interest or wishes of those who did not hold such property. They convinced themselves, first, of the divine origin of the institution and, next, that that particular institution was not safe in the hands of any body of legislators but themselves.

Meanwhile the Administration of President Buchanan looked helplessly on and proclaimed that the general government had no power to interfere; that the Nation had no power to save its own life. Mr. Buchanan had in his cabinet two members at least, who were as earnest—to use a mild term—in the cause of secession as Mr. Davis or any Southern statesman. One of them, Floyd, the Secretary of War, scattered the army so that much of it could be captured when hostilities should commence, and distributed the cannon and small arms from Northern arsenals throughout the South so as to be on hand when treason wanted them. The navy was scattered in like manner. The President did not prevent his cabinet preparing for war upon their government, either by destroying its resources or storing them in the South until a de facto government was established with Jefferson Davis as its President, and Montgomery, Alabama, as the Capital. The secessionists had then to leave the cabinet. In their own estimation they were aliens in the country which had given them birth. Loyal men were put into their places. Treason in the executive branch of the government was estopped. But the harm had already been done. The stable door was locked after the horse had been stolen.

During all of the trying winter of 1860–1, when the Southerners were so defiant that they would not allow within their borders the expression of a sentiment hostile to their views, it was a brave man indeed who could stand up and proclaim his loyalty to the Union. On the other hand men at the North— prominent men—proclaimed that the government had no power to coerce the South into submission to the laws of the land; that if the North undertook to raise armies to go south, these armies would have to march over the dead bodies of the speakers. A portion of the press of the North was constantly proclaiming similar views. When the time arrived for the President-elect to go to the capital of the Nation to be sworn into office, it was deemed unsafe for him to travel, not only as a President-elect, but as any private citizen should be allowed to do. Instead of going in a special car, receiving the good wishes of his constituents at all the stations along the road, he was obliged to stop on the way and to be smuggled into the capital. He disappeared from public view on his journey, and the next the country knew, his arrival was announced at the capital. There is little doubt that he would have been assassinated if he had attempted to travel openly throughout his journey.

Chapter XVII.

OUTBREAK OF THE REBELLION—PRESIDING AT A UNION
MEETING—MUSTERING OFFICER OF STATE TROOPS—
LYON AT CAMP JACKSON—SERVICES TENDERED
TO THE GOVERNMENT.

THE 4TH OF MARCH, 1861, came, and Abraham Lincoln was sworn to maintain the Union against all its enemies. The secession of one State after another followed, until eleven had gone out. On the 11th of April Fort Sumter, a National fort in the harbor of Charleston, South Carolina, was fired upon by the Southerners and a few days after was captured. The Confederates proclaimed themselves aliens, and thereby debarred themselves of all right to claim protection under the Constitution of the United States. We did not admit the fact that they were aliens, but all the same, they debarred themselves of the right to expect better treatment than people of any other foreign state who make war upon an independent nation. Upon the firing on Sumter President Lincoln issued his first call for troops and soon after a proclamation convening Congress in extra session. The call was for 75,000 volunteers for ninety days' service. If the shot fired at Fort Sumter "was heard around the world," the call of the President for 75,000 men was heard throughout the Northern States. There was not a state in the North of a million of inhabitants that would not have furnished the entire number faster than arms could have been supplied to them, if it had been necessary.

As soon as the news of the call for volunteers reached Galena, posters were stuck up calling for a meeting of the citizens at the court-house in the evening. Business ceased entirely; all was excitement; for a time there were no party distinctions; all were Union men, determined to avenge the insult to the national flag. In the evening the court-house was packed. Although a comparative stranger I was called upon to preside; the sole reason, possibly, was that I had been in the army and had seen service. With much embarrassment and some prompting I made out to announce the object of the meeting. Speeches were in order, but it is doubtful whether it would have been safe just then to make other than patriotic ones. There was probably no one in the house, however, who felt like making any other. The two principal speeches were by B. B. Howard, the post-master and a Breckinridge Democrat at the November election the fall before, and John A. Rawlins, an elector on the Douglas ticket. E. B. Washburne, with whom I was not acquainted at that time, came in after the meeting had been organized, and expressed, I understood afterwards, a little surprise that Galena could not furnish a presiding officer for such an occasion without taking a stranger. He came forward and was introduced, and made a speech appealing to the patriotism of the meeting.

After the speaking was over volunteers were called for to form a company. The quota of Illinois had been fixed at six regiments; and it was supposed that one company would be as much as would be accepted from Galena. The company was raised and the officers and non-commissioned officers elected before the meeting adjourned. I declined the captaincy before the balloting, but announced that I would aid the company in every way I could and would be found in the service in some position if there should be a war. I never went into our leather store after that meeting, to put up a package or do other business.

The ladies of Galena were quite as patriotic as the men. They could not enlist, but they conceived the idea of sending their first company to the field uniformed. They came to me to get a description of the United States uniform for infantry; subscribed and bought the material; procured tailors to cut out the garments, and the ladies made them up. In a few days the company was in uniform and ready to report at the State capital for assignment. The men all turned out the morning after their enlistment, and I took charge, divided them into squads and superintended their drill. When they were ready to go to Springfield I went with them and remained there until they were assigned to a regiment.

There were so many more volunteers than had been called for that the question whom to accept was quite embarrassing to the governor, Richard Yates. The legislature was in session at the time, however, and came to his relief. A law was enacted authorizing the governor to accept the services of ten additional regiments, one from each congressional district, for one month, to be paid by the State, but pledged to go into the service of the United States if there should be a further call during their term. Even with this relief the governor was still very much embarrassed. Before the war was over he was like the President when he was taken with the varioloid: "at last he had something he could give to all who wanted it."

In time the Galena company was mustered into the United States service, forming a part of the 11th Illinois volunteer infantry. My duties, I thought, had ended at Springfield, and I was prepared to start home by the evening train, leaving at nine o'clock. Up to that time I do not think I had been introduced to Governor Yates, or had ever spoken to him. I knew him by sight, however, because he was living at the same hotel and I often saw him at table. The evening I was to quit the capital I left the supper room before the governor and was standing at the front door when he came out. He spoke to me, calling me by my old army title "Captain," and said he understood that I was about leaving the city. I answered that I was. He said he would be glad if I would remain over-night and call at the Executive office the next morning. I complied with his request, and was asked to go into the Adjutant-General's office and render such assistance as I could, the governor saying that my army experience would be of great service there. I accepted the proposition.

My old army experience I found indeed of very great service. I was no clerk, nor had I any capacity to become one. The only place I ever found in my life to put a paper so as to find it again was either a side coat-pocket or the hands of a clerk or secretary more careful than myself. But I had been quartermaster, commissary and adjutant in the field. The army forms were familiar to me and I could direct how they should be made out. There was a clerk in the office of the Adjutant-General who supplied my deficiencies. The ease with which the State of Illinois settled its accounts with the government at the close of the war is evidence of the efficiency of Mr. Loomis as an accountant on a large scale. He remained in the office until that time.

As I have stated, the legislature authorized the governor to accept the services of ten additional regiments. I had charge of mustering these regiments into the State service. They were assembled at the most convenient railroad centres in their respective congressional districts. I detailed officers to muster in a portion of them, but mustered three in the southern part of the State myself. One of these was to assemble at Belleville, some eighteen miles south-east of St. Louis. When I got there I found that only one or two companies had arrived. There was no probability of the regiment coming together under five days. This gave me a few idle days which I concluded to spend in St. Louis.

There was a considerable force of State militia at Camp Jackson, on the outskirts of St. Louis, at the time. There is but little doubt that it was the design of Governor Claiborn Jackson to have these troops ready to seize the United States arsenal and the city of St. Louis. Why they did not do so I do not know. There was but a small garrison, two companies I think, under Captain N. Lyon at the arsenal, and but for the timely services of the Hon. F. P. Blair, I have little doubt that St. Louis would have gone into rebel hands, and with it the arsenal with all its arms and ammunition.

Blair was a leader among the Union men of St. Louis in 1861. There was no State government in Missouri at the time that would sanction the raising of troops or commissioned officers to protect United States property, but Blair had probably procured some form of authority from the President to raise troops in Missouri and to muster them into the service of the United States. At all events, he did raise a regiment and took command himself as Colonel. With this force he reported to Captain Lyon and placed himself and regiment under his orders. It was whispered that Lyon thus reinforced intended to break up Camp Jackson and capture the militia. I went down to the arsenal in the morning to see the troops start out. I had known Lyon for two years at West Point and in the old army afterwards. Blair I knew very well by sight. I had heard him speak in the canvass of 1858, possibly several times, but I had never spoken to him. As the troops marched out of the enclosure around the arsenal, Blair was on his horse outside forming them into line preparatory to their march. I introduced myself to him and had a few moments' conversation and expressed my sympathy with his purpose.

This was my first personal acquaintance with the Honorable—afterwards Major-General F. P. Blair. Camp Jackson surrendered without a fight and the garrison was marched down to the arsenal as prisoners of war.

Up to this time the enemies of the government in St. Louis had been bold and defiant, while Union men were quiet but determined. The enemies had their head-quarters in a central and public position on Pine Street, near Fifth—from which the rebel flag was flaunted boldly. The Union men had a place of meeting somewhere in the city, I did not know where, and I doubt whether they dared to enrage the enemies of the government by placing the national flag outside their head-quarters. As soon as the news of the capture of Camp Jackson reached the city the condition of affairs was changed. Union men became rampant, aggressive, and, if you will, intolerant. They proclaimed their sentiments boldly, and were impatient at anything like disrespect for the Union. The secessionists became quiet but were filled with suppressed rage. They had been playing the bully. The Union men ordered the rebel flag taken down from the building on Pine Street. The command was given in tones of authority and it was taken down, never to be raised again in St. Louis.

I witnessed the scene. I had heard of the surrender of the camp and that the garrison was on its way to the arsenal. I had seen the troops start out in the morning and had wished them success. I now determined to go to the arsenal and await their arrival and congratulate them. I stepped on a car standing at the corner of 4th and Pine streets, and saw a crowd of people standing quietly in front of the head-quarters, who were there for the purpose of hauling down the flag. There were squads of other people at intervals down the street. They too were quiet but filled with suppressed rage, and muttered their resentment at the insult to, what they called, "their" flag. Before the car I was in had started, a dapper little fellow—he would be called a dude at this day—stepped in. He was in a great state of excitement and used adjectives freely to express his contempt for the Union and for those who had just perpetrated such an outrage upon the rights of a free people. There was only one other passenger in the car besides myself when this young man entered. He evidently expected to find nothing but sympathy when he got away from the "mud sills" engaged in compelling a "free people" to pull down a flag they adored. He turned to me saying: "Things have come to a —— pretty pass when a free people can't choose their own flag. Where I came from if a man dares to say a word in favor of the Union we hang him to a limb of the first tree we come to." I replied that "after all we were not so intolerant in St. Louis as we might be; I had not seen a single rebel hung yet, nor heard of one; there were plenty of them who ought to be, however." The young man subsided. He was so crestfallen that I believe if I had ordered him to leave the car he would have gone quietly out, saying to himself: "More Yankee oppression."

By nightfall the late defenders of Camp Jackson were all within the walls of the St. Louis arsenal, prisoners of war. The next day I left St. Louis for Mattoon, Illinois, where I was to muster in the regiment from that congressional district. This was the 21st Illinois infantry, the regiment of which I subsequently became colonel. I mustered one regiment afterwards, when my services for the State were about closed.

Brigadier-General John Pope was stationed at Springfield, as United States mustering officer, all the time I was in the State service. He was a native of Illinois and well acquainted with most of the prominent men in the State. I was a carpet-bagger and knew but few of them. While I was on duty at Springfield the senators, representatives in Congress, ex-governors and the State legislators were nearly all at the State capital. The only acquaintance I made among them was with the governor, whom I was serving, and, by chance, with Senator S. A. Douglas. The only members of Congress I knew were Washburne and Philip Foulk. With the former, though he represented my district and we were citizens of the same town, I only became acquainted at the meeting when the first company of Galena volunteers was raised. Foulk I had known in St. Louis when I was a citizen of that city. I had been three years at West Point with Pope and had served with him a short time during the Mexican war, under General Taylor. I saw a good deal of him during my service with the State. On one occasion he said to me that I ought to go into the United States service. I told him I intended to do so if there was a war. He spoke of his acquaintance with the public men of the State, and said he could get them to recommend me for a position and that he would do all he could for me. I declined to receive endorsement for permission to fight for my country.

Going home for a day or two soon after this conversation with General Pope, I wrote from Galena the following letter to the Adjutant-General of the Army.

> GALENA, ILLINOIS,
> *May* 24, 1861.

COL. L. THOMAS,
> Adjt. Gen. U. S. A.,
>> Washington, D. C.

SIR:—Having served for fifteen years in the regular army, including four years at West Point, and feeling it the duty of every one who has been educated at the Government expense to offer their services for the support of that Government, I have the honor, very respectfully, to tender my services, until the close of the war, in such capacity as may be offered. I would say, in view of my present age and length of service, I feel myself competent to command a regiment, if the President, in his judgment, should see fit to intrust one to me

Since the first call of the President I have been serving on the staff of the Governor of this State, rendering such aid as I could in the organization of our State militia, and am still engaged in that capacity. A letter addressed to me at Springfield, Illinois, will reach me.

> I am very respectfully,
>> Your obt. svt.,
>>> U. S. GRANT.

This letter failed to elicit an answer from the Adjutant-General of the Army. I presume it was hardly read by him, and certainly it could not have been submitted to higher authority. Subsequent to the war General Badeau having heard of this letter applied to the War Department for a copy of it. The letter could not be found and no one recollected ever having seen it. I took no copy when it was written. Long after the application of General Badeau, General Townsend, who had become Adjutant-General of the Army, while packing up papers preparatory to the removal of his office, found this letter in some out-of-the-way place. It had not been destroyed, but it had not been regularly filed away.

I felt some hesitation in suggesting rank as high as the colonelcy of a regiment, feeling somewhat doubtful whether I would be equal to the position. But I had seen nearly every colonel who had been mustered in from the State of Illinois, and some from Indiana, and felt that if they could command a regiment properly, and with credit, I could also.

Having but little to do after the muster of the last of the regiments authorized by the State legislature, I asked and obtained of the governor leave of absence for a week to visit my parents in Covington, Kentucky, immediately opposite Cincinnati. General McClellan had been made a major-general and had his headquarters at Cincinnati. In reality I wanted to see him. I had known him slightly at West Point, where we served one year together, and in the Mexican war. I was in hopes that when he saw me he would offer me a position on his staff. I called on two successive days at his office but failed to see him on either occasion, and returned to Springfield.

Chapter XVIII.

APPOINTED COLONEL OF THE 21ST ILLINOIS—PERSONNEL
OF THE REGIMENT—GENERAL LOGAN—MARCH TO
MISSOURI—MOVEMENT AGAINST HARRIS AT
FLORIDA, MO.—GENERAL POPE IN COMMAND—
STATIONED AT MEXICO, MO.

W HILE I WAS ABSENT from the State capital on this occasion the President's second call for troops was issued.
This time it was for 300,000 men, for three years or the war.
This brought into the United States service all the regiments
then in the State service. These had elected their officers from
highest to lowest and were accepted with their organizations
as they were, except in two instances. A Chicago regiment,
the 19th infantry, had elected a very young man to the colonelcy. When it came to taking the field the regiment asked to
have another appointed colonel and the one they had previously chosen made lieutenant-colonel. The 21st regiment of
infantry, mustered in by me at Mattoon, refused to go into
the service with the colonel of their selection in any position.
While I was still absent Governor Yates appointed me colonel
of this latter regiment. A few days after I was in charge of it
and in camp on the fair grounds near Springfield.

My regiment was composed in large part of young men of
as good social position as any in their section of the State. It
embraced the sons of farmers, lawyers, physicians, politicians,
merchants, bankers and ministers, and some men of maturer
years who had filled such positions themselves. There were
also men in it who could be led astray; and the colonel,
elected by the votes of the regiment, had proved to be fully
capable of developing all there was in his men of recklessness.
It was said that he even went so far at times as to take the
guard from their posts and go with them to the village near
by and make a night of it. When there came a prospect of
battle the regiment wanted to have some one else to lead
them. I found it very hard work for a few days to bring all the
men into anything like subordination; but the great majority
favored discipline, and by the application of a little regular

army punishment all were reduced to as good discipline as one could ask.

The ten regiments which had volunteered in the State service for thirty days, it will be remembered, had done so with a pledge to go into the National service if called upon within that time. When they volunteered the government had only called for ninety days' enlistments. Men were called now for three years or the war. They felt that this change of period released them from the obligation of re-volunteering. When I was appointed colonel, the 21st regiment was still in the State service. About the time they were to be mustered into the United States service, such of them as would go, two members of Congress from the State, McClernand and Logan, appeared at the capital and I was introduced to them. I had never seen either of them before, but I had read a great deal about them, and particularly about Logan, in the newspapers. Both were democratic members of Congress, and Logan had been elected from the southern district of the State, where he had a majority of eighteen thousand over his Republican competitor. His district had been settled originally by people from the Southern States, and at the breaking out of secession they sympathized with the South. At the first outbreak of war some of them joined the Southern army; many others were preparing to do so; others rode over the country at night denouncing the Union, and made it as necessary to guard railroad bridges over which National troops had to pass in southern Illinois, as it was in Kentucky or any of the border slave states. Logan's popularity in this district was unbounded. He knew almost enough of the people in it by their Christian names, to form an ordinary congressional district. As he went in politics, so his district was sure to go. The Republican papers had been demanding that he should announce where he stood on the questions which at that time engrossed the whole of public thought. Some were very bitter in their denunciations of his silence. Logan was not a man to be coerced into an utterance by threats. He did, however, come out in a speech before the adjournment of the special session of Congress which was convened by the President soon after his inauguration, and announced his undying loyalty and devotion to the Union. But I had not happened to see that speech, so that when I first met Logan my impressions were those formed from reading denunciations of him. McClernand, on the other hand, had early taken strong grounds for the maintenance of the Union and had been praised accordingly by the Republican papers. The gentlemen who presented these two members of Congress asked me if I would have any objections to their addressing my regiment. I hesitated a little before answering. It was but a few days before the time set for mustering into the United States service such of the men as were willing to volunteer for three years or the war. I had some doubt as to the effect a speech from Logan might have; but as he was with McClernand, whose sentiments on the all-absorbing questions of the day were well known, I gave my consent. McClernand spoke first; and Logan followed in a speech which he has hardly equalled since for force and eloquence. It breathed a loyalty and devotion to the Union which inspired my men to such a point that they would have volunteered to remain in the army as long as an enemy of the country continued to bear arms against it. They entered the United States service almost to a man.

General Logan went to his part of the State and gave his attention to raising troops. The very men who at first made it necessary to guard the roads in southern Illinois became the defenders of the Union. Logan entered the service himself as colonel of a regiment and rapidly rose to the rank of major-general. His district, which had promised at first to give much trouble to the government, filled every call made upon it for troops, without resorting to the draft. There was no call made when there were not more volunteers than were asked for. That congressional district stands credited at the War Department to-day with furnishing more men for the army than it was called on to supply.

I remained in Springfield with my regiment until the 3d of July, when I was ordered to Quincy, Illinois. By that time the regiment was in a good state of discipline and the officers and men were well up in the company drill. There was direct railroad communication between Springfield and Quincy, but I thought it would be good preparation for the troops to march there. We had no transportation for our camp and garrison equipage, so wagons were hired for the occasion and on the 3d of July we started. There was no hurry, but fair marches were made every day until the Illinois River was crossed. There I was overtaken by a dispatch saying that the destination of the regiment had been changed to Ironton, Missouri, and ordering me to halt where I was and await the arrival of a steamer which had been dispatched up the Illinois River to take the regiment to St. Louis. The boat, when it did come, grounded on a sand-bar a few miles below where we were in camp. We remained there several days waiting to have the boat get off the bar, but before this occurred news came that an Illinois regiment was surrounded by rebels at a point on the Hannibal and St. Joe Railroad some miles west of Palmyra, in Missouri, and I was ordered to proceed with all dispatch to their relief. We took the cars and reached Quincy in a few hours.

When I left Galena for the last time to take command of the 21st regiment I took with me my oldest son, Frederick D. Grant, then a lad of eleven years of age. On receiving the order to take rail for Quincy I wrote to Mrs. Grant, to relieve what I supposed would be her great anxiety for one so young going into danger, that I would send Fred home from Quincy by river. I received a prompt letter in reply decidedly disapproving my proposition, and urging that the lad should be allowed to accompany me. It came too late. Fred was already on his way up the Mississippi bound for Dubuque, Iowa, from which place there was a railroad to Galena.

My sensations as we approached what I supposed might be "a field of battle" were anything but agreeable. I had been in all the engagements in Mexico that it was possible for one person to be in; but not in command. If some one else had been colonel and I had been lieutenant-colonel I do not think I would have felt any trepidation. Before we were prepared to cross the Mississippi River at Quincy my anxiety was relieved; for the men of the besieged regiment came straggling into town. I am inclined to think both sides got frightened and ran away.

I took my regiment to Palmyra and remained there for a few days, until relieved by the 19th Illinois infantry. From Palmyra I proceeded to Salt River, the railroad bridge over which had been destroyed by the enemy. Colonel John M.

Palmer at that time commanded the 13th Illinois, which was acting as a guard to workmen who were engaged in rebuilding this bridge. Palmer was my senior and commanded the two regiments as long as we remained together. The bridge was finished in about two weeks, and I received orders to move against Colonel Thomas Harris, who was said to be encamped at the little town of Florida, some twenty-five miles south of where we then were.

At the time of which I now write we had no transportation and the country about Salt River was sparsely settled, so that it took some days to collect teams and drivers enough to move the camp and garrison equipage of a regiment nearly a thousand strong, together with a week's supply of provision and some ammunition. While preparations for the move were going on I felt quite comfortable; but when we got on the road and found every house deserted I was anything but easy. In the twenty-five miles we had to march we did not see a person, old or young, male or female, except two horsemen who were on a road that crossed ours. As soon as they saw us they decamped as fast as their horses could carry them. I kept my men in the ranks and forbade their entering any of the deserted houses or taking anything from them. We halted at night on the road and proceeded the next morning at an early hour. Harris had been encamped in a creek bottom for the sake of being near water. The hills on either side of the creek extend to a considerable height, possibly more than a hundred feet. As we approached the brow of the hill from which it was expected we could see Harris' camp, and possibly find his men ready formed to meet us, my heart kept getting higher and higher until it felt to me as though it was in my throat. I would have given anything then to have been back in Illinois, but I had not the moral courage to halt and consider what to do; I kept right on. When we reached a point from which the valley below was in full view I halted. The place where Harris had been encamped a few days before was still there and the marks of a recent encampment were plainly visible, but the troops were gone. My heart resumed its place. It occurred to me at once that Harris had been as much afraid of me as I had been of him. This was a view of the question I had never taken before; but it was one I never forgot afterwards. From that event to the close of the war, I never experienced trepidation upon confronting an enemy, though I always felt more or less anxiety. I never forgot that he had as much reason to fear my forces as I had his. The lesson was valuable.

Inquiries at the village of Florida divulged the fact that Colonel Harris, learning of my intended movement, while my transportation was being collected took time by the forelock and left Florida before I had started from Salt River. He had increased the distance between us by forty miles. The next day I started back to my old camp at Salt River bridge. The citizens living on the line of our march had returned to their houses after we passed, and finding everything in good order, nothing carried away, they were at their front doors ready to greet us now. They had evidently been led to believe that the National troops carried death and devastation with them wherever they went.

In a short time after our return to Salt River bridge I was ordered with my regiment to the town of Mexico. General Pope was then commanding the district embracing all of the State of Missouri between the Mississippi and Missouri rivers, with his headquarters in the village of Mexico. I was assigned to the command of a sub-district embracing the troops in the immediate neighborhood, some three regiments of infantry and a section of artillery. There was one regiment encamped by the side of mine. I assumed command of the whole and the first night sent the commander of the other regiment the parole and countersign. Not wishing to be outdone in courtesy, he immediately sent me the countersign for his regiment for the night. When he was informed that the countersign sent to him was for use with his regiment as well as mine, it was difficult to make him understand that this was not an unwarranted interference of one colonel over another. No doubt he attributed it for the time to the presumption of a graduate of West Point over a volunteer pure and simple. But the question was soon settled and we had no further trouble.

My arrival in Mexico had been preceded by that of two or three regiments in which proper discipline had not been maintained, and the men had been in the habit of visiting houses without invitation and helping themselves to food and drink, or demanding them from the occupants. They carried their muskets while out of camp and made every man they found take the oath of allegiance to the government. I at once published orders prohibiting the soldiers from going into private houses unless invited by the inhabitants, and from appropriating private property to their own or to government uses. The people were no longer molested or made afraid. I received the most marked courtesy from the citizens of Mexico as long as I remained there.

Up to this time my regiment had not been carried in the school of the soldier beyond the company drill, except that it had received some training on the march from Springfield to the Illinois River. There was now a good opportunity of exercising it in the battalion drill. While I was at West Point the tactics used in the army had been Scott's and the musket the flint lock. I had never looked at a copy of tactics from the time of my graduation. My standing in that branch of studies had been near the foot of the class. In the Mexican war in the summer of 1846, I had been appointed regimental quartermaster and commissary and had not been at a battalion drill since. The arms had been changed since then and Hardee's tactics had been adopted. I got a copy of tactics and studied one lesson, intending to confine the exercise of the first day to the commands I had thus learned. By pursuing this course from day to day I thought I would soon get through the volume.

We were encamped just outside of town on the common, among scattering suburban houses with enclosed gardens, and when I got my regiment in line and rode to the front I soon saw that if I attempted to follow the lesson I had studied I would have to clear away some of the houses and garden fences to make room. I perceived at once, however, that Hardee's tactics—a mere translation from the French with Hardee's name attached—was nothing more than common sense and the progress of the age applied to Scott's system. The commands were abbreviated and the movement expedited. Under the old tactics almost every change in the order of march was preceded by a "halt," then came the change, and then the "forward march." With the new tactics all these changes could be made while in motion. I found no trouble in giving commands that would take my regiment where I wanted it to go and carry it around all obstacles. I do not believe that the officers of the regiment ever discovered that I had never studied the tactics that I used.

Chapter XIX.

COMMISSIONED BRIGADIER-GENERAL — COMMAND
AT IRONTON, MO. — JEFFERSON CITY — CAPE
GIRARDEAU — GENERAL PRENTISS — SEIZURE
OF PADUCAH — HEADQUARTERS AT CAIRO.

I HAD NOT BEEN in Mexico many weeks when, reading a St. Louis paper, I found the President had asked the Illinois delegation in Congress to recommend some citizens of the State for the position of brigadier-general, and that they had unanimously recommended me as first on a list of seven. I was very much surprised because, as I have said, my acquaintance with the Congressmen was very limited and I did not know of anything I had done to inspire such confidence. The papers of the next day announced that my name, with three others, had been sent to the Senate, and a few days after our confirmation was announced.

When appointed brigadier-general I at once thought it proper that one of my aides should come from the regiment I had been commanding, and so selected Lieutenant C. B. Lagow. While living in St. Louis, I had had a desk in the law office of McClellan, Moody and Hillyer. Difference in views between the members of the firm on the questions of the day, and general hard times in the border cities, had broken up this firm. Hillyer was quite a young man, then in his twenties, and very brilliant. I asked him to accept a place on my staff. I also wanted to take one man from my new home, Galena. The canvass in the Presidential campaign the fall before had brought out a young lawyer by the name of John A. Rawlins, who proved himself one of the ablest speakers in the State. He was also a candidate for elector on the Douglas ticket. When Sumter was fired upon and the integrity of the Union threatened, there was no man more ready to serve his country than he. I wrote at once asking him to accept the position of assistant adjutant-general with the rank of captain, on my staff. He was about entering the service as major of a new regiment then organizing in the north-western part of the State; but he threw this up and accepted my offer.

Neither Hillyer nor Lagow proved to have any particular taste or special qualifications for the duties of the soldier, and the former resigned during the Vicksburg campaign; the latter I relieved after the battle of Chattanooga. Rawlins remained with me as long as he lived, and rose to the rank of brigadier-general and chief-of-staff to the General of the Army—an office created for him—before the war closed. He was an able man, possessed of great firmness, and could say "no" so emphatically to a request which he thought should not be granted that the person he was addressing would understand at once that there was no use of pressing the matter. General Rawlins was a very useful officer in other ways than this. I became very much attached to him.

Shortly after my promotion I was ordered to Ironton, Missouri, to command a district in that part of the State, and took the 21st Illinois, my old regiment, with me. Several other regiments were ordered to the same destination about the same time. Ironton is on the Iron Mountain railroad, about seventy miles south of St. Louis, and situated among hills rising almost to the dignity of mountains. When I reached there, about the 8th of August, Colonel B. Gratz Brown—afterwards Governor of Missouri and in 1872 Vice-Presidential candidate—was in command. Some of his troops were ninety days' men and their time had expired some time before. The men had no clothing but what they had volunteered in, and much of this was so worn that it would hardly stay on. General Hardee—the author of the tactics I did not study—was at Greenville, some twenty-five miles further south, it was said, with five thousand Confederate troops. Under these circumstances Colonel Brown's command was very much demoralized. A squadron of cavalry could have ridden into the valley and captured the entire force. Brown himself was gladder to see me on that occasion than he ever has been since. I relieved him and sent all his men home, within a day or two, to be mustered out of service.

Within ten days after reaching Ironton I was prepared to take the offensive against the enemy at Greenville. I sent a column east out of the valley we were in, with orders to swing around to the south and west and come into the Greenville road ten miles south of Ironton. Another column marched on the direct road and went into camp at the point designated for the two columns to meet. I was to ride out the next morning and take personal command of the movement. My experience against Harris, in northern Missouri, had inspired me with confidence. But when the evening train came in, it brought General B. M. Prentiss with orders to take command of the district. His orders did not relieve me, but I knew that by law I was senior, and at that time even the President did not have the authority to assign a junior to command a senior of the same grade. I therefore gave General Prentiss the situation of the troops and the general condition of affairs, and started for St. Louis the same day. The movement against the rebels at Greenville went no further.

From St. Louis I was ordered to Jefferson City, the capital of the State, to take command. General Sterling Price, of the Confederate army, was thought to be threatening the capital, Lexington, Chillicothe and other comparatively large towns in the central part of Missouri. I found a good many troops in Jefferson City, but in the greatest confusion, and no one person knew where they all were. Colonel Mulligan, a gallant man, was in command, but he had not been educated as yet to his new profession and did not know how to maintain discipline. I found that volunteers had obtained permission from the department commander, or claimed they had, to raise, some of them, regiments; some battalions; some companies—the officers to be commissioned according to the number of men they brought into the service. There were recruiting stations all over town, with notices, rudely lettered on boards over the doors, announcing the arm of service and length of time for which recruits at that station would be received. The law required all volunteers to serve for three years or the war. But in Jefferson City in August, 1861, they were recruited for different periods and on different conditions; some were enlisted for six months, some for a year, some without any condition as to where they were to serve, others were not to be sent out of the State. The recruits were principally men from regiments stationed there and already in the service, bound for three years if the war lasted that long.

The city was filled with Union fugitives who had been driven by guerilla bands to take refuge with the National troops. They were in a deplorable condition and must have starved but for the support the government gave them. They had generally made their escape with a team or two, sometimes a yoke of oxen with a mule or a horse in the lead. A little bedding besides their clothing and some food had been thrown into the wagon. All else of their worldly goods were abandoned and appropriated by their former neighbors; for the Union man in Missouri who staid at home during the rebellion, if he was not immediately under the protection of the National troops, was at perpetual war with his neighbors. I stopped the recruiting service, and disposed the troops about the outskirts of the city so as to guard all approaches. Order was soon restored.

I had been at Jefferson City but a few days when I was directed from department headquarters to fit out an expedition to Lexington, Booneville and Chillicothe, in order to take from the banks in those cities all the funds they had and send them to St. Louis. The western army had not yet been supplied with transportation. It became necessary therefore to press into the service teams belonging to sympathizers with the rebellion or to hire those of Union men. This afforded an opportunity of giving employment to such of the refugees within our lines as had teams suitable for our purposes. They accepted the service with alacrity. As fast as troops could be got off they were moved west some twenty miles or more. In seven or eight days from my assuming command at Jefferson City, I had all the troops, except a small garrison, at an advanced position and expected to join them myself the next day.

But my campaigns had not yet begun, for while seated at my office door, with nothing further to do until it was time to start for the front, I saw an officer of rank approaching, who proved to be Colonel Jefferson C. Davis. I had never met him before, but he introduced himself by handing me an order for him to proceed to Jefferson City and relieve me of the command. The orders directed that I should report at department headquarters at St. Louis without delay, to receive important special instructions. It was about an hour before the only regular train of the day would start. I therefore turned over to Colonel Davis my orders, and hurriedly stated to him the progress that had been made to carry out the department instructions already described. I had at that time but one staff officer,* doing myself all the detail work usually performed by an adjutant-general. In an hour after being relieved from the command I was on my way to St. Louis, leaving my single staff officer to follow the next day with our horses and baggage.

The "important special instructions" which I received the next day, assigned me to the command of the district of south-east Missouri, embracing all the territory south of St. Louis, in Missouri, as well as all southern Illinois. At first I was to take personal command of a combined expedition that had been ordered for the capture of Colonel Jeff. Thompson, a sort of independent or partisan commander who was disputing with us the possession of south-east Missouri. Troops had been ordered to move from Ironton to Cape Girardeau, sixty or seventy miles to the south-east, on the Mississippi River; while the forces at Cape Girardeau had been ordered to move to Jacksonville, ten miles out towards Ironton; and troops at Cairo and Bird's Point, at the junction of the Ohio and Mississippi rivers, were to hold themselves in readiness to go down the Mississippi to Belmont, eighteen miles below, to be moved west from there when an officer should come to command them. I was the officer who had been selected for this purpose. Cairo was to become my headquarters when the expedition terminated.

In pursuance of my orders I established my temporary headquarters at Cape Girardeau and sent instructions to the commanding officer at Jackson, to inform me of the approach of General Prentiss from Ironton. Hired wagons were kept moving night and day to take additional rations to Jackson, to supply the troops when they started from there. Neither General Prentiss nor Colonel Marsh, who commanded at Jackson, knew their destination. I drew up all the instructions for the contemplated move, and kept them in my pocket until I should hear of the junction of our troops at Jackson. Two or three days after my arrival at Cape Girardeau, word came that General Prentiss was approaching that place (Jackson). I

---

*C. B. Lagow, the others not yet having joined me.

started at once to meet him there and to give him his orders. As I turned the first corner of a street after starting, I saw a column of cavalry passing the next street in front of me. I turned and rode around the block the other way, so as to meet the head of the column. I found there General Prentiss himself, with a large escort. He had halted his troops at Jackson for the night, and had come on himself to Cape Girardeau, leaving orders for his command to follow him in the morning. I gave the General his orders—which stopped him at Jackson—but he was very much aggrieved at being placed under another brigadier-general, particularly as he believed himself to be the senior. He had been a brigadier, in command at Cairo, while I was mustering officer at Springfield without any rank. But we were nominated at the same time for the United States service, and both our commissions bore date May 17th, 1861. By virtue of my former army rank I was, by law, the senior. General Prentiss failed to get orders to his troops to remain at Jackson, and the next morning early they were reported as approaching Cape Girardeau. I then ordered the General very peremptorily to countermarch his command and take it back to Jackson. He obeyed the order, but bade his command adieu when he got them to Jackson, and went to St. Louis and reported himself. This broke up the expedition. But little harm was done, as Jeff. Thompson moved light and had no fixed place for even nominal headquarters. He was as much at home in Arkansas as he was in Missouri and would keep out of the way of a superior force. Prentiss was sent to another part of the State.

General Prentiss made a great mistake on the above occasion, one that he would not have committed later in the war. When I came to know him better, I regretted it much. In consequence of this occurrence he was off duty in the field when the principal campaign at the West was going on, and his juniors received promotion while he was where none could be obtained. He would have been next to myself in rank in the district of south-east Missouri, by virtue of his services in the Mexican war. He was a brave and very earnest soldier. No man in the service was more sincere in his devotion to the cause for which we were battling; none more ready to make sacrifices or risk life in it.

On the 4th of September I removed my headquarters to Cairo and found Colonel Richard Oglesby in command of the post. We had never met, at least not to my knowledge. After my promotion I had ordered my brigadier-general's uniform from New York, but it had not yet arrived, so that I was in citizen's dress. The Colonel had his office full of people, mostly from the neighboring States of Missouri and Kentucky, making complaints or asking favors. He evidently did not catch my name when I was presented, for on my taking a piece of paper from the table where he was seated and writing the order assuming command of the district of south-east Missouri, Colonel Richard J. Oglesby to command the post at Bird's Point, and handing it to him, he put on an expression of surprise that looked a little as if he would like to have some one identify me. But he surrendered the office without question.

The day after I assumed command at Cairo a man came to me who said he was a scout of General Fremont. He reported that he had just come from Columbus, a point on the Mississippi twenty miles below on the Kentucky side, and that troops had started from there, or were about to start, to seize Paducah, at the mouth of the Tennessee. There was no time for delay; I reported by telegraph to the department commander the information I had received, and added that I was taking steps to get off that night to be in advance of the enemy in securing that important point. There was a large number of steamers lying at Cairo and a good many boatmen were staying in the town. It was the work of only a few hours to get the boats manned, with coal aboard and steam up. Troops were also designated to go aboard. The distance from Cairo to Paducah is about forty-five miles. I did not wish to get there before daylight of the 6th, and directed therefore that the boats should lie at anchor out in the stream until the time to start. Not having received an answer to my first dispatch, I again telegraphed to department headquarters that I should start for Paducah that night unless I received further orders. Hearing nothing, we started before midnight and arrived early the following morning, anticipating the enemy by probably not over six or eight hours. It proved very fortunate that the expedition against Jeff. Thompson had been broken up. Had it not been, the enemy would have seized Paducah and fortified it, to our very great annoyance.

When the National troops entered the town the citizens were taken by surprise. I never after saw such consternation depicted on the faces of the people. Men, women and children came out of their doors looking pale and frightened at the presence of the invader. They were expecting rebel troops that day. In fact, nearly four thousand men from Columbus were at that time within ten or fifteen miles of Paducah on their way to occupy the place. I had but two regiments and one battery with me; but the enemy did not know this and returned to Columbus. I stationed my troops at the best points to guard the roads leading into the city, left gunboats to guard the river fronts and by noon was ready to start on my return to Cairo. Before leaving, however, I addressed a short printed proclamation to the citizens of Paducah assuring them of our peaceful intentions, that we had come among them to protect them against the enemies of our country, and that all who chose could continue their usual avocations with assurance of the protection of the government. This was evidently a relief to them; but the majority would have much preferred the presence of the other army. I reinforced Paducah rapidly from the troops at Cape Girardeau; and a day or two later General C. F. Smith, a most accomplished soldier, reported at Cairo and was assigned to the command of the post at the mouth of the Tennessee. In a short time it was well fortified and a detachment was sent to occupy Smithland, at the mouth of the Cumberland.

The State government of Kentucky at that time was rebel in sentiment, but wanted to preserve an armed neutrality between the North and the South, and the governor really seemed to think the State had a perfect right to maintain a neutral position. The rebels already occupied two towns in the State, Columbus and Hickman, on the Mississippi; and at the very moment the National troops were entering Paducah from the Ohio front, General Lloyd Tilghman—a Confederate—with his staff and a small detachment of men, were getting out in the other direction, while, as I have already said, nearly four thousand Confederate troops were on Kentucky soil on their way to take possession of the town. But, in the estimation of the governor and of those who thought with him, this did not justify the National authorities in invading the soil of Kentucky. I informed the legislature of the State of what I was doing, and my action was approved by the majority of that body. On my return to Cairo I found authority from department headquarters for me to take Paducah "if I felt strong enough," but very soon after I was reprimanded from the same quarters for my correspondence with the legislature and warned against a repetition of the offence.

Soon after I took command at Cairo, General Fremont entered into arrangements for the exchange of the prisoners captured at Camp Jackson in the month of May. I received orders to pass them through my lines to Columbus as they presented themselves with proper credentials. Quite a number of these prisoners I had been personally acquainted with before the war. Such of them as I had so known were received at my headquarters as old acquaintances, and ordinary routine business was not disturbed by their presence. On one occasion when several were present in my office my intention to visit Cape Girardeau the next day, to inspect the troops at that point, was mentioned. Something transpired which postponed my trip; but a steamer employed by the government was passing a point some twenty or more miles above Cairo, the next day, when a section of rebel artillery with proper escort brought her to. A major, one of those who had been at my headquarters the day before, came at once aboard and after some search made a direct demand for my delivery. It was hard to persuade him that I was not there. This officer was Major Barrett, of St. Louis. I had been acquainted with his family before the war.

Chapter XX.

GENERAL FREMONT IN COMMAND—MOVEMENT AGAINST
BELMONT—BATTLE OF BELMONT—A NARROW
ESCAPE—AFTER THE BATTLE.

F ROM THE OCCUPATION of Paducah up to the early part of
November nothing important occurred with the troops
under my command. I was reinforced from time to time and
the men were drilled and disciplined preparatory for the service which was sure to come. By the 1st of November I had
not fewer than 20,000 men, most of them under good drill
and ready to meet any equal body of men who, like themselves, had not yet been in an engagement. They were growing impatient at lying idle so long, almost in hearing of the
guns of the enemy they had volunteered to fight against. I
asked on one or two occasions to be allowed to move against
Columbus. It could have been taken soon after the occupation of Paducah; but before November it was so strongly
fortified that it would have required a large force and a long
siege to capture it.

In the latter part of October General Fremont took the field
in person and moved from Jefferson City against General
Sterling Price, who was then in the State of Missouri with a
considerable command. About the first of November I was
directed from department headquarters to make a demonstration on both sides of the Mississippi River with the view of
detaining the rebels at Columbus within their lines. Before
my troops could be got off, I was notified from the same
quarter that there were some 3,000 of the enemy on the St.
Francis River about fifty miles west, or south-west, from
Cairo, and was ordered to send another force against them. I
dispatched Colonel Oglesby at once with troops sufficient to
compete with the reported number of the enemy. On the 5th
word came from the same source that the rebels were about
to detach a large force from Columbus to be moved by boats
down the Mississippi and up the White River, in Arkansas, in
order to reinforce Price, and I was directed to prevent this
movement if possible. I accordingly sent a regiment from

Bird's Point under Colonel W. H. L. Wallace to overtake and reinforce Oglesby, with orders to march to New Madrid, a point some distance below Columbus, on the Missouri side. At the same time I directed General C. F. Smith to move all the troops he could spare from Paducah directly against Columbus, halting them, however, a few miles from the town to await further orders from me. Then I gathered up all the troops at Cairo and Fort Holt, except suitable guards, and moved them down the river on steamers convoyed by two gunboats, accompanying them myself. My force consisted of a little over 3,000 men and embraced five regiments of infantry, two guns and two companies of cavalry. We dropped down the river on the 6th to within about six miles of Columbus, debarked a few men on the Kentucky side and established pickets to connect with the troops from Paducah.

I had no orders which contemplated an attack by the National troops, nor did I intend anything of the kind when I started out from Cairo; but after we started I saw that the officers and men were elated at the prospect of at last having the opportunity of doing what they had volunteered to do— fight the enemies of their country. I did not see how I could maintain discipline, or retain the confidence of my command, if we should return to Cairo without an effort to do something. Columbus, besides being strongly fortified, contained a garrison much more numerous than the force I had with me. It would not do, therefore, to attack that point. About two o'clock on the morning of the 7th, I learned that the enemy was crossing troops from Columbus to the west bank to be dispatched, presumably, after Oglesby. I knew there was a small camp of Confederates at Belmont, immediately opposite Columbus, and I speedily resolved to push down the river, land on the Missouri side, capture Belmont, break up the camp and return. Accordingly, the pickets above Columbus were drawn in at once, and about daylight the boats moved out from shore. In an hour we were debarking on the west bank of the Mississippi, just out of range of the batteries at Columbus.

The ground on the west shore of the river, opposite Columbus, is low and in places marshy and cut up with sloughs.

The soil is rich and the timber large and heavy. There were some small clearings between Belmont and the point where we landed, but most of the country was covered with the native forests. We landed in front of a cornfield. When the debarkation commenced, I took a regiment down the river to post it as a guard against surprise. At that time I had no staff officer who could be trusted with that duty. In the woods, at a short distance below the clearing, I found a depression, dry at the time, but which at high water became a slough or bayou. I placed the men in the hollow, gave them their instructions and ordered them to remain there until they were properly relieved. These troops, with the gunboats, were to protect our transports.

Up to this time the enemy had evidently failed to divine our intentions. From Columbus they could, of course, see our gunboats and transports loaded with troops. But the force from Paducah was threatening them from the land side, and it was hardly to be expected that if Columbus was our object we would separate our troops by a wide river. They doubtless thought we meant to draw a large force from the east bank, then embark ourselves, land on the east bank and make a sudden assault on Columbus before their divided command could be united.

About eight o'clock we started from the point of debarkation, marching by the flank. After moving in this way for a mile or a mile and a half, I halted where there was marshy ground covered with a heavy growth of timber in our front, and deployed a large part of my force as skirmishers. By this time the enemy discovered that we were moving upon Belmont and sent out troops to meet us. Soon after we had started in line, his skirmishers were encountered and fighting commenced. This continued, growing fiercer and fiercer, for about four hours, the enemy being forced back gradually until he was driven into his camp. Early in this engagement my horse was shot under me, but I got another from one of my staff and kept well up with the advance until the river was reached.

The officers and men engaged at Belmont were then under fire for the first time. Veterans could not have behaved better than they did up to the moment of reaching the rebel camp.

At this point they became demoralized from their victory and failed to reap its full reward. The enemy had been followed so closely that when he reached the clear ground on which his camp was pitched he beat a hasty retreat over the river bank, which protected him from our shots and from view. This precipitate retreat at the last moment enabled the National forces to pick their way without hinderance through the abatis—the only artificial defence the enemy had. The moment the camp was reached our men laid down their arms and commenced rummaging the tents to pick up trophies. Some of the higher officers were little better than the privates. They galloped about from one cluster of men to another and at every halt delivered a short eulogy upon the Union cause and the achievements of the command.

All this time the troops we had been engaged with for four hours, lay crouched under cover of the river bank, ready to come up and surrender if summoned to do so; but finding that they were not pursued, they worked their way up the river and came up on the bank between us and our transports. I saw at the same time two steamers coming from the Columbus side towards the west shore, above us, black—or gray—with soldiers from boiler-deck to roof. Some of my men were engaged in firing from captured guns at empty steamers down the river, out of range, cheering at every shot. I tried to get them to turn their guns upon the loaded steamers above and not so far away. My efforts were in vain. At last I directed my staff officers to set fire to the camps. This drew the fire of the enemy's guns located on the heights of Columbus. They had abstained from firing before, probably because they were afraid of hitting their own men; or they may have supposed, until the camp was on fire, that it was still in the possession of their friends. About this time, too, the men we had driven over the bank were seen in line up the river between us and our transports. The alarm "surrounded" was given. The guns of the enemy and the report of being surrounded, brought officers and men completely under control. At first some of the officers seemed to think that to be surrounded was to be placed in a hopeless position, where there was nothing to do but surrender. But when I announced that we had cut our way in and could cut our way out just as well, it seemed a

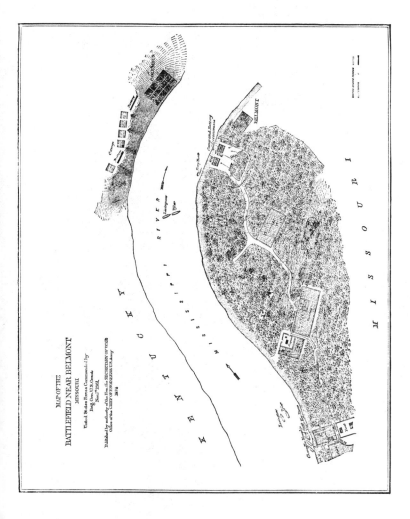

MAP OF THE
BATTLEFIELD NEAR BELMONT
MISSOURI

United States Forces Commanded by
Brig. Gen. U.S. Grant
Nov. 7th 1861

Published by authority of the Hon. the SECRETARY OF WAR
Office of the CHIEF OF ENGINEERS, U.S. Army
1876

new revelation to officers and soldiers. They formed line rapidly and we started back to our boats, with the men deployed as skirmishers as they had been on entering camp. The enemy was soon encountered, but his resistance this time was feeble. Again the Confederates sought shelter under the river banks. We could not stop, however, to pick them up, because the troops we had seen crossing the river had debarked by this time and were nearer our transports than we were. It would be prudent to get them behind us; but we were not again molested on our way to the boats.

From the beginning of the fighting our wounded had been carried to the houses at the rear, near the place of debarkation. I now set the troops to bringing their wounded to the boats. After this had gone on for some little time I rode down the road, without even a staff officer, to visit the guard I had stationed over the approach to our transports. I knew the enemy had crossed over from Columbus in considerable numbers and might be expected to attack us as we were embarking. This guard would be encountered first and, as they were in a natural intrenchment, would be able to hold the enemy for a considerable time. My surprise was great to find there was not a single man in the trench. Riding back to the boat I found the officer who had commanded the guard and learned that he had withdrawn his force when the main body fell back. At first I ordered the guard to return, but finding that it would take some time to get the men together and march them back to their position, I countermanded the order. Then fearing that the enemy we had seen crossing the river below might be coming upon us unawares, I rode out in the field to our front, still entirely alone, to observe whether the enemy was passing. The field was grown up with corn so tall and thick as to cut off the view of even a person on horseback, except directly along the rows. Even in that direction, owing to the overhanging blades of corn, the view was not extensive. I had not gone more than a few hundred yards when I saw a body of troops marching past me not fifty yards away. I looked at them for a moment and then turned my horse towards the river and started back, first in a walk, and when I thought myself concealed from the view of the enemy, as fast as my horse could carry me.

When at the river bank I still had to ride a few hundred yards to the point where the nearest transport lay.

The cornfield in front of our transports terminated at the edge of a dense forest. Before I got back the enemy had entered this forest and had opened a brisk fire upon the boats. Our men, with the exception of details that had gone to the front after the wounded, were now either aboard the transports or very near them. Those who were not aboard soon got there, and the boats pushed off. I was the only man of the National army between the rebels and our transports. The captain of a boat that had just pushed out but had not started, recognized me and ordered the engineer not to start the engine; he then had a plank run out for me. My horse seemed to take in the situation. There was no path down the bank and every one acquainted with the Mississippi River knows that its banks, in a natural state, do not vary at any great angle from the perpendicular. My horse put his fore feet over the bank without hesitation or urging, and with his hind feet well under him, slid down the bank and trotted aboard the boat, twelve or fifteen feet away, over a single gang plank. I dismounted and went at once to the upper deck.

The Mississippi River was low on the 7th of November, 1861, so that the banks were higher than the heads of men standing on the upper decks of the steamers. The rebels were some distance back from the river, so that their fire was high and did us but little harm. Our smoke-stack was riddled with bullets, but there were only three men wounded on the boats, two of whom were soldiers. When I first went on deck I entered the captain's room adjoining the pilot-house, and threw myself on a sofa. I did not keep that position a moment, but rose to go out on the deck to observe what was going on. I had scarcely left when a musket ball entered the room, struck the head of the sofa, passed through it and lodged in the foot.

When the enemy opened fire on the transports our gunboats returned it with vigor. They were well out in the stream and some distance down, so that they had to give but very little elevation to their guns to clear the banks of the river. Their position very nearly enfiladed the line of the enemy while he was marching through the cornfield. The execution was very great, as we could see at the time and as I afterwards learned more positively. We were very soon out of range and went peacefully on our way to Cairo, every man feeling that Belmont was a great victory and that he had contributed his share to it.

Our loss at Belmont was 485 in killed, wounded and missing. About 125 of our wounded fell into the hands of the enemy. We returned with 175 prisoners and two guns, and spiked four other pieces. The loss of the enemy, as officially reported, was 642 men, killed, wounded and missing. We had engaged about 2,500 men, exclusive of the guard left with the transports. The enemy had about 7,000; but this includes the troops brought over from Columbus who were not engaged in the first defence of Belmont.

The two objects for which the battle of Belmont was fought were fully accomplished. The enemy gave up all idea of detaching troops from Columbus. His losses were very heavy for that period of the war. Columbus was beset by people looking for their wounded or dead kin, to take them home for medical treatment or burial. I learned later, when I had moved further south, that Belmont had caused more mourning than almost any other battle up to that time. The National troops acquired a confidence in themselves at Belmont that did not desert them through the war.

The day after the battle I met some officers from General Polk's command, arranged for permission to bury our dead at Belmont and also commenced negotiations for the exchange of prisoners. When our men went to bury their dead, before they were allowed to land they were conducted below the point where the enemy had engaged our transports. Some of the officers expressed a desire to see the field; but the request was refused with the statement that we had no dead there.

While on the truce-boat I mentioned to an officer, whom I had known both at West Point and in the Mexican war, that I was in the cornfield near their troops when they passed; that I had been on horseback and had worn a soldier's overcoat at the time. This officer was on General Polk's staff. He said both he and the general had seen me and that Polk had said to his men, "There is a Yankee; you may try your marksmanship on him if you wish," but nobody fired at me.

Belmont was severely criticised in the North as a wholly unnecessary battle, barren of results, or the possibility of them from the beginning. If it had not been fought, Colonel Oglesby would probably have been captured or destroyed with his three thousand men. Then I should have been culpable indeed.

Chapter XXI.

GENERAL HALLECK IN COMMAND—COMMANDING THE
DISTRICT OF CAIRO—MOVEMENT ON FORT
HENRY—CAPTURE OF FORT HENRY.

WHILE AT CAIRO I had frequent opportunities of meeting the rebel officers of the Columbus garrison. They seemed to be very fond of coming up on steamers under flags of truce. On two or three occasions I went down in like manner. When one of their boats was seen coming up carrying a white flag, a gun would be fired from the lower battery at Fort Holt, throwing a shot across the bow as a signal to come no farther. I would then take a steamer and, with my staff and occasionally a few other officers, go down to receive the party. There were several officers among them whom I had known before, both at West Point and in Mexico. Seeing these officers who had been educated for the profession of arms, both at school and in actual war, which is a far more efficient training, impressed me with the great advantage the South possessed over the North at the beginning of the rebellion. They had from thirty to forty per cent. of the educated soldiers of the Nation. They had no standing army and, consequently, these trained soldiers had to find employment with the troops from their own States. In this way what there was of military education and training was distributed throughout their whole army. The whole loaf was leavened.

The North had a greater number of educated and trained soldiers, but the bulk of them were still in the army and were retained, generally with their old commands and rank, until the war had lasted many months. In the Army of the Potomac there was what was known as the "regular brigade," in which, from the commanding officer down to the youngest second lieutenant, every one was educated to his profession. So, too, with many of the batteries; all the officers, generally four in number to each, were men educated for their profession. Some of these went into battle at the beginning under division commanders who were entirely without military training. This state of affairs gave me an idea which I expressed while at Cairo; that the government ought to disband the regular army, with the exception of the staff corps, and notify the disbanded officers that they would receive no compensation while the war lasted except as volunteers. The register should be kept up, but the names of all officers who were not in the volunteer service at the close, should be stricken from it.

On the 9th of November, two days after the battle of Belmont, Major-General H. W. Halleck superseded General Fremont in command of the Department of the Missouri. The limits of his command took in Arkansas and west Kentucky east to the Cumberland River. From the battle of Belmont until early in February, 1862, the troops under my command did little except prepare for the long struggle which proved to be before them.

The enemy at this time occupied a line running from the Mississippi River at Columbus to Bowling Green and Mill Springs, Kentucky. Each of these positions was strongly fortified, as were also points on the Tennessee and Cumberland rivers near the Tennessee state line. The works on the Tennessee were called Fort Heiman and Fort Henry, and that on the Cumberland was Fort Donelson. At these points the two rivers approached within eleven miles of each other. The lines of rifle pits at each place extended back from the water at least two miles, so that the garrisons were in reality only seven miles apart. These positions were of immense importance to the enemy; and of course correspondingly important for us to possess ourselves of. With Fort Henry in our hands we had a navigable stream open to us up to Muscle Shoals, in Alabama. The Memphis and Charleston Railroad strikes the Tennessee at Eastport, Mississippi, and follows close to the banks of the river up to the shoals. This road, of vast importance to the enemy, would cease to be of use to them for through traffic the moment Fort Henry became ours. Fort Donelson was the gate to Nashville—a place of great military and political importance—and to a rich country extending far east in Kentucky. These two points in our possession the enemy would necessarily be thrown back to the Memphis and Charleston road, or to the boundary of the cotton states, and, as before stated, that road would be lost to them for through communication.

The designation of my command had been changed after Halleck's arrival, from the District of South-east Missouri to the District of Cairo, and the small district commanded by General C. F. Smith, embracing the mouths of the Tennessee and Cumberland rivers, had been added to my jurisdiction. Early in January, 1862, I was directed by General McClellan, through my department commander, to make a reconnoissance in favor of Brigadier-General Don Carlos Buell, who commanded the Department of the Ohio, with headquarters at Louisville, and who was confronting General S. B. Buckner with a larger Confederate force at Bowling Green. It was supposed that Buell was about to make some move against the enemy, and my demonstration was intended to prevent the sending of troops from Columbus, Fort Henry or Donelson to Buckner. I at once ordered General Smith to send a force up the west bank of the Tennessee to threaten forts Heiman and Henry; McClernand at the same time with a force of 6,000 men was sent out into west Kentucky, threatening Columbus with one column and the Tennessee River with another. I went with McClernand's command. The weather was very bad; snow and rain fell; the roads, never good in that section, were intolerable. We were out more than a week splashing through the mud, snow and rain, the men suffering very much. The object of the expedition was accomplished. The enemy did not send reinforcements to Bowling Green, and General George H. Thomas fought and won the battle of Mill Springs before we returned.

As a result of this expedition General Smith reported that he thought it practicable to capture Fort Heiman. This fort stood on high ground, completely commanding Fort Henry on the opposite side of the river, and its possession by us, with the aid of our gunboats, would insure the capture of Fort Henry. This report of Smith's confirmed views I had previously held, that the true line of operations for us was up the Tennessee and Cumberland rivers. With us there, the enemy would be compelled to fall back on the east and west entirely out of the State of Kentucky. On the 6th of January, before receiving orders for this expedition, I had asked permission of the general commanding the department to go to see him at St. Louis. My object was to lay this plan of campaign before him. Now that my views had been confirmed by so able a general as Smith, I renewed my request to go to St. Louis on what I deemed important military business. The leave was granted, but not graciously. I had known General Halleck but very slightly in the old army, not having met him either at West Point or during the Mexican war. I was received with so little cordiality that I perhaps stated the object of my visit with less clearness than I might have done, and I had not uttered many sentences before I was cut short as if my plan was preposterous. I returned to Cairo very much crestfallen.

Flag-officer Foote commanded the little fleet of gunboats then in the neighborhood of Cairo and, though in another branch of the service, was subject to the command of General Halleck. He and I consulted freely upon military matters and he agreed with me perfectly as to the feasibility of the campaign up the Tennessee. Notwithstanding the rebuff I had received from my immediate chief, I therefore, on the 28th of January, renewed the suggestion by telegraph that "if permitted, I could take and hold Fort Henry on the Tennessee." This time I was backed by Flag-officer Foote, who sent a similar dispatch. On the 29th I wrote fully in support of the proposition. On the 1st of February I received full instructions from department headquarters to move upon Fort Henry. On the 2d the expedition started.

In February, 1862, there were quite a good many steamers laid up at Cairo for want of employment, the Mississippi River being closed against navigation below that point. There were also many men in the town whose occupation had been following the river in various capacities, from captain down to deck hand. But there were not enough of either boats or men to move at one time the 17,000 men I proposed to take with me up the Tennessee. I loaded the boats with more than half the force, however, and sent General McClernand in command. I followed with one of the later boats and found McClernand had stopped, very properly, nine miles below Fort Henry. Seven gunboats under Flag-officer Foote had accompanied the advance. The transports we had with us had to return to Paducah to bring up a division from there, with General C. F. Smith in command.

Before sending the boats back I wanted to get the troops as near to the enemy as I could without coming within range of their guns. There was a stream emptying into the Tennessee on the east side, apparently at about long range distance below the fort. On account of the narrow watershed separating the Tennessee and Cumberland rivers at that point, the stream must be insignificant at ordinary stages, but when we were there, in February, it was a torrent. It would facilitate the investment of Fort Henry materially if the troops could be landed south of that stream. To test whether this could be done I boarded the gunboat *Essex* and requested Captain Wm. Porter commanding it, to approach the fort to draw its fire. After we had gone some distance past the mouth of the stream we drew the fire of the fort, which fell much short of us. In consequence I had made up my mind to return and bring the troops to the upper side of the creek, when the enemy opened upon us with a rifled gun that sent shot far beyond us and beyond the stream. One shot passed very near where Captain Porter and I were standing, struck the deck near the stern, penetrated and passed through the cabin and so out into the river. We immediately turned back, and the troops were debarked below the mouth of the creek.

When the landing was completed I returned with the transports to Paducah to hasten up the balance of the troops. I got back on the 5th with the advance, the remainder following as rapidly as the steamers could carry them. At ten o'clock at night, on the 5th, the whole command was not yet up. Being anxious to commence operations as soon as possible before the enemy could reinforce heavily, I issued my orders for an advance at 11 A.M. on the 6th. I felt sure that all the troops would be up by that time.

Fort Henry occupies a bend in the river which gave the guns in the water battery a direct fire down the stream. The camp outside the fort was intrenched, with rifle pits and outworks two miles back on the road to Donelson and Dover. The garrison of the fort and camp was about 2,800, with strong reinforcements from Donelson halted some miles out. There were seventeen heavy guns in the fort. The river was very high, the banks being overflowed except where the bluffs come to the water's edge. A portion of the ground on which Fort Henry stood was two feet deep in water. Below, the water extended into the woods several hundred yards back from the bank on the east side. On the west bank Fort Heiman stood on high ground, completely commanding Fort Henry. The distance from Fort Henry to Donelson is but eleven miles. The two positions were so important to the enemy, *as he saw his interest*, that it was natural to suppose that reinforcements would come from every quarter from which they could be got. Prompt action on our part was imperative.

The plan was for the troops and gunboats to start at the same moment. The troops were to invest the garrison and the gunboats to attack the fort at close quarters. General Smith was to land a brigade of his division on the west bank during the night of the 5th and get it in rear of Heiman.

At the hour designated the troops and gunboats started. General Smith found Fort Heiman had been evacuated before his men arrived. The gunboats soon engaged the water batteries at very close quarters, but the troops which were to invest Fort Henry were delayed for want of roads, as well as by the dense forest and the high water in what would in dry weather have been unimportant beds of streams. This delay made no difference in the result. On our first appearance Tilghman had sent his entire command, with the exception of about one hundred men left to man the guns in the fort, to the outworks on the road to Dover and Donelson, so as to have them out of range of the guns of our navy; and before any attack on the 6th he had ordered them to retreat on Donelson. He stated in his subsequent report that the defence was intended solely to give his troops time to make their escape.

Tilghman was captured with his staff and ninety men, as well as the armament of the fort, the ammunition and whatever stores were there. Our cavalry pursued the retreating column towards Donelson and picked up two guns and a few stragglers; but the enemy had so much the start, that the pursuing force did not get in sight of any except the stragglers.

All the gunboats engaged were hit many times. The damage, however, beyond what could be repaired by a small expenditure of money, was slight, except to the *Essex*. A shell penetrated the boiler of that vessel and exploded it, killing

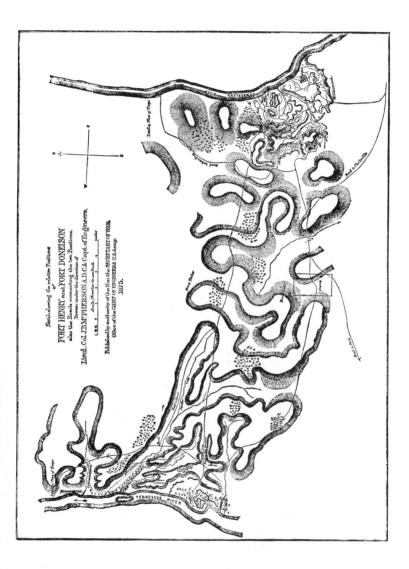

Sketch showing the relative Positions
of
FORT HENRY and FORT DONELSON
also the Roads connecting the two Positions,
Drawn under the direction of
Lieut. Col. J.B.M.PHERSON A.D.C.& Capt. of Engineers.

Scale 2½ miles to one inch.

Published by authority of the Hon. the SECRETARY OF WAR
Office of the CHIEF OF ENGINEERS U.S. Army.
1875.

TENNESSEE RIVER

and wounding forty-eight men, nineteen of whom were soldiers who had been detailed to act with the navy. On several
occasions during the war such details were made when the
complement of men with the navy was insufficient for the
duty before them. After the fall of Fort Henry Captain Walke,
commanding the iron-clad *Carondelet*, at my request ascended
the Tennessee River and thoroughly destroyed the bridge of
the Memphis and Ohio Railroad.

Chapter XXII

INVESTMENT OF FORT DONELSON—THE NAVAL
OPERATIONS—ATTACK OF THE ENEMY—ASSAULTING
THE WORKS—SURRENDER OF THE FORT.

I INFORMED the department commander of our success at
Fort Henry and that on the 8th I would take Fort Donelson. But the rain continued to fall so heavily that the roads
became impassable for artillery and wagon trains. Then, too,
it would not have been prudent to proceed without the gunboats. At least it would have been leaving behind a valuable
part of our available force.

On the 7th, the day after the fall of Fort Henry, I took my
staff and the cavalry—a part of one regiment—and made a
reconnoissance to within about a mile of the outer line of
works at Donelson. I had known General Pillow in Mexico,
and judged that with any force, no matter how small, I could
march up to within gunshot of any intrenchments he was
given to hold. I said this to the officers of my staff at the time.
I knew that Floyd was in command, but he was no soldier,
and I judged that he would yield to Pillow's pretensions. I
met, as I expected, no opposition in making the reconnoissance and, besides learning the topography of the country on
the way and around Fort Donelson, found that there were
two roads available for marching; one leading to the village of
Dover, the other to Donelson.

Fort Donelson is two miles north, or down the river,
from Dover. The fort, as it stood in 1861, embraced about
one hundred acres of land. On the east it fronted the Cumberland; to the north it faced Hickman's creek, a small
stream which at that time was deep and wide because of the
back-water from the river; on the south was another small
stream, or rather a ravine, opening into the Cumberland.
This also was filled with back-water from the river. The fort
stood on high ground, some of it as much as a hundred feet
above the Cumberland. Strong protection to the heavy guns
in the water batteries had been obtained by cutting away
places for them in the bluff. To the west there was a line of

rifle-pits some two miles back from the river at the farthest point. This line ran generally along the crest of high ground, but in one place crossed a ravine which opens into the river between the village and the fort. The ground inside and outside of this intrenched line was very broken and generally wooded. The trees outside of the rifle-pits had been cut down for a considerable way out, and had been felled so that their tops lay outwards from the intrenchments. The limbs had been trimmed and pointed, and thus formed an abatis in front of the greater part of the line. Outside of this intrenched line, and extending about half the entire length of it, is a ravine running north and south and opening into Hickman creek at a point north of the fort. The entire side of this ravine next to the works was one long abatis.

General Halleck commenced his efforts in all quarters to get reinforcements to forward to me immediately on my departure from Cairo. General Hunter sent men freely from Kansas, and a large division under General Nelson, from Buell's army, was also dispatched. Orders went out from the War Department to consolidate fragments of companies that were being recruited in the Western States so as to make full companies, and to consolidate companies into regiments. General Halleck did not approve or disapprove of my going to Fort Donelson. He said nothing whatever to me on the subject. He informed Buell on the 7th that I would march against Fort Donelson the next day; but on the 10th he directed me to fortify Fort Henry strongly, particularly to the land side, saying that he forwarded me intrenching tools for that purpose. I received this dispatch in front of Fort Donelson.

I was very impatient to get to Fort Donelson because I knew the importance of the place to the enemy and supposed he would reinforce it rapidly. I felt that 15,000 men on the 8th would be more effective than 50,000 a month later. I asked Flag-officer Foote, therefore, to order his gunboats still about Cairo to proceed up the Cumberland River and not to wait for those gone to Eastport and Florence; but the others got back in time and we started on the 12th. I had moved McClernand out a few miles the night before so as to leave the road as free as possible.

Just as we were about to start the first reinforcement reached me on transports. It was a brigade composed of six full regiments commanded by Colonel Thayer, of Nebraska. As the gunboats were going around to Donelson by the Tennessee, Ohio and Cumberland rivers, I directed Thayer to turn about and go under their convoy.

I started from Fort Henry with 15,000 men, including eight batteries and part of a regiment of cavalry, and, meeting with no obstruction to detain us, the advance arrived in front of the enemy by noon. That afternoon and the next day were spent in taking up ground to make the investment as complete as possible. General Smith had been directed to leave a portion of his division behind to guard forts Henry and Heiman. He left General Lew. Wallace with 2,500 men. With the remainder of his division he occupied our left, extending to Hickman creek. McClernand was on the right and covered the roads running south and south-west from Dover. His right extended to the back-water up the ravine opening into the Cumberland south of the village. The troops were not intrenched, but the nature of the ground was such that they were just as well protected from the fire of the enemy as if rifle-pits had been thrown up. Our line was generally along the crest of ridges. The artillery was protected by being sunk in the ground. The men who were not serving the guns were perfectly covered from fire on taking position a little back from the crest. The greatest suffering was from want of shelter. It was midwinter and during the siege we had rain and snow, thawing and freezing alternately. It would not do to allow camp-fires except far down the hill out of sight of the enemy, and it would not do to allow many of the troops to remain there at the same time. In the march over from Fort Henry numbers of the men had thrown away their blankets and overcoats. There was therefore much discomfort and absolute suffering.

During the 12th and 13th, and until the arrival of Wallace and Thayer on the 14th, the National forces, composed of but 15,000 men, without intrenchments, confronted an intrenched army of 21,000, without conflict further than what was brought on by ourselves. Only one gunboat had arrived. There was a little skirmishing each day, brought on by the

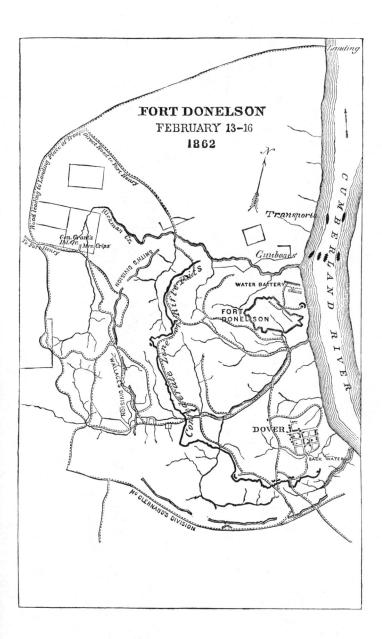

FORT DONELSON
FEBRUARY 13–16
1862

N

Landing

Road leading to Landing Place of Troops

Direct Road to Fort Henry

To Fort Henry

Hickman Cr.

Gen. Grant's Hd. Qr.

Mrs. Crisp

SMITH'S DIVISION

WALLACE'S DIVISION

Confederate Line Rifle Pits

Transports

Gunboats

WATER BATTERY

FORT DONELSON

DOVER

BACK WATER

McCLERNAND'S DIVISION

CUMBERLAND RIVER

movement of our troops in securing commanding positions; but there was no actual fighting during this time except once, on the 13th, in front of McClernand's command. That general had undertaken to capture a battery of the enemy which was annoying his men. Without orders or authority he sent three regiments to make the assault. The battery was in the main line of the enemy, which was defended by his whole army present. Of course the assault was a failure, and of course the loss on our side was great for the number of men engaged. In this assault Colonel William Morrison fell badly wounded. Up to this time the surgeons with the army had no difficulty in finding room in the houses near our line for all the sick and wounded; but now hospitals were over-crowded. Owing, however, to the energy and skill of the surgeons the suffering was not so great as it might have been. The hospital arrangements at Fort Donelson were as complete as it was possible to make them, considering the inclemency of the weather and the lack of tents, in a sparsely settled country where the houses were generally of but one or two rooms.

On the return of Captain Walke to Fort Henry on the 10th, I had requested him to take the vessels that had accom-panied him on his expedition up the Tennessee, and get pos-session of the Cumberland as far up towards Donelson as possible. He started without delay, taking, however, only his own gunboat, the *Carondelet*, towed by the steamer *Alps*. Captain Walke arrived a few miles below Donelson on the 12th, a little after noon. About the time the advance of troops reached a point within gunshot of the fort on the land side, he engaged the water batteries at long range. On the 13th I informed him of my arrival the day before and of the establishment of most of our batteries, requesting him at the same time to attack again that day so that I might take advantage of any diversion. The attack was made and many shots fell within the fort, creating some consternation, as we now know. The investment on the land side was made as complete as the number of troops engaged would ad-mit of.

During the night of the 13th Flag-officer Foote arrived with the iron-clads *St. Louis*, *Louisville* and *Pittsburg* and the wooden gunboats *Tyler* and *Conestoga*, convoying Thayer's brigade. On the morning of the 14th Thayer was landed. Wallace, whom I had ordered over from Fort Henry, also arrived about the same time. Up to this time he had been commanding a brigade belonging to the division of General C. F. Smith. These troops were now restored to the division they belonged to, and General Lew. Wallace was assigned to the command of a division composed of the brigade of Colonel Thayer and other reinforcements that arrived the same day. This new division was assigned to the centre, giving the two flanking divisions an opportunity to close up and form a stronger line.

The plan was for the troops to hold the enemy within his lines, while the gunboats should attack the water batteries at close quarters and silence his guns if possible. Some of the gunboats were to run the batteries, get above the fort and above the village of Dover. I had ordered a reconnoissance made with the view of getting troops to the river above Dover in case they should be needed there. That position attained by the gunboats it would have been but a question of time—and a very short time, too—when the garrison would have been compelled to surrender.

By three in the afternoon of the 14th Flag-officer Foote was ready, and advanced upon the water batteries with his entire fleet. After coming in range of the batteries of the enemy the advance was slow, but a constant fire was delivered from every gun that could be brought to bear upon the fort. I occupied a position on shore from which I could see the advancing navy. The leading boat got within a very short distance of the water battery, not further off I think than two hundred yards, and I soon saw one and then another of them dropping down the river, visibly disabled. Then the whole fleet followed and the engagement closed for the day. The gunboat which Flag-officer Foote was on, besides having been hit about sixty times, several of the shots passing through near the water-line, had a shot enter the pilot-house which killed the pilot, carried away the wheel and wounded the flag-officer himself. The tiller-ropes of another vessel were carried away and she, too, dropped helplessly back. Two others had their pilot-houses so injured that they scarcely formed a protection to the men at the wheel.

The enemy had evidently been much demoralized by the assault, but they were jubilant when they saw the disabled vessels dropping down the river entirely out of the control of the men on board. Of course I only witnessed the falling back of our gunboats and felt sad enough at the time over the repulse. Subsequent reports, now published, show that the enemy telegraphed a great victory to Richmond. The sun went down on the night of the 14th of February, 1862, leaving the army confronting Fort Donelson anything but comforted over the prospects. The weather had turned intensely cold; the men were without tents and could not keep up fires where most of them had to stay, and, as previously stated, many had thrown away their overcoats and blankets. Two of the strongest of our gunboats had been disabled, presumably beyond the possibility of rendering any present assistance. I retired this night not knowing but that I would have to intrench my position, and bring up tents for the men or build huts under the cover of the hills.

On the morning of the 15th, before it was yet broad day, a messenger from Flag-officer Foote handed me a note, expressing a desire to see me on the flag-ship and saying that he had been injured the day before so much that he could not come himself to me. I at once made my preparations for starting. I directed my adjutant-general to notify each of the division commanders of my absence and instruct them to do nothing to bring on an engagement until they received further orders, but to hold their positions. From the heavy rains that had fallen for days and weeks preceding and from the constant use of the road between the troops and the landing four to seven miles below, these roads had become cut up so as to be hardly passable. The intense cold of the night of the 14th–15th had frozen the ground solid. This made travel on horseback even slower than through the mud; but I went as fast as the roads would allow.

When I reached the fleet I found the flag-ship was anchored out in the stream. A small boat, however, awaited my arrival and I was soon on board with the flag-officer. He explained to me in short the condition in which he was left by the engagement of the evening before, and suggested that I should intrench while he returned to Mound City with his disabled boats, expressing at the time the belief that he could have the necessary repairs made and be back in ten days. I saw the absolute necessity of his gunboats going into hospital and did not know but I should be forced to the alternative of going through a siege. But the enemy relieved me from this necessity.

When I left the National line to visit Flag-officer Foote I had no idea that there would be any engagement on land unless I brought it on myself. The conditions for battle were much more favorable to us than they had been for the first two days of the investment. From the 12th to the 14th we had but 15,000 men of all arms and no gunboats. Now we had been reinforced by a fleet of six naval vessels, a large division of troops under General L. Wallace and 2,500 men brought over from Fort Henry belonging to the division of C. F. Smith. The enemy, however, had taken the initiative. Just as I landed I met Captain Hillyer of my staff, white with fear, not for his personal safety, but for the safety of the National troops. He said the enemy had come out of his lines in full force and attacked and scattered McClernand's division, which was in full retreat. The roads, as I have said, were unfit for making fast time, but I got to my command as soon as possible. The attack had been made on the National right. I was some four or five miles north of our left. The line was about three miles long. In reaching the point where the disaster had occurred I had to pass the divisions of Smith and Wallace. I saw no sign of excitement on the portion of the line held by Smith; Wallace was nearer the scene of conflict and had taken part in it. He had, at an opportune time, sent Thayer's brigade to the support of McClernand and thereby contributed to hold the enemy within his lines.

I saw everything favorable for us along the line of our left and centre. When I came to the right appearances were different. The enemy had come out in full force to cut his way out and make his escape. McClernand's division had to bear the brunt of the attack from this combined force. His men had stood up gallantly until the ammunition in their cartridge-boxes gave out. There was abundance of ammunition near by lying on the ground in boxes, but at that stage of the war it was not all of our commanders of regiments, brigades, or even divisions, who had been educated up to the point of seeing that their men were constantly supplied with ammunition during an engagement. When the men found themselves without ammunition they could not stand up against troops who seemed to have plenty of it. The division broke and a portion fled, but most of the men, as they were not pursued, only fell back out of range of the fire of the enemy. It must have been about this time that Thayer pushed his brigade in between the enemy and those of our troops that were without ammunition. At all events the enemy fell back within his intrenchments and was there when I got on the field.

I saw the men standing in knots talking in the most excited manner. No officer seemed to be giving any directions. The soldiers had their muskets, but no ammunition, while there were tons of it close at hand. I heard some of the men say that the enemy had come out with knapsacks, and haversacks filled with rations. They seemed to think this indicated a determination on his part to stay out and fight just as long as the provisions held out. I turned to Colonel J. D. Webster, of my staff, who was with me, and said: "Some of our men are pretty badly demoralized, but the enemy must be more so, for he has attempted to force his way out, but has fallen back: the one who attacks first now will be victorious and the enemy will have to be in a hurry if he gets ahead of me." I determined to make the assault at once on our left. It was clear to my mind that the enemy had started to march out with his entire force, except a few pickets, and if our attack could be made on the left before the enemy could redistribute his forces along the line, we would find but little opposition except from the intervening abatis. I directed Colonel Webster to ride with me and call out to the men as we passed: "Fill your cartridge-boxes, quick, and get into line; the enemy is trying to escape and he must not be permitted to do so." This acted like a charm. The men only wanted some one to give them a command. We rode rapidly to Smith's quarters, when I explained the situation to him and directed him to charge the enemy's works in his front with his whole division, saying at the same time that he would find nothing but a very thin line to contend with. The general was off in an incredibly short time, going in advance himself to keep his men from firing while they were working their way through the abatis intervening between them and the enemy. The outer line of rifle-pits was passed, and the night of the 15th General Smith, with much of his division, bivouacked within the lines of the enemy. There was now no doubt but that the Confederates must surrender or be captured the next day.

There seems from subsequent accounts to have been much consternation, particularly among the officers of high rank, in Dover during the night of the 15th. General Floyd, the commanding officer, who was a man of talent enough for any civil position, was no soldier and, possibly, did not possess the elements of one. He was further unfitted for command, for the reason that his conscience must have troubled him and made him afraid. As Secretary of War he had taken a solemn oath to maintain the Constitution of the United States and to uphold the same against all its enemies. He had betrayed that trust. As Secretary of War he was reported through the northern press to have scattered the little army the country had so that the most of it could be picked up in detail when secession occurred. About a year before leaving the Cabinet he had removed arms from northern to southern arsenals. He continued in the Cabinet of President Buchanan until about the 1st of January, 1861, while he was working vigilantly for the establishment of a confederacy made out of United States territory. Well may he have been afraid to fall into the hands of National troops. He would no doubt have been tried for misappropriating public property, if not for treason, had he been captured. General Pillow, next in command, was conceited, and prided himself much on his services in the Mexican war. He telegraphed to General Johnston, at Nashville, after our men were within the rebel rifle-pits, and almost on the eve of his making his escape, that the Southern troops had had great success all day. Johnston forwarded the dispatch to Richmond. While the authorities at the capital were reading it Floyd and Pillow were fugitives.

A council of war was held by the enemy at which all agreed

that it would be impossible to hold out longer. General Buckner, who was third in rank in the garrison but much the most capable soldier, seems to have regarded it a duty to hold the fort until the general commanding the department, A. S. Johnston, should get back to his headquarters at Nashville. Buckner's report shows, however, that he considered Donelson lost and that any attempt to hold the place longer would be at the sacrifice of the command. Being assured that Johnston was already in Nashville, Buckner too agreed that surrender was the proper thing. Floyd turned over the command to Pillow, who declined it. It then devolved upon Buckner, who accepted the responsibility of the position. Floyd and Pillow took possession of all the river transports at Dover and before morning both were on their way to Nashville, with the brigade formerly commanded by Floyd and some other troops, in all about 3,000. Some marched up the east bank of the Cumberland; others went on the steamers. During the night Forrest also, with his cavalry and some other troops, about a thousand in all, made their way out, passing between our right and the river. They had to ford or swim over the back-water in the little creek just south of Dover.

Before daylight General Smith brought to me the following letter from General Buckner:

HEADQUARTERS, FORT DONELSON,
February 16, 1862.

SIR:—In consideration of all the circumstances governing the present situation of affairs at this station, I propose to the Commanding Officer of the Federal forces the appointment of Commissioners to agree upon terms of capitulation of the forces and fort under my command, and in that view suggest an armistice until 12 o'clock to-day.

I am, sir, very respectfully,
Your ob't se'v't,
S. B. BUCKNER,
Brig. Gen. C. S. A.

To Brigadier-General U. S. GRANT,
Com'ding U. S. Forces,
Near Fort Donelson.

To this I responded as follows:

HEADQUARTERS ARMY IN THE FIELD,
Camp near Donelson,
February 16, 1862.

General S. B. BUCKNER,
Confederate Army.

SIR: — Yours of this date, proposing armistice and appointment of Commissioners to settle terms of capitulation, is just received. No terms except an unconditional and immediate surrender can be accepted. I propose to move immediately upon your works.

I am, sir, very respectfully,
Your ob't se'v't,
U. S. GRANT,
Brig. Gen.

To this I received the following reply:

HEADQUARTERS, DOVER, TENNESSEE,
February 16, 1862.

To Brig. Gen'l U. S. GRANT,
U. S. Army.

SIR: — The distribution of the forces under my command, incident to an unexpected change of commanders, and the overwhelming force under your command, compel me, notwithstanding the brilliant success of the Confederate arms yesterday, to accept the ungenerous and unchivalrous terms which you propose.

I am, sir,
Your very ob't se'v't,
S. B. BUCKNER,
Brig. Gen. C. S. A.

General Buckner, as soon as he had dispatched the first of the above letters, sent word to his different commanders on the line of rifle-pits, notifying them that he had made a proposition looking to the surrender of the garrison, and directing them to notify National troops in their front so that all fighting might be prevented. White flags were stuck at intervals along the line of rifle-pits, but none over the fort. As soon as the last letter from Buckner was received I mounted my horse and rode to Dover. General Wallace, I found, had preceded me an hour or more. I presume that, seeing white flags exposed in his front, he rode up to see what they meant and,

Hd. Qrs. Fort Donelson,
Feby 16 1862.

Sir :

In consideration of all the
circumstances governing the present
situation of affairs at this station
I propose to the commanding officer
of the Federal forces the appointment
of Commissioners to agree upon terms
of Capitulation of the forces, and post under my
command, and in that view suggest
an armistice until 12 O'clock today.
    I am, Sir, very respectfully,
        Your obb.svt.
To   S.B. Buckner.
Brig.Gen. U.S. Grant   Brig.Gen. C.S.A.
Comdg. U.S.Forces,
near Fort Donelson.

Hd Qrs, Army in the Field
Camp near Donelson, Feby 16th 1862

Gen. S. B. Buckner,
Confed. Army,

   Sir,

    Yours of this date proposing
Armistice, and appointment of Commissioners
to settle terms of Capitulation is just received.
No terms except an unconditional and immediate
Surrender can be accepted.

  I propose to move immediately upon
your works.

    I am Sir: very respectfully
     your obt. Sert.
      U. S. Grant
      Brig. Gen.

Head Quarters, Dover, Tenn,
Febry. 16. 1862.

To Brig. Gen. U.S. Grant, U.S. Army.
    Sir.
                The ~~condition~~ distribution
of the forces under my command, incident
to an unexpected change of commanders, and
the overwhelming force under your command,
compel me, notwithstanding the brilliant
success of the Confederate arms yesterday, to
accept the ungenerous and unchivalrous
terms which you propose.
        I am, sir,
        Your very obt. st.
        S.B. Buckner.
        Brig. Gen. C.S.A.

not being fired upon or halted, he kept on until he found himself at the headquarters of General Buckner.

I had been at West Point three years with Buckner and afterwards served with him in the army, so that we were quite well acquainted. In the course of our conversation, which was very friendly, he said to me that if he had been in command I would not have got up to Donelson as easily as I did. I told him that if he had been in command I should not have tried in the way I did: I had invested their lines with a smaller force than they had to defend them, and at the same time had sent a brigade full 5,000 strong, around by water; I had relied very much upon their commander to allow me to come safely up to the outside of their works. I asked General Buckner about what force he had to surrender. He replied that he could not tell with any degree of accuracy; that all the sick and weak had been sent to Nashville while we were about Fort Henry; that Floyd and Pillow had left during the night, taking many men with them; and that Forrest, and probably others, had also escaped during the preceding night: the number of casualties he could not tell; but he said I would not find fewer than 12,000, nor more than 15,000.

He asked permission to send parties outside of the lines to bury his dead, who had fallen on the 15th when they tried to get out. I gave directions that his permit to pass our limits should be recognized. I have no reason to believe that this privilege was abused, but it familiarized our guards so much with the sight of Confederates passing to and fro that I have no doubt many got beyond our pickets unobserved and went on. The most of the men who went in that way no doubt thought they had had war enough, and left with the intention of remaining out of the army. Some came to me and asked permission to go, saying that they were tired of the war and would not be caught in the ranks again, and I bade them go.

The actual number of Confederates at Fort Donelson can never be given with entire accuracy. The largest number admitted by any writer on the Southern side, is by Colonel Preston Johnston. He gives the number at 17,000. But this must be an underestimate. The commissary general of prisoners reported having issued rations to 14,623 Fort Donelson prisoners at Cairo, as they passed that point. General Pillow reported the killed and wounded at 2,000; but he had less opportunity of knowing the actual numbers than the officers of McClernand's division, for most of the killed and wounded fell outside their works, in front of that division, and were buried or cared for by Buckner after the surrender and when Pillow was a fugitive. It is known that Floyd and Pillow escaped during the night of the 15th, taking with them not less than 3,000 men. Forrest escaped with about 1,000 and others were leaving singly and in squads all night. It is probable that the Confederate force at Donelson, on the 15th of February, 1862, was 21,000 in round numbers.

On the day Fort Donelson fell I had 27,000 men to confront the Confederate lines and guard the road four or five miles to the left, over which all our supplies had to be drawn on wagons. During the 16th, after the surrender, additional reinforcements arrived.

During the siege General Sherman had been sent to Smithland, at the mouth of the Cumberland River, to forward reinforcements and supplies to me. At that time he was my senior in rank and there was no authority of law to assign a junior to command a senior of the same grade. But every boat that came up with supplies or reinforcements brought a note of encouragement from Sherman, asking me to call upon him for any assistance he could render and saying that if he could be of service at the front I might send for him and he would waive rank.

Chapter XXIII.

PROMOTED MAJOR-GENERAL OF VOLUNTEERS—
UNOCCUPIED TERRITORY—ADVANCE UPON NASHVILLE
—SITUATION OF THE TROOPS—CONFEDERATE RETREAT
—RELIEVED OF THE COMMAND—RESTORED TO THE
COMMAND—GENERAL SMITH.

THE NEWS of the fall of Fort Donelson caused great delight all over the North. At the South, particularly in Richmond, the effect was correspondingly depressing. I was promptly promoted to the grade of Major-General of Volunteers, and confirmed by the Senate. All three of my division commanders were promoted to the same grade and the colonels who commanded brigades were made brigadier-generals in the volunteer service. My chief, who was in St. Louis, telegraphed his congratulations to General Hunter in Kansas for the services he had rendered in securing the fall of Fort Donelson by sending reinforcements so rapidly. To Washington he telegraphed that the victory was due to General C. F. Smith; "promote him," he said, "and the whole country will applaud." On the 19th there was published at St. Louis a formal order thanking Flag-officer Foote and myself, and the forces under our command, for the victories on the Tennessee and the Cumberland. I received no other recognition whatever from General Halleck. But General Cullum, his chief of staff, who was at Cairo, wrote me a warm congratulatory letter on his own behalf. I approved of General Smith's promotion highly, as I did all the promotions that were made.

My opinion was and still is that immediately after the fall of Fort Donelson the way was opened to the National forces all over the South-west without much resistance. If one general who would have taken the responsibility had been in command of all the troops west of the Alleghanies, he could have marched to Chattanooga, Corinth, Memphis and Vicksburg with the troops we then had, and as volunteering was going on rapidly over the North there would soon have been force enough at all these centres to operate offensively against any body of the enemy that might be found near them. Rapid movements and the acquisition of rebellious territory would have promoted volunteering, so that reinforcements could have been had as fast as transportation could have been obtained to carry them to their destination. On the other hand there were tens of thousands of strong able-bodied young men still at their homes in the South-western States, who had not gone into the Confederate army in February, 1862, and who had no particular desire to go. If our lines had been extended to protect their homes, many of them never would have gone. Providence ruled differently. Time was given the enemy to collect armies and fortify his new positions; and twice afterwards he came near forcing his north-western front up to the Ohio River.

I promptly informed the department commander of our success at Fort Donelson and that the way was open now to Clarksville and Nashville; and that unless I received orders to the contrary I should take Clarksville on the 21st and Nashville about the 1st of March. Both these places are on the Cumberland River above Fort Donelson. As I heard nothing from headquarters on the subject, General C. F. Smith was sent to Clarksville at the time designated and found the place evacuated. The capture of forts Henry and Donelson had broken the line the enemy had taken from Columbus to Bowling Green, and it was known that he was falling back from the eastern point of this line and that Buell was following, or at least advancing. I should have sent troops to Nashville at the time I sent to Clarksville, but my transportation was limited and there were many prisoners to be forwarded north.

None of the reinforcements from Buell's army arrived until the 24th of February. Then General Nelson came up, with orders to report to me with two brigades, he having sent one brigade to Cairo. I knew General Buell was advancing on Nashville from the north, and I was advised by scouts that the rebels were leaving that place, and trying to get out all the supplies they could. Nashville was, at that time, one of the best provisioned posts in the South. I had no use for reinforcements now, and thinking Buell would like to have his troops again, I ordered Nelson to proceed to Nashville without debarking at Fort Donelson. I sent a gunboat also as a convoy. The Cumberland River was very high at the time; the railroad bridge at Nashville had been burned, and all river craft had been destroyed, or would be before the enemy left. Nashville is on the west bank of the Cumberland, and Buell was approaching from the east. I thought the steamers carrying Nelson's division would be useful in ferrying the balance of Buell's forces across. I ordered Nelson to put himself in communication with Buell as soon as possible, and if he found him more than two days off from Nashville to return below the city and await orders. Buell, however, had already arrived in person at Edgefield, opposite Nashville, and Mitchell's division of his command reached there the same day. Nelson immediately took possession of the city.

After Nelson had gone and before I had learned of Buell's arrival, I sent word to department headquarters that I should go to Nashville myself on the 28th if I received no orders to the contrary. Hearing nothing, I went as I had informed my superior officer I would do. On arriving at Clarksville I saw a fleet of steamers at the shore—the same that had taken Nelson's division—and troops going aboard. I landed and called on the commanding officer, General C. F. Smith. As soon as he saw me he showed an order he had just received from Buell in these words:

NASHVILLE, *February* 25, 1862.

GENERAL C. F. SMITH,
    Commanding U. S. Forces, Clarksville.

GENERAL:—The landing of a portion of our troops, contrary to my intentions, on the south side of the river has compelled me to hold this side at every hazard. If the enemy should assume the offensive, and I am assured by reliable persons that in view of my position such is his intention, my force present is altogether inadequate, consisting of only 15,000 men. I have to request you, therefore, to come forward with all the available force under your command. So important do I consider the occasion that I think it necessary to give this communication all the force of orders, and I send four boats, the *Diana*, *Woodford*, *John Rain*, and *Autocrat*, to bring you up. In five or six days my force will probably be sufficient to relieve you.

Very respectfully, your ob't srv't,
D. C. BUELL,
Brigadier-General Comd'g.

P. S.—The steamers will leave here at 12 o'clock to-night.

General Smith said this order was nonsense. But I told him it was better to obey it. The General replied, "of course I must obey," and said his men were embarking as fast as they could. I went on up to Nashville and inspected the position taken by Nelson's troops. I did not see Buell during the day, and wrote him a note saying that I had been in Nashville since early morning and had hoped to meet him. On my return to the boat we met. His troops were still east of the river, and the steamers that had carried Nelson's division up were mostly at Clarksville to bring Smith's division. I said to General Buell my information was that the enemy was retreating as fast as possible. General Buell said there was fighting going on then only ten or twelve miles away. I said: "Quite probably; Nashville contained valuable stores of arms, ammunition and provisions, and the enemy is probably trying to carry away all he can. The fighting is doubtless with the rearguard who are trying to protect the trains they are getting away with." Buell spoke very positively of the danger Nashville was in of an attack from the enemy. I said, in the absence of positive information, I believed my information was correct. He responded that he "knew." "Well," I said, "I do not know; but as I came by Clarksville General Smith's troops were embarking to join you."

Smith's troops were returned the same day. The enemy were trying to get away from Nashville and not to return to it.

At this time General Albert Sidney Johnston commanded all the Confederate troops west of the Alleghany Mountains, with the exception of those in the extreme south. On the National side the forces confronting him were divided into, at first three, then four separate departments. Johnston had greatly the advantage in having supreme command over all troops that could possibly be brought to bear upon one point, while the forces similarly situated on the National side, divided into independent commands, could not be brought into harmonious action except by orders from Washington.

At the beginning of 1862 Johnston's troops east of the Mississippi occupied a line extending from Columbus, on his left, to Mill Springs, on his right. As we have seen, Columbus, both banks of the Tennessee River, the west bank of the Cumberland and Bowling Green, all were strongly fortified. Mill

Springs was intrenched. The National troops occupied no territory south of the Ohio, except three small garrisons along its bank and a force thrown out from Louisville to confront that at Bowling Green. Johnston's strength was no doubt numerically inferior to that of the National troops; but this was compensated for by the advantage of being sole commander of all the Confederate forces at the West, and of operating in a country where his friends would take care of his rear without any detail of soldiers. But when General George H. Thomas moved upon the enemy at Mill Springs and totally routed him, inflicting a loss of some 300 killed and wounded, and forts Henry and Heiman fell into the hands of the National forces, with their armaments and about 100 prisoners, those losses seemed to dishearten the Confederate commander so much that he immediately commenced a retreat from Bowling Green on Nashville. He reached this latter place on the 14th of February, while Donelson was still besieged. Buell followed with a portion of the Army of the Ohio, but he had to march and did not reach the east bank of the Cumberland opposite Nashville until the 24th of the month, and then with only one division of his army.

The bridge at Nashville had been destroyed and all boats removed or disabled, so that a small garrison could have held the place against any National troops that could have been brought against it within ten days after the arrival of the force from Bowling Green. Johnston seemed to lie quietly at Nashville to await the result at Fort Donelson, on which he had staked the possession of most of the territory embraced in the States of Kentucky and Tennessee. It is true, the two generals senior in rank at Fort Donelson were sending him encouraging dispatches, even claiming great Confederate victories up to the night of the 16th when they must have been preparing for their individual escape. Johnston made a fatal mistake in intrusting so important a command to Floyd, who he must have known was no soldier even if he possessed the elements of one. Pillow's presence as second was also a mistake. If these officers had been forced upon him and designated for that particular command, then he should have left Nashville with a small garrison under a trusty officer, and with the remainder of his force gone to Donelson himself. If he had been captured the result could not have been worse than it was.

Johnston's heart failed him upon the first advance of National troops. He wrote to Richmond on the 8th of February, "I think the gunboats of the enemy will probably take Fort Donelson without the necessity of employing their land force in co-operation." After the fall of that place he abandoned Nashville and Chattanooga without an effort to save either, and fell back into northern Mississippi, where, six weeks later, he was destined to end his career.

From the time of leaving Cairo I was singularly unfortunate in not receiving dispatches from General Halleck. The order of the 10th of February directing me to fortify Fort Henry strongly, particularly to the land side, and saying that intrenching tools had been sent for that purpose, reached me after Donelson was invested. I received nothing direct which indicated that the department commander knew we were in possession of Donelson. I was reporting regularly to the chief of staff, who had been sent to Cairo, soon after the troops left there, to receive all reports from the front and to telegraph the substance to the St. Louis headquarters. Cairo was at the southern end of the telegraph wire. Another line was started at once from Cairo to Paducah and Smithland, at the mouths of the Tennessee and Cumberland respectively. My dispatches were all sent to Cairo by boat, but many of those addressed to me were sent to the operator at the end of the advancing wire and he failed to forward them. This operator afterwards proved to be a rebel; he deserted his post after a short time and went south taking his dispatches with him. A telegram from General McClellan to me of February 16th, the day of the surrender, directing me to report in full the situation, was not received at my headquarters until the 3d of March.

On the 2d of March I received orders dated March 1st to move my command back to Fort Henry, leaving only a small garrison at Donelson. From Fort Henry expeditions were to be sent against Eastport, Mississippi, and Paris, Tennessee. We started from Donelson on the 4th, and the same day I was back on the Tennessee River. On March 4th I also received the following dispatch from General Halleck:

Maj.-Gen. U. S. Grant,
    Fort Henry:
  You will place Maj.-Gen. C. F. Smith in command of expedition, and remain yourself at Fort Henry. Why do you not obey my orders to report strength and positions of your command?

H. W. HALLECK,
Major-General.

  I was surprised. This was the first intimation I had received that General Halleck had called for information as to the strength of my command. On the 6th he wrote to me again. "Your going to Nashville without authority, and when your presence with your troops was of the utmost importance, was a matter of very serious complaint at Washington, so much so that I was advised to arrest you on your return." This was the first I knew of his objecting to my going to Nashville. That place was not beyond the limits of my command, which, it had been expressly declared in orders, were "not defined." Nashville is west of the Cumberland River, and I had sent troops that had reported to me for duty to occupy the place. I turned over the command as directed and then replied to General Halleck courteously, but asked to be relieved from further duty under him.

  Later I learned that General Halleck had been calling lustily for more troops, promising that he would do something important if he could only be sufficiently reinforced. McClellan asked him what force he then had. Halleck telegraphed me to supply the information so far as my command was concerned, but I received none of his dispatches. At last Halleck reported to Washington that he had repeatedly ordered me to give the strength of my force, but could get nothing out of me; that I had gone to Nashville, beyond the limits of my command, without his authority, and that my army was more demoralized by victory than the army at Bull Run had been by defeat. General McClellan, on this information, ordered that I should be relieved from duty and that an investigation should be made into any charges against me. He even authorized my arrest. Thus in less than two weeks after the victory at Donelson, the two leading generals in the army were in correspondence as to what disposition should be made of me, and in less than three weeks I was virtually in arrest and without a command.

On the 13th of March I was restored to command, and on the 17th Halleck sent me a copy of an order from the War Department which stated that accounts of my misbehavior had reached Washington and directed him to investigate and report the facts. He forwarded also a copy of a detailed dispatch from himself to Washington entirely exonerating me; but he did not inform me that it was his own reports that had created all the trouble. On the contrary, he wrote to me, "Instead of relieving you, I wish you, as soon as your new army is in the field, to assume immediate command, and lead it to new victories." In consequence I felt very grateful to him, and supposed it was his interposition that had set me right with the government. I never knew the truth until General Badeau unearthed the facts in his researches for his history of my campaigns.

General Halleck unquestionably deemed General C. F. Smith a much fitter officer for the command of all the forces in the military district than I was, and, to render him available for such command, desired his promotion to antedate mine and those of the other division commanders. It is probable that the general opinion was that Smith's long services in the army and distinguished deeds rendered him the more proper person for such command. Indeed I was rather inclined to this opinion myself at that time, and would have served as faithfully under Smith as he had done under me. But this did not justify the dispatches which General Halleck sent to Washington, or his subsequent concealment of them from me when pretending to explain the action of my superiors.

On receipt of the order restoring me to command I proceeded to Savannah on the Tennessee, to which point my troops had advanced. General Smith was delighted to see me and was unhesitating in his denunciation of the treatment I had received. He was on a sick bed at the time, from which he never came away alive. His death was a severe loss to our western army. His personal courage was unquestioned, his judgment and professional acquirements were unsurpassed, and he had the confidence of those he commanded as well as of those over him.

Chapter XXIV.

THE ARMY AT PITTSBURG LANDING—INJURED BY A
FALL—THE CONFEDERATE ATTACK AT SHILOH—THE
FIRST DAY'S FIGHT AT SHILOH—GENERAL SHERMAN—
CONDITION OF THE ARMY—CLOSE OF THE FIRST DAY'S
FIGHT—THE SECOND DAY'S FIGHT—RETREAT AND
DEFEAT OF THE CONFEDERATES.

W HEN I REASSUMED command on the 17th of March I
found the army divided, about half being on the east
bank of the Tennessee at Savannah, while one division was at
Crump's landing on the west bank about four miles higher
up, and the remainder at Pittsburg landing, five miles above
Crump's. The enemy was in force at Corinth, the junction of
the two most important railroads in the Mississippi valley—
one connecting Memphis and the Mississippi River with the
East, and the other leading south to all the cotton states. Still another railroad connects Corinth with Jackson, in west Tennessee. If we obtained possession of Corinth the enemy would have
no railroad for the transportation of armies or supplies until
that running east from Vicksburg was reached. It was the
great strategic position at the West between the Tennessee and
the Mississippi rivers and between Nashville and Vicksburg.

I at once put all the troops at Savannah in motion for Pittsburg landing, knowing that the enemy was fortifying at
Corinth and collecting an army there under Johnston. It was
my expectation to march against that army as soon as Buell,
who had been ordered to reinforce me with the Army of the
Ohio, should arrive; and the west bank of the river was the
place to start from. Pittsburg is only about twenty miles from
Corinth, and Hamburg landing, four miles further up the
river, is a mile or two nearer. I had not been in command
long before I selected Hamburg as the place to put the Army
of the Ohio when it arrived. The roads from Pittsburg and
Hamburg to Corinth converge some eight miles out. This
disposition of the troops would have given additional roads
to march over when the advance commenced, within supporting distance of each other.

Before I arrived at Savannah, Sherman, who had joined the Army of the Tennessee and been placed in command of a division, had made an expedition on steamers convoyed by gunboats to the neighborhood of Eastport, thirty miles south, for the purpose of destroying the railroad east of Corinth. The rains had been so heavy for some time before that the low-lands had become impassable swamps. Sherman debarked his troops and started out to accomplish the object of the expedition; but the river was rising so rapidly that the back-water up the small tributaries threatened to cut off the possibility of getting back to the boats, and the expedition had to return without reaching the railroad. The guns had to be hauled by hand through the water to get back to the boats.

On the 17th of March the army on the Tennessee River consisted of five divisions, commanded respectively by Generals C. F. Smith, McClernand, L. Wallace, Hurlbut and Sherman. General W. H. L. Wallace was temporarily in command of Smith's division, General Smith, as I have said, being confined to his bed. Reinforcements were arriving daily and as they came up they were organized, first into brigades, then into a division, and the command given to General Prentiss, who had been ordered to report to me. General Buell was on his way from Nashville with 40,000 veterans. On the 19th of March he was at Columbia, Tennessee, eighty-five miles from Pittsburg. When all reinforcements should have arrived I expected to take the initiative by marching on Corinth, and had no expectation of needing fortifications, though this subject was taken into consideration. McPherson, my only military engineer, was directed to lay out a line to intrench. He did so, but reported that it would have to be made in rear of the line of encampment as it then ran. The new line, while it would be nearer the river, was yet too far away from the Tennessee, or even from the creeks, to be easily supplied with water, and in case of attack these creeks would be in the hands of the enemy. The fact is, I regarded the campaign we were engaged in as an offensive one and had no idea that the enemy would leave strong intrenchments to take the initiative when he knew he would be attacked where he was if he remained. This view, however, did not prevent every precaution being taken and every effort made to keep advised of all movements of the enemy.

Johnston's cavalry meanwhile had been well out towards our front, and occasional encounters occurred between it and our outposts. On the 1st of April this cavalry became bold and approached our lines, showing that an advance of some kind was contemplated. On the 2d Johnston left Corinth in force to attack my army. On the 4th his cavalry dashed down and captured a small picket guard of six or seven men, stationed some five miles out from Pittsburg on the Corinth road. Colonel Buckland sent relief to the guard at once and soon followed in person with an entire regiment, and General Sherman followed Buckland taking the remainder of a brigade. The pursuit was kept up for some three miles beyond the point where the picket guard had been captured, and after nightfall Sherman returned to camp and reported to me by letter what had occurred.

At this time a large body of the enemy was hovering to the west of us, along the line of the Mobile and Ohio railroad. My apprehension was much greater for the safety of Crump's landing than it was for Pittsburg. I had no apprehension that the enemy could really capture either place. But I feared it was possible that he might make a rapid dash upon Crump's and destroy our transports and stores, most of which were kept at that point, and then retreat before Wallace could be reinforced. Lew. Wallace's position I regarded as so well chosen that he was not removed.

At this time I generally spent the day at Pittsburg and returned to Savannah in the evening. I was intending to remove my headquarters to Pittsburg, but Buell was expected daily and would come in at Savannah. I remained at this point, therefore, a few days longer than I otherwise should have done, in order to meet him on his arrival. The skirmishing in our front, however, had been so continuous from about the 3d of April that I did not leave Pittsburg each night until an hour when I felt there would be no further danger before the morning.

On Friday the 4th, the day of Buckland's advance, I was very much injured by my horse falling with me, and on me, while I was trying to get to the front where firing had been heard. The night was one of impenetrable darkness, with rain pouring down in torrents; nothing was visible to the eye except as revealed by the frequent flashes of lightning. Under these circumstances I had to trust to the horse, without guidance, to keep the road. I had not gone far, however, when I met General W. H. L. Wallace and Colonel (afterwards General) McPherson coming from the direction of the front. They said all was quiet so far as the enemy was concerned. On the way back to the boat my horse's feet slipped from under him, and he fell with my leg under his body. The extreme softness of the ground, from the excessive rains of the few preceding days, no doubt saved me from a severe injury and protracted lameness. As it was, my ankle was very much injured, so much so that my boot had to be cut off. For two or three days after I was unable to walk except with crutches.

On the 5th General Nelson, with a division of Buell's army, arrived at Savannah and I ordered him to move up the east bank of the river, to be in a position where he could be ferried over to Crump's landing or Pittsburg as occasion required. I had learned that General Buell himself would be at Savannah the next day, and desired to meet me on his arrival. Affairs at Pittsburg landing had been such for several days that I did not want to be away during the day. I determined, therefore, to take a very early breakfast and ride out to meet Buell, and thus save time. He had arrived on the evening of the 5th, but had not advised me of the fact and I was not aware of it until some time after. While I was at breakfast, however, heavy firing was heard in the direction of Pittsburg landing, and I hastened there, sending a hurried note to Buell informing him of the reason why I could not meet him at Savannah. On the way up the river I directed the dispatch-boat to run in close to Crump's landing, so that I could communicate with General Lew. Wallace. I found him waiting on a boat apparently expecting to see me, and I directed him to get his troops in line ready to execute any orders he might receive. He replied that his troops were already under arms and prepared to move.

Up to that time I had felt by no means certain that Crump's landing might not be the point of attack. On reaching the front, however, about eight A.M., I found that the attack on Pittsburg was unmistakable, and that nothing more than a small guard, to protect our transports and stores, was needed at Crump's. Captain Baxter, a quartermaster on my staff, was accordingly directed to go back and order General Wallace to march immediately to Pittsburg by the road nearest the river. Captain Baxter made a memorandum of this order. About one P.M., not hearing from Wallace and being much in need of reinforcements, I sent two more of my staff, Colonel McPherson and Captain Rowley, to bring him up with his division. They reported finding him marching towards Purdy, Bethel, or some point west from the river, and farther from Pittsburg by several miles than when he started. The road from his first position to Pittsburg landing was direct and near the river. Between the two points a bridge had been built across Snake Creek by our troops, at which Wallace's command had assisted, expressly to enable the troops at the two places to support each other in case of need. Wallace did not arrive in time to take part in the first day's fight. General Wallace has since claimed that the order delivered to him by Captain Baxter was simply to join the right of the army, and that the road over which he marched would have taken him to the road from Pittsburg to Purdy where it crosses Owl Creek on the right of Sherman; but this is not where I had ordered him nor where I wanted him to go.

I never could see and do not now see why any order was necessary further than to direct him to come to Pittsburg landing, without specifying by what route. His was one of three veteran divisions that had been in battle, and its absence was severely felt. Later in the war General Wallace would not have made the mistake that he committed on the 6th of April, 1862. I presume his idea was that by taking the route he did he would be able to come around on the flank or rear of the enemy, and thus perform an act of heroism that would re-dound to the credit of his command, as well as to the benefit of his country.

Some two or three miles from Pittsburg landing was a log meeting-house called Shiloh. It stood on the ridge which di-vides the waters of Snake and Lick creeks, the former empty-ing into the Tennessee just north of Pittsburg landing, and the latter south. This point was the key to our position and was held by Sherman. His division was at that time wholly raw, no part of it ever having been in an engagement; but I thought this deficiency was more than made up by the superiority of the commander. McClernand was on Sherman's left, with troops that had been engaged at forts Henry and Donelson and were therefore veterans so far as western troops had become such at that stage of the war. Next to McClernand came Prentiss with a raw division, and on the extreme left, Stuart with one brigade of Sherman's division. Hurlbut was in rear of Prentiss, massed, and in reserve at the time of the onset. The division of General C. F. Smith was on the right, also in reserve. General Smith was still sick in bed at Savannah, but within hearing of our guns. His services would no doubt have been of inestimable value had his health permitted his presence. The command of his division devolved upon Brigadier-General W. H. L. Wallace, a most estimable and able officer; a veteran too, for he had served a year in the Mexican war and had been with his command at Henry and Donelson. Wallace was mortally wounded in the first day's engagement, and with the change of commanders thus necessarily effected in the heat of battle the efficiency of his division was much weakened.

The position of our troops made a continuous line from Lick Creek on the left to Owl Creek, a branch of Snake Creek, on the right, facing nearly south and possibly a little west. The water in all these streams was very high at the time and contributed to protect our flanks. The enemy was compelled, therefore, to attack directly in front. This he did with great vigor, inflicting heavy losses on the National side, but suffering much heavier on his own.

The Confederate assaults were made with such a disregard of losses on their own side that our line of tents soon fell into their hands. The ground on which the battle was fought was undulating, heavily timbered with scattered clearings, the woods giving some protection to the troops on both sides. There was also considerable underbrush. A number of attempts were made by the enemy to turn our right flank, where Sherman was posted, but every effort was repulsed with heavy loss. But the front attack was kept up so vigorously that, to prevent the success of these attempts to get on our flanks, the National troops were compelled, several times, to take positions to the rear nearer Pittsburg landing. When the firing ceased at night the National line was all of a mile in rear of the position it had occupied in the morning.

In one of the backward moves, on the 6th, the division commanded by General Prentiss did not fall back with the others. This left his flanks exposed and enabled the enemy to capture him with about 2,200 of his officers and men. General Badeau gives four o'clock of the 6th as about the time this capture took place. He may be right as to the time, but my recollection is that the hour was later. General Prentiss himself gave the hour as half-past five. I was with him, as I was with each of the division commanders that day, several times, and my recollection is that the last time I was with him was about half-past four, when his division was standing up firmly and the General was as cool as if expecting victory. But no matter whether it was four or later, the story that he and his command were surprised and captured in their camps is without any foundation whatever. If it had been true, as currently reported at the time and yet believed by thousands of people, that Prentiss and his division had been captured in their beds, there would not have been an all-day struggle, with the loss of thousands killed and wounded on the Confederate side.

With the single exception of a few minutes after the capture of Prentiss, a continuous and unbroken line was maintained all day from Snake Creek or its tributaries on the right to Lick Creek or the Tennessee on the left above Pittsburg. There was no hour during the day when there was not heavy firing and generally hard fighting at some point on the line, but seldom at all points at the same time. It was a case of Southern dash against Northern pluck and endurance. Three of the five divisions engaged on Sunday were entirely raw, and many of the men had only received their arms on the way from their States to the field. Many of them had arrived but a day or two before and were hardly able to load their muskets according to the manual. Their officers were equally ignorant of their duties. Under these circumstances it is not astonishing that many of the regiments broke at the first fire. In two cases, as I now

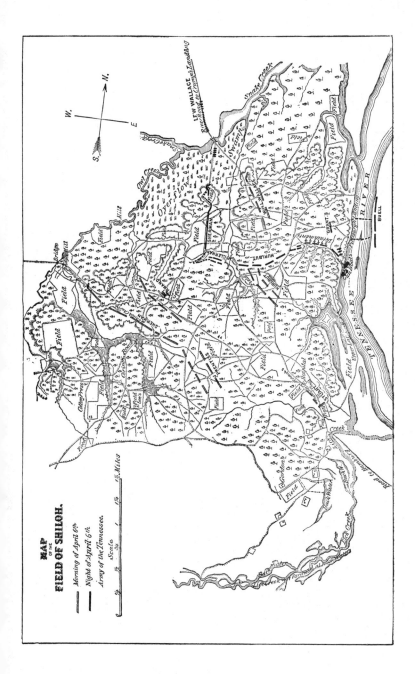

MAP
OF THE
FIELD OF SHILOH.

Morning of April 6th
Night of April 6th
Army of the Tennessee.

Scale
¼   ½   ¾   1   1¼   1½ Miles

N.
W.   E.
S.

LEW WALLACE
Riverp[?]

Snake Creek

Owl Creek

Overflow

Owl Creek

TENNESSEE RIVER

BUELL

SHERMAN

McCLERNAND

HURLBUT

PRENTISS

Field
Field
Field
Field
Field

Crump's Landing

remember, colonels led their regiments from the field on first hearing the whistle of the enemy's bullets. In these cases the colonels were constitutional cowards, unfit for any military position; but not so the officers and men led out of danger by them. Better troops never went upon a battle-field than many of these, officers and men, afterwards proved themselves to be, who fled panic-stricken at the first whistle of bullets and shell at Shiloh.

During the whole of Sunday I was continuously engaged in passing from one part of the field to another, giving directions to division commanders. In thus moving along the line, however, I never deemed it important to stay long with Sherman. Although his troops were then under fire for the first time, their commander, by his constant presence with them, inspired a confidence in officers and men that enabled them to render services on that bloody battle-field worthy of the best of veterans. McClernand was next to Sherman, and the hardest fighting was in front of these two divisions. McClernand told me on that day, the 6th, that he profited much by having so able a commander supporting him. A casualty to Sherman that would have taken him from the field that day would have been a sad one for the troops engaged at Shiloh. And how near we came to this! On the 6th Sherman was shot twice, once in the hand, once in the shoulder, the ball cutting his coat and making a slight wound, and a third ball passed through his hat. In addition to this he had several horses shot during the day.

The nature of this battle was such that cavalry could not be used in front; I therefore formed ours into line in rear, to stop stragglers—of whom there were many. When there would be enough of them to make a show, and after they had recovered from their fright, they would be sent to reinforce some part of the line which needed support, without regard to their companies, regiments or brigades.

On one occasion during the day I rode back as far as the river and met General Buell, who had just arrived; I do not remember the hour, but at that time there probably were as many as four or five thousand stragglers lying under cover of the river bluff, panic-stricken, most of whom would have been shot where they lay, without resistance, before they

would have taken muskets and marched to the front to protect themselves. This meeting between General Buell and myself was on the dispatch-boat used to run between the landing
and Savannah. It was brief, and related specially to his getting
his troops over the river. As we left the boat together, Buell's
attention was attracted by the men lying under cover of the
river bank. I saw him berating them and trying to shame
them into joining their regiments. He even threatened them
with shells from the gunboats near by. But it was all to no
effect. Most of these men afterward proved themselves as gallant as any of those who saved the battle from which they had
deserted. I have no doubt that this sight impressed General
Buell with the idea that a line of retreat would be a good
thing just then. If he had come in by the front instead of
through the stragglers in the rear, he would have thought and
felt differently. Could he have come through the Confederate
rear, he would have witnessed there a scene similar to that at
our own. The distant rear of an army engaged in battle is not
the best place from which to judge correctly what is going on
in front. Later in the war, while occupying the country between the Tennessee and the Mississippi, I learned that the
panic in the Confederate lines had not differed much from
that within our own. Some of the country people estimated
the stragglers from Johnston's army as high as 20,000. Of
course this was an exaggeration.

The situation at the close of Sunday was as follows: along
the top of the bluff just south of the log-house which stood at
Pittsburg landing, Colonel J. D. Webster, of my staff, had
arranged twenty or more pieces of artillery facing south or up
the river. This line of artillery was on the crest of a hill overlooking a deep ravine opening into the Tennessee. Hurlbut
with his division intact was on the right of this artillery, extending west and possibly a little north. McClernand came
next in the general line, looking more to the west. His division was complete in its organization and ready for any duty.
Sherman came next, his right extending to Snake Creek. His
command, like the other two, was complete in its organization and ready, like its chief, for any service it might be called
upon to render. All three divisions were, as a matter of
course, more or less shattered and depleted in numbers from

the terrible battle of the day. The division of W. H. L. Wallace, as much from the disorder arising from changes of division and brigade commanders, under heavy fire, as from any other cause, had lost its organization and did not occupy a place in the line as a division. Prentiss' command was gone as a division, many of its members having been killed, wounded or captured; but it had rendered valiant services before its final dispersal, and had contributed a good share to the defence of Shiloh.

The right of my line rested near the bank of Snake Creek, a short distance above the bridge which had been built by the troops for the purpose of connecting Crump's landing and Pittsburg landing. Sherman had posted some troops in a log-house and out-buildings which overlooked both the bridge over which Wallace was expected and the creek above that point. In this last position Sherman was frequently attacked before night, but held the point until he voluntarily abandoned it to advance in order to make room for Lew. Wallace, who came up after dark.

There was, as I have said, a deep ravine in front of our left. The Tennessee River was very high and there was water to a considerable depth in the ravine. Here the enemy made a last desperate effort to turn our flank, but was repelled. The gunboats *Tyler* and *Lexington*, Gwin and Shirk commanding, with the artillery under Webster, aided the army and effectually checked their further progress. Before any of Buell's troops had reached the west bank of the Tennessee, firing had almost entirely ceased; anything like an attempt on the part of the enemy to advance had absolutely ceased. There was some artillery firing from an unseen enemy, some of his shells passing beyond us; but I do not remember that there was the whistle of a single musket-ball heard. As his troops arrived in the dusk General Buell marched several of his regiments part way down the face of the hill where they fired briskly for some minutes, but I do not think a single man engaged in this firing received an injury. The attack had spent its force.

General Lew. Wallace, with 5,000 effective men, arrived after firing had ceased for the day, and was placed on the right. Thus night came, Wallace came, and the advance of Nelson's division came; but none—unless night—in time to be of material service to the gallant men who saved Shiloh on that first day against large odds. Buell's loss on the 6th of April was two men killed and one wounded, all members of the 36th Indiana infantry. The Army of the Tennessee lost on that day at least 7,000 men. The presence of two or three regiments of Buell's army on the west bank before firing ceased had not the slightest effect in preventing the capture of Pittsburg landing.

So confident was I before firing had ceased on the 6th that the next day would bring victory to our arms if we could only take the initiative, that I visited each division commander in person before any reinforcements had reached the field. I directed them to throw out heavy lines of skirmishers in the morning as soon as they could see, and push them forward until they found the enemy, following with their entire divisions in supporting distance, and to engage the enemy as soon as found. To Sherman I told the story of the assault at Fort Donelson, and said that the same tactics would win at Shiloh. Victory was assured when Wallace arrived, even if there had been no other support. I was glad, however, to see the reinforcements of Buell and credit them with doing all there was for them to do. During the night of the 6th the remainder of Nelson's division, Buell's army, crossed the river and were ready to advance in the morning, forming the left wing. Two other divisions, Crittenden's and McCook's, came up the river from Savannah in the transports and were on the west bank early on the 7th. Buell commanded them in person. My command was thus nearly doubled in numbers and efficiency.

During the night rain fell in torrents and our troops were exposed to the storm without shelter. I made my headquarters under a tree a few hundred yards back from the river bank. My ankle was so much swollen from the fall of my horse the Friday night preceding, and the bruise was so painful, that I could get no rest. The drenching rain would have precluded the possibility of sleep without this additional cause. Some time after midnight, growing restive under the storm and the continuous pain, I moved back to the log-house under the bank. This had been taken as a hospital, and all night wounded men were being brought in, their wounds dressed, a leg or an arm amputated as the case might require, and everything being done to save life or alleviate suffering. The sight was more unendurable than encountering the enemy's fire, and I returned to my tree in the rain.

The advance on the morning of the 7th developed the enemy in the camps occupied by our troops before the battle began, more than a mile back from the most advanced position of the Confederates on the day before. It is known now that they had not yet learned of the arrival of Buell's command. Possibly they fell back so far to get the shelter of our tents during the rain, and also to get away from the shells that were dropped upon them by the gunboats every fifteen minutes during the night.

The position of the Union troops on the morning of the 7th was as follows: General Lew. Wallace on the right; Sherman on his left; then McClernand and then Hurlbut. Nelson, of Buell's army, was on our extreme left, next to the river. Crittenden was next in line after Nelson and on his right; McCook followed and formed the extreme right of Buell's command. My old command thus formed the right wing, while the troops directly under Buell constituted the left wing of the army. These relative positions were retained during the entire day, or until the enemy was driven from the field.

In a very short time the battle became general all along the line. This day everything was favorable to the Union side. We had now become the attacking party. The enemy was driven back all day, as we had been the day before, until finally he beat a precipitate retreat. The last point held by him was near the road leading from the landing to Corinth, on the left of Sherman and right of McClernand. About three o'clock, being near that point and seeing that the enemy was giving way everywhere else, I gathered up a couple of regiments, or parts of regiments, from troops near by, formed them in line of battle and marched them forward, going in front myself to prevent premature or long-range firing. At this point there was a clearing between us and the enemy favorable for charging, although exposed. I knew the enemy were ready to break and only wanted a little encouragement from us to go quickly and join their friends who had started earlier. After marching to within musket-range I stopped and let the troops pass. The command, *Charge*, was given, and was executed with loud cheers and with a run; when the last of the enemy broke.

NOTE.—Since writing this chapter I have received from Mrs. W. H. L. Wallace, widow of the gallant general who was killed in the first day's fight on the field of Shiloh, a letter from General Lew. Wallace to him dated the morning of the 5th. At the date of this letter it was well known that the Confederates had troops out along the Mobile & Ohio railroad west of Crump's landing and Pittsburg landing, and were also collecting near Shiloh. This letter shows that at that time General Lew. Wallace was making preparations for the emergency that might happen for the passing of reinforcements between Shiloh and his position, extending from Crump's landing westward, and he sends it over the road running from Adamsville to the Pittsburg landing and Purdy road. These two roads intersect nearly a mile west of the crossing of the latter over Owl Creek, where our right rested. In this letter General Lew. Wallace advises General W. H. L. Wallace that he will send "to-morrow" (and his letter also says "April 5th," which is the same day the letter was dated and which, therefore, must have been written on the 4th) some cavalry to report to him at his headquarters, and suggesting the propriety of General W. H. L. Wallace's sending a company back with them for the purpose of having the cavalry at the two landings familiarize themselves with the road so that they could "act promptly in case of emergency as guides to and from the different camps."

This modifies very materially what I have said, and what has been said by others, of the conduct of General Lew. Wallace at the battle of Shiloh. It shows that he naturally, with no more experience than he had at the time in the profession of arms, would take the particular road that he did start upon in the absence of orders to move by a different road.

The mistake he made, and which probably caused his apparent dilatoriness, was that of advancing some distance after he found that the firing, which would be at first directly to his front and then off to the left, had fallen back until it had got very much in rear of the position of his advance. This falling back had taken place before I sent General Wallace orders to move up to Pittsburg landing and, naturally, my order was to follow the road nearest the river. But my order was verbal, and to a staff officer who was to deliver it to General Wallace, so that I am not competent to say just what order the General actually received.

General Wallace's division was stationed, the First brigade at Crump's landing, the Second out two miles, and the Third two and a half miles out. Hearing the sounds of battle General Wallace early ordered his First and Third brigades to concentrate on the Second. If the position of our front had not changed, the road which Wallace took would have been somewhat shorter to our right than the River road.

U. S. GRANT.

MOUNT MACGREGOR, NEW YORK, *June* 21, 1885.

Chapter XXV.

D**URING THIS SECOND DAY** of the battle I had been moving from right to left and back, to see for myself the progress made. In the early part of the afternoon, while riding with Colonel McPherson and Major Hawkins, then my chief commissary, we got beyond the left of our troops. We were moving along the northern edge of a clearing, very leisurely, toward the river above the landing. There did not appear to be an enemy to our right, until suddenly a battery with musketry opened upon us from the edge of the woods on the other side of the clearing. The shells and balls whistled about our ears very fast for about a minute. I do not think it took us longer than that to get out of range and out of sight. In the sudden start we made, Major Hawkins lost his hat. He did not stop to pick it up. When we arrived at a perfectly safe position we halted to take an account of damages. McPherson's horse was panting as if ready to drop. On examination it was found that a ball had struck him forward of the flank just back of the saddle, and had gone entirely through. In a few minutes the poor beast dropped dead; he had given no sign of injury until we came to a stop. A ball had struck the metal scabbard of my sword, just below the hilt, and broken it nearly off; before the battle was over it had broken off entirely. There were three of us: one had lost a horse, killed; one a hat and one a sword-scabbard. All were thankful that it was no worse.

After the rain of the night before and the frequent and heavy rains for some days previous, the roads were almost impassable. The enemy carrying his artillery and supply trains over them in his retreat, made them still worse for troops following. I wanted to pursue, but had not the heart to order the men who had fought desperately for two days, lying in the mud and rain whenever not fighting, and I did not feel disposed to positively order Buell, or any part of his command, to pursue. Although the senior in rank at the time I had been so only a few weeks. Buell was, and had been for some time past, a department commander, while I commanded only a district. I did not meet Buell in person until too late to get troops ready and pursue with effect; but had I seen him at the moment of the last charge I should have at least requested him to follow.

I rode forward several miles the day after the battle, and found that the enemy had dropped much, if not all, of their provisions, some ammunition and the extra wheels of their caissons, lightening their loads to enable them to get off their guns. About five miles out we found their field hospital abandoned. An immediate pursuit must have resulted in the capture of a considerable number of prisoners and probably some guns.

Shiloh was the severest battle fought at the West during the war, and but few in the East equalled it for hard, determined fighting. I saw an open field, in our possession on the second day, over which the Confederates had made repeated charges the day before, so covered with dead that it would have been possible to walk across the clearing, in any direction, stepping

---

NOTE: In an article on the battle of Shiloh which I wrote for the *Century* Magazine, I stated that General A. McD. McCook, who commanded a division of Buell's army, expressed some unwillingness to pursue the enemy on Monday, April 7th, because of the condition of his troops. General Badeau, in his history, also makes the same statement, on my authority. Out of justice to General McCook and his command, I must say that they left a point twenty-two miles east of Savannah on the morning of the 6th. From the heavy rains of a few days previous and the passage of trains and artillery, the roads were necessarily deep in mud, which made marching slow. The division had not only marched through this mud the day before, but it had been in the rain all night without rest. It was engaged in the battle of the second day and did as good service as its position allowed. In fact an opportunity occurred for it to perform a conspicuous act of gallantry which elicited the highest commendation from division commanders in the Army of the Tennessee. General Sherman both in his memoirs and report makes mention of this fact. General McCook himself belongs to a family which furnished many volunteers to the army. I refer to these circumstances with minuteness because I did General McCook injustice in my article in the *Century*, though not to the extent one would suppose from the public press. I am not willing to do any one an injustice, and if convinced that I have done one, I am always willing to make the fullest admission.

on dead bodies, without a foot touching the ground. On our side National and Confederate troops were mingled together in about equal proportions; but on the remainder of the field nearly all were Confederates. On one part, which had evidently not been ploughed for several years, probably because the land was poor, bushes had grown up, some to the height of eight or ten feet. There was not one of these left standing unpierced by bullets. The smaller ones were all cut down.

Contrary to all my experience up to that time, and to the experience of the army I was then commanding, we were on the defensive. We were without intrenchments or defensive advantages of any sort, and more than half the army engaged the first day was without experience or even drill as soldiers. The officers with them, except the division commanders and possibly two or three of the brigade commanders, were equally inexperienced in war. The result was a Union victory that gave the men who achieved it great confidence in themselves ever after.

The enemy fought bravely, but they had started out to defeat and destroy an army and capture a position. They failed in both, with very heavy loss in killed and wounded, and must have gone back discouraged and convinced that the "Yankee" was not an enemy to be despised.

After the battle I gave verbal instructions to division commanders to let the regiments send out parties to bury their own dead, and to detail parties, under commissioned officers from each division, to bury the Confederate dead in their respective fronts and to report the numbers so buried. The latter part of these instructions was not carried out by all; but they were by those sent from Sherman's division, and by some of the parties sent out by McClernand. The heaviest loss sustained by the enemy was in front of these two divisions.

The criticism has often been made that the Union troops should have been intrenched at Shiloh. Up to that time the pick and spade had been but little resorted to at the West. I had, however, taken this subject under consideration soon after re-assuming command in the field, and, as already stated, my only military engineer reported unfavorably. Besides this, the troops with me, officers and men, needed discipline and drill more than they did experience with the pick, shovel and axe. Reinforcements were arriving almost daily, composed of troops that had been hastily thrown together into companies and regiments—fragments of incomplete organizations, the men and officers strangers to each other. Under all these circumstances I concluded that drill and discipline were worth more to our men than fortifications.

General Buell was a brave, intelligent officer, with as much professional pride and ambition of a commendable sort as I ever knew. I had been two years at West Point with him, and had served with him afterwards, in garrison and in the Mexican war, several years more. He was not given in early life or in mature years to forming intimate acquaintances. He was studious by habit, and commanded the confidence and respect of all who knew him. He was a strict disciplinarian, and perhaps did not distinguish sufficiently between the volunteer who "enlisted for the war" and the soldier who serves in time of peace. One system embraced men who risked life for a principle, and often men of social standing, competence, or wealth and independence of character. The other includes, as a rule, only men who could not do as well in any other occupation. General Buell became an object of harsh criticism later, some going so far as to challenge his loyalty. No one who knew him ever believed him capable of a dishonorable act, and nothing could be more dishonorable than to accept high rank and command in war and then betray the trust. When I came into command of the army in 1864, I requested the Secretary of War to restore General Buell to duty.

After the war, during the summer of 1865, I travelled considerably through the North, and was everywhere met by large numbers of people. Every one had his opinion about the manner in which the war had been conducted: who among the generals had failed, how, and why. Correspondents of the press were ever on hand to hear every word dropped, and were not always disposed to report correctly what did not confirm their preconceived notions, either about the conduct of the war or the individuals concerned in it. The opportunity frequently occurred for me to defend General Buell against what I believed to be most unjust charges. On one occasion a correspondent put in my mouth the very charge I had so often refuted—of disloyalty. This brought from General Buell a very severe retort, which I saw in the New York *World* some time before I received the letter itself. I could very well understand his grievance at seeing untrue and disgraceful charges apparently sustained by an officer who, at the time, was at the head of the army. I replied to him, but not through the press. I kept no copy of my letter, nor did I ever see it in print; neither did I receive an answer.

General Albert Sidney Johnston, who commanded the Confederate forces at the beginning of the battle, was disabled by a wound on the afternoon of the first day. This wound, as I understood afterwards, was not necessarily fatal, or even dangerous. But he was a man who would not abandon what he deemed an important trust in the face of danger and consequently continued in the saddle, commanding, until so exhausted by the loss of blood that he had to be taken from his horse, and soon after died. The news was not long in reaching our side and I suppose was quite an encouragement to the National soldiers.

I had known Johnston slightly in the Mexican war and later as an officer in the regular army. He was a man of high character and ability. His contemporaries at West Point, and officers generally who came to know him personally later and who remained on our side, expected him to prove the most formidable man to meet that the Confederacy would produce.

I once wrote that nothing occurred in his brief command of an army to prove or disprove the high estimate that had been placed upon his military ability; but after studying the orders and dispatches of Johnston I am compelled to materially modify my views of that officer's qualifications as a soldier. My judgment now is that he was vacillating and undecided in his actions.

All the disasters in Kentucky and Tennessee were so discouraging to the authorities in Richmond that Jefferson Davis wrote an unofficial letter to Johnston expressing his own anxiety and that of the public, and saying that he had made such defence as was dictated by long friendship, but that in the absence of a report he needed facts. The letter was not a reprimand in direct terms, but it was evidently as much felt as though it had been one. General Johnston raised another army as rapidly as he could, and fortified or strongly intrenched at Corinth. He knew the National troops were preparing to attack him in his chosen position. But he had evidently become so disturbed at the results of his operations that he resolved to strike out in an offensive campaign which would restore all that was lost, and if successful accomplish still more. We have the authority of his son and biographer for saying that his plan was to attack the forces at Shiloh and crush them; then to cross the Tennessee and destroy the army of Buell, and push the war across the Ohio River. The design was a bold one; but we have the same authority for saying that in the execution Johnston showed vacillation and indecision. He left Corinth on the 2d of April and was not ready to attack until the 6th. The distance his army had to march was less than twenty miles. Beauregard, his second in command, was opposed to the attack for two reasons: first, he thought, if let alone the National troops would attack the Confederates in their intrenchments; second, we were in ground of our own choosing and would necessarily be intrenched. Johnston not only listened to the objection of Beauregard to an attack, but held a council of war on the subject on the morning of the 5th. On the evening of the same day he was in consultation with some of his generals on the same subject, and still again on the morning of the 6th. During this last consultation, and before a decision had been reached, the battle began by the National troops opening fire on the enemy. This seemed to settle the question as to whether there was to be any battle of Shiloh. It also seems to me to settle the question as to whether there was a surprise.

I do not question the personal courage of General Johnston, or his ability. But he did not win the distinction predicted for him by many of his friends. He did prove that as a general he was over-estimated.

General Beauregard was next in rank to Johnston and succeeded to the command, which he retained to the close of the battle and during the subsequent retreat on Corinth, as well as in the siege of that place. His tactics have been severely criticised by Confederate writers, but I do not believe his fallen chief could have done any better under the circumstances.

Some of these critics claim that Shiloh was won when Johnston fell, and that if he had not fallen the army under me would have been annihilated or captured. *If* defeated the Confederates at Shiloh. There is little doubt that we would have been disgracefully beaten *if* all the shells and bullets fired by us had passed harmlessly over the enemy and *if* all of theirs had taken effect. Commanding generals are liable to be killed during engagements; and the fact that when he was shot Johnston was leading a brigade to induce it to make a charge which had been repeatedly ordered, is evidence that there was neither the universal demoralization on our side nor the unbounded confidence on theirs which has been claimed. There was, in fact, no hour during the day when I doubted the eventual defeat of the enemy, although I was disappointed that reinforcements so near at hand did not arrive at an earlier hour.

The description of the battle of Shiloh given by Colonel Wm. Preston Johnston is very graphic and well told. The reader will imagine that he can see each blow struck, a demoralized and broken mob of Union soldiers, each blow sending the enemy more demoralized than ever towards the Tennessee River, which was a little more than two miles away at the beginning of the onset. If the reader does not stop to inquire why, with such Confederate success for more than twelve hours of hard fighting, the National troops were not all killed, captured or driven into the river, he will regard the pen picture as perfect. But I witnessed the fight from the National side from eight o'clock in the morning until night closed the contest. I see but little in the description that I can recognize. The Confederate troops fought well and deserve commendation enough for their bravery and endurance on the 6th of April, without detracting from their antagonists or claiming anything more than their just dues.

The reports of the enemy show that their condition at the end of the first day was deplorable; their losses in killed and wounded had been very heavy, and their stragglers had been quite as numerous as on the National side, with the difference that those of the enemy left the field entirely and were not brought back to their respective commands for many days. On the Union side but few of the stragglers fell back further than the landing on the river, and many of these were in line for duty on the second day. The admissions of the highest Confederate officers engaged at Shiloh make the claim of a victory for them absurd. The victory was not to either party until the battle was over. It was then a Union victory, in which the Armies of the Tennessee and the Ohio both participated. But the Army of the Tennessee fought the entire rebel army on the 6th and held it at bay until near night; and night alone closed the conflict and not the three regiments of Nelson's division.

The Confederates fought with courage at Shiloh, but the particular skill claimed I could not and still cannot see; though there is nothing to criticise except the claims put forward for it since. But the Confederate claimants for superiority in strategy, superiority in generalship and superiority in dash and prowess are not so unjust to the Union troops engaged at Shiloh as are many Northern writers. The troops on both sides were American, and united they need not fear any foreign foe. It is possible that the Southern man started in with a little more dash than his Northern brother; but he was correspondingly less enduring.

The endeavor of the enemy on the first day was simply to hurl their men against ours—first at one point, then at another, sometimes at several points at once. This they did with daring and energy, until at night the rebel troops were worn out. Our effort during the same time was to be prepared to resist assaults wherever made. The object of the Confederates on the second day was to get away with as much of their army and material as possible. Ours then was to drive them from our front, and to capture or destroy as great a part as possible of their men and material. We were successful in driving them back, but not so successful in captures as if farther pursuit could have been made. As it was, we captured or recaptured on the second day about as much artillery as we lost on the first; and, leaving out the one great capture of Prentiss, we took more prisoners on Monday than the enemy gained from us on Sunday. On the 6th Sherman lost seven pieces of artillery, McClernand six, Prentiss eight, and Hurlbut two batteries. On the 7th Sherman captured seven guns, McClernand three and the Army of the Ohio twenty.

At Shiloh the effective strength of the Union forces on the morning of the 6th was 33,000 men. Lew. Wallace brought 5,000 more after nightfall. Beauregard reported the enemy's strength at 40,955. According to the custom of enumeration in the South, this number probably excluded every man enlisted as musician or detailed as guard or nurse, and all commissioned officers—everybody who did not carry a musket or serve a cannon. With us everybody in the field receiving pay from the government is counted. Excluding the troops who fled, panic-stricken, before they had fired a shot, there was not a time during the 6th when we had more than 25,000 men in line. On the 7th Buell brought 20,000 more. Of his remaining two divisions, Thomas's did not reach the field during the engagement; Wood's arrived before firing had ceased, but not in time to be of much service.

Our loss in the two days' fight was 1,754 killed, 8,408 wounded and 2,885 missing. Of these, 2,103 were in the Army of the Ohio. Beauregard reported a total loss of 10,699, of whom 1,728 were killed, 8,012 wounded and 957 missing. This estimate must be incorrect. We buried, by actual count, more of the enemy's dead in front of the divisions of McClernand and Sherman alone than here reported, and 4,000 was the estimate of the burial parties for the whole field. Beauregard reports the Confederate force on the 6th at over 40,000, and their total loss during the two days at 10,699; and at the same time declares that he could put only 20,000 men in battle on the morning of the 7th.

The navy gave a hearty support to the army at Shiloh, as indeed it always did both before and subsequently when I was in command. The nature of the ground was such, however, that on this occasion it could do nothing in aid of the troops until sundown on the first day. The country was broken and heavily timbered, cutting off all view of the battle from the river, so that friends would be as much in danger from fire from the gunboats as the foe. But about sundown, when the National troops were back in their last position, the right of the enemy was near the river and exposed to the fire of the two gun-boats, which was delivered with vigor and effect. After nightfall, when firing had entirely ceased on land, the commander of the fleet informed himself, approximately, of the position of our troops and suggested the idea of dropping a shell within the lines of the enemy every fifteen minutes during the night. This was done with effect, as is proved by the Confederate reports.

Up to the battle of Shiloh I, as well as thousands of other citizens, believed that the rebellion against the Government would collapse suddenly and soon, if a decisive victory could be gained over any of its armies. Donelson and Henry were such victories. An army of more than 21,000 men was captured or destroyed. Bowling Green, Columbus and Hickman, Kentucky, fell in consequence, and Clarksville and Nashville, Tennessee, the last two with an immense amount of stores, also fell into our hands. The Tennessee and Cumberland rivers, from their mouths to the head of navigation, were secured. But when Confederate armies were collected which not only attempted to hold a line farther south, from Memphis to Chattanooga, Knoxville and on to the Atlantic, but assumed the offensive and made such a gallant effort to regain what had been lost, then, indeed, I gave up all idea of saving the Union except by complete conquest. Up to that time it had been the policy of our army, certainly of that portion commanded by me, to protect the property of the citizens whose territory was invaded, without regard to their sentiments, whether Union or Secession. After this, however, I regarded it as humane to both sides to protect the persons of those found at their homes, but to consume everything that could be used to support or supply armies. Protection was still continued over such supplies as were within lines held by us and which we expected to continue to hold; but such supplies within the reach of Confederate armies I regarded as much contraband as arms or ordnance stores. Their destruction was accomplished without bloodshed and tended to the same result as the destruction of armies. I continued this policy to the close of the war. Promiscuous pillaging, however, was discouraged and punished. Instructions were always given to take provisions and forage under the direction of commissioned officers who should give receipts to owners, if at home, and turn the property over to officers of the quartermaster or commissary departments to be issued as if furnished from our Northern dépôts. But much was destroyed without receipts to owners, when it could not be brought within our lines and would otherwise have gone to the support of secession and rebellion.

This policy I believe exercised a material influence in hastening the end.

The battle of Shiloh, or Pittsburg landing, has been perhaps less understood, or, to state the case more accurately, more persistently misunderstood, than any other engagement between National and Confederate troops during the entire rebellion. Correct reports of the battle have been published, notably by Sherman, Badeau and, in a speech before a meeting of veterans, by General Prentiss; but all of these appeared long subsequent to the close of the rebellion and after public opinion had been most erroneously formed.

I myself made no report to General Halleck, further than was contained in a letter, written immediately after the battle informing him that an engagement had been fought and announcing the result. A few days afterwards General Halleck moved his headquarters to Pittsburg landing and assumed command of the troops in the field. Although next to him in rank, and nominally in command of my old district and army, I was ignored as much as if I had been at the most distant point of territory within my jurisdiction; and although I was in command of all the troops engaged at Shiloh I was not permitted to see one of the reports of General Buell or his subordinates in that battle, until they were published by the War Department long after the event. For this reason I never made a full official report of this engagement.

Chapter XXVI.

HALLECK ASSUMES COMMAND IN THE FIELD—THE ADVANCE UPON CORINTH—OCCUPATION OF CORINTH—THE ARMY SEPARATED.

GENERAL HALLECK arrived at Pittsburg landing on the 11th of April and immediately assumed command in the field. On the 21st General Pope arrived with an army 30,000 strong, fresh from the capture of Island Number Ten in the Mississippi River. He went into camp at Hamburg landing five miles above Pittsburg. Halleck had now three armies: the Army of the Ohio, Buell commanding; the Army of the Mississippi, Pope commanding; and the Army of the Tennessee. His orders divided the combined force into the right wing, reserve, centre and left wing. Major-General George H. Thomas, who had been in Buell's army, was transferred with his division to the Army of the Tennessee and given command of the right wing, composed of all of that army except McClernand's and Lew. Wallace's divisions. McClernand was assigned to the command of the reserve, composed of his own and Lew. Wallace's divisions. Buell commanded the centre, the Army of the Ohio; and Pope the left wing, the Army of the Mississippi. I was named second in command of the whole, and was also supposed to be in command of the right wing and reserve.

Orders were given to all the commanders engaged at Shiloh to send in their reports without delay to department headquarters. Those from officers of the Army of the Tennessee were sent through me; but from the Army of the Ohio they were sent by General Buell without passing through my hands. General Halleck ordered me, verbally, to send in my report, but I positively declined on the ground that he had received the reports of a part of the army engaged at Shiloh without their coming through me. He admitted that my refusal was justifiable under the circumstances, but explained that he had wanted to get the reports off before moving the command, and as fast as a report had come to him he had forwarded it to Washington.

Preparations were at once made upon the arrival of the new commander for an advance on Corinth. Owl Creek, on our right, was bridged, and expeditions were sent to the northwest and west to ascertain if our position was being threatened from those quarters; the roads towards Corinth were corduroyed and new ones made; lateral roads were also constructed, so that in case of necessity troops marching by different routes could reinforce each other. All commanders were cautioned against bringing on an engagement and informed in so many words that it would be better to retreat than to fight. By the 30th of April all preparations were complete; the country west to the Mobile and Ohio railroad had been reconnoitred, as well as the road to Corinth as far as Monterey twelve miles from Pittsburg. Everywhere small bodies of the enemy had been encountered, but they were observers and not in force to fight battles.

Corinth, Mississippi, lies in a south-westerly direction from Pittsburg landing and about nineteen miles away as the bird would fly, but probably twenty-two by the nearest wagon-road. It is about four miles south of the line dividing the States of Tennessee and Mississippi, and at the junction of the Mississippi and Chattanooga railroad with the Mobile and Ohio road which runs from Columbus to Mobile. From Pittsburg to Corinth the land is rolling, but at no point reaching an elevation that makes high hills to pass over. In 1862 the greater part of the country was covered with forest with intervening clearings and houses. Underbrush was dense in the low grounds along the creeks and ravines, but generally not so thick on the high land as to prevent men passing through with ease. There are two small creeks running from north of the town and connecting some four miles south, where they form Bridge Creek which empties into the Tuscumbia River. Corinth is on the ridge between these streams and is a naturally strong defensive position. The creeks are insignificant in volume of water, but the stream to the east widens out in front of the town into a swamp, impassable in the presence of an enemy. On the crest of the west bank of this stream the enemy was strongly intrenched.

Corinth was a valuable strategic point for the enemy to

hold, and consequently a valuable one for us to possess ourselves of. We ought to have seized it immediately after the
fall of Donelson and Nashville, when it could have been
taken without a battle, but failing then it should have been
taken, without delay, on the concentration of troops at Pittsburg landing after the battle of Shiloh. In fact the arrival of
Pope should not have been awaited. There was no time from
the battle of Shiloh up to the evacuation of Corinth when
the enemy would not have left if pushed. The demoralization among the Confederates from their defeats at Henry and
Donelson; their long marches from Bowling Green, Columbus, and Nashville, and their failure at Shiloh; in fact from
having been driven out of Kentucky and Tennessee, was so
great that a stand for the time would have been impossible.
Beauregard made strenuous efforts to reinforce himself and
partially succeeded. He appealed to the people of the South-
west for new regiments, and received a few. A. S. Johnston
had made efforts to reinforce in the same quarter, before the
battle of Shiloh, but in a different way. He had negroes sent
out to him to take the place of teamsters, company cooks
and laborers in every capacity, so as to put all his white men
into the ranks. The people, while willing to send their sons
to the field, were not willing to part with their negroes. It is
only fair to state that they probably wanted their blacks to
raise supplies for the army and for the families left at home.

Beauregard, however, was reinforced by Van Dorn immediately after Shiloh with 17,000 men. Interior points, less exposed, were also depleted to add to the strength at Corinth.
With these reinforcements and the new regiments, Beauregard had, during the month of May, 1862, a large force on
paper, but probably not much over 50,000 effective men. We
estimated his strength at 70,000. Our own was, in round
numbers, 120,000. The defensible nature of the ground at
Corinth, and the fortifications, made 50,000 then enough to
maintain their position against double that number for an indefinite time but for the demoralization spoken of.

On the 30th of April the grand army commenced its advance from Shiloh upon Corinth. The movement was a siege
from the start to the close. The National troops were always

behind intrenchments, except of course the small reconnoitring parties sent to the front to clear the way for an advance.
Even the commanders of these parties were cautioned, "not to
bring on an engagement." "It is better to retreat than to
fight." The enemy were constantly watching our advance, but
as they were simply observers there were but few engagements that even threatened to become battles. All the engagements fought ought to have served to encourage the
enemy. Roads were again made in our front, and again corduroyed; a line was intrenched, and the troops were advanced
to the new position. Cross roads were constructed to these
new positions to enable the troops to concentrate in case of
attack. The National armies were thoroughly intrenched all
the way from the Tennessee River to Corinth.

For myself I was little more than an observer. Orders were
sent direct to the right wing or reserve, ignoring me, and
advances were made from one line of intrenchments to another without notifying me. My position was so embarrassing
in fact that I made several applications during the siege to be
relieved.

General Halleck kept his headquarters generally, if not all
the time, with the right wing. Pope being on the extreme
left did not see so much of his chief, and consequently got
loose as it were at times. On the 3d of May he was at Seven
Mile Creek with the main body of his command, but threw
forward a division to Farmington, within four miles of
Corinth. His troops had quite a little engagement at Farmington on that day, but carried the place with considerable
loss to the enemy. There would then have been no difficulty
in advancing the centre and right so as to form a new line
well up to the enemy, but Pope was ordered back to conform with the general line. On the 8th of May he moved
again, taking his whole force to Farmington, and pushed out
two divisions close to the rebel line. Again he was ordered
back. By the 4th of May the centre and right wing reached
Monterey, twelve miles out. Their advance was slow from
there, for they intrenched with every forward movement.
The left wing moved up again on the 25th of May and intrenched itself close to the enemy. The creek, with the

marsh before described, separated the two lines. Skirmishers thirty feet apart could have maintained either line at this point.

Our centre and right were, at this time, extended so that the right of the right wing was probably five miles from Corinth and four from the works in their front. The creek, which was a formidable obstacle for either side to pass on our left, became a very slight obstacle on our right. Here the enemy occupied two positions. One of them, as much as two miles out from his main line, was on a commanding elevation and defended by an intrenched battery with infantry supports. A heavy wood intervened between this work and the National forces. In rear to the south there was a clearing extending a mile or more, and south of this clearing a log-house which had been loop-holed and was occupied by infantry. Sherman's division carried these two positions with some loss to himself, but with probably greater to the enemy, on the 28th of May, and on that day the investment of Corinth was complete, or as complete as it was ever made. Thomas' right now rested west of the Mobile and Ohio railroad. Pope's left commanded the Memphis and Charleston railroad east of Corinth.

Some days before I had suggested to the commanding general that I thought if he would move the Army of the Mississippi at night, by the rear of the centre and right, ready to advance at daylight, Pope would find no natural obstacle in his front and, I believed, no serious artificial one. The ground, or works, occupied by our left could be held by a thin picket line, owing to the stream and swamp in front. To the right the troops would have a dry ridge to march over. I was silenced so quickly that I felt that possibly I had suggested an unmilitary movement.

Later, probably on the 28th of May, General Logan, whose command was then on the Mobile and Ohio railroad, said to me that the enemy had been evacuating for several days and that if allowed he could go into Corinth with his brigade. Trains of cars were heard coming in and going out of Corinth constantly. Some of the men who had been engaged in various capacities on railroads before the war claimed that they could tell, by putting their ears to the rail, not only which

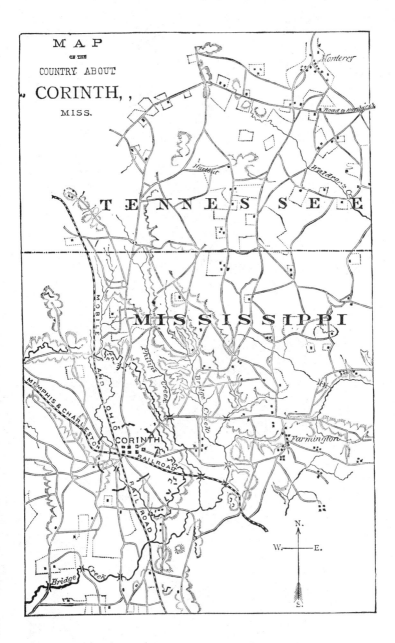

MAP
OF THE
COUNTRY ABOUT
CORINTH,
MISS.

Monterey

Road to Purdy

TENNESSEE

MISSISSIPPI

Hamburg

Waldron

MOBILE AND OHIO

MEMPHIS & CHARLESTON

Phillips Creek

Bridge Creek

CORINTH

RAILROAD

RAIL ROAD

Farmington

Bridge Creek

N.
W. E.
S.

way the trains were moving but which trains were loaded and which were empty. They said loaded trains had been going out for several days and empty ones coming in. Subsequent events proved the correctness of their judgment. Beauregard published his orders for the evacuation of Corinth on the 26th of May and fixed the 29th for the departure of his troops, and on the 30th of May General Halleck had his whole army drawn up prepared for battle and announced in orders that there was every indication that our left was to be attacked that morning. Corinth had already been evacuated and the National troops marched on and took possession without opposition. Everything had been destroyed or carried away. The Confederate commander had instructed his soldiers to cheer on the arrival of every train to create the impression among the Yankees that reinforcements were arriving. There was not a sick or wounded man left by the Confederates, nor stores of any kind. Some ammunition had been blown up—not removed—but the trophies of war were a few Quaker guns, logs of about the diameter of ordinary cannon, mounted on wheels of wagons and pointed in the most threatening manner towards us.

The possession of Corinth by the National troops was of strategic importance, but the victory was barren in every other particular. It was nearly bloodless. It is a question whether the *morale* of the Confederate troops engaged at Corinth was not improved by the immunity with which they were permitted to remove all public property and then withdraw themselves. On our side I know officers and men of the Army of the Tennessee—and I presume the same is true of those of the other commands—were disappointed at the result. They could not see how the mere occupation of places was to close the war while large and effective rebel armies existed. They believed that a well-directed attack would at least have partially destroyed the army defending Corinth. For myself I am satisfied that Corinth could have been captured in a two days' campaign commenced promptly on the arrival of reinforcements after the battle of Shiloh.

General Halleck at once commenced erecting fortifications around Corinth on a scale to indicate that this one point must be held if it took the whole National army to do it. All commanding points two or three miles to the south, south-east and south-west were strongly fortified. It was expected in case of necessity to connect these forts by rifle-pits. They were laid out on a scale that would have required 100,000 men to fully man them. It was probably thought that a final battle of the war would be fought at that point. These fortifications were never used. Immediately after the occupation of Corinth by the National troops, General Pope was sent in pursuit of the retreating garrison and General Buell soon followed. Buell was the senior of the two generals and commanded the entire column. The pursuit was kept up for some thirty miles, but did not result in the capture of any material of war or prisoners, unless a few stragglers who had fallen behind and were willing captives. On the 10th of June the pursuing column was all back at Corinth. The Army of the Tennessee was not engaged in any of these movements.

The Confederates were now driven out of West Tennessee, and on the 6th of June, after a well-contested naval battle, the National forces took possession of Memphis and held the Mississippi river from its source to that point. The railroad from Columbus to Corinth was at once put in good condition and held by us. We had garrisons at Donelson, Clarksville and Nashville, on the Cumberland River, and held the Tennessee River from its mouth to Eastport. New Orleans and Baton Rouge had fallen into the possession of the National forces, so that now the Confederates at the west were narrowed down for all communication with Richmond to the single line of road running east from Vicksburg. To dispossess them of this, therefore, became a matter of the first importance. The possession of the Mississippi by us from Memphis to Baton Rouge was also a most important object. It would be equal to the amputation of a limb in its weakening effects upon the enemy.

After the capture of Corinth a movable force of 80,000 men, besides enough to hold all the territory acquired, could have been set in motion for the accomplishment of any great campaign for the suppression of the rebellion. In addition to this fresh troops were being raised to swell the effective force. But the work of depletion commenced. Buell with the Army of the Ohio was sent east, following the line of the Memphis and Charleston railroad. This he was ordered to repair as he advanced—only to have it destroyed by small guerilla bands or other troops as soon as he was out of the way. If he had been sent directly to Chattanooga as rapidly as he could march, leaving two or three divisions along the line of the railroad from Nashville forward, he could have arrived with but little fighting, and would have saved much of the loss of life which was afterwards incurred in gaining Chattanooga. Bragg would then not have had time to raise an army to contest the possession of middle and east Tennessee and Kentucky; the battles of Stone River and Chickamauga would not necessarily have been fought; Burnside would not have been besieged in Knoxville without the power of helping himself or escaping; the battle of Chattanooga would not have been fought. These are the negative advantages, if the term negative is applicable, which would probably have resulted from prompt movements after Corinth fell into the possession of the National forces. The positive results might have been: a bloodless advance to Atlanta, to Vicksburg, or to any other desired point south of Corinth in the interior of Mississippi.

Chapter XXVII.

HEADQUARTERS MOVED TO MEMPHIS—ON THE ROAD TO
MEMPHIS—ESCAPING JACKSON—COMPLAINTS AND
REQUESTS—HALLECK APPOINTED COMMANDER-IN-
CHIEF—RETURN TO CORINTH—MOVEMENTS OF
BRAGG—SURRENDER OF CLARKSVILLE—THE ADVANCE
UPON CHATTANOOGA—SHERIDAN COLONEL OF A
MICHIGAN REGIMENT.

M Y POSITION at Corinth, with a nominal command and
yet no command, became so unbearable that I asked
permission of Halleck to remove my headquarters to Memphis. I had repeatedly asked, between the fall of Donelson and
the evacuation of Corinth, to be relieved from duty under
Halleck; but all my applications were refused until the occupation of the town. I then obtained permission to leave the
department, but General Sherman happened to call on me as I
was about starting and urged me so strongly not to think of
going, that I concluded to remain. My application to be permitted to remove my headquarters to Memphis was, however,
approved, and on the 21st of June I started for that point with
my staff and a cavalry escort of only a part of one company.
There was a detachment of two or three companies going
some twenty-five miles west to be stationed as a guard to the
railroad. I went under cover of this escort to the end of their
march, and the next morning proceeded to La Grange with
no convoy but the few cavalry men I had with me.

From La Grange to Memphis the distance is forty-seven
miles. There were no troops stationed between these two
points, except a small force guarding a working party which
was engaged in repairing the railroad. Not knowing where
this party would be found I halted at La Grange. General
Hurlbut was in command there at the time and had his headquarters tents pitched on the lawn of a very commodious
country house. The proprietor was at home and, learning of
my arrival, he invited General Hurlbut and me to dine with
him. I accepted the invitation and spent a very pleasant afternoon with my host, who was a thorough Southern gentleman

fully convinced of the justice of secession. After dinner, seated in the capacious porch, he entertained me with a recital of the services he was rendering the cause. He was too old to be in the ranks himself—he must have been quite seventy then—but his means enabled him to be useful in other ways. In ordinary times the homestead where he was now living produced the bread and meat to supply the slaves on his main plantation, in the low-lands of Mississippi. Now he raised food and forage on both places, and thought he would have that year a surplus sufficient to feed three hundred families of poor men who had gone into the war and left their families dependent upon the "patriotism" of those better off. The crops around me looked fine, and I had at the moment an idea that about the time they were ready to be gathered the "Yankee" troops would be in the neighborhood and harvest them for the benefit of those engaged in the suppression of the rebellion instead of its support. I felt, however, the greatest respect for the candor of my host and for his zeal in a cause he thoroughly believed in, though our views were as wide apart as it is possible to conceive.

The 23d of June, 1862, on the road from La Grange to Memphis was very warm, even for that latitude and season. With my staff and small escort I started at an early hour, and before noon we arrived within twenty miles of Memphis. At this point I saw a very comfortable-looking white-haired gentleman seated at the front of his house, a little distance from the road. I let my staff and escort ride ahead while I halted and, for an excuse, asked for a glass of water. I was invited at once to dismount and come in. I found my host very genial and communicative, and staid longer than I had intended, until the lady of the house announced dinner and asked me to join them. The host, however, was not pressing, so that I declined the invitation and, mounting my horse, rode on.

About a mile west from where I had been stopping a road comes up from the south-east, joining that from La Grange to Memphis. A mile west of this junction I found my staff and escort halted and enjoying the shade of forest trees on the lawn of a house located several hundred feet back from the road, their horses hitched to the fence along the line of the road. I, too, stopped and we remained there until the cool of the afternoon, and then rode into Memphis.

The gentleman with whom I had stopped twenty miles from Memphis was a Mr. De Loche, a man loyal to the Union. He had not pressed me to tarry longer with him because in the early part of my visit a neighbor, a Dr. Smith, had called and, on being presented to me, backed off the porch as if something had hit him. Mr. De Loche knew that the rebel General Jackson was in that neighborhood with a detachment of cavalry. His neighbor was as earnest in the southern cause as was Mr. De Loche in that of the Union. The exact location of Jackson was entirely unknown to Mr. De Loche; but he was sure that his neighbor would know it and would give information of my presence, and this made my stay unpleasant to him after the call of Dr. Smith.

I have stated that a detachment of troops was engaged in guarding workmen who were repairing the railroad east of Memphis. On the day I entered Memphis, Jackson captured a small herd of beef cattle which had been sent east for the troops so engaged. The drovers were not enlisted men and he released them. A day or two after one of these drovers came to my headquarters and, relating the circumstances of his capture, said Jackson was very much disappointed that he had not captured me; that he was six or seven miles south of the Memphis and Charleston railroad when he learned that I was stopping at the house of Mr. De Loche, and had ridden with his command to the junction of the road he was on with that from La Grange and Memphis, where he learned that I had passed three-quarters of an hour before. He thought it would be useless to pursue with jaded horses a well-mounted party with so much of a start. Had he gone three-quarters of a mile farther he would have found me with my party quietly resting under the shade of trees and without even arms in our hands with which to defend ourselves.

General Jackson of course did not communicate his disappointment at not capturing me to a prisoner, a young drover; but from the talk among the soldiers the facts related were learned. A day or two later Mr. De Loche called on me in Memphis to apologize for his apparent incivility in not insisting on my staying for dinner. He said that his wife accused him of marked discourtesy, but that, after the call of his neighbor, he had felt restless until I got away. I never met General Jackson before the war, nor during it, but have met him since at his very comfortable summer home at Manitou Springs, Colorado. I reminded him of the above incident, and this drew from him the response that he was thankful now he had not captured me. I certainly was very thankful too.

My occupation of Memphis as district headquarters did not last long. The period, however, was marked by a few incidents which were novel to me. Up to that time I had not occupied any place in the South where the citizens were at home in any great numbers. Dover was within the fortifications at Fort Donelson, and, as far as I remember, every citizen was gone. There were no people living at Pittsburg landing, and but very few at Corinth. Memphis, however, was a populous city, and there were many of the citizens remaining there who were not only thoroughly impressed with the justice of their cause, but who thought that even the "Yankee soldiery" must entertain the same views if they could only be induced to make an honest confession. It took hours of my time every day to listen to complaints and requests. The latter were generally reasonable, and if so they were granted; but the complaints were not always, or even often, well founded. Two instances will mark the general character. First: the officer who commanded at Memphis immediately after the city fell into the hands of the National troops had ordered one of the churches of the city to be opened to the soldiers. Army chaplains were authorized to occupy the pulpit. Second: at the beginning of the war the Confederate Congress had passed a law confiscating all property of "alien enemies" at the South, including the debts of Southerners to Northern men. In consequence of this law, when Memphis was occupied the provost-marshal had forcibly collected all the evidences he could obtain of such debts.

Almost the first complaints made to me were these two outrages. The gentleman who made the complaints informed me first of his own high standing as a lawyer, a citizen and a Christian. He was a deacon in the church which had been defiled by the occupation of Union troops, and by a Union chaplain filling the pulpit. He did not use the word "defile," but he expressed the idea very clearly. He asked that the church be restored to the former congregation. I told him that no order had been issued prohibiting the congregation attending the church. He said of course the congregation could not hear a Northern clergyman who differed so radically with them on questions of government. I told him the troops would continue to occupy that church for the present, and that they would not be called upon to hear disloyal sentiments proclaimed from the pulpit. This closed the argument on the first point.

Then came the second. The complainant said that he wanted the papers restored to him which had been surrendered to the provost-marshal under protest; he was a lawyer, and before the establishment of the "Confederate States Government" had been the attorney for a number of large business houses at the North; that "his government" had confiscated all debts due "alien enemies," and appointed commissioners, or officers, to collect such debts and pay them over to the "government": but in his case, owing to his high standing, he had been permitted to hold these claims for collection, the responsible officials knowing that he would account to the "government" for every dollar received. He said that his "government," when it came in possession of all its territory, would hold him personally responsible for the claims he had surrendered to the provost-marshal. His impudence was so sublime that I was rather amused than indignant. I told him, however, that if he would remain in Memphis I did not believe the Confederate government would ever molest him. He left, no doubt, as much amazed at my assurance as I was at the brazenness of his request.

On the 11th of July General Halleck received telegraphic orders appointing him to the command of all the armies, with headquarters in Washington. His instructions pressed him to proceed to his new field of duty with as little delay as was consistent with the safety and interests of his previous command. I was next in rank, and he telegraphed me the same day to report at department headquarters at Corinth. I was not informed by the dispatch that my chief had been ordered to a different field and did not know whether to move my headquarters or not. I telegraphed asking if I was to take my staff with me, and received word in reply: "This place will be your headquarters. You can judge for yourself." I left Memphis for my new field without delay, and reached Corinth on the 15th of the month. General Halleck remained until the 17th of July; but he was very uncommunicative, and gave me no information as to what I had been called to Corinth for.

When General Halleck left to assume the duties of general-in-chief I remained in command of the district of West Tennessee. Practically I became a department commander, because no one was assigned to that position over me and I made my reports direct to the general-in-chief; but I was not assigned to the position of department commander until the 25th of October. General Halleck while commanding the Department of the Mississippi had had control as far east as a line drawn from Chattanooga north. My district only embraced West Tennessee and Kentucky west of the Cumberland River. Buell, with the Army of the Ohio, had, as previously stated, been ordered east towards Chattanooga, with instructions to repair the Memphis and Charleston railroad as he advanced. Troops had been sent north by Halleck along the line of the Mobile and Ohio railroad to put it in repair as far as Columbus. Other troops were stationed on the railroad from Jackson, Tennessee, to Grand Junction, and still others on the road west to Memphis.

The remainder of the magnificent army of 120,000 men which entered Corinth on the 30th of May had now become so scattered that I was put entirely on the defensive in a territory whose population was hostile to the Union. One of the first things I had to do was to construct fortifications at Corinth better suited to the garrison that could be spared to man them. The structures that had been built during the months of May and June were left as monuments to the skill of the engineer, and others were constructed in a few days, plainer in design but suited to the command available to defend them.

I disposed the troops belonging to the district in conformity with the situation as rapidly as possible. The forces at Donelson, Clarksville and Nashville, with those at Corinth and along the railroad eastward, I regarded as sufficient for protection against any attack from the west. The Mobile and

Ohio railroad was guarded from Rienzi, south of Corinth, to Columbus; and the Mississippi Central railroad from Jackson, Tennessee, to Bolivar. Grand Junction and La Grange on the Memphis railroad were abandoned.

South of the Army of the Tennessee, and confronting it, was Van Dorn, with a sufficient force to organize a movable army of thirty-five to forty thousand men, after being reinforced by Price from Missouri. This movable force could be thrown against either Corinth, Bolivar or Memphis; and the best that could be done in such event would be to weaken the points not threatened in order to reinforce the one that was. Nothing could be gained on the National side by attacking elsewhere, because the territory already occupied was as much as the force present could guard. The most anxious period of the war, to me, was during the time the Army of the Tennessee was guarding the territory acquired by the fall of Corinth and Memphis and before I was sufficiently reinforced to take the offensive. The enemy also had cavalry operating in our rear, making it necessary to guard every point of the railroad back to Columbus, on the security of which we were dependent for all our supplies. Headquarters were connected by telegraph with all points of the command except Memphis and the Mississippi below Columbus. With these points communication was had by the railroad to Columbus, then down the river by boat. To reinforce Memphis would take three or four days, and to get an order there for troops to move elsewhere would have taken at least two days. Memphis therefore was practically isolated from the balance of the command. But it was in Sherman's hands. Then too the troops were well intrenched and the gunboats made a valuable auxiliary.

During the two months after the departure of General Halleck there was much fighting between small bodies of the contending armies, but these encounters were dwarfed by the magnitude of the main battles so as to be now almost forgotten except by those engaged in them. Some of them, however, estimated by the losses on both sides in killed and wounded, were equal in hard fighting to most of the battles of the Mexican war which attracted so much of the attention of the public when they occurred. About the 23d of July Colonel Ross, commanding at Bolivar, was threatened by a large force of the enemy so that he had to be reinforced from Jackson and Corinth. On the 27th there was skirmishing on the Hatchie River, eight miles from Bolivar. On the 30th I learned from Colonel P. H. Sheridan, who had been far to the south, that Bragg in person was at Rome, Georgia, with his troops moving by rail (by way of Mobile) to Chattanooga and his wagon train marching overland to join him at Rome. Price was at this time at Holly Springs, Mississippi, with a large force, and occupied Grand Junction as an outpost. I proposed to the general-in-chief to be permitted to drive him away, but was informed that, while I had to judge for myself, the best use to make of my troops *was not to scatter them*, but hold them ready to reinforce Buell.

The movement of Bragg himself with his wagon trains to Chattanooga across country, while his troops were transported over a long round-about road to the same destination, without need of guards except when in my immediate front, demonstrates the advantage which troops enjoy while acting in a country where the people are friendly. Buell was marching through a hostile region and had to have his communications thoroughly guarded back to a base of supplies. More men were required the farther the National troops penetrated into the enemy's country. I, with an army sufficiently powerful to have destroyed Bragg, was purely on the defensive and accomplishing no more than to hold a force far inferior to my own.

On the 2d of August I was ordered from Washington to live upon the country, on the resources of citizens hostile to the government, so far as practicable. I was also directed to "handle rebels within our lines without gloves," to imprison them, or to expel them from their homes and from our lines. I do not recollect having arrested and confined a citizen (not a soldier) during the entire rebellion. I am aware that a great many were sent to northern prisons, particularly to Joliet, Illinois, by some of my subordinates with the statement that it was my order. I had all such released the moment I learned of their arrest; and finally sent a staff officer north to release every prisoner who was said to be confined by my order. There were many citizens at home who deserved punishment because they were soldiers when an opportunity was afforded to inflict an injury to the National cause. This class was not of the kind that were apt to get arrested, and I deemed it better that a few guilty men should escape than that a great many innocent ones should suffer.

On the 14th of August I was ordered to send two more divisions to Buell. They were sent the same day by way of Decatur. On the 22d Colonel Rodney Mason surrendered Clarksville with six companies of his regiment.

Colonel Mason was one of the officers who had led their regiments off the field at almost the first fire of the rebels at Shiloh. He was by nature and education a gentleman, and was terribly mortified at his action when the battle was over. He came to me with tears in his eyes and begged to be allowed to have another trial. I felt great sympathy for him and sent him, with his regiment, to garrison Clarksville and Donelson. He selected Clarksville for his headquarters, no doubt because he regarded it as the post of danger, it being nearer the enemy. But when he was summoned to surrender by a band of guerillas, his constitutional weakness overcame him. He inquired the number of men the enemy had, and receiving a response indicating a force greater than his own he said if he could be satisfied of that fact he would surrender. Arrangements were made for him to count the guerillas, and having satisfied himself that the enemy had the greater force he surrendered and informed his subordinate at Donelson of the fact, advising him to do the same. The guerillas paroled their prisoners and moved upon Donelson, but the officer in command at that point marched out to meet them and drove them away.

Among other embarrassments, at the time of which I now write, was the fact that the government wanted to get out all the cotton possible from the South and directed me to give every facility toward that end. Pay in gold was authorized, and stations on the Mississippi River and on the railroad in our possession had to be designated where cotton would be received. This opened to the enemy not only the means of converting cotton into money, which had a value all over the world and which they so much needed, but it afforded them means of obtaining accurate and intelligent information in regard to our position and strength. It was also demoralizing to the troops. Citizens obtaining permits from the treasury department had to be protected within our lines and given facilities to get out cotton by which they realized enormous profits. Men who had enlisted to fight the battles of their country did not like to be engaged in protecting a traffic which went to the support of an enemy they had to fight, and the profits of which went to men who shared none of their dangers.

On the 30th of August Colonel M. D. Leggett, near Bolivar, with the 20th and 29th Ohio volunteer infantry, was attacked by a force supposed to be about 4,000 strong. The enemy was driven away with a loss of more than one hundred men. On the 1st of September the bridge guard at Medon was attacked by guerillas. The guard held the position until reinforced, when the enemy were routed leaving about fifty of their number on the field dead or wounded, our loss being only two killed and fifteen wounded. On the same day Colonel Dennis, with a force of less than 500 infantry and two pieces of artillery, met the cavalry of the enemy in strong force, a few miles west of Medon, and drove them away with great loss. Our troops buried 179 of the enemy's dead, left upon the field. Afterwards it was found that all the houses in the vicinity of the battle-field were turned into hospitals for the wounded. Our loss, as reported at the time, was forty-five killed and wounded. On the 2d of September I was ordered to send more reinforcements to Buell. Jackson and Bolivar were yet threatened, but I sent the reinforcements. On the 4th I received direct orders to send Granger's division also to Louisville, Kentucky.

General Buell had left Corinth about the 10th of June to march upon Chattanooga; Bragg, who had superseded Beauregard in command, sent one division from Tupelo on the 27th of June for the same place. This gave Buell about seventeen days' start. If he had not been required to repair the railroad as he advanced, the march could have been made in eighteen days at the outside, and Chattanooga must have been reached by the National forces before the rebels could have possibly got there. The road between Nashville and Chattanooga could easily have been put in repair by other troops, so that communication with the North would have been opened in a short time after the occupation of the place by the National troops. If Buell had been permitted to move in the first instance, with the whole of the Army of the Ohio and that portion of the Army of the Mississippi afterwards sent to him, he could have thrown four divisions from his own command along the line of road to repair and guard it.

Granger's division was promptly sent on the 4th of September. I was at the station at Corinth when the troops reached that point, and found General P. H. Sheridan with them. I expressed surprise at seeing him and said that I had not expected him to go. He showed decided disappointment at the prospect of being detained. I felt a little nettled at his desire to get away and did not detain him.

Sheridan was a first lieutenant in the regiment in which I had served eleven years, the 4th infantry, and stationed on the Pacific coast when the war broke out. He was promoted to a captaincy in May, 1861, and before the close of the year managed in some way, I do not know how, to get East. He went to Missouri. Halleck had known him as a very successful young officer in managing campaigns against the Indians on the Pacific coast, and appointed him acting-quartermaster in south-west Missouri. There was no difficulty in getting supplies forward while Sheridan served in that capacity; but he got into difficulty with his immediate superiors because of his stringent rules for preventing the use of public transportation for private purposes. He asked to be relieved from further duty in the capacity in which he was engaged and his request was granted. When General Halleck took the field in April, 1862, Sheridan was assigned to duty on his staff. During the advance on Corinth a vacancy occurred in the colonelcy of the 2d Michigan cavalry. Governor Blair, of Michigan, telegraphed General Halleck asking him to suggest the name of a professional soldier for the vacancy, saying he would appoint a good man without reference to his State. Sheridan was named; and was so conspicuously efficient that when Corinth was reached he was assigned to command a cavalry brigade in the Army of the Mississippi. He was in command at Booneville on the 1st of July with two small regiments, when he was attacked by a force full three times as numerous as his own. By very skilful manœuvres and boldness of attack he completely routed the enemy. For this he was made a brigadier-general and became a conspicuous figure in the army about Corinth. On this account I was sorry to see him leaving me. His departure was probably fortunate, for he rendered distinguished services in his new field.

Granger and Sheridan reached Louisville before Buell got there, and on the night of their arrival Sheridan with his command threw up works around the railroad station for the defence of troops as they came from the front.

Chapter XXVIII.

ADVANCE OF VAN DORN AND PRICE—PRICE
ENTERS IUKA—BATTLE OF IUKA.

A T THIS TIME, September 4th, I had two divisions of the
Army of the Mississippi stationed at Corinth, Rienzi,
Jacinto and Danville. There were at Corinth also Davies' division and two brigades of McArthur's, besides cavalry and
artillery. This force constituted my left wing, of which
Rosecrans was in command. General Ord commanded the
centre, from Bethel to Humboldt on the Mobile and Ohio
railroad and from Jackson to Bolivar where the Mississippi
Central is crossed by the Hatchie River. General Sherman
commanded on the right at Memphis with two of his brigades back at Brownsville, at the crossing of the Hatchie
River by the Memphis and Ohio railroad. This made the
most convenient arrangement I could devise for concentrating all my spare forces upon any threatened point. All the
troops of the command were within telegraphic communication of each other, except those under Sherman. By bringing
a portion of his command to Brownsville, from which point
there was a railroad and telegraph back to Memphis, communication could be had with that part of my command within a
few hours by the use of couriers. In case it became necessary
to reinforce Corinth, by this arrangement all the troops at
Bolivar, except a small guard, could be sent by rail by the way
of Jackson in less than twenty-four hours; while the troops
from Brownsville could march up to Bolivar to take their
place.

On the 7th of September I learned of the advance of Van
Dorn and Price, apparently upon Corinth. One division was
brought from Memphis to Bolivar to meet any emergency
that might arise from this move of the enemy. I was much
concerned because my first duty, after holding the territory
acquired within my command, was to prevent further reinforcing of Bragg in Middle Tennessee. Already the Army of
Northern Virginia had defeated the army under General Pope
and was invading Maryland. In the Centre General Buell was

on his way to Louisville and Bragg marching parallel to him with a large Confederate force for the Ohio River.

I had been constantly called upon to reinforce Buell until at this time my entire force numbered less than 50,000 men, of all arms. This included everything from Cairo south within my jurisdiction. If I too should be driven back, the Ohio River would become the line dividing the belligerents west of the Alleghanies, while at the East the line was already farther north than when hostilities commenced at the opening of the war. It is true Nashville was never given up after its first capture, but it would have been isolated and the garrison there would have been obliged to beat a hasty retreat if the troops in West Tennessee had been compelled to fall back. To say at the end of the second year of the war the line dividing the contestants at the East was pushed north of Maryland, a State that had not seceded, and at the West beyond Kentucky, another State which had been always loyal, would have been discouraging indeed. As it was, many loyal people despaired in the fall of 1862 of ever saving the Union. The administration at Washington was much concerned for the safety of the cause it held so dear. But I believe there was never a day when the President did not think that, in some way or other, a cause so just as ours would come out triumphant.

Up to the 11th of September Rosecrans still had troops on the railroad east of Corinth, but they had all been ordered in. By the 12th all were in except a small force under Colonel Murphy of the 8th Wisconsin. He had been detained to guard the remainder of the stores which had not yet been brought in to Corinth.

On the 13th of September General Sterling Price entered Iuka, a town about twenty miles east of Corinth on the Memphis and Charleston railroad. Colonel Murphy with a few men was guarding the place. He made no resistance, but evacuated the town on the approach of the enemy. I was apprehensive lest the object of the rebels might be to get troops into Tennessee to reinforce Bragg, as it was afterwards ascertained to be. The authorities at Washington, including the general-in-chief of the army, were very anxious, as I have said, about affairs both in East and Middle Tennessee; and my anxiety was quite as great on their account as for any danger threatening my command. I had not force enough at Corinth to attack Price even by stripping everything; and there was danger that before troops could be got from other points he might be far on his way across the Tennessee. To prevent this all spare forces at Bolivar and Jackson were ordered to Corinth, and cars were concentrated at Jackson for their transportation. Within twenty-four hours from the transmission of the order the troops were at their destination, although there had been a delay of four hours resulting from the forward train getting off the track and stopping all the others. This gave a reinforcement of near 8,000 men, General Ord in command. General Rosecrans commanded the district of Corinth with a movable force of about 9,000, independent of the garrison deemed necessary to be left behind. It was known that General Van Dorn was about a four days' march south of us, with a large force. It might have been part of his plan to attack at Corinth, Price coming from the east while he came up from the south. My desire was to attack Price before Van Dorn could reach Corinth or go to his relief.

General Rosecrans had previously had his headquarters at Iuka, where his command was spread out along the Memphis and Charleston railroad eastward. While there he had a most excellent map prepared showing all the roads and streams in the surrounding country. He was also personally familiar with the ground, so that I deferred very much to him in my plans for the approach. We had cars enough to transport all of General Ord's command, which was to go by rail to Burnsville, a point on the road about seven miles west of Iuka. From there his troops were to march by the north side of the railroad and attack Price from the north-west, while Rosecrans was to move eastward from his position south of Corinth by way of the Jacinto road. A small force was to hold the Jacinto road where it turns to the north-east, while the main force moved on the Fulton road which comes into Iuka further east. This plan was suggested by Rosecrans.

Bear Creek, a few miles to the east of the Fulton road, is a formidable obstacle to the movement of troops in the absence of bridges, all of which, in September, 1862, had been destroyed in that vicinity. The Tennessee, to the north-east, not many miles away, was also a formidable obstacle for an army

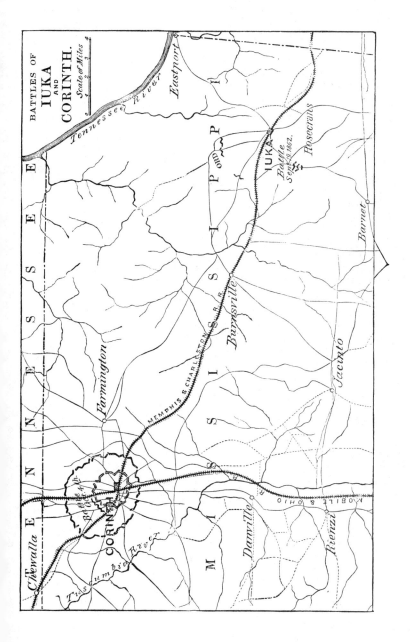

BATTLES OF
IUKA
AND
CORINTH.

Scale of Miles
0 1 2 3 4

followed by a pursuing force. Ord was on the north-west, and even if a rebel movement had been possible in that direction it could have brought only temporary relief, for it would have carried Price's army to the rear of the National forces and isolated it from all support. It looked to me that, if Price would remain in Iuka until we could get there, his annihilation was inevitable.

On the morning of the 18th of September General Ord moved by rail to Burnsville, and there left the cars and moved out to perform his part of the programme. He was to get as near the enemy as possible during the day and intrench himself so as to hold his position until the next morning. Rosecrans was to be up by the morning of the 19th on the two roads before described, and the attack was to be from all three quarters simultaneously. Troops enough were left at Jacinto and Rienzi to detain any cavalry that Van Dorn might send out to make a sudden dash into Corinth until I could be notified. There was a telegraph wire along the railroad, so there would be no delay in communication. I detained cars and locomotives enough at Burnsville to transport the whole of Ord's command at once, and if Van Dorn had moved against Corinth instead of Iuka I could have thrown in reinforcements to the number of 7,000 or 8,000 before he could have arrived. I remained at Burnsville with a detachment of about 900 men from Ord's command and communicated with my two wings by courier. Ord met the advance of the enemy soon after leaving Burnsville. Quite a sharp engagement ensued, but he drove the rebels back with considerable loss, including one general officer killed. He maintained his position and was ready to attack by daylight the next morning. I was very much disappointed at receiving a dispatch from Rosecrans after midnight from Jacinto, twenty-two miles from Iuka, saying that some of his command had been delayed, and that the rear of his column was not yet up as far as Jacinto. He said, however, that he would still be at Iuka by two o'clock the next day. I did not believe this possible because of the distance and the condition of the roads, which was bad; besides, troops after a forced march of twenty miles are not in a good condition for fighting the moment they get through. It might do in marching to relieve a beleaguered garrison, but

not to make an assault. I immediately sent Ord a copy of
Rosecrans' dispatch and ordered him to be in readiness to
attack the moment he heard the sound of guns to the south or
south-east. He was instructed to notify his officers to be on
the alert for any indications of battle. During the 19th the
wind blew in the wrong direction to transmit sound either
towards the point where Ord was, or to Burnsville where I
had remained.

A couple of hours before dark on the 19th Rosecrans arrived with the head of his column at Barnets, the point where
the Jacinto road to Iuka leaves the road going east. He here
turned north without sending any troops to the Fulton road.
While still moving in column up the Jacinto road he met a
force of the enemy and had his advance badly beaten and
driven back upon the main road. In this short engagement his
loss was considerable for the number engaged, and one battery was taken from him. The wind was still blowing hard
and in the wrong direction to transmit sound towards either
Ord or me. Neither he nor I nor any one in either command
heard a gun that was fired upon the battle-field. After the
engagement Rosecrans sent me a dispatch announcing the result. This was brought by a courier. There was no road between Burnsville and the position then occupied by Rosecrans
and the country was impassable for a man on horseback. The
courier bearing the message was compelled to move west
nearly to Jacinto before he found a road leading to Burnsville.
This made it a late hour of the night before I learned of the
battle that had taken place during the afternoon. I at once
notified Ord of the fact and ordered him to attack early in the
morning. The next morning Rosecrans himself renewed the
attack and went into Iuka with but little resistance. Ord also
went in according to orders, without hearing a gun from the
south of town but supposing the troops coming from the
south-west must be up by that time. Rosecrans, however, had
put no troops upon the Fulton road, and the enemy had
taken advantage of this neglect and retreated by that road
during the night. Word was soon brought to me that our
troops were in Iuka. I immediately rode into town and found
that the enemy was not being pursued even by the cavalry. I
ordered pursuit by the whole of Rosecrans' command and

went on with him a few miles in person. He followed only a few miles after I left him and then went into camp, and the pursuit was continued no further. I was disappointed at the result of the battle of Iuka—but I had so high an opinion of General Rosecrans that I found no fault at the time.

Chapter XXIX.

VAN DORN'S MOVEMENTS—BATTLE OF CORINTH—COMMAND OF THE DEPARTMENT OF THE TENNESSEE.

O N THE 19TH of September General Geo. H. Thomas was ordered east to reinforce Buell. This threw the army at my command still more on the defensive. The Memphis and Charleston railroad was abandoned, except at Corinth, and small forces were left at Chewalla and Grand Junction. Soon afterwards the latter of these two places was given up and Bolivar became our most advanced position on the Mississippi Central railroad. Our cavalry was kept well to the front and frequent expeditions were sent out to watch the movements of the enemy. We were in a country where nearly all the people, except the negroes, were hostile to us and friendly to the cause we were trying to suppress. It was easy, therefore, for the enemy to get early information of our every move. We, on the contrary, had to go after our information in force, and then often returned without it.

On the 22d Bolivar was threatened by a large force from south of Grand Junction, supposed to be twenty regiments of infantry with cavalry and artillery. I reinforced Bolivar, and went to Jackson in person to superintend the movement of troops to whatever point the attack might be made upon. The troops from Corinth were brought up in time to repel the threatened movement without a battle. Our cavalry followed the enemy south of Davis' mills in Mississippi.

On the 30th I found that Van Dorn was apparently endeavoring to strike the Mississippi River above Memphis. At the same time other points within my command were so threatened that it was impossible to concentrate a force to drive him away. There was at this juncture a large Union force at Helena, Arkansas, which, had it been within my command, I could have ordered across the river to attack and break up the Mississippi Central railroad far to the south. This would not only have called Van Dorn back, but would have compelled the retention of a large rebel force far to the south to prevent a repetition of such raids on the enemy's line of supplies. Geographical lines between the commands during the rebellion were not always well chosen, or they were too rigidly adhered to.

Van Doren did not attempt to get upon the line above Memphis, as had apparently been his intention. He was simply covering a deeper design; one much more important to his cause. By the 1st of October it was fully apparent that Corinth was to be attacked with great force and determination, and that Van Dorn, Lovell, Price, Villepigue and Rust had joined their strength for this purpose. There was some skirmishing outside of Corinth with the advance of the enemy on the 3d. The rebels massed in the north-west angle of the Memphis and Charleston and the Mobile and Ohio railroads, and were thus between the troops at Corinth and all possible reinforcements. Any fresh troops for us must come by a circuitous route.

On the night of the 3d, accordingly, I ordered General McPherson, who was at Jackson, to join Rosecrans at Corinth with reinforcements picked up along the line of the railroad equal to a brigade. Hurlbut had been ordered from Bolivar to march for the same destination; and as Van Dorn was coming upon Corinth from the north-west some of his men fell in with the advance of Hurlbut's and some skirmishing ensued on the evening of the 3d. On the 4th Van Dorn made a dashing attack, hoping, no doubt, to capture Rosecrans before his reinforcements could come up. In that case the enemy himself could have occupied the defences of Corinth and held at bay all the Union troops that arrived. In fact he could have taken the offensive against the reinforcements with three or four times their number and still left a sufficient garrison in the works about Corinth to hold them. He came near success, some of his troops penetrating the National lines at least once, but the works that were built after Halleck's departure enabled Rosecrans to hold his position until the troops of both McPherson and Hurlbut approached towards the rebel front and rear. The enemy was finally driven back with great slaughter: all their charges, made with great gallantry, were repulsed. The loss on our side was heavy, but nothing to compare with Van Dorn's. McPherson came up with the train of cars bearing his command as close to the enemy as was prudent, debarked on the rebel flank and got in to the support of Rosecrans just after the repulse. His approach, as well as that of Hurlbut, was known to the enemy and had a moral effect. General Rosecrans, however, failed to follow up the victory, although I had given specific orders in advance of the battle for him to pursue the moment the enemy was repelled. He did not do so, and I repeated the order after the battle. In the first order he was notified that the force of 4,000 men which was going to his assistance would be in great peril if the enemy was not pursued.

General Ord had joined Hurlbut on the 4th and being senior took command of his troops. This force encountered the head of Van Dorn's retreating column just as it was crossing the Hatchie by a bridge some ten miles out from Corinth. The bottom land here was swampy and bad for the operations of troops, making a good place to get an enemy into. Ord attacked the troops that had crossed the bridge and drove them back in a panic. Many were killed, and others were drowned by being pushed off the bridge in their hurried retreat. Ord followed and met the main force. He was too weak in numbers to assault, but he held the bridge and compelled the enemy to resume his retreat by another bridge higher up the stream. Ord was wounded in this engagement and the command devolved on Hurlbut.

Rosecrans did not start in pursuit till the morning of the 5th and then took the wrong road. Moving in the enemy's country he travelled with a wagon train to carry his provisions and munitions of war. His march was therefore slower than that of the enemy, who was moving towards his supplies. Two or three hours of pursuit on the day of battle, without anything except what the men carried on their persons, would have been worth more than any pursuit commenced the next day could have possibly been. Even when he did start, if Rosecrans had followed the route taken by the enemy, he would have come upon Van Dorn in a swamp with a stream in front and Ord holding the only bridge; but he took the road leading north and towards Chewalla instead of west, and, after having marched as far as the enemy had moved to get to the Hatchie, he was as far from battle as when he started. Hurlbut had not the numbers to meet any such force as Van Dorn's if they had been in any mood for fighting, and he might have been in great peril.

I now regarded the time to accomplish anything by pursuit as past and, after Rosecrans reached Jonesboro, I ordered him to return. He kept on to Ripley, however, and was persistent in wanting to go farther. I thereupon ordered him to halt and submitted the matter to the general-in-chief, who allowed me to exercise my judgment in the matter, but inquired "why not pursue?" Upon this I ordered Rosecrans back. Had he gone much farther he would have met a greater force than Van Dorn had at Corinth and behind intrenchments or on chosen ground, and the probabilities are he would have lost his army.

The battle of Corinth was bloody, our loss being 315 killed, 1,812 wounded and 232 missing. The enemy lost many more. Rosecrans reported 1,423 dead and 2,225 prisoners. We fought behind breastworks, which accounts in some degree for the disparity. Among the killed on our side was General Hackelman. General Oglesby was badly, it was for some time supposed mortally, wounded. I received a congratulatory letter from the President, which expressed also his sorrow for the losses.

This battle was recognized by me as being a decided victory, though not so complete as I had hoped for, nor nearly so complete as I now think was within the easy grasp of the commanding officer at Corinth. Since the war it is known that the result, as it was, was a crushing blow to the enemy, and felt by him much more than it was appreciated at the North. The battle relieved me from any further anxiety for the safety of the territory within my jurisdiction, and soon after receiving reinforcements I suggested to the general-in-chief a forward movement against Vicksburg.

On the 23d of October I learned of Pemberton's being in command at Holly Springs and much reinforced by conscripts and troops from Alabama and Texas. The same day General Rosecrans was relieved from duty with my command, and shortly after he succeeded Buell in the command of the army in Middle Tennessee. I was delighted at the promotion of General Rosecrans to a separate command, because I still believed that when independent of an immediate superior the qualities which I, at that time, credited him with possessing, would show themselves. As a subordinate I found that I could not make him do as I wished, and had determined to relieve him from duty that very day.

At the close of the operations just described my force, in round numbers, was 48,500. Of these 4,800 were in Kentucky and Illinois, 7,000 in Memphis, 19,200 from Mound City south, and 17,500 at Corinth. General McClernand had been authorized from Washington to go north and organize troops to be used in opening the Mississippi. These new levies with other reinforcements now began to come in.

On the 25th of October I was placed in command of the Department of the Tennessee. Reinforcements continued to come from the north and by the 2d of November I was prepared to take the initiative. This was a great relief after the two and a half months of continued defence over a large district of country, and where nearly every citizen was an enemy ready to give information of our every move. I have described very imperfectly a few of the battles and skirmishes that took place during this time. To describe all would take more space than I can allot to the purpose; to make special mention of all the officers and troops who distinguished themselves, would take a volume.

NOTE. — For gallantry in the various engagements, from the time I was left in command down to 26th of October and on my recommendation, Generals McPherson and C. S. Hamilton were promoted to be Major-Generals, and Colonels C. C. Marsh, 20th Illinois, M. M. Crocker, 13th Iowa, J. A. Mower, 11th Missouri, M. D. Leggett, 78th Ohio, J. D. Stevenson, 7th Missouri, and John E. Smith, 45th Illinois, to be Brigadiers.

Chapter XXX.

THE CAMPAIGN AGAINST VICKSBURG—EMPLOYING THE
FREEDMEN—OCCUPATION OF HOLLY SPRINGS—
SHERMAN ORDERED TO MEMPHIS—SHERMAN'S
MOVEMENTS DOWN THE MISSISSIPPI—VAN DORN
CAPTURES HOLLY SPRINGS—COLLECTING
FORAGE AND FOOD.

VICKSBURG WAS IMPORTANT to the enemy because it occupied the first high ground coming close to the river below Memphis. From there a railroad runs east, connecting with other roads leading to all points of the Southern States. A railroad also starts from the opposite side of the river, extending west as far as Shreveport, Louisiana. Vicksburg was the only channel, at the time of the events of which this chapter treats, connecting the parts of the Confederacy divided by the Mississippi. So long as it was held by the enemy, the free navigation of the river was prevented. Hence its importance. Points on the river between Vicksburg and Port Hudson were held as dependencies; but their fall was sure to follow the capture of the former place.

The campaign against Vicksburg commenced on the 2d of November as indicated in a dispatch to the general-in-chief in the following words: "I have commenced a movement on Grand Junction, with three divisions from Corinth and two from Bolivar. Will leave here [Jackson, Tennessee] to-morrow, and take command in person. If found practicable, I will go to Holly Springs, and, may be, Grenada, completing railroad and telegraph as I go."

At this time my command was holding the Mobile and Ohio railroad from about twenty-five miles south of Corinth, north to Columbus, Kentucky; the Mississippi Central from Bolivar north to its junction with the Mobile and Ohio; the Memphis and Charleston from Corinth east to Bear Creek, and the Mississippi River from Cairo to Memphis. My entire command was no more than was necessary to hold these lines, and hardly that if kept on the defensive. By moving against the enemy and into his unsubdued, or not yet captured, territory, driving their army before us, these lines would nearly hold themselves; thus affording a large force for field operations. My moving force at that time was about 30,000 men, and I estimated the enemy confronting me, under Pemberton, at about the same number. General McPherson commanded my left wing and General C. S. Hamilton the centre, while Sherman was at Memphis with the right wing. Pemberton was fortified at the Tallahatchie, but occupied Holly Springs and Grand Junction on the Mississippi Central railroad. On the 8th we occupied Grand Junction and La Grange, throwing a considerable force seven or eight miles south, along the line of the railroad. The road from Bolivar forward was repaired and put in running order as the troops advanced.

Up to this time it had been regarded as an axiom in war that large bodies of troops must operate from a base of supplies which they always covered and guarded in all forward movements. There was delay therefore in repairing the road back, and in gathering and forwarding supplies to the front.

By my orders, and in accordance with previous instructions from Washington, all the forage within reach was collected under the supervision of the chief quartermaster and the provisions under the chief commissary, receipts being given when there was any one to take them; the supplies in any event to be accounted for as government stores. The stock was bountiful, but still it gave me no idea of the possibility of supplying a moving column in an enemy's country from the country itself.

It was at this point, probably, where the first idea of a "Freedman's Bureau" took its origin. Orders of the government prohibited the expulsion of the negroes from the protection of the army, when they came in voluntarily. Humanity forbade allowing them to starve. With such an army of them, of all ages and both sexes, as had congregated about Grand Junction, amounting to many thousands, it was impossible to advance. There was no special authority for feeding them unless they were employed as teamsters, cooks and pioneers with the army; but only able-bodied young men were suitable for such work. This labor would support but a very limited percentage of them. The plantations were all deserted; the cotton and corn were ripe: men, women and children above ten years of age could be employed in saving these crops. To do this work with contrabands, or to have it done, organization under a competent chief was necessary. On inquiring for such a man Chaplain Eaton, now and for many years the very able United States Commissioner of Education, was suggested. He proved as efficient in that field as he has since done in his present one. I gave him all the assistants and guards he called for. We together fixed the prices to be paid for the negro labor, whether rendered to the government or to individuals. The cotton was to be picked from abandoned plantations, the laborers to receive the stipulated price (my recollection is twelve and a half cents per pound for picking and ginning) from the quartermaster, he shipping the cotton north to be sold for the benefit of the government. Citizens remaining on their plantations were allowed the privilege of having their crops saved by freedmen on the same terms.

At once the freedmen became self-sustaining. The money was not paid to them directly, but was expended judiciously and for their benefit. They gave me no trouble afterwards.

Later the freedmen were engaged in cutting wood along the Mississippi River to supply the large number of steamers on that stream. A good price was paid for chopping wood used for the supply of government steamers (steamers chartered and which the government had to supply with fuel). Those supplying their own fuel paid a much higher price. In this way a fund was created not only sufficient to feed and clothe all, old and young, male and female, but to build them comfortable cabins, hospitals for the sick, and to supply them with many comforts they had never known before.

At this stage of the campaign against Vicksburg I was very much disturbed by newspaper rumors that General McClernand was to have a separate and independent command within mine, to operate against Vicksburg by way of the Mississippi River. Two commanders on the same field are always one too many, and in this case I did not think the general selected had either the experience or the qualifications to fit him for so important a position. I feared for the safety of the troops intrusted to him, especially as he was to raise new levies, raw troops, to execute so important a trust. But on the 12th I received a dispatch from General Halleck saying that I had command of all the troops sent to my department and authorizing me to fight the enemy where I pleased. The next day my cavalry was in Holly Springs, and the enemy fell back south of the Tallahatchie.

Holly Springs I selected for my dépôt of supplies and munitions of war, all of which at that time came by rail from Columbus, Kentucky, except the few stores collected about La Grange and Grand Junction. This was a long line (increasing in length as we moved south) to maintain in an enemy's country. On the 15th of November, while I was still at Holly Springs, I sent word to Sherman to meet me at Columbus. We were but forty-seven miles apart, yet the most expeditious way for us to meet was for me to take the rail to Columbus and Sherman a steamer for the same place. At that meeting, besides talking over my general plans I gave him his orders to join me with two divisions and to march them down the Mississippi Central railroad if he could. Sherman, who was always prompt, was up by the 29th to Cottage Hill, ten miles north of Oxford. He brought three divisions with him, leaving a garrison of only four regiments of infantry, a couple of pieces of artillery and a small detachment of cavalry. Further reinforcements he knew were on their way from the north to Memphis. About this time General Halleck ordered troops from Helena, Arkansas (territory west of the Mississippi was not under my command then) to cut the road in Pemberton's rear. The expedition was under Generals Hovey and C. C. Washburn and was successful so far as reaching the railroad was concerned, but the damage done was very slight and was soon repaired.

The Tallahatchie, which confronted me, was very high, the railroad bridge destroyed and Pemberton strongly fortified on the south side. A crossing would have been impossible in the presence of an enemy. I sent the cavalry higher up the stream and they secured a crossing. This caused the enemy to evacuate their position, which was possibly accelerated by the expedition of Hovey and Washburn. The enemy was followed as far south as Oxford by the main body of troops, and some seventeen miles farther by McPherson's command. Here the pursuit was halted to repair the railroad from the Tallahatchie northward, in order to bring up supplies. The piles on which the railroad bridge rested had been left standing. The work of constructing a roadway for the troops was but a short matter, and, later, rails were laid for cars.

During the delay at Oxford in repairing railroads I learned that an expedition down the Mississippi now was inevitable and, desiring to have a competent commander in charge, I ordered Sherman on the 8th of December back to Memphis to take charge. The following were his orders:

Headquarters 13th Army Corps, Department of the Tennessee.
OXFORD, MISSISSIPPI, *December* 8, 1862.
MAJOR-GENERAL W. T. SHERMAN,
    Commanding Right Wing:
You will proceed, with as little delay as possible, to Memphis, Tennessee, taking with you one division of your present command. On your arrival at Memphis you will assume command of all the troops there, and that portion of General Curtis's forces at present east of the Mississippi River, and organize them into brigades and divisions in your own army. As soon as possible move with them down the river to the vicinity of Vicksburg, and with the co-operation of the gunboat fleet under command of Flag-officer Porter proceed to the reduction of that place in such manner as circumstances, and your own judgment, may dictate.

The amount of rations, forage, land transportation, etc., necessary to take, will be left entirely with yourself. The Quartermaster at St. Louis will be instructed to send you transportation for 30,000 men; should you still find yourself deficient, your quartermaster will be authorized to make up the deficiency from such transports as may come into the port of Memphis.

On arriving in Memphis, put yourself in communication with Admiral Porter, and arrange with him for his co-operation.

Inform me at the earliest practicable day of the time when you will embark, and such plans as may then be matured. I will hold the forces here in readiness to co-operate with you in such manner as the movements of the enemy may make necessary.

Leave the District of Memphis in the command of an efficient officer, and with a garrison of four regiments of infantry, the siege guns, and whatever cavalry may be there.

U. S. GRANT,
Major-General.

This idea had presented itself to my mind earlier, for on the 3d of December I asked Halleck if it would not be well to hold the enemy south of the Yallabusha and move a force from Helena and Memphis on Vicksburg. On the 5th again I suggested, from Oxford, to Halleck that if the Helena troops were at my command I thought it would be possible to take them and the Memphis forces south of the mouth of the Yazoo River, and thus secure Vicksburg and the State of Mississippi. Halleck on the same day, the 5th of December, directed me not to attempt to hold the country south of the Tallahatchie, but to collect 25,000 troops at Memphis by the 20th for the Vicksburg expedition. I sent Sherman with two divisions at once, informed the general-in-chief of the fact, and asked whether I should command the expedition down the river myself or send Sherman. I was authorized to do as I thought best for the accomplishment of the great object in view. I sent Sherman and so informed General Halleck.

As stated, my action in sending Sherman back was expedited by a desire to get him in command of the forces separated from my direct supervision. I feared that delay might bring McClernand, who was his senior and who had authority from the President and Secretary of War to exercise that particular command,—and independently. I doubted McClernand's fitness; and I had good reason to believe that in forestalling him I was by no means giving offence to those whose authority to command was above both him and me.

Neither my orders to General Sherman, nor the correspondence between us or between General Halleck and myself, contemplated at the time my going further south than the Yallabusha. Pemberton's force in my front was the main part of the garrison of Vicksburg, as the force with me was the defence of the territory held by us in West Tennessee and Kentucky. I hoped to hold Pemberton in my front while Sherman should get in his rear and into Vicksburg. The further north the enemy could be held the better.

It was understood, however, between General Sherman and myself that our movements were to be co-operative; if Pemberton could not be held away from Vicksburg I was to follow him; but at that time it was not expected to abandon the railroad north of the Yallabusha. With that point as a secondary base of supplies, the possibility of moving down the Yazoo until communications could be opened with the Mississippi was contemplated.

It was my intention, and so understood by Sherman and his command, that if the enemy should fall back I would follow him even to the gates of Vicksburg. I intended in such an event to hold the road to Grenada on the Yallabusha and cut loose from there, expecting to establish a new base of supplies on the Yazoo, or at Vicksburg itself, with Grenada to fall back upon in case of failure. It should be remembered that at the time I speak of it had not been demonstrated that an army could operate in an enemy's territory depending upon the country for supplies. A halt was called at Oxford with the advance seventeen miles south of there, to bring up the road to the latter point and to bring supplies of food, forage and munitions to the front.

On the 18th of December I received orders from Washington to divide my command into four army corps, with General McClernand to command one of them and to be assigned to that part of the army which was to operate down the Mississippi. This interfered with my plans, but probably resulted in my ultimately taking the command in person. McClernand was at that time in Springfield, Illinois. The order was obeyed without any delay. Dispatches were sent to him the same day in conformity.

On the 20th General Van Dorn appeared at Holly Springs, my secondary base of supplies, captured the garrison of 1,500 men commanded by Colonel Murphy, of the 8th Wisconsin regiment, and destroyed all our munitions of war, food and forage. The capture was a disgraceful one to the officer commanding but not to the troops under him. At the same time Forrest got on our line of railroad between Jackson, Tennessee, and Columbus, Kentucky, doing much damage to it. This cut me off from all communication with the north for more than a week, and it was more than two weeks before rations or forage could be issued from stores obtained in the regular way. This demonstrated the impossibility of maintaining so long a line of road over which to draw supplies for an army moving in an enemy's country. I determined, therefore, to abandon my campaign into the interior with Columbus as a base, and returned to La Grange and Grand Junction destroying the road to my front and repairing the road to Memphis, making the Mississippi river the line over which to draw supplies. Pemberton was falling back at the same time.

The moment I received the news of Van Dorn's success I sent the cavalry at the front back to drive him from the country. He had start enough to move north destroying the railroad in many places, and to attack several small garrisons intrenched as guards to the railroad. All these he found warned of his coming and prepared to receive him. Van Dorn did not succeed in capturing a single garrison except the one at Holly Springs, which was larger than all the others attacked by him put together. Murphy was also warned of Van Dorn's approach, but made no preparations to meet him. He did not even notify his command.

Colonel Murphy was the officer who, two months before, had evacuated Iuka on the approach of the enemy. General Rosecrans denounced him for the act and desired to have him tried and punished. I sustained the colonel at the time because his command was a small one compared with that of the enemy—not one-tenth as large—and I thought he had done well to get away without falling into their hands. His leaving large stores to fall into Price's possession I looked upon as an oversight and excused it on the ground of inexperience in military matters. He should, however, have destroyed them. This last surrender demonstrated to my mind that Rosecrans' judgment of Murphy's conduct at Iuka was correct. The surrender of Holly Springs was most reprehensible and showed either the disloyalty of Colonel Murphy to the cause which he professed to serve, or gross cowardice.

After the war was over I read from the diary of a lady who accompanied General Pemberton in his retreat from the Tallahatchie, that the retreat was almost a panic. The roads were bad and it was difficult to move the artillery and trains. Why there should have been a panic I do not see. No expedition had yet started down the Mississippi River. Had I known the demoralized condition of the enemy, or the fact that central Mississippi abounded so in all army supplies, I would have been in pursuit of Pemberton while his cavalry was destroying the roads in my rear.

After sending cavalry to drive Van Dorn away, my next order was to dispatch all the wagons we had, under proper escort, to collect and bring in all supplies of forage and food from a region of fifteen miles east and west of the road from our front back to Grand Junction, leaving two months' supplies for the families of those whose stores were taken. I was amazed at the quantity of supplies the country afforded. It showed that we could have subsisted off the country for two months instead of two weeks without going beyond the limits designated. This taught me a lesson which was taken advantage of later in the campaign when our army lived twenty days with the issue of only five days' rations by the commissary. Our loss of supplies was great at Holly Springs, but it was more than compensated for by those taken from the country and by the lesson taught.

The news of the capture of Holly Springs and the destruction of our supplies caused much rejoicing among the people remaining in Oxford. They came with broad smiles on their faces, indicating intense joy, to ask what I was going to do now without anything for my soldiers to eat. I told them that I was not disturbed; that I had already sent troops and wagons to collect all the food and forage they could find for fifteen miles on each side of the road. Countenances soon changed, and so did the inquiry. The next was, "What are *we* to do?" My response was that we had endeavored to feed ourselves from our own northern resources while visiting them; but their friends in gray had been uncivil enough to destroy what we had brought along, and it could not be expected that men, with arms in their hands, would starve in the midst of plenty. I advised them to emigrate east, or west, fifteen miles and assist in eating up what we left.

Chapter XXXI.

HEADQUARTERS MOVED TO HOLLY SPRINGS—GENERAL
M'CLERNAND IN COMMAND—ASSUMING COMMAND
AT YOUNG'S POINT—OPERATIONS ABOVE
VICKSBURG—FORTIFICATIONS ABOUT VICKSBURG—
THE CANAL—LAKE PROVIDENCE—OPERATIONS
AT YAZOO PASS.

THIS INTERRUPTION in my communications north—I was really cut off from communication with a great part of my own command during this time—resulted in Sherman's moving from Memphis before McClernand could arrive, for my dispatch of the 18th did not reach McClernand. Pemberton got back to Vicksburg before Sherman got there. The rebel positions were on a bluff on the Yazoo River, some miles above its mouth. The waters were high so that the bottoms were generally overflowed, leaving only narrow causeways of dry land between points of debarkation and the high bluffs. These were fortified and defended at all points. The rebel position was impregnable against any force that could be brought against its front. Sherman could not use one-fourth of his force. His efforts to capture the city, or the high ground north of it, were necessarily unavailing.

Sherman's attack was very unfortunate, but I had no opportunity of communicating with him after the destruction of the road and telegraph to my rear on the 20th. He did not know but what I was in the rear of the enemy and depending on him to open a new base of supplies for the troops with me. I had, before he started from Memphis, directed him to take with him a few small steamers suitable for the navigation of the Yazoo, not knowing but that I might want them to supply me after cutting loose from my base at Grenada.

On the 23d I removed my headquarters back to Holly Springs. The troops were drawn back gradually, but without haste or confusion, finding supplies abundant and no enemy following. The road was not damaged south of Holly Springs by Van Dorn, at least not to an extent to cause any delay. As I had resolved to move headquarters to Memphis, and to repair the road to that point, I remained at Holly Springs until this work was completed.

On the 10th of January, the work on the road from Holly Springs to Grand Junction and thence to Memphis being completed, I moved my headquarters to the latter place. During the campaign here described, the losses (mostly captures) were about equal, crediting the rebels with their Holly Springs capture, which they could not hold.

When Sherman started on his expedition down the river he had 20,000 men, taken from Memphis, and was reinforced by 12,000 more at Helena, Arkansas. The troops on the west bank of the river had previously been assigned to my command. McClernand having received the orders for his assignment reached the mouth of the Yazoo on the 2d of January, and immediately assumed command of all the troops with Sherman, being a part of his own corps, the 13th, and all of Sherman's, the 15th. Sherman, and Admiral Porter with the fleet, had withdrawn from the Yazoo. After consultation they decided that neither the army nor navy could render service to the cause where they were, and learning that I had withdrawn from the interior of Mississippi, they determined to return to the Arkansas River and to attack Arkansas Post, about fifty miles up that stream and garrisoned by about five or six thousand men. Sherman had learned of the existence of this force through a man who had been captured by the enemy with a steamer loaded with ammunition and other supplies intended for his command. The man had made his escape. McClernand approved this move reluctantly, as Sherman says. No obstacle was encountered until the gunboats and transports were within range of the fort. After three days' bombardment by the navy an assault was made by the troops and marines, resulting in the capture of the place, and in taking 5,000 prisoners and 17 guns. I was at first disposed to disapprove of this move as an unnecessary side movement having no especial bearing upon the work before us; but when the result was understood I regarded it as very important. Five thousand Confederate troops left in the rear might have caused us much trouble and loss of property while navigating the Mississippi.

Immediately after the reduction of Arkansas Post and the capture of the garrison, McClernand returned with his entire force to Napoleon, at the mouth of the Arkansas River. From here I received messages from both Sherman and Admiral Porter, urging me to come and take command in person, and expressing their distrust of McClernand's ability and fitness for so important and intricate an expedition.

On the 17th I visited McClernand and his command at Napoleon. It was here made evident to me that both the army and navy were so distrustful of McClernand's fitness to command that, while they would do all they could to insure success, this distrust was an element of weakness. It would have been criminal to send troops under these circumstances into such danger. By this time I had received authority to relieve McClernand, or to assign any person else to the command of the river expedition, or to assume command in person. I felt great embarrassment about McClernand. He was the senior major-general after myself within the department. It would not do, with his rank and ambition, to assign a junior over him. Nothing was left, therefore, but to assume the command myself. I would have been glad to put Sherman in command, to give him an opportunity to accomplish what he had failed in the December before; but there seemed no other way out of the difficulty, for he was junior to McClernand. Sherman's failure needs no apology.

On the 20th I ordered General McClernand with the entire command, to Young's Point and Milliken's Bend, while I returned to Memphis to make all the necessary preparation for leaving the territory behind me secure. General Hurlbut with the 16th corps was left in command. The Memphis and Charleston railroad was held, while the Mississippi Central was given up. Columbus was the only point between Cairo and Memphis, on the river, left with a garrison. All the troops and guns from the posts on the abandoned railroad and river were sent to the front.

On the 29th of January I arrived at Young's Point and assumed command the following day. General McClernand took exception in a most characteristic way—for him. His correspondence with me on the subject was more in the nature of a reprimand than a protest. It was highly insubordinate, but I overlooked it, as I believed, for the good of the service. General McClernand was a politician of very considerable prominence in his State; he was a member of Congress when the secession war broke out; he belonged to that political party which furnished all the opposition there was to a vigorous prosecution of the war for saving the Union; there was no delay in his declaring himself for the Union at all hazards, and there was no uncertain sound in his declaration of where he stood in the contest before the country. He also gave up his seat in Congress to take the field in defence of the principles he had proclaimed.

The real work of the campaign and siege of Vicksburg now began. The problem was to secure a footing upon dry ground on the east side of the river from which the troops could operate against Vicksburg. The Mississippi River, from Cairo south, runs through a rich alluvial valley of many miles in width, bound on the east by land running from eighty up to two or more hundred feet above the river. On the west side the highest land, except in a few places, is but little above the highest water. Through this valley the river meanders in the most tortuous way, varying in direction to all points of the compass. At places it runs to the very foot of the bluffs. After leaving Memphis, there are no such highlands coming to the water's edge on the east shore until Vicksburg is reached.

The intervening land is cut up by bayous filled from the river in high water—many of them navigable for steamers. All of them would be, except for overhanging trees, narrowness and tortuous course, making it impossible to turn the bends with vessels of any considerable length. Marching across this country in the face of an enemy was impossible; navigating it proved equally impracticable. The strategical way according to the rule, therefore, would have been to go back to Memphis; establish that as a base of supplies; fortify it so that the storehouses could be held by a small garrison, and move from there along the line of railroad, repairing as we advanced, to the Yallabusha, or to Jackson, Mississippi. At this time the North had become very much discouraged. Many strong Union men believed that the war must prove a failure. The elections of 1862 had gone against the party which was for the prosecution of the war to save the Union if it took the last man and the last dollar. Voluntary enlistments had ceased throughout the greater part of the North, and the draft had been resorted to to fill up our ranks. It was my judgment at the time that to make a backward movement as long as that from Vicksburg to Memphis, would be interpreted, by many of those yet full of hope for the preservation of the Union, as a defeat, and that the draft would be resisted, desertions ensue and the power to capture and punish deserters lost. There was nothing left to be done but to *go forward to a decisive victory.* This was in my mind from the moment I took command in person at Young's Point.

The winter of 1862–3 was a noted one for continuous high water in the Mississippi and for heavy rains along the lower river. To get dry land, or rather land above the water, to encamp the troops upon, took many miles of river front. We had to occupy the levees and the ground immediately behind. This was so limited that one corps, the 17th, under General McPherson, was at Lake Providence, seventy miles above Vicksburg.

It was in January the troops took their position opposite Vicksburg. The water was very high and the rains were incessant. There seemed no possibility of a land movement before the end of March or later, and it would not do to lie idle all this time. The effect would be demoralizing to the troops and injurious to their health. Friends in the North would have grown more and more discouraged, and enemies in the same section more and more insolent in their gibes and denunciation of the cause and those engaged in it.

I always admired the South, as bad as I thought their cause, for the boldness with which they silenced all opposition and all croaking, by press or by individuals, within their control. War at all times, whether a civil war between sections of a common country or between nations, ought to be avoided, if possible with honor. But, once entered into, it is too much for human nature to tolerate an enemy within their ranks to give aid and comfort to the armies of the opposing section or nation.

Vicksburg, as stated before, is on the first high land coming to the river's edge, below that on which Memphis stands. The bluff, or high land, follows the left bank of the Yazoo for some distance and continues in a southerly direction to the Mississippi River, thence it runs along the Mississippi to

Warrenton, six miles below. The Yazoo River leaves the high land a short distance below Haines' Bluff and empties into the Mississippi nine miles above Vicksburg. Vicksburg is built on this high land where the Mississippi washes the base of the hill. Haines' Bluff, eleven miles from Vicksburg, on the Yazoo River, was strongly fortified. The whole distance from there to Vicksburg and thence to Warrenton was also intrenched, with batteries at suitable distances and rifle-pits connecting them.

From Young's Point the Mississippi turns in a north-easterly direction to a point just above the city, when it again turns and runs south-westerly, leaving vessels, which might attempt to run the blockade, exposed to the fire of batteries six miles below the city before they were in range of the upper batteries. Since then the river has made a cut-off, leaving what was the peninsula in front of the city, an island. North of the Yazoo was all a marsh, heavily timbered, cut up with bayous, and much overflowed. A front attack was therefore impossible, and was never contemplated; certainly not by me. The problem then became, how to secure a landing on high ground east of the Mississippi without an apparent retreat. Then commenced a series of experiments to consume time, and to divert the attention of the enemy, of my troops and of the public generally. I, myself, never felt great confidence that any of the experiments resorted to would prove successful. Nevertheless I was always prepared to take advantage of them in case they did.

In 1862 General Thomas Williams had come up from New Orleans and cut a ditch ten or twelve feet wide and about as deep, straight across from Young's Point to the river below. The distance across was a little over a mile. It was Williams' expectation that when the river rose it would cut a navigable channel through; but the canal started in an eddy from both ends, and, of course, it only filled up with water on the rise without doing any execution in the way of cutting. Mr. Lincoln had navigated the Mississippi in his younger days and understood well its tendency to change its channel, in places, from time to time. He set much store accordingly by this canal. General McClernand had been, therefore, directed before I went to Young's Point to push the work of widening and deepening this canal. After my arrival the work was diligently pushed with about 4,000 men—as many as could be used to advantage—until interrupted by a sudden rise in the river that broke a dam at the upper end, which had been put there to keep the water out until the excavation was completed. This was on the 8th of March.

Even if the canal had proven a success, so far as to be navigable for steamers, it could not have been of much advantage to us. It runs in a direction almost perpendicular to the line of bluffs on the opposite side, or east bank, of the river. As soon as the enemy discovered what we were doing he established a battery commanding the canal throughout its length. This battery soon drove out our dredges, two in number, which were doing the work of thousands of men. Had the canal been completed it might have proven of some use in running transports through, under the cover of night, to use below; but they would yet have to run batteries, though for a much shorter distance.

While this work was progressing we were busy in other directions, trying to find an available landing on high ground on the east bank of the river, or to make water-ways to get below the city, avoiding the batteries.

On the 30th of January, the day after my arrival at the front, I ordered General McPherson, stationed with his corps at Lake Providence, to cut the levee at that point. If successful in opening a channel for navigation by this route, it would carry us to the Mississippi River through the mouth of the Red River, just above Port Hudson and four hundred miles below Vicksburg by the river.

Lake Providence is a part of the old bed of the Mississippi, about a mile from the present channel. It is six miles long and has its outlet through Bayou Baxter, Bayou Macon, and the Tensas, Washita and Red Rivers. The last three are navigable streams at all seasons. Bayous Baxter and Macon are narrow and tortuous, and the banks are covered with dense forests overhanging the channel. They were also filled with fallen timber, the accumulation of years. The land along the Mississippi River, from Memphis down, is in all instances highest next to the river, except where the river washes the bluffs which form the boundary of the valley through which it winds. Bayou Baxter, as it reaches lower land, begins to spread out and disappears entirely in a cypress swamp before it reaches the Macon. There was about two feet of water in this swamp at the time. To get through it, even with vessels of the lightest draft, it was necessary to clear off a belt of heavy timber wide enough to make a passage way. As the trees would have to be cut close to the bottom—under water—it was an undertaking of great magnitude.

On the 4th of February I visited General McPherson, and remained with him several days. The work had not progressed so far as to admit the water from the river into the lake, but the troops had succeeded in drawing a small steamer, of probably not over thirty tons' capacity, from the river into the lake. With this we were able to explore the lake and bayou as far as cleared. I saw then that there was scarcely a chance of this ever becoming a practicable route for moving troops through an enemy's country. The distance from Lake Providence to the point where vessels going by that route would enter the Mississippi again, is about four hundred and seventy miles by the main river. The distance would probably be greater by the tortuous bayous through which this new route would carry us. The enemy held Port Hudson, below where the Red River debouches, and all the Mississippi above to Vicksburg. The Red River, Washita and Tensas were, as has been said, all navigable streams, on which the enemy could throw small bodies of men to obstruct our passage and pick off our troops with their sharpshooters. I let the work go on, believing employment was better than idleness for the men. Then, too, it served as a cover for other efforts which gave a better prospect of success. This work was abandoned after the canal proved a failure.

Lieutenant-Colonel Wilson of my staff was sent to Helena, Arkansas, to examine and open a way through Moon Lake and the Yazoo Pass if possible. Formerly there was a route by way of an inlet from the Mississippi River into Moon Lake, a mile east of the river, thence east through Yazoo Pass to Cold-water, along the latter to the Tallahatchie, which joins the Yallabusha about two hundred and fifty miles below Moon Lake and forms the Yazoo River. These were formerly navigated by steamers trading with the rich plantations along their banks; but the State of Mississippi had built a strong levee across the inlet some years before, leaving the only entrance for vessels into this rich region the one by way of the mouth of the Yazoo several hundreds of miles below.

On the 2d of February this dam, or levee, was cut. The river being high the rush of water through the cut was so great that in a very short time the entire obstruction was washed away. The bayous were soon filled and much of the country was overflowed. This pass leaves the Mississippi River but a few miles below Helena. On the 24th General Ross, with his brigade of about 4,500 men on transports, moved into this new water-way. The rebels had obstructed the navigation of Yazoo Pass and the Coldwater by felling trees into them. Much of the timber in this region being of greater specific gravity than water, and being of great size, their removal was a matter of great labor; but it was finally accomplished, and on the 11th of March Ross found himself, accompanied by two gunboats under the command of Lieutenant-Commander Watson Smith, confronting a fortification at Greenwood, where the Tallahatchie and Yallabusha unite and the Yazoo begins. The bends of the rivers are such at this point as to almost form an island, scarcely above water at that stage of the river. This island was fortified and manned. It was named Fort Pemberton after the commander at Vicksburg. No land approach was accessible. The troops, therefore, could render no assistance towards an assault further than to establish a battery on a little piece of ground which was discovered above water. The gunboats, however, attacked on the 11th and again on the 13th of March. Both efforts were failures and were not renewed. One gunboat was disabled and we lost six men killed and twenty-five wounded. The loss of the enemy was less.

Fort Pemberton was so little above the water that it was thought that a rise of two feet would drive the enemy out. In hope of enlisting the elements on our side, which had been so much against us up to this time, a second cut was made in the Mississippi levee, this time directly opposite Helena, or six miles above the former cut. It did not accomplish the desired result, and Ross, with his fleet, started back. On the 22d he met Quinby with a brigade at Yazoo Pass. Quinby was the senior of Ross, and assumed command. He was not satisfied with returning to his former position without seeing for himself whether anything could be accomplished. Accordingly Fort Pemberton was revisited by our troops; but an inspection was sufficient this time without an attack. Quinby, with his command, returned with but little delay. In the meantime I was much exercised for the safety of Ross, not knowing that Quinby had been able to join him. Reinforcements were of no use in a country covered with water, as they would have to remain on board of their transports. Relief had to come from another quarter. So I determined to get into the Yazoo below Fort Pemberton.

Steel's Bayou empties into the Yazoo River between Haines' Bluff and its mouth. It is narrow, very tortuous, and fringed with a very heavy growth of timber, but it is deep. It approaches to within one mile of the Mississippi at Eagle Bend, thirty miles above Young's Point. Steel's Bayou connects with Black Bayou, Black Bayou with Deer Creek, Deer Creek with Rolling Fork, Rolling Fork with the Big Sunflower River, and the Big Sunflower with the Yazoo River about ten miles above Haines' Bluff in a right line but probably twenty or twenty-five miles by the winding of the river. All these waterways are of about the same nature so far as navigation is concerned, until the Sunflower is reached; this affords free navigation.

Admiral Porter explored this waterway as far as Deer Creek on the 14th of March, and reported it navigable. On the next day he started with five gunboats and four mortar-boats. I went with him for some distance. The heavy, overhanging timber retarded progress very much, as did also the short turns in so narrow a stream. The gunboats, however, ploughed their way through without other damage than to their appearance. The transports did not fare so well although they followed behind. The road was somewhat cleared for them by the gunboats. In the evening I returned to headquarters to hurry up reinforcements. Sherman went in person on the 16th, taking with him Stuart's division of the 15th corps. They took large river transports to Eagle Bend on the Mississippi, where they debarked and marched across to Steel's Bayou, where they re-embarked on the transports. The river steamers, with their tall smoke-stacks and light guards extending out, were so much impeded that the gunboats got far ahead. Porter, with his fleet, got within a few hundred yards of where the sailing would have been clear and free from the obstructions caused by felling trees into the water, when he encountered rebel sharp-shooters, and his progress was delayed by obstructions in his front. He could do nothing with gunboats against sharp-shooters. The rebels, learning his route, had sent in about 4,000 men—many more than there were sailors in the fleet.

Sherman went back, at the request of the admiral, to clear out Black Bayou and to hurry up reinforcements, which were far behind. On the night of the 19th he received notice from the admiral that he had been attacked by sharp-shooters and was in imminent peril. Sherman at once returned through Black Bayou in a canoe, and passed on until he met a steamer, with the last of the reinforcements he had, coming up. They tried to force their way through Black Bayou with their steamer, but, finding it slow and tedious work, debarked and pushed forward on foot. It was night when they landed, and intensely dark. There was but a narrow strip of land above water, and that was grown up with underbrush or cane. The troops lighted their way through this with candles carried in their hands for a mile and a half, when they came to an open plantation. Here the troops rested until morning. They made twenty-one miles from this resting-place by noon the next day, and were in time to rescue the fleet. Porter had fully made up his mind to blow up the gunboats rather than have them fall into the hands of the enemy. More welcome visitors he probably never met than the "boys in blue" on this occasion. The vessels were backed out and returned to their rendezvous on the Mississippi; and thus ended in failure the fourth attempt to get in rear of Vicksburg.

Chapter XXXII.

THE BAYOUS WEST OF THE MISSISSIPPI—CRITICISMS OF
THE NORTHERN PRESS—RUNNING THE BATTERIES—LOSS
OF THE INDIANOLA—DISPOSITION OF THE TROOPS.

THE ORIGINAL canal scheme was also abandoned on the 27th of March. The effort to make a waterway through Lake Providence and the connecting bayous was abandoned as wholly impracticable about the same time.

At Milliken's Bend, and also at Young's Point, bayous or channels start, which, connecting with other bayous passing Richmond, Louisiana, enter the Mississippi at Carthage twenty-five or thirty miles above Grand Gulf. The Mississippi levee cuts the supply of water off from these bayous or channels, but all the rainfall behind the levee, at these points, is carried through these same channels to the river below. In case of a crevasse in this vicinity, the water escaping would find its outlet through the same channels. The dredges and laborers from the canal having been driven out by overflow and the enemy's batteries, I determined to open these other channels, if possible. If successful the effort would afford a route, away from the enemy's batteries, for our transports. There was a good road back of the levees, along these bayous, to carry the troops, artillery and wagon trains over whenever the water receded a little, and after a few days of dry weather. Accordingly, with the abandonment of all the other plans for reaching a base heretofore described, this new one was undertaken.

As early as the 4th of February I had written to Halleck about this route, stating that I thought it much more practicable than the other undertaking (the Lake Providence route), and that it would have been accomplished with much less labor if commenced before the water had got all over the country.

The upper end of these bayous being cut off from a water supply, further than the rainfall back of the levees, was grown up with dense timber for a distance of several miles from their source. It was necessary, therefore, to clear this out before letting in the water from the river. This work was continued until the waters of the river began to recede and the road to Richmond, Louisiana, emerged from the water. One small steamer and some barges were got through this channel, but no further use could be made of it because of the fall in the river. Beyond this it was no more successful than the other experiments with which the winter was whiled away. All these failures would have been very discouraging if I had expected much from the efforts; but I had not. From the first the most I hoped to accomplish was the passage of transports, to be used below Vicksburg, without exposure to the long line of batteries defending that city.

This long, dreary and, for heavy and continuous rains and high water, unprecedented winter was one of great hardship to all engaged about Vicksburg. The river was higher than its natural banks from December, 1862, to the following April. The war had suspended peaceful pursuits in the South, further than the production of army supplies, and in consequence the levees were neglected and broken in many places and the whole country was covered with water. Troops could scarcely find dry ground on which to pitch their tents. Malarial fevers broke out among the men. Measles and small-pox also attacked them. The hospital arrangements and medical attendance were so perfect, however, that the loss of life was much less than might have been expected. Visitors to the camps went home with dismal stories to relate; Northern papers came back to the soldiers with these stories exaggerated. Because I would not divulge my ultimate plans to visitors, they pronounced me idle, incompetent and unfit to command men in an emergency, and clamored for my removal. They were not to be satisfied, many of them, with my simple removal, but named who my successor should be. McClernand, Fremont, Hunter and McClellan were all mentioned in this connection. I took no steps to answer these complaints, but continued to do my duty, as I understood it, to the best of my ability. Every one has his superstitions. One of mine is that in positions of great responsibility every one should do his duty to the best of his ability where assigned by competent authority, without application or the use of influence to change his position. While at Cairo I had watched with very great interest the operations of the Army of the Potomac, looking upon that as the main field of the war. I had no idea, myself, of ever having any large command, nor did I suppose that I was equal to one; but I had the vanity to think that as a cavalry officer I might succeed very well in the command of a brigade. On one occasion, in talking about this to my staff officers, all of whom were civilians without any military education whatever, I said that I would give anything if I were commanding a brigade of cavalry in the Army of the Potomac and I believed I could do some good. Captain Hillyer spoke up and suggested that I make application to be transferred there to command the cavalry. I then told him that I would cut my right arm off first, and mentioned this superstition.

In time of war the President, being by the Constitution Commander-in-chief of the Army and Navy, is responsible for the selection of commanders. He should not be embarrassed in making his selections. I having been selected, my responsibility ended with my doing the best I knew how. If I had sought the place, or obtained it through personal or political influence, my belief is that I would have feared to undertake any plan of my own conception, and would probably have awaited direct orders from my distant superiors. Persons obtaining important commands by application or political influence are apt to keep a written record of complaints and predictions of defeat, which are shown in case of disaster. Somebody must be responsible for their failures.

With all the pressure brought to bear upon them, both President Lincoln and General Halleck stood by me to the end of the campaign. I had never met Mr. Lincoln, but his support was constant.

At last the waters began to recede; the roads crossing the peninsula behind the levees of the bayous, were emerging from the waters; the troops were all concentrated from distant points at Milliken's Bend preparatory to a final move which was to crown the long, tedious and discouraging labors with success.

I had had in contemplation the whole winter the movement by land to a point below Vicksburg from which to operate, subject only to the possible but not expected success of some one of the expedients resorted to for the purpose of giving us a different base. This could not be undertaken until the waters receded. I did not therefore communicate this plan, even to an officer of my staff, until it was necessary to make preparations for the start. My recollection is that Admiral Porter was the first one to whom I mentioned it. The co-operation of the navy was absolutely essential to the success (even to the contemplation) of such an enterprise. I had no more authority to command Porter than he had to command me. It was necessary to have part of his fleet below Vicksburg if the troops went there. Steamers to use as ferries were also essential. The navy was the only escort and protection for these steamers, all of which in getting below had to run about fourteen miles of batteries. Porter fell into the plan at once, and suggested that he had better superintend the preparation of the steamers selected to run the batteries, as sailors would probably understand the work better than soldiers. I was glad to accept his proposition, not only because I admitted his argument, but because it would enable me to keep from the enemy a little longer our designs. Porter's fleet was on the east side of the river above the mouth of the Yazoo, entirely concealed from the enemy by the dense forests that intervened. Even spies could not get near him, on account of the undergrowth and overflowed lands. Suspicions of some mysterious movements were aroused. Our river guards discovered one day a small skiff moving quietly and mysteriously up the river near the east shore, from the direction of Vicksburg, towards the fleet. On overhauling the boat they found a small white flag, not much larger than a handkerchief, set up in the stern, no doubt intended as a flag of truce in case of discovery. The boat, crew and passengers were brought ashore to me. The chief personage aboard proved to be Jacob Thompson, Secretary of the Interior under the administration of President Buchanan. After a pleasant conversation of half an hour or more I allowed the boat and crew, passengers and all, to return to Vicksburg, without creating a suspicion that there was a doubt in my mind as to the good faith of Mr. Thompson and his flag.

Admiral Porter proceeded with the preparation of the steamers for their hazardous passage of the enemy's batteries.

The great essential was to protect the boilers from the ene-my's shot, and to conceal the fires under the boilers from view. This he accomplished by loading the steamers, between the guards and boilers on the boiler deck up to the deck above, with bales of hay and cotton, and the deck in front of the boilers in the same way, adding sacks of grain. The hay and grain would be wanted below, and could not be trans-ported in sufficient quantity by the muddy roads over which we expected to march.

Before this I had been collecting, from St. Louis and Chi-cago, yawls and barges to be used as ferries when we got below. By the 16th of April Porter was ready to start on his perilous trip. The advance, flagship *Benton*, Porter command-ing, started at ten o'clock at night, followed at intervals of a few minutes by the *Lafayette* with a captured steamer, the *Price*, lashed to her side, the *Louisville, Mound City, Pittsburgh* and *Carondelet*—all of these being naval vessels. Next came the transports—*Forest Queen, Silver Wave* and *Henry Clay*, each towing barges loaded with coal to be used as fuel by the naval and transport steamers when below the batteries. The gunboat *Tuscumbia* brought up the rear. Soon after the start a battery between Vicksburg and Warrenton opened fire across the intervening peninsula, followed by the upper batteries, and then by batteries all along the line. The gunboats ran up close under the bluffs, delivering their fire in return at short distances, probably without much effect. They were under fire for more than two hours and every vessel was struck many times, but with little damage to the gunboats. The transports did not fare so well. The *Henry Clay* was disabled and de-serted by her crew. Soon after a shell burst in the cotton packed about the boilers, set the vessel on fire and burned her to the water's edge. The burning mass, however, floated down to Carthage before grounding, as did also one of the barges in tow.

The enemy were evidently expecting our fleet, for they were ready to light up the river by means of bonfires on the east side and by firing houses on the point of land opposite the city on the Louisiana side. The sight was magnificent, but terrible. I witnessed it from the deck of a river transport, run out into the middle of the river and as low down as it was prudent to go. My mind was much relieved when I learned that no one on the transports had been killed and but few, if any, wounded. During the running of the batteries men were stationed in the holds of the transports to partially stop with cotton shot-holes that might be made in the hulls. All damage was afterwards soon repaired under the direction of Admiral Porter.

The experiment of passing batteries had been tried before this, however, during the war. Admiral Farragut had run the batteries at Port Hudson with the flagship *Hartford* and one iron-clad and visited me from below Vicksburg. The 13th of February Admiral Porter had sent the gunboat *Indianola*, Lieutenant-Commander George Brown commanding, below. She met Colonel Ellet of the Marine brigade below Natchez on a captured steamer. Two of the Colonel's fleet had previously run the batteries, producing the greatest consternation among the people along the Mississippi from Vicksburg* to the Red River.

The *Indianola* remained about the mouth of the Red River some days, and then started up the Mississippi. The Confederates soon raised the *Queen of the West*,† and repaired her. With this vessel and the ram *Webb*, which they had had for some time in the Red River, and two other steamers, they followed the *Indianola*. The latter was encumbered with barges of coal in tow, and consequently could make but little speed against the rapid current of the Mississippi. The Confederate fleet overtook her just above Grand Gulf, and attacked her after dark on the 24th of February. The *Indianola* was superior to all the others in armament, and probably would have destroyed them or driven them away, but for her encumbrance. As it was she fought them for an hour

---

*Colonel Ellet reported having attacked a Confederate battery on the Red River two days before with one of his boats, the *De Soto*. Running aground, he was obliged to abandon his vessel. However, he reported that he set fire to her and blew her up. Twenty of his men fell into the hands of the enemy. With the balance he escaped on the small captured steamer, the *New Era*, and succeeded in passing the batteries at Grand Gulf and reaching the vicinity of Vicksburg.

†One of Colonel Ellet's vessels which had run the blockade on February the 2d and been sunk in the Red River.

and a half, but, in the dark, was struck seven or eight times by the ram and other vessels, and was finally disabled and reduced to a sinking condition. The armament was thrown overboard and the vessel run ashore. Officers and crew then surrendered.

I had started McClernand with his corps of four divisions on the 29th of March, by way of Richmond, Louisiana, to New Carthage, hoping that he might capture Grand Gulf before the balance of the troops could get there; but the roads were very bad, scarcely above water yet. Some miles from New Carthage the levee to Bayou Vidal was broken in several places, overflowing the roads for the distance of two miles. Boats were collected from the surrounding bayous, and some constructed on the spot from such material as could be collected, to transport the troops across the overflowed interval. By the 6th of April McClernand had reached New Carthage with one division and its artillery, the latter ferried through the woods by these boats. On the 17th I visited New Carthage in person, and saw that the process of getting troops through in the way we were doing was so tedious that a better method must be devised. The water was falling, and in a few days there would not be depth enough to use boats; nor would the land be dry enough to march over. McClernand had already found a new route from Smith's plantation where the crevasse occurred, to Perkins' plantation, eight to twelve miles below New Carthage. This increased the march from Milliken's Bend from twenty-seven to nearly forty miles. Four bridges had to be built across bayous, two of them each over six hundred feet long, making about two thousand feet of bridging in all. The river falling made the current in these bayous very rapid, increasing the difficulty of building and permanently fastening these bridges; but the ingenuity of the "Yankee soldier" was equal to any emergency. The bridges were soon built of such material as could be found near by, and so substantial were they that not a single mishap occurred in crossing all the army with artillery, cavalry and wagon trains, except the loss of one siege gun (a thirty-two pounder). This, if my memory serves me correctly, broke through the only pontoon bridge we had in all our march across the peninsula. These bridges were all built by McClernand's command, under the supervision of Lieutenant Hains of the Engineer Corps.

I returned to Milliken's Bend on the 18th or 19th, and on the 20th issued the following final order for the movement of troops:

HEADQUARTERS DEPARTMENT OF THE TENNESSEE,
MILLIKEN'S BEND, LOUISIANA,
April 20, 1863.

Special Orders, No. 110.

*   *   *   *   *   *   *

VIII. The following orders are published for the information and guidance of the "Army in the Field," in its present movement to obtain a foothold on the east bank of the Mississippi River, from which Vicksburg can be approached by practicable roads.

First.—The Thirteenth army corps, Major-General John A. McClernand commanding, will constitute the right wing.

Second.—The Fifteenth army corps, Major-General W. T. Sherman commanding, will constitute the left wing.

Third.—The Seventeenth army corps, Major-General James B. McPherson commanding, will constitute the centre.

Fourth.—The order of march to New Carthage will be from right to left.

Fifth.—Reserves will be formed by divisions from each army corps; or, an entire army corps will be held as a reserve, as necessity may require. When the reserve is formed by divisions, each division will remain under the immediate command of its respective corps commander, unless otherwise specially ordered for a particular emergency.

Sixth.—Troops will be required to bivouac, until proper facilities can be afforded for the transportation of camp equipage.

Seventh.—In the present movement, one tent will be allowed to each company for the protection of rations from rain; one wall tent for each regimental headquarters; one wall tent for each brigade headquarters; and one wall tent for each division headquarters; corps commanders having the books and blanks of their respective commands to provide for, are authorized to take such tents as are absolutely necessary, but not to exceed the number allowed by General Orders No. 160, A. G. O., series of 1862.

Eighth.—All the teams of the three army corps, under the immediate charge of the quartermasters bearing them on their returns, will constitute a train for carrying supplies and ordnance and the authorized camp equipage of the army.

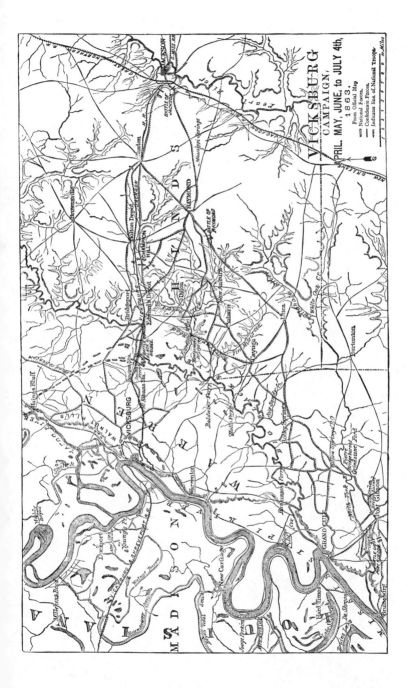

VICKSBURG
CAMPAIGN,
APRIL, MAY, JUNE, to JULY 4th,
1863.
From Official Map.
══ National Forces.
━━ Confederate Forces.
┅┅ Indicate line of National Troops
1 2 3 4 5 6 7 8 9 10 Miles

Ninth. — As fast as the Thirteenth army corps advances, the Seventeenth army corps will take its place; and it, in turn, will be followed in like manner by the Fifteenth army corps.

Tenth. — Two regiments from each army corps will be detailed by corps commanders, to guard the lines from Richmond to New Carthage.

Eleventh. — General hospitals will be established by the medical director, between Duckport and Milliken's Bend. All sick and disabled soldiers will be left in these hospitals. Surgeons in charge of hospitals will report convalescents as fast as they become fit for duty. Each corps commander will detail an intelligent and good drill officer, to remain behind and take charge of the convalescents of their respective corps; officers so detailed will organize the men under their charge into squads and companies, without regard to the regiments they belong to; and in the absence of convalescent commissioned officers to command them, will appoint non-commissioned officers or privates. The force so organized will constitute the guard of the line from Duckport to Milliken's Bend. They will furnish all the guards and details required for general hospitals, and with the contrabands that may be about the camps, will furnish all the details for loading and unloading boats.

Twelfth. — The movement of troops from Milliken's Bend to New Carthage will be so conducted as to allow the transportation of ten days' supply of rations, and one-half the allowance of ordnance, required by previous orders.

Thirteenth. — Commanders are authorized and enjoined to collect all the beef cattle, corn and other necessary supplies on the line of march; but wanton destruction of property, taking of articles useless for military purposes, insulting citizens, going into and searching houses without proper orders from division commanders, are positively prohibited. All such irregularities must be summarily punished.

Fourteenth. — Brigadier-General J. C. Sullivan is appointed to the command of all the forces detailed for the protection of the line from here to New Carthage. His particular attention is called to General Orders, No. 69, from Adjutant-General's Office, Washington, of date March 20, 1863.

By order of
MAJOR-GENERAL U. S. GRANT.

McClernand was already below on the Mississippi. Two of McPherson's divisions were put upon the march immediately. The third had not yet arrived from Lake Providence; it was on its way to Milliken's Bend and was to follow on arrival.

Sherman was to follow McPherson. Two of his divisions were at Duckport and Young's Point, and the third under Steele was under orders to return from Greenville, Mississippi, where it had been sent to expel a rebel battery that had been annoying our transports.

It had now become evident that the army could not be rationed by a wagon train over the single narrow and almost impassable road between Milliken's Bend and Perkins' plantation. Accordingly six more steamers were protected as before, to run the batteries, and were loaded with supplies. They took twelve barges in tow, loaded also with rations. On the night of the 22d of April they ran the batteries, five getting through more or less disabled while one was sunk. About half the barges got through with their needed freight.

When it was first proposed to run the blockade at Vicksburg with river steamers there were but two captains or masters who were willing to accompany their vessels, and but one crew. Volunteers were called for from the army, men who had had experience in any capacity in navigating the western rivers. Captains, pilots, mates, engineers and deck-hands enough presented themselves to take five times the number of vessels we were moving through this dangerous ordeal. Most of them were from Logan's division, composed generally of men from the southern part of Illinois and from Missouri. All but two of the steamers were commanded by volunteers from the army, and all but one so manned. In this instance, as in all others during the war, I found that volunteers could be found in the ranks and among the commissioned officers to meet every call for aid whether mechanical or professional. Colonel W. S. Oliver was master of transportation on this occasion by special detail.

Chapter XXXIII.

ATTACK ON GRAND GULF — OPERATIONS BELOW
VICKSBURG.

O N THE 24TH my headquarters were with the advance at Perkins' plantation. Reconnoissances were made in boats to ascertain whether there was high land on the east shore of the river where we might land above Grand Gulf. There was none practicable. Accordingly the troops were set in motion for Hard Times, twenty-two miles farther down the river and nearly opposite Grand Gulf. The loss of two steamers and six barges reduced our transportation so that only 10,000 men could be moved by water. Some of the steamers that had got below were injured in their machinery, so that they were only useful as barges towed by those less severely injured. All the troops, therefore, except what could be transported in one trip, had to march. The road lay west of Lake St. Joseph. Three large bayous had to be crossed. They were rapidly bridged in the same manner as those previously encountered.

On the 27th McClernand's corps was all at Hard Times, and McPherson's was following closely. I had determined to make the attempt to effect a landing on the east side of the river as soon as possible. Accordingly, on the morning of the 29th, McClernand was directed to embark all the troops from his corps that our transports and barges could carry. About 10,000 men were so embarked. The plan was to have the navy silence the guns at Grand Gulf, and to have as many men as possible ready to debark in the shortest possible time under cover of the fire of the navy and carry the works by storm. The following order was issued:

NOTE. — On this occasion Governor Richard Yates, of Illinois, happened to be on a visit to the army, and accompanied me to Carthage. I furnished an ambulance for his use and that of some of the State officers who accompanied him.

PERKINS' PLANTATION, LA., ⎱
April 27, 1863.   ⎰

MAJOR-GENERAL J. A. MCCLERNAND,
      Commanding 13th A. C.

Commence immediately the embarkation of your corps, or so much of it as there is transportation for. Have put aboard the artillery and every article authorized in orders limiting baggage, except the men, and hold them in readiness, with their places assigned, to be moved at a moment's warning.

All the troops you may have, except those ordered to remain behind, send to a point nearly opposite Grand Gulf, where you see, by special orders of this date, General McPherson is ordered to send one division.

The plan of the attack will be for the navy to attack and silence all the batteries commanding the river. Your corps will be on the river, ready to run to and debark on the nearest eligible land below the promontory first brought to view passing down the river. Once on shore, have each commander instructed beforehand to form his men the best the ground will admit of, and take possession of the most commanding points, but avoid separating your command so that it cannot support itself. The first object is to get a foothold where our troops can maintain themselves until such time as preparations can be made and troops collected for a forward movement.

Admiral Porter has proposed to place his boats in the position indicated to you a few days ago, and to bring over with them such troops as may be below the city after the guns of the enemy are silenced.

It may be that the enemy will occupy positions back from the city, out of range of the gunboats, so as to make it desirable to run past Grand Gulf and land at Rodney. In case this should prove the plan, a signal will be arranged and you duly informed, when the transports are to start with this view. Or, it may be expedient for the boats to run past, but not the men. In this case, then, the transports would have to be brought back to where the men could land and move by forced marches to below Grand Gulf, re-embark rapidly and proceed to the latter place. There will be required, then, three signals; one, to indicate that the transports can run down and debark the troops at Grand Gulf; one, that the transports can run by without the troops; and the last, that the transports can run by with the troops on board.

Should the men have to march, all baggage and artillery will be left to run the blockade.

If not already directed, require your men to keep three days' rations in their haversacks, not to be touched until a movement commences.

U. S. GRANT,
Major-General.

At 8 o'clock A.M., 29th, Porter made the attack with his entire strength present, eight gunboats. For nearly five and a half hours the attack was kept up without silencing a single gun of the enemy. All this time McClernand's 10,000 men were huddled together on the transports in the stream ready to attempt a landing if signalled. I occupied a tug from which I could see the effect of the battle on both sides, within range of the enemy's guns; but a small tug, without armament, was not calculated to attract the fire of batteries while they were being assailed themselves. About half-past one the fleet withdrew, seeing their efforts were entirely unavailing. The enemy ceased firing as soon as we withdrew. I immediately signalled the Admiral and went aboard his ship. The navy lost in this engagement eighteen killed and fifty-six wounded. A large proportion of these were of the crew of the flagship, and most of those from a single shell which penetrated the ship's side and exploded between decks where the men were working their guns. The sight of the mangled and dying men which met my eye as I boarded the ship was sickening.

Grand Gulf is on a high bluff where the river runs at the very foot of it. It is as defensible upon its front as Vicksburg and, at that time, would have been just as impossible to capture by a front attack. I therefore requested Porter to run the batteries with his fleet that night, and to take charge of the transports, all of which would be wanted below.

There is a long tongue of land from the Louisiana side extending towards Grand Gulf, made by the river running nearly east from about three miles above and nearly in the opposite direction from that point for about the same distance below. The land was so low and wet that it would not have been practicable to march an army across but for a levee. I had had this explored before, as well as the east bank below to ascertain if there was a possible point of debarkation north of Rodney. It was found that the top of the levee afforded a good road to march upon.

Porter, as was always the case with him, not only acquiesced in the plan, but volunteered to use his entire fleet as transports. I had intended to make this request, but he anticipated me. At dusk, when concealed from the view of the enemy at Grand Gulf, McClernand landed his command on the west bank. The navy and transports ran the batteries successfully. The troops marched across the point of land under cover of night, unobserved. By the time it was light the enemy saw our whole fleet, iron-clads, gunboats, river steamers and barges, quietly moving down the river three miles below them, black, or rather blue, with National troops.

When the troops debarked, the evening of the 29th, it was expected that we would have to go to Rodney, about nine miles below, to find a landing; but that night a colored man came in who informed me that a good landing would be found at Bruinsburg, a few miles above Rodney, from which point there was a good road leading to Port Gibson some twelve miles in the interior. The information was found correct, and our landing was effected without opposition.

Sherman had not left his position above Vicksburg yet. On the morning of the 27th I ordered him to create a diversion by moving his corps up the Yazoo and threatening an attack on Haines' Bluff.

My object was to compel Pemberton to keep as much force about Vicksburg as I could, until I could secure a good footing on high land east of the river. The move was eminently successful and, as we afterwards learned, created great confusion about Vicksburg and doubts about our real design. Sherman moved the day of our attack on Grand Gulf, the 29th, with ten regiments of his command and eight gunboats which Porter had left above Vicksburg.

He debarked his troops and apparently made every preparation to attack the enemy while the navy bombarded the main forts at Haines' Bluff. This move was made without a single casualty in either branch of the service. On the first of May Sherman received orders from me (sent from Hard Times the evening of the 29th of April) to withdraw from the front of Haines' Bluff and follow McPherson with two divisions as fast as he could.

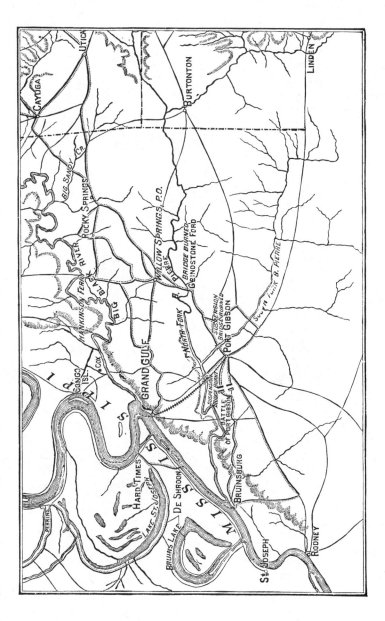

I had established a depot of supplies at Perkins' plantation. Now that all our gunboats were below Grand Gulf it was possible that the enemy might fit out boats in the Big Black with improvised armament and attempt to destroy these supplies. McPherson was at Hard Times with a portion of his corps, and the depot was protected by a part of his command. The night of the 29th I directed him to arm one of the transports with artillery and send it up to Perkins' plantation as a guard; and also to have the siege guns we had brought along moved there and put in position.

The embarkation below Grand Gulf took place at De Shroon's, Louisiana, six miles above Bruinsburg, Mississippi. Early on the morning of 30th of April McClernand's corps and one division of McPherson's corps were speedily landed.

When this was effected I felt a degree of relief scarcely ever equalled since. Vicksburg was not yet taken it is true, nor were its defenders demoralized by any of our previous moves. I was now in the enemy's country, with a vast river and the stronghold of Vicksburg between me and my base of supplies. But I was on dry ground on the same side of the river with the enemy. All the campaigns, labors, hardships and exposures from the month of December previous to this time that had been made and endured, were for the accomplishment of this one object.

I had with me the 13th corps, General McClernand commanding, and two brigades of Logan's division of the 17th corps, General McPherson commanding—in all not more than twenty thousand men to commence the campaign with. These were soon reinforced by the remaining brigade of Logan's division and Crocker's division of the 17th corps. On the 7th of May I was further reinforced by Sherman with two divisions of his, the 15th corps. My total force was then about thirty-three thousand men.

The enemy occupied Grand Gulf, Haines' Bluff and Jackson with a force of nearly sixty thousand men. Jackson is fifty miles east of Vicksburg and is connected with it by a railroad. My first problem was to capture Grand Gulf to use as a base.

Bruinsburg is two miles from high ground. The bottom at that point is higher than most of the low land in the valley of the Mississippi, and a good road leads to the bluff. It was natural to expect the garrison from Grand Gulf to come out to meet us and prevent, if they could, our reaching this solid base. Bayou Pierre enters the Mississippi just above Bruinsburg and, as it is a navigable stream and was high at the time, in order to intercept us they had to go by Port Gibson, the nearest point where there was a bridge to cross upon. This more than doubled the distance from Grand Gulf to the high land back of Bruinsburg. No time was to be lost in securing this foothold. Our transportation was not sufficient to move all the army across the river at one trip, or even two; but the landing of the 13th corps and one division of the 17th was effected during the day, April 30th, and early evening. McClernand was advanced as soon as ammunition and two days' rations (to last five) could be issued to his men. The bluffs were reached an hour before sunset and McClernand was pushed on, hoping to reach Port Gibson and save the bridge spanning the Bayou Pierre before the enemy could get there; for crossing a stream in the presence of an enemy is always difficult. Port Gibson, too, is the starting point of roads to Grand Gulf, Vicksburg and Jackson.

McClernand's advance met the enemy about five miles west of Port Gibson at Thompson's plantation. There was some firing during the night, but nothing rising to the dignity of a battle until daylight. The enemy had taken a strong natural position with most of the Grand Gulf garrison, numbering about seven or eight thousand men, under General Bowen. His hope was to hold me in check until reinforcements under Loring could reach him from Vicksburg; but Loring did not come in time to render much assistance south of Port Gibson. Two brigades of McPherson's corps followed McClernand as fast as rations and ammunition could be issued, and were ready to take position upon the battle-field whenever the 13th corps could be got out of the way.

The country in this part of Mississippi stands on edge, as it were, the roads running along the ridges except when they occasionally pass from one ridge to another. Where there are no clearings the sides of the hills are covered with a very heavy growth of timber and with undergrowth, and the ravines are filled with vines and canebrakes, almost impenetrable. This makes it easy for an inferior force to delay, if not defeat, a far superior one.

Near the point selected by Bowen to defend, the road to Port Gibson divides, taking two ridges which do not diverge more than a mile or two at the widest point. These roads unite just outside the town. This made it necessary for McClernand to divide his force. It was not only divided, but it was separated by a deep ravine of the character above described. One flank could not reinforce the other except by marching back to the junction of the roads. McClernand put the divisions of Hovey, Carr and A. J. Smith upon the right-hand branch and Osterhaus on the left. I was on the field by ten A.M., and inspected both flanks in person. On the right the enemy, if not being pressed back, was at least not repulsing our advance. On the left, however, Osterhaus was not faring so well. He had been repulsed with some loss. As soon as the road could be cleared of McClernand's troops I ordered up McPherson, who was close upon the rear of the 13th corps, with two brigades of Logan's division. This was about noon. I ordered him to send one brigade (General John E. Smith's was selected) to support Osterhaus, and to move to the left and flank the enemy out of his position. This movement carried the brigade over a deep ravine to a third ridge and, when Smith's troops were seen well through the ravine, Osterhaus was directed to renew his front attack. It was successful and unattended by heavy loss. The enemy was sent in full retreat on their right, and their left followed before sunset. While the movement to our left was going on, McClernand, who was with his right flank, sent me frequent requests for reinforcements, although the force with him was not being pressed. I had been upon the ground and knew it did not admit of his engaging all the men he had. We followed up our victory until night overtook us about two miles from Port Gibson; then the troops went into bivouac for the night.

Chapter XXXIV.

CAPTURE OF PORT GIBSON — GRIERSON'S RAID —
OCCUPATION OF GRAND GULF — MOVEMENT UP THE BIG
BLACK — BATTLE OF RAYMOND.

W E STARTED next morning for Port Gibson as soon as it was light enough to see the road. We were soon in the town, and I was delighted to find that the enemy had not stopped to contest our crossing further at the bridge, which he had burned. The troops were set to work at once to construct a bridge across the South Fork of the Bayou Pierre. At this time the water was high and the current rapid. What might be called a raft-bridge was soon constructed from material obtained from wooden buildings, stables, fences, etc., which sufficed for carrying the whole army over safely. Colonel J. H. Wilson, a member of my staff, planned and superintended the construction of this bridge, going into the water and working as hard as any one engaged. Officers and men generally joined in this work. When it was finished the army crossed and marched eight miles beyond to the North Fork that day. One brigade of Logan's division was sent down the stream to occupy the attention of a rebel battery, which had been left behind with infantry supports to prevent our repairing the burnt railroad bridge. Two of his brigades were sent up the bayou to find a crossing and reach the North Fork to repair the bridge there. The enemy soon left when he found we were building a bridge elsewhere. Before leaving Port Gibson we were reinforced by Crocker's division, McPherson's corps, which had crossed the Mississippi at Bruinsburg and come up without stopping except to get two days' rations. McPherson still had one division west of the Mississippi River, guarding the road from Milliken's Bend to the river below until Sherman's command should relieve it.

On leaving Bruinsburg for the front I left my son Frederick, who had joined me a few weeks before, on board one of the gunboats asleep, and hoped to get away without him until after Grand Gulf should fall into our hands; but on waking up he learned that I had gone, and being guided by the sound of the battle raging at Thompson's Hill—called the Battle of Port Gibson—found his way to where I was. He had no horse to ride at the time, and I had no facilities for even preparing a meal. He, therefore, foraged around the best he could until we reached Grand Gulf. Mr. C. A. Dana, then an officer of the War Department, accompanied me on the Vicksburg campaign and through a portion of the siege. He was in the same situation as Fred so far as transportation and mess arrangements were concerned. The first time I call to mind seeing either of them, after the battle, they were mounted on two enormous horses, grown white from age, each equipped with dilapidated saddles and bridles.

Our trains arrived a few days later, after which we were all perfectly equipped.

My son accompanied me throughout the campaign and siege, and caused no anxiety either to me or to his mother, who was at home. He looked out for himself and was in every battle of the campaign. His age, then not quite thirteen, enabled him to take in all he saw, and to retain a recollection of it that would not be possible in more mature years.

When the movement from Bruinsburg commenced we were without a wagon train. The train still west of the Mississippi was carried around with proper escort, by a circuitous route from Milliken's Bend to Hard Times seventy or more miles below, and did not get up for some days after the battle of Port Gibson. My own horses, headquarters' transportation, servants, mess chest, and everything except what I had on, was with this train. General A. J. Smith happened to have an extra horse at Bruinsburg which I borrowed, with a saddle-tree without upholstering further than stirrups. I had no other for nearly a week.

It was necessary to have transportation for ammunition. Provisions could be taken from the country; but all the ammunition that can be carried on the person is soon exhausted when there is much fighting. I directed, therefore, immediately on landing that all the vehicles and draft animals, whether horses, mules, or oxen, in the vicinity should be collected and loaded to their capacity with ammunition. Quite a train was collected during the 30th, and a motley train it was. In it could be found fine carriages, loaded nearly to the top

with boxes of cartridges that had been pitched in promiscu-
ously, drawn by mules with plough-harness, straw collars,
rope-lines, etc.; long-coupled wagons, with racks for carrying
cotton bales, drawn by oxen, and everything that could be
found in the way of transportation on a plantation, either for
use or pleasure. The making out of provision returns was
stopped for the time. No formalities were to retard our
progress until a position was secured when the time could be
spared to observe them.

It was at Port Gibson I first heard through a Southern
paper of the complete success of Colonel Grierson, who was
making a raid through central Mississippi. He had started
from La Grange April 17th with three regiments of about
1,700 men. On the 21st he had detached Colonel Hatch with
one regiment to destroy the railroad between Columbus and
Macon and then return to La Grange. Hatch had a sharp fight
with the enemy at Columbus and retreated along the railroad, destroying it at Okalona and Tupelo, and arriving in La
Grange April 26. Grierson continued his movement with
about 1,000 men, breaking the Vicksburg and Meridian railroad and the New Orleans and Jackson railroad, arriving at
Baton Rouge May 2d. This raid was of great importance, for
Grierson had attracted the attention of the enemy from the
main movement against Vicksburg.

During the night of the 2d of May the bridge over the
North Fork was repaired, and the troops commenced crossing
at five the next morning. Before the leading brigade was over
it was fired upon by the enemy from a commanding position;
but they were soon driven off. It was evident that the enemy
was covering a retreat from Grand Gulf to Vicksburg. Every
commanding position from this (Grindstone) crossing to
Hankinson's ferry over the Big Black was occupied by the
retreating foe to delay our progress. McPherson, however,
reached Hankinson's ferry before night, seized the ferry boat,
and sent a detachment of his command across and several
miles north on the road to Vicksburg. When the junction of
the road going to Vicksburg with the road from Grand Gulf
to Raymond and Jackson was reached, Logan with his division was turned to the left towards Grand Gulf. I went with
him a short distance from this junction. McPherson had en-

countered the largest force yet met since the battle of Port Gibson and had a skirmish nearly approaching a battle; but the road Logan had taken enabled him to come up on the enemy's right flank, and they soon gave way. McPherson was ordered to hold Hankinson's ferry and the road back to Willow Springs with one division; McClernand, who was now in the rear, was to join in this as well as to guard the line back down the bayou. I did not want to take the chances of having an enemy lurking in our rear.

On the way from the junction to Grand Gulf, where the road comes into the one from Vicksburg to the same place six or seven miles out, I learned that the last of the enemy had retreated past that place on their way to Vicksburg. I left Logan to make the proper disposition of his troops for the night, while I rode into the town with an escort of about twenty cavalry. Admiral Porter had already arrived with his fleet. The enemy had abandoned his heavy guns and evacuated the place.

When I reached Grand Gulf May 3d I had not been with my baggage since the 27th of April and consequently had had no change of underclothing, no meal except such as I could pick up sometimes at other headquarters, and no tent to cover me. The first thing I did was to get a bath, borrow some fresh underclothing from one of the naval officers and get a good meal on the flag-ship. Then I wrote letters to the general-in-chief informing him of our present position, dispatches to be telegraphed from Cairo, orders to General Sullivan commanding above Vicksburg, and gave orders to all my corps commanders. About twelve o'clock at night I was through my work and started for Hankinson's ferry, arriving there before daylight. While at Grand Gulf I heard from Banks, who was on the Red River, and who said that he could not be at Port Hudson before the 10th of May and then with only 15,000 men. Up to this time my intention had been to secure Grand Gulf, as a base of supplies, detach McClernand's corps to Banks and co-operate with him in the reduction of Port Hudson.

The news from Banks forced upon me a different plan of campaign from the one intended. To wait for his co-operation would have detained me at least a month. The reinforcements would not have reached ten thousand men after deducting casualties and necessary river guards at all high points close to the river for over three hundred miles. The enemy would have strengthened his position and been reinforced by more men than Banks could have brought. I therefore determined to move independently of Banks, cut loose from my base, destroy the rebel force in rear of Vicksburg and invest or capture the city.

Grand Gulf was accordingly given up as a base and the authorities at Washington were notified. I knew well that Halleck's caution would lead him to disapprove of this course; but it was the only one that gave any chance of success. The time it would take to communicate with Washington and get a reply would be so great that I could not be interfered with until it was demonstrated whether my plan was practicable. Even Sherman, who afterwards ignored bases of supplies other than what were afforded by the country while marching through four States of the Confederacy with an army more than twice as large as mine at this time, wrote me from Hankinson's ferry, advising me of the impossibility of supplying our army over a single road. He urged me to "stop all troops till your army is partially supplied with wagons, and then act as quick as possible; for this road will be jammed, as sure as life." To this I replied: "I do not calculate upon the possibility of supplying the army with full rations from Grand Gulf. I know it will be impossible without constructing additional roads. What I do expect is to get up what rations of hard bread, coffee and salt we can, and make the country furnish the balance." We started from Bruinsburg with an average of about two days' rations, and received no more from our own supplies for some days; abundance was found in the mean time. A delay would give the enemy time to reinforce and fortify.

McClernand's and McPherson's commands were kept substantially as they were on the night of the 2d, awaiting supplies sufficient to give them three days' rations in haversacks. Beef, mutton, poultry and forage were found in abundance. Quite a quantity of bacon and molasses was also secured from the country, but bread and coffee could not be obtained in quantity sufficient for all the men. Every plantation, however, had a run of stone, propelled by mule power, to grind corn for the owners and their slaves. All these were kept running while we were stopping, day and night, and when we were marching, during the night, at all plantations covered by the troops. But the product was taken by the troops nearest by, so that the majority of the command was destined to go without bread until a new base was established on the Yazoo above Vicksburg.

While the troops were awaiting the arrival of rations I ordered reconnoissances made by McClernand and McPherson, with the view of leading the enemy to believe that we intended to cross the Big Black and attack the city at once.

On the 6th Sherman arrived at Grand Gulf and crossed his command that night and the next day. Three days' rations had been brought up from Grand Gulf for the advanced troops and were issued. Orders were given for a forward movement the next day. Sherman was directed to order up Blair, who had been left behind to guard the road from Milliken's Bend to Hard Times with two brigades.

The quartermaster at Young's Point was ordered to send two hundred wagons with Blair, and the commissary was to load them with hard bread, coffee, sugar, salt and one hundred thousand pounds of salt meat.

On the 3d Hurlbut, who had been left at Memphis, was ordered to send four regiments from his command to Milliken's Bend to relieve Blair's division, and on the 5th he was ordered to send Lauman's division in addition, the latter to join the army in the field. The four regiments were to be taken from troops near the river so that there would be no delay.

During the night of the 6th McPherson drew in his troops north of the Big Black and was off at an early hour on the road to Jackson, viâ Rocky Springs, Utica and Raymond. That night he and McClernand were both at Rocky Springs ten miles from Hankinson's ferry. McPherson remained there during the 8th, while McClernand moved to Big Sandy and Sherman marched from Grand Gulf to Hankinson's ferry. The 9th, McPherson moved to a point within a few miles west of Utica; McClernand and Sherman remained where they were. On the 10th McPherson moved to Utica, Sherman to Big

Sandy; McClernand was still at Big Sandy. The 11th, McClernand was at Five Mile Creek; Sherman at Auburn; McPherson five miles advanced from Utica. May 12th, McClernand was at Fourteen Mile Creek; Sherman at Fourteen Mile Creek; McPherson at Raymond after a battle.

After McPherson crossed the Big Black at Hankinson's ferry Vicksburg could have been approached and besieged by the south side. It is not probable, however, that Pemberton would have permitted a close besiegement. The broken nature of the ground would have enabled him to hold a strong defensible line from the river south of the city to the Big Black, retaining possession of the railroad back to that point. It was my plan, therefore, to get to the railroad east of Vicksburg, and approach from that direction. Accordingly, McPherson's troops that had crossed the Big Black were withdrawn and the movement east to Jackson commenced.

As has been stated before, the country is very much broken and the roads generally confined to the tops of the hills. The troops were moved one (sometimes two) corps at a time to reach designated points out parallel to the railroad and only from six to ten miles from it. McClernand's corps was kept with its left flank on the Big Black guarding all the crossings. Fourteen Mile Creek, a stream substantially parallel with the railroad, was reached and crossings effected by McClernand and Sherman with slight loss. McPherson was to the right of Sherman, extending to Raymond. The cavalry was used in this advance in reconnoitring to find the roads: to cover our advances and to find the most practicable routes from one command to another so they could support each other in case of an attack. In making this move I estimated Pemberton's movable force at Vicksburg at about eighteen thousand men, with smaller forces at Haines' Bluff and Jackson. It would not be possible for Pemberton to attack me with all his troops at one place, and I determined to throw my army between his and fight him in detail. This was done with success, but I found afterwards that I had entirely under-estimated Pemberton's strength.

Up to this point our movements had been made without serious opposition. My line was now nearly parallel with the Jackson and Vicksburg railroad and about seven miles south of it. The right was at Raymond eighteen miles from Jackson, McPherson commanding; Sherman in the centre on Fourteen Mile Creek, his advance thrown across; McClernand to the left, also on Fourteen Mile Creek, advance across, and his pickets within two miles of Edward's station, where the enemy had concentrated a considerable force and where they undoubtedly expected us to attack. McClernand's left was on the Big Black. In all our moves, up to this time, the left had hugged the Big Black closely, and all the ferries had been guarded to prevent the enemy throwing a force on our rear.

McPherson encountered the enemy, five thousand strong with two batteries under General Gregg, about two miles out of Raymond. This was about two P.M. Logan was in advance with one of his brigades. He deployed and moved up to engage the enemy. McPherson ordered the road in rear to be cleared of wagons, and the balance of Logan's division, and Crocker's, which was still farther in rear, to come forward with all dispatch. The order was obeyed with alacrity. Logan got his division in position for assault before Crocker could get up, and attacked with vigor, carrying the enemy's position easily, sending Gregg flying from the field not to appear against our front again until we met at Jackson.

In this battle McPherson lost 66 killed, 339 wounded, and 37 missing—nearly or quite all from Logan's division. The enemy's loss was 100 killed, 305 wounded, besides 415 taken prisoners.

I regarded Logan and Crocker as being as competent division commanders as could be found in or out of the army and both equal to a much higher command. Crocker, however, was dying of consumption when he volunteered. His weak condition never put him on the sick report when there was a battle in prospect, as long as he could keep on his feet. He died not long after the close of the rebellion.

Chapter XXXV.

MOVEMENT AGAINST JACKSON — FALL OF
JACKSON — INTERCEPTING THE ENEMY — BATTLE
OF CHAMPION'S HILL.

W HEN THE NEWS reached me of McPherson's victory at
Raymond about sundown my position was with Sherman. I decided at once to turn the whole column towards
Jackson and capture that place without delay.

Pemberton was now on my left, with, as I supposed, about
18,000 men; in fact, as I learned afterwards, with nearly
50,000. A force was also collecting on my right, at Jackson,
the point where all the railroads communicating with Vicksburg connect. All the enemy's supplies of men and stores
would come by that point. As I hoped in the end to besiege
Vicksburg I must first destroy all possibility of aid. I therefore
determined to move swiftly towards Jackson, destroy or drive
any force in that direction and then turn upon Pemberton.
But by moving against Jackson, I uncovered my own communication. So I finally decided to have none — to cut loose altogether from my base and move my whole force eastward. I
then had no fears for my communications, and if I moved
quickly enough could turn upon Pemberton before he could
attack me in the rear.

Accordingly, all previous orders given during the day for
movements on the 13th were annulled by new ones. McPherson was ordered at daylight to move on Clinton, ten miles
from Jackson; Sherman was notified of my determination to
capture Jackson and work from there westward. He was ordered to start at four in the morning and march to Raymond.
McClernand was ordered to march with three divisions by
Dillon's to Raymond. One was left to guard the crossing of
the Big Black.

On the 10th I had received a letter from Banks, on the
Red River, asking reinforcements. Porter had gone to his assistance with a part of his fleet on the 3d, and I now wrote
to him describing my position and declining to send any
troops. I looked upon side movements as long as the enemy

held Port Hudson and Vicksburg as a waste of time and material.

General Joseph E. Johnston arrived at Jackson in the night of the 13th from Tennessee, and immediately assumed command of all the Confederate troops in Mississippi. I knew he was expecting reinforcements from the south and east. On the 6th I had written to General Halleck: "Information from the other side leaves me to believe the enemy are bringing forces from Tullahoma."

Up to this time my troops had been kept in supporting distances of each other, as far as the nature of the country would admit. Reconnoissances were constantly made from each corps to enable them to acquaint themselves with the most practicable routes from one to another in case a union became necessary.

McPherson reached Clinton with the advance early on the 13th and immediately set to work destroying the railroad. Sherman's advance reached Raymond before the last of McPherson's command had got out of the town. McClernand withdrew from the front of the enemy, at Edward's station, with much skill and without loss, and reached his position for the night in good order. On the night of the 13th, McPherson was ordered to march at early dawn upon Jackson, only fifteen miles away. Sherman was given the same order; but he was to move by the direct road from Raymond to Jackson, which is south of the road McPherson was on and does not approach within two miles of it at the point where it crossed the line of intrenchments which, at that time, defended the city. McClernand was ordered to move one division of his command to Clinton, one division a few miles beyond Mississippi Springs following Sherman's line, and a third to Raymond. He was also directed to send his siege guns, four in number, with the troops going by Mississippi Springs. McClernand's position was an advantageous one in any event. With one division at Clinton he was in position to reinforce McPherson, at Jackson, rapidly if it became necessary; the division beyond Mississippi Springs was equally available to reinforce Sherman; the one at Raymond could take either road. He still had two other divisions farther back, now that Blair had come up, available within a day at Jackson. If this last command should not be wanted at Jackson, they were already one day's march from there on their way to Vicksburg and on three different roads leading to the latter city. But the most important consideration in my mind was to have a force confronting Pemberton if he should come out to attack my rear. This I expected him to do; as shown further on, he was directed by Johnston to make this very move.

I notified General Halleck that I should attack the State capital on the 14th. A courier carried the dispatch to Grand Gulf through an unprotected country.

Sherman and McPherson communicated with each other during the night and arranged to reach Jackson at about the same hour. It rained in torrents during the night of the 13th and the fore part of the day of the 14th. The roads were intolerable, and in some places on Sherman's line, where the land was low, they were covered more than a foot deep with water. But the troops never murmured. By nine o'clock Crocker, of McPherson's corps, who was now in advance, came upon the enemy's pickets and speedily drove them in upon the main body. They were outside of the intrenchments in a strong position, and proved to be the troops that had been driven out of Raymond. Johnston had been reinforced during the night by Georgia and South Carolina regiments, so that his force amounted to eleven thousand men, and he was expecting still more.

Sherman also came upon the rebel pickets some distance out from the town, but speedily drove them in. He was now on the south and south-west of Jackson confronting the Confederates behind their breastworks, while McPherson's right was nearly two miles north, occupying a line running north and south across the Vicksburg railroad. Artillery was brought up and reconnoissances made preparatory to an assault. McPherson brought up Logan's division while he deployed Crocker's for the assault. Sherman made similar dispositions on the right. By eleven A.M. both were ready to attack. Crocker moved his division forward, preceded by a strong skirmish line. These troops at once encountered the enemy's advance and drove it back on the main body, when they returned to their proper regiment and the whole division charged, routing the enemy completely and driving him into

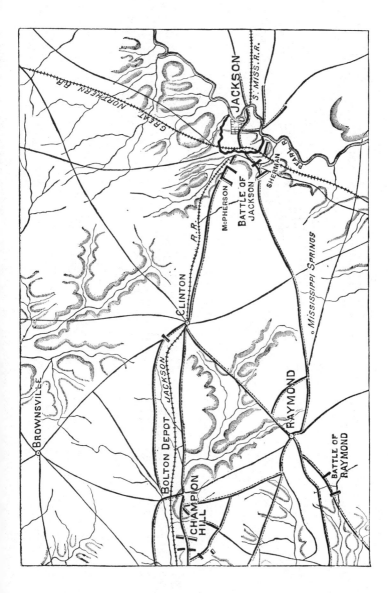

this main line. This stand by the enemy was made more than two miles outside of his main fortifications. McPherson followed up with his command until within range of the guns of the enemy from their intrenchments, when he halted to bring his troops into line and reconnoitre to determine the next move. It was now about noon.

While this was going on Sherman was confronting a rebel battery which enfiladed the road on which he was marching—the Mississippi Springs road—and commanded a bridge spanning a stream over which he had to pass. By detaching right and left the stream was forced and the enemy flanked and speedily driven within the main line. This brought our whole line in front of the enemy's line of works, which was continuous on the north, west and south sides from the Pearl River north of the city to the same river south. I was with Sherman. He was confronted by a force sufficient to hold us back. Appearances did not justify an assault where we were. I had directed Sherman to send a force to the right, and to reconnoitre as far as to the Pearl River. This force, Tuttle's division, not returning I rode to the right with my staff, and soon found that the enemy had left that part of the line. Tuttle's movement or McPherson's pressure had no doubt led Johnston to order a retreat, leaving only the men at the guns to retard us while he was getting away. Tuttle had seen this and, passing through the lines without resistance, came up in the rear of the artillerists confronting Sherman and captured them with ten pieces of artillery. I rode immediately to the State House, where I was soon followed by Sherman. About the same time McPherson discovered that the enemy was leaving his front, and advanced Crocker, who was so close upon the enemy that they could not move their guns or destroy them. He captured seven guns and, moving on, hoisted the National flag over the rebel capital of Mississippi. Stevenson's brigade was sent to cut off the rebel retreat, but was too late or not expeditious enough.

Our loss in this engagement was: McPherson, 37 killed, 228 wounded; Sherman, 4 killed and 21 wounded and missing. The enemy lost 845 killed, wounded and captured. Seventeen guns fell into our hands, and the enemy destroyed by fire their store-houses, containing a large amount of commissary stores.

On this day Blair reached New Auburn and joined McClernand's 4th division. He had with him two hundred wagons loaded with rations, the only commissary supplies received during the entire campaign.

I slept that night in the room that Johnston was said to have occupied the night before.

About four in the afternoon I sent for the corps commanders and directed the dispositions to be made of their troops. Sherman was to remain in Jackson until he destroyed that place as a railroad centre, and manufacturing city of military supplies. He did the work most effectually. Sherman and I went together into a manufactory which had not ceased work on account of the battle nor for the entrance of Yankee troops. Our presence did not seem to attract the attention of either the manager or the operatives, most of whom were girls. We looked on for a while to see the tent cloth which they were making roll out of the looms, with "C. S. A." woven in each bolt. There was an immense amount of cotton, in bales, stacked outside. Finally I told Sherman I thought they had done work enough. The operatives were told they could leave and take with them what cloth they could carry. In a few minutes cotton and factory were in a blaze. The proprietor visited Washington while I was President to get his pay for this property, claiming that it was private. He asked me to give him a statement of the fact that his property had been destroyed by National troops, so that he might use it with Congress where he was pressing, or proposed to press, his claim. I declined.

On the night of the 13th Johnston sent the following dispatch to Pemberton at Edward's station: "I have lately arrived, and learn that Major-General Sherman is between us with four divisions at Clinton. It is important to establish communication, that you may be reinforced. If practicable, come up in his rear at once. To beat such a detachment would be of immense value. All the troops you can quickly assemble should be brought. Time is all-important." This dispatch was sent in triplicate, by different messengers. One of the messengers happened to be a loyal man who had been expelled from

Memphis some months before by Hurlbut for uttering disloyal and threatening sentiments. There was a good deal of
parade about his expulsion, ostensibly as a warning to those
who entertained the sentiments he expressed; but Hurlbut
and the expelled man understood each other. He delivered his
copy of Johnston's dispatch to McPherson who forwarded it
to me.

Receiving this dispatch on the 14th I ordered McPherson
to move promptly in the morning back to Bolton, the nearest
point where Johnston could reach the road. Bolton is about
twenty miles west of Jackson. I also informed McClernand of
the capture of Jackson and sent him the following order: "It is
evidently the design of the enemy to get north of us and cross
the Big Black, and beat us into Vicksburg. We must not allow
them to do this. Turn all your forces towards Bolton station,
and make all dispatch in getting there. Move troops by the
most direct road from wherever they may be on the receipt of
this order."

And to Blair I wrote: "Their design is evidently to cross the
Big Black and pass down the peninsula between the Big Black
and Yazoo rivers. We must beat them. Turn your troops
immediately to Bolton; take all the trains with you. Smith's
division, and any other troops now with you, will go to the
same place. If practicable, take parallel roads, so as to divide
your troops and train."

Johnston stopped on the Canton road only six miles north
of Jackson, the night of the 14th. He sent from there to Pemberton dispatches announcing the loss of Jackson, and the following order:

"As soon as the reinforcements are all up, they must be
united to the rest of the army. I am anxious to see a force
assembled that may be able to inflict a heavy blow upon the
enemy. Can Grant supply himself from the Mississippi? Can
you not cut him off from it, and above all, should he be compelled to fall back for want of supplies, beat him."

The concentration of my troops was easy, considering the
character of the country. McPherson moved along the road
parallel with and near the railroad. McClernand's command
was, one division (Hovey's) on the road McPherson had to
take, but with a start of four miles. One (Osterhaus) was at

Raymond, on a converging road that intersected the other near Champion's Hill; one (Carr's) had to pass over the same road with Osterhaus, but being back at Mississippi Springs, would not be detained by it; the fourth (Smith's) with Blair's division, was near Auburn with a different road to pass over. McClernand faced about and moved promptly. His cavalry from Raymond seized Bolton by half-past nine in the morning, driving out the enemy's pickets and capturing several men.

The night of the 15th Hovey was at Bolton; Carr and Osterhaus were about three miles south, but abreast, facing west; Smith was north of Raymond with Blair in his rear.

McPherson's command, with Logan in front, had marched at seven o'clock, and by four reached Hovey and went into camp; Crocker bivouacked just in Hovey's rear on the Clinton road. Sherman with two divisions, was in Jackson, completing the destruction of roads, bridges and military factories. I rode in person out to Clinton. On my arrival I ordered McClernand to move early in the morning on Edward's station, cautioning him to watch for the enemy and not bring on an engagement unless he felt very certain of success.

I naturally expected that Pemberton would endeavor to obey the orders of his superior, which I have shown were to attack us at Clinton. This, indeed, I knew he could not do; but I felt sure he would make the attempt to reach that point. It turned out, however, that he had decided his superior's plans were impracticable, and consequently determined to move south from Edward's station and get between me and my base. I, however, had no base, having abandoned it more than a week before. On the 15th Pemberton had actually marched south from Edward's station, but the rains had swollen Baker's Creek, which he had to cross, so much that he could not ford it, and the bridges were washed away. This brought him back to the Jackson road, on which there was a good bridge over Baker's Creek. Some of his troops were marching until midnight to get there. Receiving here early on the 16th a repetition of his order to join Johnston at Clinton, he concluded to obey, and sent a dispatch to his chief, informing him of the route by which he might be expected.

About five o'clock in the morning (16th) two men, who had been employed on the Jackson and Vicksburg railroad, were brought to me. They reported that they had passed through Pemberton's army in the night, and that it was still marching east. They reported him to have eighty regiments of infantry and ten batteries; in all, about twenty-five thousand men.

I had expected to leave Sherman at Jackson another day in order to complete his work; but getting the above information I sent him orders to move with all dispatch to Bolton, and to put one division with an ammunition train on the road at once, with directions to its commander to march with all possible speed until he came up to our rear. Within an hour after receiving this order Steele's division was on the road. At the same time I dispatched to Blair, who was near Auburn, to move with all speed to Edward's station. McClernand was directed to embrace Blair in his command for the present. Blair's division was a part of the 15th army corps (Sherman's); but as it was on its way to join its corps, it naturally struck our left first, now that we had faced about and were moving west. The 15th corps, when it got up, would be on our extreme right. McPherson was directed to get his trains out of the way of the troops, and to follow Hovey's division as closely as possible. McClernand had two roads about three miles apart, converging at Edward's station, over which to march his troops. Hovey's division of his corps had the advance on a third road (the Clinton) still farther north. McClernand was directed to move Blair's and A. J. Smith's divisions by the southernmost of these roads, and Osterhaus and Carr by the middle road. Orders were to move cautiously with skirmishers to the front to feel for the enemy.

Smith's division on the most southern road was the first to encounter the enemy's pickets, who were speedily driven in. Osterhaus, on the middle road, hearing the firing, pushed his skirmishers forward, found the enemy's pickets and forced them back to the main line. About the same time Hovey encountered the enemy on the northern or direct wagon road from Jackson to Vicksburg. McPherson was hastening up to join Hovey, but was embarrassed by Hovey's trains occupying the roads. I was still back at Clinton. McPherson sent me word of the situation, and expressed the wish that I was up. By half-past seven I was on the road and proceeded rapidly to the front, ordering all trains that were in front of troops off the road. When I arrived Hovey's skirmishing amounted almost to a battle.

McClernand was in person on the middle road and had a shorter distance to march to reach the enemy's position than McPherson. I sent him word by a staff officer to push forward and attack. These orders were repeated several times without apparently expediting McClernand's advance.

Champion's Hill, where Pemberton had chosen his position to receive us, whether taken by accident or design, was well selected. It is one of the highest points in that section, and commanded all the ground in range. On the east side of the ridge, which is quite precipitous, is a ravine running first north, then westerly, terminating at Baker's Creek. It was grown up thickly with large trees and undergrowth, making it difficult to penetrate with troops, even when not defended. The ridge occupied by the enemy terminated abruptly where the ravine turns westerly. The left of the enemy occupied the north end of this ridge. The Bolton and Edward's station wagon-road turns almost due south at this point and ascends the ridge, which it follows for about a mile; then turning west, descends by a gentle declivity to Baker's Creek, nearly a mile away. On the west side the slope of the ridge is gradual and is cultivated from near the summit to the creek. There was, when we were there, a narrow belt of timber near the summit west of the road.

From Raymond there is a direct road to Edward's station, some three miles west of Champion's Hill. There is one also to Bolton. From this latter road there is still another, leaving it about three and a half miles before reaching Bolton and leads direct to the same station. It was along these two roads that three divisions of McClernand's corps, and Blair of Sherman's, temporarily under McClernand, were moving. Hovey of McClernand's command was with McPherson, farther north on the road from Bolton direct to Edward's station. The middle road comes into the northern road at the point where the latter turns to the west and descends to Baker's Creek; the southern road is still several miles south and does

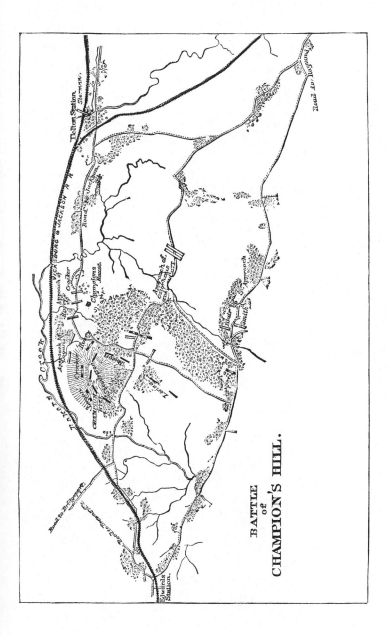

BATTLE
of
CHAMPION'S HILL.

not intersect the others until it reaches Edward's station. Pemberton's lines covered all these roads, and faced east. Hovey's line, when it first drove in the enemy's pickets, was formed parallel to that of the enemy and confronted his left.

By eleven o'clock the skirmishing had grown into a hard-contested battle. Hovey alone, before other troops could be got to assist him, had captured a battery of the enemy. But he was not able to hold his position and had to abandon the artillery. McPherson brought up his troops as fast as possible, Logan in front, and posted them on the right of Hovey and across the flank of the enemy. Logan reinforced Hovey with one brigade from his division; with his other two he moved farther west to make room for Crocker, who was coming up as rapidly as the roads would admit. Hovey was still being heavily pressed, and was calling on me for more reinforcements. I ordered Crocker, who was now coming up, to send one brigade from his division. McPherson ordered two batteries to be stationed where they nearly enfiladed the enemy's line, and they did good execution.

From Logan's position now a direct forward movement carried him over open fields, in rear of the enemy and in a line parallel with them. He did make exactly this move, attacking, however, the enemy through the belt of woods covering the west slope of the hill for a short distance. Up to this time I had kept my position near Hovey where we were the most heavily pressed; but about noon I moved with a part of my staff by our right around, until I came up with Logan himself. I found him near the road leading down to Baker's Creek. He was actually in command of the only road over which the enemy could retreat; Hovey, reinforced by two brigades from McPherson's command, confronted the enemy's left; Crocker, with two brigades, covered their left flank; McClernand two hours before, had been within two miles and a half of their centre with two divisions, and the two divisions, Blair's and A. J. Smith's, were confronting the rebel right; Ransom, with a brigade of McArthur's division of the 17th corps (McPherson's), had crossed the river at Grand Gulf a few days before, and was coming up on their right flank. Neither Logan nor I knew that we had cut off the retreat of the enemy. Just at this juncture a messenger came from Hovey, asking for more reinforcements. There were none to spare. I then gave an order to move McPherson's command by the left flank around to Hovey. This uncovered the rebel line of retreat, which was soon taken advantage of by the enemy.

During all this time, Hovey, reinforced as he was by a brigade from Logan and another from Crocker, and by Crocker gallantly coming up with two other brigades on his right, had made several assaults, the last one about the time the road was opened to the rear. The enemy fled precipitately. This was between three and four o'clock. I rode forward, or rather back, to where the middle road intersects the north road, and found the skirmishers of Carr's division just coming in. Osterhaus was farther south and soon after came up with skirmishers advanced in like manner. Hovey's division, and McPherson's two divisions with him, had marched and fought from early dawn, and were not in the best condition to follow the retreating foe. I sent orders to Osterhaus to pursue the enemy, and to Carr, whom I saw personally, I explained the situation and directed him to pursue vigorously as far as the Big Black, and to cross it if he could; Osterhaus to follow him. The pursuit was continued until after dark.

The battle of Champion's Hill lasted about four hours, hard fighting, preceded by two or three hours of skirmishing, some of which almost rose to the dignity of battle. Every man of Hovey's division and of McPherson's two divisions was engaged during the battle. No other part of my command was engaged at all, except that as described before. Osterhaus's and A. J. Smith's divisions had encountered the rebel advanced pickets as early as half-past seven. Their positions were admirable for advancing upon the enemy's line. McClernand, with two divisions, was within a few miles of the battlefield long before noon, and in easy hearing. I sent him repeated orders by staff officers fully competent to explain to him the situation. These traversed the wood separating us, without escort, and directed him to push forward; but he did not come. It is true, in front of McClernand there was a small force of the enemy and posted in a good position behind a ravine obstructing his advance; but if he had moved to the right by the road my staff officers had followed the enemy must either have fallen back or been cut off. Instead of this he sent orders to Hovey, who belonged to his corps, to join on to his right flank. Hovey was bearing the brunt of the battle at the time. To obey the order he would have had to pull out from the front of the enemy and march back as far as McClernand had to advance to get into battle, and substantially over the same ground. Of course I did not permit Hovey to obey the order of his intermediate superior.

We had in this battle about 15,000 men absolutely engaged. This excludes those that did not get up, all of McClernand's command except Hovey. Our loss was 410 killed, 1,844 wounded and 187 missing. Hovey alone lost 1,200 killed, wounded and missing—more than one-third of his division.

Had McClernand come up with reasonable promptness, or had I known the ground as I did afterwards, I cannot see how Pemberton could have escaped with any organized force. As it was he lost over three thousand killed and wounded and about three thousand captured in battle and in pursuit. Loring's division, which was the right of Pemberton's line, was cut off from the retreating army and never got back into Vicksburg. Pemberton himself fell back that night to the Big Black River. His troops did not stop before midnight and many of them left before the general retreat commenced, and no doubt a good part of them returned to their homes. Logan alone captured 1,300 prisoners and eleven guns. Hovey captured 300 under fire and about 700 in all, exclusive of 500 sick and wounded whom he paroled, thus making 1,200.

McPherson joined in the advance as soon as his men could fill their cartridge-boxes, leaving one brigade to guard our wounded. The pursuit was continued as long as it was light enough to see the road. The night of the 16th of May found McPherson's command bivouacked from two to six miles west of the battle-field, along the line of the road to Vicksburg. Carr and Osterhaus were at Edward's station, and Blair was about three miles south-east; Hovey remained on the field where his troops had fought so bravely and bled so freely. Much war material abandoned by the enemy was picked up on the battle-field, among it thirty pieces of artillery. I pushed through the advancing column with my staff and kept in advance until after night. Finding ourselves alone we stopped and took possession of a vacant house. As no troops came up we moved back a mile or more until we met the head of the column just going into bivouac on the road. We had no tents, so we occupied the porch of a house which had been taken for a rebel hospital and which was filled with wounded and dying who had been brought from the battle-field we had just left.

While a battle is raging one can see his enemy mowed down by the thousand, or the ten thousand, with great composure; but after the battle these scenes are distressing, and one is naturally disposed to do as much to alleviate the suffering of an enemy as a friend.

Chapter XXXVI.

BATTLE OF BLACK RIVER BRIDGE—CROSSING THE BIG
BLACK—INVESTMENT OF VICKSBURG—ASSAULTING
THE WORKS.

WE WERE now assured of our position between Johnston and Pemberton, without a possibility of a junction of their forces. Pemberton might have made a night march to the Big Black, crossed the bridge there and, by moving north on the west side, have eluded us and finally returned to Johnston. But this would have given us Vicksburg. It would have been his proper move, however, and the one Johnston would have made had he been in Pemberton's place. In fact it would have been in conformity with Johnston's orders to Pemberton.

Sherman left Jackson with the last of his troops about noon on the 16th and reached Bolton, twenty miles west, before halting. His rear guard did not get in until two A.M. the 17th, but renewed their march by daylight. He paroled his prisoners at Jackson, and was forced to leave his own wounded in care of surgeons and attendants. At Bolton he was informed of our victory. He was directed to commence the march early next day, and to diverge from the road he was on to Bridgeport on the Big Black River, some eleven miles above the point where we expected to find the enemy. Blair was ordered to join him there with the pontoon train as early as possible.

This movement brought Sherman's corps together, and at a point where I hoped a crossing of the Big Black might be effected and Sherman's corps used to flank the enemy out of his position in our front, thus opening a crossing for the remainder of the army. I informed him that I would endeavor to hold the enemy in my front while he crossed the river.

The advance division, Carr's (McClernand's corps), resumed the pursuit at half-past three A.M. on the 17th, followed closely by Osterhaus, McPherson bringing up the rear with his corps. As I expected, the enemy was found in position on the Big Black. The point was only six miles from that where my advance had rested for the night, and was reached at an early hour. Here the river makes a turn to the

349

west, and has washed close up to the high land; the east side is a low bottom, sometimes overflowed at very high water, but was cleared and in cultivation. A bayou runs irregularly across this low land, the bottom of which, however, is above the surface of the Big Black at ordinary stages. When the river is full water runs through it, converting the point of land into an island. The bayou was grown up with timber, which the enemy had felled into the ditch. At this time there was a foot or two of water in it. The rebels had constructed a parapet along the inner bank of this bayou by using cotton bales from the plantation close by and throwing dirt over them. The whole was thoroughly commanded from the height west of the river. At the upper end of the bayou there was a strip of uncleared land which afforded a cover for a portion of our men. Carr's division was deployed on our right, Lawler's brigade forming his extreme right and reaching through these woods to the river above. Osterhaus' division was deployed to the left of Carr and covered the enemy's entire front. McPherson was in column on the road, the head close by, ready to come in wherever he could be of assistance.

While the troops were standing as here described an officer from Banks' staff came up and presented me with a letter from General Halleck, dated the 11th of May. It had been sent by the way of New Orleans to Banks to be forwarded to me. It ordered me to return to Grand Gulf and to co-operate from there with Banks against Port Hudson, and then to return with our combined forces to besiege Vicksburg. I told the officer that the order came too late, and that Halleck would not give it now if he knew our position. The bearer of the dispatch insisted that I ought to obey the order, and was giving arguments to support his position when I heard great cheering to the right of our line and, looking in that direction, saw Lawler in his shirt sleeves leading a charge upon the enemy. I immediately mounted my horse and rode in the direction of the charge, and saw no more of the officer who delivered the dispatch; I think not even to this day.

The assault was successful. But little resistance was made. The enemy fled from the west bank of the river, burning the

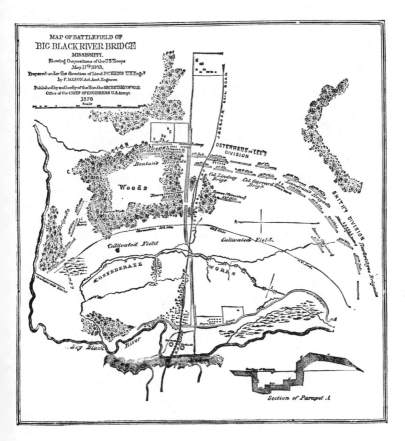

MAP OF BATTLEFIELD OF
BIG BLACK RIVER BRIDGE
MISSISSIPPI.
Showing the positions of the U S Troops
May 17th 1863.
Prepared under the direction of Lieut. P. C. HAINS U. S. Eng.[r]
by F. MASON Act. Asst. Engineer

Published by authority of the Hon. the SECRETARY OF WAR
Office of the CHIEF OF ENGINEERS U. S. Army.
1876
Scale

Section of Parapet A.

bridge behind him and leaving the men and guns on the east side to fall into our hands. Many tried to escape by swimming the river. Some succeeded and some were drowned in the attempt. Eighteen guns were captured and 1,751 prisoners. Our loss was 39 killed, 237 wounded and 3 missing. The enemy probably lost but few men except those captured and drowned. But for the successful and complete destruction of the bridge, I have but little doubt that we should have followed the enemy so closely as to prevent his occupying his defences around Vicksburg.

As the bridge was destroyed and the river was high, new bridges had to be built. It was but little after nine o'clock A.M. when the capture took place. As soon as work could be commenced, orders were given for the construction of three bridges. One was taken charge of by Lieutenant Hains, of the Engineer Corps, one by General McPherson himself and one by General Ransom, a most gallant and intelligent volunteer officer. My recollection is that Hains built a raft bridge; McPherson a pontoon, using cotton bales in large numbers, for pontoons; and that Ransom felled trees on opposite banks of the river, cutting only on one side of the tree, so that they would fall with their tops interlacing in the river, without the trees being entirely severed from their stumps. A bridge was then made with these trees to support the roadway. Lumber was taken from buildings, cotton gins and wherever found, for this purpose. By eight o'clock in the morning of the 18th all three bridges were complete and the troops were crossing.

Sherman reached Bridgeport about noon of the 17th and found Blair with the pontoon train already there. A few of the enemy were intrenched on the west bank, but they made little resistance and soon surrendered. Two divisions were crossed that night and the third the following morning.

On the 18th I moved along the Vicksburg road in advance of the troops and as soon as possible joined Sherman. My first anxiety was to secure a base of supplies on the Yazoo River above Vicksburg. Sherman's line of march led him to the very point on Walnut Hills occupied by the enemy the December before when he was repulsed. Sherman was equally anxious with myself. Our impatience led us to move in advance of the column and well up with the advanced skirmishers. There were some detached works along the crest of the hill. These were still occupied by the enemy, or else the garrison from Haines' Bluff had not all got past on their way to Vicksburg. At all events the bullets of the enemy whistled by thick and fast for a short time. In a few minutes Sherman had the pleasure of looking down from the spot coveted so much by him the December before on the ground where his command had lain so helpless for offensive action. He turned to me, saying that up to this minute he had felt no positive assurance of success. This, however, he said was the end of one of the greatest campaigns in history and I ought to make a report of it at once. Vicksburg was not yet captured, and there was no telling what might happen before it was taken; but whether captured or not, this was a complete and successful campaign. I do not claim to quote Sherman's language; but the substance only. My reason for mentioning this incident will appear further on.

McPherson, after crossing the Big Black, came into the Jackson and Vicksburg road which Sherman was on, but to his rear. He arrived at night near the lines of the enemy, and went into camp. McClernand moved by the direct road near the railroad to Mount Albans, and then turned to the left and put his troops on the road from Baldwin's ferry to Vicksburg. This brought him south of McPherson. I now had my three corps up to the works built for the defence of Vicksburg, on three roads—one to the north, one to the east and one to the south-east of the city. By the morning of the 19th the investment was as complete as my limited number of troops would allow. Sherman was on the right, and covered the high ground from where it overlooked the Yazoo as far south-east as his troops would extend. McPherson joined on to his left, and occupied ground on both sides of the Jackson road. McClernand took up the ground to his left and extended as far towards Warrenton as he could, keeping a continuous line.

On the 19th there was constant skirmishing with the enemy while we were getting into better position. The enemy had been much demoralized by his defeats at Champion's Hill and the Big Black, and I believed he would not make much effort to hold Vicksburg. Accordingly, at two o'clock I ordered an assault. It resulted in securing more advanced positions for all our troops where they were fully covered from the fire of the enemy.

The 20th and 21st were spent in strengthening our position and in making roads in rear of the army, from Yazoo River or Chickasaw Bayou. Most of the army had now been for three weeks with only five days' rations issued by the commissary. They had an abundance of food, however, but began to feel the want of bread. I remember that in passing around to the left of the line on the 21st, a soldier, recognizing me, said in rather a low voice, but yet so that I heard him, "Hard tack." In a moment the cry was taken up all along the line, "Hard tack! Hard tack!" I told the men nearest to me that we had been engaged ever since the arrival of the troops in building a road over which to supply them with everything they needed. The cry was instantly changed to cheers. By the night of the 21st all the troops had full rations issued to them. The bread and coffee were highly appreciated.

I now determined on a second assault. Johnston was in my rear, only fifty miles away, with an army not much inferior in numbers to the one I had with me, and I knew he was being reinforced. There was danger of his coming to the assistance of Pemberton, and after all he might defeat my anticipations of capturing the garrison if, indeed, he did not prevent the capture of the city. The immediate capture of Vicksburg would save sending me the reinforcements which were so much wanted elsewhere, and would set free the army under me to drive Johnston from the State. But the first consideration of all was—the troops believed they could carry the works in their front, and would not have worked so patiently in the trenches if they had not been allowed to try.

The attack was ordered to commence on all parts of the line at ten o'clock A.M. on the 22d with a furious cannonade from every battery in position. All the corps commanders set their time by mine so that all might open the engagement at the same minute. The attack was gallant, and portions of each of the three corps succeeded in getting up to the very parapets of the enemy and in planting their battle flags upon them; but at no place were we able to enter. General McClernand reported that he had gained the enemy's intrenchments at several points, and wanted reinforcements. I occupied a position from which I believed I could see as well as he what took place in his front, and I did not see the success he reported. But his request for reinforcements being repeated I could not ignore it, and sent him Quinby's division of the 17th corps. Sherman and McPherson were both ordered to renew their assaults as a diversion in favor of McClernand. This last attack only served to increase our casualties without giving any benefit whatever. As soon as it was dark our troops that had reached the enemy's line and been obliged to remain there for security all day, were withdrawn; and thus ended the last assault upon Vicksburg.

Chapter XXXVII.

SIEGE OF VICKSBURG.

I NOW DETERMINED upon a regular siege—to "out-camp the enemy," as it were, and to incur no more losses. The experience of the 22d convinced officers and men that this was best, and they went to work on the defences and approaches with a will. With the navy holding the river, the investment of Vicksburg was complete. As long as we could hold our position the enemy was limited in supplies of food, men and munitions of war to what they had on hand. These could not last always.

The crossing of troops at Bruinsburg commenced April 30th. On the 18th of May the army was in rear of Vicksburg. On the 19th, just twenty days after the crossing, the city was completely invested and an assault had been made: five distinct battles (besides continuous skirmishing) had been fought and won by the Union forces; the capital of the State had fallen and its arsenals, military manufactories and everything useful for military purposes had been destroyed; an average of about one hundred and eighty miles had been marched by the troops engaged; but five days' rations had been issued, and no forage; over six thousand prisoners had been captured, and as many more of the enemy had been killed or wounded; twenty-seven heavy cannon and sixty-one field-pieces had fallen into our hands; and four hundred miles of the river, from Vicksburg to Port Hudson, had become ours. The Union force that had crossed the Mississippi River up to this time was less than forty-three thousand men. One division of these, Blair's, only arrived in time to take part in the battle of Champion's Hill, but was not engaged there; and one brigade, Ransom's of McPherson's corps, reached the field after the battle. The enemy had at Vicksburg, Grand Gulf, Jackson, and on the roads between these places, over sixty thousand men. They were in their own country, where no rear guards were necessary. The country is admirable for defence, but difficult for the conduct of an offensive campaign. All their troops had to be met. We were fortunate, to say the least, in meeting them in detail: at Port Gibson seven or eight thousand; at Raymond, five thousand; at Jackson, from eight to eleven thousand; at Champion's Hill, twenty-five thousand; at the Big Black, four thousand. A part of those met at Jackson were all that was left of those encountered at Raymond. They were beaten in detail by a force smaller than their own, upon their own ground. Our loss up to this time was:

AT	KILLED.	WOUNDED.	MISSING.
Port Gibson	131	719	25
South Fork Bayou Pierre .	. .	1	. .
Skirmishes, May 3	1	9	. .
Fourteen Mile Creek . . .	6	24	. .
Raymond	66	339	37
Jackson	42	251	7
Champion's Hill	410	1,844	187
Big Black	39	237	3
Bridgeport	. .	1	. .
Total	695	3,425	259

Of the wounded many were but slightly so, and continued on duty. Not half of them were disabled for any length of time.

After the unsuccessful assault of the 22d the work of the regular siege began. Sherman occupied the right starting from the river above Vicksburg, McPherson the centre (McArthur's division now with him) and McClernand the left, holding the road south to Warrenton. Lauman's division arrived at this time and was placed on the extreme left of the line.

In the interval between the assaults of the 19th and 22d, roads had been completed from the Yazoo River and Chickasaw Bayou, around the rear of the army, to enable us to bring up supplies of food and ammunition; ground had been selected and cleared on which the troops were to be encamped, and tents and cooking utensils were brought up. The troops had been without these from the time of crossing the Mississippi up to this time. All was now ready for the pick and spade. Prentiss and Hurlbut were ordered to send forward every man that could be spared. Cavalry especially was wanted to watch the fords along the Big Black, and to observe Johnston. I knew that Johnston was receiving reinforcements from Bragg, who was confronting Rosecrans in Tennessee. Vicksburg was so important to the enemy that I believed he would make the most strenuous efforts to raise the siege, even at the risk of losing ground elsewhere.

My line was more than fifteen miles long, extending from Haines' Bluff to Vicksburg, thence to Warrenton. The line of the enemy was about seven. In addition to this, having an enemy at Canton and Jackson, in our rear, who was being constantly reinforced, we required a second line of defence facing the other way. I had not troops enough under my command to man these. General Halleck appreciated the situation and, without being asked, forwarded reinforcements with all possible dispatch.

The ground about Vicksburg is admirable for defence. On the north it is about two hundred feet above the Mississippi River at the highest point and very much cut up by the washing rains; the ravines were grown up with cane and underbrush, while the sides and tops were covered with a dense forest. Farther south the ground flattens out somewhat, and was in cultivation. But here, too, it was cut up by ravines and small streams. The enemy's line of defence followed the crest of a ridge from the river north of the city eastward, then southerly around to the Jackson road, full three miles back of the city; thence in a southwesterly direction to the river. Deep ravines of the description given lay in front of these defences. As there is a succession of gullies, cut out by rains along the side of the ridge, the line was necessarily very irregular. To follow each of these spurs with intrenchments, so as to command the slopes on either side, would have lengthened their line very much. Generally therefore, or in many places, their line would run from near the head of one gully nearly straight to the head of another, and an outer work triangular in shape, generally open in the rear, was thrown up on the point; with a few men in this outer work they commanded the approaches to the main line completely.

The work to be done, to make our position as strong against the enemy as his was against us, was very great. The problem was also complicated by our wanting our line as near that of the enemy as possible. We had but four engineer officers with us. Captain Prime, of the Engineer Corps, was the chief, and the work at the beginning was mainly directed by him. His health soon gave out, when he was succeeded by Captain Comstock, also of the Engineer Corps. To provide assistants on such a long line I directed that all officers who had graduated at West Point, where they had necessarily to study military engineering, should in addition to their other duties assist in the work.

The chief quartermaster and the chief commissary were graduates. The chief commissary, now the Commissary-General of the Army, begged off, however, saying that there was nothing in engineering that he was good for unless he would do for a sap-roller. As soldiers require rations while working in the ditches as well as when marching and fighting, and as we would be sure to lose him if he was used as a sap-roller, I let him off. The general is a large man; weighs two hundred and twenty pounds, and is not tall.

We had no siege guns except six thirty-two pounders, and there were none at the West to draw from. Admiral Porter, however, supplied us with a battery of navy-guns of large calibre, and with these, and the field artillery used in the campaign, the siege began. The first thing to do was to get the artillery in batteries where they would occupy commanding positions; then establish the camps, under cover from the fire of the enemy but as near up as possible; and then construct rifle-pits and covered ways, to connect the entire command by the shortest route. The enemy did not harass us much while we were constructing our batteries. Probably their artillery ammunition was short; and their infantry was kept down by our sharpshooters, who were always on the alert and ready to fire at a head whenever it showed itself above the rebel works.

In no place were our lines more than six hundred yards from the enemy. It was necessary, therefore, to cover our men

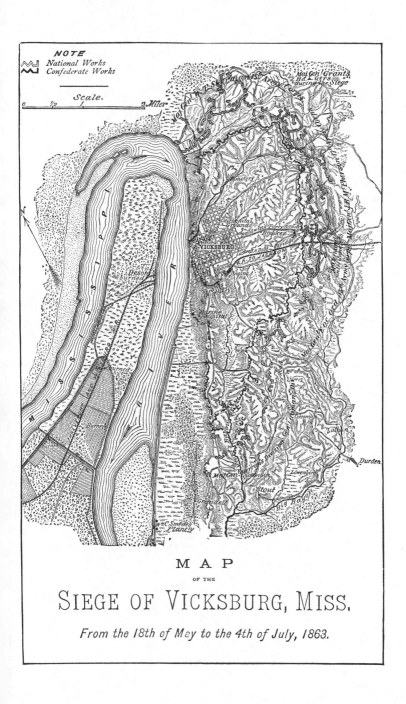

MAP

OF THE

SIEGE OF VICKSBURG, MISS.

From the 18th of May to the 4th of July, 1863.

by something more than the ordinary parapet. To give additional protection sand bags, bullet-proof, were placed along the tops of the parapets far enough apart to make loop-holes for musketry. On top of these, logs were put. By these means the men were enabled to walk about erect when off duty, without fear of annoyance from sharpshooters. The enemy used in their defence explosive musket-balls, no doubt thinking that, bursting over our men in the trenches, they would do some execution; but I do not remember a single case where a man was injured by a piece of one of these shells. When they were hit and the ball exploded, the wound was terrible. In these cases a solid ball would have hit as well. Their use is barbarous, because they produce increased suffering without any corresponding advantage to those using them.

The enemy could not resort to our method to protect their men, because we had an inexhaustible supply of ammunition to draw upon and used it freely. Splinters from the timber would have made havoc among the men behind.

There were no mortars with the besiegers, except what the navy had in front of the city; but wooden ones were made by taking logs of the toughest wood that could be found, boring them out for six or twelve pound shells and binding them with strong iron bands. These answered as coehorns, and shells were successfully thrown from them into the trenches of the enemy.

The labor of building the batteries and intrenching was largely done by the pioneers, assisted by negroes who came within our lines and who were paid for their work; but details from the troops had often to be made. The work was pushed forward as rapidly as possible, and when an advanced position was secured and covered from the fire of the enemy the batteries were advanced. By the 30th of June there were two hundred and twenty guns in position, mostly light field-pieces, besides a battery of heavy guns belonging to, manned and commanded by the navy. We were now as strong for defence against the garrison of Vicksburg as they were against us; but I knew that Johnston was in our rear, and was receiving constant reinforcements from the east. He had at this time a larger force than I had had at any time prior to the battle of Champion's Hill.

As soon as the news of the arrival of the Union army behind Vicksburg reached the North, floods of visitors began to pour in. Some came to gratify curiosity; some to see sons or brothers who had passed through the terrible ordeal; members of the Christian and Sanitary Associations came to minister to the wants of the sick and the wounded. Often those coming to see a son or brother would bring a dozen or two of poultry. They did not know how little the gift would be appreciated. Many of the soldiers had lived so much on chickens, ducks and turkeys without bread during the march, that the sight of poultry, if they could get bacon, almost took away their appetite. But the intention was good.

Among the earliest arrivals was the Governor of Illinois, with most of the State officers. I naturally wanted to show them what there was of most interest. In Sherman's front the ground was the most broken and most wooded, and more was to be seen without exposure. I therefore took them to Sherman's headquarters and presented them. Before starting out to look at the lines—possibly while Sherman's horse was being saddled—there were many questions asked about the late campaign, about which the North had been so imperfectly informed. There was a little knot around Sherman and another around me, and I heard Sherman repeating, in the most animated manner, what he had said to me when we first looked down from Walnut Hills upon the land below on the 18th of May, adding: "Grant is entitled to every bit of the credit for the campaign; I opposed it. I wrote him a letter about it." But for this speech it is not likely that Sherman's opposition would have ever been heard of. His untiring energy and great efficiency during the campaign entitle him to a full share of all the credit due for its success. He could not have done more if the plan had been his own.

NOTE.—When General Sherman first learned of the move I proposed to make, he called to see me about it. I recollect that I had transferred my headquarters from a boat in the river to a house a short distance back from the levee. I was seated on the piazza engaged in conversation with my staff when Sherman came up. After a few moments' conversation he said that he would like to see me alone. We passed into the house together and shut the door after us. Sherman then expressed his alarm at the move I had ordered, saying that I was putting myself in a position voluntarily which an enemy

On the 26th of May I sent Blair's division up the Yazoo to drive out a force of the enemy supposed to be between the Big Black and the Yazoo. The country was rich and full of supplies of both food and forage. Blair was instructed to take all of it. The cattle were to be driven in for the use of our army, and the food and forage to be consumed by our troops or destroyed by fire; all bridges were to be destroyed, and the roads rendered as nearly impassable as possible. Blair went

---

would be glad to manœuvre a year—or a long time—to get me in. I was going into the enemy's country, with a large river behind me and the enemy holding points strongly fortified above and below. He said that it was an axiom in war that when any great body of troops moved against an enemy they should do so from a base of supplies, which they would guard as they would the apple of the eye, etc. He pointed out all the difficulties that might be encountered in the campaign proposed, and stated in turn what would be the true campaign to make. This was, in substance, to go back until high ground could be reached on the east bank of the river; fortify there and establish a depot of supplies, and move from there, being always prepared to fall back upon it in case of disaster. I said this would take us back to Memphis. Sherman then said that was the very place he would go to, and would move by railroad from Memphis to Grenada, repairing the road as we advanced. To this I replied, the country is already disheartened over the lack of success on the part of our armies; the last election went against the vigorous prosecution of the war, voluntary enlistments had ceased throughout most of the North and conscription was already resorted to, and if we went back so far as Memphis it would discourage the people so much that bases of supplies would be of no use: neither men to hold them nor supplies to put in them would be furnished. The problem for us was to move forward to a decisive victory, or our cause was lost. No progress was being made in any other field, and we had to go on.

Sherman wrote to my adjutant general, Colonel J. A. Rawlins, embodying his views of the campaign that should be made, and asking him to advise me to at least get the views of my generals upon the subject. Colonel Rawlins showed me the letter, but I did not see any reason for changing my plans. The letter was not answered and the subect was not subsequently mentioned between Sherman and myself to the end of the war, that I remember of. I did not regard the letter as official, and consequently did not preserve it. General Sherman furnished a copy himself to General Badeau, who printed it in his history of my campaigns. I did not regard either the conversation between us or the letter to my adjutant-general as protests, but simply friendly advice which the relations between us fully justified. Sherman gave the same energy to make the campaign a success that he would or could have done if it had been ordered by himself. I make this statement here to correct an impression which was circulated at the close of the war to Sherman's prejudice, and for which there was no fair foundation.

forty-five miles and was gone almost a week. His work was effectually done. I requested Porter at this time to send the marine brigade, a floating nondescript force which had been assigned to his command and which proved very useful, up to Haines' Bluff to hold it until reinforcements could be sent.

On the 26th I also received a letter from Banks, asking me to reinforce him with ten thousand men at Port Hudson. Of course I could not comply with his request, nor did I think he needed them. He was in no danger of an attack by the garrison in his front, and there was no army organizing in his rear to raise the siege.

On the 3d of June a brigade from Hurlbut's command arrived, General Kimball commanding. It was sent to Mechanicsburg, some miles north-east of Haines' Bluff and about midway between the Big Black and the Yazoo. A brigade of Blair's division and twelve hundred cavalry had already, on Blair's return from the Yazoo, been sent to the same place with instructions to watch the crossings of the Big Black River, to destroy the roads in his (Blair's) front, and to gather or destroy all supplies.

On the 7th of June our little force of colored and white troops across the Mississippi, at Milliken's Bend, were attacked by about 3,000 men from Richard Taylor's trans-Mississippi command. With the aid of the gunboats they were speedily repelled. I sent Mower's brigade over with instructions to drive the enemy beyond the Tensas Bayou; and we had no further trouble in that quarter during the siege. This was the first important engagement of the war in which colored troops were under fire. These men were very raw, having all been enlisted since the beginning of the siege, but they behaved well.

On the 8th of June a full division arrived from Hurlbut's command, under General Sooy Smith. It was sent immediately to Haines' Bluff, and General C. C. Washburn was assigned to the general command at that point.

On the 11th a strong division arrived from the Department of the Missouri under General Herron, which was placed on our left. This cut off the last possible chance of communication between Pemberton and Johnston, as it enabled

Lauman to close up on McClernand's left while Herron intrenched from Lauman to the water's edge. At this point the
water recedes a few hundred yards from the high land.
Through this opening no doubt the Confederate commanders
had been able to get messengers under cover of night.

On the 14th General Parke arrived with two divisions of
Burnside's corps, and was immediately dispatched to Haines'
Bluff. These latter troops—Herron's and Parke's—were the
reinforcements already spoken of sent by Halleck in anticipation of their being needed. They arrived none too soon.

I now had about seventy-one thousand men. More than
half were disposed across the peninsula, between the Yazoo at
Haines' Bluff and the Big Black, with the division of Osterhaus watching the crossings of the latter river farther south
and west from the crossing of the Jackson road to Baldwin's
ferry and below.

There were eight roads leading into Vicksburg, along
which and their immediate sides, our work was specially
pushed and batteries advanced; but no commanding point
within range of the enemy was neglected.

On the 17th I received a letter from General Sherman and
one on the 18th from General McPherson, saying that their
respective commands had complained to them of a fulsome,
congratulatory order published by General McClernand to
the 13th corps, which did great injustice to the other troops
engaged in the campaign. This order had been sent North
and published, and now papers containing it had reached our
camps. The order had not been heard of by me, and certainly
not by troops outside of McClernand's command until
brought in this way. I at once wrote to McClernand, directing him to send me a copy of this order. He did so, and I at
once relieved him from the command of the 13th army corps
and ordered him back to Springfield, Illinois. The publication
of his order in the press was in violation of War Department
orders and also of mine.

Chapter XXXVIII.

JOHNSTON'S MOVEMENTS — FORTIFICATIONS AT
HAINES' BLUFF — EXPLOSION OF THE MINE — EXPLOSION
OF THE SECOND MINE — PREPARING FOR THE
ASSAULT — THE FLAG OF TRUCE — MEETING
WITH PEMBERTON — NEGOTIATIONS FOR
SURRENDER — ACCEPTING THE TERMS —
SURRENDER OF VICKSBURG.

O N THE 22D of June positive information was received
that Johnston had crossed the Big Black River for
the purpose of attacking our rear, to raise the siege and release Pemberton. The correspondence between Johnston and
Pemberton shows that all expectation of holding Vicksburg had by this time passed from Johnston's mind. I
immediately ordered Sherman to the command of all the
forces from Haines' Bluff to the Big Black River. This
amounted now to quite half the troops about Vicksburg. Besides these, Herron and A. J. Smith's divisions were ordered
to hold themselves in readiness to reinforce Sherman.
Haines' Bluff had been strongly fortified on the land side,
and on all commanding points from there to the Big Black
at the railroad crossing batteries had been constructed. The
work of connecting by rifle-pits where this was not already
done, was an easy task for the troops that were to defend
them.

We were now looking west, besieging Pemberton, while
we were also looking east to defend ourselves against an expected siege by Johnston. But as against the garrison of
Vicksburg we were as substantially protected as they were
against us. Where we were looking east and north we were
strongly fortified, and on the defensive. Johnston evidently
took in the situation and wisely, I think, abstained from
making an assault on us because it would simply have inflicted loss on both sides without accomplishing any result.
We were strong enough to have taken the offensive against
him; but I did not feel disposed to take any risk of losing
our hold upon Pemberton's army, while I would have re-

joiced at the opportunity of defending ourselves against an attack by Johnston.

From the 23d of May the work of fortifying and pushing forward our position nearer to the enemy had been steadily progressing. At three points on the Jackson road, in front of Leggett's brigade, a sap was run up to the enemy's parapet, and by the 25th of June we had it undermined and the mine charged. The enemy had countermined, but did not succeed in reaching our mine. At this particular point the hill on which the rebel work stands rises abruptly. Our sap ran close up to the outside of the enemy's parapet. In fact this parapet was also our protection. The soldiers of the two sides occasionally conversed pleasantly across this barrier; sometimes they exchanged the hard bread of the Union soldiers for the tobacco of the Confederates; at other times the enemy threw over hand-grenades, and often our men, catching them in their hands, returned them.

Our mine had been started some distance back down the hill; consequently when it had extended as far as the parapet it was many feet below it. This caused the failure of the enemy in his search to find and destroy it. On the 25th of June at three o'clock, all being ready, the mine was exploded. A heavy artillery fire all along the line had been ordered to open with the explosion. The effect was to blow the top of the hill off and make a crater where it stood. The breach was not sufficient to enable us to pass a column of attack through. In fact, the enemy having failed to reach our mine had thrown up a line farther back, where most of the men guarding that point were placed. There were a few men, however, left at the advance line, and others working in the countermine, which was still being pushed to find ours. All that were there were thrown into the air, some of them coming down on our side, still alive. I remember one colored man, who had been under ground at work when the explosion took place, who was thrown to our side. He was not much hurt, but terribly frightened. Some one asked him how high he had gone up. "Dun no, massa, but t'ink 'bout t'ree mile," was his reply. General Logan commanded at this point and took this colored man to his quarters, where he did service to the end of the siege.

As soon as the explosion took place the crater was seized by two regiments of our troops who were near by, under cover, where they had been placed for the express purpose. The enemy made a desperate effort to expel them, but failed, and soon retired behind the new line. From here, however, they threw hand-grenades, which did some execution. The compliment was returned by our men, but not with so much effect. The enemy could lay their grenades on the parapet, which alone divided the contestants, and roll them down upon us; while from our side they had to be thrown over the parapet, which was at considerable elevation. During the night we made efforts to secure our position in the crater against the missiles of the enemy, so as to run trenches along the outer base of their parapet, right and left; but the enemy continued throwing their grenades, and brought boxes of field ammunition (shells), the fuses of which they would light with portfires, and throw them by hand into our ranks. We found it impossible to continue this work. Another mine was consequently started which was exploded on the 1st of July, destroying an entire rebel redan, killing and wounding a considerable number of its occupants and leaving an immense chasm where it stood. No attempt to charge was made this time, the experience of the 25th admonishing us. Our loss in the first affair was about thirty killed and wounded. The enemy must have lost more in the two explosions than we did in the first. We lost none in the second.

From this time forward the work of mining and pushing our position nearer to the enemy was prosecuted with vigor, and I determined to explode no more mines until we were ready to explode a number at different points and assault immediately after. We were up now at three different points, one in front of each corps, to where only the parapet of the enemy divided us.

At this time an intercepted dispatch from Johnston to Pemberton informed me that Johnston intended to make a determined attack upon us in order to relieve the garrison at Vicksburg. I knew the garrison would make no formidable effort to relieve itself. The picket lines were so close to each other—where there was space enough between the lines to post pickets—that the men could converse. On the 21st of

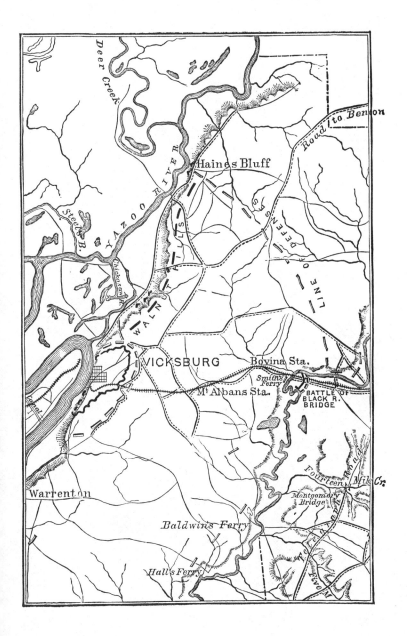

June I was informed, through this means, that Pemberton was preparing to escape, by crossing to the Louisiana side under cover of night; that he had employed workmen in making boats for that purpose; that the men had been canvassed to ascertain if they would make an assault on the "Yankees" to cut their way out; that they had refused, and almost mutinied, because their commander would not surrender and relieve their sufferings, and had only been pacified by the assurance that boats enough would be finished in a week to carry them all over. The rebel pickets also said that houses in the city had been pulled down to get material to build these boats with. Afterwards this story was verified: on entering the city we found a large number of very rudely constructed boats.

All necessary steps were at once taken to render such an attempt abortive. Our pickets were doubled; Admiral Porter was notified, so that the river might be more closely watched; material was collected on the west bank of the river to be set on fire and light up the river if the attempt was made; and batteries were established along the levee crossing the peninsula on the Louisiana side. Had the attempt been made the garrison of Vicksburg would have been drowned, or made prisoners on the Louisiana side. General Richard Taylor was expected on the west bank to co-operate in this movement, I believe, but he did not come, nor could he have done so with a force sufficient to be of service. The Mississippi was now in our possession from its source to its mouth, except in the immediate front of Vicksburg and of Port Hudson. We had nearly exhausted the country, along a line drawn from Lake Providence to opposite Bruinsburg. The roads west were not of a character to draw supplies over for any considerable force.

By the 1st of July our approaches had reached the enemy's ditch at a number of places. At ten points we could move under cover to within from five to one hundred yards of the enemy. Orders were given to make all preparations for assault on the 6th of July. The debouches were ordered widened to afford easy egress, while the approaches were also to be widened to admit the troops to pass through four abreast. Plank, and bags filled with cotton packed in tightly, were ordered prepared, to enable the troops to cross the ditches.

On the night of the 1st of July Johnston was between Brownsville and the Big Black, and wrote Pemberton from there that about the 7th of the month an attempt would be made to create a diversion to enable him to cut his way out. Pemberton was a prisoner before this message reached him.

On July 1st Pemberton, seeing no hope of outside relief, addressed the following letter to each of his four division commanders:

"Unless the siege of Vicksburg is raised, or supplies are thrown in, it will become necessary very shortly to evacuate the place. I see no prospect of the former, and there are many great, if not insuperable obstacles in the way of the latter. You are, therefore, requested to inform me with as little delay as possible, as to the condition of your troops and their ability to make the marches and undergo the fatigues necessary to accomplish a successful evacuation."

Two of his generals suggested surrender, and the other two practically did the same. They expressed the opinion that an attempt to evacuate would fail. Pemberton had previously got a message to Johnston suggesting that he should try to negotiate with me for a release of the garrison with their arms. Johnston replied that it would be a confession of weakness for him to do so; but he authorized Pemberton to use his name in making such an arrangement.

On the 3d about ten o'clock A.M. white flags appeared on a portion of the rebel works. Hostilities along that part of the line ceased at once. Soon two persons were seen coming towards our lines bearing a white flag. They proved to be General Bowen, a division commander, and Colonel Montgomery, aide-de-camp to Pemberton, bearing the following letter to me:

"I have the honor to propose an armistice for —— hours, with the view to arranging terms for the capitulation of Vicksburg. To this end, if agreeable to you, I will appoint three commissioners, to meet a like number to be named by yourself, at such place and hour to-day as you may find convenient. I make this proposition to save the further effusion of blood, which must otherwise be shed to a frightful extent, feeling myself fully able to maintain my position for a yet indefinite period. This communication will be handed you under a flag of truce, by Major-General John S. Bowen."

It was a glorious sight to officers and soldiers on the line where these white flags were visible, and the news soon spread to all parts of the command. The troops felt that their long and weary marches, hard fighting, ceaseless watching by night and day, in a hot climate, exposure to all sorts of weather, to diseases and, worst of all, to the gibes of many Northern papers that came to them saying all their suffering was in vain, that Vicksburg would never be taken, were at last at an end and the Union sure to be saved.

Bowen was received by General A. J. Smith, and asked to see me. I had been a neighbor of Bowen's in Missouri, and knew him well and favorably before the war; but his request was refused. He then suggested that I should meet Pemberton. To this I sent a verbal message saying that, if Pemberton desired it, I would meet him in front of McPherson's corps at three o'clock that afternoon. I also sent the following written reply to Pemberton's letter:

"Your note of this date is just received, proposing an armistice for several hours, for the purpose of arranging terms of capitulation through commissioners, to be appointed, etc. The useless effusion of blood you propose stopping by this course can be ended at any time you may choose, by the unconditional surrender of the city and garrison. Men who have shown so much endurance and courage as those now in Vicksburg, will always challenge the respect of an adversary, and I can assure you will be treated with all the respect due to prisoners of war. I do not favor the proposition of appointing commissioners to arrange the terms of capitulation, because I have no terms other than those indicated above."

At three o'clock Pemberton appeared at the point suggested in my verbal message, accompanied by the same officers who had borne his letter of the morning. Generals Ord, McPherson, Logan and A. J. Smith, and several officers of my staff, accompanied me. Our place of meeting was on a hillside within a few hundred feet of the rebel lines. Near by stood a stunted oak-tree, which was made historical by the event. It was but a short time before the last vestige of its body, root and limb had disappeared, the fragments taken as trophies. Since then the same tree has furnished as many cords of wood, in the shape of trophies, as "The True Cross."

Pemberton and I had served in the same division during part of the Mexican War. I knew him very well therefore, and greeted him as an old acquaintance. He soon asked what terms I proposed to give his army if it surrendered. My answer was the same as proposed in my reply to his letter. Pemberton then said, rather snappishly, "The conference might as well end," and turned abruptly as if to leave. I said, "Very well." General Bowen, I saw, was very anxious that the surrender should be consummated. His manner and remarks while Pemberton and I were talking, showed this. He now proposed that he and one of our generals should have a conference. I had no objection to this, as nothing could be made binding upon me that they might propose. Smith and Bowen accordingly had a conference, during which Pemberton and I, moving a short distance away towards the enemy's lines were in conversation. After a while Bowen suggested that the Confederate army should be allowed to march out with the honors of war, carrying their small arms and field artillery. This was promptly and unceremoniously rejected. The interview here ended, I agreeing, however, to send a letter giving final terms by ten o'clock that night.

Word was sent to Admiral Porter soon after the correspondence with Pemberton commenced, so that hostilities might be stopped on the part of both army and navy. It was agreed on my parting with Pemberton that they should not be renewed until our correspondence ceased.

When I returned to my headquarters I sent for all the corps and division commanders with the army immediately confronting Vicksburg. Half the army was from eight to twelve miles off, waiting for Johnston. I informed them of the contents of Pemberton's letters, of my reply and the substance of the interview, and that I was ready to hear any suggestion; but would hold the power of deciding entirely in my own hands. This was the nearest approach to a "council of war" I ever held. Against the general, and almost unanimous judgment of the council I sent the following letter:

"In conformity with agreement of this afternoon, I will submit the following proposition for the surrender of the City of Vicksburg, public stores, etc. On your accepting the terms proposed, I will march in one division as a guard, and take possession at eight A.M. to-morrow. As soon as rolls can be made out, and paroles be signed by officers and men, you will be allowed to march out of our lines, the officers taking with them their side-arms and clothing, and the field, staff and cavalry officers one horse each. The rank and file will be allowed all their clothing, but no other property. If these conditions are accepted, any amount of rations you may deem necessary can be taken from the stores you now have, and also the necessary cooking utensils for preparing them. Thirty wagons also, counting two two-horse or mule teams as one, will be allowed to transport such articles as cannot be carried along. The same conditions will be allowed to all sick and wounded officers and soldiers as fast as they become able to travel. The paroles for these latter must be signed, however, whilst officers present are authorized to sign the roll of prisoners."

By the terms of the cartel then in force, prisoners captured by either army were required to be forwarded as soon as possible to either Aiken's landing below Dutch Gap on the James River, or to Vicksburg, there to be exchanged, or paroled until they could be exchanged. There was a Confederate commissioner at Vicksburg, authorized to make the exchange. I did not propose to take him a prisoner, but to leave him free to perform the functions of his office. Had I insisted upon an unconditional surrender there would have been over thirty thousand men to transport to Cairo, very much to the inconvenience of the army on the Mississippi. Thence the prisoners would have had to be transported by rail to Washington or Baltimore; thence again by steamer to Aiken's—all at very great expense. At Aiken's they would have had to be paroled, because the Confederates did not have Union prisoners to give in exchange. Then again Pemberton's army was largely composed of men whose homes were in the South-west; I knew many of them were tired of the war and would get home just as soon as they could. A large number of them had voluntarily come into our lines during the siege, and requested to be sent north where they could get employment until the war was over and they could go to their homes.

Late at night I received the following reply to my last letter:

"I have the honor to acknowledge the receipt of your communication of this date, proposing terms of capitulation for this garrison and post. In the main your terms are accepted; but, in justice both to the honor and spirit of my troops, manifested in the defence of Vicksburg, I have to submit the following amendments, which, if acceded to by you, will perfect the agreement between us. At ten o'clock A.M. to-morrow, I propose to evacuate the works in and around Vicksburg, and to surrender the city and garrison under my command, by marching out with my colors and arms, stacking them in front of my present lines. After which you will take possession. Officers to retain their side-arms and personal property, and the rights and property of citizens to be respected."

This was received after midnight. My reply was as follows:

"I have the honor to acknowledge the receipt of your communication of 3d July. The amendment proposed by you cannot be acceded to in full. It will be necessary to furnish every officer and man with a parole signed by himself, which, with the completion of the roll of prisoners, will necessarily take some time. Again, I can make no stipulations with regard to the treatment of citizens and their private property. While I do not propose to cause them any undue annoyance or loss, I cannot consent to leave myself under any restraint by stipulations. The property which officers will be allowed to take with them will be as stated in my proposition of last evening; that is, officers will be allowed their private baggage and side-arms, and mounted officers one horse each. If you mean by your proposition for each brigade to march to the front of the lines now occupied by it, and stack arms at ten o'clock A.M., and then return to the inside and there remain as prisoners until properly paroled, I will make no objection to it. Should no notification be received of your acceptance of my terms by nine o'clock A.M. I shall regard them as having been rejected, and shall act accordingly. Should these terms be accepted, white flags should be displayed along your lines to prevent such of my troops as may not have been notified, from firing upon your men."

Pemberton promptly accepted these terms.

During the siege there had been a good deal of friendly sparring between the soldiers of the two armies, on picket and where the lines were close together. All rebels were known as "Johnnies," all Union troops as "Yanks." Often "Johnny" would call: "Well, Yank, when are you coming into town?"

The reply was sometimes: "We propose to celebrate the 4th of July there." Sometimes it would be: "We always treat our prisoners with kindness and do not want to hurt them;" or, "We are holding you as prisoners of war while you are feeding yourselves." The garrison, from the commanding general down, undoubtedly expected an assault on the fourth. They knew from the temper of their men it would be successful when made; and that would be a greater humiliation than to surrender. Besides it would be attended with severe loss to them.

The Vicksburg paper, which we received regularly through the courtesy of the rebel pickets, said prior to the fourth, in speaking of the "Yankee" boast that they would take dinner in Vicksburg that day, that the best receipt for cooking a rabbit was "First ketch your rabbit." The paper at this time and for some time previous was printed on the plain side of wall paper. The last number was issued on the fourth and announced that we had "caught our rabbit."

I have no doubt that Pemberton commenced his correspondence on the third with a two-fold purpose: first, to avoid an assault, which he knew would be successful, and second, to prevent the capture taking place on the great national holiday, the anniversary of the Declaration of American Independence. Holding out for better terms as he did he defeated his aim in the latter particular.

At the appointed hour the garrison of Vicksburg marched out of their works and formed line in front, stacked arms and marched back in good order. Our whole army present witnessed this scene without cheering. Logan's division, which had approached nearest the rebel works, was the first to march in; and the flag of one of the regiments of his division was soon floating over the court-house. Our soldiers were no sooner inside the lines than the two armies began to fraternize. Our men had had full rations from the time the siege commenced, to the close. The enemy had been suffering, particularly towards the last. I myself saw our men taking bread from their haversacks and giving it to the enemy they had so recently been engaged in starving out. It was accepted with avidity and with thanks.

Pemberton says in his report:

"If it should be asked why the 4th of July was selected as the day for surrender, the answer is obvious. I believed that upon that day I should obtain better terms. Well aware of the vanity of our foe, I knew they would attach vast importance to the entrance on the 4th of July into the stronghold of the great river, and that, to gratify their national vanity, they would yield then what could not be extorted from them at any other time."

This does not support my view of his reasons for selecting the day he did for surrendering. But it must be recollected that his first letter asking terms was received about 10 o'clock A.M., July 3d. It then could hardly be expected that it would take twenty-four hours to effect a surrender. He knew that Johnston was in our rear for the purpose of raising the siege, and he naturally would want to hold out as long as he could. He knew his men would not resist an assault, and one was expected on the fourth. In our interview he told me he had rations enough to hold out for some time—my recollection is two weeks. It was this statement that induced me to insert in the terms that he was to draw rations for his men from his own supplies.

On the 4th of July General Holmes, with an army of eight or nine thousand men belonging to the trans-Mississippi department, made an attack upon Helena, Arkansas. He was totally defeated by General Prentiss, who was holding Helena with less than forty-two hundred soldiers. Holmes reported his loss at 1,636, of which 173 were killed; but as Prentiss buried 400, Holmes evidently understated his losses. The Union loss was 57 killed, 127 wounded, and between 30 and 40 missing. This was the last effort on the part of the Confederacy to raise the siege of Vicksburg.

On the third, as soon as negotiations were commenced, I notified Sherman and directed him to be ready to take the offensive against Johnston, drive him out of the State and destroy his army if he could. Steele and Ord were directed at the same time to be in readiness to join Sherman as soon as the surrender took place. Of this Sherman was notified.

I rode into Vicksburg with the troops, and went to the river to exchange congratulations with the navy upon our joint victory. At that time I found that many of the citizens had been living under ground. The ridges upon which Vicksburg is built, and those back to the Big Black, are composed of a deep yellow clay of great tenacity. Where roads and streets are cut through, perpendicular banks are left and stand as well as if composed of stone. The magazines of the enemy were made by running passage-ways into this clay at places where there were deep cuts. Many citizens secured places of safety for their families by carving out rooms in these embankments. A door-way in these cases would be cut in a high bank, starting from the level of the road or street, and after running in a few feet a room of the size required was carved out of the clay, the dirt being removed by the door-way. In some instances I saw where two rooms were cut out, for a single family, with a door-way in the clay wall separating them. Some of these were carpeted and furnished with considerable elaboration. In these the occupants were fully secure from the shells of the navy, which were dropped into the city night and day without intermission.

I returned to my old headquarters outside in the afternoon, and did not move into the town until the sixth. On the afternoon of the fourth I sent Captain Wm. M. Dunn of my staff to Cairo, the nearest point where the telegraph could be reached, with a dispatch to the general-in-chief. It was as follows:

"The enemy surrendered this morning. The only terms allowed is their parole as prisoners of war. This I regard as a great advantage to us at this moment. It saves, probably, several days in the capture, and leaves troops and transports ready for immediate service. Sherman, with a large force, moves immediately on Johnston, to drive him from the State. I will send troops to the relief of Banks, and return the 9th army corps to Burnside."

This news, with the victory at Gettysburg won the same day, lifted a great load of anxiety from the minds of the President, his Cabinet and the loyal people all over the North. The fate of the Confederacy was sealed when Vicksburg fell. Much hard fighting was to be done afterwards and many precious lives were to be sacrificed; but the *morale* was with the supporters of the Union ever after.

I at the same time wrote to General Banks informing him of the fall and sending him a copy of the terms; also saying I would send him all the troops he wanted to insure the capture of the only foothold the enemy now had on the Mississippi River. General Banks had a number of copies of this letter printed, or at least a synopsis of it, and very soon a copy fell into the hands of General Gardner, who was then in command of Port Hudson. Gardner at once sent a letter to the commander of the National forces saying that he had been informed of the surrender of Vicksburg and telling how the information reached him. He added that if this was true, it was useless for him to hold out longer. General Banks gave him assurances that Vicksburg had been surrendered, and General Gardner surrendered unconditionally on the 9th of July. Port Hudson with nearly 6,000 prisoners, 51 guns, 5,000 small-arms and other stores fell into the hands of the Union forces: from that day to the close of the rebellion the Mississippi River, from its source to its mouth, remained in the control of the National troops.

Pemberton and his army were kept in Vicksburg until the whole could be paroled. The paroles were in duplicate, by organization (one copy for each, Federals and Confederates), and signed by the commanding officers of the companies or regiments. Duplicates were also made for each soldier and signed by each individually, one to be retained by the soldier signing and one to be retained by us. Several hundred refused to sign their paroles, preferring to be sent to the North as prisoners to being sent back to fight again. Others again kept out of the way, hoping to escape either alternative.

Pemberton appealed to me in person to compel these men to sign their paroles, but I declined. It also leaked out that many of the men who had signed their paroles, intended to desert and go to their homes as soon as they got out of our lines. Pemberton hearing this, again appealed to me to assist him. He wanted arms for a battalion, to act as guards in keeping his men together while being marched to a camp of instruction, where he expected to keep them until exchanged. This request was also declined. It was precisely what I expected and hoped that they would do. I told him, however, that I would see that they marched beyond our lines in good order. By the eleventh, just one week after the surrender, the paroles were completed and the Confederate garrison marched out. Many deserted, and fewer of them were ever returned to the ranks to fight again than would have been the case had the surrender been unconditional and the prisoners sent to the James River to be paroled.

As soon as our troops took possession of the city guards were established along the whole line of parapet, from the river above to the river below. The prisoners were allowed to occupy their old camps behind the intrenchments. No restraint was put upon them, except by their own commanders. They were rationed about as our own men, and from our supplies. The men of the two armies fraternized as if they had been fighting for the same cause. When they passed out of the works they had so long and so gallantly defended, between lines of their late antagonists, not a cheer went up, not a remark was made that would give pain. Really, I believe there was a feeling of sadness just then in the breasts of most of the Union soldiers at seeing the dejection of their late antagonists.

The day before the departure the following order was issued:

"Paroled prisoners will be sent out of here to-morrow. They will be authorized to cross at the railroad bridge, and move from there to Edward's Ferry,* and on by way of Raymond. Instruct the commands to be orderly and quiet as these prisoners pass, to make no offensive remarks, and not to harbor any who fall out of ranks after they have passed."

---

*Meant Edward's Station.

Chapter XXXIX.

RETROSPECT OF THE CAMPAIGN — SHERMAN'S
MOVEMENTS — PROPOSED MOVEMENT UPON MOBILE — A
PAINFUL ACCIDENT — ORDERED TO REPORT AT CAIRO.

THE CAPTURE of Vicksburg, with its garrison, ordnance
and ordnance stores, and the successful battles fought in
reaching them, gave new spirit to the loyal people of the
North. New hopes for the final success of the cause of the
Union were inspired. The victory gained at Gettysburg, upon
the same day, added to their hopes. Now the Mississippi
River was entirely in the possession of the National troops;
for the fall of Vicksburg gave us Port Hudson at once. The
army of northern Virginia was driven out of Pennsylvania and
forced back to about the same ground it occupied in 1861. The
Army of the Tennessee united with the Army of the Gulf,
dividing the Confederate States completely.

The first dispatch I received from the government after the
fall of Vicksburg was in these words:

"I fear your paroling the prisoners at Vicksburg, without actual
delivery to a proper agent as required by the seventh article of the
cartel, may be construed into an absolute release, and that the men
will immediately be placed in the ranks of the enemy. Such has been
the case elsewhere. If these prisoners have not been allowed to de-
part, you will detain them until further orders."

Halleck did not know that they had already been delivered
into the hands of Major Watts, Confederate commissioner for
the exchange of prisoners.

At Vicksburg 31,600 prisoners were surrendered, together
with 172 cannon, about 60,000 muskets and a large amount of
ammunition. The small-arms of the enemy were far superior
to the bulk of ours. Up to this time our troops at the West
had been limited to the old United States flint-lock muskets
changed into percussion, or the Belgian musket imported
early in the war — almost as dangerous to the person firing it
as to the one aimed at — and a few new and improved arms.
These were of many different calibers, a fact that caused much

trouble in distributing ammunition during an engagement. The enemy had generally new arms which had run the blockade and were of uniform caliber. After the surrender I authorized all colonels whose regiments were armed with inferior muskets, to place them in the stack of captured arms and replace them with the latter. A large number of arms turned in to the Ordnance Department as captured, were thus arms that had really been used by the Union army in the capture of Vicksburg.

In this narrative I have not made the mention I should like of officers, dead and alive, whose services entitle them to special mention. Neither have I made that mention of the navy which its services deserve. Suffice it to say, the close of the siege of Vicksburg found us with an army unsurpassed, in proportion to its numbers, taken as a whole of officers and men. A military education was acquired which no other school could have given. Men who thought a company was quite enough for them to command properly at the beginning, would have made good regimental or brigade commanders; most of the brigade commanders were equal to the command of a division, and one, Ransom, would have been equal to the command of a corps at least. Logan and Crocker ended the campaign fitted to command independent armies.

General F. P. Blair joined me at Milliken's Bend a fullfledged general, without having served in a lower grade. He commanded a division in the campaign. I had known Blair in Missouri, where I had voted against him in 1858 when he ran for Congress. I knew him as a frank, positive and generous man, true to his friends even to a fault, but always a leader. I dreaded his coming; I knew from experience that it was more difficult to command two generals desiring to be leaders than it was to command one army officered intelligently and with subordination. It affords me the greatest pleasure to record now my agreeable disappointment in respect to his character. There was no man braver than he, nor was there any who obeyed all orders of his superior in rank with more unquestioning alacrity. He was one man as a soldier, another as a politician.

The navy under Porter was all it could be, during the entire campaign. Without its assistance the campaign could not have been successfully made with twice the number of men engaged. It could not have been made at all, in the way it was, with any number of men without such assistance. The most perfect harmony reigned between the two arms of the service. There never was a request made, that I am aware of, either of the flag-officer or any of his subordinates, that was not promptly complied with.

The campaign of Vicksburg was suggested and developed by circumstances. The elections of 1862 had gone against the prosecution of the war. Voluntary enlistments had nearly ceased and the draft had been resorted to; this was resisted, and a defeat or backward movement would have made its execution impossible. A forward movement to a decisive victory was necessary. Accordingly I resolved to get below Vicksburg, unite with Banks against Port Hudson, make New Orleans a base and, with that base and Grand Gulf as a starting point, move our combined forces against Vicksburg. Upon reaching Grand Gulf, after running its batteries and fighting a battle, I received a letter from Banks informing me that he could not be at Port Hudson under ten days, and then with only fifteen thousand men. The time was worth more than the reinforcements; I therefore determined to push into the interior of the enemy's country.

With a large river behind us, held above and below by the enemy, rapid movements were essential to success. Jackson was captured the day after a new commander had arrived, and only a few days before large reinforcements were expected. A rapid movement west was made; the garrison of Vicksburg was met in two engagements and badly defeated, and driven back into its stronghold and there successfully besieged. It looks now as though Providence had directed the course of the campaign while the Army of the Tennessee executed the decree.

Upon the surrender of the garrison of Vicksburg there were three things that required immediate attention. The first was to send a force to drive the enemy from our rear, and out of the State. The second was to send reinforcements to Banks near Port Hudson, if necessary, to complete the triumph of opening the Mississippi from its source to its mouth to the free navigation of vessels bearing the Stars and Stripes. The third was to inform the authorities at Washington and the North of the good news, to relieve their long suspense and strengthen their confidence in the ultimate success of the cause they had so much at heart.

Soon after negotiations were opened with General Pemberton for the surrender of the city, I notified Sherman, whose troops extended from Haines' Bluff on the left to the crossing of the Vicksburg and Jackson road over the Big Black on the right, and directed him to hold his command in readiness to advance and drive the enemy from the State as soon as Vicksburg surrendered. Steele and Ord were directed to be in readiness to join Sherman in his move against General Johnston, and Sherman was advised of this also. Sherman moved promptly, crossing the Big Black at three different points with as many columns, all concentrating at Bolton, twenty miles west of Jackson.

Johnston heard of the surrender of Vicksburg almost as soon as it occurred, and immediately fell back on Jackson. On the 8th of July Sherman was within ten miles of Jackson and on the 11th was close up to the defences of the city and shelling the town. The siege was kept up until the morning of the 17th, when it was found that the enemy had evacuated during the night. The weather was very hot, the roads dusty and the water bad. Johnston destroyed the roads as he passed and had so much the start that pursuit was useless; but Sherman sent one division, Steele's, to Brandon, fourteen miles east of Jackson.

The National loss in the second capture of Jackson was less than one thousand men, killed, wounded and missing. The Confederate loss was probably less, except in captured. More than this number fell into our hands as prisoners.

Medicines and food were left for the Confederate wounded and sick who had to be left behind. A large amount of rations was issued to the families that remained in Jackson. Medicine and food were also sent to Raymond for the destitute families as well as the sick and wounded, as I thought it only fair that we should return to these people some of the articles we had taken while marching through the country. I wrote to Sherman: "Impress upon the men the importance of going through the State in an orderly manner, abstaining from taking anything not absolutely necessary for their subsistence while travelling. They should try to create as favorable an impression as possible upon the people." Provisions and forage, when called for by them, were issued to all the people, from Bruinsburg to Jackson and back to Vicksburg, whose resources had been taken for the supply of our army. Very large quantities of groceries and provisions were so issued.

Sherman was ordered back to Vicksburg, and his troops took much the same position they had occupied before—from the Big Black to Haines' Bluff.

Having cleaned up about Vicksburg and captured or routed all regular Confederate forces for more than a hundred miles in all directions, I felt that the troops that had done so much should be allowed to do more before the enemy could recover from the blow he had received, and while important points might be captured without bloodshed. I suggested to the General-in-chief the idea of a campaign against Mobile, starting from Lake Pontchartrain. Halleck preferred another course. The possession of the trans-Mississippi by the Union forces seemed to possess more importance in his mind than almost any campaign east of the Mississippi. I am well aware that the President was very anxious to have a foothold in Texas, to stop the clamor of some of the foreign governments which seemed to be seeking a pretext to interfere in the war, at least so far as to recognize belligerent rights to the Confederate States. This, however, could have been easily done without wasting troops in western Louisiana and eastern Texas, by sending a garrison at once to Brownsville on the Rio Grande.

Halleck disapproved of my proposition to go against Mobile, so that I was obliged to settle down and see myself put again on the defensive as I had been a year before in west Tennessee. It would have been an easy thing to capture Mobile at the time I proposed to go there. Having that as a base of operations, troops could have been thrown into the interior to operate against General Bragg's army. This would necessarily have compelled Bragg to detach in order to meet this fire in his rear. If he had not done this the troops from Mobile could have inflicted inestimable damage upon much of the country from which his army and Lee's were yet receiving their supplies. I was so much impressed with this idea that I renewed my request later in July and again about the 1st of August, and proposed sending all the troops necessary, asking only the assistance of the navy to protect the debarkation of troops at or near Mobile. I also asked for a leave of absence to visit New Orleans, particularly if my suggestion to move against Mobile should be approved. Both requests were refused. So far as my experience with General Halleck went it was very much easier for him to refuse a favor than to grant one. But I did not regard this as a favor. It was simply in line of duty, though out of my department.

The General-in-chief having decided against me, the depletion of an army, which had won a succession of great victories, commenced, as had been the case the year before after the fall of Corinth when the army was sent where it would do the least good. By orders, I sent to Banks a force of 4,000 men; returned the 9th corps to Kentucky and, when transportation had been collected, started a division of 5,000 men to Schofield in Missouri where Price was raiding the State. I also detached a brigade under Ransom to Natchez, to garrison that place permanently. This latter move was quite fortunate as to the time when Ransom arrived there. The enemy happened to have a large number, about 5,000 head, of beef cattle there on the way from Texas to feed the Eastern armies, and also a large amount of munitions of war which had probably come through Texas from the Rio Grande and which were on the way to Lee's and other armies in the East.

The troops that were left with me around Vicksburg were very busily and unpleasantly employed in making expeditions against guerilla bands and small detachments of cavalry which infested the interior, and in destroying mills, bridges and rolling stock on the railroads. The guerillas and cavalry were not there to fight but to annoy, and therefore disappeared on the first approach of our troops.

The country back of Vicksburg was filled with deserters from Pemberton's army and, it was reported, many from Johnston's also. The men determined not to fight again while the war lasted. Those who lived beyond the reach of the Confederate army wanted to get to their homes. Those who did not, wanted to get North where they could work for their support till the war was over. Besides all this there was quite a peace feeling, for the time being, among the citizens of that part of Mississippi, but this feeling soon subsided. It is not probable that Pemberton got off with over 4,000 of his army to the camp where he proposed taking them, and these were in a demoralized condition.

On the 7th of August I further depleted my army by sending the 13th corps, General Ord commanding, to Banks. Besides this I received orders to co-operate with the latter general in movements west of the Mississippi. Having received this order I went to New Orleans to confer with Banks about the proposed movement. All these movements came to naught.

During this visit I reviewed Banks' army a short distance above Carrollton. The horse I rode was vicious and but little used, and on my return to New Orleans ran away and, shying at a locomotive in the street, fell, probably on me. I was rendered insensible, and when I regained consciousness I found myself in a hotel near by with several doctors attending me. My leg was swollen from the knee to the thigh, and the swelling, almost to the point of bursting, extended along the body up to the arm-pit. The pain was almost beyond endurance. I lay at the hotel something over a week without being able to turn myself in bed. I had a steamer stop at the nearest point possible, and was carried to it on a litter. I was then taken to Vicksburg, where I remained unable to move for some time afterwards.

While I was absent General Sherman declined to assume command because, he said, it would confuse the records; but he let all the orders be made in my name, and was glad to render any assistance he could. No orders were issued by my staff, certainly no important orders, except upon consultation with and approval of Sherman.

On the 13th of September, while I was still in New Orleans, Halleck telegraphed to me to send all available forces to Memphis and thence to Tuscumbia, to co-operate with Rosecrans for the relief of Chattanooga. On the 15th he telegraphed again for all available forces to go to Rosecrans. This was received on the 27th. I was still confined to my bed, unable to rise from it without assistance; but I at once ordered Sherman to send one division to Memphis as fast as transports could be provided. The division of McPherson's corps, which had got off and was on the way to join Steele in Arkansas, was recalled and sent, likewise, to report to Hurlbut at Memphis. Hurlbut was directed to forward these two divisions with two others from his own corps at once, and also to send any other troops that might be returning there. Halleck suggested that some good man, like Sherman or McPherson, should be sent to Memphis to take charge of the troops going east. On this I sent Sherman, as being, I thought, the most suitable person for an independent command, and besides he was entitled to it if it had to be given to any one. He was directed to take with him another division of his corps. This left one back, but having one of McPherson's divisions he had still the equivalent.

Before the receipt by me of these orders the battle of Chickamauga had been fought and Rosecrans forced back into Chattanooga. The administration as well as the General-in-chief was nearly frantic at the situation of affairs there. Mr. Charles A. Dana, an officer of the War Department, was sent to Rosecrans' headquarters. I do not know what his instructions were, but he was still in Chattanooga when I arrived there at a later period.

It seems that Halleck suggested that I should go to Nashville as soon as able to move and take general direction of the troops moving from the west. I received the following dispatch dated October 3d: "It is the wish of the Secretary of War that as soon as General Grant is able he will come to Cairo and report by telegraph." I was still very lame, but started without delay. Arriving at Columbus on the 16th I reported by telegraph: "Your dispatch from Cairo of the 3d directing me to report from Cairo was received at 11.30 on the 10th. Left the same day with staff and headquarters and am here en route for Cairo."

END OF VOL. I.

PERSONAL MEMOIRS

OF

U. S. GRANT.

IN TWO VOLUMES.

VOL. II.

Contents.

VOLUME II.

Chapter XL.
FIRST MEETING WITH SECRETARY STANTON—
GENERAL ROSECRANS—COMMANDING
MILITARY DIVISION OF MISSISSIPPI—ANDREW
JOHNSON'S ADDRESS—ARRIVAL AT
CHATTANOOGA 403–412

Chapter XLI.
ASSUMING THE COMMAND AT CHATTANOOGA—
OPENING A LINE OF SUPPLIES—BATTLE OF
WAUHATCHIE—ON THE PICKET LINE 413–421

Chapter XLII.
CONDITION OF THE ARMY—REBUILDING THE
RAILROAD—GENERAL BURNSIDE'S SITUATION—
ORDERS FOR BATTLE—PLANS FOR THE
ATTACK—HOOKER'S POSITION—SHERMAN'S
MOVEMENTS 422–432

Chapter XLIII.
PREPARATIONS FOR BATTLE—THOMAS CARRIES
THE FIRST LINE OF THE ENEMY—SHERMAN
CARRIES MISSIONARY RIDGE—BATTLE OF
LOOKOUT MOUNTAIN—GENERAL HOOKER'S
FIGHT. 433–442

Chapter XLIV.
BATTLE OF CHATTANOOGA—A GALLANT
CHARGE—COMPLETE ROUT OF THE ENEMY—
PURSUIT OF THE CONFEDERATES—GENERAL
BRAGG—REMARKS ON CHATTANOOGA 443–451

Chapter XLV.
THE RELIEF OF KNOXVILLE—HEADQUARTERS
MOVED TO NASHVILLE—VISITING KNOXVILLE—
CIPHER DISPATCHES—WITHHOLDING ORDERS . 452–462

Chapter XLVI.
OPERATIONS IN MISSISSIPPI—LONGSTREET IN
EAST TENNESSEE—COMMISSIONED LIEUTENANT-
GENERAL—COMMANDING THE ARMIES OF THE
UNITED STATES—FIRST INTERVIEW WITH
PRESIDENT LINCOLN 463–474

Chapter XLVII.
THE MILITARY SITUATION—PLANS FOR THE
CAMPAIGN—SHERIDAN ASSIGNED TO
COMMAND OF THE CAVALRY—FLANK
MOVEMENTS—FORREST AT FORT PILLOW—
GENERAL BANKS'S EXPEDITION—COLONEL
MOSBY—AN INCIDENT OF THE WILDERNESS
CAMPAIGN 475–488

Chapter XLVIII.
COMMENCEMENT OF THE GRAND CAMPAIGN—
GENERAL BUTLER'S POSITION—SHERIDAN'S
FIRST RAID 489–497

Chapter XLIX.
SHERMAN'S CAMPAIGN IN GEORGIA—SIEGE OF
ATLANTA—DEATH OF GENERAL MCPHERSON—
ATTEMPT TO CAPTURE ANDERSONVILLE—
CAPTURE OF ATLANTA 498–511

Chapter L.
GRAND MOVEMENT OF THE ARMY OF THE
POTOMAC—CROSSING THE RAPIDAN—
ENTERING THE WILDERNESS—BATTLE OF
THE WILDERNESS 512–533

Chapter LI.
AFTER THE BATTLE—TELEGRAPH AND SIGNAL
SERVICE—MOVEMENT BY THE LEFT FLANK . . 534–543

Chapter LII.
BATTLE OF SPOTTSYLVANIA—HANCOCK'S POSITION
—ASSAULT OF WARREN'S AND WRIGHT'S
CORPS—UPTON PROMOTED ON THE FIELD—
GOOD NEWS FROM BUTLER AND SHERIDAN . . 544–551

Chapter LIII.
HANCOCK'S ASSAULT—LOSSES OF THE
CONFEDERATES—PROMOTIONS RECOMMENDED—
DISCOMFITURE OF THE ENEMY—EWELL'S
ATTACK—REDUCING THE ARTILLERY 552–561

Chapter LIV.
MOVEMENT BY THE LEFT FLANK—BATTLE OF
NORTH ANNA—AN INCIDENT OF THE
MARCH—MOVING ON RICHMOND—SOUTH OF
THE PAMUNKEY—POSITION OF THE NATIONAL
ARMY 562–578

Chapter LV.
ADVANCE ON COLD HARBOR—AN ANECDOTE
OF THE WAR—BATTLE OF COLD HARBOR—
CORRESPONDENCE WITH LEE—
RETROSPECTIVE 579–589

Chapter LVI.
LEFT FLANK MOVEMENT ACROSS THE
CHICKAHOMINY AND JAMES—GENERAL LEE—
VISIT TO BUTLER—THE MOVEMENT ON
PETERSBURG—THE INVESTMENT OF
PETERSBURG 590–602

Chapter LVII.
RAID ON THE VIRGINIA CENTRAL RAILROAD—
RAID ON THE WELDON RAILROAD—EARLY'S
MOVEMENT UPON WASHINGTON—MINING THE
WORKS BEFORE PETERSBURG—EXPLOSION OF
THE MINE BEFORE PETERSBURG—CAMPAIGN
IN THE SHENANDOAH VALLEY—CAPTURE OF
THE WELDON RAILROAD 603–619

Chapter LVIII.
SHERIDAN'S ADVANCE—VISIT TO SHERIDAN—
SHERIDAN'S VICTORY IN THE SHENANDOAH
—SHERIDAN'S RIDE TO WINCHESTER—
CLOSE OF THE CAMPAIGN FOR THE
WINTER 620–631

Chapter LIX.
THE CAMPAIGN IN GEORGIA—SHERMAN'S
MARCH TO THE SEA—WAR ANECDOTES—
THE MARCH ON SAVANNAH—INVESTMENT
OF SAVANNAH—CAPTURE OF
SAVANNAH 632–653

Chapter LX.
THE BATTLE OF FRANKLIN—THE BATTLE OF
NASHVILLE 654–661

Chapter LXI.
EXPEDITION AGAINST FORT FISHER—ATTACK
ON THE FORT—FAILURE OF THE EXPEDITION—
SECOND EXPEDITION AGAINST THE FORT—
CAPTURE OF FORT FISHER 662–670

Chapter LXII.
SHERMAN'S MARCH NORTH—SHERIDAN
ORDERED TO LYNCHBURG—CANBY ORDERED
TO MOVE AGAINST MOBILE—MOVEMENTS OF
SCHOFIELD AND THOMAS—CAPTURE OF
COLUMBIA, SOUTH CAROLINA—SHERMAN IN
THE CAROLINAS 671–684

Chapter LXIII.
ARRIVAL OF THE PEACE COMMISSIONERS—
LINCOLN AND THE PEACE COMMISSIONERS—
AN ANECDOTE OF LINCOLN—THE WINTER
BEFORE PETERSBURG—SHERIDAN DESTROYS
THE RAILROAD—GORDON CARRIES THE
PICKET LINE—PARKE RECAPTURES THE
LINE—THE BATTLE OF WHITE OAK ROAD . . 685–694

Chapter LXIV.
INTERVIEW WITH SHERIDAN—GRAND
MOVEMENT OF THE ARMY OF THE POTOMAC—
SHERIDAN'S ADVANCE ON FIVE FORKS—
BATTLE OF FIVE FORKS—PARKE AND WRIGHT
STORM THE ENEMY'S LINE—BATTLES BEFORE
PETERSBURG 695–706

Chapter LXV.
THE CAPTURE OF PETERSBURG—MEETING
PRESIDENT LINCOLN IN PETERSBURG—THE
CAPTURE OF RICHMOND—PURSUING THE
ENEMY—VISIT TO SHERIDAN AND MEADE. . . 707–718

Chapter LXVI.
BATTLE OF SAILOR'S CREEK—ENGAGEMENT AT
FARMVILLE—CORRESPONDENCE WITH GENERAL
LEE—SHERIDAN INTERCEPTS THE ENEMY . . . 719–729

Chapter LXVII.
NEGOTIATIONS AT APPOMATTOX—INTERVIEW
WITH LEE AT MCLEAN'S HOUSE—THE TERMS
OF SURRENDER—LEE'S SURRENDER—
INTERVIEW WITH LEE AFTER THE SURRENDER . 730–744

Chapter LXVIII.
MORALE OF THE TWO ARMIES—RELATIVE
CONDITIONS OF THE NORTH AND SOUTH—
PRESIDENT LINCOLN VISITS RICHMOND—
ARRIVAL AT WASHINGTON—PRESIDENT
LINCOLN'S ASSASSINATION—PRESIDENT
JOHNSON'S POLICY 745–753

Chapter LXIX.
SHERMAN AND JOHNSTON—JOHNSTON'S
SURRENDER TO SHERMAN—CAPTURE OF
MOBILE—WILSON'S EXPEDITION—CAPTURE OF
JEFFERSON DAVIS—GENERAL THOMAS'S
QUALITIES—ESTIMATE OF GENERAL CANBY . . 754–763

Chapter LXX.
THE END OF THE WAR—THE MARCH TO
WASHINGTON—ONE OF LINCOLN'S
ANECDOTES—GRAND REVIEW AT
WASHINGTON—CHARACTERISTICS OF
LINCOLN AND STANTON—ESTIMATE OF THE
DIFFERENT CORPS COMMANDERS 764–772

Conclusion 773–780

Appendix 781–848

Index 851–866

Maps and Illustrations.

VOLUME II.

Lieutenant-General U. S. Grant, Engraved on Steel, by Wm. E. Marshall 394

Map of Knoxville, Nashville and Chattanooga 407

Map of Chattanooga and Vicinity 415

Map of the Battlefield of Chattanooga 437

Map of the Meridian Campaign. 467

Map of Bermuda Hundred 491

Map of Sherman's Campaign, Chattanooga to Atlanta 501

Map Illustrating Siege of Atlanta 509

Map of Wilderness Campaign. 513

Map of the Battle of the Wilderness 525

Map of the Country between the Wilderness and Spottsylvania Court House 537

Map of the Battle of Spottsylvania 547

Map of the Battle of North Anna 565

Map of the Operations Between the Pamunkey and the James Rivers 573

Map of Central Virginia. 577

Map of the Battle of Cold Harbor 581

Map of Richmond 609

Map of the Shenandoah Valley Campaign 623

Map of Sherman's March to the Sea 643

Map of the Nashville Campaign South 657

Map of Fort Fisher 665

Map of Sherman's March North 677

Map of Petersburg and Five Forks 699

Map of the Appomattox Campaign. 709

Map of Jetersville and Sailor's Creek   721

Map of High Bridge and Farmville   725

Map of Appomattox Court House   733

Etching of McLean's House at Appomattox where
    General Lee's Surrender took Place   737

Fac-simile of the Original Terms of Lee's Surrender
    as Written by General Grant   742

Map of the Defences of the City of Mobile   759

Map of the Seat of War — 1861 to 1865   849

Chapter XL.

FIRST MEETING WITH SECRETARY STANTON—GENERAL
ROSECRANS—COMMANDING MILITARY DIVISION OF
MISSISSIPPI—ANDREW JOHNSON'S ADDRESS—ARRIVAL
AT CHATTANOOGA.

THE REPLY (to my telegram of October 16, 1863, from Cairo, announcing my arrival at that point) came on the morning of the 17th, directing me to proceed immediately to the Galt House, Louisville, where I would meet an officer of the War Department with my instructions. I left Cairo within an hour or two after the receipt of this dispatch, going by rail via Indianapolis. Just as the train I was on was starting out of the depot at Indianapolis a messenger came running up to stop it, saying the Secretary of War was coming into the station and wanted to see me.

I had never met Mr. Stanton up to that time, though we had held frequent conversations over the wires the year before, when I was in Tennessee. Occasionally at night he would order the wires between the War Department and my headquarters to be connected, and we would hold a conversation for an hour or two. On this occasion the Secretary was accompanied by Governor Brough of Ohio, whom I had never met, though he and my father had been old acquaintances. Mr. Stanton dismissed the special train that had brought him to Indianapolis, and accompanied me to Louisville.

Up to this time no hint had been given me of what was wanted after I left Vicksburg, except the suggestion in one of Halleck's dispatches that I had better go to Nashville and superintend the operation of troops sent to relieve Rosecrans. Soon after we started the Secretary handed me two orders, saying that I might take my choice of them. The two were identical in all but one particular. Both created the "Military Division of the Mississippi," (giving me the command) composed of the Departments of the Ohio, the Cumberland, and the Tennessee, and all the territory from the Alleghanies to the Mississippi River north of Banks's command in the southwest. One order left the department commanders as they

were, while the other relieved Rosecrans and assigned Thomas
to his place. I accepted the latter. We reached Louisville after
night and, if I remember rightly, in a cold, drizzling rain.
The Secretary of War told me afterwards that he caught a cold
on that occasion from which he never expected to recover.
He never did.

A day was spent in Louisville, the Secretary giving me the
military news at the capital and talking about the disappointment at the results of some of the campaigns. By the evening
of the day after our arrival all matters of discussion seemed
exhausted, and I left the hotel to spend the evening away,
both Mrs. Grant (who was with me) and myself having relatives living in Louisville. In the course of the evening Mr.
Stanton received a dispatch from Mr. C. A. Dana, then in
Chattanooga, informing him that unless prevented Rosecrans
would retreat, and advising peremptory orders against his
doing so.

As stated before, after the fall of Vicksburg I urged strongly
upon the government the propriety of a movement against
Mobile. General Rosecrans had been at Murfreesboro', Tennessee, with a large and well-equipped army from early in the
year 1863, with Bragg confronting him with a force quite
equal to his own at first, considering it was on the defensive.
But after the investment of Vicksburg Bragg's army was
largely depleted to strengthen Johnston, in Mississippi, who
was being reinforced to raise the siege. I frequently wrote
General Halleck suggesting that Rosecrans should move
against Bragg. By so doing he would either detain the latter's
troops where they were or lay Chattanooga open to capture.
General Halleck strongly approved the suggestion, and finally
wrote me that he had repeatedly ordered Rosecrans to advance, but that the latter had constantly failed to comply with
the order, and at last, after having held a council of war, had
replied in effect that it was a military maxim "not to fight two
decisive battles at the same time." If true, the maxim was not
applicable in this case. It would be bad to be defeated in two
decisive battles fought the same day, but it would not be bad
to win them. I, however, was fighting no battle, and the siege
of Vicksburg had drawn from Rosecrans' front so many of
the enemy that his chances of victory were much greater than

they would be if he waited until the siege was over, when these troops could be returned. Rosecrans was ordered to move against the army that was detaching troops to raise the siege. Finally he did move, on the 24th of June, but ten days afterwards Vicksburg surrendered, and the troops sent from Bragg were free to return.

It was at this time that I recommended to the general-in-chief the movement against Mobile. I knew the peril the Army of the Cumberland was in, being depleted continually, not only by ordinary casualties, but also by having to detach troops to hold its constantly extending line over which to draw supplies, while the enemy in front was as constantly being strengthened. Mobile was important to the enemy, and in the absence of a threatening force was guarded by little else than artillery. If threatened by land and from the water at the same time the prize would fall easily, or troops would have to be sent to its defence. Those troops would necessarily come from Bragg. My judgment was overruled, and the troops under my command were dissipated over other parts of the country where it was thought they could render the most service.

Soon it was discovered in Washington that Rosecrans was in trouble and required assistance. The emergency was now too immediate to allow us to give this assistance by making an attack in rear of Bragg upon Mobile. It was therefore necessary to reinforce directly, and troops were sent from every available point.

Rosecrans had very skilfully manœuvred Bragg south of the Tennessee River, and through and beyond Chattanooga. If he had stopped and intrenched, and made himself strong there, all would have been right and the mistake of not moving earlier partially compensated. But he pushed on, with his forces very much scattered, until Bragg's troops from Mississippi began to join him. Then Bragg took the initiative. Rosecrans had to fall back in turn, and was able to get his army together at Chickamauga, some miles south-east of Chattanooga, before the main battle was brought on. The battle was fought on the 19th and 20th of September, and Rosecrans was badly defeated, with a heavy loss in artillery and some sixteen thousand men killed, wounded and captured. The corps under

Major-General George H. Thomas stood its ground, while Rosecrans, with Crittenden and McCook, returned to Chattanooga. Thomas returned also, but later, and with his troops in good order. Bragg followed and took possession of Missionary Ridge, overlooking Chattanooga. He also occupied Lookout Mountain, west of the town, which Rosecrans had abandoned, and with it his control of the river and the river road as far back as Bridgeport. The National troops were now strongly intrenched in Chattanooga Valley, with the Tennessee River behind them and the enemy occupying commanding heights to the east and west, with a strong line across the valley from mountain to mountain, and with Chattanooga Creek, for a large part of the way, in front of their line.

On the 29th Halleck telegraphed me the above results, and directed all the forces that could be spared from my department to be sent to Rosecrans. Long before this dispatch was received Sherman was on his way, and McPherson was moving east with most of the garrison of Vicksburg.

A retreat at that time would have been a terrible disaster. It would not only have been the loss of a most important strategic position to us, but it would have been attended with the loss of all the artillery still left with the Army of the Cumberland and the annihilation of that army itself, either by capture or demoralization.

All supplies for Rosecrans had to be brought from Nashville. The railroad between this base and the army was in possession of the government up to Bridgeport, the point at which the road crosses to the south side of the Tennessee River; but Bragg, holding Lookout and Raccoon mountains west of Chattanooga, commanded the railroad, the river and the shortest and best wagon-roads, both south and north of the Tennessee, between Chattanooga and Bridgeport. The distance between these two places is but twenty-six miles by rail; but owing to the position of Bragg, all supplies for Rosecrans had to be hauled by a circuitous route north of the river and over a mountainous country, increasing the distance to over sixty miles.

This country afforded but little food for his animals, nearly ten thousand of which had already starved, and not enough

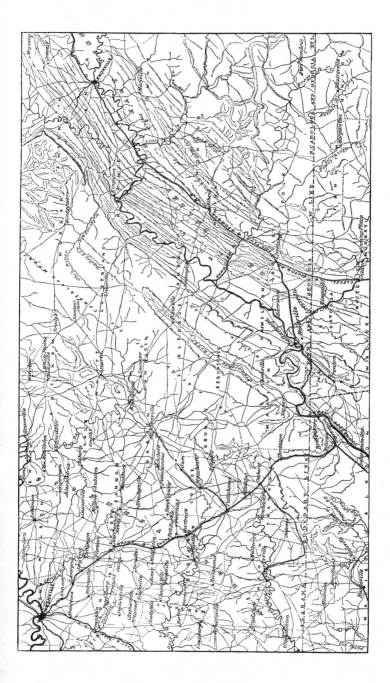

were left to draw a single piece of artillery or even the ambulances to convey the sick. The men had been on half rations of hard bread for a considerable time, with but few other supplies except beef driven from Nashville across the country. The region along the road became so exhausted of food for the cattle that by the time they reached Chattanooga they were much in the condition of the few animals left alive there—"on the lift." Indeed, the beef was so poor that the soldiers were in the habit of saying, with a faint facetiousness, that they were living on "half rations of hard bread and *beef dried on the hoof.*"

Nothing could be transported but food, and the troops were without sufficient shoes or other clothing suitable for the advancing season. What they had was well worn. The fuel within the Federal lines was exhausted, even to the stumps of trees. There were no teams to draw it from the opposite bank, where it was abundant. The only way of supplying fuel, for some time before my arrival, had been to cut trees on the north bank of the river at a considerable distance up the stream, form rafts of it and float it down with the current, effecting a landing on the south side within our lines by the use of paddles or poles. It would then be carried on the shoulders of the men to their camps.

If a retreat had occurred at this time it is not probable that any of the army would have reached the railroad as an organized body, if followed by the enemy.

On the receipt of Mr. Dana's dispatch Mr. Stanton sent for me. Finding that I was out he became nervous and excited, inquiring of every person he met, including guests of the house, whether they knew where I was, and bidding them find me and send me to him at once. About eleven o'clock I returned to the hotel, and on my way, when near the house, every person met was a messenger from the Secretary, apparently partaking of his impatience to see me. I hastened to the room of the Secretary and found him pacing the floor rapidly in his dressing-gown. Saying that the retreat must be prevented, he showed me the dispatch. I immediately wrote an order assuming command of the Military Division of the Mississippi, and telegraphed it to General Rosecrans. I then telegraphed to him the order from Washington assigning Thomas to the command of the Army of the Cumberland; and to Thomas that he must hold Chattanooga at all hazards, informing him at the same time that I would be at the front as soon as possible. A prompt reply was received from Thomas, saying, "We will hold the town till we starve." I appreciated the force of this dispatch later when I witnessed the condition of affairs which prompted it. It looked, indeed, as if but two courses were open: one to starve, the other to surrender or be captured.

On the morning of the 20th of October I started, with my staff, and proceeded as far as Nashville. At that time it was not prudent to travel beyond that point by night, so I remained in Nashville until the next morning. Here I met for the first time Andrew Johnson, Military Governor of Tennessee. He delivered a speech of welcome. His composure showed that it was by no means his maiden effort. It was long, and I was in torture while he was delivering it, fearing something would be expected from me in response. I was relieved, however, the people assembled having apparently heard enough. At all events they commenced a general handshaking, which, although trying where there is so much of it, was a great relief to me in this emergency.

From Nashville I telegraphed to Burnside, who was then at Knoxville, that important points in his department ought to be fortified, so that they could be held with the least number of men; to Admiral Porter at Cairo, that Sherman's advance had passed Eastport, Mississippi, that rations were probably on their way from St. Louis by boat for supplying his army, and requesting him to send a gunboat to convoy them; and to Thomas, suggesting that large parties should be put at work on the wagon-road then in use back to Bridgeport.

On the morning of the 21st we took the train for the front, reaching Stevenson, Alabama, after dark. Rosecrans was there on his way north. He came into my car and we held a brief interview, in which he described very clearly the situation at Chattanooga, and made some excellent suggestions as to what should be done. My only wonder was that he had not carried them out. We then proceeded to Bridgeport, where we stopped for the night. From here we took horses and made our way by Jasper and over Waldron's Ridge to Chattanooga.

There had been much rain, and the roads were almost impassable from mud, knee-deep in places, and from wash-outs on the mountain sides. I had been on crutches since the time of my fall in New Orleans, and had to be carried over places where it was not safe to cross on horseback. The roads were strewn with the *débris* of broken wagons and the carcasses of thousands of starved mules and horses. At Jasper, some ten or twelve miles from Bridgeport, there was a halt. General O. O. Howard had his headquarters there. From this point I telegraphed Burnside to make every effort to secure five hundred rounds of ammunition for his artillery and small-arms. We stopped for the night at a little hamlet some ten or twelve miles farther on. The next day we reached Chattanooga a little before dark. I went directly to General Thomas's headquarters, and remaining there a few days, until I could establish my own.

During the evening most of the general officers called in to pay their respects and to talk about the condition of affairs. They pointed out on the map the line, marked with a red or blue pencil, which Rosecrans had contemplated falling back upon. If any of them had approved the move they did not say so to me. I found General W. F. Smith occupying the position of chief engineer of the Army of the Cumberland. I had known Smith as a cadet at West Point, but had no recollection of having met him after my graduation, in 1843, up to this time. He explained the situation of the two armies and the topography of the country so plainly that I could see it without an inspection. I found that he had established a saw-mill on the banks of the river, by utilizing an old engine found in the neighborhood; and, by rafting logs from the north side of the river above, had got out the lumber and completed pontoons and roadway plank for a second bridge, one flying bridge being there already. He was also rapidly getting out the materials and constructing the boats for a third bridge. In addition to this he had far under way a steamer for plying between Chattanooga and Bridgeport whenever we might get possession of the river. This boat consisted of a scow, made of the plank sawed out at the mill, housed in, and a stern wheel attached which was propelled by a second engine taken from some shop or factory.

I telegraphed to Washington this night, notifying General Halleck of my arrival, and asking to have General Sherman assigned to the command of the Army of the Tennessee, headquarters in the field. The request was at once complied with.

Chapter XLI.

ASSUMING THE COMMAND AT CHATTANOOGA—OPENING
A LINE OF SUPPLIES—BATTLE OF WAUHATCHIE—
ON THE PICKET LINE.

THE NEXT DAY, the 24th, I started out to make a personal inspection, taking Thomas and Smith with me, besides most of the members of my personal staff. We crossed to the north side of the river, and, moving to the north of detached spurs of hills, reached the Tennessee at Brown's Ferry, some three miles below Lookout Mountain, unobserved by the enemy. Here we left our horses back from the river and approached the water on foot. There was a picket station of the enemy on the opposite side, of about twenty men, in full view, and we were within easy range. They did not fire upon us nor seem to be disturbed by our presence. They must have seen that we were all commissioned officers. But, I suppose, they looked upon the garrison of Chattanooga as prisoners of war, feeding or starving themselves, and thought it would be inhuman to kill any of them except in self-defence.

That night I issued orders for opening the route to Bridgeport—*a cracker line*, as the soldiers appropriately termed it. They had been so long on short rations that my first thought was the establishment of a line over which food might reach them.

Chattanooga is on the south bank of the Tennessee, where that river runs nearly due west. It is at the northern end of a valley five or six miles in width, through which Chattanooga Creek runs. To the east of the valley is Missionary Ridge, rising from five to eight hundred feet above the creek and terminating somewhat abruptly a half mile or more before reaching the Tennessee. On the west of the valley is Lookout Mountain, twenty-two hundred feet above-tide water. Just below the town the Tennessee makes a turn to the south and runs to the base of Lookout Mountain, leaving no level ground between the mountain and river. The Memphis and Charleston Railroad passes this point, where the mountain stands nearly perpendicular. East of Missionary Ridge flows the South Chickamauga River; west of Lookout Mountain is Lookout Creek; and west of that, Raccoon Mountains. Lookout Mountain, at its northern end, rises almost perpendicularly for some distance, then breaks off in a gentle slope of cultivated fields to near the summit, where it ends in a palisade thirty or more feet in height. On the gently sloping ground, between the upper and lower palisades, there is a single farmhouse, which is reached by a wagon-road from the valley east.

The intrenched line of the enemy commenced on the north end of Missionary Ridge and extended along the crest for some distance south, thence across Chattanooga valley to Lookout Mountain. Lookout Mountain was also fortified and held by the enemy, who also kept troops in Lookout valley west, and on Raccoon Mountain, with pickets extending down the river so as to command the road on the north bank and render it useless to us. In addition to this there was an intrenched line in Chattanooga valley extending from the river east of the town to Lookout Mountain, to make the investment complete. Besides the fortifications on Mission Ridge, there was a line at the base of the hill, with occasional spurs of rifle-pits half-way up the front. The enemy's pickets extended out into the valley towards the town, so far that the pickets of the two armies could converse. At one point they were separated only by the narrow creek which gives its name to the valley and town, and from which both sides drew water. The Union lines were shorter than those of the enemy.

Thus the enemy, with a vastly superior force, was strongly fortified to the east, south, and west, and commanded the river below. Practically, the Army of the Cumberland was besieged. The enemy had stopped with his cavalry north of the river the passing of a train loaded with ammunition and medical supplies. The Union army was short of both, not having ammunition enough for a day's fighting.

General Halleck had, long before my coming into this new field, ordered parts of the 11th and 12th corps, commanded respectively by Generals Howard and Slocum, Hooker in command of the whole, from the Army of the Potomac to reinforce Rosecrans. It would have been folly to send them to

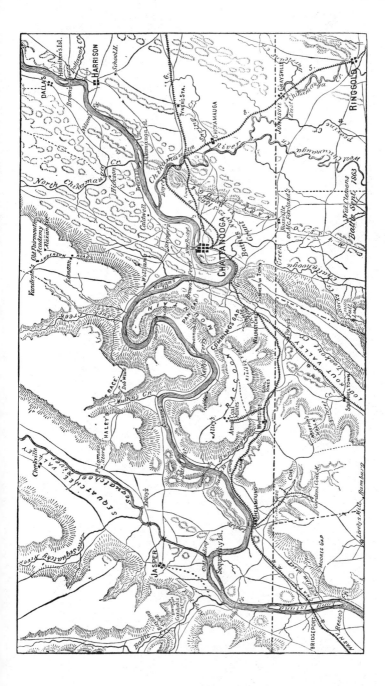

Chattanooga to help eat up the few rations left there. They were consequently left on the railroad, where supplies could be brought to them. Before my arrival, Thomas ordered their concentration at Bridgeport.

General W. F. Smith had been so instrumental in preparing for the move which I was now about to make, and so clear in his judgment about the manner of making it, that I deemed it but just to him that he should have command of the troops detailed to execute the design, although he was then acting as a staff officer and was not in command of troops.

On the 24th of October, after my return to Chattanooga, the following details were made: General Hooker, who was now at Bridgeport, was ordered to cross to the south side of the Tennessee and march up by Whitesides and Wauhatchie to Brown's Ferry. General Palmer, with a division of the 14th corps, Army of the Cumberland, was ordered to move down the river on the north side, by a back road, until opposite Whitesides, then cross and hold the road in Hooker's rear after he had passed. Four thousand men were at the same time detailed to act under General Smith directly from Chattanooga. Eighteen hundred of them, under General Hazen, were to take sixty pontoon boats, and under cover of night float by the pickets of the enemy at the north base of Lookout, down to Brown's Ferry, then land on the south side and capture or drive away the pickets at that point. Smith was to march with the remainder of the detail, also under cover of night, by the north bank of the river to Brown's Ferry, taking with him all the material for laying the bridge as soon as the crossing was secured.

On the 26th, Hooker crossed the river at Bridgeport and commenced his eastward march. At three o'clock on the morning of the 27th, Hazen moved into the stream with his sixty pontoons and eighteen hundred brave and well-equipped men. Smith started enough in advance to be near the river when Hazen should arrive. There are a number of detached spurs of hills north of the river at Chattanooga, back of which is a good road parallel to the stream, sheltered from the view from the top of Lookout. It was over this road Smith marched. At five o'clock Hazen landed at Brown's Ferry, surprised the picket guard, and captured most of it. By seven o'clock the whole of Smith's force was ferried over and in possession of a height commanding the ferry. This was speedily fortified, while a detail was laying the pontoon bridge. By ten o'clock the bridge was laid, and our extreme right, now in Lookout valley, was fortified and connected with the rest of the army. The two bridges over the Tennessee River—a flying one at Chattanooga and the new one at Brown's Ferry—with the road north of the river, covered from both the fire and the view of the enemy, made the connection complete. Hooker found but slight obstacles in his way, and on the afternoon of the 28th emerged into Lookout valley at Wauhatchie. Howard marched on to Brown's Ferry, while Geary, who commanded a division in the 12th corps, stopped three miles south. The pickets of the enemy on the river below were now cut off, and soon came in and surrendered.

The river was now opened to us from Lookout valley to Bridgeport. Between Brown's Ferry and Kelly's Ferry the Tennessee runs through a narrow gorge in the mountains, which contracts the stream so much as to increase the current beyond the capacity of an ordinary steamer to stem it. To get up these rapids, steamers must be cordelled; that is, pulled up by ropes from the shore. But there is no difficulty in navigating the stream from Bridgeport to Kelly's Ferry. The latter point is only eight miles from Chattanooga and connected with it by a good wagon-road, which runs through a low pass in the Raccoon Mountains on the south side of the river to Brown's Ferry, thence on the north side to the river opposite Chattanooga. There were several steamers at Bridgeport, and abundance of forage, clothing and provisions.

On the way to Chattanooga I had telegraphed back to Nashville for a good supply of vegetables and small rations, which the troops had been so long deprived of. Hooker had brought with him from the east a full supply of land transportation. His animals had not been subjected to hard work on bad roads without forage, but were in good condition. In five days from my arrival in Chattanooga the way was open to Bridgeport and, with the aid of steamers and Hooker's teams, in a week the troops were receiving full rations. It is hard for any one not an eye-witness to realize the relief this brought.

The men were soon reclothed and also well fed; an abundance of ammunition was brought up, and a cheerfulness prevailed not before enjoyed in many weeks. Neither officers nor men looked upon themselves any longer as doomed. The weak and languid appearance of the troops, so visible before, disappeared at once. I do not know what the effect was on the other side, but assume it must have been correspondingly depressing. Mr. Davis had visited Bragg but a short time before, and must have perceived our condition to be about as Bragg described it in his subsequent report. "These dispositions," he said, "faithfully sustained, insured the enemy's speedy evacuation of Chattanooga for want of food and forage. Possessed of the shortest route to his depot, and the one by which reinforcements must reach him, we held him at our mercy, and his destruction was only a question of time." But the dispositions were not "faithfully sustained," and I doubt not but thousands of men engaged in trying to "sustain" them now rejoice that they were not. There was no time during the rebellion when I did not think, and often say, that the South was more to be benefited by its defeat than the North. The latter had the people, the institutions, and the territory to make a great and prosperous nation. The former was burdened with an institution abhorrent to all civilized people not brought up under it, and one which degraded labor, kept it in ignorance, and enervated the governing class. With the outside world at war with this institution, they could not have extended their territory. The labor of the country was not skilled, nor allowed to become so. The whites could not toil without becoming degraded, and those who did were denominated "poor white trash." The system of labor would have soon exhausted the soil and left the people poor. The non-slaveholders would have left the country, and the small slaveholder must have sold out to his more fortunate neighbor. Soon the slaves would have outnumbered the masters, and, not being in sympathy with them, would have risen in their might and exterminated them. The war was expensive to the South as well as to the North, both in blood and treasure, but it was worth all it cost.

The enemy was surprised by the movements which secured to us a line of supplies. He appreciated its importance, and hastened to try to recover the line from us. His strength on Lookout Mountain was not equal to Hooker's command in the valley below. From Missionary Ridge he had to march twice the distance we had from Chattanooga, in order to reach Lookout Valley; but on the night of the 28th and 29th an attack was made on Geary at Wauhatchie by Longstreet's corps. When the battle commenced, Hooker ordered Howard up from Brown's Ferry. He had three miles to march to reach Geary. On his way he was fired upon by rebel troops from a foot-hill to the left of the road and from which the road was commanded. Howard turned to the left, charged up the hill and captured it before the enemy had time to intrench, taking many prisoners. Leaving sufficient men to hold this height, he pushed on to reinforce Geary. Before he got up, Geary had been engaged for about three hours against a vastly superior force. The night was so dark that the men could not distinguish one from another except by the light of the flashes of their muskets. In the darkness and uproar, Hooker's teamsters became frightened and deserted their teams. The mules also became frightened, and breaking loose from their fastenings stampeded directly towards the enemy. The latter, no doubt, took this for a charge, and stampeded in turn. By four o'clock in the morning the battle had entirely ceased, and our "cracker line" was never afterward disturbed.

In securing possession of Lookout Valley, Smith lost one man killed and four or five wounded. The enemy lost most of his pickets at the ferry, captured. In the night engagement of the 28th—9th Hooker lost 416 killed and wounded. I never knew the loss of the enemy, but our troops buried over one hundred and fifty of his dead and captured more than a hundred.

After we had secured the opening of a line over which to bring our supplies to the army, I made a personal inspection to see the situation of the pickets of the two armies. As I have stated, Chattanooga Creek comes down the centre of the valley to within a mile or such a matter of the town of Chattanooga, then bears off westerly, then north-westerly, and enters the Tennessee River at the foot of Lookout Mountain. This creek, from its mouth up to where it bears off west, lay between the two lines of pickets, and the guards of both armies drew their water from the same stream. As I would be under short-range fire and in an open country, I took nobody with me, except, I believe, a bugler, who stayed some distance to the rear. I rode from our right around to our left. When I came to the camp of the picket guard of our side, I heard the call, "Turn out the guard for the commanding general." I replied, "Never mind the guard," and they were dismissed and went back to their tents. Just back of these, and about equally distant from the creek, were the guards of the Confederate pickets. The sentinel on their post called out in like manner, "Turn out the guard for the commanding general," and, I believe, added, "General Grant." Their line in a moment front-faced to the north, facing me, and gave a salute, which I returned.

The most friendly relations seemed to exist between the pickets of the two armies. At one place there was a tree which had fallen across the stream, and which was used by the soldiers of both armies in drawing water for their camps. General Longstreet's corps was stationed there at the time, and wore blue of a little different shade from our uniform. Seeing a soldier in blue on this log, I rode up to him, commenced conversing with him, and asked whose corps he belonged to. He was very polite, and, touching his hat to me, said he belonged to General Longstreet's corps. I asked him a few questions—but not with a view of gaining any particular information—all of which he answered, and I rode off.

Chapter XLII.

CONDITION OF THE ARMY—REBUILDING THE
RAILROAD—GENERAL BURNSIDE'S SITUATION—ORDERS
FOR BATTLE—PLANS FOR THE ATTACK—HOOKER'S
POSITION—SHERMAN'S MOVEMENTS.

HAVING GOT the Army of the Cumberland in a comfortable position, I now began to look after the remainder of my new command. Burnside was in about as desperate a condition as the Army of the Cumberland had been, only he was not yet besieged. He was a hundred miles from the nearest possible base, Big South Fork of the Cumberland River, and much farther from any railroad we had possession of. The roads back were over mountains, and all supplies along the line had long since been exhausted. His animals, too, had been starved, and their carcasses lined the road from Cumberland Gap, and far back towards Lexington, Ky. East Tennessee still furnished supplies of beef, bread and forage, but it did not supply ammunition, clothing, medical supplies, or small rations, such as coffee, sugar, salt and rice.

Sherman had started from Memphis for Corinth on the 11th of October. His instructions required him to repair the road in his rear in order to bring up supplies. The distance was about three hundred and thirty miles through a hostile country. His entire command could not have maintained the road if it had been completed. The bridges had all been destroyed by the enemy, and much other damage done. A hostile community lived along the road; guerilla bands infested the country, and more or less of the cavalry of the enemy was still in the West. Often Sherman's work was destroyed as soon as completed, and he only a short distance away.

The Memphis and Charleston Railroad strikes the Tennessee River at Eastport, Mississippi. Knowing the difficulty Sherman would have to supply himself from Memphis, I had previously ordered supplies sent from St. Louis on small steamers, to be convoyed by the navy, to meet him at Eastport. These he got. I now ordered him to discontinue his work of repairing roads and to move on with his whole force to Stevenson, Alabama, without delay. This order was borne to Sherman by a messenger, who paddled down the Tennessee in a canoe and floated over Muscle Shoals; it was delivered at Iuka on the 27th. In this Sherman was notified that the rebels were moving a force towards Cleveland, East Tennessee, and might be going to Nashville, in which event his troops were in the best position to beat them there. Sherman, with his characteristic promptness, abandoned the work he was engaged upon and pushed on at once. On the 1st of November he crossed the Tennessee at Eastport, and that day was in Florence, Alabama, with the head of column, while his troops were still crossing at Eastport, with Blair bringing up the rear.

Sherman's force made an additional army, with cavalry, artillery, and trains, all to be supplied by the single track road from Nashville. All indications pointed also to the probable necessity of supplying Burnside's command in East Tennessee, twenty-five thousand more, by the same route. A single track could not do this. I gave, therefore, an order to Sherman to halt General G. M. Dodge's command, of about eight thousand men, at Athens, and subsequently directed the latter to arrange his troops along the railroad from Decatur north towards Nashville, and to rebuild that road. The road from Nashville to Decatur passes over a broken country, cut up with innumerable streams, many of them of considerable width, and with valleys far below the road-bed. All the bridges over these had been destroyed, and the rails taken up and twisted by the enemy. All the cars and locomotives not carried off had been destroyed as effectually as they knew how to destroy them. All bridges and culverts had been destroyed between Nashville and Decatur, and thence to Stevenson, where the Memphis and Charleston and the Nashville and Chattanooga roads unite. The rebuilding of this road would give us two roads as far as Stevenson over which to supply the army. From Bridgeport, a short distance farther east, the river supplements the road.

General Dodge, besides being a most capable soldier, was an experienced railroad builder. He had no tools to work with except those of the pioneers—axes, picks, and spades. With these he was able to intrench his men and protect them against surprises by small parties of the enemy. As he had no base of supplies until the road could be completed back to Nashville, the first matter to consider after protecting his men was the getting in of food and forage from the surrounding country. He had his men and teams bring in all the grain they could find, or all they needed, and all the cattle for beef, and such other food as could be found. Millers were detailed from the ranks to run the mills along the line of the army. When these were not near enough to the troops for protection they were taken down and moved up to the line of the road. Blacksmith shops, with all the iron and steel found in them, were moved up in like manner. Blacksmiths were detailed and set to work making the tools necessary in railroad and bridge building. Axemen were put to work getting out timber for bridges and cutting fuel for locomotives when the road should be completed. Car-builders were set to work repairing the locomotives and cars. Thus every branch of railroad building, making tools to work with, and supplying the workmen with food, was all going on at once, and without the aid of a mechanic or laborer except what the command itself furnished. But rails and cars the men could not make without material, and there was not enough rolling stock to keep the road we already had worked to its full capacity. There were no rails except those in use. To supply these deficiencies I ordered eight of the ten engines General McPherson had at Vicksburg to be sent to Nashville, and all the cars he had except ten. I also ordered the troops in West Tennessee to points on the river and on the Memphis and Charleston road, and ordered the cars, locomotives and rails from all the railroads except the Memphis and Charleston to Nashville. The military manager of railroads also was directed to furnish more rolling stock and, as far as he could, bridge material. General Dodge had the work assigned him finished within forty days after receiving his orders. The number of bridges to rebuild was one hundred and eighty-two, many of them over deep and wide chasms; the length of road repaired was one hundred and two miles.

The enemy's troops, which it was thought were either moving against Burnside or were going to Nashville, went no farther than Cleveland. Their presence there, however, alarmed the authorities at Washington, and, on account of our helpless condition at Chattanooga, caused me much uneasiness. Dispatches were constantly coming, urging me to do something for Burnside's relief; calling attention to the importance of holding East Tennessee; saying the President was much concerned for the protection of the loyal people in that section, etc. We had not at Chattanooga animals to pull a single piece of artillery, much less a supply train. Reinforcements could not help Burnside, because he had neither supplies nor ammunition sufficient for them; hardly, indeed, bread and meat for the men he had. There was no relief possible for him except by expelling the enemy from Missionary Ridge and about Chattanooga.

On the 4th of November Longstreet left our front with about fifteen thousand troops, besides Wheeler's cavalry, five thousand more, to go against Burnside. The situation seemed desperate, and was more aggravating because nothing could be done until Sherman should get up. The authorities at Washington were now more than ever anxious for the safety of Burnside's army, and plied me with dispatches faster than ever, urging that something should be done for his relief. On the 7th, before Longstreet could possibly have reached Knoxville, I ordered Thomas peremptorily to attack the enemy's right, so as to force the return of the troops that had gone up the valley. I directed him to take mules, officers' horses, or animals wherever he could get them, to move the necessary artillery. But he persisted in the declaration that he could not move a single piece of artillery, and could not see how he could possibly comply with the order. Nothing was left to be done but to answer Washington dispatches as best I could; urge Sherman forward, although he was making every effort to get forward, and encourage Burnside to hold on, assuring him that in a short time he should be relieved. All of Burnside's dispatches showed the greatest confidence in his ability to hold his position as long as his ammunition held out. He even suggested the propriety of abandoning the territory he held south and west of Knoxville, so as to draw the enemy farther from his base and make it more difficult for him to get back to Chattanooga when the battle should begin.

Longstreet had a railroad as far as Loudon; but from there to Knoxville he had to rely on wagon trains. Burnside's suggestion, therefore, was a good one, and it was adopted. On the 14th I telegraphed him:

"Sherman's advance has reached Bridgeport. His whole force will be ready to move from there by Tuesday at farthest. If you can hold Longstreet in check until he gets up, or by skirmishing and falling back can avoid serious loss to yourself and gain time, I will be able to force the enemy back from here and place a force between Longstreet and Bragg that must inevitably make the former take to the mountain-passes by every available road, to get to his supplies. Sherman would have been here before this but for high water in Elk River driving him some thirty miles up that river to cross."

And again later in the day, indicating my plans for his relief, as follows:

"Your dispatch and Dana's just received. Being there, you can tell better how to resist Longstreet's attack than I can direct. With your showing you had better give up Kingston at the last moment and save the most productive part of your possessions. Every arrangement is now made to throw Sherman's force across the river, just at and below the mouth of Chickamauga Creek, as soon as it arrives. Thomas will attack on his left at the same time, and together it is expected to carry Missionary Ridge, and from there push a force on to the railroad between Cleveland and Dalton. Hooker will at the same time attack, and, if he can, carry Lookout Mountain. The enemy now seems to be looking for an attack on his left flank. This favors us. To further confirm this, Sherman's advance division will march direct from Whiteside to Trenton. The remainder of his force will pass over a new road just made from Whiteside to Kelly's Ferry, thus being concealed from the enemy, and leave him to suppose the whole force is going up Lookout Valley. Sherman's advance has only just reached Bridgeport. The rear will only reach there on the 16th. This will bring it to the 19th as the earliest day for making the combined movement as desired. Inform me if you think you can sustain yourself until this time. I can hardly conceive of the enemy breaking through at Kingston and pushing for Kentucky. If they should, however, a new problem would be left for solution. Thomas has ordered a division of cavalry to the vicinity of Sparta. I will ascertain if they have started, and inform you. It will be entirely out of the question to send you ten thousand men, not because they cannot be spared, but how would they be fed after they got even one day east from here?"

Longstreet, for some reason or other, stopped at Loudon until the 13th. That being the terminus of his railroad communications, it is probable he was directed to remain there awaiting orders. He was in a position threatening Knoxville, and at the same time where he could be brought back speedily to Chattanooga. The day after Longstreet left Loudon, Sherman reached Bridgeport in person and proceeded on to see me that evening, the 14th, and reached Chattanooga the next day.

My orders for battle were all prepared in advance of Sherman's arrival,* except the dates, which could not be fixed while troops to be engaged were so far away. The possession of Lookout Mountain was of no special advantage to us now. Hooker was instructed to send Howard's corps to the north side of the Tennessee, thence up behind the hills on the north side, and to go into camp opposite Chattanooga; with the remainder of the command, Hooker was, at a time to be afterwards appointed, to ascend the western slope between the upper and lower palisades, and so get into Chattanooga valley.

The plan of battle was for Sherman to attack the enemy's right flank, form a line across it, extend our left over South Chickamauga River so as to threaten or hold the railroad in Bragg's rear, and thus force him either to weaken his lines elsewhere or lose his connection with his base at Chickamauga Station. Hooker was to perform like service on our right. His problem was to get from Lookout Valley to Chattanooga Valley in the most expeditious way possible; cross the

---

*CHATTANOOGA, *November* 18, 1863.

MAJOR-GENERAL W. T. SHERMAN:

Enclosed herewith I send you copy of instructions to Major-General Thomas. You having been over the ground in person, and having heard the whole matter discussed, further instructions will not be necessary for you. It is particularly desirable that a force should be got through to the railroad between Cleveland and Dalton, and Longstreet thus cut off from communication with the South; but being confronted by a large force here, strongly located, it is not easy to tell how this is to be effected until the result of our first effort is known.

I will add, however, what is not shown in my instructions to Thomas, that

latter valley rapidly to Rossville, south of Bragg's line on Missionary Ridge, form line there across the ridge facing north, with his right flank extended to Chickamauga Valley east of the ridge, thus threatening the enemy's rear on that flank and compelling him to reinforce this also. Thomas, with the Army of the Cumberland, occupied the centre, and was to assault while the enemy was engaged with most of his forces on his two flanks.

To carry out this plan, Sherman was to cross the Tennessee at Brown's Ferry and move east of Chattanooga to a point opposite the north end of Mission Ridge, and to place his command back of the foot-hills out of sight of the enemy on the ridge. There are two streams called Chickamauga emptying into the Tennessee River east of Chattanooga — North Chickamauga, taking its rise in Tennessee, flowing south, and emptying into the river some seven or eight miles east; while the South Chickamauga, which takes its rise in Georgia, flows

---

a brigade of cavalry has been ordered here which, if it arrives in time, will be thrown across the Tennessee above Chickamauga, and may be able to make the trip to Cleveland or thereabouts.

U. S. GRANT,
Maj.-Gen'l.

CHATTANOOGA, *November* 18, 1863.
MAJOR-GENERAL GEO. H. THOMAS,
   Chattanooga:

All preparations should be made for attacking the enemy's position on Missionary Ridge by Saturday at daylight. Not being provided with a map giving names of roads, spurs of the mountains, and other places, such definite instructions cannot be given as might be desirable. However, the general plan, you understand, is for Sherman, with the force brought with him strengthened by a division from your command, to effect a crossing of the Tennessee River just below the mouth of Chickamauga; his crossing to be protected by artillery from the heights on the north bank of the river (to be located by your chief of artillery), and to secure the heights on the northern extremity to about the railroad tunnel before the enemy can concentrate against him. You will co-operate with Sherman. The troops in Chattanooga Valley should be well concentrated on your left flank, leaving only the necessary force to defend fortifications on the right and centre, and a movable column of one division in readiness to move wherever ordered. This division should show itself as threateningly as possible on the most practicable

northward, and empties into the Tennessee some three or four miles above the town. There were now one hundred and sixteen pontoons in the North Chickamauga River, their presence there being unknown to the enemy.

At night a division was to be marched up to that point, and at two o'clock in the morning moved down with the current, thirty men in each boat. A few were to land east of the mouth of the South Chickamauga, capture the pickets there, and then lay a bridge connecting the two banks of the river. The rest were to land on the south side of the Tennessee, where Missionary Ridge would strike it if prolonged, and a sufficient number of men to man the boats were to push to the north side to ferry over the main body of Sherman's command while those left on the south side intrenched themselves. Thomas was to move out from his lines facing the ridge, leaving enough of Palmer's corps to guard against an attack down the valley. Lookout Valley being of no present value to us, and being untenable by the enemy if we should secure Missionary Ridge, Hooker's orders were changed. His revised orders brought him to Chattanooga by the established

---

line for making an attack up the valley. Your effort then will be to form a junction with Sherman, making your advance well towards the northern end of Missionary Ridge, and moving as near simultaneously with him as possible. The junction once formed and the ridge carried, communications will be at once established between the two armies by roads on the south bank of the river. Further movements will then depend on those of the enemy. Lookout Valley, I think, will be easily held by Geary's division and what troops you may still have there belonging to the old Army of the Cumberland. Howard's corps can then be held in readiness to act either with you at Chattanooga or with Sherman. It should be marched on Friday night to a position on the north side of the river, not lower down than the first pontoon-bridge, and there held in readiness for such orders as may become necessary. All these troops will be provided with two days' cooked rations in haversacks, and one hundred rounds of ammunition on the person of each infantry soldier. Special care should be taken by all officers to see that ammunition is not wasted or unnecessarily fired away. You will call on the engineer department for such preparations as you may deem necessary for carrying your infantry and artillery over the creek.

U. S. GRANT,
Major-General.

route north of the Tennessee. He was then to move out to the right to Rossville.

Hooker's position in Lookout Valley was absolutely essential to us so long as Chattanooga was besieged. It was the key to our line for supplying the army. But it was not essential after the enemy was dispersed from our front, or even after the battle for this purpose was begun. Hooker's orders, therefore, were designed to get his force past Lookout Mountain and Chattanooga Valley, and up to Missionary Ridge. By crossing the north face of Lookout the troops would come into Chattanooga Valley in rear of the line held by the enemy across the valley, and would necessarily force its evacuation. Orders were accordingly given to march by this route. But days before the battle began the advantages as well as the disadvantages of this plan of action were all considered. The passage over the mountain was a difficult one to make in the face of an enemy. It might consume so much time as to lose us the use of the troops engaged in it at other points where they were more wanted. After reaching Chattanooga Valley, the creek of the same name, quite a formidable stream to get an army over, had to be crossed. I was perfectly willing that the enemy should keep Lookout Mountain until we got through with the troops on Missionary Ridge. By marching Hooker to the north side of the river, thence up the stream, and recrossing at the town, he could be got in position at any named time; when in this new position, he would have Chattanooga Creek behind him, and the attack on Missionary Ridge would unquestionably cause the evacuation by the enemy of his line across the valley and on Lookout Mountain. Hooker's order was changed accordingly. As explained elsewhere, the original order had to be reverted to, because of a flood in the river rendering the bridge at Brown's Ferry unsafe for the passage of troops at the exact juncture when it was wanted to bring all the troops together against Missionary Ridge.

The next day after Sherman's arrival I took him, with Generals Thomas and Smith and other officers, to the north side of the river, and showed them the ground over which Sherman had to march, and pointed out generally what he was expected to do. I, as well as the authorities in Washington, was still in a great state of anxiety for Burnside's safety. Burnside himself, I believe, was the only one who did not share in this anxiety. Nothing could be done for him, however, until Sherman's troops were up. As soon, therefore, as the inspection was over, Sherman started for Bridgeport to hasten matters, rowing a boat himself, I believe, from Kelly's Ferry. Sherman had left Bridgeport the night of the 14th, reached Chattanooga the evening of the 15th, made the above-described inspection on the morning of the 16th, and started back the same evening to hurry up his command, fully appreciating the importance of time.

His march was conducted with as much expedition as the roads and season would admit of. By the 20th he was himself at Brown's Ferry with the head of column, but many of his troops were far behind, and one division (Ewing's) was at Trenton, sent that way to create the impression that Lookout was to be taken from the south. Sherman received his orders at the ferry, and was asked if he could not be ready for the assault the following morning. News had been received that the battle had been commenced at Knoxville. Burnside had been cut off from telegraphic communications. The President, the Secretary of War, and General Halleck, were in an agony of suspense. My suspense was also great, but more endurable, because I was where I could soon do something to relieve the situation. It was impossible to get Sherman's troops up for the next day. I then asked him if they could not be got up to make the assault on the morning of the 22d, and ordered Thomas to move on that date. But the elements were against us. It rained all the 20th and 21st. The river rose so rapidly that it was difficult to keep the pontoons in place.

General Orlando B. Willcox, a division commander under Burnside, was at this time occupying a position farther up the valley than Knoxville—about Maynardville—and was still in telegraphic communication with the North. A dispatch was received from him saying that he was threatened from the east. The following was sent in reply:

"If you can communicate with General Burnside, say to him that our attack on Bragg will commence in the morning. If successful, such a move will be made as I think will relieve East Tennessee, if he can hold out. Longstreet passing through our lines to Kentucky need not cause alarm. He would find the country so bare that he would lose his transportation and artillery before reaching Kentucky, and would meet such a force before he got through, that he could not return."

Meantime, Sherman continued his crossing without intermission as fast as his troops could be got up. The crossing had to be effected in full view of the enemy on the top of Lookout Mountain. Once over, however, the troops soon disappeared behind the detached hills on the north side, and would not come to view again, either to watchmen on Lookout Mountain or Missionary Ridge, until they emerged between the hills to strike the bank of the river. But when Sherman's advance reached a point opposite the town of Chattanooga, Howard, who, it will be remembered, had been concealed behind the hills on the north side, took up his line of march to join the troops on the south side. His crossing was in full view both from Missionary Ridge and the top of Lookout, and the enemy of course supposed these troops to be Sherman's. This enabled Sherman to get to his assigned position without discovery.

Chapter XLIII.

PREPARATIONS FOR BATTLE—THOMAS CARRIES THE
FIRST LINE OF THE ENEMY—SHERMAN CARRIES
MISSIONARY RIDGE—BATTLE OF LOOKOUT
MOUNTAIN—GENERAL HOOKER'S FIGHT.

ON THE 20TH, when so much was occurring to discourage—rains falling so heavily as to delay the passage of
troops over the river at Brown's Ferry and threatening the
entire breaking of the bridge; news coming of a battle raging
at Knoxville; of Willcox being threatened by a force from the
east—a letter was received from Bragg which contained these
words: "As there may still be some non-combatants in Chattanooga, I deem it proper to notify you that prudence would
dictate their early withdrawal." Of course, I understood that
this was a device intended to deceive; but I did not know
what the intended deception was. On the 22d, however, a
deserter came in who informed me that Bragg was leaving
our front, and on that day Buckner's division was sent to
reinforce Longstreet at Knoxville, and another division
started to follow but was recalled. The object of Bragg's
letter, no doubt, was in some way to detain me until Knoxville could be captured, and his troops there be returned to
Chattanooga.

During the night of the 21st the rest of the pontoon boats,
completed, one hundred and sixteen in all, were carried up to
and placed in North Chickamauga. The material for the roadway over these was deposited out of view of the enemy within
a few hundred yards of the bank of the Tennessee, where the
north end of the bridge was to rest.

Hearing nothing from Burnside, and hearing much of the
distress in Washington on his account, I could no longer defer
operations for his relief. I determined, therefore, to do on the
23d, with the Army of the Cumberland, what had been intended to be done on the 24th.

The position occupied by the Army of the Cumberland had
been made very strong for defence during the months it had
been besieged. The line was about a mile from the town, and

extended from Citico Creek, a small stream running near the base of Missionary Ridge and emptying into the Tennessee about two miles below the mouth of the South Chickamauga, on the left, to Chattanooga Creek on the right. All commanding points on the line were well fortified and well equipped with artillery. The important elevations within the line had all been carefully fortified and supplied with a proper armament. Among the elevations so fortified was one to the east of the town, named Fort Wood. It owed its importance chiefly to the fact that it lay between the town and Missionary Ridge, where most of the strength of the enemy was. Fort Wood had in it twenty-two pieces of artillery, most of which would reach the nearer points of the enemy's line. On the morning of the 23d Thomas, according to instructions, moved Granger's corps of two divisions, Sheridan and T. J. Wood commanding, to the foot of Fort Wood, and formed them into line as if going on parade, Sheridan on the right, Wood to the left, extending to or near Citico Creek. Palmer, commanding the 14th corps, held that part of our line facing south and south-west. He supported Sheridan with one division (Baird's), while his other division under Johnson remained in the trenches, under arms, ready to be moved to any point. Howard's corps was moved in rear of the centre. The picket lines were within a few hundred yards of each other. At two o'clock in the afternoon all were ready to advance. By this time the clouds had lifted so that the enemy could see from his elevated position all that was going on. The signal for advance was given by a booming of cannon from Fort Wood and other points on the line. The rebel pickets were soon driven back upon the main guards, which occupied minor and detached heights between the main ridge and our lines. These too were carried before halting, and before the enemy had time to reinforce their advance guards. But it was not without loss on both sides. This movement secured to us a line fully a mile in advance of the one we occupied in the morning, and the one which the enemy had occupied up to this time. The fortifications were rapidly turned to face the other way. During the following night they were made strong. We lost in this preliminary action about eleven hundred killed and wounded, while the enemy probably lost quite as heavily, including the prisoners that were captured. With the exception of the firing of artillery, kept up from Missionary Ridge and Fort Wood until night closed in, this ended the fighting for the first day

The advantage was greatly on our side now, and if I could only have been assured that Burnside could hold out ten days longer I should have rested more easily. But we were doing the best we could for him and the cause.

By the night of the 23d Sherman's command was in a position to move, though one division (Osterhaus's) had not yet crossed the river at Brown's Ferry. The continuous rise in the Tennessee had rendered it impossible to keep the bridge at that point in condition for troops to cross; but I was determined to move that night even without this division. Orders were sent to Osterhaus accordingly to report to Hooker, if he could not cross by eight o'clock on the morning of the 24th. Because of the break in the bridge, Hooker's orders were again changed, but this time only back to those first given to him.

General W. F. Smith had been assigned to duty as Chief Engineer of the Military Division. To him were given the general direction of moving troops by the boats from North Chickamauga, laying the bridge after they reached their position, and generally all the duties pertaining to his office of chief engineer. During the night General Morgan L. Smith's division was marched to the point where the pontoons were, and the brigade of Giles A. Smith was selected for the delicate duty of manning the boats and surprising the enemy's pickets on the south bank of the river. During this night also General J. M. Brannan, chief of artillery, moved forty pieces of artillery, belonging to the Army of the Cumberland, and placed them on the north side of the river so as to command the ground opposite, to aid in protecting the approach to the point where the south end of the bridge was to rest. He had to use Sherman's artillery horses for this purpose, Thomas having none.

At two o'clock in the morning, November 24th, Giles A. Smith pushed out from the North Chickamauga with his one hundred and sixteen boats, each loaded with thirty brave and well-armed men. The boats with their precious freight dropped down quietly with the current to avoid attracting the attention of any one who could convey information to the enemy, until arriving near the mouth of South Chickamauga. Here a few boats were landed, the troops debarked, and a rush was made upon the picket guard known to be at that point. The guard were surprised, and twenty of their number captured. The remainder of the troops effected a landing at the point where the bridge was to start, with equally good results. The work of ferrying over Sherman's command from the north side of the Tennessee was at once commenced, using the pontoons for the purpose. A steamer was also brought up from the town to assist. The rest of M. L. Smith's division came first, then the division of John E. Smith. The troops as they landed were put to work intrenching their position. By daylight the two entire divisions were over, and well covered by the works they had built.

The work of laying the bridge, on which to cross the artillery and cavalry, was now begun. The ferrying over the infantry was continued with the steamer and the pontoons, taking the pontoons, however, as fast as they were wanted to put in their place in the bridge. By a little past noon the bridge was completed, as well as one over the South Chickamauga connecting the troops left on that side with their comrades below, and all the infantry and artillery were on the south bank of the Tennessee.

Sherman at once formed his troops for assault on Missionary Ridge. By one o'clock he started with M. L. Smith on his left, keeping nearly the course of Chickamauga River; J. E. Smith next to the right and a little to the rear; and Ewing still farther to the right and also a little to the rear of J. E. Smith's command, in column, ready to deploy to the right if an enemy should come from that direction. A good skirmish line preceded each of these columns. Soon the foot of the hill was reached; the skirmishers pushed directly up, followed closely by their supports. By half-past three Sherman was in possession of the height without having sustained much loss. A brigade from each division was now brought up, and artillery was dragged to the top of the hill by hand. The enemy did not seem to be aware of this movement until the top of the hill was gained. There had been a drizzling rain during the

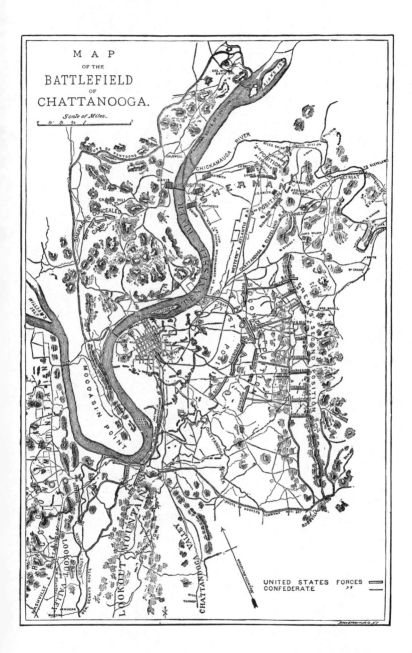

MAP
OF THE
BATTLEFIELD
OF
CHATTANOOGA.

Scale of Miles.

UNITED STATES FORCES
CONFEDERATE.

day, and the clouds were so low that Lookout Mountain and the top of Missionary Ridge were obscured from the view of persons in the valley. But now the enemy opened fire upon their assailants, and made several attempts with their skirmishers to drive them away, but without avail. Later in the day a more determined attack was made, but this, too, failed, and Sherman was left to fortify what he had gained.

Sherman's cavalry took up its line of march soon after the bridge was completed, and by half-past three the whole of it was over both bridges and on its way to strike the enemy's communications at Chickamauga Station. All of Sherman's command was now south of the Tennessee. During the afternoon General Giles A. Smith was severely wounded and carried from the field.

Thomas having done on the 23d what was expected of him on the 24th, there was nothing for him to do this day except to strengthen his position. Howard, however, effected a crossing of Citico Creek and a junction with Sherman, and was directed to report to him. With two or three regiments of his command he moved in the morning along the banks of the Tennessee, and reached the point where the bridge was being laid. He went out on the bridge as far as it was completed from the south end, and saw Sherman superintending the work from the north side and moving himself south as fast as an additional boat was put in and the roadway put upon it. Howard reported to his new chief across the chasm between them, which was now narrow and in a few minutes closed.

While these operations were going on to the east of Chattanooga, Hooker was engaged on the west. He had three divisions: Osterhaus's, of the 15th corps, Army of the Tennessee; Geary's, 12th corps, Army of the Potomac; and Cruft's, 14th corps, Army of the Cumberland. Geary was on the right at Wauhatchie, Cruft at the centre, and Osterhaus near Brown's Ferry. These troops were all west of Lookout Creek. The enemy had the east bank of the creek strongly picketed and intrenched, and three brigades of troops in the rear to reinforce them if attacked. These brigades occupied the summit of the mountain. General Carter L. Stevenson was in command of the whole. Why any troops, except artillery with a small infantry guard, were kept on the mountain-top, I do not see. A hundred men could have held the summit—which is a palisade for more than thirty feet down—against the assault of any number of men from the position Hooker occupied.

The side of Lookout Mountain confronting Hooker's command was rugged, heavily timbered, and full of chasms, making it difficult to advance with troops, even in the absence of an opposing force. Farther up, the ground becomes more even and level, and was in cultivation. On the east side the slope is much more gradual, and a good wagon road, zigzagging up it, connects the town of Chattanooga with the summit.

Early on the morning of the 24th Hooker moved Geary's division, supported by a brigade of Cruft's, up Lookout Creek, to effect a crossing. The remainder of Cruft's division was to seize the bridge over the creek, near the crossing of the railroad. Osterhaus was to move up to the bridge and cross it. The bridge was seized by Gross's brigade after a slight skirmish with the pickets guarding it. This attracted the enemy so that Geary's movement farther up was not observed. A heavy mist obscured him from the view of the troops on the top of the mountain. He crossed the creek almost unobserved, and captured the picket of over forty men on guard near by. He then commenced ascending the mountain directly in his front. By this time the enemy was seen coming down from their camps on the mountain slope, and filing into their rifle-pits to contest the crossing of the bridge. By eleven o'clock the bridge was complete. Osterhaus was up, and after some sharp skirmishing the enemy was driven away with considerable loss in killed and captured.

While the operations at the bridge were progressing, Geary was pushing up the hill over great obstacles, resisted by the enemy directly in his front, and in face of the guns on top of the mountain. The enemy, seeing their left flank and rear menaced, gave way, and were followed by Cruft and Osterhaus. Soon these were up abreast of Geary, and the whole command pushed up the hill, driving the enemy in advance. By noon Geary had gained the open ground on the north slope of the mountain, with his right close up to the base of the upper palisade, but there were strong fortifications in his front. The rest of the command coming up, a line was formed from the base of the upper palisade to the mouth of Chattanooga Creek.

Thomas and I were on the top of Orchard Knob. Hooker's advance now made our line a continuous one. It was in full view, extending from the Tennessee River, where Sherman had crossed, up Chickamauga River to the base of Mission Ridge, over the top of the north end of the ridge to Chattanooga Valley, then along parallel to the ridge a mile or more, across the valley to the mouth of Chattanooga Creek, thence up the slope of Lookout Mountain to the foot of the upper palisade. The day was hazy, so that Hooker's operations were not visible to us except at moments when the clouds would rise. But the sound of his artillery and musketry was heard incessantly. The enemy on his front was partially fortified, but was soon driven out of his works. During the afternoon the clouds, which had so obscured the top of Lookout all day as to hide whatever was going on from the view of those below, settled down and made it so dark where Hooker was as to stop operations for the time. At four o'clock Hooker reported his position as impregnable. By a little after five direct communication was established, and a brigade of troops was sent from Chattanooga to reinforce him. These troops had to cross Chattanooga Creek and met with some opposition, but soon overcame it, and by night the commander, General Carlin, reported to Hooker and was assigned to his left. I now telegraphed to Washington: "The fight to-day progressed favorably. Sherman carried the end of Missionary Ridge, and his right is now at the tunnel, and his left at Chickamauga Creek. Troops from Lookout Valley carried the point of the mountain, and now hold the eastern slope and a point high up. Hooker reports two thousand prisoners taken, besides which a small number have fallen into our hands from Missionary Ridge." The next day the President replied: "Your dispatches as to fighting on Monday and Tuesday are here. Well done. Many thanks to all. Remember Burnside." And Halleck also telegraphed: "I congratulate you on the success thus far of your plans. I fear that Burnside is hard pushed, and that any further delay may prove fatal. I know you will do all in your power to relieve him."

The division of Jefferson C. Davis, Army of the Cumberland, had been sent to the North Chickamauga to guard the pontoons as they were deposited in the river, and to prevent all ingress or egress of citizens. On the night of the 24th his division, having crossed with Sherman, occupied our extreme left from the upper bridge over the plain to the north base of Missionary Ridge. Firing continued to a late hour in the night, but it was not connected with an assault at any point.

Chapter XLIV.

BATTLE OF CHATTANOOGA—A GALLANT
CHARGE—COMPLETE ROUT OF THE ENEMY—PURSUIT
OF THE CONFEDERATES—GENERAL BRAGG—REMARKS
ON CHATTANOOGA.

A T TWELVE O'CLOCK at night, when all was quiet, I began to give orders for the next day, and sent a dispatch to Willcox to encourage Burnside. Sherman was directed to attack at daylight. Hooker was ordered to move at the same hour, and endeavor to intercept the enemy's retreat if he still remained; if he had gone, then to move directly to Rossville and operate against the left and rear of the force on Missionary Ridge. Thomas was not to move until Hooker had reached Missionary Ridge. As I was with him on Orchard Knob, he would not move without further orders from me.

The morning of the 25th opened clear and bright, and the whole field was in full view from the top of Orchard Knob. It remained so all day. Bragg's headquarters were in full view, and officers—presumably staff officers—could be seen coming and going constantly.

The point of ground which Sherman had carried on the 24th was almost disconnected from the main ridge occupied by the enemy. A low pass, over which there is a wagon road crossing the hill, and near which there is a railroad tunnel, intervenes between the two hills. The problem now was to get to the main ridge. The enemy was fortified on the point; and back farther, where the ground was still higher, was a second fortification commanding the first. Sherman was out as soon as it was light enough to see, and by sunrise his command was in motion. Three brigades held the hill already gained. Morgan L. Smith moved along the east base of Missionary Ridge; Loomis along the west base, supported by two brigades of John E. Smith's division; and Corse with his brigade was between the two, moving directly towards the hill to be captured. The ridge is steep and heavily wooded on the east side, where M. L. Smith's troops were advancing, but cleared and with a more gentle slope on the west side. The troops advanced rapidly and carried the extreme end of the rebel works. Morgan L. Smith advanced to a point which cut the enemy off from the railroad bridge and the means of bringing up supplies by rail from Chickamauga Station, where the main depot was located. The enemy made brave and strenuous efforts to drive our troops from the position we had gained, but without success. The contest lasted for two hours. Corse, a brave and efficient commander, was badly wounded in this assault. Sherman now threatened both Bragg's flank and his stores, and made it necessary for him to weaken other points of his line to strengthen his right. From the position I occupied I could see column after column of Bragg's forces moving against Sherman. Every Confederate gun that could be brought to bear upon the Union forces was concentrated upon him. J. E. Smith, with two brigades, charged up the west side of the ridge to the support of Corse's command, over open ground and in the face of a heavy fire of both artillery and musketry, and reached the very parapet of the enemy. He lay here for a time, but the enemy coming with a heavy force upon his right flank, he was compelled to fall back, followed by the foe. A few hundred yards brought Smith's troops into a wood, where they were speedily reformed, when they charged and drove the attacking party back to his intrenchments.

Seeing the advance, repulse, and second advance of J. E. Smith from the position I occupied, I directed Thomas to send a division to reinforce him. Baird's division was accordingly sent from the right of Orchard Knob. It had to march a considerable distance directly under the eyes of the enemy to reach its position. Bragg at once commenced massing in the same direction. This was what I wanted. But it had now got to be late in the afternoon, and I had expected before this to see Hooker crossing the ridge in the neighborhood of Rossville and compelling Bragg to mass in that direction also.

The enemy had evacuated Lookout Mountain during the night, as I expected he would. In crossing the valley he burned the bridge over Chattanooga Creek, and did all he could to obstruct the roads behind him. Hooker was off bright and early, with no obstructions in his front but distance and the destruction above named. He was detained four

hours crossing Chattanooga Creek, and thus was lost the immediate advantage I expected from his forces. His reaching
Bragg's flank and extending across it was to be the signal for
Thomas's assault of the ridge. But Sherman's condition was
getting so critical that the assault for his relief could not be
delayed any longer.

Sheridan's and Wood's divisions had been lying under arms
from early morning, ready to move the instant the signal was
given. I now directed Thomas to order the charge at once.* I
watched eagerly to see the effect, and became impatient at last
that there was no indication of any charge being made. The
centre of the line which was to make the charge was near
where Thomas and I stood, but concealed from view by an
intervening forest. Turning to Thomas to inquire what caused
the delay, I was surprised to see Thomas J. Wood, one of the
division commanders who was to make the charge, standing
talking to him. I spoke to General Wood, asking him why he
did not charge as ordered an hour before. He replied very
promptly that this was the first he had heard of it, but that he
had been ready all day to move at a moment's notice. I told
him to make the charge at once. He was off in a moment, and
in an incredibly short time loud cheering was heard, and he
and Sheridan were driving the enemy's advance before them
towards Missionary Ridge. The Confederates were strongly
intrenched on the crest of the ridge in front of us, and had a
second line half-way down and another at the base. Our men
drove the troops in front of the lower line of rifle-pits so
rapidly, and followed them so closely, that rebel and Union
troops went over the first line of works almost at the same
time. Many rebels were captured and sent to the rear under
the fire of their own friends higher up the hill. Those that
were not captured retreated, and were pursued. The retreating hordes being between friends and pursuers caused the enemy to fire high to avoid killing their own men. In fact, on
that occasion the Union soldier nearest the enemy was in the
safest position. Without awaiting further orders or stopping
to reform, on our troops went to the second line of works;

---

*In this order authority was given for the troops to reform after taking the
first line of rifle-pits preparatory to carrying the ridge.

over that and on for the crest—thus effectually carrying out my orders of the 18th for the battle and of the 24th* for this charge.

I watched their progress with intense interest. The fire along the rebel line was terrific. Cannon and musket balls filled the air: but the damage done was in small proportion to the ammunition expended. The pursuit continued until the crest was reached, and soon our men were seen climbing over the Confederate barriers at different points in front of both Sheridan's and Wood's divisions. The retreat of the enemy along most of his line was precipitate and the panic so great that Bragg and his officers lost all control over their men. Many were captured, and thousands threw away their arms in their flight.

Sheridan pushed forward until he reached the Chickamauga River at a point above where the enemy crossed. He met some resistance from troops occupying a second hill in rear of Missionary Ridge, probably to cover the retreat of the main body and of the artillery and trains. It was now getting dark, but Sheridan, without halting on that account pushed his men forward up this second hill slowly and without attracting the attention of the men placed to defend it, while he detached to the right and left to surround the position. The enemy discovered the movement before these dispositions were complete, and beat a hasty retreat, leaving artillery, wagon trains, and many prisoners in our hands. To Sheridan's

---

*CHATTANOOGA, *November* 24, 1863.
MAJOR-GENERAL GEO. H. THOMAS,
        Chattanooga:

    General Sherman carried Missionary Ridge as far as the tunnel with only slight skirmishing. His right now rests at the tunnel and on top of the hill, his left at Chickamauga Creek. I have instructed General Sherman to advance as soon as it is light in the morning, and your attack, which will be simultaneous, will be in co-operation. Your command will either carry the rifle-pits and ridge directly in front of them, or move to the left, as the presence of the enemy may require. If Hooker's position on the mountain [cannot be maintained] with a small force, and it is found impracticable to carry the top from where he is, it would be advisable for him to move up the valley with all the force he can spare, and ascend by the first practicable road.

                    U. S. GRANT,
                      Major-General.

prompt movement the Army of the Cumberland, and the nation, are indebted for the bulk of the capture of prisoners, artillery, and small-arms that day. Except for his prompt pursuit, so much in this way would not have been accomplished.

While the advance up Mission Ridge was going forward, General Thomas with staff, General Gordon Granger, commander of the corps making the assault, and myself and staff occupied Orchard Knob, from which the entire field could be observed. The moment the troops were seen going over the last line of rebel defences, I ordered Granger to join his command, and mounting my horse I rode to the front. General Thomas left about the same time. Sheridan on the extreme right was already in pursuit of the enemy east of the ridge. Wood, who commanded the division to the left of Sheridan, accompanied his men on horseback in the charge, but did not join Sheridan in the pursuit. To the left, in Baird's front where Bragg's troops had massed against Sherman, the resistance was more stubborn and the contest lasted longer. I ordered Granger to follow the enemy with Wood's division, but he was so much excited, and kept up such a roar of musketry in the direction the enemy had taken, that by the time I could stop the firing the enemy had got well out of the way. The enemy confronting Sherman, now seeing everything to their left giving way, fled also. Sherman, however, was not aware of the extent of our success until after nightfall, when he received orders to pursue at daylight in the morning.

As soon as Sherman discovered that the enemy had left his front he directed his reserves, Davis's division of the Army of the Cumberland, to push over the pontoon-bridge at the mouth of the Chickamauga, and to move forward to Chickamauga Station. He ordered Howard to move up the stream some two miles to where there was an old bridge, repair it during the night, and follow Davis at four o'clock in the morning. Morgan L. Smith was ordered to reconnoitre the tunnel to see if that was still held. Nothing was found there but dead bodies of men of both armies. The rest of Sherman's command was directed to follow Howard at daylight in the morning to get on to the railroad towards Graysville.

Hooker, as stated, was detained at Chattanooga Creek by the destruction of the bridge at that point. He got his troops over, with the exception of the artillery, by fording the stream at a little after three o'clock. Leaving his artillery to follow when the bridge should be reconstructed, he pushed on with the remainder of his command. At Rossville he came upon the flank of a division of the enemy, which soon commenced a retreat along the ridge. This threw them on Palmer. They could make but little resistance in the position they were caught in, and as many of them as could do so escaped. Many, however, were captured. Hooker's position during the night of the 25th was near Rossville, extending east of the ridge. Palmer was on his left, on the road to Graysville.

During the night I telegraphed to Willcox that Bragg had been defeated, and that immediate relief would be sent to Burnside if he could hold out; to Halleck I sent an announcement of our victory, and informed him that forces would be sent up the valley to relieve Burnside.

Before the battle of Chattanooga opened I had taken measures for the relief of Burnside the moment the way should be clear. Thomas was directed to have the little steamer that had been built at Chattanooga loaded to its capacity with rations and ammunition. Granger's corps was to move by the south bank of the Tennessee River to the mouth of the Holston, and up that to Knoxville, accompanied by the boat. In addition to the supplies transported by boat, the men were to carry forty rounds of ammunition in their cartridge-boxes, and four days' rations in haversacks.

In the battle of Chattanooga, troops from the Army of the Potomac, from the Army of the Tennessee, and from the Army of the Cumberland participated. In fact, the accidents growing out of the heavy rains and the sudden rise in the Tennessee River so mingled the troops that the organizations were not kept together, under their respective commanders, during the battle. Hooker, on the right, had Geary's division of the 12th corps, Army of the Potomac; Osterhaus's division of the 15th corps, Army of the Tennessee; and Cruft's division of the Army of the Cumberland. Sherman had three divisions of his own army, Howard's corps from the Army of the Potomac, and Jefferson C. Davis's division of the Army of the Cumberland. There was no jealousy—hardly rivalry. Indeed, I doubt whether officers or men took any note at the time of the fact of this intermingling of commands. All saw a defiant foe surrounding them, and took it for granted that every move was intended to dislodge him, and it made no difference where the troops came from so that the end was accomplished.

The victory at Chattanooga was won against great odds, considering the advantage the enemy had of position, and was accomplished more easily than was expected by reason of Bragg's making several grave mistakes: first, in sending away his ablest corps commander with over twenty thousand troops; second, in sending away a division of troops on the eve of battle; third, in placing so much of a force on the plain in front of his impregnable position.

It was known that Mr. Jefferson Davis had visited Bragg on Missionary Ridge a short time before my reaching Chattanooga. It was reported and believed that he had come out to reconcile a serious difference between Bragg and Longstreet, and finding this difficult to do, planned the campaign against Knoxville, to be conducted by the latter general. I had known both Bragg and Longstreet before the war, the latter very well. We had been three years at West Point together, and, after my graduation, for a time in the same regiment. Then we served together in the Mexican War. I had known Bragg in Mexico, and met him occasionally subsequently. I could well understand how there might be an irreconcilable difference between them.

Bragg was a remarkably intelligent and well-informed man, professionally and otherwise. He was also thoroughly upright. But he was possessed of an irascible temper, and was naturally disputatious. A man of the highest moral character and the most correct habits, yet in the old army he was in frequent trouble. As a subordinate he was always on the lookout to catch his commanding officer infringing his prerogatives; as a post commander he was equally vigilant to detect the slightest neglect, even of the most trivial order.

I have heard in the old army an anecdote very characteristic of Bragg. On one occasion, when stationed at a post of several companies commanded by a field officer, he was himself commanding one of the companies and at the same time acting as post quartermaster and commissary. He was first lieutenant at the time, but his captain was detached on other duty. As commander of the company he made a requisition upon the quartermaster—himself—for something he wanted. As quartermaster he declined to fill the requisition, and endorsed on the back of it his reasons for so doing. As company commander he responded to this, urging that his requisition called for nothing but what he was entitled to, and that it was the duty of the quartermaster to fill it. As quartermaster he still persisted that he was right. In this condition of affairs Bragg referred the whole matter to the commanding officer of the post. The latter, when he saw the nature of the matter referred, exclaimed: "My God, Mr. Bragg, you have quarrelled with every officer in the army, and now you are quarrelling with yourself!"

Longstreet was an entirely different man. He was brave, honest, intelligent, a very capable soldier, subordinate to his superiors, just and kind to his subordinates, but jealous of his own rights, which he had the courage to maintain. He was never on the lookout to detect a slight, but saw one as soon as anybody when intentionally given.

It may be that Longstreet was not sent to Knoxville for the reason stated, but because Mr. Davis had an exalted opinion of his own military genius, and thought he saw a chance of "killing two birds with one stone." On several occasions during the war he came to the relief of the Union army by means of his *superior military genius*.

I speak advisedly when I say Mr. Davis prided himself on his military capacity. He says so himself, virtually, in his answer to the notice of his nomination to the Confederate presidency. Some of his generals have said so in their writings since the downfall of the Confederacy.

My recollection is that my first orders for the battle of Chattanooga were as fought. Sherman was to get on Missionary Ridge, as he did; Hooker to cross the north end of Lookout Mountain, as he did, sweep across Chattanooga Valley and get across the south end of the ridge near Rossville. When Hooker had secured that position the Army of the Cumberland was to assault in the centre. Before Sherman arrived, however, the order was so changed as that Hooker was directed to come to Chattanooga by the north bank of the Tennessee River. The waters in the river, owing to heavy rains, rose so fast that the bridge at Brown's Ferry could not be maintained in a condition to be used in crossing troops upon it. For this reason Hooker's orders were changed by telegraph back to what they were originally.

NOTE.—From this point on this volume was written (with the exception of the campaign in the Wilderness, which had been previously written) by General Grant after his great illness in April, and the present arrangement of the subject-matter was made by him between the 10th and 18th of July, 1885.

Chapter XLV.

THE RELIEF OF KNOXVILLE—HEADQUARTERS MOVED TO
NASHVILLE—VISITING KNOXVILLE—CIPHER
DISPATCHES—WITHHOLDING ORDERS.

CHATTANOOGA now being secure to the National troops
beyond any doubt, I immediately turned my attention
to relieving Knoxville, about the situation of which the President, in particular, was very anxious. Prior to the battles, I
had made preparations for sending troops to the relief of
Burnside at the very earliest moment after securing Chattanooga. We had there two little steamers which had been built
and fitted up from the remains of old boats and put in condition to run. General Thomas was directed to have one of
these boats loaded with rations and ammunition and move up
the Tennessee River to the mouth of the Holston, keeping the
boat all the time abreast of the troops. General Granger, with
the 4th corps reinforced to make twenty thousand men, was
to start the moment Missionary Ridge was carried, and under
no circumstances were the troops to return to their old
camps. With the provisions carried, and the little that could
be got in the country, it was supposed he could hold out until
Longstreet was driven away, after which event East Tennessee
would furnish abundance of food for Burnside's army and his
own also.

While following the enemy on the 26th, and again on the
morning of the 27th, part of the time by the road to Ringgold, I directed Thomas, verbally, not to start Granger until
he received further orders from me; advising him that I was
going to the front to more fully see the situation. I was not
right sure but that Bragg's troops might be over their stampede by the time they reached Dalton. In that case Bragg
might think it well to take the road back to Cleveland, move
thence towards Knoxville, and, uniting with Longstreet, make
a sudden dash upon Burnside.

When I arrived at Ringgold, however, on the 27th, I
saw that the retreat was most earnest. The enemy had been
throwing away guns, caissons and small-arms, abandoning

provisions, and, altogether, seemed to be moving like a disorganized mob, with the exception of Cleburne's division, which was acting as rear-guard to cover the retreat.

When Hooker moved from Rossville toward Ringgold Palmer's division took the road to Graysville, and Sherman moved by the way of Chickamauga Station toward the same point. As soon as I saw the situation at Ringgold I sent a staff officer back to Chattanooga to advise Thomas of the condition of affairs, and direct him by my orders to start Granger at once. Feeling now that the troops were already on the march for the relief of Burnside I was in no hurry to get back, but stayed at Ringgold through the day to prepare for the return of our troops.

Ringgold is in a valley in the mountains, situated between East Chickamauga Creek and Taylor's Ridge, and about twenty miles south-east from Chattanooga. I arrived just as the artillery that Hooker had left behind at Chattanooga Creek got up. His men were attacking Cleburne's division, which had taken a strong position in the adjacent hills so as to cover the retreat of the Confederate army through a narrow gorge which presents itself at that point. Just beyond the gorge the valley is narrow, and the creek so tortuous that it has to be crossed a great many times in the course of the first mile. This attack was unfortunate, and cost us some men unnecessarily. Hooker captured, however, 3 pieces of artillery and 230 prisoners, and 130 rebel dead were left upon the field.

I directed General Hooker to collect the flour and wheat in the neighboring mills for the use of the troops, and then to destroy the mills and all other property that could be of use to the enemy, but not to make any wanton destruction.

At this point Sherman came up, having reached Graysville with his troops, where he found Palmer had preceded him. Palmer had picked up many prisoners and much abandoned property on the route. I went back in the evening to Graysville with Sherman, remained there over night and did not return to Chattanooga until the following night, the 29th. I then found that Thomas had not yet started Granger, thus having lost a full day which I deemed of so much importance in determining the fate of Knoxville. Thomas and Granger were aware that on the 23d of the month Burnside had telegraphed that his supplies would last for ten or twelve days and during that time he could hold out against Longstreet, but if not relieved within the time indicated he would be obliged to surrender or attempt to retreat. To effect a retreat would have been an impossibility. He was already very low in ammunition, and with an army pursuing he would not have been able to gather supplies.

Finding that Granger had not only not started but was very reluctant to go, he having decided for himself that it was a very bad move to make, I sent word to General Sherman of the situation and directed him to march to the relief of Knoxville. I also gave him the problem that we had to solve—that Burnside had now but four to six days supplies left, and that he must be relieved within that time.

Sherman, fortunately, had not started on his return from Graysville, having sent out detachments on the railroad which runs from Dalton to Cleveland and Knoxville to thoroughly destroy that road, and these troops had not yet returned to camp. I was very loath to send Sherman, because his men needed rest after their long march from Memphis and hard fighting at Chattanooga. But I had become satisfied that Burnside would not be rescued if his relief depended upon General Granger's movements.

Sherman had left his camp on the north side of the Tennessee River, near Chattanooga, on the night of the 23d, the men having two days' cooked rations in their haversacks. Expecting to be back in their tents by that time and to be engaged in battle while out, they took with them neither overcoats nor blankets. The weather was already cold, and at night they must have suffered more or less. The two days' rations had already lasted them five days; and they were now to go through a country which had been run over so much by Confederate troops that there was but little probability of finding much food. They did, however, succeed in capturing some flour. They also found a good deal of bran in some of the mills, which the men made up into bread; and in this and other ways they eked out an existence until they could reach Knoxville.

I was so very anxious that Burnside should get news of the

steps being taken for his relief, and thus induce him to hold out a little longer if it became necessary, that I determined to send a message to him. I therefore sent a member of my staff, Colonel J. H. Wilson, to get into Knoxville if he could, report to Burnside the situation fully, and give him all the encouragement possible. Mr. Charles A. Dana was at Chattanooga during the battle, and had been there even before I assumed command. Mr. Dana volunteered to accompany Colonel Wilson, and did accompany him. I put the information of what was being done for the relief of Knoxville into writing, and directed that in some way or other it must be secretly managed so as to have a copy of this fall into the hands of General Longstreet. They made the trip safely; General Longstreet did learn of Sherman's coming in advance of his reaching there, and Burnside was prepared to hold out even for a longer time if it had been necessary.

Burnside had stretched a boom across the Holston River to catch scows and flats as they floated down. On these, by previous arrangements with the loyal people of East Tennessee, were placed flour and corn, with forage and provisions generally, and were thus secured for the use of the Union troops. They also drove cattle into Knoxville by the east side, which was not covered by the enemy; so that when relief arrived Burnside had more provisions on hand than when he had last reported.

Our total loss (not including Burnside's) in all these engagements amounted to 757 killed, 4,529 wounded and 330 missing. We captured 6,142 prisoners—about 50 per cent. more than the enemy reported for their total loss—40 pieces of artillery, 69 artillery carriages and caissons and over 7,000 stands of small-arms. The enemy's loss in arms was probably much greater than here reported, because we picked up a great many that were found abandoned.

I had at Chattanooga, in round numbers, about 60,000 men. Bragg had about half this number, but his position was supposed to be impregnable. It was his own fault that he did not have more men present. He had sent Longstreet away with his corps swelled by reinforcements up to over twenty thousand men, thus reducing his own force more than one-

third and depriving himself of the presence of the ablest
general of his command. He did this, too, after our troops
had opened a line of communication by way of Brown's and
Kelly's ferries with Bridgeport, thus securing full rations and
supplies of every kind; and also when he knew reinforcements
were coming to me. Knoxville was of no earthly use to him
while Chattanooga was in our hands. If he should capture
Chattanooga, Knoxville with its garrison would have fallen
into his hands without a struggle. I have never been able to
see the wisdom of this move.

Then, too, after Sherman had arrived, and when Bragg
knew that he was on the north side of the Tennessee River,
he sent Buckner's division to reinforce Longstreet. He also
started another division a day later, but our attack having
commenced before it reached Knoxville Bragg ordered it
back. It had got so far, however, that it could not return to
Chattanooga in time to be of service there. It is possible this
latter blunder may have been made by Bragg having become
confused as to what was going on on our side. Sherman had,
as already stated, crossed to the north side of the Tennessee
River at Brown's Ferry, in full view of Bragg's troops from
Lookout Mountain, a few days before the attack. They then
disappeared behind foot hills, and did not come to the view
of the troops on Missionary Ridge until they met their assault. Bragg knew it was Sherman's troops that had crossed,
and, they being so long out of view, may have supposed that
they had gone up the north bank of the Tennessee River to
the relief of Knoxville and that Longstreet was therefore in
danger. But the first great blunder, detaching Longstreet, cannot be accounted for in any way I know of. If he had captured Chattanooga, East Tennessee would have fallen without
a struggle. It would have been a victory for us to have got our
army away from Chattanooga safely. It was a manifold greater
victory to drive away the besieging army; a still greater one to
defeat that army in his chosen ground and nearly annihilate it.

The probabilities are that our loss in killed was the heavier,
as we were the attacking party. The enemy reported his loss in
killed at 361: but as he reported his missing at 4,146 while we
held over 6,000 of them as prisoners, and there must have
been hundreds if not thousands who deserted, but little re-

liance can be placed on this report. There was certainly great dissatisfaction with Bragg on the part of the soldiers for his harsh treatment of them, and a disposition to get away if they could. Then, too, Chattanooga, following in the same half year with Gettysburg in the East and Vicksburg in the West, there was much the same feeling in the South at this time that there had been in the North the fall and winter before. If the same license had been allowed the people and press in the South that was allowed in the North, Chattanooga would probably have been the last battle fought for the preservation of the Union.

General William F. Smith's services in these battles had been such that I thought him eminently entitled to promotion. I was aware that he had previously been named by the President for promotion to the grade of major-general, but that the Senate had rejected the nomination. I was not aware of the reasons for this course, and therefore strongly recommended him for a major-generalcy. My recommendation was heeded and the appointment made.

Upon the raising of the siege of Knoxville I, of course, informed the authorities at Washington—the President and Secretary of War—of the fact, which caused great rejoicing there. The President especially was rejoiced that Knoxville had been relieved* without further bloodshed. The safety of Burnside's army and the loyal people of East Tennessee had been the subject of much anxiety to the President for several months, during which time he was doing all he could to relieve the situation; sending a new commander† with a few thousand troops by the way of Cumberland Gap, and tele-

---

*WASHINGTON, D. C.,
December 8, 1863, 10.2 A.M.

MAJ.-GENERAL U. S. GRANT:

Understanding that your lodgment at Knoxville and at Chattanooga is now secure, I wish to tender you, and all under your command, my more than thanks, my profoundest gratitude for the skill, courage, and perseverance with which you and they, over so great difficulties, have effected that important object. God bless you all.

A. LINCOLN,
President U. S.

†General John G. Foster.

graphing me daily, almost hourly, to "remember Burnside," "do something for Burnside," and other appeals of like tenor. He saw no escape for East Tennessee until after our victory at Chattanooga. Even then he was afraid that Burnside might be out of ammunition, in a starving condition, or overpowered: and his anxiety was still intense until he heard that Longstreet had been driven from the field.

Burnside followed Longstreet only to Strawberry Plains, some twenty miles or more east, and then stopped, believing that Longstreet would leave the State. The latter did not do so, however, but stopped only a short distance farther on and subsisted his army for the entire winter off East Tennessee. Foster now relieved Burnside. Sherman made disposition of his troops along the Tennessee River in accordance with instructions. I left Thomas in command at Chattanooga, and, about the 20th of December, moved my headquarters to Nashville, Tennessee.

Nashville was the most central point from which to communicate with my entire military division, and also with the authorities at Washington. While remaining at Chattanooga I was liable to have my telegraphic communications cut so as to throw me out of communication with both my command and Washington.

Nothing occurred at Nashville worthy of mention during the winter,* so I set myself to the task of having troops in positions from which they could move to advantage, and in collecting all necessary supplies so as to be ready to claim a due share of the enemy's attention upon the appearance of the first good weather in the spring. I expected to retain the command I then had, and prepared myself for the campaign against Atlanta. I also had great hopes of having a campaign made against Mobile from the Gulf. I expected after Atlanta

---

*During this winter the citizens of Jo Davies County, Ill., subscribed for and had a diamond-hilted sword made for General Grant, which was always known as the Chattanooga sword. The scabbard was of gold, and was ornamented with a scroll running nearly its entire length, displaying in engraved letters the names of the battles in which General Grant had participated.

Congress also gave him a vote of thanks for the victories at Chattanooga, and voted him a gold medal for Vicksburg and Chattanooga. All such things are now in the possession of the government at Washington.

fell to occupy that place permanently, and to cut off Lee's army from the West by way of the road running through Augusta to Atlanta and thence south-west. I was preparing to hold Atlanta with a small garrison, and it was my expectation to push through to Mobile if that city was in our possession: if not, to Savannah; and in this manner to get possession of the only east and west railroad that would then be left to the enemy. But the spring campaign against Mobile was not made.

The Army of the Ohio had been getting supplies over Cumberland Gap until their animals had nearly all starved. I now determined to go myself to see if there was any possible chance of using that route in the spring, and if not to abandon it. Accordingly I left Nashville in the latter part of December by rail for Chattanooga. From Chattanooga I took one of the little steamers previously spoken of as having been built there, and, putting my horses aboard, went up to the junction of the Clinch with the Tennessee. From that point the railroad had been repaired up to Knoxville and out east to Strawberry Plains. I went by rail therefore to Knoxville, where I remained for several days. General John G. Foster was then commanding the Department of the Ohio. It was an intensely cold winter, the thermometer being down as low as zero every morning for more than a week while I was at Knoxville and on my way from there on horseback to Lexington, Kentucky, the first point where I could reach rail to carry me back to my headquarters at Nashville.

The road over Cumberland Gap, and back of it, was strewn with *débris* of broken wagons and dead animals, much as I had found it on my first trip to Chattanooga over Waldron's Ridge. The road had been cut up to as great a depth as clay could be by mules and wagons, and in that condition frozen; so that the ride of six days from Strawberry Plains to Lexington over these holes and knobs in the road was a very cheerless one, and very disagreeable.

I found a great many people at home along that route, both in Tennessee and Kentucky, and, almost universally, intensely loyal. They would collect in little places where we would stop of evenings, to see me, generally hearing of my approach before we arrived. The people naturally expected to see the commanding general the oldest person in the party. I was then forty-one years of age, while my medical director was gray-haired and probably twelve or more years my senior. The crowds would generally swarm around him, and thus give me an opportunity of quietly dismounting and getting into the house. It also gave me an opportunity of hearing passing remarks from one spectator to another about their general. Those remarks were apt to be more complimentary to the cause than to the appearance of the supposed general, owing to his being muffled up, and also owing to the travel-worn condition we were all in after a hard day's ride. I was back in Nashville by the 13th of January, 1864.

When I started on this trip it was necessary for me to have some person along who could turn dispatches into cipher, and who could also read the cipher dispatches which I was liable to receive daily and almost hourly. Under the rules of the War Department at that time, Mr. Stanton had taken entire control of the matter of regulating the telegraph and determining how it should be used, and of saying who, and who alone, should have the ciphers. The operators possessed of the ciphers, as well as the ciphers used, were practically independent of the commanders whom they were serving immediately under, and had to report to the War Department through General Stager all the dispatches which they received or forwarded.

I was obliged to leave the telegraphic operator back at Nashville, because that was the point at which all dispatches to me would come, to be forwarded from there. As I have said, it was necessary for me also to have an operator during this inspection who had possession of this cipher to enable me to telegraph to my division and to the War Department without my dispatches being read by all the operators along the line of wires over which they were transmitted. Accordingly I ordered the cipher operator to turn over the key to Captain Cyrus B. Comstock, of the Corps of Engineers, whom I had selected as a wise and discreet man who certainly could be trusted with the cipher if the operator at my headquarters could.

The operator refused point blank to turn over the key to Captain Comstock as directed by me, stating that his orders from the War Department were not to give it to anybody—

the commanding general or any one else. I told him I would see whether he would or not. He said that if he did he would be punished. I told him if he did not he most certainly would be punished. Finally, seeing that punishment was certain if he refused longer to obey my order, and being somewhat remote (even if he was not protected altogether from the consequences of his disobedience to his orders) from the War Department, he yielded. When I returned from Knoxville I found quite a commotion. The operator had been reprimanded very severely and ordered to be relieved. I informed the Secretary of War, or his assistant secretary in charge of the telegraph, Stager, that the man could not be relieved, for he had only obeyed my orders. It was absolutely necessary for me to have the cipher, and the man would most certainly have been punished if he had not delivered it; that they would have to punish me if they punished anybody, or words to that effect.

This was about the only thing approaching a disagreeable difference between the Secretary of War and myself that occurred until the war was over, when we had another little spat. Owing to his natural disposition to assume all power and control in all matters that he had anything whatever to do with, he boldly took command of the armies, and, while issuing no orders on the subject, prohibited any order from me going out of the adjutant-general's office until he had approved it. This was done by directing the adjutant-general to hold any orders that came from me to be issued from the adjutant-general's office until he had examined them and given his approval. He never disturbed himself, either, in examining my orders until it was entirely convenient for him; so that orders which I had prepared would often lie there three or four days before he would sanction them. I remonstrated against this in writing, and the Secretary apologetically restored me to my rightful position of General-in-Chief of the Army. But he soon lapsed again and took control much as before.

After the relief of Knoxville Sherman had proposed to Burnside that he should go with him to drive Longstreet out of Tennessee; but Burnside assured him that with the troops which had been brought by Granger, and which were to be left, he would be amply prepared to dispose of Longstreet without availing himself of this offer. As before stated Sherman's command had left their camps north of the Tennessee, near Chattanooga, with two days' rations in their haversacks, without coats or blankets, and without many wagons, expecting to return to their camps by the end of that time. The weather was now cold and they were suffering, but still they were ready to make the further sacrifice, had it been required, for the good of the cause which had brought them into service. Sherman, having accomplished the object for which he was sent, marched back leisurely to his old camp on the Tennessee River.

Chapter XLVI.

OPERATIONS IN MISSISSIPPI — LONGSTREET IN EAST
TENNESSEE — COMMISSIONED LIEUTENANT-GENERAL —
COMMANDING THE ARMIES OF THE UNITED STATES —
FIRST INTERVIEW WITH PRESIDENT LINCOLN.

SOON AFTER his return from Knoxville I ordered Sherman to distribute his forces from Stevenson to Decatur and thence north to Nashville; Sherman suggested that he be permitted to go back to Mississippi, to the limits of his own department and where most of his army still remained, for the purpose of clearing out what Confederates might still be left on the east bank of the Mississippi River to impede its navigation by our boats. He expected also to have the co-operation of Banks to do the same thing on the west shore. Of course I approved heartily.

About the 10th of January Sherman was back in Memphis, where Hurlbut commanded, and got together his Memphis men, or ordered them collected and sent to Vicksburg. He then went to Vicksburg and out to where McPherson was in command, and had him organize his surplus troops so as to give him about 20,000 men in all.

Sherman knew that General (Bishop) Polk was occupying Meridian with his headquarters, and had two divisions of infantry with a considerable force of cavalry scattered west of him. He determined, therefore, to move directly upon Meridian.

I had sent some 2,500 cavalry under General Sooy Smith to Sherman's department, and they had mostly arrived before Sherman got to Memphis. Hurlbut had 7,000 cavalry, and Sherman ordered him to reinforce Smith so as to give the latter a force of about 7,000 with which to go against Forrest, who was then known to be south-east from Memphis. Smith was ordered to move about the 1st of February.

While Sherman was waiting at Vicksburg for the arrival of Hurlbut with his surplus men, he sent out scouts to ascertain the position and strength of the enemy and to bring back all the information they could gather. When these scouts returned it was through them that he got the information of General Polk's being at Meridian, and of the strength and disposition of his command.

Forrest had about 4,000 cavalry with him, composed of thoroughly well-disciplined men, who under so able a leader were very effective. Smith's command was nearly double that of Forrest, but not equal, man to man, for the lack of a successful experience such as Forrest's men had had. The fact is, troops who have fought a few battles and won, and followed up their victories, improve upon what they were before to an extent that can hardly be counted by percentage. The difference in result is often decisive victory instead of inglorious defeat. This same difference, too, is often due to the way troops are officered, and for the particular kind of warfare which Forrest had carried on neither army could present a more effective officer than he was.

Sherman got off on the 3d of February and moved out on his expedition, meeting with no opposition whatever until he crossed the Big Black, and with no great deal of opposition after that until he reached Jackson, Mississippi. This latter place he reached on the 6th or 7th, Brandon on the 8th, and Morton on the 9th. Up to this time he moved in two columns to enable him to get a good supply of forage, etc., and expedite the march. Here, however, there were indications of the concentration of Confederate infantry, and he was obliged to keep his army close together. He had no serious engagement; but he met some of the enemy who destroyed a few of his wagons about Decatur, Mississippi, where, by the way, Sherman himself came near being picked up.

He entered Meridian on the 14th of the month, the enemy having retreated toward Demopolis, Alabama. He spent several days in Meridian in thoroughly destroying the railroad to the north and south, and also for the purpose of hearing from Sooy Smith, who he supposed had met Forrest before this time and he hoped had gained a decisive victory because of a superiority of numbers. Hearing nothing of him, however, he started on his return trip to Vicksburg. There he learned that Smith, while waiting for a few of his men who had been ice-bound in the Ohio River, instead of getting off on the 1st as expected, had not left until the 11th. Smith did meet Forrest, but the result was decidedly in Forrest's favor.

Sherman had written a letter to Banks, proposing a co-operative movement with him against Shreveport, subject to my approval. I disapproved of Sherman's going himself, because I had other important work for him to do, but consented that he might send a few troops to the aid of Banks, though their time to remain absent must be limited. We must have them for the spring campaign. The trans-Mississippi movement proved abortive.

My eldest son, who had accompanied me on the Vicksburg campaign and siege, had while there contracted disease, which grew worse, until he had grown so dangerously ill that on the 24th of January I obtained permission to go to St. Louis, where he was staying at the time, to see him, hardly expecting to find him alive on my arrival. While I was permitted to go, I was not permitted to turn over my command to any one else, but was directed to keep the headquarters with me and to communicate regularly with all parts of my division and with Washington, just as though I had remained at Nashville.

When I obtained this leave I was at Chattanooga, having gone there again to make preparations to have the troops of Thomas in the southern part of Tennessee co-operate with Sherman's movement in Mississippi. I directed Thomas, and Logan who was at Scottsboro, Alabama, to keep up a threatening movement to the south against J. E. Johnston, who had again relieved Bragg, for the purpose of making him keep as many troops as possible there.

I learned through Confederate sources that Johnston had already sent two divisions in the direction of Mobile, presumably to operate against Sherman, and two more divisions to Longstreet in East Tennessee. Seeing that Johnston had depleted in this way, I directed Thomas to send at least ten thousand men, besides Stanley's division which was already to the east, into East Tennessee, and notified Schofield, who was now in command in East Tennessee, of this movement of troops into his department and also of the reinforcements Longstreet had received. My object was to drive Longstreet out of East Tennessee as a part of the preparations for my spring campaign.

About this time General Foster, who had been in command of the Department of the Ohio after Burnside until Schofield relieved him,* advised me that he thought it would be a good thing to keep Longstreet just where he was; that he was perfectly quiet in East Tennessee, and if he was forced to leave there, his whole well-equipped army would be free to go to any place where it could effect the most for their cause. I thought the advice was good, and, adopting that view, countermanded the orders for pursuit of Longstreet.

On the 12th of February I ordered Thomas to take Dalton and hold it, if possible; and I directed him to move without delay. Finding that he had not moved, on the 17th I urged him again to start, telling him how important it was, that the object of the movement was to co-operate with Sherman, who was moving eastward and might be in danger. Then again on the 21st, he not yet having started, I asked him if he could not start the next day. He finally got off on the 22d or 23d. The enemy fell back from his front without a battle, but took a new position quite as strong and farther to the rear. Thomas reported that he could not go any farther, because it was impossible with his poor teams, nearly starved, to keep up supplies until the railroads were repaired. He soon fell back.

Schofield also had to return for the same reason. He could not carry supplies with him, and Longstreet was between him and the supplies still left in the country. Longstreet, in his retreat, would be moving towards his supplies, while our forces, following, would be receding from theirs. On the 2d of March, however, I learned of Sherman's success, which eased my mind very much. The next day, the 3d, I was ordered to Washington.

---

*Washington, D. C.,
December 29, 1863.

Maj.-General U. S. Grant:

General Foster has asked to be relieved from his command on account of disability from old wounds. Should his request be granted, who would you like as his successor? It is possible that Schofield will be sent to your command.

H. W. HALLECK,
(*Official.*)   General-in-Chief.

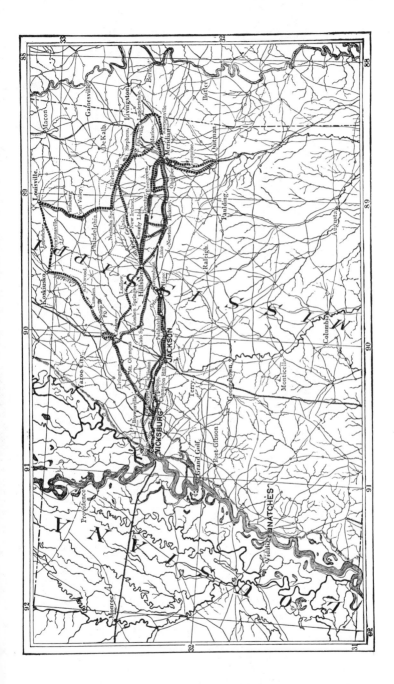

The bill restoring the grade of lieutenant-general of the army had passed through Congress and became a law on the 26th of February. My nomination had been sent to the Senate on the 1st of March and confirmed the next day (the 2d). I was ordered to Washington on the 3d to receive my commission, and started the day following that. The commission was handed to me on the 9th. It was delivered to me at the Executive Mansion by President Lincoln in the presence of his Cabinet, my eldest son, those of my staff who were with me and a few other visitors.

The President in presenting my commission read from a paper—stating, however, as a preliminary, and prior to the delivery of it, that he had drawn that up on paper, knowing my disinclination to speak in public, and handed me a copy in advance so that I might prepare a few lines of reply. The President said:

"General Grant, the nation's appreciation of what you have done, and its reliance upon you for what remains to be done in the existing great struggle, are now presented, with this commission constituting you lieutenant-general in the Army of the United States. With this high honor, devolves upon you, also, a corresponding responsibility. As the country herein trusts you, so, under God, it will sustain you. I scarcely need to add, that, with what I here speak for the nation, goes my own hearty personal concurrence."

To this I replied: "Mr. President, I accept the commission, with gratitude for the high honor conferred. With the aid of the noble armies that have fought in so many fields for our common country, it will be my earnest endeavor not to disappoint your expectations. I feel the full weight of the responsibilities now devolving on me; and I know that if they are met, it will be due to those armies, and above all, to the favor of that Providence which leads both nations and men."

On the 10th I visited the headquarters of the Army of the Potomac at Brandy Station; then returned to Washington, and pushed west at once to make my arrangements for turning over the commands there and giving general directions for the preparations to be made for the spring campaign.

It had been my intention before this to remain in the West, even if I was made lieutenant-general; but when I got to

Washington and saw the situation it was plain that here was
the point for the commanding general to be. No one else
could, probably, resist the pressure that would be brought to
bear upon him to desist from his own plans and pursue
others. I determined, therefore, before I started back to have
Sherman advanced to my late position, McPherson to Sherman's in command of the department, and Logan to the command of McPherson's corps. These changes were all made on
my recommendation and without hesitation. My commission
as lieutenant-general was given to me on the 9th of March,
1864. On the following day, as already stated, I visited General Meade, commanding the Army of the Potomac, at his
headquarters at Brandy Station, north of the Rapidan. I had
known General Meade slightly in the Mexican war, but had
not met him since until this visit. I was a stranger to most of
the Army of the Potomac, I might say to all except the officers
of the regular army who had served in the Mexican war.
There had been some changes ordered in the organization of
that army before my promotion. One was the consolidation
of five corps into three, thus throwing some officers of rank
out of important commands. Meade evidently thought that I
might want to make still one more change not yet ordered.
He said to me that I might want an officer who had served
with me in the West, mentioning Sherman specially, to take
his place. If so, he begged me not to hesitate about making
the change. He urged that the work before us was of such
vast importance to the whole nation that the feeling or wishes
of no one person should stand in the way of selecting the
right men for all positions. For himself, he would serve to the
best of his ability wherever placed. I assured him that I had
no thought of substituting any one for him. As to Sherman,
he could not be spared from the West.

This incident gave me even a more favorable opinion of
Meade than did his great victory at Gettysburg the July before. It is men who wait to be selected, and not those who
seek, from whom we may always expect the most efficient
service.

Meade's position afterwards proved embarrassing to me if
not to him. He was commanding an army and, for nearly a
year previous to my taking command of all the armies, was in

supreme command of the Army of the Potomac—except from the authorities at Washington. All other general officers occupying similar positions were independent in their commands so far as any one present with them was concerned. I tried to make General Meade's position as nearly as possible what it would have been if I had been in Washington or any other place away from his command. I therefore gave all orders for the movements of the Army of the Potomac to Meade to have them executed. To avoid the necessity of having to give orders direct, I established my headquarters near his, unless there were reasons for locating them elsewhere. This sometimes happened, and I had on occasions to give orders direct to the troops affected. On the 11th I returned to Washington and, on the day after, orders were published by the War Department placing me in command of all the armies. I had left Washington the night before to return to my old command in the West and to meet Sherman whom I had telegraphed to join me in Nashville.

Sherman assumed command of the military division of the Mississippi on the 18th of March, and we left Nashville together for Cincinnati. I had Sherman accompany me that far on my way back to Washington so that we could talk over the matters about which I wanted to see him, without losing any more time from my new command than was necessary. The first point which I wished to discuss was particularly about the co-operation of his command with mine when the spring campaign should commence. There were also other and minor points, minor as compared with the great importance of the question to be decided by sanguinary war—the restoration to duty of officers who had been relieved from important commands, namely McClellan, Burnside and Fremont in the East, and Buell, McCook, Negley and Crittenden in the West.

Some time in the winter of 1863–64 I had been invited by the general-in-chief to give my views of the campaign I thought advisable for the command under me—now Sherman's. General J. E. Johnston was defending Atlanta and the interior of Georgia with an army, the largest part of which was stationed at Dalton, about 38 miles south of Chattanooga. Dalton is at the junction of the railroad from Cleveland with the one from Chattanooga to Atlanta.

There could have been no difference of opinion as to the first duty of the armies of the military division of the Mississippi. Johnston's army was the first objective, and that important railroad centre, Atlanta, the second. At the time I wrote General Halleck giving my views of the approaching campaign, and at the time I met General Sherman, it was expected that General Banks would be through with the campaign which he had been ordered upon before my appointment to the command of all the armies, and would be ready to co-operate with the armies east of the Mississippi, his part in the programme being to move upon Mobile by land while the navy would close the harbor and assist to the best of its ability.* The plan therefore was for Sherman to attack Johnston and destroy his army if possible, to capture Atlanta and hold it, and with his troops and those of Banks to hold a line through to Mobile, or at least to hold Atlanta and command the railroad running east and west, and the troops from one or other of the armies to hold important points on the southern road, the only east and west road that would be left in the possession of the enemy. This would cut the Confederacy in two again, as our gaining possession of the Mississippi River had done before. Banks was not ready in time for the part assigned to him, and circumstances that could not be foreseen determined the campaign which was afterwards made, the success and grandeur of which has resounded throughout all lands.

In regard to restoring officers who had been relieved from important commands to duty again, I left Sherman to look after those who had been removed in the West while I looked out for the rest. I directed, however, that he should make no assignment until I could speak to the Secretary of War about the matter. I shortly after recommended to the Secretary the assignment of General Buell to duty. I received the assurance that duty would be offered to him; and afterwards the Secretary told me that he had offered Buell an assignment and that the latter had declined it, saying that it would be degradation to accept the assignment offered. I understood afterwards that he refused to serve under either Sherman or Canby because

---

*See letter to Banks, in General Grant's report, Appendix.

he had ranked them both. Both graduated before him and ranked him in the old army. Sherman ranked him as a brigadier-general. All of them ranked me in the old army, and Sherman and Buell did as brigadiers. The worst excuse a soldier can make for declining service is that he once ranked the commander he is ordered to report to.

On the 23d of March I was back in Washington, and on the 26th took up my headquarters at Culpeper Court-House, a few miles south of the headquarters of the Army of the Potomac.

Although hailing from Illinois myself, the State of the President, I never met Mr. Lincoln until called to the capital to receive my commission as lieutenant-general. I knew him, however, very well and favorably from the accounts given by officers under me at the West who had known him all their lives. I had also read the remarkable series of debates between Lincoln and Douglas a few years before, when they were rival candidates for the United States Senate. I was then a resident of Missouri, and by no means a "Lincoln man" in that contest; but I recognized then his great ability.

In my first interview with Mr. Lincoln alone he stated to me that he had never professed to be a military man or to know how campaigns should be conducted, and never wanted to interfere in them: but that procrastination on the part of commanders, and the pressure from the people at the North and Congress, *which was always with him*, forced him into issuing his series of "Military Orders"—one, two, three, etc. He did not know but they were all wrong, and did know that some of them were. All he wanted or had ever wanted was some one who would take the responsibility and act, and call on him for all the assistance needed, pledging himself to use all the power of the government in rendering such assistance. Assuring him that I would do the best I could with the means at hand, and avoid as far as possible annoying him or the War Department, our first interview ended.

The Secretary of War I had met once before only, but felt that I knew him better.

While commanding in West Tennessee we had occasionally held conversations over the wires, at night, when they were not being otherwise used. He and General Halleck both cautioned me against giving the President my plans of campaign, saying that he was so kind-hearted, so averse to refusing anything asked of him, that some friend would be sure to get from him all he knew. I should have said that in our interview the President told me he did not want to know what I proposed to do. But he submitted a plan of campaign of his own which he wanted me to hear and then do as I pleased about. He brought out a map of Virginia on which he had evidently marked every position occupied by the Federal and Confederate armies up to that time. He pointed out on the map two streams which empty into the Potomac, and suggested that the army might be moved on boats and landed between the mouths of these streams. We would then have the Potomac to bring our supplies, and the tributaries would protect our flanks while we moved out. I listened respectfully, but did not suggest that the same streams would protect Lee's flanks while he was shutting us up.

I did not communicate my plans to the President, nor did I to the Secretary of War or to General Halleck.

March the 26th my headquarters were, as stated, at Culpeper, and the work of preparing for an early campaign commenced.

Chapter XLVII.

THE MILITARY SITUATION—PLANS FOR THE CAMPAIGN—
SHERIDAN ASSIGNED TO COMMAND OF THE CAVALRY—
FLANK MOVEMENTS—FORREST AT FORT PILLOW—
GENERAL BANKS'S EXPEDITION—COLONEL MOSBY
—AN INCIDENT OF THE WILDERNESS CAMPAIGN.

WHEN I ASSUMED command of all the armies the situation was about this: the Mississippi River was guarded
from St. Louis to its mouth; the line of the Arkansas was
held, thus giving us all the North-west north of that river. A
few points in Louisiana not remote from the river were held
by the Federal troops, as was also the mouth of the Rio
Grande. East of the Mississippi we held substantially all north
of the Memphis and Charleston Railroad as far east as Chattanooga, thence along the line of the Tennessee and Holston
rivers, taking in nearly all of the State of Tennessee. West Virginia was in our hands; and that part of old Virginia north of
the Rapidan and east of the Blue Ridge we also held. On the
sea-coast we had Fortress Monroe and Norfolk in Virginia;
Plymouth, Washington and New Berne in North Carolina;
Beaufort, Folly and Morris islands, Hilton Head, Port Royal
and Fort Pulaski in South Carolina and Georgia; Fernandina,
St. Augustine, Key West and Pensacola in Florida. The balance of the Southern territory, an empire in extent, was still in
the hands of the enemy.

Sherman, who had succeeded me in the command of the
military division of the Mississippi, commanded all the troops
in the territory west of the Alleghanies and north of Natchez,
with a large movable force about Chattanooga. His command
was subdivided into four departments, but the commanders
all reported to Sherman and were subject to his orders. This
arrangement, however, insured the better protection of all
lines of communication through the acquired territory, for
the reason that these different department commanders could
act promptly in case of a sudden or unexpected raid within
their respective jurisdictions without awaiting the orders of
the division commander.

In the East the opposing forces stood in substantially the same relations towards each other as three years before, or when the war began; they were both between the Federal and Confederate capitals. It is true, footholds had been secured by us on the sea-coast, in Virginia and North Carolina, but, beyond that, no substantial advantage had been gained by either side. Battles had been fought of as great severity as had ever been known in war, over ground from the James River and Chickahominy, near Richmond, to Gettysburg and Chambersburg, in Pennsylvania, with indecisive results, sometimes favorable to the National army, sometimes to the Confederate army; but in every instance, I believe, claimed as victories for the South by the Southern press if not by the Southern generals. The Northern press, as a whole, did not discourage these claims; a portion of it always magnified rebel success and belittled ours, while another portion, most sincerely earnest in their desire for the preservation of the Union and the overwhelming success of the Federal armies, would nevertheless generally express dissatisfaction with whatever victories were gained because they were not more complete.

That portion of the Army of the Potomac not engaged in guarding lines of communication was on the northern bank of the Rapidan. The Army of Northern Virginia confronting it on the opposite bank of the same river, was strongly intrenched and commanded by the acknowledged ablest general in the Confederate army. The country back to the James River is cut up with many streams, generally narrow, deep, and difficult to cross except where bridged. The region is heavily timbered, and the roads narrow, and very bad after the least rain. Such an enemy was not, of course, unprepared with adequate fortifications at convenient intervals all the way back to Richmond, so that when driven from one fortified position they would always have another farther to the rear to fall back into.

To provision an army, campaigning against so formidable a foe through such a country, from wagons alone seemed almost impossible. System and discipline were both essential to its accomplishment.

The Union armies were now divided into nineteen de-

partments, though four of them in the West had been concentrated into a single military division. The Army of the
Potomac was a separate command and had no territorial
limits. There were thus seventeen distinct commanders. Before this time these various armies had acted separately and independently of each other, giving the enemy an opportunity
often of depleting one command, not pressed, to reinforce
another more actively engaged. I determined to stop this. To
this end I regarded the Army of the Potomac as the centre,
and all west to Memphis along the line described as our position at the time, and north of it, the right wing; the Army of
the James, under General Butler, as the left wing, and all the
troops south, as a force in rear of the enemy. Some of these
latter were occupying positions from which they could not
render service proportionate to their numerical strength. All
such were depleted to the minimum necessary to hold their
positions as a guard against blockade runners; where they
could not do this their positions were abandoned altogether.
In this way ten thousand men were added to the Army of the
James from South Carolina alone, with General Gillmore in
command. It was not contemplated that General Gillmore
should leave his department; but as most of his troops were
taken, presumably for active service, he asked to accompany
them and was permitted to do so. Officers and soldiers on
furlough, of whom there were many thousands, were ordered
to their proper commands; concentration was the order of the
day, and to have it accomplished in time to advance at the
earliest moment the roads would permit was the problem.

As a reinforcement to the Army of the Potomac, or to act
in support of it, the 9th army corps, over twenty thousand
strong, under General Burnside, had been rendezvoused at
Annapolis, Maryland. This was an admirable position for such
a reinforcement. The corps could be brought at the last moment as a reinforcement to the Army of the Potomac, or it
could be thrown on the sea-coast, south of Norfolk, in Virginia or North Carolina, to operate against Richmond from
that direction. In fact Burnside and the War Department both
thought the 9th corps was intended for such an expedition up
to the last moment.

My general plan now was to concentrate all the force

possible against the Confederate armies in the field. There were but two such, as we have seen, east of the Mississippi River and facing north. The Army of Northern Virginia, General Robert E. Lee commanding, was on the south bank of the Rapidan, confronting the Army of the Potomac; the second, under General Joseph E. Johnston, was at Dalton, Georgia, opposed to Sherman who was still at Chattanooga. Beside these main armies the Confederates had to guard the Shenandoah Valley, a great storehouse to feed their armies from, and their line of communications from Richmond to Tennessee. Forrest, a brave and intrepid cavalry general, was in the West with a large force; making a larger command necessary to hold what we had gained in Middle and West Tennessee. We could not abandon any territory north of the line held by the enemy because it would lay the Northern States open to invasion. But as the Army of the Potomac was the principal garrison for the protection of Washington even while it was moving on Lee, so all the forces to the west, and the Army of the James, guarded their special trusts when advancing from them as well as when remaining at them. Better indeed, for they forced the enemy to guard his own lines and resources at a greater distance from ours, and with a greater force. Little expeditions could not so well be sent out to destroy a bridge or tear up a few miles of railroad track, burn a storehouse, or inflict other little annoyances. Accordingly I arranged for a simultaneous movement all along the line. Sherman was to move from Chattanooga, Johnston's army and Atlanta being his objective points.* Crook, commanding in West Virginia, was to move from the mouth of the Gauley River with a cavalry force and some artillery, the Virginia and Tennessee

---

*[Private and Confidential.]

HEADQUARTERS ARMIES OF THE UNITED STATES,
WASHINGTON, D. C., April 4, 1864.

MAJOR-GENERAL W. T. SHERMAN,
     Commanding Military Division of the Mississippi.

     General:—It is my design, if the enemy keep quiet and allow me to take the initiative in the spring campaign, to work all parts of the army together, and somewhat towards a common centre. For your information I now write you my programme, as at present determined upon.

Railroad to be his objective. Either the enemy would have to keep a large force to protect their communications, or see them destroyed and a large amount of forage and provision, which they so much needed, fall into our hands. Sigel was in command in the Valley of Virginia. He was to advance up the valley, covering the North from an invasion through that channel as well while advancing as by remaining near Harper's Ferry. Every mile he advanced also gave us possession of stores on which Lee relied. Butler was to advance by the James River, having Richmond and Petersburg as his objective.

Before the advance commenced I visited Butler at Fort

I have sent orders to Banks, by private messenger, to finish up his present expedition against Shreveport with all dispatch; to turn over the defence of Red River to General Steele and the navy, and to return your troops to you and his own to New Orleans; to abandon all of Texas, except the Rio Grande, and to hold that with not to exceed four thousand men; to reduce the number of troops on the Mississippi to the lowest number necessary to hold it, and to collect from his command not less than twenty-five thousand men. To this I will add five thousand men from Missouri. With this force he is to commence operations against Mobile as soon as he can. It will be impossible for him to commence too early.

Gillmore joins Butler with ten thousand men, and the two operate against Richmond from the south side of the James River. This will give Butler thirty-three thousand men to operate with, W. F. Smith commanding the right wing of his forces and Gillmore the left wing. I will stay with the Army of the Potomac, increased by Burnside's corps of not less than twenty-five thousand effective men, and operate directly against Lee's army, wherever it may be found.

Sigel collects all his available force in two columns, one, under Ord and Averell, to start from Beverly, Virginia, and the other, under Crook, to start from Charleston on the Kanawha, to move against the Virginia and Tennessee Railroad.

Crook will have all cavalry, and will endeavor to get in about Saltville, and move east from there to join Ord. His force will be all cavalry, while Ord will have from ten to twelve thousand men of all arms.

You I propose to move against Johnston's army, to break it up and to get into the interior of the enemy's country as far as you can, inflicting all the damage you can against their war resources.

I do not propose to lay down for you a plan of campaign, but simply lay down the work it is desirable to have done and leave you free to execute it in your own way. Submit to me, however, as early as you can, your plan of operations.

Monroe. This was the first time I had ever met him. Before giving him any order as to the part he was to play in the approaching campaign I invited his views. They were very much such as I intended to direct, and as I did direct,* in writing, before leaving.

General W. F. Smith, who had been promoted to the rank of major-general shortly after the battle of Chattanooga on my recommendation, had not yet been confirmed. I found a decided prejudice against his confirmation by a majority of the Senate, but I insisted that his services had been such that he should be rewarded. My wishes were now reluctantly complied with, and I assigned him to the command of one of the corps under General Butler. I was not long in finding out that the objections to Smith's promotion were well founded.

In one of my early interviews with the President I expressed my dissatisfaction with the little that had been accomplished by the cavalry so far in the war, and the belief that it was capable of accomplishing much more than it had done if under a thorough leader. I said I wanted the very best man in the army for that command. Halleck was present and spoke up, saying: "How would Sheridan do?" I replied: "The very man I want." The President said I could have anybody I

As stated, Banks is ordered to commence operations as soon as he can. Gillmore is ordered to report at Fortress Monroe by the 18th inst., or as soon thereafter as practicable. Sigel is concentrating now. None will move from their places of rendezvous until I direct, except Banks. I want to be ready to move by the 25th inst., if possible. But all I can now direct is that you get ready as soon as possible. I know you will have difficulties to encounter in getting through the mountains to where supplies are abundant, but I believe you will accomplish it.

From the expedition from the Department of West Virginia I do not calculate on very great results; but it is the only way I can take troops from there. With the long line of railroad Sigel has to protect, he can spare no troops except to move directly to his front. In this way he must get through to inflict great damage on the enemy, or the enemy must detach from one of his armies a large force to prevent it. In other words, if Sigel can't skin himself he can hold a leg while some one else skins.

I am, general, very respectfully, your obedient servant,

U. S. GRANT,
Lieutenant-General.

*See instructions to Butler, in General Grant's report, Appendix.

wanted. Sheridan was telegraphed for that day, and on his arrival was assigned to the command of the cavalry corps with the Army of the Potomac. This relieved General Alfred Pleasonton. It was not a reflection on that officer, however, for I did not know but that he had been as efficient as any other cavalry commander.

Banks in the Department of the Gulf was ordered to assemble all the troops he had at New Orleans in time to join in the general move, Mobile to be his objective.

At this time I was not entirely decided as to whether I should move the Army of the Potomac by the right flank of the enemy, or by his left. Each plan presented advantages.*

---

*In Field, Culpeper C. H., Va.,
April 9, 1864.

Maj.-General Geo. G. Meade,
    Com'd'g Army of the Potomac.

For information and as instruction to govern your preparations for the coming campaign, the following is communicated confidentially for your own perusal alone.

So far as practicable all the armies are to move together, and towards one common centre. Banks has been instructed to turn over the guarding of the Red River to General Steele and the navy, to abandon Texas with the exception of the Rio Grande, and to concentrate all the force he can, not less than 25,000 men, to move on Mobile. This he is to do without reference to other movements. From the scattered condition of his command, however, he cannot possibly get it together to leave New Orleans before the 1st of May, if so soon. Sherman will move at the same time you do, or two or three days in advance, Jo. Johnston's army being his objective point, and the heart of Georgia his ultimate aim. If successful he will secure the line from Chattanooga to Mobile with the aid of Banks.

Sigel cannot spare troops from his army to reinforce either of the great armies, but he can aid them by moving directly to his front. This he has been directed to do, and is now making preparations for it. Two columns of his command will make south at the same time with the general move; one from Beverly, from ten to twelve thousand strong, under Major-General Ord; the other from Charleston, Va., principally cavalry, under Brig.-General Crook. The former of these will endeavor to reach the Tennessee and Virginia Railroad, about south of Covington, and if found practicable will work eastward to Lynchburg and return to its base by way of the Shenandoah Valley, or join you. The other will strike at Saltville, Va., and come eastward to join Ord. The cavalry from Ord's command will try to force a passage southward, if they are successful in reaching the Virginia and Tennessee Railroad, to cut the main lines of the road connecting Richmond with all the South and South-west.

If by his right—my left—the Potomac, Chesapeake Bay and tributaries would furnish us an easy line over which to bring all supplies to within easy hauling distance of every position the army could occupy from the Rapidan to the James River. But Lee could, if he chose, detach or move his whole army

---

Gillmore will join Butler with about 10,000 men from South Carolina. Butler can reduce his garrison so as to take 23,000 men into the field directly to his front. The force will be commanded by Maj.-General W. F. Smith. With Smith and Gillmore, Butler will seize City Point, and operate against Richmond from the south side of the river. His movement will be simultaneous with yours.

Lee's army will be your objective point. Wherever Lee goes, there you will go also. The only point upon which I am now in doubt is, whether it will be better to cross the Rapidan above or below him. Each plan presents great advantages over the other with corresponding objections. By crossing above, Lee is cut off from all chance of ignoring Richmond and going north on a raid. But if we take this route, all we do must be done whilst the rations we start with hold out. We separate from Butler so that he cannot be directed how to co-operate. By the other route Brandy Station can be used as a base of supplies until another is secured on the York or James rivers.

These advantages and objections I will talk over with you more fully than I can write them.

Burnside with a force of probably 25,000 men will reinforce you. Immediately upon his arrival, which will be shortly after the 20th inst., I will give him the defence of the road from Bull Run as far south as we wish to hold it. This will enable you to collect all your strength about Brandy Station and to the front.

There will be naval co-operation on the James River, and transports and ferries will be provided so that should Lee fall back into his intrenchments at Richmond, Butler's force and yours will be a unit, or at least can be made to act as such. What I would direct then, is that you commence at once reducing baggage to the very lowest possible standard. Two wagons to a regiment of five hundred men is the greatest number that should be allowed, for all baggage, exclusive of subsistence stores and ordnance stores. One wagon to brigade and one to division headquarters is sufficient and about two to corps headquarters.

Should by Lee's right flank be our route, you will want to make arrangements for having supplies of all sorts promptly forwarded to White House on the Pamunkey. Your estimates for this contingency should be made at once. If not wanted there, there is every probability they will be wanted on the James River or elsewhere.

If Lee's left is turned, large provision will have to be made for ordnance stores. I would say not much short of five hundred rounds of infantry ammunition would do. By the other, half the amount would be sufficient.

U. S. GRANT,
Lieutenant-General.

north on a line rather interior to the one I would have to take in following. A movement by his left—our right—would obviate this; but all that was done would have to be done with the supplies and ammunition we started with. All idea of adopting this latter plan was abandoned when the limited quantity of supplies possible to take with us was considered. The country over which we would have to pass was so exhausted of all food or forage that we would be obliged to carry everything with us.

While these preparations were going on the enemy was not entirely idle. In the West Forrest made a raid in West Tennessee up to the northern border, capturing the garrison of four or five hundred men at Union City, and followed it up by an attack on Paducah, Kentucky, on the banks of the Ohio. While he was able to enter the city he failed to capture the forts or any part of the garrison. On the first intelligence of Forrest's raid I telegraphed Sherman to send all his cavalry against him, and not to let him get out of the trap he had put himself into. Sherman had anticipated me by sending troops against him before he got my order.

Forrest, however, fell back rapidly, and attacked the troops at Fort Pillow, a station for the protection of the navigation of the Mississippi River. The garrison consisted of a regiment of colored troops, infantry, and a detachment of Tennessee cavalry. These troops fought bravely, but were overpowered. I will leave Forrest in his dispatches to tell what he did with them.

"The river was dyed," he says, "with the blood of the slaughtered for two hundred yards. The approximate loss was upward of five hundred killed, but few of the officers escaping. My loss was about twenty killed. It is hoped that these facts will demonstrate to the Northern people that negro soldiers cannot cope with Southerners." Subsequently Forrest made a report in which he left out the part which shocks humanity to read.

At the East, also, the rebels were busy. I had said to Halleck that Plymouth and Washington, North Carolina, were unnecessary to hold. It would be better to have the garrisons engaged there added to Butler's command. If success attended our arms both places, and others too, would fall into our hands naturally. These places had been occupied by Federal troops before I took command of the armies, and I knew that the Executive would be reluctant to abandon them, and therefore explained my views; but before my views were carried out the rebels captured the garrison at Plymouth. I then ordered the abandonment of Washington, but directed the holding of New Berne at all hazards. This was essential because New Berne was a port into which blockade runners could enter.

General Banks had gone on an expedition up the Red River long before my promotion to general command. I had opposed the movement strenuously, but acquiesced because it was the order of my superior at the time. By direction of Halleck I had reinforced Banks with a corps of about ten thousand men from Sherman's command. This reinforcement was wanted back badly before the forward movement commenced. But Banks had got so far that it seemed best that he should take Shreveport on the Red River, and turn over the line of that river to Steele, who commanded in Arkansas, to hold instead of the line of the Arkansas. Orders were given accordingly, and with the expectation that the campaign would be ended in time for Banks to return A. J. Smith's command to where it belonged and get back to New Orleans himself in time to execute his part in the general plan. But the expedition was a failure. Banks did not get back in time to take part in the programme as laid down. Nor was Smith returned until long after the movements of May, 1864, had been begun. The services of forty thousand veteran troops, over and above the number required to hold all that was necessary in the Department of the Gulf, were thus paralyzed. It is but just to Banks, however, to say that his expedition was ordered from Washington and he was in no way responsible except for the conduct of it. I make no criticism on this point. He opposed the expedition.

By the 27th of April spring had so far advanced as to justify me in fixing a day for the great move. On that day Burnside left Annapolis to occupy Meade's position between Bull Run and the Rappahannock. Meade was notified and directed to bring his troops forward to his advance. On the following day Butler was notified of my intended advance on the 4th of

May, and he was directed to move the night of the same day and get as far up the James River as possible by daylight, and push on from there to accomplish the task given him. He was also notified that reinforcements were being collected in Washington City, which would be forwarded to him should the enemy fall back into the trenches at Richmond. The same day Sherman was directed to get his forces up ready to advance on the 5th. Sigel was in Winchester and was notified to move in conjunction with the others.

The criticism has been made by writers on the campaign from the Rapidan to the James River that all the loss of life could have been obviated by moving the army there on transports. Richmond was fortified and intrenched so perfectly that one man inside to defend was more than equal to five outside besieging or assaulting. To get possession of Lee's army was the first great object. With the capture of his army Richmond would necessarily follow. It was better to fight him outside of his stronghold than in it. If the Army of the Potomac had been moved bodily to the James River by water Lee could have moved a part of his forces back to Richmond, called Beauregard from the south to reinforce it, and with the balance moved on to Washington. Then, too, I ordered a move, simultaneous with that of the Army of the Potomac, up the James River by a formidable army already collected at the mouth of the river.

While my headquarters were at Culpeper, from the 26th of March to the 4th of May, I generally visited Washington once a week to confer with the Secretary of War and President. On the last occasion, a few days before moving, a circumstance occurred which came near postponing my part in the campaign altogether. Colonel John S. Mosby had for a long time been commanding a partisan corps, or regiment, which operated in the rear of the Army of the Potomac. On my return to the field on this occasion, as the train approached Warrenton Junction, a heavy cloud of dust was seen to the east of the road as if made by a body of cavalry on a charge. Arriving at the junction the train was stopped and inquiries made as to the cause of the dust. There was but one man at the station, and he informed us that Mosby had crossed a few minutes before at full speed in pursuit of Federal cavalry. Had he seen our train coming, no doubt he would have let his prisoners escape to capture the train. I was on a special train, if I remember correctly, without any guard.

Since the close of the war I have come to know Colonel Mosby personally, and somewhat intimately. He is a different man entirely from what I had supposed. He is slender, not tall, wiry, and looks as if he could endure any amount of physical exercise. He is able, and thoroughly honest and truthful. There were probably but few men in the South who could have commanded successfully a separate detachment in the rear of an opposing army, and so near the border of hostilities, as long as he did without losing his entire command.

On this same visit to Washington I had my last interview with the President before reaching the James River. He had of course become acquainted with the fact that a general movement had been ordered all along the line, and seemed to think it a new feature in war. I explained to him that it was necessary to have a great number of troops to guard and hold the territory we had captured, and to prevent incursions into the Northern States. These troops could perform this service just as well by advancing as by remaining still; and by advancing they would compel the enemy to keep detachments to hold them back, or else lay his own territory open to invasion. His answer was: "Oh, yes! I see that. As we say out West, if a man can't skin he must hold a leg while somebody else does."

There was a certain incident connected with the Wilderness campaign of which it may not be out of place to speak; and to avoid a digression further on I will mention it here.

A few days before my departure from Culpeper the Honorable E. B. Washburne visited me there, and remained with my headquarters for some distance south, through the battle in the Wilderness and, I think, to Spottsylvania. He was accompanied by a Mr. Swinton, whom he presented as a literary gentleman who wished to accompany the army with a view of writing a history of the war when it was over. He assured me—and I have no doubt Swinton gave him the assurance—that he was not present as a correspondent of the press. I expressed an entire willingness to have him (Swinton) accompany the army, and would have allowed him to do so as a correspondent, restricted, however, in the character of the information he could give. We received Richmond papers with about as much regularity as if there had been no war, and knew that our papers were received with equal regularity by the Confederates. It was desirable, therefore, that correspondents should not be privileged spies of the enemy within our lines.

Probably Mr. Swinton expected to be an invited guest at my headquarters, and was disappointed that he was not asked to become so. At all events he was not invited, and soon I found that he was corresponding with some paper (I have now forgotten which one), thus violating his word either expressed or implied. He knew of the assurance Washburne had given as to the character of his mission. I never saw the man from the day of our introduction to the present that I recollect. He accompanied us, however, for a time at least.

The second night after crossing the Rapidan (the night of the 5th of May) Colonel W. R. Rowley, of my staff, was acting as night officer at my headquarters. A short time before midnight I gave him verbal instructions for the night. Three days later I read in a Richmond paper a verbatim report of these instructions.

A few nights still later (after the first, and possibly after the second, day's fighting in the Wilderness) General Meade came to my tent for consultation, bringing with him some of his staff officers. Both his staff and mine retired to the camp-fire some yards in front of the tent, thinking our conversation should be private. There was a stump a little to one side, and between the front of the tent and camp-fire. One of my staff, Colonel T. S. Bowers, saw what he took to be a man seated on the ground and leaning against the stump, listening to the conversation between Meade and myself. He called the attention of Colonel Rowley to it. The latter immediately took the man by the shoulder and asked him, in language more forcible than polite, what he was doing there. The man proved to be Swinton, the "historian," and his replies to the question were evasive and unsatisfactory, and he was warned against further eaves-dropping.

The next I heard of Mr. Swinton was at Cold Harbor. General Meade came to my headquarters saying that General Burnside had arrested Swinton, who at some previous time had given great offence, and had ordered him to be shot that afternoon. I promptly ordered the prisoner to be released, but that he must be expelled from the lines of the army not to return again on pain of punishment.

Chapter XLVIII.

COMMENCEMENT OF THE GRAND CAMPAIGN—GENERAL
BUTLER'S POSITION—SHERIDAN'S FIRST RAID.

THE ARMIES were now all ready to move for the accomplishment of a single object. They were acting as a unit so far as such a thing was possible over such a vast field. Lee, with the capital of the Confederacy, was the main end to which all were working. Johnston, with Atlanta, was an important obstacle in the way of our accomplishing the result aimed at, and was therefore almost an independent objective. It was of less importance only because the capture of Johnston and his army would not produce so immediate and decisive a result in closing the rebellion as would the possession of Richmond, Lee and his army. All other troops were employed exclusively in support of these two movements. This was the plan; and I will now endeavor to give, as concisely as I can, the method of its execution, outlining first the operations of minor detached but co-operative columns.

As stated before, Banks failed to accomplish what he had been sent to do on the Red River, and eliminated the use of forty thousand veterans whose co-operation in the grand campaign had been expected—ten thousand with Sherman and thirty thousand against Mobile.

Sigel's record is almost equally brief. He moved out, it is true, according to programme; but just when I was hoping to hear of good work being done in the valley I received instead the following announcement from Halleck: "Sigel is in full retreat on Strasburg. He will do nothing but run; never did anything else." The enemy had intercepted him about New Market and handled him roughly, leaving him short six guns, and some nine hundred men out of his six thousand.

The plan had been for an advance of Sigel's forces in two columns. Though the one under his immediate command failed ingloriously the other proved more fortunate. Under Crook and Averell his western column advanced from the Gauley in West Virginia at the appointed time, and with more happy results. They reached the Virginia and Tennessee Railroad at Dublin and destroyed a depot of supplies, besides tearing up several miles of road and burning the bridge over New River. Having accomplished this they recrossed the Alleghanies to Meadow Bluffs and there awaited further orders.

Butler embarked at Fort Monroe with all his command, except the cavalry and some artillery which moved up the south bank of the James River. His steamers moved first up Chesapeake Bay and York River as if threatening the rear of Lee's army. At midnight they turned back, and Butler by daylight was far up the James River. He seized City Point and Bermuda Hundred early in the day, without loss and, no doubt, very much to the surprise of the enemy.

This was the accomplishment of the first step contemplated in my instructions to Butler. He was to act from here, looking to Richmond as his objective point. I had given him to understand that I should aim to fight Lee between the Rapidan and Richmond if he would stand; but should Lee fall back into Richmond I would follow up and make a junction of the armies of the Potomac and the James on the James River. He was directed to secure a footing as far up the south side of the river as he could at as early a date as possible.

Butler was in position by the 6th of May and had begun intrenching, and on the 7th he sent out his cavalry from Suffolk to cut the Weldon Railroad. He also sent out detachments to destroy the railroad between Petersburg and Richmond, but no great success attended these latter efforts. He made no great effort to establish himself on that road and neglected to attack Petersburg, which was almost defenceless. About the 11th he advanced slowly until he reached the works at Drury's Bluff, about half way between Bermuda Hundred and Richmond. In the mean time Beauregard had been gathering reinforcements. On the 16th he attacked Butler with great vigor, and with such success as to limit very materially the further usefulness of the Army of the James as a distinct factor in the campaign. I afterward ordered a portion of it to join the Army of the Potomac, leaving a sufficient force with Butler to man his works, hold securely the footing he had already gained and maintain a threatening front toward the rear of the Confederate capital.

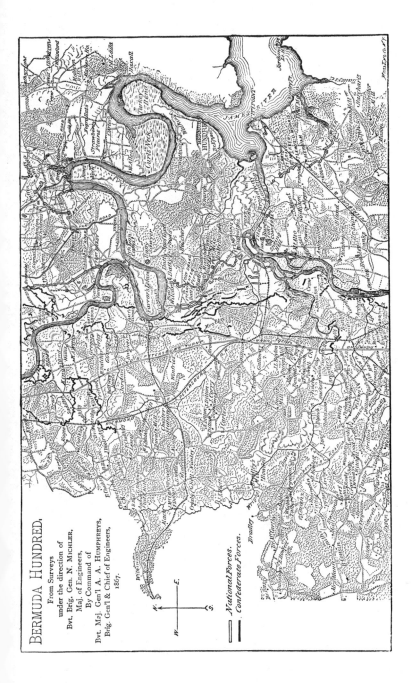

BERMUDA HUNDRED.
From Surveys
under the direction of
Bvt. Brig. Gen. N. Michler,
Maj. of Engineers,
By Command of
Bvt. Maj. Gen'l A. A. Humphreys,
Brig. Gen'l & Chief of Engineers,
1867.

National Forces.
Confederate Forces.

The position which General Butler had chosen between the two rivers, the James and Appomattox, was one of great natural strength, one where a large area of ground might be thoroughly inclosed by means of a single intrenched line, and that a very short one in comparison with the extent of territory which it thoroughly protected. His right was protected by the James River, his left by the Appomattox, and his rear by their junction—the two streams uniting near by. The bends of the two streams shortened the line that had been chosen for intrenchments, while it increased the area which the line inclosed.

Previous to ordering any troops from Butler I sent my chief engineer, General Barnard, from the Army of the Potomac to that of the James to inspect Butler's position and ascertain whether I could again safely make an order for General Butler's movement in co-operation with mine, now that I was getting so near Richmond; or, if I could not, whether his position was strong enough to justify me in withdrawing some of his troops and having them brought round by water to White House to join me and reinforce the Army of the Potomac. General Barnard reported the position very strong for defensive purposes, and that I could do the latter with great security; but that General Butler could not move from where he was, in co-operation, to produce any effect. He said that the general occupied a place between the James and Appomattox rivers which was of great strength, and where with an inferior force he could hold it for an indefinite length of time against a superior; but that he could do nothing offensively. I then asked him why Butler could not move out from his lines and push across the Richmond and Petersburg Railroad to the rear and on the south side of Richmond. He replied that it was impracticable, because the enemy had substantially the same line across the neck of land that General Butler had. He then took out his pencil and drew a sketch of the locality, remarking that the position was like a bottle and that Butler's line of intrenchments across the neck represented the cork; that the enemy had built an equally strong line immediately in front of him across the neck; and it was therefore as if Butler was in a bottle. He was perfectly safe against an attack; but, as Barnard expressed it, the enemy had corked the bottle and with a small force could hold the cork in its place. This struck me as being very expressive of his position, particularly when I saw the hasty sketch which General Barnard had drawn; and in making my subsequent report I used that expression without adding quotation marks, never thinking that anything had been said that would attract attention—as this did, very much to the annoyance, no doubt, of General Butler and, I know, very much to my own. I found afterwards that this was mentioned in the notes of General Badeau's book, which, when they were shown to me, I asked to have stricken out; yet it was retained there, though against my wishes.

I make this statement here because, although I have often made it before, it has never been in my power until now to place it where it will correct history; and I desire to rectify all injustice that I may have done to individuals, particularly to officers who were gallantly serving their country during the trying period of the war for the preservation of the Union. General Butler certainly gave his very earnest support to the war; and he gave his own best efforts personally to the suppression of the rebellion.

The further operations of the Army of the James can best be treated of in connection with those of the Army of the Potomac, the two being so intimately associated and connected as to be substantially one body in which the individuality of the supporting wing is merged.

Before giving the reader a summary of Sherman's great Atlanta campaign, which must conclude my description of the various co-operative movements preparatory to proceeding with that of the operations of the centre, I will briefly mention Sheridan's first raid upon Lee's communications which, though an incident of the operations on the main line and not specifically marked out in the original plan, attained in its brilliant execution and results all the proportions of an independent campaign. By thus anticipating, in point of time, I will be able to more perfectly observe the continuity of events occurring in my immediate front when I shall have undertaken to describe our advance from the Rapidan.

On the 8th of May, just after the battle of the Wilderness and when we were moving on Spottsylvania I directed Sheridan verbally to cut loose from the Army of the Potomac, pass around the left of Lee's army and attack his cavalry: to cut the two roads—one running west through Gordonsville, Charlottesville and Lynchburg, the other to Richmond, and, when compelled to do so for want of forage and rations, to move on to the James River and draw these from Butler's supplies. This move took him past the entire rear of Lee's army. These orders were also given in writing through Meade.

The object of this move was three-fold. First, if successfully executed, and it was, he would annoy the enemy by cutting his line of supplies and telegraphic communications, and destroy or get for his own use supplies in store in the rear and coming up. Second, he would draw the enemy's cavalry after him, and thus better protect our flanks, rear and trains than by remaining with the army. Third, his absence would save the trains drawing his forage and other supplies from Fredericksburg, which had now become our base. He started at daylight the next morning, and accomplished more than was expected. It was sixteen days before he got back to the Army of the Potomac.

The course Sheridan took was directly to Richmond. Before night Stuart, commanding the Confederate cavalry, came on to the rear of his command. But the advance kept on, crossed the North Anna, and at Beaver Dam, a station on the Virginia Central Railroad, recaptured four hundred Union prisoners on their way to Richmond, destroyed the road and used and destroyed a large amount of subsistence and medical stores.

Stuart, seeing that our cavalry was pushing towards Richmond, abandoned the pursuit on the morning of the 10th and, by a detour and an exhausting march, interposed between Sheridan and Richmond at Yellow Tavern, only about six miles north of the city. Sheridan destroyed the railroad and more supplies at Ashland, and on the 11th arrived in Stuart's front. A severe engagement ensued in which the losses were heavy on both sides, but the rebels were beaten, their leader mortally wounded, and some guns and many prisoners were captured.

Sheridan passed through the outer defences of Richmond, and could, no doubt, have passed through the inner ones. But having no supports near he could not have remained. After caring for his wounded he struck for the James River below the city, to communicate with Butler and to rest his men and horses as well as to get food and forage for them.

He moved first between the Chickahominy and the James, but in the morning (the 12th) he was stopped by batteries at Mechanicsville. He then turned to cross to the north side of the Chickahominy by Meadow Bridge. He found this barred, and the defeated Confederate cavalry, reorganized, occupying the opposite side. The panic created by his first entrance within the outer works of Richmond having subsided troops were sent out to attack his rear.

He was now in a perilous position, one from which but few generals could have extricated themselves. The defences of Richmond, manned, were to the right, the Chickahominy was to the left with no bridge remaining and the opposite bank guarded, to the rear was a force from Richmond. This force was attacked and beaten by Wilson's and Gregg's divisions, while Sheridan turned to the left with the remaining division and hastily built a bridge over the Chickahominy under the fire of the enemy, forced a crossing and soon dispersed the Confederates he found there. The enemy was held back from the stream by the fire of the troops not engaged in bridge building.

On the 13th Sheridan was at Bottom's Bridge, over the Chickahominy. On the 14th he crossed this stream and on that day went into camp on the James River at Haxall's Landing. He at once put himself into communication with General Butler, who directed all the supplies he wanted to be furnished.

Sheridan had left the Army of the Potomac at Spottsylvania, but did not know where either this or Lee's army was now. Great caution therefore had to be exercised in getting back. On the 17th, after resting his command for three days, he started on his return. He moved by the way of White House. The bridge over the Pamunkey had been burned by the enemy, but a new one was speedily improvised and the cavalry crossed over it. On the 22d he was at Aylett's on the Matapony, where he learned the position of the two armies. On the 24th he joined us on the march from North Anna to Cold Harbor, in the vicinity of Chesterfield.

Sheridan in this memorable raid passed entirely around Lee's army: encountered his cavalry in four engagements, and defeated them in all; recaptured four hundred Union prisoners and killed and captured many of the enemy; destroyed and used many supplies and munitions of war; destroyed miles of railroad and telegraph, and freed us from annoyance by the cavalry of the enemy for more than two weeks.

Chapter XLIX.

SHERMAN'S CAMPAIGN IN GEORGIA—SIEGE OF
ATLANTA—DEATH OF GENERAL McPHERSON—ATTEMPT
TO CAPTURE ANDERSONVILLE—CAPTURE OF ATLANTA.

AFTER SEPARATING from Sherman in Cincinnati I went on
to Washington, as already stated, while he returned to
Nashville to assume the duties of his new command. His military division was now composed of four departments and
embraced all the territory west of the Alleghany Mountains
and east of the Mississippi River, together with the State of
Arkansas in the trans-Mississippi. The most easterly of these
was the Department of the Ohio, General Schofield commanding; the next was the Department of the Cumberland,
General Thomas commanding; the third the Department of
the Tennessee, General McPherson commanding; and General
Steele still commanded the trans-Mississippi, or Department
of Arkansas. The last-named department was so far away that
Sherman could not communicate with it very readily after
starting on his spring campaign, and it was therefore soon
transferred from his military division to that of the Gulf,
where General Canby, who had relieved General Banks, was
in command.

The movements of the armies, as I have stated in a former
chapter, were to be simultaneous, I fixing the day to start
when the season should be far enough advanced, it was
hoped, for the roads to be in a condition for the troops to
march.

General Sherman at once set himself to work preparing for
the task which was assigned him to accomplish in the spring
campaign. McPherson lay at Huntsville with about twenty-
four thousand men, guarding those points of Tennessee which
were regarded as most worth holding; Thomas, with over
sixty thousand men of the Army of the Cumberland, was at
Chattanooga; and Schofield, with about fourteen thousand
men, was at Knoxville. With these three armies, numbering
about one hundred thousand men in all, Sherman was to
move on the day fixed for the general advance, with a view of

destroying Johnston's army and capturing Atlanta. He visited each of these commands to inform himself as to their condition, and it was found to be, speaking generally, good.

One of the first matters to turn his attention to was that of getting, before the time arrived for starting, an accumulation of supplies forward to Chattanooga sufficiently large to warrant a movement. He found, when he got to that place, that the trains over the single-track railroad, which was frequently interrupted for a day or two at a time, were only sufficient to meet the daily wants of the troops without bringing forward any surplus of any kind. He found, however, that trains were being used to transport all the beef cattle, horses for the cavalry, and even teams that were being brought to the front. He at once changed all this, and required beef cattle, teams, cavalry horses, and everything that could travel, even the troops, to be marched, and used the road exclusively for transporting supplies. In this way he was able to accumulate an abundance before the time finally fixed upon for the move, the 4th of May.

As I have said already, Johnston was at Dalton, which was nearly one-fourth of the way between Chattanooga and Atlanta. The country is mountainous all the way to Atlanta, abounding in mountain streams, some of them of considerable volume. Dalton is on ground where water drains towards Atlanta and into one of the main streams rising north-east from there and flowing south-west—this being the general direction which all the main streams of that section take, with smaller tributaries entering into them. Johnston had been preparing himself for this campaign during the entire winter. The best positions for defence had been selected all the way from Dalton back to Atlanta, and very strongly intrenched; so that, as he might be forced to fall back from one position, he would have another to fall into in his rear. His position at Dalton was so very strongly intrenched that no doubt he expected, or at least hoped, to hold Sherman there and prevent him from getting any further. With a less skilful general, and one disposed to take no risks, I have no doubt that he would have succeeded.

Sherman's plan was to start Schofield, who was farthest back, a few days in advance from Knoxville, having him move on the direct road to Dalton. Thomas was to move out to Ringgold. It had been Sherman's intention to cross McPherson over the Tennessee River at Huntsville or Decatur, and move him south from there so as to have him come into the road running from Chattanooga to Atlanta a good distance to the rear of the point Johnston was occupying; but when that was contemplated it was hoped that McPherson alone would have troops enough to cope with Johnston, if the latter should move against him while unsupported by the balance of the army. In this he was disappointed. Two of McPherson's veteran divisions had re-enlisted on the express provision that they were to have a furlough. This furlough had not yet expired, and they were not back.

Then, again, Sherman had lent Banks two divisions under A. J. Smith, the winter before, to co-operate with the trans-Mississippi forces, and this with the express pledge that they should be back by a time specified, so as to be prepared for this very campaign. It is hardly necessary to say they were not returned. That department continued to absorb troops to no purpose to the end of the war. This left McPherson so weak that the part of the plan above indicated had to be changed. He was therefore brought up to Chattanooga and moved from there on a road to the right of Thomas—the two coming together about Dalton. The three armies were abreast, all ready to start promptly on time.

Sherman soon found that Dalton was so strongly fortified that it was useless to make any attempt to carry it by assault; and even to carry it by regular approaches was impracticable. There was a narrowing up in the mountain, between the National and Confederate armies, through which a stream, a wagon road and a railroad ran. Besides, the stream had been dammed so that the valley was a lake. Through this gorge the troops would have to pass. McPherson was therefore sent around by the right, to come out by the way of Snake Creek Gap into the rear of the enemy. This was a surprise to Johnston, and about the 13th he decided to abandon his position at Dalton.

On the 15th there was very hard fighting about Resaca; but our cavalry having been sent around to the right got near the road in the enemy's rear. Again Johnston fell back, our army

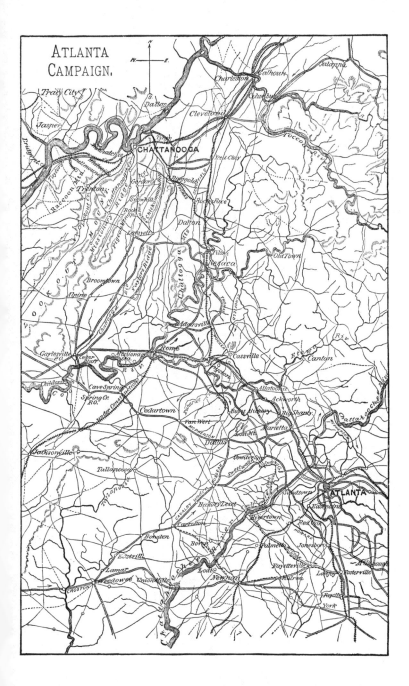

ATLANTA
CAMPAIGN.

pursuing. The pursuit was continued to Kingston, which was reached on the 19th with very little fighting, except that Newton's division overtook the rear of Johnston's army and engaged it. Sherman was now obliged to halt for the purpose of bringing up his railroad trains. He was depending upon the railroad for all of his supplies, and as of course the railroad was wholly destroyed as Johnston fell back, it had to be rebuilt. This work was pushed forward night and day, and caused much less delay than most persons would naturally expect in a mountainous country where there were so many bridges to be rebuilt.

The campaign to Atlanta was managed with the most consummate skill, the enemy being flanked out of one position after another all the way there. It is true this was not accomplished without a good deal of fighting—some of it very hard fighting, rising to the dignity of very important battles—neither were single positions gained in a day. On the contrary, weeks were spent at some; and about Atlanta more than a month was consumed.

It was the 23d of May before the road was finished up to the rear of Sherman's army and the pursuit renewed. This pursuit brought him up to the vicinity of Allatoona. This place was very strongly intrenched, and naturally a very defensible position. An assault upon it was not thought of, but preparations were made to flank the enemy out of it. This was done by sending a large force around our right, by the way of Dallas, to reach the rear of the enemy. Before reaching there, however, they found the enemy fortified in their way, and there resulted hard fighting for about a week at a place called New Hope Church. On the left our troops also were fortified, and as close up to the enemy as they could get. They kept working still farther around to the left toward the railroad. This was the case more particularly with the cavalry. By the 4th of June Johnston found that he was being hemmed in so rapidly that he drew off and Allatoona was left in our possession.

Allatoona, being an important place, was strongly intrenched for occupation by our troops before advancing farther, and made a secondary base of supplies. The railroad was finished up to that point, the intrenchments completed, storehouses provided for food, and the army got in readiness for a further advance. The rains, however, were falling in such torrents that it was impossible to move the army by the side roads which they would have to move upon in order to turn Johnston out of his new position.

While Sherman's army lay here, General F. P. Blair returned to it, bringing with him the two divisions of veterans who had been on furlough.

Johnston had fallen back to Marietta and Kenesaw Mountain, where strong intrenchments awaited him. At this latter place our troops made an assault upon the enemy's lines after having got their own lines up close to him, and failed, sustaining considerable loss. But during the progress of the battle Schofield was gaining ground to the left; and the cavalry on his left were gaining still more toward the enemy's rear. These operations were completed by the 3d of July, when it was found that Johnston had evacuated the place. He was pursued at once. Sherman had made every preparation to abandon the railroad, leaving a strong guard in his intrenchments. He had intended, moving out with twenty days' rations and plenty of ammunition, to come in on the railroad again at the Chattahoochee River. Johnston frustrated this plan by himself starting back as above stated. This time he fell back to the Chattahoochee.

About the 5th of July he was besieged again, Sherman getting easy possession of the Chattahoochee River both above and below him. The enemy was again flanked out of his position, or so frightened by flanking movements that on the night of the 9th he fell back across the river.

Here Johnston made a stand until the 17th, when Sherman's old tactics prevailed again and the final movement toward Atlanta began. Johnston was now relieved of the command, and Hood superseded him.

Johnston's tactics in this campaign do not seem to have met with much favor, either in the eyes of the administration at Richmond, or of the people of that section of the South in which he was commanding. The very fact of a change of commanders being ordered under such circumstances was an indication of a change of policy, and that now they would become the aggressors—the very thing our troops wanted.

For my own part, I think that Johnston's tactics were right. Anything that could have prolonged the war a year beyond the time that it did finally close, would probably have exhausted the North to such an extent that they might then have abandoned the contest and agreed to a separation.

Atlanta was very strongly intrenched all the way around in a circle about a mile and a half outside of the city. In addition to this, there were advanced intrenchments which had to be taken before a close siege could be commenced.

Sure enough, as indicated by the change of commanders, the enemy was about to assume the offensive. On the 20th he came out and attacked the Army of the Cumberland most furiously. Hooker's corps, and Newton's and Johnson's divisions were the principal ones engaged in this contest, which lasted more than an hour; but the Confederates were then forced to fall back inside their main lines. The losses were quite heavy on both sides. On this day General Gresham, since our Postmaster-General, was very badly wounded. During the night Hood abandoned his outer lines, and our troops were advanced. The investment had not been relinquished for a moment during the day.

During the night of the 21st Hood moved out again, passing by our left flank, which was then in motion to get a position farther in rear of him, and a desperate battle ensued, which lasted most of the day of the 22d. At first the battle went very much in favor of the Confederates, our troops being somewhat surprised. While our troops were advancing they were struck in flank, and their flank was enveloped. But they had become too thorough veterans to be thrown into irreparable confusion by an unexpected attack when off their guard, and soon they were in order and engaging the enemy, with the advantage now of knowing where their antagonist was. The field of battle continued to expand until it embraced about seven miles of ground. Finally, however, and before night, the enemy was driven back into the city.*

---

*General John A. Logan, upon whom devolved the command of the Army of the Tennessee during this battle, in his report gave our total loss in killed, wounded and missing at 3,521; and estimated that of the enemy to be not less than 10,000: and General G. M. Dodge, graphically describing to General

It was during this battle that McPherson, while passing from one column to another, was instantly killed. In his death the army lost one of its ablest, purest and best generals.

Garrard had been sent out with his cavalry to get upon the railroad east of Atlanta and to cut it in the direction of Augusta. He was successful in this, and returned about the time of the battle. Rousseau had also come up from Tennessee with a small division of cavalry, having crossed the Tennessee River about Decatur and made a raid into Alabama. Finally, when hard pressed, he had come in, striking the railroad in rear of Sherman, and reported to him about this time.

The battle of the 22d is usually known as the Battle of Atlanta, although the city did not fall into our hands until the 2d of September. Preparations went on, as before, to flank the enemy out of his position. The work was tedious, and the lines that had to be maintained were very long. Our troops were gradually worked around to the east until they struck the road between Decatur and Atlanta. These lines were strongly fortified, as were those to the north and west of the city—all as close up to the enemy's lines as practicable—in order to hold them with the smallest possible number of men, the design being to detach an army to move by our right and try to get upon the railroad down south of Atlanta.

On the 27th the movement by the right flank commenced. On the 28th the enemy struck our right flank, General Logan commanding, with great vigor. Logan intrenched himself hastily, and by that means was enabled to resist all assaults and inflict a great deal of damage upon the enemy. These assaults were continued to the middle of the afternoon, and resumed once or twice still later in the day. The enemy's losses in these unsuccessful assaults were fearful.

During that evening the enemy in Logan's front withdrew into the town. This now left Sherman's army close up to the

---

Sherman the enemy's attack, the full weight of which fell first upon and was broken by his depleted command, remarks: "The disparity of forces can be seen from the fact that in the charge made by my two brigades under Fuller and Mersy they took 351 prisoners, representing forty-nine different regiments, eight brigades and three divisions; and brought back eight battle flags from the enemy."

Confederate lines, extending from a point directly east of the city around by the north and west of it for a distance of fully ten miles; the whole of this line being intrenched, and made stronger every day they remained there.

In the latter part of July Sherman sent Stoneman to destroy the railroads to the south, about Macon. He was then to go east and, if possible, release our prisoners about Andersonville. There were painful stories current at the time about the great hardships these prisoners had to endure in the way of general bad treatment, in the way in which they were housed, and in the way in which they were fed. Great sympathy was felt for them; and it was thought that even if they could be turned loose upon the country it would be a great relief to them. But the attempt proved a failure. McCook, who commanded a small brigade, was first reported to have been captured; but he got back, having inflicted a good deal of damage upon the enemy. He had also taken some prisoners; but encountering afterwards a largely superior force of the enemy he was obliged to drop his prisoners and get back as best he could with what men he had left. He had lost several hundred men out of his small command. On the 4th of August Colonel Adams, commanding a little brigade of about a thousand men, returned reporting Stoneman and all but himself as lost. I myself had heard around Richmond of the capture of Stoneman, and had sent Sherman word, which he received. The rumor was confirmed there, also, from other sources. A few days after Colonel Adams's return Colonel Capron also got in with a small detachment and confirmed the report of the capture of Stoneman with something less than a thousand men.

It seems that Stoneman, finding the escape of all his force was impossible, had made arrangements for the escape of two divisions. He covered the movement of these divisions to the rear with a force of about seven hundred men, and at length surrendered himself and this detachment to the commanding Confederate. In this raid, however, much damage was inflicted upon the enemy by the destruction of cars, locomotives, army wagons, manufactories of military supplies, etc.

On the 4th and 5th Sherman endeavored to get upon the railroad to our right, where Schofield was in command, but these attempts failed utterly. General Palmer was charged with being the cause of this failure, to a great extent, by both General Sherman and General Schofield; but I am not prepared to say this, although a question seems to have arisen with Palmer as to whether Schofield had any right to command him. If he did raise this question while an action was going on, that act alone was exceedingly reprehensible.

About the same time Wheeler got upon our railroad north of Resaca and destroyed it nearly up to Dalton. This cut Sherman off from communication with the North for several days. Sherman responded to this attack on his lines of communication by directing one upon theirs.

Kilpatrick started on the night of the 18th of August to reach the Macon road about Jonesboro. He succeeded in doing so, passed entirely around the Confederate lines of Atlanta, and was back again in his former position on our left by the 22d. These little affairs, however, contributed but very little to the grand result. They annoyed, it is true, but any damage thus done to a railroad by any cavalry expedition is soon repaired.

Sherman made preparations for a repetition of his tactics; that is, for a flank movement with as large a force as could be got together to some point in the enemy's rear. Sherman commenced this last movement on the 25th of August, and on the 1st of September was well up towards the railroad twenty miles south of Atlanta. Here he found Hardee intrenched, ready to meet him. A battle ensued, but he was unable to drive Hardee away before night set in. Under cover of the night, however, Hardee left of his own accord. That night Hood blew up his military works, such as he thought would be valuable in our hands, and decamped.

The next morning at daylight General H. W. Slocum, who was commanding north of the city, moved in and took possession of Atlanta, and notified Sherman. Sherman then moved deliberately back, taking three days to reach the city, and occupied a line extending from Decatur on the left to Atlanta in the centre, with his troops extending out of the city for some distance to the right.

The campaign had lasted about four months, and was one of the most memorable in history. There was but little if any-

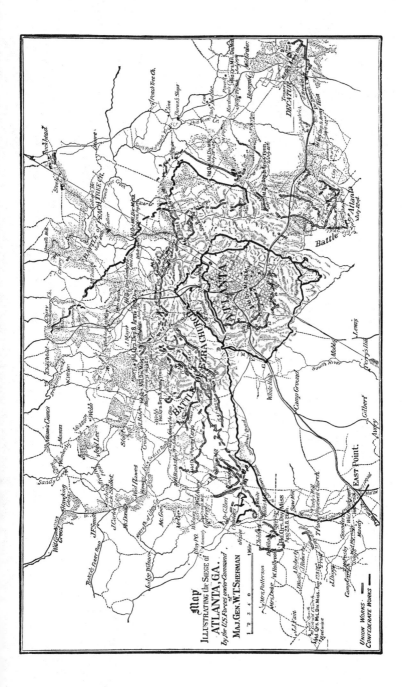

Map
ILLUSTRATING the SIEGE of
ATLANTA, GA.
By the U.S. Forces under Command
of
MAJ. GEN. W. T. SHERMAN

1 2 3 4 0   1 Mile

UNION WORKS:
CONFEDERATE WORKS:

thing in the whole campaign, now that it is over, to criticise at all, and nothing to criticise severely. It was creditable alike to the general who commanded and the army which had executed it. Sherman had on this campaign some bright, wide-awake division and brigade commanders whose alertness added a host to the efficiency of his command.

The troops now went to work to make themselves comfortable, and to enjoy a little rest after their arduous campaign. The city of Atlanta was turned into a military base. The citizens were all compelled to leave. Sherman also very wisely prohibited the assembling of the army of sutlers and traders who always follow in the wake of an army in the field, if permitted to do so, from trading with the citizens and getting the money of the soldiers for articles of but little use to them, and for which they are made to pay most exorbitant prices. He limited the number of these traders to one for each of his three armies.

The news of Sherman's success reached the North instantaneously, and set the country all aglow. This was the first great political campaign for the Republicans in their canvass of 1864. It was followed later by Sheridan's campaign in the Shenandoah Valley; and these two campaigns probably had more effect in settling the election of the following November than all the speeches, all the bonfires, and all the parading with banners and bands of music in the North.

Chapter L.

GRAND MOVEMENT OF THE ARMY OF THE POTOMAC—
CROSSING THE RAPIDAN—ENTERING THE WILDERNESS—
BATTLE OF THE WILDERNESS.

SOON AFTER MIDNIGHT, May 3d–4th, the Army of the
Potomac moved out from its position north of the Rapidan, to start upon that memorable campaign, destined to result in the capture of the Confederate capital and the army
defending it. This was not to be accomplished, however,
without as desperate fighting as the world has ever witnessed;
not to be consummated in a day, a week, a month, or a single
season. The losses inflicted, and endured, were destined to be
severe; but the armies now confronting each other had already been in deadly conflict for a period of three years, with
immense losses in killed, by death from sickness, captured and
wounded; and neither had made any real progress toward accomplishing the final end. It is true the Confederates had, so
far, held their capital, and they claimed this to be their sole
object. But previously they had boldly proclaimed their intention to capture Philadelphia, New York, and the National
Capital, and had made several attempts to do so, and once or
twice had come fearfully near making their boast good—too
near for complacent contemplation by the loyal North. They
had also come near losing their own capital on at least one
occasion. So here was a stand-off. The campaign now begun
was destined to result in heavier losses, to both armies, in a
given time, than any previously suffered; but the carnage was
to be limited to a single year, and to accomplish all that had
been anticipated or desired at the beginning in that time. We
had to have hard fighting to achieve this. The two armies had
been confronting each other so long, without any decisive result, that they hardly knew which could whip.

Ten days' rations, with a supply of forage and ammunition
were taken in wagons. Beef cattle were driven with the trains,
and butchered as wanted. Three days' rations in addition, in
haversacks, and fifty rounds of cartridges, were carried on the
person of each soldier.

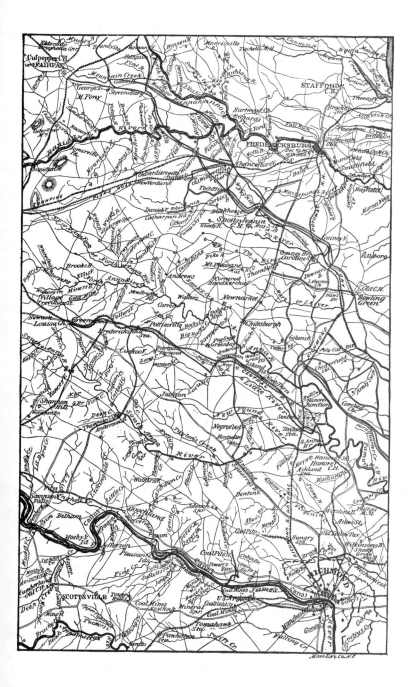

The country over which the army had to operate, from the Rapidan to the crossing of the James River, is rather flat, and is cut by numerous streams which make their way to the Chesapeake Bay. The crossings of these streams by the army were generally made not far above tide-water, and where they formed a considerable obstacle to the rapid advance of troops even when the enemy did not appear in opposition. The country roads were narrow and poor. Most of the country is covered with a dense forest, in places, like the Wilderness and along the Chickahominy, almost impenetrable even for infantry except along the roads. All bridges were naturally destroyed before the National troops came to them.

UNION ARMY ON THE RAPIDAN, MAY 5, 1864.

[COMPILED.]

LIEUTENANT-GENERAL U. S. GRANT, Commander-in-Chief.
MAJOR-GENERAL GEORGE G. MEADE, Commanding Army of the Potomac.

MAJ.-GEN. W. S. HANCOCK, commanding Second Army Corps.

First Division, Brig.-Gen. Francis C. Barlow.
- First Brigade, Col. Nelson A. Miles.
- Second Brigade, Col. Thomas A. Smyth.
- Third Brigade, Col. Paul Frank.
- Fourth Brigade, Col. John R. Brooke.

Second Division, Brig.-Gen. John Gibbon.
- First Brigade, Brig.-Gen. Alex. S. Webb.
- Second Brigade, Brig.-Gen. Joshua T. Owen.
- Third Brigade, Col. Samuel S. Carroll.

Third Division, Maj.-Gen. David B. Birney.
- First Brigade, Brig.-Gen. J. H. H. Ward.
- Second Brigade, Brig.-Gen. Alexander Hays.

Fourth Division, Brig.-Gen. Gershom Mott.
- First Brigade, Col. Robert McAllister.
- Second Brigade, Col. Wm. R. Brewster.

Artillery Brigade, Col. John C. Tidball.

The Army of the Potomac was composed of three infantry and one cavalry corps, commanded respectively by Generals W. S. Hancock, G. K. Warren, John Sedgwick and P. H. Sheridan. The artillery was commanded by General Henry J. Hunt. This arm was in such abundance that the fourth of it could not be used to advantage in such a country as we were destined to pass through. The surplus was much in the way, taking up as it did so much of the narrow and bad roads, and consuming so much of the forage and other stores brought up by the trains.

The 5th corps, General Warren commanding, was in advance on the right, and marched directly for Germania Ford, preceded by one division of cavalry, under General J. H. Wilson. General Sedgwick followed Warren with the 6th corps. Germania Ford was nine or ten miles below the right of Lee's line. Hancock, with the 2d corps, moved by another road,

MAJ.-GEN. G. K. WARREN, commanding Fifth Army Corps.	First Division, Brig.-Gen. Charles Griffin.	First Brigade, Brig.-Gen. Romeyn B. Ayres.
		Second Brigade, Col. Jacob B. Sweitzer.
		Third Brigade, Brig.-Gen. J. J. Bartlett.
	Second Division, Brig.-Gen. John C. Robinson.	First Brigade, Col. Samuel H. Leonard.
		Second Brigade, Brig.-Gen. Henry Baxter.
		Third Brigade, Col. Andrew W. Denison.
	Third Division, Brig.-Gen. Samuel W. Crawford.	First Brigade, Col. Wm. McCandless.
		Third Brigade, Col. Joseph W. Fisher.
	Fourth Division, Brig.-Gen. James S. Wadsworth.	First Brigade, Brig.-Gen. Lysander Cutler.
		Second Brigade, Brig.-Gen. James C. Rice.
		Third Brigade, Col. Roy Stone.
		Artillery Brigade, Col. C. S. Wainwright.

farther east, directly upon Ely's Ford, six miles below Germania, preceded by Gregg's division of cavalry, and followed by the artillery. Torbert's division of cavalry was left north of the Rapidan, for the time, to picket the river and prevent the

		First Brigade, Col. Henry W. Brown.
	First Division, Brig.-Gen. H. G. Wright.	Second Brigade, Col. Emory Upton.
		Third Brigade, Brig.-Gen. D. A. Russell.
		Fourth Brigade, Brig.-Gen. Alexander Shaler.
MAJ.-GEN. JOHN SEDGWICK, commanding Sixth Army Corps.	Second Division, Brig.-Gen. George W. Getty.	First Brigade, Brig.-Gen. Frank Wheaton.
		Second Brigade, Col. Lewis A. Grant.
		Third Brigade, Brig.-Gen. Thos. H. Neill.
		Fourth Brigade, Brig.-Gen. Henry L. Eustis.
	Third Division, Brig.-Gen. James B. Ricketts.	First Brigade, Brig.-Gen. Wm. H. Morris.
		Second Brigade, Brig.-Gen. T. Seymour.
	Artillery Brigade, Col. C. H. Tompkins.	
MAJ.-GEN. P. H. SHERIDAN, commanding Cavalry Corps.	First Division, Brig.-Gen. A. T. A. Torbert.	First Brigade, Brig.-Gen. G. A. Custer.
		Second Brigade, Col. Thos. C. Devin.
		Reserve Brigade, Brig.-Gen. Wesley Merritt.
	Second Division, Brig.-Gen. D. McM. Gregg.	First Brigade, Brig.-Gen. Henry E. Davies, Jr.
		Second Brigade, Col. J. Irvin Gregg.
	Third Division, Brig.-Gen. J. H. Wilson.	First Brigade, Col. T. M. Bryan, Jr.
		Second Brigade, Col. Geo. H. Chapman.

enemy from crossing and getting into our rear. The cavalry seized the two crossings before daylight, drove the enemy's pickets guarding them away, and by six o'clock A.M. had the pontoons laid ready for the crossing of the infantry and artillery. This was undoubtedly a surprise to Lee. The fact that the movement was unopposed proves this.

Burnside, with the 9th corps, was left back at Warrenton, guarding the railroad from Bull Run forward to preserve

	First Division, Brig.-Gen. T. G. Stevenson.	First Brigade, Col. Sumner Carruth. Second Brigade, Col. Daniel Leasure.
	Second Division, Brig.-Gen. Robert B. Potter.	First Brigade, Col. Zenas R. Bliss. Second Brigade, Col. Simon G. Griffin.
MAJ.-GEN. A. E. BURNSIDE, commanding Ninth Army Corps.	Third Division, Brig.-Gen. Orlando B. Willcox.	First Brigade, Col. John F. Hartranft. Second Brigade, Col. Benj. C. Christ.
	Fourth Division, Brig.-Gen. Edward Ferrero.	First Brigade, Col. Joshua K. Sigfried. Second Brigade, Col. Henry G. Thomas.
		Provisional Brigade, Col. Elisha G. Marshall.
BRIG.-GEN. HENRY J. HUNT, commanding Artillery.	Reserve, Col. H. S. Burton.	First Brigade, Col. J. H. Kitching. Second Brigade, Maj. J. A. Tompkins First Brig. Horse Art., Capt J. M. Robertson. Second Brigade Horse Art., Capt. D. R. Ransom. Third Brigade, Maj. R. H. Fitzhugh.
GENERAL HEADQUARTERS		Provost Guard, Brig.-Gen. M. R. Patrick. Volunteer Engineers, Brig.-Gen. H. W. Benham.

control of it in case our crossing the Rapidan should be long
delayed. He was instructed, however, to advance at once on

CONFEDERATE ARMY.

Organization of the Army of Northern Virginia, Commanded by GENERAL
ROBERT E. LEE, August 31st, 1864.

First Army Corps: LIEUT.-GEN. R. H. ANDERSON, Commanding.

MAJ.-GEN. GEO. E. PICKETT'S Division.	Brig.-Gen. Seth M. Barton's Brigade. (*a*) " M. D. Corse's " " Eppa Hunton's " " Wm. R. Terry's "
MAJ.-GEN. C. W. FIELD'S Division. (*b*)	Brig.-Gen. G. T. Anderson's Brigade. " E. M. Law's (*c*) " " John Bratton's "
MAJ.-GEN. J. B. KERSHAW'S Division. (*d*)	Brig.-Gen. W. T. Wofford's Brigade. " B. G. Humphrey's " " Goode Bryan's " " Kershaw's (Old) "

Second Army Corps: MAJOR-GENERAL JUBAL A. EARLY, Commanding.

MAJ.-GEN. JOHN B. GORDON'S Division.	Brig.-Gen. H. T. Hays' Brigade. (*e*) " John Pegram's " (*f*) " Gordon's " (*g*) Brig.-Gen. R. F. Hoke's "
MAJ.-GEN. EDWARD JOHNSON'S Division.	Stonewall Brig. (Brig.-Gen. J. A. Walker). (*h*) Brig.-Gen. J. M. Jones' Brigade. (*h*) " Geo. H. Stewart's " (*h*) " L. A. Stafford's " (*e*)
MAJ.-GEN. R. E. RODES' Division.	Brig.-Gen. J. Daniel's Brigade. (*i*) " Geo. Dole's " (*k*) " S. D. Ramseur's Brigade. " C. A. Battle's " " R. D. Johnston's " (*f*)

NOTE.

(*a*) Col. W. R. Aylett was in command Aug. 29th, and probably at above date.
(*b*) Inspection report of this division shows that it also contained Benning's and
      Gregg's Brigades.
(*c*) Commanded by Colonel P. D. Bowles.
(*d*) Only two brigadier-generals reported for duty; names not indicated.
(*e*) Constituting York's Brigade.
(*f*) In Ramseur's Division.
(*g*) Evan's Brigade, Colonel E. N. Atkinson commanding,
      and containing 12th Georgia Battalion.   Organization of the Army
(*h*) The Virginia regiments constituted Terry's Brigade,   of the Valley District
      Gordon's Division.
(*i*) Grimes' Brigade.
(*k*) Cook's "

receiving notice that the army had crossed; and a dispatch was sent to him a little after one P.M. giving the information that our crossing had been successful.

The country was heavily wooded at all the points of crossing, particularly on the south side of the river. The battle-field from the crossing of the Rapidan until the final movement from the Wilderness toward Spottsylvania was of the same character. There were some clearings and small farms within what might be termed the battle-field; but generally the country

---

Third Army Corps: LIEUT.-GEN. A. P. HILL, Commanding.

MAJ.-GEN. WM. MAHONE'S Division. (*l*)	Brig.-Gen. J. C. C. Sanders' Brigade.
	" Mahone's "
	Brig.-Gen. N. H. Harris's " (*m*)
	" A. R. Wright's "
	" Joseph Finegan's "
MAJ.-GEN. C. M. WILCOX'S Division.	Brig.-Gen. E. L. Thomas's Brigade (*n*)
	" James H. Lane's "
	" Sam'l McGowan's "
	" Alfred M. Scale's "
MAJ.-GEN. H. HETH'S Division. (*o*)	Brig.-Gen. J. R. Davis's Brigade.
	" John R. Cooke's "
	" D. McRae's "
	" J. J. Archer's "
	" H. H. Walker's "

Unattached: 5th Alabama Battalion.

Cavalry Corps: LIEUTENANT-GENERAL WADE HAMPTON, Commanding. (*p*)

MAJ.-GEN. FITZHUGH LEE'S Division.	Brig.-Gen. W. C. Wickham's Brigade.
	" L. L. Lomax's "
MAJ.-GEN. M. C. BUTLER'S Division.	Brig.-Gen. John Dunovant's Brigade.
	" P. M. B. Young's "
	" Thomas L. Rosser's "
MAJ.-GEN. W. H. F. LEE'S Division.	Brig.-Gen. Rufus Barringer's Brigade.
	" J. R. Chambliss's "

NOTE.

(*l*) Returns report but one general officer present for duty; name not indicated.

(*m*) Colonel Joseph M. Jayne, commanding.

(*n*) Colonel Thomas J. Simmons, commanding.

(*o*) Four brigadier-generals reported present for duty; names not indicated.

(*p*) On face of returns appears to have consisted of Hampton's, Fitz-Lee's, and W. H. F. Lee's Division, and Dearing's Brigade.

was covered with a dense forest. The roads were narrow and bad. All the conditions were favorable for defensive operations.

Artillery Reserve: Brig.-Gen. W. N. Pendleton, Commanding.

Brig.-Gen. E. P. Alexander's Division.*	Cabell's Battalion.	Manly's Battery. 1st Co. Richmond Howitzers. Carleton's Battery. Calloway's Battery.
	Haskell's Battalion.	Branch's Battery. Nelson's " Garden's " Rowan "
	Huger's Battalion.	Smith's Battery. Moody " Woolfolk " Parker's " Taylor's " Fickling's " Martin's "
	Gibb's Battalion.	Davidson's Battery. Dickenson's " Otey's "
Brig.-Gen. A. L. Long's Division.	Braxton's Battalion.	Lee Battery. 1st Md. Artillery. Stafford " Alleghany "
	Cutshaw's Battalion.	Charlotteville Artillery.- Staunton " Courtney "
	Carter's Battalion.	Morris Artillery. Orange " King William Artillery. Jeff Davis "
	Nelson's Battalion.	Amherst Artillery. Milledge " Fluvauna "
	Brown's Battalion.	Powhatan Artillery. 2d Richmond Howitzers. 3d " " Rockbridge Artillery. Salem Flying Artillery.

*But one general officer reported present for duty in the artillery, and Alexander's name not on the original.

There are two roads, good for that part of Virginia, running from Orange Court House to the battle-field. The most southerly of these roads is known as the Orange Court House Plank Road, the northern one as the Orange Turnpike. There are also roads from east of the battle-field running to Spottsylvania Court House, one from Chancellorsville, branching at Aldrich's; the western branch going by Piney Branch Church, Alsop's, thence by the Brock Road to Spottsylvania; the east branch goes by Gates's, thence to Spottsylvania. The Brock Road runs from Germania Ford through the battle-field and on to the Court House. As Spottsylvania is approached the country is cut up with numerous roads, some going to the town direct, and others crossing so as to connect the farms with roads going there.

Lee's headquarters were at Orange Court House. From there to Fredericksburg he had the use of the two roads above described running nearly parallel to the Wilderness. This gave him unusual facilities, for that country, for concentrating his forces to his right. These roads strike the road from Germania Ford in the Wilderness.

	Cutt's Battalion.	Ross's Battery. Patterson's Battery. Irwin Artillery.
	Richardson's Battalion.	Lewis Artillery. Donaldsonville Artillery. Norfolk Light " Huger "
Col. R. L. Walker's Division.	McIntosh's Battalion.	Johnson's Battery. Hardaway Artillery. Danville " 2d Rockbridge Artillery.
	Pegram's Battalion.	Peedee Artillery. Fredericksburg Artillery. Letcher Purcell Battery. Crenshaw's Battery.
	Poague's Battalion.	Madison Artillery. Albemarle " Brooke " Charlotte "

As soon as the crossing of the infantry was assured, the cavalry pushed forward, Wilson's division by Wilderness Tavern to Parker's store, on the Orange Plank Road; Gregg to the left towards Chancellorsville. Warren followed Wilson and reached the Wilderness Tavern by noon, took position there and intrenched. Sedgwick followed Warren. He was across the river and in camp on the south bank, on the right of Warren, by sundown. Hancock, with the 2d corps, moved parallel with Warren and camped about six miles east of him. Before night all the troops, and by the evening of the 5th the trains of more than four thousand wagons, were safely on the south side of the river.

There never was a corps better organized than was the quartermaster's corps with the Army of the Potomac in 1864. With a wagon-train that would have extended from the Rapidan to Richmond, stretched along in single file and separated as the teams necessarily would be when moving, we could still carry only three days' forage and about ten to twelve days' rations, besides a supply of ammunition. To overcome all difficulties, the chief quartermaster, General Rufus Ingalls, had marked on each wagon the corps badge with the division color and the number of the brigade. At a glance, the particular brigade to which any wagon belonged could be told. The wagons were also marked to note the contents: if ammunition, whether for artillery or infantry; if forage, whether grain or hay; if rations, whether bread, pork, beans, rice, sugar, coffee or whatever it might be. Empty wagons were never allowed to follow the army or stay in camp. As soon as a wagon was empty it would return to the base of supply for a load of precisely the same article that had been taken from it. Empty trains were obliged to leave the road free for loaded ones. Arriving near the army they would be parked in fields nearest to the brigades they belonged to. Issues, except of ammunition, were made at night in all cases. By this system the hauling of forage for the supply train was almost wholly dispensed with. They consumed theirs at the depots.

I left Culpeper Court House after all the troops had been put in motion, and passing rapidly to the front, crossed the Rapidan in advance of Sedgwick's corps; and established headquarters for the afternoon and night in a deserted house near the river.

Orders had been given, long before this movement began, to cut down the baggage of officers and men to the lowest point possible. Notwithstanding this I saw scattered along the road from Culpeper to Germania Ford wagon-loads of new blankets and overcoats, thrown away by the troops to lighten their knapsacks; an improvidence I had never witnessed before.

Lee, while his pickets and signal corps must have discovered at a very early hour on the morning of the 4th of May, that the Army of the Potomac was moving, evidently did not learn until about one o'clock in the afternoon by what route we would confront his army. This I judge from the fact that at 1.15 P.M., an hour and a quarter after Warren had reached Old Wilderness Tavern, our officers took off rebel signals which, when translated, were seen to be an order to his troops to occupy their intrenchments at Mine Run.

Here at night dispatches were received announcing that Sherman, Butler and Crook had moved according to programme.

On discovering the advance of the Army of the Potomac, Lee ordered Hill, Ewell and Longstreet, each commanding corps, to move to the right to attack us, Hill on the Orange Plank Road, Longstreet to follow on the same road. Longstreet was at this time—middle of the afternoon—at Gordonsville, twenty or more miles away. Ewell was ordered by the Orange Pike. He was near by and arrived some four miles east of Mine Run before bivouacking for the night.

My orders were given through General Meade for an early advance on the morning of the 5th. Warren was to move to Parker's store, and Wilson's cavalry—then at Parker's store—to move on to Craig's meeting-house. Sedgwick followed Warren, closing in on his right. The Army of the Potomac was facing to the west, though our advance was made to the south, except when facing the enemy. Hancock was to move south-westward to join on the left of Warren, his left to reach to Shady Grove Church.

At six o'clock, before reaching Parker's store, Warren discovered the enemy. He sent word back to this effect, and

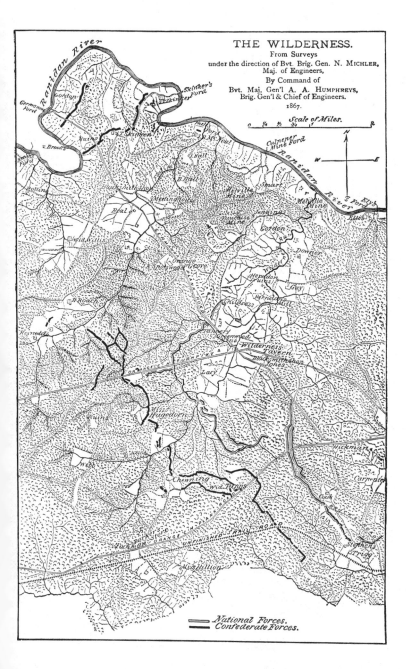

THE WILDERNESS.

From Surveys
under the direction of Bvt. Brig. Gen. N. MICHLER,
Maj. of Engineers,
By Command of
Bvt. Maj. Gen'l A. A. HUMPHREYS,
Brig. Gen'l & Chief of Engineers.
1867.

Scale of Miles.

National Forces.
Confederate Forces.

was ordered to halt and prepare to meet and attack him. Wright, with his division of Sedgwick's corps, was ordered, by any road he could find, to join on to Warren's right, and Getty with his division, also of Sedgwick's corps, was ordered to move rapidly by Warren's rear and get on his left. This was the speediest way to reinforce Warren who was confronting the enemy on both the Orange plank and turnpike roads.

Burnside had moved promptly on the 4th, on receiving word that the Army of the Potomac had safely crossed the Rapidan. By making a night march, although some of his troops had to march forty miles to reach the river, he was crossing with the head of his column early on the morning of the 5th.

Meade moved his headquarters on to Old Wilderness Tavern, four miles south of the river, as soon as it was light enough to see the road. I remained to hasten Burnside's crossing and to put him in position. Burnside at this time was not under Meade's command, and was his senior in rank. Getting information of the proximity of the enemy, I informed Meade, and without waiting to see Burnside, at once moved forward my headquarters to where Meade was.

It was my plan then, as it was on all other occasions, to take the initiative whenever the enemy could be drawn from his intrenchments if we were not intrenched ourselves. Warren had not yet reached the point where he was to halt, when he discovered the enemy near by. Neither party had any advantage of position. Warren was, therefore, ordered to attack as soon as he could prepare for it. At nine o'clock Hancock was ordered to come up to the support of Getty. He himself arrived at Getty's front about noon, but his troops were yet far in the rear. Getty was directed to hold his position at all hazards until relieved. About this hour Warren was ready, and attacked with favorable though not decisive results. Getty was somewhat isolated from Warren and was in a precarious condition for a time. Wilson, with his division of cavalry, was farther south, and was cut off from the rest of the army. At two o'clock Hancock's troops began to arrive, and immediately he was ordered to join Getty and attack the enemy. But the heavy timber and narrow roads prevented him from getting into position for attack as promptly as he generally did when receiving such orders. At four o'clock he again received his orders to attack, and General Getty received orders from Meade a few minutes later to attack whether Hancock was ready or not. He met the enemy under Heth within a few hundred yards.

Hancock immediately sent two divisions, commanded by Birney and Mott, and later two brigades, Carroll's and Owen's, to the support of Getty. This was timely and saved Getty. During the battle Getty and Carroll were wounded, but remained on the field. One of Birney's most gallant brigade commanders—Alexander Hays—was killed.

I had been at West Point with Hays for three years, and had served with him through the Mexican war, a portion of the time in the same regiment. He was a most gallant officer, ready to lead his command wherever ordered. With him it was "Come, boys," not "Go."

Wadsworth's division and Baxter's brigade of the 2d division were sent to reinforce Hancock and Getty; but the density of the intervening forest was such that, there being no road to march upon, they did not get up with the head of column until night, and bivouacked where they were without getting into position.

During the afternoon Sheridan sent Gregg's division of cavalry to Todd's Tavern in search of Wilson. This was fortunate. He found Wilson engaged with a superior force under General Rosser, supported by infantry, and falling back before it. Together they were strong enough to turn the tables upon the enemy and themselves become aggressive. They soon drove the rebel cavalry back beyond Corbin's Bridge.

Fighting between Hancock and Hill continued until night put a close to it. Neither side made any special progress.

After the close of the battle of the 5th of May my orders were given for the following morning. We knew Longstreet with 12,000 men was on his way to join Hill's right, near the Brock Road, and might arrive during the night. I was anxious that the rebels should not take the initiative in the morning, and therefore ordered Hancock to make an assault at 4.30 o'clock. Meade asked to have the hour changed to six. Deferring to his wishes as far as I was willing, the order was modified and five was fixed as the hour to move.

Hancock had now fully one-half of the Army of the Potomac. Wadsworth with his division, which had arrived the night before, lay in a line perpendicular to that held by Hill, and to the right of Hancock. He was directed to move at the same time, and to attack Hill's left.

Burnside, who was coming up with two divisions, was directed to get in between Warren and Wadsworth, and attack as soon as he could get in position to do so. Sedgwick and Warren were to make attacks in their front, to detain as many of the enemy as they could and to take advantage of any attempt to reinforce Hill from that quarter. Burnside was ordered if he should succeed in breaking the enemy's centre, to swing around to the left and envelop the right of Lee's army. Hancock was informed of all the movements ordered.

Burnside had three divisions, but one of them—a colored division—was sent to guard the wagon train, and he did not see it again until July.

Lee was evidently very anxious that there should be no battle on his right until Longstreet got up. This is evident from the fact that notwithstanding the early hour at which I had ordered the assault, both for the purpose of being the attacking party and to strike before Longstreet got up, Lee was ahead in his assault on our right. His purpose was evident, but he failed.

Hancock was ready to advance by the hour named, but learning in time that Longstreet was moving a part of his corps by the Catharpin Road, thus threatening his left flank, sent a division of infantry, commanded by General Barlow, with all his artillery, to cover the approaches by which Longstreet was expected. This disposition was made in time to attack as ordered. Hancock moved by the left of the Orange Plank Road, and Wadsworth by the right of it. The fighting was desperate for about an hour, when the enemy began to break up in great confusion.

I believed then, and see no reason to change that opinion now, that if the country had been such that Hancock and his command could have seen the confusion and panic in the lines of the enemy, it would have been taken advantage of so

effectually that Lee would not have made another stand outside of his Richmond defences.

Gibbon commanded Hancock's left, and was ordered to
attack, but was not able to accomplish much.

On the morning of the 6th Sheridan was sent to connect
with Hancock's left and attack the enemy's cavalry who were
trying to get on our left and rear. He met them at the intersection of the Furnace and Brock roads and at Todd's Tavern,
and defeated them at both places. Later he was attacked, and
again the enemy was repulsed.

Hancock heard the firing between Sheridan and Stuart, and
thinking the enemy coming by that road, still further reinforced his position guarding the entrance to the Brock Road.
Another incident happened during the day to further induce
Hancock to weaken his attacking column. Word reached him
that troops were seen moving towards him from the direction
of Todd's Tavern, and Brooke's brigade was detached to meet
this new enemy; but the troops approaching proved to be
several hundred convalescents coming from Chancellorsville,
by the road Hancock had advanced upon, to join their respective commands. At 6.50 o'clock A.M., Burnside, who had
passed Wilderness Tavern at six o'clock, was ordered to send a
division to the support of Hancock, but to continue with the
remainder of his command in the execution of his previous
order. The difficulty of making a way through the dense forests prevented Burnside from getting up in time to be of any
service on the forenoon of the sixth.

Hancock followed Hill's retreating forces, in the morning,
a mile or more. He maintained this position until, along in
the afternoon, Longstreet came upon him. The retreating column of Hill meeting reinforcements that had not yet been
engaged, became encouraged and returned with them. They
were enabled, from the density of the forest, to approach
within a few hundred yards of our advance before being discovered. Falling upon a brigade of Hancock's corps thrown
to the advance, they swept it away almost instantly. The enemy followed up his advantage and soon came upon Mott's
division, which fell back in great confusion. Hancock made
dispositions to hold his advanced position, but after holding
it for a time, fell back into the position that he had held in the

morning, which was strongly intrenched. In this engagement the intrepid Wadsworth while trying to rally his men was mortally wounded and fell into the hands of the enemy. The enemy followed up, but made no immediate attack.

The Confederate General Jenkins was killed and Longstreet seriously wounded in this engagement. Longstreet had to leave the field, not to resume command for many weeks. His loss was a severe one to Lee, and compensated in a great measure for the mishap, or misapprehensions, which had fallen to our lot during the day.

After Longstreet's removal from the field Lee took command of his right in person. He was not able, however, to rally his men to attack Hancock's position, and withdrew from our front for the purpose of reforming. Hancock sent a brigade to clear his front of all remnants that might be left of Longstreet's or Hill's commands. This brigade having been formed at right angles to the intrenchments held by Hancock's command, swept down the whole length of them from left to right. A brigade of the enemy was encountered in this move; but it broke and disappeared without a contest.

Firing was continued after this, but with less fury. Burnside had not yet been able to get up to render any assistance. But it was now only about nine in the morning, and he was getting into position on Hancock's right.

At 4.15 in the afternoon Lee attacked our left. His line moved up to within a hundred yards of ours and opened a heavy fire. This status was maintained for about half an hour. Then a part of Mott's division and Ward's brigade of Birney's division gave way and retired in disorder. The enemy under R. H. Anderson took advantage of this and pushed through our line, planting their flags on a part of the intrenchments not on fire. But owing to the efforts of Hancock, their success was but temporary. Carroll, of Gibbon's division, moved at a double quick with his brigade and drove back the enemy, inflicting great loss. Fighting had continued from five in the morning sometimes along the whole line, at other times only in places. The ground fought over had varied in width, but averaged three-quarters of a mile. The killed, and many of the severely wounded, of both armies, lay within this belt where it was impossible to reach them. The woods were set on fire by the bursting shells, and the conflagration raged. The wounded who had not strength to move themselves were either suffocated or burned to death. Finally the fire communicated with our breastworks, in places. Being constructed of wood, they burned with great fury. But the battle still raged, our men firing through the flames until it became too hot to remain longer.

Lee was now in distress. His men were in confusion, and his personal efforts failed to restore order. These facts, however, were learned subsequently, or we would have taken advantage of his condition and no doubt gained a decisive success. His troops were withdrawn now, but I revoked the order, which I had given previously to this assault, for Hancock to attack, because his troops had exhausted their ammunition and did not have time to replenish from the train, which was at some distance.

Burnside, Sedgwick, and Warren had all kept up an assault during all this time; but their efforts had no other effect than to prevent the enemy from reinforcing his right from the troops in their front.

I had, on the 5th, ordered all the bridges over the Rapidan to be taken up except one at Germania Ford.

The troops on Sedgwick's right had been sent to reinforce our left. This left our right in danger of being turned, and us of being cut off from all present base of supplies. Sedgwick had refused his right and intrenched it for protection against attack. But late in the afternoon of the 6th Early came out from his lines in considerable force and got in upon Sedgwick's right, notwithstanding the precautions taken, and created considerable confusion. Early captured several hundred prisoners, among them two general officers. The defence, however, was vigorous; and night coming on, the enemy was thrown into as much confusion as our troops, engaged, were. Early says in his Memoirs that if we had discovered the confusion in his lines we might have brought fresh troops to his great discomfort. Many officers, who had not been attacked by Early, continued coming to my headquarters even after Sedgwick had rectified his lines a little farther to the rear, with news of the disaster, fully impressed with the idea that the enemy was pushing on and would soon be upon me.

During the night all of Lee's army withdrew within their intrenchments. On the morning of the 7th General Custer drove the enemy's cavalry from Catharpin Furnace to Todd's Tavern. Pickets and skirmishers were sent along our entire front to find the position of the enemy. Some went as far as a mile and a half before finding him. But Lee showed no disposition to come out of his works. There was no battle during the day, and but little firing except in Warren's front; he being directed about noon to make a reconnoissance in force. This drew some sharp firing, but there was no attempt on the part of Lee to drive him back. This ended the Battle of the Wilderness.

Chapter LI.

AFTER THE BATTLE—TELEGRAPH AND SIGNAL SERVICE—
MOVEMENT BY THE LEFT FLANK.

MORE DESPERATE FIGHTING has not been witnessed on this continent than that of the 5th and 6th of May. Our victory consisted in having successfully crossed a formidable stream, almost in the face of an enemy, and in getting the army together as a unit. We gained an advantage on the morning of the 6th, which, if it had been followed up, must have proven very decisive. In the evening the enemy gained an advantage; but was speedily repulsed. As we stood at the close, the two armies were relatively in about the same condition to meet each other as when the river divided them. But the fact of having safely crossed was a victory.

Our losses in the Wilderness were very severe. Those of the Confederates must have been even more so; but I have no means of speaking with accuracy upon this point. The Germania Ford bridge was transferred to Ely's Ford to facilitate the transportation of the wounded to Washington.

It may be as well here as elsewhere to state two things connected with all movements of the Army of the Potomac: first, in every change of position or halt for the night, whether confronting the enemy or not, the moment arms were stacked the men intrenched themselves. For this purpose they would build up piles of logs or rails if they could be found in their front, and dig a ditch, throwing the dirt forward on the timber. Thus the digging they did counted in making a depression to stand in, and increased the elevation in front of them. It was wonderful how quickly they could in this way construct defences of considerable strength. When a halt was made with the view of assaulting the enemy, or in his presence, these would be strengthened or their positions changed under the direction of engineer officers. The second was, the use made of the telegraph and signal corps. Nothing could be more complete than the organization and discipline of this body of brave and intelligent men. Insulated wires—insulated so that they would transmit messages in a storm, on the ground or under water—were wound upon reels, making about two hundred pounds weight of wire to each reel. Two men and one mule were detailed to each reel. The pack-saddle on which this was carried was provided with a rack like a sawbuck placed crosswise of the saddle, and raised above it so that the reel, with its wire, would revolve freely. There was a wagon, supplied with a telegraph operator, battery and telegraph instruments for each division, each corps, each army, and one for my headquarters. There were wagons also loaded with light poles, about the size and length of a wall tent pole, supplied with an iron spike in one end, used to hold the wires up when laid, so that wagons and artillery would not run over them. The mules thus loaded were assigned to brigades, and always kept with the command they were assigned to. The operators were also assigned to particular headquarters, and never changed except by special orders.

The moment the troops were put in position to go into camp all the men connected with this branch of service would proceed to put up their wires. A mule loaded with a coil of wire would be led to the rear of the nearest flank of the brigade he belonged to, and would be led in a line parallel thereto, while one man would hold an end of the wire and uncoil it as the mule was led off. When he had walked the length of the wire the whole of it would be on the ground. This would be done in rear of every brigade at the same time. The ends of all the wires would then be joined, making a continuous wire in the rear of the whole army. The men, attached to brigades or divisions, would all commence at once raising the wires with their telegraph poles. This was done by making a loop in the wire and putting it over the spike and raising the pole to a perpendicular position. At intervals the wire would be attached to trees, or some other permanent object, so that one pole was sufficient at a place. In the absence of such a support two poles would have to be used, at intervals, placed at an angle so as to hold the wire firm in its place. While this was being done the telegraph wagons would take their positions near where the headquarters they belonged to were to be established, and would connect with the wire. Thus, in a few minutes longer time than it took a mule to walk the length of its coil, telegraphic communication would be effected between all the headquarters of the army. No orders ever had to be given to establish the telegraph.

The signal service was used on the march. The men composing this corps were assigned to specified commands. When movements were made, they would go in advance, or on the flanks, and seize upon high points of ground giving a commanding view of the country, if cleared, or would climb tall trees on the highest points if not cleared, and would denote, by signals, the positions of different parts of our own army, and often the movements of the enemy. They would also take off the signals of the enemy and transmit them. It would sometimes take too long a time to make translations of intercepted dispatches for us to receive any benefit from them. But sometimes they gave useful information.

On the afternoon of the 7th I received news from Washington announcing that Sherman had probably attacked Johnston that day, and that Butler had reached City Point safely and taken it by surprise on the 5th. I had given orders for a movement by the left flank, fearing that Lee might move rapidly to Richmond to crush Butler before I could get there.

My order for this movement was as follows:

> HEADQUARTERS ARMIES OF THE U. S.,
> *May* 7, 1864, 6.30 A.M.

MAJOR-GENERAL MEADE,
        Commanding A. P.

Make all preparations during the day for a night march to take position at Spottsylvania C. H. with one army corps, at Todd's Tavern with one, and another near the intersection of the Piney Branch and Spottsylvania road with the road from Alsop's to Old Court House. If this move is made the trains should be thrown forward early in the morning to the Ny River.

I think it would be advisable in making the change to leave Hancock where he is until Warren passes him. He could then follow and become the right of the new line. Burnside will move to Piney Branch Church. Sedgwick can move along the pike to Chancellorsville and on to his destination. Burnside will move on the plank road to the intersection of it with the Orange and Fredericksburg plank road, then follow Sedgwick to his place of destination.

All vehicles should be got out of hearing of the enemy before the troops move, and then move off quietly.

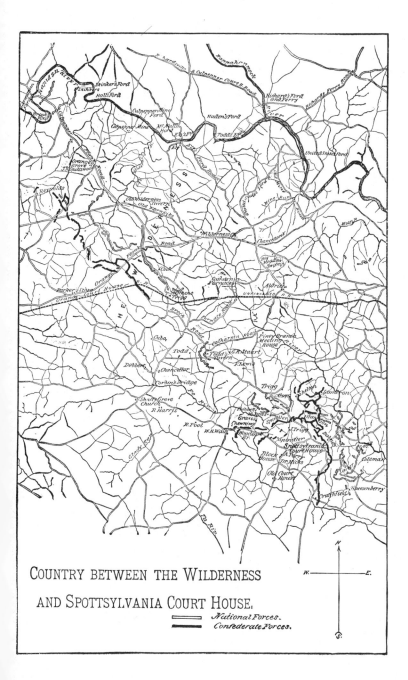

COUNTRY BETWEEN THE WILDERNESS
AND SPOTTSYLVANIA COURT HOUSE.

National Forces.
Confederate Forces.

It is more than probable that the enemy concentrate for a heavy attack on Hancock this afternoon. In case they do we must be prepared to resist them, and follow up any success we may gain, with our whole force. Such a result would necessarily modify these instructions.

All the hospitals should be moved to-day to Chancellorsville.

U. S. GRANT,
Lieut.-General.

During the 7th Sheridan had a fight with the rebel cavalry at Todd's Tavern, but routed them, thus opening the way for the troops that were to go by that route at night. Soon after dark Warren withdrew from the front of the enemy, and was soon followed by Sedgwick. Warren's march carried him immediately behind the works where Hancock's command lay on the Brock Road. With my staff and a small escort of cavalry I preceded the troops. Meade with his staff accompanied me. The greatest enthusiasm was manifested by Hancock's men as we passed by. No doubt it was inspired by the fact that the movement was south. It indicated to them that they had passed through the "beginning of the end" in the battle just fought. The cheering was so lusty that the enemy must have taken it for a night attack. At all events it drew from him a furious fusillade of artillery and musketry, plainly heard but not felt by us.

Meade and I rode in advance. We had passed but a little way beyond our left when the road forked. We looked to see, if we could, which road Sheridan had taken with his cavalry during the day. It seemed to be the right-hand one, and accordingly we took it. We had not gone far, however, when Colonel C. B. Comstock, of my staff, with the instinct of the engineer, suspecting that we were on a road that would lead us into the lines of the enemy, if he, too, should be moving, dashed by at a rapid gallop and all alone. In a few minutes he returned and reported that Lee was moving, and that the road we were on would bring us into his lines in a short distance. We returned to the forks of the road, left a man to indicate the right road to the head of Warren's column when it should come up, and continued our journey to Todd's Tavern, where we arrived after midnight.

My object in moving to Spottsylvania was twofold: first, I did not want Lee to get back to Richmond in time to attempt to crush Butler before I could get there; second, I wanted to get between his army and Richmond if possible; and, if not, to draw him into the open field. But Lee, by accident, beat us to Spottsylvania. Our wagon trains had been ordered easterly of the roads the troops were to march upon before the movement commenced. Lee interpreted this as a semi-retreat of the Army of the Potomac to Fredericksburg, and so informed his government. Accordingly he ordered Longstreet's corps—now commanded by Anderson—to move in the morning (the 8th) to Spottsylvania. But the woods being still on fire, Anderson could not go into bivouac, and marched directly on to his destination that night. By this accident Lee got possession of Spottsylvania. It is impossible to say now what would have been the result if Lee's orders had been obeyed as given; but it is certain that we would have been in Spottsylvania, and between him and his capital. My belief is that there would have been a race between the two armies to see which could reach Richmond first, and the Army of the Potomac would have had the shorter line. Thus, twice since crossing the Rapidan we came near closing the campaign, so far as battles were concerned, from the Rapidan to the James River or Richmond. The first failure was caused by our not following up the success gained over Hill's corps on the morning of the 6th, as before described: the second, when fires caused by that battle drove Anderson to make a march during the night of the 7th–8th which he was ordered to commence on the morning of the 8th. But accident often decides the fate of battle.

Sheridan's cavalry had had considerable fighting during the afternoon of the 7th, lasting at Todd's Tavern until after night, with the field his at the close. He issued the necessary orders for seizing Spottsylvania and holding the bridge over the Po River, which Lee's troops would have to cross to get to Spottsylvania. But Meade changed Sheridan's orders to Merritt—who was holding the bridge—on his arrival at Todd's Tavern, and thereby left the road free for Anderson when he came up. Wilson, who was ordered to seize the town, did so, with his division of cavalry; but he could not hold it against the Confederate corps which had not been detained at the crossing of the Po, as it would have been but for the unfortunate change in Merritt's orders. Had he been permitted to execute the orders Sheridan gave him, he would have been guarding with two brigades of cavalry the bridge over the Po River which Anderson had to cross, and must have detained him long enough to enable Warren to reinforce Wilson and hold the town.

Anderson soon intrenched himself—if indeed the intrenchments were not already made—immediately across Warren's front. Warren was not aware of his presence, but probably supposed it was the cavalry which Merritt had engaged earlier in the day. He assaulted at once, but was repulsed. He soon organized his men, as they were not pursued by the enemy, and made a second attack, this time with his whole corps. This time he succeeded in gaining a position immediately in the enemy's front, where he intrenched. His right and left divisions—the former Crawford's, the latter Wadsworth's, now commanded by Cutler—drove the enemy back some distance.

At this time my headquarters had been advanced to Piney Branch Church. I was anxious to crush Anderson before Lee could get a force to his support. To this end Sedgwick, who was at Piney Branch Church, was ordered to Warren's support. Hancock, who was at Todd's Tavern, was notified of Warren's engagement, and was directed to be in readiness to come up. Burnside, who was with the wagon trains at Aldrich's on our extreme left, received the same instructions. Sedgwick was slow in getting up for some reason—probably unavoidable, because he was never at fault when serious work was to be done—so that it was near night before the combined forces were ready to attack. Even then all of Sedgwick's command did not get into the engagement. Warren led the last assault, one division at a time, and of course it failed.

Warren's difficulty was twofold: when he received an order to do anything, it would at once occur to his mind how all the balance of the army should be engaged so as properly to co-operate with him. His ideas were generally good, but he would forget that the person giving him orders had thought of others at the time he had of him. In like manner, when he did get ready to execute an order, after giving most intelligent instructions to division commanders, he would go in with one division, holding the others in reserve until he could superintend their movements in person also, forgetting that division commanders could execute an order without his presence. His difficulty was constitutional and beyond his control. He was an officer of superior ability, quick perceptions, and personal courage to accomplish anything that could be done with a small command.

Lee had ordered Hill's corps—now commanded by Early—to move by the very road we had marched upon. This shows that even early in the morning of the 8th Lee had not yet become acquainted with my move, but still thought that the Army of the Potomac had gone to Fredericksburg. Indeed, he informed the authorities at Richmond that he had possession of Spottsylvania and was thus on my flank. Anderson was in possession of Spottsylvania, through no foresight of Lee, however. Early only found that he had been following us when he ran against Hancock at Todd's Tavern. His coming detained Hancock from the battle-field of Spottsylvania for that day; but he, in like manner, kept Early back and forced him to move by another route.

Had I ordered the movement for the night of the 7th by my left flank, it would have put Hancock in the lead. It would also have given us an hour or more earlier start. It took all that time for Warren to get the head of his column to the left of Hancock after he had got his troops out of their line confronting the enemy. This hour, and Hancock's capacity to use his whole force when necessary, would, no doubt, have enabled him to crush Anderson before he could be reinforced. But the movement made was tactical. It kept the troops in mass against a possible assault by the enemy. Our left occupied its intrenchments while the two corps to the right passed. If an attack had been made by the enemy he would have found the 2d corps in position, fortified, and, practically, the 5th and 6th corps in position as reserves, until his entire front was passed. By a left flank movement the army would have been scattered while still passing the front of the enemy, and before the extreme right had got by it would have been very much exposed. Then, too, I had not yet learned the special qualifications of the different corps commanders. At that time my judgment was that Warren was the man I would suggest to succeed Meade should anything happen to that gallant soldier to take him from the field. As I have before said, Warren was a gallant soldier, an able man; and he was beside thoroughly imbued with the solemnity and importance of the duty he had to perform.

Chapter LII.

BATTLE OF SPOTTSYLVANIA—HANCOCK'S
POSITION—ASSAULT OF WARREN'S AND WRIGHT'S
CORPS—UPTON PROMOTED ON THE FIELD—GOOD NEWS
FROM BUTLER AND SHERIDAN.

THE MATTAPONY RIVER is formed by the junction of the Mat, the Ta, the Po and the Ny rivers, the last being the northernmost of the four. It takes its rise about a mile south and a little east of the Wilderness Tavern. The Po rises southwest of the same place, but farther away. Spottsylvania is on the ridge dividing these two streams, and where they are but a few miles apart. The Brock Road reaches Spottsylvania without crossing either of these streams. Lee's army coming up by the Catharpin Road, had to cross the Po at Wooden Bridge. Warren and Hancock came by the Brock Road. Sedgwick crossed the Ny at Catharpin Furnace. Burnside coming by Aldrich's to Gates's house, had to cross the Ny near the enemy. He found pickets at the bridge, but they were soon driven off by a brigade of Willcox's division, and the stream was crossed. This brigade was furiously attacked; but the remainder of the division coming up, they were enabled to hold their position, and soon fortified it.

About the time I received the news of this attack, word came from Hancock that Early had left his front. He had been forced over to the Catharpin Road, crossing the Po at Corbin's and again at Wooden Bridge. These are the ridges Sheridan had given orders to his cavalry to occupy on the 8th, while one division should occupy Spottsylvania. These movements of the enemy gave me the idea that Lee was about to make the attempt to get to, or towards, Fredericksburg to cut off my supplies. I made arrangements to attack his right and get between him and Richmond if he should try to execute this design. If he had any such intention it was abandoned as soon as Burnside was established south of the Ny.

The Po and the Ny are narrow little streams, but deep, with abrupt banks, and bordered by heavily wooded and marshy bottoms—at the time we were there—and difficult to cross except where bridged. The country about was generally heavily timbered, but with occasional clearings. It was a much better country to conduct a defensive campaign in than an offensive one.

By noon of the 9th the position of the two armies was as follows: Lee occupied a semicircle facing north, north-west and north-east, inclosing the town. Anderson was on his left extending to the Po, Ewell came next, then Early. Warren occupied our right, covering the Brock and other roads converging at Spottsylvania; Sedgwick was to his left and Burnside on our extreme left. Hancock was yet back at Todd's Tavern, but as soon as it was known that Early had left Hancock's front the latter was ordered up to Warren's right. He formed a line with three divisions on the hill overlooking the Po early in the afternoon, and was ordered to cross the Po and get on the enemy's flank. The fourth division of Hancock's corps, Mott commanding, was left at Todd's when the corps first came up; but in the afternoon it was brought up and placed to the left of Sedgwick's—now Wright's—6th corps. In the morning General Sedgwick had been killed near the right of his intrenchments by rebel sharp-shooters. His loss was a severe one to the Army of the Potomac and to the Nation. General H. G. Wright succeeded him in the command of his corps.

Hancock was now, nine P.M. of the 9th of May, across the left flank of Lee's army, but separated from it, and also from the remainder of Meade's army, by the Po River. But for the lateness of the hour and the darkness of the night he would have attempted to cross the river again at Wooden Bridge, thus bringing himself on the same side with both friend and foe.

The Po at the points where Hancock's corps crossed runs nearly due east. Just below his lower crossing—the troops crossed at three points—it turns due south, and after passing under Wooden Bridge soon resumes a more easterly direction. During the night this corps built three bridges over the Po; but these were in rear.

The position assumed by Hancock's corps forced Lee to reinforce his left during the night. Accordingly on the morning of the 10th, when Hancock renewed his effort to get over the Po to his front, he found himself confronted by some of Early's command, which had been brought from the extreme right of the enemy during the night. He succeeded in effecting a crossing with one brigade, however, but finding the enemy intrenched in his front, no more were crossed.

Hancock reconnoitred his front on the morning of the 10th, with the view of forcing a crossing, if it was found that an advantage could be gained. The enemy was found strongly intrenched on the high ground overlooking the river, and commanding the Wooden Bridge with artillery. Anderson's left rested on the Po, where it turns south; therefore, for Hancock to cross over—although it would bring him to the same side of the stream with the rest of the army—would still farther isolate him from it. The stream would have to be crossed twice in the face of the enemy to unite with the main body. The idea of crossing was therefore abandoned.

Lee had weakened the other parts of his line to meet this movement of Hancock's, and I determined to take advantage of it. Accordingly in the morning, orders were issued for an attack in the afternoon on the centre by Warren's and Wright's corps, Hancock to command all the attacking force. Two of his divisions were brought to the north side of the Po. Gibbon was placed to the right of Warren, and Birney in his rear as a reserve. Barlow's division was left south of the stream, and Mott of the same corps was still to the left of Wright's corps. Burnside was ordered to reconnoitre his front in force, and, if an opportunity presented, to attack with vigor. The enemy seeing Barlow's division isolated from the rest of the army, came out and attacked with fury. Barlow repulsed the assault with great slaughter, and with considerable loss to himself. But the enemy reorganized and renewed the assault. Birney was now moved to the high ground overlooking the river crossings built by our troops, and covered the crossings. The second assault was repulsed, again with severe loss to the enemy, and Barlow was withdrawn without further molestation. General T. G. Stevenson was killed in this move.

Between the lines, where Warren's assault was to take place, there was a ravine grown up with large trees and underbrush,

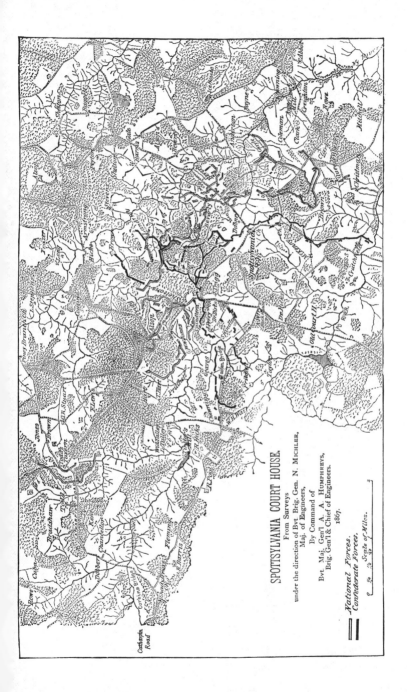

SPOTTSYLVANIA COURT HOUSE.
From Surveys
under the direction of Bvt. Brig. Gen. N. MICHLER,
Maj. of Engineers,
By Command of
Bvt. Maj. Gen'l A. A. HUMPHREYS,
Brig. Gen'l & Chief of Engineers.
1867.

National Forces.
Confederate Forces.

Scale of Miles.

making it almost impenetrable by man. The slopes on both sides were also covered with a heavy growth of timber. Warren, before noon, reconnoitred his front twice, the first time with one and the second with two divisions. He was repulsed on both occasions, but gained such information of the ground as to induce him to report recommending the assault.

Wright also reconnoitred his front and gained a considerably advanced position from the one he started from. He then organized a storming party, consisting of twelve regiments, and assigned Colonel Emory Upton, of the 121st New York Volunteers, to the command of it. About four o'clock in the afternoon the assault was ordered, Warren's and Wright's corps, with Mott's division of Hancock's corps, to move simultaneously. The movement was prompt, and in a few minutes the fiercest of struggles began. The battle-field was so densely covered with forest that but little could be seen, by any one person, as to the progress made. Meade and I occupied the best position we could get, in rear of Warren.

Warren was repulsed with heavy loss, General J. C. Rice being among the killed. He was not followed, however, by the enemy, and was thereby enabled to reorganize his command as soon as covered from the guns of the enemy. To the left our success was decided, but the advantage was lost by the feeble action of Mott. Upton with his assaulting party pushed forward and crossed the enemy's intrenchments. Turning to the right and left he captured several guns and some hundreds of prisoners. Mott was ordered to his assistance but failed utterly. So much time was lost in trying to get up the troops which were in the right position to reinforce, that I ordered Upton to withdraw; but the officers and men of his command were so averse to giving up the advantage they had gained that I withdrew the order. To relieve them, I ordered a renewal of the assault. By this time Hancock, who had gone with Birney's division to relieve Barlow, had returned, bringing the division with him. His corps was now joined with Warren's and Wright's in this last assault. It was gallantly made, many men getting up to, and over, the works of the enemy; but they were not able to hold them. At night they were withdrawn. Upton brought his prisoners with him, but the guns he had captured he was obliged to abandon.

Upton had gained an important advantage, but a lack in others of the spirit and dash possessed by him lost it to us. Before leaving Washington I had been authorized to promote officers on the field for special acts of gallantry. By this authority I conferred the rank of brigadier-general upon Upton on the spot, and this act was confirmed by the President. Upton had been badly wounded in this fight.

Burnside on the left had got up to within a few hundred yards of Spottsylvania Court House, completely turning Lee's right. He was not aware of the importance of the advantage he had gained, and I, being with the troops where the heavy fighting was, did not know of it at the time. He had gained his position with but little fighting, and almost without loss. Burnside's position now separated him widely from Wright's corps, the corps nearest to him. At night he was ordered to join on to this. This brought him back about a mile, and lost to us an important advantage. I attach no blame to Burnside for this, but I do to myself for not having had a staff officer with him to report to me his position.

The enemy had not dared to come out of his line at any point to follow up his advantage, except in the single instance of his attack on Barlow. Then he was twice repulsed with heavy loss, though he had an entire corps against two brigades. Barlow took up his bridges in the presence of this force.

On the 11th there was no battle and but little firing; none except by Mott who made a reconnoissance to ascertain if there was a weak point in the enemy's line.

I wrote the following letter to General Halleck:

NEAR SPOTTSYLVANIA C. H.,
May 11, 1864 — 8.30 A.M.
MAJOR-GENERAL HALLECK, Chief of Staff of the Army,
Washington, D. C.

We have now ended the 6th day of very hard fighting. The result up to this time is much in our favor. But our losses have been heavy as well as those of the enemy. We have lost to this time eleven general officers killed, wounded and missing, and probably twenty thousand men. I think the loss of the enemy must be greater — we having taken over four thousand prisoners in battle, whilst he has taken from us but few except a few stragglers. I am now sending back to

Belle Plain all my wagons for a fresh supply of provisions and ammunition, and purpose to fight it out on this line if it takes all summer.

The arrival of reinforcements here will be very encouraging to the men, and I hope they will be sent as fast as possible, and in as great numbers. My object in having them sent to Belle Plain was to use them as an escort to our supply trains. If it is more convenient to send them out by train to march from the railroad to Belle Plain or Fredericksburg, send them so.

I am satisfied the enemy are very shaky, and are only kept up to the mark by the greatest exertions on the part of their officers, and by keeping them intrenched in every position they take.

Up to this time there is no indication of any portion of Lee's army being detached for the defence of Richmond.

U. S. GRANT,
Lieut.-General.

And also, I received information, through the War Department, from General Butler that his cavalry under Kautz had cut the railroad south of Petersburg, separating Beauregard from Richmond, and had whipped Hill, killing, wounding and capturing many. Also that he was intrenched, and could maintain himself. On this same day came news from Sheridan to the effect that he had destroyed ten miles of the railroad and telegraph between Lee and Richmond, one and a half million rations, and most of the medical stores for his army.

On the 8th I had directed Sheridan verbally to cut loose from the Army of the Potomac and pass around the left of Lee's army and attack his cavalry and communications, which was successfully executed in the manner I have already described.

Chapter LIII.

HANCOCK'S ASSAULT—LOSSES OF THE CONFEDERATES—
PROMOTIONS RECOMMENDED—DISCOMFITURE OF THE
ENEMY—EWELL'S ATTACK—REDUCING THE ARTILLERY.

IN THE RECONNOISSANCE made by Mott on the 11th, a salient was discovered at the right centre. I determined that
an assault should be made at that point.* Accordingly in the
afternoon Hancock was ordered to move his command by the
rear of Warren and Wright, under cover of night, to Wright's
left, and there form it for an assault at four o'clock the next
morning. The night was dark, it rained heavily, and the road
was difficult, so that it was midnight when he reached the
point where he was to halt. It took most of the night to get
the men in position for their advance in the morning. The
men got but little rest. Burnside was ordered to attack† on

---

the left of the salient at the same hour. I sent two of my staff officers to impress upon him the importance of pushing forward vigorously. Hancock was notified of this. Warren and Wright were ordered to hold themselves in readiness to join in the assault if circumstances made it advisable. I occupied a central position most convenient for receiving information from all points. Hancock put Barlow on his left, in double column, and Birney to his right. Mott followed Birney, and Gibbon was held in reserve.

The morning of the 12th opened foggy, delaying the start more than half an hour.

The ground over which Hancock had to pass to reach the enemy, was ascending and heavily wooded to within two or three hundred yards of the enemy's intrenchments. In front of Birney there was also a marsh to cross. But, notwithstanding all these difficulties, the troops pushed on in quick time without firing a gun, and when within four or five hundred yards of the enemy's line broke out in loud cheers, and with a rush went up to and over the breastworks. Barlow and Birney entered almost simultaneously. Here a desperate hand-to-hand conflict took place. The men of the two sides were too close together to fire, but used their guns as clubs. The hand conflict was soon over. Hancock's corps captured some four thousand prisoners—among them a division and a brigade commander—twenty or more guns with their horses, caissons, and ammunition, several thousand stand of arms, and many colors. Hancock, as soon as the hand-to-hand conflict was over, turned the guns of the enemy against him and advanced inside the rebel lines. About six o'clock I ordered

---

inst. Let your preparations for this attack be conducted with the utmost secrecy and veiled entirely from the enemy.

I send two of my staff officers; Colonels Comstock and Babcock, in whom I have great confidence and who are acquainted with the direction the attack is to be made from here, to remain with you and General Hancock with instructions to render you every assistance in their power. Generals Warren and Wright will hold their corps as close to the enemy as possible, to take advantage of any diversion caused by yours and Hancock's attack, and will push in their whole force if any opportunity presents itself.

U. S. GRANT,
Lieut.-General.

Warren's corps to the support of Hancock's. Burnside, on the left, had advanced up east of the salient to the very parapet of the enemy. Potter, commanding one of his divisions, got over but was not able to remain there. However, he inflicted a heavy loss upon the enemy; but not without loss in return.

This victory was important, and one that Lee could not afford to leave us in full possession of. He made the most strenuous efforts to regain the position he had lost. Troops were brought up from his left and attacked Hancock furiously. Hancock was forced to fall back: but he did so slowly, with his face to the enemy, inflicting on him heavy loss, until behind the breastworks he had captured. These he turned, facing them the other way, and continued to hold. Wright was ordered up to reinforce Hancock, and arrived by six o'clock. He was wounded soon after coming up but did not relinquish the command of his corps, although the fighting lasted until one o'clock the next morning. At eight o'clock Warren was ordered up again, but was so slow in making his dispositions that his orders were frequently repeated, and with emphasis. At eleven o'clock I gave Meade written orders to relieve Warren from his command if he failed to move promptly. Hancock placed batteries on high ground in his rear, which he used against the enemy, firing over the heads of his own troops.

Burnside accomplished but little on our left of a positive nature, but negatively a great deal. He kept Lee from reinforcing his centre from that quarter. If the 5th corps, or rather if Warren, had been as prompt as Wright was with the 6th corps, better results might have been obtained.

Lee massed heavily from his left flank on the broken point of his line. Five times during the day he assaulted furiously, but without dislodging our troops from their new position. His losses must have been fearful. Sometimes the belligerents would be separated by but a few feet. In one place a tree, eighteen inches in diameter, was cut entirely down by musket balls. All the trees between the lines were very much cut to pieces by artillery and musketry. It was three o'clock next morning before the fighting ceased. Some of our troops had then been twenty hours under fire. In this engagement we did not lose a single organization, not even a company. The enemy lost one division with its commander, one brigade and one regiment, with heavy losses elsewhere.* Our losses were heavy, but, as stated, no whole company was captured. At night Lee took a position in rear of his former one, and by the following morning he was strongly intrenched in it.

Warren's corps was now temporarily broken up, Cutler's division sent to Wright, and Griffin's to Hancock. Meade ordered his chief of staff, General Humphreys, to remain with Warren and the remaining division, and authorized him to give it orders in his name.

During the day I was passing along the line from wing to wing continuously. About the centre stood a house which proved to be occupied by an old lady and her daughter. She showed such unmistakable signs of being strongly Union that I stopped. She said she had not seen a Union flag for so long a time that it did her heart good to look upon it again. She said her husband and son, being Union men, had had to leave early in the war, and were now somewhere in the Union army, if alive. She was without food or nearly so, so I ordered rations issued to her, and promised to find out if I could where the husband and son were.

There was no fighting on the 13th, further than a little skirmishing between Mott's division and the enemy. I was afraid that Lee might be moving out, and I did not want him to go without my knowing it. The indications were that he was moving, but it was found that he was only taking his new position back from the salient that had been captured. Our dead were buried this day. Mott's division was reduced to a brigade, and assigned to Birney's division.

---

*HEADQUARTERS ARMIES U. S.,
May 12, 1864, 6.30 P.M.

MAJOR-GENERAL HALLECK,
		Washington, D.C.

The eighth day of the battle closes, leaving between three and four thousand prisoners in our hands for the day's work, including two general officers, and over thirty pieces of artillery. The enemy are obstinate, and seem to have found the last ditch. We have lost no organizations, not even that of a company, whilst we have destroyed and captured one division (Johnson's), one brigade (Doles'), and one regiment entire from the enemy.

U. S. GRANT,
Lieut.-General.

During this day I wrote to Washington recommending Sherman and Meade* for promotion to the grade of Major-General in the regular army; Hancock for Brigadier-General; Wright, Gibbon and Humphreys to be Major-Generals of Volunteers; and Upton and Carroll to be Brigadiers. Upton had already been named as such, but the appointment had to be confirmed by the Senate on the nomination of the President.

The night of the 13th Warren and Wright were moved by the rear to the left of Burnside. The night was very dark and it rained heavily, the roads were so bad that the troops had to cut trees and corduroy the road a part of the way, to get through. It was midnight before they got to the point where they were to halt, and daylight before the troops could be organized to advance to their position in line. They gained their position in line, however, without any fighting, except a little in Wright's front. Here Upton had to contend for an elevation which we wanted and which the enemy was not

---

*SPOTTSYLVANIA C. H., *May* 13, 1864.
HON. E. M. STANTON, SECRETARY OF WAR,
Washington, D. C.

I beg leave to recommend the following promotions be made for gallant and distinguished services in the last eight days' battles, to wit: Brigadier-General H. G. Wright and Brigadier-General John Gibbon to be Major-Generals; Colonel S. S. Carroll, 8th Ohio Volunteers; Colonel E. Upton, 121st New York Volunteers; Colonel William McCandless, 2d Pennsylvania Reserves, to be Brigadier-Generals. I would also recommend Major-General W. S. Hancock for Brigadier-General in the regular army. His services and qualifications are eminently deserving of this recognition. In making these recommendations I do not wish the claims of General G. M. Dodge for promotion forgotten, but recommend his name to be sent in at the same time. I would also ask to have General Wright assigned to the command of the Sixth Army Corps. I would further ask the confirmation of General Humphreys to the rank of Major-General.

General Meade has more than met my most sanguine expectations. He and Sherman are the fittest officers for large commands I have come in contact with. If their services can be rewarded by promotion to the rank of Major-Generals in the regular army the honor would be worthily bestowed, and I would feel personally gratified. I would not like to see one of these promotions at this time without seeing both.

U. S. GRANT,
Lieut.-General.

disposed to yield. Upton first drove the enemy, and was then repulsed in turn. Ayres coming to his support with his brigade (of Griffin's division, Warren's corps), the position was secured and fortified. There was no more battle during the 14th. This brought our line east of the Court House and running north and south and facing west.

During the night of the 14th–15th Lee moved to cover this new front. This left Hancock without an enemy confronting him. He was brought to the rear of our new centre, ready to be moved in any direction he might be wanted.

On the 15th news came from Butler and Averill. The former reported the capture of the outer works at Drury's Bluff, on the James River, and that his cavalry had cut the railroad and telegraph south of Richmond on the Danville road: and the latter, the destruction of a depot of supplies at Dublin, West Virginia, and the breaking of New River Bridge on the Virginia and Tennessee Railroad. The next day news came from Sherman and Sheridan. Sherman had forced Johnston out of Dalton, Georgia, and was following him south. The report from Sheridan embraced his operations up to his passing the outer defences of Richmond. The prospect must now have been dismal in Richmond. The road and telegraph were cut between the capital and Lee. The roads and wires were cut in every direction from the rebel capital. Temporarily that city was cut off from all communication with the outside except by courier. This condition of affairs, however, was of but short duration.

I wrote Halleck:

> Near Spottsylvania C. H.,
> *May* 16, 1864, 8 a.m.
>
> Major-General Halleck,
> Washington, D. C.:
> We have had five days almost constant rain without any prospect yet of it clearing up. The roads have now become so impassable that ambulances with wounded men can no longer run between here and Fredericksburg. All offensive operations necessarily cease until we can have twenty-four hours of dry weather. The army is in the best of spirits, and feel the greatest confidence of ultimate success.
>
> * * * * * *
>
> You can assure the President and Secretary of War that the ele-

ments alone have suspended hostilities, and that it is in no manner due to weakness or exhaustion on our part.

U. S. GRANT,
Lieut.-General.

The condition of the roads was such that nothing was done on the 17th. But that night Hancock and Wright were to make a night march back to their old positions, and to make an assault at four o'clock in the morning. Lee got troops back in time to protect his old line, so the assault was unsuccessful. On this day (18th) the news was almost as discouraging to us as it had been two days before in the rebel capital. As stated above, Hancock's and Wright's corps had made an unsuccessful assault. News came that Sigel had been defeated at New Market, badly, and was retreating down the valley. Not two hours before, I had sent the inquiry to Halleck whether Sigel could not get to Staunton to stop supplies coming from there to Lee. I asked at once that Sigel might be relieved, and some one else put in his place. Hunter's name was suggested, and I heartily approved. Further news from Butler reported him driven from Drury's Bluff, but still in possession of the Petersburg road. Banks had been defeated in Louisiana, relieved, and Canby put in his place. This change of commander was not on my suggestion. All this news was very discouraging. All of it must have been known by the enemy before it was by me. In fact, the good news (for the enemy) must have been known to him at the moment I thought he was in despair, and his anguish had been already relieved when we were enjoying his supposed discomfiture. But this was no time for repining. I immediately gave orders for a movement by the left flank, on towards Richmond, to commence on the night of the 19th. I also asked Halleck to secure the co-operation of the navy in changing our base of supplies from Fredericksburg to Port Royal, on the Rappahannock.

Up to this time I had received no reinforcements, except six thousand raw troops under Brigadier-General Robert O. Tyler, just arrived. They had not yet joined their command, Hancock's corps, but were on our right. This corps had been brought to the rear of the centre, ready to move in any direction. Lee, probably suspecting some move on my part, and seeing our right entirely abandoned, moved Ewell's corps about five o'clock in the afternoon, with Early's as a reserve, to attack us in that quarter. Tyler had come up from Fredericksburg, and had been halted on the road to the right of our line, near Kitching's brigade of Warren's corps. Tyler received the attack with his raw troops, and they maintained their position, until reinforced, in a manner worthy of veterans.

Hancock was in a position to reinforce speedily, and was the soldier to do it without waiting to make dispositions. Birney was thrown to Tyler's right and Crawford to his left, with Gibbon as a reserve; and Ewell was whirled back speedily and with heavy loss.

Warren had been ordered to get on Ewell's flank and in his rear, to cut him off from his intrenchments. But his efforts were so feeble that under the cover of night Ewell got back with only the loss of a few hundred prisoners, besides his killed and wounded. The army being engaged until after dark, I rescinded the order for the march by our left flank that night.

As soon as it was discovered that the enemy were coming out to attack, I naturally supposed they would detach a force to destroy our trains. The withdrawal of Hancock from the right uncovered one road from Spottsylvania to Fredericksburg over which trains drew our supplies. This was guarded by a division of colored troops, commanded by General Ferrero, belonging to Burnside's corps. Ferrero was therefore promptly notified, and ordered to throw his cavalry pickets out to the south and be prepared to meet the enemy if he should come; if he had to retreat to do so towards Fredericksburg. The enemy did detach as expected, and captured twenty-five or thirty wagons which, however, were soon retaken.

In consequence of the disasters that had befallen us in the past few days, Lee could be reinforced largely, and I had no doubt he would be. Beauregard had come up from the south with troops to guard the Confederate capital when it was in danger. Butler being driven back, most of the troops could be sent to Lee. Hoke was no longer needed in North Carolina; and Sigel's troops having gone back to Cedar Creek, whipped, many troops could be spared from the valley.

The Wilderness and Spottsylvania battles convinced me that we had more artillery than could ever be brought into action at any one time. It occupied much of the road in marching, and taxed the trains in bringing up forage. Artillery is very useful when it can be brought into action, but it is a very burdensome luxury where it cannot be used. Before leaving Spottsylvania, therefore, I sent back to the defences of Washington over one hundred pieces of artillery, with the horses and caissons. This relieved the roads over which we were to march of more than two hundred six-horse teams, and still left us more artillery than could be advantageously used. In fact, before reaching the James River I again reduced the artillery with the army largely.

I believed that, if one corps of the army was exposed on the road to Richmond, and at a distance from the main army, Lee would endeavor to attack the exposed corps before reinforcements could come up; in which case the main army could follow Lee up and attack him before he had time to intrench. So I issued the following orders:

NEAR SPOTTSYLVANIA C. H., VA.,
May 18, 1864.

MAJOR-GENERAL MEADE,
    Commanding Army of the Potomac.

Before daylight to-morrow morning I propose to draw Hancock and Burnside from the position they now hold, and put Burnside to the left of Wright. Wright and Burnside should then force their way up as close to the enemy as they can get without a general engagement, or with a general engagement if the enemy will come out of their works to fight, and intrench. Hancock should march and take up a position as if in support of the two left corps. To-morrow night, at twelve or one o'clock, he will be moved south-east with all his force and as much cavalry as can be given to him, to get as far towards Richmond on the line of the Fredericksburg Railroad as he can make, fighting the enemy in whatever force he can find him. If the enemy make a general move to meet this, they will be followed by the other three corps of the army, and attacked, if possible, before time is given to intrench.

Suitable directions will at once be given for all trains and surplus artillery to conform to this movement.

U. S. GRANT.

On the 20th, Lee showing no signs of coming out of his lines, orders were renewed for a left-flank movement, to commence after night.

Chapter LIV.

WE WERE NOW to operate in a different country from
any we had before seen in Virginia. The roads were
wide and good, and the country well cultivated. No men were
seen except those bearing arms, even the black man having
been sent away. The country, however, was new to us, and
we had neither guides nor maps to tell us where the roads
were, or where they led to. Engineer and staff officers were
put to the dangerous duty of supplying the place of both
maps and guides. By reconnoitring they were enabled to locate the roads in the vicinity of each army corps. Our course
was south, and we took all roads leading in that direction
which would not separate the army too widely.

Hancock who had the lead had marched easterly to
Guiney's Station, on the Fredericksburg Railroad, thence
southerly to Bowling Green and Milford. He was at Milford
by the night of the 21st. Here he met a detachment of Pickett's division coming from Richmond to reinforce Lee. They
were speedily driven away, and several hundred captured.
Warren followed on the morning of the 21st, and reached
Guiney's Station that night without molestation. Burnside
and Wright were retained at Spottsylvania to keep up the appearance of an intended assault, and to hold Lee, if possible,
while Hancock and Warren should get start enough to interpose between him and Richmond.

Lee had now a superb opportunity to take the initiative
either by attacking Wright and Burnside alone, or by following by the Telegraph Road and striking Hancock's and
Warren's corps, or even Hancock's alone, before reinforcements could come up. But he did not avail himself of either
opportunity. He seemed really to be misled as to my designs;
but moved by his interior line—the Telegraph Road—to
make sure of keeping between his capital and the Army of the

Potomac. He never again had such an opportunity of dealing a heavy blow.

The evening of the 21st Burnside, 9th corps, moved out followed by Wright, 6th corps. Burnside was to take the Telegraph Road; but finding Stanard's Ford, over the Po, fortified and guarded, he turned east to the road taken by Hancock and Warren without an attempt to dislodge the enemy. The night of the 21st I had my headquarters near the 6th corps, at Guiney's Station, and the enemy's cavalry was between us and Hancock. There was a slight attack on Burnside's and Wright's corps as they moved out of their lines; but it was easily repulsed. The object probably was only to make sure that we were not leaving a force to follow upon the rear of the Confederates.

By the morning of the 22d Burnside and Wright were at Guiney's Station. Hancock's corps had now been marching and fighting continuously for several days, not having had rest even at night much of the time. They were, therefore, permitted to rest during the 22d. But Warren was pushed to Harris's Store, directly west of Milford, and connected with it by a good road, and Burnside was sent to New Bethel Church. Wright's corps was still back at Guiney's Station.

I issued the following order for the movement of the troops the next day:

NEW BETHEL, VA., *May* 22, 1864.

MAJOR-GENERAL MEADE,

        Commanding Army of the Potomac.

Direct corps commanders to hold their troops in readiness to march at five A.M. to-morrow. At that hour each command will send out cavalry and infantry on all roads to their front leading south, and ascertain, if possible, where the enemy is. If beyond the South Anna, the 5th and 6th corps will march to the forks of the road, where one branch leads to Beaver Dam Station, the other to Jericho Bridge, then south by roads reaching the Anna, as near to and east of Hawkins Creek as they can be found.

The 2d corps will move to Chesterfield Ford. The 9th corps will be directed to move at the same time to Jericho Bridge. The map only shows two roads for the four corps to march upon, but, no doubt, by the use of plantation roads, and pressing in guides, others can be found, to give one for each corps.

The troops will follow their respective reconnoitring parties. The trains will be moved at the same time to Milford Station.

Headquarters will follow the 9th corps.

U. S. GRANT,
Lieut.-General.

Warren's corps was moved from Harris's Store to Jericho Ford, Wright's following. Warren arrived at the ford early in the afternoon, and by five o'clock effected a crossing under the protection of sharp-shooters. The men had to wade in water up to their waists. As soon as enough troops were over to guard the ford, pontoons were laid and the artillery and the rest of the troops crossed. The line formed was almost perpendicular to the course of the river—Crawford on the left, next to the river, Griffin in the centre, and Cutler on the right. Lee was found intrenched along the front of their line. The whole of Hill's corps was sent against Warren's right before it had got in position. A brigade of Cutler's division was driven back, the enemy following, but assistance coming up the enemy was in turn driven back into his trenches with heavy loss in killed and wounded, with about five hundred prisoners left in our hands. By night Wright's corps was up ready to reinforce Warren.

On the 23d Hancock's corps was moved to the wooden bridge which spans the North Anna River just west of where the Fredericksburg Railroad crosses. It was near night when the troops arrived. They found the bridge guarded, with troops intrenched, on the north side. Hancock sent two brigades, Egan's and Pierce's, to the right and left, and when properly disposed they charged simultaneously. The bridge was carried quickly, the enemy retreating over it so hastily that many were shoved into the river, and some of them were drowned. Several hundred prisoners were captured. The hour was so late that Hancock did not cross until next morning.

Burnside's corps was moved by a middle road running between those described above, and which strikes the North Anna at Ox Ford, midway between Telegraph Road and Jericho Ford. The hour of its arrival was too late to cross that night.

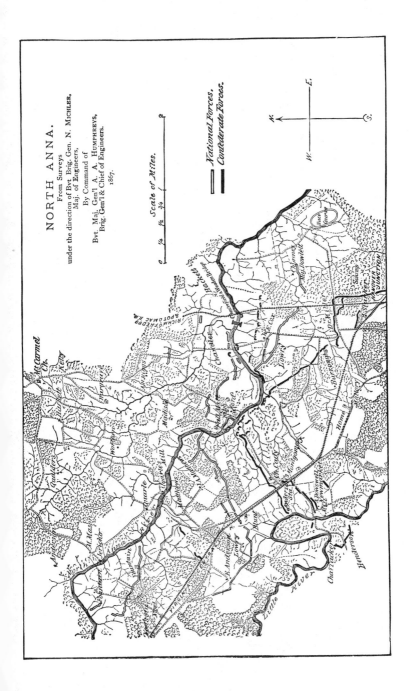

NORTH ANNA.

From Surveys

under the direction of Bvt. Brig. Gen. N. MICHLER,
Maj. of Engineers,

By Command of

Bvt. Maj. Gen'l A. A. HUMPHREYS,
Brig. Gen'l & Chief of Engineers.

1867.

Scale of Miles.

━━━ National Forces.
━━━ Confederate Forces.

On the 24th Hancock's corps crossed to the south side of the river without opposition, and formed line facing nearly west. The railroad in rear was taken possession of and destroyed as far as possible. Wright's corps crossed at Jericho early the same day, and took position to the right of Warren's corps, extending south of the Virginia Central Railroad. This road was torn up for a considerable distance to the rear (west), the ties burned, and the rails bent and twisted by heating them over the burning ties. It was found, however, that Burnside's corps could not cross at Ox Ford. Lee had taken a position with his centre on the river at this point, with the two wings thrown back, his line making an acute angle where it overlooked the river.

Before the exact position of the whole of Lee's line was accurately known, I directed Hancock and Warren each to send a brigade to Ox Ford by the south side of the river. They found the enemy too strong to justify a serious attack. A third ford was found between Ox Ford and Jericho. Burnside was directed to cross a division over this ford, and to send one division to Hancock. Crittenden was crossed by this newly-discovered ford, and formed up the river to connect with Crawford's left. Potter joined Hancock by way of the wooden bridge. Crittenden had a severe engagement with some of Hill's corps on his crossing the river, and lost heavily. When joined to Warren's corps he was no further molested. Burnside still guarded Ox Ford from the north side.

Lee now had his entire army south of the North Anna. Our lines covered his front, with the six miles separating the two wings guarded by but a single division. To get from one wing to the other the river would have to be crossed twice. Lee could reinforce any part of his line from all points of it in a very short march; or could concentrate the whole of it wherever he might choose to assault. We were, for the time, practically two armies besieging.

Lee had been reinforced, and was being reinforced, largely. About this time the very troops whose coming I had predicted, had arrived or were coming in. Pickett with a full division from Richmond was up; Hoke from North Carolina had come with a brigade; and Breckinridge was there: in all probably not less than fifteen thousand men. But he did not attempt to drive us from the field.

On the 22d or 23d I received dispatches from Washington saying that Sherman had taken Kingston, crossed the Etowah River and was advancing into Georgia.

I was seated at the time on the porch of a fine plantation house waiting for Burnside's corps to pass. Meade and his staff, besides my own staff, were with me. The lady of the house, a Mrs. Tyler, and an elderly lady, were present. Burnside seeing us, came up on the porch, his big spurs and saber rattling as he walked. He touched his hat politely to the ladies, and remarked that he supposed they had never seen so many "live Yankees" before in their lives. The elderly lady spoke up promptly saying, "Oh yes, I have; many more." "Where?" said Burnside. "In Richmond." Prisoners, of course, was understood.

I read my dispatch aloud, when it was received. This threw the younger lady into tears. I found the information she had received (and I suppose it was the information generally in circulation through the South) was that Lee was driving us from the State in the most demoralized condition, and that in the South-west our troops were but little better than prisoners of war. Seeing our troops moving south was ocular proof that a part of her information was incorrect, and she asked me if my news from Sherman was true. I assured her that there was no doubt about it. I left a guard to protect the house from intrusion until the troops should have all passed, and assured her that if her husband was in hiding she could bring him in and he should be protected also. But I presume he was in the Confederate army.

On the 25th I gave orders, through Halleck, to Hunter, who had relieved Sigel, to move up the Valley of Virginia, cross over the Blue Ridge to Charlottesville and go as far as Lynchburg if possible, living upon the country and cutting the railroads and canal as he went. After doing this he could find his way back to his base, or join me.

On the same day news was received that Lee was falling back on Richmond. This proved not to be true. But we could do nothing where we were unless Lee would assume the offensive. I determined, therefore, to draw out of our present position and make one more effort to get between him and Richmond. I had no expectation now, however, of succeeding in this; but I did expect to hold him far enough west to enable me to reach the James River high up. Sheridan was now again with the Army of the Potomac.

On the 26th I informed the government at Washington of the position of the two armies; of the reinforcements the enemy had received; of the move I proposed to make;* and directed that our base of supplies should be shifted to White House, on the Pamunkey. The wagon train and guards moved

---

*QUARLES' MILLS, VA., *May* 26, 1864.

MAJOR-GENERAL HALLECK,
      Washington, D. C.

The relative position of the two armies is now as follows: Lee's right rests on a swamp east of the Richmond and Fredericksburg road and south of the North Anna, his centre on the river at Ox Ford, and his left at Little River with the crossings of Little River guarded as far up as we have gone. Hancock with his corps and one division of the 9th corps crossed at Chesterfield Ford and covers the right wing of Lee's army. One division of the 9th corps is on the north bank of the Anna at Ox Ford, with bridges above and below at points nearest to it where both banks are held by us, so that it could reinforce either wing of our army with equal facility. The 5th and 6th corps with one division of the 9th corps run from the south bank of the Anna from a short distance above Ox Ford to Little River, and parallel with and near to the enemy.

To make a direct attack from either wing would cause a slaughter of our men that even success would not justify. To turn the enemy by his right, between the two Annas, is impossible on account of the swamp upon which his right rests. To turn him by the left leaves Little River, New Found River and South Anna River, all of them streams presenting considerable obstacles to the movement of our army, to be crossed. I have determined therefore to turn the enemy's right by crossing at or near Hanover Town. This crosses all three streams at once, and leaves us still where we can draw supplies.

During the last night the teams and artillery not in position, belonging to the right wing of our army, and one division of that wing were quietly withdrawn to the north bank of the river and moved down to the rear of the left. As soon as it is dark this division with most of the cavalry will commence a forced march for Hanover Town to seize and hold the crossings. The balance of the right wing will withdraw at the same hour, and follow as rapidly as possible. The left wing will also withdraw from the south bank of the river to-night and follow in rear of the right wing.

Lee's army is really whipped. The prisoners we now take show it, and the action of his army shows it unmistakably. A battle with them outside of intrenchments cannot be had. Our men feel that they have gained the *morale*

directly from Port Royal to White House. Supplies moved around by water, guarded by the navy. Orders had previously been sent, through Halleck, for Butler to send Smith's corps to White House. This order was repeated on the 25th, with directions that they should be landed on the north side of the Pamunkey, and marched until they joined the Army of the Potomac.

It was a delicate move to get the right wing of the Army of the Potomac from its position south of the North Anna in the presence of the enemy. To accomplish it. I issued the following order:

QUARLES' MILLS, VA., May 25, 1864.

MAJOR GENERAL MEADE,
     Commanding A. P.

Direct Generals Warren and Wright to withdraw all their teams and artillery, not in position, to the north side of the river to-morrow. Send that belonging to General Wright's corps as far on the road to Hanover Town as it can go, without attracting attention to the fact. Send with it Wright's best division or division under his ablest commander. Have their places filled up in the line so if possible the enemy will not notice their withdrawal. Send the cavalry to-morrow afternoon, or as much of it as you may deem necessary, to watch and seize, if they can, Littlepage's Bridge and Taylor's Ford, and to remain on one or other side of the river at these points until the infantry and artillery all pass. As soon as it is dark to-morrow night start the division which you withdraw first from Wright's

---

over the enemy, and attack him with confidence. I may be mistaken, but I feel that our success over Lee's army is already assured. The promptness and rapidity with which you have forwarded reinforcements has contributed largely to the feeling of confidence inspired in our men, and to break down that of the enemy.

We are destroying all the rails we can on the Central and Fredericksburg roads. I want to leave a gap on the roads north of Richmond so big that to get a single track they will have to import rail from elsewhere.

Even if a crossing is not effected at Hanover Town it will probably be necessary for us to move on down the Pamunkey until a crossing is effected. I think it advisable therefore to change our base of supplies from Port Royal to the White House. I wish you would direct this change at once, and also direct Smith to put the railroad bridge there in condition for crossing troops and artillery and leave men to hold it.

U. S. GRANT,
Lieut.-General.

corps to make a forced march to Hanover Town, taking with them no teams to impede their march. At the same time this division starts commence withdrawing all of the 5th and 6th corps from the south side of the river, and march them for the same place. The two divisions of the 9th corps not now with Hancock, may be moved down the north bank of the river where they will be handy to support Hancock if necessary, or will be that much on their road to follow the 5th and 6th corps. Hancock should hold his command in readiness to follow as soon as the way is clear for him. To-morrow it will leave nothing for him to do, but as soon as he can he should get all his teams and spare artillery on the road or roads which he will have to take. As soon as the troops reach Hanover Town they should get possession of all the crossings they can in that neighborhood. I think it would be well to make a heavy cavalry demonstration on the enemy's left, to-morrow afternoon, also.

U. S. GRANT,

Lieut.-General.

Wilson's division of cavalry was brought up from the left and moved by our right south to Little River. Here he manœuvred to give the impression that we were going to attack the left flank of Lee's army.

Under cover of night our right wing was withdrawn to the north side of the river, Lee being completely deceived by Wilson's feint. On the afternoon of the 26th Sheridan moved, sending Gregg's and Torbert's cavalry to Taylor's and Littlepage's fords towards Hanover. As soon as it was dark both divisions moved quietly to Hanover Ferry, leaving small guards behind to keep up the impression that crossings were to be attempted in the morning. Sheridan was followed by a division of infantry under General Russell. On the morning of the 27th the crossing was effected with but little loss, the enemy losing thirty or forty, taken prisoners. Thus a position was secured south of the Pamunkey.

Russell stopped at the crossing while the cavalry pushed on to Hanover Town. Here Barringer's, formerly Gordon's, brigade of rebel cavalry was encountered, but it was speedily driven away.

Warren's and Wright's corps were moved by the rear of Burnside's and Hancock's corps. When out of the way these latter corps followed, leaving pickets confronting the enemy. Wilson's cavalry followed last, watching all the fords until everything had recrossed; then taking up the pontoons and destroying other bridges, became the rear-guard.

Two roads were traversed by the troops in this move. The one nearest to and north of the North Anna and Pamunkey was taken by Wright, followed by Hancock. Warren, followed by Burnside, moved by a road farther north, and longer. The trains moved by a road still farther north, and had to travel a still greater distance. All the troops that had crossed the Pamunkey on the morning of the 27th remained quiet during the rest of the day, while the troops north of that stream marched to reach the crossing that had been secured for them.

Lee had evidently been deceived by our movement from North Anna; for on the morning of the 27th he telegraphed to Richmond: "Enemy crossed to north side, and cavalry and infantry crossed at Hanover Town." The troops that had then crossed left his front the night of the 25th.

The country we were now in was a difficult one to move troops over. The streams were numerous, deep and sluggish, sometimes spreading out into swamps grown up with impenetrable growths of trees and underbrush. The banks were generally low and marshy, making the streams difficult to approach except where there were roads and bridges.

Hanover Town is about twenty miles from Richmond. There are two roads leading there; the most direct and shortest one crossing the Chickahominy at Meadow Bridge, near the Virginia Central Railroad, the second going by New and Old Cold Harbor. A few miles out from Hanover Town there is a third road by way of Mechanicsville to Richmond. New Cold Harbor was important to us because while there we both covered the roads back to White House (where our supplies came from), and the roads south-east over which we would have to pass to get to the James River below the Richmond defences.

On the morning of the 28th the army made an early start, and by noon all had crossed except Burnside's corps. This was left on the north side temporarily to guard the large wagon train. A line was at once formed extending south from the river, Wright's corps on the right, Hancock's in the centre,

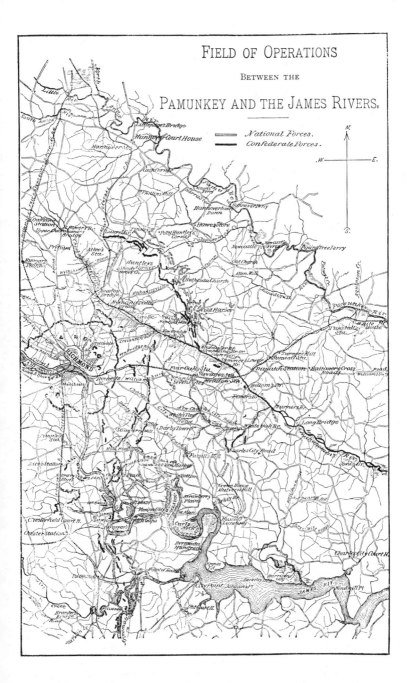

FIELD OF OPERATIONS

BETWEEN THE

PAMUNKEY AND THE JAMES RIVERS.

National Forces.
Confederate Forces.

and Warren's on the left, ready to meet the enemy if he should come.

At the same time Sheridan was directed to reconnoitre towards Mechanicsville to find Lee's position. At Hawes' Shop, just where the middle road leaves the direct road to Richmond, he encountered the Confederate cavalry dismounted and partially intrenched. Gregg attacked with his division, but was unable to move the enemy. In the evening Custer came up with a brigade. The attack was now renewed, the cavalry dismounting and charging as infantry. This time the assault was successful, both sides losing a considerable number of men. But our troops had to bury the dead, and found that more Confederate than Union soldiers had been killed. The position was easily held, because our infantry was near.

On the 29th a reconnoissance was made in force, to find the position of Lee. Wright's corps pushed to Hanover Court House. Hancock's corps pushed toward Totopotomoy Creek; Warren's corps to the left on the Shady Grove Church Road, while Burnside was held in reserve. Our advance was pushed forward three miles on the left with but little fighting. There was now an appearance of a movement past our left flank, and Sheridan was sent to meet it.

On the 30th Hancock moved to the Totopotomoy, where he found the enemy strongly fortified. Wright was moved to the right of Hancock's corps, and Burnside was brought forward and crossed, taking position to the left of Hancock. Warren moved up near Huntley Corners on the Shady Grove Church Road. There was some skirmishing along the centre, and in the evening Early attacked Warren with some vigor, driving him back at first, and threatening to turn our left flank. As the best means of reinforcing the left, Hancock was ordered to attack in his front. He carried and held the rifle-pits. While this was going on Warren got his men up, repulsed Early, and drove him more than a mile.

On this day I wrote to Halleck ordering all the pontoons in Washington to be sent to City Point. In the evening news was received of the arrival of Smith with his corps at White House. I notified Meade, in writing, as follows:

NEAR HAWES' SHOP, VA.,
6.40 P.M., *May* 30, 1864.

MAJOR-GENERAL MEADE,
    Commanding A. P.

General Smith will debark his force at the White House to-night and start up the south bank of the Pamunkey at an early hour, probably at 3 A.M. in the morning. It is not improbable that the enemy, being aware of Smith's movement, will be feeling to get on our left flank for the purpose of cutting him off, or by a dash to crush him and get back before we are aware of it. Sheridan ought to be notified to watch the enemy's movements well out towards Cold Harbor, and also on the Mechanicsville road. Wright should be got well massed on Hancock's right, so that, if it becomes necessary, he can take the place of the latter readily whilst troops are being thrown east of the Totopotomoy if necessary.

I want Sheridan to send a cavalry force of at least half a brigade, if not a whole brigade, at 5 A.M. in the morning, to communicate with Smith and to return with him. I will send orders for Smith by the messenger you send to Sheridan with his orders.

U. S. GRANT.

I also notified Smith of his danger, and the precautions that would be taken to protect him.

The night of the 30th Lee's position was substantially from Atlee's Station on the Virginia Central Railroad south and east to the vicinity of Cold Harbor. Ours was: The left of Warren's corps was on the Shady Grove Road, extending to the Mechanicsville Road and about three miles south of the Totopotomoy. Burnside to his right, then Hancock, and Wright on the extreme right, extending towards Hanover Court House, six miles south-east of it. Sheridan with two divisions of cavalry was watching our left front towards Cold Harbor. Wilson with his division on our right was sent to get on the Virginia Central Railroad and destroy it as far back as possible. He got possession of Hanover Court House the next day after a skirmish with Young's cavalry brigade. The enemy attacked Sheridan's pickets, but reinforcements were sent up and the attack was speedily repulsed and the enemy followed some distance towards Cold Harbor.

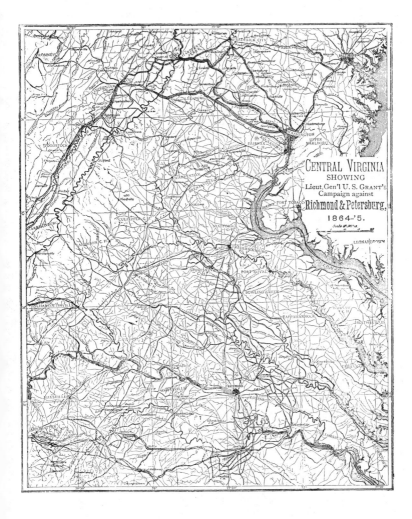

CENTRAL VIRGINIA
SHOWING
Lieut. Gen'l U. S. Grant's
Campaign against
Richmond & Petersburg,
1864-'5.
Scale of Miles.

Chapter LV.

ADVANCE ON COLD HARBOR—AN ANECDOTE OF THE
WAR—BATTLE OF COLD HARBOR—CORRESPONDENCE
WITH LEE—RETROSPECTIVE.

ON THE 31ST Sheridan advanced to near Old Cold Harbor. He found it intrenched and occupied by cavalry and
infantry. A hard fight ensued but the place was carried. The
enemy well knew the importance of Cold Harbor to us, and
seemed determined that we should not hold it. He returned
with such a large force that Sheridan was about withdrawing
without making any effort to hold it against such odds; but
about the time he commenced the evacuation he received
orders to hold the place at all hazards, until reinforcements
could be sent to him. He speedily turned the rebel works to
face against them and placed his men in position for defence.
Night came on before the enemy was ready for assault.

Wright's corps was ordered early in the evening to march
directly to Cold Harbor passing by the rear of the army. It
was expected to arrive by daylight or before; but the night
was dark and the distance great, so that it was nine o'clock the
1st of June before it reached its destination. Before the arrival
of Wright the enemy had made two assaults on Sheridan,
both of which were repulsed with heavy loss to the enemy.
Wright's corps coming up, there was no further assault on
Cold Harbor.

Smith, who was coming up from White House, was also
directed to march directly to Cold Harbor, and was expected
early on the morning of the 1st of June; but by some blunder
the order which reached Smith directed him to Newcastle instead of Cold Harbor. Through this blunder Smith did not
reach his destination until three o'clock in the afternoon, and
then with tired and worn-out men from their long and dusty
march. He landed twelve thousand five hundred men from
Butler's command, but a division was left at White House
temporarily and many men had fallen out of ranks in their
long march.

Before the removal of Wright's corps from our right, after dark on the 31st, the two lines, Federal and Confederate, were so close together at that point that either side could detect directly any movement made by the other. Finding at daylight that Wright had left his front, Lee evidently divined that he had gone to our left. At all events, soon after light on the 1st of June Anderson, who commanded the corps on Lee's left, was seen moving along Warren's front. Warren was ordered to attack him vigorously in flank, while Wright was directed to move out and get on his front. Warren fired his artillery at the enemy; but lost so much time in making ready that the enemy got by, and at three o'clock he reported the enemy was strongly intrenched in his front, and besides his lines were so long that he had no mass of troops to move with. He seemed to have forgotten that lines in rear of an army hold themselves while their defenders are fighting in their front. Wright reconnoitred some distance to his front: but the enemy finding Old Cold Harbor already taken had halted and fortified some distance west.

By six o'clock in the afternoon Wright and Smith were ready to make an assault. In front of both the ground was clear for several hundred yards, and then became wooded. Both charged across this open space and into the wood, capturing and holding the first line of rifle-pits of the enemy, and also capturing seven or eight hundred prisoners.

While this was going on, the enemy charged Warren three separate times with vigor, but were repulsed each time with loss. There was no officer more capable, nor one more prompt in acting, than Warren when the enemy forced him to it. There was also an attack upon Hancock's and Burnside's corps at the same time; but it was feeble and probably only intended to relieve Anderson who was being pressed by Wright and Smith.

During the night the enemy made frequent attacks with the view of dispossessing us of the important position we had gained, but without effecting their object.

Hancock was moved from his place in line during the night and ordered to the left of Wright. I expected to take the offensive on the morning of the 2d, but the night was so dark, the heat and dust so excessive and the roads so intricate and

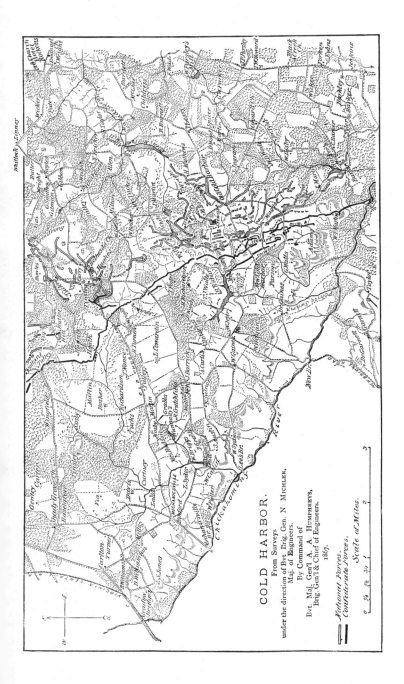

COLD HARBOR.

From Surveys
under the direction of Bvt. Brig. Gen. N. MICHLER,
Maj. of Engineers.
By Command of
Bvt. Maj. Gen'l A. A. HUMPHREYS,
Brig. Gen'l & Chief of Engineers.
1867.

National Forces.
Confederate Forces.

Scale of Miles.

0   ¼   ½   ¾   1   2   3

hard to keep, that the head of column only reached Old Cold Harbor at six o'clock, but was in position at 7.30 A.M. Preparations were made for an attack in the afternoon, but did not take place until the next morning. Warren's corps was moved to the left to connect with Smith: Hancock's corps was got into position to the left of Wright's, and Burnside was moved to Bethesda Church in reserve. While Warren and Burnside were making these changes the enemy came out several times and attacked them, capturing several hundred prisoners. The attacks were repulsed, but not followed up as they should have been. I was so annoyed at this that I directed Meade to instruct his corps commanders that they should seize all such opportunities when they occurred, and not wait for orders, all of our manœuvres being made for the very purpose of getting the enemy out of his cover.

On this day Wilson returned from his raid upon the Virginia Central Railroad, having damaged it considerably. But, like ourselves, the rebels had become experts in repairing such damage. Sherman, in his memoirs, relates an anecdote of his campaign to Atlanta that well illustrates this point. The rebel cavalry lurking in his rear to burn bridges and obstruct his communications had become so disgusted at hearing trains go whistling by within a few hours after a bridge had been burned, that they proposed to try blowing up some of the tunnels. One of them said, "No use, boys, Old Sherman carries duplicate tunnels with him, and will replace them as fast as you can blow them up; better save your powder."

Sheridan was engaged reconnoitring the banks of the Chickahominy, to find crossings and the condition of the roads. He reported favorably.

During the night Lee moved his left up to make his line correspond to ours. His lines extended now from the Totopotomoy to New Cold Harbor. Mine from Bethesda Church by Old Cold Harbor to the Chickahominy, with a division of cavalry guarding our right. An assault was ordered for the 3d, to be made mainly by the corps of Hancock, Wright and Smith; but Warren and Burnside were to support it by threatening Lee's left, and to attack with great earnestness if he should either reinforce more threatened points by drawing from that quarter or if a favorable opportunity should present itself.

The corps commanders were to select the points in their respective fronts where they would make their assaults. The move was to commence at half-past four in the morning. Hancock sent Barlow and Gibbon forward at the appointed hour, with Birney as a reserve. Barlow pushed forward with great vigor, under a heavy fire of both artillery and musketry, through thickets and swamps. Notwithstanding all the resistance of the enemy and the natural obstructions to overcome, he carried a position occupied by the enemy outside their main line where the road makes a deep cut through a bank affording as good a shelter for troops as if it had been made for that purpose. Three pieces of artillery had been captured here, and several hundred prisoners. The guns were immediately turned against the men who had just been using them. No assistance coming to him, he (Barlow) intrenched under fire and continued to hold his place. Gibbon was not so fortunate in his front. He found the ground over which he had to pass cut up with deep ravines, and a morass difficult to cross. But his men struggled on until some of them got up to the very parapet covering the enemy. Gibbon gained ground much nearer the enemy than that which he left, and here he intrenched and held fast.

Wright's corps moving in two lines captured the outer rifle-pits in their front, but accomplished nothing more. Smith's corps also gained the outer rifle-pits in its front. The ground over which this corps (18th) had to move was the most exposed of any over which charges were made. An open plain intervened between the contending forces at this point, which was exposed both to a direct and a cross fire. Smith,

---

NEAR COLD HARBOR, *June* 3, 1864, 7 A.M.
MAJOR-GENERAL MEADE,
    Commanding A. P.

The moment it becomes certain that an assault cannot succeed, suspend the offensive; but when one does succeed, push it vigorously and if necessary pile in troops at the successful point from wherever they can be taken. I shall go to where you are in the course of an hour.

U. S. GRANT,
Lieut.-General.

however, finding a ravine running towards his front, sufficiently deep to protect men in it from cross fire, and somewhat from a direct fire, put Martindale's division in it, and with Brooks supporting him on the left and Devens on the right succeeded in gaining the outer—probably picket—rifle-pits. Warren and Burnside also advanced and gained ground —which brought the whole army on one line.

This assault cost us heavily and probably without benefit to compensate: but the enemy was not cheered by the occurrence sufficiently to induce him to take the offensive. In fact, nowhere after the battle of the Wilderness did Lee show any disposition to leave his defences far behind him.

Fighting was substantially over by half-past seven in the morning. At eleven o'clock I started to visit all the corps commanders to see for myself the different positions gained and to get their opinion of the practicability of doing anything more in their respective fronts.

Hancock gave the opinion that in his front the enemy was too strong to make any further assault promise success. Wright thought he could gain the lines of the enemy, but it would require the co-operation of Hancock's and Smith's corps. Smith thought a lodgment possible, but was not sanguine: Burnside thought something could be done in his front, but Warren differed. I concluded, therefore, to make no more assaults, and a little after twelve directed in the following letter that all offensive action should cease.

COLD HARBOR, *June* 3, 1864. —12.30 P.M.
MAJOR-GENERAL MEADE,
Commanding A. P.

The opinion of corps commanders not being sanguine of success in case an assault is ordered, you may direct a suspension of farther advance for the present. Hold our most advanced positions and strengthen them. Whilst on the defensive our line may be contracted from the right if practicable. Reconnoissances should be made in front of every corps and advances made to advantageous positions by regular approaches. To aid the expedition under General Hunter it is necessary that we should detain all the army now with Lee until the former gets well on his way to Lynchburg. To do this effectually it will be better to keep the enemy out of the intrenchments of Richmond than to have them go back there.

Wright and Hancock should be ready to assault in case the enemy should break through General Smith's lines, and all should be ready to resist an assault.

U. S. GRANT,
Lieutenant-General.

The remainder of the day was spent in strengthening the line we now held. By night we were as strong against Lee as he was against us.

During the night the enemy quitted our right front, abandoning some of their wounded, and without burying their dead. These we were able to care for. But there were many dead and wounded men between the lines of the contending forces, which were now close together, who could not be cared for without a cessation of hostilities.

So I wrote the following:

COLD HARBOR, VA., *June 5,* 1864.
GENERAL R. E. LEE,
          Commanding Confederate Army.

It is reported to me that there are wounded men, probably of both armies, now lying exposed and suffering between the lines occupied respectively by the two armies. Humanity would dictate that some provision should be made to provide against such hardships. I would propose, therefore, that hereafter, when no battle is raging, either party be authorized to send to any point between the pickets or skirmish lines, unarmed men bearing litters to pick up their dead or wounded, without being fired upon by the other party. Any other method, equally fair to both parties, you may propose for meeting the end desired will be accepted by me.

U. S. GRANT,
Lieut.-General.

Lee replied that he feared such an arrangement would lead to misunderstanding, and proposed that in future, when either party wished to remove their dead and wounded, a flag of truce be sent. I answered this immediately by saying:

COLD HARBOR, VA., *June 6,* 1864.
GENERAL R. E. LEE,
          Commanding Army of N. Va.

Your communication of yesterday's date is received. I will send immediately, as you propose, to collect the dead and wounded between the lines of the two armies, and will also instruct that you be allowed to do the same. I propose that the time for doing this be between the hours of 12 M. and 3 P.M. to-day. I will direct all parties going out to bear a white flag, and not to attempt to go beyond where we have dead or wounded, and not beyond or on ground occupied by your troops.

U. S. GRANT,
Lieut.-General.

Lee's response was that he could not consent to the burial of the dead and removal of the wounded in the way I proposed, but when either party desired such permission it should be asked for by flag of truce; and he had directed that any parties I may have sent out, as mentioned in my letter, to be turned back. I answered:

COLD HARBOR, VA, *June* 6, 1864.
GENERAL R. E. LEE,
Commanding Army, N. Va.
The knowledge that wounded men are now suffering from want of attention, between the two armies, compels me to ask a suspension of hostilities for sufficient time to collect them in, say two hours. Permit me to say that the hours you may fix upon for this will be agreeable to me, and the same privilege will be extended to such parties as you may wish to send out on the same duty without further application.

U. S. GRANT,
Lieut.-General.

Lee acceded to this; but delays in transmitting the correspondence brought it to the 7th of June—forty-eight hours after it commenced—before parties were got out to collect the men left upon the field. In the meantime all but two of the wounded had died. And I wrote to Lee:

COLD HARBOR, VA., *June* 7, 1864.
10.30 A.M.
GEN. R. E. LEE,
Commanding Army of N. Va.
I regret that your note of seven P.M. yesterday should have been received at the nearest corps headquarters, to where it was delivered, after the hour which had been given for the removal of the dead and wounded had expired; 10.45 P.M. was the hour at which it was received at corps headquarters, and between eleven and twelve it reached my headquarters. As a consequence, it was not understood

by the troops of this army that there was a cessation of hostilities for the purpose of collecting the dead and wounded, and none were collected. Two officers and six men of the 8th and 25th North Carolina Regts., who were out in search of the bodies of officers of their respective regiments, were captured and brought into our lines, owing to this want of understanding. I regret this, but will state that as soon as I learned the fact, I directed that they should not be held as prisoners, but must be returned to their commands. These officers and men having been carelessly brought through our lines to the rear, I have not determined whether they will be sent back the way they came, or whether they will be sent by some other route.

Regretting that all my efforts for alleviating the sufferings of wounded men left upon the battle-field have been rendered nugatory, I remain, &c.,

U. S. GRANT,
Lieutenant-General.

I have always regretted that the last assault at Cold Harbor was ever made. I might say the same thing of the assault of the 22d of May, 1863, at Vicksburg. At Cold Harbor no advantage whatever was gained to compensate for the heavy loss we sustained. Indeed, the advantages other than those of relative losses, were on the Confederate side. Before that, the Army of Northern Virginia seemed to have acquired a wholesome regard for the courage, endurance, and soldierly qualities generally of the Army of the Potomac. They no longer wanted to fight them "one Confederate to five Yanks." Indeed, they seemed to have given up any idea of gaining any advantage of their antagonist in the open field. They had come to much prefer breastworks in their front to the Army of the Potomac. This charge seemed to revive their hopes temporarily; but it was of short duration. The effect upon the Army of the Potomac was the reverse. When we reached the James River, however, all effects of the battle of Cold Harbor seemed to have disappeared.

There was more justification for the assault at Vicksburg. We were in a Southern climate, at the beginning of the hot season. The Army of the Tennessee had won five successive victories over the garrison of Vicksburg in the three preceding weeks. They had driven a portion of that army from Port Gibson with considerable loss, after having flanked them out of their stronghold at Grand Gulf. They had attacked another portion of the same army at Raymond, more than fifty miles farther in the interior of the State, and driven them back into Jackson with great loss in killed, wounded, captured and missing, besides loss of large and small arms: they had captured the capital of the State of Mississippi, with a large amount of materials of war and manufactures. Only a few days before, they had beaten the enemy then penned up in the town first at Champion's Hill, next at Big Black River Bridge, inflicting upon him a loss of fifteen thousand or more men (including those cut off from returning) besides large losses in arms and ammunition. The Army of the Tennessee had come to believe that they could beat their antagonist under any circumstances. There was no telling how long a regular siege might last. As I have stated, it was the beginning of the hot season in a Southern climate. There was no telling what the casualties might be among Northern troops working and living in trenches, drinking surface water filtered through rich vegetation, under a tropical sun. If Vicksburg could have been carried in May, it would not only have saved the army the risk it ran of a greater danger than from the bullets of the enemy, but it would have given us a splendid army, well equipped and officered, to operate elsewhere with. These are reasons justifying the assault. The only benefit we gained—and it was a slight one for so great a sacrifice—was that the men worked cheerfully in the trenches after that, being satisfied with digging the enemy out. Had the assault not been made, I have no doubt that the majority of those engaged in the siege of Vicksburg would have believed that had we assaulted it would have proven successful, and would have saved life, health and comfort.

Chapter LVI.

LEFT FLANK MOVEMENT ACROSS THE CHICKAHOMINY
AND JAMES—GENERAL LEE—VISIT TO BUTLER—
THE MOVEMENT ON PETERSBURG—THE INVESTMENT
OF PETERSBURG.

LEE'S POSITION was now so near Richmond, and the intervening swamps of the Chickahominy so great an obstacle to the movement of troops in the face of an enemy, that I determined to make my next left flank move carry the Army of the Potomac south of the James River.* Preparations for this were promptly commenced. The move was a hazardous one to make: the Chickahominy River, with its marshy and heavily timbered approaches, had to be crossed; all the bridges over it east of Lee were destroyed; the enemy had a shorter line and better roads to travel on to confront me in crossing; more than fifty miles intervened between me and Butler, by the roads I should have to travel, with both the James and the Chickahominy unbridged to cross; and last, the Army of the Potomac had to be got out of a position but a few hundred yards from the enemy at the widest place. Lee, if he did not choose to follow me, might, with his shorter distance to travel and his bridges over the Chickahominy and the James, move rapidly on Butler and crush him before the army with me could come to his relief. Then too he might spare troops enough to send against Hunter who was approaching Lynchburg, living upon the country he passed through, and without ammunition further than what he carried with him.

---

*COLD HARBOR, *June* 5, 1864.
MAJOR-GENERAL HALLECK, Chief of Staff of the Army,
   Washington, D. C.
   A full survey of all the ground satisfies me that it would be impracticable to hold a line north-east of Richmond that would protect the Fredericksburg Railroad to enable us to use that road for supplying the army. To do so would give us a long vulnerable line of road to protect, exhausting much of our strength to guard it, and would leave open to the enemy all of his lines of communication on the south side of the James. My idea from the start has been to beat Lee's army if possible north of Richmond; then after destroying

590

But the move had to be made, and I relied upon Lee's not seeing my danger as I saw it. Besides we had armies on both sides of the James River and not far from the Confederate capital. I knew that its safety would be a matter of the first consideration with the executive, legislative and judicial branches of the so-called Confederate government, if it was not with the military commanders. But I took all the precaution I knew of to guard against all dangers.

Sheridan was sent with two divisions, to communicate with Hunter and to break up the Virginia Central Railroad and the James River Canal, on the 7th of June, taking instructions to

---

his lines of communication on the north side of the James River to transfer the army to the south side and besiege Lee in Richmond, or follow him south if he should retreat.

I now find, after over thirty days of trial, the enemy deems it of the first importance to run no risks with the armies they now have. They act purely on the defensive behind breastworks, or feebly on the offensive immediately in front of them, and where in case of repulse they can instantly retire behind them. Without a greater sacrifice of human life than I am willing to make all cannot be accomplished that I had designed outside of the city. I have therefore resolved upon the following plan:

I will continue to hold substantially the ground now occupied by the Army of the Potomac, taking advantage of any favorable circumstance that may present itself until the cavalry can be sent west to destroy the Virginia Central Railroad from about Beaver Dam for some twenty-five or thirty miles west. When this is effected I will move the army to the south side of the James River, either by crossing the Chickahominy and marching near to City Point, or by going to the mouth of the Chickahominy on north side and crossing there. To provide for this last and most possible contingency, several ferry-boats of the largest class ought to be immediately provided.

Once on the south side of the James River, I can cut off all sources of supply to the enemy except what is furnished by the canal. If Hunter succeeds in reaching Lynchburg, that will be lost to him also. Should Hunter not succeed, I will still make the effort to destroy the canal by sending cavalry up the south side of the river with a pontoon train to cross wherever they can.

The feeling of the two armies now seems to be that the rebels can protect themselves only by strong intrenchments, whilst our army is not only confident of protecting itself without intrenchments, but that it can beat and drive the enemy wherever and whenever he can be found without this protection.

U. S. GRANT,
Lieutenant-General.

Hunter to come back with him.* Hunter was also informed by way of Washington and the Valley that Sheridan was on the way to meet him. The canal and Central Road, and the regions penetrated by them, were of vast importance to the enemy, furnishing and carrying a large per cent. of all the supplies for the Army of Northern Virginia and the people of Richmond. Before Sheridan got off on the 7th news was received from Hunter reporting his advance to Staunton and successful engagement with the enemy near that place on the 5th, in which the Confederate commander, W. S. Jones, was killed. On the 4th of June the enemy having withdrawn his left corps, Burnside on our right was moved up between Warren and Smith. On the 5th Birney returned to Hancock, which extended his left now to the Chickahominy, and Warren was withdrawn to Cold Harbor. Wright was directed to send two divisions to the left to extend down the banks of that stream to Bottom's Bridge. The cavalry extended still farther east to Jones's Bridge.

---

*COLD HARBOR, VA., *June* 6, 1864.
MAJOR-GENERAL D. HUNTER,
          Commanding Dept. W. Va.
   General Sheridan leaves here to-morrow morning, with instructions to proceed to Charlottesville, Va., and to commence there the destruction of the Va. Cen. R. R., destroying this way as much as possible. The complete destruction of this road and of the canal on James River is of great importance to us. According to the instructions I sent to General Halleck for your guidance, you were to proceed to Lynchburg and commence there. It would be of great value to us to get possession of Lynchburg for a single day. But that point is of so much importance to the enemy, that in attempting to get it such resistance may be met as to defeat your getting onto the road or canal at all. I see, in looking over the letter to General Halleck on the subject of your instructions, that it rather indicates that your route should be from Staunton via Charlottesville. If you have so understood it, you will be doing just what I want. The direction I would now give is, that if this letter reaches you in the valley between Staunton and Lynchburg, you immediately turn east by the most practicable road until you strike the Lynchburg branch of the Va. Central road. From thence move eastward along the line of the road, destroying it completely and thoroughly, until you join General Sheridan. After the work laid out for General Sheridan and yourself is thoroughly done, proceed to join the Army of the Potomac by the route laid out in General Sheridan's instructions.
   If any portion of your force, especially your cavalry, is needed back in your Department, you are authorized to send it back.

On the 7th Abercrombie—who was in command at White House, and who had been in command at our base of supplies in all the changes made from the start—was ordered to take up the iron from the York River Railroad and put it on boats, and to be in readiness to move by water to City Point.

On the 8th Meade was directed to fortify a line down the bank overlooking the Chickahominy, under cover of which the army could move.

On the 9th Abercrombie was directed to send all organized troops arriving at White House, without debarking from their transports, to report to Butler. Halleck was at this time instructed to send all reinforcements to City Point.

On the 11th I wrote:

COLD HARBOR, VA., June 11, 1864.

MAJOR-GEN. B. F. BUTLER,
       Commanding Department of Va. and N. C.

The movement to transfer this army to the south side of the James River will commence after dark to-morrow night. Col. Comstock, of my staff, was sent specially to ascertain what was necessary to make your position secure in the interval during which the enemy might use most of his force against you, and also, to ascertain what point on the river we should reach to effect a crossing if it should not be practicable to reach this side of the river at Bermuda Hundred. Colonel Comstock has not yet returned, so that I cannot make instructions as definite as I would wish, but the time between this and Sunday night being so short in which to get word to you, I must do the best I can. Colonel Dent goes to make arrangements for gunboats and transportation to send up the Chickahominy to take to you the 18th corps. The corps will leave its position in the trenches as early in the evening, to-morrow, as possible, and make a forced march to Cole's Landing or Ferry, where it should reach by ten A.M. the following morning. This corps numbers now 15,300 men. They take with them neither wagons nor artillery; these latter marching with the balance of the army to the James River. The remainder of

---

If on receipt of this you should be near to Lynchburg and deem it practicable to reach that point, you will exercise your judgment about going there.

If you should be on the railroad between Charlottesville and Lynchburg, it may be practicable to detach a cavalry force to destroy the canal. Lose no opportunity to destroy the canal.

U. S. GRANT,
Lieut.-General.

the army will cross the Chickahominy at Long Bridge and at Jones's, and strike the river at the most practicable crossing below City Point.

I directed several days ago that all reinforcements for the army should be sent to you. I am not advised of the number that may have gone, but suppose you have received from six to ten thousand. General Smith will also reach you as soon as the enemy could, going by the way of Richmond.

The balance of the force will not be more than one day behind, unless detained by the whole of Lee's army, in which case you will be strong enough.

I wish you would direct the proper staff officers, your chief-engineer and your chief-quartermaster, to commence at once the collection of all the means in their reach for crossing the army on its arrival. If there is a point below City Point where a pontoon bridge can be thrown, have it laid.

Expecting the arrival of the 18th corps by Monday night, if you deem it practicable from the force you have to seize and hold Petersburg, you may prepare to start, on the arrival of troops to hold your present lines. I do not want Petersburg visited, however, unless it is held, nor an attempt to take it, unless you feel a reasonable degree of confidence of success. If you should go there, I think troops should take nothing with them except what they can carry, depending upon supplies being sent after the place is secured. If Colonel Dent should not succeed in securing the requisite amount of transportation for the 18th corps before reaching you, please have the balance supplied.

U. S. GRANT,
Lieut.-General.

P. S.—On reflection I will send the 18th corps by way of White House. The distance which they will have to march will be enough shorter to enable them to reach you about the same time, and the uncertainty of navigation on the Chickahominy will be avoided.

U. S. GRANT.

COLD HARBOR, VA., *June* 11, 1864.
MAJOR-GENERAL G. G. MEADE,
    Commanding Army of the Potomac.

Colonel Comstock, who visited the James River for the purpose of ascertaining the best point below Bermuda Hundred to which to march the army has not yet returned. It is now getting so late, however, that all preparations may be made for the move to-morrow night without waiting longer.

The movement will be made as heretofore agreed upon, that is, the 18th corps make a rapid march with the infantry alone, their wagons and artillery accompanying the balance of the army to Cole's Landing or Ferry, and there embark for City Point, losing no time for rest until they reach the latter point.

The 5th corps will seize Long Bridge and move out on the Long Bridge Road to its junction with Quaker Road, or until stopped by the enemy.

The other three corps will follow in such order as you may direct, one of them crossing at Long Bridge, and two at Jones's Bridge. After the crossing is effected, the most practicable roads will be taken to reach about Fort Powhattan. Of course, this is supposing the enemy makes no opposition to our advance. The 5th corps, after securing the passage of the balance of the army, will join or follow in rear of the corps which crosses the same bridge with themselves. The wagon trains should be kept well east of the troops, and if a crossing can be found, or made lower down than Jones's they should take it.

U. S. GRANT,
Lieut.-General.

P. S.—In view of the long march to reach Cole's Landing, and the uncertainty of being able to embark a large number of men there, the direction of the 18th corps may be changed to White House. They should be directed to load up transports, and start them as fast as loaded without waiting for the whole corps or even whole divisions to go together.

U. S. GRANT.

About this time word was received (through the Richmond papers of the 11th) that Crook and Averell had united and were moving east. This, with the news of Hunter's successful engagement near Staunton, was no doubt known to Lee before it was to me. Then Sheridan leaving with two divisions of cavalry, looked indeed threatening, both to Lee's communications and supplies. Much of his cavalry was sent after Sheridan, and Early with Ewell's entire corps was sent to the Valley. Supplies were growing scarce in Richmond, and the sources from which to draw them were in our hands. People from outside began to pour into Richmond to help eat up the little on hand. Consternation reigned there.

On the 12th Smith was ordered to move at night to White House, not to stop until he reached there, and to take boats at once for City Point, leaving his trains and artillery to move by land.

Soon after dark some of the cavalry at Long Bridge effected a crossing by wading and floundering through the water and mud, leaving their horses behind, and drove away the cavalry pickets. A pontoon bridge was speedily thrown across, over which the remainder of the army soon passed and pushed out for a mile or two to watch and detain any advance that might be made from the other side. Warren followed the cavalry, and by the morning of the 13th had his whole corps over. Hancock followed Warren. Burnside took the road to Jones's Bridge, followed by Wright. Ferrero's division, with the wagon train, moved farther east, by Window Shades and Cole's Ferry, our rear being covered by cavalry.

It was known that the enemy had some gunboats at Richmond. These might run down at night and inflict great damage upon us before they could be sunk or captured by our navy. General Butler had, in advance, loaded some vessels with stone ready to be sunk so as to obstruct the channel in an emergency. On the 13th I sent orders to have these sunk as high up the river as we could guard them, and prevent their removal by the enemy.

As soon as Warren's corps was over the Chickahominy it marched out and joined the cavalry in holding the roads from Richmond while the army passed. No attempt was made by the enemy to impede our march, however, but Warren and Wilson reported the enemy strongly fortified in their front. By the evening of the 13th Hancock's corps was at Charles City Court House on the James River. Burnside's and Wright's corps were on the Chickahominy, and crossed during the night, Warren's corps and the cavalry still covering the army. The material for a pontoon bridge was already at hand and the work of laying it was commenced immediately, under the superintendence of Brigadier-General Benham, commanding the engineer brigade. On the evening of the 14th the crossing commenced, Hancock in advance, using both the bridge and boats.

When the Wilderness campaign commenced the Army of the Potomac, including Burnside's corps—which was a separate command until the 24th of May when it was incorporated with the main army—numbered about 116,000 men. During the progress of the campaign about 40,000 reinforcements were received. At the crossing of the James River June 14th—15th the army numbered about 115,000. Besides the ordinary losses incident to a campaign of six weeks' nearly constant fighting or skirmishing, about one-half of the artillery was sent back to Washington, and many men were discharged by reason of the expiration of their term of service.* In estimating our strength every enlisted man and every commissioned officer present is included, no matter how employed; in bands, sick in field hospitals, hospital attendants, company cooks and all. Operating in an enemy's country, and being supplied always from a distant base, large detachments had at all times to be sent from the front, not only to guard the base of supplies and the roads to it, but all the roads leading to our flanks and rear. We were also operating in a country unknown to us, and without competent guides or maps showing the roads accurately.

The manner of estimating numbers in the two armies differs materially. In the Confederate army often only bayonets are taken into account, never, I believe, do they estimate more than are handling the guns of the artillery and armed with muskets or carbines. Generally the latter are far enough away to be excluded from the count in any one field. Officers and details of enlisted men are not included. In the Northern armies the estimate is most liberal, taking in all connected with the army and drawing pay.

Estimated in the same manner as ours, Lee had not less than 80,000 men at the start. His reinforcements were about equal to ours during the campaign, deducting the discharged men and those sent back. He was on the defensive, and in a country in which every stream, every road, every obstacle to

*FROM A STATEMENT OF LOSSES COMPILED IN THE ADJUTANT-GENERAL'S OFFICE.

FIELD OF ACTION AND DATE.	KILLED.	WOUNDED.	MISSING.	AGGREGATE.
Wilderness, May 5th to 7th . . .	2,261	8,785	2,902	13,948
Spottsylvania, May 8th to 21st. . .	2,271	9,360	1,970	13,601
North Anna, May 23d to 27th. . .	186	792	165	1,143
Totopotomoy, May 27th to 31st . .	99	358	52	509
Cold Harbor, May 31st to June 12th .	1,769	6,752	1,537	10,058
Total.	6,586	26,047	6,626	39,259

the movement of troops and every natural defence was familiar to him and his army. The citizens were all friendly to him and his cause, and could and did furnish him with accurate reports of our every move. Rear guards were not necessary for him, and having always a railroad at his back, large wagon trains were not required. All circumstances considered we did not have any advantage in numbers.

General Lee, who had led the Army of Northern Virginia in all these contests, was a very highly estimated man in the Confederate army and States, and filled also a very high place in the estimation of the people and press of the Northern States. His praise was sounded throughout the entire North after every action he was engaged in: the number of his forces was always lowered and that of the National forces exaggerated. He was a large, austere man, and I judge difficult of approach to his subordinates. To be extolled by the entire press of the South after every engagement, and by a portion of the press North with equal vehemence, was calculated to give him the entire confidence of his troops and to make him feared by his antagonists. It was not an uncommon thing for my staff-officers to hear from Eastern officers, "Well, Grant has never met Bobby Lee yet." There were good and true officers who believe now that the Army of Northern Virginia was superior to the Army of the Potomac man to man. I do not believe so, except as the advantages spoken of above made them so. Before the end I believe the difference was the other way. The Army of Northern Virginia became despondent and saw the end. It did not please them. The National army saw the same thing, and were encouraged by it.

The advance of the Army of the Potomac reached the James on the 14th of June. Preparations were at once commenced for laying the pontoon bridges and crossing the river. As already stated, I had previously ordered General Butler to have two vessels loaded with stone and carried up the river to a point above that occupied by our gunboats, where the channel was narrow, and sunk there so as to obstruct the passage and prevent Confederate gunboats from coming down the river. Butler had had these boats filled and put in position, but had not had them sunk before my arrival. I ordered this done, and also directed that he should turn over all material and boats not then in use in the river to be used in ferrying the troops across.

I then, on the 14th, took a steamer and ran up to Bermuda Hundred to see General Butler for the purpose of directing a movement against Petersburg, while our troops of the Army of the Potomac were crossing.

I had sent General W. F. Smith back from Cold Harbor by the way of White House, thence on steamers to City Point for the purpose of giving General Butler more troops with which to accomplish this result. General Butler was ordered to send Smith with his troops reinforced, as far as that could be conveniently done, from other parts of the Army of the James. He gave Smith about six thousand reinforcements, including some twenty-five hundred cavalry under Kautz, and about thirty-five hundred colored infantry under Hinks.

The distance which Smith had to move to reach the enemy's lines was about six miles, and the Confederate advance line of works was but two miles outside of Petersburg. Smith was to move under cover of night, up close to the enemy's works, and assault as soon as he could after daylight. I believed then, and still believe, that Petersburg could have been easily captured at that time. It only had about 2,500 men in the defences besides some irregular troops, consisting of citizens and employees in the city who took up arms in case of emergency. Smith started as proposed, but his advance encountered a rebel force intrenched between City Point and their lines outside of Petersburg. This position he carried, with some loss to the enemy; but there was so much delay that it was daylight before his troops really got off from there. While there I informed General Butler that Hancock's corps would cross the river and move to Petersburg to support Smith in case the latter was successful, and that I could reinforce there more rapidly than Lee could reinforce from his position.

I returned down the river to where the troops of the Army of the Potomac now were, communicated to General Meade, in writing, the directions I had given to General Butler and directed him (Meade) to cross Hancock's corps over under cover of night, and push them forward in the morning to Petersburg; halting them, however, at a designated point until they could hear from Smith. I also informed General Meade that I had ordered rations from Bermuda Hundred for Hancock's corps, and desired him to issue them speedily, and to lose no more time than was absolutely necessary. The rations did not reach him, however, and Hancock, while he got all his corps over during the night, remained until half-past ten in the hope of receiving them. He then moved without them, and on the road received a note from General W. F. Smith, asking him to come on. This seems to be the first information that General Hancock had received of the fact that he was to go to Petersburg, or that anything particular was expected of him. Otherwise he would have been there by four o'clock in the afternoon.

Smith arrived in front of the enemy's lines early in the forenoon of the 15th, and spent the day until after seven o'clock in the evening in reconnoitering what appeared to be empty works. The enemy's line consisted of redans occupying commanding positions, with rifle-pits connecting them. To the east side of Petersburg, from the Appomattox back, there were thirteen of these redans extending a distance of several miles, probably three. If they had been properly manned they could have held out against any force that could have attacked them, at least until reinforcements could have got up from the north of Richmond.

Smith assaulted with the colored troops, and with success. By nine o'clock at night he was in possession of five of these redans and, of course, of the connecting lines of rifle-pits. All of them contained artillery, which fell into our hands. Hancock came up and proposed to take any part assigned to him; and Smith asked him to relieve his men who were in the trenches.

Next morning, the 16th, Hancock himself was in command, and captured another redan. Meade came up in the afternoon and succeeded Hancock, who had to be relieved, temporarily, from the command of his corps on account of the breaking out afresh of the wound he had received at Gettysburg. During the day Meade assaulted and carried one more redan to his right and two to his left. In all this we lost very heavily. The works were not strongly manned, but they all had guns in them which fell into our hands, together with the men who were handling them in the effort to repel these assaults.

Up to this time Beauregard, who had commanded south of Richmond, had received no reinforcements, except Hoke's division from Drury's Bluff,* which had arrived on the morning of the 16th; though he had urged the authorities very strongly to send them, believing, as he did, that Petersburg would be a valuable prize which we might seek.

During the 17th the fighting was very severe and the losses heavy; and at night our troops occupied about the same position they had occupied in the morning, except that they held a redan which had been captured by Potter during the day. During the night, however, Beauregard fell back to the line which had been already selected, and commenced fortifying it. Our troops advanced on the 18th to the line which he had abandoned, and found that the Confederate loss had been very severe, many of the enemy's dead still remaining in the ditches and in front of them.

Colonel J. L. Chamberlain, of the 20th Maine, was wounded on the 18th. He was gallantly leading his brigade at the time, as he had been in the habit of doing in all the engagements in which he had previously been engaged. He had several times been recommended for a brigadier-generalcy for gallant and meritorious conduct. On this occasion, however, I promoted him on the spot, and forwarded a copy of my order to the War Department, asking that my act might be confirmed and Chamberlain's name sent to the Senate for confir-

---

*City Point, Va., *June* 17, 1864—11 a.m.

Major-Gen. Halleck,
    Washington, D. C.

   *   *   *   *   *   *

The enemy in their endeavor to reinforce Petersburg abandoned their intrenchments in front of Bermuda Hundred. They no doubt expected troops from north of the James River to take their place before we discovered it. General Butler took advantage of this and moved a force at once upon the railroad and plank road between Richmond and Petersburg, which I hope to retain possession of. Too much credit cannot be given to the troops and their commanders for the energy and fortitude displayed during the last five days. Day and night has been all the same, no delays being allowed on any account.

          U. S. GRANT,
            Lieut.-General.

mation without any delay. This was done, and at last a gallant and meritorious officer received partial justice at the hands of his government, which he had served so faithfully and so well.

If General Hancock's orders of the 15th had been communicated to him, that officer, with his usual promptness, would undoubtedly have been upon the ground around Petersburg as early as four o'clock in the afternoon of the 15th. The days were long and it would have given him considerable time before night. I do not think there is any doubt that Petersburg itself could have been carried without much loss; or, at least, if protected by inner detached works, that a line could have been established very much in rear of the one then occupied by the enemy. This would have given us control of both the Weldon and South Side railroads. This would also have saved an immense amount of hard fighting which had to be done from the 15th to the 18th, and would have given us greatly the advantage in the long siege which ensued.

I now ordered the troops to be put under cover and allowed some of the rest which they had so long needed. They remained quiet, except that there was more or less firing every day, until the 22d, when General Meade ordered an advance towards the Weldon Railroad. We were very anxious to get to that road, and even round to the South Side Railroad if possible.

Meade moved Hancock's corps, now commanded by Birney, to the left, with a view to at least force the enemy to stay within the limits of his own line. General Wright, with the 6th corps, was ordered by a road farther south, to march directly for the Weldon road. The enemy passed in between these two corps and attacked vigorously, and with very serious results to the National troops, who were then withdrawn from their advanced position.

The Army of the Potomac was given the investment of Petersburg, while the Army of the James held Bermuda Hundred and all the ground we possessed north of the James River. The 9th corps, Burnside's, was placed upon the right at Petersburg; the 5th, Warren's, next; the 2d, Birney's, next; then the 6th, Wright's, broken off to the left and south. Thus began the siege of Petersburg.

Chapter LVII.

RAID ON THE VIRGINIA CENTRAL RAILROAD—RAID ON
THE WELDON RAILROAD—EARLY'S MOVEMENT UPON
WASHINGTON—MINING THE WORKS BEFORE
PETERSBURG—EXPLOSION OF THE MINE BEFORE
PETERSBURG—CAMPAIGN IN THE SHENANDOAH
VALLEY—CAPTURE OF THE WELDON RAILROAD.

O N THE 7TH of June, while at Cold Harbor, I had as
already indicated sent Sheridan with two divisions of
cavalry to destroy as much as he could of the Virginia Central
Railroad. General Hunter had been operating up the Shenandoah Valley with some success, having fought a battle near
Staunton where he captured a great many prisoners, besides
killing and wounding a good many men. After the battle he
formed a junction at Staunton with Averell and Crook, who
had come up from the Kanawha, or Gauley River. It was supposed, therefore, that General Hunter would be about Charlottesville, Virginia, by the time Sheridan could get there,
doing on the way the damage that he was sent to do.

I gave Sheridan instructions to have Hunter, in case he
should meet him about Charlottesville, join and return with
him to the Army of the Potomac. Lee, hearing of Hunter's
success in the valley, started Breckinridge out for its defence
at once. Learning later of Sheridan's going with two divisions, he also sent Hampton with two divisions of cavalry, his
own and Fitz-Hugh Lee's.

Sheridan moved to the north side of the North Anna to get
out west, and learned of the movement of these troops to the
south side of the same stream almost as soon as they had
started. He pushed on to get to Trevilian Station to commence his destruction at that point. On the night of the 10th
he bivouacked some six or seven miles east of Trevilian, while
Fitz-Hugh Lee was the same night at Trevilian Station and
Hampton but a few miles away.

During the night Hampton ordered an advance on Sheridan, hoping, no doubt, to surprise and very badly cripple
him. Sheridan, however, by a counter move sent Custer on a

rapid march to get between the two divisions of the enemy and into their rear. This he did successfully, so that at daylight, when the assault was made, the enemy found himself at the same time resisted in front and attacked in rear, and broke in some confusion. The losses were probably very light on both sides in killed and wounded, but Sheridan got away with some five hundred prisoners and sent them to City Point.

During that day, the 11th, Sheridan moved into Trevilian Station, and the following day proceeded to tear up the road east and west. There was considerable fighting during the whole of the day, but the work of destruction went on. In the meantime, at night, the enemy had taken possession of the crossing which Sheridan had proposed to take to go north when he left Trevilian. Sheridan learned, however, from some of the prisoners he had captured here, that General Hunter was about Lynchburg, and therefore that there was no use of his going on to Charlottesville with a view to meet him.

Sheridan started back during the night of the 12th, and made his way north and farther east, coming around by the north side of White House, and arriving there on the 21st. Here he found an abundance of forage for his animals, food for his men, and security while resting. He had been obliged to leave about ninety of his own men in the field-hospital which he had established near Trevilian, and these necessarily fell into the hands of the enemy.

White House up to this time had been a depot; but now that our troops were all on the James River, it was no longer wanted as a store of supplies. Sheridan was, therefore, directed to break it up; which he did on the 22d of June, bringing the garrison and an immense wagon train with him. All these were over the James River by the 26th of the month, and Sheridan ready to follow.

In the meantime Meade had sent Wilson's division on a raid to destroy the Weldon and South Side roads. Now that Sheridan was safe and Hampton free to return to Richmond with his cavalry, Wilson's position became precarious. Meade therefore, on the 27th, ordered Sheridan over the river to make a demonstration in favor of Wilson. Wilson got back, though not without severe loss, having struck both roads, but the damage done was soon repaired.

After these events comparative quiet reigned about Petersburg until late in July. The time, however, was spent in strengthening the intrenchments and making our position generally more secure against a sudden attack. In the meantime I had to look after other portions of my command, where things had not been going on so favorably, always, as I could have wished.

General Hunter who had been appointed to succeed Sigel in the Shenandoah Valley immediately took up the offensive. He met the enemy on the 5th of June at Piedmont, and defeated him. On the 8th he formed a junction with Crook and Averell at Staunton, from which place he moved direct on Lynchburg, via Lexington, which he reached and invested on the 16th. Up to this time he was very successful; and but for the difficulty of taking with him sufficient ordnance stores over so long a march, through a hostile country, he would, no doubt, have captured Lynchburg. The destruction of the enemy's supplies and manufactories had been very great. To meet this movement under General Hunter, General Lee sent Early with his corps, a part of which reached Lynchburg before Hunter. After some skirmishing on the 17th and 18th, General Hunter, owing to a want of ammunition to give battle, retired from before the place. Unfortunately, this want of ammunition left him no choice of route for his return but by the way of the Gauley and Kanawha rivers, thence up the Ohio River, returning to Harper's Ferry by way of the Baltimore and Ohio Railroad. A long time was consumed in making this movement. Meantime the valley was left open to Early's troops, and others in that quarter; and Washington also was uncovered. Early took advantage of this condition of affairs and moved on Washington.

In the absence of Hunter, General Lew Wallace, with headquarters at Baltimore, commanded the department in which the Shenandoah lay. His surplus of troops with which to move against the enemy was small in number. Most of these were raw and, consequently, very much inferior to our veterans and to the veterans which Early had with him; but the situation of Washington was precarious, and Wallace moved with commendable promptitude to meet the enemy at the Monocacy. He could hardly have expected to defeat him badly, but he hoped to cripple and delay him until Washington could be put into a state of preparation for his reception. I had previously ordered General Meade to send a division to Baltimore for the purpose of adding to the defences of Washington, and he had sent Ricketts's division of the 6th corps (Wright's), which arrived in Baltimore on the 8th of July. Finding that Wallace had gone to the front with his command, Ricketts immediately took the cars and followed him to the Monocacy with his entire division. They met the enemy and, as might have been expected, were defeated; but they succeeded in stopping him for the day on which the battle took place. The next morning Early started on his march to the capital of the Nation, arriving before it on the 11th.

Learning of the gravity of the situation I had directed General Meade to also order Wright with the rest of his corps directly to Washington for the relief of that place, and the latter reached there the very day that Early arrived before it. The 19th corps, which had been stationed in Louisiana, having been ordered up to reinforce the armies about Richmond, had about this time arrived at Fortress Monroe, on their way to join us. I diverted them from that point to Washington, which place they reached, almost simultaneously with Wright, on the 11th. The 19th corps was commanded by Major-General Emory.

Early made his reconnoissance with a view of attacking on the following morning, the 12th; but the next morning he found our intrenchments, which were very strong, fully manned. He at once commenced to retreat, Wright following. There is no telling how much this result was contributed to by General Lew Wallace's leading what might well be considered almost a forlorn hope. If Early had been but one day earlier he might have entered the capital before the arrival of the reinforcements I had sent. Whether the delay caused by the battle amounted to a day or not, General Wallace contributed on this occasion, by the defeat of the troops under him a greater benefit to the cause than often falls to the lot of a commander of an equal force to render by means of a victory.

Farther west also the troubles were threatening. Some time before, Forrest had met Sturgis in command of some of our cavalry in Mississippi and handled him very roughly, gaining a very great victory over him. This left Forrest free to go almost where he pleased, and to cut the roads in rear of Sherman who was then advancing. Sherman was abundantly able to look after the army that he was immediately with, and all of his military division so long as he could communicate with it; but it was my place to see that he had the means with which to hold his rear. Two divisions under A. J. Smith had been sent to Banks in Louisiana some months before. Sherman ordered these back, with directions to attack Forrest. Smith met and defeated him very badly. I then directed that Smith should hang to Forrest and not let him go; and to prevent by all means his getting upon the Memphis and Nashville Railroad. Sherman had anticipated me in this matter, and given the same orders in substance; but receiving my directions for this order to Smith, he repeated it.

On the 25th of June General Burnside had commenced running a mine from about the centre of his front under the Confederate works confronting him. He was induced to do this by Colonel Pleasants, of the Pennsylvania Volunteers, whose regiment was mostly composed of miners, and who was himself a practical miner. Burnside had submitted the scheme to Meade and myself, and we both approved of it, as a means of keeping the men occupied. His position was very favorable for carrying on this work, but not so favorable for the operations to follow its completion. The position of the two lines at that point were only about a hundred yards apart with a comparatively deep ravine intervening. In the bottom of this ravine the work commenced. The position was unfavorable in this particular: that the enemy's line at that point was re-entering, so that its front was commanded by their own lines both to the right and left. Then, too, the ground was sloping upward back of the Confederate line for a considerable distance, and it was presumable that the enemy had, at least, a detached work on this highest point.

The work progressed, and on the 23d of July the mine was finished ready for charging; but I had this work of charging deferred until we were ready for it.

On the 17th of July several deserters came in and said that there was great consternation in Richmond, and that Lee was coming out to make an attack upon us—the object being to put us on the defensive so that he might detach troops to go to Georgia where the army Sherman was operating against was said to be in great trouble. I put the army commanders, Meade and Butler, on the lookout, but the attack was not made.

I concluded, then, a few days later, to do something in the way of offensive movement myself, having in view something of the same object that Lee had had. Wright's and Emory's corps were in Washington, and with this reduction of my force Lee might very readily have spared some troops from the defences to send West. I had other objects in view, however, besides keeping Lee where he was. The mine was constructed and ready to be exploded, and I wanted to take that occasion to carry Petersburg if I could. It was the object, therefore, to get as many of Lee's troops away from the south side of the James River as possible. Accordingly, on the 26th, we commenced a movement with Hancock's corps and Sheridan's cavalry to the north side by the way of Deep Bottom, where Butler had a pontoon bridge laid. The plan, in the main, was to let the cavalry cut loose and, joining with Kautz's cavalry of the Army of the James, get by Lee's lines and destroy as much as they could of the Virginia Central Railroad, while, in the mean time, the infantry was to move out so as to protect their rear and cover their retreat back when they should have got through with their work. We were successful in drawing the enemy's troops to the north side of the James as I expected. The mine was ordered to be charged, and the morning of the 30th of July was the time fixed for its explosion. I gave Meade minute orders* on the 24th directing

---

*CITY POINT, VA., *July* 24, 1864.

MAJOR-GENERAL MEADE,
     Commanding, etc.

The engineer officers who made a survey of the front from Bermuda Hundred report against the probability of success from an attack there. The

RICHMOND.

From Surveys
under the direction of
Bvt. Brig. Gen. N. MICHLER,
Maj. of Engineers,
By Command of
Bvt. Maj. G'l A.A. HUMPHREYS,
Brig. Gen. & Chief of Engineers,
1867.

Scale of Miles.

National Forces.
Confederate Forces.

how I wanted the assault conducted, which orders he amplified into general instructions for the guidance of the troops that were to be engaged.

Meade's instructions, which I, of course, approved most heartily, were all that I can see now was necessary. The only further precaution which he could have taken, and which he could not foresee, would have been to have different men to execute them.

The gallery to the mine was over five hundred feet long from where it entered the ground to the point where it was under the enemy's works, and with a cross gallery of something over eighty feet running under their lines. Eight chambers had been left, requiring a ton of powder each to charge them. All was ready by the time I had prescribed; and on the 29th Hancock and Sheridan were brought back near the James River with their troops. Under cover of night they started to recross the bridge at Deep Bottom, and to march directly for that part of our lines in front of the mine.

Warren was to hold his line of intrenchments with a sufficient number of men and concentrate the balance on the right

---

chances they think will be better on Burnside's front. If this is attempted it will be necessary to concentrate all the force possible at the point in the enemy's line we expect to penetrate. All officers should be fully impressed with the absolute necessity of pushing entirely beyond the enemy's present line, if they should succeed in penetrating it, and of getting back to their present line promptly if they should not succeed in breaking through.

To the right and left of the point of assault all the artillery possible should be brought to play upon the enemy in front during the assault. Their lines would be sufficient for the support of the artillery, and all the reserves could be brought on the flanks of their commands nearest to the point of assault, ready to follow in if successful. The field artillery and infantry held in the lines during the first assault should be in readiness to move at a moment's notice either to their front or to follow the main assault, as they should receive orders. One thing, however, should be impressed on corps commanders. If they see the enemy giving away on their front or moving from it to reinforce a heavily assaulted portion of their line, they should take advantage of such knowledge and act promptly without waiting for orders from army commanders. General Ord can co-operate with his corps in this movement, and about five thousand troops from Bermuda Hundred can be sent to reinforce you or can be used to threaten an assault between the Appomattox and James rivers, as may be deemed best.

This should be done by Tuesday morning, if done at all. If not at-

next to Burnside's corps, while Ord, now commanding the
18th corps, temporarily under Meade, was to form in the rear
of Burnside to support him when he went in. All were to
clear off the parapets and the *abatis* in their front so as to
leave the space as open as possible, and be able to charge the
moment the mine had been sprung and Burnside had taken
possession. Burnside's corps was not to stop in the crater at
all but push on to the top of the hill, supported on the right
and left by Ord's and Warren's corps.

Warren and Ord fulfilled their instructions perfectly so far
as making ready was concerned. Burnside seemed to have
paid no attention whatever to the instructions, and left all the
obstruction in his own front for his troops to get over in the
best way they could. The four divisions of his corps were
commanded by Generals Potter, Willcox, Ledlie and Ferrero.
The last was a colored division; and Burnside selected it to
make the assault. Meade interfered with this. Burnside then
took Ledlie's division—a worse selection than the first could
have been. In fact, Potter and Willcox were the only division
commanders Burnside had who were equal to the occasion.
Ledlie besides being otherwise inefficient, proved also to possess disqualification less common among soldiers.

There was some delay about the explosion of the mine so
that it did not go off until about five o'clock in the morning.
When it did explode it was very successful, making a crater
twenty feet deep and something like a hundred feet in length.
Instantly one hundred and ten cannon and fifty mortars,
which had been placed in the most commanding positions
covering the ground to the right and left of where the troops
were to enter the enemy's lines, commenced playing. Ledlie's
division marched into the crater immediately on the explosion, but most of the men stopped there in the absence of any

---

tempted, we will then start at the date indicated to destroy the railroad as far
as Hicksford at least, and to Weldon if possible.

*   *   *   *   *   *   *

Whether we send an expedition on the road or assault at Petersburg, Burnside's mine will be blown up. . . .

U. S. GRANT,
Lieutenant-General.

one to give directions; their commander having found some safe retreat to get into before they started. There was some delay on the left and right in advancing, but some of the troops did get in and turn to the right and left, carrying the rifle-pits as I expected they would do.

There had been great consternation in Petersburg, as we were well aware, about a rumored mine that we were going to explode. They knew we were mining, and they had failed to cut our mine off by countermining, though Beauregard had taken the precaution to run up a line of intrenchments to the rear of that part of their line fronting where they could see that our men were at work. We had learned through deserters who had come in that the people had very wild rumors about what was going on on our side. They said that we had undermined the whole of Petersburg; that they were resting upon a slumbering volcano and did not know at what moment they might expect an eruption. I somewhat based my calculations upon this state of feeling, and expected that when the mine was exploded the troops to the right and left would flee in all directions, and that our troops, if they moved promptly, could get in and strengthen themselves before the enemy had come to a realization of the true situation. It was just as I expected it would be. We could see the men running without any apparent object except to get away. It was half an hour before musketry firing, to amount to anything, was opened upon our men in the crater. It was an hour before the enemy got artillery up to play upon them; and it was nine o'clock before Lee got up reinforcements from his right to join in expelling our troops.

The effort was a stupendous failure. It cost us about four thousand men, mostly, however, captured; and all due to inefficiency on the part of the corps commander and the incompetency of the division commander who was sent to lead the assault.

After being fully assured of the failure of the mine, and finding that most of that part of Lee's army which had been drawn north of the James River were still there, I gave Meade directions to send a corps of infantry and the cavalry next morning, before Lee could get his forces back, to destroy fifteen or twenty miles of the Weldon Railroad. But misfortunes never come singly. I learned during that same afternoon that Wright's pursuit of Early was feeble because of the constant and contrary orders he had been receiving from Washington, while I was cut off from immediate communication by reason of our cable across Chesapeake Bay being broken. Early, however, was not aware of the fact that Wright was not pursuing until he had reached Strasburg. Finding that he was not pursued he turned back to Winchester, where Crook was stationed with a small force, and drove him out. He then pushed north until he had reached the Potomac, then he sent McCausland across to Chambersburg, Pa., to destroy that town. Chambersburg was a purely defenceless town with no garrison whatever, and no fortifications; yet McCausland, under Early's orders, burned the place and left about three hundred families houseless. This occurred on the 30th of July. I rescinded my orders for the troops to go out to destroy the Weldon Railroad, and directed them to embark for Washington City. After burning Chambersburg McCausland retreated, pursued by our cavalry, towards Cumberland. They were met and defeated by General Kelley and driven into Virginia.

The Shenandoah Valley was very important to the Confederates, because it was the principal store-house they now had for feeding their armies about Richmond. It was well known that they would make a desperate struggle to maintain it. It had been the source of a great deal of trouble to us heretofore to guard that outlet to the north, partly because of the incompetency of some of the commanders, but chiefly because of interference from Washington. It seemed to be the policy of General Halleck and Secretary Stanton to keep any force sent there, in pursuit of the invading army, moving right and left so as to keep between the enemy and our capital; and, generally speaking, they pursued this policy until all knowledge of the whereabouts of the enemy was lost. They were left, therefore, free to supply themselves with horses, beef cattle, and such provisions as they could carry away from Western Maryland and Pennsylvania. I determined to put a stop to this. I started Sheridan at once for that field of operation, and on the following day sent another division of his cavalry.

I had previously asked to have Sheridan assigned to that command, but Mr. Stanton objected, on the ground that he was too young for so important a command. On the 1st of August when I sent reinforcements for the protection of Washington, I sent the following orders:

CITY POINT, VA.,
August 1, 1864, 11.30 A.M.

MAJOR-GENERAL HALLECK,
       Washington, D. C.

I am sending General Sheridan for temporary duty whilst the enemy is being expelled from the border. Unless General Hunter is in the field in person, I want Sheridan put in command of all the troops in the field, with instructions to put himself south of the enemy and follow him to the death. Wherever the enemy goes let our troops go also. Once started up the valley they ought to be followed until we get possession of the Virginia Central Railroad. If General Hunter is in the field, give Sheridan direct command of the 6th corps and cavalry division. All the cavalry, I presume, will reach Washington in the course of to-morrow.

U. S. GRANT,
Lieutenant-General.

The President in some way or other got to see this dispatch of mine directing certain instructions to be given to the commanders in the field, operating against Early, and sent me the following very characteristic dispatch:

OFFICE U. S. MILITARY TELEGRAPH,
WAR DEPARTMENT,
WASHINGTON, D. C., *August* 3, 1864.

Cypher. 6 P.M.,
     LT.-GENERAL GRANT,
       City Point, Va.

I have seen your despatch in which you say, "I want Sheridan put in command of all the troops in the field, with instructions to put himself south of the enemy, and follow him to the death. Wherever the enemy goes, let our troops go also." This, I think, is exactly right, as to how our forces should move. But please look over the despatches you may have received from here, even since you made that order, and discover, if you can, that there is any idea in the head of any one here, of "putting our army *south* of the enemy," or of "following him to the *death*" in any direction. I repeat to you it will neither be done nor attempted unless you watch it every day, and hour, and force it.

A. LINCOLN.

I replied to this that "I would start in two hours for Washington," and soon got off, going directly to the Monocacy without stopping at Washington on my way. I found General Hunter's army encamped there, scattered over the fields along the banks of the Monocacy, with many hundreds of cars and locomotives, belonging to the Baltimore and Ohio Railroad, which he had taken the precaution to bring back and collect at that point. I asked the general where the enemy was. He replied that he did not know. He said the fact was, that he was so embarrassed with orders from Washington moving him first to the right and then to the left that he had lost all trace of the enemy.

I then told the general that I would find out where the enemy was, and at once ordered steam got up and trains made up, giving directions to push for Halltown, some four miles above Harper's Ferry, in the Shenandoah Valley. The cavalry and the wagon trains were to march, but all the troops that could be transported by the cars were to go in that way. I knew that the valley was of such importance to the enemy that, no matter how much he was scattered at that time, he would in a very short time be found in front of our troops moving south.

I then wrote out General Hunter's instructions.* I told him that Sheridan was in Washington, and still another division was on its way; and suggested that he establish the headquarters of the department at any point that would suit him best, Cumberland, Baltimore, or elsewhere, and give Sheridan command of the troops in the field. The general replied to this, that he thought he had better be relieved entirely. He said that General Halleck seemed so much to distrust his fitness for the position he was in that he thought somebody else ought to be there. He did not want, in any way, to embarrass the cause; thus showing a patriotism that was none too common in the army. There were not many major-generals who

---

*See letter, August 5th, Appendix.

would voluntarily have asked to have the command of a department taken from them on the supposition that for some particular reason, or for any reason, the service would be better performed. I told him, "very well then," and telegraphed at once for Sheridan to come to the Monocacy, and suggested that I would wait and meet him there.

Sheridan came at once by special train, but reached there after the troops were all off. I went to the station and remained there until he arrived. Myself and one or two of my staff were about all the Union people, except General Hunter and his staff, who were left at the Monocacy when Sheridan arrived. I hastily told Sheridan what had been done and what I wanted him to do, giving him, at the same time, the written instructions which had been prepared for General Hunter and directed to that officer.

Sheridan now had about 30,000 men to move with, 8,000 of them being cavalry. Early had about the same number, but the superior ability of the National commander over the Confederate commander was so great that all the latter's advantage of being on the defensive was more than counterbalanced by this circumstance. As I had predicted, Early was soon found in front of Sheridan in the valley, and Pennsylvania and Maryland were speedily freed from the invaders. The importance of the valley was so great to the Confederates that Lee reinforced Early, but not to the extent that we thought and feared he would.

To prevent as much as possible these reinforcements from being sent out from Richmond, I had to do something to compel Lee to retain his forces about his capital. I therefore gave orders for another move to the north side of the James River, to threaten Richmond. Hancock's corps, part of the 10th corps under Birney, and Gregg's division of cavalry were crossed to the north side of the James during the night of the 13th–14th of August. A threatening position was maintained for a number of days, with more or less skirmishing, and some tolerably hard fighting; although it was my object and my instructions that anything like a battle should be avoided, unless opportunities should present themselves which would insure great success. General Meade was left in command of the few troops around Petersburg, strongly intrenched; and was instructed to keep a close watch upon the enemy in that quarter, and himself to take advantage of any weakening that might occur through an effort on the part of the enemy to reinforce the north side. There was no particular victory gained on either side; but during that time no more reinforcements were sent to the valley.

I informed Sheridan of what had been done to prevent reinforcements being sent from Richmond against him, and also that the efforts we had made had proven that one of the divisions which we supposed had gone to the valley was still at Richmond, because we had captured six or seven hundred prisoners from that division, each of its four brigades having contributed to our list of captures. I also informed him that but one division had gone, and it was possible that I should be able to prevent the going of any more.

To add to my embarrassment at this time Sherman, who was now near Atlanta, wanted reinforcements. He was perfectly willing to take the raw troops then being raised in the North-west, saying that he could teach them more soldiering in one day among his troops than they would learn in a week in a camp of instruction. I therefore asked that all troops in camps of instruction in the North-west be sent to him. Sherman also wanted to be assured that no Eastern troops were moving out against him. I informed him of what I had done and assured him that I would hold all the troops there that it was possible for me to hold, and that up to that time none had gone. I also informed him that his real danger was from Kirby Smith, who commanded the trans-Mississippi Department. If Smith should escape Steele, and get across the Mississippi River, he might move against him. I had, therefore, asked to have an expedition ready to move from New Orleans against Mobile in case Kirby Smith should get across. This would have a tendency to draw him to the defence of that place, instead of going against Sherman.

Right in the midst of all these embarrassments Halleck informed me that there was an organized scheme on foot in the North to resist the draft, and suggested that it might become necessary to draw troops from the field to put it down. He also advised taking in sail, and not going too fast.

The troops were withdrawn from the north side of the

James River on the night of the 20th. Before they were withdrawn, however, and while most of Lee's force was on that side of the river, Warren had been sent with most of the 5th corps to capture the Weldon Railroad. He took up his line of march well back to the rear, south of the enemy, while the troops remaining in the trenches extended so as to cover that part of the line which he had vacated by moving out. From our left, near the old line, it was about three miles to the Weldon Railroad. A division was ordered from the right of the Petersburg line to reinforce Warren, while a division was brought back from the north side of the James River to take its place.

This road was very important to the enemy. The limits from which his supplies had been drawn were already very much contracted, and I knew that he must fight desperately to protect it. Warren carried the road, though with heavy loss on both sides. He fortified his new position, and our trenches were then extended from the left of our main line to connect with his new one. Lee made repeated attempts to dislodge Warren's corps, but without success, and with heavy loss.

As soon as Warren was fortified and reinforcements reached him, troops were sent south to destroy the bridges on the Weldon Railroad; and with such success that the enemy had to draw in wagons, for a distance of about thirty miles, all the supplies they got thereafter from that source. It was on the 21st that Lee seemed to have given up the Weldon Railroad as having been lost to him; but along about the 24th or 25th he made renewed attempts to recapture it; again he failed and with very heavy losses to him as compared with ours.

On the night of the 20th our troops on the north side of the James were withdrawn, and Hancock and Gregg were sent south to destroy the Weldon Railroad. They were attacked on the 25th at Reams's Station, and after desperate fighting a part of our line gave way, losing five pieces of artillery. But the Weldon Railroad never went out of our possession from the 18th of August to the close of the war.

Chapter LVIII.

SHERIDAN'S ADVANCE—VISIT TO SHERIDAN—SHERIDAN'S
VICTORY IN THE SHENANDOAH—SHERIDAN'S RIDE
TO WINCHESTER—CLOSE OF THE CAMPAIGN FOR
THE WINTER.

WE HAD our troops on the Weldon Railroad contending against a large force that regarded this road of so much importance that they could afford to expend many lives in retaking it; Sherman just getting through to Atlanta with great losses of men from casualties, discharges and detachments left along as guards to occupy and hold the road in rear of him; Washington threatened but a short time before, and now Early being strengthened in the valley so as, probably, to renew that attempt. It kept me pretty active in looking after all these points.

On the 10th of August Sheridan had advanced on Early up the Shenandoah Valley, Early falling back to Strasburg. On the 12th I learned that Lee had sent twenty pieces of artillery, two divisions of infantry and a considerable cavalry force to strengthen Early. It was important that Sheridan should be informed of this, so I sent the information to Washington by telegraph, and directed a courier to be sent from there to get the message to Sheridan at all hazards, giving him the information. The messenger, an officer of the army, pushed through with great energy and reached Sheridan just in time. The officer went through by way of Snicker's Gap, escorted by some cavalry. He found Sheridan just making his preparations to attack Early in his chosen position. Now, however, he was thrown back on the defensive.

On the 15th of September I started to visit General Sheridan in the Shenandoah Valley. My purpose was to have him attack Early, or drive him out of the valley and destroy that source of supplies for Lee's army. I knew it was impossible for me to get orders through Washington to Sheridan to make a move, because they would be stopped there and such orders as Halleck's caution (and that of the Secretary of War) would suggest would be given instead, and would, no doubt, be contradictory to mine. I therefore, without stopping at Washington, went directly through to Charlestown, some ten miles above Harper's Ferry, and waited there to see General Sheridan, having sent a courier in advance to inform him where to meet me.

When Sheridan arrived I asked him if he had a map showing the positions of his army and that of the enemy. He at once drew one out of his side pocket, showing all roads and streams, and the camps of the two armies. He said that if he had permission he would move so and so (pointing out how) against the Confederates, and that he could "whip them." Before starting I had drawn up a plan of campaign for Sheridan, which I had brought with me; but, seeing that he was so clear and so positive in his views and so confident of success, I said nothing about this and did not take it out of my pocket.

Sheridan's wagon trains were kept at Harper's Ferry, where all of his stores were. By keeping the teams at that place, their forage did not have to be hauled to them. As supplies of ammunition, provisions and rations for the men were wanted, trains would be made up to deliver the stores to the commissaries and quartermasters encamped at Winchester. Knowing that he, in making preparations to move at a given day, would have to bring up wagon trains from Harper's Ferry, I asked him if he could be ready to get off by the following Tuesday. This was on Friday. "O yes," he said, he "could be off before daylight on Monday." I told him then to make the attack at that time and according to his own plan; and I immediately started to return to the army about Richmond. After visiting Baltimore and Burlington, New Jersey, I arrived at City Point on the 19th.

On the way out to Harper's Ferry I had met Mr. Robert Garrett, President of the Baltimore and Ohio Railroad. He seemed very anxious to know when workmen might be put upon the road again so as to make repairs and put it in shape for running. It was a large piece of property to have standing idle. I told him I could not answer then positively but would try and inform him before a great while. On my return Mr. Garrett met me again with the same question and I told him I thought that by the following Wednesday he might send his workmen out on his road. I gave him no further information however, and he had no suspicion of how I expected to have the road cleared for his workmen.

Sheridan moved at the time he had fixed upon. He met Early at the crossing of Opequon Creek, and won a most decisive victory—one which electrified the country. Early had invited this attack himself by his bad generalship and made the victory easy. He had sent G. T. Anderson's division east of the Blue Ridge before I went to Harper's Ferry; and about the time I arrived there he started with two other divisions (leaving but two in their camps) to march to Martinsburg for the purpose of destroying the Baltimore and Ohio Railroad at that point. Early here learned that I had been with Sheridan and, supposing there was some movement on foot, started back as soon as he got the information. But his forces were separated and, as I have said, he was very badly defeated. He fell back to Fisher's Hill, Sheridan following.

The valley is narrow at that point, and Early made another stand there, behind works which extended across. But Sheridan turned both his flanks and again sent him speeding up the valley, following in hot pursuit. The pursuit was continued up the valley to Mount Jackson and New Market. Sheridan captured about eleven hundred prisoners and sixteen guns. The houses which he passed all along the route were found to be filled with Early's wounded, and the country swarmed with his deserters. Finally, on the 25th, Early turned from the valley eastward, leaving Sheridan at Harrisonburg in undisputed possession.

Now one of the main objects of the expedition began to be accomplished. Sheridan went to work with his command, gathering in the crops, cattle, and everything in the upper part of the valley required by our troops; and especially taking what might be of use to the enemy. What he could not take away he destroyed, so that the enemy would not be invited to come back there. I congratulated Sheridan upon his recent great victory and had a salute of a hundred guns fired in honor of it, the guns being aimed at the enemy around Petersburg. I also notified the other commanders throughout the country, who also fired salutes in honor of his victory.

I had reason to believe that the administration was a little afraid to have a decisive battle fought at that time, for fear it

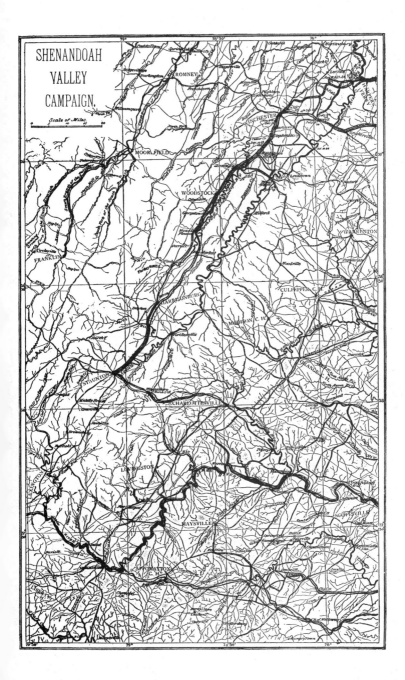

SHENANDOAH
VALLEY
CAMPAIGN.

Scale of Miles.

might go against us and have a bad effect on the November elections. The convention which had met and made its nomination of the Democratic candidate for the presidency had declared the war a failure. Treason was talked as boldly in Chicago at that convention as ever it had been in Charleston. It was a question whether the government would then have had the power to make arrests and punish those who thus talked treason. But this decisive victory was the most effective campaign argument made in the canvass.

Sheridan, in his pursuit, got beyond where they could hear from him in Washington, and the President became very much frightened about him. He was afraid that the hot pursuit had been a little like that of General Cass was said to have been, in one of our Indian wars, when he was an officer of the army. Cass was pursuing the Indians so closely that the first thing he knew he found himself in their front, and the Indians pursuing him. The President was afraid that Sheridan had got on the other side of Early and that Early was in behind him. He was afraid that Sheridan was getting so far away that reinforcements would be sent out from Richmond to enable Early to beat him. I replied to the President that I had taken steps to prevent Lee from sending reinforcements to Early, by attacking the former where he was.

On the 28th of September, to retain Lee in his position, I sent Ord with the 18th corps and Birney with the 10th corps to make an advance on Richmond, to threaten it. Ord moved with the left wing up to Chaffin's Bluff; Birney with the 10th corps took a road farther north; while Kautz with the cavalry took the Darby road, still farther to the north. They got across the river by the next morning, and made an effort to surprise the enemy. In that, however, they were unsuccessful.

The enemy's lines were very strong and very intricate. Stannard's division of the 18th corps with General Burnham's brigade leading, tried an assault against Fort Harrison and captured it with sixteen guns and a good many prisoners. Burnham was killed in the assault. Colonel Stevens who succeeded him was badly wounded; and his successor also fell in the same way. Some works to the right and left were also carried with the guns in them—six in number—and a few more prisoners. Birney's troops to the right captured the enemy's intrenched picket-lines, but were unsuccessful in their efforts upon the main line.

Our troops fortified their new position, bringing Fort Harrison into the new line and extending it to the river. This brought us pretty close to the enemy on the north side of the James, and the two opposing lines maintained their relative positions to the close of the siege.

In the afternoon a further attempt was made to advance, but it failed. Ord fell badly wounded, and had to be relieved; the command devolved upon General Heckman, and later General Weitzel was assigned to the command of the 18th corps. During the night Lee reinforced his troops about Fort Gilmer, which was at the right of Fort Harrison, by transferring eight additional brigades from Petersburg, and attempted to retake the works which we had captured by concentrating ten brigades against them. All their efforts failed, their attacks being all repulsed with very heavy loss. In one of these assaults upon us General Stannard, a gallant officer, who was defending Fort Harrison, lost an arm. Our casualties during these operations amounted to 394 killed, 1,554 wounded and 324 missing.

Whilst this was going on General Meade was instructed to keep up an appearance of moving troops to our extreme left. Parke and Warren were kept with two divisions, each under arms, ready to move, leaving their enclosed batteries manned, with a scattering line on the other intrenchments. The object of this was to prevent reinforcements from going to the north side of the river. Meade was instructed to watch the enemy closely and, if Lee weakened his lines, to make an attack.

On the 30th these troops moved out, under Warren, and captured an advanced intrenched camp at Peeble's farm, driving the enemy back to the main line. Our troops followed and made an attack in the hope of carrying the enemy's main line; but in this they were unsuccessful and lost a large number of men, mostly captured. The number of killed and wounded was not large. The next day our troops advanced again and established themselves, intrenching a new line about a mile in front of the enemy. This advanced Warren's position on the Weldon Railroad very considerably.

Sheridan having driven the enemy out of the valley, and taken the productions of the valley so that instead of going there for supplies the enemy would have to bring his provisions with him if he again entered it, recommended a reduction of his own force, the surplus to be sent where it could be of more use. I approved of his suggestion, and ordered him to send Wright's corps back to the James River. I further directed him to repair the railroad up the Shenandoah Valley towards the advanced position which we would hold with a small force. The troops were to be sent to Washington by the way of Culpeper, in order to watch the east side of the Blue Ridge, and prevent the enemy from getting into the rear of Sheridan while he was still doing his work of destruction.

The valley was so very important, however, to the Confederate army that, contrary to our expectations, they determined to make one more strike, and save it if possible before the supplies should be all destroyed. Reinforcements were sent therefore to Early, and this before any of our troops had been withdrawn. Early prepared to strike Sheridan at Harrisonburg; but the latter had not remained there.

On the 6th of October Sheridan commenced retiring down the valley, taking or destroying all the food and forage and driving the cattle before him, Early following. At Fisher's Hill Sheridan turned his cavalry back on that of Early, which, under the lead of Rosser, was pursuing closely, and routed it most completely, capturing eleven guns and a large number of prisoners. Sheridan lost only about sixty men. His cavalry pursued the enemy back some twenty-five miles. On the 10th of October the march down the valley was again resumed, Early again following.

I now ordered Sheridan to halt, and to improve the opportunity if afforded by the enemy's having been sufficiently weakened, to move back again and cut the James River Canal and Virginia Central Railroad. But this order had to go through Washington where it was intercepted; and when Sheridan received what purported to be a statement of what I wanted him to do it was something entirely different. Halleck informed Sheridan that it was my wish for him to hold a forward position as a base from which to act against Charlottesville and Gordonsville; that he should fortify this position and provision it.

Sheridan objected to this most decidedly; and I was impelled to telegraph him, on the 14th, as follows:

> CITY POINT, VA.,
> *October* 14, 1864. —12.30 P.M.
>
> MAJOR-GENERAL SHERIDAN,
>   Cedar Creek, Va.
>
> What I want is for you to threaten the Virginia Central Railroad and canal in the manner your judgment tells you is best, holding yourself ready to advance, if the enemy draw off their forces. If you make the enemy hold a force equal to your own for the protection of those thoroughfares, it will accomplish nearly as much as their destruction. If you cannot do this, then the next best thing to do is to send here all the force you can. I deem a good cavalry force necessary for your offensive, as well as defensive operations. You need not therefore send here more than one division of cavalry.
>
> U. S. GRANT,
> Lieutenant-General.

Sheridan having been summoned to Washington City, started on the 15th leaving Wright in command. His army was then at Cedar Creek, some twenty miles south of Winchester. The next morning while at Front Royal, Sheridan received a dispatch from Wright, saying that a dispatch from Longstreet to Early had been intercepted. It directed the latter to be ready to move and to crush Sheridan as soon as he, Longstreet, arrived. On the receipt of this news Sheridan ordered the cavalry up the valley to join Wright.

On the 18th of October Early was ready to move, and during the night succeeded in getting his troops in the rear of our left flank, which fled precipitately and in great confusion down the valley, losing eighteen pieces of artillery and a thousand or more prisoners. The right under General Getty maintained a firm and steady front, falling back to Middletown where it took a position and made a stand. The cavalry went to the rear, seized the roads leading to Winchester and held them for the use of our troops in falling back, General Wright having ordered a retreat back to that place.

Sheridan having left Washington on the 18th, reached Winchester that night. The following morning he started to join his command. He had scarcely got out of town, when he met his men returning in panic from the front and also heard heavy firing to the south. He immediately ordered the cavalry at Winchester to be deployed across the valley to stop the stragglers. Leaving members of his staff to take care of Winchester and the public property there, he set out with a small escort directly for the scene of battle. As he met the fugitives he ordered them to turn back, reminding them that they were going the wrong way. His presence soon restored confidence. Finding themselves worse frightened than hurt the men did halt and turn back. Many of those who had run ten miles got back in time to redeem their reputation as gallant soldiers before night.

When Sheridan got to the front he found Getty and Custer still holding their ground firmly between the Confederates and our retreating troops. Everything in the rear was now ordered up. Sheridan at once proceeded to intrench his position; and he awaited an assault from the enemy. This was made with vigor, and was directed principally against Emory's corps, which had sustained the principal loss in the first attack. By one o'clock the attack was repulsed. Early was so badly damaged that he seemed disinclined to make another attack, but went to work to intrench himself with a view to holding the position he had already gained. He thought, no doubt, that Sheridan would be glad enough to leave him unmolested; but in this he was mistaken.

About the middle of the afternoon Sheridan advanced. He sent his cavalry by both flanks, and they penetrated to the enemy's rear. The contest was close for a time, but at length the left of the enemy broke, and disintegration along the whole line soon followed. Early tried to rally his men, but they were followed so closely that they had to give way very quickly every time they attempted to make a stand. Our cavalry, having pushed on and got in the rear of the Confederates, captured twenty-four pieces of artillery, besides retaking what had been lost in the morning. This victory pretty much closed the campaigning in the Valley of Virginia. All the Confederate troops were sent back to Richmond with the exception of one division of infantry and a little cavalry. Wright's corps was ordered back to the Army of the Potomac, and two other divisions were withdrawn from the valley. Early had lost more men in killed, wounded and captured in the valley than Sheridan had commanded from first to last.

On more than one occasion in these engagements General R. B. Hayes, who succeeded me as President of the United States, bore a very honorable part. His conduct on the field was marked by conspicuous gallantry as well as the display of qualities of a higher order than that of mere personal daring. This might well have been expected of one who could write at the time he is said to have done so: "Any officer fit for duty who at this crisis would abandon his post to electioneer for a seat in Congress, ought to be scalped." Having entered the army as a Major of Volunteers at the beginning of the war, General Hayes attained by meritorious service the rank of Brevet Major-General before its close.

On the north side of the James River the enemy attacked Kautz's cavalry on the 7th of October, and drove it back with heavy loss in killed, wounded and prisoners, and the loss of all the artillery. This was followed up by an attack on our intrenched infantry line, but was repulsed with severe slaughter. On the 13th a reconnoissance was sent out by General Butler, with a view to drive the enemy from some new works he was constructing, which resulted in heavy loss to us.

On the 24th I ordered General Meade to attempt to get possession of the South Side Railroad, and for that purpose to advance on the 27th. The attempt proved a failure, however, the most advanced of our troops not getting nearer than within six miles of the point aimed for. Seeing the impossibility of its accomplishment I ordered the troops to withdraw, and they were all back in their former positions the next day.

Butler, by my directions, also made a demonstration on the north side of the James River in order to support this move, by detaining there the Confederate troops who were on that side. He succeeded in this, but failed of further results by not marching past the enemy's left before turning in on the Darby road and by reason of simply coming up against their lines in place.

This closed active operations around Richmond for the winter. Of course there was frequent skirmishing between pickets, but no serious battle was fought near either Petersburg or Richmond. It would prolong this work to give a detailed account of all that took place from day to day around Petersburg and at other parts of my command, and it would not interest the general reader if given. All these details can be found by the military student in a series of books published by the Scribners, Badeau's history of my campaigns, and also in the publications of the War Department, including both the National and Confederate reports.

In the latter part of November General Hancock was relieved from the command of the 2d corps by the Secretary of War and ordered to Washington, to organize and command a corps of veteran troops to be designated the 1st corps. It was expected that this would give him a large command to cooperate with in the spring. It was my expectation, at the time, that in the final operations Hancock should move either up the valley, or else east of the Blue Ridge to Lynchburg; the idea being to make the spring campaign the close of the war. I expected, with Sherman coming up from the South, Meade south of Petersburg and around Richmond, and Thomas's command in Tennessee with depots of supplies established in the eastern part of that State, to move from the direction of Washington or the valley towards Lynchburg. We would then have Lee so surrounded that his supplies would be cut off entirely, making it impossible for him to support his army.

General Humphreys, chief-of-staff of the Army of the Potomac, was assigned to the command of the 2d corps, to succeed Hancock.

Chapter LIX.

THE CAMPAIGN IN GEORGIA—SHERMAN'S MARCH TO THE SEA—WAR ANECDOTES—THE MARCH ON SAVANNAH—INVESTMENT OF SAVANNAH— CAPTURE OF SAVANNAH.

LET US now return to the operations in the military division of the Mississippi, and accompany Sherman in his march to the sea.

The possession of Atlanta by us narrowed the territory of the enemy very materially and cut off one of his two remaining lines of roads from east to west.

A short time after the fall of Atlanta Mr. Davis visited Palmetto and Macon and made speeches at each place. He spoke at Palmetto on the 20th of September, and at Macon on the 22d. Inasmuch as he had relieved Johnston and appointed Hood, and Hood had immediately taken the initiative, it is natural to suppose that Mr. Davis was disappointed with General Johnston's policy. My own judgment is that Johnston acted very wisely: he husbanded his men and saved as much of his territory as he could, without fighting decisive battles in which all might be lost. As Sherman advanced, as I have shown, his army became spread out, until, if this had been continued, it would have been easy to destroy it in detail. I know that both Sherman and I were rejoiced when we heard of the change. Hood was unquestionably a brave, gallant soldier and not destitute of ability; but unfortunately his policy was to fight the enemy wherever he saw him, without thinking much of the consequences of defeat.

In his speeches Mr. Davis denounced Governor Brown, of Georgia, and General Johnston in unmeasured terms, even insinuating that their loyalty to the Southern cause was doubtful. So far as General Johnston is concerned, I think Davis did him a great injustice in this particular. I had known the general before the war and strongly believed it would be impossible for him to accept a high commission for the purpose of betraying the cause he had espoused. Then, as I have said, I think that his policy was the best one that could have been pursued by the whole South—protract the war, which was all that was necessary to enable them to gain recognition in the end. The North was already growing weary, as the South evidently was also, but with this difference. In the North the people governed, and could stop hostilities whenever they chose to stop supplies. The South was a military camp, controlled absolutely by the government with soldiers to back it, and the war could have been protracted, no matter to what extent the discontent reached, up to the point of open mutiny of the soldiers themselves. Mr. Davis's speeches were frank appeals to the people of Georgia and that portion of the South to come to their relief. He tried to assure his frightened hearers that the Yankees were rapidly digging their own graves; that measures were already being taken to cut them off from supplies from the North; and that with a force in front, and cut off from the rear, they must soon starve in the midst of a hostile people. Papers containing reports of these speeches immediately reached the Northern States, and they were republished. Of course, that caused no alarm so long as telegraphic communication was kept up with Sherman.

When Hood was forced to retreat from Atlanta he moved to the south-west and was followed by a portion of Sherman's army. He soon appeared upon the railroad in Sherman's rear, and with his whole army began destroying the road. At the same time also the work was begun in Tennessee and Kentucky which Mr. Davis had assured his hearers at Palmetto and Macon would take place. He ordered Forrest (about the ablest cavalry general in the South) north for this purpose; and Forrest and Wheeler carried out their orders with more or less destruction, occasionally picking up a garrison. Forrest indeed performed the very remarkable feat of capturing, with cavalry, two gunboats and a number of transports, something the accomplishment of which is very hard to account for. Hood's army had been weakened by Governor Brown's withdrawing the Georgia State troops for the purpose of gathering in the season's crops for the use of the people and for the use of the army. This not only depleted Hood's forces but it served a most excellent purpose in gathering in supplies of food and forage for the use of our army in its subsequent march. Sherman was obliged to push on with his force and go himself with portions of it hither and thither, until it was clearly demonstrated to him that with the army he then had it would be impossible to hold the line from Atlanta back and leave him any force whatever with which to take the offensive. Had that plan been adhered to, very large reinforcements would have been necessary; and Mr. Davis's prediction of the destruction of the army would have been realized, or else Sherman would have been obliged to make a successful retreat, which Mr. Davis said in his speeches would prove more disastrous than Napoleon's retreat from Moscow.

These speeches of Mr. Davis were not long in reaching Sherman. He took advantage of the information they gave, and made all the preparation possible for him to make to meet what now became expected, attempts to break his communications. Something else had to be done: and to Sherman's sensible and soldierly mind the idea was not long in dawning upon him, not only that something else had to be done, but what that something else should be.

On September 10th I telegraphed Sherman as follows:

CITY POINT, VA., *Sept.* 10, 1864.
MAJOR-GENERAL SHERMAN,
　　　Atlanta, Georgia.

So soon as your men are sufficiently rested, and preparations can be made, it is desirable that another campaign should be commenced. We want to keep the enemy constantly pressed to the end of the war. If we give him no peace whilst the war lasts, the end cannot be distant. Now that we have all of Mobile Bay that is valuable, I do not know but it will be the best move to transfer Canby's troops to act upon Savannah, whilst you move on Augusta. I should like to hear from you, however, in this matter.

　　　　　　　　　U. S. GRANT,
　　　　　　　　　Lieutenant-General.

Sherman replied promptly:

"If I could be sure of finding provisions and ammunition at Augusta, or Columbus, Georgia, I can march to Milledgeville, and compel Hood to give up Augusta or Macon, and then turn on the other. * * * If you can manage to take the Savannah River as high up as Augusta, or the Chattahoochee as far up as Columbus, I can sweep the whole State of Georgia."

On the 12th I sent a special messenger, one of my own staff, with a letter inviting Sherman's views about the next campaign.

CITY POINT, VA., *Sept.* 12, 1864.

MAJOR-GENERAL W. T. SHERMAN,
    Commanding Mil. Division of the Mississippi.

I send Lieutenant-Colonel Porter, of my staff, with this. Colonel Porter will explain to you the exact condition of affairs here better than I can do in the limits of a letter. Although I feel myself strong enough for offensive operations, I am holding on quietly to get advantage of recruits and convalescents, who are coming forward very rapidly. My lines are necessarily very long, extending from Deep Bottom north of the James across the peninsula formed by the Appomattox and the James, and south of the Appomattox to the Weldon Road. This line is very strongly fortified, and can be held with comparatively few men, but from its great length takes many in the aggregate. I propose, when I do move, to extend my left so as to control what is known as the South Side, or Lynchburg and Petersburg Road, then if possible to keep the Danville Road cut. At the same time this move is made, I want to send a force of from six to ten thousand men against Wilmington.

The way I propose to do this is to land the men north of Fort Fisher, and hold that point. At the same time a large naval fleet will be assembled there, and the iron-clads will run the batteries as they did at Mobile. This will give us the same control of the harbor of Wilmington that we now have of the harbor of Mobile. What you are to do with the forces at your command, I do not see. The difficulties of supplying your army, except when you are constantly moving, beyond where you are, I plainly see. If it had not been for Price's movements Canby would have sent twelve thousand more men to Mobile. From your command on the Mississippi an equal number could have been taken. With these forces my idea would have been to divide them, sending one half to Mobile and the other half to Savannah. You could then move as proposed in your telegram, so as to threaten Macon and Augusta equally. Whichever was abandoned by the enemy you could take and open up a new base of supplies. My object now in sending a staff officer is not so much to suggest operations for you, as to get your views and have plans matured by the time everything can be got ready. It will probably be the 5th of October before any of the plans herein indicated will be executed.

If you have any promotions to recommend, send the names forward and I will approve them. * * *

U. S. GRANT,
Lieutenant-General.

This reached Sherman on September 20th.

On the 25th of September Sherman reported to Washington that Hood's troops were in his rear. He had provided against this by sending a division to Chattanooga and a division to Rome, Georgia, which was in the rear of Hood, supposing that Hood would fall back in the direction from which he had come to reach the railroad. At the same time Sherman and Hood kept up a correspondence relative to the exchange of prisoners, the treatment of citizens, and other matters suitable to be arranged between hostile commanders in the field. On the 27th of September I telegraphed Sherman as follows:

CITY POINT, VA.,
September 27, 1864. — 10.30 A.M.

MAJOR-GENERAL SHERMAN:

I have directed all recruits and new troops from the Western States to be sent to Nashville, to receive their further orders from you. * * *

U. S. GRANT,
Lieutenant-General.

On the 29th Sherman sent Thomas back to Chattanooga, and afterwards to Nashville, with another division (Morgan's) of the advanced army. Sherman then suggested that, when he was prepared, his movements should take place against Milledgeville and then to Savannah. His expectation at that time was, to make this movement as soon as he could get up his supplies. Hood was moving in his own country, and was moving light so that he could make two miles to Sherman's one. He depended upon the country to gather his supplies, and so was not affected by delays.

As I have said, until this unexpected state of affairs happened, Mobile had been looked upon as the objective point of Sherman's army. It had been a favorite move of mine from 1862, when I first suggested to the then commander-in-chief that the troops in Louisiana, instead of frittering away their time in the trans-Mississippi, should move against Mobile. I recommended this from time to time until I came into command of the army, the last of March 1864. Having the power in my own hands, I now ordered the concentration of supplies, stores and troops, in the department of the Gulf about New Orleans, with a view to a move against Mobile, in support of, and in conjunction with, the other armies operating in the field. Before I came into command, these troops had been scattered over the trans-Mississippi department in such a way that they could not be, or were not, gotten back in time to take any part in the original movement; hence the consideration, which had caused Mobile to be selected as the objective point for Sherman's army to find his next base of supplies after having cut loose from Atlanta, no longer existed.

General G. M. Dodge, an exceedingly efficient officer, having been badly wounded, had to leave the army about the first of October. He was in command of two divisions of the 16th corps, consolidated into one. Sherman then divided his army into the right and left wings—the right commanded by General O. O. Howard and the left by General Slocum. General Dodge's two divisions were assigned, one to each of these wings. Howard's command embraced the 15th and 17th corps, and Slocum's the 14th and 20th corps, commanded by Generals Jeff. C. Davis and A. S. Williams. Generals Logan and Blair commanded the two corps composing the right wing. About this time they left to take part in the presidential election, which took place that year, leaving their corps to Osterhaus and Ransom. I have no doubt that their leaving was at the earnest solicitation of the War Department. General Blair got back in time to resume his command and to proceed with it throughout the march to the sea and back to the grand review at Washington. General Logan did not return to his command until after it reached Savannah.

Logan felt very much aggrieved at the transfer of General Howard from that portion of the Army of the Potomac which was then with the Western Army, to the command of the Army of the Tennessee, with which army General Logan had served from the battle of Belmont to the fall of Atlanta— having passed successively through all grades from colonel commanding a regiment to general commanding a brigade, division and army corps, until upon the death of McPherson the command of the entire Army of the Tennessee devolved upon him in the midst of a hotly contested battle. He conceived that he had done his full duty as commander in that engagement; and I can bear testimony, from personal observation, that he had proved himself fully equal to all the lower positions which he had occupied as a soldier. I will not pretend to question the motive which actuated Sherman in taking an officer from another army to supersede General Logan. I have no doubt, whatever, that he did this for what he considered would be to the good of the service, which was more important than that the personal feelings of any individual should not be aggrieved; though I doubt whether he had an officer with him who could have filled the place as Logan would have done. Differences of opinion must exist between the best of friends as to policies in war, and of judgment as to men's fitness. The officer who has the command, however, should be allowed to judge of the fitness of the officers under him, unless he is very manifestly wrong.

Sherman's army, after all the depletions, numbered about sixty thousand effective men. All weak men had been left to hold the rear, and those remaining were not only well men, but strong and hardy, so that he had sixty thousand as good soldiers as ever trod the earth; better than any European soldiers, because they not only worked like a machine but the machine thought. European armies know very little what they are fighting for, and care less. Included in these sixty thousand troops, there were two small divisions of cavalry, numbering altogether about four thousand men. Hood had about thirty-five to forty thousand men, independent of Forrest, whose forces were operating in Tennessee and Kentucky, as Mr. Davis had promised they should. This part of Mr. Davis's military plan was admirable, and promised the best results of anything he could have done, according to my judgment. I say this because I have criticised his military judgment in the removal of Johnston, and also in the appointment of Hood. I am aware, however, that there was high feeling existing at that time between Davis and his subordinate, whom I regarded as one of his ablest lieutenants.

On the 5th of October the railroad back from Atlanta was again very badly broken, Hood having got on the track with his army. Sherman saw after night, from a high point, the road burning for miles. The defence of the railroad by our troops was very gallant, but they could not hold points between their intrenched positions against Hood's whole army; in fact they made no attempt to do so; but generally the intrenched positions were held, as well as important bridges, and stores located at them. Allatoona, for instance, was defended by a small force of men under the command of General Corse, one of the very able and efficient volunteer officers produced by the war. He, with a small force, was cut off from the remainder of the National army and was attacked with great vigor by many times his own number. Sherman from his high position could see the battle raging, with the Confederate troops between him and his subordinate. He sent men, of course, to raise the temporary siege, but the time that would be necessarily consumed in reaching Corse, would be so great that all occupying the intrenchments might be dead. Corse was a man who would never surrender. From a high position some of Sherman's signal corps discovered a signal flag waving from a hole in the block house at Allatoona. It was from Corse. He had been shot through the face, but he signalled to his chief a message which left no doubt of his determination to hold his post at all hazards. It was at this point probably, that Sherman first realized that with the forces at his disposal, the keeping open of his line of communications with the North would be impossible if he expected to retain any force with which to operate offensively beyond Atlanta. He proposed, therefore, to destroy the roads back to Chattanooga, when all ready to move, and leave the latter place garrisoned. Yet, before abandoning the railroad, it was necessary that he should repair damages already done, and hold the road until he could get forward such supplies, ordnance stores and small rations, as he wanted to carry with him on his proposed march, and to return to the north his surplus artillery; his object being to move light and to have no more artillery than could be used to advantage on the field.

Sherman thought Hood would follow him, though he proposed to prepare for the contingency of the latter moving the other way while he was moving south, by making Thomas strong enough to hold Tennessee and Kentucky. I, myself, was thoroughly satisfied that Hood would go north, as he did. On the 2d of November I telegraphed Sherman authorizing him definitely to move according to the plan he had proposed: that is, cutting loose from his base, giving up Atlanta and the railroad back to Chattanooga. To strengthen Thomas he sent Stanley (4th corps) back, and also ordered Schofield, commanding the Army of the Ohio, twelve thousand strong, to report to him. In addition to this, A. J. Smith, who, with two divisions of Sherman's army, was in Missouri aiding Rosecrans in driving the enemy from that State, was under orders to return to Thomas and, under the most unfavorable circumstances, might be expected to arrive there long before Hood could reach Nashville.

In addition to this, the new levies of troops that were being raised in the North-west went to Thomas as rapidly as enrolled and equipped. Thomas, without any of these additions spoken of, had a garrison at Chattanooga—which had been strengthened by one division—and garrisons at Bridgeport, Stevenson, Decatur, Murfreesboro, and Florence. There were already with him in Nashville ten thousand soldiers in round numbers, and many thousands of employees in the quartermaster's and other departments who could be put in the intrenchments in front of Nashville, for its defence. Also, Wilson was there with ten thousand dismounted cavalrymen, who were being equipped for the field. Thomas had at this time about forty-five thousand men without any of the reinforcements here above enumerated. These reinforcements gave him altogether about seventy thousand men, without counting what might be added by the new levies already spoken of.

About this time Beauregard arrived upon the field, not to supersede Hood in command, but to take general charge over the entire district in which Hood and Sherman were, or might be, operating. He made the most frantic appeals to the citizens for assistance to be rendered in every way: by sending reinforcements, by destroying supplies on the line of march of the invaders, by destroying the bridges over which they would have to cross, and by, in every way, obstructing the roads to their front. But it was hard to convince the people of the propriety of destroying supplies which were so much needed by themselves, and each one hoped that his own possessions might escape.

Hood soon started north, and went into camp near Decatur, Alabama, where he remained until the 29th of October, but without making an attack on the garrison of that place.

The Tennessee River was patrolled by gunboats, from Muscle Shoals east; and, also, below the second shoals out to the Ohio River. These, with the troops that might be concentrated from the garrisons along the river at any point where Hood might choose to attempt to cross, made it impossible for him to cross the Tennessee at any place where it was navigable. But Muscle Shoals is not navigable, and below them again is another shoal which also obstructs navigation. Hood therefore moved down to a point nearly opposite Florence, Alabama, crossed over and remained there for some time, collecting supplies of food, forage and ammunition. All of these had to come from a considerable distance south, because the region in which he was then situated was mountainous, with small valleys which produced but little, and what they had produced had long since been exhausted. On the 1st of November I suggested to Sherman, and also asked his views thereon, the propriety of destroying Hood before he started on his campaign.

On the 2d of November, as stated, I approved definitely his making his proposed campaign through Georgia, leaving Hood behind to the tender mercy of Thomas and the troops in his command. Sherman fixed the 10th of November as the day of starting.

Sherman started on that day to get back to Atlanta, and on the 15th the real march to the sea commenced. The right wing, under Howard, and the cavalry went to Jonesboro, Milledgeville, then the capital of Georgia, being Sherman's objective or stopping place on the way to Savannah. The left wing moved to Stone Mountain, along roads much farther east than those taken by the right wing. Slocum was in command, and threatened Augusta as the point to which he was moving, but he was to turn off and meet the right wing at Milledgeville.

Atlanta was destroyed so far as to render it worthless for military purposes before starting, Sherman himself remaining over a day to superintend the work, and see that it was well done. Sherman's orders for this campaign were perfect. Before starting, he had sent back all sick, disabled and weak men, retaining nothing but the hardy, well-inured soldiers to accompany him on his long march in prospect. His artillery was reduced to sixty-five guns. The ammunition carried with them was two hundred rounds for musket and gun. Small rations were taken in a small wagon train, which was loaded to its capacity for rapid movement. The army was expected to live on the country, and to always keep the wagons full of forage and provisions against a possible delay of a few days.

The troops, both of the right and left wings, made most of their advance along the line of railroads, which they destroyed. The method adopted to perform this work, was to burn and destroy all the bridges and culverts, and for a long distance, at places, to tear up the track and bend the rails. Soldiers to do this rapidly would form a line along one side of the road with crowbars and poles, place these under the rails and, hoisting all at once, turn over many rods of road at one time. The ties would then be placed in piles, and the rails, as they were loosened, would be carried and put across these log heaps. When a sufficient number of rails were placed upon a pile of ties it would be set on fire. This would heat the rails very much more in the middle, that being over the main part of the fire, than at the ends, so that they would naturally bend of their own weight; but the soldiers, to increase the damage, would take tongs and, one or two men at each end of the rail, carry it with force against the nearest tree and twist it around, thus leaving rails forming bands to ornament the forest trees of Georgia. All this work was going on at the same time, there being a sufficient number of men detailed for that purpose. Some piled the logs and built the fire; some put the rails upon the fire; while others would bend those that were sufficiently heated: so that, by the time the last bit of road was torn up, that it was designed to destroy at a certain place, the rails previously taken up were already destroyed.

The organization for supplying the army was very complete. Each brigade furnished a company to gather supplies of

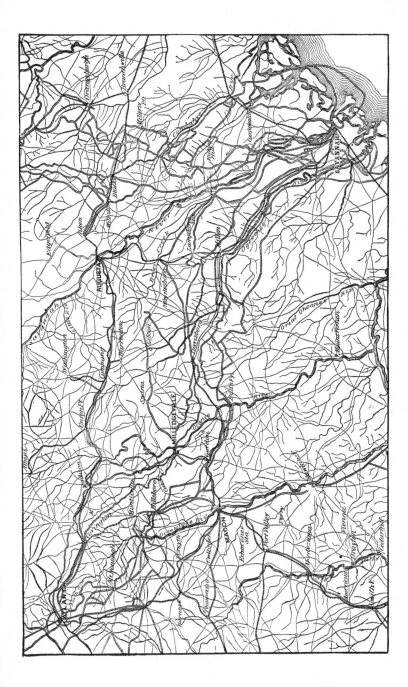

forage and provisions for the command to which they belonged. Strict injunctions were issued against pillaging, or
otherwise unnecessarily annoying the people; but everything
in shape of food for man and forage for beast was taken. The
supplies were turned over to the brigade commissary and
quartermaster, and were issued by them to their respective
commands precisely the same as if they had been purchased.
The captures consisted largely of cattle, sheep, poultry, some
bacon, cornmeal, often molasses, and occasionally coffee or
other small rations.

The skill of these men, called by themselves and the army
"bummers," in collecting their loads and getting back to their
respective commands, was marvellous. When they started out
in the morning, they were always on foot; but scarcely one of
them returned in the evening without being mounted on a
horse or mule. These would be turned in for the general use
of the army, and the next day these men would start out afoot
and return again in the evening mounted.

Many of the exploits of these men would fall under the
head of romance; indeed, I am afraid that in telling some of
their experiences, the romance got the better of the truth
upon which the story was founded, and that, in the way many
of these anecdotes are told, very little of the foundation is left.
I suspect that most of them consist chiefly of the fiction added
to make the stories better. In one instance it was reported that
a few men of Sherman's army passed a house where they discovered some chickens under the dwelling. They immediately
proceeded to capture them, to add to the army's supplies.
The lady of the house, who happened to be at home, made
piteous appeals to have these spared, saying they were a few
she had put away to save by permission of other parties who
had preceded and who had taken all the others that she had.
The soldiers seemed moved at her appeal; but looking at the
chickens again they were tempted and one of them replied:
"The rebellion must be suppressed if it takes the last chicken
in the Confederacy," and proceeded to appropriate the last
one.

Another anecdote characteristic of these times has been
told. The South, prior to the rebellion, kept bloodhounds to
pursue runaway slaves who took refuge in the neighboring

swamps, and also to hunt convicts. Orders were issued to kill all these animals as they were met with. On one occasion a soldier picked up a poodle, the favorite pet of its mistress, and was carrying it off to execution when the lady made a strong appeal to him to spare it. The soldier replied, "Madam, our orders are to kill every bloodhound." "But this is not a bloodhound," said the lady. "Well, madam, we cannot tell what it will grow into if we leave it behind," said the soldier as he went off with it.

Notwithstanding these anecdotes, and the necessary hardship they would seem to imply, I do not believe there was much unwarrantable pillaging considering that we were in the enemy's territory and without any supplies except such as the country afforded.

On the 23d Sherman, with the left wing, reached Milledgeville. The right wing was not far off: but proceeded on its way towards Savannah destroying the road as it went. The troops at Milledgeville remained over a day to destroy factories, buildings used for military purposes, etc., before resuming its march.

The governor, who had been almost defying Mr. Davis before this, now fled precipitately, as did the legislature of the State and all the State officers. The governor, Sherman says, was careful to carry away even his garden vegetables, while he left the archives of the State to fall into our hands. The only military force that was opposed to Sherman's forward march was the Georgia militia, a division under the command of General G. W. Smith, and a battalion under Harry Wayne. Neither the quality of the forces nor their numbers was sufficient to even retard the progress of Sherman's army.

The people at the South became so frantic at this time at the successful invasion of Georgia that they took the cadets from the military college and added them to the ranks of the militia. They even liberated the State convicts under promise from them that they would serve in the army. I have but little doubt that the worst acts that were attributed to Sherman's army were committed by these convicts, and by other Southern people who ought to have been under sentence—such people as could be found in every community, North and South—who took advantage of their country being invaded to commit crime. They were in but little danger of detection, or of arrest even if detected.

The Southern papers in commenting upon Sherman's movements pictured him as in the most deplorable condition: stating that his men were starving, that they were demoralized and wandering about almost without object, aiming only to reach the sea coast and get under the protection of our navy. These papers got to the North and had more or less effect upon the minds of the people, causing much distress to all loyal persons—particularly to those who had husbands, sons or brothers with Sherman. Mr. Lincoln seeing these accounts, had a letter written asking me if I could give him anything that he could say to the loyal people that would comfort them. I told him there was not the slightest occasion for alarm; that with 60,000 such men as Sherman had with him, such a commanding officer as he was could not be cut off in the open country. He might possibly be prevented from reaching the point he had started out to reach, but he would get through somewhere and would finally get to his chosen destination: and even if worst came to worst he could return North. I heard afterwards of Mr. Lincoln's saying, to those who would inquire of him as to what he thought about the safety of Sherman's army, that Sherman was all right: "Grant says they are safe with such a general, and that if they cannot get out where they want to, they can crawl back by the hole they went in at."

While at Milledgeville the soldiers met at the State House, organized a legislature, and proceeded to business precisely as if they were the legislative body belonging to the State of Georgia. The debates were exciting, and were upon the subject of the situation the South was in at that time, particularly the State of Georgia. They went so far as to repeal, after a spirited and acrimonious debate, the ordinance of secession.

The next day (24th) Sherman continued his march, going by the way of Waynesboro and Louisville, Millen being the next objective and where the two columns (the right and left wings) were to meet. The left wing moved to the left of the direct road, and the cavalry still farther off so as to make it look as though Augusta was the point they were aiming for.

They moved on all the roads they could find leading in that direction. The cavalry was sent to make a rapid march in hope of surprising Millen before the Union prisoners could be carried away; but they failed in this.

The distance from Milledgeville to Millen was about one hundred miles. At this point Wheeler, who had been ordered from Tennessee, arrived and swelled the numbers and efficiency of the troops confronting Sherman. Hardee, a native of Georgia, also came, but brought no troops with him. It was intended that he should raise as large an army as possible with which to intercept Sherman's march. He did succeed in raising some troops, and with these and those under the command of Wheeler and Wayne, had an army sufficient to cause some annoyance but no great detention. Our cavalry and Wheeler's had a pretty severe engagement, in which Wheeler was driven towards Augusta, thus giving the idea that Sherman was probably making for that point.

Millen was reached on the 3d of December, and the march was resumed the following day for Savannah, the final objective. Bragg had now been sent to Augusta with some troops. Wade Hampton was there also trying to raise cavalry sufficient to destroy Sherman's army. If he ever raised a force it was too late to do the work expected of it. Hardee's whole force probably numbered less than ten thousand men.

From Millen to Savannah the country is sandy and poor, and affords but very little forage other than rice straw, which was then growing. This answered a very good purpose as forage, and the rice grain was an addition to the soldier's rations. No further resistance worthy of note was met with, until within a few miles of Savannah. This place was found to be intrenched and garrisoned. Sherman proceeded at once on his arrival to invest the place, and found that the enemy had placed torpedoes in the ground, which were to explode when stepped on by man or beast. One of these exploded under an officer's horse, blowing the animal to pieces and tearing one of the legs of the officer so badly that it had to be amputated. Sherman at once ordered his prisoners to the front, moving them in a compact body in advance, to either explode the torpedoes or dig them up. No further explosion took place.

On the 10th of December the siege of Savannah commenced. Sherman then, before proceeding any further with operations for the capture of the place, started with some troops to open communication with our fleet, which he expected to find in the lower harbor or as near by as the forts of the enemy would permit. In marching to the coast he encountered Fort McAllister, which it was necessary to reduce before the supplies he might find on shipboard could be made available. Fort McAllister was soon captured by an assault made by General Hazen's division. Communication was then established with the fleet. The capture of Savannah then only occupied a few days, and involved no great loss of life. The garrison, however, as we shall see, was enabled to escape by crossing the river and moving eastward.

When Sherman had opened communication with the fleet he found there a steamer, which I had forwarded to him, carrying the accumulated mails for his army, also supplies which I supposed he would be in need of. General J. G. Foster, who commanded all the troops south of North Carolina on the Atlantic sea-board, visited General Sherman before he had opened communication with the fleet, with the view of ascertaining what assistance he could be to him. Foster returned immediately to his own headquarters at Hilton Head, for the purpose of sending Sherman siege guns, and also if he should find he had them to spare, supplies of clothing, hard bread, etc., thinking that these articles might not be found outside. The mail on the steamer which I sent down, had been collected by Colonel A. H. Markland of the Post Office Department, who went in charge of it. On this same vessel I sent an officer of my staff (Lieutenant Dunn) with the following letter to General Sherman:

CITY POINT, VA., *Dec.* 3, 1864.
MAJOR-GENERAL W. T. SHERMAN,
    Commanding Armies near Savannah, Ga.
    The little information gleaned from the Southern press, indicating no great obstacle to your progress, I have directed your mails (which had been previously collected at Baltimore by Colonel Markland, Special Agent of the Post Office Department) to be sent as far as the blockading squadron off Savannah, to be forwarded to you as soon as heard from on the coast.

Not liking to rejoice before the victory is assured, I abstain from congratulating you and those under your command, until bottom has been struck. I have never had a fear, however, for the result.

Since you left Atlanta, no very great progress has been made here. The enemy has been closely watched though, and prevented from detaching against you. I think not one man has gone from here, except some twelve or fifteen hundred dismounted cavalry. Bragg has gone from Wilmington. I am trying to take advantage of his absence to get possession of that place. Owing to some preparations Admiral Porter and General Butler are making to blow up Fort Fisher (which, while hoping for the best, I do not believe a particle in), there is a delay in getting this expedition off. I hope they will be ready to start by the 7th, and that Bragg will not have started back by that time.

In this letter I do not intend to give you anything like directions for future action, but will state a general idea I have, and will get your views after you have established yourself on the sea-coast. With your veteran army I hope to get control of the only two through routes from east to west possessed by the enemy before the fall of Atlanta. The condition will be filled by holding Savannah and Augusta, or by holding any other port to the east of Savannah and Branchville. If Wilmington falls, a force from there can co-operate with you.

Thomas has got back into the defences of Nashville, with Hood close upon him. Decatur has been abandoned, and so have all the roads except the main one leading to Chattanooga. Part of this falling back was undoubtedly necessary, and all of it may have been. It did not look so, however, to me. In my opinion, Thomas far outnumbers Hood in infantry. In cavalry, Hood has the advantage in *morale* and numbers. I hope yet that Hood will be badly crippled if not destroyed. The general news you will learn from the papers better than I could give it.

After all becomes quiet, and roads become so bad up here that there is likely to be a week or two when nothing can be done, I will run down the coast to see you. If you desire it, I will ask Mrs. Sherman to go with me.

Yours truly,
U. S. GRANT,
Lieutenant-General.

I quote this letter because it gives the reader a full knowledge of the events of that period.

Sherman now (the 15th) returned to Savannah to complete

its investment and insure the surrender of the garrison. The country about Savannah is low and marshy, and the city was well intrenched from the river above to the river below, and assaults could not be made except along a comparatively narrow causeway. For this reason assaults must have resulted in serious destruction of life to the Union troops, with the chance of failing altogether. Sherman therefore decided upon a complete investment of the place. When he believed this investment completed, he summoned the garrison to surrender. General Hardee, who was in command, replied in substance that the condition of affairs was not such as Sherman had described. He said he was in full communication with his department and was receiving supplies constantly.

Hardee, however, was cut off entirely from all communication with the west side of the river, and by the river itself to the north and south. On the South Carolina side the country was all rice fields, through which it would have been impossible to bring supplies—so that Hardee had no possible communication with the outside world except by a dilapidated plank road starting from the west bank of the river. Sherman, receiving this reply, proceeded in person to a point on the coast, where General Foster had troops stationed under General Hatch, for the purpose of making arrangements with the latter officer to go through by one of the numerous channels running inland along that part of the coast of South Carolina, to the plank road which General Hardee still possessed, and thus to cut him off from the last means he had of getting supplies, if not of communication.

While arranging for this movement, and before the attempt to execute the plan had been commenced, Sherman received information through one of his staff officers that the enemy had evacuated Savannah the night before. This was the night of the 21st of December. Before evacuating the place Hardee had blown up the navy yard. Some iron-clads had been destroyed, as well as other property that might have been valuable to us; but he left an immense amount of stores untouched, consisting of cotton, railroad cars, workshops, numerous pieces of artillery, and several thousand stands of small arms.

A little incident occurred, soon after the fall of Savannah, which Sherman relates in his Memoirs, and which is worthy of repetition. Savannah was one of the points where blockade runners entered. Shortly after the city fell into our possession, a blockade runner came sailing up serenely, not doubting but the Confederates were still in possession. It was not molested, and the captain did not find out his mistake until he had tied up and gone to the Custom House, where he found a new occupant of the building, and made a less profitable disposition of his vessel and cargo than he had expected.

As there was some discussion as to the authorship of Sherman's march to the sea, by critics of his book when it appeared before the public, I want to state here that no question upon that subject was ever raised between General Sherman and myself. Circumstances made the plan on which Sherman expected to act impracticable, and as commander of the forces he necessarily had to devise a new one which would give more promise of success: consequently he recommended the destruction of the railroad back to Chattanooga, and that he should be authorized then to move, as he did, from Atlanta forward. His suggestions were finally approved, although they did not immediately find favor in Washington. Even when it came to the time of starting, the greatest apprehension, as to the propriety of the campaign he was about to commence, filled the mind of the President, induced no doubt by his advisers. This went so far as to move the President to ask me to suspend Sherman's march for a day or two until I could think the matter over. My recollection is, though I find no record to show it, that out of deference to the President's wish I did send a dispatch to Sherman asking him to wait a day or two, or else the connections between us were already cut so that I could not do so. However this may be, the question of who devised the plan of march from Atlanta to Savannah is easily answered: it was clearly Sherman, and to him also belongs the credit of its brilliant execution. It was hardly possible that any one else than those on the spot could have devised a new plan of campaign to supersede one that did not promise success.*

*See Appendix, letters of Oct. 11th.

I was in favor of Sherman's plan from the time it was first submitted to me. My chief of staff, however, was very bitterly opposed to it and, as I learned subsequently, finding that he could not move me, he appealed to the authorities at Washington to stop it.

Chapter LX.

THE BATTLE OF FRANKLIN—THE BATTLE OF NASHVILLE.

A S WE have seen, Hood succeeded in crossing the Tennessee River between Muscle Shoals and the lower shoals at the end of October, 1864. Thomas sent Schofield with the 4th and 23d corps, together with three brigades of Wilson's cavalry to Pulaski to watch him. On the 17th of November Hood started and moved in such a manner as to avoid Schofield, thereby turning his position. Hood had with him three infantry corps, commanded respectively by Stephen D. Lee, Stewart and Cheatham. These, with his cavalry, numbered about forty-five thousand men. Schofield had, of all arms, about thirty thousand. Thomas's orders were, therefore, for Schofield to watch the movements of the enemy, but not to fight a battle if he could avoid it; but to fall back in case of an advance on Nashville, and to fight the enemy, as he fell back, so as to retard the enemy's movements until he could be reinforced by Thomas himself. As soon as Schofield saw this movement of Hood's, he sent his trains to the rear, but did not fall back himself until the 21st, and then only to Columbia. At Columbia there was a slight skirmish but no battle. From this place Schofield then retreated to Franklin. He had sent his wagons in advance, and Stanley had gone with them with two divisions to protect them. Cheatham's corps of Hood's army pursued the wagon train and went into camp at Spring Hill, for the night of the 29th.

Schofield retreating from Columbia on the 29th, passed Spring Hill, where Cheatham was bivouacked, during the night without molestation, though within half a mile of where the Confederates were encamped. On the morning of the 30th he had arrived at Franklin.

Hood followed closely and reached Franklin in time to ' make an attack the same day. The fight was very desperate and sanguinary. The Confederate generals led their men in the repeated charges, and the loss among them was of unusual proportions. This fighting continued with great severity until long after the night closed in, when the Confederates drew .

off. General Stanley, who commanded two divisions of the Union troops, and whose troops bore the brunt of the battle, was wounded in the fight, but maintained his position.

The enemy's loss at Franklin, according to Thomas's report, was 1,750 buried upon the field by our troops, 3,800 in the hospital, and 702 prisoners besides. Schofield's loss, as officially reported, was 189 killed, 1,033 wounded, and 1,104 captured and missing.

Thomas made no effort to reinforce Schofield at Franklin, as it seemed to me at the time he should have done, and fight out the battle there. He simply ordered Schofield to continue his retreat to Nashville, which the latter did during that night and the next day.

Thomas, in the meantime, was making his preparations to receive Hood. The road to Chattanooga was still well guarded with strong garrisons at Murfreesboro, Stevenson, Bridgeport and Chattanooga. Thomas had previously given up Decatur and had been reinforced by A. J. Smith's two divisions just returned from Missouri. He also had Steedman's division and R. S. Granger's, which he had drawn from the front. His quartermaster's men, about ten thousand in number, had been organized and armed under the command of the chief quartermaster, General J. L. Donaldson, and placed in the fortifications under the general supervision of General Z. B. Tower, of the United States Engineers.

Hood was allowed to move upon Nashville, and to invest that place almost without interference. Thomas was strongly fortified in his position, so that he would have been safe against the attack of Hood. He had troops enough even to annihilate him in the open field. To me his delay was unaccountable—sitting there and permitting himself to be invested, so that, in the end, to raise the siege he would have to fight the enemy strongly posted behind fortifications. It is true the weather was very bad. The rain was falling and freezing as it fell, so that the ground was covered with a sheet of ice, that made it very difficult to move. But I was afraid that the enemy would find means of moving, elude Thomas and manage to get north of the Cumberland River. If he did this, I apprehended most serious results from the campaign in the North, and was afraid we might even have to send troops from the East to head him off if he got there, General Thomas's movements being always so deliberate and so slow, though effective in defence.

I consequently urged Thomas in frequent dispatches sent from City Point* to make the attack at once. The country was alarmed, the administration was alarmed, and I was alarmed lest the very thing would take place which I have just described—that is, Hood would get north. It was all without avail further than to elicit dispatches from Thomas saying that he was getting ready to move as soon as he could,

---

*City Point, Va., *December* 2, 1864.

Major-General Thomas,
    Nashville, Tenn.

If Hood is permitted to remain quietly about Nashville, you will lose all the road back to Chattanooga and possibly have to abandon the line of the Tennessee. Should he attack you it is all well, but if he does not you should attack him before he fortifies. Arm and put in the trenches your quartermaster employees, citizens, etc.

U. S. GRANT,
Lieutenant-General.

City Point, Va., *December* 2, 1864.—1.30 P.M.

Major-General Thomas,
    Nashville, Tenn.

With your citizen employees armed, you can move out of Nashville with all your army and force the enemy to retire or fight upon ground of your own choosing. After the repulse of Hood at Franklin, it looks to me that instead of falling back to Nashville we should have taken the offensive against the enemy where he was. At this distance, however, I may err as to the best method of dealing with the enemy. You will now suffer incalculable injury upon your railroads if Hood is not speedily disposed of. Put forth therefore every possible exertion to attain this end. Should you get him to retreating give him no peace.

U. S. GRANT,
Lieutenant-General.

City Point, Va., *December* 5, 1864.

Major-General Thomas,
    Nashville, Tenn.

Is there not danger of Forrest moving down the Cumberland to where he can cross it? It seems to me whilst you should be getting up your cavalry as rapidly as possible to look after Forrest, Hood should be attacked where he is. Time strengthens him in all possibility as much as it does you.

U. S. GRANT,
Lieutenant-General.

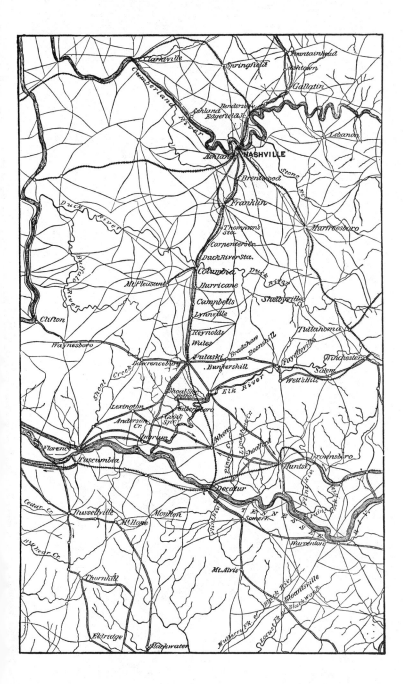

that he was making preparations, etc. At last I had to say to General Thomas that I should be obliged to remove him unless he acted promptly. He replied that he was very sorry, but he would move as soon as he could.

General Logan happening to visit City Point about that time, and knowing him as a prompt, gallant and efficient officer, I gave him an order to proceed to Nashville to relieve Thomas. I directed him, however, not to deliver the order or

---

CITY POINT, VA., *December* 6, 1864.—4 P.M.

MAJOR-GENERAL THOMAS,
   Nashville, Tenn.

Attack Hood at once and wait no longer for a remnant of your cavalry. There is great danger of delay resulting in a campaign back to the Ohio River.

U. S. GRANT,
Lieutenant-General.

CITY POINT, VA., *December* 8, 1864.—8.30 P.M.

MAJOR-GENERAL THOMAS,
   Nashville, Tenn.

Your dispatch of yesterday received. It looks to me evident the enemy are trying to cross the Cumberland River, and are scattered. Why not attack at once? By all means avoid the contingency of a foot race to see which, you or Hood, can beat to the Ohio. If you think necessary call on the governors of States to send a force into Louisville to meet the enemy if he should cross the river. You clearly never should cross except in rear of the enemy. Now is one of the finest opportunities ever presented of destroying one of the three armies of the enemy. If destroyed he never can replace it. Use the means at your command, and you can do this and cause a rejoicing that will resound from one end of the land to the other.

U. S. GRANT,
Lieutenant-General.

CITY POINT, VA., *December* 11, 1864.—4 P.M.

MAJOR-GENERAL THOMAS,
   Nashville, Tenn.

If you delay attack longer the mortifying spectacle will be witnessed of a rebel army moving for the Ohio River, and you will be forced to act, accepting such weather as you find. Let there be no further delay. Hood cannot even stand a drawn battle so far from his supplies of ordnance stores. If he retreats and you follow, he must lose his material and much of his army. I am in hopes of receiving a dispatch from you to-day announcing that you have moved. Delay no longer for weather or reinforcements.

U. S. GRANT,
Lieutenant-General.

publish it until he reached there, and if Thomas had moved, then not to deliver it at all, but communicate with me by telegraph. After Logan started, in thinking over the situation, I became restless, and concluded to go myself. I went as far as Washington City, when a dispatch was received from General Thomas announcing his readiness at last to move, and designating the time of his movement. I concluded to wait until that time. He did move, and was successful from the start. This was on the 15th of December. General Logan was at Louisville at the time this movement was made, and telegraphed the fact to Washington, and proceeded no farther himself.

The battle during the 15th was severe, but favorable to the Union troops, and continued until night closed in upon the combat. The next day the battle was renewed. After a successful assault upon Hood's men in their intrenchments the enemy fled in disorder, routed and broken, leaving their dead, their artillery and small arms in great numbers on the field, besides the wounded that were captured. Our cavalry had fought on foot as infantry, and had not their horses with them; so that they were not ready to join in the pursuit the moment the enemy retreated. They sent back, however, for their horses, and endeavored to get to Franklin ahead of Hood's broken army by the Granny White Road, but too much time was consumed in getting started. They had got but a few miles beyond the scene of the battle when they found the enemy's cavalry dismounted and behind intrenchments covering the road on which they were advancing. Here another battle ensued, our men dismounting and fighting on

---

WASHINGTON, D. C., *December 15, 1864.*

MAJOR-GENERAL THOMAS,
     Nashville, Tenn.

I was just on my way to Nashville, but receiving a dispatch from Van Dutzer detailing your splendid success of to-day, I shall go no further. Push the enemy now and give him no rest until he is entirely destroyed. Your army will cheerfully suffer many privations to break up Hood's army and render it useless for future operations. Do not stop for trains or supplies, but take them from the country as the enemy have done. Much is now expected.

          U. S. GRANT,
          Lieutenant-General.

foot, in which the Confederates were again routed and driven in great disorder. Our cavalry then went into bivouac, and renewed the pursuit on the following morning. They were too late. The enemy already had possession of Franklin, and was beyond them. It now became a chase in which the Confederates had the lead.

Our troops continued the pursuit to within a few miles of Columbia, where they found the rebels had destroyed the railroad bridge as well as all other bridges over Duck River. The heavy rains of a few days before had swelled the stream into a mad torrent, impassable except on bridges. Unfortunately, either through a mistake in the wording of the order or otherwise, the pontoon bridge which was to have been sent by rail out to Franklin, to be taken thence with the pursuing column, had gone toward Chattanooga. There was, consequently, a delay of some four days in building bridges out of the remains of the old railroad bridge. Of course Hood got such a start in this time that farther pursuit was useless, although it was continued for some distance, but without coming upon him again.

Chapter LXI.

EXPEDITION AGAINST FORT FISHER—ATTACK ON THE
FORT—FAILURE OF THE EXPEDITION—SECOND
EXPEDITION AGAINST THE FORT—CAPTURE OF
FORT FISHER.

U P TO JANUARY, 1865, the enemy occupied Fort Fisher, at the mouth of Cape Fear River and below the City of Wilmington. This port was of immense importance to the Confederates, because it formed their principal inlet for blockade runners by means of which they brought in from abroad such supplies and munitions of war as they could not produce at home. It was equally important to us to get possession of it, not only because it was desirable to cut off their supplies so as to insure a speedy termination of the war, but also because foreign governments, particularly the British Government, were constantly threatening that unless ours could maintain the blockade of that coast they should cease to recognize any blockade. For these reasons I determined, with the concurrence of the Navy Department, in December, to send an expedition against Fort Fisher for the purpose of capturing it.

To show the difficulty experienced in maintaining the blockade, I will mention a circumstance that took place at Fort Fisher after its fall. Two English blockade runners came in at night. Their commanders, not supposing the fort had fallen, worked their way through all our fleet and got into the river unobserved. They then signalled the fort, announcing their arrival. There was a colored man in the fort who had been there before and who understood these signals. He informed General Terry what reply he should make to have them come in, and Terry did as he advised. The vessels came in, their officers entirely unconscious that they were falling into the hands of the Union forces. Even after they were brought in to the fort they were entertained in conversation for some little time before suspecting that the Union troops were occupying the fort. They were finally informed that their vessels and cargoes were prizes.

I selected General Weitzel, of the Army of the James, to go with the expedition, but gave instructions through General Butler. He commanded the department within whose geographical limits Fort Fisher was situated, as well as Beaufort and other points on that coast held by our troops; he was, therefore, entitled to the right of fitting out the expedition against Fort Fisher.

General Butler conceived the idea that if a steamer loaded heavily with powder could be run up to near the shore under the fort and exploded, it would create great havoc and make the capture an easy matter. Admiral Porter, who was to command the naval squadron, seemed to fall in with the idea, and it was not disapproved of in Washington; the navy was therefore given the task of preparing the steamer for this purpose. I had no confidence in the success of the scheme, and so expressed myself; but as no serious harm could come of the experiment, and the authorities at Washington seemed desirous to have it tried, I permitted it. The steamer was sent to Beaufort, North Carolina, and was there loaded with powder and prepared for the part she was to play in the reduction of Fort Fisher.

General Butler chose to go in command of the expedition himself, and was all ready to sail by the 9th of December (1864). Very heavy storms prevailed, however, at that time along that part of the sea-coast, and prevented him from getting off until the 13th or 14th. His advance arrived off Fort Fisher on the 15th. The naval force had been already assembled, or was assembling, but they were obliged to run into Beaufort for munitions, coal, etc.; then, too, the powder-boat was not yet fully prepared. The fleet was ready to proceed on the 18th; but Butler, who had remained outside from the 15th up to that time, now found himself out of coal, fresh water, etc., and had to put into Beaufort to replenish. Another storm overtook him, and several days more were lost before the army and navy were both ready at the same time to co-operate.

On the night of the 23d the powder-boat was towed in by a gunboat as near to the fort as it was safe to run. She was then propelled by her own machinery to within about five hundred yards of the shore. There the clockwork, which was to explode her within a certain length of time, was set and she was abandoned. Everybody left, and even the vessels put out to sea to prevent the effect of the explosion upon them. At two o'clock in the morning the explosion took place—and produced no more effect on the fort, or anything else on land, than the bursting of a boiler anywhere on the Atlantic Ocean would have done. Indeed when the troops in Fort Fisher heard the explosion they supposed it was the bursting of a boiler in one of the Yankee gunboats.

Fort Fisher was situated upon a low, flat peninsula north of Cape Fear River. The soil is sandy. Back a little the peninsula is very heavily wooded, and covered with fresh-water swamps. The fort ran across this peninsula, about five hundred yards in width, and extended along the sea coast about thirteen hundred yards. The fort had an armament of 21 guns and 3 mortars on the land side, and 24 guns on the sea front. At that time it was only garrisoned by four companies of infantry, one light battery and the gunners at the heavy guns—less than seven hundred men—with a reserve of less than a thousand men five miles up the peninsula. General Whiting of the Confederate army was in command, and General Bragg was in command of the force at Wilmington. Both commenced calling for reinforcements the moment they saw our troops landing. The Governor of North Carolina called for everybody who could stand behind a parapet and shoot a gun, to join them. In this way they got two or three hundred additional men into Fort Fisher; and Hoke's division, five or six thousand strong, was sent down from Richmond. A few of these troops arrived the very day that Butler was ready to advance.

On the 24th the fleet formed for an attack in arcs of concentric circles, their heavy iron-clads going in very close range, being nearest the shore, and leaving intervals or spaces so that the outer vessels could fire between them. Porter was thus enabled to throw one hundred and fifteen shells per minute. The damage done to the fort by these shells was very slight, only two or three cannon being disabled in the fort. But the firing silenced all the guns by making it too hot for the men to maintain their positions about them and compelling them to seek shelter in the bomb-proofs.

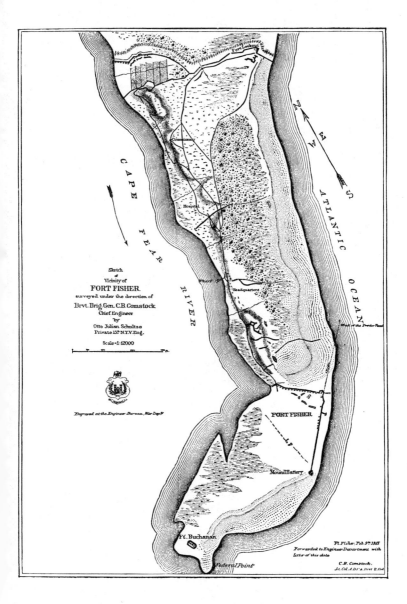

Sketch
of
Vicinity of
FORT FISHER
surveyed under the direction of
Brvt. Brig. Gen. C.B. Comstock
Chief Engineer
by
Otto Julian Schultze
Private 15t N.Y.V. Eng.

Scale = 1:12000

Engraved at the Engineer Bureau, War Dep.t

CAPE FEAR RIVER

ATLANTIC OCEAN

Fort Lookout

Commissary

Hospital

Wharf

Wharf No 2

Headquarters

Site of the Powder Boat

FORT FISHER

Mound Battery

Ft. Buchanan

Federal Point

Ft. Fisher. Feb. 5th 1865
Forwarded to Engineer Department with
letter of this date

C.B. Comstock.
Lt. Col. A.D.C. & Brvt B.Gen.

On the next day part of Butler's troops under General Adelbert Ames effected a landing out of range of the fort without difficulty. This was accomplished under the protection of gunboats sent for the purpose, and under cover of a renewed attack upon the fort by the fleet. They formed a line across the peninsula and advanced, part going north and part toward the fort, covering themselves as they did so. Curtis pushed forward and came near to Fort Fisher, capturing the small garrison at what was called the Flag Pond Battery. Weitzel accompanied him to within a half a mile of the works. Here he saw that the fort had not been injured, and so reported to Butler, advising against an assault. Ames, who had gone north in his advance, captured 228 of the reserves. These prisoners reported to Butler that sixteen hundred of Hoke's division of six thousand from Richmond had already arrived and the rest would soon be in his rear.

Upon these reports Butler determined to withdraw his troops from the peninsula and return to the fleet. At that time there had not been a man on our side injured except by one of the shells from the fleet. Curtis had got within a few yards of the works. Some of his men had snatched a flag from the parapet of the fort, and others had taken a horse from the inside of the stockade. At night Butler informed Porter of his withdrawal, giving the reasons above stated, and announced his purpose as soon as his men could embark to start for Hampton Roads. Porter represented to him that he had sent to Beaufort for more ammunition. He could fire much faster than he had been doing, and would keep the enemy from showing himself until our men were within twenty yards of the fort, and he begged that Butler would leave some brave fellows like those who had snatched the flag from the parapet and taken the horse from the fort.

Butler was unchangeable. He got all his troops aboard, except Curtis's brigade, and started back. In doing this, Butler made a fearful mistake. My instructions to him, or to the officer who went in command of the expedition, were explicit in the statement that to effect a landing would be of itself a great victory, and if one should be effected, the foothold must not be relinquished; on the contrary, a regular siege of the fort must be commenced and, to guard against interference by reason of storms, supplies of provisions must be laid in as soon as they could be got on shore. But General Butler seems to have lost sight of this part of his instructions, and was back at Fort Monroe on the 28th.

I telegraphed to the President as follows:

CITY POINT, VA.,
Dec. 28, 1864. —8.30 P.M.

The Wilmington expedition has proven a gross and culpable failure. Many of the troops are back here. Delays and free talk of the object of the expedition enabled the enemy to move troops to Wilmington to defeat it. After the expedition sailed from Fort Monroe, three days of fine weather were squandered, during which the enemy was without a force to protect himself. Who is to blame will, I hope, be known.

U. S. GRANT,
Lieutenant-General.

Porter sent dispatches to the Navy Department in which he complained bitterly of having been abandoned by the army just when the fort was nearly in our possession, and begged that our troops might be sent back again to co-operate, but with a different commander. As soon as I heard this I sent a messenger to Porter with a letter asking him to hold on. I assured him that I fully sympathized with him in his disappointment, and that I would send the same troops back with a different commander, with some reinforcements to offset those which the enemy had received. I told him it would take some little time to get transportation for the additional troops; but as soon as it could be had the men should be on their way to him, and there would be no delay on my part. I selected A. H. Terry to command.

It was the 6th of January before the transports could be got ready and the troops aboard. They sailed from Fortress Monroe on that day. The object and destination of the second expedition were at the time kept a secret to all except a few in the Navy Department and in the army to whom it was necessary to impart the information. General Terry had not the slightest idea of where he was going or what he was to do. He simply knew that he was going to sea and that he had his orders with him, which were to be opened when out at sea.

He was instructed to communicate freely with Porter and have entire harmony between army and navy, because the work before them would require the best efforts of both arms of the service. They arrived off Beaufort on the 8th. A heavy storm, however, prevented a landing at Fort Fisher until the 13th. The navy prepared itself for attack about as before, and at the same time assisted the army in landing, this time five miles away. Only iron-clads fired at first; the object being to draw the fire of the enemy's guns so as to ascertain their positions. This object being accomplished, they then let in their shots thick and fast. Very soon the guns were all silenced, and the fort showed evident signs of being much injured.

Terry deployed his men across the peninsula as had been done before, and at two o'clock on the following morning was up within two miles of the fort with a respectable *abatis* in front of his line. His artillery was all landed on that day, the 14th. Again Curtis's brigade of Ames's division had the lead. By noon they had carried an unfinished work less than a half mile from the fort, and turned it so as to face the other way.

Terry now saw Porter and arranged for an assault on the following day. The two commanders arranged their signals so that they could communicate with each other from time to time as they might have occasion. At daylight the fleet commenced its firing. The time agreed upon for the assault was the middle of the afternoon, and Ames who commanded the assaulting column moved at 3.30. Porter landed a force of sailors and marines to move against the sea-front in co-operation with Ames's assault. They were under Commander Breese of the navy. These sailors and marines had worked their way up to within a couple of hundred yards of the fort before the assault. The signal was given and the assault was made; but the poor sailors and marines were repulsed and very badly handled by the enemy, losing 280 killed and wounded out of their number.

Curtis's brigade charged successfully though met by a heavy fire, some of the men having to wade through the swamp up to their waists to reach the fort. Many were wounded, of course, and some killed; but they soon reached the palisades. These they cut away, and pushed on through. The other troops then came up, Pennypacker's following Curtis, and Bell, who commanded the 3d brigade of Ames's division, following Pennypacker. But the fort was not yet captured though the parapet was gained.

The works were very extensive. The large parapet around the work would have been but very little protection to those inside except when they were close up under it. Traverses had, therefore, been run until really the work was a succession of small forts enclosed by a large one. The rebels made a desperate effort to hold the fort, and had to be driven from these traverses one by one. The fight continued till long after night. Our troops gained first one traverse and then another, and by 10 o'clock at night the place was carried. During this engagement the sailors, who had been repulsed in their assault on the bastion, rendered the best service they could by reinforcing Terry's northern line—thus enabling him to send a detachment to the assistance of Ames. The fleet kept up a continuous fire upon that part of the fort which was still occupied by the enemy. By means of signals they could be informed where to direct their shots.

During the succeeding nights the enemy blew up Fort Caswell on the opposite side of Cape Fear River, and abandoned two extensive works on Smith's Island in the river.

Our captures in all amounted to 169 guns, besides small-arms, with full supplies of ammunition, and 2,083 prisoners. In addition to these, there were about 700 dead and wounded left there. We had lost 110 killed and 536 wounded.

In this assault on Fort Fisher, Bell, one of the brigade commanders, was killed, and two, Curtis and Pennypacker, were badly wounded.

Secretary Stanton, who was on his way back from Savannah, arrived off Fort Fisher soon after it fell. When he heard the good news he promoted all the officers of any considerable rank for their conspicuous gallantry. Terry had been nominated for major-general, but had not been confirmed. This confirmed him; and soon after I recommended him for a brigadier-generalcy in the regular army, and it was given to him for this victory.

Chapter LXII.

SHERMAN'S MARCH NORTH — SHERIDAN ORDERED TO
LYNCHBURG — CANBY ORDERED TO MOVE AGAINST
MOBILE — MOVEMENTS OF SCHOFIELD AND THOMAS —
CAPTURE OF COLUMBIA, SOUTH CAROLINA —
SHERMAN IN THE CAROLINAS.

WHEN NEWS of Sherman being in possession of Savannah reached the North, distinguished statesmen and visitors began to pour in to see him. Among others who went was the Secretary of War, who seemed much pleased at the result of his campaign. Mr. Draper, the collector of customs of New York, who was with Mr. Stanton's party, was put in charge of the public property that had been abandoned and captured. Savannah was then turned over to General Foster's command to hold, so that Sherman might have his own entire army free to operate as might be decided upon in the future. I sent the chief engineer of the Army of the Potomac (General Barnard) with letters to General Sherman. He remained some time with the general, and when he returned brought back letters, one of which contained suggestions from Sherman as to what ought to be done in co-operation with him, when he should have started upon his march northward.

I must not neglect to state here the fact that I had no idea originally of having Sherman march from Savannah to Richmond, or even to North Carolina. The season was bad, the roads impassable for anything except such an army as he had, and I should not have thought of ordering such a move. I had, therefore, made preparations to collect transports to carry Sherman and his army around to the James River by water, and so informed him. On receiving this letter he went to work immediately to prepare for the move, but seeing that it would require a long time to collect the transports, he suggested the idea then of marching up north through the Carolinas. I was only too happy to approve this; for if successful, it promised every advantage. His march through Georgia had thoroughly destroyed all lines of transportation in that State, and had completely cut the enemy off from all sources of supply to the west of it. If North and South Carolina were rendered helpless so far as capacity for feeding Lee's army was concerned, the Confederate garrison at Richmond would be reduced in territory, from which to draw supplies, to very narrow limits in the State of Virginia; and, although that section of the country was fertile, it was already well exhausted of both forage and food. I approved Sherman's suggestion therefore at once.

The work of preparation was tedious, because supplies, to load the wagons for the march, had to be brought from a long distance. Sherman would now have to march through a country furnishing fewer provisions than that he had previously been operating in during his march to the sea. Besides, he was confronting, or marching toward, a force of the enemy vastly superior to any his troops had encountered on their previous march; and the territory through which he had to pass had now become of such vast importance to the very existence of the Confederate army, that the most desperate efforts were to be expected in order to save it.

Sherman, therefore, while collecting the necessary supplies to start with, made arrangements with Admiral Dahlgren, who commanded that part of the navy on the South Carolina and Georgia coast, and General Foster, commanding the troops, to take positions, and hold a few points on the sea coast, which he (Sherman) designated, in the neighborhood of Charleston.

This provision was made to enable him to fall back upon the sea coast, in case he should encounter a force sufficient to stop his onward progress. He also wrote me a letter, making suggestions as to what he would like to have done in support of his movement farther north. This letter was brought to City Point by General Barnard at a time when I happened to be going to Washington City, where I arrived on the 21st of January. I cannot tell the provision I had already made to co-operate with Sherman, in anticipation of his expected movement, better than by giving my reply to this letter.

HEADQUARTERS ARMIES OF THE UNITED STATES,
Washington, D. C., *Jan.* 21, 1865.

MAJOR-GENERAL W. T. SHERMAN,
Commanding Mil. Div. of the Mississippi.

GENERAL: — Your letters brought by General Barnard were received at City Point, and read with interest. Not having them with me, however, I cannot say that in this I will be able to satisfy you on all points of recommendation. As I arrived here at one P.M., and must leave at six P.M., having in the meantime spent over three hours with the Secretary and General Halleck, I must be brief. Before your last request to have Thomas make a campaign into the heart of Alabama, I had ordered Schofield to Annapolis, Md., with his corps. The advance (six thousand) will reach the seaboard by the 23d, the remainder following as rapidly as railroad transportation can be procured from Cincinnati. The corps numbers over twenty-one thousand men. I was induced to do this because I did not believe Thomas could possibly be got off before spring. His pursuit of Hood indicated a sluggishness that satisfied me that he would never do to conduct one of your campaigns. The command of the advance of the pursuit was left to subordinates, whilst Thomas followed far behind. When Hood had crossed the Tennessee, and those in pursuit had reached it, Thomas had not much more than half crossed the State, from whence he returned to Nashville to take steamer for Eastport. He is possessed of excellent judgment, great coolness and honesty, but he is not good on a pursuit. He also reported his troops fagged, and that it was necessary to equip up. This report and a determination to give the enemy no rest determined me to use his surplus troops elsewhere.

Thomas is still left with a sufficient force surplus to go to Selma under an energetic leader. He has been telegraphed to, to know whether he could go, and, if so, which of the several routes he would select. No reply is yet received. Canby has been ordered to act offensively from the sea-coast to the interior, towards Montgomery and Selma. Thomas's forces will move from the north at an early day, or some of his troops will be sent to Canby. Without further reinforcements Canby will have a moving column of twenty thousand men.

Fort Fisher, you are aware, has been captured. We have a force there of eight thousand effective. At New Bern about half the number. It is rumored, through deserters, that Wilmington also has fallen. I am inclined to believe the rumor, because on the 17th we knew the enemy were blowing up their works about Fort Caswell, and that on the 18th Terry moved on Wilmington.

If Wilmington is captured, Schofield will go there. If not, he will be sent to New Bern. In either event, all the surplus forces at the two points will move to the interior toward Goldsboro' in co-operation with your movements. From either point, railroad communications can be run out, there being here abundance of rolling-stock suited to the gauge of those roads.

There have been about sixteen thousand men sent from Lee's army south. Of these, you will have fourteen thousand against you, if Wilmington is not held by the enemy, casualties at Fort Fisher having overtaken about two thousand.

All these troops are subject to your orders as you come in communication with them. They will be so instructed. From about Richmond I will watch Lee closely, and if he detaches much more, or attempts to evacuate, will pitch in. In the meantime, should you be brought to a halt anywhere, I can send two corps of thirty thousand effective men to your support, from the troops about Richmond.

To resume: Canby is ordered to operate to the interior from the Gulf. A. J. Smith may go from the north, but I think it doubtful. A force of twenty-eight or thirty thousand will co-operate with you from New Bern or Wilmington, or both. You can call for reinforcements.

This will be handed you by Captain Hudson, of my staff, who will return with any message you may have for me. If there is anything I can do for you in the way of having supplies on ship-board, at any point on the sea-coast, ready for you, let me know it.

Yours truly,

U. S. GRANT,

Lieut.-General.

I had written on the 18th of January to General Sherman, giving him the news of the battle of Nashville. He was much pleased at the result, although, like myself, he had been very much disappointed at Thomas for permitting Hood to cross the Tennessee River and nearly the whole State of Tennessee, and come to Nashville to be attacked there. He, however, as I had done, sent Thomas a warm congratulatory letter.

On the 10th of January, 1865, the resolutions of thanks to Sherman and his army passed by Congress were approved.

Sherman, after the capture, at once had the *débris* in Savannah cleared up, commencing the work by removing the piling and torpedoes from the river, and taking up all other

obstructions. He had then intrenched the city, so that it could
be held by a small garrison. By the middle of January all his
work was done, except the accumulation of supplies to commence his movements with.

He proposed to move in two columns, one from Savannah,
going along by the river of the same name, and the other by
roads farther east, threatening Charleston. He commenced
the advance by moving his right wing to Beaufort, South
Carolina, then to Pocotaligo by water. This column, in
moving north, threatened Charleston, and, indeed, it was not
determined at first that they would not have a force visit
Charleston. South Carolina had done so much to prepare the
public mind of the South for secession, and had been so active in precipitating the decision of the question before the
South was fully prepared to meet it, that there was, at that
time, a feeling throughout the North and also largely entertained by people of the South, that the State of South Carolina, and Charleston, the hot-bed of secession in particular,
ought to have a heavy hand laid upon them. In fact, nothing
but the decisive results that followed, deterred the radical portion of the people from condemning the movement, because
Charleston had been left out. To pass into the interior would,
however, be to insure the evacuation of the city, and its possession by the navy and Foster's troops. It is so situated between two formidable rivers that a small garrison could have
held it against all odds as long as their supplies would hold
out. Sherman therefore passed it by.

By the first of February all preparations were completed for
the final march, Columbia, South Carolina, being the first objective; Fayetteville, North Carolina, the second; and Goldsboro, or neighborhood, the final one, unless something
further should be determined upon. The right wing went
from Pocotaligo, and the left from about Hardeeville on the
Savannah River, both columns taking a pretty direct route for
Columbia. The cavalry, however, were to threaten Charleston
on the right, and Augusta on the left.

On the 15th of January Fort Fisher had fallen, news of
which Sherman had received before starting out on his march.
We already had New Bern and had soon Wilmington, whose
fall followed that of Fort Fisher; as did other points on the

sea coast, where the National troops were now in readiness to co-operate with Sherman's advance when he had passed Fayetteville.

On the 18th of January I ordered Canby, in command at New Orleans, to move against Mobile, Montgomery and Selma, Alabama, for the purpose of destroying roads, machine shops, etc. On the 8th of February I ordered Sheridan, who was in the Valley of Virginia, to push forward as soon as the weather would permit and strike the canal west of Richmond at or about Lynchburg; and on the 20th I made the order to go to Lynchburg as soon as the roads would permit, saying: "As soon as it is possible to travel, I think you will have no difficulty about reaching Lynchburg with a cavalry force alone. From there you could destroy the railroad and canal in every direction, so as to be of no further use to the rebellion. * * * This additional raid, with one starting from East Tennessee under Stoneman, numbering about four or five thousand cavalry; one from Eastport, Mississippi, ten thousand cavalry; Canby, from Mobile Bay, with about eighteen thousand mixed troops—these three latter pushing for Tuscaloosa, Selma and Montgomery; and Sherman with a large army eating out the vitals of South Carolina—is all that will be wanted to leave nothing for the rebellion to stand upon. I would advise you to overcome great obstacles to accomplish this. Charleston was evacuated on Tuesday last."

On the 27th of February, more than a month after Canby had received his orders, I again wrote to him, saying that I was extremely anxious to hear of his being in Alabama. I notified him, also, that I had sent Grierson to take command of his cavalry, he being a very efficient officer. I further suggested that Forrest was probably in Mississippi, and if he was there, he would find him an officer of great courage and capacity whom it would be difficult to get by. I still further informed him that Thomas had been ordered to start a cavalry force into Mississippi on the 20th of February, or as soon as possible thereafter. This force did not get off however.

All these movements were designed to be in support of Sherman's march, the object being to keep the Confederate troops in the West from leaving there. But neither Canby nor Thomas could be got off in time. I had some time before

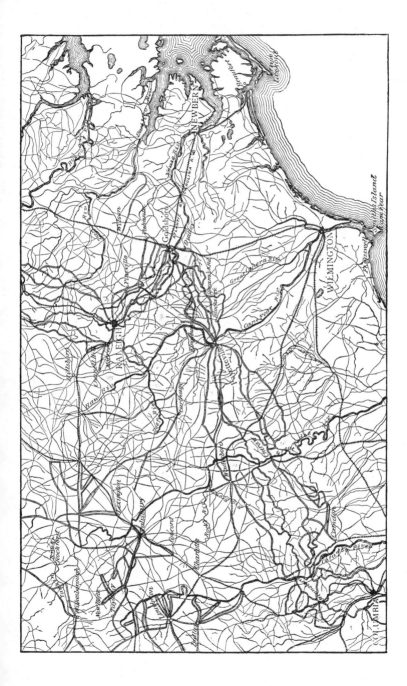

depleted Thomas's army to reinforce Canby, for the reason that Thomas had failed to start an expedition which he had been ordered to send out, and to have the troops where they might do something. Canby seemed to be equally deliberate in all of his movements. I ordered him to go in person; but he prepared to send a detachment under another officer. General Granger had got down to New Orleans, in some way or other, and I wrote Canby that he must not put him in command of troops. In spite of this he asked the War Department to assign Granger to the command of a corps.

Almost in despair of having adequate service rendered to the cause in that quarter, I said to Canby: "I am in receipt of a dispatch * * * informing me that you have made requisitions for a construction corps and material to build seventy miles of railroad. I have directed that none be sent. Thomas's army has been depleted to send a force to you that they might be where they could act in winter, and at least detain the force the enemy had in the West. If there had been any idea of repairing railroads, it could have been done much better from the North, where we already had the troops. I expected your movements to be co-operative with Sherman's last. This has now entirely failed. I wrote to you long ago, urging you to push promptly and to live upon the country, and destroy railroads, machine shops, etc., not to build them. Take Mobile and hold it, and push your forces to the interior—to Montgomery and to Selma. Destroy railroads, rolling stock, and everything useful for carrying on war, and, when you have done this, take such positions as can be supplied by water. By this means alone you can occupy positions from which the enemy's roads in the interior can be kept broken."

Most of these expeditions got off finally, but too late to render any service in the direction for which they were designated.

The enemy, ready to intercept his advance, consisted of Hardee's troops and Wheeler's cavalry, perhaps less than fifteen thousand men in all; but frantic efforts were being made in Richmond, as I was sure would be the case, to retard Sherman's movements. Everything possible was being done to raise troops in the South. Lee dispatched against Sherman the troops which had been sent to relieve Fort Fisher, which, including those of the other defences of the harbor and its neighborhood, amounted, after deducting the two thousand killed, wounded and captured, to fourteen thousand men. After Thomas's victory at Nashville what remained, of Hood's army were gathered together and forwarded as rapidly as possible to the east to co-operate with these forces; and, finally, General Joseph E. Johnston, one of the ablest commanders of the South though not in favor with the administration (or at least with Mr. Davis), was put in command of all the troops in North and South Carolina.

Schofield arrived at Annapolis in the latter part of January, but before sending his troops to North Carolina I went with him down the coast to see the situation of affairs, as I could give fuller directions after being on the ground than I could very well have given without. We soon returned, and the troops were sent by sea to Cape Fear River. Both New Bern and Wilmington are connected with Raleigh by railroads which unite at Goldsboro. Schofield was to land troops at Smithville, near the mouth of the Cape Fear River on the west side, and move up to secure the Wilmington and Charlotteville Railroad. This column took their pontoon bridges with them, to enable them to cross over to the island south of the city of Wilmington. A large body was sent by the north side to co-operate with them. They succeeded in taking the city on the 22d of February. I took the precaution to provide for Sherman's army, in case he should be forced to turn in toward the sea coast before reaching North Carolina, by forwarding supplies to every place where he was liable to have to make such a deflection from his projected march. I also sent railroad rolling stock, of which we had a great abundance, now that we were not operating the roads in Virginia. The gauge of the North Carolina railroads being the same as the Virginia railroads had been altered too; these cars and locomotives were ready for use there without any change.

On the 31st of January I countermanded the orders given to Thomas to move south to Alabama and Georgia. (I had previously reduced his force by sending a portion of it to Terry.) I directed in lieu of this movement, that he should send Stoneman through East Tennessee, and push him well down toward Columbia, South Carolina, in support of Sherman.

Thomas did not get Stoneman off in time, but, on the contrary, when I had supposed he was on his march in support of Sherman I heard of his being in Louisville, Kentucky. I immediately changed the order, and directed Thomas to send him toward Lynchburg. Finally, however, on the 12th of March, he did push down through the north-western end of South Carolina, creating some consternation. I also ordered Thomas to send the 4th corps (Stanley's) to Bull Gap and to destroy no more roads east of that. I also directed him to concentrate supplies at Knoxville, with a view to a probable movement of his army through that way toward Lynchburg.

Goldsboro is four hundred and twenty-five miles from Savannah. Sherman's march was without much incident until he entered Columbia, on the 17th of February. He was detained in his progress by having to repair and corduroy the roads, and rebuild the bridges. There was constant skirmishing and fighting between the cavalry of the two armies, but this did not retard the advance of the infantry. Four days, also, were lost in making complete the destruction of the most important railroads south of Columbia; there was also some delay caused by the high water, and the destruction of the bridges on the line of the road. A formidable river had to be crossed near Columbia, and that in the face of a small garrison under General Wade Hampton. There was but little delay, however, further than that caused by high water in the stream. Hampton left as Sherman approached, and the city was found to be on fire.

There has since been a great deal of acrimony displayed in discussions of the question as to who set Columbia on fire. Sherman denies it on the part of his troops, and Hampton denies it on the part of the Confederates. One thing is certain: as soon as our troops took possession, they at once proceeded to extinguish the flames to the best of their ability with the limited means at hand. In any case, the example set by the Confederates in burning the village of Chambersburg, Pa., a town which was not garrisoned, would seem to make a defence of the act of firing the seat of government of the State most responsible for the conflict then raging, not imperative.

The Confederate troops having vacated the city, the mayor took possession, and sallied forth to meet the commander of the National forces for the purpose of surrendering the town, making terms for the protection of property, etc. Sherman paid no attention at all to the overture, but pushed forward and took the town without making any conditions whatever with its citizens. He then, however, co-operated with the mayor in extinguishing the flames and providing for the people who were rendered destitute by this destruction of their homes. When he left there he even gave the mayor five hundred head of cattle to be distributed among the citizens, to tide them over until some arrangement could be made for their future supplies. He remained in Columbia until the roads, public buildings, work-shops and everything that could be useful to the enemy were destroyed. While at Columbia, Sherman learned for the first time that what remained of Hood's army was confronting him, under the command of General Beauregard.

Charleston was evacuated on the 18th of February, and Foster garrisoned the place. Wilmington was captured on the 22d. Columbia and Cheraw farther north, were regarded as so secure from invasion that the wealthy people of Charleston and Augusta had sent much of their valuable property to these two points to be stored. Among the goods sent there were valuable carpets, tons of old Madeira, silverware, and furniture. I am afraid much of these goods fell into the hands of our troops. There was found at Columbia a large amount of powder, some artillery, small-arms and fixed ammunition. These, of course, were among the articles destroyed. While here, Sherman also learned of Johnston's restoration to command. The latter was given, as already stated, all troops in North and South Carolina. After the completion of the destruction of public property about Columbia, Sherman proceeded on his march and reached Cheraw without any special opposition and without incident to relate. The railroads, of course, were thoroughly destroyed on the way. Sherman remained a day or two at Cheraw; and, finally, on the 6th of March crossed his troops over the Pedee and advanced straight for Fayetteville. Hardee and Hampton were there, and barely escaped. Sherman reached Fayetteville on the 11th of March. He had dispatched scouts from Cheraw with letters to General Terry, at Wilmington, asking him to send a

steamer with some supplies of bread, clothing and other articles which he enumerated. The scouts got through successfully, and a boat was sent with the mail and such articles for
which Sherman had asked as were in store at Wilmington;
unfortunately, however, those stores did not contain clothing.

Four days later, on the 15th, Sherman left Fayetteville for
Goldsboro. The march, now, had to be made with great caution, for he was approaching Lee's army and nearing the
country that still remained open to the enemy. Besides, he
was confronting all that he had had to confront in his previous march up to that point, reinforced by the garrisons along
the road and by what remained of Hood's army. Frantic appeals were made to the people to come in voluntarily and
swell the ranks of our foe. I presume, however, that Johnston
did not have in all over 35,000 or 40,000 men. The people
had grown tired of the war, and desertions from the Confederate army were much more numerous than the voluntary
accessions.

There was some fighting at Averysboro on the 16th between
Johnston's troops and Sherman's, with some loss; and at Bentonville on the 19th and 21st of March, but Johnston withdrew
from the contest before the morning of the 22d. Sherman's
loss in these last engagements in killed, wounded, and missing, was about sixteen hundred. Sherman's troops at last
reached Goldsboro on the 23d of the month and went into
bivouac; and there his men were destined to have a long rest.
Schofield was there to meet him with the troops which had
been sent to Wilmington.

Sherman was no longer in danger. He had Johnston confronting him; but with an army much inferior to his own,
both in numbers and morale. He had Lee to the north of him
with a force largely superior; but I was holding Lee with a
still greater force, and had he made his escape and gotten
down to reinforce Johnston, Sherman, with the reinforcements he now had from Schofield and Terry, would have been
able to hold the Confederates at bay for an indefinite period.
He was near the sea-shore with his back to it, and our navy
occupied the harbors. He had a railroad to both Wilmington
and New Bern, and his flanks were thoroughly protected by
streams, which intersect that part of the country and deepen

as they approach the sea. Then, too, Sherman knew that if Lee should escape me I would be on his heels, and he and Johnston together would be crushed in one blow if they attempted to make a stand. With the loss of their capital, it is doubtful whether Lee's army would have amounted to much as an army when it reached North Carolina. Johnston's army was demoralized by constant defeat and would hardly have made an offensive movement, even if they could have been induced to remain on duty. The men of both Lee's and Johnston's armies were, like their brethren of the North, as brave as men can be; but no man is so brave that he may not meet such defeats and disasters as to discourage him and dampen his ardor for any cause, no matter how just he deems it.

Chapter LXIII.

ARRIVAL OF THE PEACE COMMISSIONERS—LINCOLN
AND THE PEACE COMMISSIONERS—AN ANECDOTE
OF LINCOLN—THE WINTER BEFORE
PETERSBURG—SHERIDAN DESTROYS THE RAILROAD—
GORDON CARRIES THE PICKET LINE—PARKE
RECAPTURES THE LINE—THE BATTLE OF
WHITE OAK ROAD.

O N THE LAST of January, 1865, peace commissioners from the so-called Confederate States presented themselves on our lines around Petersburg, and were immediately conducted to my headquarters at City Point. They proved to be Alexander H. Stephens, Vice-President of the Confederacy, Judge Campbell, Assistant-Secretary of War, and R. M. T. Hunter, formerly United States Senator and then a member of the Confederate Senate.

It was about dark when they reached my headquarters, and I at once conducted them to the steamer *Mary Martin*, a Hudson River boat which was very comfortably fitted up for the use of passengers. I at once communicated by telegraph with Washington and informed the Secretary of War and the President of the arrival of these commissioners and that their object was to negotiate terms of peace between the United States and, as they termed it, the Confederate Government. I was instructed to retain them at City Point, until the President, or some one whom he would designate, should come to meet them. They remained several days as guests on board the boat. I saw them quite frequently, though I have no recollection of having had any conversation whatever with them on the subject of their mission. It was something I had nothing to do with, and I therefore did not wish to express any views on the subject. For my own part I never had admitted, and never was ready to admit, that they were the representatives of a *government*. There had been too great a waste of blood and treasure to concede anything of the kind. As long as they remained there, however, our relations were pleasant and I found them all very agreeable gentlemen. I directed the captain to furnish them with the best the boat afforded, and to administer to their comfort in every way possible. No guard was placed over them and no restriction was put upon their movements; nor was there any pledge asked that they would not abuse the privileges extended to them. They were permitted to leave the boat when they felt like it, and did so, coming up on the bank and visiting me at my headquarters.

I had never met either of these gentlemen before the war, but knew them well by reputation and through their public services, and I had been a particular admirer of Mr. Stephens. I had always supposed that he was a very small man, but when I saw him in the dusk of the evening I was very much surprised to find so large a man as he seemed to be. When he got down on to the boat I found that he was wearing a coarse gray woollen overcoat, a manufacture that had been introduced into the South during the rebellion. The cloth was thicker than anything of the kind I had ever seen, even in Canada. The overcoat extended nearly to his feet, and was so large that it gave him the appearance of being an average-sized man. He took this off when he reached the cabin of the boat, and I was struck with the apparent change in size, in the coat and out of it.

After a few days, about the 2d of February, I received a dispatch from Washington, directing me to send the commissioners to Hampton Roads to meet the President and a member of the cabinet. Mr. Lincoln met them there and had an interview of short duration. It was not a great while after they met that the President visited me at City Point. He spoke of his having met the commissioners, and said he had told them that there would be no use in entering into any negotiations unless they would recognize, first: that the Union as a whole must be forever preserved, and second: that slavery must be abolished. If they were willing to concede these two points, then he was ready to enter into negotiations and was almost willing to hand them a blank sheet of paper with his signature attached for them to fill in the terms upon which they were willing to live with us in the Union and be one people. He always showed a generous and kindly spirit toward the Southern people, and I never heard him abuse an enemy. Some of the cruel things said about President Lincoln, particularly in the North, used to pierce him to the heart; but never in my presence did he evince a revengeful disposition—and I saw a great deal of him at City Point, for he seemed glad to get away from the cares and anxieties of the capital.

Right here I might relate an anecdote of Mr. Lincoln. It was on the occasion of his visit to me just after he had talked with the peace commissioners at Hampton Roads. After a little conversation, he asked me if I had seen that overcoat of Stephens's. I replied that I had. "Well," said he, "did you see him take it off?" I said yes. "Well," said he, "didn't you think it was the biggest shuck and the littlest ear that ever you did see?" Long afterwards I told this story to the Confederate General J. B. Gordon, at the time a member of the Senate. He repeated it to Stephens, and, as I heard afterwards, Stephens laughed immoderately at the simile of Mr. Lincoln.

The rest of the winter, after the departure of the peace commissioners, passed off quietly and uneventfully, except for two or three little incidents. On one occasion during this period, while I was visiting Washington City for the purpose of conferring with the administration, the enemy's cavalry under General Wade Hampton, passing our extreme left and then going to the south, got in east of us. Before their presence was known, they had driven off a large number of beef cattle that were grazing in that section. It was a fair capture, and they were sufficiently needed by the Confederates. It was only retaliating for what we had done, sometimes for many weeks at a time, when out of supplies—taking what the Confederate army otherwise would have gotten. As appears in this book, on one single occasion we captured five thousand head of cattle which were crossing the Mississippi River near Port Hudson on their way from Texas to supply the Confederate army in the East.

One of the most anxious periods of my experience during the rebellion was the last few weeks before Petersburg. I felt that the situation of the Confederate army was such that they would try to make an escape at the earliest practicable moment, and I was afraid, every morning, that I would awake from my sleep to hear that Lee had gone, and that nothing was left but a picket line. He had his railroad by the way of

Danville south, and I was afraid that he was running off his men and all stores and ordnance except such as it would be necessary to carry with him for his immediate defence. I knew he could move much more lightly and more rapidly than I, and that, if he got the start, he would leave me behind so that we would have the same army to fight again farther south— and the war might be prolonged another year.

I was led to this fear by the fact that I could not see how it was possible for the Confederates to hold out much longer where they were. There is no doubt that Richmond would have been evacuated much sooner than it was, if it had not been that it was the capital of the so-called Confederacy, and the fact of evacuating the capital would, of course, have had a very demoralizing effect upon the Confederate army. When it was evacuated (as we shall see further on), the Confederacy at once began to crumble and fade away. Then, too, desertions were taking place, not only among those who were with General Lee in the neighborhood of their capital, but throughout the whole Confederacy. I remember that in a conversation with me on one occasion long prior to this, General Butler remarked that the Confederates would find great difficulty in getting more men for their army; possibly adding, though I am not certain as to this, "unless they should arm the slave."

The South, as we all knew, were conscripting every able-bodied man between the ages of eighteen and forty-five; and now they had passed a law for the further conscription of boys from fourteen to eighteen, calling them the junior reserves, and men from forty-five to sixty to be called the senior reserves. The latter were to hold the necessary points not in immediate danger, and especially those in the rear. General Butler, in alluding to this conscription, remarked that they were thus "robbing both the cradle and the grave," an expression which I afterwards used in writing a letter to Mr. Washburn.

It was my belief that while the enemy could get no more recruits they were losing at least a regiment a day, taking it throughout the entire army, by desertions alone. Then by casualties of war, sickness, and other natural causes, their losses were much heavier. It was a mere question of arithmetic to calculate how long they could hold out while that rate of depletion was going on. Of course long before their army would be thus reduced to nothing the army which we had in the field would have been able to capture theirs. Then too I knew from the great number of desertions, that the men who had fought so bravely, so gallantly and so long for the cause which they believed in—and as earnestly, I take it, as our men believed in the cause for which they were fighting—had lost hope and become despondent. Many of them were making application to be sent North where they might get employment until the war was over, when they could return to their Southern homes.

For these and other reasons I was naturally very impatient for the time to come when I could commence the spring campaign, which I thoroughly believed would close the war.

There were two considerations I had to observe, however, and which detained me. One was the fact that the winter had been one of heavy rains, and the roads were impassable for artillery and teams. It was necessary to wait until they had dried sufficiently to enable us to move the wagon trains and artillery necessary to the efficiency of an army operating in the enemy's country. The other consideration was that General Sheridan with the cavalry of the Army of the Potomac was operating on the north side of the James River, having come down from the Shenandoah. It was necessary that I should have his cavalry with me, and I was therefore obliged to wait until he could join me south of the James River.

Let us now take account of what he was doing.

On the 5th of March I had heard from Sheridan. He had met Early between Staunton and Charlottesville and defeated him, capturing nearly his entire command. Early and some of his officers escaped by finding refuge in the neighboring houses or in the woods.

On the 12th I heard from him again. He had turned east, to come to White House. He could not go to Lynchburg as ordered, because the rains had been so very heavy and the streams were so very much swollen. He had a pontoon train with him, but it would not reach half way across some of the streams, at their then stage of water, which he would have to get over in going south as first ordered.

I had supplies sent around to White House for him, and kept the depot there open until he arrived. We had intended to abandon it because the James River had now become our base of supplies.

Sheridan had about ten thousand cavalry with him, divided into two divisions commanded respectively by Custer and Devin. General Merritt was acting as chief of cavalry. Sheridan moved very light, carrying only four days' provisions with him, with a larger supply of coffee, salt and other small rations, and a very little else besides ammunition. They stopped at Charlottesville and commenced tearing up the railroad back toward Lynchburg. He also sent a division along the James River Canal to destroy locks, culverts, etc. All mills and factories along the lines of march of his troops were destroyed also.

Sheridan had in this way consumed so much time that his making a march to White House was now somewhat hazardous. He determined therefore to fight his way along the railroad and canal till he was as near to Richmond as it was possible to get, or until attacked. He did this, destroying the canal as far as Goochland, and the railroad to a point as near Richmond as he could get. On the 10th he was at Columbia. Negroes had joined his column to the number of two thousand or more, and they assisted considerably in the work of destroying the railroads and the canal. His cavalry was in as fine a condition as when he started, because he had been able to find plenty of forage. He had captured most of Early's horses and picked up a good many others on the road. When he reached Ashland he was assailed by the enemy in force. He resisted their assault with part of his command, moved quickly across the South and North Anna, going north, and reached White House safely on the 19th.

The time for Sherman to move had to be fixed with reference to the time he could get away from Goldsboro where he then was. Supplies had to be got up to him which would last him through a long march, as there would probably not be much to be obtained in the country through which he would pass. I had to arrange, therefore, that he should start from where he was, in the neighborhood of Goldsboro, on the 18th of April, the earliest day at which he supposed he could be ready.

Sherman was anxious that I should wait where I was until he could come up, and make a sure thing of it; but I had determined to move as soon as the roads and weather would admit of my doing so. I had been tied down somewhat in the matter of fixing any time at my pleasure for starting, until Sheridan, who was on his way from the Shenandoah Valley to join me, should arrive, as both his presence and that of his cavalry were necessary to the execution of the plans which I had in mind. However, having arrived at White House on the 19th of March, I was enabled to make my plans.

Prompted by my anxiety lest Lee should get away some night before I was aware of it, and having the lead of me, push into North Carolina to join with Johnston in attempting to crush out Sherman, I had, as early as the 1st of the month of March, given instructions to the troops around Petersburg to keep a sharp lookout to see that such a movement should not escape their notice, and to be ready to strike at once if it was undertaken.

It is now known that early in the month of March Mr. Davis and General Lee had a consultation about the situation of affairs in and about Richmond and Petersburg, and they both agreed that these places were no longer tenable for them, and that they must get away as soon as possible. They, too, were waiting for dry roads, or a condition of the roads which would make it possible to move.

General Lee, in aid of his plan of escape, and to secure a wider opening to enable them to reach the Danville Road with greater security than he would have in the way the two armies were situated, determined upon an assault upon the right of our lines around Petersburg. The night of the 24th of March was fixed upon for this assault, and General Gordon was assigned to the execution of the plan. The point between Fort Stedman and Battery No. 10, where our lines were closest together, was selected as the point of his attack. The attack was to be made at night, and the troops were to get possession of the higher ground in the rear where they supposed we had intrenchments, then sweep to the right and left, create a panic in the lines of our army, and force me to contract my lines. Lee hoped this would detain me a few days longer and give him an opportunity of escape. The plan was well conceived and the execution of it very well done indeed, up to the point of carrying a portion of our line.

Gordon assembled his troops under the cover of night, at the point at which they were to make their charge, and got possession of our picket-line, entirely without the knowledge of the troops inside of our main line of intrenchments; this reduced the distance he would have to charge over to not much more than fifty yards. For some time before the deserters had been coming in with great frequency, often bringing their arms with them, and this the Confederate general knew. Taking advantage of this knowledge he sent his pickets, with their arms, creeping through to ours as if to desert. When they got to our lines they at once took possession and sent our pickets to the rear as prisoners. In the main line our men were sleeping serenely, as if in great security. This plan was to have been executed and much damage done before daylight; but the troops that were to reinforce Gordon had to be brought from the north side of the James River and, by some accident on the railroad on their way over, they were detained for a considerable time; so that it got to be nearly daylight before they were ready to make the charge.

The charge, however, was successful and almost without loss, the enemy passing through our lines between Fort Stedman and Battery No. 10. Then turning to the right and left they captured the fort and the battery, with all the arms and troops in them. Continuing the charge, they also carried batteries Eleven and Twelve to our left, which they turned toward City Point.

Meade happened to be at City Point that night, and this break in his line cut him off from all communication with his headquarters. Parke, however, commanding the 9th corps when this breach took place, telegraphed the facts to Meade's headquarters, and learning that the general was away, assumed command himself and with commendable promptitude made all preparations to drive the enemy back. General Tidball gathered a large number of pieces of artillery and planted them in rear of the captured works so as to sweep the narrow space of ground between the lines very thoroughly. Hartranft was soon out with his division, as also was Willcox. Hartranft to the right of the breach headed the rebels off in that direction and rapidly drove them back into Fort Stedman. On the other side they were driven back into the intrenchments which they had captured, and batteries eleven and twelve were retaken by Willcox early in the morning.

Parke then threw a line around outside of the captured fort and batteries, and communication was once more established. The artillery fire was kept up so continuously that it was impossible for the Confederates to retreat, and equally impossible for reinforcements to join them. They all, therefore, fell captives into our hands. This effort of Lee's cost him about four thousand men, and resulted in their killing, wounding and capturing about two thousand of ours.

After the recapture of the batteries taken by the Confederates, our troops made a charge and carried the enemy's intrenched picket line, which they strengthened and held. This, in turn, gave us but a short distance to charge over when our attack came to be made a few days later.

The day that Gordon was making dispositions for this attack (24th of March) I issued my orders for the movement to commence on the 29th. Ord, with three divisions of infantry and Mackenzie's cavalry, was to move in advance on the night of the 27th, from the north side of the James River and take his place on our extreme left, thirty miles away. He left Weitzel with the rest of the Army of the James to hold Bermuda Hundred and the north of the James River. The engineer brigade was to be left at City Point, and Parke's corps in the lines about Petersburg.*

Ord was at his place promptly. Humphreys and Warren were then on our extreme left with the 2d and 5th corps. They were directed on the arrival of Ord, and on his getting into position in their places, to cross Hatcher's Run and extend out west toward Five Forks, the object being to get into a position from which we could strike the South Side Railroad and ultimately the Danville Railroad. There was considerable

---

*See orders to Major-Generals Meade, Ord, and Sheridan, March 24th, Appendix.

fighting in taking up these new positions for the 2d and 5th corps, in which the Army of the James had also to participate somewhat, and the losses were quite severe.

This was what was known as the battle of White Oak Road.

Chapter LXIV.

INTERVIEW WITH SHERIDAN—GRAND MOVEMENT OF
THE ARMY OF THE POTOMAC—SHERIDAN'S ADVANCE
ON FIVE FORKS—BATTLE OF FIVE FORKS—PARKE
AND WRIGHT STORM THE ENEMY'S LINE—BATTLES
BEFORE PETERSBURG.

SHERIDAN reached City Point on the 26th day of March. His horses, of course, were jaded and many of them had lost their shoes. A few days of rest were necessary to recuperate the animals and also to have them shod and put in condition for moving. Immediately on General Sheridan's arrival at City Point I prepared his instructions for the move which I had decided upon. The movement was to commence on the 29th of the month.

After reading the instructions I had given him, Sheridan walked out of my tent, and I followed to have some conversation with him by himself—not in the presence of anybody else, even of a member of my staff. In preparing his instructions I contemplated just what took place; that is to say, capturing Five Forks, driving the enemy from Petersburg and Richmond and terminating the contest before separating from the enemy. But the Nation had already become restless and discouraged at the prolongation of the war, and many believed that it would never terminate except by compromise. Knowing that unless my plan proved an entire success it would be interpreted as a disastrous defeat, I provided in these instructions that in a certain event he was to cut loose from the Army of the Potomac and his base of supplies, and living upon the country proceed south by the way of the Danville Railroad, or near it, across the Roanoke, get in the rear of Johnston, who was guarding that road, and co-operate with Sherman in destroying Johnston; then with these combined forces to help carry out the instructions which Sherman already had received, to act in co-operation with the armies around Petersburg and Richmond.

I saw that after Sheridan had read his instructions he seemed somewhat disappointed at the idea, possibly, of having to cut loose again from the Army of the Potomac, and place himself between the two main armies of the enemy. I said to him: "General, this portion of your instructions I have put in merely as a blind;" and gave him the reason for doing so, heretofore described. I told him that, as a matter of fact, I intended to close the war right here, with this movement, and that he should go no farther. His face at once brightened up, and slapping his hand on his leg he said: "I am glad to hear it, and we can do it."

Sheridan was not however to make his movement against Five Forks until he got further instructions from me.

One day, after the movement I am about to describe had commenced, and when his cavalry was on our extreme left and far to the rear, south, Sheridan rode up to where my headquarters were then established, at Dabney's Mills. He met some of my staff officers outside, and was highly jubilant over the prospects of success, giving reasons why he believed this would prove the final and successful effort. Although my chief-of-staff had urged very strongly that we return to our position about City Point and in the lines around Petersburg, he asked Sheridan to come in to see me and say to me what he had been saying to them. Sheridan felt a little modest about giving his advice where it had not been asked; so one of my staff came in and told me that Sheridan had what they considered important news, and suggested that I send for him. I did so, and was glad to see the spirit of confidence with which he was imbued. Knowing as I did from experience, of what great value that feeling of confidence by a commander was, I determined to make a movement at once, although on account of the rains which had fallen after I had started out the roads were still very heavy. Orders were given accordingly.

Finally the 29th of March came, and fortunately there having been a few days free from rain, the surface of the ground was dry, giving indications that the time had come when we could move. On that date I moved out with all the army available after leaving sufficient force to hold the line about Petersburg. It soon set in raining again however, and in a very short time the roads became practically impassable for teams, and almost so for cavalry. Sometimes a horse or mule would be standing apparently on firm ground, when all at once one foot would sink, and as he commenced scrambling to catch himself all his feet would sink and he would have to be drawn by hand out of the quicksands so common in that part of Virginia and other southern States. It became necessary therefore to build corduroy roads every foot of the way as we advanced, to move our artillery upon. The army had become so accustomed to this kind of work, and were so well prepared for it, that it was done very rapidly. The next day, March 30th, we had made sufficient progress to the south-west to warrant me in starting Sheridan with his cavalry over by Dinwiddie with instructions to then come up by the road leading north-west to Five Forks, thus menacing the right of Lee's line.

This movement was made for the purpose of extending our lines to the west as far as practicable towards the enemy's extreme right, or Five Forks. The column moving detached from the army still in the trenches was, excluding the cavalry, very small. The forces in the trenches were themselves extending to the left flank. Warren was on the extreme left when the extension began, but Humphreys was marched around later and thrown into line between him and Five Forks.

My hope was that Sheridan would be able to carry Five Forks, get on the enemy's right flank and rear, and force them to weaken their centre to protect their right so that an assault in the centre might be successfully made. General Wright's corps had been designated to make this assault, which I intended to order as soon as information reached me of Sheridan's success. He was to move under cover as close to the enemy as he could get.

It is natural to suppose that Lee would understand my design to be to get up to the South Side and ultimately to the Danville Railroad, as soon as he had heard of the movement commenced on the 29th. These roads were so important to his very existence while he remained in Richmond and Petersburg, and of such vital importance to him even in case of retreat, that naturally he would make most strenuous efforts to defend them. He did on the 30th send Pickett with five brigades to reinforce Five Forks. He also sent around to the right of his army some two or three other divisions, besides directing that other troops be held in readiness on the north side of the James River to come over on call. He came over himself to superintend in person the defence of his right flank.

Sheridan moved back to Dinwiddie Court-House on the night of the 30th, and then took a road leading north-west to Five Forks. He had only his cavalry with him. Soon encountering the rebel cavalry he met with a very stout resistance. He gradually drove them back however until in the neighborhood of Five Forks. Here he had to encounter other troops besides those he had been contending with, and was forced to give way.

In this condition of affairs he notified me of what had taken place and stated that he was falling back toward Dinwiddie gradually and slowly, and asked me to send Wright's corps to his assistance. I replied to him that it was impossible to send Wright's corps because that corps was already in line close up to the enemy, where we should want to assault when the proper time came, and was besides a long distance from him; but the 2d (Humphreys's) and 5th (Warren's) corps were on our extreme left and a little to the rear of it in a position to threaten the left flank of the enemy at Five Forks, and that I would send Warren.

Accordingly orders were sent to Warren to move at once that night (the 31st) to Dinwiddie Court House and put himself in communication with Sheridan as soon as possible, and report to him. He was very slow in moving, some of his troops not starting until after 5 o'clock next morning. When he did move it was done very deliberately, and on arriving at Gravelly Run he found the stream swollen from the recent rains so that he regarded it as not fordable. Sheridan of course knew of his coming, and being impatient to get the troops up as soon as possible, sent orders to him to hasten. He was also hastened or at least ordered to move up rapidly by General Meade. He now felt that he could not cross that creek without bridges, and his orders were changed to move so as to strike the pursuing enemy in flank or get in their rear; but he was so late in getting up that Sheridan determined to move forward without him. However, Ayres's division of Warren's corps reached him in time to be in the fight all day, most of

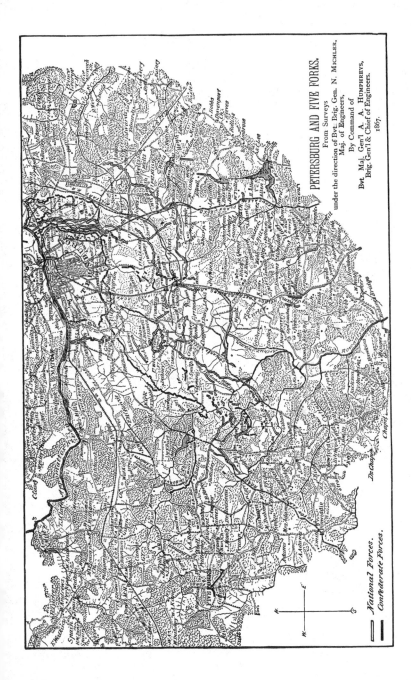

PETERSBURG AND FIVE FORKS.

From Surveys

under the direction of Bvt. Brig. Gen. N. MICHLER,
Maj. of Engineers,

By Command of

Bvt. Maj. Gen'l A. A. HUMPHREYS,
Brig. Gen'l & Chief of Engineers.
1867.

National Forces.
Confederate Forces.

the time separated from the remainder of the 5th corps and fighting directly under Sheridan.

Warren reported to Sheridan about 11 o'clock on the 1st, but the whole of his troops were not up so as to be much engaged until late in the afternoon. Griffin's division in backing to get out of the way of a severe cross fire of the enemy was found marching away from the fighting. This did not continue long, however; the division was brought back and with Ayres's division did most excellent service during the day. Crawford's division of the same corps had backed still farther off, and although orders were sent repeatedly to bring it up, it was late before it finally got to where it could be of material assistance. Once there it did very excellent service.

Sheridan succeeded by the middle of the afternoon or a little later, in advancing up to the point from which to make his designated assault upon Five Forks itself. He was very impatient to make the assault and have it all over before night, because the ground he occupied would be untenable for him in bivouac during the night. Unless the assault was made and was successful, he would be obliged to return to Dinwiddie Court-House, or even further than that for the night.

It was at this junction of affairs that Sheridan wanted to get Crawford's division in hand, and he also wanted Warren. He sent staff officer after staff officer in search of Warren, directing that general to report to him, but they were unable to find him. At all events Sheridan was unable to get that officer to him. Finally he went himself. He issued an order relieving Warren and assigning Griffin to the command of the 5th Corps. The troops were then brought up and the assault successfully made.

I was so much dissatisfied with Warren's dilatory movements in the battle of White Oak Road and in his failure to reach Sheridan in time, that I was very much afraid that at the last moment he would fail Sheridan. He was a man of fine intelligence, great earnestness, quick perception, and could make his dispositions as quickly as any officer, under difficulties where he was forced to act. But I had before discovered a defect which was beyond his control, that was very prejudicial to his usefulness in emergencies like the one just before us. He could see every danger at a glance before he had encountered it. He would not only make preparations to meet the danger which might occur, but he would inform his commanding officer what others should do while he was executing his move.

I had sent a staff officer to General Sheridan to call his attention to these defects, and to say that as much as I liked General Warren, now was not a time when we could let our personal feelings for any one stand in the way of success; and if his removal was necessary to success, not to hesitate. It was upon that authorization that Sheridan removed Warren. I was very sorry that it had been done, and regretted still more that I had not long before taken occasion to assign him to another field of duty.

It was dusk when our troops under Sheridan went over the parapets of the enemy. The two armies were mingled together there for a time in such manner that it was almost a question which one was going to demand the surrender of the other. Soon, however, the enemy broke and ran in every direction; some six thousand prisoners, besides artillery and small-arms in large quantities, falling into our hands. The flying troops were pursued in different directions, the cavalry and 5th corps under Sheridan pursuing the larger body which moved northwest.

This pursuit continued until about nine o'clock at night, when Sheridan halted his troops, and knowing the importance to him of the part of the enemy's line which had been captured, returned, sending the 5th corps across Hatcher's Run to just south-west of Petersburg, and facing them toward it. Merritt, with the cavalry, stopped and bivouacked west of Five Forks.

This was the condition which affairs were in on the night of the 1st of April. I then issued orders for an assault by Wright and Parke at four o'clock on the morning of the 2d. I also ordered the 2d corps, General Humphreys, and General Ord with the Army of the James, on the left, to hold themselves in readiness to take any advantage that could be taken from weakening in their front.

I notified Mr. Lincoln at City Point of the success of the day; in fact I had reported to him during the day and evening as I got news, because he was so much interested in the movements taking place that I wanted to relieve his mind as much as I could. I notified Weitzel on the north side of the James River, directing him, also, to keep close up to the enemy, and take advantage of the withdrawal of troops from there to promptly enter the city of Richmond.

I was afraid that Lee would regard the possession of Five Forks as of so much importance that he would make a last desperate effort to retake it, risking everything upon the cast of a single die. It was for this reason that I had ordered the assault to take place at once, as soon as I had received the news of the capture of Five Forks. The corps commanders, however, reported that it was so dark that the men could not see to move, and it would be impossible to make the assault then. But we kept up a continuous artillery fire upon the enemy around the whole line including that north of the James River, until it was light enough to move, which was about a quarter to five in the morning.

At that hour Parke's and Wright's corps moved out as directed, brushed the *abatis* from their front as they advanced under a heavy fire of musketry and artillery, and went without flinching directly on till they mounted the parapets and threw themselves inside of the enemy's line. Parke, who was on the right, swept down to the right and captured a very considerable length of line in that direction, but at that point the outer was so near the inner line which closely enveloped the city of Petersburg that he could make no advance forward and, in fact, had a very serious task to turn the lines which he had captured to the defence of his own troops and to hold them; but he succeeded in this.

Wright swung around to his left and moved to Hatcher's Run, sweeping everything before him. The enemy had traverses in rear of his captured line, under cover of which he made something of a stand, from one to another, as Wright moved on; but the latter met no serious obstacle. As you proceed to the left the outer line becomes gradually much farther from the inner one, and along about Hatcher's Run they must be nearly two miles apart. Both Parke and Wright captured a considerable amount of artillery and some prisoners— Wright about three thousand of them.

In the meantime Ord and Humphreys, in obedience to the instructions they had received, had succeeded by daylight, or very early in the morning, in capturing the intrenched picket-lines in their front; and before Wright got up to that point, Ord had also succeeded in getting inside of the enemy's intrenchments. The second corps soon followed; and the outer works of Petersburg were in the hands of the National troops, never to be wrenched from them again. When Wright reached Hatcher's Run, he sent a regiment to destroy the South Side Railroad just outside of the city.

My headquarters were still at Dabney's saw-mills. As soon as I received the news of Wright's success, I sent dispatches announcing the fact to all points around the line, including the troops at Bermuda Hundred and those on the north side of the James, and to the President at City Point. Further dispatches kept coming in, and as they did I sent the additional news to these points. Finding at length that they were all in, I mounted my horse to join the troops who were inside the works. When I arrived there I rode my horse over the parapet just as Wright's three thousand prisoners were coming out. I was soon joined inside by General Meade and his staff.

Lee made frantic efforts to recover at least part of the lost ground. Parke on our right was repeatedly assaulted, but repulsed every effort. Before noon Longstreet was ordered up from the north side of the James River, thus bringing the bulk of Lee's army around to the support of his extreme right. As soon as I learned this I notified Weitzel and directed him to keep up close to the enemy and to have Hartsuff, commanding the Bermuda Hundred front, to do the same thing, and if they found any break to go in; Hartsuff especially should do so, for this would separate Richmond and Petersburg.

Sheridan, after he had returned to Five Forks, swept down to Petersburg, coming in on our left. This gave us a continuous line from the Appomattox River below the city to the same river above. At eleven o'clock, not having heard from Sheridan, I reinforced Parke with two brigades from City Point. With this additional force he completed his captured works for better defence, and built back from his right, so as to protect his flank. He also carried in and made an *abatis* between himself and the enemy. Lee brought additional troops and artillery against Parke even after this was done, and made several assaults with very heavy losses.

The enemy had in addition to their intrenched line close up to Petersburg, two enclosed works outside of it, Fort Gregg and Fort Whitworth. We thought it had now become necessary to carry them by assault. About one o'clock in the day, Fort Gregg was assaulted by Foster's division of the 24th corps (Gibbon's), supported by two brigades from Ord's command. The battle was desperate and the National troops were repulsed several times; but it was finally carried, and immediately the troops in Fort Whitworth evacuated the place. The guns of Fort Gregg were turned upon the retreating enemy, and the commanding officer with some sixty of the men of Fort Whitworth surrendered.

I had ordered Miles in the morning to report to Sheridan. In moving to execute this order he came upon the enemy at the intersection of the White Oak Road and the Claiborne Road. The enemy fell back to Sutherland Station on the South Side Road and were followed by Miles. This position, naturally a strong and defensible one, was also strongly entrenched. Sheridan now came up and Miles asked permission from him to make the assault, which Sheridan gave. By this time Humphreys had got through the outer works in his front, and came up also and assumed command over Miles, who commanded a division in his corps. I had sent an order to Humphreys to turn to his right and move towards Petersburg. This order he now got, and started off, thus leaving Miles alone. The latter made two assaults, both of which failed, and he had to fall back a few hundred yards.

Hearing that Miles had been left in this position, I directed Humphreys to send a division back to his relief. He went himself.

Sheridan before starting to sweep down to Petersburg had sent Merritt with his cavalry to the west to attack some Confederate cavalry that had assembled there. Merritt drove them north to the Appomattox River. Sheridan then took the enemy at Sutherland Station on the reverse side from where Miles was, and the two together captured the place, with a large number of prisoners and some pieces of artillery, and put the remainder, portions of three Confederate corps, to flight. Sheridan followed, and drove them until night, when further pursuit was stopped. Miles bivouacked for the night on the ground which he with Sheridan had carried so handsomely by assault. I cannot explain the situation here better than by giving my dispatch to City Point that evening:

BOYDTON ROAD, NEAR PETERSBURG,
April 2, 1865. —4.40 P.M.

COLONEL T. S. BOWERS,
      City Point.

We are now up and have a continuous line of troops, and in a few hours will be intrenched from the Appomattox below Petersburg to the river above. Heth's and Wilcox's divisions, such part of them as were not captured, were cut off from town, either designedly on their part or because they could not help it. Sheridan with the cavalry and 5th corps is above them. Miles's division, 2d corps, was sent from the White Oak Road to Sutherland Station on the South Side Railroad, where he met them, and at last accounts was engaged with them. Not knowing whether Sheridan would get up in time, General Humphreys was sent with another division from here. The whole captures since the army started out gunning will amount to not less than twelve thousand men, and probably fifty pieces of artillery. I do not know the number of men and guns accurately however. * * * I think the President might come out and pay us a visit to-morrow.

U. S. GRANT,
Lieutenant-General.

During the night of April 2d our line was intrenched from the river above to the river below. I ordered a bombardment to be commenced the next morning at five A.M., to be followed by an assault at six o'clock; but the enemy evacuated Petersburg early in the morning.

Chapter LXV.

THE CAPTURE OF PETERSBURG—MEETING PRESIDENT
LINCOLN IN PETERSBURG—THE CAPTURE OF
RICHMOND—PURSUING THE ENEMY—VISIT TO
SHERIDAN AND MEADE.

GENERAL MEADE and I entered Petersburg on the morning of the 3d and took a position under cover of a house which protected us from the enemy's musketry which was flying thick and fast there. As we would occasionally look around the corner we could see the streets and the Appomattox bottom, presumably near the bridge, packed with the Confederate army. I did not have artillery brought up, because I was sure Lee was trying to make his escape, and I wanted to push immediately in pursuit. At all events I had not the heart to turn the artillery upon such a mass of defeated and fleeing men, and I hoped to capture them soon.

Soon after the enemy had entirely evacuated Petersburg, a man came in who represented himself to be an engineer of the Army of Northern Virginia. He said that Lee had for some time been at work preparing a strong enclosed intrenchment, into which he would throw himself when forced out of Petersburg, and fight his final battle there; that he was actually at that time drawing his troops from Richmond, and falling back into this prepared work. This statement was made to General Meade and myself when we were together. I had already given orders for the movement up the south side of the Appomattox for the purpose of heading off Lee; but Meade was so much impressed by this man's story that he thought we ought to cross the Appomattox there at once and move against Lee in his new position. I knew that Lee was no fool, as he would have been to have put himself and his army between two formidable streams like the James and Appomattox rivers, and between two such armies as those of the Potomac and the James. Then these streams coming together as they did to the east of him, it would be only necessary to close up in the west to have him thoroughly cut off from all supplies or possibility of reinforcement. It would only have been a question of days, and not many of them, if he had taken the position assigned to him by the so-called engineer, when he would have been obliged to surrender his army. Such is one of the ruses resorted to in war to deceive your antagonist. My judgment was that Lee would necessarily have to evacuate Richmond, and that the only course for him to pursue would be to follow the Danville Road. Accordingly my object was to secure a point on that road south of Lee, and I told Meade this. He suggested that if Lee was going that way we would follow him. My reply was that we did not want to follow him; we wanted to get ahead of him and cut him off, and if he would only stay in the position he (Meade) believed him to be in at that time, I wanted nothing better; that when we got in possession of the Danville Railroad, at its crossing of the Appomattox River, if we still found him between the two rivers, all we had to do was to move eastward and close him up. That we would then have all the advantage we could possibly have by moving directly against him from Petersburg, even if he remained in the position assigned him by the engineer officer.

I had held most of the command aloof from the intrenchments, so as to start them out on the Danville Road early in the morning, supposing that Lee would be gone during the night. During the night I strengthened Sheridan by sending him Humphreys's corps.

Lee, as we now know, had advised the authorities at Richmond, during the day, of the condition of affairs, and told them it would be impossible for him to hold out longer than night, if he could hold out that long. Davis was at church when he received Lee's dispatch. The congregation was dismissed with the notice that there would be no evening service. The rebel government left Richmond about two o'clock in the afternoon of the 2d.

At night Lee ordered his troops to assemble at Amelia Court House, his object being to get away, join Johnston if possible, and to try to crush Sherman before I could get there. As soon as I was sure of this I notified Sheridan and directed him to move out on the Danville Railroad to the south side of the Appomattox River as speedily as possible. He replied that he already had some of his command nine

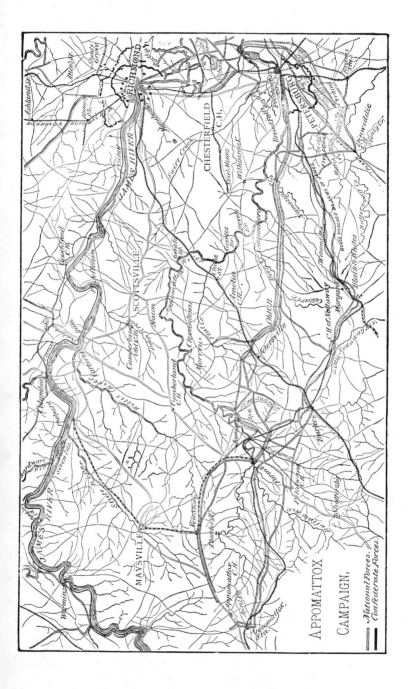

APPOMATTOX
CAMPAIGN.

National Forces. ?
Confederate Forces.

miles out. I then ordered the rest of the Army of the Potomac under Meade to follow the same road in the morning. Parke's corps followed by the same road, and the Army of the James was directed to follow the road which ran alongside of the South Side Railroad to Burke's Station, and to repair the railroad and telegraph as they proceeded. That road was a 5 feet gauge, while our rolling stock was all of the 4 feet 8½ inches gauge; consequently the rail on one side of the track had to be taken up throughout the whole length and relaid so as to conform to the gauge of our cars and locomotives.

Mr. Lincoln was at City Point at the time, and had been for some days. I would have let him know what I contemplated doing, only while I felt a strong conviction that the move was going to be successful, yet it might not prove so; and then I would have only added another to the many disappointments he had been suffering for the past three years. But when we started out he saw that we were moving for a purpose, and bidding us Godspeed, remained there to hear the result.

The next morning after the capture of Petersburg, I telegraphed Mr. Lincoln asking him to ride out there and see me, while I would await his arrival. I had started all the troops out early in the morning, so that after the National army left Petersburg there was not a soul to be seen, not even an animal in the streets. There was absolutely no one there, except my staff officers and, possibly, a small escort of cavalry. We had selected the piazza of a deserted house, and occupied it until the President arrived.

About the first thing that Mr. Lincoln said to me, after warm congratulations for the victory, and thanks both to myself and to the army which had accomplished it, was: "Do you know, general, that I have had a sort of a sneaking idea for some days that you intended to do something like this." Our movements having been successful up to this point, I no longer had any object in concealing from the President all my movements, and the objects I had in view. He remained for some days near City Point, and I communicated with him frequently and fully by telegraph.

Mr. Lincoln knew that it had been arranged for Sherman to join me at a fixed time, to co-operate in the destruction of

Lee's army. I told him that I had been very anxious to have the Eastern armies vanquish their old enemy who had so long resisted all their repeated and gallant attempts to subdue them or drive them from their capital. The Western armies had been in the main successful until they had conquered all the territory from the Mississippi River to the State of North Carolina, and were now almost ready to knock at the back door of Richmond, asking admittance. I said to him that if the Western armies should be even upon the field, operating against Richmond and Lee, the credit would be given to them for the capture, by politicians and non-combatants from the section of country which those troops hailed from. It might lead to disagreeable bickerings between members of Congress of the East and those of the West in some of their debates. Western members might be throwing it up to the members of the East that in the suppression of the rebellion they were not able to capture an army, or to accomplish much in the way of contributing toward that end, but had to wait until the Western armies had conquered all the territory south and west of them, and then come on to help them capture the only army they had been engaged with.

Mr. Lincoln said he saw that now, but had never thought of it before, because his anxiety was so great that he did not care where the aid came from so the work was done.

The Army of the Potomac has every reason to be proud of its four years' record in the suppression of the rebellion. The army it had to fight was the protection to the capital of a people which was attempting to found a nation upon the territory of the United States. Its loss would be the loss of the cause. Every energy, therefore, was put forth by the Confederacy to protect and maintain their capital. Everything else would go if it went. Lee's army had to be strengthened to enable it to maintain its position, no matter what territory was wrested from the South in another quarter.

I never expected any such bickering as I have indicated, between the soldiers of the two sections; and, fortunately, there has been none between the politicians. Possibly I am the only one who thought of the liability of such a state of things in advance.

When our conversation was at an end Mr. Lincoln mounted his horse and started on his return to City Point, while I and my staff started to join the army, now a good many miles in advance. Up to this time I had not received the report of the capture of Richmond.

Soon after I left President Lincoln I received a dispatch from General Weitzel which notified me that he had taken possession of Richmond at about 8.15 o'clock in the morning of that day, the 3d, and that he had found the city on fire in two places. The city was in the most utter confusion. The authorities had taken the precaution to empty all the liquor into the gutter, and to throw out the provisions which the Confederate government had left, for the people to gather up. The city had been deserted by the authorities, civil and military, without any notice whatever that they were about to leave. In fact, up to the very hour of the evacuation the people had been led to believe that Lee had gained an important victory somewhere around Petersburg.

Weitzel's command found evidence of great demoralization in Lee's army, there being still a great many men and even officers in the town. The city was on fire. Our troops were directed to extinguish the flames, which they finally succeeded in doing. The fire had been started by some one connected with the retreating army. All authorities deny that it was authorized, and I presume it was the work of excited men who were leaving what they regarded as their capital and may have felt that it was better to destroy it than have it fall into the hands of their enemy. Be that as it may, the National troops found the city in flames, and used every effort to extinguish them.

The troops that had formed Lee's right, a great many of them, were cut off from getting back into Petersburg, and were pursued by our cavalry so hotly and closely that they threw away caissons, ammunition, clothing, and almost everything to lighten their loads, and pushed along up the Appomattox River until finally they took water and crossed over.

I left Mr. Lincoln and started, as I have already said, to join the command, which halted at Sutherland Station, about nine miles out. We had still time to march as much farther, and time was an object; but the roads were bad and the trains belonging to the advance corps had blocked up the road so that it was impossible to get on. Then, again, our cavalry had struck some of the enemy and were pursuing them; and the orders were that the roads should be given up to the cavalry whenever they appeared. This caused further delay.

General Wright, who was in command of one of the corps which were left back, thought to gain time by letting his men go into bivouac and trying to get up some rations for them, and clearing out the road, so that when they did start they would be uninterrupted. Humphreys, who was far ahead, was also out of rations. They did not succeed in getting them up through the night; but the Army of the Potomac, officers and men, were so elated by the reflection that at last they were following up a victory to its end, that they preferred marching without rations to running a possible risk of letting the enemy elude them. So the march was resumed at three o'clock in the morning.

Merritt's cavalry had struck the enemy at Deep Creek, and driven them north to the Appomattox, where, I presume, most of them were forced to cross.

On the morning of the 4th I learned that Lee had ordered rations up from Danville for his famishing army, and that they were to meet him at Farmville. This showed that Lee had already abandoned the idea of following the railroad down to Danville, but had determined to go farther west, by the way of Farmville. I notified Sheridan of this and directed him to get possession of the road before the supplies could reach Lee. He responded that he had already sent Crook's division to get upon the road between Burkesville and Jetersville, then to face north and march along the road upon the latter place; and he thought Crook must be there now. The bulk of the army moved directly for Jetersville by two roads.

After I had received the dispatch from Sheridan saying that Crook was on the Danville Road, I immediately ordered Meade to make a forced march with the Army of the Potomac, and to send Parke's corps across from the road they were on to the South Side Railroad, to fall in the rear of the Army of the James and to protect the railroad which that army was repairing as it went along.

Our troops took possession of Jetersville and in the telegraph office, they found a dispatch from Lee, ordering two hundred thousand rations from Danville. The dispatch had not been sent, but Sheridan sent a special messenger with it to Burkesville and had it forwarded from there. In the meantime, however, dispatches from other sources had reached Danville, and they knew there that our army was on the line of the road; so that they sent no further supplies from that quarter.

At this time Merritt and Mackenzie, with the cavalry, were off between the road which the Army of the Potomac was marching on and the Appomattox River, and were attacking the enemy in flank. They picked up a great many prisoners and forced the abandonment of some property.

Lee intrenched himself at Amelia Court House, and also his advance north of Jetersville, and sent his troops out to collect forage. The country was very poor and afforded but very little. His foragers scattered a great deal; many of them were picked up by our men, and many others never returned to the Army of Northern Virginia.

Griffin's corps was intrenched across the railroad south of Jetersville, and Sheridan notified me of the situation. I again ordered Meade up with all dispatch, Sheridan having but the one corps of infantry with a little cavalry confronting Lee's entire army. Meade, always prompt in obeying orders, now pushed forward with great energy, although he was himself sick and hardly able to be out of bed. Humphreys moved at two, and Wright at three o'clock in the morning, without rations, as I have said, the wagons being far in the rear.

I stayed that night at Wilson's Station on the South Side Railroad. On the morning of the 5th I sent word to Sheridan of the progress Meade was making, and suggested that he might now attack Lee. We had now no other objective than the Confederate armies, and I was anxious to close the thing up at once.

On the 5th I marched again with Ord's command until within about ten miles of Burkesville, where I stopped to let his army pass. I then received from Sheridan the following dispatch:

"The whole of Lee's army is at or near Amelia Court House, and on this side of it. General Davies, whom I sent out to Painesville on their right flank, has just captured six pieces of artillery and some wagons. We can capture the Army of Northern Virginia if force enough can be thrown to this point, and then advance upon it. My cavalry was at Burkesville yesterday, and six miles beyond, on the Danville Road, last night. General Lee is at Amelia Court House in person. They are out of rations, or nearly so. They were advancing up the railroad towards Burkesville yesterday, when we intercepted them at this point."

It now became a life and death struggle with Lee to get south to his provisions.

Sheridan, thinking the enemy might turn off immediately towards Farmville, moved Davies's brigade of cavalry out to watch him. Davies found the movement had already commenced. He attacked and drove away their cavalry which was escorting wagons to the west, capturing and burning 180 wagons. He also captured five pieces of artillery. The Confederate infantry then moved against him and probably would have handled him very roughly, but Sheridan had sent two more brigades of cavalry to follow Davies, and they came to his relief in time. A sharp engagement took place between these three brigades of cavalry and the enemy's infantry, but the latter was repulsed.

Meade himself reached Jetersville about two o'clock in the afternoon, but in advance of all his troops. The head of Humphreys's corps followed in about an hour afterwards. Sheridan stationed the troops as they came up, at Meade's request, the latter still being very sick. He extended two divisions of this corps off to the west of the road to the left of Griffin's corps, and one division to the right. The cavalry by this time had also come up, and they were put still farther off to the left, Sheridan feeling certain that there lay the route by which the enemy intended to escape. He wanted to attack, feeling that if time was given, the enemy would get away; but Meade prevented this, preferring to wait till his troops were all up.

At this juncture Sheridan sent me a letter which had been handed to him by a colored man, with a note from himself saying that he wished I was there myself. The letter was dated Amelia Court House, April 5th, and signed by Colonel Taylor. It was to his mother, and showed the demoralization of the Confederate army. Sheridan's note also gave me the information as here related of the movements of that day. I received a second message from Sheridan on the 5th, in which he urged more emphatically the importance of my presence. This was brought to me by a scout in gray uniform. It was written on tissue paper, and wrapped up in tin-foil such as chewing tobacco is folded in. This was a precaution taken so that if the scout should be captured he could take this tin-foil out of his pocket and putting it into his mouth, chew it. It would cause no surprise at all to see a Confederate soldier chewing tobacco. It was nearly night when this letter was received. I gave Ord directions to continue his march to Burkesville and there intrench himself for the night, and in the morning to move west to cut off all the roads between there and Farmville.

I then started with a few of my staff and a very small escort of cavalry, going directly through the woods, to join Meade's army. The distance was about sixteen miles; but the night being dark our progress was slow through the woods in the absence of direct roads. However, we got to the outposts about ten o'clock in the evening, and after some little parley convinced the sentinels of our identity and were conducted in to where Sheridan was bivouacked. We talked over the situation for some little time, Sheridan explaining to me what he thought Lee was trying to do, and that Meade's orders, if carried out, moving to the right flank, would give him the coveted opportunity of escaping us and putting us in rear of him.

We then together visited Meade, reaching his headquarters about midnight. I explained to Meade that we did not want to follow the enemy; we wanted to get ahead of him, and that his orders would allow the enemy to escape, and besides that, I had no doubt that Lee was moving right then. Meade changed his orders at once. They were now given for an advance on Amelia Court House, at an early hour in the morning, as the army then lay; that is, the infantry being across the railroad, most of it to the west of the road, with the cavalry swung out still farther to the left.

Chapter LXVI.

THE APPOMATTOX, going westward, takes a long sweep to the south-west from the neighborhood of the Richmond and Danville Railroad bridge, and then trends northwesterly. Sailor's Creek, an insignificant stream, running northward, empties into the Appomattox between the High Bridge and Jetersville. Near the High Bridge the stage road from Petersburg to Lynchburg crosses the Appomattox River, also on a bridge. The railroad runs on the north side of the river to Farmville, a few miles west, and from there, recrossing, continues on the south side of it. The roads coming up from the south-east to Farmville cross the Appomattox River there on a bridge and run on the north side, leaving the Lynchburg and Petersburg Railroad well to the left.

Lee, in pushing out from Amelia Court House, availed himself of all the roads between the Danville Road and Appomattox River to move upon, and never permitted the head of his columns to stop because of any fighting that might be going on in his rear. In this way he came very near succeeding in getting to his provision trains and eluding us with at least part of his army.

As expected, Lee's troops had moved during the night before, and our army in moving upon Amelia Court House soon encountered them. There was a good deal of fighting before Sailor's Creek was reached. Our cavalry charged in upon a body of theirs which was escorting a wagon train in order to get it past our left. A severe engagement ensued, in which we captured many prisoners, and many men also were killed and wounded. There was as much gallantry displayed by some of the Confederates in these little engagements as was displayed at any time during the war, notwithstanding the sad defeats of the past week.

The armies finally met on Sailor's Creek, when a heavy engagement took place, in which infantry, artillery and cavalry were all brought into action. Our men on the right, as they were brought in against the enemy, came in on higher ground, and upon his flank, giving us every advantage to be derived from the lay of the country. Our firing was also very much more rapid, because the enemy commenced his retreat westward and in firing as he retreated had to turn around every time he fired. The enemy's loss was very heavy, as well in killed and wounded as in captures. Some six general officers fell into our hands in this engagement, and seven thousand men were made prisoners. This engagement was commenced in the middle of the afternoon of the 6th, and the retreat and pursuit were continued until nightfall, when the armies bivouacked upon the ground where the night had overtaken them.

When the move towards Amelia Court House had commenced that morning, I ordered Wright's corps, which was on the extreme right, to be moved to the left past the whole army, to take the place of Griffin's, and ordered the latter at the same time to move by and place itself on the right. The object of this movement was to get the 6th corps, Wright's, next to the cavalry, with which they had formerly served so harmoniously and so efficiently in the valley of Virginia.

The 6th corps now remained with the cavalry and under Sheridan's direct command until after the surrender.

Ord had been directed to take possession of all the roads southward between Burkesville and the High Bridge. On the morning of the 6th he sent Colonel Washburn with two infantry regiments with instructions to destroy High Bridge and to return rapidly to Burkesville Station; and he prepared himself to resist the enemy there. Soon after Washburn had started Ord became a little alarmed as to his safety and sent Colonel Read, of his staff, with about eighty cavalrymen, to overtake him and bring him back. Very shortly after this he heard that the head of Lee's column had got up to the road between him and where Washburn now was, and attempted to send reinforcements, but the reinforcements could not get through. Read, however, had got through ahead of the enemy. He rode on to Farmville and was on his way back again when he found his return cut off, and Washburn confronting apparently the advance of Lee's army. Read drew his

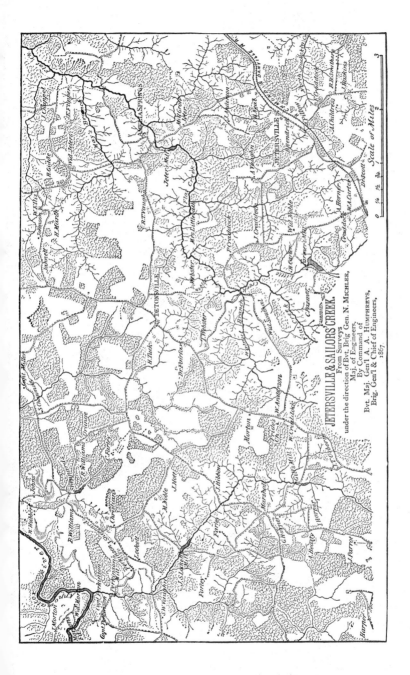

JETERSVILLE & SAILORS CREEK.
From Surveys
under the direction of Bvt. Brig. Gen. N. MICHLER,
Maj. of Engineers,
By Command of
Bvt. Maj. Gen'l A. A. HUMPHREYS,
Brig. Gen'l & Chief of Engineers,
1867

Scale of Miles

men up into line of battle, his force now consisting of less than six hundred men, infantry and cavalry, and rode along their front, making a speech to his men to inspire them with the same enthusiasm that he himself felt. He then gave the order to charge. This little band made several charges, of course unsuccessful ones, but inflicted a loss upon the enemy more than equal to their own entire number. Colonel Read fell mortally wounded, and then Washburn; and at the close of the conflict nearly every officer of the command and most of the rank and file had been either killed or wounded. The remainder then surrendered. The Confederates took this to be only the advance of a larger column which had headed them off, and so stopped to intrench; so that this gallant band of six hundred had checked the progress of a strong detachment of the Confederate army.

This stoppage of Lee's column no doubt saved to us the trains following. Lee himself pushed on and crossed the wagon road bridge near the High Bridge, and attempted to destroy it. He did set fire to it, but the flames had made but little headway when Humphreys came up with his corps and drove away the rear-guard which had been left to protect it while it was being burned up. Humphreys forced his way across with some loss, and followed Lee to the intersection of the road crossing at Farmville with the one from Petersburg. Here Lee held a position which was very strong, naturally, besides being intrenched. Humphreys was alone, confronting him all through the day, and in a very hazardous position. He put on a bold face, however, and assaulted with some loss, but was not assaulted in return.

Our cavalry had gone farther south by the way of Prince Edward's Court House, along with the 5th corps (Griffin's), Ord falling in between Griffin and the Appomattox. Crook's division of cavalry and Wright's corps pushed on west of Farmville. When the cavalry reached Farmville they found that some of the Confederates were in ahead of them, and had already got their trains of provisions back to that point; but our troops were in time to prevent them from securing anything to eat, although they succeeded in again running the trains off, so that we did not get them for some time. These troops retreated to the north side of the Appomattox to join

Lee, and succeeded in destroying the bridge after them. Considerable fighting ensued there between Wright's corps and a portion of our cavalry and the Confederates, but finally the cavalry forded the stream and drove them away. Wright built a foot-bridge for his men to march over on and then marched out to the junction of the roads to relieve Humphreys, arriving there that night. I had stopped the night before at Burkesville Junction. Our troops were then pretty much all out of the place, but we had a field hospital there, and Ord's command was extended from that point towards Farmville.

Here I met Dr. Smith, a Virginian and an officer of the regular army, who told me that in a conversation with General Ewell, one of the prisoners and a relative of his, Ewell had said that when we had got across the James River he knew their cause was lost, and it was the duty of their authorities to make the best terms they could while they still had a right to claim concessions. The authorities thought differently, however. Now the cause was lost and they had no right to claim anything. He said further, that for every man that was killed after this in the war somebody is responsible, and it would be but very little better than murder. He was not sure that Lee would consent to surrender his army without being able to consult with the President, but he hoped he would.

I rode in to Farmville on the 7th, arriving there early in the day. Sheridan and Ord were pushing through, away to the south. Meade was back towards the High Bridge, and Humphreys confronting Lee as before stated. After having gone into bivouac at Prince Edward's Court House, Sheridan learned that seven trains of provisions and forage were at Appomattox, and determined to start at once and capture them; and a forced march was necessary in order to get there before Lee's army could secure them. He wrote me a note telling me this. This fact, together with the incident related the night before by Dr. Smith, gave me the idea of opening correspondence with General Lee on the subject of the surrender of his army. I therefore wrote to him on this day, as follows:

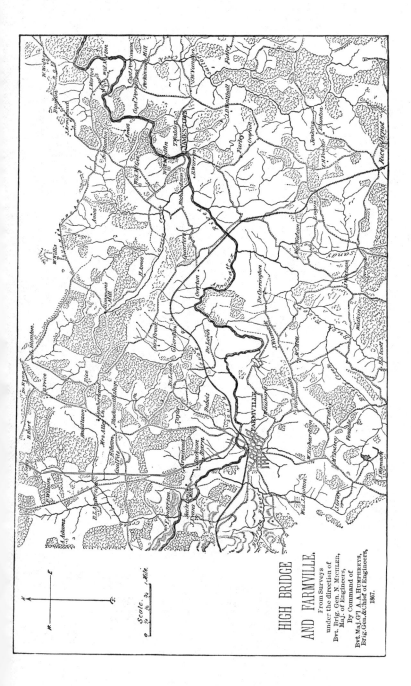

HIGH BRIDGE
AND FARMVILLE,
From Surveys
under the direction of
Bvt. Brig. Gen. N. MICHLER,
Maj. of Engineers,
By Command of
Bvt. Maj. Gⁿ¹ A. A. HUMPHREYS,
Brig. Gen. & Chief of Engineers,
1867.

Scale. ¾ ₁ Mile.
0   ½   ½

HEADQUARTERS ARMIES OF THE U. S.,
5 P.M., *April* 7, 1865.

GENERAL R. E. LEE,
    Commanding C. S. A.

The results of the last week must convince you of the hopelessness of further resistance on the part of the Army of Northern Virginia in this struggle. I feel that it is so, and regard it as my duty to shift from myself the responsibility of any further effusion of blood, by asking of you the surrender of that portion of the Confederate States army known as the Army of Northern Virginia.

U. S. GRANT,
Lieut.-General.

Lee replied on the evening of the same day as follows:

April 7, 1865.

GENERAL:—I have received your note of this day. Though not entertaining the opinion you express on the hopelessness of further resistance on the part of the Army of Northern Virginia, I reciprocate your desire to avoid useless effusion of blood, and therefore before considering your proposition, ask the terms you will offer on condition of its surrender.

R. E. LEE,
General.

LIEUT.-GENERAL U. S. GRANT,
    Commanding Armies of the U.S.

This was not satisfactory, but I regarded it as deserving another letter and wrote him as follows:

April 8, 1865.

GENERAL R. E. LEE,
    Commanding C. S. A.

Your note of last evening in reply to mine of same date, asking the condition on which I will accept the surrender of the Army of Northern Virginia is just received. In reply I would say that, peace being my great desire, there is but one condition I would insist upon, namely: that the men and officers surrendered shall be disqualified for taking up arms again against the Government of the United States until properly exchanged. I will meet you, or will designate officers to meet any officers you may name for the same purpose, at any point agreeable to you, for the purpose of arranging definitely the terms upon which the surrender of the Army of Northern Virginia will be received.

U.S. GRANT,
Lieut.-General.

Lee's army was rapidly crumbling. Many of his soldiers had enlisted from that part of the State where they now were, and were continually dropping out of the ranks and going to their homes. I know that I occupied a hotel almost destitute of furniture at Farmville, which had probably been used as a Confederate hospital. The next morning when I came out I found a Confederate colonel there, who reported to me and said that he was the proprietor of that house, and that he was a colonel of a regiment that had been raised in that neighborhood. He said that when he came along past home, he found that he was the only man of the regiment remaining with Lee's army, so he just dropped out, and now wanted to surrender himself. I told him to stay there and he would not be molested. That was one regiment which had been eliminated from Lee's force by this crumbling process.

Although Sheridan had been marching all day, his troops moved with alacrity and without any straggling. They began to see the end of what they had been fighting four years for. Nothing seemed to fatigue them. They were ready to move without rations and travel without rest until the end. Straggling had entirely ceased, and every man was now a rival for the front. The infantry marched about as rapidly as the cavalry could.

Sheridan sent Custer with his division to move south of Appomattox Station, which is about five miles south-west of the Court House, to get west of the trains and destroy the roads to the rear. They got there the night of the 8th, and succeeded partially; but some of the train men had just discovered the movement of our troops and succeeded in running off three of the trains. The other four were held by Custer.

The head of Lee's column came marching up there on the morning of the 9th, not dreaming, I suppose, that there were any Union soldiers near. The Confederates were surprised to find our cavalry had possession of the trains. However, they were desperate and at once assaulted, hoping to recover them. In the melée that ensued they succeeded in burning one of the trains, but not in getting anything from it. Custer then ordered the other trains run back on the road towards Farmville, and the fight continued.

So far, only our cavalry and the advance of Lee's army were engaged. Soon, however, Lee's men were brought up from the rear, no doubt expecting they had nothing to meet but our cavalry. But our infantry had pushed forward so rapidly that by the time the enemy got up they found Griffin's corps and the Army of the James confronting them. A sharp engagement ensued, but Lee quickly set up a white flag.

Chapter LXVII.

NEGOTIATIONS AT APPOMATTOX — INTERVIEW WITH
LEE AT McLEAN'S HOUSE — THE TERMS OF
SURRENDER — LEE'S SURRENDER — INTERVIEW
WITH LEE AFTER THE SURRENDER.

O N THE 8TH I had followed the Army of the Potomac in
rear of Lee. I was suffering very severely with a sick
headache, and stopped at a farmhouse on the road some distance in rear of the main body of the army. I spent the night
in bathing my feet in hot water and mustard, and putting
mustard plasters on my wrists and the back part of my neck,
hoping to be cured by morning. During the night I received
Lee's answer to my letter of the 8th, inviting an interview
between the lines on the following morning.* But it was for a
different purpose from that of surrendering his army, and I
answered him as follows:

> HEADQUARTERS ARMIES OF THE U. S.,
> *April 9,* 1865.
>
> GENERAL R. E. LEE,
> Commanding C. S. A.
>
> Your note of yesterday is received. As I have no authority to treat
> on the subject of peace, the meeting proposed for ten A.M. to-day
> could lead to no good. I will state, however, General, that I am
> equally anxious for peace with yourself, and the whole North enter-
> tains the same feeling. The terms upon which peace can be had are
> well understood. By the South laying down their arms they will has-
> ten that most desirable event, save thousands of human lives, and
> hundreds of millions of property not yet destroyed. Sincerely hoping
> that all our difficulties may be settled without the loss of another life,
> I subscribe myself, etc.,
>
> > U. S. GRANT,
> > Lieutenant-General.

I proceeded at an early hour in the morning, still suffering
with the headache, to get to the head of the column. I was
not more than two or three miles from Appomattox Court

---

*See Appendix.

House at the time, but to go direct I would have to pass through Lee's army, or a portion of it. I had therefore to move south in order to get upon a road coming up from another direction.

When the white flag was put out by Lee, as already described, I was in this way moving towards Appomattox Court House, and consequently could not be communicated with immediately, and be informed of what Lee had done. Lee, therefore, sent a flag to the rear to advise Meade and one to the front to Sheridan, saying that he had sent a message to me for the purpose of having a meeting to consult about the surrender of his army, and asked for a suspension of hostilities until I could be communicated with. As they had heard nothing of this until the fighting had got to be severe and all going against Lee, both of these commanders hesitated very considerably about suspending hostilities at all. They were afraid it was not in good faith, and we had the Army of Northern Virginia where it could not escape except by some deception. They, however, finally consented to a suspension of hostilities for two hours to give an opportunity of communicating with me in that time, if possible. It was found that, from the route I had taken, they would probably not be able to communicate with me and get an answer back within the time fixed unless the messenger should pass through the rebel lines.

Lee, therefore, sent an escort with the officer bearing this message through his lines to me.

April 9, 1865.

GENERAL:—I received your note of this morning on the picket-line whither I had come to meet you and ascertain definitely what terms were embraced in your proposal of yesterday with reference to the surrender of this army. I now request an interview in accordance with the offer contained in your letter of yesterday for that purpose.

R. E. LEE, General.
LIEUTENANT-GENERAL U. S. GRANT,
            Commanding U. S. Armies.

When the officer reached me I was still suffering with the sick headache; but the instant I saw the contents of the note I was cured. I wrote the following note in reply and hastened on:

April 9, 1865.

GENERAL R. E. LEE,
        Commanding C. S. Armies.

Your note of this date is but this moment (11.50 A.M.) received, in consequence of my having passed from the Richmond and Lynchburg road to the Farmville and Lynchburg road. I am at this writing about four miles west of Walker's Church and will push forward to the front for the purpose of meeting you. Notice sent to me on this road where you wish the interview to take place will meet me.

                                        U. S. GRANT,
                                        Lieutenant-General.

I was conducted at once to where Sheridan was located with his troops drawn up in line of battle facing the Confederate army near by. They were very much excited, and expressed their view that this was all a ruse employed to enable the Confederates to get away. They said they believed that Johnston was marching up from North Carolina now, and Lee was moving to join him; and they would whip the rebels where they now were in five minutes if I would only let them go in. But I had no doubt about the good faith of Lee, and pretty soon was conducted to where he was. I found him at the house of a Mr. McLean, at Appomattox Court House, with Colonel Marshall, one of his staff officers, awaiting my arrival. The head of his column was occupying a hill, on a portion of which was an apple orchard, beyond a little valley which separated it from that on the crest of which Sheridan's forces were drawn up in line of battle to the south.

Before stating what took place between General Lee and myself, I will give all there is of the story of the famous apple tree.

Wars produce many stories of fiction, some of which are told until they are believed to be true. The war of the rebellion was no exception to this rule, and the story of the apple tree is one of those fictions based on a slight foundation of fact. As I have said, there was an apple orchard on the side of the hill occupied by the Confederate forces. Running diagonally up the hill was a wagon road, which, at one point, ran very near one of the trees, so that the wheels of vehicles had, on that side, cut off the roots of this tree, leaving a little embankment. General Babcock, of my staff, reported to me that

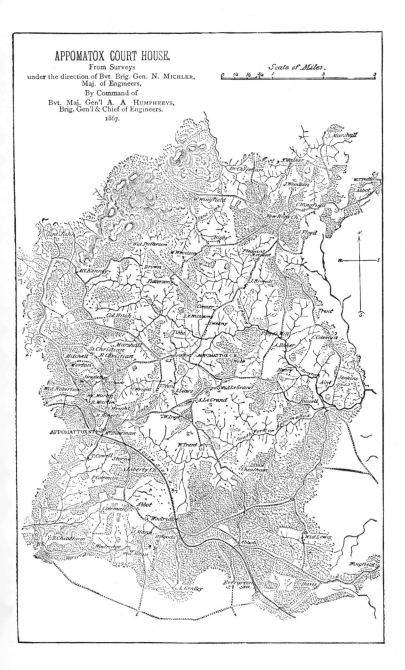

APPOMATOX COURT HOUSE.

From Surveys
under the direction of Bvt. Brig. Gen. N. MICHLER,
Maj. of Engineers,
By Command of
Bvt. Maj. Gen'l A. A HUMPHREYS,
Brig. Gen'l & Chief of Engineers.
1867.

Scale of Miles.

when he first met General Lee he was sitting upon this embankment with his feet in the road below and his back resting against the tree. The story had no other foundation than that. Like many other stories, it would be very good if it was only true.

I had known General Lee in the old army, and had served with him in the Mexican War; but did not suppose, owing to the difference in our age and rank, that he would remember me; while I would more naturally remember him distinctly, because he was the chief of staff of General Scott in the Mexican War.

When I had left camp that morning I had not expected so soon the result that was then taking place, and consequently was in rough garb. I was without a sword, as I usually was when on horseback on the field, and wore a soldier's blouse for a coat, with the shoulder straps of my rank to indicate to the army who I was. When I went into the house I found General Lee. We greeted each other, and after shaking hands took our seats. I had my staff with me, a good portion of whom were in the room during the whole of the interview.

What General Lee's feelings were I do not know. As he was a man of much dignity, with an impassible face, it was impossible to say whether he felt inwardly glad that the end had finally come, or felt sad over the result, and was too manly to show it. Whatever his feelings, they were entirely concealed from my observation; but my own feelings, which had been quite jubilant on the receipt of his letter, were sad and depressed. I felt like anything rather than rejoicing at the downfall of a foe who had fought so long and valiantly, and had suffered so much for a cause, though that cause was, I believe, one of the worst for which a people ever fought, and one for which there was the least excuse. I do not question, however, the sincerity of the great mass of those who were opposed to us.

General Lee was dressed in a full uniform which was entirely new, and was wearing a sword of considerable value, very likely the sword which had been presented by the State of Virginia; at all events, it was an entirely different sword from the one that would ordinarily be worn in the field. In my rough traveling suit, the uniform of a private with the

straps of a lieutenant-general, I must have contrasted very
strangely with a man so handsomely dressed, six feet high and
of faultless form. But this was not a matter that I thought of
until afterwards.

We soon fell into a conversation about old army times. He
remarked that he remembered me very well in the old army;
and I told him that as a matter of course I remembered him
perfectly, but from the difference in our rank and years
(there being about sixteen years' difference in our ages), I
had thought it very likely that I had not attracted his attention sufficiently to be remembered by him after such a long
interval. Our conversation grew so pleasant that I almost
forgot the object of our meeting. After the conversation had
run on in this style for some time, General Lee called my
attention to the object of our meeting, and said that he had
asked for this interview for the purpose of getting from me
the terms I proposed to give his army. I said that I meant
merely that his army should lay down their arms, not to take
them up again during the continuance of the war unless duly
and properly exchanged. He said that he had so understood
my letter.

Then we gradually fell off again into conversation about
matters foreign to the subject which had brought us together.
This continued for some little time, when General Lee again
interrupted the course of the conversation by suggesting that
the terms I proposed to give his army ought to be written
out. I called to General Parker, secretary on my staff, for
writing materials, and commenced writing out the following
terms:

APPOMATTOX C. H., VA.,

Ap l 9th, 1865.

GEN. R. E. LEE,
   Comd'g C. S. A.

 GEN: In accordance with the substance of my letter to you of the
8th inst., I propose to receive the surrender of the Army of N. Va. on
the following terms, to wit: Rolls of all the officers and men to be
made in duplicate. One copy to be given to an officer designated by
me, the other to be retained by such officer or officers as you may
designate. The officers to give their individual paroles not to take up
arms against the Government of the United States until properly

Eng. by A. Dresher

McLean's house at Appomattox in which General Lee signed the terms of surrender

exchanged, and each company or regimental commander sign a like parole for the men of their commands. The arms, artillery and public property to be parked and stacked, and turned over to the officer appointed by me to receive them. This will not embrace the side-arms of the officers, nor their private horses or baggage. This done, each officer and man will be allowed to return to their homes, not to be disturbed by United States authority so long as they observe their paroles and the laws in force where they may reside.

Very respectfully,

U. S. GRANT,

Lt. Gen.

When I put my pen to the paper I did not know the first word that I should make use of in writing the terms. I only knew what was in my mind, and I wished to express it clearly, so that there could be no mistaking it. As I wrote on, the thought occurred to me that the officers had their own private horses and effects, which were important to them, but of no value to us; also that it would be an unnecessary humiliation to call upon them to deliver their side arms.

No conversation, not one word, passed between General Lee and myself, either about private property, side arms, or kindred subjects. He appeared to have no objections to the terms first proposed; or if he had a point to make against them he wished to wait until they were in writing to make it. When he read over that part of the terms about side arms, horses and private property of the officers, he remarked, with some feeling, I thought, that this would have a happy effect upon his army.

Then, after a little further conversation, General Lee re-marked to me again that their army was organized a little differently from the army of the United States (still maintain-ing by implication that we were two countries); that in their army the cavalrymen and artillerists owned their own horses; and he asked if he was to understand that the men who so owned their horses were to be permitted to retain them. I told him that as the terms were written they would not; that only the officers were permitted to take their private property. He then, after reading over the terms a second time, remarked that that was clear.

I then said to him that I thought this would be about the last battle of the war—I sincerely hoped so; and I said further I took it that most of the men in the ranks were small farmers. The whole country had been so raided by the two armies that it was doubtful whether they would be able to put in a crop to carry themselves and their families through the next winter without the aid of the horses they were then riding. The United States did not want them and I would, therefore, instruct the officers I left behind to receive the paroles of his troops to let every man of the Confederate army who claimed to own a horse or mule take the animal to his home. Lee remarked again that this would have a happy effect.

He then sat down and wrote out the following letter:

HEADQUARTERS ARMY OF NORTHERN VIRGINIA,
April 9, 1865.

GENERAL:—I received your letter of this date containing the terms of the surrender of the Army of Northern Virginia as proposed by you. As they are substantially the same as those expressed in your letter of the 8th inst., they are accepted. I will proceed to designate the proper officers to carry the stipulations into effect.

R. E. LEE, General.

LIEUT.-GENERAL U. S. GRANT.

While duplicates of the two letters were being made, the Union generals present were severally presented to General Lee.

The much talked of surrendering of Lee's sword and my handing it back, this and much more that has been said about it is the purest romance. The word sword or side arms was not mentioned by either of us until I wrote it in the terms. There was no premeditation, and it did not occur to me until the moment I wrote it down. If I had happened to omit it, and General Lee had called my attention to it, I should have put it in the terms precisely as I acceded to the provision about the soldiers retaining their horses.

General Lee, after all was completed and before taking his leave, remarked that his army was in a very bad condition for want of food, and that they were without forage; that his men had been living for some days on parched corn exclusively, and that he would have to ask me for rations and forage. I told him "certainly," and asked for how many men he wanted rations. His answer was "about twenty-five thousand:" and I authorized him to send his own commissary and quartermaster to Appomattox Station, two or three miles away, where he could have, out of the trains we had stopped, all the provisions wanted. As for forage, we had ourselves depended almost entirely upon the country for that.

Generals Gibbon, Griffin and Merritt were designated by me to carry into effect the paroling of Lee's troops before they should start for their homes—General Lee leaving Generals Longstreet, Gordon and Pendleton for them to confer with in order to facilitate this work. Lee and I then separated as cordially as we had met, he returning to his own lines, and all went into bivouac for the night at Appomattox.

Soon after Lee's departure I telegraphed to Washington as follows:

> HEADQUARTERS APPOMATTOX C. H., VA.,
> *April 9th*, 1865, 4.30 P.M.
>
> HON. E. M. STANTON, Secretary of War,
>   Washington.
>
> General Lee surrendered the Army of Northern Virginia this afternoon on terms proposed by myself. The accompanying additional correspondence will show the conditions fully.
>
>   U. S. GRANT,
>   Lieut.-General.

When news of the surrender first reached our lines our men commenced firing a salute of a hundred guns in honor of the victory. I at once sent word, however, to have it stopped. The Confederates were now our prisoners, and we did not want to exult over their downfall.

I determined to return to Washington at once, with a view to putting a stop to the purchase of supplies, and what I now deemed other useless outlay of money. Before leaving, however, I thought I would like to see General Lee again; so next morning I rode out beyond our lines towards his headquarters, preceded by a bugler and a staff-officer carrying a white flag.

Lee soon mounted his horse, seeing who it was, and met me. We had there between the lines, sitting on horseback, a

(2)
Appomattox C.H. Va
Apl. 9th 1865.

Gen. R. E. Lee
Comdg C.S.A.

Gen.

In accordance
with the substance of my letter
to you of the 8th inst. I propose to
receive the surrender of the Army of
N. Va. on the following terms: to wit.
Rolls of all the officers and
men to be made in duplicate
One copy to be given to an officer
designated by me, the other to be
retained by such officer or officers
as you may designate. The officers
to give their individual paroles
not to take up arms against the

Government of the United States and until properly exchanged and
each Company or Regimental Commander officer sign a like
parole for the men of their
men Commands.

The Arms Artillery and public
property to be parked and stacked
and turned over to the officer
appointed by me to receive them
This will not embrace the side
arms of the officers nor their
this private horses or baggage. This done
each officer and man will be
allowed to return to their homes
not to be disturbed by United
States authority so long as they
observe their parole and the
laws in force where they may
reside.
                    Very respectfully
                    U S Grant Lt Gl

very pleasant conversation of over half an hour, in the course of which Lee said to me that the South was a big country and that we might have to march over it three or four times before the war entirely ended, but that we would now be able to do it as they could no longer resist us. He expressed it as his earnest hope, however, that we would not be called upon to cause more loss and sacrifice of life; but he could not foretell the result. I then suggested to General Lee that there was not a man in the Confederacy whose influence with the soldiery and the whole people was as great as his, and that if he would now advise the surrender of all the armies I had no doubt his advice would be followed with alacrity. But Lee said, that he could not do that without consulting the President first. I knew there was no use to urge him to do anything against his ideas of what was right.

I was accompanied by my staff and other officers, some of whom seemed to have a great desire to go inside the Confederate lines. They finally asked permission of Lee to do so for the purpose of seeing some of their old army friends, and the permission was granted. They went over, had a very pleasant time with their old friends, and brought some of them back with them when they returned.

When Lee and I separated he went back to his lines and I returned to the house of Mr. McLean. Here the officers of both armies came in great numbers, and seemed to enjoy the meeting as much as though they had been friends separated for a long time while fighting battles under the same flag. For the time being it looked very much as if all thought of the war had escaped their minds. After an hour pleasantly passed in this way I set out on horseback, accompanied by my staff and a small escort, for Burkesville Junction, up to which point the railroad had by this time been repaired.

Chapter LXVIII.

MORALE OF THE TWO ARMIES—RELATIVE CONDITIONS
OF THE NORTH AND SOUTH—PRESIDENT LINCOLN
VISITS RICHMOND—ARRIVAL AT WASHINGTON—
PRESIDENT LINCOLN'S ASSASSINATION—PRESIDENT
JOHNSON'S POLICY.

AFTER THE FALL of Petersburg, and when the armies of the Potomac and the James were in motion to head off Lee's army, the *morale* of the National troops had greatly improved. There was no more straggling, no more rear guards. The men who in former times had been falling back, were now, as I have already stated, striving to get to the front. For the first time in four weary years they felt that they were now nearing the time when they could return to their homes with their country saved. On the other hand, the Confederates were more than correspondingly depressed. Their despondency increased with each returning day, and especially after the battle of Sailor's Creek. They threw away their arms in constantly increasing numbers, dropping out of the ranks and betaking themselves to the woods in the hope of reaching their homes. I have already instanced the case of the entire disintegration of a regiment whose colonel I met at Farmville. As a result of these and other influences, when Lee finally surrendered at Appomattox, there were only 28,356 officers and men left to be paroled, and many of these were without arms. It was probably this latter fact which gave rise to the statement sometimes made, North and South, that Lee surrendered a smaller number of men than what the official figures show. As a matter of official record, and in addition to the number paroled as given above, we captured between March 29th and the date of surrender 19,132 Confederates, to say nothing of Lee's other losses, killed, wounded and missing, during the series of desperate conflicts which marked his headlong and determined flight. The same record shows the number of cannon, including those at Appomattox, to have been 689 between the dates named.

There has always been a great conflict of opinion as to the number of troops engaged in every battle, or all important battles, fought between the sections, the South magnifying the number of Union troops engaged and belittling their own. Northern writers have fallen, in many instances, into the same error. I have often heard gentlemen, who were thoroughly loyal to the Union, speak of what a splendid fight the South had made and successfully continued for four years before yielding, with their twelve million of people against our twenty, and of the twelve four being colored slaves, noncombatants. I will add to their argument. We had many regiments of brave and loyal men who volunteered under great difficulty from the twelve million belonging to the South.

But the South had rebelled against the National government. It was not bound by any constitutional restrictions. The whole South was a military camp. The occupation of the colored people was to furnish supplies for the army. Conscription was resorted to early, and embraced every male from the age of eighteen to forty-five, excluding only those physically unfit to serve in the field, and the necessary number of civil officers of State and intended National government. The old and physically disabled furnished a good portion of these. The slaves, the non-combatants, one-third of the whole, were required to work in the field without regard to sex, and almost without regard to age. Children from the age of eight years could and did handle the hoe; they were not much older when they began to hold the plough. The four million of colored non-combatants were equal to more than three times their number in the North, age for age and sex for sex, in supplying food from the soil to support armies. Women did not work in the fields in the North, and children attended school.

The arts of peace were carried on in the North. Towns and cities grew during the war. Inventions were made in all kinds of machinery to increase the products of a day's labor in the shop, and in the field. In the South no opposition was allowed to the government which had been set up and which would have become real and respected if the rebellion had been successful. No rear had to be protected. All the troops in service could be brought to the front to contest every inch of ground threatened with invasion. The press of the South, like the people who remained at home, were loyal to the Southern cause.

In the North, the country, the towns and the cities presented about the same appearance they do in time of peace. The furnace was in blast, the shops were filled with workmen, the fields were cultivated, not only to supply the population of the North and the troops invading the South, but to ship abroad to pay a part of the expense of the war. In the North the press was free up to the point of open treason. The citizen could entertain his views and express them. Troops were necessary in the Northern States to prevent prisoners from the Southern army being released by outside force, armed and set at large to destroy by fire our Northern cities. Plans were formed by Northern and Southern citizens to burn our cities, to poison the water supplying them, to spread infection by importing clothing from infected regions, to blow up our river and lake steamers—regardless of the destruction of innocent lives. The copperhead disreputable portion of the press magnified rebel successes, and belittled those of the Union army. It was, with a large following, an auxiliary to the Confederate army. The North would have been much stronger with a hundred thousand of these men in the Confederate ranks and the rest of their kind thoroughly subdued, as the Union sentiment was in the South, than we were as the battle was fought.

As I have said, the whole South was a military camp. The colored people, four million in number, were submissive, and worked in the field and took care of the families while the able-bodied white men were at the front fighting for a cause destined to defeat. The cause was popular, and was enthusiastically supported by the young men. The conscription took all of them. Before the war was over, further conscriptions took those between fourteen and eighteen years of age as junior reserves, and those between forty-five and sixty as senior reserves. It would have been an offence, directly after the war, and perhaps it would be now, to ask any able-bodied man in the South, who was between the ages of fourteen and sixty at any time during the war, whether he had been in the Confederate army. He would assert that he had, or account for his absence from the ranks. Under such circumstances it is hard to conceive how the North showed such a superiority of force in every battle fought. I know they did not.

During 1862 and '3, John H. Morgan, a partisan officer, of no military education, but possessed of courage and endurance, operated in the rear of the Army of the Ohio in Kentucky and Tennessee. He had no base of supplies to protect, but was at home wherever he went. The army operating against the South, on the contrary, had to protect its lines of communication with the North, from which all supplies had to come to the front. Every foot of road had to be guarded by troops stationed at convenient distances apart. These guards could not render assistance beyond the points where stationed. Morgan was foot-loose and could operate where his information—always correct—led him to believe he could do the greatest damage. During the time he was operating in this way he killed, wounded and captured several times the number he ever had under his command at any one time. He destroyed many millions of property in addition. Places he did not attack had to be guarded as if threatened by him. Forrest, an abler soldier, operated farther west, and held from the National front quite as many men as could be spared for offensive operations. It is safe to say that more than half the National army was engaged in guarding lines of supplies, or were on leave, sick in hospital or on detail which prevented their bearing arms. Then, again, large forces were employed where no Confederate army confronted them. I deem it safe to say that there were no large engagements where the National numbers compensated for the advantage of position and intrenchment occupied by the enemy.

While I was in pursuit of General Lee, the President went to Richmond in company with Admiral Porter, and on board his flagship. He found the people of that city in great consternation. The leading citizens among the people who had remained at home surrounded him, anxious that something should be done to relieve them from suspense. General Weitzel was not then in the city, having taken offices in one of the neighboring villages after his troops had succeeded in subduing the conflagration which they had found in progress on entering the Confederate capital. The President sent for him, and, on his arrival, a short interview was had on board the vessel, Admiral Porter and a leading citizen of Virginia being also present. After this interview the President wrote an order in about these words, which I quote from memory: "General Weitzel is authorized to permit the body calling itself the Legislature of Virginia to meet for the purpose of recalling the Virginia troops from the Confederate armies."

Immediately some of the gentlemen composing that body wrote out a call for a meeting and had it published in their papers. This call, however, went very much further than Mr. Lincoln had contemplated, as he did not say the "Legislature of Virginia" but "the body which called itself the Legislature of Virginia." Mr. Stanton saw the call as published in the Northern papers the very next issue and took the liberty of countermanding the order authorizing any meeting of the Legislature, or any other body, and this notwithstanding the fact that the President was nearer the spot than he was.

This was characteristic of Mr. Stanton. He was a man who never questioned his own authority, and who always did in war time what he wanted to do. He was an able constitutional lawyer and jurist; but the Constitution was not an impediment to him while the war lasted. In this latter particular I entirely agree with the view he evidently held. The Constitution was not framed with a view to any such rebellion as that of 1861–5. While it did not authorize rebellion it made no provision against it. Yet the right to resist or suppress rebellion is as inherent as the right of self-defence, and as natural as the right of an individual to preserve his life when in jeopardy. The Constitution was therefore in abeyance for the time being, so far as it in any way affected the progress and termination of the war.

Those in rebellion against the government of the United States were not restricted by constitutional provisions, or any other, except the acts of their Congress, which was loyal and devoted to the cause for which the South was then fighting. It would be a hard case when one-third of a nation, united in rebellion against the national authority, is entirely untrammeled, that the other two-thirds, in their efforts to maintain the Union intact, should be restrained by a Constitution prepared by our ancestors for the express purpose of insuring the permanency of the confederation of the States.

After I left General Lee at Appomattox Station, I went with my staff and a few others directly to Burkesville Station on my way to Washington. The road from Burkesville back having been newly repaired and the ground being soft, the train got off the track frequently, and, as a result, it was after midnight of the second day when I reached City Point. As soon as possible I took a dispatch-boat thence to Washington City.

While in Washington I was very busy for a time in preparing the necessary orders for the new state of affairs; communicating with my different commanders of separate departments, bodies of troops, etc. But by the 14th I was pretty well through with this work, so as to be able to visit my children, who were then in Burlington, New Jersey, attending school. Mrs. Grant was with me in Washington at the time, and we were invited by President and Mrs. Lincoln to accompany them to the theatre on the evening of that day. I replied to the President's verbal invitation to the effect, that if we were in the city we would take great pleasure in accompanying them; but that I was very anxious to get away and visit my children, and if I could get through my work during the day I should do so. I did get through and started by the evening train on the 14th, sending Mr. Lincoln word, of course, that I would not be at the theatre.

At that time the railroad to New York entered Philadelphia on Broad Street; passengers were conveyed in ambulances to the Delaware River, and then ferried to Camden, at which point they took the cars again. When I reached the ferry, on the east side of the City of Philadelphia, I found people awaiting my arrival there; and also dispatches informing me of the assassination of the President and Mr. Seward, and of the probable assassination of the Vice-President, Mr. Johnson, and requesting my immediate return.

It would be impossible for me to describe the feeling that overcame me at the news of these assassinations, more especially the assassination of the President. I knew his goodness of heart, his generosity, his yielding disposition, his desire to have everybody happy, and above all his desire to see all the people of the United States enter again upon the full privileges of citizenship with equality among all. I knew also the feeling that Mr. Johnson had expressed in speeches and conversation against the Southern people, and I feared that his course towards them would be such as to repel, and make them unwilling citizens; and if they became such they would remain so for a long while. I felt that reconstruction had been set back, no telling how far.

I immediately arranged for getting a train to take me back to Washington City; but Mrs. Grant was with me; it was after midnight and Burlington was but an hour away. Finding that I could accompany her to our house and return about as soon as they would be ready to take me from the Philadelphia station, I went up with her and returned immediately by the same special train. The joy that I had witnessed among the people in the street and in public places in Washington when I left there, had been turned to grief; the city was in reality a city of mourning. I have stated what I believed then the effect of this would be, and my judgment now is that I was right. I believe the South would have been saved from very much of the hardness of feeling that was engendered by Mr. Johnson's course towards them during the first few months of his administration. Be this as it may, Mr. Lincoln's assassination was particularly unfortunate for the entire nation.

Mr. Johnson's course towards the South did engender bitterness of feeling. His denunciations of treason and his ever-ready remark, "Treason is a crime and must be made odious," was repeated to all those men of the South who came to him to get some assurances of safety so that they might go to work at something with the feeling that what they obtained would be secure to them. He uttered his denunciations with great vehemence, and as they were accompanied with no assurances of safety, many Southerners were driven to a point almost beyond endurance.

The President of the United States is, in a large degree, or ought to be, a representative of the feeling, wishes and judgment of those over whom he presides; and the Southerners who read the denunciations of themselves and their people must have come to the conclusion that he uttered the sentiments of the Northern people; whereas, as a matter of fact, but for the assassination of Mr. Lincoln, I believe the great majority of the Northern people, and the soldiers unanimously, would have been in favor of a speedy reconstruction on terms that would be the least humiliating to the people who had rebelled against their government. They believed, I have no doubt, as I did, that besides being the mildest, it was also the wisest, policy.

The people who had been in rebellion must necessarily come back into the Union, and be incorporated as an integral part of the nation. Naturally the nearer they were placed to an equality with the people who had not rebelled, the more reconciled they would feel with their old antagonists, and the better citizens they would be from the beginning. They surely would not make good citizens if they felt that they had a yoke around their necks.

I do not believe that the majority of the Northern people at that time were in favor of negro suffrage. They supposed that it would naturally follow the freedom of the negro, but that there would be a time of probation, in which the ex-slaves could prepare themselves for the privileges of citizenship before the full right would be conferred; but Mr. Johnson, after a complete revolution of sentiment, seemed to regard the South not only as an oppressed people, but as the people best entitled to consideration of any of our citizens. This was more than the people who had secured to us the perpetuation of the Union were prepared for, and they became more radical in their views. The Southerners had the most power in the executive branch, Mr. Johnson having gone to their side; and with a compact South, and such sympathy and support as they could get from the North, they felt that they would be able to control the nation at once, and already many of them acted as if they thought they were entitled to do so.

Thus Mr. Johnson, fighting Congress on the one hand, and receiving the support of the South on the other, drove Congress, which was overwhelmingly republican, to the passing of first one measure and then another to restrict his power. There being a solid South on one side that was in accord with the political party in the North which had sympathized with the rebellion, it finally, in the judgment of Congress and of the majority of the legislatures of the States, became necessary to enfranchise the negro, in all his ignorance. In this work, I shall not discuss the question of how far the policy of Congress in this particular proved a wise one. It became an absolute necessity, however, because of the foolhardiness of the President and the blindness of the Southern people to their own interest. As to myself, while strongly favoring the course that would be the least humiliating to the people who had been in rebellion, I had gradually worked up to the point where, with the majority of the people, I favored immediate enfranchisement.

Chapter LXIX.

SHERMAN AND JOHNSTON—JOHNSTON'S SURRENDER
TO SHERMAN—CAPTURE OF MOBILE—WILSON'S
EXPEDITION—CAPTURE OF JEFFERSON DAVIS—GENERAL
THOMAS'S QUALITIES—ESTIMATE OF GENERAL CANBY.

WHEN I LEFT Appomattox I ordered General Meade to proceed leisurely back to Burkesville Station with the Army of the Potomac and the Army of the James, and to go into camp there until further orders from me. General Johnston, as has been stated before, was in North Carolina confronting General Sherman. It could not be known positively, of course, whether Johnston would surrender on the news of Lee's surrender, though I supposed he would; and if he did not, Burkesville Station was the natural point from which to move to attack him. The army which I could have sent against him was superior to his, and that with which Sherman confronted him was also superior; and between the two he would necessarily have been crushed, or driven away. With the loss of their capital and the Army of Northern Virginia it was doubtful whether Johnston's men would have had the spirit to stand. My belief was that he would make no such attempt; but I adopted this course as a precaution against what might happen, however improbable.

Simultaneously with my starting from City Point, I sent a messenger to North Carolina by boat with dispatches to General Sherman, informing him of the surrender of Lee and his army; also of the terms which I had given him; and I authorized Sherman to give the same terms to Johnston if the latter chose to accept them. The country is familiar with the terms that Sherman agreed to *conditionally*, because they embraced a political question as well as a military one and he would therefore have to confer with the government before agreeing to them definitely.

General Sherman had met Mr. Lincoln at City Point while visiting there to confer with me about our final movement, and knew what Mr. Lincoln had said to the peace commissioners when he met them at Hampton Roads, viz.: that before he could enter into negotiations with them they would have to agree to two points: one being that the Union should be preserved, and the other that slavery should be abolished; and if they were ready to concede these two points he was almost ready to sign his name to a blank piece of paper and permit them to fill out the balance of the terms upon which we would live together. He had also seen notices in the newspapers of Mr. Lincoln's visit to Richmond, and had read in the same papers that while there he had authorized the convening of the Legislature of Virginia.

Sherman thought, no doubt, in adding to the terms that I had made with General Lee, that he was but carrying out the wishes of the President of the United States. But seeing that he was going beyond his authority, he made it a point that the terms were only conditional. They signed them with this understanding, and agreed to a truce until the terms could be sent to Washington for approval; if approved by the proper authorities there, they would then be final; if not approved, then he would give due notice, before resuming hostilities. As the world knows, Sherman, from being one of the most popular generals of the land (Congress having even gone so far as to propose a bill providing for a second lieutenant-general for the purpose of advancing him to that grade), was denounced by the President and Secretary of War in very bitter terms. Some people went so far as to denounce him as a traitor—a most preposterous term to apply to a man who had rendered so much service as he had, even supposing he had made a mistake in granting such terms as he did to Johnston and his army. If Sherman had taken authority to send Johnston with his army home, with their arms to be put in the arsenals of their own States, without submitting the question to the authorities at Washington, the suspicions against him might have some foundation. But the feeling against Sherman died out very rapidly, and it was not many weeks before he was restored to the fullest confidence of the American people.

When, some days after my return to Washington, President Johnson and the Secretary of War received the terms which General Sherman had forwarded for approval, a cabinet meeting was immediately called and I was sent for. There seemed to be the greatest consternation, lest Sherman would commit the government to terms which they were not willing to accede to and which he had no right to grant. A message went out directing the troops in the South not to obey General Sherman. I was ordered to proceed at once to North Carolina and take charge of matters there myself. Of course I started without delay, and reached there as soon as possible. I repaired to Raleigh, where Sherman was, as quietly as possible, hoping to see him without even his army learning of my presence.

When I arrived I went to Sherman's headquarters, and we were at once closeted together. I showed him the instructions and orders under which I visited him. I told him that I wanted him to notify General Johnston that the terms which they had conditionally agreed upon had not been approved in Washington, and that he was authorized to offer the same terms I had given General Lee. I sent Sherman to do this himself. I did not wish the knowledge of my presence to be known to the army generally; so I left it to Sherman to negotiate the terms of the surrender solely by himself, and without the enemy knowing that I was anywhere near the field. As soon as possible I started to get away, to leave Sherman quite free and untrammelled.

At Goldsboro', on my way back, I met a mail, containing the last newspapers, and I found in them indications of great excitement in the North over the terms Sherman had given Johnston; and harsh orders that had been promulgated by the President and Secretary of War. I knew that Sherman must see these papers, and I fully realized what great indignation they would cause him, though I do not think his feelings could have been more excited than were my own. But like the true and loyal soldier that he was, he carried out the instructions I had given him, obtained the surrender of Johnston's army, and settled down in his camp about Raleigh, to await final orders.

There were still a few expeditions out in the South that could not be communicated with, and had to be left to act according to the judgment of their respective commanders. With these it was impossible to tell how the news of the surrender of Lee and Johnston, of which they must have heard, might affect their judgment as to what was best to do.

The three expeditions which I had tried so hard to get off from the commands of Thomas and Canby did finally get off: one under Canby himself, against Mobile, late in March; that under Stoneman from East Tennessee on the 20th; and the one under Wilson, starting from Eastport, Mississippi, on the 22d of March. They were all eminently successful, but without any good result. Indeed much valuable property was destroyed and many lives lost at a time when we would have liked to spare them. The war was practically over before their victories were gained. They were so late in commencing operations, that they did not hold any troops away that otherwise would have been operating against the armies which were gradually forcing the Confederate armies to a surrender. The only possible good that we may have experienced from these raids was by Stoneman's getting near Lynchburg about the time the armies of the Potomac and the James were closing in on Lee at Appomattox.

Stoneman entered North Carolina and then pushed north to strike the Virginia and Tennessee Railroad. He got upon that road, destroyed its bridges at different places and rendered the road useless to the enemy up to within a few miles of Lynchburg. His approach caused the evacuation of that city about the time we were at Appomattox, and was the cause of a commotion we heard of there. He then pushed south, and was operating in the rear of Johnston's army about the time the negotiations were going on between Sherman and Johnston for the latter's surrender. In this raid Stoneman captured and destroyed a large amount of stores, while fourteen guns and nearly two thousand prisoners were the trophies of his success.

Canby appeared before Mobile on the 27th of March. The city of Mobile was protected by two forts, besides other intrenchments—Spanish Fort, on the east side of the bay, and Fort Blakely, north of the city. These forts were invested. On the night of the 8th of April, the National troops having carried the enemy's works at one point, Spanish Fort was evacuated; and on the 9th, the very day of Lee's surrender, Blakely was carried by assault, with a considerable loss to us. On the 11th the city was evacuated.

I had tried for more than two years to have an expedition sent against Mobile when its possession by us would have been of great advantage. It finally cost lives to take it when its possession was of no importance, and when, if left alone, it would within a few days have fallen into our hands without any bloodshed whatever

Wilson moved out with full 12,000 men, well equipped and well armed. He was an energetic officer and accomplished his work rapidly. Forrest was in his front, but with neither his old-time army nor his old-time prestige. He now had principally conscripts. His conscripts were generally old men and boys. He had a few thousand regular cavalry left, but not enough to even retard materially the progress of Wilson's cavalry. Selma fell on the 2d of April, with a large number of prisoners and a large quantity of war material, machine shops, etc., to be disposed of by the victors. Tuscaloosa, Montgomery and West Point fell in quick succession. These were all important points to the enemy by reason of their railroad connections, as depots of supplies, and because of their manufactories of war material. They were fortified or intrenched, and there was considerable fighting before they were captured. Macon surrendered on the 21st of April. Here news was received of the negotiations for the surrender of Johnston's army. Wilson belonged to the military division commanded by Sherman, and of course was bound by his terms. This stopped all fighting.

General Richard Taylor had now become the senior Confederate officer still at liberty east of the Mississippi River, and on the 4th of May he surrendered everything within the limits of this extensive command. General E. Kirby Smith surrendered the trans-Mississippi department on the 26th of May, leaving no other Confederate army at liberty to continue the war.

Wilson's raid resulted in the capture of the fugitive president of the defunct confederacy before he got out of the country. This occurred at Irwinsville, Georgia, on the 11th of May. For myself, and I believe Mr. Lincoln shared the feeling, I would have been very glad to have seen Mr. Davis succeed

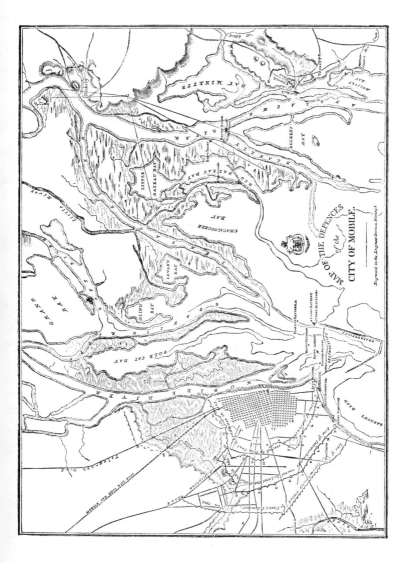

MAP OF THE DEFENCES
of the
CITY OF MOBILE.

Engraved in the Engineer Bureau Richmond

in escaping, but for one reason: I feared that if not captured, he might get into the trans-Mississippi region and there set up a more contracted confederacy. The young men now out of homes and out of employment might have rallied under his standard and protracted the war yet another year. The Northern people were tired of the war, they were tired of piling up a debt which would be a further mortgage upon their homes.

Mr. Lincoln, I believe, wanted Mr. Davis to escape, because he did not wish to deal with the matter of his punishment. He knew there would be people clamoring for the punishment of the ex-Confederate president, for high treason. He thought blood enough had already been spilled to atone for our wickedness as a nation. At all events he did not wish to be the judge to decide whether more should be shed or not. But his own life was sacrificed at the hands of an assassin before the ex-president of the Confederacy was a prisoner in the hands of the government which he had lent all his talent and all his energies to destroy.

All things are said to be wisely directed, and for the best interest of all concerned. This reflection does not, however, abate in the slightest our sense of bereavement in the untimely loss of so good and great a man as Abraham Lincoln.

He would have proven the best friend the South could have had, and saved much of the wrangling and bitterness of feeling brought out by reconstruction under a President who at first wished to revenge himself upon Southern men of better social standing than himself, but who still sought their recognition, and in a short time conceived the idea and advanced the proposition to become their Moses to lead them triumphantly out of all their difficulties.

The story of the legislation enacted during the reconstruction period to stay the hands of the President is too fresh in the minds of the people to be told now. Much of it, no doubt, was unconstitutional; but it was hoped that the laws enacted would serve their purpose before the question of constitutionality could be submitted to the judiciary and a decision obtained. These laws did serve their purpose, and now remain "a dead letter" upon the statute books of the United States, no one taking interest enough in them to give them a passing thought.

Much was said at the time about the garb Mr. Davis was wearing when he was captured. I cannot settle this question from personal knowledge of the facts; but I have been under the belief, from information given to me by General Wilson shortly after the event, that when Mr. Davis learned that he was surrounded by our cavalry he was in his tent dressed in a gentleman's dressing gown. Naturally enough, Mr. Davis wanted to escape, and would not reflect much how this should be accomplished provided it might be done successfully. If captured, he would be no ordinary prisoner. He represented all there was of that hostility to the government which had caused four years of the bloodiest war—and the most costly in other respects of which history makes any record. Every one supposed he would be tried for treason if captured, and that he would be executed. Had he succeeded in making his escape in any disguise it would have been adjudged a good thing afterwards by his admirers.

As my official letters on file in the War Department, as well as my remarks in this book, reflect upon General Thomas by dwelling somewhat upon his tardiness, it is due to myself, as well as to him, that I give my estimate of him as a soldier. The same remark will apply also in the case of General Canby. I had been at West Point with Thomas one year, and had known him later in the old army. He was a man of commanding appearance, slow and deliberate in speech and action; sensible, honest and brave. He possessed valuable soldierly qualities in an eminent degree. He gained the confidence of all who served under him, and almost their love. This implies a very valuable quality. It is a quality which calls out the most efficient services of the troops serving under the commander possessing it.

Thomas's dispositions were deliberately made, and always good. He could not be driven from a point he was given to hold. He was not as good, however, in pursuit as he was in action. I do not believe that he could ever have conducted Sherman's army from Chattanooga to Atlanta against the defences and the commander guarding that line in 1864. On the other hand, if it had been given him to hold the line which Johnston tried to hold, neither that general nor Sherman, nor any other officer could have done it better.

Thomas was a valuable officer, who richly deserved, as he has received, the plaudits of his countrymen for the part he played in the great tragedy of 1861–5.

General Canby was an officer of great merit. He was naturally studious, and inclined to the law. There have been in the army but very few, if any, officers who took as much interest in reading and digesting every act of Congress and every regulation for the government of the army as he. His knowledge gained in this way made him a most valuable staff officer, a capacity in which almost all his army services were rendered up to the time of his being assigned to the Military Division of the Gulf. He was an exceedingly modest officer, though of great talent and learning. I presume his feelings when first called upon to command a large army against a fortified city, were somewhat like my own when marching a regiment against General Thomas Harris in Missouri in 1861. Neither of us would have felt the slightest trepidation in going into battle with some one else commanding. Had Canby been in other engagements afterwards, he would, I have no doubt, have advanced without any fear arising from a sense of the responsibility. He was afterwards killed in the lava beds of Southern Oregon, while in pursuit of the hostile Modoc Indians. His character was as pure as his talent and learning were great. His services were valuable during the war, but principally as a bureau officer. I have no idea that it was from choice that his services were rendered in an office, but because of his superior efficiency there.

Chapter LXX.

THE END OF THE WAR—THE MARCH TO
WASHINGTON—ONE OF LINCOLN'S ANECDOTES—GRAND
REVIEW AT WASHINGTON—CHARACTERISTICS OF
LINCOLN AND STANTON—ESTIMATE OF THE
DIFFERENT CORPS COMMANDERS.

THINGS BEGAN to quiet down, and as the certainty that there would be no more armed resistance became clearer, the troops in North Carolina and Virginia were ordered to march immediately to the capital, and go into camp there until mustered out. Suitable garrisons were left at the prominent places throughout the South to insure obedience to the laws that might be enacted for the government of the several States, and to insure security to the lives and property of all classes. I do not know how far this was necessary, but I deemed it necessary, at that time, that such a course should be pursued. I think now that these garrisons were continued after they ceased to be absolutely required; but it is not to be expected that such a rebellion as was fought between the sections from 1861 to 1865 could terminate without leaving many serious apprehensions in the mind of the people as to what should be done.

Sherman marched his troops from Goldsboro, up to Manchester, on the south side of the James River, opposite Richmond, and there put them in camp, while he went back to Savannah to see what the situation was there.

It was during this trip that the last outrage was committed upon him. Halleck had been sent to Richmond to command Virginia, and had issued orders prohibiting even Sherman's own troops from obeying his, Sherman's, orders. Sherman met the papers on his return, containing this order of Halleck, and very justly felt indignant at the outrage. On his arrival at Fortress Monroe returning from Savannah, Sherman received an invitation from Halleck to come to Richmond and be his guest. This he indignantly refused, and informed Halleck, furthermore, that he had seen his order. He also stated that he was coming up to take command of his troops, and as he marched through it would probably be as well for Halleck not to show himself, because he (Sherman) would not be responsible for what some rash person might do through indignation for the treatment he had received. Very soon after that, Sherman received orders from me to proceed to Washington City, and to go into camp on the south side of the city pending the mustering-out of the troops.

There was no incident worth noting in the march northward from Goldsboro, to Richmond, or in that from Richmond to Washington City. The army, however, commanded by Sherman, which had been engaged in all the battles of the West and had marched from the Mississippi through the Southern States to the sea, from there to Goldsboro, and thence to Washington City, had passed over many of the battle-fields of the Army of the Potomac, thus having seen, to a greater extent than any other body of troops, the entire theatre of the four years' war for the preservation of the Union.

The march of Sherman's army from Atlanta to the sea and north to Goldsboro, while it was not accompanied with the danger that was anticipated, yet was magnificent in its results, and equally magnificent in the way it was conducted. It had an important bearing, in various ways, upon the great object we had in view, that of closing the war. All the States east of the Mississippi River up to the State of Georgia, had felt the hardships of the war. Georgia, and South Carolina, and almost all of North Carolina, up to this time, had been exempt from invasion by the Northern armies, except upon their immediate sea coasts. Their newspapers had given such an account of Confederate success, that the people who remained at home had been convinced that the Yankees had been whipped from first to last, and driven from pillar to post, and that now they could hardly be holding out for any other purpose than to find a way out of the war with honor to themselves.

Even during this march of Sherman's the newspapers in his front were proclaiming daily that his army was nothing better than a mob of men who were frightened out of their wits and hastening, panic-stricken, to try to get under the cover of our navy for protection against the Southern people. As the army was seen marching on triumphantly, however, the minds of the people became disabused and they saw the true state of affairs. In turn they became disheartened, and would have been glad to submit without compromise.

Another great advantage resulting from this march, and which was calculated to hasten the end, was the fact that the great storehouse of Georgia was entirely cut off from the Confederate armies. As the troops advanced north from Savannah, the destruction of the railroads in South Carolina and the southern part of North Carolina, further cut off their resources and left the armies still in Virginia and North Carolina dependent for supplies upon a very small area of country, already very much exhausted of food and forage.

In due time the two armies, one from Burkesville Junction and the other from the neighborhood of Raleigh, North Carolina, arrived and went into camp near the Capital, as directed. The troops were hardy, being inured to fatigue, and they appeared in their respective camps as ready and fit for duty as they had ever been in their lives. I doubt whether an equal body of men of any nation, take them man for man, officer for officer, was ever gotten together that would have proved their equal in a great battle.

The armies of Europe are machines: the men are brave and the officers capable; but the majority of the soldiers in most of the nations of Europe are taken from a class of people who are not very intelligent and who have very little interest in the contest in which they are called upon to take part. Our armies were composed of men who were able to read, men who knew what they were fighting for, and could not be induced to serve as soldiers, except in an emergency when the safety of the nation was involved, and so necessarily must have been more than equal to men who fought merely because they were brave and because they were thoroughly drilled and inured to hardships.

There was nothing of particular importance occurred during the time these troops were in camp before starting North.

I remember one little incident which I will relate as an anecdote characteristic of Mr. Lincoln. It occurred a day after I reached Washington, and about the time General Meade reached Burkesville with the army. Governor Smith of Virginia had left Richmond with the Confederate States government, and had gone to Danville. Supposing I was necessarily with the army at Burkesville, he addressed a letter to me there informing me that, as governor of the Commonwealth of the State of Virginia, he had temporarily removed the State capital from Richmond to Danville, and asking if he would be permitted to perform the functions of his office there without molestation by the Federal authorities. I give this letter only in substance. He also inquired of me whether in case he was not allowed to perform the duties of his office, he with a few others might not be permitted to leave the country and go abroad without interference. General Meade being informed that a flag of truce was outside his pickets with a letter to me, at once sent out and had the letter brought in without informing the officer who brought it that I was not present. He read the letter and telegraphed me its contents. Meeting Mr. Lincoln shortly after receiving this dispatch, I repeated its contents to him. Mr. Lincoln, supposing I was asking for instructions, said, in reply to that part of Governor Smith's letter which inquired whether he with a few friends would be permitted to leave the country unmolested, that his position was like that of a certain Irishman (giving the name) he knew in Springfield who was very popular with the people, a man of considerable promise, and very much liked. Unfortunately he had acquired the habit of drinking, and his friends could see that the habit was growing on him. These friends determined to make an effort to save him, and to do this they drew up a pledge to abstain from all alcoholic drinks. They asked Pat to join them in signing the pledge, and he consented. He had been so long out of the habit of using plain water as a beverage that he resorted to soda-water as a substitute. After a few days this began to grow distasteful to him. So holding the glass behind him, he said: "Doctor, couldn't you drop a bit of brandy in that unbeknownst to myself."

I do not remember what the instructions were the President gave me, but I know that Governor Smith was not permitted to perform the duties of his office. I also know that if Mr. Lincoln had been spared, there would have been no efforts made to prevent any one from leaving the country who desired to do so. He would have been equally willing to permit the return of the same expatriated citizens after they had time to repent of their choice.

On the 18th of May orders were issued by the adjutant-general for a grand review by the President and his cabinet of Sherman's and Meade's armies. The review commenced on the 23d and lasted two days. Meade's army occupied over six hours of the first day in passing the grand stand which had been erected in front of the President's house. Sherman witnessed this review from the grand stand which was occupied by the President and his cabinet. Here he showed his resentment for the cruel and harsh treatment that had unnecessarily been inflicted upon him by the Secretary of War, by refusing to take his extended hand.

Sherman's troops had been in camp on the south side of the Potomac. During the night of the 23d he crossed over and bivouacked not far from the Capitol. Promptly at ten o'clock on the morning of the 24th, his troops commenced to pass in review. Sherman's army made a different appearance from that of the Army of the Potomac. The latter had been operating where they received directly from the North full supplies of food and clothing regularly: the review of this army therefore was the review of a body of 65,000 well-drilled, well-disciplined and orderly soldiers inured to hardship and fit for any duty, but without the experience of gathering their own food and supplies in an enemy's country, and of being ever on the watch. Sherman's army was not so well-dressed as the Army of the Potomac, but their marching could not be excelled; they gave the appearance of men who had been thoroughly drilled to endure hardships, either by long and continuous marches or through exposure to any climate, without the ordinary shelter of a camp. They exhibited also some of the order of march through Georgia where the "sweet potatoes sprung up from the ground" as Sherman's army went marching through. In the rear of a company there would be a captured horse or mule loaded with small cooking utensils, captured chickens and other food picked up for the use of the men. Negro families who had followed the army would sometimes come along in the rear of a company, with three or four children packed upon a single mule, and the mother leading it.

The sight was varied and grand: nearly all day for two successive days, from the Capitol to the Treasury Building, could be seen a mass of orderly soldiers marching in columns of companies. The National flag was flying from almost every house and store; the windows were filled with spectators; the door-steps and side-walks were crowded with colored people and poor whites who did not succeed in securing better quarters from which to get a view of the grand armies. The city was about as full of strangers who had come to see the sights as it usually is on inauguration day when a new President takes his seat.

It may not be out of place to again allude to President Lincoln and the Secretary of War, Mr. Stanton, who were the great conspicuous figures in the executive branch of the government. There is no great difference of opinion now, in the public mind, as to the characteristics of the President. With Mr. Stanton the case is different. They were the very opposite of each other in almost every particular, except that each possessed great ability. Mr. Lincoln gained influence over men by making them feel that it was a pleasure to serve him. He preferred yielding his own wish to gratify others, rather than to insist upon having his own way. It distressed him to disappoint others. In matters of public duty, however, he had what he wished, but in the least offensive way. Mr. Stanton never questioned his own authority to command, unless resisted. He cared nothing for the feeling of others. In fact it seemed to be pleasanter to him to disappoint than to gratify. He felt no hesitation in assuming the functions of the executive, or in acting without advising with him. If his act was not sustained, he would change it—if he saw the matter would be followed up until he did so.

It was generally supposed that these two officials formed the complement of each other. The Secretary was required to prevent the President's being imposed upon. The President was required in the more responsible place of seeing that injustice was not done to others. I do not know that this view of these two men is still entertained by the majority of the people. It is not a correct view, however, in my estimation. Mr. Lincoln did not require a guardian to aid him in the fulfilment of a public trust.

Mr. Lincoln was not timid, and he was willing to trust his generals in making and executing their plans. The Secretary was very timid, and it was impossible for him to avoid interfering with the armies covering the capital when it was sought to defend it by an offensive movement against the army guarding the Confederate capital. He could see our weakness, but he could not see that the enemy was in danger. The enemy would not have been in danger if Mr. Stanton had been in the field. These characteristics of the two officials were clearly shown shortly after Early came so near getting into the capital.

Among the army and corps commanders who served with me during the war between the States, and who attracted much public attention, but of whose ability as soldiers I have not yet given any estimate, are Meade, Hancock, Sedgwick, Burnside, Terry and Hooker. There were others of great merit, such as Griffin, Humphreys, Wright and Mackenzie. Of those first named, Burnside at one time had command of the Army of the Potomac, and later of the Army of the Ohio. Hooker also commanded the Army of the Potomac for a short time.

General Meade was an officer of great merit, with drawbacks to his usefulness that were beyond his control. He had been an officer of the engineer corps before the war, and consequently had never served with troops until he was over forty-six years of age. He never had, I believe, a command of less than a brigade. He saw clearly and distinctly the position of the enemy, and the topography of the country in front of his own position. His first idea was to take advantage of the lay of the ground, sometimes without reference to the direction we wanted to move afterwards. He was subordinate to his superiors in rank to the extent that he could execute an order which changed his own plans with the same zeal he would have displayed if the plan had been his own. He was brave and conscientious, and commanded the respect of all who knew him. He was unfortunately of a temper that would get beyond his control, at times, and make him speak to officers of high rank in the most offensive manner. No one saw this fault more plainly than he himself, and no one regretted it more. This made it unpleasant at times, even in battle, for those around him to approach him even with information. In spite of this defect he was a most valuable officer and deserves a high place in the annals of his country.

General Burnside was an officer who was generally liked and respected. He was not, however, fitted to command an army. No one knew this better than himself. He always admitted his blunders, and extenuated those of officers under him beyond what they were entitled to. It was hardly his fault that he was ever assigned to a separate command.

Of Hooker I saw but little during the war. I had known him very well before, however. Where I did see him, at Chattanooga, his achievement in bringing his command around the point of Lookout Mountain and into Chattanooga Valley was brilliant. I nevertheless regarded him as a dangerous man. He was not subordinate to his superiors. He was ambitious to the extent of caring nothing for the rights of others. His disposition was, when engaged in battle, to get detached from the main body of the army and exercise a separate command, gathering to his standard all he could of his juniors.

Hancock stands the most conspicuous figure of all the general officers who did not exercise a separate command. He commanded a corps longer than any other one, and his name was never mentioned as having committed in battle a blunder for which he was responsible. He was a man of very conspicuous personal appearance. Tall, well-formed and, at the time of which I now write, young and fresh-looking, he presented an appearance that would attract the attention of an army as he passed. His genial disposition made him friends, and his personal courage and his presence with his command in the thickest of the fight won for him the confidence of troops serving under him. No matter how hard the fight, the 2d corps always felt that their commander was looking after them.

Sedgwick was killed at Spottsylvania before I had an opportunity of forming an estimate of his qualifications as a soldier from personal observation. I had known him in Mexico when both of us were lieutenants, and when our service gave no indication that either of us would ever be equal to the command of a brigade. He stood very high in the army, however, as an officer and a man. He was brave and conscientious. His ambition was not great, and he seemed to dread responsibility. He was willing to do any amount of battling, but always wanted some one else to direct. He declined the command of the Army of the Potomac once, if not oftener.

General Alfred H. Terry came into the army as a volunteer without a military education. His way was won without political influence up to an important separate command—the expedition against Fort Fisher, in January, 1865. His success there was most brilliant, and won for him the rank of brigadier-general in the regular army and of major-general of volunteers. He is a man who makes friends of those under him by his consideration of their wants and their dues. As a commander, he won their confidence by his coolness in action and by his clearness of perception in taking in the situation under which he was placed at any given time.

Griffin, Humphreys, and Mackenzie were good corps commanders, but came into that position so near to the close of the war as not to attract public attention. All three served as such, in the last campaign of the armies of the Potomac and the James, which culminated at Appomattox Court House, on the 9th of April, 1865. The sudden collapse of the rebellion monopolized attention to the exclusion of almost everything else. I regarded Mackenzie as the most promising young officer in the army. Graduating at West Point, as he did, during the second year of the war, he had won his way up to the command of a corps before its close. This he did upon his own merit and without influence.

Conclusion.

THE CAUSE of the great War of the Rebellion against the United States will have to be attributed to slavery. For some years before the war began it was a trite saying among some politicians that "A state half slave and half free cannot exist." All must become slave or all free, or the state will go down. I took no part myself in any such view of the case at the time, but since the war is over, reviewing the whole question, I have come to the conclusion that the saying is quite true.

Slavery was an institution that required unusual guarantees for its security wherever it existed; and in a country like ours where the larger portion of it was free territory inhabited by an intelligent and well-to-do population, the people would naturally have but little sympathy with demands upon them for its protection. Hence the people of the South were dependent upon keeping control of the general government to secure the perpetuation of their favorite institution. They were enabled to maintain this control long after the States where slavery existed had ceased to have the controlling power, through the assistance they received from odd men here and there throughout the Northern States. They saw their power waning, and this led them to encroach upon the prerogatives and independence of the Northern States by enacting such laws as the Fugitive Slave Law. By this law every Northern man was obliged, when properly summoned, to turn out and help apprehend the runaway slave of a Southern man. Northern marshals became slave-catchers, and Northern courts had to contribute to the support and protection of the institution.

This was a degradation which the North would not permit any longer than until they could get the power to expunge such laws from the statute books. Prior to the time of these encroachments the great majority of the people of the North had no particular quarrel with slavery, so long as they were not forced to have it themselves. But they were not willing to play the rôle of police for the South in the protection of this particular institution.

In the early days of the country, before we had railroads, telegraphs and steamboats—in a word, rapid transit of any sort—the States were each almost a separate nationality. At that time the subject of slavery caused but little or no disturbance to the public mind. But the country grew, rapid transit was established, and trade and commerce between the States got to be so much greater than before, that the power of the National government became more felt and recognized and, therefore, had to be enlisted in the cause of this institution.

It is probably well that we had the war when we did. We are better off now than we would have been without it, and have made more rapid progress than we otherwise should have made. The civilized nations of Europe have been stimulated into unusual activity, so that commerce, trade, travel, and thorough acquaintance among people of different nationalities, has become common; whereas, before, it was but the few who had ever had the privilege of going beyond the limits of their own country or who knew anything about other people. Then, too, our republican institutions were regarded as experiments up to the breaking out of the rebellion, and monarchical Europe generally believed that our republic was a rope of sand that would part the moment the slightest strain was brought upon it. Now it has shown itself capable of dealing with one of the greatest wars that was ever made, and our people have proven themselves to be the most formidable in war of any nationality.

But this war was a fearful lesson, and should teach us the necessity of avoiding wars in the future.

The conduct of some of the European states during our troubles shows the lack of conscience of communities where the responsibility does not come upon a single individual. Seeing a nation that extended from ocean to ocean, embracing the better part of a continent, growing as we were growing in population, wealth and intelligence, the European nations thought it would be well to give us a check. We might, possibly, after a while threaten their peace, or, at least, the perpetuity of their institutions. Hence, England was constantly finding fault with the administration at Washington because we were not able to keep up an effective blockade.

She also joined, at first, with France and Spain in setting up an Austrian prince upon the throne in Mexico, totally disregarding any rights or claims that Mexico had of being treated as an independent power. It is true they trumped up grievances as a pretext, but they were only pretexts which can always be found when wanted.

Mexico, in her various revolutions, had been unable to give that protection to the subjects of foreign nations which she would have liked to give, and some of her revolutionary leaders had forced loans from them. Under pretence of protecting their citizens, these nations seized upon Mexico as a foothold for establishing a European monarchy upon our continent, thus threatening our peace at home. I, myself, regarded this as a direct act of war against the United States by the powers engaged, and supposed as a matter of course that the United States would treat it as such when their hands were free to strike. I often spoke of the matter to Mr. Lincoln and the Secretary of War, but never heard any special views from them to enable me to judge what they thought or felt about it. I inferred that they felt a good deal as I did, but were unwilling to commit themselves while we had our own troubles upon our hands.

All of the powers except France very soon withdrew from the armed intervention for the establishment of an Austrian prince upon the throne of Mexico; but the governing people of these countries continued to the close of the war to throw obstacles in our way. After the surrender of Lee, therefore, entertaining the opinion here expressed, I sent Sheridan with a corps to the Rio Grande to have him where he might aid Juarez in expelling the French from Mexico. These troops got off before they could be stopped; and went to the Rio Grande, where Sheridan distributed them up and down the river, much to the consternation of the troops in the quarter of Mexico bordering on that stream. This soon led to a request from France that we should withdraw our troops from the Rio Grande and to negotiations for the withdrawal of theirs. Finally Bazaine was withdrawn from Mexico by order of the French Government. From that day the empire began to totter. Mexico was then able to maintain her independence without aid from us.

France is the traditional ally and friend of the United States. I did not blame France for her part in the scheme to erect a monarchy upon the ruins of the Mexican Republic. That was the scheme of one man, an imitator without genius or merit. He had succeeded in stealing the government of his country, and made a change in its form against the wishes and instincts of his people. He tried to play the part of the first Napoleon, without the ability to sustain that rôle. He sought by new conquests to add to his empire and his glory; but the signal failure of his scheme of conquest was the precursor of his own overthrow.

Like our own war between the States, the Franco-Prussian war was an expensive one; but it was worth to France all it cost her people. It was the completion of the downfall of Napoleon III. The beginning was when he landed troops on this continent. Failing here, the prestige of his name—all the prestige he ever had—was gone. He must achieve a success or fall. He tried to strike down his neighbor, Prussia—and fell.

I never admired the character of the first Napoleon; but I recognize his great genius. His work, too, has left its impress for good on the face of Europe. The third Napoleon could have no claim to having done a good or just act.

To maintain peace in the future it is necessary to be prepared for war. There can scarcely be a possible chance of a conflict, such as the last one, occurring among our own people again; but, growing as we are, in population, wealth and military power, we may become the envy of nations which led us in all these particulars only a few years ago; and unless we are prepared for it we may be in danger of a combined movement being some day made to crush us out. Now, scarcely twenty years after the war, we seem to have forgotten the lessons it taught, and are going on as if in the greatest security, without the power to resist an invasion by the fleets of fourth-rate European powers for a time until we could prepare for them.

We should have a good navy, and our sea-coast defences should be put in the finest possible condition. Neither of these cost much when it is considered where the money goes, and what we get in return. Money expended in a fine navy, not only adds to our security and tends to prevent war in the future, but is very material aid to our commerce with foreign nations in the meantime. Money spent upon sea-coast defences is spent among our own people, and all goes back again among the people. The work accomplished, too, like that of the navy, gives us a feeling of security.

England's course towards the United States during the rebellion exasperated the people of this country very much against the mother country. I regretted it. England and the United States are natural allies, and should be the best of friends. They speak one language, and are related by blood and other ties. We together, or even either separately, are better qualified than any other people to establish commerce between all the nationalities of the world.

England governs her own colonies, and particularly those embracing the people of different races from her own, better than any other nation. She is just to the conquered, but rigid. She makes them self-supporting, but gives the benefit of labor to the laborer. She does not seem to look upon the colonies as outside possessions which she is at liberty to work for the support and aggrandizement of the home government.

The hostility of England to the United States during our rebellion was not so much real as it was apparent. It was the hostility of the leaders of one political party. I am told that there was no time during the civil war when they were able to get up in England a demonstration in favor of secession, while these were constantly being gotten up in favor of the Union, or, as they called it, in favor of the North. Even in Manchester, which suffered so fearfully by having the cotton cut off from her mills, they had a monster demonstration in favor of the North at the very time when their workmen were almost famishing.

It is possible that the question of a conflict between races may come up in the future, as did that between freedom and slavery before. The condition of the colored man within our borders may become a source of anxiety, to say the least. But he was brought to our shores by compulsion, and he now should be considered as having as good a right to remain here as any other class of our citizens. It was looking to a settlement of this question that led me to urge the annexation of Santo Domingo during the time I was President of the United States.

Santo Domingo was freely offered to us, not only by the administration, but by all the people, almost without price. The island is upon our shores, is very fertile, and is capable of supporting fifteen millions of people. The products of the soil are so valuable that labor in her fields would be so compensated as to enable those who wished to go there to quickly repay the cost of their passage. I took it that the colored people would go there in great numbers, so as to have independent states governed by their own race. They would still be States of the Union, and under the protection of the General Government; but the citizens would be almost wholly colored.

By the war with Mexico, we had acquired, as we have seen, territory almost equal in extent to that we already possessed. It was seen that the volunteers of the Mexican war largely composed the pioneers to settle up the Pacific coast country. Their numbers, however, were scarcely sufficient to be a nucleus for the population of the important points of the territory acquired by that war. After our rebellion, when so many young men were at liberty to return to their homes, they found they were not satisfied with the farm, the store, or the work-shop of the villages, but wanted larger fields. The mines of the mountains first attracted them; but afterwards they found that rich valleys and productive grazing and farming lands were there. This territory, the geography of which was not known to us at the close of the rebellion, is now as well mapped as any portion of our country. Railroads traverse it in every direction, north, south, east, and west. The mines are worked. The high lands are used for grazing purposes, and rich agricultural lands are found in many of the valleys. This is the work of the volunteer. It is probable that the Indians would have had control of these lands for a century yet but for the war. We must conclude, therefore, that wars are not always evils unmixed with some good.

Prior to the rebellion the great mass of the people were satisfied to remain near the scenes of their birth. In fact an immense majority of the whole people did not feel secure against coming to want should they move among entire strangers. So much was the country divided into small communities that localized idioms had grown up, so that you could almost tell what section a person was from by hearing him speak. Before, new territories were settled by a "class"; people who shunned contact with others; people who, when the country began to settle up around them, would push out farther from civilization. Their guns furnished meat, and the cultivation of a very limited amount of the soil, their bread and vegetables. All the streams abounded with fish. Trapping would furnish pelts to be brought into the States once a year, to pay for necessary articles which they could not raise—powder, lead, whiskey, tobacco and some store goods. Occasionally some little articles of luxury would enter into these purchases—a quarter of a pound of tea, two or three pounds of coffee, more of sugar, some playing cards, and if anything was left over of the proceeds of the sale, more whiskey.

Little was known of the topography of the country beyond the settlements of these frontiersmen. This is all changed now. The war begot a spirit of independence and enterprise. The feeling now is, that a youth must cut loose from his old surroundings to enable him to get up in the world. There is now such a commingling of the people that particular idioms and pronunciation are no longer localized to any great extent; the country has filled up "from the centre all around to the sea"; railroads connect the two oceans and all parts of the interior; maps, nearly perfect, of every part of the country are now furnished the student of geography.

The war has made us a nation of great power and intelligence. We have but little to do to preserve peace, happiness and prosperity at home, and the respect of other nations. Our experience ought to teach us the necessity of the first; our power secures the latter.

I feel that we are on the eve of a new era, when there is to be great harmony between the Federal and Confederate. I cannot stay to be a living witness to the correctness of this prophecy; but I feel it within me that it is to be so. The universally kind feeling expressed for me at a time when it was supposed that each day would prove my last, seemed to me the beginning of the answer to "Let us have peace."

The expressions of these kindly feelings were not restricted to a section of the country, nor to a division of the people. They came from individual citizens of all nationalities; from all denominations—the Protestant, the Catholic, and the Jew; and from the various societies of the land—scientific, educational, religious, or otherwise. Politics did not enter into the matter at all.

I am not egotist enough to suppose all this significance should be given because I was the object of it. But the war between the States was a very bloody and a very costly war. One side or the other had to yield principles they deemed dearer than life before it could be brought to an end. I commanded the whole of the mighty host engaged on the victorious side. I was, no matter whether deservedly so or not, a representative of that side of the controversy. It is a significant and gratifying fact that Confederates should have joined heartily in this spontaneous move. I hope the good feeling inaugurated may continue to the end.

APPENDIX.

REPORT OF LIEUTENANT-GENERAL U. S. GRANT,
OF THE
UNITED STATES ARMIES—1864–'65.

HEADQUARTERS ARMIES OF THE UNITED STATES,
WASHINGTON, D. C., *July* 22, 1865.

HON. E. M. STANTON, Secretary of War.

SIR:—I have the honor to submit the following report of the operations of the Armies of the United States from the date of my appointment to command the same.

From an early period in the rebellion I had been impressed with the idea that active and continuous operations of all the troops that could be brought into the field, regardless of season and weather, were necessary to a speedy termination of the war. The resources of the enemy and his numerical strength were far inferior to ours; but as an offset to this, we had a vast territory, with a population hostile to the government, to garrison, and long lines of river and railroad communications to protect, to enable us to supply the operating armies.

The armies in the East and West acted independently and without concert, like a balky team, no two ever pulling together, enabling the enemy to use to great advantage his interior lines of communication for transporting troops from East to West, reinforcing the army most vigorously pressed, and to furlough large numbers, during seasons of inactivity on our part, to go to their homes and do the work of producing, for the support of their armies. It was a question whether our numerical strength and resources were not more than balanced by these disadvantages and the enemy's superior position.

From the first, I was firm in the conviction that no peace could be had that would be stable and conducive to the happiness of the people, both North and South, until the military power of the rebellion was entirely broken.

I therefore determined, first, to use the greatest number of troops practicable against the armed force of the enemy; preventing him from using the same force at different seasons against first one and then another of our armies, and the possibility of repose for refitting and producing necessary supplies for carrying on resistance. Second, to hammer continuously against the armed force of the enemy and his resources, until by mere attrition, if in no other way, there should be nothing left to him but an equal submission with the loyal section of our common country to the constitution and laws of the land.

These views have been kept constantly in mind, and orders given and campaigns made to carry them out. Whether they might have been better in conception and execution is for the people, who mourn the loss of friends fallen, and who have to pay the pecuniary cost, to say. All I can say is, that what I have done has been done conscientiously, to the best of my ability, and in what I conceived to be for the best interests of the whole country.

At the date when this report begins, the situation of the contending forces was about as follows: The Mississippi River was strongly garrisoned by Federal troops, from St. Louis, Missouri, to its mouth. The line of the Arkansas was also held, thus giving us armed possession of all west of the Mississippi, north of that stream. A few points in Southern Louisiana, not remote from the river, were held by us, together with a small garrison at and near the mouth of the Rio Grande. All the balance of the vast territory of Arkansas, Louisiana, and Texas was in the almost undisputed possession of the enemy, with an army of probably not less than eighty thousand effective men, that could have been brought into the field had there been sufficient opposition to have brought them out. The let-alone policy had demoralized this force so that probably but little more than one-half of it was ever present in garrison at any one time. But the one-half, or forty thousand men, with the bands of guerillas scattered through Missouri, Arkansas, and along the Mississippi River, and the disloyal character of much of the population, compelled the use of a large number of troops to keep navigation open on the river, and to protect the loyal people to the west of it. To the east of the Mississippi we held substantially with the line of the Tennessee and Holston rivers, running eastward to include nearly all of the State of Tennessee. South of Chattanooga, a small foothold had been obtained in Georgia, sufficient to protect East Tennessee from incursions from the enemy's force at Dalton, Georgia. West Virginia was substantially within our lines. Virginia, with the exception of the northern border, the Potomac River, a small area about the mouth of James River, covered by the troops at Norfolk and Fort Monroe, and the territory covered by the Army of the Potomac lying along the Rapidan, was in the possession of the enemy. Along the sea-coast footholds had been obtained at Plymouth, Washington, and New Bern, in North Carolina; Beaufort, Folly and Morris Islands, Hilton Head, Fort Pulaski, and Port Royal, in South Carolina; Fernandina and St. Augustine, in Florida. Key West and Pensacola were also in our possession, while all the important ports were blockaded by the navy. The accompanying map, a copy of which was sent to General Sherman and other commanders in March, 1864, shows by red lines the territory occupied by us at the beginning of the rebellion, and at the opening of the campaign of 1864, while those in blue are the lines which it was proposed to occupy.

Behind the Union lines there were many bands of guerillas and a large population disloyal to the government, making it necessary to guard every foot of road or river used in supplying our armies. In the South, a reign of military despotism prevailed, which made every man and boy capable of bearing arms a soldier; and those who could not bear arms in the field acted as provosts for collecting deserters and returning them. This enabled the enemy to bring almost his entire strength into the field.

The enemy had concentrated the bulk of his forces east of the Mississippi into two armies, commanded by Generals R. E. Lee and J. E. Johnston, his ablest and best generals. The army commanded by Lee occupied the south bank of the Rapidan, extending from Mine Run westward, strongly intrenched, covering and defending Richmond, the rebel capital, against the Army of the Potomac. The army under Johnston occupied a strongly intrenched position at Dalton, Georgia, covering and defending Atlanta, Georgia, a place of great importance as a railroad centre, against the armies under Major-General W. T. Sherman. In addition to these armies he had a large cavalry force under Forrest, in North-east Mississippi; a considerable force, of all arms, in the Shenandoah Valley, and in the western part of Virginia and extreme eastern part of Tennessee; and also confronting our sea-coast garrisons, and holding blockaded ports where we had no foothold upon land.

These two armies, and the cities covered and defended by them, were the main objective points of the campaign.

Major-General W. T. Sherman, who was appointed to the command of the Military Division of the Mississippi, embracing all the armies and territory east of the Mississippi River to the Alleghanies and the Department of Arkansas, west of the Mississippi, had the immediate command of the armies operating against Johnston.

Major-General George G. Meade had the immediate command of the Army of the Potomac, from where I exercised general supervision of the movements of all our armies.

General Sherman was instructed to move against Johnston's army, to break it up, and to go into the interior of the enemy's country as far as he could, inflicting all the damage he could upon their war resources. If the enemy in his front showed signs of joining Lee, to follow him up to the full extent of his ability, while I would prevent the concentration of Lee upon him, if it was in the power of the Army of the Potomac to do so. More specific written instructions were not given, for the reason that I had talked over with him the plans of the campaign, and was satisfied that he understood them and would execute them to the fullest extent possible.

Major-General N. P. Banks, then on an expedition up Red River against Shreveport, Louisiana (which had been organized previous to my appointment to command), was notified by me on the 15th of March, of the importance it was that Shreveport should be taken at the earliest possible day, and that if he found that the taking of it would occupy from ten to fifteen days' more time than General Sherman had given his troops to be absent from their command, he would send them back at the time specified by General Sherman, even if it led to the abandonment of the main object of the Red River expedition, for this force was necessary to movements east of the Mississippi; that should his expedition prove successful, he would hold Shreveport and the Red River with such force as he might deem necessary, and return the balance of his troops to the neighborhood of New Orleans, commencing no move for the further acquisition of territory, unless it was to make that then held by him more easily held; that it might be a part of the spring campaign to move against Mobile; that it certainly would be, if troops enough could be obtained to make it without embarrassing other movements; that New Orleans would be the point of departure for such an expedition; also, that I had directed General Steele to make a real move from Arkansas, as suggested by him (General Banks), instead of a demonstration, as Steele thought advisable.

On the 31st of March, in addition to the foregoing notification and directions, he was instructed as follows:

"1st. If successful in your expedition against Shreveport, that you turn over the defence of the Red River to General Steele and the navy.

"2d. That you abandon Texas entirely, with the exception of your hold upon the Rio Grande. This can be held with four thousand men, if they will turn their attention immediately to fortifying their positions. At least one-half of the force required for this service might be taken from the colored troops.

"3d. By properly fortifying on the Mississippi River, the force to guard it from Port Hudson to New Orleans can be reduced to ten thousand men, if not to a less number. Six thousand more would then hold all the rest of the territory necessary to hold until active operations can again be resumed west of the river. According to your last return, this would give you a force of over thirty thousand effective men with which to move against Mobile. To this I expect to add five thousand men from Missouri. If, however, you think the force here stated too small to hold the territory regarded as necessary to hold possession of, I would say concentrate at least twenty-five thousand men of your present command for operations against Mobile. With these and such additions as I can give you from elsewhere, lose no time in making a demonstration, to be followed by an attack upon Mobile. Two or more iron-clads will be ordered to report to Admiral Farragut. This gives him a strong naval fleet with which to co-operate. You can make your own arrangements with the admiral for his co-operation, and select your own line of approach. My own idea of the matter is that Pascagoula should be your base; but, from your long service in the Gulf Department, you will know best about the matter. It is intended that your movements shall be co-operative with movements elsewhere, and you cannot now start too soon. All I would now add is, that you commence the concentration of your forces at once. Preserve a profound secrecy of what you intend doing, and start at the earliest possible moment.

"U. S. GRANT, Lieutenant-General.
"Major-General N. P. Banks."

Major-General Meade was instructed that Lee's army would be his objective point; that wherever Lee went he would go also. For his movement two plans presented themselves: One to cross the Rapidan below Lee, moving by his right flank; the other above, moving by his left. Each presented advantages over the other, with corresponding objections. By crossing above, Lee would be cut off from all chance of ignoring Richmond or going north on a raid. But if we took this route, all we did would have to be done whilst the rations we started with held out; besides, it separated us from Butler, so that he could not be directed how to co-operate. If we took the other route, Brandy Station could be used as a base of supplies until another was secured on the York or James rivers. Of these, however, it was decided to take the lower route.

The following letter of instruction was addressed to Major-General B. F. Butler:

"Fort Monroe, Virginia, *April* 2, 1864.
"General:—In the spring campaign, which it is desirable shall commence at as early a day as practicable, it is proposed to have co-operative action of all the armies in the field, as far as this object can be accomplished.

"It will not be possible to unite our armies into two or three large ones to act as so many units, owing to the absolute necessity of holding on to the territory already taken from the enemy. But, generally speaking, concentration can be practically effected by armies moving to the interior of the enemy's country from the territory they have to guard. By such movement, they interpose themselves between the enemy and the country to be guarded, thereby reducing the number necessary to guard important points, or at least occupy the attention of a part of the enemy's force, if no greater object is gained. Lee's army and Richmond being the greater objects towards which our attention must be directed in the next campaign, it is desirable to unite all the force we can against them. The necessity of covering Washington with the

Army of the Potomac, and of covering your department with your army, makes it impossible to unite these forces at the beginning of any move. I propose, therefore, what comes nearest this of anything that seems practicable: The Army of the Potomac will act from its present base, Lee's army being the objective point. You will collect all the forces from your command that can be spared from garrison duty—I should say not less than twenty thousand effective men—to operate on the south side of James River, Richmond being your objective point. To the force you already have will be added about ten thousand men from South Carolina, under Major-General Gillmore, who will command them in person. Major-General W. F. Smith is ordered to report to you, to command the troops sent into the field from your own department.

"General Gillmore will be ordered to report to you at Fortress Monroe, with all the troops on transports, by the 18th instant, or as soon thereafter as practicable. Should you not receive notice by that time to move, you will make such disposition of them and your other forces as you may deem best calculated to deceive the enemy as to the real move to be made.

"When you are notified to move, take City Point with as much force as possible. Fortify, or rather intrench, at once, and concentrate all your troops for the field there as rapidly as you can. From City Point directions cannot be given at this time for your further movements.

"The fact that has already been stated—that is, that Richmond is to be your objective point, and that there is to be co-operation between your force and the Army of the Potomac—must be your guide. This indicates the necessity of your holding close to the south bank of the James River as you advance. Then, should the enemy be forced into his intrenchments in Richmond, the Army of the Potomac would follow, and by means of transports the two armies would become a unit.

"All the minor details of your advance are left entirely to your direction. If, however, you think it practicable to use your cavalry south of you, so as to cut the railroad about Hicksford, about the time of the general advance, it would be of immense advantage.

"You will please forward for my information, at the earliest practicable day, all orders, details, and instructions you may give for the execution of this order.

"U. S. GRANT, Lieutenant-General.

"MAJOR-GENERAL B. F. BUTLER."

On the 16th these instructions were substantially reiterated. On the 19th, in order to secure full co-operation between his army and that of General Meade, he was informed that I expected him to move from Fort Monroe the same day that General Meade moved from Culpeper. The exact time I was to telegraph him as soon as it was fixed, and that it would not be earlier than the 27th of April; that it was my intention to fight Lee between Culpeper and Richmond, if he would stand. Should he, however, fall back into Richmond, I would follow up and make a junction with his (General Butler's) army on the James River; that, could I be certain he would be able to invest Richmond on the south side, so as to have his left resting on the James, above the city, I would form the junction there; that circumstances might make this course advisable anyhow; that he should use every exertion to secure footing as far up the south side of the river as he could, and as soon as possible after the receipt of orders to move; that if he could not carry the city, he should at least detain as large a force there as possible.

In co-operation with the main movements against Lee and Johnston, I was desirous of using all other troops necessarily kept in departments remote from the fields of immediate operations, and also those kept in the background for the protection of our extended lines between the loyal States and the armies operating against them.

A very considerable force, under command of Major-General Sigel, was so held for the protection of West Virginia, and the frontiers of Maryland and Pennsylvania. Whilst these troops could not be withdrawn to distant fields without exposing the North to invasion by comparatively small bodies of the enemy, they could act directly to their front, and give better protection than if lying idle in garrison. By such a movement they would either compel the enemy to detach largely for the protection of his supplies and lines of communication, or he would lose them. General Sigel was therefore directed to organize all his available force into two expeditions, to move from Beverly and Charleston, under command of Generals Ord and Crook, against the East Tennessee and Virginia Railroad. Subsequently, General Ord having been relieved at his own request, General Sigel was instructed, at his own suggestion, to give up the expedition by Beverly, and to form two columns, one under General Crook, on the Kanawha, numbering about ten thousand men, and one on the Shenandoah, numbering about seven thousand men. The one on the Shenandoah to assemble between Cumberland and the Shenandoah, and the infantry and artillery advanced to Cedar Creek with such cavalry as could be made available at the moment, to threaten the enemy in the Shenandoah Valley, and advance as far as possible; while General Crook would take possession of Lewisburg with part of his force and move down the Tennessee Railroad, doing as much damage as he could, destroying the New River Bridge and the salt-works, at Saltville, Va.

Owing to the weather and bad condition of the roads, operations were delayed until the 1st of May, when, everything being in readiness and the roads favorable, orders were given for a general movement of all the armies not later than the 4th of May.

My first object being to break the military power of the rebellion, and capture the enemy's important strongholds, made me desirous that General Butler should succeed in his movement against Richmond, as that would tend more than anything else, unless it were the capture of Lee's army, to accomplish this desired result in the East. If he failed, it was my determination, by hard fighting, either to compel Lee to retreat, or to so cripple him that he could not detach a large force to go north, and still retain enough for the defence of Richmond. It was well understood, by both Generals Butler and Meade, before starting on the campaign, that it was my intention to put both their armies south of the James River, in case of failure to destroy Lee without it.

Before giving General Butler his instructions, I visited him at Fort Monroe, and in conversation pointed out the apparent importance of getting possession of Petersburg, and destroying railroad communication as far south as possible. Believing, however, in the practicability of capturing Richmond unless it was reinforced, I made that the objective point of his operations. As the Army of the Potomac was to move simultaneously with him, Lee could not detach from his army with safety, and the enemy did not have troops elsewhere to bring to the defence of the city in time to meet a rapid movement from the north of James River.

I may here state that, commanding all the armies as I did, I tried, as far as possible, to leave General Meade in independent command of the Army of the Potomac. My instructions for that army were all through him, and were general in their nature, leaving all the details and the execution to him. The campaigns that followed proved him to be the right man in the right place. His commanding always in the presence of an officer superior to him in rank, has drawn from him much of that public attention that his zeal and ability entitle him to, and which he would otherwise have received.

The movement of the Army of the Potomac commenced early on the morning of the 4th of May, under the immediate direction and orders of Major-General Meade, pursuant to instructions. Before night, the whole army was across the Rapidan (the fifth and sixth corps crossing at Germania Ford, and the second corps at Ely's Ford, the cavalry, under Major-General Sheridan, moving in advance,) with the greater part of its trains, numbering about four thousand wagons, meeting with but slight opposition. The average distance travelled by the troops that day was about twelve miles. This I regarded as a great success, and it removed from my mind the most serious apprehensions I had entertained, that of crossing the river in the face of an active, large, well-appointed, and ably commanded army, and how so large a train was to be carried through a hostile country, and protected. Early on the 5th, the advance corps (the fifth, Major-General G. K. Warren commanding,) met and engaged the enemy outside his intrenchments near Mine Run. The battle raged furiously all day, the whole army being brought into the fight as fast as the corps could be got upon the field, which, considering the density of the forest and narrowness of the roads, was done with commendable promptness.

General Burnside, with the ninth corps, was, at the time the Army of the Potomac moved, left with the bulk of his corps at the crossing of the Rappahannock River and Alexandria Railroad, holding the road back to Bull Run, with instructions not to move until he received notice that a crossing of the Rapidan was secured, but to move promptly as soon as such notice was received. This crossing he was apprised of on the afternoon of the 4th. By six o'clock of the morning of the 6th he was leading his corps into action near the Wilderness Tavern, some of his troops having marched a distance of over thirty miles, crossing both the Rappahannock and Rapidan rivers. Considering that a large proportion, probably two-thirds of his command, was composed of new troops, unaccustomed to marches, and carrying the accoutrements of a soldier, this was a remarkable march.

The battle of the Wilderness was renewed by us at five o'clock on the morning of the 6th, and continued with unabated fury until darkness set in, each army holding substantially the same position that they had on the evening of the 5th. After dark, the enemy made a feeble attempt to turn our right flank, capturing several hundred prisoners and creating considerable confusion. But the promptness of General Sedgwick, who was personally present and commanded that part of our line, soon reformed it and restored order. On the morning of the 7th, reconnoissances showed that the enemy had fallen behind his intrenched lines, with pickets to the front, covering a part of the battle-field. From this it was evident to my mind that the two days' fighting had satisfied him of his inability to further maintain the contest in the open field, notwithstanding his advantage of position, and that he would wait an attack behind his works. I therefore determined to push on and put my whole force between him and Richmond; and orders were at once issued for a movement by his right flank. On the night of the 7th, the march was commenced towards Spottsylvania Court House, the fifth corps moving on the most direct road. But the enemy having become apprised of our movement, and having the shorter line, was enabled to reach there first. On the 8th, General Warren met a force of the enemy, which had been sent out to oppose and delay his advance, to gain time to fortify the line taken up at Spottsylvania. This force was steadily driven back on the main force, within the recently constructed works, after considerable fighting, resulting in severe loss to both sides. On the morning of the 9th, General Sheridan started on a raid against the enemy's lines of communication with Richmond. The 9th, 10th, and 11th were spent in manœuvring and fighting, without decisive results. Among the killed on the 9th was that able and distinguished soldier Major-General John Sedgwick, commanding the sixth army corps. Major-General H. G. Wright succeeded him in command. Early on the morning of the 12th a general attack was made on the enemy in position. The second corps, Major-General Hancock commanding, carried a salient of his line, capturing most of Johnson's division of Ewell's corps and twenty pieces of artillery. But the resistance was so obstinate that the advantage gained did not prove decisive. The 13th, 14th, 15th, 16th, 17th, and 18th, were consumed in manœuvring and awaiting the arrival of reinforcements from Washington. Deeming it impracticable to make any further attack upon the enemy at Spottsylvania Court House, orders were issued on the 18th with a view to a movement to the North Anna, to commence at twelve o'clock on the night of the 19th. Late in the afternoon of the 19th, Ewell's corps came out of its works on our extreme right flank; but the attack was promptly repulsed, with heavy loss. This delayed the movement to the North Anna until the night of the 21st, when it was commenced. But the enemy again, having the shorter line, and being in possession of the main roads, was enabled to reach the North Anna in advance of us, and took position behind it. The fifth corps reached the North Anna on the afternoon of the 23d, closely followed by the sixth corps. The second and ninth corps got up about the same time, the second holding the railroad bridge, and the ninth lying between that and Jericho Ford. General Warren effected a crossing the same afternoon, and got a position without much opposition. Soon after getting into position he was violently attacked, but repulsed the enemy with great slaughter. On the 25th, General Sheridan rejoined the Army of the Potomac from the raid on which he started from Spottsylvania, having destroyed the depots at Beaver Dam and Ashland stations, four trains of cars, large supplies of rations, and many miles of railroad-track; recaptured about four hundred of our men on their way to Richmond as prisoners of war; met and defeated the enemy's cavalry at Yellow Tavern; carried the first line of works around Richmond (but finding the second line too strong to be carried by assault), recrossed to the north bank of the Chickahominy at Meadow Bridge under heavy fire, and moved by a detour to Haxall's Landing, on the James

River, where he communicated with General Butler. This raid had the effect of drawing off the whole of the enemy's cavalry force, making it comparatively easy to guard our trains.

General Butler moved his main force up the James River, in pursuance of instructions, on the 4th of May, General Gillmore having joined him with the tenth corps. At the same time he sent a force of one thousand eight hundred cavalry, by way of West Point, to form a junction with him wherever he might get a foothold, and a force of three thousand cavalry, under General Kautz, from Suffolk, to operate against the road south of Petersburg and Richmond. On the 5th, he occupied, without opposition, both City Point and Bermuda Hundred, his movement being a complete surprise. On the 6th, he was in position with his main army, and commenced intrenching. On the 7th he made a reconnoissance against the Petersburg and Richmond Railroad, destroying a portion of it after some fighting. On the 9th he telegraphed as follows:

> "HEADQUARTERS, NEAR BERMUDA LANDING,
> *May* 9, 1864.
>
> "HON. E. M. STANTON, Secretary of War.
>
> "Our operations may be summed up in a few words. With one thousand seven hundred cavalry we have advanced up the Peninsula, forced the Chickahominy, and have safely brought them to their present position. These were colored cavalry, and are now holding our advance pickets towards Richmond.
>
> "General Kautz, with three thousand cavalry from Suffolk, on the same day with our movement up James River, forced the Black Water, burned the railroad bridge at Stony Creek, below Petersburg, cutting into Beauregard's force at that point.
>
> "We have landed here, intrenched ourselves, destroyed many miles of railroad, and got a position which, with proper supplies, we can hold out against the whole of Lee's army. I have ordered up the supplies.
>
> "Beauregard, with a large portion of his force, was left south by the cutting of the railroads by Kautz. That portion which reached Petersburg under Hill I have whipped to-day, killing and wounding many, and taking many prisoners, after a severe and well-contested fight.
>
> "General Grant will not be troubled with any further reinforcements to Lee from Beauregard's force.
>
> "BENJ. F. BUTLER, Major-General."

On the evening of the 13th and morning of the 14th he carried a portion of the enemy's first line of defences at Drury's Bluff, or Fort Darling, with small loss. The time thus consumed from the 6th lost to us the benefit of the surprise and capture of Richmond and Petersburg, enabling, as it did, Beauregard to collect his loose forces in North and South Carolina, and bring them to the defence of those places. On the 16th, the enemy attacked General Butler in his position in front of Drury's Bluff. He was forced back, or drew back, into his intrenchments between the forks of the James and Appomattox rivers, the enemy intrenching strongly in his front, thus covering his railroads, the city, and all that was valuable to him. His army, therefore, though in a position of great security, was as completely shut off from further operations directly against Richmond as if it had been in a bottle strongly corked. It required but a comparatively small force of the enemy to hold it there.

On the 12th, General Kautz, with his cavalry, was started on a raid against the Danville Railroad, which he struck at Coalfield, Powhatan, and Chula Stations, destroying them, the railroad-track, two freight trains, and one locomotive, together with large quantities of commissary and other stores; thence, crossing to the South Side Road, struck it at Wilson's, Wellsville, and Black's and White's Stations, destroying the road and station-houses; thence he proceeded to City Point, which he reached on the 18th.

On the 19th of April, and prior to the movement of General Butler, the enemy, with a land force under General Hoke and an iron-clad ram, attacked Plymouth, N. C., commanded by General H. W. Wessells, and our gunboats there; and, after severe fighting, the place was carried by assault, and the entire garrison and armament captured. The gunboat *Smithfield* was sunk, and the *Miami* disabled.

The army sent to operate against Richmond having hermetically sealed itself up at Bermuda Hundred, the enemy was enabled to bring the most, if not all, the reinforcements brought from the south by Beauregard against the Army of the Potomac. In addition to this reinforcement, a very considerable one, probably not less than fifteen thousand men, was obtained by calling in the scattered troops under Breckinridge from the western part of Virginia.

The position of Bermuda Hundred was as easy to defend as it was difficult to operate from against the enemy. I determined, therefore, to bring from it all available forces, leaving enough only to secure what had been gained; and accordingly, on the 22d, I directed that they be sent forward, under command of Major-General W. F. Smith, to join the Army of the Potomac.

On the 24th of May, the 9th army corps, commanded by Major-General A. E. Burnside, was assigned to the Army of the Potomac, and from this time forward constituted a portion of Major-General Meade's command.

Finding the enemy's position on the North Anna stronger than either of his previous ones, I withdrew on the night of the 26th to the north bank of the North Anna, and moved *via* Hanover Town to turn the enemy's position by his right.

Generals Torbert's and Merritt's divisions of cavalry, under Sheridan, and the 6th corps, led the advance; crossed the Pamunkey River at Hanover Town, after considerable fighting, and on the 28th the two divisions of cavalry had a severe, but successful engagement with the enemy at Hawes's Shop. On the 29th and 30th we advanced, with heavy skirmishing, to the Hanover Court House and Cold Harbor Road, and developed the enemy's position north of the Chickahominy. Late on the evening of the last day the enemy came out and attacked our left, but was repulsed with very considerable loss. An attack was immediately ordered by General Meade, along his whole line, which resulted in driving the enemy from a part of his intrenched skirmish line.

On the 31st, General Wilson's division of cavalry destroyed the railroad bridges over the South Anna River, after defeating the enemy's cavalry. General Sheridan, on the same day, reached Cold Harbor, and held it until relieved by the 6th corps and General Smith's command, which had just arrived, *via* White House, from General Butler's army.

On the 1st day of June an attack was made at five P.M. by the 6th corps and the troops under General Smith, the other corps being held in readiness to advance on the receipt of orders. This resulted in our carrying and holding the enemy's first line of works in front of the right of the 6th corps, and in front of General Smith. During the attack the enemy made repeated assaults on each of the corps not engaged in the main attack, but was repulsed with heavy loss in every instance. That night he made several assaults to regain what he had lost in the day, but failed. The 2d was spent in getting troops into position for an attack on the 3d. On the 3d of June we again assaulted the enemy's works, in the hope of driving him from his position. In this attempt our loss was heavy, while that of the enemy, I have reason to believe, was comparatively light. It was the only general attack made from the Rapidan to the James which did not inflict upon the enemy losses to compensate for our own losses. I would not be understood as saying that all previous attacks resulted in victories to our arms, or accomplished as much as I had hoped from them; but they inflicted upon the enemy severe losses, which tended, in the end, to the complete overthrow of the rebellion.

From the proximity of the enemy to his defences around Richmond, it was impossible, by any flank movement, to interpose between him and the city. I was still in a condition to either move by his left flank, and invest Richmond from the north side, or continue my move by his right flank to the south side of the James. While the former might have been better as a covering for Washington, yet a full survey of all the ground satisfied me that it would be impracticable to hold a line north and east of Richmond that would protect the Fredericksburg Railroad, a long, vulnerable line, which would exhaust much of our strength to guard, and that would have to be protected to supply the army, and would leave open to the enemy all his lines of communication on the south side of the James. My idea, from the start, had been to beat Lee's army north of Richmond, if possible. Then, after destroying his lines of communication north of the James River, to transfer the army to the south side, and besiege Lee in Richmond, or follow him south if he should retreat. After the battle of the Wilderness, it was evident that the enemy deemed it of the first importance to run no risks with the army he then had. He acted purely on the defensive, behind breastworks, or feebly on the offensive immediately in front of them, and where, in case of repulse, he could easily retire behind them. Without a greater sacrifice of life than I was willing to make, all could not be accomplished that I had designed north of Richmond. I therefore determined to continue to hold substantially the ground we then occupied, taking advantage of any favorable circumstances that might present themselves, until the cavalry could be sent to Charlottesville and Gordonsville to effectually break up the railroad connection between Richmond and the Shenandoah Valley and Lynchburg; and when the cavalry got well off, to move the army to the south side of the James River, by the enemy's right flank, where I felt I could cut off all his sources of supply, except by the canal.

On the 7th, two divisions of cavalry, under General Sheridan, got off on the expedition against the Virginia Central Railroad, with instructions to Hunter, whom I hoped he would meet near Charlottesville, to join his forces to Sheridan's, and after the work laid out for them was thoroughly done, to join the Army of the Potomac by the route laid down in Sheridan's instructions.

On the 10th of June, General Butler sent a force of infantry, under General Gillmore, and of cavalry under General Kautz, to capture Petersburg, if possible, and destroy the railroad and common bridges across the Appomattox. The cavalry carried the works on the south side, and penetrated well in towards the town, but were forced to retire. General Gillmore, finding the works which he approached very strong, and deeming an assault impracticable, returned to Bermuda Hundred without attempting one.

Attaching great importance to the possession of Petersburg, I sent back to Bermuda Hundred and City Point, General Smith's command by water, *via* the White House, to reach there in advance of the Army of the Potomac. This was for the express purpose of securing Petersburg before the enemy, becoming aware of our intention, could reinforce the place.

The movement from Cold Harbor commenced after dark on the evening of the 12th. One division of cavalry, under General Wilson, and the 5th corps, crossed the Chickahominy at Long Bridge, and moved out to White Oak Swamp, to cover the crossings of the other corps. The advance corps reached James River, at Wilcox's Landing and Charles City Court House, on the night of the 13th.

During three long years the Armies of the Potomac and Northern Virginia had been confronting each other. In that time they had fought more desperate battles than it probably ever before fell to the lot of two armies to fight, without materially changing the vantage ground of either. The Southern press and people, with more shrewdness than was displayed in the North, finding that they had failed to capture Washington and march on to New York, as they had boasted they would do, assumed that they only defended their Capital and Southern territory. Hence, Antietam, Gettysburg, and all the other battles that had been fought, were by them set down as failures on our part, and victories for them. Their army believed this. It produced a morale which could only be overcome by desperate and continuous hard fighting. The battles of the Wilderness, Spottsylvania, North Anna and Cold Harbor, bloody and terrible as they were on our side, were even more damaging to the enemy, and so crippled him as to make him wary ever after of taking the offensive. His losses in men were probably not so great, owing to the fact that we were, save in the Wilderness, almost invariably the attacking party; and when he did attack, it was in the open field. The details of these battles, which for endurance and bravery on the part of the soldiery, have rarely been surpassed, are given in the report of Major-General Meade, and the subordinate reports accompanying it.

During the campaign of forty-three days, from the Rapidan to the James River, the army had to be supplied from an ever-shifting base, by wagons, over narrow roads, through a densely wooded country, with a lack of wharves at each new base from which to conveniently discharge vessels. Too much credit cannot, therefore, be awarded to the quartermaster and commissary departments for the zeal and efficiency displayed by them. Under the general supervision of the chief quartermaster, Brigadier-General R. Ingalls, the trains were made to occupy all the available roads between the army and our water-base, and but little difficulty was experienced in protecting them.

The movement in the Kanawha and Shenandoah valleys, under

General Sigel, commenced on the 1st of May. General Crook, who had the immediate command of the Kanawha expedition, divided his forces into two columns, giving one, composed of cavalry, to General Averell. They crossed the mountains by separate routes. Averell struck the Tennessee and Virginia Railroad, near Wytheville, on the 10th, and proceeding to New River and Christiansburg, destroyed the road, several important bridges and depots, including New River Bridge, forming a junction with Crook at Union on the 15th. General Sigel moved up the Shenandoah Valley, met the enemy at New Market on the 15th, and, after a severe engagement, was defeated with heavy loss, and retired behind Cedar Creek. Not regarding the operations of General Sigel as satisfactory, I asked his removal from command, and Major-General Hunter was appointed to supersede him. His instructions were embraced in the following dispatches to Major-General H. W. Halleck, chief of staff of the army:

> "NEAR SPOTTSYLVANIA COURT HOUSE, VA.,
> *May* 20, 1864.

> *   *   *   *   *   *   *

> "The enemy are evidently relying for supplies greatly on such as are brought over the branch road running through Staunton. On the whole, therefore, I think it would be better for General Hunter to move in that direction; reach Staunton and Gordonsville or Charlottesville, if he does not meet too much opposition. If he can hold at bay a force equal to his own, he will be doing good service. * * *

> "U. S. GRANT, Lieutenant-General.

> "MAJOR-GENERAL H. W. HALLECK."

> JERICHO FORD, VA., *May* 25, 1864.

> "If Hunter can possibly get to Charlottesville and Lynchburg, he should do so, living on the country. The railroads and canal should be destroyed beyond possibility of repairs for weeks. Completing this, he could find his way back to his original base, or from about Gordonsville join this army.

> "U. S. GRANT, Lieutenant-General.

> "MAJOR-GENERAL H. W. HALLECK."

General Hunter immediately took up the offensive, and, moving up the Shenandoah Valley, met the enemy on the 5th of June at Piedmont, and, after a battle of ten hours, routed and defeated him, capturing on the field of battle one thousand five hundred men, three pieces of artillery, and three hundred stand of small arms. On the 8th of the same month he formed a junction with Crook and Averell at Staunton, from which place he moved direct on Lynchburg, *via* Lexington, which place he reached and invested on the 16th day of June. Up to this time he was very successful; and but for the difficulty of taking with him sufficient ordnance stores over so long a march, through a hostile country, he would, no doubt, have captured that, to the enemy important, point. The destruction of the enemy's supplies and manufactories was very great. To meet this movement under General Hunter, General Lee sent a force, perhaps equal to a corps, a part of which reached Lynchburg a short time before Hunter. After some skirmishing on the 17th and 18th, General Hunter, owing to a want of ammunition to give battle, retired from before the place. Unfortunately, this want of ammunition left him no choice of route for his return but by way of Kanawha. This lost to us the use of his troops for several weeks from the defence of the North.

Had General Hunter moved by way of Charlottesville, instead of Lexington, as his instructions contemplated, he would have been in a position to have covered the Shenandoah Valley against the enemy, should the force he met have seemed to endanger it. If it did not, he would have been within easy distance of the James River Canal, on the main line of communication between Lynchburg and the force sent for its defence. I have never taken exception to the operations of General Hunter, and am not now disposed to find fault with him, for I have no doubt he acted within what he conceived to be the spirit of his instructions and the interests of the service. The promptitude of his movements and his gallantry should entitle him to the commendation of his country.

To return to the Army of the Potomac: The 2d corps commenced crossing the James River on the morning of the 14th by ferry-boats at Wilcox's Landing. The laying of the pontoon-bridge was completed about midnight of the 14th, and the crossing of the balance of the army was rapidly pushed forward by both bridge and ferry.

After the crossing had commenced, I proceeded by steamer to Bermuda Hundred to give the necessary orders for the immediate capture of Petersburg.

The instructions to General Butler were verbal, and were for him to send General Smith immediately, that night, with all the troops he could give him without sacrificing the position he then held. I told him that I would return at once to the Army of the Potomac, hasten its crossing, and throw it forward to Petersburg by divisions as rapidly as it could be done; that we could reinforce our armies more rapidly there than the enemy could bring troops against us. General Smith got off as directed, and confronted the enemy's pickets near Petersburg before daylight next morning, but for some reason that I have never been able to satisfactorily understand, did not get ready to assault his main lines until near sundown. Then, with a part of his command only, he made the assault, and carried the lines north-east of Petersburg from the Appomattox River, for a distance of over two and a half miles, capturing fifteen pieces of artillery and three hundred prisoners. This was about seven P.M. Between the line thus captured and Petersburg there were no other works, and there was no evidence that the enemy had reinforced Petersburg with a single brigade from any source. The night was clear—the moon shining brightly—and favorable to further operations. General Hancock, with two divisions of the 2d corps, reached General Smith just after dark, and offered the service of these troops as he (Smith) might wish, waiving rank to the named commander, who he naturally supposed knew best the position of affairs, and what to do with the troops. But instead of taking these troops and pushing at once into Petersburg, he requested General Hancock to relieve a part of his line in the captured works, which was done before midnight.

By the time I arrived the next morning the enemy was in force. An attack was ordered to be made at six o'clock that evening by the troops under Smith and the 2d and 9th corps. It required until that time for the 9th corps to get up and into position. The attack was made as ordered, and the fighting continued with but little intermission until six o'clock the next morning, and resulted in our carrying the advance and some of the main works of the enemy to the right (our left) of those previously captured by General Smith, several pieces of artillery, and over four hundred prisoners.

The 5th corps having got up, the attacks were renewed and persisted in with great vigor on the 17th and 18th, but only resulted in forcing the enemy into an interior line, from which he could not be dislodged. The advantages of position gained by us were very great. The army then proceeded to envelop Petersburg towards the South Side Railroad, as far as possible without attacking fortifications.

On the 16th the enemy, to reinforce Petersburg, withdrew from a part of his intrenchment in front of Bermuda Hundred, expecting, no doubt, to get troops from north of the James to take the place of those withdrawn before we could discover it. General Butler, taking advantage of this, at once moved a force on the railroad between Petersburg and Richmond. As soon as I was apprised of the advantage thus gained, to retain it I ordered two divisions of the 6th corps, General Wright commanding, that were embarking at Wilcox's Landing, under orders for City Point, to report to General Butler at Bermuda Hundred, of which General Butler was notified, and the importance of holding a position in advance of his present line urged upon him.

About two o'clock in the afternoon General Butler was forced back to the line the enemy had withdrawn from in the morning.

General Wright, with his two divisions, joined General Butler on the forenoon of the 17th, the latter still holding with a strong picket-line the enemy's works. But instead of putting these divisions into the enemy's works to hold them, he permitted them to halt and rest some distance in the rear of his own line. Between four and five o'clock in the afternoon the enemy attacked and drove in his pickets and re-occupied his old line.

On the night of the 20th and morning of the 21st a lodgment was effected by General Butler, with one brigade of infantry, on the north bank of the James, at Deep Bottom, and connected by pontoon-bridge with Bermuda Hundred.

On the 19th, General Sheridan, on his return from his expedition against the Virginia Central Railroad, arrived at the White House just as the enemy's cavalry was about to attack it, and compelled it to retire. The result of this expedition was, that General Sheridan met the enemy's cavalry near Trevilian Station, on the morning of the 11th of June, whom he attacked, and after an obstinate contest drove from the field in complete rout. He left his dead and nearly all his wounded in our hands, and about four hundred prisoners and several hundred horses. On the 12th he destroyed the railroad from Trevilian Station to Louisa Court House. This occupied until three o'clock P.M., when he advanced in the direction of Gordonsville. He found the enemy reinforced by infantry, behind well-constructed rifle-pits, about five miles from the latter place, and too strong to successfully assault. On the extreme right, however, his reserve brigade carried the enemy's works twice, and was twice driven therefrom by infantry. Night closed the contest. Not having sufficient ammunition to continue the engagement, and his animals being without forage (the country furnishing but inferior grazing), and hearing nothing from General Hunter, he withdrew his command to the north side of the North Anna, and commenced his return march, reaching White House at the time before stated. After breaking up the depot at that place, he moved to the James River, which he reached safely after heavy fighting. He commenced crossing on the 25th, near Fort Powhatan, without further molestation, and rejoined the Army of the Potomac.

On the 22d, General Wilson, with his own division of cavalry of the Army of the Potomac, and General Kautz's division of cavalry of the Army of the James, moved against the enemy's railroads south of Richmond. Striking the Weldon Railroad at Reams's Station, destroying the depot and several miles of the road, and the South Side road about fifteen miles from Petersburg, to near Nottoway Station, where he met and defeated a force of the enemy's cavalry. He reached Burkesville Station on the afternoon of the 23d, and from there destroyed the Danville Railroad to Roanoke Bridge, a distance of twenty-five miles, where he found the enemy in force, and in a position from which he could not dislodge him. He then commenced his return march, and on the 28th met the enemy's cavalry in force at the Weldon Railroad crossing of Stony Creek, where he had a severe but not decisive engagement. Thence he made a detour from his left with a view of reaching Reams's Station (supposing it to be in our possession). At this place he was met by the enemy's cavalry, supported by infantry, and forced to retire, with the loss of his artillery and trains. In this last encounter, General Kautz, with a part of his command, became separated, and made his way into our lines. General Wilson, with the remainder of his force, succeeded in crossing the Nottoway River and coming in safely on our left and rear. The damage to the enemy in this expedition more than compensated for the losses we sustained. It severed all connection by railroad with Richmond for several weeks.

With a view of cutting the enemy's railroad from near Richmond to the Anna rivers, and making him wary of the situation of his army in the Shenandoah, and, in the event of failure in this, to take advantage of his necessary withdrawal of troops from Petersburg, to explode a mine that had been prepared in front of the 9th corps and assault the enemy's lines at that place, on the night of the 26th of July the 2d corps and two divisions of the cavalry corps and Kautz's cavalry were crossed to the north bank of the James River and joined the force General Butler had there. On the 27th the enemy was driven from his intrenched position, with the loss of four pieces of artillery. On the 28th our lines were extended from Deep Bottom to New Market Road, but in getting this position were attacked by the enemy in heavy force. The fighting lasted for several hours, resulting in considerable loss to both sides. The first object of this move having failed, by reason of the very large force thrown there by the enemy, I determined to take advantage of the diversion made, by assaulting Petersburg before he could get his force back there. One division of the 2d corps was withdrawn on the night of the 28th, and moved during the night to the rear of the 18th corps, to relieve that corps in the line, that it might be foot-loose in the assault to be made. The other two divisions of the 2d corps and Sheridan's cavalry were crossed over on the night of the 29th and moved in front of Petersburg. On the morning of the 30th, between four and five o'clock, the mine was sprung, blowing up a battery and most of a regiment, and the advance of the assaulting column, formed of the 9th corps, immediately took possession of the crater made by the explosion, and the line for some distance to the right and left of it, and a detached line in front of it, but for some cause failed to advance promptly to the ridge beyond. Had they done this, I have every reason to believe that Petersburg would have fallen. Other troops were immediately pushed forward, but the time consumed in getting them up enabled the enemy to rally from his surprise (which had been complete), and get forces to this point for its defence. The captured line thus held being untenable, and of no advantage to us, the troops were withdrawn, but not without heavy loss. Thus terminated in disaster what promised to be the most successful assault of the campaign.

Immediately upon the enemy's ascertaining that General Hunter was retreating from Lynchburg by way of the Kanawha River, thus laying the Shenandoah Valley open for raids into Maryland and Pennsylvania, he returned northward and moved down that valley. As soon as this movement of the enemy was ascertained, General Hunter, who had reached the Kanawha River, was directed to move his troops without delay, by river and railroad, to Harper's Ferry; but owing to the difficulty of navigation by reason of low water and breaks in the railroad, great delay was experienced in getting there. It became necessary, therefore, to find other troops to check this movement of the enemy. For this purpose the 6th corps was taken from the armies operating against Richmond, to which was added the 19th corps, then fortunately beginning to arrive in Hampton Roads from the Gulf Department, under orders issued immediately after the ascertainment of the result of the Red River expedition. The garrisons of Baltimore and Washington were at this time made up of heavy-artillery regiments, hundred days' men, and detachments from the invalid corps. One division under command of General Ricketts, of the 6th corps, was sent to Baltimore, and the remaining two divisions of the 6th corps, under General Wright, were subsequently sent to Washington. On the 3d of July the enemy approached Martinsburg. General Sigel, who was in command of our forces there, retreated across the Potomac at Shepherdstown; and General Weber, commanding at Harper's Ferry, crossed the river and occupied Maryland Heights. On the 6th the enemy occupied Hagerstown, moving a strong column towards Frederick City. General Wallace, with Ricketts's division and his own command, the latter mostly new and undisciplined troops, pushed out from Baltimore with great promptness, and met the enemy in force on the Monocacy, near the crossing of the railroad bridge. His force was not sufficient to insure success, but he fought the enemy nevertheless, and although it resulted in a defeat to our arms, yet it detained the enemy, and thereby served to enable General Wright to reach Washington with two divisions of the 6th corps, and the advance of the 19th corps, before him. From Monocacy the enemy moved on Washington, his cavalry advance reaching Rockville on the evening of the 10th. On the 12th a reconnoissance was thrown out in front of Fort Stevens, to ascertain the enemy's position and force. A severe skirmish ensued, in which we lost about two hundred and eighty in killed and wounded. The enemy's loss was probably greater. He commenced retreating during the night. Learning the exact condition of affairs at Washington, I requested by telegraph, at forty-five minutes past eleven P.M., on the 12th, the assignment of Major-General H. G. Wright to the command of all the troops that could be made available to operate in the field against the enemy, and directed that he should get outside of the trenches with all the force he could, and push Early to the last moment. General Wright commenced the pursuit on the 13th; on the 18th the enemy was overtaken at Snicker's Ferry, on the Shenandoah, when a sharp skirmish occurred; and on the 20th, General Averell encountered and defeated a portion of the rebel army at Winchester, capturing four pieces of artillery and several hundred prisoners.

Learning that Early was retreating south towards Lynchburg or Richmond, I directed that the 6th and 19th corps be got back to the armies operating against Richmond, so that they might be used in a movement against Lee before the return of the troops sent by him into the valley; and that Hunter should remain in the Shenandoah Valley, keeping between any force of the enemy and Washington, acting on the defensive as much as possible. I felt that if the enemy had any notion of returning, the fact would be developed before the 6th and 19th corps could leave Washington. Subsequently, the 19th corps was excepted from the order to return to the James.

About the 25th it became evident that the enemy was again advancing upon Maryland and Pennsylvania, and the 6th corps, then at Washington, was ordered back to the vicinity of Harper's Ferry. The rebel force moved down the valley, and sent a raiding party into Pennsylvania which on the 30th burned Chambersburg, and then retreated, pursued by our cavalry, towards Cumberland. They were met and defeated by General Kelley, and with diminished numbers escaped into the mountains of West Virginia. From the time of the first raid the telegraph wires were frequently down between Washington and City Point, making it necessary to transmit messages a part of the way by boat. It took from twenty-four to thirty-six hours to get dispatches through and return answers back; so that often orders would be given, and then information would be received showing a different state of facts from those on which they were based, causing a confusion and apparent contradiction of orders that must have considerably embarrassed those who had to execute them, and rendered operations against the enemy less effective than they otherwise would have been. To remedy this evil, it was evident to my mind that some person should have the supreme command of all the forces in the Departments of West Virginia, Washington, Susquehanna, and the Middle Department, and I so recommended.

On the 2d of August, I ordered General Sheridan to report in person to Major-General Halleck, chief of staff, at Washington, with a view to his assignment to the command of all the forces against Early. At this time the enemy was concentrated in the neighborhood of Winchester, while our forces, under General Hunter, were concentrated on the Monocacy, at the crossing of the Baltimore and Ohio Railroad, leaving open to the enemy Western Maryland and Southern Pennsylvania. From where I was, I hesitated to give positive orders for the movement of our forces at Monocacy, lest by so doing I should expose Washington. Therefore, on the 4th, I left City Point to visit Hunter's command, and determine for myself what was best to be done. On arrival there, and after consultation with General Hunter, I issued to him the following instructions:

> "MONOCACY BRIDGE, MARYLAND,
> *August* 5, 1864—8 P.M.
>
> "GENERAL:—Concentrate all your available force without delay in the vicinity of Harper's Ferry, leaving only such railroad guards and garrisons for public property as may be necessary. Use, in this concentrating, the railroad, if by so doing time can be saved. From Harper's Ferry, if it is found that the enemy has moved north of the Potomac in large force, push north, following him and attacking him wherever found; follow him, if driven south of the Potomac, as long as it is safe to do so. If it is ascertained that the enemy has but a small force north of the Potomac, then push south with the main force, detaching under a competent commander a sufficient force to look after the raiders, and drive them to their homes. In detaching such a force, the brigade of cavalry now *en route* from Washington *via* Rockville may be taken into account.
>
> "There are now on their way to join you three other brigades of the best cavalry, numbering at least five thousand men and horses. These will be instructed, in the absence of further orders, to join you by the south side of the Potomac. One brigade will probably start to-morrow. In pushing up the Shenandoah Valley, where it is expected you will have to go first or last, it is desirable that nothing should be left to invite the enemy to return. Take all provisions, forage, and stock wanted for the use of your command; such as cannot be consumed, destroy. It is not desirable that the buildings should be

destroyed—they should rather be protected; but the people should be informed that, so long as an army can subsist among them, recurrences of these raids must be expected, and we are determined to stop them at all hazards.

"Bear in mind, the object is to drive the enemy south; and to do this, you want to keep him always in sight. Be guided in your course by the course he takes.

"Make your own arrangements for supplies of all kinds, giving regular vouchers for such as may be taken from loyal citizens in the country through which you march.

"U. S. GRANT, Lieutenant-General.
"MAJOR-GENERAL D. HUNTER."

The troops were immediately put in motion, and the advance reached Halltown that night.

General Hunter having, in our conversation, expressed a willingness to be relieved from command, I telegraphed to have General Sheridan, then at Washington, sent to Harper's Ferry by the morning train, with orders to take general command of all the troops in the field, and to call on General Hunter at Monocacy, who would turn over to him my letter of instructions. I remained at Monocacy until General Sheridan arrived, on the morning of the 6th, and, after a conference with him in relation to military affairs in that vicinity, I returned to City Point by way of Washington.

On the 7th of August, the Middle Department, and the Departments of West Virginia, Washington, and Susquehanna, were constituted into the "Middle Military Division," and Major-General Sheridan was assigned to temporary command of the same.

Two divisions of cavalry, commanded by Generals Torbert and Wilson, were sent to Sheridan from the Army of the Potomac. The first reached him at Harper's Ferry about the 11th of August.

His operations during the month of August and the fore part of September were both of an offensive and defensive character, resulting in many severe skirmishes, principally by the cavalry, in which we were generally successful, but no general engagement took place. The two armies lay in such a position—the enemy on the west bank of the Opequon Creek covering Winchester, and our forces in front of Berryville—that either could bring on a battle at any time. Defeat to us would lay open to the enemy the States of Maryland and Pennsylvania for long distances before another army could be interposed to check him. Under these circumstances I hesitated about allowing the initiative to be taken. Finally, the use of the Baltimore and Ohio Railroad, and the Chesapeake and Ohio Canal, which were both obstructed by the enemy, became so indispensably necessary to us, and the importance of relieving Pennsylvania and Maryland from continuously threatened invasion so great, that I determined the risk should be taken. But fearing to telegraph the order for an attack without knowing more than I did of General Sheridan's feelings as to what would be the probable result, I left City Point on the 15th of September to visit him at his headquarters, to decide, after conference with him, what should be done. I met him at Charlestown, and he pointed out so distinctly how each army lay; what he could do the moment he was authorized, and expressed such confidence of success, that I saw there were but two words of instructions necessary—Go in! For the conveniences of forage, the teams for supplying the army were kept at Harper's Ferry. I asked him if he could get out his teams and supplies in time to make an attack on the ensuing Tuesday morning. His reply was, that he could before daylight on Monday. He was off promptly to time, and I may here add, that the result was such that I have never since deemed it necessary to visit General Sheridan before giving him orders.

Early on the morning of the 19th, General Sheridan attacked General Early at the crossing on the Opequon Creek, and after a most sanguinary and bloody battle, lasting until five o'clock in the evening, defeated him with heavy loss, carrying his entire position from Opequon Creek to Winchester, capturing several thousand prisoners and five pieces of artillery. The enemy rallied, and made a stand in a strong position at Fisher's Hill, where he was attacked, and again defeated with heavy loss on the 20th [22d]. Sheridan pursued him with great energy through Harrisonburg, Staunton, and the gaps of the Blue Ridge. After stripping the upper valley of most of the supplies and provisions for the rebel army, he returned to Strasburg, and took position on the north side of Cedar Creek.

Having received considerable reinforcements, General Early again returned to the valley, and, on the 9th of October, his cavalry encountered ours near Strasburg, where the rebels were defeated, with the loss of eleven pieces of artillery and three hundred and fifty prisoners. On the night of the 18th, the enemy crossed the mountains which separate the branches of the Shenandoah, forded the North Fork, and early on the morning of the 19th, under cover of the darkness and the fog, surprised and turned our left flank, and captured the batteries which enfiladed our whole line. Our troops fell back with heavy loss and in much confusion, but were finally rallied between Middletown and Newtown. At this juncture, General Sheridan, who was at Winchester when the battle commenced, arrived on the field, arranged his lines just in time to repulse a heavy attack of the enemy, and immediately assuming the offensive, he attacked in turn with great vigor. The enemy was defeated with great slaughter, and the loss of most of his artillery and trains, and the trophies he had captured in the morning. The wreck of his army escaped during the night, and fled in the direction of Staunton and Lynchburg. Pursuit was made to Mount Jackson. Thus ended this, the enemy's last attempt to invade the North *via* the Shenandoah Valley. I was now enabled to return the 6th corps to the Army of the Potomac, and to send one division from Sheridan's army to the Army of the James, and another to Savannah, Georgia, to hold Sherman's new acquisitions on the sea-coast, and thus enable him to move without detaching from his force for that purpose.

Reports from various sources led me to believe that the enemy had detached three divisions from Petersburg to reinforce Early in the Shenandoah Valley. I therefore sent the 2d corps and Gregg's division of cavalry, of the Army of the Potomac, and a force of General Butler's army, on the night of the 13th of August, to threaten Richmond from the north side of the James, to prevent him from sending troops away, and, if possible, to draw back those sent. In this move we captured six pieces of artillery and several hundred prisoners, detained troops that were under marching orders, and ascertained that but one division (Kershaw's), of the three reputed detached, had gone.

The enemy having withdrawn heavily from Petersburg to resist this movement, the 5th corps, General Warren commanding, was moved out on the 18th, and took possession of the Weldon Railroad. During the day he had considerable fighting. To regain possession of the road, the enemy made repeated and desperate assaults, but was each time repulsed with great loss. On the night of the 20th, the troops on the north side of the James were withdrawn, and Hancock and Gregg returned to the front at Petersburg. On the 25th, the 2d corps and Gregg's division of cavalry, while at Reams's Station destroying the railroad, were attacked, and after desperate fighting, a part of our line gave way, and five pieces of artillery fell into the hands of the enemy.

By the 12th of September, a branch railroad was completed from the City Point and Petersburg Railroad to the Weldon Railroad, enabling us to supply, without difficulty, in all weather, the army in front of Petersburg.

The extension of our lines across the Weldon Railroad compelled the enemy to so extend his, that it seemed he could have but few troops north of the James for the defence of Richmond. On the night of the 28th, the 10th corps, Major-General Birney, and the 18th corps, Major-General Ord commanding, of General Butler's army, were crossed to the north side of the James, and advanced on the morning of the 29th, carrying the very strong fortifications and in-trenchments below Chaffin's Farm, known as Fort Harrison, captur-ing fifteen pieces of artillery, and the New Market Road and intrenchments. This success was followed up by a gallant assault upon Fort Gilmer, immediately in front of the Chaffin Farm fortifi-cations, in which we were repulsed with heavy loss. Kautz's cavalry was pushed forward on the road to the right of this, supported by infantry, and reached the enemy's inner line, but was unable to get further. The position captured from the enemy was so threatening to Richmond, that I determined to hold it. The enemy made several desperate attempts to dislodge us, all of which were unsuccessful, and for which he paid dearly. On the morning of the 30th, General Meade sent out a reconnoissance, with a view to attacking the ene-my's line, if it was found sufficiently weakened by withdrawal of troops to the north side. In this reconnoissance we captured and held the enemy's works near Poplar Spring Church. In the after-noon, troops moving to get to the left of the point gained were attacked by the enemy in heavy force, and compelled to fall back until supported by the forces holding the captured works. Our cav-alry under Gregg was also attacked, but repulsed the enemy with great loss.

On the 7th of October, the enemy attacked Kautz's cavalry north of the James, and drove it back with heavy loss in killed, wounded, and prisoners, and the loss of all the artillery—eight or nine pieces. This he followed up by an attack on our intrenched infantry line, but was repulsed with severe slaughter. On the 13th, a reconnoissance was sent out by General Butler, with a view to drive the enemy from some new works he was constructing, which resulted in very heavy loss to us.

On the 27th, the Army of the Potomac, leaving only sufficient men to hold its fortified line, moved by the enemy's right flank. The 2d corps, followed by two divisions of the 5th corps, with the cavalry in advance and covering our left flank, forced a passage of Hatcher's Run, and moved up the south side of it towards the South Side Railroad, until the 2d corps and part of the cavalry reached the Boyd-ton Plank Road where it crosses Hatcher's Run. At this point we were six miles distant from the South Side Railroad, which I had hoped by this movement to reach and hold. But finding that we had not reached the end of the enemy's fortifications, and no place pre-senting itself for a successful assault by which he might be doubled up and shortened, I determined to withdraw to within our fortified line. Orders were given accordingly. Immediately upon receiving a report that General Warren had connected with General Hancock, I returned to my headquarters. Soon after I left the enemy moved out across Hatcher's Run, in the gap between Generals Hancock and Warren, which was not closed as reported, and made a desperate attack on General Hancock's right and rear. General Hancock immediately faced his corps to meet it, and after a bloody combat drove the enemy within his works, and withdrew that night to his old position.

In support of this movement, General Butler made a demonstration on the north side of the James, and attacked the enemy on the Williamsburg Road, and also on the York River Railroad. In the former he was unsuccessful; in the latter he succeeded in carrying a work which was afterwards abandoned, and his forces withdrawn to their former positions.

From this time forward the operations in front of Petersburg and Richmond, until the spring campaign of 1865, were confined to the defence and extension of our lines, and to offensive movements for crippling the enemy's lines of communication, and to prevent his detaching any considerable force to send south. By the 7th of February, our lines were extended to Hatcher's Run, and the Weldon Railroad had been destroyed to Hicksford.

General Sherman moved from Chattanooga on the 6th of May, with the Armies of the Cumberland, Tennessee, and Ohio, commanded, respectively, by Generals Thomas, McPherson, and Schofield, upon Johnston's army at Dalton; but finding the enemy's position at Buzzard's Roost, covering Dalton, too strong to be assaulted, General McPherson was sent through Snake Gap to turn it, while Generals Thomas and Schofield threatened it in front and on the north. This movement was successful. Johnston, finding his retreat likely to be cut off, fell back to his fortified position at Resaca, where he was attacked on the afternoon of May 15th. A heavy battle ensued. During the night the enemy retreated south. Late on the 17th, his rear-guard was overtaken near Adairsville, and heavy skirmishing followed. The next morning, however, he had again disappeared. He was vigorously pursued, and was overtaken at Cassville on the 19th, but during the ensuing night retreated across the Etowah. While these operations were going on, General Jefferson C. Davis's division of Thomas's army was sent to Rome, capturing it with its forts and artillery, and its valuable mills and foundries. General Sherman, having given his army a few days' rest at this point, again put it in motion on the 23d, for Dallas, with a view of turning the difficult pass at Allatoona. On the afternoon of the 25th, the advance, under General Hooker, had a severe battle with the enemy, driving him back to New Hope Church, near Dallas. Several sharp encounters occurred at this point. The most important was on the 28th, when the enemy assaulted General McPherson at Dallas, but received a terrible and bloody repulse.

On the 4th of June, Johnston abandoned his intrenched position at New Hope Church, and retreated to the strong positions of Kenesaw, Pine, and Lost mountains. He was forced to yield the two last-named places, and concentrate his army on Kenesaw, where, on the 27th, Generals Thomas and McPherson made a determined but unsuccessful assault. On the night of the 2d of July, Sherman commenced moving his army by the right flank, and on the morning of the 3d, found that the enemy, in consequence of this movement, had abandoned Kenesaw and retreated across the Chattahoochee.

General Sherman remained on the Chattahoochee to give his men rest and get up stores until the 17th of July, when he resumed his operations, crossed the Chattahoochee, destroyed a large portion of the railroad to Augusta, and drove the enemy back to Atlanta. At this place General Hood succeeded General Johnston in command of the rebel army, and assuming the offensive-defensive policy, made several severe attacks upon Sherman in the vicinity of Atlanta, the most desperate and determined of which was on the 22d of July. About one P.M. of this day the brave, accomplished, and noble-hearted McPherson was killed. General Logan succeeded him, and commanded the Army of the Tennessee through this desperate battle, and until he was superseded by Major-General Howard, on the 26th, with the same success and ability that had characterized him in the command of a corps or division.

In all these attacks the enemy was repulsed with great loss. Finding it impossible to entirely invest the place, General Sherman, after securing his line of communications across the Chattahoochee, moved his main force round by the enemy's left flank upon the Montgomery and Macon roads, to draw the enemy from his fortifications. In this he succeeded, and after defeating the enemy near Rough-and-Ready, Jonesboro, and Lovejoy's, forcing him to retreat to the south, on the 2d of September occupied Atlanta, the objective point of his campaign.

About the time of this move, the rebel cavalry, under Wheeler, attempted to cut his communications in the rear, but was repulsed at Dalton, and driven into East Tennessee, whence it proceeded west to McMinnville, Murfreesboro', and Franklin, and was finally driven south of the Tennessee. The damage done by this raid was repaired in a few days.

During the partial investment of Atlanta, General Rousseau joined General Sherman with a force of cavalry from Decatur, having made a successful raid upon the Atlanta and Montgomery Railroad, and its branches near Opelika. Cavalry raids were also made by Generals McCook, Garrard, and Stoneman, to cut the remaining railroad communication with Atlanta. The first two were successful—the latter, disastrous.

General Sherman's movement from Chattanooga to Atlanta was prompt, skilful, and brilliant. The history of his flank movements and battles during that memorable campaign will ever be read with an interest unsurpassed by anything in history.

His own report, and those of his subordinate commanders, accompanying it, give the details of that most successful campaign.

He was dependent for the supply of his armies upon a single-track railroad from Nashville to the point where he was operating. This passed the entire distance through a hostile country, and every foot of it had to be protected by troops. The cavalry force of the enemy under Forrest, in Northern Mississippi, was evidently waiting for Sherman to advance far enough into the mountains of Georgia, to make a retreat disastrous, to get upon this line and destroy it beyond the possibility of further use. To guard against this danger, Sherman left what he supposed to be a sufficient force to operate against Forrest in West Tennessee. He directed General Washburn, who commanded there, to send Brigadier-General S. D. Sturgis in command of this force to attack him. On the morning of the 10th of June, General Sturgis met the enemy near Guntown, Mississippi, was badly beaten, and driven back in utter rout and confusion to Memphis, a distance of about one hundred miles, hotly pursued by the enemy. By this, however, the enemy was defeated in his designs upon Sherman's line of communications. The persistency with which he followed up this success exhausted him, and made a season for rest and repairs necessary. In the meantime, Major-General A. J. Smith, with the troops of the Army of the Tennessee that had been sent by General Sherman to General Banks, arrived at Memphis on their return from Red River, where they had done most excellent service. He was directed by General Sherman to immediately take the offensive against Forrest. This he did with the promptness and effect which has characterized his whole military career. On the 14th of July, he met the enemy at Tupelo, Mississippi, and whipped him badly. The fighting continued through three days. Our loss was small compared with that of the enemy. Having accomplished the object of his expedition, General Smith returned to Memphis.

During the months of March and April this same force under Forrest annoyed us considerably. On the 24th of March it captured Union City, Kentucky, and its garrison, and on the 24th attacked

Paducah, commanded by Colonel S. G. Hicks, 40th Illinois Volunteers. Colonel H., having but a small force, withdrew to the forts near the river, from where he repulsed the enemy and drove him from the place.

On the 13th of April, part of this force, under the rebel General Buford, summoned the garrison of Columbus, Kentucky, to surrender, but received for reply from Colonel Lawrence, 34th New Jersey Volunteers, that being placed there by his Government with adequate force to hold his post and repel all enemies from it, surrender was out of the question.

On the morning of the same day Forrest attacked Fort Pillow, Tennessee, garrisoned by a detachment of Tennessee cavalry and the 1st Regiment Alabama colored troops, commanded by Major Booth. The garrison fought bravely until about three o'clock in the afternoon, when the enemy carried the works by assault; and, after our men threw down their arms, proceeded to an inhuman and merciless massacre of the garrison.

On the 14th, General Buford, having failed at Columbus, appeared before Paducah, but was again driven off.

Guerillas and raiders, seemingly emboldened by Forrest's operations, were also very active in Kentucky. The most noted of these was Morgan. With a force of from two to three thousand cavalry, he entered the State through Pound Gap in the latter part of May. On the 11th of June they attacked and captured Cynthiana, with its entire garrison. On the 12th he was overtaken by General Burbridge, and completely routed with heavy loss, and was finally driven out of the State. This notorious guerilla was afterwards surprised and killed near Greenville, Tennessee, and his command captured and dispersed by General Gillem.

In the absence of official reports of the commencement of the Red River expedition, except so far as relates to the movements of the troops sent by General Sherman under General A. J. Smith, I am unable to give the date of its starting. The troops under General Smith, comprising two divisions of the 16th and a detachment of the 17th army corps, left Vicksburg on the 10th of March, and reached the designated point on Red River one day earlier than that appointed by General Banks. The rebel forces at Fort de Russy, thinking to defeat him, left the fort on the 14th to give him battle in the open field; but, while occupying the enemy with skirmishing and demonstrations, Smith pushed forward to Fort de Russy, which had been left with a weak garrison, and captured it with its garrison—about three hundred and fifty men, eleven pieces of artillery, and many small-arms. Our loss was but slight. On the 15th he pushed forward to Alexandria, which place he reached on the 18th. On the 21st he had an engagement with the enemy at Henderson's Hill, in which he defeated him, capturing two hundred and ten prisoners and four pieces of artillery.

On the 28th, he again attacked and defeated the enemy under the rebel General Taylor, at Cane River. By the 26th, General Banks had assembled his whole army at Alexandria, and pushed forward to Grand Ecore. On the morning of April 6th he moved from Grand Ecore. On the afternoon of the 7th, he advanced and met the enemy near Pleasant Hill, and drove him from the field. On the same afternoon the enemy made a stand eight miles beyond Pleasant Hill, but was again compelled to retreat. On the 8th, at Sabine Cross Roads and Peach Hill, the enemy attacked and defeated his advance, capturing nineteen pieces of artillery and an immense amount of transportation and stores. During the night, General Banks fell back to Pleasant Hill, where another battle was fought on the 9th, and the enemy repulsed with great loss. During the night, General Banks continued his retrograde movement to Grand Ecore, and thence to Alexandria, which he reached on the 27th of April. Here a serious difficulty arose in getting Admiral Porter's fleet which accompanied the expedition, over the rapids, the water having fallen so much since they passed up as to prevent their return. At the suggestion of Colonel (now Brigadier-General) Bailey, and under his superintendence, wing-dams were constructed, by which the channel was contracted so that the fleet passed down the rapids in safety.

The army evacuated Alexandria on the 14th of May, after considerable skirmishing with the enemy's advance, and reached Morganzia and Point Coupée near the end of the month. The disastrous termination of this expedition, and the lateness of the season, rendered impracticable the carrying out of my plans of a movement in force sufficient to insure the capture of Mobile.

On the 23d of March, Major-General Steele left Little Rock with the 7th army corps, to co-operate with General Banks's expedition on the Red River, and reached Arkadelphia on the 28th. On the 16th of April, after driving the enemy before him, he was joined, near Elkin's Ferry, in Washita County, by General Thayer, who had marched from Fort Smith. After several severe skirmishes, in which the enemy was defeated, General Steele reached Camden, which he occupied about the middle of April.

On learning the defeat and consequent retreat of General Banks on Red River, and the loss of one of his own trains at Mark's Mill, in Dallas County, General Steele determined to fall back to the Arkansas River. He left Camden on the 26th of April, and reached

Little Rock on the 2d of May. On the 30th of April, the enemy attacked him while crossing Saline River at Jenkins's Ferry, but was repulsed with considerable loss. Our loss was about six hundred in killed, wounded and prisoners.

Major-General Canby, who had been assigned to the command of the "Military Division of the West Mississippi," was therefore directed to send the 19th army corps to join the armies operating against Richmond, and to limit the remainder of his command to such operations as might be necessary to hold the positions and lines of communications he then occupied.

Before starting General A. J. Smith's troops back to Sherman, General Canby sent a part of it to disperse a force of the enemy that was collecting near the Mississippi River. General Smith met and defeated this force near Lake Chicot on the 5th of June. Our loss was about forty killed and seventy wounded.

In the latter part of July, General Canby sent Major-General Gordon Granger, with such forces as he could collect, to co-operate with Admiral Farragut against the defences of Mobile Bay. On the 8th of August, Fort Gaines surrendered to the combined naval and land forces. Fort Powell was blown up and abandoned.

On the 9th, Fort Morgan was invested, and, after a severe bombardment, surrendered on the 23d. The total captures amounted to one thousand four hundred and sixty-four prisoners, and one hundred and four pieces of artillery.

About the last of August, it being reported that the rebel General Price, with a force of about ten thousand men, had reached Jacksonport, on his way to invade Missouri, General A. J. Smith's command, then *en route* from Memphis to join Sherman, was ordered to Missouri. A cavalry force was also, at the same time, sent from Memphis, under command of Colonel Winslow. This made General Rosecrans's forces superior to those of Price, and no doubt was entertained he would be able to check Price and drive him back; while the forces under General Steele, in Arkansas, would cut off his retreat. On the 26th day of September, Price attacked Pilot Knob and forced the garrison to retreat, and thence moved north to the Missouri River, and continued up that river towards Kansas. General Curtis, commanding Department of Kansas, immediately collected such forces as he could to repel the invasion of Kansas, while General Rosecrans's cavalry was operating in his rear.

The enemy was brought to battle on the Big Blue and defeated, with the loss of nearly all his artillery and trains and a large number of prisoners. He made a precipitate retreat to Northern Arkansas. The impunity with which Price was enabled to roam over the State of Missouri for a long time, and the incalculable mischief done by him, shows to how little purpose a superior force may be used. There is no reason why General Rosecrans should not have concentrated his forces, and beaten and driven Price before the latter reached Pilot Knob.

September 20th, the enemy's cavalry, under Forrest, crossed the Tennessee near Waterloo, Alabama, and on the 23d attacked the garrison at Athens, consisting of six hundred men, which capitulated on the 24th. Soon after the surrender two regiments of reinforcements arrived, and after a severe fight were compelled to surrender. Forrest destroyed the railroad westward, captured the garrison at Sulphur Branch trestle, skirmished with the garrison at Pulaski on the 27th, and on the same day cut the Nashville and Chattanooga Railroad near Tullahoma and Dechard. On the morning of the 30th, one column of Forrest's command, under Buford, appeared before Huntsville, and summoned the surrender of the garrison. Receiving an answer in the negative, he remained in the vicinity of the place until next morning, when he again summoned its surrender, and received the same reply as on the night before. He withdrew in the direction of Athens, which place had been regarrisoned, and attacked it on the afternoon of the 1st of October, but without success. On the morning of the 2d he renewed his attack, but was handsomely repulsed.

Another column under Forrest appeared before Columbia on the morning of the 1st, but did not make an attack. On the morning of the 3d he moved towards Mount Pleasant. While these operations were going on, every exertion was made by General Thomas to destroy the forces under Forrest before he could recross the Tennessee, but was unable to prevent his escape to Corinth, Mississippi.

In September, an expedition under General Burbridge was sent to destroy the salt-works at Saltville, Virginia. He met the enemy on the 2d of October, about three miles and a half from Saltville, and drove him into his strongly intrenched position around the salt-works, from which he was unable to dislodge him. During the night he withdrew his command and returned to Kentucky.

General Sherman, immediately after the fall of Atlanta, put his armies in camp in and about the place, and made all preparations for refitting and supplying them for future service. The great length of road from Atlanta to the Cumberland River, however, which had to be guarded, allowed the troops but little rest.

During this time Jefferson Davis made a speech in Macon, Georgia, which was reported in the papers of the South, and soon became known to the whole country, disclosing the plans of the enemy, thus enabling General Sherman to fully meet them. He exhibited the weakness of supposing that an army that had been beaten and fearfully decimated in a vain attempt at the defensive, could successfully undertake the offensive against the army that had so often defeated it.

In execution of this plan, Hood, with this army, was soon reported to the south-west of Atlanta. Moving far to Sherman's right, he succeeded in reaching the railroad about Big Shanty, and moved north on it.

General Sherman, leaving a force to hold Atlanta, with the remainder of his army fell upon him and drove him to Gadsden, Alabama. Seeing the constant annoyance he would have with the roads to his rear if he attempted to hold Atlanta, General Sherman proposed the abandonment and destruction of that place, with all the railroads leading to it, and telegraphed me as follows:

"CENTREVILLE, GEORGIA,
October 10—noon.

"Dispatch about Wilson just received. Hood is now crossing Coosa River, twelve miles below Rome, bound west. If he passes over the Mobile and Ohio road, had I not better execute the plan of my letter sent by Colonel Porter, and leave General Thomas with the troops now in Tennessee, to defend the State? He will have an ample force when the reinforcements ordered reach Nashville.

"W. T. SHERMAN, Major-General.

"LIEUTENANT-GENERAL GRANT."

For a full understanding of the plan referred to in this dispatch, I quote from the letter sent by Colonel Porter: "I will therefore give my opinion, that your army and Canby's should be reinforced to the maximum; that after you get Wilmington, you strike for Savannah and the river; that Canby be instructed to hold the Mississippi River, and send a force to get Columbus, Georgia, either by the way of the Alabama or the Appalachicola, and that I keep Hood employed and put my army in final order for a march on Augusta, Columbia, and Charleston, to be ready as soon as Wilmington is sealed as to commerce, and the city of Savannah is in our possession." This was in reply to a letter of mine of date September 12th, in answer to a dispatch of his containing substantially the same proposition, and in which I informed him of a proposed movement against Wilmington, and of the situation in Virginia, etc.

"CITY POINT, VIRGINIA,
October 11, 1864—11 A.M.

"Your dispatch of October 10th received. Does it not look as if Hood was going to attempt the invasion of Middle Tennessee, using the Mobile and Ohio and Memphis and Charleston roads to supply his base on the Tennessee

River, about Florence or Decatur? If he does this, he ought to be met and prevented from getting north of the Tennessee River. If you were to cut loose, I do not believe you would meet Hood's army, but would be bushwhacked by all the old men and little boys, and such railroad guards as are still left at home. Hood would probably strike for Nashville, thinking that by going north he could inflict greater damage upon us than we could upon the rebels by going south. If there is any way of getting at Hood's army, I would prefer that, but I must trust to your own judgment. I find I shall not be able to send a force from here to act with you on Savannah. Your movements, therefore, will be independent of mine; at least until the fall of Richmond takes place. I am afraid Thomas, with such lines of road as he has to protect, could not prevent Hood from going north. With Wilson turned loose, with all your cavalry, you will find the rebels put much more on the defensive than heretofore.

"U. S. GRANT, Lieutenant-General.
"MAJOR-GENERAL W. T. SHERMAN."

"KINGSTON, GEORGIA,
October 11—11 A.M.
"Hood moved his army from Palmetto Station across by Dallas and Cedartown, and is now on the Coosa River, south of Rome. He threw one corps on my road at Acworth, and I was forced to follow. I hold Atlanta with the 20th corps, and have strong detachments along my line. This reduces my active force to a comparatively small army. We cannot remain here on the defensive. With the twenty-five thousand men, and the bold cavalry he has, he can constantly break my roads. I would infinitely prefer to make a wreck of the road, and of the country from Chattanooga to Atlanta, including the latter city—send back all my wounded and worthless, and with my effective army, move through Georgia, smashing things, to the sea. Hood may turn into Tennessee and Kentucky, but I believe he will be forced to follow me. Instead of my being on the defensive, I would be on the offensive; instead of guessing at what he means to do, he would have to guess at my plans. The difference in war is full twenty-five per cent. I can make Savannah, Charleston, or the mouth of the Chattahoochee.

"Answer quick, as I know we will not have the telegraph long.
"W. T. SHERMAN, Major-General.
"LIEUTENANT-GENERAL GRANT."

"CITY POINT, VIRGINIA,
October 11, 1864—11.30 P.M.
"Your dispatch of to-day received. If you are satisfied the trip to the seacoast can be made, holding the line of the Tennessee River firmly, you may make it, destroying all the railroad south of Dalton or Chattanooga, as you think best.

"U. S. GRANT, Lieutenant-General.
"MAJOR-GENERAL W. T. SHERMAN."

It was the original design to hold Atlanta, and by getting through to the coast, with a garrison left on the southern railroads, leading east and west, through Georgia, to effectually sever the east from the west. In other words, cut the would-be Confederacy in two again, as it had been cut once by our gaining possession of the Mississippi River. General Sherman's plan virtually effected this object.

General Sherman commenced at once his preparations for his proposed movement, keeping his army in position in the meantime to watch Hood. Becoming satisfied that Hood had moved westward from Gadsden across Sand Mountain, General Sherman sent the 4th corps, Major-General Stanley commanding, and the 23d corps, Major-General Schofield commanding, back to Chattanooga to report to Major-General Thomas, at Nashville, whom he had placed in command of all the troops of his military division, save the four army corps and cavalry division he designed to move with through Georgia. With the troops thus left at his disposal, there was little doubt that General Thomas could hold the line of the Tennessee, or, in the event Hood should force it, would be able to concentrate and beat him in battle. It was therefore readily consented to that Sherman should start for the sea-coast.

Having concentrated his troops at Atlanta by the 14th of November, he commenced his march, threatening both Augusta and Macon. His coming-out point could not be definitely fixed. Having to gather his subsistence as he marched through the country, it was not impossible that a force inferior to his own might compel him to head for such point as he could reach, instead of such as he might prefer. The blindness of the enemy, however, in ignoring his movement, and sending Hood's army, the only considerable force he had west of Richmond and east of the Mississippi River, northward on an offensive campaign, left the whole country open, and Sherman's route to his own choice.

How that campaign was conducted, how little opposition was met with, the condition of the country through which the armies passed, the capture of Fort McAllister, on the Savannah River, and the occupation of Savannah on the 21st of December, are all clearly set forth in General Sherman's admirable report.

Soon after General Sherman commenced his march from Atlanta, two expeditions, one from Baton Rouge, Louisiana, and one from Vicksburg, Mississippi, were started by General Canby to cut the enemy's lines of communication with Mobile and detain troops in that field. General Foster, commanding Department of the South, also sent an expedition, *via* Broad River, to destroy the railroad between Charleston and Savannah. The expedition from Vicksburg, under command of Brevet Brigadier-General E. D. Osband (colonel 3d United States colored cavalry), captured, on the 27th of November, and destroyed the Mississippi Central Railroad bridge and trestle-work over Big Black River, near Canton, thirty miles of the road, and two locomotives, besides large amounts of stores. The expedition from Baton Rouge was without favorable results. The expedition from the Department of the South, under the immediate command of Brigadier-General John P. Hatch, consisting of about five thousand men of all arms, including a brigade from the navy, proceeded up Broad River and debarked at Boyd's Neck on the 29th of November, from where it moved to strike the railroad at Grahamsville. At Honey Hill, about three miles from Grahamsville, the enemy was found and attacked in a strongly fortified position, which resulted, after severe fighting, in our repulse with a loss of seven hundred and forty-six in killed, wounded, and missing. During the night General Hatch withdrew. On the 6th of December General Foster obtained a position covering the Charleston and Savannah Railroad, between the Coosawhatchie and Tulifinny rivers.

Hood, instead of following Sherman, continued his move northward, which seemed to me to be leading to his certain doom. At all events, had I had the power to command both armies, I should not have changed the orders under which he seemed to be acting. On the 26th of October, the advance of Hood's army attacked the garrison at Decatur, Alabama, but failing to carry the place, withdrew towards Courtland, and succeeded, in the face of our cavalry, in effecting a lodgment on the north side of the Tennessee River, near Florence. On the 28th, Forrest reached the Tennessee, at Fort Heiman, and captured a gunboat and three transports. On the 2d of November he planted batteries above and below Johnsonville, on the opposite side of the river, isolating three gunboats and eight transports. On the 4th the enemy opened his batteries upon the place, and was replied to from the gunboats and the garrison. The gunboats becoming disabled were set on fire, as also were the transports, to prevent their falling into the hands of the enemy. About a million and a half dollars' worth of stores and property on the levee and in storehouses was consumed by fire. On the 5th the enemy disappeared and crossed to the north side of the Tennessee River, above Johnsonville, moving towards Clifton, and subsequently joined Hood. On the night of the 5th, General Schofield, with the advance of the 23d corps, reached Johnsonville, but finding the enemy gone, was ordered to Pulaski, and put in command of all the troops there, with instructions to watch the movements of Hood and retard his advance, but not to risk a general engagement until the arrival of

General A. J. Smith's command from Missouri, and until General Wilson could get his cavalry remounted.

On the 19th, General Hood continued his advance. General Thomas, retarding him as much as possible, fell back towards Nashville for the purpose of concentrating his command and gaining time for the arrival of reinforcements. The enemy coming up with our main force, commanded by General Schofield, at Franklin, on the 30th, assaulted our works repeatedly during the afternoon until late at night, but were in every instance repulsed. His loss in this battle was one thousand seven hundred and fifty killed, seven hundred and two prisoners, and three thousand eight hundred wounded. Among his losses were six general officers killed, six wounded, and one captured. Our entire loss was two thousand three hundred. This was the first serious opposition the enemy met with, and I am satisfied was the fatal blow to all his expectations. During the night, General Schofield fell back towards Nashville. This left the field to the enemy—not lost by battle, but voluntarily abandoned—so that General Thomas's whole force might be brought together. The enemy followed up and commenced the establishment of his line in front of Nashville on the 2d of December.

As soon as it was ascertained that Hood was crossing the Tennessee River, and that Price was going out of Missouri, General Rosecrans was ordered to send to General Thomas the troops of General A. J. Smith's command, and such other troops as he could spare. The advance of this reinforcement reached Nashville on the 30th of November.

On the morning of the 15th December, General Thomas attacked Hood in position, and, in a battle lasting two days, defeated and drove him from the field in the utmost confusion, leaving in our hands most of his artillery and many thousand prisoners, including four general officers.

Before the battle of Nashville I grew very impatient over, as it appeared to me, the unnecessary delay. This impatience was increased upon learning that the enemy had sent a force of cavalry across the Cumberland into Kentucky. I feared Hood would cross his whole army and give us great trouble there. After urging upon General Thomas the necessity of immediately assuming the offensive, I started West to superintend matters there in person. Reaching Washington City, I received General Thomas's dispatch announcing his attack upon the enemy, and the result as far as the battle had progressed. I was delighted. All fears and apprehensions were dispelled. I am not yet satisfied but that General Thomas, immediately upon the appearance of Hood before Nashville, and before he had time to fortify, should have moved out with his whole force and given him battle, instead of waiting to remount his cavalry, which delayed him until the inclemency of the weather made it impracticable to attack earlier than he did. But his final defeat of Hood was so complete, that it will be accepted as a vindication of that distinguished officer's judgment.

After Hood's defeat at Nashville he retreated, closely pursued by cavalry and infantry, to the Tennessee River, being forced to abandon many pieces of artillery and most of his transportation. On the 28th of December our advanced forces ascertained that he had made good his escape to the south side of the river.

About this time, the rains having set in heavily in Tennessee and North Alabama, making it difficult to move army transportation and artillery, General Thomas stopped the pursuit by his main force at the Tennessee River. A small force of cavalry, under Colonel W. J. Palmer, 15th Pennsylvania Volunteers, continued to follow Hood for some distance, capturing considerable transportation and the enemy's pontoon-bridge. The details of these operations will be found clearly set forth in General Thomas's report.

A cavalry expedition, under Brevet Major-General Grierson, started from Memphis on the 21st of December. On the 25th he surprised and captured Forrest's dismounted camp at Verona, Mississippi, on the Mobile and Ohio Railroad, destroyed the railroad, sixteen cars loaded with wagons and pontoons for Hood's army, four thousand new English carbines, and large amounts of public stores. On the morning of the 28th he attacked and captured a force of the enemy at Egypt, and destroyed a train of fourteen cars; thence turning to the south-west, he struck the Mississippi Central Railroad at Winona, destroyed the factories and large amounts of stores at Bankston, and the machine-shops and public property at Grenada, arriving at Vicksburg January 5th.

During these operations in Middle Tennessee, the enemy, with a force under General Breckinridge, entered East Tennessee. On the 13th of November he attacked General Gillem, near Morristown, capturing his artillery and several hundred prisoners. Gillem, with what was left of his command, retreated to Knoxville. Following up his success, Breckinridge moved to near Knoxville, but withdrew on the 18th, followed by General Ammen. Under the directions of General Thomas, General Stoneman concentrated the commands of Generals Burbridge and Gillem near Bean's Station, to operate against Breckinridge, and destroy or drive him into Virginia—destroy the salt-works at Saltville, and the railroad into Virginia as far as he could go without endangering his command. On the 12th of December he commenced his movement, capturing and dispersing the enemy's forces wherever he met them. On the 16th he struck the enemy, under Vaughn, at Marion, completely routing and pursuing him to Wytheville, capturing all his artillery, trains, and one hundred and ninety-eight prisoners; and destroyed Wytheville, with its stores and supplies, and the extensive lead-works near there. Returning to Marion, he met a force under Breckinridge, consisting, among other troops, of the garrison of Saltville, that had started in pursuit. He at once made arrangements to attack it the next morning; but morning found Breckinridge gone. He then moved directly to Saltville, and destroyed the extensive salt-works at that place, a large amount of stores, and captured eight pieces of artillery. Having thus successfully executed his instructions, he returned General Burbridge to Lexington and General Gillem to Knoxville.

Wilmington, North Carolina, was the most important sea-coast port left to the enemy through which to get supplies from abroad, and send cotton and other products out by blockade-runners, besides being a place of great strategic value. The navy had been making strenuous exertions to seal the harbor of Wilmington, but with only partial effect. The nature of the outlet of Cape Fear River was such, that it required watching for so great a distance that, without possession of the land north of New Inlet, or Fort Fisher, it was impossible for the navy to entirely close the harbor against the entrance of blockade-runners.

To secure the possession of this land required the co-operation of a land force, which I agreed to furnish. Immediately commenced the assemblage in Hampton Roads, under Admiral D. D. Porter, of the most formidable armada ever collected for concentration upon one given point. This necessarily attracted the attention of the enemy, as well as that of the loyal North; and through the imprudence of the public press, and very likely of officers of both branches of service, the exact object of the expedition became a subject of common discussion in the newspapers both North and South. The enemy, thus warned, prepared to meet it. This caused a postponement of the expedition until the later part of November, when, being again called upon by Hon. G. V. Fox, Assistant Secretary of the Navy, I agreed to furnish the men required at once, and went myself, in company with Major-General Butler, to Hampton Roads, where we had a conference with Admiral Porter as to the force required and the time of starting. A force of six thousand five hundred men was regarded as sufficient. The time of starting was not definitely arranged, but it was thought all would be ready by the 6th of December, if not before. Learning, on the 30th of

November, that Bragg had gone to Georgia, taking with him most of the forces about Wilmington, I deemed it of the utmost importance that the expedition should reach its destination before the return of Bragg, and directed General Butler to make all arrangements for the departure of Major-General Weitzel, who had been designated to command the land forces, so that the navy might not be detained one moment.

On the 6th of December, the following instructions were given:

"CITY POINT, VIRGINIA, *December* 6, 1864.

"GENERAL:—The first object of the expedition under General Weitzel is to close to the enemy the port of Wilmington. If successful in this, the second will be to capture Wilmington itself. There are reasonable grounds to hope for success, if advantage can be taken of the absence of the greater part of the enemy's forces now looking after Sherman in Georgia. The directions you have given for the numbers and equipment of the expedition are all right, except in the unimportant matter of where they embark and the amount of intrenching tools to be taken. The object of the expedition will be gained by effecting a landing on the main land between Cape Fear River and the Atlantic, north of the north entrance to the river. Should such landing be effected while the enemy still holds Fort Fisher and the batteries guarding the entrance to the river, then the troops should intrench themselves and, by co-operating with the navy, effect the reduction and capture of those places. These in our hands, the navy could enter the harbor, and the port of Wilmington would be sealed. Should Fort Fisher and the point of land on which it is built fall into the hands of our troops immediately on landing, then it will be worth the attempt to capture Wilmington by a forced march and surprise. If time is consumed in gaining the first object of the expedition, the second will become a matter of after consideration.

"The details for execution are intrusted to you and the officer immediately in command of the troops.

"Should the troops under General Weitzel fail to effect a landing at or near Fort Fisher, they will be returned to the armies operating against Richmond without delay.

"U. S. GRANT, Lieutenant-General.

"MAJOR-GENERAL B. F. BUTLER."

General Butler commanding the army from which the troops were taken for this enterprise, and the territory within which they were to operate, military courtesy required that all orders and instructions should go through him. They were so sent; but General Weitzel has since officially informed me that he never received the foregoing instructions, nor was he aware of their existence, until he read General Butler's published official report of the Fort Fisher failure, with my indorsement and papers accompanying it. I had no idea of General Butler's accompanying the expedition until the evening before it got off from Bermuda Hundred, and then did not dream but that General Weitzel had received all the instructions, and would be in command. I rather formed the idea that General Butler was actuated by a desire to witness the effect of the explosion of the powder-boat. The expedition was detained several days at Hampton Roads, awaiting the loading of the powder-boat.

The importance of getting the Wilmington expedition off without any delay, with or without the powder-boat, had been urged upon General Butler, and he advised to so notify Admiral Porter.

The expedition finally got off on the 13th of December, and arrived at the place of rendezvous, off New Inlet, near Fort Fisher, on the evening of the 15th. Admiral Porter arrived on the evening of the 18th, having put in at Beaufort to get ammunition for the monitors. The sea becoming rough, making it difficult to land troops, and the supply of water and coal being about exhausted, the transport fleet put back to Beaufort to replenish; this, with the state of the weather, delayed the return to the place of rendezvous until the 24th. The powder-boat was exploded on the morning of the 24th, before the return of General Butler from Beaufort; but it would seem, from the notice taken of it in the Southern newspapers, that the enemy were never enlightened as to the object of the explosion until they were informed by the Northern press.

On the 25th a landing was effected without opposition, and a reconnoissance, under Brevet Brigadier-General Curtis, pushed up towards the fort. But before receiving a full report of the result of this reconnoissance, General Butler, in direct violation of the instructions given, ordered the re-embarkation of the troops and the return of the expedition. The re-embarkation was accomplished by the morning of the 27th.

On the return of the expedition, officers and men — among them Brevet Major-General (then Brevet Brigadier-General) N. M. Curtis, First-Lieutenant G. W. Ross, 117th Regiment New York Volunteers, First-Lieutenant William H. Walling, and Second-Lieutenant George Simpson, 142d New York Volunteers — voluntarily reported to me that when recalled they were nearly into the fort, and, in their opinion, it could have been taken without much loss.

Soon after the return of the expedition, I received a dispatch from the Secretary of the Navy, and a letter from Admiral Porter, informing me that the fleet was still off Fort Fisher, and expressing the conviction that, under a proper leader, the place could be taken. The natural supposition with me was, that when the troops abandoned the expedition, the navy would do so also. Finding it had not, however, I answered on the 30th of December, advising Admiral Porter to hold on, and that I would send a force and make another attempt to take the place. This time I selected Brevet Major-General (now Major-General) A. H. Terry to command the expedition. The troops composing it consisted of the same that composed the former, with the addition of a small brigade, numbering about one thousand five hundred, and a small siege train. The latter it was never found necessary to land. I communicated direct to the commander of the expedition the following instructions:

"CITY POINT, VIRGINIA, *January* 3, 1865.

"GENERAL:—The expedition intrusted to your command has been fitted out to renew the attempt to capture Fort Fisher, N. C., and Wilmington ultimately, if the fort falls. You will then proceed with as little delay as possible to the naval fleet lying off Cape Fear River, and report the arrival of yourself and command to Admiral D. D. Porter, commanding North Atlantic Blockading Squadron.

"It is exceedingly desirable that the most complete understanding should exist between yourself and the naval commander. I suggest, therefore, that you consult with Admiral Porter freely, and get from him the part to be performed by each branch of the public service, so that there may be unity of action. It would be well to have the whole programme laid down in writing. I have served with Admiral Porter, and know that you can rely on his judgment and his nerve to undertake what he proposes. I would, therefore, defer to him as much as is consistent with your own responsibilities. The first object to be attained is to get a firm position on the spit of land on which Fort Fisher is built, from which you can operate against that fort. You want to look to the practicability of receiving your supplies, and to defending yourself against superior forces sent against you by any of the avenues left open to the enemy. If such a position can be obtained, the siege of Fort Fisher will not be abandoned until its reduction is accomplished, or another plan of campaign is ordered from these headquarters.

"My own views are, that if you effect a landing, the navy ought to run a portion of their fleet into Cape Fear River, while the balance of it operates on the outside. Land forces cannot invest Fort Fisher, or cut it off from supplies or reinforcements, while the river is in possession of the enemy.

"A siege-train will be loaded on vessels and sent to Fort Monroe, in readiness to be sent to you if required. All other supplies can be drawn from Beaufort as you need them.

"Keep the fleet of vessels with you until your position is assured. When you find they can be spared, order them back, or such of them as you can spare, to Fort Monroe, to report for orders.

"In case of failure to effect a landing, bring your command back to Beaufort, and report to these headquarters for further instructions. You will not debark at Beaufort until so directed.

"General Sheridan has been ordered to send a division of troops to Baltimore and place them on sea-going vessels. These troops will be brought to

Fort Monroe and kept there on the vessels until you are heard from. Should you require them, they will be sent to you.

"U.S. GRANT, Lieutenant-General.
"Brevet Major-General A. H. Terry."

Lieutenant-Colonel C. B. Comstock, aide-de-camp (now brevet brigadier-general), who accompanied the former expedition, was assigned, in orders, as chief-engineer to this.

It will be seen that these instructions did not differ materially from those given for the first expedition; and that in neither instance was there an order to assault Fort Fisher. This was a matter left entirely to the discretion of the commanding officer.

The expedition sailed from Fort Monroe on the morning of the 6th, arriving at the rendezvous, off Beaufort, on the 8th, where, owing to the difficulties of the weather, it lay until the morning of the 12th, when it got under way and reached its destination that evening. Under cover of the fleet, the disembarkation of the troops commenced on the morning of the 13th, and by three o'clock P.M. was completed without loss. On the 14th a reconnoissance was pushed to within five hundred yards of Fort Fisher, and a small advance work taken possession of and turned into a defensive line against any attempt that might be made from the fort. This reconnoissance disclosed the fact that the front of the work had been seriously injured by the navy fire. In the afternoon of the 15th the fort was assaulted, and after most desperate fighting was captured, with its entire garrison and armament. Thus was secured, by the combined efforts of the navy and army, one of the most important successes of the war. Our loss was: killed, one hundred and ten; wounded, five hundred and thirty-six. On the 16th and 17th the enemy abandoned and blew up Fort Caswell and the works on Smith's Island, which were immediately occupied by us. This gave us entire control of the mouth of the Cape Fear River.

At my request, Major-General B. F. Butler was relieved, and Major-General E. O. C. Ord assigned to the Department of Virginia and North Carolina.

The defence of the line of the Tennessee no longer requiring the force which had beaten and nearly destroyed the only army now threatening it, I determined to find other fields of operation for General Thomas's surplus troops—fields from which they would cooperate with other movements. General Thomas was therefore directed to collect all troops, not essential to hold his communications at Eastport, in readiness for orders. On the 7th of January, General Thomas was directed, if he was assured of the departure of Hood south from Corinth, to send General Schofield with his corps east with as little delay as possible. This direction was promptly complied with, and the advance of the corps reached Washington on the 23d of the same month, whence it was sent to Fort Fisher and New Bern. On the 26th he was directed to send General A. J. Smith's command and a division of cavalry to report to General Canby. By the 7th of February the whole force was *en route* for its destination.

The State of North Carolina was constituted into a military department, and General Schofield assigned to command, and placed under the orders of Major-General Sherman. The following instructions were given him:

"City Point, Va., *January* 31, 1865.

"General: — * * * Your movements are intended as co-operative with Sherman's through the States of South and North Carolina. The first point to be attained is to secure Wilmington. Goldsboro' will then be your objective point, moving either from Wilmington or New Bern, or both, as you deem best. Should you not be able to reach Goldsboro', you will advance on the line or lines of railway connecting that place with the sea-coast—as near to it as you can, building the road behind you. The enterprise under you has two objects: the first is to give General Sherman material aid, if needed, in his march north; the second, to open a base of supplies for him on his line of march. As soon, therefore, as you can determine which of the two points, Wilmington or New Bern, you can best use for throwing supplies from, to the interior, you will commence the accumulation of twenty days' rations and forage for sixty thousand men and twenty thousand animals. You will get of these as many as you can house and protect to such point in the interior as you may be able to occupy. I believe General Palmer has received some instructions direct from General Sherman on the subject of securing supplies for his army. You will learn what steps he has taken, and be governed in your requisitions accordingly. A supply of ordnance stores will also be necessary.

"Make all requisitions upon the chiefs of their respective departments in the field with me at City Point. Communicate with me by every opportunity, and should you deem it necessary at any time, send a special boat to Fortress Monroe, from which point you can communicate by telegraph.

"The supplies referred to in these instructions are exclusive of those required for your own command.

"The movements of the enemy may justify, or even make it your imperative duty, to cut loose from your base, and strike for the interior to aid Sherman. In such case you will act on your own judgment without waiting for instructions. You will report, however, what you purpose doing. The details for carrying out these instructions are necessarily left to you. I would urge, however, if I did not know that you are already fully alive to the importance of it, prompt action. Sherman may be looked for in the neighborhood of Goldsboro' any time from the 22d to the 28th of February; this limits your time very materially.

"If rolling-stock is not secured in the capture of Wilmington, it can be supplied from Washington. A large force of railroad men have already been sent to Beaufort, and other mechanics will go to Fort Fisher in a day or two. On this point I have informed you by telegraph.

"U. S. GRANT, Lieutenant-General.

"MAJOR GENERAL J. M. SCHOFIELD."

Previous to giving these instructions I had visited Fort Fisher, accompanied by General Schofield, for the purpose of seeing for myself the condition of things, and personally conferring with General Terry and Admiral Porter as to what was best to be done.

Anticipating the arrival of General Sherman at Savannah—his army entirely foot-loose, Hood being then before Nashville, Tennessee, the Southern railroads destroyed, so that it would take several months to re-establish a through line from west to east, and regarding the capture of Lee's army as the most important operation towards closing the rebellion—I sent orders to General Sherman on the 6th of December, that after establishing a base on the sea-coast, with necessary garrison, to include all his artillery and cavalry, to come by water to City Point with the balance of his command.

On the 18th of December, having received information of the defeat and utter rout of Hood's army by General Thomas, and that, owing to the great difficulty of procuring ocean transportation, it would take over two months to transport Sherman's army, and doubting whether he might not contribute as much towards the desired result by operating from where he was, I wrote to him to that effect, and asked him for his views as to what would be best to do. A few days after this I received a communication from General Sherman, of date 16th December, acknowledging the receipt of my order of the 6th, and informing me of his preparations to carry it into effect as soon as he could get transportation. Also that he had expected, upon reducing Savannah, instantly to march to Columbia, South Carolina, thence to Raleigh, and thence to report to me; but that this would consume about six weeks' time after the fall of Savannah, whereas by sea he could probably reach me by the middle of January. The confidence he manifested in this letter of being able to march up and join me pleased me, and, without waiting for a reply to my letter of the 18th, I directed him, on the 28th of December, to make preparations to start, as he proposed, without delay, to break up the railroads in North and South Carolina, and join the armies operating against Richmond as soon as he could.

On the 21st of January I informed General Sherman that I had ordered the 23d corps, Major-General Schofield commanding, east; that it numbered about twenty-one thousand men; that we had at Fort Fisher, about eight thousand men; at New Bern, about four thousand; that if Wilmington was captured, General Schofield would go there; if not, he would be sent to New Bern; that, in either event, all the surplus force at both points would move to the interior towards Goldsboro', in co-operation with his movement; that from either point railroad communication could be run out; and that all these troops would be subject to his orders as he came into communication with them.

In obedience to his instructions, General Schofield proceeded to reduce Wilmington, North Carolina, in co-operation with the navy under Admiral Porter, moving his forces up both sides of the Cape Fear River. Fort Anderson, the enemy's main defence on the west bank of the river, was occupied on the morning of the 19th, the enemy having evacuated it after our appearance before it.

After fighting on 20th and 21st, our troops entered Wilmington on the morning of the 22d, the enemy having retreated towards Goldsboro' during the night. Preparations were at once made for a movement on Goldsboro' in two columns—one from Wilmington, and the other from New Bern—and to repair the railroad leading there from each place, as well as to supply General Sherman by Cape Fear River, towards Fayetteville, if it became necessary. The column from New Bern was attacked on the 8th of March, at Wise's Forks, and driven back with the loss of several hundred prisoners. On the 11th the enemy renewed his attack upon our intrenched position, but was repulsed with severe loss, and fell back during the night. On the 14th the Neuse River was crossed and Kinston occupied, and on the 21st Goldsboro' was entered. The column from Wilmington reached Cox's Bridge, on the Neuse River, ten miles above Goldsboro', on the 22d.

By the 1st of February, General Sherman's whole army was in motion from Savannah. He captured Columbia, South Carolina, on the 17th; thence moved on Goldsboro', North Carolina, *via* Fayetteville, reaching the latter place on the 12th of March, opening up communication with General Schofield by way of Cape Fear River. On the 15th he resumed his march on Goldsboro'. He met a force of the enemy at Averysboro', and after a severe fight defeated and compelled it to retreat. Our loss in this engagement was about six hundred. The enemy's loss was much greater. On the 18th the combined forces of the enemy, under Joe Johnston, attacked his advance at Bentonville, capturing three guns and driving it back upon the main body. General Slocum, who was in the advance, ascertaining that the whole of Johnston's army was in the front, arranged his troops on the defensive, intrenched himself and awaited reinforcements, which were pushed forward. On the night of the 21st the enemy retreated to Smithfield, leaving his dead and wounded in our hands. From there Sherman continued to Goldsboro', which place had been occupied by General Schofield on the 21st (crossing the Neuse River ten miles above there, at Cox's Bridge, where General Terry had got possession and thrown a pontoon-bridge on the 22d), thus forming a junction with the columns from New Bern and Wilmington.

Among the important fruits of this campaign was the fall of Charleston, South Carolina. It was evacuated by the enemy on the night of the 17th of February, and occupied by our forces on the 18th.

On the morning of the 31st of January, General Thomas was directed to send a cavalry expedition, under General Stoneman, from East Tennessee, to penetrate South Carolina well down towards Columbia, to destroy the railroads and military resources of the country, and return, if he was able, to East Tennessee by way of Salisbury, North Carolina, releasing our prisoners there, if possible. Of the feasibility of this latter, however, General Stoneman was to judge. Sherman's movements, I had no doubt, would attract the attention of all the force the enemy could collect, and facilitate the execution of this. General Stoneman was so late in making his start on this expedition (and Sherman having passed out of the State of South Carolina), on the 27th of February I directed General Thomas to change his course, and order him to repeat his raid of last fall, destroying the railroad towards Lynchburg as far as he could. This would keep him between our garrisons in East Tennessee and the enemy. I regarded it not impossible that in the event of the enemy being driven from Richmond, he might fall back to Lynchburg and attempt a raid north through East Tennessee. On the 14th of February the following communication was sent to General Thomas:

"CITY POINT, VA., *February* 14, 1865.

"General Canby is preparing a movement from Mobile Bay against Mobile and the interior of Alabama. His force will consist of about twenty thousand men, besides A. J. Smith's command. The cavalry you have sent to Canby will be debarked at Vicksburg. It, with the available cavalry already in that section, will move from there eastward, in co-operation. Hood's army has been terribly reduced by the severe punishment you gave it in Tennessee, by desertion consequent upon their defeat, and now by the withdrawal of many of them to oppose Sherman. (I take it a large portion of the infantry has been so withdrawn. It is so asserted in the Richmond papers, and a member of the rebel Congress said a few days since in a speech, that one-half of it had been brought to South Carolina to oppose Sherman.) This being true, or even if it is not true, Canby's movement will attract all the attention of the enemy, and leave the advance from your standpoint easy. I think it advisable, therefore, that you prepare as much of a cavalry force as you can spare, and hold it in readiness to go south. The object would be threefold: first, to attract as much of the enemy's force as possible, to insure success to Canby; second, to destroy the enemy's line of communications and military resources; third, to destroy or capture their forces brought into the field. Tuscaloosa and Selma would probably be the points to direct the expedition against. This, however, would not be so important as the mere fact of penetrating deep into Alabama. Discretion should be left to the officer commanding the expedition to go where, according to the information he may receive, he will best secure the objects named above.

"Now that your force has been so much depleted, I do not know what number of men you can put into the field. If not more than five thousand men, however, all cavalry, I think it will be sufficient. It is not desirable that you should start this expedition until the one leaving Vicksburg has been three or four days out, or even a week. I do not know when it will start, but will inform you by telegraph as soon as I learn. If you should hear through other sources before hearing from me, you can act on the information received.

"To insure success your cavalry should go with as little wagon-train as possible, relying upon the country for supplies. I would also reduce the number of guns to a battery, or the number of batteries, and put the extra teams to the guns taken. No guns or caissons should be taken with less than eight horses.

"Please inform me by telegraph, on receipt of this, what force you think you will be able to send under these directions.

"U. S. GRANT, Lieutenant-General.

"MAJOR-GENERAL G. H. THOMAS."

On the 15th, he was directed to start the expedition as soon after the 20th as he could get it off.

I deemed it of the utmost importance, before a general movement of the armies operating against Richmond, that all communications with the city, north of James River, should be cut off. The enemy having withdrawn the bulk of his force from the Shenandoah Valley and sent it south, or replaced troops sent from Richmond, and desiring to reinforce Sherman, if practicable, whose cavalry was greatly inferior in numbers to that of the enemy, I determined to make a move from the Shenandoah, which, if successful, would accomplish the first at least, and possibly the latter of these objects. I therefore telegraphed General Sheridan as follows:

"CITY POINT, VA., *February* 20, 1865—1 P.M.

"GENERAL:—As soon as it is possible to travel, I think you will have no difficulty about reaching Lynchburg with a cavalry force alone. From there you could destroy the railroad and canal in every direction, so as to be of no further use to the rebellion. Sufficient cavalry should be left behind to look after Mosby's gang. From Lynchburg, if information you might get there would justify it, you will strike south, heading the streams in Virginia to the westward of Danville, and push on and join General Sherman. This additional raid, with one now about starting from East Tennessee under Stoneman, numbering four or five thousand cavalry, one from Vicksburg, numbering seven or eight thousand cavalry, one from Eastport, Mississippi, ten thousand cavalry, Canby from Mobile Bay, with about thirty-eight thousand mixed troops, these three latter pushing for Tuscaloosa, Selma, and Montgomery, and Sherman with a large army eating out the vitals of South Carolina, is all that will be wanted to leave nothing for the rebellion to stand upon. I would advise you to overcome great obstacles to accomplish this. Charleston was evacuated on Tuesday last.

"U. S. GRANT, Lieutenant-General.
"MAJOR-GENERAL P. H. SHERIDAN."

On the 25th I received a dispatch from General Sheridan, inquiring where Sherman was aiming for, and if I could give him definite information as to the points he might be expected to move on, this side of Charlotte, North Carolina. In answer, the following telegram was sent him:

"CITY POINT, VA., *February* 25, 1865.
"GENERAL: — Sherman's movements will depend on the amount of opposition he meets with from the enemy. If strongly opposed, he may possibly have to fall back to Georgetown, S. C., and fit out for a new start. I think, however, all danger for the necessity of going to that point has passed. I believe he has passed Charlotte. He may take Fayetteville on his way to Goldsboro'. If you reach Lynchburg, you will have to be guided in your after movements by the information you obtain. Before you could possibly reach Sherman, I think you would find him moving from Goldsboro' towards Raleigh, or engaging the enemy strongly posted at one or the other of these places, with railroad communications opened from his army to Wilmington or New Bern.

"U. S. GRANT, Lieutenant-General.
"MAJOR-GENERAL P. H. SHERIDAN."

General Sheridan moved from Winchester on the 27th of February, with two divisions of cavalry, numbering about five thousand each. On the 1st of March he secured the bridge, which the enemy attempted to destroy, across the middle fork of the Shenandoah, at Mount Crawford, and entered Staunton on the 2d, the enemy having retreated on Waynesboro'. Thence he pushed on to Waynesboro', where he found the enemy in force in an intrenched position, under General Early. Without stopping to make a reconnoissance, an immediate attack was made, the position was carried, and sixteen hundred prisoners, eleven pieces of artillery, with horses and caissons complete, two hundred wagons and teams loaded with subsistence, and seventeen battle-flags, were captured. The prisoners, under an escort of fifteen hundred men, were sent back to Winchester. Thence he marched on Charlottesville, destroying effectually the railroad and bridges as he went, which place he reached on the 3d. Here he remained two days, destroying the railroad towards Richmond and Lynchburg, including the large iron bridges over the north and south forks of the Rivanna River and awaited the arrival of his trains. This necessary delay caused him to abandon the idea of capturing Lynchburg. On the morning of the 6th, dividing his force into two columns, he sent one to Scottsville, whence it marched up the James River Canal to New Market, destroying every lock, and in many places the bank of the canal. From here a force was pushed out from this column to Duiguidsville, to obtain possession of the bridge across the James River at that place, but failed. The enemy burned it on our approach. The enemy also burned the bridge across the river at Hardwicksville. The other column moved down the railroad towards Lynchburg, destroying it as far as Amherst Court House, sixteen miles from Lynchburg; thence across the country, uniting with the column at New Market. The river being very high, his pontoons would not reach across it; and the enemy having destroyed the bridges by which he had hoped to cross the river and get on the South Side Railroad about Farmville, and destroy it to Appomattox Court House, the only thing left for him was to return to Winchester or strike a base at the White House. Fortunately, he chose the latter. From New Market he took up his line of march, following the canal towards Richmond, destroying every lock upon it and cutting the banks wherever practicable, to a point eight miles east of Goochland, concentrating the whole force at Columbia on the 10th. Here he rested one day, and sent through by scouts information of his whereabouts and purposes, and a request for supplies to meet him at White House, which reached me on the night of the 12th. An infantry force was immediately sent to get possession of White House, and supplies were forwarded. Moving from Columbia in a direction to threaten Richmond, to near Ashland Station, he crossed the Annas, and after having destroyed all the bridges and many miles of the railroad, proceeded down the north bank of the Pamunkey to White House, which place he reached on the 19th.

Previous to this the following communication was sent to General Thomas:

"CITY POINT, VIRGINIA,
March 7, 1865 — 9.30 A.M.

"GENERAL.: — I think it will be advisable now for you to repair the railroad in East Tennessee, and throw a good force up to Bull's Gap and fortify there. Supplies at Knoxville could always be got forward as required. With Bull's Gap fortified, you can occupy as outposts about all of East Tennessee, and be prepared, if it should be required of you in the spring, to make a campaign towards Lynchburg, or into North Carolina. I do not think Stoneman should break the road until he gets into Virginia, unless it should be to cut off rolling-stock that may be caught west of that.

"U. S. GRANT, Lieutenant-General.
"MAJOR GENERAL G. H. THOMAS."

Thus it will be seen that in March, 1865, General Canby was moving an adequate force against Mobile and the army defending it under General Dick Taylor; Thomas was pushing out two large and well-appointed cavalry expeditions—one from Middle Tennessee under Brevet Major-General Wilson against the enemy's vital points in Alabama, the other from East Tennessee, under Major-General Stoneman, towards Lynchburg—and assembling the remainder of his available forces, preparatory to commence offensive operations from East Tennessee; General Sheridan's cavalry was at White House; the armies of the Potomac and James were confronting the enemy, under Lee, in his defences of Richmond and Petersburg; General Sherman with his armies, reinforced by that of General Schofield, was at Goldsboro'; General Pope was making preparations for a spring campaign against the enemy under Kirby Smith and Price, west of the Mississippi; and General Hancock was concentrating a force in the vicinity of Winchester, Virginia, to guard against invasion or to operate offensively, as might prove necessary.

After the long march by General Sheridan's cavalry over winter roads, it was necessary to rest and refit at White House. At this time the greatest source of uneasiness to me was the fear that the enemy would leave his strong lines about Petersburg and Richmond for the purpose of uniting with Johnston, before he was driven from them by battle, or I was prepared to make an effectual pursuit. On the 24th of March, General Sheridan moved from White House, crossed the James River at Jones's Landing, and formed a junction with the Army of the Potomac in front of Petersburg on the 27th. During this move, General Ord sent forces to cover the crossings of the Chickahominy.

On the 24th of March the following instructions for a general movement of the armies operating against Richmond were issued:

"CITY POINT, VIRGINIA,
March 24, 1865.

"GENERAL:—On the 29th instant the armies operating against Richmond will be moved by our left, for the double purpose of turning the enemy out of his present position around Petersburg, and to insure the success of the cavalry under General Sheridan, which will start at the same time, in its efforts to reach and destroy the South Side and Danville railroads. Two corps of the Army of the Potomac will be moved at first in two columns, taking the two roads crossing Hatcher's Run, nearest where the present line held by us strikes that stream, both moving towards Dinwiddie Court House.

"The cavalry under General Sheridan, joined by the division now under General Davies, will move at the same time by the Weldon Road and the Jerusalem Plank Road, turning west from the latter before crossing the Nottoway, and west with the whole column before reaching Stony Creek. General Sheridan will then move independently, under other instructions which will be given him. All dismounted cavalry belonging to the Army of the Potomac, and the dismounted cavalry from the Middle Military Division not required for guarding property belonging to their arm of service, will report to Brigadier-General Benham, to be added to the defences of City Point. Major-General Parke will be left in command of all the army left for holding the lines about Petersburg and City Point, subject of course to orders from the commander of the Army of the Potomac. The 9th army corps will be left intact, to hold the present line of works so long as the whole line now occupied by us is held. If, however, the troops to the left of the 9th corps are withdrawn, then the left of the corps may be thrown back so as to occupy the position held by the army prior to the capture of the Weldon Road. All troops to the left of the 9th corps will be held in readiness to move at the shortest notice by such route as may be designated when the order is given.

"General Ord will detach three divisions, two white and one colored, or so much of them as he can, and hold his present lines, and march for the present left of the Army of the Potomac. In the absence of further orders, or until further orders are given, the white divisions will follow the left column of the Army of the Potomac, and the colored division the right column. During the movement Major-General Weitzel will be left in command of all the forces remaining behind from the Army of the James.

"The movement of troops from the Army of the James will commence on the night of the 27th instant. General Ord will leave behind the minimum number of cavalry necessary for picket duty, in the absence of the main army. A cavalry expedition, from General Ord's command, will also be started from Suffolk, to leave there on Saturday, the 1st of April, under Colonel Sumner, for the purpose of cutting the railroad about Hicksford. This, if accomplished, will have to be a surprise, and therefore from three to five hundred men will be sufficient. They should, however, be supported by all the infantry that can be spared from Norfolk and Portsmouth, as far out as to where the cavalry crosses the Blackwater. The crossing should probably be at Uniten. Should Colonel Sumner succeed in reaching the Weldon Road, he will be instructed to do all the damage possible to the triangle of roads between Hicksford, Weldon, and Gaston. The railroad bridge at Weldon being fitted up for the passage of carriages, it might be practicable to destroy any accumulation of supplies the enemy may have collected south of the Roanoke. All the troops will move with four days' rations in haversacks and eight days' in wagons. To avoid as much hauling as possible, and to give the Army of the James the same number of days' supplies with the Army of the Potomac, General Ord will direct his commissary and quartermaster to have sufficient supplies delivered at the terminus of the road to fill up in passing. Sixty rounds of ammunition per man will be taken in wagons, and as much grain as the transportation on hand will carry, after taking the specified amount of other supplies. The densely wooded country in which the army has to operate making the use of much artillery impracticable, the amount taken with the army will be reduced to six or eight guns to each division, at the option of the army commanders.

"All necessary preparations for carrying these directions into operation may be commenced at once. The reserves of the 9th corps should be massed as much as possible. While I would not now order an unconditional attack on the enemy's line by them, they should be ready and should make the attack if the enemy weakens his line in their front, without waiting for orders. In case they carry the line, then the whole of the 9th corps could follow up so as to join or co-operate with the balance of the army. To prepare for this, the 9th corps will have rations issued to them, same as the balance of the army. General Weitzel will keep vigilant watch upon his front, and if found at all practicable to break through at any point, he will do so. A success north of the James should be followed up with great promptness. An attack will not be feasible unless it is found that the enemy has detached largely. In that case it may be regarded as evident that the enemy are relying upon their local reserves principally for the defence of Richmond. Preparations may be made for abandoning all the line north of the James, except inclosed works—only to be abandoned, however, after a break is made in the lines of the enemy.

"By these instructions a large part of the armies operating against Richmond is left behind. The enemy, knowing this, may, as an only chance, strip their lines to the merest skeleton, in the hope of advantage not being taken of it, while they hurl everything against the moving column, and return. It cannot be impressed too strongly upon commanders of troops left in the trenches not to allow this to occur without taking advantage of it. The very fact of the enemy coming out to attack, if he does so, might be regarded as almost conclusive evidence of such a weakening of his lines. I would have it particularly enjoined upon corps commanders that, in case of an attack from the enemy, those not attacked are not to wait for orders from the commanding officer of the army to which they belong, but that they will move promptly, and notify the commander of their action. I would also enjoin the same action on the part of division commanders when other parts of their corps are engaged. In like manner, I would urge the importance of following up a repulse of the enemy.

"U. S. GRANT, Lieutenant-General.
"MAJOR-GENERALS MEADE, ORD, and SHERIDAN."

Early on the morning of the 25th the enemy assaulted our lines in front of the 9th corps (which held from the Appomattox River towards our left), and carried Fort Stedman, and a part of the line to the right and left of it, established themselves and turned the guns of the fort against us; but our troops on either flank held their ground until the reserves were brought up, when the enemy was driven back with a heavy loss in killed and wounded, and one thousand nine hundred prisoners. Our loss was sixty-eight killed, three hundred and thirty-seven wounded, and five hundred and six missing. General Meade at once ordered the other corps to advance and feel the enemy in their respective fronts. Pushing forward, they captured and held the enemy's strongly intrenched picket-line in front of the 2d and 6th corps, and eight hundred and thirty-four prisoners. The enemy made desperate attempts to retake this line, but without success. Our loss in front of these was fifty-two killed, eight hundred and sixty-four wounded, and two hundred and seven missing. The enemy's loss in killed and wounded was far greater.

General Sherman having got his troops all quietly in camp about Goldsboro', and his preparations for furnishing supplies to them perfected, visited me at City Point on the 27th of March, and stated that he would be ready to move, as he had previously written me, by the 10th of April, fully equipped and rationed for twenty days, if it should become necessary to bring his command to bear against Lee's army, in co-operation with our forces in front of Richmond and Petersburg. General Sherman proposed in this movement to threaten Raleigh, and then, by turning suddenly to the right, reach the Roanoke at Gaston or thereabouts, whence he could move on to the Richmond and Danville Railroad, striking it in the vicinity of Burkesville, or join the armies operating against Richmond, as might be deemed best. This plan he was directed to carry into execution, if he received no further directions in the meantime. I explained to him the movement I had ordered to commence on the 29th of March. That if it should not prove as entirely successful as I hoped, I would cut the cavalry loose to destroy the Danville and South Side railroads, and thus deprive the enemy of further supplies, and also to prevent the rapid concentration of Lee's and Johnston's armies.

I had spent days of anxiety lest each morning should bring the report that the enemy had retreated the night before. I was firmly convinced that Sherman's crossing the Roanoke would be the signal for Lee to leave. With Johnston and him combined, a long, tedious, and expensive campaign, consuming most of the summer, might become necessary. By moving out I would put the army in better condition for pursuit, and would at least, by the destruction of the Danville Road, retard the concentration of the two armies of Lee and Johnston, and cause the enemy to abandon much material that he might otherwise save. I therefore determined not to delay the movement ordered.

On the night of the 27th, Major-General Ord, with two divisions of the 24th corps, Major-General Gibbon commanding, and one division of the 25th corps, Brigadier-General Birney commanding, and Mackenzie's cavalry, took up his line of march in pursuance of the foregoing instructions, and reached the position assigned him near Hatcher's Run on the morning of the 29th. On the 28th the following instructions were given to General Sheridan:

"CITY POINT, VA., *March* 28, 1865.

"GENERAL:—The 5th army corps will move by the Vaughn Road at three A.M. to-morrow morning. The 2d moves at about nine A.M., having but about three miles to march to reach the point designated for it to take on the right of the 5th corps, after the latter reaching Dinwiddie Court House. Move your cavalry at as early an hour as you can, and without being confined to any particular road or roads. You may go out by the nearest roads in rear of the 5th corps, pass by its left, and passing near to or through Dinwiddie, reach the right and rear of the enemy as soon as you can. It is not the intention to attack the enemy in his intrenched position, but to force him out, if possible. Should he come out and attack us, or get himself where he can be attacked, move in with your entire force in your own way, and with the full reliance that the army will engage or follow, as circumstances will dictate. I shall be on the field, and will probably be able to communicate with you. Should I not do so, and you find that the enemy keeps within his main intrenched line, you may cut loose and push for the Danville Road. If you find it practicable, I would like you to cross the South Side Road, between Petersburg and Burkesville, and destroy it to some extent. I would not advise much detention, however, until you reach the Danville Road, which I would like you to strike as near to the Appomattox as possible. Make your destruction on that road as complete as possible. You can then pass on to the South Side Road, west of Burkesville, and destroy that in like manner.

"After having accomplished the destruction of the two railroads, which are now the only avenues of supply to Lee's army, you may return to this army, selecting your road further south, or you may go on into North Carolina and join General Sherman. Should you select the latter course, get the information to me as early as possible, so that I may send orders to meet you at Goldsboro'.

"U. S. GRANT, Lieutenant-General.

"MAJOR-GENERAL P. H. SHERIDAN."

On the morning of the 29th the movement commenced. At night the cavalry was at Dinwiddie Court House, and the left of our infantry line extended to the Quaker Road, near its intersection with the Boydton Plank Road. The position of the troops from left to right was as follows: Sheridan, Warren, Humphreys, Ord, Wright, Parke.

Everything looked favorable to the defeat of the enemy and the capture of Petersburg and Richmond, if the proper effort was made. I therefore addressed the following communication to General Sheridan, having previously informed him verbally not to cut loose for the raid contemplated in his orders until he received notice from me to do so:

"GRAVELLY CREEK, *March* 29, 1865.

"GENERAL: — Our line is now unbroken from the Appomattox to Dinwiddie. We are all ready, however, to give up all, from the Jerusalem Plank Road to Hatcher's Run, whenever the forces can be used advantageously. After getting into line south of Hatcher's, we pushed forward to find the enemy's position. General Griffin was attacked near where the Quaker Road intersects the Boydton Road, but repulsed it easily, capturing about one hundred men. Humphreys reached Dabney's Mill, and was pushing on when last heard from.

"I now feel like ending the matter, if it is possible to do so, before going back. I do not want you, therefore, to cut loose and go after the enemy's roads at present. In the morning push around the enemy, if you can, and get on to his right rear. The movements of the enemy's cavalry may, of course, modify your action. We will act all together as one army here, until it is seen what can be done with the enemy. The signal-officer at Cobb's Hill reported, at half-past eleven A.M., that a cavalry column had passed that point from Richmond towards Petersburg, taking forty minutes to pass.

"U. S. GRANT, Lieutenant-General.
"MAJOR-GENERAL P. H. SHERIDAN."

From the night of the 29th to the morning of the 31st the rain fell in such torrents as to make it impossible to move a wheeled vehicle, except as corduroy roads were laid in front of them. During the 30th, Sheridan advanced from Dinwiddie Court House towards Five Forks, where he found the enemy in full force. General Warren advanced and extended his line across the Boydton Plank Road to near the White Oak Road, with a view of getting across the latter; but, finding the enemy strong in his front and extending beyond his left, was directed to hold on where he was, and fortify. General Humphreys drove the enemy from his front into his main line on the Hatcher, near Burgess's Mills. Generals Ord, Wright, and Parke made examinations in their fronts to determine the feasibility of an assault on the enemy's lines. The two latter reported favorably. The enemy confronting us as he did, at every point from Richmond to our extreme left, I conceived his lines must be weakly held, and could be penetrated if my estimate of his forces was correct. I determined, therefore, to extend our line no farther, but to reinforce General Sheridan with a corps of infantry, and thus enable him to cut loose and turn the enemy's right flank, and with the other corps assault the enemy's lines. The result of the offensive effort of the enemy the week before, when he assaulted Fort Stedman, particularly favored this. The enemy's intrenched picket-line captured by us at that time threw the lines occupied by the belligerents so close together at some points that it was but a moment's run from one to the other. Preparations were at once made to relieve General Humphreys's corps, to report to General Sheridan; but the condition of the roads prevented immediate movement. On the morning of the 31st, General Warren reported favorably to getting possession of the White Oak Road, and was directed to do so. To accomplish this, he moved with one division, instead of his whole corps, which was attacked by the enemy in superior force and driven back on the 2d division before it had time to form, and it, in turn, forced back upon the 3d division, when the enemy was checked. A division of the 2d corps was immediately sent to his support, the enemy driven back with heavy loss, and possession of the White Oak Road gained. Sheridan advanced, and with a portion of his cavalry got possession of the Five Forks; but the enemy, after the affair with the 5th corps, reinforced the rebel cavalry, defending that point with infantry, and forced him back towards Dinwiddie Court House. Here General Sheridan displayed great generalship. Instead of retreating with his whole command on the main army, to tell the story of superior forces encountered, he deployed his cavalry on foot, leaving only mounted men enough to take charge of the horses. This compelled the enemy to deploy over a vast extent of wooded and broken country, and made his progress slow. At this juncture he dispatched to me what had taken place, and that he was dropping back slowly on Dinwiddie Court House. General Mackenzie's cavalry and one division of the 5th corps were immediately ordered to his assistance. Soon after receiving a report from General Meade that Humphreys could hold our position on the Boydton Road, and that the other two divisions of the 5th corps could go to Sheridan, they were so ordered at once. Thus the operations of the day necessitated the sending of Warren, because of his accessibility, instead of Humphreys, as was intended, and precipitated intended movements. On the morning of the 1st of April, General Sheridan, reinforced by General Warren, drove the enemy back on Five Forks, where, late in the evening, he assaulted and carried his strongly fortified position, capturing all his artillery and between five and six thousand prisoners.

About the close of this battle, Brevet Major-General Charles Griffin relieved Major-General Warren in command of the 5th corps. The report of this reached me after nightfall. Some apprehensions filled my mind lest the enemy might desert his lines during the night, and by falling upon General Sheridan before assistance could reach him, drive him from his position and open the way for retreat. To guard against this, General Miles's division of Humphreys's corps was sent to reinforce him, and a bombardment was commenced and kept up until four o'clock in the morning (April 2), when an assault was ordered on the enemy's lines. General Wright penetrated the lines with his whole corps, sweeping everything before him, and to his left towards Hatcher's Run, capturing many guns and several thousand prisoners. He was closely followed by two divisions of General Ord's command, until he met the other division of General Ord's that had succeeded in forcing the enemy's lines near Hatcher's Run. Generals Wright and Ord immediately swung to the right, and closed all of the enemy on that side of them in Petersburg, while General Humphreys pushed forward with two divisions and joined General Wright on the left. General Parke succeeded in carrying the enemy's main line, capturing guns and prisoners, but was unable to carry his inner line. General Sheridan being advised of the condition of affairs, returned General Miles to his proper command. On reaching the enemy's lines immediately surrounding Petersburg, a portion of General Gibbon's corps, by a most gallant charge, captured two strong inclosed works—the most salient and commanding south of Petersburg—thus materially shortening the line of investment necessary for taking in the city. The enemy south of Hatcher's Run retreated westward to Sutherland's Station, where they were overtaken by Miles's division. A severe engagement ensued, and lasted until both his right and left flanks were threatened by the approach of General Sheridan, who was moving from Ford's Station towards Petersburg, and a division sent by General Meade from the front of Petersburg, when he broke in the utmost confusion, leaving in our hands his guns and many prisoners. This force retreated by the main road along the Appomattox River. During the night of the 2d the enemy evacuated Petersburg and Richmond, and retreated towards Danville. On the morning of the 3d pursuit was commenced. General Sheridan pushed for the Danville Road, keeping near the Appomattox, followed by General Meade with the 2d and 6th corps, while General Ord moved for Burkesville, along the South Side Road; the 9th corps stretched along that road behind him. On the 4th, General Sheridan struck the Danville Road near Jetersville, where he learned that Lee was at Amelia Court House. He immediately intrenched himself and awaited the arrival of General Meade, who reached there the next day. General Ord reached Burkesville on the evening of the 5th.

On the morning of the 5th, I addressed Major-General Sherman the following communication:

"WILSON'S STATION, *April* 5, 1865.

"GENERAL: — All indications now are that Lee will attempt to reach Danville with the remnant of his force. Sheridan, who was up with him last night, reports all that is left, horse, foot, and dragoons, at twenty thousand, much demoralized. We hope to reduce this number one-half. I shall push on to Burkesville, and if a stand is made at Danville, will in a very few days go there. If you can possibly do so, push on from where you are, and let us see if we cannot finish the job with Lee's and Johnston's armies. Whether it will be better for you to strike for Greensboro', or nearer to Danville, you will be better able to judge when you receive this. Rebel armies now are the only strategic points to strike at.

"U. S. GRANT, Lieutenant-General.
"MAJOR-GENERAL W. T. SHERMAN."

On the morning of the 6th, it was found that General Lee was moving west of Jetersville, towards Danville. General Sheridan moved with his cavalry (the 5th corps having been returned to General Meade on his reaching Jetersville) to strike his flank, followed by the 6th corps, while the 2d and 5th corps pressed hard after, forcing him to abandon several hundred wagons and several pieces of artillery. General Ord advanced from Burkesville towards Farmville, sending two regiments of infantry and a squadron of cavalry, under Brevet Brigadier-General Theodore Read, to reach and destroy the bridges. This advance met the head of Lee's column near Farmville, which it heroically attacked and detained until General Read was killed and his small force overpowered. This caused a delay in the enemy's movements, and enabled General Ord to get well up with the remainder of his force, on meeting which, the enemy immediately intrenched himself. In the afternoon, General Sheridan struck the enemy south of Sailors' Creek, captured sixteen pieces of artillery and about four hundred wagons, and detained him until the 6th corps got up, when a general attack of infantry and cavalry was made, which resulted in the capture of six or seven thousand prisoners, among whom were many general officers. The movements of the 2d corps and General Ord's command contributed greatly to the day's success.

On the morning of the 7th the pursuit was renewed, the cavalry, except one division, and the 5th corps moving by Prince Edward's Court House; the 6th corps, General Ord's command, and one division of cavalry, on Farmville; and the 2d corps by the High Bridge Road. It was soon found that the enemy had crossed to the north side of the Appomattox; but so close was the pursuit, that the 2d corps got possession of the common bridge at High Bridge before the enemy could destroy it, and immediately crossed over.

The 6th corps and a division of cavalry crossed at Farmville to its support.

Feeling now that General Lee's chance of escape was utterly hopeless, I addressed him the following communication from Farmville:

"April 7, 1865.

"GENERAL:—The result of the last week must convince you of the hopelessness of further resistance on the part of the Army of Northern Virginia in this struggle. I feel that it is so, and regard it as my duty to shift from myself the responsibility of any further effusion of blood, by asking of you the surrender of that portion of the Confederate States army known as the Army of Northern Virginia.

"U. S. GRANT, Lieutenant-General.

"GENERAL R. E. LEE."

Early on the morning of the 8th, before leaving, I received at Farmville the following:

"April 7, 1865.

"GENERAL:—I have received your note of this date. Though not entertaining the opinion you express on the hopelessness of further resistance on the part of the Army of Northern Virginia, I reciprocate your desire to avoid useless effusion of blood, and therefore, before considering your proposition, ask the terms you will offer on condition of its surrender.

"R. E. LEE, General.

"LIEUTENANT-GENERAL U. S. GRANT."

To this I immediately replied:

"April 8, 1865.

"GENERAL:—Your note of last evening, in reply to mine of same date, asking the condition on which I will accept the surrender of the Army of Northern Virginia, is just received. In reply, I would say, that *peace* being my great desire, there is but one condition I would insist upon—namely, That the men and officers surrendered shall be disqualified for taking up arms again against the Government of the United States until properly exchanged. I will meet you, or will designate officers to meet any officers you may name for the same purpose, at any point agreeable to you, for the purpose of arranging definitely the terms upon which the surrender of the Army of Northern Virginia will be received.

"U. S. GRANT, Lieutenant-General.

"GENERAL R. E. LEE."

Early on the morning of the 8th the pursuit was resumed. General Meade followed north of the Appomattox, and General Sheridan, with all the cavalry, pushed straight for Appomattox Station, followed by General Ord's command and the 5th corps. During the day General Meade's advance had considerable fighting with the enemy's rear-guard, but was unable to bring on a general engagement. Late in the evening General Sheridan struck the railroad at Appomattox Station, drove the enemy from there, and captured twenty-five pieces of artillery, a hospital-train, and four trains of cars loaded with supplies for Lee's army. During this day I accompanied General Meade's column, and about midnight received the following communication from General Lee:

"*April* 8, 1865.

"GENERAL:—I received, at a late hour, your note of to-day. In mine of yesterday I did not intend to propose the surrender of the Army of Northern Virginia, but to ask the terms of your proposition. To be frank, I do not think the emergency has arisen to call for the surrender of this army; but as the restoration of peace should be the sole object of all, I desired to know whether your proposals would lead to that end. I cannot, therefore, meet you with a view to surrender the Army of Northern Virginia; but as far as your proposal may affect the Confederates States forces under my command, and tend to the restoration of peace, I should be pleased to meet you at ten A.M. tomorrow on the old stage-road to Richmond, between the picket-lines of the two armies.

"R. E. LEE, General.

"LIEUTENANT-GENERAL U. S. GRANT."

Early on the morning of the 9th I returned him an answer as follows, and immediately started to join the column south of the Appomattox:

"*April* 9, 1865.

"GENERAL:—Your note of yesterday is received. I have no authority to treat on the subject of peace; the meeting proposed for ten A.M. to-day could lead to no good. I will state, however, general, that I am equally anxious for peace with yourself, and the whole North entertains the same feeling. The terms upon which peace can be had are well understood. By the South laying down their arms they will hasten that most desirable event, save thousands of human lives, and hundreds of millions of property not yet destroyed. Seriously hoping that all our difficulties may be settled without the loss of another life. I subscribe myself, etc.

"U. S. GRANT, Lieutenant-General.

"GENERAL R. E. LEE."

On the morning of the 9th, General Ord's command and the 5th corps reached Appomattox Station just as the enemy was making a desperate effort to break through our cavalry. The infantry was at once thrown in. Soon after a white flag was received, requesting a suspension of hostilities pending negotiations for a surrender.

Before reaching General Sheridan's headquarters, I received the following from General Lee:

"April 9, 1865.

"GENERAL:—I received your note of this morning on the picket-line, whither I had come to meet you, and ascertain definitely what terms were embraced in your proposal of yesterday with reference to the surrender of this army. I now ask an interview, in accordance with the offer contained in your letter of yesterday, for that purpose.

"R. E. LEE, General.

"LIEUTENANT-GENERAL U. S. GRANT."

The interview was held at Appomattox Court-House, the result of which is set forth in the following correspondence:

APPOMATTOX COURT-HOUSE, Virginia, *April* 9, 1865.

"GENERAL:—In accordance with the substance of my letter to you of the 8th instant, I propose to receive the surrender of the Army of Northern Virginia on the following terms, to wit: Rolls of all the officers and men to be made in duplicate, one copy to be given to an officer to be designated by me, the other to be retained by such officer or officers as you may designate. The officers to give their individual paroles not to take up arms against the Government of the United States until properly exchanged; and each company or regimental commander sign a like parole for the men of their commands. The arms, artillery, and public property to be parked and stacked, and turned over to the officers appointed by me to receive them. This will not embrace the side-arms of the officers, nor their private horses or baggage. This done, each officer and man will be allowed to return to his home, not to be disturbed by United States authority so long as they observe their paroles and the laws in force where they may reside.

"U. S. GRANT, Lieutenant-General.

"GENERAL R. E. LEE."

"HEADQUARTERS ARMY OF NORTHERN VIRGINIA, *April* 9, 1865.

"GENERAL:—I have received your letter of this date containing the terms of surrender of the Army of Northern Virginia as proposed by you. As they are substantially the same as those expressed in your letter of the 8th instant, they are accepted. I will proceed to designate the proper officers to carry the stipulations into effect.

"R. E. LEE, General.

"LIEUTENANT-GENERAL U. S. GRANT."

The command of Major-General Gibbon, the 5th army corps under Griffin, and Mackenzie's cavalry, were designated to remain at Appomattox Court-House until the paroling of the surrendered army was completed, and to take charge of the public property. The remainder of the army immediately returned to the vicinity of Burkesville.

General Lee's great influence throughout the whole South caused his example to be followed, and to-day the result is that the armies lately under his leadership are at their homes, desiring peace and quiet, and their arms are in the hands of our ordnance officers.

On the receipt of my letter of the 5th, General Sherman moved directly against Joe Johnston, who retreated rapidly on and through Raleigh, which place General Sherman occupied on the morning of the 13th. The day preceding, news of the surrender of General Lee reached him at Smithfield.

On the 14th a correspondence was opened between General Sherman and General Johnston, which resulted on the 18th in an agreement for a suspension of hostilities, and a memorandum or basis for peace, subject to the approval of the President. This agreement was disapproved by the President on the 21st, which disapproval, together with your instructions, was communicated to General Sherman by me in person on the morning of the 24th, at Raleigh, North Carolina, in obedience to your orders. Notice was at once given by him to General Johnston for the termination of the truce that had been entered into. On the 25th another meeting between them was agreed upon, to take place on the 26th, which terminated in the surrender and disbandment of Johnston's army upon substantially the same terms as were given to General Lee.

The expedition under General Stoneman from East Tennessee got off on the 20th of March, moving by way of Boone, North Carolina, and struck the railroad at Wytheville, Chambersburg, and Big Lick. The force striking it at Big Lick pushed on to within a few miles of Lynchburg, destroying the important bridges, while with the main force he effectually destroyed it between New River and Big Lick, and then turned for Greensboro', on the North Carolina Railroad; struck that road and destroyed the bridges between Danville and Greensboro', and between Greensboro' and the Yadkin, together with the depots of supplies along it, and captured four hundred prisoners. At Salisbury he attacked and defeated a force of the enemy under General Gardiner, capturing fourteen pieces of artillery and one thousand three hundred and sixty-four prisoners, and destroyed large amounts of army stores. At this place he destroyed fifteen miles of railroad and the bridges towards Charlotte. Thence he moved to Slatersville.

General Canby, who had been directed in January to make preparations for a movement from Mobile Bay against Mobile and the interior of Alabama, commenced his movement on the 20th of March. The 16th corps, Major-General A. J. Smith commanding, moved from Fort Gaines by water to Fish River; the 13th corps, under Major-General Gordon Granger, moved from Fort Morgan and joined the 16th corps on Fish River, both moving thence on

Spanish Fort and investing it on the 27th; while Major-General Steele's command moved from Pensacola, cut the railroad leading from Tensas to Montgomery, effected a junction with them, and partially invested Fort Blakely. After a severe bombardment of Spanish Fort, a part of its line was carried on the 8th of April. During the night the enemy evacuated the fort. Fort Blakely was carried by assault on the 9th, and many prisoners captured; our loss was considerable. These successes practically opened to us the Alabama River, and enabled us to approach Mobile from the north. On the night of the 11th the city was evacuated, and was taken possession of by our forces on the morning of the 12th.

The expedition under command of Brevet Major-General Wilson, consisting of twelve thousand five hundred mounted men, was delayed by rains until March 22d, when it moved from Chickasaw, Alabama. On the 1st of April, General Wilson encountered the enemy in force under Forrest near Ebenezer Church, drove him in confusion, captured three hundred prisoners and three guns, and destroyed the central bridge over the Cahawba River. On the 2d he attacked and captured the fortified city of Selma, defended by Forrest, with seven thousand men and thirty-two guns, destroyed the arsenal, armory, naval foundry, machine-shops, vast quantities of stores, and captured three thousand prisoners. On the 4th he captured and destroyed Tuscaloosa. On the 10th he crossed the Alabama River, and after sending information of his operations to General Canby, marched on Montgomery, which place he occupied on the 14th, the enemy having abandoned it. At this place many stores and five steamboats fell into our hands. Thence a force marched direct on Columbus, and another on West Point, both of which places were assaulted and captured on the 16th. At the former place we got one thousand five hundred prisoners and fifty-two field-guns, destroyed two gunboats, the navy yard, foundries, arsenal, many factories, and much other public property. At the latter place we got three hundred prisoners, four guns, and destroyed nineteen locomotives and three hundred cars. On the 20th he took possession of Macon, Georgia, with sixty field-guns, one thousand two hundred militia, and five generals, surrendered by General Howell Cobb. General Wilson, hearing that Jeff. Davis was trying to make his escape, sent forces in pursuit and succeeded in capturing him on the morning of May 11th.

On the 4th day of May, General Dick Taylor surrendered to General Canby all the remaining rebel forces east of the Mississippi.

A force sufficient to insure an easy triumph over the enemy under Kirby Smith, west of the Mississippi, was immediately put in motion for Texas, and Major-General Sheridan designated for its immediate command; but on the 26th day of May, and before they reached their destination, General Kirby Smith surrendered his entire command to Major-General Canby. This surrender did not take place, however, until after the capture of the rebel President and Vice-President; and the bad faith was exhibited of first disbanding most of his army and permitting an indiscriminate plunder of public property.

Owing to the report that many of those lately in arms against the government had taken refuge upon the soil of Mexico, carrying with them arms rightfully belonging to the United States, which had been surrendered to us by agreement—among them some of the leaders who had surrendered in person—and the disturbed condition of affairs on the Rio Grande, the orders for troops to proceed to Texas were not changed.

There have been severe combats, raids, expeditions, and movements to defeat the designs and purposes of the enemy, most of them reflecting great credit on our arms, and which contributed greatly to our final triumph, that I have not mentioned. Many of these will be found clearly set forth in the reports herewith submitted; some in the telegrams and brief dispatches announcing them, and others, I regret to say, have not as yet been officially reported.

For information touching our Indian difficulties, I would respectfully refer to the reports of the commanders of departments in which they have occurred.

It has been my fortune to see the armies of both the West and the East fight battles, and from what I have seen I know there is no difference in their fighting qualities. All that it was possible for men to do in battle they have done. The Western armies commenced their battles in the Mississippi Valley, and received the final surrender of the remnant of the principal army opposed to them in North Carolina. The armies of the East commenced their battles on the river from which the Army of the Potomac derived its name, and received the final surrender of their old antagonists at Appomattox Court House, Virginia. The splendid achievements of each have nationalized our victories, removed all sectional jealousies (of which we have unfortunately experienced too much), and the cause of crimination and recrimination that might have followed had either section failed in its duty. All have a proud record, and all sections can well congratulate themselves and each other for having done their full share in restoring the supremacy of law over every foot of territory belonging to the United States. Let them hope for perpetual peace and harmony with that enemy, whose manhood, however mistaken the cause, drew forth such herculean deeds of valor.

I have the honor to be,

Very respectfully, your obedient servant,

U. S. GRANT,

Lieutenant-General.

THE END

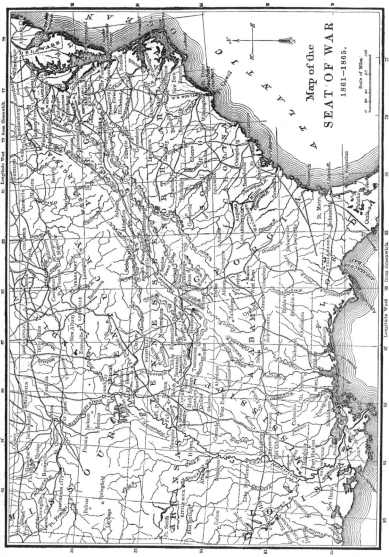

Map of the
SEAT OF WAR
1861–1865.

Index

ABERCROMBIE, GENERAL, 593.

Adams, Colonel, 507.

Albertis, Major, death of, 87.

Ames, Adelbert, General, 667; at capture of Fort Fisher, 669, 670.

Anderson, G. T., General, 662.

Anderson, R. H., General, at battle of Wilderness, 531; 540; 541; 542; at battle of Spottsylvania, 545; 580.

Anderson, Richard, Lieutenant, 122; 124.

Arkansas Post, capture of, 293.

Army of Invasion, organization of, 69.

Army of Northern Virginia, composition of, 519–522.

Army of Occupation, character of, 50–51.

Army of the Potomac, composition of, 515–518; quartermaster's corps of, 523; intrenchments of, 534; telegraph system of, 535–536; signal service of, 536; losses of, 597.

Atlanta, Ga, Sherman's campaign against, 500–511; battle of, 505; capture of, 508.

Augur, Lieutenant, 54; 56.

Averell, General, 479; 489; 557; 595; 603; 605.

Ayres, General, 557; 698; 701.

BABCOCK, COLONEL, 553; General, 732–733.

Badeau, General, applies to War Department for copy of letter from Grant offering his services to Government, 158; unearths facts in relation to Halleck's removal of Grant from command, 221; statements made by, 228, 237, 247, 365, 494, 631.

Bailey, Doctor, 28.

Bailey, Major, 30.

Baird, General, 434; at battle of Chattanooga, 444, 447.

Banks, Major-General, 327; 332; 350; 366; receives surrender of Port Hudson, 382; 386; 389; 390; 403; 463; 465; 472; 479; 480; 481; his Red River expedition, 484; 489; 498; 500; 558; 607.

Barlow, General, at battle of Wilderness, 529; at battle of Spottsylvania, 546, 549, 550; 553; at battle of Cold Harbor, 584.

Barnard, General, 493; 494; 671; 672.

Barrett, Major, attempts to capture Grant, 176.

Barringer, General, 571.

Baxter, Captain, 226.

Baxter, General, at battle of Wilderness, 528.

Bazaine, General, 775.

Beauregard, P. G. T., Lieutenant, at battle of Cerro Gordo, 90; differs with A. S. Johnston in views, 242; succeeds Johnston in command at Shiloh, 242; his reports of losses, 245; makes efforts to obtain reinforcements, 250; is reinforced, 250; orders the evacuation of Corinth, 255; is superseded by Bragg, 267; 485; 490; 551; 559; 601; 613; 640; 682.

Belknap, Colonel, 117.

Bell, General, at capture of Fort Fisher, 670; is killed, 670.

Belmont, battle of, 177–185.

Benham, Brigadier-General, 596.

Benjamin, Lieutenant, 54; 55; 56.

Benton, Thomas H., Senator, 84; 117.

Big Black River Bridge, battle of, 349–353.

Birney, General, at battle of Wilderness, 528, 531; at battle of Spottsylvania, 546, 549; 553; 555;

at battle of Cold Harbor, 559; 584; 592; 602; 617; 625.

Blair, Frank P., leads Free-soil Democracy of St. Louis, 142; prevents St. Louis from going into rebel hands, 155; raises a regiment and takes command of it, 155–156; at occupation of Grand Gulf, 329; 333; 338; 339; 340; 341; 342; at battle of Champion Hill, 345, 347; at battle of Big Black River Bridge, 349, 353; at siege of Vicksburg, 357, 365, 366; General, his bravery and obedience, 385; 423; 637.

Blair, Governor, 268.

Bliss, Captain, 59; Colonel, 139.

Boggs, Harry, 141; 142.

Bowen, General, 322; 323; at surrender of Vicksburg, 374, 375, 376.

Bowers, T. S., Colonel, 487; 706.

Bragg, General, 257; 265; 267; 270; 271; 359; 388; 404; 405; 406; 419; 426; 428; 431; 433; 443; at battle of Chattanooga, 444, 445, 446, 447; 448; his character and disposition, 449; 450; 452; 455; 456; 465; 648; 650; 664.

Brannan, J. M., General, 435.

Breckinridge, Mr., 144; General, 567; 603.

Breese, Commander, at capture of Fort Fisher, 669.

Brooke, Colonel, at battle of Wilderness, 530.

Brooks, Captain Horace, 106.

Brooks, General, at battle of Cold Harbor, 585.

Brough, Governor, 403.

Brown, B. Gratz, Colonel, 169.

Brown, George, Lieutenant-Commander, 308.

Brown, Governor, 632; 633; 646.

Brown, Jacob, Major, 64; 69.

Brown, John, character of, 18–19.

Buchanan, James, 144; President, helplessness of administration of, 150; 206; 306.

Buckland, Colonel, 224.

Buckner, S. B., 122; 124; General, 189; surrenders Fort Donelson, 207, 208, 212, 213; 433; 456.

Buell, Don Carlos, Brigadier-General, commands Department of the Ohio, 189; 215; 216; 217; 218; 222; 223; 224; 225; at battle of Shiloh, 231, 232, 233, 234, 235, 238; character of, 240, 241; 242; 245; 247; 248; 256; 257; 263; 265; 266; 267; 269; 270; 271; 278; is succeeded by Rosecrans, 281; 471; 472.

Bull-fighting, 119–120.

Bureau, Freedman's, origin of, 284–285.

Burnham, General, is killed, 625.

Burnside, General, 257; 367; 410; 422; 423; 424; 425; 426; 431; 433; 435; 441; 443; 448; 452; 453; 454; 455; 458; 461; 466; 471; 477; 479; 482; 484; 487; 518; 527; at battle of Wilderness, 529, 530, 531, 532; 536; 541; at battle of Spottsylvania, 544, 545, 546, 550; 552; 554; 556; 559; 560; 562; 563; at battle of North Anna, 563; 564; 567; 568; 571; 572; 575; 576; 580; 583; at battle of Cold Harbor, 585; 592; 596; 602; 607; 611; 612; 770; his ability, 771.

Butler, B. F., General, 477; 479; 480; 481; 482; 483; operates on James River, 490, 493; his earnestness, 494; 495; 496; 524; captures City Point, 536; 540; 551; 557; 558; 559; 570; 579; 590; 593; 596; 598; 599; 601; 608; 630; 650; 663; 667; 668; 688.

Butler, William O., General, 75; 117.

Campbell, Judge, 685.

Camp Salubrity, 40; 42–45.

Canby, General, 472; 498; 558; 634; 635; 673; 674; 676; 679; 757; 758; his character and ability, 763.

Capron, Colonel, 507.

Carlin, General, 441.

Carr, General, 323; 340; 341; at battle of Champion's Hill, 346, 347; 349; 350.

Carroll, Colonel, at battle of Wilderness, 528; 531; 556.

Casey, Captain, at battle of Chapultepec, 104.

Cass, General, 625.

Caves of Mexico, visit to, 124–127.

Cerro Gordo, battle of, 91–92.

Chamberlain, J. L., Colonel, 601; promoted to brigadier-generalcy on the field, 601–602.

Champion's Hill, battle of, 345–348.

Chandler, Zachariah, elected mayor of Detroit, 130.

Chapultepec, battle of, 104.

Charleston, S. C., evacuation of, 682.

Chattanooga, Tenn., 413.

Chattanooga, battle of, 443–447.

Cheatham, General, 654.

Childs, Lieutenant-Colonel, at battle of Palo Alto, 66.

Church, Professor, 39.

Churubusco, battle of, 99.

Clarke, General, at capture of San Antonio, 98.

Clay, Mr., Grant's admiration for, 142.

Cleburne, General, 453.

Cold Harbor, battle of, 579–588; reflections upon, 588.

Columbia, S. C., burning of, 681.

Comstock, Captain, at siege of Vicksburg, 360; 460; 461; Colonel, 539; 553; 593; 594.

Contreras, battle of, 100.

Corinth, Miss., occupation of, 252–256; battle of, 279–281.

Corpus Christi, Texas, 47.

Corse, General, at battle of Chattanooga, 443; his efficiency, 444, 639.

Courage, 44; 65; 163–165.

Crawford, General, 541; 559; 564; at battle of North Anna, 567; at battle of Five Forks, 701.

Crittenden, George, Captain, 122.

Crittenden, General, at battle of Shiloh, 234; 235; 406; 471; at battle of North Anna, 567.

Crocker, M. M., Brigadier-General, 282; 321; 324; at battle of Raymond, 331; his ability, 331; at capture of Jackson, 334, 337; 340; at battle of Champion's Hill, 345, 346; 385.

Crook, Brigadier-General, 478; 479; 489; 524; 595; 603; 605; 614; 714; 723.

Cross, Major, 63.

Cruft, General, 439; at battle of Lookout Mountain, 440; 448.

Cullum, General, 214.

Curtis, General, 287.

Curtis, N. M., General, 667; at capture of Fort Fisher, 669, 670; seriously wounded, 670.

Cushing, Brigadier-General, 117.

Custer, General, at battle of Wilderness, 533; 575; 603; 629; 690; 728.

Cutler, General, 541; 555; 564.

Dahlgren, Admiral, 672.

Dana, C. A., 325; 391; 404; 409; 426; 455.

Davies, General, 270; 716.

Davis, Jefferson, 148; is elected president of Confederacy, 151; 241; 419; 449; his military capacity, 450; 632; 633; 634; 638; 646; 680; 691; 708; 724; 744; is captured, 761; 762.

Davis, Jefferson C., Colonel, 171; 442; 447; 448; 637.

De Loche, Mr., 260.

Dennis, Colonel, 267.

Dent, F. T., 36; Colonel, 593; 594.

Dent, Julia, becomes acquainted with Grant, 36; is engaged to Grant, 39; corresponds with Grant, 39; marries Grant, 130.

Devens, General, at battle of Cold Harbor, 585.

Devin, Colonel, 690.

Dix, Major, 54.

Dodge, G. M., General, 423; 424; 505; 555; his efficiency, 637.

Dole, General, 555.

Donaldson, J. L., General, 655.

Donelson, Fort, capture of, 196–213.

Douglas, Stephen A., 144; Senator, 157; 473.

Draper, Mr., 671.

Dueling, Grant's opinion of, 44.

Duncan, Colonel, opposes Scott, 117.

Dunn, William M., Captain, 381; Lieutenant, 649.

Duty, Grant's ideas of, 304–305.

EARLY, GENERAL, at battle of Wilderness, 532; 542; at battle of Spottsylvania, 245; 546; 559; 575; 595; 605; 606; 614; 615; 617; 620; 622; 625; 627; 628; 629; 689; 690; 770.

Eaton, Chaplain, organizes labor of freedmen, 285.

Egan, General, at battle of North Anna, 564.

Ellet, Colonel, 308.

Emory, Major-General, 606; 608; 629.

England, attitude of, 777.

Ewell, Lieutenant, 38; General, 524; at battle of Spottsylvania, 545; 559; 595; 724.

Ewing, General, 431; at battle of Missionary Ridge, 436.

FARRAGUT, ADMIRAL, runs batteries at Port Hudson, 308.

Ferrero, General, 559; 596; 612.

Five Forks, battle of, 701–703.

Floyd, Secretary, scatters army and sends arms South, 150; General, his inefficiency as a soldier, 196, 206; his unfaithfulness as a civil officer, 206; escapes from Fort Donelson, 207, 212, 213; 218.

Foote, Flag-officer, 190; at capture of Fort Henry, 190; at capture of Fort Donelson, 197, 201, 202, 203, 204; 214.

Forrest, General, escapes from Fort Donelson, 207, 212, 213; 289;
464; 465; his bravery, 478; captures Fort Pillow, 483; 607; his ability, 633; 638; 656; his courage and capacity, 676; 748.

Fort Fisher, capture of, 669–670.

Fort Henry, capture of, 190–195.

Fort Pillow, Forrest's capture of, 483.

Foster, John G., Lieutenant, 90; General, 457; 459; 466; 649; 651; 671; 672; 675; 682; 705.

Foulk, Philip, 157.

France, attitude of, 776.

Franklin, battle of, 654–655.

Fremont, General, 174; 176; takes command in field, 177; is superseded by Halleck, 188; 304; 471.

Fuller, General, 506.

Fyffe, Colonel, 30.

GAINES, GENERAL, 83.

Galena, Ill., Grant's residence at, 141–153.

Gardner, Frank, 56; General, surrenders Port Hudson, 382.

Garland, Lieutenant-Colonel, 72; at battle of Monterey, 77; 97; 98; is seriously wounded, 111.

Garrard, General, 506.

Garrett, Robert, 621.

Geary, General, 418; at battle of Wauhatchie, 420; 429; at battle of Lookout Mountain, 440; 448.

Georgetown, O., Grant's boyhood at, 21–27; notable facts in regard to, 30.

Getty, General, 527; at battle of Wilderness, 528; 628; 629.

Gibbon, General, at battle of Wilderness, 530; 531; at battle of Spottsylvania, 546; 553; 556; 559; at battle of Cold Harbor, 584; 705; 741.

Gillmore, General, 477; 479; 480; 481.

Gore, Captain, 105.

Gordon, J. B., General, 571; 687; 692; 693; 741.

Grand Gulf, occupation of, 327.

Granger, Gordon, General, 267; 268; 269; 434; at battle of Chattanooga, 447; 448; 452; 453; 454; 461; 679.

Granger, R. S., General, 655.

Grant, Frederick D., assists in preparing Memoirs, 6; 163; is with Grant in campaign and siege of Vicksburg, 324, 325; 465; 469.

Grant, Jesse R., lives with Judge Tod, 18, 19; his education, 19; establishes himself in business at Ravenna, O., 19; moves to Point Pleasant, O., 19; contributes to newspapers, 19; his interest in politics, 19; marries Hannah Simpson, 21; his interest in education of his children, 22; cultivates land, 22; moves to Bethel, O., 32; 142; 144.

Grant, Lawson, 20.

Grant, Matthew, 17.

Grant, Noah, 17.

Grant, Noah, Captain, 17; 18.

Grant, Peter, 18.

Grant, Samuel, 17.

Grant, Solomon, 17; 18.

Grant, U. S., is injured by a fall, 5; loses financial resources, 5; writes for *Century Magazine*, 5; is seriously ill, 5; his ancestry, 17–18; his birth, at Point Pleasant, O., 21; moves to Georgetown, O., 21; his early educational opportunities, 21–22; his progress at school, 22; his early tastes and occupations, 22–27; is appointed to West Point, 28; goes to West Point, 31; is admitted to West Point, 31; is discontented, 31–32; his class rank, 32; enjoys his first furlough, 32–33; has a presentiment of future greatness, 33; chooses between arms of service, 34; leaves West Point, 34; serves at Jefferson

Barracks, 36–39; becomes acquainted with Julia Dent, 36; is engaged to Julia Dent, 39; corresponds with Julia Dent, 39; applies for assistant professorship at West Point, 39; serves at Camp Salubrity, 40–45; goes to Corpus Christi with his regiment, 46–47; visits Austin, 54–55; marches to the Rio Grande, 60–62; is promoted to second-lieutenancy, 56; at battle of Palo Alto, 66–68; commands a company, 68; at battle of Resaca de la Palma, 68–69; his reflections on his destiny, 71; acts as quartermaster and commissary, 72–73; at battle of Monterey, 76–82; at siege of Vera Cruz, 87–88; at battle of Cerro Gordo, 90–92; at battle of Contreras, 97; at battle of Churubusco, 99; at battle of Molino del Rey, 102–104; at battle of Chapultepec, 105–108; at San Cosme, 105–110; is promoted to first-lieutenancy, 111; visits Popocatapetl, 122–124; visits Caves of Mexico, 124–127; marries Julia Dent, 130; serves at Detroit, 130; goes to Pacific coast with his regiment, 130–134; is stationed in California, 135–136; in Oregon Territory, 136–138; is promoted to captaincy, 139; resigns his position in army and joins his family, 141; builds a house, 141; engages in real estate business in St. Louis, 141; is candidate for office of county engineer, 142; enters his father's store at Galena, Ill., as clerk, 142; casts his first vote, 142, presides at a Union meeting, 152; declines a captaincy of volunteers, 153; assists the adjutant-general of Illinois, 154–157; offers his services to the Government, 158; is appointed colonel of 21st Illinois regiment, 160; moves in various directions with his regiment, 162–165; takes command of a sub-district, 165; is stationed at Mexico, Mo., 165–166; is appointed brigadier-general, 168; at Ironton, Mo., 169–170; at Jefferson City, Mo., 170–171; is assigned to command of District of South-east Missouri, 172; seizes Paducah, 174–175; at battle of Belmont, 177–185; narrowly escapes death, 184; captures Fort Henry, 190–195; captures Fort Donelson, 196–213; is promoted to major-generalship of volunteers, 214; is relieved of command, 219–220; is restored to command, 221; is injured by fall of a horse, 224–225; at battle of Shiloh, 226–236; is struck by a bullet, 237; narrowly escapes being made a prisoner, 259–261; at battle of Iuka, 275–277; at battle of Corinth, 279–281; is put in command of Department of the Tennessee, 282; begins campaign against Vicksburg, 283; employs freedmen, 284–285; is criticised by newspapers, 304–305; at attack on Grand Gulf, 315–317; captures Port Gibson, 324; occupies Grand Gulf, 327; at battle of Raymond, 331; captures Jackson, Miss., 332–338; at battle of Champion's Hill, 345–348; at battle of Black River Bridge, 350–353; relieves McClernand of command, 367; receives surrender of Vicksburg, 378–379; is injured by fall of a horse, 390; is ordered to Cairo, 391; is appointed to command of Military Division of the Mississippi, 403; at battle of Wauhatchie, 420; at battle of Missionary Ridge, 436–439; at battle of Lookout Mountain, 440–442; at battle of Chattanooga, 443–447; is thanked by President Lincoln, 457; receives thanks of Congress, 458; antagonizes Stanton, 460–461; is commissioned lieutenant-general, 469–470; narrowly escapes capture, 485–488; at battle of Wilderness, 527–533; at battle of Spottsylvania, 544–551; at battle of North Anna, 564–567; at battle of Cold Harbor, 579–588; receives surrender of Lee, 735–741.

Grant, U. S., Mrs., 130; 163; 404; 750; 751.

Gregg, General, 331; 496; 517; 523; at battle of Wilderness, 528; 571; 575; 617; 619.

Gresham, General, 505.

Grierson, Colonel, 326; 676.

Griffin, General, 555; 557; 564; at battle of Five Forks, 701; 716; 720; 723; 729; 741; 770; 772.

Grose, Colonel, at battle of Lookout Mountain, 440.

Gwin, Commander, 233.

HACKELMAN, GENERAL, 281.

Hains, Lieutenant, 310; 353.

Halleck, H. W., Major-General, supersedes Fremont, 188; 189; 190; 197; 214; 219; removes Grant from command of an expedition, 219; 220; 221; 248; assumes command in field, 248; 251; 255; occupies Corinth, 256; 258; is appointed to command of all the Union armies, 262; 263; 264; 268; 279; 285; 286; 287; 288; 303; supports Grant against newspaper criticism, 305; 328; 333; 334; 350; 359; 367; 384; 388; his disposition, 389; 390; 391; 403; 404; 406; 412; 414; 431; 441; 448; 466; 472; 473; 480; 483; 484; 489; 550; 555; 557; 568; 569; 575; 590; 592;

593; 601; 615; 616; 618; 620; 627; 673; 764.

Hamer, Thomas L., secures Grant's appointment to West Point, 28, 29; his ability, 71.

Hamilton, C. S., Major-General, 282; 284.

Hampton, Wade, General, 603; 604; 648; 681; 682; 687.

Hancock, W. S., General, 516; 523; 524; 527; at battle of Wilderness, 528, 529, 530, 531, 532; 539; 541; 542; at battle of Spottsylvania, 545, 546, 549; 552; 553; 554; 555; 556; 557; 558; 559; 560; 562; at battle of North Anna, 564, 565; 567; 571; 572; 575; 580; at battle of Cold Harbor, 583, 584; 592; 596; 599; 600; 602; 608; 611; 617; 619; 631; 770; his ability and courage, 771.

Hardee, Captain, 63; General, 169; 508; 648; 651; 679; 682.

Harney, General, 94.

Harris, Thomas, Colonel, 164; 165; General, 763.

Hartranft, General, 693.

Hartsuff, General, 704.

Haslett, Lieutenant, 40.

Hatch, Colonel, 326.

Hatch, General, 651.

Hawkins, Major, 237.

Hayes, R. B., General, his gallantry and efficiency, 630.

Hays, Alexander, General, at battle of Wilderness, his gallantry, 528.

Hazen, General, 417; captures Fort McAllister, 649.

Hebert, Colonel, 129.

Heckman, General, 626.

Herron, General, at siege of Vicksburg, 366, 367, 368.

Heth, General, at battle of Wilderness, 528; 706.

Hill, General, 524; at battle of Wilderness, 528, 529, 530; 540; 542; 551; 564; at battle of North Anna, 567.

Hillyer, Captain, 168; 204.

Hinks, General, 599.

Hoffman, Colonel, at capture of San Antonio, 98.

Hoke, General, 559; 567; 601; 664; 667.

Holly Springs, Miss., occupation of, 286; loss of, 289.

Holmes, Captain, 56; 129; General, 380.

Hood, General, supersedes Johnston, 504; 505; 508; his methods, 632; 633; 634; 636; 640; 641; 650; at battle of Franklin, 654, 655, 656; at battle of Nashville, 660, 661; 673; 674; 680; 682; 683.

Hooker, General, 414; 417; 418; 420; at battle of Wauhatchie, 420; 426; 427; 428; 429; 430; 435; 439; at battle of Lookout Mountain, 440; 441; at battle of Chattanooga, 444; 447; 448; 450; 451; 453; 505; 770; his character, 771.

Horses, Grant's experience with, 26–27; 38–39; 60–61; 390.

Hoskins, Lieutenant, at battle of Monterey, 76.

Hovey, General, 286; 323; 339; 340; 341; 342; at battle of Champion's Hill, 345, 346, 347.

Howard, B. B., 155.

Howard, O. O., General, 411; 414; 420; at battle of Wauhatchie, 427; 432; 434; 439; 447; 448; 637; 641.

Hudson, Captain, 674.

Humphreys, General, 555; 556; 631; at battle of White Oak Road, 693; 697; 698; 702; 704; 705; 706; 708; 714; 715; 723; 724; 770; 772.

Hunt, Henry J., General, 516.

Hunter, General, 197; 214; 304; 558; 568; 585; 590; 591; 592; 595; 603; 604; 605; 615; 616; 617.

Hunter, R. M. T., 685.

Hurlbut, General, 223; at battle of Shiloh, 227, 235, 244, 258; at battle of Corinth, 279, 280; 294; 329; 339; 359; 366; 391; 463.

INDIANS, their treatment by Hudson's Bay Company, their

manner of trading, 137; their
    remedy for disease, 138.
Ingalls, Rufus, General, 523.
Intrigue, political, 83–85.
Iuka, battle of, 275–277.

JACKSON, CLAIBORN, GOVERNOR,
    150; 155.
Jackson, General, attempts to
    capture Grant, 260, 261.
Jackson, Miss., capture of, 332–338.
Jefferson Barracks, St. Louis, 36.
Jenkins, General, at battle of
    Wilderness, 531.
Johnson, Andrew, Governor, 410;
    Vice-President, 750; President,
    751; his course toward the
    South, 751; 752; 754; 755; 761;
    768.
Johnson, R. D., General, 555.
Johnson, Richard W., General, 434;
    505.
Johnston, A. S., General, 129; 206;
    207; 217; 218; 219; 222; 224;
    232; his ability, 241, 242, 243;
    250.
Johnston, Joseph E., General, 129;
    333; 334; 337; 338; 339; 340; 349;
    355; 363; 367; 368; 369; 374; 376;
    380; 381; 389; 404; 465; 471;
    472; 478; 479; 481; 489; 499;
    500; 503; 504; is relieved from
    command, his tactics, 504; 536;
    557; 632; his policy, 633; his
    ability, is put in command of
    troops in North and South
    Carolina, 680; 682; 683; 684;
    691; 695; 708; 754; 755;
    surrenders to Sherman, 756;
    757; 758; 762.
Johnston, William Preston, Colonel,
    212; 243.
Jones, W. S., General, 592.
Juarez, President, 775.
Judah, Lieutenant, at battle of San
    Cosme, 105.

KAUTZ, A. V., GENERAL, 30; 551;
    599; 608; 625; 630.

Kearney, Philip, Captain, 99; 129.
Kearney, Steven, Colonel, 36.
Kelley, General, 614.
Kelly, Miss, 18.
Kilpatrick, General, 508.
Kimball, General, 366.
King, Major, 30.
Kitching, Colonel, 559.

LAGOW, C. B., LIEUTENANT, 168;
    169.
Lake Providence, 298–299.
Lauman, General, 329; at siege of
    Vicksburg, 358, 367.
Lawler, General, 350; at battle of
    Black River Bridge, 350.
Ledlie, General, 612.
Lee, Fitz-Hugh, General, 603.
Lee, Robert E., Captain, 90; 129;
    General, 388; 389; 459; 474;
    478; 479; 482; 485; 489; 490;
    494; 496; 516; 518; 522; 524; at
    battle of Wilderness, 529, 530,
    531, 532, 533; 536; 540; 541; 542;
    at battle of Spottsylvania, 544,
    545, 546, 550; 551; 554; 555; 557;
    558; 559; 560; 562; 564; at battle
    of North Anna, 567; 568; 569;
    571; 572; 575; 576; 580; 583; at
    battle of Cold Harbor, 585; 586;
    587; 590; 591; 594; 595; his
    advantages as a commander,
    597; 598; 599; 603; 605; 608; 613;
    617; 619; 620; 625; 626; 672;
    674; 679; 683; 684; 687; 688;
    691; 692; 693; 697; 703; 704;
    707; 708; 712; 713; 714; 715; 716;
    717; 719; 720; 723; 724; 727; 728;
    729; 730; 731; 732; surrenders
    Army of Northern Virginia,
    735, 738, 739, 740, 741; 744; 745;
    748; 754; 755; 756; 757; 775.
Lee, Stephen D., General, 654.
Leggett, M. D., Colonel, 677;
    Brigadier-General, 282; 369.
Lincoln, Abraham, 144–145; goes to
    Washington as President elect,
    151; takes oath to maintain
    Union, 152; 168; his hopefulness
    of Union cause, 271; sends

congratulatory letter to Grant,
281; 288; 297; 305; supports
Grant against newspaper
criticism, 305; 388; 425; 431;
441; 452; thanks Grant, 457;
469; 473; 474; 480; 485; 486;
556; 557; 615; 625; 647; 652; 668;
685; 686; his generosity and
kindness, 687; 702; 703; 704;
706; 711; 712; 713; 714; 748; 749;
is assassinated, 750; 751; 752;
754; 755; reflections in regard
to, 761; anecdote about, 766,
767; contrasted with Stanton,
769, 770; 775.
Lincoln, Mrs., 750.
Logan, John A., is elected to
Congress, 161; his political
attitude, 161; General, his
influence in his Congressional
district, 162; 252; 314; 321; 323;
324; at occupation of Grand
Gulf, 327; his ability, 331; 334;
340; at battle of Champion's
Hill, 345, 346, 347; at siege of
Vicksburg, 369; 375; 379; 385;
465; 470; 505; 506; 637; 638;
659; 660.
Longstreet, General, at battle of
Wauhatchie, 420; 421; 425; 426;
427; 432; 433; 449; his
character, 450; 452; 454; 455;
456; 458; 461; 465; 466; 524; at
battle of Wilderness, 528, 529,
530, 531; is seriously wounded,
531; 540; 628; 704; 741.
Lookout Mountain, battle of,
440–441.
Loomis, General, at battle of
Chattanooga, 443.
Loomis, Mr., 154.
Loring, General, 322; 347.
Loudon, Colonel, 30.
Lovell, Mansfield, 122; General, 279.
Luther, Lieutenant, 67.
Lyon, N., Captain, 155.

MACKENZIE, GENERAL, 693; 715;
770; his ability, 772.
Macon, Ga., capture of, 758.

Mansfield, Major, 75; 129.
Markland, A. H., Colonel, 649.
Marshall, Colonel, 30.
Marshall, Colonel, 732.
Marsh, C. C., Colonel, 172;
Brigadier-General, 282.
Mason, Rodney, Colonel,
surrenders Clarksville, 266.
Matamoras, Mex., skirmish at, 63.
Martindale, General, at battle of
Cold Harbor, 585.
McArthur, General, 270; 345; at
siege of Vicksburg, 358.
McCall, Captain, 56–57; 60–61; at
battle of Resaca de la Palma,
68; 129.
McCandless, William, Colonel, 556.
McCausland, General, 614.
McClellan, George B., Lieutenant,
at battle of Cerro Gordo, 90;
General, 159; 189; 219; orders
Grant relieved from duty, 220;
304; 471.
McClernand, John A., 161; 162;
General, 189; at capture of Fort
Henry, 190; at capture of Fort
Donelson, 198, 201, 204, 205;
213; 223; at battle of Shiloh,
227, 231, 232, 235, 239, 244, 245;
248; 282; 285; 288; 289; 292; at
capture of Arkansas Post, 293;
his fitness to command, 294;
295; 297; 304; 309; 310; 313; 315;
316; 318; 321; 322; 323; at
occupation of Grand Gulf, 327;
328; 329; 330; 331; 332; 333; 338;
339; 340; 341; 342; 345; 346;
347; 349; 354; at siege of
Vicksburg, 355, 358, 367.
McCook, A. McD., General, at
battle of Shiloh, 234, 235, 237,
238; 406; 471; 507.
McGroierty, General, 30.
McKinzie, Captain, at battle of
Chapultepec, 104.
McLean, Mr., 732; 744.
McPherson, Colonel, 223; 225; 226;
at battle of Shiloh, 237;
General, at battle of Corinth,
279, 280; is promoted to major-
generalcy, 282; 284; 286; 296;

298; 299; 310; 313; 314; 316; 321; 322; 323; 324; 326; at occupation of Grand Gulf, 327; 329; 330; at battle of Raymond, 331; at capture of Jackson, 332, 333, 334, 337, 339; 340; 341; at battle of Champion's Hill, 342, 345, 346; 347; at battle of Black River Bridge, 349; 350; 353; 354; 356; at siege of Vicksburg, 357, 358, 367, 375; 391; 406; 424; 463; 470; 498; 500; is killed, his character and ability, 506; 637.

Meade, George G., Lieutenant, 75; General, 470; 471; 481; 484; 487; 495; 524; 527; at battle of Wilderness, 528, 529; 536; 539; 540; 543; at battle of Spottsylvania, 545, 549; 552; 554; 555; 556; 560; 563; 568; 570; 576; 583; 584; 585; 593; 594; 599; 600; 602; 604; 606; 607; 608; 611; 612; 613; 617; 626; 630; 631; 692; 693; 698; 704; at capture of Petersburg, 707; 708; 711; 714; 715; 716; 717; 724; 731; 754; 766; 767; 768; his character and ability, 770.

Merritt, General, 541; 690; 702; 705; 714; 715; 741.

Mersy, Colonel, 506.

Mexicans, their bravery and patriotism, 114–115; their amusements, 119–121; 126–127.

Mexico under Spanish rule, 48–50.

Mexico, City of, capture of, 111.

Miles, General, 705; 706.

Missionary Ridge, battle of, 436; 439.

Mitchell, General, 216.

Mobile, Ala., capture of, 757–758.

Molino del Rey, battle of, 102–104.

Monterey, Mex., movement of forces to, 72–73; preparation for attacking, 75; battle of, 76–82.

Montgomery, Ala., capture of, 758.

Montgomery, Colonel, 374.

Morales, General, surrenders Vera Cruz, 88.

Morgan, General, 636.

Morgan, John H., General, 748.

Morrison, William R., Colonel, 201.

Morris, Thomas, 28; 29.

Mosby, John S., Colonel, 485; his character and ability, 486.

Mott, General, at battle of Wilderness, 528, 530, 531; at battle of Spottsylvania, 545, 546, 549, 550; 552; 553; 555.

Mower, J. A., Brigadier-General, 282; 366.

Mules, branding and breaking, 57–59.

Mulligan, Colonel, 170.

Murphy, Colonel, 271; 289; his character, 290.

Napoleon I, 776.

Napoleon III, 776.

Nashville, battle of, 659–660.

Navy under Admiral Porter, efficiency of, 385–386.

Negley, General, 471.

Nelson, General, 197; 215; 216; 217; 225; 233; at battle of Shiloh, 235; 244.

Newton, General, 503; 505.

North Anna, battle of, 564–567.

O'Fallon, John, Colonel, 37.

Oglesby, Richard J., Colonel, 174; 177; 178; 186; at battle of Corinth, 281.

Oliver, W. S., Colonel, 314.

Ord, General, 270; 272; at battle of Iuka, 275, 276; at battle of Corinth, 280; at capture of Vicksburg, 375; 380; 387; 390; 479; 481; 611; 612; 625; is seriously wounded, 626; at battle of White Oak Road, 693; 702; 704; 705; 715; 717; 720; 723; 724.

Osterhaus, General, 323; 339; 340; 341; at battle of Champion's Hill, 346, 347; 349; 350; 367; 435; 439; at battle of Lookout Mountain, 440; 448; 637.

Owen, General, at battle of Wilderness, 528.

PADUCAH, KY., capture of, 174–175.

Page, Captain, at battle of Palo Alto, 67.

Palmer, John M., Colonel, 163–164; General, 417; 429; 434; 448; 453; 508.

Palo Alto, battle of, 65–67.

Parke, General, 367; 626; 693; 702; 703; 704; 705; 711; 714.

Parker, General, 736.

Parties, secret political, Grant's opinion of, 142–143.

Patterson, General, 90.

Payne, Mr., 25.

Pemberton, Lieutenant, 109; General, 281; 284; 286; 288; 290; 292; 318; 330; 332; 334; 338; 339; 340; 341; at battle of Champion's Hill, 342, 347; 349; 355; 367; 368; 370; 374; 375; 376; 377; surrenders Vicksburg, 378; 379; 380; 382; 387; 389; 390.

Pendelton, General, 741.

Pennybacker, Colonel, at capture of Fort Fisher, 670; is seriously wounded, 670.

Perote, Mex., capture of, 92.

Petersburg, Va., investment of, 602; explosion of mine before, 612; capture of, 707.

Pleasonton, Alfred, General, 481.

Pleasants, Colonel, 607.

Pickett, General, 562; 567; 697.

Pierce, Colonel, at battle of North Anna, 564.

Pierce, General Franklin, 99; 100.

Pillow, General, at battle of Cerro Gordo, 91; 94; at battle of Chapultepec, 104; opposes Scott, 117; 196; 206; escapes from Fort Donelson, 207; 212; 213; 218.

Pittsburg Landing, Tenn., 222–226.

Prime, Captain, at siege of Vicksburg, 360.

Point Pleasant, O., Grant's birth at, 21.

Politics before War of Rebellion, 142–151; Grant's participation in, 142–145.

Polk, Bishop, General, 185; 463.

Polk, President, 84; 117.

Pope, John, General, 157; 165; 248; 250; 251; 252; 256; 270.

Porter, Admiral, 287; at capture of Arkansas Post, 293; 301; 302; 306; runs Vicksburg batteries, 307, 308; attacks Grand Gulf, 316, 317; 318; 327; 332; at siege of Vicksburg, 360, 366, 373, 376; 385; 410; 663; 664; 667; 668; at capture of Fort Fisher, 669; 748.

Porter, Andrew, Captain, 122; 125.

Porter, Lieutenant-Colonel, 635.

Porter, Theodric, Lieutenant, 63.

Porter, William, Captain, 191.

Port Gibson, Miss., capture of, 324.

Port Hudson, La., surrender of, 382.

Potter, General, 554; at battle of North Anna, 567; 601; 612.

Prentiss, B. M., General, supersedes Grant, 170; is disaffected, 172; his bravery and devotion, 173; 223; at battle of Shiloh, 227; is captured, 228; 233; 247; defends Helena, 359; 380.

Price, Sterling, General, 170; 177; 264; 265; 270; captures Iuka, 271, 272; 275; 279; 290; 389; 635.

QUINBY, GENERAL, 301; 356.

Quitman, General, 94; 98; 105; 110.

RALSTON, MR., 26.

Ransom, General, 345; his ability, 353; 357; 385; 389; 637.

Rawlins, John A., 153; 169; Colonel, 365.

Raymond, battle of, 331.

Read, Colonel, 720.

Resaca de la Palma, battle of, 67–69.

Revolution, right of, 146.

Reynolds, Lieutenant-Governor, 150.

Rice, J. C., General, at battle of Spottsylvania, killed, 549.

Richmond, Va., capture of, 713.

Ricketts, General, 606.

Riley, General, at capture of San Antonio, 98.
Ringgold, Major, at battle of Palo Alto, 67.
Rockwell, Mrs., 17.
Rosecrans, General, 270; 271; 272; at battle of Iuka, 275; 276; 277; at battle of Corinth, 279, 280, 281; 290; 359; 390; 391; 403; 404; 405; 406; is superseded by Thomas, 409; 410; 414; 640.
Ross, Colonel, 264; General, 300; 301.
Rosser, General, at battle of Wilderness, 528; 627.
Rousseau, General, 506.
Rowley, Captain, 226; 487.
Russell, General, 571.
Rust, General, at battle of Corinth, 279.

SAILOR'S CREEK, battle of, 719–720.
San Antonio, Mex., capture of, 98.
San Cosme, battle of, 105–110.
Sanders, Captain, 75.
San Francisco, Cal., early days of, 135–137; 139–140.
Santa Anna, President, 41; 42; 90; 91; 92; 100; 101; evacuates City of Mexico, 109; 116.
Santo Domingo, 778.
Savannah, Ga., siege of, 648–651; capture of, 651.
Schenck, Captain, 131.
Schofield, General, 389; 465; 466; 498; 499; 504; 507; 508; 640; 654; 655; 673; 674; 680; 683.
Scott, Winfield S., General, his personal appearance, 33; his aspirations, 83; political opposition to, 83, 84; assumes command of army of invasion, 85; 89; 90; 91; 92; contrasted with Taylor, 94, 95; 97; his tactics, 99; 100; 101; 102; 104; 110; his wisdom and discretion, 111; 112; his generalship, 113, 114; 116; is relieved of command in field, 117; 118; 121; 735.
Sedgwick, John, General, 516; 523;

524; 527; at battle of Wilderness, 529, 532; 536; 539; 541; 544; at battle of Spottsylvania, is killed, 545; 770; his bravery and conscientiousness, 771–772.
Slavery, 773.
Selma, Ala., capture of, 758.
Semmes, Lieutenant, at battle of San Cosme, 105.
Seward, Mr., 148; is assassinated, 750.
Sheridan, P. H., Colonel, 265; General, 268; 269; 434; at battle of Chattanooga, 445, 446, 447; 480; makes first raid against Lee, 494, 495, 496, 497; 511; 516; at battle of Wilderness, 528, 530; 539; 540; 541; 544; 551; 557; 569; 571; 575; 576; 579; 583; 591; 592; 595; 603; 604; 608; 611; 615; 616; 617; 618; 620; 621; is congratulated by Grant, 622; 625; 627; his ride to Winchester, 628; 629; 676; 689; 690; 691; 693; 695; 696; 697; 698; at battle of Five Forks, 701, 702, 703; 704; 705; 706; 708; 714; 715; 716; 717; 720; 724; 728; 731; 732; 775.
Sherman, General, offers assistance to Grant, 213; 223; 224; 226; 227; his ability, is wounded, 231; at battle of Shiloh, 232, 233, 234, 235, 238, 239, 244, 245, 247; 252; 258; 264; 270; 284; 286; 287; 288; 289; attempts to capture Vicksburg, 292; captures Arkansas Post, 293; 294; 301; 302; 310; 314; 318; 321; 324; 328; 329; 330; 331; at capture of Jackson, 332, 333, 334, 337; 338; 340; 341; 342; 349; 353; 354; 356; at siege of Vicksburg, 358, 364, 365, 367, 368; 380; 381; 387; 388; 390; 391; 406; 410; is assigned to command of Army of the Tennessee, 412; 422; 423; 425; 426; 427; 428; 429; 430; 431; 432; 435; at battle of Missionary Ridge, 436; 439;

441; 442; at battle of
Chattanooga, 443, 444, 446;
447; 448; 450; 453; 454; 456;
458; 461; 462; 463; 464; 465;
466; 470; succeeds Grant in
command of Division of the
Mississippi, 471; 472; 473; 475;
478; 479; 480; 481; 483; 484;
485; 489; 494; 498; 499;
conducts campaign against
Atlanta, 500, 503, 504, 506, 507;
captures Atlanta, 508; 509; 536;
555; 556; 557; 568; 583; 607; 608;
618; 620; 631; his march to the
sea, 632–653; 671; 672; 673;
receives resolutions of thanks
from Congress, 674; 675; 676;
679; 680; 681; 682; 683; 684;
690; 691; 695; 708; 709; 754;
755; receives surrender of
Johnston, his loyalty, 756; 757;
758; 762; 764; 765; 768.
Sherman, Mrs., 650.
Shields, General, at battle of
Churubusco, 99.
Shiloh, battle of, 227–247.
Shirk, Commander, at battle of
Shiloh, 233.
Sibley, Captain, 122; 125.
Sigel, General, 479; 480; 481; 485;
489; 558; 559; 568; 605.
Simpson, Hannah, ancestry of, 20;
marries Jesse R. Grant, 21.
Simpson, John, 20.
Slaughter, Lieutenant, 133.
Slocum, H. W., General, 414; 508;
637; 641.
Smith, A. J., General, 323; 325; 339;
340; 341; at battle of
Champion's Hill, 345; at siege
of Vicksburg, 368, 375, 376;
484; 500; 607; 640; 655; 674.
Smith, C. F., Captain, 33; 68;
General, 175; 178; 189; his
ability, 190; 192; 198; 202; at
capture of Fort Donelson, 204,
205, 214; 215; 216; 217; Halleck's
estimate of, 221; 223; 227.
Smith, Dr., 260.
Smith, Dr., 724.
Smith, Giles A., General, 435; 439.

Smith, Governor, 766; 767.
Smith, G. W., Lieutenant, 90;
General, 646.
Smith, John E., Brigadier-General,
282; 323; at battle of Missionary
Ridge, 436; at battle of
Chattanooga, 443, 444.
Smith, Kirby, General, 618;
surrenders, 758.
Smith, Morgan L., General, 435; at
capture of Missionary Ridge,
436; at battle of Chattanooga,
443, 444; 447.
Smith, Sidney, Lieutenant, 86; 111.
Smith, Sooy, General, 366; 463;
464.
Smith, Watson, Lieutenant-
Commander, 300.
Smith, W. F., Brigadier-General,
411; 413; 417; 418; at battle of
Wauhatchie, 420; 430; 435;
Major-General, 457; 479; 480;
482; 570; 576; 579; 580; 583; at
battle of Cold Harbor, 584, 585;
586; 592; 594; 595.
South, attitude of, before War,
146–151; advantages of, at
beginning of War, 187–188;
boldness of, during War, 296;
benefit of War to, 419; bravery
and gallantry of, 688.
Spottsylvania, battle of, 544–550.
Stager, General, 460; 461.
Stanley, General, 465; 640; at battle
of Franklin, 655; 681.
Stannard, General, 625; 626.
Stanton, Secretary, 403; 404; 409;
431; 457; 460; his disposition,
461; 472; 473; 474; 485; 556; 557;
615; 620; 631; 670; 671; 673; 685;
741; 749; 755; 756; 768;
contrasted with Lincoln, 769,
770; 775.
States, European, conduct of,
774–777.
Steedman, General, 655.
Steele, General, 314; 341; 380; 387;
479; 481; 489; 498; 618.
Stephens, Alexander H., 685; 686;
687.
Stevens, Colonel, 625.

Stevens, Isaac I., Lieutenant, 90.
Stevenson, Carter L., General, 439.
Stevenson, J. D., Brigadier-General, 282; 337.
Stevenson, T. G., General, at battle of Spottsylvania, is killed, 546.
Stewart, General, 654.
Stone, C. P., Lieutenant, 122; 124.
Stoneman, General, 507; 676; 680; 757.
Stuart, General, at battle of Shiloh, 227; 301.
Stuart, J. E. B., General, 495; at battle of Wilderness, 530.
Sturgis, General, 607.
Sullivan, J. C., Brigadier-General, 313; 327.
Swinton, Mr., 486; 487; 488.

Taylor, Colonel, 717.
Taylor, Richard, General, 366; 373; surrenders, 758.
Taylor, Zachary, General, commands army of occupation, 50; 52; prevents plundering, 60; 65; 66; 67; 69; his bravery and modesty, 70, 71; 74; 75; 83; 84; 85; 91; contrasted with Scott, 94, 95; 112; his generalship, 113; 114; is elected President, 118.
Territt, Lieutenant, at battle of Monterey, 81.
Terry, Alfred H., General, 662; 668; at capture of Fort Fisher, 669, 670; promoted to brigadier-generalcy in regular army, 670; 673; 680; 682; 683; 770; his character, 772.
Texas, condition of, before Mexican War, 41; occupation of, by United States troops, 49; transportation in, 50–51; game in, 54–55; wild horses in, 61–62.
Thayer, Colonel, at capture of Fort Donelson, 198; 202; 204; 205.
Thomas, George H., Major-General, 189; 218; 245; 248; 252; 278; 404; 406; supersedes Rosecrans, 409, 410; 411; 413; 417; 425; 427; 429; 430; 431;

434; 439; battle of Lookout Mountain, 441; 443; at battle of Chattanooga, 444, 445, 446, 447; 448; 452; 453; 458; 465; 466; 498; 500; 631; 636; 640; 641; 650; 654; 655; 656; 659; 660; 673; 674; 676; 677; 678; 679; 680; 757; his ability, 762, 763.
Thompson, Jacob, 306.
Thompson, Jeff., Colonel, 172; 173.
Thornton, Captain, 63.
Tidball, General, 692.
Tilghman, Lloyd, General, 175; is captured, 192.
Tod, Governor, 18.
Tod, Judge, 18; 19.
Tod, Mrs., 18.
Torbert, A. T. A., Brigadier-General, 517; 571.
Tower, Z. B., Lieutenant, 90; 122; General, 655.
Townsend, General, 158.
Towson, Brevet Brigadier-General, 117.
Trist, Nicholas P., negotiates treaty with Mexico, 100; 116.
Tuscaloosa, Ala., capture of, 758.
Tuttle, General, 337.
Twiggs, Colonel, 70; 75; General, 89; 94.
Tyler, Mrs., 568.
Tyler, President, approves bill for annexation of Texas, 44.
Tyler, Robert O., Brigadier-General, 558.

Upton, Emory, Colonel, at battle of Spottsylvania, 549; is promoted to brigadier-generalcy and seriously wounded, 550; 556; 557.

Van Buren, Martin, President, 33.
Van Dorn, General, 250; 264; 270; at battle of Iuka, 272; 275; 278; at battle of Corinth, 279, 280, 281; captures Holly Springs, 289; 290; 291; 292.

Van Duzer, 660.
Vera Cruz, siege of 87–88.
Vicksburg, Miss., movements against, 283–356; siege of 357–378; surrender of, 379.
Villepigue, General, at battle of Corinth, 279.
Vose, Colonel, 45.

WADSWORTH, GENERAL, at battle of Wilderness, 528, 529; is mortally wounded and captured, 531; 541.
Walke, Captain, 195; 201.
Wallace, Lew., General, at capture of Fort Donelson, 198; 202; 204, 208; 223; 224; 225; 226; at battle of Shiloh, 233; 234; 235; 236; 248; 605; 606.
Wallace, W. H. L., Colonel, 270; Brigadier-General, 223; 225; his ability, 227; 233; 236.
Wallace, W. H. L., Mrs., 236.
Wallen, Lieutenant, 67.
Ward, General, at battle of Wilderness, 531.
War, Mexican, injustice of, 40–43; assemblage of troops for, 49; acts of troops to provoke, 50; forces at beginning of, 60; first movement of troops in, 60–63; skirmish at Matamoras, 63; battle of Palo Alto, 66–67; armaments of contending forces, 67; battle of Resaca de la Palma, 67–69; movement of forces to Monterey, 72–73; preparation for attacking Monterey, 75–76; battle of Monterey, 76–81; movement of army to Vera Cruz, 84–87; siege of Vera Cruz, 87–88; battle of Cerro Gordo, 90–92; capture of Perote, 92; raising of additional troops, 94; battle of Contreras, 97–98; capture of San Antonio, 98; battle of Churubusco, 99; negotiations for peace, 100; battle of Molino del Rey, 102–104; battle of

Chapultepec, 104; battle of San Cosme, 105–110; capture of City of Mexico, 111; treaty of peace signed, 117; treaty of peace ratified, 130.
War of Rebellion, Reflections on, 115–116; secession of States, 152; loss of Fort Sumter, 152; first call for troops, 152–153; second call for troops, 160; battle of Belmont, 178–185; capture of Fort Henry, 190–195; capture of Fort Donelson, 196–213; battle of Shiloh, 227–247; occupation of Corinth, 255; discouraging indications, 271; battle of Iuka, 275–277; battle of Corinth, 279–281; loss of Holly Springs, 289; capture of Arkansas Post, 293; capture of Port Gibson, 324; occupation of Grand Gulf, 327; battle of Raymond, 331; capture of Jackson, 332–338; battle of Champion's Hill, 345–348; battle of Black River Bridge, 350–353; capture of Vicksburg, 357–379; battle of Gettysburg, 381; capture of Port Hudson, 382; battle of Wauhatchie, 419–420; battle of Missionary Ridge, 436–439; battle of Lookout Mountain, 440–441; battle of Chatta-nooga, 443–447; loss of Fort Pillow, 483; battle of Atlanta, 505; occupation of Atlanta, 508; battle of Wilderness, 527–533; battle of Spottsylvania, 544–550; battle of North Anna, 564–567; battle of Cold Harbor, 584–588; Sherman's march to the sea, 632–653; capture of Savannah, 651; battle of Franklin, 654–655; battle of Nashville, 660–661; capture of Fort Fisher, 669–670; attempt to negotiate peace, 685–687; battle of White Oak Road, 693–694; battle of Five Forks, 701–702; capture of Richmond, 713; battle of

Sailor's Creek, 719–720;
surrender of Lee, 732–741;
surrender of Johnston, 756;
capture of Mobile, 757–758;
capture of Selma, Tuscaloosa,
Montgomery, West Point, and
Macon, 758; surrender of
Taylor, 758; surrender of E.
Kirby Smith, 758; capture of
Jefferson Davis, 758–759; review
of Sherman's and Meade's
armies, 768–769; cause of,
773–774; reflections on, 774–780.

Warren, G. K., General, 516; 523;
524; at battle of Wilderness,
527, 529, 532, 533; 536; 539; 541,
542; his methods, 543; at battle
of Spottsylvania, 544, 546, 549;
552; 553; 554; 555; 556; 557; 558;
563; 564; at battle of North
Anna, 567; 570; 571; 572; 575;
576; 580; 583; at battle of Cold
Harbor, 584, 585; 592; 596; 602;
611; 612; 619; 626; at battle of
White Oak Road, 693; 697;
698; is relieved of command,
701; his defects, 701, 702.

Washburn, C. C., General, 286; 366.

Washburn, Colonel, 720; 723.

Washburne, E. B., 153; 157; 486; 487;
688.

Watts, Major, 384.

Wauhatchie, battle of, 420.

Wayne, Harry, General, 646; 648.

Webster, J. D., Colonel, at capture
of Fort Donelson, 205; at battle
of Shiloh, 232, 233.

West Point, Ala., capture of, 758.

West Point, N. Y., Grant's stay at,
31–35.

Wheeler, General, 425; 508; 633;
648; 679.

White, Chilton, 26; Colonel, 30.

White, John D., 26; 27.

Whiting, General, 664.

White Oak Road, battle of,
693–694.

Wilcox, Cadmus M., General,
706.

Wilderness, battle of, 527–533;
comments on, 534.

Willcox, Orlando B., General, 431;
433; 443; 448; at battle of
Spottsylvania, 544; 612; 693.

Williams, A. S., General, 637.

Williams, Captain, 81.

Williams, Thomas, General, 297.

Wilmington, N. C., capture of, 682.

Wilson, J. H., Lieutenant-Colonel,
299; 324; 455; General, 496; 516;
523; 524; at battle of
Wilderness, 527, 528; 541; 571;
576; 583; 596; 604; 640; 654;
757; 758; 762.

Wolves, 55–56.

Wood, T. J., General, 245; 434; at
battle of Chattanooga, 445,
446, 447.

Worth, William J., General, 70; 75;
at battle of Monterey, 77; his
temperament, 85, 86; 89; 93;
94; 97; 98; 101; his relations
with Scott, 102; at battle of
Molino del Rey, 102–103; at
battle of San Cosme, 105, 106,
109; 110; opposes Scott, 117.

Wright, H. G., General, 527; at
battle of Spottsylvania, 545,
546; 549; 552; 553; 554; 555; 556;
558; 560; 562; 563; 564; at battle
of North Anna, 567; 570; 571;
572; 575; 576; 579; 580; 583; 584;
585; at battle of Cold Harbor,
592; 596; 602; 606; 608; 614;
627; 628; 629; 697; 698; 702;
703; 704; 714; 715; 720; 723;
724; 770.

YATES, RICHARD, GOVERNOR, 154;
160.

Yazoo Pass, operations at, 299–302.

Young, P. M. B., General, 576.

SELECTED LETTERS
1839 – 1865

Contents

To R. McKinstry Griffith, September 22, 1839 877

To Julia Dent, June 4, 1844 879

To Mrs. George B. Bailey, June 6, 1844 882

To Julia Dent, July 28, 1844 884

To Julia Dent, August 31, 1844 887

To Julia Dent, January 12, 1845 890

To Julia Dent, May 6, 1845 892

To Julia Dent, July 6, 1845 894

To Julia Dent, July 11, 1845 896

To Julia Dent, September 14, 1845 898

To Julia Dent, October 1845 900

To Julia Dent, February 5, 1846 902

To Julia Dent, February 7, 1846 904

To Julia Dent, March 3, 1846 905

To Julia Dent, March 29, 1846 907

To Julia Dent, May 11, 1846 909

To John W. Lowe, June 26, 1846 912

To Julia Dent, July 25, 1846 917

To Julia Dent, October 3, 1846 918

To Julia Dent, April 24, 1847 920

To John W. Lowe, May 3, 1847 923

To Julia Dent, September 1847 925

To Julia Dent, January 9, 1848 927

To Julia Dent Grant, April 27, 1849 929

To Julia Dent Grant, May 28, 1851 930

To Julia Dent Grant, August 10, 1851 932

To Julia Dent Grant, July 15, 1852 933

To Julia Dent Grant, August 9, 1852 935

To Julia Dent Grant, August 20, 1852 937

To Julia Dent Grant, December 19, 1852 939

To Julia Dent Grant, January 3, 1853 941

To Julia Dent Grant, March 31, 1853 943

To Julia Dent Grant, July 13, 1853 945

To Osborn Cross, July 25, 1853 947

To Julia Dent Grant, February 2, 1854 949

To Julia Dent Grant, February 6, 1854 951

To Julia Dent Grant, March 6, 1854 953

To Frederick Dent, April 19, 1861 955

To Jesse Root Grant, April 21, 1861 956

To Julia Dent Grant, April 27, 1861 957

To Mary Grant, April 29, 1861 959

To Julia Dent Grant, May 1, 1861 960

To Jesse Root Grant, May 2, 1861 962

To Julia Dent Grant, May 3, 1861 963

To Julia Dent Grant, May 21, 1861 964

Orders No. 7, June 18, 1861 965

To Julia Dent Grant, June 26, 1861 965

To Julia Dent Grant, July 7, 1861 967

To Jesse Root Grant, July 13, 1861 968

To Julia Dent Grant, July 13, 1861 970

To Jesse Root Grant, August 3, 1861 971

To Julia Dent Grant, August 3, 1861 973

To Julia Dent Grant, August 10, 1861 974

To Mary Grant, August 12, 1861 975

To Julia Dent Grant, August 26, 1861 977

To Eleazer A. Paine, January 11, 1862 978

General Orders No. 3, January 13, 1862 979

To Julia Dent Grant, February 5, 1862 980

To Mary Grant, February 9, 1862 981

To George W. Cullum, February 16, 1862 982

To Julia Dent Grant, February 16, 1862 985

To Julia Dent Grant, February 24, 1862 985

To Julia Dent Grant, February 26, 1862 986

To Julia Dent Grant, March 11, 1862 987

To Julia Dent Grant, March 18, 1862 988

To Elihu B. Washburne, March 22, 1862 989

To Julia Dent Grant, March 23, 1862 991

To Henry W. Halleck, March 24, 1862 993

To Julia Dent Grant, March 29, 1862 994

To Julia Dent Grant, April 3, 1862 996

To William T. Sherman, April 4, 1862 997

To Henry W. Halleck, April 5, 1862 997

To Don Carlos Buell, April 6, 1862 998

To Commanding Officer, Advance Forces, April 6, 1862 999

To Henry W. Halleck, April 7, 1862 999

To Henry W. Halleck, April 8, 1862 1000

To Julia Dent Grant, April 8, 1862 1000

To Nathaniel H. McLean, April 9, 1862 1001

To Jesse Root Grant, April 26, 1862 1004

To Mrs. Charles F. Smith, April 26, 1862. 1005

To Julia Dent Grant, April 30, 1862 1006

To Elihu B. Washburne, May 14, 1862 1007

To Julia Dent Grant, June 12, 1862 1009

To Henry W. Halleck, July 7, 1862 1010

To Salmon P. Chase, July 31, 1862 1010

Fragment on Shiloh, August–September 1862?. 1011

To Jesse Root Grant, September 17, 1862 1013

To Stephen A. Hurlbut, November 9, 1862 1015

To Jesse Root Grant, November 23, 1862 1015

To John C. Pemberton, December 14, 1862 1016

To Henry W. Halleck, February 18, 1863 1017

To David D. Porter, February 26, 1863. 1018

To Isaac F. Quinby, March 23, 1863. 1019

To Thomas W. Knox, April 6, 1863 1020

To Stephen A. Hurlbut, April 9, 1863 1021

To Julia Dent Grant, April 20, 1863 1022

To Jesse Root Grant, April 21, 1863 1023

To Peter J. Osterhaus, May 29, 1863 1025

To Jesse Root Grant, July 6, 1863 1025

To Lorenzo Thomas, July 11, 1863 1026

To Salmon P. Chase, July 21, 1863 1028

To Charles W. Ford, July 28, 1863 1029

To Abraham Lincoln, August 23, 1863 1030

To John G. Thompson, August 29, 1863 1032

To Elihu B. Washburne, August 30, 1863 1033

To Henry W. Halleck, October 26, 1863 1034

To Julia Dent Grant, October 27, 1863 1036

To Julia Dent Grant, November 2, 1863 1037

To J. Russell Jones, December 5, 1863 1038

To Barnabas Burns, December 17, 1863 1039

To Henry W. Halleck, January 15, 1864 1040

To George H. Thomas, January 16, 1864 1043

To Henry W. Halleck, January 19, 1864 1043

To Rufus Ingalls, February 16, 1864 1045

To William T. Sherman, March 4, 1864 1046

To Julia Dent Grant, March 25, 1864 1047

To Benjamin F. Butler, April 17, 1864 1048

To Julia Dent Grant, April 17, 1864 1049

To William T. Sherman, April 19, 1864 1050

To Julia Dent Grant, April 24, 1864 1051

To Henry W. Halleck, April 29, 1864 1051

To Henry W. Halleck, May 7, 1864 1053

To Julia Dent Grant, May 13, 1864 1054

To *Julia Dent Grant, June 1, 1864* 1055

To *Ellen Wrenshall Grant, June 4, 1864* 1055

To *Julia Dent Grant, June 7, 1864* 1056

To *Julia Dent Grant, June 15, 1864* 1057

To *Elihu B. Washburne, June 23, 1864* 1057

To *Henry W. Halleck, July 1, 1864* 1058

To *Julia Dent Grant, July 7, 1864* 1059

To *Charles E. Fuller, July 16, 1864* 1060

To *Abraham Lincoln, July 19, 1864* 1060

To *Edwin M. Stanton, July 20, 1864* 1061

To *Henry W. Halleck, July 21, 1864* 1061

To *Winfield Scott, July 23, 1864* 1062

To *Henry W. Halleck, August 1, 1864* 1062

To *Lydia Slocum, August 10, 1864* 1063

To *Elihu B. Washburne, August 16, 1864* 1064

To *William H. Seward, August 19, 1864* 1065

To *Philip H. Sheridan, August 26, 1864* 1067

To *William T. Sherman, September 4, 1864* 1067

To *Frederick Dent Grant and Ulysses S. Grant, Jr.,*
   September 13, 1864 1068

To *Julia Dent Grant, September 14, 1864* 1068

To *Edwin M. Stanton, September 20, 1864* 1069

To *Elihu B. Washburne, September 21, 1864* 1069

To *Julia Dent Grant, October 26, 1864* 1070

To *Isaac S. Stewart, December 1, 1864* 1071

To William T. Sherman, December 6, 1864 1071

To Abraham Lincoln, December 7, 1864 1072

To Henry W. Halleck, December 8, 1864 1073

To Henry W. Halleck, December 9, 1864 1073

To Henry W. Halleck, December 9, 1864 1073

To George H. Thomas, December 9, 1864 1074

To Edwin M. Stanton, December 18, 1864 1074

To George H. Thomas, December 18, 1864 1075

To George H. Thomas, December 22, 1864 1075

To Julia Dent Grant, January 1, 1865 1076

To Julia Dent Grant, January 11, 1865 1076

To Abraham Lincoln, January 31, 1865 1077

To Abraham Lincoln, February 1, 1865 1077

To William T. Sherman, February 1, 1865 1078

To Edwin M. Stanton, February 6, 1865 1079

To Abraham Lincoln, March 2, 1865 1080

To Edwin M. Stanton, March 3, 1865 1080

To Jesse Root Grant, March 19, 1865 1081

To Edwin M. Stanton, March 21, 1865 1082

To Philip H. Sheridan, March 21, 1865 1082

To William T. Sherman, March 22, 1865 1083

To Abraham Lincoln, March 29, 1865 1085

To George G. Meade, April 9, 1865 1085

To Julia Dent Grant, April 16, 1865 1085

To Edward O. C. Ord, April 17, 1865 1086

To William T. Sherman, April 21, 1865 1087

To Julia Dent Grant, April 21, 1865. 1088

To Julia Dent Grant, April 25, 1865. 1089

Index 1091

To R. McKinstry Griffith

Military Academy
West Point N.Y.
Sept. 22d 1839

Dear Coz.

I was just thinking that you would be right glad to hear from one of your relations who is so far away as I am so, I have put asaid my Algebra and French and am going to tell you a long story about this prettiest of places West Point. So far as it regards natural attractions it is decidedly the most beautiful place that I have ever seen; here are hills and dales, rocks and river; all pleasant to look upon. From the window near I can see the Hudson; that far famed, that beautiful river with its bosom studded with hundreds of snow sails. Again if I look another way I can see Fort Putnan frowning far above; a stern monument of a sterner age which seems placed there on purpose to tell us of the glorious deeds of our fathers and to bid us remember *their* sufferings—to follow their examples. In short this is the best of all places—the *place* of all *places* for an institution like this. I have not told you *half* its attractions. here is the house Washington used to live in—there Kosisuseko used to walk and think of *his* country and of *ours*. Over the river we are shown the duelling house of Arnold, that *base* and *heartless* traiter *to* his country and his God. I do love the *place*. it seems as though I could live here ferever if my friends would only come too. You might search the wide world over and then not find a better. Now all this sounds nice, very nice, "what a happy fellow you are" you will say, but I am not one to show fals colers the brightest side of the picture. So I will tell you about a few of the *drawbacks*. First, I slept for two months upon one single pair of blankets, now this sounds romantic and you may think it very easy. but I tell you what coz, it is *tremendeus hard*. suppose you try it by way of experiment for a night or two. I am pretty shure that you would be perfectly satisfied that is no easy matter. but glad am I these things are over. we are now in our quarters. I have a spleanded bed and get along very well. Our pay is nomonally about twenty eight dollars a month. but we never see one cent of it. if we want any thing from a shoestring to a coat we must go to the commandant of the post and get an order fer it or we cannot have it. We have tremendous long and hard lessons to get in both French and Algebra. I study hard and hope to get along so as to pass the examination in January. this examination is a hard one they say, but I am not frightened *yet*. If I am successful here you will not see me fer two long years. it seems a long while to me. but time passes off very fast. it seems but a few days since I came here. it is because every hour has it duty which must be performed. On the whole I like the place very much. so much that I would not go away on any account. The fact is if a man graduates here he safe fer life. let him go where he will. There is much to dislike but more to like. I mean to study hard and stay if it be possible. if I cannot—very well—the world is wide. I have now been here about four months and have not seen a single familier face or *spoken* to a single lady. I wish some of the pretty girles of Bethel were here just so I might look at them. but fudge! confound the girles. I have seen great men plenty of them. let us see. Gen Scott. M. Van Buren. Sec. of War and Navy. Washington Irving and lots of other big bugs. If I were to come home now with my uniform on. they way you would laugh at my appearance would be curious. My pants sit as tight to my skin as the bark to a tree and if I do not walk *military*. that is if I bend over quickly or run. they are very apt to crack with a report as loud as a pistol. my coat must always be buttoned up tight to the chin. it is made of sheeps grey cloth all covered with big round buttens. it makes me look very singulir. If you were to see me at a distance. the first question you would ask would be. "is that a Fish or an animal"? You must give my very best love and respects to all my friends particulaly you brothers. Uncle Ross & Sam'l Simpson. You must also write me a long. long letter in reply to this and till me about evry thing and every body including yourself. If you happen to see my folks just till them that I am happy, *alive* and *kicking*.

> I am truly your cousin
> and obedand servant
> U. H. GRANT

McKinstrey Griffith

N.B. In coming on I stopped five days in Philidelpha with my friends they are all well. Tell Grandmother Simpson that they always have expected to see here before. but have almost given up the idea now. they hope to hear from her often. U. H. GRANT

My very best respects to Grandmother Simpson. I think often her, I put this on the margen so that you may remember it better. I want you to show this letter and all others that I may write to you, to her

I am going to write to some of my friends in Philadelphia soon when they answer I shall write you again to tell you about them &c. &c. remember and write me very soon fer I want to here much

I came near forgetting to tell you about our demerit or "black marks" They give a man one of these "black marks" for almost nothing and if he gets 200 a year they dismiss him. To show how easy one can get these a man by the name of *Grant* of this state got *eight* of these "marks" fer not going to Church today. he was also put under arrest so he cannot leave his room perhaps fer a month, all this fer not going to Church. We are not only obliged to go to church but must *march* there by companys. This is not exactly republican. It is an Episcopal Church

Contrary to the prediction of you and rest of my Bethel friends I have not yet been the least *homesick* no! I would not go home on any account whatever. When I come home in two years (if I live) they way I shall astonish you *natives* will be *curious*. I hope you wont take me for a Babboon

To Julia Dent

Camp Salubrity
Near Nachitoches Louisiana
June 4th 1844

My Dear Julia

I have at length arrived here with the most pleasing recollections of the short leave of absence which prevented my accompanying my Regiment; and as well, with the conse-

quences of the leave. I arrived here on Monday the 3d Ins; I
believe just the day that I told you I thought I should arrive.
My journey to N. Orleans was a pleasant one, on a pleasant
boat, with pleasant passengers and officers, but was marked
with no incident worth relating, except that as we approached
the South the Musquetoes become troublesome, and by the
time I left N. Orleans my hands and face bore the strongest
testamony of their numbers and magnitude.—I spent something over a day in N. Orleans, and its being a tolerably large
place, and my Bump of Acquisitiveness prompting me on to
see as much of the place as possible, the result was that I went
over the town just fast enough to see nothing as I went,
stoped long enough at a time to find out nothing atall and at
the end found found myself perfectly tired out. But I saw
enough to convince me that a very pleasant season might be
passed there; and if I *cant* get back to *Jeff. Bks* again will make
no objections to the contemplated change which sends me
there. But I am not disposed to give up a known good for an
untried one, and as I *know* the climate &c. (&c. meaning
much more than what precedes it) about St. Louis suits me
well, I will by no means fail to take up with any offer which
will take me back.—My journey up the Red River was not so
pleasant as the other. The boat was quite small and considerably crouded with passengers, and they not of the most pleasant sort; a number of them being what are usually called *Black
Legs* or Gamblers; and some of them with very cut throat
appearances. There was some of them that I should very
much dislike to meet unarmed, and in a retired place, their
knowing I had a hundred dollars about me. Likely I judge
harshly. The monotony of the Journey though was somewhat
broken by the great difference in the appearance of the Red
River country and anything else I had ever seen. The first
hundred miles looks like a little deep and winding canal finding its way through a forest so thickly set, and of such heavy
foliage that the eye cannot penetrate. The country is low and
flat and overflown to the first limbs of the trees. Aligators and
other revolting looking things occupy the swamps in thousands; and no doubt the very few people who live there shake
with the ague all Summer. As far up the river as where we are

the land is high and healthy, but too poor to bear any thing
but one vast pine forest. Since Mr. Hazlitt wrote to you our
Encampment has been moved to a much more pleasant and
higher situation. We are on the top of a high ridge, with
about the best spring of water in Louisiana runing near.
There is nothing but pine woods surrounding us and they
infested to an inormaus degree with Ticks, Red bugs, and a
little creeping thing looking like a Lizard, that I dont know
the name of. This last vermin is singularly partial to society,
and become so very intimate and sociable on a short acquaintance as to visit our tents, crawl into our beds &c. &c. Tis said
they are very innocent but I dont like the looks of them. —
Nearly the first person I met here was Hazlitt, or Sly Bob,
with one of those Stage driver's round top wool hats and a
round jacket, trying to take the heat as comfortably as possible. He drew me into his tent; which by the way is a little
linen affair just like your Fishing tent, with the ground covered with Pine leaves for a floore. It took me one day
to answer his questions, and you may rest assured that a
number of them were about Ellen and yourself together with
the rest of the family. When you write to him tell him how
Clarra is comeing on. — Since I first set down to write we
have had a hard shower and I can tell you my tent is a poor
protection. The rain run through in streams. But I will have a
shed built in a few days then I will do better. You have been
to Camp Meeting, and know just how the people cook, and
sleep, and live there? Our life here is just about the same.
Hazlitt probably told you all about how we live here. While I
think of it he sends his love to you and Ellen and the rest of
the family, and to Wrenshall Dent's family. Mine must go to
the same. —

I was detained a day longer in St. Louis than I expected
and to make time pleasantly pass away I called on Joe Shurlds
and had a long talk of three or four hours, about — about! —
let me see: What was the subject? I believe it was the usual
topic. Nothing in particular, but matters generally. She pre-
tends to have made a great discovery. Can you concieve what
it was?

Julia! I cannot express the regrets that I feel at having to leave Jeff. Bks. at the time that I did. I was just learning how to enjoy the place and the *Society*, at least a part of it. Blank

—— —— —— —— —— —— ——

—— —— —— —— —— —— ——

—— —— —— —— —— —— —— Read these blank lines just as I intend them and they will express more than words.— You must not forget to write soon and what to seal with. Until I hear from you I shall be,— I dont know what I was going to say— but I recon it was your most humble [. . . . .] and Obt. Friend.

ULYSSES S GRANT

Miss Julia Dent
Gravois Mo.

P.S. Did you get the Magazines I sent you, one from Memphis the other from N. Orleans?   usg

To Mrs. George B. Bailey

Camp Salubrity
Near Nachitoches Louisiana
June 6th 1844

Mrs. Bailey

My journey fortunately is at an end, and agreeably to your request, and my own pleasure, I hasten to notify you of my safe arrival here   It always affords me pleasure to write to old acquaintances, and much more to hear from them, so I would be pleased if the correspondence would not stop here. As long as my letters are answered, if agreeable to you I will continue to write.—

My trip to this place "forty days journey in the wilderness" was marked with no incident, Save one, worth relating and that one is *laughable curious, important, surprising* &c. &c. but I cant tell it now. It is for the present a secret, but I will tell it to you some time. You must not guess what it is for you will go wrong. On my route I called arroune by the way of St Louis and Jefferson Barrack where I spent four or five days very pleasantly among my newly made acquaintances   From St Louis to N Orleans I had a very pleasant trip on a large and splendid boat, with pleasant passengers and not much crouded. As we approached the South the sun become sensibly warmer, and the Musquetoes desidedly more numerous   By the time we got to N Orleans my hands and face bore the strongest evidence of the number and size of this insect in a Southern climate   I was but one day in Orleans which was spent in runing over the city just fast enough to tire myself out and get but little good of my visit   But from what I saw I think it would be a pleasant place to live, and it is now contemplated that my Regiment will go in that neighborhood in case Texas should not be anexed to the U States, but in case of the anexation we will probably have to go much farther West than we are now. Probably to the Rio Colorado. From N. Orleans to Nachitoches I had the bad fortune to travel on a small boat considerably crouded, through a hot country, with gambling going on day and night. Some of the passengers had very cut throat appearances. From Nachitoches I had to walk (or pay an extravigant price for a conveyance) three miles through the hotest sun I think I ever felt   I found my Regiment Camping out in small linen tents on the top of a high Sandy ridge and in the midst of a pine forest   The great elevation of our situation and the fact that one of the best springs of water in the state puts out here are the only recommendations the place has. We are about three miles from any place, there is no conveyance to take us from on place to another and evry thing is so high that we cant afford to keep a horse or other conveyance of our own. I could walk myself but for the intensity of the heat. As for lodgings I have a small tent that the rain runs through as it would through a seive. For a bedstead I have four short pine sticks set upright and plank runing from the two at one end to the other. For chairs I use my trunk and bed, and as to a floor we have no such a luxury yet. Our meals are cooked in the woods by servants that know no more about culinary matters than I do myself. But with all these disadvantages my appetite is becoming extravigant. I would like to have our old West Point board again that you may have heard so much about. As for the troublesome insects of creation they abound here. The swamps are full of Aligators, and the wood full of Red bugs and ticks; insects the you are not trouble with in Ohio, but are the plague of this country. They crawl entirely unde the skin when they git on a person and it is impossible to keep them off.—So much for Camp Salubrity.—I should be happy to get an answer to this as early as possible; and if nothing more, a Post Script from the Young ladies. Ladies are always so much better at giving the news than others, and then there is nothing doing or said about Georgetown that I would not like to hear. They could tell me of all the weddings &c. &c. that are talked of. Give my love to evry body in Georgetown.

LT. U S GRANT
4th Infantry

To Mrs. G. B. Bailey
Georgetown Ohio

P. S. I give my title in signing this not because I wish people to know what it is, but because I want to get an answer to this and put it there that a letter may be directed so as to get to me

To Julia Dent

Camp Salubrity La.
Near Nachitoches
July 28th 1844

My Dear Julia.

Mr. Higgins has just arrived from Jefferson Barracks and brings word that he saw you well on the 4th Inst. He delivered your message and says that he promised to bring some letters from you but supposes that you expected him out at your house to recieve them. You can hardly immagine how acceptable your message was but when I found that I might have expected a letter from you by his calling for it, I took the Blues (You told me that you had experienced the same complaint) so badly that I could resort to no other means of expelling the dire feeling than by writing to My *Dear Julia*. It has been but few days since I wrote to you but I must write again. Be as punctual in writing to me Julia and then I will be compensated in a slight degree,—nothing could fully compensate—for your absence.—In my mind I am constantly turning over plans to get back to Missouri, and until today there has been strong grounds for hoping that the whole of the 4th Regiment would be ordered back there; but that hope is blasted now. Orders have arrive from Washington City that no troops on the frontier will be removed. Fred's Regiment as well as mine will have to remain. Mexico has appropriated four millions of dollars for the purpose of raising an Army of thirty thousand men for the re-conquering of Texas, and we are to remain here to preserve neutrality between the United States and the belligerent parties. Who knows but Fred. and me may have something to do yet? though it may be something short of the conquest of Mexico, or the overpowering of some other big country. Would you not be glad to hear of something of the kind after the difficulty was all over and we were safely out? I think there is no danger however, from any present causes, of anything of the kind taking place. Fred. and me are doomed to stay safe and quietly in the woods for some time yet. I may be able to get to the same post with Fred. by transfering with Lt. Elting   I have written to Towson on the subject. If I should get there Fred. and me will be great friends as we always have been, and no doubt will spend many pleasant hours together talking over the pleasant times both of us have spent on the Gravois. No doubt your brother will have many pleasant things to relate of the place, and to me they will be doubly interesting because Julia Dent is there. Many a pleasant hour have I spent at Camp Salubrity thinking over my last visit to Mo. and its results. Never before was I satisfied that my love for you was returned, but you then assured me that it was. Does Mrs. Dent know of the engagement between us? I believe from Freds letter that he half suspects it, though he mentions nothing of the kind. I would be perfectly willing that he should be acquainted with the fact though of course, would not tell him myself.—Mr. Higgins gives us an account of the Barbecue on the Gravois the 4th of July. No doubt Miss Fanny Morrison was in all her glory with her returned intended! Does Fanny call out to see you often? What does she say about me? What is the reason I cant be there myself to hear? evry body els is going. Col. Garland, Captain Morris & Capt. Barber are just starting, and in a few days Capt. Morrison will be off.—Julia write to me soon and give a long account of how you pass your time. No doubt it is much more pleasantly spent than mine in the hot pine woods of Louisiana. Hazlitt and me visit each other, at our linen Mansions about three times per day, and our calls are so unfashionable that the three calls lasts from morning until bed time. The subjects of our conversations are usually Missouri   Turn over and commence reading the cross lines on the first page.

To Miss Julia Dent.   Yours most Constantly U S GRANT and the people of Missouri—Miss J. & E Dent in particular and our future prospects and plans. We have big plans laid for visiting Mixico and Texas this winter and Missouri too soon. Sometimes we get to talking about your house I almost immagine myself there. While speaking of Mr. Hazlitt let me tell you that he has just left my tent and the last words he said was for me to be sure and give you and Ellen, and the rest of the family his very best love. He says that he expects a partnership letter from you two.—I wish Julia that you and Ellen could be here for one hour to see our mode of living. When any body calls to see me we have very cozily to take our seats side by side on the bed for I have no chair. If I could only be in your parlor an hour per day what a recreation it would be. Since I arrived here it has been so very hot that I but seldom go out of Camp. Once I was over at Fort Jesup and saw Mr. Jarvis. Tell Ellen that he fell a good deal more than half in love with her. He seemed very anxious to know what word she had sent him by me. Has Miss Fanny ever tried to convince you *since*, that she is in possession of all my secrets and knows just who I love best? Dont you think it strange that a young lady will talk so. I am affraid that you will find difficulty in reading the crossed lines. I will therefore conclude on the page left for directing the letter. u.s.g.

Julia I would not presume so much as to send this letter without having recieved an answer to either of my others if Mr. Higgins had not mentioned that you told him you had rec'd letters from Mr Hazlitt and me, which led me to suppose that Mr. & Mrs. Dent knew of your recieving them and made no objection. I have too an opportunity of sending it to Jeff. Bks. to be mailed.—Be sure and answer it and all my others soon—and I am sorry Julia that I wrote the letter sent in one of Mrs. Porters. Burn it up wont you? I would feel much freer if the consent desired in that letter was obtained, but as it is not, I will have to wait until I get back there to get it; unless you can satisfy me that there is no parental objection.—What is the reason that John Dent has not written to me? He must have been much engaged electioneering this Summer! Give my love to Ellen and the rest of the family. Again, be sure and write soon and relieve from suspense your most *Devoted* and *Constant l*——

U S G

P. S. I have carefully preserved the lock of hair you gave me. Recollect when you write to seal with the ring I used to wear: I am anxious to see an impression of it once more.

u s g

To Julia Dent

Camp Necessity La.
Grand Ecore & Texas Road
Aug. 31st 1844

My Dear Julia

Your two letters of July and August have just been recieved and read you can scarsely immagine with how much pleasure. I have waited so long for an answer to my three letters (I have written you three times Julia one of them you probably had not time to get when you wrote yours) that I began to dispare of ever recieving a line from you; but it come at last and how agreeable the surprise! Take example in punctuality by me Julia, I have rec'd your letters only to day and now I am answering them. But I can forgive you since the tone of your last letter, the one in pencil, is so conclusive of constancy. I am sorry to hear that Mrs. Dent thinks there is nothing serious in our engagement with me nothing is more serious or half as pleasant to think of—Since the arrival of your letters I have read them over and over again and will continue to do so until another comes. I have not been into Camp Salubrity yet to deliver to Mr. Hazlitt verbally the messages you sent him, but I wrote him a note this morning containing them. Mr. Hazlitt has been quite unwell for a few days past—You probably have heard from Mr Porters letters that for the last three weeks my company have been road making—The day we came out it rained very hard all day—the men had heavy Knap sacks to carry through the mud and rain for a distance of about five miles and no shelter to go under at the end of their journey—My fare was just the same only I had nothing but myself to carry—The first night we had to lay our wet beds on the still damper ground and make out the best we could—Musketoes and Wood ticks by the hundreds pestered us—On the whole I spent a few miserable nights and not much better days at the begining of my first experience at campaigning, but now I find it much better—We will probably be through and return to Camp Salubrity in ten days more—I have just rec'd a letter from Fred, he is about my most punctual correspondent, he speaks of Louise Stribling. I think she certainly is not married nor wont be unless she gets Fred—Fred is very well but hartily tired of Fort Towson— He proposes that him and me should each get a leave of absence next Spring and go to Missouri I would accept his proposal but I intend going sooner—I shall try very hard to go in the Fall—The happiness of seeing you again can hardly be realized, and then like you I have so much that I would like to say and dont want to write.—Julia do tell me the secrets that Georgia M disclosed to you—I think I can guess them from what follows in your letter—Georgia M is a very nice modest and inexperienced girl and can very easily be made to believe anything her oldest sister tells her—I know very well that Fanny has told her that I was in love with her and she foundes her reasons for thinking so upon what took place at you house—You remember the occurrence of the apple seeds? Fany has tried to find out from Mr. Hazlitt which I loved best Georgia or Julia—Mr. Hazlitt would not tell her which he thought because to please her he would have to tell what he believed to be a story, and to have said you (as he believed though of course he new nothing about certain) he thought would give an unnecessary offense. Hazlitt told me of the conversation he had and it displeased me so much with

Miss F. that I said things of her which I would not commit to paper—Believe me my dear Julia what ever Miss Georgia may have told you she no doubt believed herself, but in believing she has allowed herself to be the dupe of one older than she is, but whose experience *in love affairs*, ought to be worth a great deel more than it is.—Tell me what she said in your next letter—Dont let Mrs. Dent see this part of my letter for of all things I dont like to have to speak ill of a third person, and if I do have to speak so I would like as few as possible to know it.—I am very far from having forgotten our promise to think of each other at sun seting—At that time I am most always on parade and no doubt I sometimes appear very absent minded—You say you were at a loss to ascribe a meaning to the blank lines in my first letter! Nothing is easyer, they were only intended to express an attachment which words would fail to express Julia do not keep anything a secret from me with persons standing in the relation that we do to each other there should be no backwardness about making any request—You commenced to make a request of me and checked yourself—Do not be affraid that any thing you may request will not be granted, and just think too the good you might do by giving good advice—No one is so capable of giving good advice as a lady, for they always practice just what they would preach—No doubt you have laid down to Fred. just the course he ought to take, and if he follows the advice he must do well—How fortunate he must feel himself to have a sister to correspond with I know I should have been proud to have had such a one to write to me all the years of my absence. My oldest sister is old enough to write now and I intend to direct all my home letters to her—She loves you and Ellen already without ever having seen you just from what she has heard me say—You say Julia that you often dream of me! do tell me some of your good ones; dont tell me any more of the bad ones; but it is an old saying that dreams go by contraries so I shall hope you will never find me in the condition you drempt I was in—And to think too that while I am writing this the ring I used to wear is on your hand—Parting with that ring Julia was the strongest evidence I could have given you (that is—in the way of a present) of the depth and sincerity of my love for you—Write to me soon, much than the last time and if Mrs. Porter is not there, or not writing at the time take a little ride and put your letter in the Post Office — On the road think of some of the conversations we used to have when we rode out together

Most Truly and Devotedly Your Lover
ULYSSES

To Julia

P S I think in the course of a few days Julia I will write to Col. Dent to obtain his consent to our correspondence; I will ask nothing more at present but when I get back to St. Louis I will lay the whole subject before him Julia do not let any disclosed secrets such as Miss Georgia told you, make you doubt for a moment the sincerity depth & constancy of my feeling, for you and you alone out of the whole acquaintance. Find some name beginning with "S" for me Julia You know I have an 'S in my name and dont know what it stand for.

U.S.G.

P.P.S. Tell Ellen that I have not been into Camp yet to see the playthings she sent Mr. Hazlitt but I will go tomorrow morning if I have to walk. I think there is no danger of us quarreling since we have agreed so long together; but if we do get into a scrape I will let her know it. Remember me to Miss Ellen, Mrs. Porter Mrs. Mary Dent and your Fathers family all.

USG

To Julia Dent

Camp Salubrity
Near Nachitoches La.
January 12th 1845

My Dear Julia

It has now been nearly two months since I heard from you and about four since I wrote the letter to your parents to which I hoped so speedy an answer. Of course I cannot argue any thing very strong in favor of my request being granted from their not answering it, but at the same time they do not say that I shall not write to you, at least as a friend, and therfore I write you this Julia, and direct it to Sappington P. O. expecting your Pa & Ma to know that you get it. The fact is I thought I must hear from you again—The more than ordinary attachment that I formed for *yourself* and family during my stay at Jeff. Bks. cannot be changed to forgetfulness by a few months absence. But why should I use to you here the language of flattery Julia, when we have spoken so much more plainly of our feeling for each other? Indeed I have not changed since and shall hope that you have not, nor will not, at least untill I have seen all of you once more. I intend to apply for a leave in the spring again and will go to St. Louis. For three months now I have been the only officer with my company and of course cannot leave even for one week. Julia can we hope that you pa will be induced to change his opinion of an army life? I think he is mistaken about the army life being such an unpleasant one. It is true the movements of the troops from Jeff. Bks. so suddenly and to so outlandish a place would rather create that opinion, but then such a thing hardly occurs once a lifetime.

Mr. Hazlitt returned about one month ago looking as lazy and healthy as ever. I was away from camp when he returned and did not get home until about midnight. I woke him up and him and me had a long talk from that until morning. He told me all about what a pleasant visit he had at Jeff. Bks. or rather on the Gravois. Was he plagued much about Miss Clara while there? You dont know how much I wished to be along with him! He regrets very much that he didnot return by St Louis.—I must tell you something about Mr. Hazlitt since he returned. He has got him a little pony about the size of the one I had at Jeff. Bks. it is a little "Jim a long Josy" of a thing and if you were to see it you would think it was going to drawl out "*y-e-s im* hisn" just as you know Mr. Hazlitt does himself; he rode his pony to a Ball four or five mile from camp a few days ago and as he was joging along the road, neither pony nor man thinking of anything I suppose, the little thing stumbled and away went Hazlitt over its head rolling in the dust and dirt. When he got up he found the pony laying with its head in the other direction so it must have turned a complete summer-set. I was not at the Ball myself, and therefore didnot see Hazlitts exhibition and it was several days before he told me of it. He could'nt keep it a secret. You ought to be here a short time to see how we all live in our winter houses. They are built by puting posts in the ground as if for a fence and nailing up the outside with shingles. I have plank for my house but there is but one or two other officers that have. The chimneys are of mud and sticks and generally are completed by puting a barrel or two on top to make them high enough. Mr. Porter, Wallen, & Ridgley have built themselves fine houses expecting their families here. Mr. Porter went three or four weeks ago to visit his wife [. . . . .] the mouth of Red river. If they were here they might live very pleasantly for the weather is so warm that we need but little or no fires. Mr. Hazlitt and me keep bachilors hall on a small scale and get along very pleasantly. We have an old woman about fifty years old to cook for us and a boy to take care of our horses so that we live as well as though we were out of the woods—Mr. Hazlitt wishes to be remembered to all of you. He says that you must write to him right off.—I hear from Fred. very often. He was well the last time he wrote. Julia you must answer this quick wont you? I know you can. Give my love to all the family

Fare well
ULYSSES

To Julia Dent

Camp Salubrity
Near Nachitoches La.
Tuesday, May 6th 1845

My Dear Julia

I have just arrived at Camp Salubrity after a tolerably pleasant trip of only one week from St. Louis, with one days detention at the mouth of Red River. I am here just in time; one day later I would have probably an excuse to write. Whilst at the mouth of Red river I met with Lt. Baker who is strait from Fort Towson. He left there only about one week ago. Fred. is very well, and would have been in Missouri with me but his commanding officer refused him a leave. It was right mean in him was'nt it?—Evry thing at Camp Salubrity Looks as usual only much greener from the contrast between the advancement of the season here and in the North. Though we are so far South and vegetation so far advanced a fire this evening is very comfortable. The officers are all collected in little parties discussing affairs of the nation. Annexation of Texas, war with Mexico, occupation of Orregon and difficulties with England are the general topics. Some of them expect and seem to contemplate with a great deal of pleasure some difficulty where they may be able to gain laurels and *advance a little in rank.* Any moove would be pleasant to me since I am so near promotion that a change of post would not affect me long. I have advanced three in rank very lately, leaving only five between me and promotion.—Mr. Hazlitt has gone to Fort Jesup and wont be back for a week; he left this morning before I got here.— It seems very strange for me to be siting here at Camp Salubrity writing to you when only a little more than one short week ago I was spending my time so pleasantly on the Gravois.—Mrs. Porter started a few days ago for Washita and of course took little Dave. along so that I could not give him the kiss you sent him. Mr. Porter was very particular in his enquiries about all of you, and if he knew that I was writing would send his love. When I got to Nachitoches I found Mr. Higgins and Beaman there just ready to start on a leave of absence. I am sorry that Miss Fanny dont know that he is on the way. I wanted him to tell me if he intended to bring her to Salubrity with him but he would not say yes nor no. Tell me what the probabilities are.—Have you heard yet from Col. Dent? I supose Brand must have written you a very amusing account of his adventuries in the East.—I supose Capt. Cotton has taken Lizzy to Green Bay before this. Does John pretend to be as much as ever in love?—The first thing I did after geting here was to get my letters from the Post Office. I found one from Miss J. B. D. that afforded me a great deel of pleasure, and one from home that had come by the way of St. Louis.— Is Miss Jemima Sappington married yet? —Tell John not to take it so hard as he appeared inclined to when he first heard of it. —I wrote to Fred. on my way down the Mississippi and told

him of the pleasant visit I had, and how disappointed you all
were that he was not along. I shall always look back to my
short visit to Mo. as the most pleasant part of my life. In fact
it seems more like a pleasant dream than reality. I can scarsely
convince myself of the fact that I was there so short a time
ago. My mind must be on this subject something like what
Hercules Hardy's was whilst he was a prisoner among the
Piannakataws in Guiana. I send you the story that you may
read it.—Remember me very kindly to Mrs. Dent and Ellen
and Emmy and your brothers and to your Aunt Fielding and
your Cousins. Dont neglect to write as soon as you get this.

I am most devotedly your
ULYSSES S. GRANT

Julia

P. S. I promised to write to Lewis Dent as soon as I got here
but I am so busily engaged building myself a new house that I
will not have much time for a while. Mrs. Wallen is here safe
and looks very delicate.—I am going to follow your advice
Julia and have me a good and comfortable house.

U.

The letter you wrote me before I went to Mo. was very
different from what I expected to find it. It was not near so
cold and formal as you led me to believe. I should not have
written this last Post script should I?

u

To Julia Dent

N. Orleans Barracks La.
July 6th 1845

My Dear Julia

I recieved your letter a day or two before leaving Camp Salubrity but after we knew that we were to go. You dont know
how glad I was to get it at that time. A weeks longer delay in
writing to me and I probably would not have heard from you
for months, for there is no telling where we are going or how

letters will have to be directed so as to reach us. Our orders are for the Western borders of Texas but how far up the Rio Grand is hard to tell. My prediction that I would recieve but few letters more at Camp Salubrity has proven very true. I hope you have sent me a letter by Mr. Higgins. How unfortune Miss Fanny has been. The Brevets that are going to Texas are probably better off than those of higher rank. I am perfectly rejoiced at the idea of going there myself for the reason that in the course of five or six months I expect to be promoted and there are seven chances out of eight that I will not be promoted in the 4th so that at the end of that time I shall hope to be back to the U. States, unless of course there should be active service there to detain me and to take many others there.—I was very much in hopes Julia that I would recieve a letter from your pa before leaving Camp Salubrity giving his full consent to our engagement. Now—that I am going so far away and dont know how long it may be before I can hear from you I shall be in a greatdeal of suspense on the subject. Soldiering is a very pleasant occupation generally and is so even on this occation except so far as it may be an obsticle in the way of our gaining the unconditional consent of your parents to what *we*, or at least I, believe is for our happiness.—Mrs. Wallen will soon go to Jefferson Barracks to remain until her husband has quarters comfortably arranged for her where the troops may be posted. She will be writing to Mr. Wallen, wont you ask her how she directs her letters and write to me? If you knew how happy I am to get a letter from you you would write often. Mrs. Wallen asked me if I would not have a letter for her to carry when she went to St. Louis and I told her that I would so if you will call on her when she arrives which will probably be about the 1st of August you may find another letter from me.—From what I have seen N. Orleans Barracks is the most pleasant place I have ever been stationed at. It is about four miles below the city, but it is so thickly settled all the way along that we appear to be in town from the start. The place is much more handsomely fixed than Jeff. Bks.—In a few days the 3d Infantry will join us here, and not long after two companies are expected from Fort Scott. I dont know what the probabilities are for Fred. going to Texas, I know he is anxious to go and I

should be happy to meet him there.—You ask if Fred. has
done any thing out of the way that his commanding officer
would not give him a leave! Certainly he has not; the comd.g
off. probably thinks that he has not been long enough in service to have a leave, or els there is too many officers absent
already, or something of the kind. There are but few Commanding officers as indulgent about giving young officers
leaves of absence as the one I am serving under. (Col. Vose). I
recieved a letter from Fred. but a few weeks ago and he said
nothing to me about being ordered farther into the wilderness. probably some of the Indians in those parts have been
pestering the frontier setlers. Dont be frightened about his
geting home again and I shall hope too to be with him. Next
time I ask for a leave of absence it will be for six months, *to
take a trip North*.

Give my love to all your family, and your Aunt Fieldings
also. Mr. Hazlitt wishes to be remembered. He says that he
was not two months in answering your letter.

Write without failing and I will trust to providence for geting the letter. for ever yours most devotedly

u s GRANT

Julia

P. S. Remind your pa about writing to me and you plead for
us wont you Julia? I will keep an account of all the Mexicans
and Comanches that we take in battle and give you a full
account. I have a black boy to take along as my servant that
has been in Mexico. He speaks English Spanish and French I
think he may be very useful where we are going. fare well my
Dear Julia for a scout among the Mexicans

U

To Julia Dent

N. Orleans Barracks La.
July 11th 1845

My Dear Julia

I wrote you a letter a few days ago in which I promised to
write again by Mrs. Wallen. It was my intention then to write

you a very long one but she starts much sooner than I expected so that I will only trouble you with a short note, and it too will probably reach you before the letter sent by Mail. There is now no doubt Julia but we will all be in Texas in a very short time. The 3d Infantry have arrived on their way and in a week or so we will all be afloat on the Gulf of Mexico. When I get so far away you will still think of and write to me I know and for my part I will avail my self of evry opportunity to send you a letter. It cannot well be many months that I will be detained in that country unless I be promoted to one of the Regiments stationed there and the chances are much against that. I have never mentioned any thing about *love* in any of the letters I have ever written you Julia, and indeed it is not necessary that I should, for you know as well as I can tell you that you alone have a place in my *my*—What an out I make at expressing any thing like love or sentiment: You know what I mean at all events, and you know too how acquerdly I made known to you for the first time my love. It is a scene that I often think of, and with how much pleasure did I hear that my offer was not entirely unacceptable? In going away now I feel as if I had some one els than myself to live and strive to do well for. You can have but little idea of the influance you have over me Julia, even while so far away. If I feel tempted to do any thing that I think is not right I am shure to think, "Well now if Julia saw me would I do so" and thus it is absent or present I am more or less governed by what I think is your will.

Julia you know I have never written anything like this befor and wont you keep any one from seeing it. It may not be exactly right to keep it from your parents, but then you will get a letter from me by Mail about the same time which they will probably see. Am I giving you bad advice? if you think so act just as you think you ought.—Mrs. Wallen will give you all the news afloat here. Dont forget to ask her how she intends to direct her letters to Mr. Wallen and send mine to the same address, and now I must close with sending the most devotional love of

U S G

To Julia

To Julia Dent

Corpus Christi Texas
Sept. 14th 1845

My Dear Julia

I have just recieved your letter of the 21st ultimo in which you reproach me so heavily for not writing to you oftener. You know my Dear Julia that I never let two days pass over after recieving a letter from you without answering it; But we are so far separated now that we should not be contented with writing a letter and waiting an answer before we write again. Hereafter I will write evry two or three weeks at farthest, and wont you do the same Julia? I recieved your letter before the last only about three weeks ago and answered it immediately. Your letters always afford me a greatdeal of happiness because they assure me again that you love me still; I never doubted your love Julia for one instant but it is so pleasant to hear it repeated, for my own part I would sacrifice evrything Earthly [. . .] to make my Dear Julia my own forever. All that I would ask would be that my Regiment should be at a healthy post and you be with me, then I would be content though I might be out of the world. There are two things that you are mistaken in Julia, you say you know that I am in an unhealthy climate and in hourly expectation of War: The climate is delightful and very healthy, as much so as any climate in the world and as for war we dont believe a word of it. We are so numerous here now that we are in no fear of an attack upon our present ground. There are some such heavy storms here on the coast the later part of Sept. and October however that we will probably be moved up the Nuices river to San Patricio, an old deserted town, that the Indians have compelled the inhabitants to leave.—Since the troops have been at Corpus Christi there has not been a single death from sickness, but there has been two or three terrible visitations of providence. There has been one man drownd in the breakers; a few weeks ago a storm passed over camp and a flash of lightning struck a tent occupied by two black boys killing one and stuning the other, and day before yesterday the most terrible accidents of all occured. For the last few weeks there has been an old worn out Steam Boat, chartered by

government, runing across the bay here, and day before yesterday there happened to be several officers and a number of
soldiers aboard crossing the bay; the boat had scarsely got out
of sight when the boilers bursted tearing the boat into atoms
and througing almost evry one aboard from twenty to fifty
yards from the wreck into the Briny Deep. Some were struck
with iron bars and splinters and killed immediately others
swam and got hold of pieces of the wreck and were saved.
Among the killed was Lt. Higgins and Lt. Berry both of the
4th Infantry. It will drive Fanny almost mad I fear. Capt.
Morrison takes Mr. Higgins' death very hard. When he was
killed he was standing talking with several officers; the others
were uninjured. The number killed and wounded I have not
heard accurately stated, but I believe there was 9 killed and
about 17 wounded one or two probably mortally.

Do you hear much about War with Mexico? From the accounts we get here one would supposed that you all thought
the Mexicans were devouring us. The vacancies that have
lately occured brings me about first for promotion and if by
chance I should go back to the States I may have the pleasure
of seeing my Dear Julia again before the end of the year; what
happiness it would be to see you again so soon! I feel as
though my good fortune would take me back. If I should be
promoted to a Regt. in Texas I will have to remain untill
na[. . . .] affairs look a little more settled and we become
permanent in this country, which is a delightful one so far as
climate and soil is concerned, but where no one lives scarsely
except the troops, and then I will go back and either remain
there, or—May I flatter myself that one who I love so much
would return with me to this country, when all the families
that are now absent join there husbands?—If so Julia you
know what I would say.

The mail is just going to close so I must stop writing. I intended to have written another sheet but I will have to put off
my long letter until next time. Give my very best love to all
your family and also Mrs. Fieldings. Dont neglect writing to
me very soon Julia for you dont know anxious I always am to
get a letter from my *Dear Dear* Julia and how disappointed I
always feel when I am a long time without one from her. I
very often look at the name in the ring I wear and think how

much I would like to see again the one who gave it to me. I must close, so good by my Dear Julia

U S GRANT

To Julia Dent

Corpus Christi Texas

My Dear Julia

In my last letter I promised to write to you evry two or three weeks and it is now about that time since I wrote and you see how punctual I am. I fear Julia that there was a long time between the receipt of my letters from N. Orleans and my first from Texas but you must reflect that I had writen you three without having recieved an answer and before writing again I wanted to hear from my *Dear Dear* Julia. I always do and always will answer your letters immediately and if you knew how delighted I always am to hear from yourself you would write often too.

The late casualty in the 4th Infantry promotes me so that I am now permanently at home in this Regiment. I should have prefered being promoted to a Regiment that is now in the States, because then I would get to see again, *soon*, one who is much dearer to me than my commission, and because too, there is hardly a probability of active service in this remote quarter of our country, and there is nothing els, excepting a fine climate and soil, to make one wish to stay here.—There is now over half of the Army of the U. States at Corpus Christi, and there must of course be a breaking up and scatterment of this large force as soon as it is found that their services will not be required in this part of the country. It is the general opinion that on account of the length of time the 4th has already been encamped, here and at Camp Salubrity, and the general unsettled position that it has been in since the begining of the Florida war, that we will be the first out of Texas. Once in quarters again no doubt we will remain for a good long time.

The most of the talk of war now comes from the papers of the old portion of the U. States. There are constantly bands of Mexican Smugglers coming to this place to trade, and they seem to feel themselvs as secure from harm here as though they were citizens of Texas, and we on the other hand, although we are occupying disputed Territory, even acknowedging our right to Texas, feel as secure from attack as you do off in Missouri. There was a time since we have been here when we were in about half expectation of a fight and with a fare prospect of being whipped too; that was when there was but few of us here and we learned that General Arista and other officers of rank were on the Rio Grande ready to march down upon us. We began to make preparations to make as stout a defence as possible. Evry working man was turned out and an intrenchment began and continued for about a week and then abandoned.

Now my Dear Julia that a prospect is ahead for some perminancy in my situation dont you think it time for us to begin to settle upon some plan for consumating what we believe is for our mutual happiness? After an engagement of sixteen or seventeen months ought we not to think of bringing that engagement to an end, in the way that all true and constant lovers should? I have always expressed myself willing you know my Dear Julia to resign my appointment in the army for the sake of overcomeing the objections of your parents, and I would still do so; at the same time I think they mistake an army life very much. No set of ladies that I ever saw are better contented or more unwilling to change their condition than those of the Army; and you Julia would be contented knowing how much and how dearly devoted I am to you—I cannot help writing thus affectionately since you told me that no one but yourself reads my letters.

Your Pa asks what I could do out of the Army? I can tell you: I have at this time the offer of a professorship of mathematics in a tolerably well endowed College in Hillsboro, Ohio, a large and flourishing town, where my salery would probably equal or exceed my present pay. The Principle of the Institution got my father to write to me on the subject; he says I can have until next spring to think of this matter. The last letter I wrote was to make all the enquiries I could about the situation and if the answer proves favorable I shall give this matter serious concideration.

I am now reading the Wandering Jew, the copy that belonged to Mr. Higgins and the very same numbers read by
yourself. How often I think of you whilst reading it. I think
well Julia has read the very same words that I am now reading
and not long before me. Yesterday in reading the 9th No I saw
a sentence marked around with a pencil and the word *good*
written after it. I thought it had been marked by you and before I knew it I had read it over three or four times. The sentence was a sentiment expressed by the Indian Prince Djalmo
on the subject of the marriage of two loving hearts, making a
compareison you may recollect. Was it you that marked the
place. I have written so long a letter that I must close. Remember me to evry body on the Gravois. Mr. Hazlitt also
wishes to be remembered.

Give my love to Ellen. How is Ellen's soft eyed lover comeing on that she wanted me to quiz somebody down here
about? She did not say so but I know she wanted some of her
friends here to hear of him just to see how jealous she could
make them.

Good bye my Dear Julia and dont forget to write soon.

Yours most affectionately
ULYSSES

Julia

October 1845

To Julia Dent

Corpus Christi Texas
Feb 5th 1846

My Dear Julia

Two or three Mails have arrived at Corpus Christi in the
last few days and by each I confidently expected a letter from
you, but each time I was disappointed. As a consolation then
I come to my tent and got out all the letters you have ever
written me—How many do you think they amounted to?
only 11 Julia, and it is now twenty months that we have been
engaged. I read all of them over but two and now write to
you again Julia in hopes that hereafter I will get a letter from

you evry two or three weeks. You dont know with what pleasure I read your letters or you would write much oftener.

At present the prospect of the 4th Infantry, or any other
Regiment, geting back to civilization is by no means flattering. Our march is still onwards to the West. Orders have been
recieved here for the removal of the troops to the Rio Grand
(to Francis Isabel) and before you get this no doubt we will
be on our way.—Continue to direct your letters as before,
the care of Col. Hunt N. Orleans and they will reach me. In
all probability this movement to the Rio Grande will hasten
the settlement of the boundary question, either by treaty or
the sword, and in eather case we may hope for early peace and
a more settled life in the army, and then may *we—you and
I Julia*—hope for as speedy a consent on the part of your
parents to our union? You say they certainly will not refuse it.
I shall continue to hope and believe that it will be as you say.

I wrote to you a short time ago that I thought our engagement should be carried into effect as early as possible. I still
think so and would be very happy to have you set the time at
no very distant day, with the condition if the troops are not
actively emploid. Of course Julia I never even dremed of such
a thing as asking you to come to a Camp or a temporary and
distant post with me. I would not wish to take you from a
home where you are surrounded by evry comfort and where
you are among friends that you know and love. That is not
what I proposed. If you should consent that I might "clasp
that little hand and call it mine" while the troops are still in
their present unsettled state I would either resign as my father
is anxious to have me do, or return by myself leaving my Dear
Julia at a comfortable home while I was fighting the battles of
our Country.—Has John made application for an appointment in one of the new Regiments that are to be raised   I
hope he has not let the oportunity slip. With Mr. Bentons
influance he could probably get a Captaincy.—I got a letter
from Fred. a few days ago. He is well and is now looking out
for promotion. He is anxious to get to the 4th Inf.y and says
that if he is not promoted to it he intends to make a transfer
to get to it if he can.—Dont neglect to write to me often
Julia. If you have but a little to write say that, it gives me so
much pleasure even to see your name in your own hand

writing. About the time you get this I will be on the march (on foot of course) between this and San Isabel or Francis Isabel. In the evenings just think that one who loves you above all on this Earth is then resting on the ground (thinking of Julia) after a hard days march.—Give my love to Ellen Emmy and the rest at White Haven.

> Your most affectionately
> U S GRANT

Julia

To Julia Dent

> Corpus Christi Texas
> Feb. 7th 1846

Dearest Julia

I have just been delighted by a long and interesting letter from my Dear Julia and although I wrote to you but two or three days ago I answer this with my usual punctuality. You say you write me letter for letter well I am satisfied that my love is returned and you know how anxious one is to hear often from the one they love and it may appear to me that you do not write as often as you really do. Your letter was one of the sweetest you have ever written me and your answer to the question I have so often asked was so much like yourself, it was just what I wanted to hear you say; boldness indeed: no my Dear Julia that is a charge that can never be laid to you.—There is a part of your letter that is entirely incomprehensible to me. I dont know whether you are jesting or if you are serious. *** I first loved Julia I have loved no one els.— The chance of any of the troops geting out of Texas this spring is worse than ever, before long we will be on our way farther West but no doubt it will be but a few months until the boundary question will be settled and then we may look for a general dispersion of troops and I for one at least will see Missouri again.—Does your pa ever speak of me or of our engagement? I am so glad to hear you say that you think his consent will be given when asked for. I shall never let an oportuntiy to do so pass.—As to resigning it would not be right in the present state of affairs and I shall not think of it again for the present.—So John is again a Bachilor without a string to his bow. no doubt he will remain single all his life The extract from some newspaper you send me is a gross exageration of the morals and health of Corpus Christi. I do not believe that there is a more healthy spot in the world. So much exposure in the winter season is of course attended with a goodeal of sickness but not of a serious nature. The letter was written I believe by a soldier of the 3d Inf.y. As to the poisning and robberies I believe they are entirely false. There has been several soldiers murdered since we have been here, but two of the number were shot by soldiers and there is no knowing that the others were not. Soldiers are a class of people who will drink and gamble let them be where they may, and they can always find houses to visit for these purposes. Upon the whole Corpus Christi is just the same as any other plase would be where there were so many troops. I think the man who wrote the letter you have been reading deservs to be put in the Guard house and kept there until we leave the country. There he would not see so much to write about.— Do you get the paper I send you evry week?—I know Julia if you could see me now you would not know me, I have allowed my beard to grow two or three inches long. Ellen would not have to be told now that I am trying to raise whiskers. Give my love to all at White Haven.

Your Devoted lover
ULYSSES

Julia

To Julia Dent

Corpus Christi Texas
March 3d 1846

My Dear Julia

    I have not recieved a letter from you since my last, but as I may not have an opportunity of writing to you again for several weeks I must avail my self of this chance of writing to my dear Julia. This morning before I got awake I dreamed that I was some place away from Corpus Christi walking with you leaning upon my arm, your hand was in mine and I felt very happy. How disappointed when I awoke and found that it was but a dream. However I shall continue to hope that it will not be a great while befor such enjoyment will be real and no dream. — The troops have not yet left this place but the movement is to commence now in a few days. The 4th Inf.y is the last to leave. We are to go into camp on this side of the Rio Grande just opposite to Matamoras, a town of considerable importance in Mexico, and as we are informed, occupied by several thousand troops who it is believed by many will make us fight for our ground before we will be allowed to occupy it. But fight or no fight evry one rejoises at the idea of leaving Corpus Christi. It is to be hoped that our troops being so close on the borders of Mexico will bring about a speedy settlement of the boundary question; at all events it is some consolation to know that we have now got as far as we can go in this direction by any order from Government and therefore the next move will be for the better. We may be taken prisoners it is true and taken to the City of Mexico and then when we will be able to get away is entirely uncertain. From the accounts recieved here I think the chances of a fight on our first arrival on the Rio Grand are about equal to the chances for peace, and if we are attacked in the present reduced state of the troops here the consequences may be much against us. — Fred is now about 2d or 3d for promotion and I have no doubt but this moove will make him a 2d Lieut. — But I have said enough on this subject for the present. A few weeks more and we will know exactly what is to take place and then the first thing, I will write to one who in all difficulties is not out of my mind. My Dear Julia as long as I must be separated from your dear self evry moove that takes place I hail with joy. I am always rejoised when an order comes for any change of position hoping that soon a change will take place that will bring the 4th Inf.y to a post where there are comfortable quarters, and where my Dear Julia will be willing to accompany me. In my previous letters I have spoken a great deal of resigning but of course I could not think of such a thing now just at a time when it is probable that the services of evry officer will be called into requisition; but I do not think that I will stand another year of idleness in camp.—You must write to me often Julia and direct your letters as heretofore. I will write to you very often and look forward with a great deal of anxiety—to the time when I may see you again and claim a kiss for my long absence.—Do you wear the ring with the letters U. S. G. in it Julia. I often take yours off to look at the name engraved in it.—While writing this I am on guard of course for the last time at this place.—Give my love to all at White Haven.

Mr. Hazlitt is well and also Capt Morrison. Tell John not to let his chance of geting into one of the new Reg.t that will probably be raised, slip by unimproved.

> Your Most Devoted
> ULYSSES

Julia

To Julia Dent

Camp Near Matamoras
March 29th 1846

My Dear Julia

A long and laborious march, and one that was threatened with opposition from the enemy too, has just been completed, and the Army now in this country are laying in camp just opposite to the town of Matamoras. The city from this side of the river bears a very imposing appearance and no doubt contains from four to five thousand inhabitants. Apparently there are a large force of Mexican troops preparing to attack us. Last night during the night they threw up a small Breast work of Sand Bags and this morning they have a piece of Artillery mounted on it and directed toward our camp. Whether they really intend anything or not is doubtful. Already they have boasted and threatened so much and executed so little that it is generally believed that all they are doing is mere bombast and show, intended to intimidate our troops. When our troops arrived at the Little Colorado, (a river of about 100 yards in width and near five feet deep where we forded it) they were met by a Mexican force, which was represented by there commander to be large and ready for an attack. A parly took place between Gen. Taylor and their commanding officer, whose name I have forgotten, the result of which was, that if we attempted to cross they would fire upon us. The Mexican officer said that however much he might be prepossessed in our favor himself he would have to obey the orders of his own Government, which were peremptory and left him but one course, and that was to defend the Colorado against our passing, and he pledged his honor that the moment we put foot into the water to cross he would fire upon us and war would commence. Gen. Taylor replied that he was going over and that he would allow them fifteen minuets to withdraw their troop and if one of them should show his head after he had started over, that he would fire upon them; whereupon they left and were seen no more until we were safely landed on this side. I think after making such threats and speaking so positivly of what they would do and then let so fine an opportunity to execute what they had threatened pass unimproved, shows anything but a decided disposition to drive us from the soil. When the troops were in the water up to their necks a small force on shore might have given them a greatdeel of trouble. — During our whole march we have been favored with fine weather, and alltogether the march has been a pleasant one. There are about forty miles between the Nuices and the Colorado rivers that is one continuous sandy desert waste, almost without wood, or water with the exception of Salt Lakes. Passing this the troops of course suffered considerably. — Here the soil is rich and the country beautiful for cultivation. When peace is established the most pleasant Military posts in our country I believe will be on the Banks of the Rio Grande. No doubt you suppose the Rio Grande, from its name and appearance on the map to be a large and magnificent stream, but instead of that it is a small muddy stream of probably from 150 to 200 yards in width and navigable for only small sized steamers. I forgot to mention that we recieved before we arrived here, the proclamation of Col. Majia the Commander-in-Chief I believe, of the Mexican forces. It was a long wordy and threatning document. He said that the citizens of Mexico were ready to expose their bare breasts to the Rifles of the Hunters of the

Mississippi, that the Invaders of the North would have to reap their Laurels at the points of their sharpened swords; if we continued our march the deep waters of the Rio Grande would be our Sepulcher the people of our Government should be driven East of the Sabine and Texas re-conquered &c. &c. all of which is thought to mean but very little.

The most beliggerent move that has taken place yet occured yesterday. When we had arrived near this place a party of Mexican soldiers siezed upon two of our Dragoons and the horse of a Bugler boy who had been sent in advance to keep an eye in the direction of the enemy and to communicate if they saw any movement towards our column. The prisoners are now confined in the city. It is quite possible that Gen. Taylor will demand the prisoners and if they are not given up march over and take the city or attempt it.

I am still in hopes notwithstand all warlike appearances that in a few months all difficulties will be settled and I will be permitted to see again My Dear Dear Julia. The time will appear long to me until this event but hope that has so long borne me out, the hope that one day we will meet to part no more for so long a time, will sustain me again. Give my love to all at White Haven and be sure to write soon and often. I have not heard from Fred. very lately. Vacancies have occured here which make him I think 2d from promotion and another will probably take place soon in the case of an officer who is to be tried for being drunk on duty.—I will write again in a few days, but dont put of answering this until you get my next.

ULYSSES

Julia

To Julia Dent

Head Quarters Mexican Army
May 11th 1846

My Dear Julia
After two hard fought battles against a force far superior to our own in numbers, Gen. Taylor has got possesion of the

Enemy's camp and now I am writing on the head of one of the captured drums. I wrote to you from Point Isabel and told you of the march we had and of the suspected attack upon the little force left near Matamoras. About two days after I wrote we left Point Isabel with about 300 waggons loaded with Army supplies. For the first 18 miles our course was uninterrupted but at the end of that distance we found the Mexican Army, under the command of General Arista drawn up in line of battle waiting our approach. Our waggons were immediately parked and Gen. Taylor marched us up towards them. When we got in range of their Artillery they let us have it right and left. They had I believe 12 pieces. Our guns were then rounded at them and so the battle commenced. Our Artillery amounted to 8 guns of six pound calibre and 2 Eighteen pounders. Evry moment we could see the charges from our pieces cut a way through their ranks making a perfect road, but they would close up the interval without showing signs of retreat. Their officers made an attempt to charge upon us but the havoc had been so great that their soldiers could not be made to advance. Some of the prisoners that we have taken say that their officers cut and slashed among them with their Sabres at a dreadful rate to make them advance but it was no use, they would not come. This firing commenced at ½ past 2 o'clock and was nearly constant from that until Sun down.

Although the balls were whizing thick and fast about me I did not feel a sensation of fear until nearly the close of the firing a ball struck close by me killing one man instantly, it nocked Capt. Page's under Jaw entirely off and broke in the roof of his mouth, and nocked Lt. Wallen and one Sergeant down besides, but they were not much hurt. Capt. Page is still alive. When it become to dark to see the enemy we encamped upon the field of battle and expected to conclude the fight the next morning. Morning come and we found that the enemy had retreated under cover of the night. So ended the battle of the 8th of May. The enemy numbered three to our one besides we had a large waggon train to guard. It was a terrible sight to go over the ground the next day and see the amont of life that had been destroyed. The ground was litterally strewed with the bodies of dead men and horses. The loss of the enemy is variously estimated from about 300 to 500. Our loss was comparitively small. But two officers were badly wounded, two or three slightly. About 12 or 15 of our men were killed and probably 50 wounded. When I can learn the exact amount of loss I will write and correct the statements I have made if they are not right. On the 9th of May about noon we left the field of battle and started on our way to Matamoras. When we advanced about six miles we found that the enemy had taken up a new position in the midst of a dense wood, and as we have since learned they had recieved a reinforcement equal to our whole numbers. Grape shot and musket balls were let fly from both sides making dreadful havoc. Our men continued to advance and did advance in spite of their shots, to the very mouths of the cannon and killed and took prisoner the Mexicans with them, and drove off with their own teams, taking cannon ammunition and all, to our side. In this way nine of their big guns were taken and their own ammunition turned against them. The Mexicans fought very hard for an hour and a half but seeing their means of war fall from their hands in spite of all their efforts they finally commenced to retreat helter skelter. A great many retreated to the banks of the Rio Grande and without looking for means of crossing plunged into this water and no doubt many of them were dround. Among the prisoners we have taken there are 14 officers and I have no idea how many privates. I understand that General Lavega, who is a prisoner in our camp has said that he has fought against several different nations but ours are the first that he ever saw who would charge up to the very mouths of cannon.

In this last affray we had we had three officers killed and some 8 or ten wounded. how many of our men suffered has not yet been learned. The Mexicans were so certain of sucsess that when we took their camp we found thir dinners on the fire cooking. After the battle the woods was strued with the dead. Waggons have been engaged drawing the bodies to bury. How many waggon loads have already come in and how many are still left would be hard to guess. I saw 3 large waggon loads at one time myself. We captured, besides the prisoners, 9 cannon, with a small amount of ammunition for them, probably 1000 or 1500 stand of fire arms sabres swords &c. Two hundred and fifty thousand rounds of ammunition for them over four hundred mules and pack saddles or harness. Drums, musical instruments camp equipage &c, &c. innumerable. The victory for us has been a very great one. No doubt you will see accounts enough of it in the papers. There is no great sport in having bullets flying about one in evry direction but I find they have less horror when among them than when in anticipation. Now that the war has commenced with such vengence I am in hopes my Dear Julia that we will soon be able to end it. In the thickest of it I thought of Julia. How much I should love to see you now to tell you all that happened. Mr. Hazlitt come out alive and whole. When we have another engagement, if we do have another atall, I will write again; that is if I am not one of the victims. Give my love to all at White Haven and do write soon my Dear Julia. I think you will find that history will count the victory just achieved one of the greatest on record. But I do not want to say to much about it until I see the accounts given by others. Dont forget to write soon to your most Devoted

ULYSSES

P. S. I forgot to tell you that the Fortifications left in charge of Maj. Brown in command of the 7th Inf.y was attacked while we were at Point Isabel and for five days the Mexicans continued to throw in shells. There was but 2 killed, Maj. Brown & one soldier, and 2 wounded.

To John W. Lowe

Matamoras Mexico
June 26th 1846

Dear Lowe

I have just recieved your letter of the 6th of June,: the first I have had from you since my Reg.t took the field in anticipation of the Annexation of Texas. Since that time the 4th Infantry has experienced but little of that ease and luxury of which the Hon. Mr. Black speaks so much. Besides hard marching, a great part of the time we have not even been blessed with a good tent as a protection against wind and weather. At Corpus Christi our troops were much exposed last winter which the citizens say was the severest season they have had for many years. From Corpus Christi to this place (a distance of about 180 miles) they had to march through a low sandy desert covered with salt ponds and in one or two instances ponds of drinkable water were separated by a whole days March. The troops suffered much but stood it like men who were able to fight many such battles as those of the 8th & 9th of May, that is without a murmur. On our arrival at the Rio Grande we found Matamoras occupied by a force superior to ours (in numbers) who might have made our march very uncomfortable if they had have had the spirit and courage to attempt it. But they confined their hostilities (except their paper ones) to small detached parties and single individuals as in the cases you mention in your letter, until they had their force augmented to thrible or quadrouple ours and then they made the bold efforts of which the papers are so full. About the last of April we got word of the enemy crossing the river no doubt with the intention of cuting us off from our supplies at Point Isabel. On the 1st of April at 3 o'clock General Taylor started with about 2000 men to go after and escort the Waggon train from Point Isabel and with the determination to cut his way, no matter how superior their numbers. Our march on this occation was as severe as could be made. Until 3 o'clock at night we scarsely halted, then we laid down in the grass and took a little sleep and marched the ballance of the way the next morning. Our March was mostly through grass up to the waist with a wet and uneven bottom yet we made 30 miles in much less than a day. I consider my march on that occation equal to a walk of sixty miles in one day on good roads and unencumbered with troops. The next morning after our arrival at Point Isabel we heard the enemies Artillery playing upon the little Field work which we had left Garrisoned by the 7th Inf.y and two Companies of Artillery. This bombardment was kept up for seven days with a loss of but two killed and four or five wounded on our side. The loss of the enemy was much greater though not serious. On the

7th of May General Taylor started from P. I. with his little force encumbered with a train of about 250 waggons loaded with provisions and ammunition. Although we knew the enemy was between us and Matamoras and in large numbers too, yet I did not believe, I was not able to appreciate the possibility of an attack from them. We had heard so much bombast and so many threats from the Mexicans that I began to believe that they were good for paper wars alone, but they stood up to their work manfully. On the 8th when within about 14 miles of Matamoras we found the enemy drawn up in line of battle on the edge of the prairie next a piece of woods Called Palo Alto. (Which is the Spanish for Tall Trees.) Even then I did not believe they were going to give battle. Our troops were halted out of range of Artillery and the waggons parked and the men allowed to fill their canteens with water. All preparations being made we marched forward in line of battle until we recieved a few shots from the enemy and then we were halted and our Artillery commenced. The first shot was fired about 3 o'clock P. M. and was kept up pretty equally on both sides until sun down or after, we then encamped on our own ground and the enemy on theirs. We supposed that the loss of the enemy had not been much greater than our own and expected of course that the fight would be renewed in the morning. During that night I believe all slept as soundly on the ground at Palo Alto as if they had been in a palace. For my own part I dont think I even dreamed of battles. During the days fight I scarsely thought of the probability or possibility of being touched myself (although 9 lb. shots were whistling all round,) until near the close of the evening a shot struck the ranks a little ways in front of me and nocked one man's head off, nocked the under Jaw of Capt. Page entirely away, and brought several others to the ground. Although Capt. Page rec'd so terrible a wound he is recovering from it. The under jaw is gone to the wind pipe and the tongue hangs down upon the throat. He will never be able to speak or to eat. The next morning we found to our surprise that the last rear guard of the enemy was just leaving their ground, the main body having left during the night. From Palo Alto to Matamoras there is for a great part of the way a dense forest of under growth, here called chapparel. The

Mexicans after having marched a few miles through this were reinforced by a conciderable body of troops. They chose a place on the opposite side from us of a long but narrow pond (called Resaca de la Palma) which gave them greatly the advantage of position Here they made a stand. The fight was a pel mel affair evry body for himself. The chapparel is so dense that you may be within five feet of a person and not know it. Our troops rushed forward with shouts of victory and would kill and drive away the Mexicans from evry piece of Artillery they could get their eyes upon. The Mexicans stood this hot work for over two hours but with a great loss. When they did retreat there was such a panic among them that they only thought of safty in flight. They made the best of their way for the river and where ever they [. . . . .] it they would rush in. Many of them no doubt were drowned. Our loss in the two days was 182 killed & wounded. What the loss of the enemy was cannot be certainly ascertained but I know that acres of ground was strewed with the bodies of the dead and wounded. I think it would not be an over estimate to say that their loss from killed wounded, take prisoners, and missing was over 2,000; and of the remainder nothing now scarsely remains. So precipitate was their flight when they found that we were going to cross the river and take the town, that sickness broke out among them and as we have understood, they have but little effective force left. News has been recieved that Parades is about taking the field with a very large force. Daily, volunteers are arriving to reinforce us and soon we will be able to meet them in what ever force they choose to come. What will be our course has not been announced in orders, but no doubt we will carry the war into the interior. Monteray, distant about 300 miles from here, will no doubt be the first place where difficulties with an enemy await us. You want to know what my feelings were on the field of battle! I do not know that I felt any peculiar sensation. War seems much less horrible to persons engaged in it than to those who read of the battles. I forgot to tell you in the proper place of the amount of property taken. We took on the 9th Eight pieces of Artillery with all their ammunition something like 2,000 stand of arms, muskets, pistols, swords sabres Lances & 500 mules with their packs, camp equipage & provisions and in fact about evry thing they had. When we got into the camp of the enemy evrything showed the great confidence they had of sucsess. They were actually cooking their meal during the fight, and as we have since learned, the women of Matamoras were making preparations for a great festival upon the return of their victorious Army.—The people of Mexico are a very different race of people from ours. The better class are very proud and tyrinize over the lower and much more numerous class as much as a hard master does over his negroes, and they submit to it quite as humbly. The great majority inhabitants are either pure or more than half blooded Indians, and show but little more signs of neatness or comfort in their miserable dwellings than the uncivilized Indian.—Matamoras contains probably about 7,000 inhabitants, a great majority of them of the lower order. It is not a place of as much business importance as our little towns of 1,000. But no doubt I will have an opportunity of knowing more of Mexico and the Mexicans before I leave the country and I will take another occation of telling you more of them.

Dont you think Mr. Polk has done the Officers of the Army injustice by filling up the new Regt. of Riflemen from citizens? It is plain to be seen that we have but little to expect from him.—I have now written you a long letter; as soon as any thing more is done I will write again. If you have an opportunity I wish you would let them know at home that I am well. I dont think I have written in the last few weeks.—I should like very much to see you here in command of a volunteer company. I think you would not be affected by the climate. So far our troops have had their health remarkably well—

Remember me to your own and Judge Fishback's family. I suppose Tom has grown so much that he almost thinks of volunteering for the Mexican Wars himself.—I shall be pleased to hear from you as often as you will make it convenient to write and will answer all your letters—

Yours Truly
U S GRANT
4th Inf.y

J. W. Lowe Esq.
Batavia O——

To Julia Dent

Matamoras Mexico
July 25th 1846

My Dearest Julia

It must be about two weeks since I have written to you, and as I am determined that a longer time shall never pass with my Dearest hearing from me, whilst I am in an enemie's country, I write to you again, notwithstanding I have not heard from you for some time. Do not understand me though to cast any censure upon you, for you may have written me a dozen letters and me not recieved one of them yet, for I believe it is about two weeks since we have had a Mail, and there is no telling when we will have another. You must not neglect to write often Dearest so that whenever a mail does reach this far-out-of-the-way country I can hear from the one single person who of all others occupies my thoughts. This is my last letter from Matamoras Julia. Already the most of the troops have left for Camargo and a very few days more will see the remainder of us off. Whether we will have much more fighting is a matter of much speculation. At present we are bound for Camargo and from thence to Monteray, where it is reported that there is several thousand Mexican troops engaged in throwing up Fortifications, and there is no doubt either but that Parades has left Mexico at the head of nine thousand more to reinforce them, but the latest news says that he has been obliged to return to the City of Mexico on account of some rupture there. But a few months more will determine what we have to do, and I will be careful to keep my Dear Julia advised of what the army in this quarter is about. Fred. has not arrived here yet but I am looking for him daily. His commission arrived some time ago, and also a letter from St. Louis for him. I have them both in my possession, and wrote to him to hasten on. His Reg.t. (the 5th Infantry) is already in Camargo. A few months more of fatigue and privation, I am much in hopes, will bring our difficulties to such a crisis that I will be able to see you again Julia, and then if my wishes prevailed, we would never part again as merely engaged, but as, — you know what I would say. — No doubt a hard march awaits us between Camargo and Monteray. The distance is over two hundred miles, and as I have understood, a great part of it without water. But a person cannot expect to make a Campaign without meeting with some privations.

Fred. and me will probably be near each other during the time and between us I am in hopes that I will hear from my Dear Julia evry week, but write oftener to me than to Fred. — Since we have been in Matamoras a great many murders have been committed, and what is strange there seemes to be but very week means made use of to prevent frequent repetitions. Some of the volunteers and about all the Texans seem to think it perfectly right to impose upon the people of a conquered City to any extent, and even to murder them where the act can be covered by the dark. And how much they seem to enjoy acts of violence too! I would not pretend to guess the number of murders that have been committed upon the persons of poor Mexicans and our soldiers, since we have been here, but the number would startle you. — Is Ellen married yet? I never hear you mention her name any more. John I suppose is on his way for the seat of war by this time. If we have to fight we may all meet next winter in the City of Mexico.

There is no telling whether it will be as prisoners of war or as a conquering force. From my experience I judge the latter much the most probable. — How pleasant it would be now for me to spend a day with you at White Haven. I envy you all very much, but still hope on that better times are coming. Remember me to all at White Haven and write very soon and very often to

                              ULYSSES
Julia

To Julia Dent

                    Camp Near Monteray Mex.
                             Oct. 3d 1846
My Dearest Julia

I wrote to you while we were still storming the city of Monteray and told you then that the town was not yet taken but that I thought the worst part was then over. I was right for the next day the Mexicans capitulated and we have been ever since the uninterupted holders of the beautiful city of Monteray. Monteray is a beautiful city enclosed on three sides by the mountains with a pass through them to the right and to the left. There are points around the city which command it and these the Mexicans fortified and armed. The city is built almost entirely of stone and with very thick walls. We found all their streets baricaded and the whole place well defended with artillery, and taking together the strength of the place and the means the Mexicans had of defending it it is almost incredible that the American army now are in possession here. But our victory was not gained without loss. 500, or near abouts, brave officers and men fell in the attack. Many of them were only wounded and will recover, but many is the leg or arm that will be buryed in this country while the owners will live to relate over and over again the scenes they witnessed during the siege of Monteray. I told you in my last letter the officers that you were acquainted with that suffered, but for fear the letter may not reach you I will inumerate them again. Capt. Morris of the 3d Inf.y Maj. Barbour Capt. Field Lt. Irwin Lt. Hazlitt Lt. Hoskins and Lt. Terrett & Dilworth since dead. Lt. Graham & Maj. Lier dangerously wounded. It is to be hoped that we are done fighting with Mexico for we have shown them now that we can whip them under evry disadvantage. I dont believe that we will ever advance beyond this place, for it is generally believed that Mexico has rec'd our Minister and a few months more will restore us to amity. I hope it may be so for fighting is no longer a pleasure. Fred. has not joined us yet and I think it a great pity too, for his Regiment was engaged at a point where they done the enemy as much harm probably as any other Reg.t but lost but very few men and no officer. Monteray is so full of Orange Lime and Pomgranite trees that the houses can scarsly be seen until you get into the town. If it was an American city I have no doubt it would be concidered the handsomest one in the Union. The climate is excellent and evry thing might be produced that any one could want *** I have written two pages and have not told you that I got a letter a few days ago from my Dear Dear Julia. It has been a long long time since I got one before but I do not say that you have not written often for I can very well conceive of letters loosing their way following us up. What made you ask me the question Dearest Julia "if I thought absence could conquer love"? You ought to be just as good a judge as me! I can only answer for myself alone, that Julia is as *dear* to me to-day as she was the day we visited St. Louis together, more than two years ago, when I first told her of my love. From that day to this I have loved you constantly and the same and with the hope too that long before this time I would have been able to call you *Wife*. Dearest Julia if you have been just as constant in your love it *shall not* [. . . .] long until I will be entitled to call you by the [. . . .] affectionate title. You have not told me for a long time Julia that you still loved me, but I never thought to doubt it. Write soon to me and continue to write often. Now that we are going to stay here some time I am in hopes that I will get a number of letters from you. I forgot to tell you that by the terms of the capitulation the Mexicans were to retire beyond Linariz within seven days and were not to fight again for eight weeks and we were not to advance for the same time. Fred. certainly will join soon and then I will make him write often. Give my love to all at White Haven

ULYSSES

Julia

P. S. I am going to write to you evry two weeks if I have an opportunity to write so you may know if you dont get letters that often that some of them are lost

U.

To Julia Dent

Castle of Perote Mexico
April 24th 1847

My Dear Julia

You see from the above that the great and long talked of Castle of Perote is at last in the hands of the Americans. On the 13th of this month the rear Division of Gen. Scott's army left Vera Cruz to drive Santa Anna and his army from the strong mountain passes which they had fortified, with the determination of driving back the Barbarians of the North, at all hazards. On the morning of the 17th our army met them at a pass called Cierra Gorda a mountain pass which to look at one would suppose impregnable. The road passes between mountains of rock the tops of which were all fortified and well armed with artillery. The road was Barricaded by a strong work with five pieces of artillery. Behind this was a peak of the mountains much higher than all the others and commanded them so that the Enemy calculated that even if the Americans should succeed in taking all the other hights, from this one they could fire upon us and be out of reach themselvs. But they were disappointed. Gen. Twiggs' Division worked its way around with a great deel of laibor and made the attack in the rear. With some loss on our side and great loss on the part of the Enemy this highest point was taken and soon the White flag of the enemy was seen to float. Of Generals and other officers and soldiers some Six thousand surrendered as prisoners of war   Their Artillery ammunition supplies and most of their small arms were captured. As soon as Santa Anna saw that the day was lost he made his escape with a portion of his army but he was pursued so closely that his carriage, a splendid affair, was taken and in it was his cork leg and some Thirty thousand dollars in gold. The pursuit was so close that the Mexicans could not establish themselvs in another strong pass which they had already fortified, and when they got to the strong Castle of Perote they passed on leaving it too with all of its artillery to fall into our hands. After so many victories on our part and so much defeat on the part of the Mexicans they certainly will agree to treat. For my part I do not believe there will be another fight unless we should pursue with a very small force.—From Vera Cruz to this place it is an almost constant rize Perote being about Eight thousand feet above the ocean. Around us are mountains covered with eternal snow and greatly the influance is felt too. Although we are in the Torrid zone it is never so warm as to be uncomfortable nor so cold as to make a fire necessary. From Vera Cruz to this place the road is one of the best and one that cost more laibor probably than any other in the world. It was made a great many years ago when Mexico was a province of Spain. On the road there a great many specimens of beautiful table land and a decided improvement in the appearance of the people and the stile of building over any thing I had seen before in Mexico. Jalapa is decidedly the most beautiful place I ever saw in my life. From its low Latitude and great elevation it is never hot nor never cold. The climate is said to be the best in the world and from what I saw I would be willing to make Jalapa my home for life with only one condition and that would be that I should be permitted to go and bring my Dearest Julia.—The 5th Inf.y, Fred's Reg.t was was not present at the fight of Cierra Gorda. A few days before we left Vera Cruz the 5th Inf.y was ordered down the coast to Alvarado to procure horses and mules for the use of the army, and when we left they had not returned. My Dearest Julia how very long it seems since we were together and still our march is onward. In a few days no doubt we will start for Puebla and then we will be within from Eighty to a Hundred miles of the City of Mexico; there the march must end. Three years now the 4th Inf.y has been on the tented field and I think it is high time that I should have a leave of absence. Just think Julia it is now three long years that we have been engaged. Do you think I could endure another years separation loving you as I do now and believing my love returned? At least commission and all will go in less time or I will be permitted to see the one I have loved so much for three long years. My Dearest dont you think a soldiers life a hard one! But after a storm there must be a calm. This war must end some time and the army scattered to occupy different places and I will be satisfied with any place wher I can have you with me. Would you be willing to go with me to some out-of-the-way post Dearest? But I know you would for you have said so so often.—Your next letter will probably reach me in Puebla the 3d city in size in the Republic of Mexico. Write to me often Julia I always get your letters. I will write again as soon as the army makes another halt Has your pa ever said anything more about our engagement? You know in one of your sweet letters you told me something he had said which argued that his consent would be given. Remember me affectionately to you father and mother Miss Ellen & Emmy.

ULYSSES

Julia

P. S. Among the wounded on our side was Lt. Dana very dangerously. In the Rifle Reg.t one officer, Lt. Ewell, was killed Mr. Maury lost his hand Mason and Davis a leg each. A great many Volunteer officers were killed and wounded. I have not had a letter from you since the one I answered from Vera Cruz but there have been but few mails arrived since. I hope to get one soon.

U

To John W. Lowe

Tepey Ahualco Mexico
May 3d 1847

Dear Lowe

Just as the troops were leaving Vera Cruz I recieved a letter from my young friend Tom and yourself. Now that we will probably be stationary for four or five days I avail my self of the opportunity of answering. I see that you have written me several letters which you have not recieved answers to. I always make it a point to answer all your letters and am only sorry that I dont get more of them. You say you would like to hear more about the war. If you had seen as much of it as I have you would be tired of the subject. Of our success at Vera Cruz you have read evry thing. The strength of the town its Forts and Castle the papers are full and they do not exagerate. On the 13th of April the rear Division of Gen. Scotts army left Vera Cruze to ascend the mountains and drive Santa Anna from his strong position in one of the Passes. On the night of the 15th Gen. Worth arrived at Plana del Rio three miles from the Battle ground. Gen. Twiggs with his Division had been there several days prepairing for an attack. By the morning of the 17th the way was completed to go arround the Pass, Cierra Gordo, and make the attack in the rear as well as in front. The difficulties to surmount made the undertaking almost equal to Bonapartes Crossing the Alps. Cierra Gorda is a long narrow Pass the mountains towring far above the road on either side. Some five of the peaks were fortified and armed with Artillery and Infantry. At the outlett of the Mountain Gorge a strong Breast work was thrown up and 5 pieces placed into embrasure sweeping the road so that it would have been impossible for any force in the world to have advanced. Immediately behind this is a peak of the Mountains several hundred feet higher than any of the others and commanding them. It was on this hight that Gen. Twiggs made his attack. As soon as the Mexicans saw this hight taken they knew the day was up with them. Santa Anna Vamoused with a small part of his force leaving about 6000 to be taken prisoner with all their arms supplies &c. Santa Anna's loss could not have been less than 8000 killed, wounded taken prisoners and misen. The pursuit was so close upon the retreating few that Santa Anna's carriage and mules were taken and with them his wooden leg and some 20 or 30 thousand dollars in money. Between the thrashing the Mexicans have got at Buon Vista, Vera Cruz and Cierra Gorde they are so completely broken up that if we only had transportation we could go to the City of Mexico and where ever els we liked without resistance. Garrisons could be established in all the important towns and the Mexicans prevented from ever raising another army. Santa Anna is said to be at Orazaba, at the foot of a mountain always covered with snow and of the same name. He has but a small force. Orazaba looks from here as if you could almost throw a stone to it, but it looked the same from Jalapa some fifty miles back and was even visable from Vera Cruze. Since we left the Sea Coast the improvement in the appearance of the people and the stile of building has been very visable over any thing I had seen in Mexico before. The road is one of the best in the world. The scenery is beautiful and a great deal of magnificent table land spreads out above you and below you. Jalapa is the most beautiful place that I ever saw. It is about 4000 feet above the sea and being in the Torrid zone, they have there everlasting spring. Fruit and vegitables the year around. I saw there a great many handsome ladies and more well dressed men than I had ever seen before in the Republic. From Jalapa we marched to Perote and walked quietly into the strong Castle that you no doubt have read about. It is a great work. One Brigade, the one I belong to is now 20 miles in advance of Perote. Soon no doubt we will advance upon Puebla. I am Regtl Quarter Master appointed under the new law allowing one to each Reg.t and giving extra allowances.—Remember me to all your family and Judge Fishbacks. Tel Tom he must write to me again

I will be much pleased to recieve all the letters you will write to me and all that Tom will write too. I will write to Tom from Puebla. I suppose we will be there in a few days. If you see any of the Bethel people please remember me to them. Tell them I am hartily tired of the wars. If you were to see me now you would never recognize me in the world. I have a beard more than four inches long and it is red.

Your Friend   U. S. GRANT
4th Inf.y

To Julia Dent

City of Mexico
September 1847

My Dearest Julia

Because you have not heard from me for so long a time you must not think that I have neglected to write or in the least forgotten one who is so ever dear to me. For several months no mail has gone to Vera Cruz except such as Editors of papers send by some Mexican they hire and these generally fall into the hands of the enemy who infest the wole line from here to the sea coast. Since my last letter to you four of the hardest fougt battles that the world ever witnessed have taken place, and the most astonishing victories have crowned the American arms. But dearly have they paid for it! The loss of officers and men killed and wounded is frightful. Among the wounded you will find Fred's name but he is now walking about and in the course of two wecks more will be entirely well. I saw Fred. a moment after he received his wound but escaped myself untouched. It is to be hoped that such fights it

will not be our misfortune to witness again during the war,
and how can be? The whole Mexican army is destroyed or
disbursed, they have lost nearly all their artillery and other
munitions of war; we are occupying the rich and populace
valley from which the great part of their revenues are collected and all their sea ports are cut off from them. Evry thing
looks as if peace should be established soon; but perhaps my
anxiety to get back to see again my Dearest Julia makes me
argue thus. The idea of staying longer in this country is to me
insupportable. Just think of the three long years that have
passed since we met. My health has always been good, but
exposure to weather and a Tropicle Sun had added ten years
to my apparent age. At this rate I will soon be old.—Out of
all the officers that left Jefferson Barracks with the 4th Infantry but three besides myself now remains with us, besides this
four or five who joined since, are gone. Poor Sidney Smith
was the last one killed. He was shot from one of the houses
after we entered the city.

Mexico is one of the most beautiful cities in the world and
being the capital no wonder that the Mexicans should have
fought desperately to save it. But they deserve no credit. They
fought us with evry advantage on their side. They doubled us
in numbers, doubled us and more in artillery, they behind
strong Breast-works had evry advantage and then they were
fighting for their homes.*** It *** truly a great country. No
country was ever so blessed by nature. There is no fruit nor
no grain that cant be raised here nor no temperature that cant
be found at any season. You have only to choose the degree of
elevation to find perpetual snow or the hotest summer. But
with all these advantages how anxious I am to get out of
Mexico. You can redily solve the problem of my discontent
Julia. If you were but here and me in the United States my
anxiety would be just as great to come to Mexico as it now is
to get out.

Oct. 25th   At last a mail is to leave here for the U States   I
am glad at finally having an opportunity of leting you hear
from me. A train is going to Vera Cruz and with it many of
the wounded officers and men. Fred. is geting too well to
be one of them. I am almost sorry that I was not one of
the unfortunates so that now I could be going back. It is to

be hoped that in future mails will be much more frequent though in fact it is generally believed that as soon as congress meets the whole army will be ordered from this valey of Mexico. There is no use of my teling you any more that I will take the first opportunity of geting back to Mo. for I have told you that so often, and yet no chance has occured. At present Gen. Scott will let no officer leave who is able for duty not even if he tenders his resignation. So you see it is not so easy to get out of the wars as it is to get into them. — Write to me often dearest Julia so if I cant have the pleasure of sending letters often to you let me at least enjoy the receipt of one from you by evry Mail coming this way. — No doubt before this the papers are teaming with accounts of the different battles and the courage and science shown by individuals. Even here one hears of individual exploits (which were never performed) sufficient to account for the taking of Mexico throwing out about four fifths of the army to do nothing. One bit of credit need not be given to accounts that are given except those taken from the reports of the different commanders.

Remember me my Dearest Julia to you father & mother and the rest of the family and pray that the time may not be far distant when we may take our walks again up and down the banks of the Gravois. Truly it will be a happy time for me when I see that stram again.

Farewell My Dearest Julia
U S GRANT

To Julia Dent

Tacabaya Mexico
January 9th 1848

My Dear Julia

Since I wrote to you last one Brigade has moved to this place which is about four miles from the City of Mexico and from being so much higher than the City is much more healthy. One Brigade has gone to Toluca and it is rumored that before a great while we will move to some distant part, either Queretero, Zacetecus, San Louis Potosi or Guernivaca unless there is a strong probability of peace. It is now how-

ever strongly believed that peace will be established before
many months. I hope it may be so for it is scarsely suportible
for me to be separated from you so long my dearest Julia. A
few weeks ago I went to the commanding officer of my Regiment and represented to him that when the 4th Inf.y left
Jefferson Barracks, three years ago last May, I was engaged,
and that I thought it high time that I should have a leave of
absence to go back. He told me that he would approve it but
I found that it would be impossible to get the Comd.g Gen.
to give the leave so I never made the application. I have
strong hopes though of going back in a few months. If peace
is not made it is at all events about my turn to go on recruiting service. As to geting a sick leave that is out of the question for I am never sick a day. Mexico is a very pleasant place
to live because it is never hot nor never cold, but I believe
evry one is hartily tired of the war. There is no amusements
except the Theatre and as the actors & actresses are Spanish
but few of the officers can understand them. The better class
of Mexicans dare not visit the Theatre or associate with the
Americans lest they should be assassinated by their own people or banished by their Government as soon as we leave. A
few weeks ago a Benefit was given to a favorite actress and the
Govorner of Queretero hearing of it sent secret spies to take
the names of such Mexicans as might be caught in indulging
in amusements with the Americans for the purpose of banish-
ing them as soon as the *Magnanimous Mexican Republic*
should drive away the Barbarians of the North. I pity poor
Mexico. With a soil and climate scarsely equaled in the world
she has more poor and starving subjects who are willing and
able to work than any country in the world. The rich keep
down the poor with a hardness of heart that is incredible.
Walk through the streets of Mexico for one day and you will
see hundreds of begars, but you never see them ask alms of
their own people, it is always of the Americans that they expect to recieve. I wish you could be here for one short day
then I should be doubly gratified. Gratified at seeing you my
dearest Julia, and gratified that you might see too the manners
and customs of these people. You would see what you never
dreamed of nor can you form a correct idea from reading.***
All gamble Priests & civilians, male & female and particularly

so on Sundays.—But I will tell you all that I know about Mexico and the Mexicans when I see you which I do hope will not be a great while now. Fred. is in the same Brigade with me. I see him evry day. He like myself is in excellent health and has no prospect of geting out of the country on the plea of sickness.—I have one chance of geting out of Mexico soon besides going on recruiting service. Gen. Scott will grant leaves of absence to officers where there is over two to a Company. In my Reg.t there are three or four vacancies which will be filled soon [. . . .] h and will give an oportunity for one or two now here to go out. Give my love to all at White Haven and do not fail to write often dearest Julia. I write but seldom myself but it is because a mail but seldom goes from here to the sea coast. Coming this way it is different for the Volunteers are constantly arriving.

When you write next tell me if Mrs. Porter and Mrs. Higgins are married or likely to be.

Adieu My Dearest Julia
ULYSSES

To Julia Dent Grant

Detroit Michigan
April 27th 1849

My Dearest Julia

I recieved your Telagraphic dispach yesterday morning from which I see that you are on your way to St. Louis. I hope you may find all at home well, and get this soon after your arrival. This you know is my Birth day and I doubt if you will think of it once.—I have a room and am staying at present with Mr. Wallen. Wallen and family are as well as can be expected under present circumstances.

I have rented a neat little house in the same neighborhood with Wallen and Gore   In the lower part of the house there is a neat double parlour, a dining room, one small bedroom and kitchen. There is a nice upstares and a garden filled with the best kind of fruit. There is a long arbour grown over with vines that will bear fine grapes in abundance for us and to give away. There are currents and plum & peach trees and infact evrything that the place could want to make it comfortable.

I will have a soldier at work in the garden next week so that by the time you get here evrything will be in the nicest order. I find Detroit very dull as yet but I hope that it will appear better when I get better acquainted and you know dearest without *you* no place, or home, can be very pleasant to me. Now that we are fixed to go to hous keeping I will be after you sooner than we expected when you left. I think about the 1st of June you may look for me. Very likely Ellen will come along and spend the Summer with us. — I hope dearest that you had a very pleasant trip. I know that you have thought of me very often. *** I have dreamed of you several times since we parted.

I have nothing atal to do here. I have no company and consequently do not go on Guard or to Drills. Mr. Gore and myself are to commence fishing in a day or two and if sucsessful we will spend a great many pleasant hours in that way.

When I commence housekeeping I will probably get a soldier to cook for me, but in the mean time if any good girl offers I will engage her to come when you return.

Dearest I nothing more to write except to tell you how very very dear you are to me and how much I think of you. Give my love to all at home and write to me very soon and often. Yours devotedly

ULYS

P. S. I recieved two letters here for you which I opened and read; the one from Annie Walker I forwarded to you at Bethel. One from Elen I did not send inasmuch as you would be at home so soon. Give my love to Sallie & Annie.

U

To Julia Dent Grant

Detroit Michigan
Wednesday 28th May 1851

Dearest Julia

You will no doubt be astonished to learn that we have all been ordered away from Detroit. Maj. Gore goes with his

company to Fort Gratioit. Col. Whistler is ordered to move
his Head quarters to Fort Niagara; but as there are not sufficient quarters there he has represented the matter to Washington and no doubt our destination will be changed to Sacket's
Harbor. Wont this be pleasant. I will write to you again before we leave here and tell you all about it. Dr. Tripler goes
with us and Capt. McDowell goes to Jefferson Barracks. I will
send your scarf by him.

Mrs. Gore is thoroughly disgusted at the idea of going to
Gratiot. She seems really distressed at the idea of being separated from you. She starts to-day so as to be there before her
troubles come on.

I think now I will send for you sooner than you expected to
return when you left. When you come I will meet you at
Detroit and we will spend a week here and at Fort Gratiot. If
Ellen is not to be married this Fall get her to come with you
and spend this Winter.

There is no possible news in Detroit. Evry thing is about as
when you left. People all pretend to regret our depature very
much and I presume some of them are sincere. For my part I
am glad to go to Sackets Harbor. I anticipate pleasant housekeeping for the next year or two. I shall provide nothing in
the way of furnature until you arrive except a carpet for one
room.

I hope dearest Julia you have not been as unfortunate about
geting letters this time as you was the last time you left me. I
have had but one from you yet but I am expecting another
now evry day.

You have none idea dearest how much I miss little Fred. I
think I can see the little dog todeling along by himself and
looking up and laughing as though it was something smart.
Aint he walking? I know they will all dislike to see him leave
Bethel.

Write to me very soon dearest and tell me all about what
kind of a trip you had from Cincinnati, how you found all in
St. Louis &c. &c.

Give my love to all of them and kiss them for me. Kiss
Freddy and learn him to say papa before he comes back. Dont
let him learn to say any bad words. — Mrs. Gore says Jim is

learning to talk but I guess he talks about as he did when you left.

Good buy dearest Julia and dont forget to write very often. I will write punctually evry week as I promised.

ULYSSES

P. S. I am about selling my horse and if I do I will send you $50.00 by my next letter.

U

To Julia Dent Grant

Sacket's Harbor N. Y.
August 10th 1851

My Dearest Julia

My regular day for writing has come again but this time I have no letter of yours to answer. I am looking for a long letter now evry day. I am so sorry that you are not here now. Sacket's Harbor is one of the most pleasant places in the country to spend a summer. It is always cool and healthy. There are several pleasant families in garrison and the parade ground would be such a nice place for Fred. to run. I want to see the little dog very much. You will start now very soon will you not? Evry letter I get now I shall expect to hear that you are geting ready to start. I have not got a particle of news to write you only that I am well and want to see Fred. and you very much.

I have had some very nice furnature made in garrison and otherwise our quarters look very nice. All that we want now to go to housekeeping is the table furnature. That I will not buy until you come on lest I should not please you. The furnature made in garrison is nicer than I could buy in Watertown and more substantial. It consists of lounges, chairs and a center table.

I know dearest Julia you will dislike very much to leave home, and I know that they will miss you and Fred. very much; but you know that you must come after while and you might just as well leave soon as late. Write to Virginia and see if she will not come with you if you come that way. I have told you to ask Nelly two or three times but you never say anything about whether she can come or whether she is to be married this fall or anything about it. I suppose however from your always sending your letters by McKeever to the post office that she is to be married to him soon.—What news do the boys send from California? Are they doing as well as formerly? I suppose they say nothing more about comeing home now.

Col. Whistler confidantly expects to be ordered away from here in the spring. What leads him to think we will go I dont know. I hope his prediction may not prove true.

Tell Fred. to be a good boy and not annoy his grandpa & ma. Is he geting big enough to whip when he is a bad boy? I expect his aunt Ell. annoys him so as to make him act bad evry day. When he comes here I will get him his dog and little wagon so that he can ride about the garrison all day. You dont tell me, though I have asked so often, how many teeth he has.

I have not heard from home now for a long time, and to tell the truth I have not written since I was at Quebec.

I hope all are well at your house. Give my love to them all and write soon.

Dont forget to avail yourself of the first good opportunity to come on here.

Adieu dearest Julia. A thousand kisses to you and Fred.

ULYS.

To Julia Dent Grant

Steamer Ohio
July 15th 1852

My Dearest Julia;

What would I not give to know that you are well at this time? This is about the date when you expected to be sick and my being so far away I am afraid may affect you. I am very well, only sea-sick, and so are all the passengers, notwithstanding we are in latitude 10° North. We have been blessed

with remarkably fine weather from the begining; a very fortunate thing for a vessel coming to this latitude in July, with
1100 persons on board.

You see dearest Julia how bad it would have been had you
accompanied me to New York. The Regiment had but two
days notice before sailing and I had but a few hours. You
know I wrote to you Sunday afternoon from Philadelphia
when I knew nothing, nor suspected nothing, of the move.
The orders to sail were sent by Telegraph and obeyed before
there was time to correspond.

There is no insident of the voyage to relate that would interest you much, and then dearest I do not know how this
letter will find you. I hope for the best of course, but cannot
help fearing the worst. When I get on land and hear that you
are all over your troubles I will write you some long letters. I
cannot say when you may look for another letter from me.
This goes to New York by the vessel we come out upon. To-
morrow we commence crossing the Isthmus and I write you
this to-day because then I may not have an opportunity. I
write this on deck, standing up, because in the cabin it is so
insufferably hot that no one can stay there.

The vessel on the Pacific puts in at Acapulco, Mexico, and I
may find an opportunity of mailing a letter from there. If I do
you will hear from me again in about three weeks or less.

Before recieving this dearest I the little one will be born.
If it is a girl name it what you like, but if a boy name it after
me. I know you will do this Julia of your own choise but then
I want you to know it will please me too.

Dear little Fred. how is he now? I want to see him very
much. I imagine that he is begining to talk quite well. Is he
not? I know he is a great favorite with his Grandpa & ma and
his Aunts. Does he like them all? Kiss the little rascal for me.

My dearest Julia if I could only hear from you daily for the
next [. . .] days I would have nothing to regret in this move.
I expect by it to do something for myself.

The only ladies with us are Mrs. Gore, Mrs. Wallen, Mrs.
Slaughter, Mrs. Collins & Mrs. Underwood. They poor
things I fear will regret it before twenty four hours. It is now
in the midst of the rainy season and we have to cross the
mountains on mules, through passes which are too narrow

for two abreast, and the ascent and descent to precipitate for
any other animal. Give my love to all at home dearest Julia. I
hope you recieved the check for one hundred that I sent you.
I have one hundred & fifty dollars in the hands of Col.
Swords, Qr. Master in New York which I will direct him to
send you.

Adieu Dearest, A thousand kisses for yourself, Fred. and
our other little one. I will let no opportunity of mailing a
letter pass unimproved. Write often dearest to your affectionate husband

ULYSS

To Julia Dent Grant

Steamer Golden Gate
Near Acapulco, Mexico, Aug. 9th 1852

My Dearest Julia;

I wish I could only know that you, and our dear little ones
were as well as I am. Although we have had terrible sickness
among the troops, and have lost one hundred persons, counting men, women & children, yet I have enjoyed good health.
It has been the province of my place as Quarter Master to be
exposed to the weather and climate on the Isthmus, while
most of the others were quietly aboard ship, but to that very
activity probably may be ascribed my good health. It no
doubt will be a relief to you to know that we have been out
from Panama over four days and no sickness has broken out
aboard. All are healthy and evry minuet brings us towards a
better climate.

Among the deaths was that of poor Maj. Gore. The Maj.
was taken before daylight in the morning and in the afternoon was dead. Mrs. Gore took his death very hard and then
to think too of the trip she had to undergo crossing the Isthmus again! My dearest you never could have crossed the Isthmus at this season, for the first time, let alone the second. The
horrors of the road, in the rainy season, are beyond description.—Mrs. Gore will be at home, if she is so fortunate as to
stand the trip, before you get this. I hope father and Gennie

will go and see her soon. Lieut. Macfeely, 2d Lt. of Maj. Gore's Comp.y, accompanied Mrs. Gore and may go to our house to see you. He promised me that he would. I gave him an order on the Qr. Mr. in New York for $150 00 Mr. Hooker owes me which he gets he will send you.

Mrs. Wallen and the other ladies along are tollerably well, but a goodeal reduced. Mrs. Wallens weight when she got across the Isthmus was 84 lbs. Her children, Harry Nanny & Eddy look quite differently from what they did when they left New York. But thank fortune we are fas approaching a better climate. The Golden Gate takes us nearly 300 miles per day.

We have seen from a Calafornia paper our destination. All but one company goes to Oregon. Head Quarters (and of course me with it) goes to Columbia Barracks, Fort Van Couver, Oregon. In consequence of one company of the Reg.t, and all the sick being left at the Island Flamingo, near Panama, to follow on an other steamer, we will remain at Benecia Cal. for probably a month. Benecia is within a days travels of where John is and of course I shall see him.

You must not give yourself any uneasiness about me now dearest for the time has passed for danger. I know you have borrowed a goodeal of trouble and from the exagerated accounts which the papers will give you could not help it. From Mrs. Gore however you can get the facts which are terrible enough.

I have not given you any discription of any part of our journey, and as I told you in all my letters dearest, I will not until I hear of your being well. I will say however that there is a great accountability some where for the loss which we have sustained. — Out of the troops at Sackets Harbor some twelve or fifteen are dead, none that you would recollect however except O'Maley, and Sgt. Knox, the one you thought looked so much like Maloney.

Elijah Camp is with us. He goes as sutler, probably with Head Quarters.

Give my love to all at home dearest and kiss our dear little ones for me. Fred, the little dog I know talks quite well by this time. Is he not a great pet? You must not let them spoil him dearest. A thousand kisses for yourself dear Julia. Dont

forget to write often and Direct, Hd Qrs. 4th Inf.y Columbia
Barracks Fort Van Couver, Oregon.

Adieu dear wife,
Your affectionate husband
ULYS.

P. S. You may be anxious to hear from Maggy. She looks wors
than ever. She has been sea-sick ever since she started. She
regrets very much that she had not staid with you.

Mrs. Wallen was going to write to you from Panama but
Maj. Gore's taking sick prevented.

Again adieu dear dear wife.
U.

To Julia Dent Grant

Benecia Calafornia
August 20th 1852

My Dear Wife.

We have arrived, all safely, at this place where we will remain, probably, for some three weeks. When we leave here it
will be for Fort Van Couver as I have told you in all my
previous letters from Panama up to this place.—Benecia is a
nice healthy place where our troops will pick up what they
lost on the Isthmus in a very short time. I can assure you it
was no little that all lost in the way of flesh. Capt. McConnell
and myself when we got across were in prime order for riding
a race or doing anything where a light weight was required. I
have not been sick but the degree of prostration that I felt
could not be produced in any other latitude except that of the
tropics, and near the equator at that.

I should not write you now because there is no Mail going
for several days but I am going up to the Stanislands, to-
morrow, to see John and before I get back the Mail may leave,
and I can assure you dearest Julia that I shall never allow a
Mail to leave here without carrying a letter to you.

I am staying with Fred. Steel, a class-mate of mine, who
was at our wedding, and when I told him we had a little boy

named Fred. he was very much elated. McConnell, Russell and Underwood all joined in telling what a nice boy Fred. is. I really believe Fred. was much more of a favorite with the officers than we thought.

I spent an hour or two with Mrs. Stevens in San Francisco, and she would have come up with us only Stevens was sick. They will be here in a day or two and make this their home. Mrs. Stevens seemed very much disappointed at not seeing you and Mrs. Gore. She sayd that she had heard you say so much about Mrs. Gore that she felt almost like she was an old acquaintance.

I have seen enough of Calafornia to know that it is a different country from any thing that a person in the states could imagine in their wildes dreams. There is no reason why an active energetic person should not make a fortune evry year. For my part I feel that I could quit the Army to-day and in one year go home with enough to make us comfortable, on Gravois, all our life. Of course I do not contemplate doing any thing of the sort, because what I have is a certainty, and what I might expect to do, might prove a dream.

Jim. de Camp come aboard at San Francisco to see Mrs. Wallen and he told her that John was making one hundred dollars per day. This is Friday night and on Sunday night I expect to be with John and then I will write to you, and make him write also, and it is more than probable that you will get the letters at the same time as you get this.

I wish dearest Julia that I could hear from you.—I cannot hope to hear from, after your confinement, for at least a month yet. It distresses me very much. If I could only know that you and our little ones were well I would be perfectly satisfied. Kiss them both for me dearest and dont let Fred. forget his pa. No person can know the attachment that exists between parent and child until they have been seperated for some time. I am almost crazy sometimes to see Fred. I cannot be seperated from him and his Ma for a long time.

Dearest I hope you have been well taken care of and contented at our house. I know they would do evrything to make you comfortable. I have often feared that you would fret and give yourself trouble because I was not there.

Give my love to all at home dear and kiss our little ones for their pa. Write me all about both of them.

Adieu dear dear Julia,

Your affectionate husband
ULYSS.

To Julia Dent Grant

Columbia Bks. Fort Vancouver O. T.
December 19th 1852

My Dear Wife;

The Mail Steamer very unexpectedly arrived this morning before I had half my correspondence completed. It brings no Mail however to this point but leaves it at Astoria to be brought up by the river steamer. As the Mail Steamer starts back before we will get the last Mail I cannot tell you whether I will recieve any letters or not; but I am very sure that there are letters for me.

I am, and have been, perfectly well in body since our arrival at Vancouver, but for the last few weeks I have suffered terribly from cramp in my feet and legs, and in one hand. You know I have always been subject to this affliction. I would recover from it entirely in a very short time if I could keep in the house and remain dry. My duties however have kept me out of doors a great deel, and as this is the rainy season I must necessarily suffer from wet and cold. I am now intending to spend one or two weeks indoors, on toast and tea, only going out once per day to see if the supply of wood is kept complete.

This is said by the old inhabitants of Origon to be a most terrible winter; the snow is now some ten inches in depth, and still snowing more, with a strong probability of much more falling. The Thermometer has been from Eigteen to twenty two degrees for several days. Ice has formed in the river to such an extent that it is extremly doubtful whether the Mail Steamer can get back here to take off the Mail by which I have been hoping to send this. You must know the Steamer comes here first, and then goes down the Columbia

about four miles, to the mouth of the Willamett river, and up
that some fifteen miles to Portland, the largest town in the
Territory, though an insignificant little place of but a few hundred inhabitants. I do not know enough of this country to
give you the account of it I would like to, having a desire to
say nothing that is calculated to mislead others in their opinions of it, but this I can say; so far as I have seen it it opens
the richest chances for poor persons who are willing, and
able, to work, either in cuting wood, saw logs, raising vegitables, poultry or stock of any kind, of any place I have ever
seen. Timber stands close to the banks of the river free for all.
Wood is worth five dollars per cord for steamers. The soil
produces almost double it does any place I have been before
with the finest market in the world for it after it is raised. For
instance beef gets fat without feeding and is worth at the
door from seventy to one hundred dollars per head, chickens
one dollar each, butter one dollar per pound, milk twenty five
cents per quart, wheat five dollars a bushel, oats two dollars,
onions four dollars, potatoes two dollars and evry thing in
the same proportion. You can see from this that mess bills
amount to something to speak of. I could not mess alone for
less than one hundred dollars per month, but by living as we
do, five or six together it does not cost probably much over
fifty. *** I have nearly filled this sheet dear Julia without saying one word about our dear little ones about whom I think
so much. If I could see Fred. and hear him talk, and see little
Ulys. I could then be contented for a month provided their
mother was with them. Learn them to be good boys and to
think of their Pa. If your brother does not come out there is
no telling when I am to see them and you. It cannot be a
great while however because I would prefer sacrifising my
commission and try something to continuing this seperation.
My hope is to get promotion and then orders to go to washington to settle my accounts. If you, Fred. and Ulys. were
only here I would not care to ever go back only to visit our
friends. Remember me most affectionately to all of them. Kiss
Fred. and Ulys. for their Pa and tell them to kiss their ma for
me. Maggy and Getz enquire a greatdeel after you and Fred.
They evidently think the world and all of him. I hope he is a
favorite with his grandpa and all his Uncles and Aunts. I have

no dought though the little rascal bothers them enough. When you write to me again dear Julia say a goodeal about Fred. and Ulys. You dont know what pleasure it gave me to read yours and Clara's account of them.

Has Jennie left yet? I suppose so however. How did they like her at your house? Adieu dear dear wife; think of me and dream of me often. I but seldom dream myself but I think of you none the less often.

> Your affectionate husband
> ULYS. to his dear wife Julia.

To Julia Dent Grant

Columbia Barracks O. T.
January 3d 1853

I wrote you a letter two weeks ago upon the arrival of the Mail Steamer at this place and told you that I had no doubt but that I would find letters. I was disappointed.

The weather has been very cold here and what is most unusual, the Colum river has been frozen over. Captain Ingalls and myself were the first to cross on it. It is now open however so you need not feel any alarm about my falling through. It either rains or snows here all the time at this place so I scarsely ever get a mile from home, and half the time do not go out of the house during the day. I am situated quite as comfortable as any body here, or in the Territory. The house I am living in is probably the best one in Oregon. Capt. Brent & Ingalls and their two clerks Mr. Bomford & myself live to gether and Maggy cooks for us and Getz assists about the house. Evry one says they are the best servants in the whole Territory. With Getz's pay, the sale of his rations, the wages we give and Maggy's washing, they get about 75 dollars per month. Living together as we do I suppose board, washing, and servant hire does not cost us over 61 dollars per month each, but alone it would require economy to get along inside of near twice that amount. For instance flour is 42 dollars per barrel and evry thing is proportionally dear. I expect to go to San Francisco in two or four weeks now, under orders to bring up public funds, and if I do I shall stay over one trip of the Steamer and go up and spend ten days with John and Wrenshall. You need not be atall surprised if my next letter should be from San Francisco.

I promised you to tell you all about Oregon, but I have seen so little of it that I know nothing that I have not told you. The country is very new but almost doubling its population yearly. The soil is generally very fertile but then there is but a very small proportion of it that can be cultivated.

My dearest I wish, if I am to be separated from you, and our little ones, that I could at least be where it did not take two months to get a letter. Just think, you write to me and tell me all Fred s pranks and how finely Ulys. is coming on all of which interests me exceedingly, but then I think what improvements must have taken place since the letter was written. I suppose that Ulys will be seting alone by the time you get this. Is Fred. very patronising towards him? I expect he wants to nurse him? The dear little dogs how much I wish I could see them. Is Fred. as fond of riding as he was in Bethel? How was Jennie pleased with her visit? and how were they all pleased with her? As a matter of course she had left before you will get this. Fred. and his bride no doubt have gone too. Does your Brother Lewis intend remaining in Missouri? or will he return to Calafornia? I have never recieved a line from your brother John since my arrival at Van-Couver although I wrote to him soon after we got here.

All the ladies here are quite well and the gentlemen also. Mrs. Wallen stays at home all the time and in fact she could not well do otherwise. She always enquires very particularly after you evry mail.

Give my love dearest Julia to your Pa & Ma and all the rest of the family. Tell Fred. to be a good boy and recollect his pa and mind evry thing his grand pa & ma tells him. Kiss him and Ulys for me and write a great deel about them. I will close here for the present hoping that before the Mail closes we will get the mail which has just come up and then I can let you know if I get anything.

Adieu dear wife

ULYS.

P. S. There is not a particle of hope of geting the Mail that come up in time to add anything to this If the Mail should come in time to give me five minuets I will write you another letter if it is only to tell you whether or not I have heard from you. Do not fret dear Julia about me. I am perfectly well and have entirely recovered from those attacks of cramp which I had a few weeks since. They amounted to nothing except they were painful. Adieu again dear dear Julia.

Your affectionate husband
Ulys

To Julia Dent Grant

Columbia Barracks
Washington Territory
March 31st 1853

My Dearest Wife;

The Mail has just arrived bringing me a very short and very unsatisfactory letter. You speak of not joining me on this coast in a manner that would indicate that you have been reflecting upon a dream which you say you have had until you really imagine that it is true. Do not write so any more dearest. It is hard enough for us to be seperated so far without borrowing immaginary troubles. You know that it was entirely out of the question for you to have come with me at the time I had to come. I am doing all I can to put up a penny not only to enable you and our dear little boys to get here comfortably, but to enable you to be comfortable after you do get here.

You ask why I do not live with the bachilors? I do: that is there are two "messes" and I am in one. Capt.s Brent & Ingalls, Mr. Bomford, Brooke and Eastman are in the same mess that I am. If it is economy you think I should consult all I have to say is that my expenses are about twenty dollars per month less than if I was in the other. We all live and eat in the same house so that Maggy & Getz wash for us and wait upon us; and besides Maggy wastes nothing. The other "mess" is seperated from evry officer so that all expenses of servant hire &c. is surplus.

I am farming now in good earnest. All the ploughing and furrowing I do myself. There are two things that I have found out by working myself. One is that I can do as much, and do it better, than I can hire it done. The other is that by working myself those that are hired do a third more than if left alone.

I was surprised to find that I could run as strait a furrow now as I could fifteen years ago and work all day quite as well. I never worked before with so much pleasure either, because now I feel sure that evry day will bring a large reward.

I believe I told you that I have to do that detestable Quarter Master business this Summer? I dislike it very much. Mr. Camp become very much dissatisfied here and sold out. He was making money *** much faster than he will ever do again. Notwithstanding his bad luck having his store blown up he has cleared in the few months he has been here more than six thousand dollars, this without two thousand capital to start with.

Mrs. Wallen is quite well and so are all the officers. Capt. McConnell is here. Mr. Hunt is at Humbolt Bay, Russell at Fort Reading Calafornia. All were well when last heard from. Capt. Wallen met with a serious accident a few days since. He was riding in a wagon and the horse commenced kicking so to save himself he jumped out and fell throughing his right rist entirely out of joint. He will probably be lame in it all Summer.

You can tell your brother that we have had the news all the time that long beards were allowed, at least, on this coast. I have not shaved since I left Calafornia consequently my beard is several inches long. Why did you not tell me more about our dear little boys? I would like to hear some of Fred's sayings. I wish I could have him and his brother here. What does Fred. call Ulys.? What does the S stand for in Ulys.'s name? in mine you know it does not stand for anything! Give my love to all at your house. When you write again dearest write in better spirits.

Does Fred. and his Aunt Ellen get on harmoniously together? I expect she teases him. Cant you have your Dagueriotype taken with Fred. & Ulys. along? if you can send it by

Adam's and Co's Express, to Portland, O. T. I presume you have recieved your watch ere this? I have no opportunity of buying any pretty presents here to send you.

Adieu dear dear wife. I shall hope to get a long sweet letter from you next Mail. Kiss our little boys for their pa. A thousand kisses for yourself dear wife.

Your affectionate husband.
ULYS.

To Julia Dent Grant

Columbia Bks. W. T.
July 13th 1853

My Dearest Julia;

It is about 12 o'clock at night, but as the Mail is to leave here early in the morning I must write to-night.—I got your long sweet letter giving an account of our dear little boys at the pic nic where Fred. started behind his Grand ma, but wanted her to ride behinde him before he got through. You know before he could talk he would always persist in having his hands in front of mine when driving. The loose end of the lines never satisfied him.

My dear Julia if you could see the letters they write from my home about our dear little boys it would make you as proud as it does me. I am sure there never was one of my own brothers or sisters who have been more thought of than Fred. & Ulys. In the long letter I got from father he speaks of him as something more than boys of his age. You understand though that I can make allowances for his prejudices either in favor or against; where prejudices are strong predilections are generally right, so I must conclude that Fred. & Ulys. are more than I ever dreamed they were. I dreamed of you last night but not of either of our dear little boys. I mearly saw you for a minuet without having an opportunity of speaking to you and you were gone.

My dear julia I have spoken of speculations so much that the subject is becoming painful, but yet I know you feel interested in what I am doing.—In a former letter I told you, for the first time, of the *downs* of all I had done. (Before I had never met with a *down*.) Since that I have made several hundreds in speculations of various sorts. In groceries which I do not sell, and which are not retailed. I have now a large quantity of pork on hand which is worth to-day ten dollars pr. barrel more than I gave for it at the very place where it was bought. All this will help to buy dresses for Fred. & Ulys. but what interests me most is to know how it is to let their pa see them wear them, and their ma put them on to advantage.

I wrote you that Scott was appointed Inspector General and that it would take me to Fort Reading.—It turns out that he has not been appointed so I must await my place either for Alden's resignation, or for Col. Buchanan's promotion. The first would take me to Fort Jones, of which I have spoken, in former letters: the latter to a detestible place where the mails reach occationally. I should however have command of of the post, with double rations and two companies. Wallen is going to San Francisco before you recieve this letter with the intention of seting up a Dairy, Pigery, and market Garden, if practicable,. He will go on leave for a few months and then, if sucsessfull, strike out for himself.

You ask how many children Laura has? Before this you know. She has but two; Harry who is a healthy & smart boy, and Nancy who has always, until lately, been heathy.

My dear Julia I have said nothing about the pink leaves upon each of which you say you presed a sweet kiss. I cannot, in this, return the favor on flowers but you may rest assured that I will imprint them when we first meet upon your lips and those of our dear babes.

How can your pa & ma think that they are going to keep Fred. & Ulys always with them? I am growing impatient to see them myself.—Tell Fred. to say *Ugly Aunt Ell* I wont let you learn me anything. *** so Fred. might say the same to his Uncle. If you cant go your self send him to his other Grandpa's for tuition for a few months.—Indeed dear Julia you must either go with the children or make a very good excuse. Thy want to see you so much. If you have not got means enough I have still some in N. Y. I shall never draw it so long as I remain in this country except in your favor. I hope you got the hundred which I sent you, and also the begining of what Calender was to send you! Give my love to all at your house. I got the pink leaves that you kissed. A thousand kisses for our little boys and yourself.

Adieu dear julia. the Steamer is in sight that is to take this.

Your affectionate husband
ULYS.

To Osborn Cross

R. Q. Mrs. Office
Columbia Bks. W. T.
July 25th 1853

Maj;

The constant, and unremiting, calls upon the time, both of myself and clerk, consequent upon the fiting out of the expiditions connected with the Northern Pacific R. R. survey, in addition to the current duties of the office, have prevented the making out, and forwarding, of the annual report called for, by you, at an earlier date; and obliges me to enter far less than I should have done into detail had I not feared that the delay of another mail would be too late to serve your purposes.

As I have only been on duty at this Post, as Post Qr. Mr., since the first of May last (my previous duties here, in the Q. M. D, being merely nominal having neither funds nor stores in my charge) my Report can only embrace the operations of the Department here for the last two months of the past fical year.

I enclose a plan of the post marked "A" and a statement of the public buildings marked "B". With the exception of the shops, office & Qrs. in the immediate occupation of the Qr. Mr's Dept. & one cook house, the public buildings at this post are log buildings and most of them requiring repairs to make them comfortable.

By direction of the Com.g Genl. the Qrs. of the officers, and men, were chinked and daubed with mud, with a little lime to improve its consistency. The first heavy rains of winter swept this away and made new repairs necessary.

These Qrs. can only be made comfortable, permanently, by being ceiled inside in a manner similar to those of the Comd.g Officer & either weatherboarded, or at least chinked & daubed with mortar made with plenty of lime & hair.

The Mechanics & Laborers employed have been one clerk, two herdsmen, one blacksmith and one carpenter & boat-builder—and the amount in round number paid—$670 00

The transportation furnished has been for Capt. Brent's party, and "H" Co. hence to the Dalles at say a cost of $10 per man and twenty five tons of public property, between the same ponts, at an average cost of $60 00 per ton—with about twelve tons from Portland at $8 00 per ton.

The manner of transportation has been by steamer between Portland and this point, and between this point and the Cascades. Across the Cascade portage by R. R. & wagons; from the Cascades to the Dalles by boats & steamer, all private transportation.

The amt. of Lumber, Materials, Barley &c. is $2.342 00. The lumber was required for repairs &c. at this post; the materials & forage for the post & Depot.

The principle disbursments have been on account of other posts and expiditions fitted out at this point. The amount expended for the Dept. purposes of the post has been very small.

The soil on the borders of the river, where the banks are not precipitous, and the lands are level for some distance back, is exceedingly rich and productive, giving extraordinary yieald of oats, wheat and potatoes, but unfortunately subject to overflow during the June freshets. Farther back from the river the soil is of a more gravely or sandy nature, easily cultivated when once cleared, but far less productive than the bottom lands.

The country is heavily timbered, being, with the exception of the river bottom, occational plains, and now and then an occational clearing, almost entirely covered with a heavy growth of fir with here and there a cedar, and on the banks of the streams, groves of Oak, Cottonwood & Maple. The prevailing growth however is fir.

There are but few Indians in the vicinity of the post. These few are of the Clickitat tribe with occational passing visits

from the Cowlitz and the Dalles, easily controlled and altogether to insignificant in prowess & numbers to need much
care or attention, and even this poor remnant of a once
powerful tribe is fast wasting away before those blessings of
civilization "whisky and Small pox.

There are no outstanding debts of the Department, at this
post, at the end of the fiscal year.

Very Respectfully
I am Maj.

To Maj. O. Cross   Your Obt. Svt.
Chf. Q. M. Pacific Div.   U. S. GRANT
San Francisco Cal.   Bvt. Capt. & R. Q. M. 4th Infy

To Julia Dent Grant

Fort Humboldt,
Humboldt Bay, Cal.
February 2d 1854

My Dear Wife.

You do not know how forsaken I feel here! The place is
good enough but I have interests at others which I cannot
help thinking about day and night; then to it is a long time
since I made application for orders to go on to Washington to
settle my accounts but not a word in reply do I get. Then I
feel again as if I had been separated from you. and Fred. long
enough and as to Ulys. I have never seen him. He must by
this time be talking about as Fred. did when I saw him last.
How very much I want to see all of you. I have made up
my mind what Ulys. looks like and I am anxious to see if
my presentiment is correct. Does he advance rapidly? Tell
me a great deel about him and Fred. and Freds pranks
with his Grandpa. How does he get along with his Uncle
Lewis?

I do nothing here but set in my room and read and occationally take a short ride on one of the public horses. There is
game here such as ducks, geese &c. which some of the officers
amuse themselves by shooting but I have not entered into the
sport. Within eight or ten miles Deer and occationally Elk

and black Bear are found. Further back the Grisley Bear are quite numerous. I do not know if I have told you what officers are at this post? Col. Buchanan, Hunt, Collins, Dr. Potts and Lt. Latimer to join. Expected soon. Col. B expects promotion by evry Mail which, if he gets, will bring Montgomery, and leave me in command of the post. Mrs. Collins is the only lady at the post. Dr. Potts however will have his wife here in a short time. The quarters are comfortable frame buildings, backed by a dense forest of immense trees. In front is the Bay. We are on a bluff which gives us one of the most commanding views that can be had from almost any point on the whole Bay. Besides having a view of the Bay itself we can look out to sea as far as the eye can extend. There are four villeges on the Bay. One at the outlet, Humbolt Point is the name, where there are probably not more than 50 inhabitants. What they depend upon for support I do'nt know. They are probably persons who supposed that it would be the point for a City and they would realize a California fortune by the rise of lots. Three miles up the Bay is Bucksport and this garrison Here geting out lumber is the occupation, and as it finds a ready market in San Francisco this is a flourishing little place of about 200. Three miles further up is Euricka with a population of about 500 with the same resourses. The mills in these two villeges have, for the last year, loaded an average of 19 vessels per month with lumber, and as they are building several additional mills they will load a greater number this year. Twelve miles further up, and at the head of the Bay, is Union, the larges and best built town of the whole. From there they pack provisions to the gold mines, and return with the dust. Taking all of these villeges together there are about enough ladies to get up a small sized Ball. There has been several of them this winter.

I got one letter from you since I have been here but it was some three months old. I fear very much that I shall loose some before they get in the regular way of coming. There is no regular mail between here and San Francisco so the only way we have of geting letters off is to give them to some Captain of a vessel to mail them after he gets down. In the same way mails are recieved. This makes it very uncertain as to the time a letter may be on the way. Sometimes, owing to advers winds, vessels are 40 and even 60 days making the passage, while at others they make it in less than two days. So you need not be surprised if sometimes you would be a great while without a letter and then likely enough get three or four at once. I hope the next mail we get to have several from you. Be particular to pay postage on yours for otherwise they may refuse to deliver them at the San Francisco Post Office. I cant pay the postage here having no stamps and not being able to get them. I have sent below however for some.

I must finish by sending a great deel of love to all of you, your Pa. Ma. brother and sisters, niece and nepews. I have not yet fulfilled my promise to Emmy to write her a long letter from Humboldt.

Kiss our little ones for me. A thousand kisses for yourself dear Julia.

Your affectionate husband
ULYS

To Julia Dent Grant

Fort Humboldt
Humboldt Bay, Cal.
Feb. 6th 1854.

My Dear Wife;

A mail come in this evening but brought me no news from you nor nothing in reply to my application for orders to go home. I cannot concieve what is the cause of the delay. The state of suspense that I am in is scarsely bearable. I think I have been from my family quite long enough and sometimes I feel as though I could almost *** go home "nolens volens." I presume, under ordinary circumstances, Humboldt would be a good enough place but the suspense I am in would make paradice form a bad picture. There is but one thing to console; misery loves company and there are a number in just the same fix with myself, and, with other Regiments, some who have been seperated much longer from their families than I have been.

It has only been a few days since I wrote to you but it will not do to let an opportunity pass of geting a letter into the San Francisco Post Office, and there is a vessel to leave here to-morrow. It is not all the vessels that it will do to entrust letters with. A few that come take the trouble, and expense, of going to the Post Office in San Francisco and geting all the mail directed to this bay and bring it without any remuneration either from the Post Office Department, or from individuals.

I have been suffering for the last few days most terribly. I am certain that if you were to see me now you would not know me. That tooth I had set in in Wattertown (You remember how much I suffered at the time) has been giving me the same trouble over again. Last evening I had it drawn and it was much harder to get out than any other tooth would have been. My face is swolen until it is as round as an apple and so tender that I do not feel as if I could shave, so, looking at the glass, I think I could pass readily for a person of forty five. Otherwise I am very well. You know what it is to suffer with teeth.

I am very much pleased with my company. All the men I have are old soldiers and very neat in their appearance. The contrast between them and the other company here is acknowledged as very great by the officers of the other company. The reason is that all my men are old soldiers while the other were recruits when they come here. I have however less than one third of the complement allowed by law and all of them will be discharged about the same time. I wish their times were out now so that I could go on recruiting service if no other way.

My dear wife you do not tell me whether you are contented or not! I hope you enjoy yourself very much. — Has Capt. Calender continued to send you money? Some three or four months since I bought two land warrants, one of which I want to send you but when I got to San Francisco I found that they were not negociable on account of not having on the transfer the Seal of the County Clerk. I sent them back to Vancouver to have this fixed and when I get them I will send you one. They are worth about forty dollars more there than I gave for them.

Do you think of going to Ohio this Spring? I hope you will

go. They want to see you very much. Evry letter I get from home they speak of it.

In my letter written a few days ago I told you what officers we had here, the amusements &c. so I have nothing more on that head. Living here is extravigantly high besides being very poor. Col. Buchanan, the Dr. and myself live together at an expense of about $50 per month each including servant hire and washing. Mr. Hunt lives by himself. Give my love to all at home. Write me a great deel about our little boys. Tell me all their pranks. I suppose Ulys. speaks a great many words distinctly? Kiss both of them for me.—I believe I told you that Mrs. Wallen had lost another child. I do not think Wallen will ever raise either of his children. Harry & Nanny are large fat children but they do not look right and they are forever sick. If Wallen was out of the Army and had to pay his Doctor's bill it would amount to about as much as our entire living.—Kiss Fred. and Ulys. for their pa. A great many kisses for you dear wife.

Your affectionate husband
ULYS.

To Julia Dent Grant

Fort Humboldt
Humboldt Bay, Cal.
March 6th 1854.

My Dear Wife;

I have only had one letter from you in three months and that had been a long time on the way so you may know how anxious I am to hear from you. I know there are letters for me in the Post Office department, someplace, but when shall I get them. I sometimes get so anxious to see you, and our little boys, that I am almost tempted to resign and trust to Providence, and my own exertions, for a living where I can have you and them with me. It would only require the certainty of a moderate competency to make me take the step. Whenever I get to thinking upon the subject however *poverty, poverty,* begins to stare me in the face and then I think what would

I do if you and our little ones should want for the necessaries of life.

I could be contented at Humboldt if it was possible to have you here but it is not. You could not do without a servant and a servant you could not have   This is to bad is it not? But you never complain of being lonesome so I infer that you are quite contented. I dreamed of you and our little boys the other night the first time for a long time I thought you were at a party when I arrived and before paying any attention to my arrival you said you must go you were engaged for that dance. Fred. and Ulys. did not seem half so large as I expected to see them. If I should see you it would not be as I dreamed, would it dearest? I know it would not.

I am geting to be as great a hand for staying in the house now as I used to be to run about. I have not been a hundred yards from my door but once in the last two weeks. I get so tired and out of patience with the lonliness of this place that I feel like volunteering for the first service that offers. It is likely a party will have to go from here for Cape Mendeceno in the course of a week and if so I think I shall go. I would be absent about two weeks. In the Summer I will try and make an exkursion out into the mines and in the fall another out on the immigrant trail. This will help pass off so much of the time.

This seems to be a very healthy place; all here are enjoying excellent health. The post has been occupied now for about fourteen months, by two Companies, and I believe there has been but two deaths. One by accidentally shooting himself and the other by a limb from a tree falling on a man.

Wallen has made up his mind to resign. Mrs. W. declared she would not go back to Vancouver that if he went he would go without her. W. has gone into the Coal business.— Stevens is going ahead at a rapid stride. A recent decission of the Courts in a land case made him one hundred thousand dollars better off than before. Mrs. Stevens & husband intended to have gone home last January but S. could not find time to go. Mrs. S. will soon be confined again. You recollect what she said at Sackets Harbor?

Mr. Hunt has just recently returned from San Francisco. While there he met John looking well.—There is no news here only occationally a disater at sea. A few days since a steamer went down just inside the Columbia river bar; vessel with all on board except one lost. I am in a great hurry to get this ready for the Mail so I must bid you all good buy for the present. Give my love to your pa, ma, sisters and brother. Kiss our little boys for me. Talk to them a great deel about their pa. A thousand kisses for yourself dearest.

I have some land warrants one of which I want to send you to sell but I am afraid to trust it to the mail. I will send it by the first favorable opportunity. They are worth about $180.00 in N. York; I do not know what you will be able to get in St. Louis.

Adieu dear wife.
ULYS.

To Frederick Dent

Galena, April 19th 1861

Mr. F. Dent;
Dear Sir:

I have but very little time to write but as in these exciting times we are very anxious to hear from you, and know of no other way but but by writing first to you, I must make time.—We get but little news, by telegraph, from St. Louis but from most all other points of the Country we are hearing all the time. The times are indeed startling but now is the time, particularly in the border Slave states, for men to prove their love of country. I know it is hard for men to apparently work with the Republican party but now all party distinctions should be lost sight of and evry true patriot be for maintaining the integrity of the glorious old *Stars & Stripes*, the Constitution and the Union. The North is responding to the Presidents call in such a manner that the rebels may truly quaik. I tell you there is no mistaking the feelings of the people. The Government can call into the field not only 75000 troops but ten or twenty times 75000 if it should be necessary and find the means of maintaining them too. It is all a mistake about the Northern pocket being so sensative. In times like the present no people are more ready to give their own time or of their abundant means. No impartial man can conceal from himself the fact that in all these troubles the South have been the aggressors and the Administration has stood purely on the defensive, more on the defensive than she would dared to have done but for her consiousness of strength and the certainty of right prevailing in the end. The news to-day is that Virginia has gone out of the Union. But for the influance she will have on the other border slave states this is not much to be regreted. Her position, or rather that of Eastern Virginia, has been more reprehensible from the begining than that of South Carolina. She should be made to bear a heavy portion of the burthen of the War for her guilt.—In all this I can but see the doom of Slavery. The North do not want, nor will they want, to interfere with the institution. But they will refuse for all time to give it protection unless the South shall return soon to their allegiance, and then too this disturbance will give such an impetus to the production of their staple, cotton, in other parts of the world that they can never recover the controll of the market again for that comodity. This will reduce the value of negroes so much that they will never be worth fighting over again.—I have just rec'd a letter from Fred. He breathes forth the most patriotic sentiments. He is for the old Flag as long as there is a Union of two states fighting under its banner and when they desolve he will go it alone. This is not his language but it is the idea not so well expressed as he expresses it.

Julia and the children are all well and join me in love to you all. I forgot to mention that Fred. has another heir, with some novel name that I have forgotten.

> Yours Truly
> U. S. GRANT

Get John or Lewis Sheets to write to me.

To Jesse Root Grant

Galena, April 21st 1861

Dear Father;

We are now in the midst of trying times when evry one must be for or against his country, and show his colors too, by his every act. Having been educated for such an emergency, at the expense of the Government, I feel that it has upon me superior claims, such claims as no ordinary motives of self-interest can surmount. I do not wish to act hastily or unadvisadly in the matter, and as there are more than enough to respond to the first call of the President, I have not yet offered myself. I have promised and am giving all the assistance I can in organizing the Company whose services have been accepted from this place. I have promised further to go with them to the state Capital and if I can be of service to the Governer in organizing his state troops to do so. What I ask now is your approval of the course I am taking, or advice in the matter. A letter written this week will reach me in Springfield. I have not time to write you but a hasty line for though Sunday as it is we are all busy here. In a few minuets I shall be engaged in directing tailors in the style and trim of uniforms for our men.

Whatever may have been my political opinions before I have but one sentiment now. That is we have a Government, and laws and a flag and they must all be sustained. There are but two parties now, Traitors & Patriots and I want hereafter to be ranked with the latter, and I trust, the stronger party. — I do not know but you may be placed in an awkward position, and a dangerous one pecuniarily, but costs can not now be counted. My advice would be to leave where you are if you are not safe with the veiws you entertain. I would never stultify my opinions for the sake of a little security.

I will say nothing about our business. Orvil & Lank will keep you posted as to that.

Write soon and direct as above.

> Yours Truly
> U. S. GRANT.

To Julia Dent Grant

Springfield, Apl. 27th/61

Dear Julia;

On account of the cars not connecting promptly we did not arrive here until evening yesterday, and as no mail gets through as fast as passengers you will not probably get this until Tuesday morning. I fully made up my mind last night, and had not changed it this morning, to start home to-day and consequently did not intend to write to you atall. Mr. Washburn however come to me this morning and prevailed upon me to remain over for a day or two to see the result of a bill now before the legislature and which will no doubt pass to-day, authorizing the Governer to ration and pay the surplus troops now here, and to arrive, and to appoint suitable persons to take charge of them until such times as they may be organized into Companies and Regiments. All the Companies that have arrived so far, and that is near the whole number called for, have brought with them from twenty to sixty men more each than the law allows. The overplus have as a matter of course, to be cut off. These are the men the Legislature are providing for. The Governer told Mr Washburn last night that should the legislature pass the provision for them, he wanted me to take the command and drill them until they are organized into Companies and placed in Regiments. In case I should accept such a position I may remain here several weeks. In any event however I shall go home, if but for a day or two, so as to be there on next Sunday morning.—Our trip here was a perfect ovation, at evry station the whole population seemed to be out to greet the troops. There is such a feeling arroused through the country now as has not been known since the Revolution. Evry company called for in the Presidents proclimation has been organized, and filled to near double the amount that can be recieved. In addition to that evry town of 1000 inhabitants and over has from one to four additional companies organized ready to answer the next call that will be made.—I find but few old acquaintances here except from Galena. Capt. Pope of the army is here mustering in the volunteers.—I see by Telegraphic dispatch that K McKenzie died yesterday. So they go one at a time. I shall write to your father about Monday. Kiss all the children for me. Write as soon as you get this.

ULYS.

To Mary Grant

Springfield, April 29th, 1861

Dear Sister;

I come to this place several days ago fully expecting to find a letter here for me from father. As yet I have rec'd none. It was my intention to have returned to Galena last evening but the Governer detained, and I presume will want me to remain with him, until all the troops now called into service, or to be so called, are fully mustered in and completely organized. The enthusiasm through this state surpasses anything that could have been imagined three weeks ago. Only six Regiments are called for here while at least thirty could be promptly raised. The Governer, and all others in authority, are harrassed from morning until night with Patriotic men, and such political influance as they can bring, to obtain first promises of acceptance of their companies if there should be another call for troops. The eagerness to enter companies that were accepted by the Governer was so great that it has been impossible for commanders of companies to keep their numbers within the limits of the law consequently companies that have arrived here have all had from ten to sixty men more than can be accepted. The Legislature on Saturday last passed a bill providing for the maintenance and discipline of these surplus troops for one month, unless sooner mustered into service of the United States under a second call.—I am convinced that if the South knew the entire unanimity of the North for the Union and maintenance of Law, and how freely men and money are offered to the cause, they would lay down their arms at once in humble submission. There is no disposition to compromise now. Nearly every one is anxious to see the Government fully tested as to its strength, and see if it is not worth preserving. The conduct of eastern Virginia has been so abominable through the whole contest that there would be a great deal of disappointment here if matters should be settled before she is thoroughly punished. This is my feeling, and I believe it universal. Great allowance should be made for South Carolinians, for the last generation have been educated, from their infancy, to look upon their Government as oppressive and tyrannical and only to be endured till such time as they might have sufficient strength to strike it down. Virginia, and other border states, have no such excuse and are therefore traitors at heart as well as in act. I should like very much to see the letter Aunt Rachel wrote Clara! or a copy of it. Can't you send it?

When I left Galena, Julia and the children were very well. Jesse had been very sick for a few days but was getting much better. I have been very anxious that you should spend the summer with us. You have never visited us and I don't see why you can't. Two of you often travel together, and you might do so again, and come out with Clara. I do not like to urge anything of the kind, lest you should think that I ignored entirely the question of economy, but I do not do so. The fact is I have had my doubts whether or not it would not be more prudent for all of you to lock up and leave, until the present excitement subsides. If father were younger and Simpson strong and healthy, I would not advise such a course. On the contrary, I would like to see every Union man in the border slave states remain firm at his post. Every such man is equal to an armed volunteer at this time in defence of his country. There is very little that I can tell you that you do not get from the papers.

Remember me to all at home and write to me at once, to this place.

BROTHER ULYSSES.

To Julia Dent Grant

GENERAL HEAD QUARTERS—STATE OF ILLINOIS.
ADJUTANT GENERAL'S OFFICE,
SPRINGFIELD, MAY 1st *1861*.

Dear Julia;

I have an opportunity of sending a letter direct to Galena by Mr. Corwith and as it will probably reach you a day or two earlyer than if sent by Mail I avail myself of the chance. I enclose also a letter from father for you to read. As I shall probably be home on Saturday evening I shall say nothing about what my intentions are for the future, in fact my plans will have to mature from circumstances as they develop themselvs. At present I am on duty with the Governer, at his request, occupation principally smoking and occationally giving advice as to how an order should be communicated &c. I am going this morning however into the Adjutant General's Office to remain until some regularity is established there, if I can bring about that regularity. The fact is however, as I told the Governer, my bump of order is not largely developed and papers are not my forte and therefore my services may not be as valuable as he anticipates. However I am in to do all I can and will do my best.

We recieve the St. Louis morning papers here at 10 O'Clock a.m. evry day of the day issued and evry day some one is here from the city. The state of affairs there is terrible and no doubt a terrible calamity awaits them. Stationing Ill. Troops within striking distance of St Louis may possibly save the city. Business is entirely prostrated and the best houses are forced to close. I see by the Mo. Republican that Charless Blow & Co are among the number. But for the little piece of stratagem used to get the arms out of the arsenal, to this place, they would have fallen into the hands of the Secessionests and with their hands strengthened with these an attempt would have been made to take the city entirely under controll and terrible slaughter would have taken place. Great numbers of people are leaving Missouri now in evry direction, except South. In some of the Northern towns of the state merchants and business men are leaving with all their personal property. Missouri will be a great state ultimately but she is set back now for years. It will end in more rapid advancement however for she will be left a free state. Negroes are stampeding already and those who do not will be carried further South so that the destiny of the state, in that respect, may now be considered settled by fate and not political parties. Kiss the children for me. You need not write as I will be home so soon

ULYS.

To Jesse Root Grant

GENERAL HEAD QUARTERS—STATE OF ILLINOIS.
ADJUTANT GENERAL'S OFFICE,
SPRINGFIELD, May 2nd, *1861*.

Dear Father:

Your letter of the 24th inst was received the same evening one I had written to Mary was mailed. I would have answered earlier but for the fact I had just written.

I am not a volunteer, and indeed could not be, now that I did not go into the first Company raised in Galena. The call of the President was so promptly responded to that only those companies that organized at once, and telegraphed their application to come in, were received. All other applications were filed, and there are enough of them to furnish Illinois quota if the Army should be raised to 300,000 men. I am serving on the Governor's staff at present at his request, but suppose I shall not be here long.

I should have offered myself for the Colonelcy of one of the Regiments, but I find all those places are wanted by politicians who are up to log-rolling, and I do not care to be under such persons.

The war feeling is not abating here much, although hostilities appear more remote than they did a few days ago. Three of the six Regiments mustered in from this state are now at Cairo, and probably will be reinforced with two others within a few days.

Galena has several more companies organized but only one of them will be able to come in under a new call for ten regiments. Chicago has raised companies enough nearly to fill all the first call. The Northern feeling is so fully aroused that they will stop at no expense of money and men to insure the success of their cause.

I presume the feeling is just as strong on the other side, but they are infinitely in the minority in resources.

I have not heard from Galena since coming down here, but presume all is moving along smoothly. My advice was not to urge collections from such men as we knew to be good, and to make no efforts to sell in the present distracted state of our currency. The money will not buy Eastern exchange and is liable to become worse; I think that thirty days from this we shall have specie, and the bills of good foreign banks to do business on, and then will be the time to collect.

If Mary writes to me any time next week she may direct here to

ULYSSES.

To Julia Dent Grant

Springfield, May 3d/61

Dear Julia;

I thought I was going home this evening but when I told the Governer of it he objected because he had important duties for me in connexion with the organization of new Regiments provided for by the Legislature a day or two ago. I presume I shall be put on duty in Freeport mustering in a Regiment from that Congressional district. If so I will be within a few hours travel of Galena and can go down most any afternoon and return in the morning. It may be that I will remain there two or three weeks and then retire from the service. This place is within four hours travel of St. Louis and the Cars run here so that I could start at 5 o'clock a.m. be in St. Louis at 9, get a horse and buggy and go out and spend the day at your fathers and return here for breakfast the next morning. If I can get sent down to Alton on business I will try and go out and spend one day. All is buzz and excitement here, as well as confusion, and I dont see really that I am doing any good. But when I speak of going it is objected to by not only Governer Yates, but others. — I imagine it will do me no harm the time I spend here, for it has enabled me to become acquainted with the principle men in the state. I do not know that I shall receive any benefit from this but it does no harm.

Orvil enquires what compensation I receive: I presume it will be the pay of Capt. or $140 00 per month. At present I am at the Principle Hotel where I presume my board will be 10 or 12 dollars per week but if I remain I shall leave it. I have not had a line from you since I come here, how does this happen?

Kiss all the children for me. Tell Mary Duncan her beaux takes to soldiering very naturally. I have no doubt but he will send her a kiss by me when I go back.

Write to me Sunday the day you will get this.

ULYS.

To Julia Dent Grant

Anna, Ill.
May 21st 1861

Dear Julia;

I am through at this place and will leave in about one hour for Cairo, where I shall only remain until evening. I will then return to Springfield when I may be released from further duty. I am not however by any means certain of that for I know that I have been applied for for other service. I will write you again on Thirsday if I am not at home. I might about as well volunteered in the first instance as to be detained the way I have and then I should have got the Colonelcy of a Regt. However my services have been quite as valuable, I presume the state thinks, as if I had been at the head of a Regt. and the duties are much more pleasant to me.—I have been agreeably disappointed in the people of Egypt. It is the prevailing opinion abroad that the people of this section of the State are ignorant, disloyal, intemperate and generally heathenish. The fact is the Regt. formed here is the equal, if not the superior, of any of the Regiments raised in the State, for all the virtues of which they are charged with being deficient. I have had no letter from you here but expect to find one at Springfield when I get there. I am anxious to·hear from you and the children as well as see you. Somehow though I feel as if I was in for the War and cannot divest myself of the feeling. I will not go though for a position which I look upon as inferior to that of Col. of a Regt. and will not seek that. How much soever I might deem it my duty to give my services at this time I do not feel that the obligation, at present, calls for me to accept a lower position. —I see Jo Reynolds is in with the Indiana Volunteers. I do not expect to see Emma at Cairo but presume Jim. is there. My stay will be but about five hours there and my duties will occupy about half that time.

I hope you are geting along happily without me. I presume the last crash among the banks has startled Orvil. I expected it to come and when they wrote me that business was dull and collections ditto I was glad of it. No debts can be paid with the money they are geting and there is no use holding the depreciated stuff. Kiss the children for me and give my love to all our relations.

ULYS.

Orders No. 7

Head Quarters, Camp Yates June 18 1861.

Orders No. 7.

The undersigned having been duly appointed Colonel of the 7th Congl Dist Regt. of Ills Volts. Militia by order of Govr Richard Yates, duly promulgated hereby assumes command.

In accepting this command, your Commander will require the co-operation of all the commissioned and non-commissioned Officers in instructing the command, and in maintaining discipline, and hopes to receive also the hearty support of every enlisted man.

All orders now in force at this camp will be continued until countermanded.

By Order
U. S. GRANT Col. Comdg.

To Julia Dent Grant

Camp Yates, June 26th 1861

Dear Julia;

We arrived here on Monday evening all well. Fred. was delighted with his trip but I think is not so pleased here as while

traveling. When I get a horse however so that he can ride out
with me he will make up.

The probabilities are that we will not remain here longer
than next week. I will write again before leaving here.—I am
very much pleased with my officers generally. They are sober
and attentive and anxious to learn their duties. The men I
believe are pleased with the change that has taken place in
their commander, or at least the greatest change has taken
place in the order in camp. For Lieut. Colonel and Major I
have two men that I think a greatdeal of but I can never have
a game of Eucre with them. One is a preacher and the other a
member of Church. For the Field officers of my regt. the 21st
Ill. Volunteers one pint of liquor will do to the end of the
war.

I am kept very busy from morning until night and no time
for making acquaintances. No ladies have yet been to see me
in camp and although I have been here most of the time for
over two months I have not made the acquaintance of a single
family.

Has Buck got used to being without Fred? When we get
over to Quincy all of you will have an opportunity of trying
camp life for a while.

Tell Orvil that I shall not buy another horse until I get to
Quincy, in the mean time if he should see a very fine one in
Galena I would rather buy there. Rondy will do me for the
march, if we should make it which is by no means certain.
Fred. will ride in a waggon if we should march. That part he
will enjoy very much. It is a very uphill business for me to
write this evening.—Is Simp. & Mother with you yet? When
they come be sure and write me at once and tell me how
Simp. stood the trip. I am very anxious that he should get out
for I believe the trip will do him good if he can stand it.—
Have you heard from any of your people since I left? I should
like to hear from Dr. Sharp. I feel a little anxious to his sentiments on the present issues.

If you have an opportunity I wish you would send me
McClellands report of battles in the Crimea. You will find it
about the house.—Kiss all the children for me. Tell Mary
Duncan to give you back that kiss you caught me giving

her. The next time I write you may take back the one from Hellen.

This is a very poor letter but I have not written scarsely a single sentence without interruption.

Your Dodo

To Julia Dent Grant

Naples, Ill.
July 7th 1861

Dear Julia;

We are now laying in camp on the Illinois river spending sunday and will leave to-morrow on our way to Quincy. Up to this time my regiment have made their marches as well as troops ever do and the men have been very orderly. There have been a few men who show a disposition not to respect private property such as hen roosts and gardens, but I have kept such a watch on them, and punished offenders so, that I will venture that the same number of troops never marched through a thickly settled country like this committing fewer depridations. Fred. enjoys it hugely. Our Lieut. Col. was left behind and I am riding his horse so that Fred. has Rondy to ride. The Soldiers and officers call him Colonel and he seems to be quite a favorite.

From Springfield here is one of the most beautiful countries in the world. It is all settled and highly improved. It is all of it the district of the State that sends so much fine stock to St. Louis fair.

Passing through the towns the whole population would turn out to receive us. At Jacksonville, one of the prettyest towns with the most tasty houses that I ever saw, the ladies were all out waving their handkerchiefs, and one of them (I know she must be pretty) made up a boquet and sent me with her name, which by the way the messenger forgot before it come to me. So you see I shall probably never find who the fair donor was.

From present indications we will not remain long at

Quincy. There was four regiments ordered there with the expectation of remaining until frost. Two have arrived and been ordered into Missouri. I think my regiment cannot be ordered so soon because we have yet to get all our uniforms & equipments and a part of our arms. It will be at least two weeks before my regt. can be of much service and a month before it can do good service. It was in a terribly disorganized state when I took it but a very great change has taken place. Evry one says so and to me it is very observable. I dont believe there is a more orderly set of troops now in the volunteer service. I have been very strict with them and the men seem to like it. They appreciate that it is all for their own benefit. — Kiss the children for me. Fred. would send his love to all of you but he is out. He says he will answer Susy Felts letter but I am affraid that he will be slow about it. He writes sometimes but never copys letter.

Kisses to you.

ULYS.

To Jesse Root Grant

East Quincy, Mo.,
July 13th, 1861.

Dear Father:

I have just received yours and Mary's letters and really did not know that I had been so negligent as not to have written to you before. I did write from Camp Yates, but since receiving yours remember that I did not get to finish it at the time, and have neglected it since. The fact is that since I took command of this regiment I have had no spare time, and flatter myself, and believe I am sustained in my judgment by my officers and men, that I have done as much for the improvement and efficiency of this regiment as was ever done for a command in the same length of time. — You will see that I am in Missouri. Yesterday I went out as far as Palmyra and stationed my regiment along the railroad for the protection of the bridges, trestle work, etc. The day before I sent a small command, all I could spare, to relieve Colonel Smith who was surrounded by secessionists. He effected his relief, however, before they got there. Tomorrow I start for Monroe, where I shall fall in with Colonel Palmer and one company of horse and two pieces of artillery. One regiment and a battalion of infantry will move on to Mexico, North Missouri road, and all of us together will try to nab the notorious Tom Harris with his 1200 secessionists. His men are mounted, and I have but little faith in getting many of them. The notorious Jim Green who was let off on his parole of honor but a few days ago, has gone towards them with a strong company well armed. If he is caught it will prove bad work for him.

You no doubt saw from the papers that I started to march across the country for Quincy. My men behaved admirably, and the lesson has been a good one for them. They can now go into camp after a day's march with as much promptness as veteran troops; they can strike their tents and be on the march with equal celerity. At the Illinois River, I received a dispatch at eleven o'clock at night that a train of cars would arrive at half past eleven to move my regiment. All the men were of course asleep, but I had the drum beaten, and in forty minutes every tent and all the baggage was at the water's edge ready to put aboard the ferry to cross the river.

I will try to keep you posted from time to time, by writing either to you or to Mary, of my whereabouts and what I am doing. I hope you will have only a good account of me and the command under my charge. I assure you my heart is in the cause I have espoused, and however I may have disliked party Republicanism there has never been a day that I would not have taken up arms for a Constitutional Administration.

You ask if I should not like to go in the regular army. I should not. I want to bring my children up to useful employment, and in the army the chance is poor. There is at least the same objection that you find where slavery exists. Fred. has been with me until yesterday; I sent him home on a boat.

Yours &c.
U. S. GRANT.

To Julia Dent Grant

West Quincy, Mo.
July 13th 1861

Dear Julia;

A letter from you has just reached me. I join you in disappointment that you will not likely be able to make a trip to visit me this Summer. But our country calls me elswhere and I must obey. Secessionests are thick through this part of Missouri but so far they show themselves very scary about attacking. Their depridations are confined more to burning R. R. bridges, tearing up the track and where they can, surround small parties of Union troops. I come here to release Col. Smith who was surrounded but he effected his release too soon for me to assist him. Yesterday I went out as far as Palmyra and stationed my Regt. along at different points for the protection of the road. To-morrow I will be relieved by Col. Terchin and will start for Monroe where I will meet Col. Palmer with his Regt. and one company of horse & two pieces of Artillery. There will also be a Regt. & a half over at Mexico on the North Missouri road and all of us together will try and surround the notorious Tom Harris and his band. After that my Regt. goes down to St. Charles where we take a steamer for Alton there to go into Camp. I have no idea however that we will be allowed to remain long. I am kept very busy but with such a set of officers as I have they will learn their duties rapidly and relieve me of many of the cares I now have. My Regt. is a good one and deserves great credit for the progress it has made in the last three weeks. Our March from Springfield was conducted with as much dicipline, and our geting into camp at night and starting in the morning, was as prompt as I ever saw with regular troops. I have been strict with my men but it seems to have met with the approbation of them all. — Fred. started home yesterday and I did not telegraph you because I thought you would be in a perfect stew until he arrived. He did not want to go atall and I felt lothe at sending him but now that we are in the enemies country I thought you would be alarmed if he was with me. Fred. is a good boy and behaved very manly. Last night we had an alarm which kept me out all night with one of those terrible headaches which you know I am subject to. To-day I have laid up all day and taken medicine so that I feel pretty well.

Write your next letter to me at Alton. Fred. will have a budget of news to tell you. You must not fret about me. Of course there is more or less exposure in a call of the kind I am now obeying but the justness of it is a consolation.—It is geting late and I must go to bed. give my love to all at home. I hope Simp. will not abandon the idea of going to Lake Superior. I think it will do him a greatdeel of good. Kisses for yourself & children.

ULYS.

To Jesse Root Grant

Mexico Mo.
Aug 3, 1861

Dear Father;

I have written to you once from this place and received no answer, but as Orvil writes to me that you express great anxiety to hear from me often I will try and find time to drop you a line twice a month, and oftener when anything of special interest occurs.

The papers keep you posted as to Army Movements and as you are already in possession of my notions on Secession nothing more is wanted on that point. I find here however a different state of feeling from what I expected existed in any part of the South. The majority in this part of the State are Secessionists, as we would term them, but deplore the present state of affairs. They would make almost any sacrifice to have the Union restored, but regard it as disolved and nothing is left for them but to choose between two evils. Many too seem to be entirely ignorant of the object of present hostilities. You can't convince them but what the ultimate object is to extinguish, by force, slavery. Then too they feel that the Southern Confederacy will never consent to give up their State and as they, the South, are the strong party it is prudent to favor them from the start. There is never a movement of troops made that the Secession journals through the Country do not give a startling account of their almost annihilation at the hands of the States troops, whilst the facts are there are no engagements. My Regt. has been reported cut to pieces once that I know of, and I dont know but oftener, whilst a gun has not been fired at us. These reports go uncontradicted here and give confirmation to the conviction already entertained that one Southron is equal to five Northerners. We believe they are deluded and know that if they are not we are.

Since I have been in Command of this Military District (two weeks) I have received the greatest hospitality and attention from the Citizens about here. I have had every opportunity of conversing with them freely and learning their sentiments and although I have confined myself strictly to the truth as to what has been the result of the different engagements, the relative strength etc. and the objects of the Administration, and the North Generally, yet they dont believe a word I dont think.

I see from the papers that my name has been sent in for Brigadier Gen.! This is certainly very complimentary to me particularly as I have never asked a friend to intercede in my behalf. My only acquaintance with men of influence in the State was whilst on duty at Springfield and I then saw much pulling and hauling for favors that I determined never to ask for anything, and never have, not even a Colonelcy. I wrote a letter to Washington tendering my services but then declined Gov. Yates' & Mr. Trumbull's endorsement.

My services with the Regt. I am now with have been highly satisfactory to me. I took it in a very disorganized, demoralized and insubordinate condition and have worked it up to a reputation equal to the best, and I believe with the good will of all the officers and all the men. Hearing that I was likely to be promoted the officers, with great unanimity, have requested to be attached to my Command. This I dont want you to read to others for I very much dislike speaking of myself.

We are now breaking up Camp here gradually. In a few days the last of us will be on our way for the Mo. River, at what point cannot be definitely determined, wood & water being a concideration, as well as a healthy fine sight for a large encampment. A letter addressed to me at Galena will

probably find me there. If I get my promotion I shall expect
to go there for a few days.

Remember me to all at home and write to me.

Yours Truly
U. S. GRANT

To Julia Dent Grant

Mexico, Mo.
August 3d 1861

Dear Julia;

This is the last letter you will get from me from this point.
We are now breaking up camp preparitory to moving on to
the Missouri river. At what point I cannot yet say. From the
accounts in the papers I may not go along however. I see
some kind friends have been working to get me the Appointment of Brigadier General which, if confirmed may send me
any place where there are Ill. troops.

I am glad to get away from here. The people have been
remarkably polite if they are seceshers, but the weather is
intolerably warm and dry and as there is neither wells nor
springs in this country we have drank the whole place dry.
People here will be glad to get clear of us notwithstanding
their apparent hospitality. They are great fools in this section
of country and will never rest until they bring upon themselvs
all the horrors of war in its worst form. The people are inclined to carry on a guerilla Warfare that must eventuate in
retaliation and when it does commence it will be hard to control. I hope from the bottom of my heart I may be mistaken
but since the defeat of our troops at Manassas things look
more gloomy here.

How long has it been since I wrote to you before? I am
kept very busy and time passes off rapidly so that it seems but
a day or two. I have received two letters from you since our
arrival, one in which you gave me fits for sending Fred. home
by himself and one of later date. Fred. will make a good General some day and I think you had better pack his valise and
start him on now. I should like very much to see you and the

children again.—The weather has been intolerably warm here for the last week.***

You need not write to me until you hear from me again. I will write soon and often if I do write short letters. Give my love to all at home. Kiss the children for me. Does Jess. talk about his pa or has he forgotten me. Little rascal I want to see him. Love and kisses for yourself.

U. S. GRANT

To Julia Dent Grant

Ironton Mo.
August 10th 1861

Dear Julia;

Night before last I come down to Jefferson Bks. with my old Regt. leaving my trunk at the Planter's House flattering myself that at 9 O'Clock the next day I would return to St. Louis, get a leave of absence for a few days and pop down upon you taking you by surprize. But my destination was suddenly changed, 9 O'Clock brought me orders, (and cars to carry a regiment) to proceed at once to this place and assume command. My present command here numbers about 3000 and will be increased to 4000 to-morrow and probably much larger the next day. When I come there was great talk of an attack upon this place and it was represented that there was 8000 rebels within a few miles but I am not ready to credit the report.

I have envited Mr. Rollins of Galena to accept a place on my Staff. I wish you would tell Orvil to say to him that I would like to have him come as soon as possible if he accepts the position.

I sent you some money the other day and requested Ford to write to you. Did he do it? The four gold dollars were thrown in extra for the four children. Bless their hearts I wish I could see them.

I certainly feel very greatful to the people of Ill. for the interest they seem to have taken in me and unasked too. Whilst I was about Springfield I certainly never blew my own trumpet and was not aware that I attracted any attention but it seems from what I have heard from there the people, who were perfect strangers to me up to the commencement of our present unhappy national difficulties, were very unanimous in recommending me for my present position. I shall do my very best not to disappoint them and shall hope by dilligence to render good account of some of the Ill. Vols. All my old Regt. expressed great regret at my leaving them and applied to be attached to my Brigade.

I called to see Harry Boggs the other day as I passed through St. Louis. He cursed and went on like a Madman. Told me that I would never be welcom in his hous; that the people of Illinois were a poor misserable set of Black Republicans, Abolition paupers that had to invade their state to get something to eat. Good joke that on something to eat. Harry is such a pittiful insignificant fellow that I could not get mad at him and told him so where upon he set the Army of Flanders far in the shade with his profanity.

Give my love to all the good people of Galena. I hope to be at home a day or two soon but dont you be disappointed if I am. Kiss the children for me.—Dont act upon the permission I gave you to go to Covington to board until you hear from me again on the subject.

ULYS.

To Mary Grant

Ironton Mo.
August 12th 1861

Dear Sister;

Your letter directed to me at Mexico, Mo. come to hand yesterday at this place. A glance at the map will show you where I am. When I come here it was reported that this place was to be attacked by 8,000 secessionests, under Gen. Hardee, within a day or two. Now Hardee's force seems to have reduced and his distance from here to have increased. Scouting parties however are constantly seen within a few miles of our Pickets. I have here about 3000 Vols. nearly all

Infantry, but our position being strong and our cause a good one, it would trouble a much larger force of the enemy to dislodge us. — You ask my views about the continuance of the war &c. Well I have changed my mind so much that I dont know what to think. That the Rebels will be so badly whipped by April next that they cannot make a stand anywhere I dont doubt. But they are so dogged that there is no telling when they may be subdued. Send Union troops among them and respect all their rights, pay for evrything you get and they become desperate and reckless because their state sovereignty is invaded. Troops of the opposite side march through and take evrything they want, leaving no pay but script, and they become desperate secession partisans because they have nothing more to loose. Evry change makes them more desperate. I should like to be sent to Western Virginia but my lot seems to be cast in this part of the world. I wanted to remain in St. Louis a day or two to get some books to read that might help me in my profession, and get my uniform &c. made. Mine has been a busy life from the begining and my new made friends in Ill. seem to give me great credit. I hope to deserve it and shall spare no pains on my part to do so.

It is precious little time I shall have for writing letters but I have subscribed for the Daily St. Louis Democrat to be sent to you, through which you may occationally hear from me.

Write to me often even though your letters are not answered. As I told father in my last, I will try and have you hear from me twice a month if I have to write after midnight.

I told Julia she might go to Covington and board whilst I am away but I dont know but she had better stay where she is. The people of Galena have always shown the greatest friendship for me and I would prefer keeping my home there. I would like very much though if you would go and stay with Julia.

If I get a uniform, and get where I can have my Dagueareotype taken your wish in that respect shall be gratified.

Your Brother

ULYS.

To Julia Dent Grant

Head Quarters, Jefferson City, Mo
August 26th 1861

Dear Julia;

The day Orvil arrived here I got a big batch of letters from you the first for a long time. I was surprised to learn that you had not heard from me for so long a time. I have been very particular to write often, and I think a single week has not passed without my writing at least once and generally twice.—Orvil can tell you how busy I have been. Evry night I am kept from 12 O'Clock to 2 in the morning. I stand it first rate however and never enjoyed better health in my life.

I receive a great many letters that I cannot answer and many that I do. Josh Sharp has applied to go on my Staff. He says that he will go on without pay and without position if I will let him go along.

My Staff are, J. A. Rawlins Clark B Lagow & W. S. Hillyer, three of the cleverest men that can be found anywhere. Father's recommendation come too late. I know the father of the young man he recommends and if the son is like him I could not get one that would suit better.

I am sorry that I did not keep Fred with me. He would have enjoyed it very much.

How long we will be here and whether I will get to go home is hard to tell. Gen. Fremont promised that I should but if a forward movement is to take place I fear I shall not.— When I was ordered away from Ironton nearly all the commanders of regiments expressed regret I am told. The fact is my whole career since the begining of present unhappy difficulties has been complimented in a very flattering manner. All my old friends in the Army and out seem to heartily congratulate me. I scarsely ever get to go out of the house and consequently see but little of the people here. There seems to be no stir however except among the troops and they are quiet. There is considerable apprehension of an attack soon but my means of information are certainly better than can be had by most others and my impression is that there is no force sufficiently strong to attempt anything of the kind under a weeks march.

I sent you ten dollars by Orvil to carry you through a few days until I can draw a months pay when I will send $75 or $100 more. I want you to have evrything comfortable and when I get some debts paid will supply you more liberally. My outfit costs $900 00 without being anything extra. This includes three horses saddles & bridles at $600 00.

Give my love to all at home. Remember me to the neighbors around you. I am very much in hopes I shall be able to pay you a short visit but fear I shall not. Kiss the children for me and accept the same for yourself.

> Good night.
> ULYS.

To Eleazer A. Paine

Head Quarters, Dist of Cairo
Cairo, Jany 11th 1862.

Brig Gen. E. A. Paine
Commdg Bird's Point, Mo.
General:

I undestand that four of our pickets were shot this morning. If this is so, and appearances indicate that the assassins were citizens, not regularly organized in the rebel Army, the whole country should be cleaned out, for six miles around, and word given that all citizens making their appearance within those limits are liable to be shot. To execute this, patrols should be sent out, in all directions, and bring into camp at Bird's Point all citizens, together with their Subsistence, and require them to remain, under pain of death and destruction of their property until properly relieved.

Let no harm befall these people, if they quietly submit but bring them in, and place them in camp below the breastworks and have them properly guarded.

The intention is not to make political prisoners of these people, but to cut off a dangerous class of spies.

This applies to all classes and conditions, Age and Sex. If however, Woman and Children, prefer other protection than we can afford them, they may be allowed to retire, beyond the limits indicated, not to return until authorized.

Report to me as soon as possibe every important occurrence within your command.

> Very Respectfully,
> Your Obt. Servant,
> U. S. GRANT.
> Brig. Gen'l. Commdg.

General Orders No. 3

Head Quarters Dist of Cairo
Cairo Ill. January 13. 1862

General Order No. 3

During the absence of the Expedition now starting upon soil hitherto occupied almost solely by the Rebel Army, and where it is a fair inference that every stranger met is our enemy, the following orders will be observed.

Troops, in marching, will be kept in the ranks, Company officers being held strictly accountable for all stragglers from their Companies.

No firing will be allowed in camp or on the march, not strictly required in the performance of duty.

Whilst in Camp, no permits will be granted to officers or soldiers to leave their regimental grounds, and all violations of this order must be promptly and summarily punished.

Disrepute having been brought upon our brave soldiers by the bad conduct of some of their numbers, showing on all occasions, when marching through territory occupied by sympathisers of the enemy, a total disregard of rights of citizens, and being guilty of wanton destruction of private propety the Genl. commanding, desires and intends to enforce a change in this respect.

Interpreting Confiscation Acts by troops themselves, has a demoralizing effect, weakens them in exact proportion to the demoralization and makes open and armed enemies of many who, from opposite treatment would become friends or at worst non-combatants.

It is orded, therefore that the severest punishment, be inflicted upon every soldier, who is guilty of taking or dstroying private property, and any commissioned officer guilty of like conduct, or of countenancing it shall be deprived of his sword and expelled from the camp, not to be permitted to return.

On the march, Cavalry Advance guards will be well thrown out, also flank guards of Cavalry or Infantry when practicable.

A rear guard of Infantry will be required to see that no teams, baggage or disabled soldiers are left behind

It will be the duty of Company Commanders to see that rolls of their Companies are called immediatly upon going into camp each day and every member accounted for

By order
U. S. GRANT Brig. Gen'l Comdg.

To Julia Dent Grant

Camp Near Fort Henry, Ten.
Feb.y 5th 1862

Dear Julia,

We returned to-day with most of the remainder of our troops. The sight of our camp fires on either side of the river is beautiful and no doubt inspires the enemy, who is in full view of them, with the idea that we have full 4,000 men. To-morrow will come the tug of war. One side or the other must to-morrow night rest in quiet possession of Fort Henry. What the strength of Fort Henry is I do not know accurately, probably 10,000 men.

To-day our reconnoitering parties had a little skirmishing resulting in one killed & two slightly wounded on our side and one killed and a number wounded on the side of the rebels, and the balance badly frightened and driven into their fortifications.

I am well and in good spirits yet feeling confidance in the success of our enterprise. Probably by the time you receive this you will receive another announcing the result.

I received your letter last night just after I had written to you.

I have just written my order of battle. I hope it will be a report of the battle after it is fought.

Kiss the children for me. Kisses for yourself.

ULYS.

P. S. I was up til 5 o'clock this morning and awoke at 8 so I must try and get rest to-night. It is now 10½ however, and I cannot go to bed for some time yet.

U.

To Mary Grant

Fort Henry, Ten.
Feb.y 9th 1862.

Dear Sister,

I take my pen in hand "away down in Dixie" to let you know that I am still alive and well. What the next few days may bring forth however I cant tell you. I intend to keep the ball moving as lively as possible and have only been detained here from the fact that the Tennessee is very high and has been raising ever since we have been here overflowing the back land making it necessary to bridge it before we could move. — Before receiving this you will hear, by telegraph, of Fort Donaldson being attacked. — Yesterday I went up the Ten. river twenty odd miles and to-day crossed over to near the Cumberland river at Fort Donaldson. — Our men had a little engagement with the enemie's pickets killing five of them, wounding a number and, expressively speaking, "gobbeling up" some twenty-four more.

If I had your last letter at hand I would answer it. But I have not and therefore write you a very hasty and random letter simply to let you know that I believe you still remember me and am carrying on a conversation whilst writing with my Staff and others.

Julia will be with you in a few days and possibly I may accompany her. This is bearly possible, depending upon having full possession of the line from Fort Henry to Fort Donaldson and being able to quit for a few days without retarding any contemplated movement. This would not leave me free more than one day however.

You have no conception of the amount of labor I have to perform. An army of men all helpless looking to the commanding officer for every supply. Your plain brother however has, as yet, had no reason to feel himself unequal to the task and fully believes that he will carry on a successful campaign against our rebel enemy. I do not speak boastfully but utter a presentiment. The scare and fright of the rebels up here is beyond conception. Twenty three miles above here some were drowned in their haste to retreat thinking us such Vandals that neither life nor property would be respected. G. J. Pillow commands at Fort Donaldson. I hope to give him a tug before you receive this.

U. S. G.

To George W. Cullum

Head Quarters, Army in the Field
Fort Donelson, Feb. 16th 1862

Gen. G. W. Cullum
Chief of Staff, Dept. of the Mo.
Gen.

I am pleased to announce to you the unconditional surrender this morning of Fort Donelson, with twelve to fifteen thousand prisoners, at least forty pieces of Artillery and a large amount of stores, horses, mules and other public property. I left Fort Henry on the 12th inst. with a force of about 15000 men, divided into two Divisions under the commands of Gens. McClernand and Smith. Six regiments were sent around by water the day before, convoyed by a gun boat, or rather started one day later than one of the gunboats, and with instructions not to pass it.

The troops made the march in good order, the head of the colum arriving within two miles of the Fort, at 12 o'clock M. At this point the enemies pickets were met and driven in.

The fortifications of the enemy were from this point gradually approached and surrounded with occational skirmishing on the line. The following day owing to the nonarrival of the Gunboats and reinforcements sent by water no attack was made but the investment was extended on the flanks of the enemy and drawn closer to his works, with skirmishing all day. The evening of the 13th the Gunboats and reinforcements arrived. On the 14th a gallant attack was made by Flag Officer Foote, upon the enemies works, with his fleet. The engagement lasted probably one hour and a half and bid fair to result favorably to the cause of the Union when two unlucky shots disabled two of the Armoured boats so that they were carrid back by the tide. The remaining two were very much disabled also having received a number of heavy shots about the pilot houses and other parts of the vessels.

After these mishaps I concluded to make the investment of Fort Donelson as perfect as possible and partially fortify and await repairs to the gunboats. This plan was frustrated however by the enemy making a most vigorous attack upon our right wing, commanded by Gen. J. A. McClernands with a portion of the force under Gen. L. Wallace. The enemy were repelled after a closely contested battle of several hours in which our loss was heavy. The officers, and particularly field officers, suffered out of proportion. I have not the means yet of determining our loss even approximately but it cannot fall far short of 1200 killed wounded and missing. Of the latter I understand through Gen. Buckner about 250 were taken prisoners.—I shall retain enough of the enemy to exchange for them as they were immediately shipped off and not left for recapture.—About the close of this action the ammunition in cartridge boxes gave out, which with the loss of many of the Field officers produced great confusion in the ranks. Seeing that the enemy did not take advantage of it convinced me that equal confusion, and possibly great demoralization, existed with him. Taking advantage of this fact I ordered a charge upon the left,—Enemies right,—with the Division under Gen. C. F. Smith which was most brilliantly executed and gave to our arms full assurance of victory. The battle lasted until dark giving us possession of part of the entrenchments. — An attack was ordered from the other flank, after the charge by Gen. Smith was commenced, by the Divisions under Gens. McClernand & Wallace, which, notwithstanding the hours of exposure to a heavy fire in the fore part of the day, was gallantly made and the enemy further repulsed.

At the points thus gained, night having come on, all the troops encamped for the night feeling that a complete victory would crown their labors at an early hour in the morning.

This morning at a very early hour a note was received from Gen. S. B. Buckner, under a flag of truce, proposing an armistice &c. A copy of the correspondence which ensued is herewith accompanying.

I cannot mention individuals who specially distinguished themselvs but leave that to Division and Brigade Commanders, whos reports will be forwarded as soon as received.

To Division Commanders however, Gens McClernand, Smith and Wallace I must do the justice to say that each of them were with their commands in the midst of danger and were always ready to execute all orders no matter what the exposure to themselvs.

At the hour the attack was made on Gen. McClernand's command I was absent, having received a note from Flag Officer Foote requesting me to go and see him he being unable to call in consequence of a wound received the day before

My personal staff, Col. J. T. Webster, Chief of Staff Col. J. Riggin Jr Vol. Aid. Capt. J. A. Rawlins, A. A. Gen. Capts C. B Lagow & W. S. Hillyer Aids, and Lt. Col. J. B. McPherson Chief Engineer all are deserving of personal mention for their gallantry and services.

For full details see reports of Engineers, Medical Director and Commanders of Brigades & Divisions to follow.

I am Gen. very respectfully
your obt. svt.
U. S. GRANT
Brig. Gen

To Julia Dent Grant

Head Quarters, Fort Donelson Ten.
Feb.y 16th 1862

Dear Wife

I am most happy to write you from this very strongly fortified place, now in my possession, after the greatest victory of the season. Some 12 or 15 thousand prisoners have fallen into our possession to say nothing of 5 to 7 thousand that escaped in the darkness of the night last night.

This is the largest capture I believe ever made on the continent.

You warn me against Capt. Kountz. He can do me no harm. He is known as a venimous man whose hand is raised against every man and is without friends or influance.*** —My impression is that I shall have one hard battle more to fight and will find easy sailing after that. No telling though. This was one of the most desperate affairs fought during this war. Our men were out three terrible cold nights and fighting through the day, without tents. Capt. Hillyer will explain all to you. Kiss the children for me. I will direct my next letter to Covington.

ULYS.

To Julia Dent Grant

Fort Donelson, Feb. 24th 1862.

Dear Julia,

I have just returned from Clarkesville. Yesterday some citizens of Nasville come down there ostensibly to bring surgeons to attend their wounded at that place but in reality no doubt to get assurances that they would not be molested. Johnson with his army of rebels have fallen back about forty miles south from Nashville leaving the river clear to our troops   To-day a Division of Gen. Buells Army reported to me for orders. As they were on Steamers I ordered them immediately up to Nashville. "Secesh" is now about on its last legs in Tennessee. I want to push on as rapidly as possible to save hard fighting. These terrible battles are very good things to read about for persons who loose no friends but I am decidedly in favor of having as little of it as possible. The way to avoid it is to push forward as vigorously as possible.

Gen. Halleck is clearly the same way of thinking and with his clear head I think the Congressional Committee for investigating the Conduct of the War will have nothing to enquire about in the West.

I am writing you in great haste a boat being about leaving here. I will write you often to make up for the very short letters I send.

Give my love to all at home and write frequently. Tell me all about the children. I want to see rascal Jess already. Tell Mary she must write to me often. Kiss the children for me and the same for yourself

ULYS.

To Julia Dent Grant

Fort Donelson, Feby. 26th, 1862.

Dear Julia:

I am just starting to Nashville and will drop you a line before starting. Gen. Buell is there, or at least a portion of his command is, and I want to have an interview with the comdg. officer and learn what I can of the movements of the enemy. I shall be back here to-morrow evening and remain until some movement takes place. Since my promotion some change may take place in my command, but I do not know. I want however to remain in the field and be actively employed. But I shall never ask a favor or change. Whatever is ordered I will do independantly and as well as I know how. If a command inferior to my rank is given me it shall make no difference in my zeal. In spite of enemies, I have so far progressed satisfactorily to myself and the country and in reviewing the past can see but few changes that could have bettered the result. Perhaps I have done a little too much of the office duties and thereby lost time that might have been better employed in inspecting and reviewing troops.

I want to hear from you. I have not had a word since you left Cairo. My clothing &c. came up all right except the saddle cover. Do you know anything about it? Those covers cost $30 00 and I shall be compelled to buy another if that one is lost. I have written to Gen. Cullum to look it up. I am anxious to get a letter from Father to see his criticisms. I see his paper the Gazette gets off whole numbers without mentioning my name   That paper and the Cincinnati Commercial for some reason inexplicable to me have always apparently been my enemies   It never disturbed me however

Give my love to all at home. I write to you so often that you must be satisfied with short letters.

ULYS.

To Julia Dent Grant

Fort Henry Mach 11th/62

My Dear Julia,

I am just going down to Paducah looking after the interest of the expedition now gone up the Tennessee. Soon more troops will join us then I will go in command of the whole. What you are to look out for I cannot tell you but you may rely upon it that your husband will never disgrace you nor leave a defeated field. We all volunteered to be killed, if needs be, and whilst any of us are living there should be no feeling other than we are so far successful. This is my feeling and believe it is well inculcated among the troops.

My dear Julia I have but little idea from what point I shall next write you. If I knew I would hardly tell but I hope another mark will be made against rebelion.

There is a greatdeel that might be said, in a Military way, but that cannot be properly discussed. If I was ahead of the telegraph however I might say that I believe that I have the whole Tennessee river, to Florance Alabama, safe from any immediate attack. The enemy have preserved one Gunboat, the Dunbar, and may have run her up some creek, during the present high water, to bring out and destroy our transports. That would be my policy yet I do not think it has been adopted. Of course the steamer would be lost but she is lost anyhow and individuals should never take that into account. — We have such an inside track of the enemy that by following up our success we can go anywhere. To counteract us Tennessee at least is trying to bring out all her men. She is doing so so much against the feeling of the men themselvs that within my limited sphere I am giving all the protection possible to prevent forced enlistments. I have written you a military letter when only my love and kisses to the children, and to yourself, was intended. Tell Mary that her last letter was received and she must continue to write. Some day I will find a chance of answering

ULYS.

To Julia Dent Grant

Savanna Tennessee
March 18th 1862

My Dear Julia,

You will see by the above that I am far up South in the State of Ten. When you will hear of another great and important strike I cant tell you but it will be a big lick so far as numbers engaged is concerned. I have no misgivings myself as to the result and you must not feel the slightest alarm. — It is now 3 O'Clock in the morning but as a boat will be going down to-morrow and having just arrived I will have to much to do to write private letters in the morning. We got here about 4 O'Clock in the afternoon and I had necessarily many orders to write.

There is a strong manifestation of Union feeling in this section. Already some 500 have come in voluntarily and enlisted to prevent being drafted on the other side. Many more have come in to get the protection of our army for the same purpose. — With one more great success I do not see how the rebellion is to be sustained. War matters however must be an uninteresting subject to you so I will close on that.—I have been poorly for several weeks but began to feel better the very moment of arriving where there is so much to do and where it is so important that I should be able to do it.

I will try and have you hear from me often but it will not be possible to communicate as often as heretofore. I'm getting further from home. You are spending a pleasant time in Covington are you not? I should love very much to be there a day or two with you and the children. Does Jess talk of his pa? Kiss all the children for me and give my love to all at home.

Good night dear Julia.

ULYS.

To Elihu B. Washburne

Savanna, Tennessee
March 22d 1862.

Hon. E. B. Washburn
Washington D. C.
Dear Sir:

I have received two or three letters from you which I have not answered, because, at the time they were received I was unwell, and busy, and because at the time they were received either your brother or Rowley were about writing. I am now getting nearly well and ready for any immmergency that may arise. A severe contest may be looked for in this quarter before many weeks, but of the result feel no alarm.

There are some things which I wish to say to you in my own vindication, not that I care one straw for what is said, individually, but because you have taken so much interest in my wellfare that I think you entitled to all facts connected with my acts.

I see by the papers that I am charged with giving up a certain number of slaves captured at Fort Donelson!

My published order on the occasion shows that citizens were not permitted to pass through our camps to look for their slaves. There were some six or seven negroes at Donelson who represented that they had been brought from Ky. to work for officers, and had been kept a number of months without receiving pay. They expressed great anxiety to get back to their families and protested that they were free men. These I let go and none others.—I have studiously tried to prevent the running off of negroes from all outside places as I have tried to prevent all other marauding and plundering.

So long as I hold a commission in the Army I have no views of my own to carry out. Whatever may be the orders of my superiors, and law, I will execute. No man can be efficient as a commander who sets his own notions above law and those whom he is sworn to obey. When Congress enacts anything too odious for me to execute I will resign.

I see the credit of attacking the enemy by the way of the Tennessee and Cumberland is variously attributed! It is little to talk about it being the great wisdom of any Gen. that first brought forth this plan of attack.

Our gunboats were running up the Ten. and Cumberland rivers all fall and winter watching the progress of the rebels on these works. Gen. Halleck no doubt thought of this route long ago and I am shure I did. As to how the battles should be fought both McClellan and Halleck are too much of soldiers to suppose that they can plan how that should be done at a distance. This would presuppose that the enemy would make just the moves laid down for them. It would be a game of Chess the right hand against the left determining before hand that the right should win.

The job being an important one neither of the above Generals would have entrusted it to an officer who they had not confidance in. So far I was highly complimented by both.

After geting into Donelson Gen. Halleck did not hear from me for near two weeks. It was about the same time before I heard from him. I was writing every day and sometimes as often as three times a day. Reported every move and change, the condition of my troops &c. Not getting these Gen. Halleck very justly become dissatisfied and was, as I have since learned, sending me daily repremands. Not receiving them they lost their sting. When one did reach me not seeing the justice of it I retorted and asked to be relieved. Three telegrams passed in this way each time ending by my requesting to be relieved. All is now understood however and I feel assured that Gen. Halleck is fully satisfied. In fact he wrote me a letter saying that I could not be relieved and otherwise quite complimentary. I will not tire you with a longer letter but assure you again that you shall not be disappointed in me if it is in my power to prevent it.

> I am sir, very respectfully
> your obt. svt.
> U. S. GRANT

To Julia Dent Grant

Savanna, March 23d/62

Dear Julia,

Two letters from you are just received. One of them a business letter and the other not. You do not say a word about the $700 00 I sent you since you left Cairo. I see plainly from your letter that it will be impossible for you to stay in Covington. Such unmittigated meanness as is shown by the girls makes me ashamed of them. You may go to Columbus and board or to Galena and keep house. It will be impossible for you to join me. It will be but a short time before I shall be in the tented field, *without a tent*, and after the enemy.

What the papers say about relieving me is all a falshood. For some reason to me entirely inexplicable Gen. Halleck did not hear from me for about two weeks after the fall of Donelson, nor did I hear from him for about the same time. I was writing daily and sometimes two or three times a day and the Gen. doing the same. At last a repremand come for not reporting as I had been frequently ordered.

I replied sharply that that was the first order I had but to relieve me. Gen. Halleck declined though he said my course had caused him to be repremanded from Washington. As I had been reporting daily I stated so and again asked to be relieved, and so again for the third time. All was understood however afterwards and though I say it myself I believe that I am the very last man in the Dept. Gen. Halleck would want to see taken out of it. Through some misrepresentations of jealous and disappointed persons, not belonging with my Army, false rumors were set afloat about what was done with captured property. I done all in my power to prevent any of it being carried off. I had sentinels placed to prevent it being carried aboard of boats, and send persons aboard of boats leaving to search and bring off all captured property they could find. This maddened the rascals engaged in the business and as much escaped my vigilence they have no doubt given currency to reports prejudicial to me. I am so consious of having done all things right myself that I borrow no trouble from the lies published. I say I dont care for what the papers say but I do. It annoys me very much when I see such barefaced falshoods published and then it distresses you.

I want to whip these rebels once more in a big fight and see what will then be said. I suppose such a result would make me a host of enemies.

I wrote to you last night and Capt. Lagow wrote the night before. Some day a big lot of letters will be turning up as I write from two to four letters a week.

If you go to Columbus to spend the summer put the children to school at once. I am sorry you cannot stay in Covington pleasantly for it is such a good place for the children. But it is too mortifying to me to hear of my sisters complaining about the amount paid for the board of their brothers children. If I should name the subject of board for one of them I could not raise my head again. How much better it would appear if they should never say a word on the subject. It would cost nothing either for them to hold their tongues.

You had better leave at once for some place. Tell them I direct it and the reason why.

Kiss the children for me and accept the same for yourself. It looks now as if the first place you could join me would be far down in Dixie.

ULYS.

To Henry W. Halleck

Savanna, March 24th 1862

Maj. Gen. H. W. Halleck
Comd.g Dept. of the Miss.
St. Louis Mo.
Gen.

Your letter enclosing correspondence between yourself and Adj. Gen. Thomas is just received. In regard to the plundering at Fort Donelson it is very much overestimated by disappointed persons who failed in getting off the trophies they had gathered. My orders of the time show that I did all in my power to prevent marauding. To execute these orders I kept a company on duty searching boats about leaving and to bring off all captured property found.

My great difficulty was with the rush of citizens, particularly the sanitary committee, who infested Donelson after its fall. They thought it an exceedingly hard case that patriotic gentleman like themselvs, who had gone to tender their services to the sick and wounded could not carry off what they pleased. Most of the wounded had reached hospitals before these gentlemen left Cairo. One of these men, a Dr. Fowler of Springfield, swore vengeance against me for this very act, of preventing trophies being carried off. How many more did the same thing I cant tell.

My going to Nashville I did not regard particularly as going beyond my District. After the fall of Donelson from information I had I knew that the way was clear to Clarkesville & Nashville. Accordingly I wrote to you, directed to your Chief of Staff, as was all my correspondence from the time of leaving Fort Henry until I learned you were not hearing from me, that by Friday following the fall of Donelson I should occupy Clarkesville, and by Saturday week following should be in Nashville if not prevented by orders from Hd Qrs. of the Dept. During all this time not one word was received from you and I accordingly occupied Clarkesville on the day indicated and two days after the time I was to occupy Nashville Gen. Nelson reported to me with a Division of Buell's Army. They being already on transports and knowing that Buells Column should have arrived opposite Nashville the day before, and having no use for these troops myself I ordered them immediately to Nashville.

It is perfectly plain to me that designing enemies are the cause of all the publications that appear and are the means of getting extracts sent to you. It is also a little remarkable that the Adj. Gen. should learn of my presence in Nashville before it was known in St. Louis where I reported that I was going before starting.

I do not feel that I have neglected a single duty. My reports to you have averaged at least one a day since leaving Cairo and there has been scarsely a single day that I have not either written or telegraphed to Hd Qrs.

I most fully appreciate your justness Gen. in the part you have taken and you may rely upon me to the utmost of my capacity for carrying out all your orders.

I Am Gen. very respectfully
your obt. svt.
U. S. GRANT
Maj. Gen. Com

To Julia Dent Grant

Savanna, March 29th 1862

Dear Julia,

I am again fully well. I have had the Diaoreah for several weeks and an inclination to Chills & Fever. We are all in *statu qua*. Dont know when we will move. Troops are constantly arriving so that I will soon have a very large army. A big fight may be looked for someplace before a great while which it appears to me will be the last in the West. This is all the time supposing that we will be successful which I never doubt for a single moment.

I heard of your arrival at Louisville several days ago through some Steamboat Capt. and before your letter was received stating that you would start the next day.

All my Staff are now well though most of them have suffered same as myself. Rawlins & myself both being very unwell at the same time made our labors hard upon us. All that were with me at Cairo are with me here, substuting Dr. Brinton for Dr. Simons, and in addition Capt. Hawkins & Capt. Rowley. Rowley has also been very unwell. Capt. Hillyer will probably return home and go to Washington. His position on my Staff is not recognized and he will have to quit or get it recognized.

Capt. Brinck is in the same category. All the slanders you have seen against me originated away from where I was. The only foundation was from the fact that I was ordered to remain at Fort Henry and send the expedition under command of Maj. Gen. Smith. This was ordered because Gen. Halleck received no report from me for near two weeks after the fall of Fort Donelson. The same occured with me I received nothing from him. The consequence was I apparently totally disregarded his orders. The fact was he was ordering me every day to report the condition of my command, I was not receiving the orders but knowing my duties was reporting daily, and when anything occured to make it necessary, two or three times a day. When I was ordered to remain behind it was the cause of much astonishment among the troops of my command and also disappointment. When I was again ordered to join them they showed, I believe, heartfelt joy. Knowing that for some reason I was relieved of the most important part of my command the papers began to surmize the cause, and the Abolition press, the New York Tribune particularly, was willing to hear to no solution not unfavorable to me. Such men as Kountz busyed themselvs very much. I never allowed a word of contridiction to go out from my Head Quarters, thinking this the best course. I know, though I do not like to speak of myself, that Gen. Halleck would regard this army badly off if I was relieved. Not but what there are Generals with it abundantly able to command but because it would leave inexperienced officers senior in rank. You need not fear but what I will come out triumphantly. I am pulling no wires, as political Generals do, to advance myself. I have no future ambition. My object is to carry on my part of this war successfully and I am perfectly willing that others may make all the glory they can out of it.

Give my love to all at home. Kiss the children for me.

ULYS.

To Julia Dent Grant

Savanna, April 3d 1862

Dear Julia,

Letters from you drop along occationally, generally two or three at a time; sometimes one will be three weeks old whilst another will come in as many days.

I have received three written from Louisville one of them by Charles Page. I am very glad you are having a pleasant visit. I wish I could make a visit anywhere for a week or two. It would be a great relief not to have to think for a short time. Soon I hope to be permitted to move from here and when I do there will probably be the greatest battle fought of the War. I do not feel that there is the slightest doubt about the result and therefore, individually, feel as unconcerned about it as if nothing more than a review was to take place. Knowing however that a terrible sacrifice of life must take place I feel conserned for my army and their friends at home.

It will be impossible for you to join me at present. There are constantly ladies coming up here to see their husbands and consequencely destroying the efficiency of the army until I have determined to publish an order entirely excluding females from our lines. This is ungallant but necessary.

Mr. & Miss Safford were up here and returned a few days ago. I sent my watch by him to be expressed to you. I want you to keep it and not leave it with anyone els. I sent for a plain silver watch for myself. There would be no great danger in keeping the other but if it should be lost I never could forgive myself. I want to preserve it to the last day of my life, and want my children to do the same thing, in remembrance of poor Simp. who carried it in his lifetime.

Kiss Jess & Buck for me, and your cousin also, I mean the

young lady, if you want. *** Remember me kindly to Uncle
& Aunt Page

ULYS.

To William T. Sherman

Head Quarters, Dist of West. Tenn.
Pittsburg, April 4th 1862.

Gen. W. T. Sherman
Commdg 5th Division
Gen:

Information just received would indicate that the enemy
are sending a force to Purdy, and it may be with a view to
attack Gen. Wallace at Crumps Landing. I have directed Gen.
W. H. L. Wallace, Commdg 2nd Division, temporarily, to reinforce Gen. L. Wallace in case of an attack with his entire
Division, although, I look for nothing of the kind, but it is
best to be prepared.

I would direct, therefore, that you advise your advance
guards to keep a sharp look out for any movement in that
direction, and should such a thing be attempted, give all the
support of your Division, and Gen. Hurlbut's if necessary. I
will return to Pittsburg at an early hour tomorrow, and will
ride out to your camp.

I am, Gen, Very Respectfully
Your Obt Servant.
U. S. GRANT.
Major. Gen. Commdg

To Henry W. Halleck

Head Quarters, Dist. of West Ten.
Savanna, April 5th 1862.

Maj. Gen. H. W. Halleck,
Comd.g Dept. of the Miss.
St. Louis, Mo.
Gen.

Just as my letter of yesterday to Capt. McLean, A. A. Gen.
was finished notes from Gens. McClernand's & Sherman's

A. A. Gens. were received stating that our outposts had been attacked by the enemy apparently in conciderable force. I immediately went up but found all quiet. The enemy took two officers and four or five of our men prisoners and wounded four. We took eight prisoners and killed several. Number of the enemy wounded not know.

They had with them three pieces of Artillery and Cavalry and Infantry. How much cannot of course be estimated.

I have scarsely the faintest idea of an attack, (general one,) being made upon us but will be prepared should such a thing take place.

Gen. Nelsons Division has arrived. The other two of Gen. Buells Column will arrive to-morrow and next day. It is my present intention to send them to Hamburg, some four miles above Pittsburg, when they all get here. From that point to Corinth the road is good and a junction can be formed with the troops from Pittsburg at almost any point.

Col. McPherson has gone with an escort to-day to examine the defensibility of the ground about Hamburg and to lay out the position of the Camps if advisable to occupy that place.

> I am Gen. very respectfully
> your obt. svt.
> U. S. GRANT
> Maj. Gen.

To Don Carlos Buell

Savanna, April 6th 1862

Gen. D. C. Buell,

Heavy firing is heard up the indicating plainly that an attack has been made upon our most advance positions. I have been looking for this but did not believe the attack could be made before Monday or Teusday.

This necessitates my joining the forces up the river instead of meeting you to-day as I had contemplated.

I have directed Gen. Nelson to move to the river with his Division. He can march to opposite Pittsburg.

> Respectfully your obt. svt.
> U. S. GRANT
> Maj. Gen Com

To Commanding Officer, Advance Forces

Pittsburg, April 6th 1862

Comd.g Officer
Advance Forces Near Pittsburg, Ten.
Gen.

The attack on my forces has been very spirited from early this morning. The appearance of fresh troops on the field now would have a powerful effect both by inspiring our men and disheartining the enemy. If you will get upon the field leaving all your baggage on the East bank of the river it will be a move to our advantage and possibly save the day to us.

The rebel forces is estimated at over 100.000 men.

My Hd Qrs. will be in the log building on top of the hill where you will be furnished a staff officer to guide you to your place on the field.

> Respectfully &c
> U. S. GRANT
> Maj. Gen.

To Henry W. Halleck

BY TELEGRAPH FROM Pittsburgh Tennessee 7th April *1862*
To Maj Gen Halleck

Yesterday the rebels attacked us here with an overwhelming force driving our troops in from their advanced position nearer to the landing—General Wallace was immy. ordered up from Crumps landing and in the evening one division of Buells Army and D C. Buell in person arrived, during the night one other division arrived, and still another today. This

morning at the break of day I ordered an attack which resulted in a fight that continued until late this afternoon with a
very heavy loss on both sides but a complete repulse of the
enemy. I shall follow tomorrow far enough to see that no
immediate renewal of attack is contemplated

U S GRANT

To Henry W. Halleck

BY TELEGRAPH FROM Pittsburg Tenn   *186*
To Maj. Genl. Halleck
Comdg. Dept.

Enemy badly routed & fleeing towards Corinth Our
Cavalry supported by Infy. are now pursuing him with in-
structions to pursue to the swampy grounds near Pea Ridge.
I want transports sent here for our wounded.

U. S. GRANT

April 8, 1862

To Julia Dent Grant

Pittsburg, Ten. April 8th 1862

Dear Julia,

Again another terrible battle has occured in which our arms
have been victorious. For the number engaged and the tenacity with which both parties held on for two days, during an
incessant fire of musketry and artillery, it has no equal on this
continent. The best troops of the rebels were engaged to the
number of 162 regiments as stated by a deserter from their
camp, and their ablest generals. Beaurigard commanded in
person aided by A. S. Johnson, Bragg, Breckenridge and hosts
of other generals of less note but possibly of quite as much
merit. Gen. Johnson was killed and Bragg wounded. The loss
on both sides was heavy probably not less than 20,000 killed
and wounded altogether. The greatest loss was sustained by
the enemy. They suffered immensly by demoralization also

many of their men leaving the field who will not again be of value on the field.

I got through all safe having but one shot which struck my sword but did not touch me.

I am detaining a steamer to carry this and must cut it short.

Give my love to all at home. Kiss the children for me. The same for yourself.

Good night dear Julia.

ULYS.

To Nathaniel H. McLean

Head Quarters Disct of West Tenn
Pittsburgh April 9th 1862

Capt N H McLean
A A Genl Dept of the Mississippi
Saint Louis. Mo.
Capt

It becomes my duty again to report another battle fought between two great armies, one contending for the maintainance of the best Government ever devised the other for its destruction. It is pleasant to record the success of the army contending for the former principle.

On Sunday morning our pickets were attacked and driven in by the enemy. Immediately the five Divisions stationed at this place were drawn up in line of battle ready to meet them. The battle soon waxed warm on the left and center, varying at times to all parts of the line.

The most continuous firing of musketry and artillery ever heard on this Continent was kept up until night fall, the enemy having forced the entire line to fall back nearly half way from their Camps to the Landing. At a late hour in the afternoon a desperate effort was made by the enemy to turn our left and get possession of the Landing, transports &c. This point was guarded by the Gun boats Tyler and Lexington, Capt's Gwinn & Shirk U S N commanding Four 20 pounder Parrott guns and a battery of rifled guns. As there is a deep and impassable ravine for artillery or Cavalry and very

difficult for Infantry at this point. No troops were stationed
here except the neccessary Artillerists and a small Infantry
force for their support   Just at this moment the advance of
Maj Genl Buells Column (a part of the Division under Genl
Nelson) arrived, the two Generals named both being present. An advance was immediately made upon the point of
attack and the enemy soon driven back.

In this repulse much is due to the presence of the Gun
boats Tyler and Lexington and their able Commanders Capt
Gwinn and Shirk.

During the night the Divisions under Genl Crittenden and
McCook arrived. Genl Lew Wallace, at Crumps Landing six
miles below, was ordered at an early hour in the morning to
hold his Division in readiness to be moved in any direction to
which it might be ordered. At about 11 oClock the order was
delivered to move it up to Pittsburgh, but owing to its being
led by a circuitous route did not arrive in time to take part in
Sundays action.

During the night all was quiet, and feeling that a great
moral advantage would be gained by becoming the attacking
party, an advance was ordered as soon as day dawned. The
result was a gradual repulse of the enemy at all parts of the
line from morning until probably 5 oClock in the afternoon
when it became evident the enemy was retreating. Before the
close of the action the advance of Genl T J Woods Division
arrived in time to take part in the action.

My force was too much fatigued from two days hard fighting and exposure in the open air to a drenching rain during
the intervening night to pursue immediately.

Night closed in cloudy and with heavy rain making the
roads impracticable for artillery by the next morning. Genl
Sherman however followed the enemy finding that the main
part of the army had retreated in good order.

Hospitals of the enemies wounded were found all along the
road as far as pursuit was made. Dead bodies of the enemy
and many graves were also found.

I enclose herewith report of Genl Sherman which will explain more fully the result of this pursuit.

Of the part taken by each seperate Command I cannot take

special notice in this report, but will do so more fully when reports of Division Commanders are handed in.

Genl Buell, coming on the Field with a distinct army, long under his command, and which did such efficient service, commanded by himself in person on the field, will be much better able to notice those of his command who particularly distinguished themselves than I possibly can.

I feel it a duty however to a gallant and able officer Brig Genl W T Sherman to make special mention. He not only was with his Command during the entire of the two days action, but displayed great judgment and skill in the management of his men. Altho severely wounded in the hand the first day, his place was never vacant. He was again wounded and had three horses killed under him. In making this mention of a gallant officer no disparagement is intended to the other Division Commanders Major Generals John A McClernand and Lew Wallace, and Brig Generals S A Hurlbut, B M. Prentiss and W H L Wallace, all of whom maintained their places with credit to themselves and the cause Genl Prentiss was taken prisoner in the first days action, and Genl W H L Wallace severely, probably mortally wounded. His Ass Adj Genl Capt William McMichael is missing, probably taken prisoner.

My personal Staff are all deserving of particular mention, they having been engaged during the entire two days in conveying orders to every part of the field. It consists of Col J D Webster, Chief of Staff, Lt Col J B McPherson Chief Engineer assisted by Lieuts W L B Jenney and William Kossack, Capt J A Rawlins A A Genl Capts W S Hillyer, W R Rowley and C B Lagow aides-de-Camp Col G. G. Pride Volunteer aide and Capt J P Hawkins Chief Commissary who accompanied me upon the field.

The Medical Department under the direction of Surgeon Hewitt Medical Director, showed great energy in providing for the wounded and in getting them from the field regardless of danger

Col Webster was placed in special charge of all the artillery and was constantly upon the field. He displayed, as always heretofore, both skill and bravery. At least in one instance he was the means of placing an entire Regiment in a position of doing most valuable service, and where it would not have been but for his exertions.

Lt Col McPherson attached to my staff as Chief Engineer deserves more than a passing notice for his activity and courage. All the grounds beyond our Camps for miles have been reconnoitred by him, and plats carefully prepared under his supervision, give accurate information of the nature of approaches to our lines. During the two days battle he was constantly in the saddle leading troops as they arrived to points where their services were required. During the engagement he had one horse shot under him.

The Country will have to mourn the loss of many brave men who fell at the battle of Pittsburgh, or Chilo more properly. The exact loss in killed and wounded will be known in a day or two. At present I can only give it approximately at 1500 killed and 3500 wounded.

The loss of Artillery was great, many pieces being disabled by the enemies shots and some loosing all their horses and many men. There was probably not less than two hundred horses killed.

The loss of the enemy in killed and left upon the field was greater than ours. In wounded the estimate cannot be made as many of them must have been sent back to Corinth and other points.

The enemy suffered terribly from demorilization and desertion. A flag of Truce was sent in to day from Genl Beaurigard. I enclose herewith a copy of the Correspondence.

> I am. Very Respectfully
> Your Obt Servt
> U. S. GRANT
> Major General Comdg

To Jesse Root Grant

Pittsburg Landing, Tenn., April 26, 1862.
I will go on, and do my duty to the very best of my ability, without praise, and do all I can to bring this war to a speedy

close. I am not an aspirant for any thing at the close of the war.

There is one thing I feel well assured of; that is, that I have the confidence of every brave man in my command. Those who showed the white feather will do all in their power to attract attention from themselves. I had perhaps a dozen officers arrested for cowardice in the first day's fight at this place. These men are necessarily my enemies.

As to the talk about a surprise here, nothing could be more false. If the enemy had sent us word when and where they would attack us, we could not have been better prepared. Skirmishing had been going on for two days between our reconnoitering parties and the enemy's advance. I did not believe, however, that they intended to make a determined attack, but simply that they were making a reconnoisance in force.

My headquarters were in Savannah, though I usually spent the day here. Troops were constantly arriving to be assigned to brigades and divisions, all ordered to report at Savannah, making it necessary to keep an office and some one there. I was also looking for Buell to arrive, and it was important that I should have every arrangement complete for his speedy transit to this side of the river.

U. S. GRANT.

To Mrs. Charles F. Smith

Pittsburg Landing Tenn
April 26th 1862

Mrs C F Smith
No 191 East 4th St New York

It becomes my painful duty to announce to you the death of your lamented husband Major General Charles F Smith. He died at 4 Oclock P M yesterday at Savanna Tennessee

In his death the nation has lost one of its most gallant and most able defenders

It was my fortune to have gone through West Point with the Gen. (then Captain & Commandant of Cadets) and to have served with him in all his battles in Mexico, And in this rebellion, And I can bear honest testimony to his great worth as a soldier and friend. Where an entire nation condoles with you in your bereavement. no one can do so with more heartfelt grief than myself

> Very Truly Yours
> U S GRANT
> Maj Genl.

To Julia Dent Grant

> Camp in the Field
> Near Pittsburg Ten.
> April 30th 1862

Dear Julia,

I move from here to-morrow. Before this reaches you probably another battle, and I think the last big one, will have taken place or be near at hand. I mean the last in the Mississippi Valley and this of course implies if we are successful which no doubt we will be. You need give yourself no trouble about newspaper reports. They will all be understood and me come out all right without a single contradiction. Most or all that you have seen has been written by persons who were not here and thos few items collected from persons nominally present, eye witnesses, was from those who disgraced themselvs and now want to draw off public attention. I am very sorry to say a greatdeel originates in jealousy. This is very far from applying however, I think, to our Chief, Halleck, who I look upon as one of the greatest men of the age. You enquire how I was hurt? For several days before the battle of Pittsburg our out Pickets were skirmishing with the enemies advance. I would remain up here all day and go back to Savanna in the evening where I was anxiously looking for the advance of Gen. Buell's column. My object was, if possible, to keep off an attack until Buell arrived otherwise I would have gone out and met the enemy on Friday before they could have got in position to use all their forces advantageously. Friday evening I went back to Savanna as usual and soon after dark a messenger arrived informing that we were attacked. I immediately returned here and started out onto the field on horseback, my staff with me. The night was intensely dark. I soon found that the firing had seased and started to go back to the river. Being very dark and in the woods we had to ride in a slow walk and at that got off the road. In geting back to it my horse's foot either cought or struck something and he fell flat on his side with my leg under him. Being wet and muddy I was not hurt much at the time but being in the saddle all of Sunday and Monday, and in the rain the intervening night without taking off boots or spurs my ancle swelled terribly and kept me on crutches for several days, unable to get on a boot. Col. Riggin is not with me. The rest of the gentlemen are. In addition I have Col. McPherson of the regular Army and one of the nicest gentleman you ever saw, Capt. Reynolds, regular, Lieuts Bowers & Rowley. We are all well and me as sober as a deacon no matter what is said to the contrary. Mrs. Turner & Miss Hadley run on the steamer Memphis carrying sick soldiers to hospital. As I am out from the river and they are only here about one day in eight or ten I rarely see them. There are no inhabitants here atall

Kiss all the children for me. Tell Jess I have a five shooter pistol for him. When you hear of me being on the Mississippi river join me leaving all the children except Jess. Draw the hundred dollars you have as a matter of course. If I had an opportunity I would send you $200 00 now. Give my love to all at home. Kisses for yourself.

Good buy
ULYS.

To Elihu B. Washburne

Camp Near Corinth, Miss.
May 14th 1862

Hon. E. B. Washburn,
Dear Sir:

The great number of attacks made upon me by the press of the country is my apology for not writing to you oftener, not desiring to give any contradiction to them myself.—You have interested yourself so much as my friend that should I say anything it would probably be made use of in my behalf. I would scorn being my own defender against such attacks except through the record which has been kept of all my official acts and which can be examined at Washington at any time.

To say that I have not been distressed at these attacks upon me would be false, for I have a father, mother, wife & children who read them and are distressed by them and I necessarily share with them in it. Then too all subject to my orders read these charges and it is calculated to weaken their confidance in me and weaken my ability to render efficient service in our present cause. One thing I will assure you of however; I can not be driven from rendering the best service within my ability to suppress the present rebellion, and when it is over retiring to the same quiet it, the rebellion, found me enjoying.

Notoriety has no charms for me and could I render the same services that I hope it has been my fortune to render our just cause, without being known in the matter, it would be infinately prefferable to me.

Those people who expect a field of battle to be maintained, for a whole day, with about 30,000 troops, most of them entirely raw, against 70,000, as was the case at Pittsburg Landing, whilst waiting for reinforcements to come up, without loss of life, know little of War. To have left the field of Pittsburg for the enemy to occupy until our force was sufficient to have gained a bloodless victory would have been to left the Tennessee to become a second Potomac.—There was nothing left for me but to occupy the West bank of the Tennessee and to hold it at all hazards. It would have set this war back six months to have failed and would have caused the necessity of raising, as it were, a new Army.

Looking back at the past I cannot see for the life of me any important point that could be corrected.—Many persons who have visited the different fields of battle may have gone away displeased because they were not permitted to carry off horses, fire arms, or other valuables as trophies. But they are no patriots who would base their enmity on such grounds. Such I assure you are the grounds of many bitter words that have been said against me by persons who at this day would not know me by sight yet profess to speak from a personal acquaintance.

I am sorry to write such a letter, infinately sorry that there should be grounds for it. My own justification does not demand it, but you, a friend, are entitled to know my feelings.

As a friend I would be pleased to give you a record, weekly at furthest, of all that transpires in that portion of the army that I am, or may be, connected with, but not to make public use of.

I am very truly Yours
U. S. GRANT.

To Julia Dent Grant

Corinth Miss.
June 12th 1862

Dear Julia

It is bright and early (before the morning mail leaves) and I thought to write you that in a few days, Monday the 16th probably, I would leave here. I hope to be off on Monday for Memphis and if so want you to join me there. I will write again however just before starting and it may be will have arranged to go after you instead of you coming by yourself.— I would love most dearly to get away from care for a week or two.

I am very well. This is apparently an exceedingly fine climate and one to enjoy health in.—Citizens are begining to return to Corinth and seem to think the Yankees a much less bloody, revengeful and to be dreaded people, than they had been led to think.

In my mind there is no question but that this war could be ended at once if the whole Southern people could express their unbiased feeling untramelled by by leaders. The feeling is kept up however by crying out Abolitionest against us and this is unfortunately sustained by the acts of a very few among us.—There has been instances of negro stealing, persons going to the houses of farmers who have remained at home, being inclined to Union sentiments, and before their eyes perswaid their blacks to mount up behind them and go off. Of course I can trace such conduct to no individual but believe the guilty parties have never heard the whistle of a single bullet nor intentionally never will.

Give my love to all at home. Kisses for yourself and children.

Your husband
ULYS.

To Henry W. Halleck

Memphis Tenn July 8 /62

Maj Gen Halleck

I commenced gathering contrabands last Saturday to work on fortifications   They are now at work. On account of the limited force here we are only fortifying south end of city to protect stores & our own troops. Col Webster has been too unwell to push this matter & I have no other engineer.

Secessionists here have news from Richmond by the South which makes them jubilant. I would like to hear the truth

U S. GRANT
Maj Gen

July 7, 1862

To Salmon P. Chase

Head Qrs Disct of West Tenn
Corinth, Miss. July 31, 1862

To Hon S P Chase
Secretary of the Treasury
Washington, D. C.
Sir

Large quantities of salt flour, liquors and other articles of use and luxury are being shipped by the way of the Tennessee river and other lines of communication, to different points within our lines. It is presumed that these come under authority of regular permits from agents of the Treasury Department, and that the trade is so far legitimate. The collateral

smuggling that goes on undoubtedly to a large extent is another matter not now under notice. It is however a very grave
question in my mind whether this policy of "letting trade follow the flag" is not working injuriously to the Union Cause.
Practically and really I think it is benefitting almost exclusively, first, a class of greedy traders whose first and only desire is gain, and to whom it would be idle to attribute the
least patriotism, and secondly our enemies south of our lines.
The quantities in which these goods are shipped clearly intimate that they are intended to be worked off into the enemys
country thus administering to him the most essential "aid and
comfort." Our lines are so extended that it is impossible for
any military surveillance to contend successfully with the cun-
ning of the traders, aided by the local knowledge and eager
interest of the residents along the border. The enemy are thus
receiving supplies of most necessary and useful articles which
relieve their sufferings and strengthens them for resistance to
our authority; while we are sure that the benefits thus conferred, tend in no degree to abate their rancorous hostility to
our flag and Government. If any hopes have been entertained
that a liberal commercial policy might have a conciliatory effect, I fear they will not be realized. The method of correcting
the evil which first suggests itself is restriction of the quantity
of these articles which may be allowed to be shipped under
one invoice, together with more careful investigation of the
loyalty of persons permitted to trade. Very limited amounts
will be sufficient to supply the wants of the truly loyal men of
the Districts within our lines, for unfortunately they are not
numerous, and outside (south) of our lines, I fear it is little
better than a unanimous rebellion. The evil is a great and
growing one, and needs immediate attention.

> I am sir, your obt. svt
> U. S. GRANT
> Maj. Gen. Com

Fragment on Shiloh

I cannot close this report without paying particular attention to the report of Brig. Gen (now Maj. Gen.) Nelson,

commanding the 4th Division of the Army of the Ohio. Not having seen the report until within a few days attention could not be paid it before.—The report is a tissue of unsupported romance from begining to end some of which I will point out.—Gen. Nelson says that "I left Savanna at 1.30 p.m. on Sunday the 6th by my order, reiterated by Gen. Buell." My order was given Gen. Nelson not later than 7 O'clock, must have reached him not later than that hour, and was accompanied by a guide to show him the road. If not much mistaken the most of his Division must have been on the march before the arrival of Gen. Buell at Savanna. To say the least he showed great want of promptness in not leaving Savanna until 1.30 p.m. after receiving my orders and they given at so early an hour.

In the second paragraph four days are mentioned as the time consumed in making the march over most dreadful roads resulting from previously overflowed bottoms. Four hours were probably intended. Taking this charitable view of the matter the head of his column had made the distance from Savanna to Pittsburg Landing, had made the difficult ferrage at that point and were marching up the bank in just 30 minuets less time than the Gen.'s own statements show, that through great exertion, and anxiety to participate in a battle which they heard raging, took to march up the East bank of the river.

The fire of the rebel artillery began to reach the landing after the head of Gen. Nelsons column had assended the hill at Pittsburg Landing.

The semicircle of artillery spoken of had been established at an early hour in the day and were not unsupported at any time. The left of the artillery spoken of was not turned at any time and the abrupt nature of the ground and depth of backwater in the slew immediately in front of the artillery would have completely checked any attempt at such a movement. The gunners never fled from their pieces.

The Gen. shows great fluancy in guessing at the large numbers he found cowering under the river bank when he crossed placing the number at from 7000 to 10,000. I cannot see that he was called on to make any report in this matter but if he did he should have informed himself somewhat of the necessity of men taking that position. He should recollect that large armies had been engaged in a terrible conflict all day compared with which the second days fight was mere childs play, and that the wounded were habitually carried back to the bank of the river. With them necessarily had to come men as nurses and supports who were not injured. This made a very large number; nearly equal to the Generals speculation who were back there lagitimately. In this I do not wish to shield the conduct of many who behaved badly and left the field on the first fire. Some excuse is to be found for them however, in the fact that they were perfectly raw having reached the ground but a few days before and having received their arms for the first time on their way to that scene of conflict.

Gen. Nelson claims to have directed Capt. Guinn of the gunboat service to throw an 8-inch shell in to the enemies camp every ten minuets during the night. This was great presumption in him if true his command being limited to a single division. The fact is I directed the gunboats to fire a shot into where we supposed the enemies camps to be every fifteen minuets and this is the order which was obeyed.

These are some of the glaring misstatements I would call attention. There are others with regard to who gave orders simply personal to myself which I abstain from noticing.

The statement of the killing of Gen. Johnson in front of the 4th Division of the Army of the Ohio on the 7th and of his body being in possession of the Federal troops might be mentioned. Southern official reports show that he was killed at about ½ past 2 O'clock on the day previous and was buried by his own friends.

August – September 1862?

To Jesse Root Grant

Corinth Mississippi
September 17th 1862

Dear Father,

A letter from you and one from Mary was received some time ago which I commenced answer in a letter addressed to

Mary, but being frequently interrupted by matters of business it was laid aside for some days, and finally torn up.—I now have all my time taxed. Although occupying a position attracting but little attention at this time there is probably no garrison more threatened to-day than this.

I expect to hold it and have never had any other feeling either here or elswhere but that of success. I would write you many particulars but you are so imprudent that I dare not trust you with them; and while on this subject let me say a word. I have not an enemy in the world who has done me so much injury as you in your efforts in my defence. I require no defenders and for my sake let me alone. I have heard this from various sources and persons who have returned to this Army and did not know that I had parents living near Cincinnati have said that they found the best feeling existing towards every place except there. You are constantly denouncing other General officers and the inference with people naturally is that you get your impressions for me.

Do nothing to correct what you have already done but for the future keep quiet on this subject.

Mary wrote to me about an appointment for Mr. Nixon! I have nothing in the world to do with any appointments, no power to make and nothing to do with recommending except for my own Staff. That is now already full.

If I can do anthing in the shape of lending any influence I may possess in Mr. Nixons behalf I will be most happy to do so on the strength of what Mary says in commendation, and should be most happy if it could so be that our lot would cast us near each other.

I do not know what Julia is going to do. I want her to go to Detroit and board. She has many pleasant acquaintances there and she would find good schools for the children.

I have no time for writing and scarsely to look over the telegraphic columns of the newspapers.

My love to all at home.

ULYS.

To Stephen A. Hurlbut

By Telegraph from Lagrange   *9 1862*

To Maj Gen Hurlbut

Refuse all permits to come south of Jackson for the present The Isrealites especially should be kept out   what troops have you now exclusive of stevensons brigade

U S Grant
Maj Genl

November 9, 1862

To Jesse Root Grant

Lagrange Ten.
Nov. 23d 1862

Dear Father,

A batch of letters from Covington, and among them one from you is just received.

I am only sorry your letter, and all that comes from you speaks so condescendingly of every thing Julia says, writes or thinks. You without probably being aware of it are so prejudiced against her that she could not please you. This is not pleasing to me.

Your letter speaks of Fred.s illness. Fred is a big stout looking boy but he is not healthy. The difference that has always been made between him and the other children has had a very bad influence on him. He is sensitive and notices these things. I hope no distinction will be made and he will in time recover from his diffidence caused by being scolded so much.

I wish you would have a bottle of Cod liver oil bought and have Fred. take a table spoonful three times a day in part of a glass of ale each dose. Dr. Pope of St. Louis says that he requires that treatment every little while and will continue to do so whilst he is growing. One of Mary's letters asks me for some explaination, about the Iuka battle. You can say that my report of that battle, and also of Corinth & the Hatchee went to Washington several weeks ago and I suppose will be printed. These will answer her question fully.

Before you receive this I will again be in motion. I feel every confidance of success but I know that a heavy force is now to my front. If it is my good fortune to come out successfully I will try and find time to write Mary a long letter.

Julia joins me in sending love to all of you.

ULYSSES.

To John C. Pemberton

Head Quarters, 13th Army Corps.
Dept of the Tennessee.
Oxford, Miss. Dec 14, 1862

Lieut. Gen. Pemberton,
Commdg Confederate Forces
Jackson, Tenn.
Genl:

Your communication in relation to the case of Col. Hedgepath is just received.

I did not even know that Col. Hedgepath was in the Hospital at Memphis and cannot answer as to the misfortunes that may possibly have befallen him in the way of losses sustained. Where there are large Armies, and particularly in large cities, there are always persons ready to *steal* where there is an opportunity occurs and especially have many of our Federal troops who have been so unfortunate as to fall into the hands of the Southern Army found this true.

As to the other, or any other bad treatment towards Col. Hedgepath you will find, when the facts are before you he has received none.

All prisoners of War are humanely treated by the Federal authorities and many a wounded or sick soldier has remonstrated against being sent back for exchange on the ground that the treatment received at the hands of the Union authorities was so much better than they could get among what they denominated their friends.

All prisoners who desire it are sent by the first opportunity that occurs to Vicksburg for exchange. Sick and wounded are paroled in Hospital and as soon as able to travel are furnished passes out of our lines, or are sent with other prisoners to the Depot agreed upon for exchange.

Unless there is some good reason for it Col. Hedgepath has not nor will not be made an exception to the rule

I am, Sir, Very Respectfully
Your Obt. Servant.
U. S. GRANT
Maj Genl.

To Henry W. Halleck

Head Quarters, Dept. of the Ten.
Before Vicksburg, Feb.y 18th 1863.

Maj. Gen. H. W. Halleck,
Gen. in Chief, Washington D. C.
Gen.

The work upon the canal here is progressing as well as possible with the excessively bad weather and high water we have had to contend against. Most of the time that troops could be out atall has been expended in keeping the water out of our camps. Five good working days would enable the force here to complete the canal sixty feet wide and of sufficient depth to admit any vessel here. Judging from the past it is fare to calculate that it will take ten or twelve days in which to get these five working days. Three more perhaps should be allowed from the fact that the work is being done by soldiers the most of whom under the most favorable circumstances could not come up to the calculations of the Engineer officers. McPherson's Army Corps is at Lake Providence prossecuting the work there. They could not be of any service in helping on the work here because there are already as many men as can be employed on it, and then he would have to go five or six miles above to find land above water to encamp on. I am using a few hundred contrabands on the work here, but have been compelled to prohibit any more coming in. Humanity dictates this policy. Planters have mostly deserted their plantations taking with them all their able bodied negroes and leaving the old and very young. Here they could not have shelter nor assurances of transportation when we leave.

I have sent one Division of troops from Helena to join the Yazoo expedition under Lt. Col. Wilson. Col. Wilson's last report was sent you a few days ago. If successful they will destroy the rail-road bridges at Grenada and capture or destroy all the transports in the Yazoo and tributaries.

The health of this command is not what is represented in the public press. It is as good as any previous calculation could have prognosticated. I believe too there is the best of feeling and greatest confidance of success among them. The greatest draw back to the spirits of the troops has been the great delay in paying them. Many of them have families at home who are no doubt in a suffering condition for want of the amounts due those bound for their support.

> I am Gen. very respectfully
> your obt. svt.
> U. S. GRANT
> Maj. Gen. Com

To David D. Porter

> Feb.y 26th 1863.

Admiral,

I have changed the signal to the following. One rocket will denote the presence, in sight, of a rebel boat; two guns the presence of more than one. The same signals with the addition of a single gun that they are passing up stream above Warrenton and rapid firing that they are passing the batteries. Three rockets will indicate that rebel boats have turned back and followed by a single gun afterwards that. they have come to anchor below. Entire silence after three rockets will indicate that they have passed out of sight.

> Very respectfully
> U. S. GRANT
> Maj. Gen.

To Isaac F. Quinby

Before Vicksburgh March 23d 1863

Brig Gen J. F. Quinby
Comm'dg. Yazoo Expedition

Learning of the slow progress in getting small steamers suitable for your expedition, I wrote to Gen McPherson to collect all of his forces not already in the Yazoo Pass and bring them to where he is.

Since sending this order I have learned of the arrival of a number of small boats at Helena and the probability that Smith's Division had started. As he may have made a start but not got so far but what orders could readily be sent for his return I hasten to change this and will instruct Gen Prentiss if Smith has gone to let him go. You will understand from Prentiss at the same time you receive this what force you are to expect. It is highly desirable that your expedition should clear out the Yazoo river and if possible effect a a lodgment from which we could act against Haines Bluff. You will be the best judge whether this can be done. You will also have to be governed by the disposition of the Navy to co-operate. We cannot order them but only ask their co-operation. I leave to you judgment to say whether the expedition with you should return from Greenwood or prosecute the attack further   It may be necessary for you to take more or less supplies from the citizens along the route but in doing so prevent all the plundering and destruction of property you can and only permit such things to be taken as are actually required for the use of the Army. Admiral Porter started about one week ago to try and reach the Yazoo river below Yazoo City with five Gunboats. His route was by way of Yazoo river to Steele's Bayou up the latter to Black Bayou through that to Deer Creek and up it to Rolling Fork thence across to Big Sunflower and down the Sunflower to the Yazoo. I sent Sherman with an army force of about equal to yours to co-operate. If successful they will come in below the enemy you contending against and between the two forces you would find no further difficulty before reaching the ground I so much desire. I have not heard from this expedition for several days. At last accounts they had got up Deer Creek but had not got through Rolling

Fork I cannot promise success to this expedition but it is possible that if it does get through such consternation will be created among the inhabitants and the troops on the Yazoo that you will hear of it. Feeling great anxiety for your success or speedy return if the object of the expedition shall prove impraticable

U S GRANT
Maj Genl

P. S. If not sanguine of success return immediately with your entire force and fleet. Banks is at Port Hudson but he writes with a force inadequate to the task. If I now had the forces in the Yazoo river upper and lower and I could send an army corps to co-operate with Banks and the two to-gether would easily take the place and every thing on the river from there to Warrenton just below Vicksburgh. The Lake Providence route through to Red river has proven a success and it is by this route I would send them I have neither transports or Gunboats suitable for this expedition all of them being in the Yazoo

U. S. G

To Thomas W. Knox

Head Quarters, Department of the Tennessee,
Before Vicksburg, April 6th 1863.

Thomas W. Knox,
Correspondent New York Herald.—
Sir.—

The letter of the President of the United States, authorizing you to return to these Head Quarters, and remain, with my consent, or leave if such consent is withheld, has been shown me.

You came here first in positive violation of an order from General Sherman. Because you were not pleased with his treatment of Army followers, who had violated his order, you attempted to break down his influence with his command, and to blast his reputation with the public. You made insinuations against his sanity, and said many things which were untrue, and so far as your letter had influence, calculated to effect the public service unfavorably.

General Sherman is one of the ablest Soldiers and purest men in the country. You have attacked him, and been sentenced to expulsion from this Department for the offence. Whilst I would conform to the slightest wish of the President, where it was founded upon a fair representation of both sides of any question, my respect for General Sherman is such, that in this case I must decline unless General Sherman first gives his consent to your remaining.

> I am, Sir,
> Yours &c.
> U. S. GRANT
> Maj. Gen.

To Stephen A. Hurlbut

> Head Quarters, Dept. of the Ten.
> Millikin's Bend, La, Apl. 9th/63

Maj. Gen. S. A. Hurlbut,
Comd.g 16th Army Corps,
Gen.

Suppress the entire press of Memphis for giving aid and comfort to the enemy by publishing in their columns every move made here by troops and every work commenced. Arrest the Editors of the Bulliten and send him here a prisoner, under guard, for his publication of present plans via New Carthage & Grand Gulf.

I am satisfied that much has found its way into the public press through that incoragibly gassy man Col. Bissell of the Eng. Regt. I sent him to you thinking he could not do so much harm there as here. His tongue will have to be tied if there is anything going on where he is which you dont want made public. I feel a strong inclination to arrest him and trust to find evidence against him afterwards.

> Very respectfully
> U. S. GRANT
> Maj. Gen Com

To Julia Dent Grant

Millikin's Bend La.
April 20th 1863.

Dear Julia,

I want you to go to St. Louis and stay there until you get the deed from your brother John for the 60 acres of land *where our house* is, and have it recorded. Also get the deed for 40 acres where your brother Lew's. house is and have it recorded. Be shure and have this done right. Then lease out the farm to some good and prompt tenant, for five years, giving them the privilege of taking off every stick of timber and puting the whole place in cultivation. Bind them to take care of the house, fences and fruit trees. Place Bass Sappington or Pardee in charge to collect the rent and when all is done say to your father that the house is for his use as long as he wants it and the rents are to go to him for the other place.

If John Dent wants to go to Calafornia you may offer him $1600 for 40 acres adjoining the 60 acres. If he desires this have this deed recorded also before you leave. I want it distinctly understood however that I do not desire this trade and only make the offer to enable him to go and look after other property he has. If it was not that I am poor and have not a dollar except my savings in the last two years I would not hesitate to furnish him all the necessary money without any other guarantee than the conciousnous that I had done him a favor.

In case you make this trade it will be necessary for you to go to Galena to get the money. You can explain to Orvil that I have purchased property and paid $3000 on it and have to pay $1600 more. You can settle the difference they make out against me at the store but try and have Lank. who kept the books, to make up the account. Ask Orvil how brother Simps estate was settled. Inform him that I should never have mentioned it in the world but some of them are seting so much higher merit upon money than any other earthly consideration that I feel it a duty to protect myself. If you go to Galena be patient and even tempered. Do not expose yourself to any misconstruction from a hasty remark. Be firm however. Give up no notes except what you get cashed unless they pay the whole with the interest accrued. In that case you can allow them for what they say I owe with the same interest upon the debt they pay you. Should you however get but a part of the money give only the notes they pay. Tell Orvil that on final settlement I will allow the same interest that I receive. So long as they hold money of mine they need not be afraid to trust me.

This business all settled you can visit any of your friends until you hear that I am in Vicksburg when you can join me as soon as possible. Try and engage a Governess to teach the children, one who speaks German if possible. Do not make a possitive bargain however until you write to me.

U. S. GRANT

To Jesse Root Grant

Millikins Bend La
April 21st 1863.

Dear Father,

Your letter of the 7th of April has just this day reached me. I hasten to answer your interogitories.

When I left Memphis with my past experiance I prohibited trade below Helena. Trade to that point had previously been opened by the Treasury Department. I give no permits to buy Cotton and if I find any one engaged in the business I send them out of the Department and seize their Cotton for the Government. I have given a few families permission to leave the country and to take with them as far as Memphis their Cotton. In doing this I have been decieved by unprincipled speculators who have smuggled themselves along with the Army in spite of orders prohibiting them and have been compelled to suspend this favor to persons anxious to get out of Dixie.

I understand that Govt has adopted some plan to regulate geting the Cotton out of the country. I do not know what plan they have adopted but am satisfied than any that can be adopted, except for Government to take the Cotton themselves, and rule out speculators altogether will be a bad one. I feel all Army followers who are engaged in speculating off the misfortunes of their country, and really aiding the enemy more than they possibly could do by open treason, should be drafted at once and put in the first forlorn hope.

I move my Head Quarters to New Carthage to-morrow. This whole country is under water except strips of land behind the levees along the river and bayous and makes opperations almost impossible. I struck upon a plan which I thought would give me a foot hold on the East bank of the Miss. before the enemy could offer any great resistance. But the difficulty of the last one & a half miles next to Carthage makes it so tedious that the enemy cannot fail to discover my plans. I am doing my best and am full of hope for complete success. Time has been consumed but it was absolutely impossible to avoid it. An attack upon the rebel works at any time since I arrived here must inevitably resulted in the loss of a large portion of my Army if not in an entire defeat. There was but two points of land, Hains Bluff & Vicksburg itself, out of water any place from which troops could march. These are thoroughly fortified and it would be folly to attack them as long as there is a prospect of turning their position. I never expect to have an army under my command whipped unless it is very badly whipped and cant help it but I have no idea of being driven to do a desperate or foolish act by the howlings of the press. It is painful to me as a matter of course to see the course pursued by some of the papers. But there is no one less disturbed by them than myself. I have never saught a large command and have no ambitious ends to accomplish. Was it not for the very natural desire of proving myself equal to anything expected of me, and the evidence my removal would afford that I was not thought equal to it, I would gladly accept a less responsible position. I have no desire to be an object of envy or jealousy, nor to have this war continue. I want, and will do my part towards it, to put down the rebellion in the shortest possible time without expecting or desiring any other recognition than a quiet approval of my course. I beg that you will destroy this letter. At least do not show it.

Julia and the children are here but will go up by the first good boat. I sent for her to come down and get instructions about some business I want attended to and see no immediate prospect of being able to attend to myself.

ULYSSES

To Peter J. Osterhaus

Head Quarters, Dept. of the Ten.
Near Vicksburg, May 29th 1863,

Brig. Gen. Osterhaus,
Comd.g at Black River Bridge,
Gen.

Burn up the remainder of Black River Bridge. Make details from the Negroes collected about your camp, and also from the troops and have as much of the road taken up, East of the river, as you can. Pile the ties up and lay the rails across them and burn them up. Wherever there is a bridge, or trestle work, as far East as you send troops have them destroyed. Effectually destroy the road, and particularly the rails, as far East as you can.

Very respectfully
U. S. GRANT
Maj. Gen. Com

To Jesse Root Grant

Vicksburg, July 6th 1863

Dear Father,

Vicksburg has at last surrendered after a siege of over forty days. The surrender took place on the morning of the 4th of July. I found I had continuously underestimated the force of the enemy both in men and Artillery. The number of prisoners surrendered was Thirty thousand & two hundred. The process of parolling is so tedious however that many who are desirous of getting to their homes will escape before the paroling officers get around to them. The Arms taken is about 180 pieces of Artillery and over 30 000 stand of small arms.

The enemy still had about four days rations of flour & meat and a large quantity of sugar.

The weather now is excessively warm and the roads intolerably dusty. It can not be expected under these circumstances that the health of this command can keep up as it has done. My troops were not allowed one hours idle time after the surrender but were at once started after other game.

My health has continued very good during the campaign which has just closed. — Remember me to all at home.

ULYSSES

To Lorenzo Thomas

Vicksburg, Mississippi
July 11th, 1863.

Brig.-Genl. L. Thomas,
Adj. Gen. of the Army.
General:

Your letter of the 26th of last month, enclosing a letter from Mrs Duncan, was received on the 9th. I have ordered an investigation of the matters complained of but think there must be some mistake about the acts complained of having been committed. About the date of your letter Mr Duncan the husband of Mrs Mary Duncan, called on me for a permit to ship from the north, supplies of various kinds for the use of his negroes. He then thanked me for the protection and courtesy that had been extended to him by the Federal Authorities in this Department. He made no complaint of even having been annoyed.

All new organizations of negro regiments have been broken up and their men transferred to those regiments for which you had appointed officers. I found that the old regiments never could be filled so long as authority was granted to form new ones. I am anxious to get as many of these negro regiments as possible and to have them full and completely equipped. The large amount of arms and equipments captured here will enable me to equip these regiments as rapidly as they can be formed.

I am particularly desirous of organizing a regiment of Heavy Artillerists from the negroes to garrison this place, and shall do so as soon as possible, asking the authority and commissions for the officers named after it is organized. I will ask now if this course will be approved.

I caused an informal investigation to be had in the case of Col. Shepard. The result of it was, his release and restoration to duty. I will send the proceedings to your office for your information. I am satisfied that the whole difficulty arose from the outrageous treatment of the Black troops by some of the white ones, and the failure of their officers to punish the perpetrators when they were reported. Becoming exasperated Col. Shepard took the punishment in his own hands.

The long line of Plantations from Lake Providence to Millikens Bend, it has been perfectly impossible to give perfect protection to, during the siege of Vicksburg. Besides the gunboats, negro troops and six regiments of white troops left west of the Mississippi River in consequence of these Plantations being there, I sent an additional Brigade from the investing Army, and that at a time when the government was straining every nerve to send me troops to insure the success of the enterprise against Vicksburg. All has not been availing. I can now clean out the Tensas, and Bayou Macon country so that there will be but little difficulty in protecting what is left of the Plantations.

There are two of the Commissioners appointed by you, Field and Livermore who are doing a great deal of harm. The limits of a private letter would not suffice to describe their character, selfishness misrepresentations and impracticable characteristics for doing good to any cause. I have thought seriously of removing them from my Department and appointing officers to act in their stead until successors could be appointed by proper authority. Capt. Strickle I believe to be honest and enthusiastic in the cause which he is serving. He is probaby influenced by old theories of abolishing slavery and elevating the negro but withal very well qualified to carry out orders as he receives them without reference to his private views. The capture of Vicksburg has proved a bigger thing than I supposed it would. There was over thirty one thousand rebel troops still left when we entered the city. The number of small arms will reach 50,000 stands I think, and the amount of Ordnance and Ordnance stores is enormous. Since crossing the Miss. River an army of (60,000) sixty thousand men has, in the various battles been killed wounded, captured, and scattered so as to be lost to the Confederacy, and an armament for an army of (100,000) one hunderd thousand men has departed from there forever.

My surplus troops were held in a position menacing Johnston ready to move at a moments notice when Vicksburg should fall. The moment a surrendered was agreed upon the order was given. I hope to hear to day that Johnston's forces have been broken to pieces and much of his munition of War abandoned   I have not heard from Sherman since the morning of 9th. He was then near Jackson skirmishing with the cavalry of the enemy. What was intended as a private letter General has spun out into a long semi official one which I hope you will excuse

Thanking you kindly for the assurance given in your letter of the satisfaction my course has given the Administration I remain

Your very oddt Servt
U. S. GRANT
Major General

To Salmon P. Chase

Head Qrs. Dept. of the Ten.
Vicksburg Miss. July 21st 1863.

Hon. S. P. Chase
Sec. of the Treasury,
Sir:

Your letter of the 4th inst. to me, enclosing copy of letter of same date to Mr. Mellen; Spl. Agt. of the Treasury is just received.—My Asst. Adj. Gen. by whom I shall send this letter is about starting for Washington hence I shall be very short in my reply.

My experiance in West Tennessee has convinced me that any trade whatever with the rebellious states is weakening to us of at least Thirty three per cent of our force. No matter what the restrictions thrown around trade if any whatever is allowed it will be made the means of supplying to the enemy all they want. Restrictions if lived up to make trade unproffit-able and hence none but dishonest men go into it. I will ven-ture that no honest man has made money in West Tennessee in the last year whilst many fortunes have been made there during the time.

The people in the Mississippi Valley are now nearly subju-gated. Keep trade out for but a few months and I doubt not but that the work of subjugation will be so complete that trade can be opened freely with the states of Arkansas, La. & Mississippi. That the people of these states will be more anx-ious for the enforcement, and protection, of our laws than the people of the loyal states. They have experienced the misfor-tune of being without them and are now in a most happy condition to appreciate their blessing.

No theory of my own will ever stand in the way of my executing, in good faith, any order I may receive from those in authority over me. But my position has given me an op-portunity of seeing what could not be know by persons away from the scene of War and I venture therefore to suggest great caution in opening trade with rebels.

I am sir, very respectfully
your obt. svt.
U. S. GRANT
Maj. Gen. Com

To Charles W. Ford

Vicksburg Mississippi,
July 28th 1863.

Dear Ford,

It will soon be time now for schools to open and as I am entirely broken up of a home from which to send my children I must look around for a placc for them in time. If possible I would rather place my two oldest boys with Mr. Wyman of St. Louis. Not knowing his initials or address I want to ask the favor of you to see Mr. Wyman for me and know if he can take them and his conditions.

The oldest boy is thirteen years old and the other eleven. I want them to board with Mr. Wyman and have their washing done there also. My little girl I will send to Mrs. Boggs.

If you will attend to this for me you will place me under renewed obligations.

This breaking up of families is hard. But such is War. I have much less to complain of however than the majority. In this worlds goods I had nothing to loose, and in escaping wounds, or loss of health, I have been so far fortunate.

Everything is now quiet along the Mississippi. But there is still work for the Army. Little side expeditions will be required to clean out the country West of the Miss.—The state of Miss. is now completely subjugated. It would be easyer to preserve law and order in this state now than in Mo. or Ky. so far as the inhabitants are concerned. Ark. & Louisiana will soon be in the same happy frame of mind.

I shall hope to hear from you soon.

Yours Truly
U. S. GRANT

To Abraham Lincoln

Cairo Illinois
August 23d 1863,

His Excellency A. Lincoln
President of the United States,
Sir:

Your letter of the 9th inst. reached me at Vicksburg just as I was about starting for this place. Your letter of the 13th of July was also duly received.

After the fall of Vicksburg I did incline very much to an immediate move on Mobile. I believed then the place could be taken with but little effort, and with the rivers debouching there, in our possession, we would have such a base to opperate from on the very center of the Confederacy as would make them abandon entirely the states bound West by the Miss. I see however the importance of a movement into Texas just at this time.

I have reinforced Gen. Banks with the 13th Army Corps comprising ten Brigades of Infantry with a full proportion of Artillery.

I have given the subject of arming the negro my hearty support. This, with the emancipation of the negro, is the heavyest blow yet given the Confederacy. The South rave a greatdeel about it and profess to be very angry. But they were united in their action before and with the negro under subjection could spare their entire white population for the field. Now they complain that nothing can be got out of their negroes.

There has been great difficulty in getting able bodied negroes to fill up the colored regiments in consequence of the rebel cavalry runing off all that class to Georgia and Texas. This is especially the case for a distance of fifteen or twenty miles on each side of the river. I am now however sending two expeditions into Louisiana, one from Natchez to Harrisonburg and one from Goodriche's Landing to Monroe, that I expect will bring back a large number. I have ordered recruiting officers to accompany these expeditions. I am also moving a Brigade of Cavalry from Tennessee to Vicksburg which will enable me to move troops to a greater distance into the interior and will facilitate materially the *recruiting service*.

Gen. Thomas is now with me and you may rely on it I will give him all the aid in my power. I would do this whether the arming the negro seemed to me a wise policy or not, because it is an order that I am bound to obey and do not feel that in my position I have a right to question any policy of the Government. In this particular instance there is no objection however to my expressing an honest conviction. That is, by arming the negro we have added a powerful ally. They will make good soldiers and taking them from the enemy weaken him in the same proportion they strengthen us. I am therefore most decidedly in favor of pushing this policy to the enlistment of a force sufficient to hold all the South falling into our hands and to aid in capturing more.

Thanking you very kindly for the great favors you have ever shown me I remain, very truly and respectfully

> your obt. svt.
> U. S. GRANT
> Maj. Gn.

To John G. Thompson

> Head Quarters, Dept. of the Ten.
> Vicksburg Miss. Aug. 29th 1863,

Jno. G. Thompson, Esq.
Sir:

Your letter of the 10th inst. asking if "Democratic" newspapers, pamphlets &c. will be allowed to circulate within this Army, and stating that it is reported that such documents are destroyed by Postmasters, Provost Marshals &c. is received.

There can scarsely be a foundation for the report you speak of. If such a thing has ever been done in any one instance it has been without authority and has never been reported to me. This Army is composed of intelligent, reading, thinking men, capable of forming their own judgement, and acting accordingly. Papers of all pursuasions, political and religious, are received and freely read. Even those from Mobile & Selma are some times received and no effort is made to keep them out of the hands of soldiers. I will state however that whilst the troops in this command are left free to vote the ticket of their choice no electioneering or circulation of speaches of a disloyal character, or those calculated to create dissentions, will be tolerated if it can be avoided.

Disloyalty in the North should not be tolerated whilst such an expenditure of blood and treasure is going on to punish it in the South.

> I have the honor to be
> very respectfully
> your obt. svt.
> U. S. GRANT
> Maj. Gen Commanding

To Elihu B. Washburne

Vicksburg Mississippi
August 30th 1863.

Hon. E. B. Washburn,
Dear Sir;

Your letter of the 8th of August, enclosing one from Senator Wilson to you, reached here during my temporary absence to the Northern part of my command; hence my apparent delay in answering. I fully appreciate all Senator Wilson says. Had it not been for Gen. Halleck & Dana I think it altogether likely I would have been ordered to the Potomac. My going could do no possible good. They have there able officers who have been brought up with that army and to import a commander to place over them certainly could produce no good. Whilst I would not possitively disobey an order I would have objected most vehemently to taking that command, or any other except the one I have. I can do more with this army than it would be possible for me to do with any other without time to make the same acquaintance with others I have with this. I know that the soldiers of the Army of the Ten. can be relied on to the fullest extent. I believe I know the exact capacity of every General in my command to command troops, and just where to place them to get from them their best services. This is a matter of no small importance.

Your letter to Gen. Thomas has been delivered to him. I will make an effort to secure a Brigadiership for Col. Chetlain with the colored troops Before such a position will be open however more of these troops will have to be raised. This work will progress rapidly.

The people of the North need not quarrel over the institution of Slavery. What Vice President Stevens acknowledges the corner stone of the Confederacy is already knocked out. Slavery is already dead and cannot be resurrected. It would take a standing Army to maintain slavery in the South if we were to make peace to-day guaranteeing to the South all their former constitutional privileges.

I never was an Abolitionest, not even what could be called anti slavery, but I try to judge farely & honestly and it become patent to my mind early in the rebellion that the North & South could never live at peace with each other except as one nation, and that without Slavery. As anxious as I am to see peace reestablished I would not therefore be willing to see any settlement until this question is forever settled.

Rawlins & Maltby have been appointed Brigadier Generals. These are richly deserved promotions. Rawlins especially is no ordinary man. The fact is had he started in this war in the Line instead of in the Staff there is every probability he would be to-day one of our shining lights. As it is he is better and more favorably know than probably any other officer in the Army who has filled only staff appointments. Some men, to many of them, are only made by their Staff appointments whilst others give respectability to the position. Rawlins is of the latter class.

My kind regards to the citizens of Galena.

Your sincere friend
U. S. GRANT

To Henry W. Halleck

Head Quarters Military Div. of the Miss.
Chattanooga Ten. Oct. 26th 1863.

Maj. Gen. H. W. Halleck,
Gen. in Chief, Washington,
General,

I arrived here in the night of the 23d inst. after a ride on horseback of fifty miles, from Bridgeport, over the worst roads it is possible to concieve of, and through a continuous drenching rain. It is now clear and so long as it continues so it is bearly possible to supply this Army from its present base. But when Winter rains set in it will be impossible.—To guard against the possible contingency of having to abandon Chattanooga for want of supplies every precaution is being taken. The fortifications are being pushed to completion and when done a large part of the troops could be removed back near to their supplies. The troops at Bridgeport are engaged on the rail-road to Jaspar and can finish it in about two weeks. Rails are taken from one of the branch roads which we do not use. This shortens the distance to supplies twelve miles and avoids the worst part of the road in wet weather. Gen. Thomas had also set on foot, before my arrival, a plan for geting possession of the river from a point below Lookout Mountain to Bridgeport. If successful, and I think it will be the question of supplies will be fully settled.

The greatest apprehension I now have is that the enemy will move a large force up the river and force a passage through our line between Blyhe's Ferry and Cotton Port. Should he do this our Artillery horses are not in a condition to enable us to follow and neither is our larder. This part of the line is well watched but I cannot say guarded. To guard against this, in addition to the troops now on that part of the river, I have directed Gen. Thomas to increase the force at McMinnville immediately by one regiment of Cavalry with instructions to collect all the provisions and forage which the enemy would have to depend on for his subsistence, giving vouches payable at once when taken from loyal citizens, and payable at the end of the war, on proof of good conduct, when disloyal. As soon as the fortifications here are sufficiently defensable a Division will be sent there. I have also ordered Sherman to move Easward towards Stevenson until he recieved further orders, guarding nothing this side of Bear Creek, with the view of having his forces in a position to use if the enemy should attempt this move. Should this not be attempted when Sherman gets well up there will be force enough to insure a line for our supplies and enable me to move Thomas to the left thus securing Burnside's position and give a strong hold upon that part of the line from which I suppose a move will finally have to be made to turn Bragg. I think this will have to be done from the Northeast.

This leaves a gap to the West for the enemy to get into Middle Tennessee by, but he has no force to avail himself of this opportunity with except Cavalry, and our Cavalry can be held ready to oppose this.

I will endeavor to study up my position well and post the troops to the best of my judgement to meet all contingencies. I will also endeavor to get the troops in a state of readiness for a forward movement at the earlyest possible day.

What force the enemy have to my front I have no means of judging accurately. Deserters come in every day but their information is limited to their own Brigades or Divisions at furthest. The camps of the enemy are in sight and for the last few days there seems to have been some moving of troops. But where to I cannot tell. Some seem to have gone towards Cleveland whilst others moved in exactly an opposite direction.

> I am Gen. very respectfully
> your obt. svt.
> U. S. GRANT
> Maj. Gen.

To Julia Dent Grant

Chattanooga Tennessee
October 27th 1863.

Dear Julia,

The very hard ride over here and necessary exercise since to gain a full knowledge of location instead of making my injury worse has almost entirely cured me. I now walk without the use of a crutch or cane and mount my horse from the ground without difficulty. This is one of the wildest places you ever saw and without the use of rail-roads one of the most out-of-the way places. To give you an idea of its inaccessibility I have only to state that the waggons with our baggage left Bridge-port, the present rail-road turminus, fifty miles distant by the road they have to travel, on the 23d inst. It is now 10 O'Clock at night of the 27th and they have not yet arrived and I hardly expect them to-morrow. Then too six-mule teams are not loaded with what two would easily pull on ordinary dirt roads. We have not consequently been able to start Messes.— Ross remained back at Nashville to lay in supplies but as he has not yet come up to Bridgeport I suspect he has had to go, or send, to Louisville for them. When they will get up is hard to surmise. I am making a desperate effort however to get possession of the river from here to Bridgeport and if I do it will facilitate bringing supplies very much.

There are but very few people here and those few will have to leave soon. People about Vicksburg have not seen War yet, or at least not the suffering brought on by war.

I have received no line from you yet. I feel very anxious to hear from the children. Tell Fred and Buck they must write at least one letter each week to you or me.

Kisses for yourself and Jess.

ULYS.

When do you think of starting on your trip to Ohio? You ought to start soon or you will not be able to go this Fall.

U.

To Julia Dent Grant

Chattanooga Tennessee,
November 2d 1863,

Dear Julia,

I have received your second letter stating that you had not yet heard from me. Dr. Kittoe wrote to you the next day after our arrival and I wrote the same or next day. Since that I have written several times. You still ask to come to Nashville! I do not know what in the world you will do there. There is not a respectable hotel and I leave no one of my Staff there. You would be entirely among strangers and at an expensive and disagreeable place to live. Bowers is there now, but is there only to close up unfinished business and to pack up and dispose of papers useless to carry into the field. This is just as unsuitable a place for you to be as as Millikins Bend. More so for there you could get by Steamer and here you cannot.

I see the papers again team with all sorts of rumors of the reason for recent changes. This time however I do not see myself abused. I do not know whether this is a good omen or not. I have been so accustomed to seeing at least a portion of the press against me that I rather feel lost when not attacked from some quarter. The best of feeling seems to prevail with the Army here since the change. Thomas has the confidance of all the troops of Rosecrans late command. The consolidation of the three Departments into one command also seems to give general satisfaction.

I hope you have had a pleasant visit to Ohio. If I had thought of it I would have advised you to have asked Alice Tweed to have accompanied you. I hope you saw father & mother as you passed through Cincinnati? I would not have asked you to cross the river to see them. I know mother will feel very badly if she does not get to see you & Jess. Kiss the little rascal for me. Tell him to be a good boy and learn his lessons so that he can write letters to me. Kisses for yourself dear Julia.

ULYS.

To J. Russell Jones

Chattanooga Dec. 5th 1863,

Dear Jones,

Your letter of the 25th reached here about the time closing scenes of the late battles were taking place. I regret that you could not be here to witness the grand panorama. I presume a battle never took place on so large a scale where so much of it could be seen, or where every move proved so successful; and out of doors where there was an outlet to retreat by. An Army never was whipped so badly as Bragg was. So far as any opposition the enemy could make I could have marched to Atlanta or any other place in the Confederacy. But I was obliged to rescue Burnside. Again I had not rations to take nor the means of taking them and this mountain country will not support an Army. Altogether I feel well satisfied and the Army feel that they have accomplished great things. Well they may. By the end of this month I will have enough due me to pay you what you have laid out for me. In the mean time can you borrow, at my expense, the amount? It is rather hard to ask a friend to make an investment for you and then get him to borrow the money to make it. But I am so situated that I cannot attend to my own private affairs and hope I am not giving you too much trouble.

J. E. Smith, Rawlins, Dr. Kittoe, and the Galenaites are well and desire to be remembered.

Yours Truly
U. S. GRANT
Maj. Gen.

To Barnabas Burns

Chattanooga Tennessee,
December 17th 1863.

B. Burns, Esq.
Chairman Dem. Cen. Com.
Dear Sir:

Your letter of the 7th inst. asking if you will be at liberty to use my name before the convention of the "War Democracy", as candidate for the office of the Presidency is just received. —The question astonishes me. I do not know of anything I have ever done or said which would indicate that I could be a candidate for any office whatever within the gift of the people.

I shall continue to do my duty, to the best of my ability, so long as permitted to remain in the Army, supporting whatever Administration may be in power, in their endeavor to suppress the rebellion and maintain National unity, and never desert it because my vote, if I had one, might have been cast for different candidates.

Nothing likely to happen would pain me so much as to see my name used in connection with a political office. I am not a candidate for any office nor for favors from any party. Let us succeed in crushing the rebellion, in the shortest possible time, and I will be content with whatever credit may then be given me, feeling assured that a just public will award all that is due.

Your letter I take to be private. Mine is also private. I wish to avoid notoriety as far as possible, and above all things desire to be spaired the pain of seeing my name mixed with politics. Do not therefore publish this letter but wherever, and by whatever party, you hear my name mentioned in connection with the candidacy for any office, say that you know from me direct that I am not "in the field," and cannot allow my name to be used before any convention.

> I am, with great respect,
> your obt. svt.
> U. S. GRANT

To Henry W. Halleck

Head Quarters Mil. Div. of the Miss.
Nashville Ten. Jan.y 15th 1864

Maj. Gen. H. W. Halleck,
Gen. in Chief, Washington D.C.
General,

I reached here the evening of the 12th on my return from East Tennessee. I felt a particular anxiety to have Longstreet driven from East Tennessee, and went there with the intention of taking such steps as would secure this end. I found however a large part of Foster's command suffering for want of clothing, especially shoes, so that in any advance not to exceed two thirds of his men could be taken. The difficulties of supplying them are such that to send reinforcements, at present, would be to put the whole on insufficient rations for their support. Under these circumstances I only made such changes of position of troops as would place Foster nearer the enemy when he did get in a condition to move, and would open to us new foraging grounds and diminish those held by the enemy. Having done this and seen the move across the Holston, at Strawberry Plains, commenced, I started on my return via Cumberland Gap, Barboursville, London & Richmond to Lexington Ky. The weather was intensly cold the thermometer standing a portion of the time below zero. But being desirous of seeing what portion of our supplies might be depended upon over that route, and it causing no loss of time, I determined to make the trip. From the personal inspection made I am satisfied that no portion of our supplies can be hawled by teams from Camp Nelson. Whilst forage could be got from the country to supply teams at the different stations on the road some supplies could be got through in this way. But the time is nearly at an end when this can be done.

On the first rise of the Cumberland 1.200,000 rations will be sent to the mouth of the Big South Fork. These I hope teams will be able to take. The distance to hawl is materially shortened, the road is said to be better than that by Cumberland Gap, and it is a new route and will furnish forage for a time. In the mean time troops in East Tennessee must depend for subsistence on what they can get from the country, and the little we can send them from Chattanooga. The rail road is now complete into Chattanooga and in a short time, say three weeks, the road by Decatur & Huntsville will be complete. Steamers then can be spared to supply the present force in E. Ten. well and to accumulate a store to support a large army for a short time if it should become necessary to send one there in the Spring. This contingency however I will do every thing in my power to avert.

Two steamers ply now tolerably regularly between Chattanooga and Loudon. From the latter place to Mossy Creek we have rail road. Some clothing has already reached Knoxville since my departure. A good supply will be got there with all dispatch. These, if necessary, and subsistence can by possibility be obtained, I will send force enough to secure Longstreets expulsion.

Sherman has gone down the Miss. to collect at Vicksburg all the force that can be spared for a separate movement from the Miss. He will probably have ready by the 24th of this month a force of 20.000 men that could be used East of the river. But to go West so large a force could not be spared.

The Red River, and all the streams West of the Miss. are now too low for navigation. I shall direct Sherman therefore to move out to Meredian with his spare force, the Cavalry going from Corinth and destroy the roads East & South of there so effectually that the enemy will not attempt to rebuild them during the rebellion. He will then return unless the opportunity of going into Mobile with the force he has appears perfectly plain. Owing to the large number of veterans furloughed I will not be able to do more at Chattanooga than to threaten an advance and try to detain the force now in Thomas' front.

Sherman will be instructed, whilst left with large discretionary powers, to take no extra hazard of loosing his army, or of getting it crippled too much for efficient service in the Spring.

I look upon the next line for me to secure to be that from Chattanooga to Mobile, Montgomery & Atlanta being the important intermediate points. To do this large supplies must be secured on the Tennessee River so as to be independent of the rail-roads from here to the Tennessee for a conciderable length of time. Mobile would be a second base. The destruction which Sherman will do the roads around Meredian will be of material importance to us in preventing the enemy from drawing supplies from Mississippi and in clearing that section of all large bodies of rebel troops.

I do not look upon any points except Mobile in the South and the Tennessee in the North as presenting practicable starting points from which to opperate against Atlanta and Montgomery. They are objectionable as starting points, to be all under one command from the fact that the time it will take to communicate from one to the other will be so great. But Sherman or McPherson, one of whom would be entrusted with the distant command, are officers of such experience and reliability that all objection on this score, except that of enabling the two armies to act as one unit, would be removed. The same objection will exist, probably not to so great an extent however, if a movement is made in more than one column. This will have to be with an army of the size we will be compelled to use.

Heretofore I have abstained from suggesting what might be done in other commands than my own, in co-operation with it, or even to think much over the matter. But as you have kindly asked me in your letter of the 8th of Jan.y, only just received, for an interchange of views on our present situation, I will write you again, in a day or two, going out side of my own operations.

> I am General, very respectfully,
> your obt. svt.
> U. S. GRANT
> Maj. Gen.

To George H. Thomas

Nashville Jany 16th 12 30 a m

Maj Genl Thomas

Longstreet is said to be marching towards Knoxville.

Enemy reinforced by one Div from Ewells Corps with another expected.

I have advised Foster to keep his force between Longstreet and you.

Should he be forced back south of the Tenn it may become necessary to reinforce him from your command.

In that case I would fill the place of troops taken away from Maj Genl W T Shermans Command

Send Foster all the provisions you can.

The question of provisions alone may decide the fate of East Tenn

Maj Genl GRANT

To Henry W. Halleck

Confidential   Head Quarters, Mil. Div. of the Miss.

Nashville Ten. Jan.y 19th 1864,

Maj. Gen. H. W. Halleck,
Gen. in Chief of the Army,
Washington, D. C.
General,

I would respectfully suggest whether an abandonment of all previously attempted lines to Richmond is not advisable, and in line of these one be taken further South. I would suggest Raleigh North Carolina as the objective point and Suffolk as the starting point. Raleigh once secured I would make New Bern the base of supplies until Wilmington is secured. A moving force of sixty thousand men would probably be required to start on such an expedition. This force would not have to be increased unless Lee should withdraw from his present position. In that case the necessity for so large a force on the Potomac would not exist.

A force moving from Suffolk would destroy first all the roads about Weldon, or even as far north as Hicksford. From Weldon to Raleigh they would scarsely meet with serious opposition. Once there the most interior line of rail way still left to the enemy, in fact the only one they would then have, would be so threatened as to force him to use a large portion of his army in guarding it. This would virtually force an evacuation of Virginia and indirectly of East Tennessee. It would throw our Armies into new fields where they could partially live upon the country and would reduce the stores of the enemy. It would cause thousands of the North Carolina troops to desert and return to their homes. It would give us possession of many Negroes who are now indirectly aiding the rebellion. It would draw the enemy from Campaigns of their own choosing, and for which they are prepared, to new lines of operations never expected to become necessary. It would effectually blockade Wilmington, the port now of more value to the enemy than all the balance of their sea coast. It would enable operations to commence at once by removing the war to a more southern climate instead of months of inactivity in winter quarters. Other advantages might be cited which would be likely to grow out of this plan, but these are enough. From your better opportunities of studying the country, and the Armies, that would be involved in this plan, you will be better able to judge of the practicability of it than I possibly can.

I have written this in accordance with what I understood to be an invitation from you to express my views about Military operations and not to insist that any plan of mine should be carried out. Whatever course is agreed upon I shall always believe is at least intended for the best and until fully tested will hope to have it prove so.

> I am General, very respectfully your obt. svt.
> U. S. GRANT
> Maj. Gen.

To Rufus Ingalls

Nashville, Ten.
Feb.y 16th 1864.

Dear Ruf,

Your very welcom letter was received by due course of Mail and read with great interest and full intention to answer it right off. But since that time I have been moving about so much that I have neglected it. I have often wished that I could have you here to run the machinery of your department. This was on account of old acquaintance however. The Quartermaster's Dept. here has been well and satisfactorily managed so far as the heads are concerned. I did once apply to have you sent here as chief but it was thought you could not be spared from where you are. I have never had any cause of complaint either on account of deficiency in the Staff Deptmts or embarassments trown in the way by the Authorities at Washington. The fact is I believe complaints are generally made to shift responsibility of inaction from commanders to Staff Departments or Washington Authorities. Of course I only speak for the West. I am thankful my lot has not been cast where I could judge for any other section.

I am begining now to make preparations for attack or defence when Spring opens. Two important expeditions are now out, one under Sherman and the other under Thomas, which, if as successful as I expect them to be will have an important bearing on the Spring Campaign.

This war has developed some of our old acquaintances much differently from what we would have expected. Fred. Steele, a good fellow always but you would have supposed not much more, is really a splendid officer and would be fully capable of the management of the Army of the Potomac or any of the Departments. Some who much would have been expected from have proven rather failures. This class I do not like to mention by name.

I believe Ruf. you are still leading a bachilor's life? Don't you regret it? Now I have four children, three boys and one girl, in whos society I feel more enjoyment than I possibly can with any other company. They are a responsibility giving much more pleasure than anxiety. It may not be too late for you yet.

    My respects to such old acquaintances as are with you.

Yours Truly

U. S. GRANT

To William T. Sherman

Nashville Tennessee,

March 4th 1864.

Dear Sherman,

    The bill reviving the grade of Lieut. Gen. in the Army has become a law and my name has been sent to the Senate for the place. I now receive orders to report to Washington, *in person*, immediately, which indicates either a confirmation or a likelyhood of confirmation. I start in the morning to comply with the order but I shall say very distinctly on my arrival there that I accept no appointment which will require me to make that city my Hd Qrs. This however is not what I started out to write about.

    Whilst I have been eminently successful in this War, in at least gaining the confidence of the public, no one feels more than me how much of this success is due to the energy, skill, and harmonious puting forth of that energy and skill, of those who it has been my good fortune to have occupying a subordinate position under me. There are many officers to whom these remarks are applicable to a greater or less degree, proportionate to their ability as soldiers, but what I want is to express my thanks to you and McPherson as *the men* to whom, above all others, I feel indebted for whatever I have had of success. How far your advice and suggestions have been of assistance you know. How far your execution of whatever has been given you to do entitles you to the reward I am receiving you cannot know as well as me. I feel all the gratitude this letter would express, giving it the most flattering construction.

The word *you* I use in the plural intending it for Mc. also. I should write to him, and will some day, but starting in the morning I do not know that I will find time just now.

Your friend
U. S. GRANT
Maj. Gen.

To Julia Dent Grant

Culpepper C. H. Va
March 25th 1864

Dear Julia,

I arrived here yesterday well but as on my former trip brought wet and bad weather. I have not been out of the house today and from appearances shall not be able to go out for several days. At present however I shall find enough to do in doors. From indications I would judge the best of feelings animate all the troops here towards the changes that have been made.—I find mails follow me up with remarkable promptitude. More letters reach me than I can answer.—I hope you have entirely recovered? It is poor enjoyment confined to bed in Washington.—There is one thing I learned in Washington just on leaving that wants attending to. You know breakfast lasts from early in the morning until about noon, and dinner from that time until night. Jess runs about the house loose and seeing the guests at meals thinks each time it is a new meal and that he must necessarily eat. In this way he eats five or six times each day and dips largely into deserts. If not looked after he will make himself sick.—Have you heard from Fred.? No doubt he got home safely. I shall go down to Washington on Sunday. You need not mention it however.—I have sent in my recommendations for staff appointments placing Fred's name among them. I will know by to-morrow if they are approved. No doubt they will be however. I have put in the name of Capt. H. Porter, a very valuable regular officer, about such as Comstock, and still left one vacancy so that if Wilson should fail in his confirmation

I can appoint him. I do not apprehend however any danger of his confirmation.

Kisses for yourself & Jess.

ULYS.

To Benjamin F. Butler

In field Culpeper C. H. Va. Apr. 17th 1864

Maj. Gen. B. F. Butler,
Com'd'g Dept. Va. & N. C.
Fortress Monroe, Va.
General:

Your report of negotiations with Mr. Ould, Confederate States Agent, touching the exchange of prisoners, has been referred to me by the Secretary of War, with directions to furnish you such instructions on the subject, as I may deem proper.

After a careful examination of your report, the only points on which I deem instructions necessary, are—

1st.: Touching the validity of the paroles of the prisoners captured at Vicksburg and Port Hudson.

2nd.: The status of colored prisoners.

As to the *first*. No Arrangement for the exchange of prisoners will be acceded to that does not fully recognize the validity of these paroles, and provide for the release to us, of a sufficient number of prisoners now held by the Confederate Authorities to cancel any balance that may be in our favor by virtue of these paroles. Until there is released to us an equal number of officers and men as were captured and paroled at Vicksburg and Port Hudson, not another Confederate prisoner of war will be paroled or exchanged.

As to the *second*. No distinction whatever will be made in the exchange between white and colored prisoners; the only question being, were they, at the time of their capture, in the military service of the United States. If they were, the same terms as to treatment while prisoners and conditions of release and exchange must be exacted and had, in the case of colored soldiers as in the case of white soldiers.

Non-acquiescence by the Confederate Authorities in both

or either of these propositions, will be regarded as a refusal on their part to agree to the further exchange of prisoners, and will be so treated by us.

> I am General
> Very Respectfully
> Your Obt. Servant
> U. S. GRANT
> Lieut. General

To Julia Dent Grant

Culpepper Apl. 17th 1864

Dear Julia,

Bowers will leave here on Teusday, (Washington on Wednesday) for the West. If your mind is made up to accompany him telegraph me and I will go in to see you off. I dislike however very much going in again. In the first place I do not like being seen so much about Washington. In the second it is not altogether safe. I cannot move without it being known all over the country, and to the enemy who are hovering within a few miles of the rail-road all the time. I do not know that the enemy's attack on the road last Friday was with the view of ketching me, but it was well timed. If you intend going either get Mr. Stanton or Mr. Chadwick to telegraph me.

I understand Jess has been having a fight in the hall! How is that?—Fred has said nothing about Helen coming East. He told me that when you went out she would have to leave your fathers. Kisses for yourself and Jess. Gen. Hunter will deliver this and tell you how we are living. Plain and well, surrounded with mud. I do not say you must go but I see no particular reason for your remaining longer. I shall certainly go to Washington but once more and that will be to see you off. As soon as it is possible for me to settle I will send for you and the children. Should we be so fortunate as to whip the enemy well, I feel that after that there will be no campaigning that I cannot direct from some one place.

Kisses again.

ULYS.

To William T. Sherman

Head Quarters, Armies in the Field,
Culpepper C. H. Va. Apl. 19th 1864

Maj. Gen. W. T. Sherman,
Comd.g Mil. Div. of the Miss.
General,

Since my letter to you I have seen no reason to change any portion of the general plan of Campaign if the enemy remain still and allow us to take the initiative. Rain has continued so uninteruptedly until the last day or two that it will be impossible to move however before the 27th even if no more should fall in the mean time. I think Saturday the 30th will probably be the day for our general move.

Col. Comstock, who will take this, can spend a day with you and fill up many little gaps of information not given in any of my letters.

What I now want more particularly to say is, that if the two main attacks, yours and the one from here, should promise great success the enemy may in a fit of desperation, abandon one part of their line of defence and throw their whole strength upon a single army, believing that a defeat with one victory to sustain them better than a defeat all along their line, and hoping too at the same time that the army meeting with no resistince will rest perfectly satisfied with their laurels having penetrated to a given point south thereby enabling them to throw their force first upon one and then on the other.

With the majority of Military commanders they might do this. But you have had too much experience in traveling light and subsisting upon the country to be caught by any such ruse. I hope my experience has not been thrown away. My directions then would be if the enemy in your front show signs of joining Lee follow him up to the full extent of your ability. I will prevent the concentration of Lee upon your front if it is in the power of this Army to do it.

The Army of the Potomac looks well and so far as I can judge officers and men feel well.

Yours Truly
U. S. GRANT
Lt. Gen.

To Julia Dent Grant

Culpepper April 24th/64

Dear Julia,

I see by the papers you are having a good time in New York. Hope you will enjoy it. But don't forget Jess and loose him in the streets in all the excitement, New York is a big place and you might not find him.—A telegraph dispatch announces that the sword has been voted to me! I am rather sorry for it, or rather regret that my name has been mixed up in such a contest. I could not help it however and therefore have nothing to blame myself for in the matter.

The weather has been very fine here for a few days and dried the roads up so as to make them quite passable. It has commenced raining again however, and is now raining so hard, that it will take a week to bring them back to what they were this afternoon.

Remember me kindly to Col. and Mrs. Hillyer and the children. Kisses for yourself and Jess. I rather expected a letter from you this evening, but none came. I will write to the children to-morrow evening. Don't forget to send me any letters you receive from them. I know they must be anxious to see you back.

ULYS.

To Henry W. Halleck

Head Qrs. Armies in the Field,
Culpepper C. H. Va. Apl. 29th 1864

Maj. Gen. Halleck,
Chief of Staff of the Army,
General,

If General Gilmore reaches Fortress Monroe in time, and if four of the Iron Clads promised by the Navy are also there, our advance will commence on the 4th of May. Gen. Butler will operate on the South side of James River, Richmond being his objective point. I will move against Lee's Army attempting to turn him by one flank or the other. Should Lee fall back within his fortifications at Richmond, either before or after giving battle, I will form a junction with Butler, and the two forces will draw supplies from the James River. My own notions about our line of march are entirely made up. But, as circumstances beyond my controll may change them I will only state that my effort will be to bring Butler's and Meade's forces together.

The Army will start with fifteen days supplies. All the country affords will be gathered as we go along. This will no doubt enable us to go twenty or twenty-five days, without further supplies, unless we should be forced to keep in the country between the Rapidan and Chickahominy, in which case supplies might be required by way of the York or the Rappahannock River. To provide for this contingency I would like to have about one million rations, and two hundred thousand forage rations, afloat to be sent wherever it may prove they will be required.

The late call for one hundred day men ought to give us all the old troops in the Northern States for the field. I think full two thousand of those in the West ought to be got to Nashville as soon as possible. Probably it would be as well to assemble all the balance of the reinforcements for the West at Cairo. Those that come to the East I think should come to Washington unless movements of the enemy, yet to develope, should require them elswhere. With all our reserves at two or three points you will know what to do with them when they come to be needed in the field.

If the enemy fall back it is probable General Butler will want all the force that can be sent to him. I have instructed him however to keep you constantly advised of his own movements, and those of the enemy, so far as he can.

General Burnside will not leave his present position, between Bull Run and the Rappahannock, until the 5th of May. By that time the troops to occupy the Blockhouses, with their rations, should be out. If they cannot be sent from Washington I will have to require Gen. Burnside to furnish the detail from his Corps. When we get once established on the James River there will be no further necessity of occupying the road South of Bull Run. I do not know even that it will be necessary to go so far South as that. In this matter your

opportunity for knowing what is required being so far superior to mine I will leave it entirely to you.

> I am General, Very respectfully
> your obt. svt.
> U. S. GRANT
> Lt. Gen.

To Henry W. Halleck

> Hd Qrs "Wilderness"
> 11 a. m. May 7. 1864.
> By mail from Alexandria Va.

Maj Gen. H. W. Halleck,
Chief of Staff

We were engaged with the enemy nearly all day both on the
5th & 6th. Yesterday the enemy attacked our lines vigorously
first at one point and then another from right to left. They
were repulsed at all points before reaching our lines, except
once during the afternoon on Hancock's front, and just after
night on Sedgwick's front In the former instance they were
promptly and handsomely repulsed. The latter, Milroy's old
brigade, was attacked & gave way in the greatest confusion
almost without resistance, carrying good troops with them.
Had there been daylight the enemy could have injured us very
much in the confusion that prevailed, they however instead of
getting through the break, attacked Gen Wright's Div of
Sedgwick's Corps & were beaten back.

Our losses to this time in killed, wounded & prisoners
will not probably exceed 12.000. of whom an unusually
large proportion are but slightly wounded. Among the
killed we have to deplore the loss of Genls Wadsworth &
Hays, Genls Getty & Bartlett wounded & Genls Seymour &
Shaler taken prisoners. We have about 2.000 prisoners. They
report Gen Jenkins killed & Longstreet wounded. I think the
loss of the enemy must exceed ours, but this is only a guess
based upon the fact that they attacked & were repulsed so
often.

I wish you would send me all the information you have of

Gen Sherman by Bull Run & also care of Genl Butler. Send by way of Bull Run all the information from the James River expedition.

At present we can claim no victory over the enemy, neither have they gained a single advantage

Enemy pushed out of their fortifications to prevent their position being turned & have been sooner or later driven back in every instance.

Up to this hour enemy have not shown themselves in force within a mile of our lines.

U. S. GRANT
Lt Genl

To Julia Dent Grant

Near Spotsylvania C. H. Va.
May 13th 1864

Dear Julia,

The ninth day of battle is just closing with victory so far on our side. But the enemy are fighting with great desperation entrenching themselves in every position they take up. We have lost many thousand men killed and wounded and the enemy have no doubt lost more. We have taken about eight thousand prisoners and lost likely three thousand. Among our wounded the great majority are but slightly hurt but most of them will be unfit for service in this battle. I have reinforcements now coming up which will greatly encourage our men and discourage the enemy correspondingly.

I am very well and full of hope. I see from the papers the country is also hopeful.

Remember me to your father and Aunt Fanny. Kisses for yourself and the children. The world has never seen so bloody or so protracted a battle as the one being fought and I hope never will again. The enemy were really whipped yesterday but their situation is desperate beyond anything heretofore known. To loose this battle they loose their cause. As bad as it is they have fought for it with a gallantry worthy of a better.

ULYS.

To Julia Dent Grant

June 1st 1864

Dear Julia,

There has been a very severe battle this afternoon and as I write, now 9 O'clock at night firing is still continued on some parts of the battle line. What the result of the days fighting has been I will know but little about before midnight and possibly not then. The rebels are making a desperate fight and I presume will continue to do so as long as they can get a respectable number of men to stand.

I send pay accounts for May to Washington by Col. Bowers, who starts in the morning, with directions to send you $800 00 of it. April pay I sent all to Jones in liquidation of my indebtedness. In June I hope to pay all up. — I see by the papers dear little Nellie acquitted herself very handsomely at the Sanitary Fair. I would like very much to see you and the children but cannot hope to do so until this Campaign is over. How long it will last is a problem. I can hardly hope to get through this month. — With the night booming of Artillery and musketry I do not feel much like writing so you must excuse a short letter this time. Dr. Sharp is with me apparently enjoying himself very much. Fred. has been suffering intensely for several days with rheumatism. He has to lay upon his back in the ambulance unable to turn himself. I think he will be well in a day or two. Orvil Grant is at the White House and will probably be here to morrow.

My love to all. Kisses for yourself and the children.

ULYS.

To Ellen Wrenshall Grant

Cold Harbor Va. June 4th 1864

My Dear little Nelly,

I received your pretty well written letter more than a week ago. You do not know how happy it made me feel to see how well my little girl not yet nine years old could write. I expect by the end of the year you and Buck will be able to speak

German and then I will have to buy you those nice gold watches I promised. I see in the papers, and also from Mamas letter, that you have been representing "the Old Woman that lived in a Shoe" at the Fair! I know you must have enjoyed it very much. You must send me one of your photographs taken at the Fair.

We have been fighting now for thirty days and have every prospect of still more fighting to do before we get into Richmond. When we do get there I shall go home to see you and Ma Fred, Buck and Jess. I expect Jess rides Little Rebel every day! I think when I go home I will get a little buggy to work Rebel in so that you and Jess can ride about the country during vacation. Tell Ma to let Fred learn French as soon as she thinks he is able to study it. It will be a great help to him when he goes to West Point. You must send this letter to Ma to read because I will not write to her to-day. Kiss Ma, Cousin Louisa and all the young ladies for pa. Be a good little girl as you have always been, study your lessons and you will be contented and happy.

From
PAPA

To Julia Dent Grant

June 7th/64

Dear Julia,

I wrote to you last night but having had my hair cut to-day and remembering that you asked me to send you a lock I now write again to send it. I have nothing to add. To-day has been the quietest since leaving Culpepper. There has been no fighting except a little Artillery firing and some skirmishing driving the enemy's pickets south of the Chickahominy at two of the bridges below our main line. War will get to be so common with me if this thing continues much longer that I will not be able to sleep after a while unless there is an occational gun shot near me during the night.

Love and kisses for you and the children.

ULYS.

To Julia Dent Grant

City Point Va. June 15th/64

Dear Julia,

Since Sunday we have been engaged in one of the most perilous movements ever executed by a large army, that of withdrawing from the front of an enemy and moving past his flank crossing two rivers over which the enemy has bridges and rail-roads whilst we have bridges to improvise. So far it has been eminently successful and I hope will prove so to the end. About one half my troops are now on the South side of James River. A few days now will enable me to form a judgement of the work before me. It will be hard and may be tedious however.

I am in excellent health and feel no doubt about holding the enemy in much greater alarm than I ever felt in my life. They are now on a strain that no people ever endured for any great length of time. As soon as I get a little settled I will write Buck and Missy. each a letter in answer to theirs and will write to Cousin Louisa who I have received another short letter from enclosing Buck's. I want the children to write to me often. It improves them very much. I forgot that I had received a letter from Fred. since I wrote to him. I will answer his first.

Give my love to all at home. Did you receive the draft for $800 00? It is all I can send you until the end of July.—Kisses for you and the children.

ULYS.

To Elihu B. Washburne

City Point Va. June 23d *1864*.

Hon. E. B. Washburn,
Dear Sir.

In answer to your letter of a few days ago asking what "S" stands for in my name I can only state *nothing*. It was a mistake made by Senator Morris of Ohio when application was first made for my appointment as Cadet to West Point. My mother's family name is Simpson and having a brother of that name Mr. Morris, who knew both of us as children, got the matter confounded and sent in the application for Cadet-ship for Ulysses S. Grant. I tried on entering West Point to correct this mistake but failing, after I received my Diploma and Commission, with the "S" inserted, adopted it and have so signed my name ever since.

Every thing progresses here slowly. The dispatches given by the Sec. of War contains all the news.

Yours Truly
U. S. GRANT

To Henry W. Halleck

City Point, Va. July 1st 1864.

Maj. Gen H. W. Halleck,
Chief of Staff of the Army
General,

Mr. Dana Asst. Sec. of War, has just returned. He informs me that he called attention to the necessity of sending Gen. Butler to another field of duty. Whilst I have no difficulty with Gen. Butler, finding him always clear in his conception of orders, and prompt to obey, yet there is a want of knowledge how to execute, and particularly a prejudice against him, as a commander, that operates against his usefulness. I have feared that it might become necessary to separate him and Gen. Smith. The latter is really one of the most efficient officers in service, readiest in expedients and most skilful in the management of troops in action. I would dislike removing him from his present command unless it was to increase it, but as I say, may have it to do yet if Gen. Butler remains.

As an administrative officer Gen. Butler has no superior. In taking charge of a Dept.mt where there are no great battles to be fought, but a dissatisfied element to controll no one could manage it better than he. If a command could be cut out such as Mr Dana proposed, namely Ky. Ill. & Ia. or if the Depts. of the Mo. Kansas and the states of Ill. & Ia. could be merged together and Gen. Butler put over it I believe the good of the service would be subserved.

I regret the necessity of asking for a change in commander here, but Gen. Butler not being a soldier by education or experience, is in the hands of his subordinates in the execution of all operations Military. I would feel strengthened with Smith, Franklin or J. J. Reynolds commanding the right wing of this Army. At the same time, as I have here stated, Gen. Butler has always been prompt in his obedience to orders, with me, and clear in his understanding of them. I would not therefore be willing to recommend his retirement.

I send this by Mail for consideration but will telegraph if I think it absolutely necessary to make a change.

I am General, very respectf.
your obt. svt.
U. S. GRANT
Lt. Gen

To Julia Dent Grant

City Point, Va. July 7th *1864*.

Dear Julia,

I received two letters from you this evening, written after you had received mine stating that you could come to Fortress Monroe to spend the Summer. I am satisfied it is best you should not come. It would be expensive to furnish a house there and difficult supplying it afterwards. The camp life we are leading you would not be able to be where I am often and then only to come up and go immediately back, with an express boat that might be running at the time.

I wrote to you in my last why not make the same arrangement for the children as last year? Permanency is a great thing for children at school and you could not have a better home for them than with Louisa Boggs. If they were with her I should always feel easy for you to leave them for two or three months to stay with me if I was where you could possibly be with me. I want the children to prossecute their studies, and especially in languages. Speaking languages is a much greater accomplishment than the little parapharnalias of society such as music, dancing &c. I would have no objection to music being added to Nellies studies but with the boys I would never have it occupy one day of their time, or thought.

If you think it advisable to go some place where you can keep the children with you, and where they will be at a good school, I will not object. But I cannot settle for you where such a place would be, probably the City of St. Louis would be as good as any other, for the present. Love and Kisses for yourself and the children. How much I wish I could see you all.

ULYS.

To Charles E. Fuller

City Point July 16th 1864

Col. C. E. Fuller A. Q. M.
Bermuda Hundred

My Brother-in-law, who is now a prisoner in the south, is named John C. Dent. He was captured some place on the Miss. River not far from Vicksburg, and is now, or was when I last heard from him, at Columbia S. C. He is a citizen, never connected with the army since the breaking out of the War and I regret to say not a loyal man, otherwise I should have interested myself long ago for his exchange

U. S. GRANT Lt. Gen.

To Abraham Lincoln

(Cipher)   City Point Va. July 19th *1864*
A. Lincoln, President,

In my opinion there ought to be an immediate call for say 300.000 men to be put in the field in the shortest possible time. The presence of this number of reinforcements would save the annoyance of raids and would enable us to drive the enemy back from his present front, particularly from Richmond, without attacking fortifications. The enemy now have their last man in the field. Every depletion of their Army is an irreparable loss. Desertions from it are now rapid. With the prospect of large additions to our force these desertions would increase. The greater number of men we have the shorter and less sanguinary will be the war.

I give this entirely as my view and not in any spirit of dictation, always holding myself in readiness to use the material given me to the best advantage I know how.

U. S. GRANT
Lt. Gen.

To Edwin M. Stanton

(Cipher)   City Point July 20th/64
E. M. Stanton Sec. of War

I must enter my protest against States sending recruiting Agents into the Southern States for the purpose of filling their quotas. The negroes brought within our lines are rightfully recruits to the United States Service and should not go to benefit any particular state. It is simply allowing Massachusetts (I mention Mass. because I see the order of the Governor of that state for establishing recruiting agencies in the South and see no such order from any other state authority.) to fill her quota by paying an amount of money to recruits the United States have already got. I must also enter my protest against recruiting from prisoners of War. Each one enlisted robs us of a soldier and adds one to the enemy with a bounty paid in loyal money.

U. S. GRANT
Lt. Gen.

To Henry W. Halleck

City Point July 21st *1864*.
Maj. Gen. Halleck, Washington

There is no indication of any troops having been sent from here North. Deserters coming in daily indicate nearly the position of every Division of Hill's Longstreet's and Beaurigard's forces. Hill's Corps has withdrawn from its position on the extreme right and was yesterday in rear of the other part of the line held by the enemy. There is a rumor of some force having been sent to Georgia but if this is so it is most likely only regiments detached from their command.

> U. S. GRANT
> Lt. Gen.

To Winfield Scott

HEADQUARTERS, ARMIES OF THE UNITED STATES,
CITY POINT, Va, July 23, 1864.
Lieutenant General Winfield Scott, U. S. A.:—

My Dear General—Your letter of the 2d inst., addressed to the Hon. E. B Washburne, in which you informed him that you had heard that some one had told me that you had spoken slightingly of my appointment to my present rank, is just received. Allow me to assure you, General, that no one has ever given me such information. I have never heard of any speech of yours in connection with the present rebellion which did not show the great interest felt by you, both in our eminent success and in the success of all our commanders. In fact, all that I have heard of your saying in relation to myself has been more flattering to me than I probably deserve.

With assurance of great esteem for you personally, General, as well as for the services you have rendered our country throughout a long and eventful public career, I subscribe myself, very respectfully and truly, your obedient servant,

> U. S. GRANT,
> Lieutenant General U. S. A.

To Henry W. Halleck

(Cipher)   City Point Va. Aug. 1st *1864*
Maj. Gen Halleck, Washington,

The loss in the disaster of saturday last foots up about 3500 of whom 450 were killed and 2000 wounded. It was the saddest affair I have witnessed in this war. Such opportunity for carrying fortifications I have never seen and do not expect again to have. The enemy with a line of works five miles long had been reduced by our previous movements to the North side of James River to a force of only three Divisions. This line was undermined and blown up carrying a battery and most of a regiment with it. The enemy were taken completely by surprise and did not recover from it for more than an hour. The crater and several hundred yards of the enemys line to the right & left of it, and a short detached line in front of the crater, were occupied by our troops without opposition. Immediately in front of this and not 150 yards off, with clear ground intervening, was the crest of the ridge leading into town and which if carried the enemy would have made no resistance but would have continued a flight already commenced. It was three hours from the time our troops first occupied their works before the enemy took possession of this crest. I am constrained to believe that had instructions been promptly obeyed that Petersburg would have been carried with all the Artillery and a large number of prisoners without a loss of 300 men. It was in getting back to our lines that the loss was sustained. The enemy attempted to charge and retake the line captured from them and were repulsed, with heavy loss, by our Artillery. Their loss in killed must be greater than ours whilst our loss in wounded and captured is four times that of the enemy.

U. S. GRANT
Lt. Gn.

To Lydia Slocum

HEADQ'RS ARMIES OF THE UNITED STATES,
CITY POINT, VA., August 10.

Mrs. Lydia Slocum:

My Dear Madam: Your very welcome letter of the 3d instant has reached me. I am glad to know the relatives of the lamented Major General McPherson are aware of the more than friendship existing between him and myself. A nation grieves at the loss of one so dear to our nation's cause. It is a selfish grief, because the nation had more to expect from him than from almost any one living. I join in this selfish grief, and add the grief of personal love for the departed. He formed for some time one of my military family. I knew him well. To know him was but to love him. It may be some consolation to you, his aged grandmother, to know that every officer and every soldier who served under your grandson felt the highest reverence for his patriotism, his zeal, his great, almost unequalled ability, his amiability, and all the manly virtues that can adorn a commander. Your bereavement is great, but cannot exceed mine.

> Yours truly,
> U. S. GRANT,
> Lieutenant General.

To Elihu B. Washburne

City Point Va. Aug. 16th *1864*.

Hon. E. B. Washburn,
Dear Sir:

Your letter asking for Autographs to send to Mrs. Adams, the wife of our Minister to England, was duly received. She had also sent to Mr. Dana for the same thing and his requisition, he being with me at the time, was at once filled. I have directed Col. Bowers to send with this a few of the original dispatches telegraphed from here. They have all been hastily written and not with the expectation of ever being seen afterwards but will, I suppose, answer as well as any thing els, or as if they had been written specially for the purpose of sending.

We are progressing here slowly. The weather has been intolerably warm, so much so that marching troops is nearly death.

I state to all Citizens who visit me that all we want now to insure an early restoration of the Union is a determined unity of sentiment North. The rebels have now in their ranks their last man. The little boys and old men are guarding prisoners, guarding rail-road bridges and forming a good part of their garrisons for intrenched positions. A man lost by them can not be replaced. They have robbed the cradle and the grave equally to get their present force. Besides what they lose in frequent skirmishes and battles they are now loosing from desertions and other causes at least one regiment per day. With this drain upon them the end is visible if we will but be true to ourselves. Their only hope now is in a divided North. This might give them reinforcements from Tenn. Ky. Maryland and Mo. whilst it would weaken us. With the draft quietly enforced the enemy would become dispondent and would make but little resistence.

I have no doubt but the enemy are exceedingly anxious to hold out until after the Presidential election. They have many hopes from its effects. They hope a counter revolution. They hope the election of the peace candidate. In fact, like McCawber, the hope *something* to turn up.

Our peace friends, if they expect peace from separation, are much mistaken. It would be but the begining of war with thousands of Northern men joining the South because of our disgrace allowing separation. To have peace "on any terms" the South would demand the restoration of their slaves already freed. They would demand indemnity for losses sustained, and they would demand a treaty which would make the North slave hunters for the South. They would demand pay or the restoration of every slave escaping to the North.

Your Truly

U. S. GRANT

To William H. Seward

City Point, Va, Aug. 19th 1864.

Hon. W. H. Seward,
Sec. of State,
Washington D. C.
Dear Sir:

I am in receipt of copy of F. W. Morse letter of the 22d of July to you inclosing copy of statement of C. W. G. in relation to desertions from this Army. There are constant desertions, though but few of them go over to the enemy. Unlike the enemy however we do not loose our veterans and men who entered the service through patriotic motives. The men who desert are those who have just arrived and who have never done any fighting and never intended to when they enlisted. They are a class known as "Bounty Jumpers" or "Substitute" men, men who enlist for the money, desert and enlist again. After they have done this until they become fearful of punishment they join their regiments, in the field, and desert to the enemy.

Of this class of recruits we do not get one for every eight bounties paid to do good service. My Provost Marshal Gn. is preparing a statement on this subject which will show the reinforcements received from this class of recruits. Take the other side: the desertions from the enemy to us. Not a day passes but men come into our lines and men too who have been fighting for the South for more than three years. Not unfrequently a commissioned officer comes with them. Only a few days ago I sent a regiment, numbering one thousand men for duty, to Gen. Popes Department composed wholly of deserters from the rebel Army and prisoners who took the oath of allegiance and joined them.

There is no doubt but many prisoners of War have taken the oath of allegiance and enlisted as substitutes to get the bounty and effect their return to the South. These men are paraded abroad as deserters who want to join the south and fight her battles, and it is through our leniency that the South expects to reap great advantages.

We ought not to make a single exchange nor release a prisoner on any pretext whatever until the war closes. We have got to fight until the Military power of the South is exhausted and if we release or exchange prisoners captured it simply becomes a War of extermination.

> I have the honor to be
> Very respectfully
> your obt. svt.
> U. S. GRANT
> Lt. Gn

To Philip H. Sheridan

(Cipher)   City Point Va. Aug. 26th *1864*. *2:30* P.M.
Maj. Gen. Sheridan, Halltown Va.

I telegraphed you that I had good reason for believing that Fitz Lee had been ordered back here? I now think it likely that all troops will be ordered back from the Valley except what they beleive to be the minimum number to detain you. My reason for supposing this is based upon the fact that yealding up the Welden road seems to be a blow to the enemy he can not stand. I think I do not overstate the loss of the enemy in the last two weeks at 10,000 killed & wounded. We have lost heavily but ours has been mostly in captures when the enemy gained temporay advantages.

Watch closely and if you find this theory correct push will all vigor   Give the enemy no rest and if it is possible to follow to the Va Central road follow that far. Do all the damage to rail-roads & crops you can. Carry off stock of all discreptions and negroes so as to prevent further planting. If the War is to last another year we want the Shenandoah valley to remain a barren waste.

U. S. GRANT
Lt. Gn.

To William T. Sherman

(Cipher)   City Point Va. Sept. 4th *1864*. 9 p. m.
Maj. Gen. Sherman, Atlanta Ga.

I have just received your dispatch announcing the capture of Atlanta. In honor of your great victory I have ordered a salute to be fired with shotted guns from every battery bearing upon the enemy. The salute will be fired within an hour amidst great rejoicing.

U. S. GRANT
Lt. Gen.

To Frederick Dent Grant
and Ulysses S. Grant, Jr.

City Point Va. Sept. 13th *1864.*

Dear Fred. & Buck,

I was very glad to get your letters the other day and still better pleased to see so few mistakes. There was some mistakes though. Write often to me and when you do write always keep a dictionary by you. When you feel any doubt about how a word should be spelled look at your dictionary and be sure to get it right. Missy did not write? Why did she not? She writes very pretty letters and by writing often now she will write a better letter at twelve years of age than most grown up yong ladies.

I have sent to get Jess' pony brought into town from your grand pa's. If he is left there long I am afraid he will be stolen.

I hope to be up to see you all before many weeks and before many months to be with you most of the time. Is Jess sorry he run off and left his pa the way he did? I thought he was going to be a brave boy and stay with me and ride Jeff Davis. Ask Jess if Jeff aint a bully horse.

Kiss your Ma, little Nelly & Jess for your

PA

To Julia Dent Grant

City Point Va. Sept. 14th *1864.*

Dear Julia,

Your letter speaking of the new embarassment which has arisen in not being able to send the boys to College without having them board away from home has just reached me. As school does not commence until the begining of next month it will not be necessary for me to write to the principle about it as I shall try to slip up there for a day and see him in person. As to Jess refusing to go to school I think you will have to show him that you are *boss.* How does he expect ever to write letters to his Pa, or get to be Aide de Camp if he does not go to school and learn to write. He will go I know. He was only joking when he said he would not. I hope you will be pleasantly situated. Burlington is said to be a very nice place and nice people. You will soon be more at home there than in Gravois where there is no body except your own family for whom you have much reason to care. — I hope Jennie will come on and at least spend the Winter with you. I have written to your father asking him to make his home with us. Love and kisses for you and the children. Good night.

ULYS.

To Edwin M. Stanton

(Cipher)   City Point Va. Sept. 20th *1864. 11:00* A.M.
Hon. E. M. Stanton, Sec. of War, Washington.

Please advise the President not to attempt to doctor up a state government for Georgia by the appointment of citizens in any capacity whatever. Leave Sherman to treat on all questions in his own way the President reserving his power to approve or disapprove of his action. Through Treasury Agents on the Mississippi and a very bad civil policy in Louisianna I have no doubt the war has been very conciderably protracted and the states bordering on that river thrown further from sympathy with the Government than they were before the river was opened to commerse. This is given as my private views.

U. S. GRANT
Lt. Gn.

To Elihu B. Washburne

City Point Va
Sept 21st 1864

Hon. E. B. Washburne—

I have no objection to the President using any thing I have ever written to him as he sees fit—I think however for him to attempt to answer all the charges the opposition will bring against him will be like setting a maiden to work to prove her chastity—

U. S. GRANT
Lieut. Genl

To Julia Dent Grant

City Point Va. Oct. 26th *1864*

Dear Julia,

To-morrow a great battle will probably be fought. At all events I have made all the arrangements for one and unless I conclude through the day to change my programme it will take place. I do not like to predict results therefore will say nothing about what I expect to accomplish. The cake you sent by Mr. Smith come to hand but the other you speak of having sent by Express has not. In one of your letters you ask if I accepted the house in Chicago? I did not accept or decline. I stated that I had no disposition to give up Ill. as my place of residence but the probability being that my duties hereafter would keep me most of the time in the East I had selected Phila as a place where my children could have the benefit of good schools and I could expect often to visit my family. If they were in Chicago I could not expect to see them often. I have heard nothing further since.

All are well here. Rawlins appears to have entirely recovered. Shall I have Little Rebel sent to you? If you had him you could get a little buggy and sleigh expressly for him and the children could then ride as much as they pleased. I expect when this campaign ends to send all my horses home and stay there most of the time myself when I am not visiting the different Armies. I do wish I could tell when that would be.— Love and kisses for you and the children.

ULYS.

To Isaac S. Stewart

City Point, Va, Dec. 1st *1864*

Dear Major,

Your favor of the 29th ultimo enclosing draft for $47.50 and accounts for signature is just received. As I draw forage in kind I am not entitled to the $50 00 per month for horses. The accounts upon which you paid are therefore correct. Enclosed you will please find the draft returned.

The following is a discriptive list of my servants which you can have inserted in the accounts paid upon to perfect them

		ft	in	Eyes	Hair
James Guard,	White	5.	11	Dark	
William	Black	5.	7	"	
Douglass	"	5.	9	"	
Georgianna	"	5.	4	"	

I am under obligations to you Major for your concideration and favor.

Yours Truly
U. S. GRANT
Lt. Gen

To Maj. I. S. Stewart
Paymaster U. S. A.

To William T. Sherman

Confidential—   City Point, Va, Dec. 6th *1864.*

Maj. Gen. W. T. Sherman,
Comd.g Mil. Div. of the Miss.

General,

On reflection since sending my letter by the hands of Lieut. Dunn I have concluded that the most important operation towards closing out the rebellion will be to close out Lee and his Army. You have now destroyed the roads of the South so that it will probably take three months, without interruption, to reestablish a through line from East to West. In that time I think the job here will be effectually completed. My idea now then is that you establish a base on the Sea Coast. Fortify and leave in it all your Artillery and Cavalry and enough Infantry to protect them, and at the same time so threaten the interior that the Militia of the South will have to be kept at home. With the balance of your command come here by water with all dispatch. Select yourself the officer to leave in command, but you I want in person.

Unless you see objections to this plan which I can not see use every vessel going to you for purposes of transportation.

Hood has Thomas close in Nashville. I have said all I could to force him to attack without giving the possitive order until to-day. To-day however I could stand it no longer and gave the order without any reserve. I think the battle will take place to-morrow. The result will probably be known in New York before Col. Babcock, the bearer of this, will leaves New York. Col. B. will give you full information of all operations now in progress.

> Very respectfully
> your obt. svt.
> U. S. GRANT
> Lt. Gn.

To Abraham Lincoln

(Cipher)　　　　　　　　City Point, Va, Dec. 7th 1864 *3:30* P.M.
A. Lincoln, President, Washington,

The best interests of the service require that the troops of the Northwest, Departments of the N. W. Mo. & Kansas, should all be under one head. Properly they should all be in one Department. Knowing however the difficulty of displacing Department commanders I have recommended these Departments be thrown together into a Military Division and Gen. Pope put in command. This is advisable for the fact that as a rule only one point is threatened at a time and if all that territory is commanded by one man he can take troops from one point to satisfy the wants of another. With separate Department commanders they want to keep what they have and get all they can. This will not be the case with Dodge who has been apponted to command Mo. nor will it be with Pope.

> U. S. GRANT
> Lt. Gn

To Henry W. Halleck

(Cipher)   City Point, Va, Dec. 8th *1864. 10:00* P.M.
Maj. Gen. Halleck, Washington,

Your dispatch of 9 p. m. just received. I want Gen. Thomas reminded of the importance of immediate action. I sent him a dispatch this evening which will probably urge him on. I would not say relieve him until I hear further from him.

U. S. GRANT
Lt. Gn.

To Henry W. Halleck

(Cipher)   City Point Va. Dec. 9th *1864. 11:00* A.M.
Maj. Gen. Halleck, Washington.

Dispatch of 8 p. m, last evening from Nashville shews the enemy scattered for more than seventy miles down the river and no attack yet made by Thomas. Please telegraph orders relieving him at once and placing Schofield in command. Thomas should be directed to turn over all orders and dispatches received since the battle of Franklin to Schofield.

U. S. GRANT
Lt. Gn.

To Henry W. Halleck

(Cipher)   City Point, Va. Dec. 9th *1864. 5:30* P.M.
Maj. Gen. Halleck, Washington.

Gen. Thomas has been urged in every way possible to attack the enemy even to the giving the possitive order. He did say he thought he would be able to attack on the 7th but did not do so nor has he given a reason for not doing it. I am very unwilling to do injustice to an officer who has done as much good service as Gen. Thomas has, however and will therefore suspend the order relieving him until it is seen whether he will do anything.

U. S. GRANT
Lt. Gen.

To George H. Thomas

(Cipher)   City Point, Va, Dec. 9th 1864 *7:30* P.M.
Maj. Gn. Thomas, Nashville Tenn.

Your dispatch of 1 P. M. to-day received. I have as much confidence in your conducting a battle rightly as I have in any other officer. But it has seemed to me that you have been slow and I have had no explaination of affairs to convince me otherwise. Receiving your dispatch to Gen. Halleck of 2 p. m. before I did the one to me, I telegraphed to suspend the order relieving you until we should hear further. I hope most sincerely that there will be no necessity of repeating the order and that the facts will show that you have been right all the time.

U. S. GRANT
Lt. Gn.

To Edwin M. Stanton

Washington City,
Dec. 18th *1864*

Hon E M Stanton

In my opinion no General Order should be issued which would authorize subordinate Military Commanders to invade a foreign country, with which we are at peace, at their discretion. If such officers should pursue Marauders fitted out in Canada, to depridate upon our frontier, it should be the act of the officer himself to be justified or condemned afterwards upon the merits of the case. In all instances where to much delay will not ensue they should wait for the authority of the Comd.g Gn. of the Dept. at least, and then his action should be reported, through the proper channel, to the President at once.

U. S. GRANT
Lt. Gn.

To George H. Thomas

Washington City,
December 18th *1864*

Major General Thomas
Nashville, Tenn.

The armies operating against Richmond have fired two hundred guns in honor of your great victory. Sherman has fully established his base on Ossabaw Sound with Savannah fully invested. I hope to be able to fire a salute to-morrow in honor of the fall of Savannah. In all your operations we hear nothing of Forrest; Great precaution should be taken to prevent him crossing the Cumberland or Tennessee below Eastport. After Hood is driven as far as it is possible to follow him, you want to re-occupy Decatur and all other abandoned points.

U. S. GRANT
Lt. Gen.

To George H. Thomas

(Cipher)   City Point, Va, Dec. 22d *1864*. *11:00* P.M.
Maj. Gen. Thomas, Nashville Tenn.

You have the congratulations of the public for the energy with which you are pushing Hood. I hope you will succeed in reaching his pontoon bridge at Tuscumbia before he gets there. Should you do so it looks to me that Hood is cut off. If you succeed in destroying Hood's Army there will be but one Army left to the so called Confederacy capable of doing us harm. I will take care of that and try to draw the sting from it so that in the Spring we shall have easy sailing. You now have a big oportunity which I know you are availing yourself of. Let us push and do all we can before the enemy can derive benefit either from the rasing of Negro troops or the concentration of white troops now in the field.

U. S. GRANT
Lt. Gen.

To Julia Dent Grant

City Point, Va Jan 1st *1865*.

Dear Julia,

Happy New Year to you. Fred. starts home this morning and will tell you I am quite well. I must commence taking quinine however. Every one on the Staff have been sick, Col. Badeau and Col. Porter so much so that they had to be sent home.

I inclose you two strips of paper which I want you to read and preserve. Sherman's letter shows how noble a man he is. How few there are who when rising to popular favor as he now is would stop to say a word in defence of the only one between himself and the highest in command. I am glad to say that I appreciated Sherman from the first feeling him to be what he has proven to the world he is. Good buy.

Ulys.

Kisses for you and the children.

U.

To Julia Dent Grant

City Point, Va, Jan. 11th *1865*.

Dear Julia,

I have just rec'd a letter from Jones saying he had sent you $475 00 This however includes the gold which I do not want you to spend. If it is necessary for you to have more money I will try to send it. I have received a letter from Jim. Casey saying that $1400 00 back taxes are due on your fathers place and unless paid this month the place will be sold. Now I cannot afford to send $1400 there and get no return for it. I know if I pay up the taxes it will be the last I shall ever see of the money. Looking to my own interest in the matter I wrote to Ford to attend to the matter for me and to let the farm be sold for taxes and him to buy it in in my name. I at the same time arranged for borrowing the money to send to him. A tax title amounts to no title atall but it is good until the money paid is refunded. If I can I will force John to make Nelly and Emma deeds to their land and probably to Fred. also.

I receive all your letters. Some of them are rather cross.— Love and kisses for you and the children.

ULYS.

To Abraham Lincoln

(Cipher)   City Point, Va. Jan. 31st *1865. 10:00* A.M.
A. Lincoln President
Washington

The following communication was received here last evening. Petersburg, Va, Jan. 30th 1865   LIEUT. GN. U. S. GRANT, SIR: We desire to pass your lines under safe conduct, and to proceed to Washington, to hold a conference with President Lincoln, upon the subject of the existing War, and with a view of ascertaining upon what terms it may be terminated, in pursuance of the course indicated by him in his letter to Mr. F. P. Blair of 18th of Jan.y 1865 of which we presume you have a copy; and if not we wish to see you in person, if convenient, and to confer with you upon the subject. (Signed) Yours very respectfully, ALEXANDER STEPHENS, J. A. CAMPBELL, R. M. T. HUNTER. I have sent directions to receive these gentlemen and expect to have them at my quarters this evening awaiting your instructions.

U. S. GRANT
Lt. Gn.

To Abraham Lincoln

From City Point Va Feb'y 1st 12 30 P. M *1865.*
His Excellency A. Lincoln
Prest U. S.

Your despatch received; there will be no armistice in consequence of the presence of Mr Stephens and others within our lines. The troops are kept in readiness to move at the shortest notice if occasion should justify it

U. S. GRANT
Lieut Genl

To William T. Sherman

City Point, Va, Feb.y *1865*.

Maj. Gen. W. T. Sherman,
Comd.g Mil. Div. of the Miss.
General.

Without much expectation of it reaching you in time to be of any service I have mailed to you copies of instructions to Schofield and Thomas. I had informed Schofield by telegraph of the departure of Mahones Division, South, from the Petersburg front. These troops marched down the Weldon road and as they apparently went without baggage it is doubtful whether they have not returned. I was absent from here when they left. Just returned yesterday morning from Cape Fear River. I went there to determine where Schofields Corps had better go to operate against Wilmington & Goldsboro The instructions with this will inform you of the conclution arrived at. Schofield was with me and the plan of the movement against Wilmington fully determined before we started back, hence the absence of more detailed instructions to him. He will land one Division at Smithville and move rapidly up the south side of the river and secure the W & C rail-road and with his Pontoon train cross onto the Island south of the City if he can. With the aid of the gunboats there is no doubt but this move will drive the enemy from their position eight miles East of the City either back to their inner line or away altogether. There will be a large force on the North bank of Cape Fear river ready to follow up and invest the garrison if they should go inside.

The rail-roads of N. C. are 4 ft. 8½ in. gauge. I have sent large parties of rail-road men there to build them up and have ordered stock to run them. We have abundance of it idle from the non use of the Va. roads.

I have taken every precaution to have supplies ready for you wherever you may turn up. I did this before when you left Atlanta and regret that they did not reach you promptly when you reached Saltwater. The fact is Foster, from physical disability is entirely unfit for his command. I would like to change him for a man that can get about and see for himself.

Alexander Stevens, R. M. T. Hunter & Judge Campbelle are now at my Hd Qrs. very desirous of going to Washington to see Mr. Lincoln, informally, on the subject of peace. The Peace feeling within the rebel lines is gaining ground rapidly. This however should not relax our energies in the least, but should stimulate us to greater activity.

I have received your very kind letter in which you say you would decline, or are opposed, to promotion. No one would be more pleased at your advancement than I, and if you should be placed in my position and I put subordinate it would not change our personal relations in the least. I would make the same exertions to support you that you have ever done to support me, and would do all in my power to make our cause win

Yours Truly. U. S. GRANT, Lt. Gn

February 1, 1865

To Edwin M. Stanton

CITY POINT, VA., *February 6, 1865.*

Hon. E. M. Stanton:

The Richmond Dispatch to-day says that a rumor was current yesterday that Sherman had reached and was destroying the rail-road at Midway, ten miles west of Branchville. The Whig, however, says that the rumor was without foundation, as the tenor of official dispatches received at the War Department last evening renders it certain that such was not the case. On Saturday telegraphic communication was temporarily suspended with Augusta, but was resumed on yesterday. The Whig remarks that a repulse of Sherman, who is now apparently presumptuous on account of his unimpeded march through Georgia, would work wonders in bringing the North to its senses. The Confederate generals and the men under their commands on his front are commissioners to whose pacific exertions the country may well look with anxious and prayerful solicitude. The Enquirer reports that the salt-works are again in successful operation. C. C. Clay, jr., is reported having arrived in the Confederacy. The Peace Commissioners arrived in Richmond Saturday evening. The same evening a large war meeting was held, which was addressed by Henry A. Wise. Governor Smith issues a notice to-day to the citizens of Richmond, Va., and citizens of other States sojourning in Richmond, to meet this evening to respond to the answer made by President Lincoln to the Confederate deputies sent to confer with him on the subject of peace. It is expected that Stephens will be invited by the Confederate Congress to address them before leaving for Georgia, whither it is rumored he intends going to arouse the people of that State to renewed vigor in prosecuting the war. The general tone of all the Richmond papers to-day says that there is nothing left for the South to do but to fight it out.

U. S. GRANT,
Lieutenant-General.

To Abraham Lincoln

City Point, Va, March 2d 1865 *1:00* P.M.

A. Lincoln President, Washington,

Richmond papers are received daily. No bullitins were sent Teusday or Wednsday because there was not an item of either good or bad news in them. There is every indication that Sherman is perfectly safe. I am looking every day for direct news from him.

U. S. GRANT
Lt. Gen.

To Edwin M. Stanton

City Point Va, March 3d 1865 *12:30* P.M.

Hon, E, M, Stanton
Sec, of War, Washington

A great many deserters are coming in from the enemy bringing their Arms with them expecting the pay for them as the means of a little ready cash, Would there be any objection to amending my order so as to allow this? Now that the sources of supply are cutt off from the enemy it is a great object to deprive the enemy of present supply of Arms

U. S. GRANT
Lieut, General

To Jesse Root Grant

City Point, Va, March 19th *1865*

Dear Father,

I received your two letters announcing the death of Clara. Although I had known for some time that she was in a decline yet I was not expecting to hear of her death at this time.—I have had no heart to write earlyer. Your last letter made me feel very badly. I will not state the reason and hope I may be wrong in my judgement of its meaning.

We are now having fine weather and I think will be able to wind up matters about Richmond soon. I am anxious to have Lee hold on where he is a short time longer so that I can get him in a position where he must loose a great portion of his Army. The rebellion has lost its vitality and if I am not much mistaken there will be no rebel Army of any great dimentions a few weeks hence. Any great catastrophy to any one of our Armies would of course revive the enemy for a short time. But I expect no such thing to happen.

I do not know what I can do either for Will. Griffith's son or for Belville Simpson. I sent orders last Fall for John Simpson to come to these Hd Qrs. to run between here and Washington as a Mail Messenger. But he has not come. I hope this service to end now soon.

I am in excellent health but would enjoy a little respite from duty wonderfully. I hope it will come soon.

My kindest regards to all at home. I shall expect to make you a visit the coming Summer.

Yours Truly
ULYSSES.

To Edwin M. Stanton

(Cipher)   City Point, Va, March 21st *1865* *2:30* P.M.
Hon. E. M. Stanton, Sec. of War, Washington.

I would recommend releiving Gen. Crook from command of his Dept. and ordering him to command the Cavalry of the A. P. I would call attention to the fact that our White troops are being paid whilst the Colored troops are not. If paymasters could be ordered here immediately to commence paying them it would have a fine affect.

U. S. GRANT
Lt. Gn.

To Philip H. Sheridan

City Point, Va. March 21, 1865

Maj. Gen. P. H. Sheridan
Com'dg Middle Military Division
General:

I do not wish to hurry you, and besides fully appreciate the necessity of both having your horses well shod and well rested before starting again on another long march. But there is now such a possibility, if not probability of Lee and Johnston attempting to unite, that I feel extremely desirous not only of cutting the lines of communication between them but of having a large and properly commanded cavalry force ready to act with in case such an attempt is made. I think that by Saturday next you had better start, even if you have to stop here to finish shoeing up

I will have a force moved out from north of the James, to take possession of Long Bridge crossing, and to lay a pontoon for you. Some of the troops will push up as far as Bottom Bridge if they do not meet with too much opposition. This move will not be made at the date indicated unless it is known that you are ready to start. It will be made earlier if you indicate a readiness to start earlier.

Stoneman started yesterday from Knoxville with a Cavalry force of probably 5000 men to penetrate S. W. Virginia as far towards Lynchburg as possible. Under his instructions he may strike from New river towards Danville. This however I do not expect him to do. Wilson started at the same time from Eastport towards Selma with a splendidly equipped Cavalry force of 12000 men. Canby is in motion and I have reason to believe that Sherman and Schofield have formed a junction at Goldsboro.

U. S. Grant

To William T. Sherman

City Point, Va. March 22d *1865*

Maj. Gen. W. T. Sherman,
Comd.g Mil. Div. of the Miss.
General,

Although the Richmond papers do not communicate the fact yet I saw enough in them to satisfy me that you occupied Goldsboro on the 19th inst. I congratulate you and the Army on what may be regarded as the sucsessful termination of the third Campaign since leaving the Tenn. river less than one year ago.

Since Sheridan's very sucsessful raid North of the James the enemy are left dependent on the South Side and Danville roads for all of their supplies. These I hope to cut next week. Sheridan is at "White House" shoeing up and resting his Cavalry. I expect him to finish by Friday night and to start the following morning via Long Bridge, New Market, Bermuda Hundred and the extreme left of the Army around Petersburg. He will make no halt with the Armies operating here, but will be joined by a Division of Cav.y, 5500 strong, from the Army of the Potomac, and will proceed directly to the S. S. & Danville roads. His instructions will be to strike the S. S. road as near Petersburg as he can and destroy it so that it cannot be repaired for three or four days, and push on to the Danville road as near to the Appomattox as he can get. Then I want him to destroy the road towards Burkesville as far as he can; then push on to the S. S. road, West of Burkesville, and destroy it effectually. From that point I shall probably leave it to

his discretion either to return to this Army crossing the Danville road South of Burkeville, or go and join you passing
between Danville and Greensboro?

When this movement commences I shall move out by
my left with all the force I can, holding present intrenched
lines. I shall start with no distinct view further than holding Lee's forces from following Sheridan. But I shall be
along myself and will take advantage of any thing that
turns up. If Lee detaches I will attack or if he comes out of
his lines I will endeavor to repulse him and follow it up
to the best advantage. It is most difficult to understand what
the rebels intend to do. So far but few troops have been detached from Lee's Army. Much Machinery has been removed
and materiel has been sent to Lynchburg showing a disposition to go there. Points too have been fortified on the Danville road.

Lee's Army is much demoralized and are deserting in great
numbers. Probably from returned prisoners and such conscripts as can be picked up his numbers may be kept up. I
estimate his force now at about 65.000 men.

Wilson started on Monday with 12.000 Cavalry from Eastport. Stoneman started on the same day from East Tenn. toward Lynchburg. Thomas is moving the 4th Corps to Bulls
Gap. Canby is moving with a formidable force on Mobile and
the interior of Alabama.

I ordered Gilmore, as soon as the fall of Charleston was
known, to hold all important posts on the Seacoast and to
send to Wilmington all surplus forces. Thomas was also directed to forward to New Berne all troops belonging to the
corps with you. I understand this will give you about 5000
men besides those brought East by Meagher.

I have been telegraphing Gen. Meigs to hasten up locomotives and cars for you. Gen. McCallum he informs me is
attending to it. I fear they are not going forward as fast as I
would like.

Let me know if you want more troops or anything else.

> Very respectfully
> your obt. svt.
> U. S. GRANT
> Lt. Gn.

To Abraham Lincoln

Gravely Run, March 29th *1865*

A. Lincoln, President, City Point

Griffin was attacked near where the Quaker road intersects the Boydton plank road. At 5.50 p m. Warren reports the fighting pretty severe but the enemy repulsed leaving 100 prisoners in our hands. Warren advanced to attack at the hour named but found the enemy gone, he thinks inside of his main works. Warrens pickets on his left along Boydton plank road reported the enemy's Cavalry moving rapidly Northward and they though Sheridan after them. Sheridan was in Dinwiddie this afternoon—

U. S. GRANT
Lt. Gn—

To George G. Meade

Appomattox C. H.
April 9th 1865.

Agreement having been made for the Surrender of the Army of North Va. hostilities will not be resumed. General Lee desires that during the time the two Armies are laying near each other, the men of the two Armies be Kept separate, the sole object being to prevent unpleasant individual rencontres that may take place with a too free intercourse.

U. S. GRANT.

To Julia Dent Grant

Washington Apl. 16th *1865*

Dear Julia,

I got back here about 1 p. m. yesterday and was called immediately into the presence of our new President, who had already been qualified, and the Cabinet. I telegraphed you from Baltimore and told Beckwith to do the same thing from here. You no doubt received the dispatches. All seems very quiet here. There is but little doubt but that the plot contemplated the distruction of more than the President and Sec. of State. I think now however it has expended itself and there is but little to fear. For the present I shall occupy a room in the office which is well guarded and will be occupied by Bowers and probably two or three others. I shall only go to the Hotel twice a day for my meals and will stay indoors of evenings. The change which has come upon the country so suddenly will make it necessary for me to remain in the City for several days yet. Gen. Halleck will go to Richmond to command there and Ord to Charleston. Other changes which will have to be made, and the apparent feeling that I should remain here until everything gets into working order under the new régime will probably detain me here until next Saturday. If I can get home sooner I will do so. I hope you will be in your house in Phila when I do go home. The inconvenience of getting from the Phila depot to Burlington is about equal to the balance of the trip.

Love and kisses for you and the children.

Ulys.

To Edward O. C. Ord

Apl. 17th *1865* *5:00* P.M.

Maj. Gen. Ord, Richmond, Va

Ford, Manager of the theatre where the President was assassinated is now in Richmond. Have him arrested and sent under guard to Washington. Do not let it be noised about that he is to be arrested until the work is done lest he escapes.

U. S. Grant
Lt. Gn

To William T. Sherman

Washington, D. C., Apl. 21st 1865.

Maj. Gen. W. T. Sherman,
Comd.g Mil. Div. of the Miss.
General,

The basis of agreement entered into between yourself and Gen. J. E. Johnston for the disbandment of the Southern Army and the extension of the authority of the general government over all the territory belonging to it, sent for the approval of the President, is received.

I read it carefully myself before submitting it to the President and secretary of War and felt satisfied that it could not possibly be approved. My reasons for these views I will give you at another time in a more extended letter.

Your agreement touches upon questions of such vital importance that as soon as read I addressed a note to the Sec. of War notifying him of their receipt and the importance of immediate action by the President, and suggested in view of their importance that the entire Cabinet be called together that all might give an expression of their opinions upon the matter. The result was a disapproval by the President of the basis laid down, a disapproval of the negotiations altogether, except for the surrender of the Army commanded by Johnston, and directions to me to notify you of this decission. I cannot do so better than by sending you the enclosed copy of a dispatch penned by the late President, though signed by the Sec. of War, in answer to me on sending a letter received from Gen. Lee proposing to meet me for the purpose of submitting the question of peace to a convention of Officers.

Please notify General Johnston immediately on receipt of this of the termination of the truce and resume hostilities against his Army at the earlyest moment you can, acting in in good faith.

The rebels know well the terms upon which they can have peace and just where negotiations can commence, namely: when they lay down their Arms and submit to the laws of the United States. Mr. Lincoln gave them full assurances of what he would do I believe in his conference with commissioners met in Hampton Roads.

>Very respectfully
>your obt. svt.
>U. S. GRANT
>Lt. Gn.

To Julia Dent Grant

Apl. 21st *1865*

Dear Julia,

It is now nearly 11 O'Clock at night and I have received directions from the Sec. of War, and President, to start at once for Raleigh North Carolina. I start in an hour. Gen. Meigs, Maj. Leet, Capt. Dunn, (Dunn is Capt. and Asst. Adj. Gn.) and Major Hudson go with me. I will write to you from Morehead City or New Berne.—I do hope you will have moved to Phila by the time I return. I can run up to Philadelphia easily; but to get to Burlington I have to give notice of my going to secure a train to take me the last end of the way.

I find my duties, anxieties, and the necessity for having all my wits about me, increasing instead of diminishing. I have a Herculean task to perform and shall endeavor to do it, not to please any one, but for the interests of our great country that is now begining to loom far above all other countries, modern or ancient. What a spectacle it will be to see a country able to put down a rebellion able to put half a Million of soldiers in the field, at one time, and maintain them! That will be done and is almost done already. That Nation, united, will have a strength which will enable it to dictate to all others, *conform to justice and right.* Power I think can go no further. The moment conscience leaves, physical strength will avail nothing, in the long run.

I only sat down to write you that I was suddenly required to leave on important duty, and not feeling willing to say what that duty is, you must await my return to know more.

Love and kisses for you and the children.

>U. S. GRANT

To Julia Dent Grant

In the Field Raleigh Apl. 25th *1865*

Dear Julia,

We arrived here yesterday and as I expected to return to-day did not intend to write until I returned. Now however matters have taken such a turn that I suppose Sherman will finish up matters by to-morrow night and I shall wait to see the result.

Raleigh is a very beautiful place. The grounds are large and filled with the most beautiful spreading oaks I ever saw. Nothing has been destroyed and the people are anxious to see peace restored so that further devastation need not take place in the country. The suffering that must exist in the South the next year, even with the war ending now, will be beyond conception. People who talk now of further retalliation and punishment, except of the political leaders, either do not conceive of the suffering endured already or they are heartless and unfeeling and wish to stay at home, out of danger, whilst the punishment is being inflicted.

Love and Kisses for you and the children,

ULYS,

Index to the Letters

Abolitionists
  USG and, 1033
  sustain anti-Northern feelings,
    1009
Acapulco, Mexico, 934, 935
Adams, Mrs. Charles F., 1064
Alabama
  campaign of 1864 in, 1041, 1042
  campaign of 1865 in, 1084
  see also Mobile; Selma; Stevenson;
    Tuscumbia
Alden, Capt. Bradford R., 946
Alexander, Lt. Col. John W. S., 966,
    967
Alton, Ill., 970, 971
Alvarado, Mexico, 922
Anna, Ill.: USG at, 964–65
Appomattox Court House, Va.
  surrender at, 1085
  threatened, 1083
Arista, Gen. Mariano, 901, 910
Arkansas, 1029, 1030
Army career of USG
  alternatives to, 901
  pay/compensation, 963, 1071
  promotions, see Rank and
    promotions of USG
  as quartermaster, 935, 944, 947–49
  resignation considered, 901, 903,
    904–5, 906, 938, 940, 953
Army life of USG
  Dents' opinion of, 891, 900
  expenses, 940, 941, 943, 953, 963,
    978, 987
  (Julia) Grant at USG's army
    quarters, 903, 906, 922, 932, 943,
    953, 954, 966, 970, 991, 992, 996,
    1007, 1009, 1023, 1024, 1037, 1049,
    1059
  USG's opinion of, 891, 895, 922
  horses for, 966, 1070
  housing, 883, 892, 929–30, 941, 950,
    963
  road-building, 888
  social life, 966
Arnold, Benedict, 877

Astoria, Oregon Territory, 939
Atlanta, Ga., 1042
  Sherman's capture of, 1067

Babcock, Col. Orville E. (staff officer
    of USG), 1072
Badeau, Col. Adam (staff officer of
    USG), 1076
Bailey, Mrs. George B.: letter to,
    882–84
Baker, Lt. Charles T., 892
Banks, Gen. Nathaniel P., 1020
  reinforced, 1031
Barbour, Capt. Philip N., 885
  at Monterey, 919
Barboursville, Ky., 1040
Bartlett, Gen. Joseph J., 1053
Bass, Mr. (of St. Louis), 1022
Bayou Macon (La.), 1027
Beaman, Lt. Jenks, 893
Bear Creek (Ala.), 1035
Beauregard, Gen. P.G.T. (C.S.
    Army)
  desertions from his army,
    1061–62
  at Shiloh, 1000, 1004
Beckwith, Samuel H., 1085
Benicia Barracks, Calif., 936, 937
Benton, Thomas Hart, 903
Bermuda Hundred, Va., 1083
Berry, Lt. Benjamin A., 899
Bethel, Ohio: Julia Grant urged to
    visit, 946, 952
Big Black River (Miss.), bridge, 1025
Big South Fork (Cumberland River),
    1041
Bird's Point, Mo., 978
Bissell, Col. Josiah W., 1021
Black Bayou (Miss.), 1019
Black River, see Big Black River
    (Miss.)
Blair, Francis P., Sr., 1077
Blythe's Ferry, Tenn., 1035
Boggs, Harry, 975
Boggs, Louisa, 1056, 1057, 1059

Bomford, George (quartermaster
    agent), 941, 943
Bottom's Bridge (Chickahominy
    River), 1082
Bowers, Col. Theodore S. (staff officer
    of USG), 1007, 1037, 1064
  carries USG's pay accounts, 1055
  (Julia) Grant's plan to accompany,
    1049
  guards USG after Lincoln
    assassination, 1086
Boydton Plank Road (Va.), 1085
Bragg, Gen. Braxton (C.S. Army)
  defeat of, 1038
  at Shiloh, 1000
  threatened, 1035
Branchville, S.C., 1079
Breckinridge, Gen. John C. (C.S.
    Army), 1000
Brent, Capt. Thomas L., 941, 943
Bridgeport, Ala., 1034, 1036
Brinck, Capt. Wilbur F. (staff officer
    of USG), 995
Brinton, Dr. John H., 995
Brook, Lloyd (quartermaster clerk),
    943
Brown, Maj. Jacob, 912
Buchanan, Col. Robert C.
  at Humboldt Bay, 950, 953
  promotion likely, 946
Buckner, Gen. Simon B. (C.S. Army),
    983, 984
Bucksport, Calif., 950
Buell, Gen. Don Carlos
  expected at Savannah, 998
  letter to, 998–99
  occupies Nashville, 985, 986, 993–94
  at Shiloh, 999, 1002, 1003, 1005,
    1006, 1012
Buena Vista, battle of (Feb. 1847), 924
Bull Run (Va.), 1052, 1054
  first battle of (July 1861), 973
Bull's Gap (Tenn.), 1084
Burke, M. T. ("Lank"), 957
Burkeville, Va., 1083, 1084
Burlington, N.J., 1069, 1086, 1088
Burns, Barnabas: letter to, 1039–40
Burnside, Gen. Ambrose E., 1035, 1038,
    1052
Butler, Gen. Benjamin F.
  letter to, 1048–49

possible removal of, 1058–59
spring campaign plans for, 1051–52
    (mentioned), 1054

Cairo, Ill., 964, 978–80, 1052
California
  USG describes, 949–50
  USG in (1852), 937–39, 947–55
  USG praises, 938
  see also Humboldt Bay; San
    Francisco
Callender, Capt. Franklin D., 952
Camargo, Mexico, 917
Camp, Elijah (sutler), 936, 944
Campbell, John A., 1077, 1079
Camp Necessity, La., 887
Camp Nelson, Ky., 1040
Camp Salubrity, La., 879–87
  USG arrival (1844), 879–80; (1845),
    892
  USG describes, 881, 883–84, 893
  USG leaves (1845), 894
Camp Yates, Springfield, Ill., 965–67
Canada, pursuit of marauders in,
    1074
Canby, Gen. Edward R. S., 1083,
    1084
Cape Fear River (N.C.), 1078
Casey, Emily (Emma) Dent (sister-in-
    law of USG), 951, 965
  USG's regards to, 894, 904, 923
Casey, James F. (brother-in-law of
    USG), 965, 1076
Cerro Gordo, battle of (Apr. 1847),
    921, 923–24
Chadwick, C. A. (of Washington,
    D.C.), 1049
Charless, Blow & Co. (St. Louis), 961
Charleston, S.C., 1084, 1086
Chase, Salmon P.: letters to, 1010–11,
    1028–29
Chattanooga, Tenn.
  fortified, 1034, 1035
  USG in, 1034–40
  inaccessibility of, 1036
  in strategic planning, 1041–42
Chicago
  as place for USG's family to live,
    1070
  volunteer troops organized, 962

Chickahominy River (Va.), 1052, 1056
  Long Bridge and Bottom's Bridge,
    1082
Children of USG
  USG's correspondence with, 1051,
    1057, 1068
  USG sends money to, 974
  USG writes Ingalls about, 1045–46
  their health, 960
  schooling of, 992, 1014, 1023,
    1029–30, 1055–56, 1059–60,
    1068–69, 1070
  see also Grant, Ellen Wrenshall;
    Grant, Frederick Dent; Grant,
    Jesse Root, Jr.; Grant, Ulysses S.,
    Jr.
Cincinnati: Julia Grant visits, 1038
Cincinnati Commercial (newspaper),
    987
Cincinnati Gazette (newspaper), 987
City Point, Va.: USG in, 1057–84
Civil War
  arms and ammunition, captured and
    lost, 982, 1004, 1025, 1027–28, 1063
  casualties, 983, 998, 1000, 1002,
    1004, 1028, 1053, 1054, 1062–63,
    1067
  USG assesses probable duration,
    976, 1055
  peace prospects and negotiations,
    1034, 1065, 1077, 1079, 1080,
    1087–88
  press and publicity, 971–72, 987, 991,
    992, 995, 1006, 1007–9, 1018, 1024,
    1037, 1079
  prisoners, 982, 983, 985, 1016–17,
    1025, 1027, 1053, 1054, 1067
  and private property, 978–79, 992,
    993
  public opinion and, 955, 959, 962,
    988, 1009
  see also Confederate Army; Union
    Army; specific battles, campaigns,
    and generals
Civil War, battles
  Corinth, Miss., 1015
  Fort Donelson, 982–84
  Hatchie River, 1015
  Iuka, 1015
  Petersburg, 1062–63
  Shiloh, 1000–1004, 1006–7

  Spotsylvania Court House, 1054
  Vicksburg, 1025–26
  Wilderness, the, 1053–54
Civil War, naval aspects
  at Fort Donelson, 983
  at Shiloh, 1001, 1002, 1013
  in Virginia campaign, 1051
  and Yazoo expedition, 1019
Clarksville, Tenn., 985, 993
Clay, Clement C., Jr., 1079–80
Cleveland, Tenn., 1036
Clickitat Indians, 948
Collins, Lt. Joseph B., 950
Collins, Mrs. Joseph B., 934, 950
Columbia, S.C.: John Dent prisoner
    in, 1060
Columbia Barracks, Oregon Territory
  4th Infantry assigned to, 936
  USG at, 939–49
Columbia River, 939–40, 941, 955
Columbus, Ohio, 991, 992
Comanche Indians, 896
Commercial enterprises, USG's
  and currency difficulties, 962–63, 965
  as quartermaster, 946
  see also Land warrants, deeds, and
    deals (USG's)
Comstock, Col. Cyrus B., 1047, 1050
Confederate Army
  desertions, 1036, 1044, 1061–62, 1065,
    1066, 1080–81, 1084
  forced enlistments, 988
  USG comments on, 982, 1054,
    1064–65
  morale of, 1084
  peace sentiments in, 1079
  supply lines, 1081, 1083
  surrender negotiations, 1085,
    1087–88
Confederate States Congress: Stephens
    to address, 1080
Confederate States of America
  Missouri and, 971
  peace proposals, 1077
  public opinion in, 988, 1009
Confiscation Acts, 979
Corinth, Miss.
  citizens return to, 1009
  C.S. Army flees toward, 1000
  expedition from, to destroy
    railroads, 1041

USG in, 1007–14
USG's report of battle, 1015
plans to attack, 998
Corpus Christi, Tex.
climate, 898, 913
conduct of troops at, 905
USG at, 898–907
steamboat explosion, 898–99
troops happy to leave, 906
troops may leave, 898, 900, 906
Corwith, Mr., 960
Cotton, Capt. John W., 893
Cotton Port, Tenn., 1035
Cotton trade, regulated, 1023–24
Covington, Ky.: as place for Julia
    Grant to board, 976, 991, 992
Cowlitz Indians, 949
Crimean War, 966
Crittenden, Gen. Thomas L., 1002
Crook, Gen. George, 1082
Cross, Maj. Osborn: letter to, 947–49
Crump's Landing, Tenn., 997, 999, 1002
Cullum, Gen. George W.: letter to,
    982–84
Culpepper Court House, Va.
USG in, 1047–53
troop movements, 1050
Cumberland Gap (Tenn.), 1040, 1041
Cumberland River, 981, 990, 1041, 1075
Currency: secession and, 962–63, 965

Dalles Indians, 949
Dana, Charles A., 1033, 1058, 1064
Dana, Lt. Napoleon Jackson
    Tecumseh, 923
Danville, Va., 1083, 1084
Davis, Lt. Thomas, 923
De Camp, Jim, 938
Decatur, Ala., 1041, 1075
Deer Creek (Miss.), 1019
Dent, Ellen, see Sharp, Ellen Dent
    (sister-in-law of USG)
Dent, Ellen Wrenshall (mother-in-law
    of USG)
and (Julia) Dent's engagement, 885,
    886, 887
USG's letter unanswered, 890
USG's regards to, 894
Dent, Emily (Emma) Marbury, see
    Casey, Emily (Emma) Dent

Dent, Frederick (father-in-law of
    USG)
and (Julia) Dent's engagement, 886,
    887, 891, 895, 896, 903, 904,
    922–23
USG invites to live with family,
    1069
USG sends greetings to, 1054
USG's letters unanswered, 890, 895,
    896
USG will write to, 890
letter to, 955–56
taxes due on his land, 1076–77
Dent, Frederick T. (brother-in-law of
    USG), 1049
children of, 956
and Civil War, 956, 1055, 1076
(Julia) Grant and, 889
USG writes to, 893
health, 892–93, 903, 925, 926, 929,
    1055
letters to USG, 888, 892, 896, 903,
    956
marriage, 942
and Mexican War, 917, 918, 919, 920,
    922
military assignments, 885, 888,
    895–96, 1047
military promotions, 906, 917
no letters from, 909
and (Louise) Stribling, 888
Dent, George Wrenshall (brother-in-
    law of USG), 881, 942
Dent, Helen Louise Lynde (sister-in-
    law of USG), 1049
Dent, John C. (brother-in-law of
    USG), 887, 893, 905, 918
in California, USG and, 936, 937,
    938, 942, 954
USG asks for letter from, 956
USG impugns loyalty of, 1060
land deals with USG, 1022, 1077
as prisoner of war, 1060
urged to join new regiment, 903,
    907
Dent, Julia, see Grant, Julia Dent
Dent, Lewis (brother-in-law of USG)
and (Frederick Dent) Grant, 949
USG inquires about, 942
USG will write to, 894
land deal with, 1022

Dent, Mary Shurlds, 890
Deserters
  from Confederate army, 1036, 1044,
    1061–62, 1065, 1066, 1080–81,
    1084
  from Union army, 1065–66
Detroit, Mich.
  4th Infantry ordered away,
    930–31
  USG at, 929–32
  USG rents house, 929–30
  as place for Julia Grant to board,
    1014
Diaz de la Vega, Gen. R., 911
Dilworth, Lt. Rankin, 919
Dinwiddie Court House, Va., 1085
Dodge, Gen. Grenville M., 1072
Dunbar (gunboat), 987–88
Duncan, Henry P. (of Miss.), 1026
Duncan, Mary (Mrs. Henry P.), 1026
Duncan, Mary E., 964, 966
Dunn, Capt. William M., Jr. (staff
  officer of USG), 1071, 1088

Eastman, C. A. (quartermaster clerk),
  943
Eastport, Miss., 1075, 1083, 1084
Education
  teaching offer in Ohio, 901
  see also Children of USG: schooling
Election, presidential (1864), 1065;
  see also Presidency (U.S.),
  USG and
Elting, Lt. Norman, 885
Eureka, Calif., 950
Ewell, Gen. Richard S. (C.S. Army),
  1043
Ewell, Lt. Thomas, 923

Farming, USG and, 944
Felt, Susan M., 968
Field, George B. (commissioner of
  plantations), 1027
Field, Capt. George P., 919
Fielding, Mrs. John (aunt of Julia
  Grant): USG's regards to, 894,
  896, 899
Financial situation of USG
  arrangements with Julia Grant, 932,

    935, 936, 946–47, 952, 955, 974,
    978, 991, 1007, 1055, 1057, 1076
  in California, as quartermaster, 946
  in Civil War, army accounts, 1071
  fear of poverty, 953–54
  lack of funds, 1022, 1030, 1038
  see also Army life of USG: expenses;
    Commercial enterprises, USG's
Fishback, Owen T., 916, 925
Flamingo Island, New Granada, 936
Florence, Ala., 987
Foote, Comm. Andrew H. (U.S.
  Navy), 983, 984
Ford, Charles W., 974, 1076
  letter to, 1029–30
Ford, John T., 1086
Ford's Theatre, Washington, D.C.,
  1086
Forrest, Gen. Nathaniel B. (C.S.
  Army), 1075
Fort Donelson, Tenn.
  communications problem, 990–91,
    991–92, 995
  C.S.A. commander, 982
  USG at, 982–87
  USG plans to capture, 981–82
  plundering at, 992, 993
  reconnaissances toward, 981
  siege and surrender of (Feb. 1862),
    982–84, 985
  skirmish near, 981
  slaves at, 989–90
Fort Gratiot, Mich., 931
Fort Henry, Tenn.
  attack prepared, 980
  USG in or near, 980–82, 987–88,
    995
Fort Humboldt, Calif., *see* Humboldt
  Bay, Calif.
Fort Jesup, La., 886, 893
Fort Jones, Calif., 946
Fort Monroe, Va.
  forces concentrate at, 1051
  (Julia) Grant discouraged from
    visiting USG at, 1059
  ships at, 1051
Fort Niagara, N.Y., 931
Fort Reading, Calif., 944, 946
Fort Scott, Kans., 895
Fort Towson, Indian Territory, 885,
  888, 892

Fort Vancouver, Oregon Territory,
    936, 937, 954; *see also* Columbia
    Barracks, Oregon Territory
Fort Washita, Indian Territory, 893
Foster, Gen. John G., 1040, 1043, 1078
Fowler, Dr., 993
Francis Isabel, *see* Point Isabel, Tex.
Franklin, Gen. William B., 1059
Freeport, Ill., 963
Frémont, Gen. John C., 977
Fuller, Col. Charles E.: letter to, 1060

Galena, Ill.
    (Julia) Grant to raise money for
        land in, 1022–23
    USG expects to go to, 972–73
    as place for Julia Grant to live, 976,
        991
    volunteers raised in, 956–57, 962
Garland, Col. John, 885
General Orders No. 3, signed by USG
    (Jan. 1862), 979–80
Georgetown, Ohio, 884
Georgia
    C.S.A. troops in, 1062
    USG advises Lincoln on
        government of, 1069
    Sherman's march through, 1079
    see also Atlanta; Savannah
Getty, Gen. George W., 1053
Getz (husband of Margaret), 940, 941,
    943
Getz, Margaret (Maggy), 937, 940,
    941, 943
Gillmore, Gen. Quincy A., 1051, 1084
Golden Gate (steamship), 935, 936
Goldsboro, N.C., 1078, 1083
Goodrich's Landing, La., 1031
Gore, Maj. John H., 929, 930–31, 937
    death, 935
Gore, Mrs. John H., 931, 934, 935, 936,
    938
Graham, Lt. Richard H., 919
Grant, Clara Rachel (sister of USG),
    881, 889, 891
    death, 1081
    (Rachel) Tompkins' letter to, 960
Grant, Ellen Wrenshall (Nelly;
    daughter of USG), 1045
    education of, 1060

    fails to write to USG, 1068
    USG requests photograph of, 1056
    letter to, 1055–56
    letter to USG, 1055
    at sanitary fair, 1055
Grant, Frederick Dent (son of USG)
    and Civil War military maneuvers,
        965–66, 967, 969, 970, 977
    and Dent family, 946, 949
    USG inquires about and sends
        greetings, 931, 933, 934, 938, 940,
        941, 942, 944, 945, 947, 949, 953,
        1047
    USG praises, 970, 973
    USG requests letters from, 1037
    USG requests picture of, 944
    and USG's family, 932, 940–41, 945,
        946
    health, 1015
    to learn French, 1056
    letter to, 1068
    letters to USG, 968, 1057, 1068
    officers' comments on, 938
    (Ellen Dent) Sharp and, 933, 944,
        946
    (mentioned), 932, 936, 940
Grant, Gennie (or Jennie), *see* Grant,
    Virginia Paine
Grant, Hannah Simpson (mother of
    USG)
    family name, 1058
    and (Julia) Grant, 1038
    USG inquires about, 966
Grant, Jesse Root (father of USG)
    age, 960
    and (Mrs.) Gore, 935–36
    and (Frederick Dent) Grant, 945
    and (Julia) Grant, 952–53, 1015, 1038
    USG awaits letters from, 959, 987
    USG criticizes, 1014, 1015
    USG seeks his approval of plans, 957
    letters to, 956–57, 962–63, 968–69,
        971–73, 1004–5, 1013–14, 1015–16,
        1023–25, 1025–26, 1081
    letters to USG, 960, 968, 1013, 1015,
        1023, 1081
Grant, Jesse Root, Jr. (son of USG)
    and (Hannah) Grant, 1038
    USG inquires about, 974, 989
    USG sends greetings to, 996, 1037,
        1038, 1048, 1049, 1051

USG urges discipline of, 1047, 1049,
1051
illness, 960
refuses to attend school, 1068–69
(mentioned), 986, 1007, 1056
Grant, Julia Dent
childbearing, 933, 934, 938
and (Frederick T.) Dent, 889
engagement to USG, 885, 886, 887,
891, 895, 901, 903, 904, 922
financial arrangements with USG,
932, 935, 936, 946–47, 952, 955,
974, 978, 991, 1007, 1055, 1057,
1076
USG requests picture of, 944
at USG's army quarters, 903, 906,
922, 932, 943, 953, 954, 966, 970,
991, 992, 996, 1007, 1009, 1023,
1024, 1037, 1049, 1059
USG sends lock of hair to, 1056
USG sends watch to, 996
and USG's family, 946, 952–53, 992,
1015, 1038
health, 1047
letters to, 879–82, 884–87, 887–90,
890–92, 892–94, 894–96, 896–97,
898–900, 900–902, 902–4, 904–5,
905–7, 907–9, 909–12, 917–18,
918–20, 920–23, 925–27, 927–29,
929–30, 930–32, 932–33, 933–35,
935–37, 937–39, 939–41, 941–43,
943–45, 945–47, 949–51, 951–53,
953–55, 957–58, 960–61, 963–64,
964–65, 965–67, 967–68, 970–71,
973–74, 974–75, 977–78, 980–81,
985, 985–86, 986–87, 987–88,
988–89, 991–92, 994–96, 996–97,
1000–1001, 1006–7, 1009–10,
1022–23, 1036–37, 1037–38,
1047–48, 1049, 1051, 1054, 1055,
1056, 1057, 1059–60, 1068–69, 1070,
1076, 1076–77, 1085–86, 1088, 1089
rings exchanged with USG, 887,
889, 899, 907
Grant, Mary Frances (sister of
USG)
(Julia) Grant visits, 981
USG asks to stay with Julia, 976
USG intends to write to, 969
USG requests letters from, 986
USG urges to visit, 960

letters to, 959–60, 975–76, 981–82
letters to USG, 968, 975, 988,
1013
requests appointment for Nixon,
1014
Grant, Orvil Lynch (brother of
USG), 966
asked to urge Rawlins to join
USG, 974
asks USG about pay, 963
and family business, 965, 1022–23
visits USG, 977, 1055
will write to Jesse R. Grant, 957
writes to USG, 971
Grant, Rachel B., see Tompkins,
Rachel Grant
Grant, Samuel Simpson (Simp;
brother of USG)
estate of, 1022
USG inquires about, 966
USG preserves watch of, 996
in poor health, 960, 971
Grant, Ulysses S., Jr. (Buck; son of
USG)
and Dent family, 946
USG inquires about, 941, 942, 944,
949, 953
USG requests letters from, 1037
USG requests picture of, 944
USG sends greetings to, 940, 942,
945, 947, 953, 996
USG will write to, 1057
letter to, 1068
Grant, Virginia Paine (sister of USG)
USG wants her to visit, 932–33,
1069
USG wants her to visit Mrs. Gore,
935–36
visits Julia Grant, 941, 942
Gravelly Run (Va.), 1085
Gravois Creek region, 885, 891, 893,
927, 938, 1069
Great Britain, 893
Green, James S., 969
Green Bay, Wis., 893
Greensboro, N.C., 1084
Greenwood, Miss., 1019
Grenada, Miss., expedition to, 1018
Griffin, Gen. Charles, 1085
Griffith, R. McKinstry: letter to,
877–79

Griffith, William L. (cousin of USG), 1081
Guerrilla warfare, 973
Gwinn, Lt. William (U.S. Navy), 1001, 1002, 1013

Hadley, Miss (nurse), 1007
Haines's Bluff, Miss., 1019, 1024
Halleck, Gen. Henry W., 986, 1033, 1086
    communications problem with USG, 990–91, 991–92, 995
    conflict with USG, 993–94
    USG praises, 1006
    letters to, 993–94, 997–98, 999–1000, 1000, 1010, 1017–18, 1034–36, 1040–42, 1043–44, 1051–53, 1053–54, 1058–59, 1061–62, 1062–63, 1073
Hamburg, Tenn., 998
Hampton Roads, Va., 1088
Hancock, Gen. Winfield S., 1053
Hardee, Gen. William J. (C.S. Army), 975
Harris, Gen. Thomas A. (Mo. State Guard), 969, 970
Harrisonburg, La., 1031
Hatchie River, battle of, 1015
Hawkins, Capt. John P. (staff officer of USG), 995, 1003
Hays, Gen. Alexander, 1053
Hazlitt, Robert
    at Camp Salubrity, 881, 886, 891–92
    death of, 919
    and (Ellen) Dent, 881, 890
    and (Julia) Dent, 886, 888, 892, 896, 902
    to Fort Jesup, 893
    in Mexican War, 911, 919
    and (Fanny) Morrison, 888
    (mentioned), 907
Health (USG's), 926, 928, 933, 935, 936, 937, 939, 943, 952, 970–71, 977, 989, 994–95, 1001, 1006–7, 1026, 1036, 1057, 1076, 1081
Hedgpeth, Col. Isaac N., 1016–17
Helena, Ark., 1018, 1019
Hewit, Dr. Henry S., 1003
Hicksford, Va., 1044

Higgins, Fanny Morrison, 886, 888–89, 895
    and (Thaddeus) Higgins, 885, 893, 899
    may remarry, 929
Higgins, Lt. Thaddeus, 885, 893
    at Camp Salubrity, 884
    death, 899
    and USG correspondence with Julia Dent, 884, 895
Hill, Gen. Ambrose P. (C.S. Army), 1061–62
Hillsboro, Ohio, 901
Hillyer, Col. William S. (staff officer of USG), 977, 995
    at Fort Donelson, 984
    USG sends greetings to, 1051
    at Shiloh, 1003
    (mentioned), 985
Holston River (Tenn.), 1040
Hood, Gen. John B. (C.S. Army), 1072, 1075
Hooker, Samuel T., 936
Hoskins, Lt. Charles, 919
Hudson, Maj. Peter T. (staff officer of USG), 1088
Humboldt Bay, Calif.
    environs described, 949–50
    USG at, 949–55
    USG praises his company at, 952
    as healthy environment, 954
    (Lewis C.) Hunt at, 944
    sea disasters at, 954–55
Hunt, Lt. Lewis C., 944, 950, 953, 954
Hunt, Col. Thomas F., 903
Hunter, Gen. David, 1049
Hunter, R.M.T., 1077, 1079
Huntsville, Ala., 1041
Hurlbut, Gen. Stephen A.
    letter to, 1021
    at Pittsburg Landing, 997
    at Shiloh, 1003
    telegram to, 1015

Illinois, see Alton; Chicago; Freeport; Galena; Illinois Volunteers; Jacksonville, Ill.; Naples; Springfield
Illinois River, 967, 969

Illinois Volunteers
  USG appointed colonel in, 965
  USG considers serving in, 957, 962, 964–65
  USG disciplines and trains his regiment, 966, 967, 968, 969, 970, 979–80
  USG organizes, 957–64 *passim*
  USG prefers to regular army, 969
  USG's staff, 977
Indiana Volunteers, 965
Indians
  and frontier settlers, 896
  in Oregon Territory, 948–49
  see also Comanche Indians
Ingalls, Gen. Rufus, 941, 943
  letter to, 1045–46
Ironton, Mo.: USG in, 974–76
Irving, Washington, 878
Irwin, Lt. Douglass S., 919
Isthmus of Panama, *see* Panama, Isthmus of
Iuka, Miss., 1015

Jackson, Miss.: expedition to, 1028
Jackson, Tenn., 1015
Jacksonville, Ill., 967
Jalapa, Mexico, 922, 924
James River (Va.), 1051, 1052, 1054, 1057, 1063, 1082
Jarvis, Lt. Charles E., 886
Jasper, Tenn., 1034
Jefferson Barracks, Mo.
  USG leaves for La., 882
  USG letter mailed from, 886
  USG regrets leaving, 881–82, 891
  USG visits, 974
  USG wishes to return to, 880
  McDowell goes to, 931
  (Mrs.) Wallen returns to, 895
Jefferson City, Mo., 977–78
Jenkins, Gen. Micah (C.S. Army), 1053
Jenney, Lt. William L. B., 1003
Jews: USG's orders regarding, 1015
Johnson, Andrew
  USG meets with, 1085
  and terms of Confederate surrender, 1087
Johnston, Gen. A. S. (C.S. Army), 985
  death, at Shiloh, 1000, 1013

Johnston, Gen. Joseph E. (C.S. Army), 1028, 1082, 1087
Jones, J. Russell
  and USG's financial affairs, 1038, 1055, 1076
  letter to, 1038–39

Kentucky
  USG campaigns in, 1040–41
  see also Louisville; Paducah
Kittoe, Dr. Edward D., 1037, 1039
Knox, Sgt. (4th Infantry), 936
Knox, Thomas W.: letter to, 1020–21
Knoxville, Tenn., 1041, 1043, 1082
Kosciuszko, Tadeusz, 877
Kossak, Lt. William, 1003
Kountz, Capt. William J., 985, 995

Lagow, Lt. Clark B. (staff officer of USG), 977
  at Fort Donelson, 984
  at Shiloh, 1003
  writes to Julia Grant, 992
La Grange, Tenn.: USG at, 1015–16
Lake Providence, La., 1017, 1020
  plantations near, 1027
Land warrants, deeds, and deals (USG's), 952, 955, 1022–23, 1076–77
Latimer, Lt. Alfred E., 950
Lavega, Gen., *see* Diaz de la Vega, Gen. R.
Lear, Maj. William W., 919
Lee, Gen. Fitzhugh (C.S. Army), 1067
Lee, Gen. Robert E. (C.S. Army)
  USG's strategy against, 1043, 1050, 1051–52, 1071, 1081, 1084
  Sheridan urged to hasten against, 1082
  in surrender negotiations, 1085, 1087
Leet, Maj. George K., 1088
Lexington (gunboat), 1001, 1002
Lexington, Ky., 1040
Lincoln, Abraham
  assassination of, 1086
  calls for troops, 955, 957, 958, 962
  USG advises on civil rule in Georgia, 1069
  USG permits to publish letter, 1069

letters to, 1030–32, 1060–61, 1072,
    1077, 1080, 1085
letters to USG, 1030
and peace negotiations, 1077, 1079,
    1080, 1087–88
Little Colorado River (Tex.), 907–8
Livermore, Lark S., 1027
London, Ky., 1040
Long Bridge (Chickahominy River),
    1082, 1083
Longstreet, Gen. James (C.S. Army)
    desertions from, 1061–62
    USG moves against, 1040, 1041,
        1043
    threatens Knoxville, 1043
    wounded, 1053
Lookout Mountain, Tenn., 1035
Loudon, Tenn., 1041
Louisiana
    Northern civil policy in, 1069
    Northern subjugation of, 1029,
        1030
    recruitment of Negro troops in,
        1031
    see also Camp Salubrity; Fort Jesup;
        Lake Providence; Milliken's Bend;
        New Orleans; Port Hudson
Louisville, Ky: Julia Grant in, 994
Lowe, John W.: letters to, 912–16,
    923–25
Lowe, Tom, 916, 923, 925
Lynchburg, Va., 1083, 1084

McCallum, Gen. Daniel C., 1084
McClellan, Gen. George B.
    campaign on Tennessee and
        Cumberland rivers, 990
    report on Crimean War, 966
McClernand, Gen. John A.
    in Fort Donelson campaign, 982,
        983, 984
    at Pittsburg Landing, 997
    at Shiloh, 1003
McConnell, Capt. Thomas R., 937,
    938, 944
McCook, Gen. Alexander McD., 1002
McDowell, Capt. Irvin, 931
Macfeely, Lt. Robert, 936
McKeever (friend of Ellen Dent), 933
MacKenzie, Kenneth, 958

McLean, Capt. Nathaniel H., 997
    letter to, 1001–4
McMackin, Maj. Warren E., 966
McMichael, Capt. William, 1003
McMinnville, Tenn., 1035
McPherson, Gen. James B.
    Alabama campaign, 1042
    as engineer officer, 998, 1017
    at Fort Donelson, 984
    USG praises, 1046–47, 1064
    USG's condolences to his
        grandmother, 1063–64
    at Shiloh, 1003, 1004, 1007
    and Yazoo Pass expedition, 1019
Mahone, Gen. William (C.S. Army),
    1078
Majia, Gen. Francisco, 908–9
Maloney, Capt. Maurice, 936
Maltby, Gen. Jasper A., 1034
Manassas (Va.), 1st battle of (July
    1861), 973
Mason, Capt. Stevens T., 923
Massachusetts: recruits Negro troops,
    1061
Matamoros, Mexico
    USG based at, 912–18
    USG describes, 916
    U.S. troops camp opposite, 906,
        907
    U.S. troops march to, 907, 908, 913
    violence in, 918
Maury, Lt. Dabney H., 923
Meade, Gen. George G., 1052
Meagher, Gen. Thomas F., 1084
Meigs, Gen. Montgomery C., 1084,
    1088
Mellen, William P., 1028
Memphis, Tenn.
    fortification of, 1010
    USG disciplines press, 1021
    USG intends to go to, 1009
Memphis Bulletin (newspaper), 1021
Mendocino Cape, Calif., 954
Meridian, Miss., 1041, 1042
Mexican War (1846–48)
    accounts and reports of, 899,
        900–901, 912
    arms and ammunition, captured and
        lost, 911–12, 915–16, 921
    casualties, 910–11, 913, 915, 919, 921,
        923, 924, 925, 926

USG comments on Mexican troops,
911, 926
USG in, 905–29
Mexico threatens reconquest of
Texas, 885
peace prospects discussed, 919, 926,
928
possibility of war discussed, 893
prisoners, 909, 923, 924
U.S. troops opposite Matamoros,
906, 907
U.S. troops seized, 909
U.S. troops threatened at Little
Colorado River, 907–8
weariness of, 928
Mexican War (1846–48), battles
Buena Vista (Feb. 1847), 924
Cerro Gordo (Apr. 1847), 921,
923–24
Monterrey (May 1846), 918–19
Palo Alto (May 1846), 909, 910,
914
Resaca de la Palma (May 1846), 909,
911, 915
Mexico, 927
boundary issue with Texas, 903,
904, 906
USG comments on people, 916, 922,
928
USG comments on soil, climate,
928
USG may visit, 886
see also Matamoros; Mexico City;
Monterrey
Mexico, Mo., 969, 970
USG in, 971–74
Mexico City, Mexico, 918, 922, 924
described by USG, 926, 928
USG camped near, 927
Micawber, Mr. (character in David
Copperfield), 1065
Military life, see Army life of USG
Milliken's Bend, La.
USG at, 1021–25
plantations near, 1027
as unsuitable for Julia Grant, 1037
Milroy, Gen. Robert H., 1053
Mississippi
Northern civil policy in, 1069
Northern subjugation of, 1029, 1030
see also Corinth; Eastport; Jackson;

Oxford; Vicksburg; Warrenton;
Yazoo Pass
Mississippi River, trade policy,
1069
Missouri
USG remembers visit fondly, 894
USG wishes to return to, 885, 886
secessionist sentiments in, 971
slavery doomed in, 961
unsettled conditions in, 961
see also Ironton; Jefferson Barracks;
Palmyra; St. Louis
Missouri Democrat (newspaper), 976
Missouri River, 972, 973
Mobile, Ala., 1030, 1041, 1042, 1084
newspapers, 1032
Monroe, La., 1031
Monroe, Mo., 969, 970
Monterrey, Mexico
battle expected, 915
battle of, 918–19
climate and appearance praised,
919
destination of U.S. troops, 917
fortifications, 917, 919
U.S. troops march to, 917–18
Montgomery, Lt. Thomas J., 950
Montgomery, Ala., 1042
Morris, Capt. Gouverneur, 885
at Monterrey, 919
Morris, Thomas, 1058
Morrison, Fanny, see Higgins, Fanny
Morrison
Morrison, Georgia, 888, 889, 890
Morrison, Capt. Pitcairn, 886, 907
and Higgins' death, 899
Morse, Freeman H., 1065
Mossy Creek, (Tenn.), 1041

Name, USG's, 944, 1057–58
Naples, Ill.: USG in, 967–68
Nashville, Tenn.
Buell occupies, 985, 986, 993–94
(Julia) Grant asks to join USG at,
1037
USG goes to, 986, 993
USG in, 1040–47
occupied, 985
Ross remains in, 1036
Thomas vs. Hood at, 1072–75

Natchez, Miss., 1031
Natchitoches, La.
  USG at/near, 879–87
  USG goes to, 883, 893
Negroes
  Confederacy deprived of labor of,
    1031, 1044
  as soldiers, *see* Negro troops
  see also Slavery; Slaves
Negro troops
  advantages of raising, 1031
  C.S. Army may raise, 1075
  USG's personal support of, 1031
  mistreatment of, 1027
  organization of, 1026–27, 1031,
    1033
  payment of, 1082
  as prisoners of war, 1048–49
  recruitment of, 1031, 1033, 1061
Nelson, Gen. William, 993
  USG disputes his report on Shiloh,
    1011–13
  joins USG at Savannah, 998
  at Shiloh, 999, 1002
New Berne, N.C., 1043, 1084
New Carthage, La., 1024
New Market, Va., 1083
New Orleans, La.
  4th Infantry stationed at barracks,
    894–97
  USG visits (1844), 880, 882, 883
New River (Va.), 1083
Newspapers
  circulated among Union troops,
    1032
  of Mobile, 1032
  of Richmond, 1079, 1080, 1083
  of St. Louis, 961
  of Selma, 1032
  see also Press
New York City: Julia Grant visits,
  1051
New York *Herald* (newspaper):
  correspondent refused permission
  to return to USG's command,
  1020–21
New-York Tribune (newspaper), 995
Nixon, John S., 1014
North Carolina
  strategy for subjugation of,
    1043–44, 1078, 1084

  see also Goldsboro; Raleigh;
    Wilmington
Nueces River (Tex.), 898, 908

Ohio
  (Julia) Grant visits, 1037, 1038
  see also Bethel; Columbus;
    Georgetown; Hillsboro
Ohio (steamship), 933–34
O'Maley (4th Infantry), 936
Ord, Gen. Edward O. C., 1086
  letter to, 1086
Oregon Territory
  climate, 939, 941
  USG describes, 940, 942
  occupation discussed, 893
  see also Columbia Barracks; Fort
    Vancouver; Portland
Orizaba, Mexico, 924
Ossabaw Sound (Ga.), 1075
Osterhaus, Gen. Peter J.: letter to, 1025
Ould, Robert, 1048
Oxford, Miss.: USG in, 1016–17

Paducah, Ky., 987
Page, Charles A., 996
Page, Ellen, 996–97
Page, Emily Wrenshall, 997
Page, Capt. John, 910, 914
Page, Samuel K., 997
Paine, Gen. Eleazar A.: letter to,
  978–79
Palmer, Col. John M., 969, 970
Palmyra, Mo.: Ill. Volunteers occupy,
  968, 970
Palo Alto, battle of (May 1846), 909,
  910, 914
Panama, Isthmus of, 934, 935, 936,
  937
Pardee, Mr. (of St. Louis), 1022
Paredes y Arillaga, Gen. Mariano, 915,
  917
Pea Ridge, Tenn., 1000
Pemberton, Gen. John C.: letter to,
  1016–17
Perote, Castle of (Mexico), 920, 921,
  925
Petersburg, Va., 1078, 1083
  assaulted, 1062–63

Philadelphia, Pa.
  USG plans to visit family at, 1086,
    1088
  as place for USG's family to live,
    1070
Physical appearance of USG, 905, 925,
    926, 944, 952
Pillow, Gen. Gideon J. (C.S. Army),
    982
Pittsburg Landing, Tenn.
  attacked by C.S.A., 998–99, 1000
  USG at/near, 997–1007
  Nelson marches to, 1012
  skirmishes at, 997–98
  see also Shiloh (Tenn.), battle of
Plan del Rio, Mexico, 923
Point Isabel, Tex., 903, 904, 910, 912,
    913
Political views, USG's, 957
  refuses candidacy for presidency
    (1863), 1039–40
Polk, James K.: criticized, 916
Pope, Dr. Charles A. (of St. Louis),
    1015
Pope, Gen. John, 958, 1066, 1072
Porter, David, 893
Porter, Adm. David D. (U.S. Navy)
  letter to, 1018
  and Yazoo expedition, 1019
Porter, Col. Horace (staff officer of
    USG), 1047, 1076
Porter, Lt. Theodoric H., 888, 892,
    893
Porter, Mrs. Theodoric H., 887, 893
  USG's regards to, 890
  may remarry, 929
Port Hudson, La., 1020, 1048
Portland, Oregon Territory, 940
Potomac, Army of the
  Crook proposed to command
    cavalry, 1082
  USG and, 1033
  morale of, 1050
Potts, Dr. Richard, 950, 953
Prentiss, Gen. Benjamin M., 1003, 1019
Presidency (U.S.), USG and, 1039–40
Press
  USG disciplines Memphis press,
    1021
  USG evicts New York *Herald*
    correspondent, 1020–21

reports Civil War, 971–72, 987, 991,
    992, 995, 1006, 1007–9, 1018, 1024,
    1037, 1079
reports Mexican War, 899, 900–901,
    912
Pride, Col. George G., 1003
Prisoners of war, in Civil War, 982,
    983, 985, 1016–17, 1025, 1027, 1053,
    1054, 1067
  as deserters, 1066
  exchange of, 1016, 1048–49, 1066
  Negro, 1048–49
  recruiting among, 1061
  treatment of, 1016–17
Prisoners of war, in Mexican War,
    909, 923
Promotions, see Rank and promotions
    of USG
Property, private: Civil War and,
    978–79, 992, 993
Puebla, Mexico, 922, 925

Quaker Road (Va.), 1085
Quinby, Gen. Isaac F.: letter to,
    1019–20
Quincy, Ill.: 21st Volunteers march
    toward, 966, 967, 969

Railroads
  building, 1034–35, 1041, 1078
  destruction of, 1025, 1041, 1067,
    1079, 1083
  strategic to Confederacy, 1044
  for Union military transport, 1035,
    1041, 1078, 1084
  see also Weldon Railroad
Raleigh, N.C., 1043, 1044
  USG in, 1089
  USG ordered to, 1088
Rank and promotions of USG, 884,
    893, 895, 899, 900, 940, 962, 964,
    965, 972–73, 986, 1046
Rapidan River (Va.), 1052
Rappahannock River (Va.), 1052
Rawlins, Gen. John A.
  at Fort Donelson, 984
  on USG's staff, 974, 977
  health, 995, 1070
  promoted, 1034

at Shiloh, 1003
(mentioned), 1039
Red River, 880, 892, 1020, 1041
Republican party: USG comments on,
955, 969
Resaca de la Palma, battle of (May
1846), 909, 911, 915
Reynolds, Capt. Charles A., 1007
Reynolds, Capt. Joseph J., 965, 1059
Richmond, Ky., 1040
Richmond, Va.
assault on, 1056
battle at, 1010
Halleck commands, 1086
meetings to discuss peace, 1080
newspapers, 1079, 1080, 1083
Ord ordered to arrest Ford at,
1086
strategy against, 1043, 1051–52, 1081
Richmond Dispatch (newspaper), 1079
Richmond Enquirer (newspaper),
1079
Richmond Whig (newspaper), 1079
Riggin, Col. John, Jr., 984, 1007
Rio Grande (river), 895, 901
4th Infantry ordered to, 903, 906
USG praises countryside, 908
Rolling Fork River (Miss.), 1019–20
Rosecrans, Gen. William S., 1037
Ross, Orlando H. (cousin of USG),
1036
Ross, James (uncle of USG), 878
Rowley, Capt. William R. (staff officer
of USG), 989, 995, 1003, 1007
Russell, Lt. Edmund, 938, 944

Sackets Harbor, N.Y., 931, 932–33
Safford, Alfred B., 996
Safford, Mary Jane, 996
St. Charles, Mo., 970
St. Louis, Mo.
(Julia) Grant visits, 929
USG in, 881, 882, 892, 920
USG reads newspapers from, 961
USG urges Julia Grant to go to,
1022, 1060
USG wishes to return to, 880
unsettled conditions, 961
*St. Louis Democrat, see Missouri
Democrat*

San Francisco
USG expects to visit, 941–42
lumber trade, 950
Wallen goes to, 946
San Isabel, *see* Point Isabel, Tex.
San Patricio, Tex., 898
Santa Anna, Antonio López de, 921,
923–24
Sappington, Jemima, 893
Sappington, Sebastian, 1022
Sappington Post Office, Mo., 891
Savannah, Ga.: Sherman and, 1075
Savannah, Tenn.
USG in, 988–99, 1005, 1006
Nelson leaves, 1012
Schofield, Gen. John M., 1073, 1078,
1083
Scott, Capt. Henry L., 946
Scott, Gen. Winfield
letter about USG, 1062
letter to, 1062
in Mexican War, 920–21, 923
his policy on leaves, 927, 929
(mentioned), 878
Secession and secessionists, 971
impact on currency, 962–63, 965
Virginia and, 959, 960
Sedgwick, Gen. John, 1053
Selma, Ala., 1083
newspapers, 1032
Servants
in California, 953
at Camp Salubrity, 892
in Civil War, 1071
at Detroit, 930
(Julia) Grant and, 954
USG takes to Texas, 896
in Oregon, 941, 943
Seward, William H.
letter to, 1065–66
wounded, 1086
Seymour, Gen. Truman, 1053
Shaler, Gen. Alexander, 1053
Sharp, Dr. Alexander (brother-in-law
of USG), 966, 1055
Sharp, Ellen Dent (sister-in-law of
USG)
and (Frederick Dent) Grant, 933,
944, 946
USG's regards to, 886, 887, 890,
894, 902, 904, 923

and (Robert) Hazlitt, 881, 890
marriage plans, 931
may visit USG and Julia, 930, 931
writes to Julia Grant, 930
(mentioned), 905, 918
Sharp, Josh, 977
Sheets, Lewis, 956
Shenandoah Valley (Va.), 1067
Shepard, Col. Isaac F., 1027
Sheridan, Gen. Philip H.
   USG urges haste, 1082
   letters to, 1067, 1082–83
   Virginia campaign (1865), 1083–84,
      1085
Sherman, Gen. William Tecumseh
   campaigns in Miss., 1028, 1041, 1042,
      1045
   at Goldsboro, 1083
   USG awaits news of, 1054, 1080,
      1089
   USG commends to Lincoln, 1069
   USG discusses strategy with, 1050,
      1071–72, 1078–79, 1083–84
   USG praises, 1021, 1046–47, 1067,
      1076
   letters to, 997, 1046–47, 1050, 1067,
      1071–72, 1078–79, 1083–84,
      1087–88
   marches to Chattanooga, 1035
   marches through Georgia, 1079
   press and, 1020–21
   and promotion, 1079
   at Savannah, 1075
   at Shiloh, 1002, 1003
   and skirmishes near Pittsburg
      Landing, 997–98
   and terms of surrender
      (Confederate), 1087–88
   victory at Atlanta, 1067
   and Yazoo expedition, 1019
Shiloh (Tenn.), battle of
   beginning of, 999–1000, 1001
   casualties, 1000, 1004, 1013
   USG defends conduct of, 1005,
      1008–9, 1011–13
   USG injured, 1006–7
   number of troops at, 999, 1000
   reported, 1000–1004, 1006–7
   troops ordered toward, 999
Shirk, Lt. James W. (U.S. Navy), 1001,
   1002

Shurlds, Joe, 881
Shurlds, Mary Isabella, see Dent, Mary
   Shurlds
Simons, Dr. James, 995
Simpson, John (cousin of USG), 1081
Simpson, Rebecca Weir (grandmother
   of USG), 879
Simpson, Robert B. (cousin of USG),
   1081
Simpson, Samuel (uncle of USG),
   878
Slaughter, Mrs. William A., 934
Slavery
   defeat of, as object of Civil War,
      971
   USG discusses, 956, 1033–34
   and peace terms of Civil War, 1065
Slaves
   captured at Fort Donelson,
      989–90
   leaving Mo., 961
   runaway, at Memphis, 1010
   runaway, at Vicksburg, 1017
   theft/liberation of, 1009–10
Slocum, Lydia: letter to, 1063–64
Smith, Gen. Charles F.
   in Fort Donelson campaign, 982,
      983, 984, 995
   USG consoles widow on his death,
      1005–6
Smith, Mrs. Charles F.: letter to,
   1005–6
Smith, Gen. John E., 1019, 1039
Smith, Col. Robert F., 968–69,
   970
Smith, Lt. Sidney, 926
Smith, William (governor of Va.),
   1080
Smith, Gen. William F.
   USG supports, 1058, 1059
   quarrels with Butler, 1058
Smith, William W. (cousin of Julia
   Grant), 1070
Smithville, N.C., 1078
Smugglers and speculators, 1023–24
South Carolina, 959–60; see also
   Charleston
Speculators, 1023–24
Spies, guarded against, 978
Spotsylvania Court House (Va.), battle
   of, 1054

Springfield, Ill.
    USG organizes troops in, 957–64
        passim
    see also Camp Yates, Springfield, Ill.
Staff (military) of USG, 977, 995, 1014
    (Frederick T.) Dent nominated to,
        1047
    USG praises, 984, 1003, 1034
    health, 994–95, 1076
Stanislaus River (Calif.), 937
Stanton, Edwin M.
    letters to, 1061, 1069, 1074, 1079–80,
        1080–81, 1082
    and peace negotiations, 1087
    (mentioned), 1049
Steele, Capt. Frederick, 937, 1045
Steele's Bayou (Miss.), 1019
Stephens, Alexander H., 1033
    and peace negotiations, 1077, 1079,
        1080
Stevens, Lt. Thomas H. (U.S. Navy),
    938, 954
Stevens, Mrs. Thomas H., 938, 954
Stevenson, Col. John D. (Mo.
    Volunteers), 1015
Stevenson, Ala., 1035
Stewart, Maj. Isaac S.: letter to, 1071
Stoneman, Gen. George, 1082–83,
    1084
Strawberry Plains, Tenn., 1040
Stribling, Louise, 888
Strickle, Capt. Abraham E., 1027
Sue, Eugène: *Le Juif errant
    (Wandering Jew)*, 902
Suffolk, Va., 1043
Sunflower River (Miss.), 1019
Sword, awarded to USG, 1051
Swords, Col. Thomas, 935

Tacubaya, Mexico: USG in, 927–29
Taylor, Gen. Zachary
    attacked while returning to
        Matamoros, 909–10, 913
    at battle of Palo Alto, 910
    crosses Little Colorado River, 908
Tennessee
    Union sentiment in, 988
    see also Chattanooga; Crump's
        Landing; Fort Donelson; Fort
        Henry; Knoxville; Memphis;

Nashville; Pittsburg Landing;
        Savannah, Tenn.; Shiloh
Tennessee, Army of the: USG and,
    1033
Tennessee River, 981, 987, 990, 1042,
    1075
    trade on, 1010
Tensas River (La.), 1027
Tepeyahualco, Mexico, 923
Terchin, Col., *see* Turchin, Col.
    John B.
Terrett, Lt. John C., 919
Texas
    annexation discussed, 883, 893, 912
    boundary issue, 903, 904, 906
    chances USG will leave, 899, 900,
        904
    Civil War in, 1031
    country praised, 899
    4th Infantry ordered to, 895, 897
    USG may visit, 886
    see also Corpus Christi; Point Isabel
Thomas, Gen. George H.
    USG orders to attack, 1072, 1073
    USG plans movements for, 1035,
        1042, 1045, 1078
    vs. Hood in Tenn. and Ala., 1072,
        1075
    letters to, 1043, 1074, 1075
    relieved of command, and order
        suspended, 1073, 1074
    in Tenn., 1072, 1084
    troops' confidence in, 1037
    victory in Nashville, 1075
Thomas, Gen. Lorenzo
    letter to, 1026–28
    organizes Negro troops, 1031,
        1033
Thompson, John G.: letter to, 1032
Toluca, Mexico, 927
Tompkins, Rachel Grant (aunt of
    USG), 960
Trade, regulated, 1010–11, 1023–24,
    1028–29
    on Mississippi River, 1069
Tripler, Dr. Charles, 931
Trumbull, Lyman, 972
Turchin, Col. John B., 970
Turner, Mrs. William D., 1007
Tuscumbia, Ala., 1075
Tweed, Alice (of Cincinnati), 1038

Twiggs, Gen. David E., 921,
    923–24
Tyler (gunboat), 1001, 1002

Underwood, Lt. Edmund, 938
Underwood, Mrs. Edmund, 934
Union, Calif., 950
Union Army
    desertions, 1065–66
    morale of, 1018
    Negro troops, *see* Negro troops
    organization and commands, 1042,
        1058–59, 1072, 1082
    payment of, 1018, 1082
    supply lines and problems, 1034,
        1035, 1036, 1038, 1040–41, 1042,
        1043, 1052, 1078
    see also Illinois Volunteers
Union Army, conscription, 955, 957,
    958, 962, 1052, 1060–61, 1065
    Negro troops, 1031, 1033, 1061
    recruiting agents from states, 1061
U.S. Congress, Committee to
    Investigate the Conduct of the
    War, 986
U.S. Military Academy, West Point,
    N.Y.
    described by USG, 877–78, 879
    USG expects son Fred to attend,
        1056
    USG's name change on entering,
        1057–58

Van Buren, Martin, 878
Veracruz, Mexico, 921, 923, 924,
    925
Vicksburg, Miss.
    arms captured, 1025, 1027–28
    citizens of, 1037
    fortified, 1017, 1024
    USG in/near, 1017, 1019–21, 1025–30,
        1032–34
    naval preparations, 1018
    prisoners, 1025, 1027, 1048
    prisoners exchanged in, 1016, 1048
    siege of, and safety of nearby
        plantations, 1027
    siege of, and surrender, 1025–26
    troop movements, 1031, 1041

Virginia
    campaign of 1864 in, 1051–75
    campaign of 1865 in, 1082–84
    USG wants to be assigned to, 976
    secedes, 956
    secession deplored, 959, 960
    see also Appomattox Court House;
        City Point; James River;
        Petersburg; Richmond;
        Shenandoah Valley; Wilderness
        (Va.), battle of
Vose, Col. Josiah H., 896

Wadsworth, Gen. James S., 1053
Walker, Annie (of St. Louis), 930
Wallace, Gen. Lew
    at Crump's Landing, 997
    in Fort Donelson campaign, 983, 984
    at Shiloh, 999, 1002, 1003
Wallace, Gen. W. H. L., 997, 1003
Wallen, Capt. Henry D.
    at Camp Salubrity, 892
    in Detroit, lives with USG, 929
    injured, in Oregon, 944
    in Mexican War, 910
    plans private enterprise, 946, 954
Wallen, Laura
    in California, 938
    at Camp Salubrity, 894, 895
    children of, 936, 946, 953
    and USG's correspondence with
        Julia Dent, 896–97
    intends writing to Julia Grant, 937
    on journey to Calif., 934, 936
    in Oregon, 942, 944
    refuses return to Fort Vancouver,
        954
    returns to Jefferson Barracks, 895
War: USG comments on, 915, 927, 986,
    1056
Warren, Gen. Gouverneur K., 1085
Warrenton, Miss., 1020
Washburne, Elihu B.
    letters to, 989–91, 1007–9, 1033–34,
        1057–58, 1064–65, 1069–70
    (Winfield) Scott writes to, about
        USG, 1062
    urges USG to stay in Springfield,
        958
    writes to USG, 989, 1033

Washington, George, 877
Washington, D.C.
    USG plans to visit, 1047, 1049
    USG stays in, after Lincoln
        assassination, 1085–88
    USG unwilling to have headquarters
        in, 1046
    troops in, 1052
Webster, Col. Joseph D. (staff officer
        of USG), 984, 1010
    at Shiloh, 1003–4
Weldon, N.C., 1044
Weldon Railroad, 1067, 1078
West Point, N.Y., see U.S. Military
    Academy, West Point, N.Y.
West Quincy, Mo., 968–71
Whistler, Col. William, 931, 933
Wilderness (Va.), battle of the
    casualties and prisoners, 1053, 1054
    planning for, 1051–53
Willamette River, 940
Wilmington, N.C., 1043, 1044
    Gillmore sent against, 1084
    Schofield sent against, 1078

Wilson, Henry, 1033
Wilson, Gen. James H., 1083, 1084
    on USG's staff, 1047
    on Yazoo Pass expedition, 1018
Wise, Henry A., 1080
Wood, Gen. Thomas J., 1002
Worth, Gen. William J., 923
Wright, Gen. Horatio G., 1053
Wyman, Edward (of St. Louis),
    1029–30

Yates, Richard
    appoints USG as colonel in Ill.
        Volunteers, 965
    asks USG to organize and drill
        volunteers, 957, 958, 959, 961, 962,
        963
    offers to endorse USG, 972
Yazoo City, Miss., 1019
Yazoo Pass (Miss.), expedition
    through, 1018, 1019–20
Yazoo River, 1018, 1019, 1020

Notes to the Doctor

*written while completing the Memoirs
at Mount McGregor, June – July 1885*

Notes to the Doctor

Dr. Since coming to this beautiful climate and getting a complete rest for about ten hours, I have watched my pains and compared them with those of the past few weeks. I can feel plainly that my system is preparing for dissolution in three ways; one by hemhorages, one by strangulation and the third by exaustion. The first and second are liable to come at any moment to relieve me of my earthly sufferings; the time for the arrival of the third can be computed with almost mathematical certainty. With an increase of daily food I have fallen off in weight and strength very rapidly for the last two weeks. There can not be a hope of going far beyond this time. All any physician, or any number of them do for me now is to make my burden of pain as light as possible. I do not want any physician but yourself but I tell you so that if you are unwilling to have me go without consultation with other professional men, you can send for them. I dread them however knowing that it means another desperate effort to save me, and more suffering.

June 17, 1885

I said I had been adding to my book and to my coffin. I presume every strain of the mind or body is one more nail in the coffin.

. . . . .

Several more pages since, a portion of which I wrote out.

. . . . .

I have now worked off all that I had notes of, and which often kept me thinking at night.

I will not push to make more notes for the present.

June 23, 1885, 5:30 P.M.

If this goes on I do not know but it will be best for me to take my first injection early. Three days ago I would scarsily have been able to endure the pain of to-day.

June 27, 1885

I am about as I every day at this hour. Papers are all read. I am drowsy without being able to sleep, and time passes heavily. No worse however only that my mouth has not been washed out to-day and the cocaine does not seem to relieve the pain.

June 29, 1885

This is always the trouble. No matter how well I get along the balance of the 24 hours, when the middle of the afternoon comes I begin to feel stuffy, stopped up and generally uncomfortable.

. . . . .

I do not feel the slightest desire to take morphine now. In fact when I do take it it is not from craving, but merely from a knowledge of the relief it gives. If I should go without it all night I would become restless I know, partly from the loss of it, and partly from the continuous pain I would have to endure.

June 29, 1885, 4:00 P.M.

I was frightened this morning because I felt so sleepy. I forgot that I had had nothing like the rest a well man requires. My feeling this am was what we want to produce: one that enables me to rest. But I was not quite conscious enough to reason correctly about what produced it.

June 30, 1885, 8:00 A.M.

12^{05} I will try to observe the effect of the last injection. Pain has ceased and slight drowsyness set in. Nothing however to indicate heavyness or the use of too much morphine.—At this hour, or a few minutes later, was given the minim of morphine. Went to sleep almost immediately. Awoke at 3^{30} feeling no effect of the injection.

. . . . .

It is a little hard giving up the use of cocoane when it gives so much relief. But I suppose that it may be used two or three times a day, without injury, and possibly with benefit, when the overuse of it has been counteracted.

. . . . .

It will probably take several days to see the effect of discontinuing the use of cocoan? It might then be used once a day, might it not? say when I am retiring for the night. It is no trouble however to quit outright for the present.

June 30, 1885

I see the Times man keeps up the character of his dispatches to the paper. They are quite as untrue as they would be if he described me as getting better from day to day. I think he might spare my family at least from reading such stuff.

June 30, 1885, P.M.

I will have to be careful about my writing. I see ever person I give a piece of paper to puts it in his pocket. Some day they will be coming up against my English

June – July 1885

But you intend to go back to the hotel to-night whether I want an injection or not?

I think then you had better run now. But we will see better in a few minuets. The probabilities are that I shall feel no more inclination to sleep for the next hour in any event, injection or no injection. I think my tongue has commenced to diminish.

June – July 1885

I see no effect whatever from the gas as yet. Mine is a different case from ordinary suffering.

June – July 1885

There was a week or such matter when I had but little acute pain. The newspapers gave that as a sure indication that I was declining rapidly.

June – July 1885

I feel weak from my exertions last night in throwing up. Then since that I can not help repeating two advertisements of the B & O railroad when I am half awake. The houses on their place at Deer Park are advertised as a sure cure for Malaria, or the place is signed Robt Garrett, Pres. The other is that the water—I think—is a sure cure for Catarrh. Signed same. There may be no such advertisement, but I keep dreaming them all the same. It strikes me as a very sharp dodge for a gentleman to advertise his own wares in such a way. When you consider Garrett owns the water and buildings at the park; is Pres. of the road over which invalids must pass to get to the place, and is a very large owner in the stock of the road it strikes me as another instance of what a man will do for money.

July 1, 1885, 8:00 A.M.

I have not taken any wine in six days. So far as I have tried I do not think alcoholic drinks agree with me. They seem to heat me up and have no other effect.

July 1, 1885, 10:00 A.M.

I talked a goodeal with my pencil. The wine I did take was not Madiera but Tokay, but since leaving N.Y. three small wine glasses of Old Port. I do not need or want either. Mrs. Grant and Fred thought they would help me.

July 1, 1885

I do not care about the doors being closed. I thought after coming down you might want to sit with me awhile. I have worked and feel a little weak from it, but I cannot sleep— since seven this am I have dosed off a few times, but not half hour in the aggregate.

July 2, 1885, A.M.

This is the first of the "jim-cracks" that has seemed to have real merit. I found it easy to-day to write upon for an hour without stopping. It also makes a good invalid table to get ones meals off of.

July 2, 1885

Cocain is a failure in my case now. It hurts very much to apply it and I do not feel that it does me much good. I do not see why it should have afforded so much relief heretofore and now stopped.

.   .   .   .   .

I have been writing up my views of some of our generals, and of the character of Lincoln & Stanton. I do not place Stanton as high as some people do. Mr. Lincoln cannot be extolled too highly.

July 2, 1885, P.M.

Dr. I ask you not to show this to any one, unless physicians you consult with, until the end. Particularly I want it kept from my family. If known to one man the papers will get it and they will get it. It would only distress them almost beyond endurance to know it, and, by reflex, would distress me.

I have not changed my mind materially since I wrote you before in the same strain. (Now however I know that I gain in strength some days, but when I do go back it is beyond when I started to improve.) I think the chances are very decidedly in favor of your being able to keep me alive until the change of weather towards the winter. Of course there are contingencies that might arise at any time that would carry me off very suddenly. The most probable of these are choking. Under these circumstances life is not worth living. I am very thankful to have been spared this long because it has enabled me to practically complete the work in which I take so much interest. I can not stir up strength enough to review it and make additions and subtractions that would suggest themselves to me and are not likely to to any one els.

Under the above circumstances I will be the happiest the most pain I can avoid. If there is to be an extraordinary cure, such as some people believe there is to be, it will develope itself. I would say therefore to you and your collegues to make me as comfortable as you can. If it is within Gods providence that I should go now I am ready to obey His call without a murmur. I should prefer going now to enduring my present suffering for a single day without hope of recovery. As I have stated I am thankful for the providential extension of my time to enable me to continue my work. I am further thankful, and in a much greater degree thankful, because it has enabled me to see for myself the happy harmony which has so suddenly sprung up between those engaged but a few short years ago in deadly conflict. It has been an inestimable blessing to me to hear the kind expressions towards me in person from all parts of our country; from people of all nationalities of all religions and of no religion, of Confederate and National troops alike; of soldiers organizations; of mechanical, scientific religious and all other societies, embracing almost every Citizen in the land. They have brought joy to my heart, if they have not effected a cure. To you and your collegues I acknowledge my indebtedness for having brought me through the "valley of the shadow of death" to enable me to witness these things.

U. S. GRANT

Mt. McGregor, N. Y.
July 2d 1885.

I have found so much difficulty in getting my breath this morning that I tried laudanum a few minuets ago, but with the same result as for some time past. The injection has not yet had any effect. The douche has not acted well for some time. Do you think it worth the experiment of trying. I imagine I feel the morphine commencing to act.

July 3, 1885

In coughing a while ago much blood came up— Has Dr. Sands gone. He takes a much more hopeful view of my case than I do— How old is he— I had to use the cocoan several times in quick succession this morning. I have not had to use it since. You used it once in the mean time, but that was more to let Dr. Sands see than for anything els. I did not need it.

July 4, 1885

I feel much relieved this morning. I had begun to feel that the work of getting my book to-gether was making but slow progress. I find it about completed, and the work now to be done is mostly after it gets back in gallies. It can be sent to the printer faster than he is ready for it. There from one hundred and fifty to two hundred pages more of it than I intended. Will not cut out anything of interest. It is possible we may find a little repetition. The whole of that however is not likely to amount to many pages. Then too there is more likelyhood of omissions.

July 5, 1885

I know that what you are doing will be as likely to cure me as any think els. Nature is given a good opportunity to act and if a cure is possible it will develope itself. All the medical scill in America, including Dr. Bron, could not find a cure.

July 6, 1885

I feel very badly probably because of a cross fire between opium and laudanum. If relieved of that I half hope to feel better.

I feel as if I cannot endure it any longer. The alcoholic stimulants must absolutely be given up.

July 7, 1885

If I live long enough I will become a sort of specialist in the use of certain medicines if not in the treatment of disease. It seems that one mans destiny in this world is quite as much a mystery as it is likely to be in the next. I never thought of acquiring rank in the profession I was educated for; yet it came with two grades higher prefixed to the rank of General officer for me. I certainly never had either ambition or taste for a political life; yet I was twice president of the United States. If any one had suggested the idea of my becoming an author, as they frequently did I was not sure whether they were making sport of me or not. I have now written a book which is in the hands of the manufacturers. I ask that you keep these notes very private lest I become authority with treatment of diseases. I have already to many trades to be proficent in any. Of course I feel very much better from your application of cocain, the first in three days, or I should never have thought of saying what I have said above.

July 8, 1885, 4:00 A.M.

I feel pretty well but get sleepy sitting in the air. Took a half hours nap. Do you want me to go in the house. I am as bright and well now, for a time at least, as I ever will be.

Will you tell Harrison to bring me the larger pad I have been using in my room.

July 8, 1885, 11:00 A.M.

Buck has brought up the last of first vol. in print. In two weeks if they work hard they can have the second vol. copied ready to go to the printer. I will then feel that my work is done.

.   .   .   .   .

Gen. Buckner — Fort Donelson — will be here on the next train. He is coming up specially to pay his respects.

July 10, 1885, 11:30 A.M.

I do not feel a great deal of pain, but more than through the day. Not much pain but enough to be unpleasant. It is confined principally to the side of the tongue which cocain does not help, and to the place about where the right nostril enters the mouth.

I must try to get some soft pencils. I could then write plainer and more rapidly.

July 1885

Not sleeping does not disturb me because I have had so much sleep. And then too I have been comparitively free from pain. I know a sick person cannot feel just as he would like all the time; but I think it a duty to let the physician know from time to time just my feelings. It may benefit some other fellow sufferer hereafter. Wake the Dr. up and advise with him whether anything should be done. I cleared my mouth and throat very well just before twelve. I feel very well but have nearly a constant hicup. Whether this indicates anything or not I do not know, but it is inconvenient. I have not felt a desire or need of cocain since taking it to-day.

July 11, 1885, 1:00 A.M.

7⁴⁵ am, July 11th woke up by biting my tongue, feeling perfectly fresh however as if I had had a good nights natural sleep. My breathing is less obstructed than usual at the same time of day and the head less filled up. In fact my breathing is not obstructed in the least. Have used no cocain during the night nor do I require any yet.

July 11, 1885, 7:45 A.M.

After all that however the disease is still there and must be fatal in the end. My life is precious of course to my family and would be to me if I could recover entirely. There never was one more willing to go than I am. I know most people have first one and then another little thing to fix up, and never get quite through. This was partially my case. I first wanted so many days to work on my book so the authorship would be clearly mine. It was graciously granted to me, after being apparently much lower than since, and with a capacity to do more work than I ever did in the same time. My work had been done so hastily that much was left out and I did all of it over from the crossing of the James river in June/64, to Appomattox in /65. Since that I have added as much as fifty pages to the book I should think. There is nothing more I should do to it now, and therefore I am not likely to be more ready to go than at this moment.

July 16, 1885

I have tried to study the question of the use of cocain as impartially as possible considering that I am the person effected by its use. The conclusion I have come to in my case is; taken properly it gives a wonderfull amount of relief from pain. Gradually the parts near those where the medicine is applied become numb and partially paralized. The feeling is unpleasant but not painful. Without the use of it the parts not effected with disease are pliable but of no use because their exercise moves the diseased parts and produces pain. When the medicine is being applied the tendency is to take more than there is any necessity for, and oftener. On the whole my conclusion is to take it when it seems to be so much needed as it was at times yesterday. I will try to limit its use. The latter you know how hard it is to do.

July 19, 1885

I can however write better seated with the board before me. I do not think I should take my medicine now. I might try to go to sleep and when I want the medicine call you.

July 19, 1885

What do you think of my taking the bath wagon and going down to overlook the south view?

July 20, 1885, 4:00 P.M.

I do not sleep though I sometimes dose off a little. If up I am talked to and in my efforts to answer cause pain. The fact is I think I am a verb instead of a personal pronoun. A verb is anything that signifies to be; to do; or to suffer. I signify all three.

July 1885

Chronology

1822   Born April 27 at Point Pleasant, Ohio, a small village along the Ohio River, first child of Jesse Root Grant and Hannah Simpson Grant. (Grandfather Noah Grant, a farmer and cobbler, moved from Connecticut to Westmoreland County in western Pennsylvania, where father, Jesse Root Grant, was born in 1794, and then to northeastern Ohio in 1799. After death of grandmother Rachel Kelly Grant in 1805 the family broke up, and father eventually was apprenticed to his half-brother Peter Grant's tannery in Maysville, Kentucky. In 1820 father began working in tannery at Point Pleasant and on June 24, 1821, married Hannah Simpson, b. 1798, the daughter of farmers who had moved to Ohio from eastern Pennsylvania in 1817.) Named Hiram Ulysses Grant and called Ulysses by his family (his father and mother's stepmother had read Fénelon's *Telemachus*).

1823   Father establishes tannery at Georgetown, Ohio, village 25 miles east of Point Pleasant and five miles from the Ohio River, and has two-story brick house built for his family, who move there in autumn.

1825   Brother Samuel Simpson Grant (called Simpson by family) born September 23.

1828   Begins attending subscription schools in Georgetown (may have started in 1827). Sister Clara Rachel Grant born December 11.

1830   Hauls cut wood from land owned by father. Enjoys working with horses; detests tannery.

1832   Sister Virginia Paine (Jennie) Grant born February 20.

1833   Begins working on family farm.

1835   Brother Orvil Lynch Grant born May 15.

1836–37   Attends Maysville Seminary, Maysville, Kentucky, living with father's relatives there.

1837–38   Attends subscription school in Georgetown.

1838–39   Attends Presbyterian Academy in Ripley, Ohio.

1839   Father arranges with Congressman Thomas L. Hamer
           for Grant to enter the U.S. Military Academy, and he is
           appointed on March 22. Arrives at West Point, New York,
           on May 29; however, due to Hamer's error, his appoint-
           ment is in the name of U. S. Grant, and he is officially
           registered under that name, though he will sign himself
           Ulysses H. (or U. H.) Grant while at the Academy. Passes
           entrance examination and spends summer in training
           encampment. Sister Mary Frances Grant born July 28.
           Studies mathematics and French when classes begin in
           fall. Reads novels and stories by Edward Bulwer (later Ed-
           ward Bulwer-Lytton), James Fenimore Cooper, Frederick
           Marryat, Walter Scott, and Washington Irving (later will
           read works of Charles Lever and Eugène Sue). Becomes a
           friend of roommate Rufus Ingalls (later quartermaster of
           the Army of the Potomac) and others, including Frederick
           Steele (later a Union major general) and James Longstreet
           (later a Confederate lieutenant general).

1840   Ranks 16th in mathematics and 49th in French in class of
           60 members and 147th in conduct in corps of 233 cadets;
           achieves overall standing of 27th in his class. Spends sum-
           mer in training encampment (will do so again in 1842).
           Studies mathematics, French, topographical and anatomi-
           cal drawing, and ethics. Does watercolor paintings for
           drawing class taught by well-known painter Robert Walter
           Weir. Distinguishes himself as a horseman, often riding
           difficult mounts.

1841   Ranks 10th in mathematics, 44th in French, 23rd in draw-
           ing, and 46th in ethics out of class of 53, and 144th in
           conduct out of corps of 219; stands 24th in his class over-
           all. Visits family, now living in Bethel, Ohio, ten miles
           northwest of Georgetown, and friends during ten-week
           summer furlough. Studies philosophy (physics), chemis-
           try, and landscape drawing.

1842   Ranks 15th in philosophy, 22nd in chemistry, and 19th in
           drawing in class of 41 and 157th in conduct in corps of 217;

achieves overall standing of 20th in his class. Studies military and civil engineering, ethics, artillery, infantry tactics, and mineralogy and geology. Rooms with friend Frederick T. Dent.

1843   Serves as president of Dialectic Society, cadet literary society. Ranks 16th in engineering, 28th in ethics, 25th in artillery, 28th in infantry tactics, and 17th in mineralogy and geology in class of 39, and 156th in conduct in corps of 223. Graduates 21st in his class in June and is commissioned brevet (provisional) second lieutenant in the 4th Infantry Regiment. Begins signing name as Ulysses S. Grant. Reports to Jefferson Barracks, outside of St. Louis, Missouri, on September 30. Visits White Haven, Dent family home near Jefferson Barracks (White Haven is adjacent to present-day Grantwood, Missouri). Meets Dent's parents, Frederick F. Dent, a slaveholding planter who had moved to Missouri from Maryland, and Ellen Wrenshall Dent. Grant studies mathematics in hopes of becoming assistant professor at the Military Academy.

1844   Begins courting Julia Boggs Dent (b. 1826), eldest daughter in the family, when she returns in late winter from stay in St. Louis. They often go riding together. While on leave in Bethel in early May, Grant learns that the 4th Infantry has been ordered to Louisiana. Returns to Missouri and proposes marriage to Julia Dent; she accepts. Joins regiment in June at Camp Salubrity, outside Natchitoches, Louisiana, near the Texas border. Plays cards with fellow officers and enjoys watching and betting on horse races.

1845   Congress votes to annex Texas, March 1. Grant takes leave in April to visit Julia Dent and receives her father's conditional consent to their marriage. Regiment is sent to Corpus Christi, Texas, in September. Grant is promoted to second lieutenant on September 30. Offered position as professor of mathematics at college in Hillsboro, Ohio, and considers resigning from the army to accept it. Visits San Antonio and Austin in December. Texas is admitted to the Union as a state, December 29.

1846   As part of force under Brevet Brigadier General Zachary Taylor (whom Grant will come to admire), Grant's regiment moves south on March 11 into territory between Nueces and Rio Grande rivers claimed by both Texas and Mexico. Troops reach Rio Grande opposite Matamoras on March 28. Mexico declares war, April 24. While on supply assignment at Point Isabel on the Gulf Coast, Grant hears sounds of fighting at Matamoros on May 3. Fights in battle of Palo Alto, May 8, and temporarily commands his company at battle of Resaca de la Palma, May 9. Mexicans retreat and Americans occupy Matamoros, May 18. Taylor's army begins advance on Monterrey on August 5. Grant becomes regimental quartermaster and commissary. Takes part in first American assault on Monterrey, September 21. Volunteers to ride through streets during heavy fighting on September 23, carrying message requesting ammunition resupply. Mexican defenders surrender, September 24. Grant remains in camp near Monterrey for remainder of the year.

1847   Regiment is assigned to Major General Winfield Scott's expedition against Veracruz and embarks at Point Isabel on February 13. Lands outside of Veracruz on March 9 and joins siege of the city, which surrenders March 27. Scott begins advance on Mexico City April 8. Grant takes part in the battle of Cerro Gordo, April 18, an American victory. Learns that Frederick F. Dent has given his final consent to his marriage to Julia. Fights at battles of Churubusco, August 20, and Molino del Rey, September 8, outside of Mexico City, and takes part in assault on the city, September 13; city surrenders on September 14. Promoted to first lieutenant September 16. Spends remainder of year outside of Mexico City as part of occupying force. (During the Mexican War, Grant serves with and gets to know many officers he will later command or fight against during the Civil War.)

1848   Peace negotiators sign Treaty of Guadalupe Hidalgo, February 2, and it is ratified by the U.S. Senate, March 10. Tours Valley of Mexico during armistice. Climbs Mount Popocatépetl, 17,887-foot volcano, in April with fellow officers, including his friend Simon Bolivar Buckner, but does not reach its summit because of bad weather; suffers temporary snow blindness. Visits Cacahuamilpa caverns near Cuernavaca. Mexican National Congress ratifies peace treaty May 30, officially ending war. On June 16, during the 4th Infantry's return to the United States, $1,000 in quartermaster's funds are stolen from the trunk of Grant's friend, Captain John H. Gore. Board of inquiry called at Grant's request exonerates him of blame for the theft, but he is not relieved of his obligation to reimburse the government. Returns to United States on July 23 and takes leave. Sees Julia Dent at White Haven, visits his family at Bethel, and then returns to Missouri. Marries Julia at Dent home at Fourth and Cerre streets in St. Louis on August 22; among the guests are Longstreet, Steele, and Cadmus M. Wilcox (later a Confederate major general). Returns to Bethel with Julia for extended stay, visiting Georgetown, Maysville, and Cincinnati. Reports for duty at Detroit, Michigan, on November 17, and is assigned to Madison Barracks at Sackets Harbor, New York, on the eastern shore of Lake Ontario near the Canadian border. Serves as company commander and post quartermaster. Plays chess and checkers with citizens of nearby Watertown.

1849   Successfully requests transfer back to regimental headquarters in Detroit and returns in April when lakes become navigable. Rents house at 253 E. Fort Street and is joined by Julia when she returns from visit to her family. Enjoys racing and betting on horses, plays cards, and entertains fellow officers and their wives at his home.

1850   On advice of regimental surgeon, Julia returns to her parents' home for the birth of her first child. Son Frederick Dent Grant (called "Fred" by the family) born May 30 in St. Louis. Grant takes extended leave to visit Missouri and Ohio and then returns to Detroit with wife and child.

1851   Reassigned to Sackets Harbor in June. Julia and son Frederick spend summer at White Haven. Grant takes leave in July and visits Quebec City, Montreal, Lake Champlain, New York City, and West Point. Rejoined by Julia and Frederick in late summer.

1852   4th Infantry is ordered to Pacific Northwest in May. Grant leaves Sackets Harbor in June and goes to Governor's Island in New York harbor; Julia, who is awaiting the birth

of their second child, and Frederick go to stay with
Grant's family in Bethel after Grant insists that they not
accompany him. Grant goes to Washington, D.C., on July
1, seeking relief from his obligation to repay the quartermaster funds stolen in 1848. Finds government offices
closed for Henry Clay's funeral; is later able to see several
congressmen, but issue of lost funds remains unresolved.
Sails from New York July 5 and reaches Aspinwall (now
Colón, Panama) on July 16, where he makes arrangements
for regiment and its dependents to cross the Isthmus.
Helps tend the sick when cholera breaks out (about 100
people in regimental party die, including Captain John H.
Gore and 17 children). Sails from Panama City on August 5
and arrives in San Francisco on August 18. Writes favorably to Julia about California. Reports on September 20 to
Columbia Barracks (renamed Fort Vancouver in July 1853)
on the Columbia River, near Portland, Oregon Territory
(post becomes part of Washington Territory when it is
created in March 1853). Serves as commissary officer. Likes
Oregon but finds cost of living high. Realizes $1,500 profit
from investment in store and speculates in cattle and hogs.
Starts 100-acre farm with three fellow officers and plants
potatoes and oats. Learns in early December of birth of
Ulysses S. Grant, Jr., (later called "Buck" by the family) in
Bethel on July 22.

1853   Sells cut wood to steamboats and rents out horses. Columbia floods in June, destroying much of his crop.
Equips railroad surveying parties, including one led by
Brevet Captain George B. McClellan. Promoted to captain
on August 5. Resigns as regimental quartermaster and asks
permission to go to Washington, D.C., to settle his accounts (including matter of stolen funds), hoping to return with his wife and children. Request is denied, and he
is ordered to Fort Humboldt, California.

1854   Arrives at Fort Humboldt on January 5, and becomes commander of Company F of the 4th Infantry under Brevet
Lieutenant Colonel Robert C. Buchanan, an officer he dislikes. Fort receives little mail; Grant is uncertain of status
of his request for orders to return East and he becomes
bored, lonely, and depressed (is alleged to have drunk
heavily while at Fort Humboldt). Receives official com-

mission as captain on April 11 and resigns from the army the same day, effective July 31. Settles army accounts, but is unable to collect $1,750 owed to him in San Francisco. Sails from San Francisco, June 1, and arrives in New York City by way of Nicaragua on June 25. Goes to Sackets Harbor in unsuccessful attempt to collect $800 owed to him by Elijah Camp, an army sutler Grant had invested with in Oregon. Army friend Captain Simon Bolivar Buckner lends him money. Joins wife and children at White Haven in late summer. Begins clearing 60 acres of land given to Julia by her father, cuts wood, and sells it on the streets of St. Louis (continues for several years to sell firewood as principal means of earning money).

1855   Plants wheat and corn and continues to clear land. Moves in spring to Wish-ton-wish, house on Dent property owned by brother-in-law Lewis Dent, who is in California. Hires and works with free blacks to cut and haul wood; in addition, Julia owns three slaves. Daughter Ellen Wrenshall (Nellie) Grant born July 4. Occasionally sees army friends in St. Louis who are stationed at Jefferson Barracks or traveling to and from western posts.

1856   Plants oats, corn, and potatoes, but is hampered by lack of money for seed. Builds two-story, six-room house (which Julia dislikes), names it Hardscrabble, and moves family into it in summer. Casts his first ballot in a presidential election, voting for Democrat James Buchanan over Whig-American party candidate Millard Fillmore (Republican John C. Frémont is not on the ballot in Missouri).

1857   Mother-in-law Ellen Wrenshall Dent dies January 14. Grant writes to father on February 7, asking for $500 loan with which to buy farm implements and seed for market crops. Financial panic in late August leads to nationwide economic depression. Meets William Tecumseh Sherman in St. Louis, where Sherman is helping close down the bank he had worked for since resigning from the army in 1853. Grant pawns gold watch for $22 on December 23.

1858   Son Jesse Root Grant born February 6. Father-in-law rents White Haven and 200 acres of ploughed land to Grant and moves into St. Louis; Grant rents out his 60 acres and Hardscrabble. Plants potatoes, corn, oats, and wheat, but farm suffers from unseasonably cold weather. Frederick is dangerously ill with typhoid fever in summer, and Grant develops recurrent fever and chills. Decides, with father-in-law, to auction off farm equipment and animals in fall, rent out cleared land, and sell woods on Dent property. Goes to work in St. Louis for Julia's cousin Harry Boggs in real estate firm, acting primarily as a rent collector.

1859   Lives in room in Boggs house until early March, then moves with family to rented cottage at Seventh and Lynch streets. Frees slave William Jones, whom he had bought from father-in-law (probably in 1858), on March 29. Seeks position as St. Louis County engineer, but is rejected by free-soil majority on county commission, which identifies him politically with the Democrats. Leaves real estate business, which has become increasingly unprofitable. Exchanges Hardscrabble for house on Ninth and Barton streets and note for $3,000, and moves there in October. Works briefly as clerk in the customhouse.

1860   Visits father (now living in Covington, Kentucky, across the Ohio from Cincinnati) and arranges to work as a clerk in his prosperous Galena, Illinois, leather-goods store, managed by younger brothers Simpson (who is suffering from tuberculosis) and Orvil. Moves to Galena with his family in May, renting house at 121 High Street. Becomes acquainted with attorney John A. Rawlins, an elector pledged to Democrat Stephen A. Douglas in the presidential race. Travels on business through northern Illinois, southern Wisconsin and Minnesota, and eastern Iowa. Does not meet Illinois residency requirement for voting in November 6 presidential election. In response to Abraham Lincoln's election, South Carolina secedes from the Union, December 20 (Mississippi, Florida, Alabama, Georgia, Louisiana, and Texas follow within two months).

1861   Confederates open fire on Fort Sumter on April 12. President Lincoln calls forth 75,000 militia on April 15. Grant attends public meeting in Galena on April 16 and presides at recruiting rally held on April 18. Declines to become captain of local company of volunteers, but agrees to drill them in Galena and at Camp Yates, Springfield, Illinois. Becomes military aide to Republican governor Richard Yates, April 29, partially through influence of Republican congressman Elihu B. Washburne, who represents Galena. Makes brief visit to Dent family in Missouri and watches as Union forces move against Confederate militia in St. Louis on May 10. Musters in three regiments of volunteers in central and southern Illinois. Applies on May 24 for commission as colonel and appointment as commander of regiment in regular army; request is not acted upon. Appointed commander of militia infantry regiment by Yates on June 15; troops are mustered into United States service as 21st Illinois Volunteers on June 28. Trains and disciplines troops at Springfield before crossing into northeastern Missouri on July 11. Guards railroad bridges and trestles against secessionist raids. Assigned command of several regiments in vicinity of Mexico, Missouri, on July 24. Appointed brigadier general of volunteers on August 5 at same time as several other colonels, after being recommended for promotion by Washburne. Names John A. Rawlins of Galena as his adjutant (Rawlins, whose wife is dying, does not join Grant's headquarters until early September, after her death). Commands troops at Ironton, Jefferson City, and Cape Girardeau, Missouri, before being appointed commander of the District of Southeast Missouri on September 1. Establishes his headquarters at Cairo, Illinois, at junction of Mississippi and Ohio rivers. Learns on September 5 that Confederates have entered previously neutral Kentucky and begun fortifying positions along the Mississippi at Columbus. Organizes expedition to occupy Paducah, Kentucky, near junction of Ohio and Tennessee rivers, and reaches town on September 6. Brother Samuel Simpson Grant dies of tuberculosis on September 13. Continues to train, discipline, and equip his forces and has fortifications built along the Ohio and the Mississippi. Attacks Confederate camp at Belmont, Missouri, on November 7. Joined in Cairo by Julia and their children. (Julia and some or all of the children will continue to stay with him during the war whenever it is practicable.) Major General Henry W. Halleck assumes command of the Department of the Missouri on November 19, becoming Grant's immediate superior. Grant attempts to stop contraband trade between Union and

Confederate-held territory and investigates corruption among army contractors. Tells subordinates to obey Department orders forbidding the sheltering of fugitive slaves in army camps, but also instructs them not to act as slave-catchers. Allegations begin circulating that Grant is often drunk. (Charge will recur throughout the war, although evidence indicates that, with a few exceptions, Grant abstained from drinking during the war.)

1862   Goes to St. Louis on January 23 and proposes immediate offensive up the Tennessee River against Fort Henry, Tennessee, to Halleck. Returns to Cairo on January 28 and sends telegram requesting permission to make attack, with the endorsement of Flag Officer Andrew H. Foote, commander of the Union riverboat flotilla. Halleck telegraphs his approval on January 30. Grant's expedition leaves Cairo on February 2. Confederates begin evacuating partially flooded Fort Henry on February 5, and the fort is surrendered to Foote after brief gunboat bombardment on February 6. Grant plans immediate attack on Fort Donelson, Tennessee, on the Cumberland River ten miles to the east, but it is delayed by bad roads and heavy rains. Writes to Washburne defending Brigadier General Charles F. Smith against accusations of disloyalty. (Smith, now a divisional commander under Grant, had been commandant of cadets when Grant was at West Point.) Union forces advance on Fort Donelson, February 12; their position outside the fort becomes difficult when temperature falls below freezing on February 13. Grant receives reinforcements and supplies sent from Paducah by Brigadier General William Tecumseh Sherman. On February 14 Grant is appointed commander of the District of West Tennessee; his troops become the Army of the Tennessee. Naval assault on Fort Donelson is repulsed on February 14. Confederates attack Grant's right on February 15; he orders counterattack along entire Union line, which captures portion of Confederate outer works. Confederate Brigadier General Simon Bolivar Buckner seeks terms of capitulation for the garrison before daybreak on February 16; Grant sends message demanding "unconditional and immediate surrender," which Buckner gives. Victory is hailed throughout North. Lincoln promotes Grant to major general of volunteers on February 19, making him second to Halleck in seniority in the western theater. Union forces move up the Cumberland and occupy Clarksville, Tennessee, on February 19. Grant orders occupation of Nashville on February 24; Union troops enter on February 25. Move angers Brigadier General Don Carlos Buell, commander of the Army of the Ohio, who had made Nashville the objective of his own advance. Halleck orders Grant on March 1 to send force up the Tennessee to disrupt Confederate railroads, then relieves him of command of expedition on March 4, accusing him of failing to report his strength and positions and naming Smith to command the river advance. Grant denies charge and stays at Fort Henry, making arrangements for expedition. Halleck repeats reprimand in telegram on March 6. Grant replies on March 7, defending his conduct and requesting to be relieved from further duty in Halleck's department; renews application on March 8. Halleck responds that he has been under pressure from Major General George B. McClellan, the Union general-in-chief, to forward reports and tells Grant that he will soon be restored to field command. Grant agrees on March 14 to serve in field under Halleck. Goes upriver (southward) to Savannah, Tennessee, on March 17. Sends reinforcements farther south to Pittsburg Landing, Tennessee, where Sherman, now a division commander, is organizing them for an advance against Corinth, Mississippi, while Grant awaits the arrival of Buell and the Army of the Ohio. On morning of April 6, Confederate army under General Albert Sidney Johnston attacks Union forces at Pittsburg Landing, beginning battle of Shiloh. Grant goes to Pittsburg Landing and takes command as Union troops fall back toward river. Johnston is killed in afternoon and General Pierre G. T. Beauregard assumes command of Confederates. By nightfall Union troops have been driven back to high ground along the river, but Confederates break off attack and reinforcements from Buell's army begin arriving. Grant orders counterattack on morning of April 7, and Confederates retreat toward Corinth in afternoon. Casualties during the two days at Shiloh are greater than the total losses in the four costliest battles of the Civil War until that time. Halleck arrives at Pittsburg Landing on April 11 and personally assumes command of Grant's and Buell's armies. Several newspapers severely criticize Grant for having been taken by surprise and suffering heavy losses at Shiloh. Washburne, Sherman, and his brother, Ohio senator John Sherman, publicly defend Grant's conduct. Grant mourns death on April 25 of Smith, who had fallen ill after injuring his leg in a minor boating accident. Halleck reorganizes his forces on April 30, making Grant his second in command while relieving him of authority over the Army of the Tennessee, and begins slow advance toward Corinth. Grant writes Halleck on May 11, asking to be either restored to field command or relieved from further duty; Halleck declines to do either. Confederates evacuate Corinth, May 29–30. Grant obtains leave of absence to visit his family and considers requesting transfer to another theater of operations, but is persuaded by Sherman to remain with army in hopes of being restored to independent command. Restored by Halleck to command of the Army of the Tennessee on June 10. Congress enacts legislation on June 17 relieving Grant of his obligations for missing Mexican War funds. Grant establishes headquarters in Memphis, June 23, and issues order on July 3 warning that Confederate guerillas captured out of uniform will not be treated as prisoners of war, and that Confederate sympathizers will have their property seized to compensate for losses caused by guerilla action. Halleck is appointed general-in-chief on July 11, and on July 16 appoints Grant to command all troops between the Mississippi and the Tennessee. Grant moves his headquarters to Corinth. Issues order, July 25, prohibiting government-licensed cotton dealers from making purchases with gold or silver (ban is soon countermanded by the administration). Repairs and guards railroads and begins to employ large numbers of escaped slaves as laborers. Sends reinforcements to Buell, who is deploying against Confederate advance through eastern Tennessee. Redeploys his troops to guard against Confederate forces in northern Mississippi under Major Generals Sterling Price and Earl Van Dorn, then attacks Price at Iuka, Mississippi, on September 19. Union forces capture town on September 20, but Price escapes and joins Van Dorn in attack on Corinth, which is repulsed, October 3–4. Grant is unhappy with his subordinate Major General William S. Rosecran's pursuit of the retreating Confederates and is pleased when Rosecrans replaces Buell on October 24 as commander of the

Army of the Ohio (command is renamed the Army of the Cumberland). Grant begins concentrating forces at Grand Junction, Tennessee, in early November, in preparation for advance south along the Mississippi Central Railroad. Directs John Eaton, chaplain of the 27th Ohio Volunteers, to set up camps for black refugees and to pay them to pick, bale, and ship cotton for the government. Angered by speculators in his military department, issues order on November 19 requiring all cotton traders to obtain permits from the army as well the Treasury Department; repeatedly criticizes the activities of Jewish cotton traders in his correspondence. Confers with Sherman in Oxford, Mississippi, on December 8, and orders him to move down the Mississippi against Vicksburg, while Grant advances south along the Mississippi Central Railroad against the Confederate forces under Lieutenant General John C. Pemberton. Issues General Order 11, December 17, expelling all Jews from the Department of the Tennessee. Recommends to the War Department that all cotton be purchased by the government at a fixed rate. Sherman leaves Memphis on December 19. Confederate cavalry under Van Dorn destroys Grant's main supply depot at Holly Springs, Mississippi, December 20. Grant orders a retreat but is unable to tell Sherman that he is turning back due to the cutting of telegraph lines by Confederate raiders. Sherman attacks Confederate positions along the Yazoo River, north of Vicksburg, on December 29 and is repulsed.

1863 Lincoln signs final Emancipation Proclamation on January 1. In response to protests, Lincoln revokes, through Halleck, General Order 11, expelling Jews, on January 4. Major General John A. McClernand, a politically influential War Democrat and former Illinois congressman who had been authorized by Lincoln to raise and lead troops against Vicksburg, assumes command of Sherman's expedition on January 4. Grant arrives in Memphis, January 10, and receives Halleck's approval on January 12 to relieve McClernand as commander of the Vicksburg expedition. Goes downriver and assumes personal command of the expedition on January 30, making his headquarters at Young's Point, Louisiana, several miles above Vicksburg. Assigns McClernand to lead one of the three corps in the river force (Sherman and Major General James B. McPherson

command the other two). Grant attempts to bypass the
Confederate batteries at Vicksburg by having a canal dug
across a peninsula opposite the city and by opening a water route through Louisiana lakes, rivers, and bayous to
the Mississippi below the city, and attempts to reach the
Yazoo River above Vicksburg by opening two water
routes through the rivers and bayous of the Mississippi
Delta. Abandons all of these approaches by the end of
March and begins preparing to cross the Mississippi below Vicksburg. Charles A. Dana, special emissary sent by
Secretary of War Edwin M. Stanton, arrives on April 6
and begins to report favorably on Grant's performance to
Stanton and Lincoln. Sherman advises Grant on April 8 to
take the army back to Memphis and again approach Vicksburg overland along the line of the Mississippi Central
Railroad. Instead, Grant has Acting Rear Admiral David
D. Porter run his fleet past the Vicksburg shore batteries
on April 16. Orders all commanders on April 22 to cooperate with efforts to raise black troops, and endorses the
dismissal of three officers who sought to resign in protest
against such a policy. Moves most of the army down the
west bank of the Mississippi below Vicksburg, and then
has Sherman feint attack north of the city on April 29.
Grant crosses the river on April 30 and his troops win
battle of Port Gibson, May 1. Sherman's corps crosses on
May 7, and Grant's troops advance on Jackson, Mississippi, supplying themselves by foraging on the countryside. Jackson falls on May 14. Union forces win the battle
of Champion's Hill, May 16, and capture crossings on the
Big Black River, May 17, forcing Confederates back toward Vicksburg fortifications. Orders assault on Vicksburg defenses, May 19, which fails, and a second assault on
May 22, which also fails. Begins siege operations against
Vicksburg. Criticizes McClernand in letter to Halleck,
May 24, as unfit to command his corps. After Sherman
and McPherson strongly protest McClernand's publication of a self-congratulatory order in the newspapers without authorization, Grant removes him from command on
June 18 and appoints Major General Edward O. C. Ord as
his successor. Pemberton opens negotiations, July 3, and
surrenders Vicksburg and its garrison on July 4. Grant
is made a major general in the regular army on July 7.
Sherman forces Confederates under General Joseph E.

Johnston to retreat east of Jackson, then breaks off pursuit. Grant rests his troops and works to secure Mississippi Valley. Sends Rawlins to Washington in late July to explain to Lincoln his reasons for removing McClernand. Goes to New Orleans to discuss strategy with Major General Nathaniel P. Banks, arriving on September 2. Injured when his horse falls on him, September 4. Returns to Vicksburg on September 16. Army of the Cumberland, commanded by Major General William S. Rosecrans, is defeated in battle of Chickamauga, September 19–20, and retreats to Chattanooga, Tennessee, which Confederates under General Braxton Bragg then besiege. On Halleck's orders, Grant begins sending troops to reinforce Rosecrans on September 22. Meets Secretary of War Stanton at the train station in Indianapolis, Indiana, on October 17, and goes with him to Louisville, Kentucky, where they confer on October 18. Grant is appointed commander of the Military Division of the Mississippi, covering territory between the Alleghenies and the Mississippi, except for Louisiana; replaces Rosecrans with Major General George H. Thomas and makes Sherman the new commander of the Army of the Tennessee. Still suffering effects of New Orleans injury, arrives in Chattanooga on October 23 after difficult ride over mountain trail, the only route still open into the town. Approves and implements plan drawn up by Thomas and his chief engineer, Brigadier General William F. Smith, to open new supply line into Chattanooga. Siege is broken on October 30, and Chattanooga garrison is reinforced by troops from the armies of the Potomac and the Tennessee. Grant plans offensive against Bragg, whose troops are entrenched on Missionary Ridge overlooking Chattanooga. Thomas's forces begin attack on November 23, capturing Confederate outposts below the ridge. On November 24 troops under Major General Joseph Hooker seize Lookout Mountain, overlooking southern end of Confederate position, while Sherman's troops occupy hill near northern end of ridge. Sherman's attack on November 25 makes little headway and Hooker's advance is delayed, but Thomas's troops break the Confederate center in the afternoon and Bragg's men retreat into northern Georgia. Grant sends force under Sherman to Knoxville, Tennessee, which is besieged by Confederates under Lieutenant General

James Longstreet; the Confederates begin retreating toward Virginia on December 3. Proposes winter campaign against Mobile and the interior of Alabama to Halleck on December 7, but administration does not act on plan because of concern over situation in East Tennessee and desire to mount campaign west of the Mississippi. Washburne introduces bill in Congress, December 14, to revive rank of lieutenant general, previously held only by George Washington and, by brevet, Winfield Scott. Responding on December 17 to letter from Barnabas Burns, an Ohio War Democrat, Grant privately disclaims any interest in the presidency.

1864 Returns to Nashville headquarters, January 12. Suggests abandoning attempts to take Richmond from the north or east in letter to Halleck on January 19, and proposes instead an advance from Suffolk, Virginia, toward Raleigh, North Carolina, with the aim of cutting rail lines into Virginia and forcing its evacuation. Learns that his son Frederick is dangerously ill in St. Louis and visits him there, January 27–February 1; Frederick begins to recover and Grant returns to Nashville. Continues to disavow any interest in the presidency in private letters, but considers a public statement to be incompatible with his military position. Halleck writes Grant on February 17 that proposed attack into North Carolina would open Maryland to Confederate invasion. Lincoln signs bill reviving rank of lieutenant general and nominates Grant for the position, February 29; he is confirmed by the U.S. Senate on March 2, with pay of $8,640 a year. Arrives in Washington on March 8 to receive commission and at the White House meets Lincoln for the first time. Assigned command of all Union armies, March 10. Confers in Virginia with Major General George G. Meade and decides to retain him as commander of the Army of the Potomac. Halleck becomes chief of staff and Sherman succeeds Grant as commander of the Military Division of the Mississippi. Grant plans spring campaign involving simultaneous advances by all Union forces in the field, with the Confederate armies in northern Georgia defending Atlanta and in northern Virginia defending Richmond as the main objectives. Returns to Nashville to consult with Sherman and other western commanders, goes back to Washington on March 23, and then joins the Army of the Potomac at Culpeper, Virginia. Orders halt in prisoner exchanges until the Confederates agree to recognize validity of the paroles given the Vicksburg garrison and to exchange black prisoners as well as white prisoners. On May 4 Grant and the Army of the Potomac cross the Rapidan River and begin advance on Richmond. Confederate General Robert E. Lee orders counteroffensive by the Army of Northern Virginia, leading to heavy losses on both sides in the battle of the Wilderness, May 5–6. Grant orders move southeast toward Spotsylvania Court House on May 7. Sherman begins advance toward Atlanta, May 7. Lee's troops reach Spotsylvania ahead of Union forces, May 8, and the two armies begin fighting there. Union assaults on May 10, 12, and 18 fail to achieve decisive break in Confederate line. Union forces are defeated in the Shenandoah Valley, May 15, and Union advance on Richmond along the James River is repulsed, May 16–17. Grant moves Army of the Potomac toward Richmond, May 20. Reaches the new Confederate lines near the North Anna River, May 23, but does not order a major attack. Begins disengaging on the night of May 26–27, and again moves toward Richmond, reaching new positions around Cold Harbor on May 31. Union attack on June 1 makes limited gains, and Grant orders second assault for June 2, which he then postpones until June 3. Attack is repulsed with severe loss. Army withdraws from Cold Harbor lines on June 12 and begins crossing the James River on June 14. Union troops attack Petersburg, rail center south of Richmond, June 15–18, capturing several Confederate defensive positions but failing to take the city itself. Grant decides against further frontal assaults and begins siege operations. Establishes headquarters at City Point, Virginia, sending and receiving most of his messages to and from other Union commanders through Washington. Makes unsuccessful attempt on June 22 to cut railroad running south from Petersburg (will make further attacks on Lee's flanks and supply routes into late October, resulting in the extension of siege lines to the north and west of Petersburg). Begins sending reinforcements to Washington on July 5 as Confederate force under Lieutenant General Jubal A. Early advances north through the Shenandoah Valley. Unsuccessfully tries to have politically influential Major General Benjamin F. Butler removed from active command of Union forces along the James River. After series of flanking maneuvers along the Chattanooga–Atlanta railroad, Sherman forces the Confederates to retreat inside Atlanta's fortifications on July 9. Early's troops skirmish with Union forces on outskirts of Washington, July 11–12, and then withdraw. Grant mourns death of Major General James B. McPherson, Sherman's successor as commander of the Army of the Tennessee, who is killed outside of Atlanta on July 22. Union engineers explode mine at Petersburg on July 30, creating gap in Confederate line, but Union troops fail to exploit it and are severely repulsed; Grant describes it to Halleck as "the saddest affair I have witnessed in this war." On August 1, orders Major General Philip H. Sheridan to take command of Union field forces in the Shenandoah Valley and, on Lincoln's suggestion, goes to Washington, August 5–7, to simplify command arrangements in the upper Potomac region. Recommends to Stanton on August 15 that Halleck be made commander of the Pacific Division, but Halleck is retained in Washington as chief of staff. Writes Halleck on August 15 that he is unwilling to send troops away from Petersburg to guard against possible uprisings in the North against the draft, and receives telegram from Lincoln on August 17 endorsing his decision. Sherman's troops capture Atlanta, September 2. Confers with Sheridan in West Virginia, September 16–17, and approves his plans for taking the offensive in the Shenandoah Valley. Visits his family at Burlington, New Jersey, where they have rented a house, before returning to City Point on September 19. Sheridan wins battles at Winchester, September 19, Fisher's Hill, September 22, and Cedar Creek, October 19, and devastates large parts of the Shenandoah Valley, a major source of supplies for Lee's army; his success, along with the fall of Atlanta, raises hopes of the administration's supporters for victory in the fall elections. Approves on October 12 Sherman's proposed march from Atlanta to the sea and endorses it in letter to Lincoln and Stanton on October 13. Reconsiders when Confederate army under General John B. Hood reaches the Tennessee River, but is assured by Sherman that Hood can be defeated by forces in Tennessee under Thomas and gives his final approval to Sherman's plan on November 2. Lincoln is reelected, November 8. Sherman leaves Atlanta, November 16. Hood reaches outskirts of Nashville, Tennessee, on December 2. Grant repeatedly urges Thomas to attack Hood, issues and cancels order relieving him on December 9, orders Major General John A. Logan to Nashville on December 13 to replace Thomas, then decides on December 14 to go to Nashville himself and reaches Washington on December 15. Thomas attacks and decisively defeats Hood, December 15–16; Grant congratulates Thomas and retains him in command. Visits his family in Burlington on December 17. Sherman captures Savannah, Georgia, December 21. Union expedition under Butler attacks Fort Fisher, guarding entrance to Wilmington, North Carolina, on December 25 and is repulsed. Grant approves on December 27 Sherman's proposal to march his army north through the Carolinas.

1865   Has Butler relieved from command and orders new expedition against Fort Fisher under Brigadier General Alfred H. Terry. Receives furnished house in Philadelphia as gift from group of citizens. Fort Fisher is captured January 15; Grant goes there, January 27–31, to plan attack on Wilmington. Sherman begins march through South Carolina, February 1. Grant recommends on February 1 that Lincoln meet with Confederate peace commissioners who had come to City Point on January 31. Lincoln has unsuccessful conference with them at Hampton Roads, February 3. Receives letter from Lee, March 3, proposing that they meet to negotiate peace terms. Asks Stanton for instructions, and is told by Lincoln that he has authority only to accept Lee's capitulation. Sister Clara Grant dies March 6. Sherman reaches Goldsboro, North Carolina, March 23. Grant meets with Lincoln, Sherman, and Porter at City Point, March 27, to discuss spring campaign and possible terms of Confederate surrender. Begins offensive southwest of Petersburg, March 29, leading to Union victory at Five Forks, April 1, and capture of much of the Petersburg entrenchments, April 2. Confederates evacuate Petersburg and Richmond, April 2, and Grant begins pursuit of retreating Army of Northern Virginia. Lee surrenders the Army of Northern Virginia to Grant at Appomattox Court House, Virginia, April 9. Grant meets with Lee, Longstreet, and other Confederate generals on April 10. Goes to Washington and confers with Stanton on April 13 and with Lincoln and the Cabinet on April 14. Declines invitation to join Lincolns at Ford's Theatre that evening and goes with Julia to visit their children in Burlington. Learns in Philadelphia that Lincoln has been fatally shot, and returns to Washington at Stanton's request on April 15. Stands at the catafalque during White House funeral service on April 19. Receives on April 21 an agreement signed by Sherman and General Joseph E. Johnston on April 18 that proposes political and military terms for the surrender of the remaining Confederate armies. Submits agreement to President Andrew Johnson and the Cabinet that evening; it is disapproved and Grant is ordered by Stanton and Johnson to go to Raleigh, North Carolina, and resume hostilities against Johnston's army. Arrives on April 24 and confers with Sherman, who on April 26 accepts Johnston's surrender under terms similar to those given to Lee at Appomattox. Grant returns to Washington, April 29. Family moves into Philadelphia home in early May. Confederates in Alabama, Mississippi, and eastern Louisiana surrender on May 4. Orders Sheridan to Texas on May 17 to force surrender of remaining Confederates and to exert pressure on the French to withdraw their army from Mexico. Watches grand review of the Union armies in Washington, May 23–24. Confederates in western Louisiana and Texas surrender on May 26. Endorses Lee's application for presidential pardon and amnesty, June 16, and protests his recent indictment for treason, arguing that it violates the Appomattox surrender terms (indictment is dropped). Directs mustering out of volunteer troops and the reorganization of the army; Sherman is assigned to command new Military Division of the Mississippi, covering the western plains. Urges President Johnson to sell arms and send officers to the liberal forces in Mexico fighting against Emperor Maximilian (will continue to advocate interventionist Mexican policy and oppose Secretary of State William H. Seward's attempts to achieve a French withdrawal through diplomacy). Makes extensive tour through the East and Midwest, July 24–October 6; is presented with a house by the citizens of Galena and cheered by crowds throughout his travels. Submits report on October 20 recommending establishment of peacetime army of 80,000 men. Stanton asks for reduction, and Grant submits new figure of 53,000 on November 3. Buys house in Washington at 205 I Street, N.W., for $30,000. Instructs military commanders to prevent Fenians (Irish nationalists) from attacking Canada (Fenian border incidents continue until 1871). Makes tour of South at Johnson's request, November 27–December 11, visiting Raleigh, North Carolina, Charleston, South Carolina, and Savannah and Augusta, Georgia. Submits report describing the majority of Southerners as submissive to the government's authority, recommending the withdrawal of black troops from the interior of the South, and criticizing some agents of the Freedmen's Bureau for encouraging blacks to believe that they will be given land by the government. Johnson sends report to the Senate on December 18 and cites it in his accompanying message describing the South as reconciled to its defeat.

1866   Issues order on January 12 protecting army officers, soldiers, and federal officials (including agents of the Freedmen's Bureau) acting in their official capacity, as well as Unionists charged for their wartime actions against the Confederates, from prosecution or suit in Southern local and state courts. Order also forbids the prosecution of blacks for offenses for which whites are not punished in the same manner or degree. Receives $50,000 in government bonds and $20,000 in cash as gift from committee of New York businessmen, who also pay mortgage on his Washington house. Son Frederick is appointed to the U.S. Military Academy in March. Concerned by increasing violence against freed blacks, issues orders on July 6 directing commanders in the South to arrest and hold for trial persons engaged in violence in cases where the civil authorities fail to act. Promoted on July 25 to rank of general, previously held only by George Washington. Strength of army is set by act of Congress, July 28, at approximately 54,000 men. Accompanies Johnson on tour of the North, August 28–September 17, ostensibly connected with the dedication in Chicago of a monument to Stephen A. Douglas. Johnson uses tour to rally support for National Union congressional candidates who support him in his struggle with the Republicans over Reconstruction and gives speeches violently attacking Republican leaders. Grant writes Julia that Johnson's speeches are disgraceful, but that his opinion of the President must be kept private. Orders surplus arms removed from Southern arsenals, and writes to Sheridan on October 12 expressing fear that Johnson's opposition to congressional Reconstruction policy may result in renewed rebellion against the Union. Repeatedly refuses Johnson's requests in late October that he accompany diplomatic mission to Mexico; Sherman goes in his place. Grant negotiates agreement between rival parties in Baltimore that prevents election-day violence. Urges Brigadier General Edward O. C. Ord to use his influence with the Arkansas legislature to gain ratification of the Fourteenth Amendment.

1867   Congress passes Reconstruction Act over Johnson's veto on March 2; it declares that no legal state governments exist in the former Confederate states (excluding Tennessee), divides these states into five military districts, and sets conditions necessary for their regaining congressional representation, including ratification of the Fourteenth Amendment and adoption of state constitutions providing for black suffrage. Congress also passes Command of the Army Act, requiring that all orders to the army go through Grant and protecting him from being removed against his will, and the Tenure of Office Act, restricting the power of the president to remove certain government officials without Senate approval. Johnson appoints district commanders recommended by Grant. Further legislation passed in March and July increases the role of Grant and the district commanders in implementing the Reconstruction Act. Grant rents seaside cottage at Long Branch, New Jersey (later buys summer home there, and family will return whenever possible for much of remainder of Grant's life). Congress adjourns July 20. Grant advises Johnson on August 1 not to remove Stanton as secretary of war for his support of congressional Reconstruction policy, but accepts appointment as secretary of war *ad interim* when Johnson suspends Stanton on August 12. When Johnson removes Sheridan as district commander for Louisiana and Texas for his forceful implementation of the Reconstruction acts, Grant protests in a letter that is soon made public, and continues to advise district commanders to execute congressional Reconstruction policy. Endorsements of Grant for the presidency increase in the Republican press after the Democrats make gains in the fall elections. Congress reconvenes on November 21 and begins considering Stanton's suspension.

1868   Grant tells Johnson on January 11 that he has recently learned that violation of the Tenure of Office Act is punishable by fine and imprisonment and therefore will not continue as secretary of war against the wishes of the Senate. Senate votes on January 13 not to sustain Stanton's suspension. Grant vacates office at the War Department on January 14 and Stanton reoccupies it. In exchange of letters, Johnson accuses Grant of breaking an earlier promise to retain the office so that Stanton would be forced to test constitutionality of Tenure of Office Act in court, and of not making his intentions known during their January 11 meeting; Grant denies accusations of bad faith. Correspondence is published, making their breach public. On February 21 Johnson appoints Adjutant General Lorenzo Thomas secretary of war *ad interim*, but Stanton refuses to leave his office in the War Department. House of Representatives votes eleven articles of impeachment of Johnson, March 2–3, nine of which concern his attempt to replace Stanton with Lorenzo Thomas. Senate acquits Johnson of the most comprehensive article of impeachment by one vote on May 16. Republican national convention meeting in Chicago unanimously nominates Grant for president on the first ballot, May 21, and nominates Speaker of the House Schuyler Colfax of Indiana for vice-president. Grant learns of his nomination at army headquarters in Washington. Johnson is acquitted of two further articles by one vote, May 26, and his trial is adjourned indefinitely. Stanton resigns and is succeeded as secretary of war by Brigadier General John M. Schofield. Grant accepts nomination on May 29 in letter that concludes, "Let us have peace"; phrase becomes main slogan of Republican campaign. On July 9 the Democrats nominate Horatio Seymour, former governor of New York, for president and Francis P. Blair, Jr., a former Missouri congressman who had commanded a division under Grant during the Vicksburg campaign, for vice-president. Fourteenth Amendment is declared ratified on July 28. Grant makes inspection tour of the West with Sherman and Sheridan in July, traveling mostly by train through Kansas, Nebraska, Wyoming, and Colorado. Visits Denver before returning to Galena, where he receives reports from Republican leaders. Makes no public political statements during campaign. Follows election returns at Washburne's home in Galena, November 3. Defeats Seymour, receiving 214 of 294 electoral votes and 52.7 percent of the popular vote. Returns to Washington in early November.

1869   On February 26 Congress proposes ratification of the Fifteenth Amendment, forbidding the denial of suffrage on account of race, color, or previous condition of servitude. Grant is inaugurated March 4. Delivers short address advocating full repayment of the national debt, redemption of government bonds and payment of their interest in gold, eventual restoration of the currency to a specie basis, and ratification of the Fifteenth Amendment. Names Sherman as commanding general of the army and issues order giving him authority over its administrative bureaus and staff corps. Makes Cabinet appointments without consulting Republican leaders or, in some cases, the nominees themselves. Washburne receives one-week courtesy appointment as secretary of state before becoming minister to France, and is succeeded by former New York governor, congressman, and senator Hamilton Fish. Grant withdraws nomination of wealthy New York department store owner Alexander T. Stewart to be secretary of the treasury because of 1789 law barring persons engaged in trade from holding the office, and names Massachusetts congressman George S. Boutwell in his place. Remainder of Cabinet includes Rawlins (secretary of war), Massachusetts state supreme court judge Ebenezer R. Hoar (attorney general), Maryland senator John A. J. Creswell (postmaster general), Philadelphia businessman Adolph E. Borie (secretary of the navy), who resigns in June and is succeeded by New Jersey state attorney general George E. Robeson, and former Ohio governor Jacob D. Cox (secretary of the interior). At Rawlins' request, Grant rescinds his earlier order and instructs the army administrative bureaus and staff corps to report to the secretary of war instead of the commanding general. On April 7 Grant proposes that referendums on new Virginia and Mississippi state constitutions be held with separate votes taken on disqualification clauses barring many former Confederates from voting or holding office. Signs appropriate legislation, April 10; act gives him power to schedule and supervise elections previously held by district commanders. (Virginia and Mississippi approve constitutions and reject disqualification clauses, July 6 and November 30; Texas also adopts new constitution on November 30, and all three states are readmitted, January–March 1870.) Grant appoints Colonel Ely S. Parker (Donehogawa), a Seneca Indian sachem and a member of his staff since 1864, as commissioner of Indian affairs, and begins reforming federal Indian policy. (New approach, known as Grant's "peace policy," intended to resolve status of western Indian tribes, eventually includes their concentration on reservations under the supervision of religious denominations, the conversion of nomadic hunting tribes to an agricultural way of life, and the abolition of the treaty system that recognized tribes as separate nations; it is partially opposed by Sherman, who favors giving the army sole control over Indian affairs and using force to drive Indians onto the reservations. Despite new policy, however, fighting and raiding between Indians and settlers and the army occur throughout Grant's administration.) Financiers Jay Gould and James Fisk, Jr., plot with Abel R. Corbin, who had recently married Grant's sister Virginia, to corner the gold market and in June begin attempts to persuade Grant to stop further government sale of gold. Responding to overtures from President Buenaventura Báez, Grant sends his personal secretary, Colonel Orville E. Babcock, to the Dominican Republic (widely known in the United States as Santo Domingo) on July 17 to investigate possible annexation of the country. Despite Rawlins' advocacy of the cause of Cubans rebelling against Spain, Grant agrees with Fish that the United States should not support the rebels by granting them recognition as belligerents. (Diplomatic tensions caused by Americans involved in the Cuban rebellion persist for remainder of Grant's presidency.) Rawlins dies of tuberculosis, September 6, and Grant loses closest adviser. Sherman serves as secretary of war until confirmation in November of William W. Belknap of Iowa, who had commanded a brigade under Sherman during the war. Babcock returns from the Dominican Republic on September 14, having signed treaty of annexation without diplomatic authority. Gould, Fisk, and Corbin's speculations create gold market panic in New York, September 24. Grant and Boutwell decide to sell $4 million in government gold, restoring financial stability. (Fish subsequently tells congressional investigators that Julia Grant had been speculating in gold with Gould and Corbin, but investigation exonerates both her and Grant of wrongdoing in their contacts with the conspirators.) Supports Radical Republicans for governor in Mississippi, where brother-in-law Lewis Dent is conservative National Union candidate, and in Texas (Radicals win in both states). Babcock returns to the Dominican Republic carrying proper diplomatic credentials and signs second treaty of annexation with Báez on November 29. Grant nominates Stanton and Hoar to the Supreme Court. Stanton is confirmed but dies on December 24; Hoar fails to receive Senate confirmation. After months of political unrest caused by the expulsion of black members from the state legislature, Grant restores military rule in Georgia on December 24 (black legislators regain their seats and the state ratifies the Fifteenth Amendment before being readmitted in July 1870).

1870   Grant submits treaty for annexation of the Dominican Republic to the Senate for ratification, January 10. Massachusetts Republican Charles Sumner, chairman of the Senate Foreign Relations Committee, leads opposition to annexation, warning that it will involve the United States in Dominican civil strife and threaten the independence of Haiti. Grant nominates William Strong of Pennsylvania and Joseph P. Bradley of New Jersey to the Supreme Court on February 7; both are soon confirmed. Foreign Relations Committee unfavorably reports treaty to the Senate on March 15. Fifteenth Amendment is declared ratified, March 30. Grant signs first Enforcement Act, passed under the enforcement provision of the Fifteenth Amendment, on May 31. Act makes the denial of suffrage on racial grounds through force, fraud, bribery, and intimidation a federal offense. (Further acts, signed on July 14, 1870, and February 28, 1871, extend federal powers over elections, especially in large cities; however, execution of the enforcement acts, particularly in the South, is sporadic and often ineffectual.) Grant sends message to the Senate, May 31, arguing that the annexation of the Dominican Republic will prevent further European intervention in the Caribbean, guard American commerce through the Gulf of Mexico and the Isthmus of Panama, hasten the end of slavery in Cuba, Puerto Rico, and Brazil, provide a market for American goods, and reduce the trade deficit. In bid for Southern Republican support for Dominican treaty, Grant asks for Hoar's resignation and names Amos T. Akerman of Georgia as new attorney general. Signs bill on June 22 establishing Department of Justice, increasing power of the federal government to enforce Reconstruction legislation. Senate fails to ratify Dominican treaty by vote of 28–28, June 30. Defeat embitters Grant's relations with Sumner and Missouri senator Carl Schurz and draws him into closer political alliance with congressional supporters, including Indiana senator Oliver P. Morton, New York senator Roscoe Conkling, and Benjamin F. Butler, now a Massachusetts congressman and Sumner's rival in that state's Republican party. Son Ulysses, Jr., enters Harvard College (graduates in 1874). Cox resigns as secretary of the interior in October to protest lack of civil service reform in Grant's administration and is replaced by Columbus Delano of Ohio, the commissioner of internal revenue. In his annual message to Congress, December 5, Grant agains advocates acquiring the Dominican Republic and asks Congress to authorize a commission to negotiate a new treaty. (Congress funds commission for investigatory purposes only; it reports favorably on annexation in spring 1871, but Grant does not propose further action.)

1871   Grant submits report to Congress, January 13, on Ku Klux Klan outrages in the South; Congress begins investigation of Klan activities and debate over new enforcement law. Grant appoints Fish and four other commissioners on February 9 to negotiate American claims against Great Britain for damages caused by Confederate raiders built in British shipyards during the Civil War (popularly known as the *Alabama* claims, after a famous Confederate warship). Commissioners are also empowered to negotiate the water boundary between Washington Territory and British Columbia, disputes between the United States and Canada over trade, navigation on the St. Lawrence River, fishing rights, and claims against the United States resulting from the Fenian raids on Canada. Grant has administration's Senate supporters remove Sumner, who had advocated settling Civil War claims against Britain by annexing Canada, as chairman of the Foreign Relations Committee on March 10. Urges the passage of new enforcement bill in message to Congress, March 23, and signs it into law, April 20; act establishes criminal penalties for individuals who conspire to deprive citizens of their rights under the Fourteenth and Fifteenth Amendments, provides for prosecution in federal court in cases where state authorities fail to act, and gives the president power to suspend the writ of habeas corpus and declare martial law. Attorney General Akerman begins prosecution of Klansmen, concentrating on cases in North and South Carolina and Mississippi. Treaty of Washington, signed on May 8, submits commerce raider claims and western boundary dispute to arbitration, rejects claims arising from Fenian raids, and resolves other U.S.-Canadian issues. (Arbitration tribunal composed of American, British, Brazilian, Italian, and Swiss members awards the United States $15.5 million and Great Britain $1.9 million in Civil War claims on August 25, 1872; Emperor William I of Germany, the sole arbitrator of boundary dispute, settles it in favor of the United States on October 21, 1872.) Commissioner of Indian Affairs Parker submits his resignation on June 29 despite having been cleared in February of corruption charges brought before a congressional committee. Grant suspends the writ of habeas corpus in nine counties in South Carolina, October 17, and dispatches federal troops; Akerman supervises arrests of hundreds of suspected Klansmen (several dozen are eventually convicted). Grant replaces Akerman, who had ruled against western railroad companies in land-grant cases, as attorney general in December with former Oregon senator George H. Williams, who continues Klan prosecutions until 1873. (Klan declines as result of prosecutions, but other white supremacist groups continue acts of violence against blacks and white Republicans.)

1872   Signs act on March 1 establishing Yellowstone National Park (the first national park in the world). Convention of Liberal Republicans opposed to Grant's administration meets in Cincinnati on May 1. It nominates Horace Greeley, editor of the *New-York Tribune*, for president and Benjamin Gratz Brown, governor of Missouri, for vice-president, and adopts platform denouncing corruption in government and calling for civil service reform, universal political amnesty for former Confederates, and an end to federal intervention in the South. Grant is nominated for president on the first ballot by the Republican convention meeting in Philadelphia, June 5–6, which nominates Senator Henry Wilson of Massachusetts for vice-president. Democratic convention endorses Greeley and Brown on July 9. Grant is reelected on November 5, winning 286 of 352 electoral votes and over 55 percent of the popular vote. Voting in Louisiana results in two sets of election returns. On December 3 Grant authorizes use of the army to enforce U.S. circuit court orders regarding the Louisiana election. Attends funeral of Greeley, who died on November 29. Circuit court judge Edward H. Durell declares the Republican election returns valid, December 5, and orders statehouse seized; troops occupy it and admit Republican legislators, who declare William P. Kellogg to be the governor-elect. Grant appoints Ward Hunt of New York to the Supreme Court, December 11 (confirmed by the Senate, he is seated in 1873).

1873   Orders army to protect Kellogg's inauguration, but forbids it to disperse conservative group who declare themselves to be the legitimate state legislature and claim John McEnery to be governor. Signs Coinage Act, February 12, demonetizing the silver dollar, and salary act, March 3, which raises the president's salary from $25,000 to $50,000 and increases the pay of the vice-president, Cabinet members, Supreme Court justices, and members of Congress (measure is widely criticized and becomes known as the "Salary Grab" act). Inaugurated for second term on March 4. Concludes his address by describing his reelection as vindication against the abuse and slander to which he had been subjected during the war and his first term. Boutwell is elected to the Senate from Massachusetts and is replaced as secretary of the treasury by his assistant secretary, William A. Richardson, also from Massachusetts. Chief Justice Salmon P. Chase dies May 7. After months of worsening violence in Louisiana, Grant sends troop reinforcements to state and issues proclamation on May 22 ordering pro-McEnery forces to disperse. Father dies in Covington, Kentucky, on June 29. Series of financial failures in New York, September 8–18, leads to widespread panic and severe national economic depression (which continues to worsen for remainder of Grant's term). Grant and Richardson confer with bankers in New York in late September and moderately increase the supply of paper money irredeemable in gold ("greenbacks"). In December Grant nominates Attorney General Williams to be Chief Justice of the Supreme Court. Father-in-law dies in Washington on December 15.

1874   Withdraws nomination of Williams because of Senate opposition focusing on his wife's purchase of a carriage with government funds. Nominates Caleb Cushing of Massachusetts in his place, then withdraws nomination when letter Cushing wrote to Jefferson Davis in March 1861, recommending a former clerk for a Confederate position, is made public. Appoints Morrison R. Waite of Ohio, who is confirmed on January 21. On April 22 Grant vetoes bill to further increase the supply of irredeemable paper money. Sherman, frustrated by Belknap's increasing control of the army and Grant's reluctance to clearly define the commanding general's authority, receives permission from Belknap and Grant to move his headquarters from Washington, D.C., to St. Louis. Daughter Nellie marries Englishman Algernon Sartoris at the White House, May 21. Secretary of the Treasury Richardson resigns after being linked to a Massachusetts tax collection scandal; Grant nominates Benjamin H. Bristow of Kentucky, a former solicitor general, to replace him. Postmaster General Creswell resigns in June and is replaced in August by former Connecticut governor Marshall Jewell. White League militia overthrows Kellogg government in Louisiana and seizes control of New Orleans, September 14. Grant orders 5,000 troops sent to New Orleans, September 16. White League forces disperse and Kellogg is restored as governor. Fall elections give the Democrats a majority in the House of Representatives and reduce the Republican majority in the Senate. Louisiana legislative election again results in disputed count. Grant withdraws troops from the statehouse in New Orleans, November 17, but orders Sheridan to Louisiana on December 24 to observe situation there.

1875   Democrats attempt to gain control of Louisiana legislature on January 4 by forcibly installing five members in its lower chamber. At Kellogg's request, federal troops eject the five Democrats from the statehouse. Sheridan defends their removal and requests authority to try White League

leaders by military tribunal. Action is widely denounced as
an illegitimate military intervention in civil affairs. In message to the Senate, January 13, Grant reviews history of
electoral fraud and violence in Louisiana, defends his previous interventions as constitutionally justified, states his
belief that the military did not commit an "intentional
wrong" by ousting the disputed legislators, and asks Congress to resolve the matter. (Congressional compromise,
implemented in April 1875, gives control of the lower
chamber of the legislature to the Democrats, the state senate to the Republicans, and retains Kellogg as governor.)
Signs Specie Resumption Act, January 14, setting January
1, 1879, as date for restoration of currency to a specie basis.
In message to Congress, February 8, Grant describes the
revocation in 1874 of Arkansas's Reconstruction constitution as the illegal result of fraud and intimidation and asks
Congress not to recognize it; instead, the House passes
resolution accepting the new Arkansas state constitution
and the Senate refuses to endorse federal intervention.
Signs Civil Rights Act, March 1, which forbids racial dis-
crimination in public accommodations, travel, and jury
duty (law is overturned by Supreme Court in 1883). Attorney General Williams resigns and is replaced by New York
lawyer Edwards Pierrepont. Bristow's investigation of the
"whiskey rings" defrauding the treasury of excise taxes results in massive raids, May 10, and the subsequent indictment of over 200 distillers and revenue agents. Grant
writes letter, published May 31, disavowing interest in a
third term. First grandchild, Grant Sartoris, born at Long
Branch on July 11 (child dies in England, May 21, 1876).
Pierrepont warns Grant that Babcock is implicated in the
St. Louis "whiskey ring"; Grant writes note directing the
investigation to continue: "Let no guilty man escape if it
can be avoided." Babcock and others tell Grant that the
prosecutions are politically motivated. Mississippi governor Adelbert Ames calls on September 8 for federal troops
to suppress violence by "White Liners" attempting to intimidate Republican voters in the state election. Pierrepont forwards message to Grant at Long Branch. Grant
writes to Pierrepont on September 13 describing federal
intervention in the South as unpopular but necessary and
reluctantly agreeing to send troops. Pierrepont selectively
quotes from Grant's letter in his reply to Ames on Sep-

tember 14, encouraging Ames to suppress disorders with the state militia and promising federal intervention only in case of direct rebellion against the state government. (Democrats win control of Mississippi legislature in November, and Ames resigns in 1876 to avoid impeachment.) Secretary of the Interior Delano resigns amid accusations of nepotism and corruption in his department and is replaced in October by former Michigan senator Zachariah Chandler. Grant abandons efforts to keep gold prospectors out of the Black Hills despite treaty ceding it to the Sioux. Democratic majority in House begins investigating corruption in Grant's administration when new Congress meets, December 6. Babcock is indicted in St. Louis "whiskey ring" case, December 9.

1876   Grant has Pierrepont order U.S. attorneys prosecuting "whiskey ring" cases not to grant immunity to suspects in return for testimony. After being persuaded by his Cabinet not to testify at Babcock's trial, Grant gives sworn deposition praising Babcock's character and Babcock is acquitted, February 24, but is forced to leave the White House staff. Secretary of War Belknap, under congressional investigation for taking bribes from an army post trader, resigns on the morning of March 2 and is impeached by the House that afternoon; Grant is criticized for accepting his resignation. (Belknap is later acquitted by the Senate on the grounds that his resignation removed him from their jurisdiction.) Grant appoints Ohio attorney Alphonso Taft as new secretary of war; Taft restores Sherman's operational control of the army, and Sherman returns to Washington. Grant opens International Centennial Exposition in Philadelphia, May 10. Attorney General Pierrepont is made minister to Great Britain, and is succeeded in May by Taft, who is replaced as secretary of war by James D. Cameron of Pennsylvania. First surviving grandchild, Julia Grant, daughter of Frederick Dent Grant, born June 7 (eight more grandchildren are born during Grant's lifetime). Secretary of the Treasury Bristow resigns on June 17 and is succeeded by Maine senator Lot M. Morrill. Lieutenant Colonel George A. Custer and 262 of his men are killed in Montana, June 25, by the Sioux and Northern Cheyenne in the battle of the Little Big Horn (army soon resumes offensive, which continues until surviving Indians surrender in 1877). Postmaster

General Jewell resigns in July and is replaced by James N. Tyner of Connecticut. In October Grant sends troops to South Carolina and issues proclamation in attempt to control violence by white supremacist rifle clubs before the election. Presidential election between Democrat Samuel J. Tilden and Republican Rutherford B. Hayes on November 7 results in conflicting election returns in South Carolina, Florida, and Louisiana, and disqualification controversy over an Oregon elector, causing a disputed electoral count. Grant orders troops to guard the capitals of the three Southern states, allowing their Republican-controlled election boards to prepare and certify official returns, and promises to maintain order and work for a fair resolution of the electoral dispute. Reviews his administration's record in his final annual message to Congress, December 5, and describes his failures as "errors of judgment, not of intent." Defends his attempt to annex the Dominican Republic by arguing that it would have served as a refuge for persecuted Southern blacks and allowed them to secure their rights in the South by threatening to emigrate there.

1877   Supports creation of electoral commission to resolve presidential election and signs bill establishing 15-member panel on January 29. In series of 8–7 votes, commission awards all disputed electoral votes to Hayes, giving him electoral majority of one. Joint session of Congress declares Hayes the victor, March 2. Hayes privately takes oath of office on Saturday, March 3, and Grants leave the White House after public inaugural on March 5. Plans European tour. Visits Galena before sailing from Philadelphia on May 17 with Julia, son Jesse, and John Russell Young of the New York *Herald*. (Young's reports of Grant's travels and of their conversations about the Civil War and politics are widely reprinted in newspapers and are published in 1879 as part of travel account *Around the World with General Grant*.) Arrives in Liverpool, May 28, and visits Manchester and Leicester before going to London. Attends numerous banquets, receptions, and welcoming ceremonies, and meets prominent aristocrats and political leaders (will do so in many of the countries he visits). Sees Nellie and new grandson Algernon Edward Sartoris at her home in Southampton, and has dinner with Queen Victoria at Windsor Castle on June 27. Sails to

Ostend, July 5, and tours Belgium, western Germany, Switzerland, northern Italy, and Alsace and Lorraine before returning to Britain for tour of Scotland. Arrives in Edinburgh, August 31, and visits Glasgow and the Highlands. Goes to Newcastle-on-Tyne in northern England, September 20, where he watches procession of approximately 80,000 Northumberland and Durham miners, workers, and artisans in his honor on September 22 and is hailed for his role in ending slavery and upholding "the rights of man and the dignity of labor." Tours steel mills in Sheffield and factories in Birmingham and then stays with Nellie in Southampton for ten days. Arrives in Paris, October 24. Meets French republican leader Léon Gambetta, but is unable to see Victor Hugo, who considers Grant to have favored Prussia in the 1870–71 war. Remains in Paris until December, then sails for Italy from Marseilles. Arrives in Naples, December 17, goes up Mt. Vesuvius, and tours Pompeii. Spends Christmas in Palermo harbor, then sails for Egypt by way of Malta. Reads Mark Twain's *The Innocents Abroad* and Petroleum V. Nasby's *The Nasby Papers* on board ship.

1878   Arrives in Alexandria January 5. Meets explorer Henry Morton Stanley, who is returning from his recent expedition down the Congo River. Goes up the Nile to Cairo, Karnak, and Luxor, then sails for Palestine from Port Said in February 9, landing at Jaffa. Visits Jerusalem, Bethlehem, Nablus, Nazareth, and Damascus before sailing from Beirut. Arrives in Constantinople, March 5, and after short stay goes to Athens and Rome. Has audience with Pope Leo XIII, then goes to Florence, Venice, Milan, and Paris with Nellie. Jesse returns to the United States. Grant tours the Netherlands before arriving in Berlin on June 26 where congress of European powers is meeting to revise the peace terms of the Russo-Turkish War of 1877–78. Discusses the American Civil War with German chancellor Prince Otto von Bismarck, who equates the preservation of the Union with the wars of German unification (Grant later says that Gambetta and Bismarck were the two men in Europe he found most impressive). Meets sister Mary and brother-in-law Michael John Cramer, American minister to Denmark, in Copenhagen on July 6. Tours Norway and Sweden before sailing for Russia from Stockholm. Arrives in St. Petersburg July 30. Discusses American Indian warfare with Tsar Alexander II, answers Grand Duke Alexis' questions about Custer, and meets with Chancellor Aleksandr M. Gorchakov. Visits Moscow and Warsaw before arriving in Vienna August 18. Tours Bavaria, southern France, and northern Spain, reaching Madrid on October 28. Fall elections give Democrats control of both houses of Congress and increase public speculation about Grant seeking a third presidential term. Grant visits Lisbon, Cordova, Seville, Cadiz, and Gibraltar before returning to London by way of Paris.

1879 Grant arrives in Dublin, January 3, for tour of Ireland while Julia stays with Nellie in England. Son Frederick joins Grant and Julia, and they sail for India from Marseilles on January 24. Arrives in Bombay, February 13, and visits Allahabad, Agra, Jaipur, Delhi, Lucknow, and Benares before reaching Calcutta on March 10, where he is received by the viceroy, Lord Lytton (son of novelist Edward Bulwer-Lytton). Sails from Calcutta to Rangoon, and then travels to Penang, Malacca, Singapore, Bangkok, and Saigon before arriving in Hong Kong on April 30. Goes to Canton and Macao, then north to Shanghai and Tientsin. Discusses railroad and telegraph construction in China with the viceroy of Tientsin, General Li Hung-chang, who had helped suppress the Taiping rebellion in 1864. Meets Prince Kung, co-regent of the child emperor Tsai-t'ien, in Peking. Kung and Li ask Grant for help in Sino-Japanese dispute caused by the recent Japanese annexation of the Ryukyu Islands; Grant promises to raise issue during his visit to Japan. Arrives on June 21 in Nagasaki, where Grant and Julia plant trees in fairgrounds before sailing through Inland Sea to Yokohama. Meets Emperor Mutsuhito (the Meiji emperor) and Empress Haruko in Tokyo, July 4; the emperor and Grant shake hands (reported to be the first time an emperor of Japan had ever done so). In later private interview with the emperor, Grant recommends the gradual introduction of suffrage and a legislature to Japan, warns against incurring foreign debt, condemns European control of Asian commerce, and urges a peaceful resolution of the Ryukyu dispute without European intervention (conveys similar advice to Kung and Li, and China eventually accepts Japanese annexation of islands; Grant will later write to Li about Chinese-American issues). Visits shrines of early

Tokugawa shoguns at Nikko, but is unable to tour widely because of cholera outbreak. Praises Japanese schools and advises country to seek foreign investment while resisting unfair trade treaties. Unable to book passage for Australia, sails for California. Reads Victor Hugo's *Les Misérables* during voyage. Greeted by thousands of people in San Francisco, September 20. Visits Portland, Oregon, Fort Vancouver, and Yosemite, and descends with Julia into silver mine in Virginia City, Nevada. Returns to Galena, then attends reunion of Army of the Tennessee in Chicago on November 13, where he begins friendship with Samuel L. Clemens, who is the final speaker at the banquet. Travels to Philadelphia on December 16, completing his around-the-world trip.

1880   Continues traveling as supporters, including Conkling, Washburne, and Illinois senator John A. Logan, work for his nomination for a third term. Grant visits Florida and Cuba before going to Mexico in February. Lands at Vera-cruz and travels to Mexico City, where he shows Julia sites of 1847 battles. Returns to Galena in April by way of Texas, New Orleans, and the Mississippi Valley. Grant leads major rivals, Maine senator James G. Blaine and Ohio senator John Sherman, for 35 ballots in voting for presidential nomination at Republican national convention in Chicago, June 7–8, but loses on 36th ballot to dark-horse candidate, Ohio congressman James A. Garfield. Washburne receives small number of votes, angering Grant and causing permanent breach between them. Visits Colorado in August to investigate possible mining investments. Grant and Conkling meet with Garfield in September at Mentor, Ohio, in attempt to reconcile Republican factions, and Grant campaigns for Garfield in New Jersey, New York, and Connecticut in October. Garfield defeats Democratic nominee Winfield S. Hancock, November 2. Grants go to New York City for the winter, staying at the Fifth Avenue Hotel.

1881   Grant makes recommendations on appointments to Garfield. Becomes president of the Mexican Southern Railroad on March 23, new company formed to build railroad from Mexico City to Pacific Coast in Oaxaca, and goes to Mexico City to obtain government concessions. Partners in company include Grenville M. Dodge, for-

merly a Union major general and chief engineer of the
Union Pacific, and financier Russell Sage, both of whom
are business associates of Jay Gould, and Matías Romero,
former Mexican minister to the United States and a friend
of Grant's. Writes public letter protesting appointment by
Garfield of one of Conkling's opponents as collector of
customs in New York City. Returns from Mexico in late
spring and goes to Long Branch for the summer. Brother
Orvil dies August 4. Moves in fall to house at 3 East 66th
Street, New York City, bought with funds raised by group
of businessmen, and works at office at 2 Wall Street. Railroad does not attract sufficient capital to begin significant
track laying. Grant invests $100,000, his entire liquid cap-
ital, in Grant & Ward, private banking firm founded by
Ulysses, Jr., and Ferdinand Ward; Julia, Jesse, sister Virginia, and other family members also invest in the bank.
Firm appears to flourish, and Grant considers himself to
be financially secure.

1882   President Chester A. Arthur appoints Grant as one of
two American commissioners to negotiate commercial
treaty with Mexico; Romero is one of two Mexican commissioners. Publishes article "An Undeserved Stigma," defending Major General Fitz-John Porter, who had been
cashiered in 1863 for his role in the Union defeat at the
second battle of Bull Run, in the December *North American Review*.

1883   Commercial treaty eliminating tariffs on variety of goods
is signed on January 20. Critics charge that treaty favors
interests of Mexican Southern Railroad, and agreement is
never put into effect by the U.S. Senate. Mother dies May
11. Grant takes part in excursion made by group of political and business figures in late summer along newly completed Northern Pacific Railroad. Leaves from Chicago
and travels through Minnesota, North Dakota, Montana,
Idaho, and Oregon to Tacoma, Washington. Shares platform with Sitting Bull in Bismarck, North Dakota. Visits
British Columbia and Yellowstone National Park before
returning to the East. Slips on sidewalk in New York City,
December 24, and injures left leg and hip, which had
been badly hurt in his 1863 riding accident in New Orleans
(will regularly use crutches or cane for the remainder
of his life).

1884   Develops pleurisy in January and is confined to bed for several weeks. Ward tells Grant on May 4 that he needs one-day loan of $150,000 to meet temporary demands on Marine National Bank, with which Grant & Ward is associated. Grant obtains personal check for the full amount from William H. Vanderbilt. Marine National Bank fails on May 6 and Grant & Ward suspends operations a few hours later (failures cause Mexican Southern Railroad to go bankrupt). Ward is revealed to have been defrauding his investors. Grant is financially ruined and is accused by some newspapers of being implicated in Ward's dishonesty. Gives Vanderbilt the deeds to all of his properties, his Civil War swords and trophies, and the gifts he had received on his world tour (move protects property from other creditors; Vanderbilt later gives Civil War collection and gifts to the Smithsonian). Agrees in June to write articles for *The Century Magazine* series on the Civil War, receiving $500 per article, and begins work at his Long Branch cottage. Submits draft of article on Shiloh, July 1, then rewrites it when *Century* editors ask him to provide a more personal perspective on the battle (article appears as "The Battle of Shiloh" in February 1885). Begins article on Vicksburg campaign, writing four hours a day. Discusses further articles on the Wilderness campaign and Lee's surrender with *Century* editor Robert U. Johnson on July 22, and tells Johnson that he intends to write a book about his campaigns. Begins suffering from dryness and pain in his throat during the summer, but postpones seeking medical attention until his family doctor returns from Europe. Works on draft of Vicksburg article with the assistance of Frederick, Johnson, and Adam Badeau, one of his former staff aides and author of the three-volume *Military History of Ulysses S. Grant*. Submits Vicksburg manuscript to *Century* in August and begins writing account of Chattanooga campaign. Meets with Roswell Smith, president of the Century Company, in early September and discusses his memoirs with him. Returns to New York in October and hires Badeau to assist him by locating documents, checking facts, and reviewing the manuscript. Family physician Dr. Fordyce Barker refers Grant to Dr. John H. Douglas, a leading throat specialist. Douglas finds inflammation on Grant's palate during examination on October 22. Grant asks if it is cancerous; Douglas tells him that he has a serious "epithelial" disease "sometimes capable of being cured." Continues work on his book and sees Douglas regularly for topical treatments. Receives draft contract from Century, offering him 10 percent royalty with expected sale of 25,000 copies. Grant gives up smoking in late November. Clemens learns of the Century offer and tells Grant that it is inadequate. Encourages Grant to sign with the company Clemens had recently founded with Charles L. Webster to publish *Adventures of Huckleberry Finn*. Grant makes no commitment to Clemens, and does not accept Webster's offer in early December of a $50,000 advance. Enjoys visits by Sherman.

1885   Receives extra $1,000 from *Century* for article on Shiloh. On February 3 Webster offers Grant choice of 20 percent royalty or 70 percent of net profits from his book. Grant develops throat ulcers, which doctors determine on February 19 to be cancerous and inoperable. Clemens learns during February 21 visit that Grant is dying, but renews offer to publish book. Grant signs contract with Charles L. Webster & Co., February 27, and chooses to receive 70 percent of the net profits; Clemens and Webster begin selling book by subscription canvassing (60,000 sets are ordered by May 1). After weeks of conflicting press reports concerning Grant's health, *The New York Times* confirms on March 1 that he has fatal cancer. Congress passes bill on March 4 placing Grant on army retired list as full general, with pay. Nellie arrives from Europe, March 20. Grant gives deposition on March 26 for trial of James D. Fish, an associate of Ferdinand Ward (Fish is convicted and sent to prison). Receives local injections of cocaine for pain and morphine to help him sleep. Has first of several violent choking and coughing fits on night of March 28, and is close to death for several days. Douglas and Dr. George F. Shrady keep his throat clear and Shrady administers brandy injections as stimulants. To please his family, receives baptism from Methodist minister John P. Newman. Press maintains vigil outside of house. Grant's condition unexpectedly improves after coughing fit brings on hemorrhage, and he is able to take carriage rides by late April. Webster & Co. begins printing proofs of first half of first volume. New York *World* reports on April 29 that Badeau is writing the memoirs from rough notes provided

by Grant. Clemens wants to sue paper for libel, but instead Grant writes public letter declaring that the composition of the book is entirely his own. Begins giving
dictation to a stenographer. Badeau writes Grant, May 2,
offering to complete memoirs for $1,000 a month and 10
percent of the profits, and tells Grant that he is incapable
of finishing the book on his own. Grant replies on May 5,
dismissing Badeau as his assistant and insisting that he will
finish the book himself. Continues dictation, giving
10,000 words in one session, then develops difficulty
speaking and reverts to writing. Finishes draft of chapters
covering the campaign from the Wilderness to Appomattox by early June. On advice of his doctors, goes to Mount
McGregor, summer resort in Adirondacks near Saratoga
Springs, New York, on June 16. Travels by special train in
Vanderbilt's private car; crowds gather at stations along
the route, and he is cheered by veterans while changing
trains at Saratoga Springs. Stays in cottage with Julia, their
children, and three grandchildren and is attended by Dr.
Douglas. Newspapers print daily reports on his condition.
Tells Douglas in note on June 17 that he does not expect to
live much longer, but continues to work on memoirs, having proofs read aloud and writing revisions on slips of
paper. Mostly communicates by writing notes, but man-
ages to dictate extensive changes in proofs in a whisper on
June 23. Clemens arrives on June 29. Grant tells him that
second volume is nearly done, then writes preface and new
section evaluating wartime generals and political leaders.
Clemens leaves on July 2. Robert U. Johnson visits on July
8 and confirms arrangements, negotiated earlier by Clemens, for publishing three remaining articles in *Century
Magazine* (they appear posthumously in September and
November 1885 and February 1886). Simon Bolivar Buckner visits July 10; tells reporters his meeting with Grant is
"too sacred" to recount. Last proofs of first volume are returned to the printer on July 11. Frederick prepares manuscript of second volume for the printer and discourages
Grant from making further changes. Grant sits on porch
of cottage, reading newspapers as visitors intent on seeing
him pass by. Writes notes to doctors describing effects of
medication. Manuscript of second volume is delivered to
Webster on July 18. (First volume of *Personal Memoirs of
U. S. Grant* is published by Charles L. Webster & Co. on

December 1, 1885, and the second volume on March 1, 1886. Over 300,000 sets are sold, and Julia eventually receives between $420,000 and $450,000 in royalties.) On July 20 Grant has himself pushed in invalid's chair to outlook facing Hudson River and Green Mountains of Vermont; returns to cottage exhausted. Condition worsens on July 21. Dies surrounded by family at around 8:00 A.M., July 23. After funeral services at Mount McGregor on August 4 body is taken by train to New York City, where it lies in state at City Hall for two days. Funeral procession on August 8 carries body through Manhattan to Riverside Park, where it is interred in a temporary brick tomb (reinterred in permanent granite and marble tomb overlooking the Hudson River in 1897).

Note on the Texts

This volume presents the text of the *Personal Memoirs of U. S. Grant*, published in two volumes by Charles L. Webster & Company, 1885–86, and a selection of 175 letters, orders, and reports, written by Grant from 1839 to 1865, taken from the first 14 volumes of *The Papers of Ulysses S. Grant*, edited by John Y. Simon and published by Southern Illinois University Press, 1967–85.

Grant's *Personal Memoirs* grew out of the articles he had agreed to contribute to *The Century* as part of a series on the Civil War. He had earlier declined the offer, but after Grant & Ward, the private banking firm with which he was associated, failed on May 6, 1884, he was deeply in debt and in need of money. The agreement was for him to write four articles covering the battle of Shiloh, the Vicksburg and Wilderness campaigns, and Appomattox, for each of which he would be paid $500. He began writing in the middle of June 1884, and by July 1, 1884, he had sent a completed draft of "Shiloh" to *The Century*. This first version was very much like the official reports he had written during the Civil War. Robert U. Johnson, editor of *The Century*, visited him and explained that the readers of the series wanted a more personal story, told from his own point of view. Grant rewrote the article, and then began work on "Vicksburg." When Johnson visited him on July 22 and asked him if he had thought of turning the articles into a book, Grant replied that he had already "formed the intention" of writing a book during the coming winter. By mid-August, the Vicksburg article was given to *The Century*, and Grant had decided to contribute an article on his Chattanooga campaign rather than one on Appomattox. Aware that other publishers were beginning to hear about Grant's prospective book, Roswell Smith, president of the Century Company, accompanied by Johnson, visited Grant early in September to tentatively propose book publication. Though no definite arrangement was concluded, Grant said he would give them a chance to see the work when it was done. On October 22, 1884, the same day on which he learned that the sore throat he had been suffering from for several months was caused by a serious ailment (later diagnosed as cancer), Grant visited the Century office and said he would like the firm to publish his book. A contract was drawn up in November, offering him ten percent royalty on an expected sale of some 25,000 sets.

Grant was still considering this offer when his friend Samuel L. Clemens (Mark Twain) heard about the book. Clemens had recently formed his own subscription publishing company with his nephew and business associate, Charles L. Webster, whose name he used for the firm, in order to publish his own works, beginning with *Adventures of Huckleberry Finn.* Clemens told Grant that the terms offered in the Century's contract were not good enough and that he should not sign anything until he had had the chance to consider the offer Charles L. Webster & Co. would make. In early December 1884, Webster offered Grant a $50,000 advance: $25,000 for each volume. But Grant was still undecided; he had verbally agreed to let the Century Company publish his memoirs, and Johnson had helped him in the writing of the Shiloh article and had also encouraged him to write the book. Finally, Webster offered Grant on February 3, 1885, a choice of a twenty percent royalty or seventy percent of the profits. Grant chose seventy percent of the profits because that way, he said, no one would lose money on the deal. The contract was signed on February 27, 1885.

Grant's method of writing the book was similar to the way he had prepared his official reports during the Civil War. He would write the narrative, then his aides would read it over, suggest revisions, check the facts, and locate and insert the relevant documents. For this purpose, he had engaged in October the services of Adam Badeau, his former military secretary and the author of a three-volume history of Grant's war service; in addition, his son Frederick Dent Grant was already at work on the copying and researching. Meanwhile, Grant's health continued to deteriorate, and it was uncertain whether he would live to complete the work. When Clemens reviewed the progress of the manuscript in mid-March, he found that the first volume still lacked the last chapters and decided that, if necessary, the volume would end there, so ensuring that at least one volume would have been written by Grant. The second volume would be finished by someone else (presumably Badeau). By the end of March, the first volume was complete, and parts of the second volume were also done: Grant had finished writing the Chattanooga section and drafted an account of the Wilderness campaign. But then his condition seriously worsened, and he was unable to work for almost a month.

The Century series on the Civil War had begun in the November 1884 number. Grant's article, "The Battle of Shiloh," appearing in the February 1885 number, immediately increased the magazine's circulation, and the Century Company voluntarily paid him an additional sum of $1,000. (In July, they paid him an additional $1,500.) Clemens had looked over the completed section on Vicksburg that Grant had submitted to *The Century* and saw that it was at least twice as long as the other articles. With the help of Frederick Grant he convinced Grant that half the article, the section dealing with the siege of Vicksburg, would be enough. Clemens was worried that Grant's contributions to *The Century* series would not be recognized as excerpts from his forthcoming book. On April 15, 1885, Webster made an agreement with *The Century* that all future articles by Grant appearing in the magazine would acknowledge that they were copyrighted by Grant and taken from the *Personal Memoirs of U. S. Grant*. In return, Webster was to allow all articles to appear before book publication: the first volume was to be published December 1, 1885, and the second to follow in March 1886. ("Vicksburg" appeared in the September 1885 number, "Chattanooga" in the November 1885 number, and "Preparing for the Wilderness Campaign" in the February 1886 number.)

By the middle of April 1885 the first part of Volume I was in galleys. Proofs were sent to Clemens at the same time they were sent to the Grant family, Clemens correcting only punctuation and grammar. To encourage Grant, he wrote him that some of his chapters were like *Caesar's Commentaries* in their "simplicity, naturalness & purity" of style. Grant's health improved enough to continue work, and on April 30, using a stenographer supplied by Webster & Co., he dictated for three hours on the Appomattox campaign. On May 5

Clemens wrote to his friend William Dean Howells that Grant had dictated 50 pages, and thus "the Wilderness & Appomatox stand for all time in his own words."

Meanwhile, a disturbing story had appeared in late April in the New York *World* claiming that Grant was not writing his *Memoirs* himself, but only supplying information to Adam Badeau, who was actually doing the composition. With the knowledge that returns from the subscription canvass now showed that 60,000 sets of the *Personal Memoirs* were already sold, and Webster & Co. expected the total sales would be more than 300,000 sets, Adam Badeau wrote Grant a letter on May 2, 1885, asking that the terms of agreement between them be changed. Instead of the promise that he would receive $10,000 if the profits exceeded $30,000, he wanted to be paid $1,000 in advance each month until the work was finished, and then receive ten percent of the profits. He also preferred to have direct communication with Grant rather than through the stenographer. Grant, he said, did not have the strength to do his own research, and Badeau was the only one who could finish the book if Grant were not able to do so. Grant wrote to his publishers denying that anyone but himself was writing the book (this letter was printed in the newspapers), and privately wrote Badeau that he no longer needed his services and telling him that he was too petulant and demanded too much. He also said there had been a time when he was not sure that he would live to finish the book himself and had "supposed some one, whose name would necessarily be given to the public, and that name yours, would finish the book."

Though illness continued to interrupt his work, Grant could tell Clemens on May 26 that he had made the book too long by 200 pages. As proofs were received they were read to him; he made revisions, either dictating or writing them. By early June a great part of the Wilderness and Appomattox sections were set in galleys. A prospectus for the book, containing material from the early years to Appomattox, was given to the canvassers on June 8. Grant's son Frederick now acted as chief researcher, checking facts and finding particular letters and dispatches written during the war. Grant's other sons, Ulysses, Jr., and Jesse, also helped. This pattern of work continued even after Grant left New York on June 16 to spend the summer at Mount McGregor, New York. The Webster stenographer, Noble E. Dawson, accompanied the family and not only took dictation but helped Frederick Grant in copying and inserting new additions and revisions into the proofs. There were very few days now when Grant could dictate to the stenographer because the cancer in his throat made speaking too painful; instead, using a pencil and a special lap table, he wrote out his new sections and made notes for revisions. Clemens came to Mount McGregor the evening of June 29 and stayed until July 2, during which time Grant wrote the Preface. The first volume was completely set in type, but Grant continued to make last-minute revisions and notes for it until the first week of July. He was also organizing and rewriting the second volume. He was pleased with his revisions of the Appomattox section but felt that he did not have the time to revise other sections. At one point, in a note to his son Frederick, he wrote: "I should change Spotts. if I was able and could improve N. Ana and Cold Harbor." He also went over the contents of the Appendix with Frederick. The last two chapters were written at Mount McGregor. By July 10, all of Volume I was in page proofs and ready for the press, and by July 18, the text of Volume II was copied and ready for the printers, except for the documents that still had to be inserted, both in the work itself and in the Appendix. Grant died at Mount McGregor on July 23, 1885.

The first volume went to press in mid-July, but because more than 300,000 copies were needed, the total printing was not completed until December. Seven binderies were employed to bind the books. The first volume was published December 1, 1885, in five bindings: cloth at $7.00 a set; sheep, $9.00; half-morocco, $11.00; full-morocco, $18.00; and tree calf, $25.00. The second volume was still being set and revised in November. Clemens gave orders that "All on the Wilderness from the Rapidan to the James to come back in galleys. Insertions to be made in *corrected* galleys, & then printed *again* in galleys." This was the section that Grant had earlier wished he had more time to work on and improve. The insertions seem to be letters and dispatches; there are more of them in the second volume than in the first, and more of them are included as footnotes rather than inserted into the text. An index to both volumes was prepared. In addition, Frederick Grant was trying to make more revisions than Webster and Clemens wanted him to do. Webster reported to Clemens on December 25 that he had reversed some of Frederick's alterations, and Clemens agreed, saying, "It won't *do* to leave things out & make unnecessary alterations in the General's text." Though the full order of 300,000 copies of Volume II was not ready because of last-minute alterations, the publication date of March 1, 1886, was not officially changed. In all, over 300,000 sets were sold. Charles L. Webster & Co. paid Mrs. Grant $200,000, the largest single royalty payment ever made until then, on February 27, 1886, the anniversary of the signing of the contract. She later received another check for $150,000, and eventually received from $420,000 to $450,000.

The second volume of the *Personal Memoirs* contains an errata page correcting errors in the first volume, and these corrections, with one exception, are incorporated in the text printed here: at 62.8 and 63.3, "Little Colorado" replaces "Colorado"; at 65.24, "May" replaces "March"; at 75.3, "1846" replaces "1847"; at 117.23, "paymaster-general" replaces "surgeon-general"; at 121.11, "*tlacos*" replaces "*clackos*"; at 127.4, "tlacos" replaces "clackos"; at 170.15, "Sterling" replaces "Stirling"; at 198.19, "Cumberland" replaces "Tennessee"; and at 329.38, "9th" replaces "8th". Only at 195.6, where the errata page lists "Phelps" to replace "Walke", is the correction not made, since "Walke" is correct.

The letters, orders, and reports selected for this volume are from the years covered in Grant's *Personal Memoirs*, beginning with the earliest available letter written from West Point on September 22, 1839, and ending with a letter written to Julia Dent Grant from Raleigh, North Carolina, on April 25, 1865, where Grant had gone to confer with W. T. Sherman. *The Papers of Ulysses S. Grant*, edited by John Y. Simon, from which the texts of the 175 items included in this volume are taken, is the first inclusive collection of Grant's writings ever to be published. Eighty percent of the material contained in these volumes had never been published before. Except for his *Personal Memoirs* and two heavily edited volumes of his private letters—*General Grant's Letters to a Friend, 1861–1880*, edited by James Grant Wilson (New York, 1897), containing letters to Elihu Washburne, and *Letters of Ulysses S. Grant to his Father and his Youngest Sister, 1857–78*, edited by Jesse Grant Cramer (New York and London, 1912)—almost nothing outside of compilations of official documents was available to the interested reader. The largest repository of his official writings has been *The War of the Rebellion: A Compilation of the Official Records of the Union and Confederate Armies* (Washington, D.C., 1880–1901), and some of his presidential messages and addresses were available in various compilations made over the years. Most of the original material remained hidden, and the full extent of Grant's writings was unknown. This situation changed during the years 1953 to 1960 when Grant's grandson, Major General Ulysses S. Grant 3rd, gave to the Library of Congress his grandfather's headquarters records in 111 volumes and the letters Grant wrote his wife, Julia Dent Grant. In addition, new material in private hands, or owned by dealers, has been acquired by libraries across the country. In 1962, the Ulysses S. Grant Association was founded to collect, edit, and publish an edition of the Grant papers. John Y. Simon was made editor of the edition, and the first volume of *The Papers of Ulysses S. Grant* was published in 1967.

Simon's editorial policy in *The Papers* is to remain faithful to the original document. The items included in the edition are transcribed, whenever possible, from Grant's original manuscripts, and preserve Grant's own spelling, grammar, and punctuation. Some letters exist only in copies, and in these cases Simon has selected the one that he believes is the earliest. During the Civil War, aides copied out orders and dispatches by hand, and these were then copied in other quarters as well; the further removed a copy is from the original source, the more likely that it contains elements not originating with Grant. Beginning in the fall of 1864, Grant used a "Philp & Salomons' Highly Improved Manifold Writer," which allowed him to write multiple copies of his dispatches and reports, so a higher proportion of documents from this period are still extant in Grant's own handwriting.

Some of the original manuscript letters are in imperfect condition. Simon uses certain conventions to indicate particular problems, such as missing material and reconstructed texts. These conventions are adapted to suit the needs of the present volume in several ways. In *The Papers of Ulysses S. Grant*, when a word or letter is damaged, torn, or otherwise illegible, but there is no question about what the missing word or letter is, the missing material is set in roman type and enclosed in brackets; in these cases, the present volume accepts this editorial reconstruction and prints the word without brackets. When letters are missing, and reconstruction is not possible, Simon uses [. . .], the number of dots representing the missing letters; this practice is retained in the present volume. Grant also crossed out words. The *Papers* shows cancellations by printing the canceled words with lines through them; this volume does not print the crossed-out words. In addition, Julia Dent Grant deleted some sentences from Grant's letters to her, and her descendants requested that her wishes be followed. The *Papers* indicates these places in footnotes; the present volume uses three asterisks. *The Papers of Ulysses S. Grant* also indicates and offers corrections of errors, such as missing or incorrect dates and words, by printing corrections and conjectures in italic within brackets. The present volume omits the bracketed italic correction and usually prints the text as Grant wrote it; in some cases, however, the corrections are accepted and the word or date is printed without brackets. The following is a list of the corrections accepted in this volume, cited by page and line number: 888.19, [*s*]he; 913.1, ha[*r*]d; 920.9, ~~be~~fofore; 949.16, 1853 [*1854*]; 963.21, her[*e*]; 966.4, next [*week*]; 966.7, taken [*place*] in; 972.39, sigh[*t*]; 990.14, to[*o*]; 990.39, d[*a*]ily; 994.23, sever[*al*]. In addition, at 1065.17, "the" has been changed to "they."

This volume presents the texts of the editions chosen for inclusion here but does not attempt to reproduce features of their typographic design. The texts are printed without alteration except for the changes previously discussed and for the correction of typographical errors. Spelling, punctuation, and capitalization are often expressive features, and they are not altered, even when inconsistent or irregular. The following is a list of typographical errors corrected, cited by page and line number: 76.24, run,/ning; 121.2–3, as be; 191.3, empting; 376.32, suggest/tion; 480.41, Generals; 493.33, sameline; 498.2, SEIGE; 558.28, discomfiture,; 586.38, "Your; 707.8, enemies; 765.40, however; 773.36, rolé; 776.8, rolé; 797.32, vere; 816.10, ndependent; 839.6, possesions; 852.3b, surenders.

Notes

In the notes below, the numbers refer to page and line of this volume (the line count includes chapter headings). No note is made for information available in a standard desk-reference book. All notes in the text appeared in the Charles L. Webster edition and are either Grant's own or were supplied by the publisher. For more detailed notes and references to other studies, see John Y. Simon, ed., *The Papers of Ulysses S. Grant* (16 vols. to date, Carbondale: University of Southern Illinois Press, 1967–88). For further identification of persons mentioned in the text, see E. B. Long and Barbara Long, *Civil War Day by Day: An Almanac, 1861–1865* (New York: Doubleday, 1971), and Mark Mayo Boatner III, *The Civil War Dictionary*, revised edition (New York: David McKay, 1988). For further biographical background than is provided in the Chronology, see Bruce Catton, *Grant Moves South* (Boston: Little, Brown, 1960) and *Grant Takes Command* (Boston: Little, Brown, 1969); William S. McFeely, *Grant: A Biography* (New York: Norton, 1981); and Thomas L. Pitkin, *The Captain Departs: Ulysses S. Grant's Last Campaign* (Carbondale: University of Southern Illinois Press, 1973).

PERSONAL MEMOIRS OF U. S. GRANT

5.2   MAN . . . disposes."]   Early appearances of this proverb are in *Piers Plowman* by William Langland (c. 1332–c. 1400) and in *Imitation of Christ* by Thomas à Kempis (1379–1471).

5.10–11   rascality . . . failure.]   Ferdinand Ward had formed the private banking firm of Grant & Ward with Ulysses S. Grant, Jr., in 1881. Grant then invested his entire liquid capital in his son's firm, which suspended its operations on May 6, 1884. Ward was subsequently imprisoned for fraud in connection with the bank's operations.

15.32   *Bridge* . . . 371]   In the Charles L. Webster edition the following note appeared at this point:
    "The Daguerreotype from which the frontispiece was engraved was furnished the publishers through the courtesy of Mr. George W. Childs.
    "The fac-similes of General Buckner's dispatches at Fort Donelson are copied from the originals furnished the publishers through the courtesy of Mr. Ferdinand J. Dreer. General Grant's dispatch, 'I propose to move immediately upon your works,' was copied from the original document in the possession of the publishers."

18.25–26   Judge . . . Ohio]   George Tod (1773–1841) of Youngstown served as a judge of the state supreme court, 1806–10, and state court of appeals, 1816–29, as well as a state senator, 1804–6, 1810–12. His son David (1805–68), a Democrat, was elected governor of Ohio on the Union party ticket in 1861 but was not renominated in 1863. When asked by Lincoln to succeed Salmon P. Chase as secretary of the treasury in 1864, he declined because of poor health.

18.40–19.1   John . . . on."] The Civil War song most often known as "John Brown's Body," authorship unknown, was set to the music of a hymn (c. 1856) ascribed to the North Carolina musician William Steffe. "The Battle Hymn of the Republic" (1862), by Julia Ward Howe, is sung to the same tune.

19.25   Western Reserve] A section of land in the northeast corner of Ohio reserved by the state of Connecticut when it dropped its claims to other western lands in 1786. In 1800 Connecticut transferred jurisdiction over the reserve to the federal government, and it became part of the newly created Ohio Territory.

21.37–22.2   Two . . . Brewster.] William Henry Wadsworth (1821–93) of Kentucky served as a Unionist member of the House of Representatives, 1861–65, and as a Republican, 1885–87. No Brewster from the Richardson and Rand school is known to have served in the United States Congress.

28.6–7   Thomas . . . Senator] Morris (1776–1844), elected as a Democrat, served from 1833 to 1839. He ran for vice-president with James G. Birney on the antislavery Liberty party ticket in 1844.

28.35–36   Thomas . . . Congress] Thomas Hamer (1800–46) of Georgetown served in the House of Representatives from 1833 to 1839.

29.7   removal . . . moneys] President Andrew Jackson withdrew all federal deposits from the Bank of the United States on October 1, 1833.

30.7–8   John . . . Ohio] Confederate Brigadier General John Hunt Morgan (1825–64) led a large cavalry raid across the Ohio River into Indiana on July 8, 1863, then turned east and rode into southern Ohio. His troops passed through the area of Cincinnati and Georgetown on July 13–14, but were unable to elude their Union pursuers and find an unguarded ford across the Ohio. Morgan surrendered the remnants of his force at Salineville in northeastern Ohio on July 26 and was imprisoned in the Ohio state penitentiary at Columbus. He escaped on November 26, 1863, and rejoined the Confederate army, but was killed at Greeneville, Tennessee, on September 4, 1864.

31.26   Girard College] The college—a home and primary and secondary schools—was built and endowed with the six million dollars in cash and real estate left in trust to the city of Philadelphia by Stephen Girard (1750–1831) for the education of orphaned white boys. It opened in 1848.

34.23−24   brother . . . rebellion]   Samuel Simpson Grant (called Simpson by his family), born September 23, 1825, died on September 13, 1861, in St. Paul, Minnesota, and Clara Rachel Grant, born December 11, 1828, died on March 6, 1865, in Covington, Kentucky.

36.27   F. T. Dent]   Frederick Tracy Dent (1820−92) fought in the Mexican War and served on the western frontier until 1863. He was on Grant's staff from March 1864 until April 1865, and retired from the army as a colonel in 1883.

37.2   Colonel John O'Fallon]   John O'Fallon (1791−1865), a nephew of Revolutionary War commander George Rogers Clark and explorer William Clark, was wounded at the battle of Tippecanoe in 1811 and served in the War of 1812. He resigned from the army in 1818 and became a wealthy St. Louis merchant and philanthropist.

39.36   Professor Church]   Albert E. Church had been professor of mathematics at the Academy while Grant was a cadet there.

42.5−6   treaty . . . Santa Anna]   President Antonio López de Santa Anna (1794−1876) was captured by the Texans after the battle of San Jacinto on April 21, 1836, and signed an armistice withdrawing the Mexican army beyond the Rio Grande.

42.14   Alamo . . . Goliad]   On March 6, 1836, Santa Anna's army stormed the Alamo mission in San Antonio, Texas, and killed all 187 of its defenders. Another Mexican force captured about 400 men near the village of Goliad on March 20, most of whom were volunteers from the southern United States. Having previously decreed that all foreigners caught under arms on Mexican soil would be treated as pirates, Santa Anna ordered their execution, and about 330 of the prisoners were shot on March 27, 1836.

63.18−19   Hardee . . . tactics]   *Rifle and Light Infantry Tactics* (1855) by William J. Hardee (1815−73).

63.20   Theodric Porter]   A younger brother of naval officer David D. Porter (1813−91), who commanded the Union riverboat squadron during the Vicksburg campaign in 1863.

71.31   died . . . days]   Hamer died of dysentery on December 2, 1846.

98.34−35   tête-de-pont]   Bridgehead.

105.20−21   Lieutenant Semmes]   Raphael Semmes (1809−77), an officer of the U.S. Navy, accompanied Winfield Scott's expedition to Mexico City on a mission to secure the parole of an American midshipman, captured during a shore raid, whom the Mexican authorities had threatened to treat as a spy. Although the midshipman successfully escaped in July 1847, Semmes remained with the army, serving as a volunteer aide to Brevet Major General William J. Worth. Semmes joined the Confederate navy in 1861 and commanded the commerce raider *Alabama* from its commissioning in August

1862 until its sinking off Cherbourg, France, by the U.S.S. *Kearsarge* on June 19, 1864.

105.38   carry . . . trail]   A weapon carried in trail position is held by the right hand along the side of the body, with its muzzle inclined obliquely upwards.

106.32   voltigeurs]   Skirmishers, sharpshooters.

109.38   Mentioned . . . Garland]   Grant received a brevet promotion to captain for his actions on September 13, 1847. Major Francis Lee commanded the 4th Infantry during the battle while Lieutenant Colonel John Garland of the 4th led a brigade.

117.5–6   the whole . . . California]   The treaty of Guadalupe Hidalgo, ratified in 1848, ended the Mexican War by ceding to the United States Nuevo Mexico, a territory including all of what is now Nevada and Utah, almost all of Arizona and New Mexico, and part of present-day Colorado and Wyoming, and Upper California, corresponding to the present-day American state.

118.8   party . . . defeat.]   Winfield Scott, the Whig party candidate, was defeated in 1852 by Democrat Franklin Pierce. In 1856 the Whig party endorsed Millard Fillmore, the nominee of the nativist American (Know-Nothing) party, although by then many Whigs had joined the new anti-slavery Republican party.

120.40–121.1   During . . . Mexico]   Grant visited Mexico in 1880 and in 1881.

124.3   excruciating . . . eyes]   The group was probably experiencing snow blindness.

130.31–33   Chandler's . . . success]   Zachariah Chandler (1813–79) was a Republican senator from Michigan from 1857 to 1875. He served as secretary of the interior, 1875–77, during Grant's second term, and was again elected to the U.S. Senate in 1879.

130.36   Sackett's Harbor]   A village on the eastern shore of Lake Ontario in upstate New York, near Watertown and about 20 miles from the Canadian border.

131.3–26   Aspinwall . . . Panama]   Aspinwall, now called Colón, was founded in 1850 and named for the railroad builder William H. Aspinwall. Grant's crossing of the Isthmus roughly followed the future route of the Panama Canal.

136.22   Benicia barracks]   Situated on a strait linking two northern extensions of San Francisco Bay, Benicia was the site of the army's main arsenal on the Pacific Coast.

139.3−4   Bliss . . . promoted]   Captain William Wallace Smith Bliss (1815−53), a brevet lieutenant colonel, had been commissioned in the 4th Infantry after graduating from the Military Academy in 1833 and at the time of his death on August 5, 1853, was still officially an officer of that regiment, even though he had taught mathematics at the Academy from 1834 to 1840 and then served in the adjutant general's department for the remainder of his life.

141.5   two children]   Frederick Dent Grant, born May 30, 1850, and Ulysses S. ("Buck") Grant, Jr., born July 22, 1852.

142.19   Know-Nothing party]   Know-Nothing was the popular name of the nativist American party, organized in the 1850s to oppose Catholic and immigrant influence in American public life.

142.24−25   Free-Soil . . . Blair]   Free-Soil Democrats opposed the extension of slavery into the western territories. Francis P. Blair, Jr. (1821−75), elected to Congress as a Free-Soiler in 1856, supported Abraham Lincoln in 1860 and was a Republican during the Civil War, but returned to the Democratic party during Reconstruction and was its nominee for vice-president in 1868.

144.18   my two brothers]   Samuel Simpson Grant (1825−61) and Orvil Lynch Grant (1835−81).

144.39−40   Douglas . . . Lincoln]   The Democratic national convention split along sectional lines in June 1860. Northern Democrats nominated Douglas for president while Southern Democrats chose John C. Breckinridge as their candidate. In the election Abraham Lincoln, the Republican candidate, won a majority of 180 of 303 electoral votes (all from free states) and a plurality of approximately 40 percent of the popular vote. Douglas received 12 electoral votes (from both slave and free states) and 21 percent of the popular vote, Breckinridge 72 electoral votes (all from slave states) and 14 percent of the popular vote, and John Bell of the Constitutional Union party 39 electoral votes (also all from slave states) and 12 percent of the popular vote. About 13 percent of the popular vote went to anti-Lincoln fusion tickets in the free states.

145.8   time . . . nomination]   Lincoln won the nomination for president on May 18, 1860, on the third ballot taken at the Republican national convention.

149.35−36   States . . . acts]   Emancipation measures were seriously debated in the Kentucky state constitutional conventions of 1792 and 1799 and in the Virginia House of Delegates in 1832. No record exists of their defeat by a tie or by one vote.

150.33   two . . . least]   John B. Floyd (1806−63) of Virginia, who resigned on December 29, 1860, and Secretary of the Interior Jacob Thompson (1820−85) of Mississippi, who resigned January 8, 1861, were accused of using their Cabinet posts to aid secession. Secretary of the Treasury Howell Cobb

(1815–68) of Georgia resigned on December 10, 1860, so that he could return
to his state in expectation of its secession; he was not accused of having acted
in bad faith.

151.3–4   de facto . . . Capital.] Delegates chosen by elected state conventions in South Carolina, Georgia, Florida, Alabama, Mississippi, and
Louisiana met in Montgomery, Alabama, on February 4–9, 1861 (the Texas
delegates arrived on February 8). Acting as the provisional Congress of the
Confederate States of America, they adopted a provisional constitution and
elected Jefferson Davis as president for a provisional one-year term. Davis was
inaugurated on February 18; the Confederate capital was shifted to Richmond, Virginia, on May 21, 1861.

151.22–30   President-elect . . . capital.] After leaving Springfield, Illinois, by train on February 11, 1861, Abraham Lincoln made brief speeches in
Indiana, Ohio, Pennsylvania, New York, and New Jersey before being warned
in Philadelphia of a possible attempt to assassinate him in Baltimore. Lincoln
then traveled secretly to Washington, D.C., on the night of February 22–23.

152.22   "was . . . world,"] Cf. Ralph Waldo Emerson, "Concord Hymn:
Sung at the Completion of the Battle Monument, April 19, 1836," Stanza 1:
"Here once the embattled farmers stood, / And fired the shot heard round the
world."

153.6   Rawlins . . . Washburne] Rawlins (1831–69) was appointed assistant adjutant general on Grant's staff with the rank of captain on August 30,
1861; see pp. 168.25–169.13 in this volume. Elihu B. Washburne (1816–87), a
Galena resident, served in the U.S. House of Representatives as a Whig,
1853–56, and then as a Republican, 1856–69. By arrangement with Grant he
served as secretary of state for a few days in March 1869 before becoming
minister to France from 1869 to 1877.

154.6–7   President . . . wanted it."] This remark is attributed to President Lincoln, who fell ill with varioloid, a mild form of smallpox, on his
return to Washington after delivering his dedicatory address at Gettysburg on
November 19, 1863.

157.31   Philip Foulk] Philip B. Fouke (1818–76), Democratic congressman from Illinois, 1859–63, became a colonel in the Illinois volunteer infantry
and served under Grant at the battle of Belmont, where he was wounded.

158.32   General Badeau] Brevet Brigadier General Adam Badeau
(1831–95), Grant's military secretary, was writing *Military History of Ulysses S.
Grant* (3 vols., 1868–1881).

166.15   tactics . . . Scott's] *Infantry Tactics,* revised and expanded by
Winfield Scott (3 vols., 1835).

169.22–23   1872 . . . candidate] Benjamin Gratz Brown (1826–75) was
nominated by the Liberal Republicans to run with Horace Greeley against

Grant. The Liberal ticket was endorsed by the Democrats, but was decisively defeated in the election.

189.26–27   General . . . Mill Springs]   The battle was fought on January 19, 1862.

236.4   Since . . . chapter]   Chapters XXIV and XXV of the *Personal Memoirs of U. S. Grant* are a revised version of the article "The Battle of Shiloh," written by Grant in the summer of 1884, which appeared in the February 1885 *Century Magazine*.

238.23–24   I stated . . . unwillingness]   In his *Century* article Grant wrote: "The enemy had hardly started in retreat from his last position, when, looking back toward the river, I saw a division of troops coming up in beautiful order, as if going on parade or review. The commander was at the head of the column, and the staff seemed to be disposed about as they would have been had they been going on parade. When the head of the column came near where I was standing, it was halted, and the commanding officer, General A. McD. McCook, rode up to where I was and appealed to me not to send his division any farther, saying that they were worn out with marching and fighting. This division had marched on the 6th from a point ten or twelve miles east of Savanna, over bad roads. The men had also lost rest during the night while crossing the Tennessee, and had been engaged in the battle of the 7th. It was not, however, the rank and file or the junior officers who asked to be excused, but the division commander." This passage preceded the sentence beginning on p. 238.8 in this volume ("I rode forward several miles . . .").

238.34–36   conspicuous . . . report]   In his report of April 10, 1862, later printed in the *Memoirs of General William T. Sherman* (1875), Sherman praised McCook's division for driving the Confederates back along the Corinth road and singled out one of its brigades for capturing a heavily defended wood.

238.37–38   family . . . volunteers]   McCook's father, uncle, eight of his brothers, and four of his cousins served in the Union army, while another brother recruited and trained Ohio volunteers as a civilian and another cousin served as a Union naval officer. His father and three of his brothers were killed during the war.

240.40–241.2   correspondent . . . *World*]   Grant was reported in the New York *Herald* of August 3, 1865, as saying that Buell "was thoroughly versed in the theory of war, but knew nothing about handling men in an emergency," that his "heart was never in the war from the first," and that Buell's troops might have reached Pittsburg Landing several days earlier than they did. Buell wrote Grant on August 5 and December 27, asking for an explanation. Grant replied on December 29, 1865, that while he had no recollection of the conversation reported in the *Herald*, he was certain that he had been misquoted. Buell subsequently wrote a letter to Grant defending his movements before the battle of Shiloh, which appeared in the New York *World* on April 6, 1866.

241.27   I . . . wrote] In his *Century* article Grant wrote: "Nothing occurred in his brief command of an army to prove or disprove the high estimate that had been placed upon his military ability." This sentence was
followed by the paragraph beginning at p. 242.35 in this volume.

242.8   son and biographer] William Preston Johnston (1831–99) wrote
The Life of Albert Sidney Johnston (1880) and drew upon it in preparing "Albert
Sidney Johnston and the Shiloh Campaign," which appeared in the February
1885 *Century* immediately following Grant's article on Shiloh.

247.28   full . . . report] A fragment of the draft of a report appears on
pp. 1011–13 in this volume.

284.29   "Freedman's Bureau"] The Bureau of Refugees, Freedmen, and
Abandoned Lands was established in the War Department by act of Congress
on March 3, 1865. It provided provisions, clothing, and fuel to destitute
former slaves and white refugees, leased abandoned and confiscated land (almost all of which was eventually restored to its former owners), founded
schools and hospitals, regulated labor contracts, and attempted to mediate
cases of racial conflict. President Andrew Johnson vetoed a bill extending its
lifetime and expanding its powers on February 19, 1866, but another bill re-
newing the Bureau was passed over his veto on July 16, 1866. The Bureau
ceased operations on July 1, 1869, except for its educational activities, which
continued until June 30, 1872.

285.4   Chaplain Eaton] John Eaton, Jr. (1829–1906) became an army
chaplain in 1861. In May 1865 he was endorsed by Grant for commissioner of
the Freedman's Bureau, but the post was given to Major General Oliver O.
Howard, and Eaton was made assistant commissioner in charge of Washington, D.C., Maryland, and parts of Virginia. Grant appointed him commissioner of education in 1870, and he served until 1886.

286.26–27   C. C. Washburn] Cadwallader C. Washburn (1818–82), a
brother of Congressman Elihu B. Washburne.

306.32–33   Jacob Thompson] See note 150.33.

313.34–35   General . . . No. 69] An order providing for the organization
of detachments of hospital invalids for limited duties.

360.16–17   chief . . . Army] Robert Macfeely became commissary general in 1875.

360.19   sap-roller] A large wickerwork cylinder filled with sticks that was
rolled in front of trenches (saps) being dug toward enemy fortifications to
protect the soldiers digging them from hostile fire.

363.23   coehorns]   Small portable mortars, named after their Dutch inventor Baron Menno van Coehoorn (1641–1704).

370.20   redan]   A V-shaped earthwork fortification, with its point projecting toward the enemy.

384.25–27   Halleck . . . prisoners.]   A dispute over the validity of the paroles given to the Vicksburg garrison contributed to the eventual suspension of prisoner exchanges under the cartel. See Grant's letter to Benjamin F. Butler of April 17, 1864, pp. 1048–49 in this volume.

403.22   Governor Brough]   John Brough (1811–65), a War Democrat nominated by the Republicans, was elected governor of Ohio on October 13, 1863, and was inaugurated on January 11, 1864.

409.35–36   pacing . . . dressing-gown]   Grant wrote in his manuscript that Stanton had been "pacing the room rapidly in about the garb Mr. Davis was supposed to be wearing subsequently, when he was captured in a dressing gown," but then changed the passage in proof. Several Union officers who had helped capture Jefferson Davis near Irwinville, Georgia, on May 10, 1865, had described him as attempting to escape with a shawl over his head and a woman's waterproof cloak or robe, gathered at the waist, over his clothes.

458.33   Jo Davies County]   Galena is the seat of Jo Daviess County.

461.32–33   remonstrated . . . writing]   Grant wrote Stanton on January 29, 1866, that in his opinion "the Gen. in Chief stands between the President and the Army in all official matters and the Secretary of War is between the Army, (through the General in Chief,) and the President." He requested that Stanton adhere to this chain of command and not issue orders directly to the army through the adjutant general.

463.22   General (Bishop) Polk]   Leonidas Polk (1806–64) graduated from the Military Academy in 1827 before resigning from the army to become an Episcopal minister. He became Bishop of Louisiana in 1841 and joined the Confederate army in 1861. Polk was killed by a Union shell at Pine Mountain, Georgia, on June 14, 1864.

469.1   restoring . . . lieutenant-general]   George Washington was the only American previously to have held the permanent rank of lieutenant-general in the army; Winfield Scott had held it by brevet after 1855.

471.31–32   McClellan . . . Crittenden]   Major General George B. McClellan (1826–85) had been relieved by Lincoln as commander of the Army of the Potomac on November 5, 1862. He received no further command during the war and was the Democratic candidate for president in 1864. Major General Ambrose E. Burnside (1824–81), McClellan's immediate successor as commander of the Army of the Potomac, was relieved by Lincoln on January 25, 1863. After commanding the Department of the Ohio for most of 1863,

Burnside returned to the East in April 1864 as commander of the 9th Corps. Major General John C. Frémont (1813–80) was relieved of his command in northwestern Virginia on June 28, 1862, when he refused to serve under Major General John Pope, and held no further command during the war; in 1864 he was briefly the presidential nominee of a splinter group of Republican radicals. Major General Don C. Buell (1818–98), relieved as commander of the Army of the Ohio on October 24, 1862, held no further command and resigned his commission on June 1, 1864 (see pp. 472.32–473.6 in this volume). Major General Alexander M. McCook (1831–1903), Major General James S. Negley (1826–1901), and Major General Thomas L. Crittenden (1815–93) all lost control of their commands in the rout of the Union right wing during the second day of the battle of Chickamauga, September 20, 1863. They were exonerated by a court of inquiry, but only Crittenden, who commanded a division in the Army of the Potomac in 1864, subsequently held a field command during the war.

480.36–37   In . . . skins.]   See p. 486.13–25 and note 486.24–25 in this volume.

486.24–25   "Oh . . . does."]   Cf. the version of this remark retold by Lincoln to his personal secretary John Hay and recorded by Hay in his diary on April 30, 1864: "Those not skinning, can hold a leg."

494.4–5   making . . . expression]   See p. 792.7–9 in this volume.

507.14   McCook]   Brigadier General Edward M. McCook (1833–1909), a cousin of Major General Alexander M. McCook.

519.23   Stonewall Brig.]   The brigade, recruited from the Shenandoah Valley of Virginia in April 1861, was trained by Thomas J. Jackson and commanded by him at the first battle of Bull Run, July 21, 1861, where both the unit and its commander gained the nickname "Stonewall"; it became the brigade's official designation after Jackson's death in May 1863. After being reduced to regimental strength by the May 12, 1864, fighting at Spotsylvania, 210 survivors of the unit surrendered at Appomattox. Of the seven men who commanded it at brigade strength (including Jackson), five were killed during the war.

531.5–6   Jenkins . . . engagement.]   In the confusion and poor visibility of the Wilderness battle, Jenkins and Longstreet were accidentally shot by Confederate troops, only a few miles from where Lieutenant General Thomas J. Jackson was mortally wounded by his own men on the night of May 2, 1863, during the battle of Chancellorsville.

532.26   refused his right]   Moved it back, away from the enemy line.

612.17   Meade interfered]   In his testimony about the Petersburg mine before the Congressional Joint Committee on the Conduct of the War on December 20, 1864, Grant said: "General Burnside wanted to put his colored division in front, and I believe if he had done so it would have been a success.

Still I agreed with General Meade in his objection to that plan. General Meade said that if we put the colored troops in front (we had only that one division) and it should prove a failure, it would then be said, and very properly, that we were shoving those people ahead to get killed because we did not care anything about them. But that could not be said if we put white troops in front. That is the only point he changed, to my knowledge, after he had given his orders to General Burnside. It was then that General Burnside left his three division commanders to toss coppers or draw straws which should and which should not go in front."

615.3   too young]   Sheridan was 33 years old.

621.29   Burlington, New Jersey]   The Grants had rented a house in Burlington.

631.6−9   series . . . reports]   "Campaigns of the Civil War," published by Charles Scribner's Sons, volume 12 of which is Andrew A. Humphreys' *The Virginia Campaign of '64 and '65; The Army of the Potomac and the Army of the James* (1883); Badeau's *Military History of Ulysses S. Grant* (1868−81); the Union and Confederate reports were later printed in *The War of the Rebellion: A Compilation of the Official Records of the Union and Confederate Armies* (70 vols., 1880−1901).

635.31   Price's movements]   See pp. 813.25−814.5 in this volume.

636.13   treatment of citizens]   Sherman had ordered the expulsion of all civilians from Atlanta so that it could be held solely as a military depot.

653.2   chief of staff]   John A. Rawlins.

685.13−15   Stephens . . . Hunter]   Alexander H. Stephens (1812−83) of Georgia served in the House of Representatives as a Whig, 1843−52, and then as a Democrat, 1852−59. He was vice-president of the Confederate States of America from 1861 to 1865. John A. Campbell (1811−89) of Alabama was an associate justice of the U.S. Supreme Court, 1853−61, and a Confederate assistant secretary of war, 1862−65. Robert M. T. Hunter (1809−87) of Virginia served in the House of Representatives from 1837 to 1843, first as a Whig and then as Democrat, and was its Speaker from 1839 to 1841. He returned to the House as a Democrat, 1845−47, before serving in the Senate from 1847 to 1861. Hunter was Confederate secretary of state, 1861−62, and a Confederate senator, 1862−65.

702.11   authorization . . . Warren.]   Gouverneur K. Warren (1830−82) held other commands before resigning his commission in the volunteers on May 27, 1865. He then served in the regular army as a major, and later lieutenant colonel, of engineers, and repeatedly asked for a court of inquiry into his relief at the battle of Five Forks. His request was finally granted on December 9, 1879, by President Rutherford B. Hayes. The court criticized Warren's performance in getting his troops into position on March 31, 1865, but exonerated him of misconduct in the battle on April 1. On November 21, 1881,

President Chester A. Arthur ordered the findings of the court published, but they were not made public until after Warren's death.

732.29–30   story . . . tree.]   According to a widespread report, Lee surrendered to Grant under an apple tree.

742.1   /2/ . . . Va.]   In the Charles L. Webster edition, the following publisher's note appeared at the bottom of the page facing the facsimile, which was printed on a fold-out page:

"The fac-simile of the terms of Lee's surrender inserted at this place, was copied from the original document furnished the publishers through the courtesy of General Ely S. Parker, Military Secretary on General Grant's staff at the time of the surrender.

"Three pages of paper were prepared in General Grant's manifold order book on which he wrote the terms, and the interlineations and erasures were added by General Parker at the suggestion of General Grant. After such alteration it was handed to General Lee, who put on his glasses, read it, and handed it back to General Grant. The original was then transcribed by General Parker upon official headed paper and a copy furnished to General Lee.

"The fac-simile herewith shows the color of the paper of the original document and all interlineations and erasures.

"There is a popular error to the effect that Generals Grant and Lee each signed the articles of surrender. The document in the form of a letter was signed only by General Grant, in the parlor of McLean's house while General Lee was sitting in the room, and General Lee immediately wrote a letter accepting the terms and handed it to General Grant. This letter is copied on page 494."

Lee's letter accepting the terms appears on p. 740.14–22 in this volume. The facsimile of the surrender terms in this volume does not reproduce the color of the original.

749.2   leading . . . Virginia]   Gustavus Myers, a member of the Confederate legislature of Virginia, accompanied by John A. Campbell, conferred with Lincoln.

754.29–30   terms . . . *conditionally*]   On April 18, 1865, Sherman and Johnston signed a "Memorandum, or Basis of Agreement" near Durham's Station, North Carolina, which set the following terms:

"1. The contending armies now in the field to maintain the *statu quo* until notice is given by the commanding general of any one to its opponent, and reasonable time—say, forty-eight hours—allowed.

"2. The Confederate armies now in existence to be disbanded and conducted to their several State capitals, there to deposit their arms and public property in the State Arsenal; and each officer and man to execute and file an agreement to cease from acts of war, and to abide the action of the State and Federal authority. The number of arms and munitions of war to be reported to the Chief of Ordnance at Washington City, subject to the future action of the Congress of the United States, and, in the mean time, to be used solely to maintain peace and order within the borders of the States respectively.

"3. The recognition, by the Executive of the United States, of the several State governments, on their officers and Legislatures taking the oaths prescribed by the Constitution of the United States, and, where conflicting State governments have resulted from the war, the legitimacy of all shall be submitted to the Supreme Court of the United States.

"4. The reëstablishment of all the Federal Courts in the several States, with powers as defined by the Constitution of the United States and of the States respectively.

"5. The people and inhabitants of all the States to be guaranteed, so far as the Executive can, their political rights and franchises, as well as their rights of person and property, as defined by the Constitution of the United States and of the States respectively.

"6. The Executive authority of the Government of the United States not to disturb any of the people by reason of the late war, so long as they live in peace and quiet, abstain from acts of armed hostility, and obey the laws in existence at the place of their residence.

"7. In general terms—the war to cease; a general amnesty, so far as the Executive of the United States can command, on condition of the disbandment of the Confederate armies, the distribution of arms, and the resumption of peaceful pursuits by the officers and men hitherto composing said armies.

"Not being fully empowered by our respective principals to fulfill these terms, we individually and officially pledge ourselves to promptly obtain the necessary authority, and to carry out the above programme."

762.1–2   garb . . . wearing]   See note 409.35–36.

768.33   "sweet . . . ground"]   Cf. the song "Marching through Georgia" (1865), words by Henry C. Work: "How the sweet potatoes even started from the ground."

772.23–26   Mackenzie . . . corps]   Ranald Slidell Mackenzie (1840–89), who graduated first in his class at the Military Academy in 1862, commanded the cavalry division of the Army of the James during the Appomattox campaign. After the Civil War he led the 4th Cavalry in campaigns against the Comanche, Kickapoo, and Cheyenne Indians. Wounded several times in action, Mackenzie was made a brigadier general in the regular army in 1882, but retired on disability in 1884 after having been judged insane. He was the son of Commander Alexander Slidell Mackenzie (1803–48), who had provoked a fierce controversy by hanging three suspected mutineers on board the brig *Somers* in 1842, and the nephew of John Slidell (1793–1871), the Confederate commissioner in France, 1862–65.

773.25   Fugitive . . . Law.]   Congress passed a new fugitive slave law in 1850.

774.40   effective blockade]   Under the Declaration of Paris, signed by
France and Great Britain in 1856, a blockade had to be "maintained by a force
sufficient really to prevent access to the coast of the enemy" in order to be
considered legitimate by neutral powers; otherwise, the blockading power
had no right to stop and search neutral shipping on the high seas, and attempts to do so became potential grounds for war.

775.2   Austrian prince]   After French troops captured Mexico City in June
1863, Napoleon III arranged for the Hapsburg archduke Maximilian
(1832–67) to be offered the imperial throne of Mexico in July 1863. Maximilian was crowned in 1864 and ruled until 1867, when he was overthrown and
executed by Mexicans led by Benito Juárez.

777.25   leaders . . . party]   Prime Minister Viscount Palmerston, Foreign
Secretary Lord John Russell, and Chancellor of the Exchequer William E.
Gladstone, leaders of the Liberal government in office from 1859 to 1865, were
criticized in the North for taking actions and making statements favorable to
the Confederate cause. Other prominent Liberals, including John Bright and
Richard Cobden, were supporters of the Union.

778.1–2   annexation . . . President]   On January 10, 1870, Grant submitted a treaty calling for the annexation of the Dominican Republic for ratification by the Senate. It was defeated by a 28–28 vote on June 30, 1870. The
opposition was led by Republicans Charles Sumner of Massachusetts, chairman of the Senate Foreign Relations Committee, and Carl Schurz of
Missouri.

779.25–26   "from . . . sea"]   William Cowper (1731–1800), "Verses Supposed to be Written by Alexander Selkirk" (1782).

779.40   "Let . . . peace."]   The conclusion of Grant's letter of May 29,
1868, accepting the Republican nomination for the presidency, which became
the party's main slogan during the ensuing campaign.

783.1   accompanying map]   This map was not printed in the Charles L.
Webster edition of the *Personal Memoirs of U. S. Grant*.

801.28   hundred . . . men]   Men serving for 100 days were generally used
to guard supply depots, rail lines, and prisoner-of-war camps.

SELECTED LETTERS 1839–1865

877.1   *R. McKinstry Griffith*]   Son of James Griffith and Mary Simpson
Griffith, Grant's maternal aunt.

877.22   Kosisuseko]   Tadeusz Andrzej Bonawentura Kościuszko (1746–
1817), a Polish officer, served as colonel of engineers with the Conti-

nental Army, 1776–83, and directed the fortification of West Point from 1778 to 1780. In 1794 he led an unsuccessful revolt against Russian rule in Poland.

880.10   Bump of Acquisitiveness]   A reference to phrenology, in which the conformation of the skull reveals character traits and mental faculties, different "bumps" signifying specific attributes.

881.2   Mr. Hazlitt]   Robert Hazlitt was an Academy classmate of Grant's. He was killed in the battle of Monterrey on September 21, 1846. See p. 919.20–23 in this volume.

881.20   Ellen]   Julia Dent's sister, Ellen (Nellie) Wrenshall Dent (1824–1904).

881.30   Wrenshall Dent's family]   George Wrenshall Dent (1819–99), Julia's brother, had married Mary Isabella Shurlds in 1841.

882.10   [. . . . .]]   Bracketed ellipses indicate lost material in the original manuscripts that could not be reconstructed by the editors of *The Papers of Ulysses S. Grant*. The number of dots indicates the approximate number of missing letters.

882.16   *Mrs. George B. Bailey*]   A Georgetown neighbor and the mother of Bartlett Bailey, whose departure from the Military Academy created the vacancy Grant filled.

884.24   Mr. Higgins]   Second Lieutenant Thaddeus Higgins, an 1840 Military Academy graduate from Pennsylvania.

885.6–7   Fred's Regiment]   Brevet Second Lieutenant Frederick T. Dent (1820–92), Julia's brother and Grant's roommate during his last year at the Military Academy, was stationed with the 6th Infantry at Fort Towson in Indian Territory (later Oklahoma).

885.36   Miss Fanny Morrison]   Fanny Morrison, daughter of Captain Pitcairn Morrison of the 4th Infantry, married Lieutenant Higgins in 1845.

887.6   John Dent]   Julia Dent's brother.

888.4   Mr. Porters]   Second Lieutenant Theodoric H. Porter of the 4th Infantry. See p. 63.20–21 and note 63.20 in this volume.

889.29   My oldest sister]   Clara Rachel Grant (1828–65).

890.9   Col. Dent]   The title was honorific.

890.23   Mrs. Mary Dent]   See note 881.30.

891.3   Sappington P. O.] Sappington Post Office, the mailing address of White Haven, the Dent family home outside of St. Louis.

891.32   "Jim a long Josy"] "Jim Along Josey" was the title of a minstrel song by Edward Harper, published in 1840.

893.9   occupation . . . England] Treaties signed in 1818 and 1827 established joint Anglo-American occupation of the region west of the Rockies between 42° and 54°40′ latitude. In 1844–45 expansionist Democrats advocated annexation of the Pacific northwest up to the 54°40′ line and expressed the willingness to go to war with Great Britain over the issue. The question was resolved when the administration of President James K. Polk signed a treaty with Great Britain on June 18, 1846, that extended the boundary along the 49th parallel westward from the Rockies to the Strait of Georgia.

893.26   Beaman] Second Lieutenant Jenks Beaman, an 1842 graduate of the Military Academy, was an officer in the 4th Infantry. He died of disease in Mexico in May 1848.

894.10   Emmy] Julia's sister, Emily Marbury Dent (b. 1836).

900.17   promotes me] Grant was promoted from brevet second lieutenant to second lieutenant on September 30, 1845.

900.32   Florida war] Attempts by the United States to remove the Seminole Indians, and the Negroes who found refuge from slavery among them, from Florida Territory led to the outbreak of war in 1835. Fighting continued until 1842, by which time almost all of the surviving Seminoles had been sent to Indian Territory. The conflict, also known as the second Seminole War, cost the lives of approximately 1,500 American soldiers.

902.1   Wandering Jew] *The Wandering Jew* (1844–45) by French novelist Eugène Sue (1804–75).

902.8–10   sentence . . . hearts,] ". . . for two drops of dew blending in the cup of a flower are as hearts that mingle in a pure and virgin love; and two rays of light united in one inextinguishable flame, are as the burning and eternal joys of lovers joined in wedlock."

902.24   *October 1845*] This letter, not dated by Grant, was postmarked in New Orleans on October 13, 1845.

903.33–34   Mr. Benton's influance] Thomas Hart Benton (1782–1858) was a Democratic senator from Missouri, 1821–51.

904.27   ***] In this volume, three asterisks indicate places where Julia Dent Grant later crossed out words or passages in the letters. The editors of *The Papers of Ulysses S. Grant* did not print this material at the request of Grant's descendants.

908.37   Col. Majia]   General Francisco Mejía.

910.31–32   Capt. Page . . . alive.]   Captain John Page died of his wounds on July 12, 1846.

911.26   General Lavega]   General R. Díaz de la Vega.

912.28   *John W. Lowe*]   Lowe, an Ohio lawyer and associate of Congressman Thomas L. Hamer, was a longtime friend of Grant and his father.

915.26   Paredes]   General Mariano Paredes y Arrillaga (1797–1849), who opposed any compromise with the United States over territorial issues, overthrew President José Joaquín Herrera in December 1845 and became acting president on January 4, 1846. He stepped down on July 28, 1846, to lead troops in the field, but quickly lost all power. Santa Anna then returned from exile and assumed command of the Mexican army in September 1846.

916.21   new . . . Riflemen]   Congress added a regiment of Mounted Riflemen to the regular army on May 19, 1846.

919.22–23   Graham . . . wounded.]   First Lieutenant Richard H. Graham and Major William W. Lear died of their wounds in October 1846.

924.2   Bonapartes . . . Alps]   Napoleon Bonaparte led his reserve army from Switzerland through the Great St. Bernard Pass into Italy between May 14 and 25, 1800, and then moved on the rear of the Austrian army in Piedmont, defeating it at Marengo on June 14, 1800.

925.33   wounded . . . Fred's]   Frederick T. Dent was wounded in the thigh during the battle of Molino del Rey on September 8, 1847.

931.29   little Fred]   Grant's first child, Frederick Dent Grant, born May 30, 1850.

932.35   Virginia]   Grant's sister Virginia (Gennie, Jennie) Paine Grant (b. 1832).

933.33   date . . . sick]   Julia was expecting their second child. A son, Ulysses S. Grant, Jr., was born on July 22, 1852.

936.20   where John is]   Grant's brother-in-law John Dent (1816–89) operated a ferry, tavern, and stables at Knight's Ferry, California.

936.35   Elijah Camp]   Camp had been a special contractor at Sackets Harbor. He left Oregon Territory in 1853 owing Grant $800 from a joint business venture.

937.6   Maggy]   Margaret Getz and her husband, an enlisted soldier, had worked for the Grants at Sackets Harbor and now were with him in Oregon.

937.34 Fred. Steel] Frederick Steele (1819–68) became a Union major general of volunteers during the Civil War.

938.5 Mrs. Stevens] The wife of Lieutenant Thomas H. Stevens, a naval officer Grant had known at Sackets Harbor.

943.13 Washington Territory] On March 2, 1853, Congress created a new territory out of the northern portion of Oregon Territory.

944.21 Mr. Hunt . . . Russell] Unknown to Grant, first lieutenants Lewis C. Hunt and Edmund Russell had been killed on March 24, 1853, in a fight with Indians at Red Bluff, California.

946.22 Laura] Laura Wallen, the wife of First Lieutenant Henry Davies Wallen.

947.27–28 enclose . . . "B".] These attachments to Grant's report are not known to be extant.

948.40–949.1 Clickitat . . . Dalles] The Klikitat, a tribe in the Sahaptin linguistic group, lived north of the Columbia. In an adjacent region were the Cowlitz, a Salish tribe. The Dalles, a branch of the Wascos, a tribe in the Chinook linguistic group, lived upriver on the Columbia in The Dalles region.

949.20–21 long . . . application] Grant had made his request on September 8, 1853, in letters to the quartermaster general and the commissary general.

950.4–5 Col. B . . . promotion] Brevet Lieutenant Colonel Robert C. Buchanan (1811–78) held the permanent rank of captain until his promotion to major on February 3, 1855. He commanded a brigade in the Army of the Potomac, 1862–63.

952.31–32 Capt. Calender . . . money?] Grant had sold his stock in the Detroit & Saline and the Plymouth railroads to Franklin D. Callender, who was paying for it with interest.

955.14 *Frederick Dent*] Frederick F. Dent (1786–1873), Grant's father-in-law.

956.28 novel name] Sidney Johnston Dent was born in Walla Walla, Washington Territory, on February 18, 1861.

957.25–26 leave . . . safe] Jesse Root Grant (1794–1873) continued to live in Covington, Kentucky, across the Ohio River from Cincinnati, until his death.

957.28 Orvil] Grant's brother, Orvil Lynch Grant (1835–81).

958.16   The Governer]   Richard Yates (1818–73) was Republican governor of Illinois from 1861 to 1865.

958.32   Capt. Pope]   John Pope (1822–92) was appointed brigadier general of volunteers on May 17, 1861, and made a major general in 1862.

958.34   K McKenzie]   Kenneth MacKenzie was a St. Louis merchant who had endorsed Grant in 1859 for the position of county engineer.

960.5   Aunt . . . Clara!]   Rachel B. Grant Tompkins, a sister of Grant's father, lived in Charleston, Virginia (now West Virginia). She had written to Grant's sister Clara, "If you are with the accursed Lincolnites, the ties of consanguinity shall be forever severed." In a subsequent letter of June 5, 1861, she criticized Grant for "drawing his sword against those connected by the ties of blood."

960.17–18   Simpson]   See p. 144.18–28 in this volume.

961.10   bump of order]   See note 880.10.

961.20–21   Charless Blow & Co]   A wholesale drug firm in St. Louis.

964.3   Mary Duncan]   The stepdaughter of a Galena grain merchant and a neighbor of the Grant family.

964.24   Egypt]   A colloquial name for the southern, or southernmost, counties of Illinois.

965.2   Jo Reynolds]   Joseph Jones Reynolds (1822–99), a friend and classmate of Grant's at the Military Academy, resigned from the army in 1857 to become professor of mechanics and engineering at Washington University in St. Louis and in 1859 endorsed Grant's unsuccessful candidacy for the post of St. Louis County engineer. After serving as a major general of volunteers in the Civil War, Reynolds rejoined the regular army as a colonel. He was court-martialed and convicted in January 1877 on charges stemming from the failure of his March 17, 1876, attack on an Indian village along the Powder River in Montana, and sentenced to one year's suspension of rank and pay. President Grant remitted the sentence, however, and Reynolds retired on disability in July 1877.

965.3   Emma . . . Jim]   Julia's sister Emily had married James F. Casey February 14, 1861. In 1869 Grant appointed Casey collector of customs at New Orleans, where he took part in the bitter feuding within the Louisiana Republican party and was accused of running a corrupt ring in the custom-house.

965.15   Camp Yates]   The camp was located in a fairgrounds outside of Springfield, Illinois.

966.34   Dr. Sharp]   Dr. Alexander Sharp, husband of Julia's sister Ellen and a resident of Lincoln County, Missouri. He remained loyal to the Union.

966.37   McClellands . . . Crimea.]   "Report of the Secretary of War, communicating the Report of Captain George B. McClellan (First Regiment United States Cavalry.) one of the Officers sent to the Seat of War in Europe in 1855 and 1856," published in *Senate Executive Documents* (1857).

968.14   Susy Felts] Susan M. Felt was the eight-year-old daughter of a Galena grocer.

968.20   East Quincy, Mo.] West Quincy, Missouri. This letter is taken from *Letters of Ulysses S. Grant to his Father and his Youngest Sister, 1857–78* (1912), edited by J. G. Cramer; the error may have occurred in transcription.

969.9   notorious Jim Green] James S. Green (1817–70) was a Democratic congressman from Missouri, 1847–51, and then served in the U.S. Senate, 1857–61, where he defended the Buchanan administration's policy in Kansas.

972.26   Mr. Trumbull's] Lyman Trumbull (1817–96) was a Republican senator from Illinois, 1855–73.

973.28   Manassas] The first battle of Manassas (or Bull Run) was fought in northern Virginia on July 21, 1861.

974.26   Mr. Rollins] John A. Rawlins. See note 153.6.

974.30   Ford] Charles W. Ford, a lawyer, first met Grant at Sackets Harbor. Their friendship continued after Ford moved to St. Louis, and Ford often assisted Grant in business and financial transactions.

975.10   Harry Boggs] Harry Boggs was Julia's cousin. Grant had worked for several months in 1858–59 as a bill collector in Boggs's real estate firm.

975.17–18   set . . . profanity.] Cf. Laurence Sterne (1713–68), *Tristram Shandy*, Book III (1761–62), Chapter 11: " 'Our armies swore terribly in Flanders,' cried my uncle Toby—'But nothing to this.' "

975.22   Covington] See note 957.25–26.

979.3   Report to me] Paine reported on January 12, 1862, that his patrols would probably bring in 100 citizens by nightfall. On January 19, 1862, Grant ordered the release of all civilian prisoners at Bird's Point who had not been charged with a specific offense.

985.12   Capt. Kountz] Captain William J. Kountz, the owner of a Pennsylvania steamboat fleet, had been reprimanded by Grant on December 21, 1861, for inspecting the river transportation at Cairo, Illinois, without first reporting to Grant and presenting his authorizing papers. Kountz was subsequently assigned by Major Robert Allen, quartermaster of the Department of the Missouri, to serve as master of river transportation at Cairo, where he quarreled with the civilian boatmen serving with the Union flotilla and caused several army officers to petition for his replacement. On January 14, 1862, Grant ordered his arrest for disobeying orders and applied to have him removed from his military district. Kountz then prepared charges against Grant, which Grant saw on January 30 before forwarding them to higher headquarters, accusing him of having been "beastly drunk" while meeting with Confederate officers under flag of truce and of having set an "evil example" to his command by repeated public drunkenness. These charges reached the War Department in Washington, D.C., but were never acted upon, and Kountz resigned his commission on March 13, 1862.

989.23   your brother] Colonel Cadwallader C. Washburn (1818–82), commander of the 2nd Wisconsin Cavalry. Washburn later became a major general of volunteers.

993.8   Thomas] Brigadier General Lorenzo Thomas (1804–75).

996.12   Charles Page] Charles Page was the son of Samuel K. Page, a prosperous Louisville builder, and Ellen Wrenshall Page, Julia's maternal aunt.

997.12   Gen. Wallace] Major General Lewis Wallace (1827–1905).

1004.27   the Correspondence] On April 8, 1862, Confederate General Pierre G. T. Beauregard wrote Grant, requesting permission to send a burial party to the Shiloh battlefield. Grant replied on April 9 that the warm weather had already caused him to order the immediate burial of the dead of both armies.

1004.32   *To Jesse Root Grant*] This letter appeared in the *Cincinnati Commercial* on May 2, 1862. Grant wrote to Julia on May 11, 1862, that he had seen "with pain" a letter to his father in the press and that its publication "should never have occured."

1010.16   news . . . Richmond] Confederate General Robert E. Lee had attacked the Army of the Potomac outside of Richmond in the Seven Days' Battles, June 25–July 1, 1862, causing Major General George B. McClellan to retreat to Harrison's Landing on the north bank of the James River.

1011.35   *Fragment on Shiloh*] This is printed from an undated manuscript draft, probably written between July 17, 1862, when William Nelson was confirmed as a major general of volunteers, and September 29, 1862, when Nelson was shot to death in Louisville, Kentucky, by Brigadier General Jefferson C. Davis during a quarrel.

1014.22   Mr. Nixon] John S. Nixon was a Covington, Kentucky, lawyer. With the help of Grant's father, he had written two letters praising Grant that were published in the *Cincinnati Gazette* in May 1862.

1015.1   *Stephen A. Hurlbut*] Hurlbut commanded the military district around Jackson, Tennessee. On November 10, 1862, Grant ordered that no Jews be allowed to travel south by railroad from any point within his department, and on December 17, 1862, authorized the issue of General Order No. 11, which expelled "Jews, as a class" from the Department of the Tennessee for "violating every regulation of trade established by the Treasury Department." President Lincoln, through Halleck, revoked General Order No. 11 on

January 4, 1863. For Grant's objections to the cotton trade, see pp. 266.30–267.8 in this volume.

1016.15–16   Col. Hedgepath]   Confederate Lieutenant Colonel Isaac N. Hedgpeth of the 6th Missouri Infantry was wounded and captured at Corinth, Mississippi, on October 3, 1862. Pemberton wrote Grant on December 10 that he had been "credibly informed" that Hedgpeth had been subjected to "unusually harsh treatment" and had had his parole, watch, and money taken from him.

1020.21   *Thomas W. Knox*]   Knox had accompanied Sherman's December 1862 movement against Vicksburg in violation of orders intended to exclude newspaper correspondents from the expedition. His dispatch in the New York *Herald* of January 18, 1863, criticized Sherman both for his failed attack against the bluffs above Chickasaw Bayou and for attempting to ban reporters from his operations. Sherman had Knox court-martialed for publishing military news without permission, making false accusations against army officers, and violating the exclusion order. On February 18, 1863, Knox was convicted of the third charge and expelled from the army's lines.

1020.27   letter . . . President]   In his letter of March 20, 1863, Lincoln wrote that he was conditionally revoking Knox's expulsion because Brigadier General John M. Thayer, president of the court-martial, Major General John McClernand, and "many other respectable persons" were of the opinion that Knox's offense was "technical, rather than wilfully wrong."

1021.9–10   Sherman . . . consent]   Sherman wrote Knox on April 7, 1863, that he would be allowed to rejoin Sherman's command as a soldier, but never as a correspondent.

1026.17–18   letter . . . Mrs Duncan]   Mary Duncan was the wife of Henry P. Duncan and the daughter-in-law of Dr. Stephen Duncan of Natchez, Mississippi, a wealthy planter and investor and staunch Unionist. She wrote Thomas on June 2, 1863, that despite protection papers issued by Grant and other Union commanders, freedmen now working for wages on her family's plantations had been forcibly removed by Union troops. On July 11 Grant ordered an investigation, which subsequently found that a number of soldiers in the 8th Louisiana Volunteers of African Descent claimed to have been forced into service from the Duncan plantations, but that the officer responsible had been killed in action on May 27. However, the commander of the 8th Louisiana Volunteers denied the charge of impressment and suggested that the claims had been made by soldiers who wanted to return to their families. Grant is not known to have taken any further action in this matter.

1027.13   Col. Shepard . . . punishment]   Colonel Isaac F. Shepard had ordered a white soldier tied to a tree and whipped by black soldiers under his command. In a letter of October 5, 1863, Thomas told Secretary of War Edwin M. Stanton that white troops had committed "acts of wantoness" against Shepard's soldiers and their families and that the "flagrant case under consideration" had been "one calling for the severest punishment, even to the loss of life . . ."

1027.26   Commissioners]   Commissioners in charge of plantations abandoned by their owners.

1028.30–31   Your letter . . . Mellen]   Chase asked Grant to confer with treasury agent William P. Mellen about the possibility of allowing civilians to trade in areas under military occupation after posting bonds to ensure their compliance with regulations.

1030.29   letter . . . 13th]   Lincoln had written to Grant from the White House on July 13, 1863:
   "I do not remember that you and I ever met personally. I write this now as a grateful acknowledgment for the almost inestimable service you have done the country. I wish to say a word further. When you first reached the vicinity of Vicksburg, I thought you should do, what you finally did—march the troops across the neck, run the batteries with the transports, and thus go below; and I never had any faith, except a general hope that you knew better than I, that the Yazoo Pass expedition, and the like, could succeed. When you got below, and took Port-Gibson, Grand Gulf, and vicinity, I thought you should go down the river and join Gen. Banks; and when you turned Northward East of the Big Black, I feared it was a mistake. I now wish to make the personal acknowledgment that you were right, and I was wrong."

1031.1–2   importance . . . time]   See p. 388.11–28 in this volume and note 775.2.

1031.6–8   arming . . . Confederacy]   Cf. Lincoln's letter to a public meeting held in Springfield, Illinois, on September 3, 1863: "I know as fully as one can know the opinions of others, that some of the commanders of our armies in the field who have given us our most important successes, believe the emancipation policy, and the use of colored troops, constitute the heaviest blow yet dealt to the rebellion; . . ." This passage was part of a paragraph Lincoln added by telegram on August 31 to the main text of the letter, which he had sent to his friend James C. Conkling on August 26.

1032.6   *John G. Thompson*]   Thompson, a Columbus, Ohio, merchant, was chairman of the Ohio Democratic State Central Committee.

1032.24–26   vote . . . dissentions]   The Democratic nominee for governor of Ohio was Clement L. Vallandigham (1820–71), who had been exiled from the North by the administration in May 1863 for denouncing the prosecution of the war.

1033.7–9   Wilson . . . says]   Henry Wilson (1812–75), a Republican senator from Massachusetts from 1855 to 1873, was chairman of the Senate Military Affairs Committee. Wilson had written Washburne on July 25, 1863, praising Grant for favoring the overthrow of slavery and hoping that he would remain with the Army of the Tennessee and not accept a reported offer of the command of the Army of the Potomac, where, Wilson warned, Grant would be "ruined" by envious men "in and out of that army."

1036.18   my injury]   See p. 390.13–26 in this volume.

1038.13   *J. Russell Jones*]   Jones was a friend of Grant's from Galena, now living in Chicago, who advised Grant on investments.

1039.6   *Barnabas Burns*]   Burns was chairman of the State Central Committee of the Ohio "War Democracy," organized in opposition to the supporters of Clement L. Vallandigham (see note 1032.24–26). He had written Grant on December 7, 1863, asking permission to place Grant's name in nomination for the presidency at a state convention to be held in Columbus on January 8, 1864.

1044.25   you . . . judge]   On February 17, 1864, Halleck wrote Grant that an attack into North Carolina with 60,000 men would seriously weaken the Army of the Potomac and leave Maryland and Pennsylvania open to Confederate invasion. Halleck expressed his conviction that Lee's army, not Richmond, should be the objective of the next campaign and suggested that supply considerations favored making the advance over land through northern Virginia.

1045.1   *Rufus Ingalls*]   Ingalls (1820–93) was a friend and classmate of Grant's at the Military Academy and served with him at Fort Vancouver. He was chief quartermaster of the Army of the Potomac, 1862–64, and of the armies of the Potomac and the James, 1864–65.

1046.7   *To . . . Sherman*]   Sherman replied to Grant on March 10, 1864:
    "Dear General: I have your more than kind and characteristic letter of the 4th—I will send a copy to General McPherson at once. You do yourself injustice and us too much honor in assigning to us so large a share of the merits which have led to your high advancement. I know you approve the friendship I have ever professed to you, and permit me to continue as heretofore to manifest it on all proper occasions. You are now Washington's legitimate successor and occupy a position of almost dangerous elevation, but if you can continue as heretofore to be yourself, simple, honest, and unpretending, you will enjoy through life the respect and love of friends, and the homage of millions of human beings that will award to you a large share in securing to them and their descendants a Government of Law and Stability. I repeat you do General McPherson and myself too much honor. At Belmont you manifested your traits, neither of us being near—at Donelson also you illustrated your whole character. I was not near, and Gen'l McPherson in too subordinate a capacity to influence you. Until you had won Donelson, I confess I was almost cowed by the terrible array of anarchial elements that presented themselves at every point, but that victory admitted the ray of light which I have followed ever since   I believe you are as brave, patriotic, and just, as the great prototype Washington—as unselfish, kindhearted and honest, as a man should be, but the chief characteristic in your nature is the

simple faith in success you have always manifested, which I can liken to nothing else than the faith a Christian has in a Savior. This faith gave you victory at Shiloh and Vicksburg. Also when you have completed your best preparations you go into Battle without hesitation, as at Chattanooga—no doubts—no reserve, and I tell you that it was this that made us act with confidence. I knew wherever I was that you thought of me, and if I got in a tight place you would come if alive My only points of doubt were in your knowledge of Grand Strategy and of Books of Science and History. But I confess your common sense seems to have supplied all these. Now as to the future. Dont stay in Washington. Halleck is better qualified than you are to stand the buffets of Intrigue and Policy. Come out West, take to yourself the whole Mississippi Valley. Let us make it dead sure, and I tell you the Atlantic slope and Pacific shores will follow its destiny as sure as the limbs of a tree live or die with the main trunk. We have done much, but still much remains to be done. Time and times influences are all with us. We could almost afford to sit still and let these influences work. Even in the Seceded States your word now would go further than a Presidents Proclamation or an Act of Congress. For Gods sake and for your Countrys sake come out of Washington. I foretold to Gen'l Halleck before he left Corinth the inevitable result to him, and I now exhort you to come out West. Here lies the seat of the coming Empire, and from the West when our task is done, we will make short work of Charleston, and Richmond, and the impoverished coast of the Atlantic. Your sincere friend,

"W. T. Sherman"

1049.22   Mr. Chadwick]   A proprietor of Willard's Hotel in Washington, D.C.

1049.24   Helen]   Helen Louise Lynde Dent was the wife of Frederick T. Dent.

1051.8   sword . . . voted]   Julia had been attending the New York Sanitary Fair, where donors of a dollar could vote to award an ornate sword to either Grant or Major General George B. McClellan.

1052.18–19   one hundred . . . field]   See note 801.28.

1055.25–26   the White House]   White House, Virginia, a Union supply base on the Pamunkey River.

1057.4   Sunday]   Sunday was June 12, 1864.

1058.24   Gen. Smith]   Major General William F. Smith (1824–1903), commander of the 18th Corps, part of Butler's Army of the James.

1059.11   make a change]   Halleck suggested on July 3 retaining Butler as commander of the Department of Virginia and North Carolina while assigning his troops along the James to Smith. Grant agreed on July 6, but found the wording of the subsequent order issued from Washington unsatisfactory and eventually abandoned his attempt to displace the politically influential

Butler. Instead, Grant relieved Smith, who had become increasingly critical of Major General George G. Meade, from command of the 18th Corps on July 19, 1864, replacing him with Major General Edward O. C. Ord.

1060.26–27   immediate call . . . 300.000]   On July 20, 1864, Lincoln telegraphed in reply: "Yours of yesterday about a call for 300,000 is received. I suppose you had not seen the call for 500,000 made the day before, and which I suppose covers the case. Always glad to have your suggestions."

1061.12   E. M. . . . War]   When drafting this telegram, Grant first addressed it to "A. Lincoln, President," but then changed its recipient to Stanton.

1061.13–15   protest . . . quotas.]   Stanton telegraphed Grant on July 20 that this practice was "neither reccommended nor sanctioned" by the War Department but was favored by the President. Later that day Stanton forwarded to Grant a copy of a telegram sent by Lincoln to Sherman on July 18, 1864:

"I have seen your despatches objecting to agents of Northern States opening recruiting stations near your camps. An act of congress authorizes this, giving the appointment of agents to the States, and not to this Executive government. It is not for the War Department, or myself, to restrain, or modify the law, in it's execution, further than actual necessity may require. To be candid, I was for the passage of the law, not apprehending at the time that it would produce such inconvenience to the armies in the field, as you now cause me to fear. Many of the States were very anxious for it, and I hoped that, with their State bounties, and active exertions, they would get out substantial additions to our colored forces, which, unlike white recruits, help us where they come from, as well as where they go to. I still hope advantage from the law; and being a law, it must be treated as such by all of us. We here, will do what we consistently can to save you from difficulties arising out of it. May I ask therefore that you will give your hearty co-operation?"

1061.22–23   protest . . . War.]   Stanton replied that the President had authorized Major General Benjamin F. Butler to recruit from prisoners of war. On August 9, 1864, Grant wrote Halleck that he was sending the first regiment recruited from Confederate prisoners to the northwest Indian frontier, where they would not risk punishment for desertion if taken prisoner. See Grant's letter to William H. Seward of August 19, 1864, pp. 1065–66 in this volume.

1063.29   To Lydia Slocum]   This letter was printed in the Washington Chronicle on August 29, 1864. Mrs. Slocum was the 87-year-old grandmother of Major General James B. McPherson, who was killed in the battle of Atlanta on July 22, 1864.

1064.20   Mrs. Adams]   Abigail Brooks Adams (1808–89), wife of Charles

Francis Adams, Sr., and mother of Charles Francis Adams, Jr., a captain serving in the Army of the Potomac, and Henry and Brooks Adams.

1064.33   I state]   The last three paragraphs of this letter were widely circulated in Republican campaign broadsides during the 1864 election.

1065.16–17   McCawber]   Wilkins Micawber, a character in Charles Dickens' *David Copperfield* (1849–50).

1065.35–36   F. W. Morse . . . C. W. G.]   Freeman H. Morse, a Whig (1843–45) and later a Republican (1857–61) congressman from Maine, was United States consul in London. C. W. Geddes, a Union agent, quoted the secretary at the Confederate legation in London as saying that Union deserters wanted to fight against Grant because he had treated them so badly.

1066.21   Gen. Popes Department]   Major General John Pope commanded the Department of the Northwest, which covered Iowa, Wisconsin, Minnesota, and the Nebraska and Dakota territories.

1069.2   Burlington]   See note 621.29.

1069.31   written to him]   Washburne telegraphed Grant on September 20, 1864, that publication of an exchange of letters between Grant and Lincoln in the spring of 1864 would refute charges that the President had interfered with Grant's arrangements. Lincoln had written Grant on April 30, 1864, expressing his "entire satisfaction with what you have done up to this time . . ." The President continued: "The particulars of your plans I neither know, or seek to know. You are vigilant and self-reliant; and, pleased with this, I wish not to obtrude any constraints or restraints upon you." Grant replied on May 1, 1864, from his headquarters at Culpeper, Virginia, as follows:
    "Your very kind letter of yesterday is just received. The confidence you express for the future, and satisfaction with the past, in my Military administration is acknowledged with pride. It will be my earnest endeavor that you, and the country, shall not be disappointed.
    "From my first entrance into the volunteer service of the country, to the present day, I have never had cause of complaint, have never expressed or implied a complaint, against the Administration, or the Sec. of War, for throwing any embarassment in the way of my vigerously prossecuting what appeared to me my duty. Indeed since the promotion which placed me in command of all the Armies, and in view of the great responsibility, and importance of success, I have been astonished at the readiness with which every thing asked for has been yielded without even an explaination being asked. Should my success be less than I desire, and expect, the least I can say is, the fault is not with you."

1072.13   Col. Babcock]   Orville E. Babcock (1835–84) was an aide-de-camp on Grant's staff. He served as President Grant's private secretary until

1876, when he was forced to resign because of his involvement in the "whiskey ring" tax fraud scandal.

1072.26–29   Knowing . . . command.]   On February 3, 1865, Pope assumed command of the new Division of the Missouri, covering the Department of the Missouri (into which the Department of Kansas had been merged) and the Department of the Northwest. Pope was succeeded in the Department of the Northwest by Major General Samuel R. Curtis (1805–66), previously the commander of the Department of Kansas.

1072.34–35   Dodge . . . Mo.]   Major General Grenville M. Dodge (1831–1916) was replacing Major General William S. Rosecrans (1819–98). Grant had long been critical of Curtis's and Rosecrans's performance as department commanders.

1073.4   dispatch of 9 p. m.]   Halleck had expressed his belief that while no one in Washington wished Thomas to be removed, no one there would interfere if Grant relieved Thomas on his own responsibility.

1074.4   dispatch of 1 P. M.]   Thomas telegraphed that a "terrible storm of freezing rain" had forced him to postpone an attack scheduled for the morning of December 10.

1074.8   dispatch . . . 2 p. m.]   Thomas justified his delay in his telegram to Halleck, but said he would "submit without a murmur" if Grant ordered his removal.

1079.8   decline . . . promotion.]   In a letter to Grant on January 21, 1865, Sherman expressed his disapproval of moves in Congress to create a second lieutenant general in the U.S. Army.

1079.35   C. C. Clay, jr.,]   Clement C. Clay, Jr. (1816–82) was a Democratic senator from Alabama, 1853–61, and served in the Confederate Senate, 1862–64. He was sent to Canada as a confidential agent of the Confederate government in April 1864, where he conferred with Northern opponents of the war. In July 1864 he met with newspaper editor Horace Greeley in an unsuccessful bid to open peace negotiations with the Lincoln administration.

1081.2   amending my order]   Grant had printed for circulation among Confederate troops his Special Order No. 82 of August 28, 1864, which offered subsistence and free transportation home, or to any point in the North, to Confederate deserters who took an oath not to take up arms again, and paid employment in the quartermaster department to deserters who took an oath of allegiance. The order promised that deserters would not be forced into military service, or into any service endangering them to capture by the Confederate army.

1081.10   death of Clara.]   See note 34.23–24.

1082.25   Saturday next]   March 25, 1865.

1086.28–29   arrested . . . escapes.]   Ord replied that Ford had left for Baltimore on the morning of April 17. Ford was eventually arrested and jailed for 39 days before being released.

1087.6   basis of agreement]   See note 754.29–30.

1087.26   copy . . . dispatch]   This message, sent on March 3, 1865, read: "The President directs me to say to you that he wishes you to have no conference with General Lee unless it be for the capitulation of Gen. Lee's army, or on some minor, and purely, military matter. He instructs me to say that you are not to decide, discuss, or confer upon any political question. Such questions the President holds in his own hands; and will submit them to no military conferences or conventions. Meantime you are to press to the utmost, your military advantages."

APPENDIX

1111.1   Notes . . . Doctor]   Dr. John Hancock Douglas (1824–92) was the throat specialist who diagnosed Grant's cancer on October 22, 1884, and attended him personally until his death. Dr. Douglas preserved these notes, written at Mount McGregor, New York, by Grant when he was unable to speak, describing the final stages of his illness. They are now in the Douglas Collection in the Library of Congress. The following are a selection from the Douglas Collection, transcribed from the originals, which were written in pencil. Grant's own spelling and punctuation have been preserved.

1116.31–32   Dr. Sands]   Henry B. Sands, called in for consultation in February 1885, was nearby in case of emergency during part of the time Grant was at Mount McGregor.

1118.10   Harrison]   Harrison Tyrrell, Grant's valet.

1119.2   the Dr.]   Dr. George F. Shrady, also attending Grant.

1120.18   bath wagon]   Bath chair; a large chair on wheels for invalids. The name derives from Bath, England, a fashionable health resort.

CATALOGING INFORMATION

Grant, Ulysses S., 1822–1885.
    Memoirs and selected letters: personal memoirs
    of U. S. Grant, selected letters 1839–1865 / Ulysses
    S. Grant.
    Edited by Mary Drake McFeely and William S. McFeely.

    (The Library of America ; 50)
    1. Grant, Ulysses S., 1822–1885. 2. Grant, Ulysses S.,
1822–1865—Correspondence. 3. Generals—United States—
Biography. 4. Presidents—United States—Biography.
5. United States. Army—Biography. I. Title. II. Series.

E660.G7562   1990   973.8'2'092—dc20   90–60013
ISBN 0–940450–58–5 (alk. paper)

For a list of titles in The Library of America, write:
The Library of America
14 East 60th Street
New York, New York 10022

This book is set in 10 point Linotron Galliard,
a face designed for photocomposition by Matthew Carter
and based on the sixteenth-century face Granjon. The paper
is acid-free Ecusta Nyalite and meets the requirements for perma-
nence of the American National Standards Institute. The binding
material is Brillianta, a 100% woven rayon cloth made by
Van Heek-Scholco Textielfabrieken, Holland. The com-
position is by Haddon Craftsmen, Inc., and The
Clarinda Company. Printing and binding
by R. R. Donnelley & Sons Company.
Designed by Bruce Campbell.

THE LIBRARY OF AMERICA SERIES

1. Herman Melville, *Typee, Omoo, Mardi* (1982)
2. Nathaniel Hawthorne, *Tales and Sketches* (1982)
3. Walt Whitman, *Poetry and Prose* (1982)
4. Harriet Beecher Stowe, *Three Novels* (1982)
5. Mark Twain, *Mississippi Writings* (1982)
6. Jack London, *Novels and Stories* (1982)
7. Jack London, *Novels and Social Writings* (1982)
8. William Dean Howells, *Novels 1875–1886* (1982)
9. Herman Melville, *Redburn, White-Jacket, Moby-Dick* (1983)
10. Nathaniel Hawthorne, *Novels* (1983)
11. Francis Parkman, *France and England in North America* vol. I, (1983)
12. Francis Parkman, *France and England in North America* vol. II, (1983)
13. Henry James, *Novels 1871–1880* (1983)
14. Henry Adams, *Novels, Mont Saint Michel, The Education* (1983)
15. Ralph Waldo Emerson, *Essays and Lectures* (1983)
16. Washington Irving, *History, Tales and Sketches* (1983)
17. Thomas Jefferson, *Writings* (1984)
18. Stephen Crane, *Prose and Poetry* (1984)
19. Edgar Allan Poe, *Poetry and Tales* (1984)
20. Edgar Allan Poe, *Essays and Reviews* (1984)
21. Mark Twain, *The Innocents Abroad, Roughing It* (1984)
22. Henry James, *Essays, American & English Writers* (1984)
23. Henry James, *European Writers & The Prefaces* (1984)
24. Herman Melville, *Pierre, Israel Potter, The Confidence-Man, Tales & Billy Budd* (1985)
25. William Faulkner, *Novels 1930–1935* (1985)
26. James Fenimore Cooper, *The Leatherstocking Tales* vol. I, (1985)
27. James Fenimore Cooper, *The Leatherstocking Tales* vol. II, (1985)
28. Henry David Thoreau, *A Week, Walden, The Maine Woods, Cape Cod* (1985)
29. Henry James, *Novels 1881–1886* (1985)
30. Edith Wharton, *Novels* (1986)
31. Henry Adams, *History of the United States during the Administrations of Jefferson* (1986)
32. Henry Adams, *History of the United States during the Administrations of Madison* (1986)
33. Frank Norris, *Novels and Essays* (1986)
34. W. E. B. Du Bois, *Writings* (1986)
35. Willa Cather, *Early Novels and Stories* (1987)
36. Theodore Dreiser, *Sister Carrie, Jennie Gerhardt, Twelve Men* (1987)
37. Benjamin Franklin, *Writings* (1987)
38. William James, *Writings 1902–1910* (1987)
39. Flannery O'Connor, *Collected Works* (1988)
40. Eugene O'Neill, *Complete Plays 1913–1920* (1988)
41. Eugene O'Neill, *Complete Plays 1920–1931* (1988)
42. Eugene O'Neill, *Complete Plays 1932–1943* (1988)
43. Henry James, *Novels 1886–1890* (1989)
44. William Dean Howells, *Novels 1886–1888* (1989)
45. Abraham Lincoln, *Speeches and Writings 1832–1858* (1989)
46. Abraham Lincoln, *Speeches and Writings 1859–1865* (1989)
47. Edith Wharton, *Novellas and Other Writings* (1990)
48. William Faulkner, *Novels 1936–1940* (1990)
49. Willa Cather, *Later Novels* (1990)
50. Ulysses S. Grant, *Personal Memoirs and Selected Letters* (1990)
51. William Tecumseh Sherman, *Memoirs* (1990)

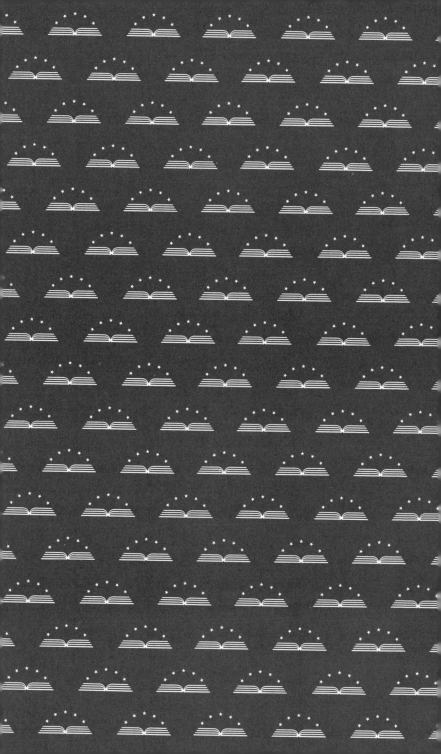